An Introduction to Mathematical Statistics and Its Applications

Third Edition

Richard J. Larsen
Vanderbilt University

Morris L. Marx
University of West Florida

PRENTICE HALL, Upper Saddle River, NJ 07458

Library of Congress Cataloging-in-Publication Data

Larsen, Richard J.
   An Introduction to mathematical statistics and its applications / Richard J. Larsen,
   Morris L. Marx,—3rd ed.
      p. cm.
   Includes bibliographical references and index
   ISBN 0-13-922303-7
      1. Mathematical statistics   I. Marx, Morris L.   II. Title.
   QA276.L314   2001
   519.5–dc.21

                                              00-025176

Acquisitions Editor: *Kathleen Boothby Sestak*
Assistant Vice President of Production and Manufacturing: *David W. Riccardi*
Executive Managing Editor: *Kathleen Schiaparelli*
Senior Managing Editor: *Linda Mihatov Behrens*
Production Editor: *Betsy Williams*
Manufacturing Buyer: *Alan Fischer*
Manufacturing Manager: *Trudy Pisciotti*
Marketing Manager: *Angela Battle*
Marketing Assistant: *Vince Jansen*
Director of Marketing: *John Tweeddale*
Editorial Assistant/Supplements Editor: *Joanne Wendelken*
Art Director: *Jayne Conte*
PrePress: *Preparé Inc. / Emilcomp srl*

 © 2001, 1986, 1981 by Prentice-Hall, Inc.
Upper Saddle River, NJ 07458

Printed in the United States of America
10   9   8   7   6   5   4   3

ISBN 0-13-922303-7

Prentice-Hall International (UK) Limited, *London*
Prentice-Hall of Australia Pty. Limited, *Sydney*
Prentice-Hall of Canada, Inc., *Toronto*
Prentice-Hall Hispanoamericana, S.A., *Mexico*
Prentice-Hall of India Private Limited, *New Delhi*
Prentice-Hall of Japan, Inc., *Tokyo*
Pearson Education Asia Pte. Ltd.
Editora Prentice-Hall do Brasil, Ltda., *Rio de Janeiro*

Contents

Preface

Changes in this third edition have been primarily motivated by our own teaching experiences as well as by the comments of others who use the text. Technology, though, has also dictated certain revisions. The widespread use of statistical software packages has brought certain topics and concepts to the fore, while diminishing the relevance of others. All in all, we feel that this new edition has a sharper focus and that students will find it more accessible and easier to use.

Many of the major changes come in the middle third of the book, much of which has been rewritten. These are the chapters that make the critical transition from probability to statistics. We have taken a variety of steps to make that material come more alive, ranging from the addition of more helpful examples to the frequent use of computer simulations.

Chapter 4, for example, now addresses more fully the important question of *why* certain measurements are modeled by particular probability functions. Relationships that exist between pdfs are given more attention, and the connection between theoretical models and sample data is explored in greater depth. Chapter 5 has been restructured. In the new edition, methods of estimation come first and the underlying theory is taken up last. That arrangement makes it easier for instructors to adjust the amount of time spent on estimation to whatever suits their individual needs. In Chapter 6, the principles of decision-making are now introduced in the context of testing $H_0: \mu = \mu_0$ rather than $H_0: p = p_0$. The result is a more steamlined presentation that avoids the complications inherent in a test statistic whose pdf is discrete.

Positioned between Chapter 7, which deals with the normal distribution, and Chapters 9 through 14, where the various techniques for analyzing data are introduced, is a new chapter on experimental design. Chapter 8 profiles seven of the most frequently encountered "data models." The basic characteristics of each design are discussed as well as the types of questions each seeks to answer. By providing a framework and a theme, Chapter 8 brings cohesion and a sense of order to the chapters that follow.

Chapter 11 (*Regression*) has also been changed substantially. It now begins with curve-fitting, then introduces the linear model, and eventually concludes with the bivariate normal. Regression "diagnostics" have been added to the new edition, and the various inference procedures associated with the linear model have been explained and delineated more carefully.

Our overriding motivation in deciding which topics to present—and in what order—stem from our objective to write a book that emphasizes the interrelation between probability theory, mathematical statistics, and data analysis. We believe that integrating all three is vitally important, particularly for those students who take only one statistics course during their college careers. Our experience in the classroom has certainly strengthened our faith in this approach: Students can more clearly see the importance of each of the three when viewed in the context of the other two.

Pedagogical Enhancements

Other changes have been implemented throughout the book as well. New case studies and examples have been added; others have been updated, revised, or replaced. The number of exercises has been substantially expanded, a 50% increase in some sections. Many chapters have a "MINITAB Applications" Appendix. Included is the syntax for doing whatever procedures appear in that chapter, along with a discussion of the output. Answers to most odd-numbered exercises are given at the end of the book.

Supplements

Instructor's Solutions Manual. This resource contains worked-out solutions to all text exercises (0-13-922311-8).

Student Solutions Manual: Featuring complete solutions to odd-numbered exercises, this is a great tool for students as they study and work through the problem material (0-13-031015-8).

Acknowledgments

We would like to express our indebtedness to the editors at J.R. Geigy, Biometrika, and McGraw-Hill for letting us use tables that appear in the Appendix and to the many researchers whose data we have used for examples. And for their detailed comments, criticisms, and suggestions, we thank the reviewers:

Dane Wu, Pacific Lutheran University; Pantelis K. Vlachos, Carnegie Mellon University; Lee K. Jones, University of Massachusetts–Lowell; Daniel W. Chambers, Boston College; Josephine S. Hamer, Western Connecticut State University; Raisa E. Feldman, University of California–Santa Barbara.

Finally, we would like to convey our gratitude to our editor, Kathy Boothby Sestak, and production editor, Betsy Williams. Their counsel on matters of design, form, and style was sincerely appreciated.

Richard J. Larsen
Nashville, Tennessee

Morris L. Marx
Pensacola, Florida

CHAPTER 1

Introduction

Francis Galton

"Some people hate the very name of statistics, but I find them full of beauty and interest. Whenever they are not brutalized, but delicately handled by the higher methods, and are warily interpreted, their power of dealing with complicated phenomena is extraordinary. They are the only tools by which an opening can be cut through the formidable thicket of difficulties that bars the path of those who pursue the Science of man."

1.1 A BRIEF HISTORY

Statistics is the science of sampling. How one set of measurements differs from another and what the implications of those differences might be are its primary concerns. Conceptually, the subject is rooted in the mathematics of probability, but its applications are everywhere. Statisticians are as likely to be found in a research lab or a field station as they are in a government office, an advertising firm, or a college classroom.

Properly applied, statistical techniques can be enormously effective in clarifying and quantifying natural phenomena. Figure 1.1.1 illustrates a case in point. Pictured at the top is a facsimile of the kind of data routinely recorded by a seismograph—listed chronologically are the occurrence times and Richter magnitudes for a series of earthquakes. Viewed in that format, the numbers are largely meaningless: No patterns are evident, nor is there any obvious connection between the frequencies of tremors and their severities.

Episode number	Date	Time	Severity (Richter scale)
⋮	⋮	⋮	⋮
217	6/19	4:53 P.M.	2.7
218	7/2	6:07 A.M.	3.1
219	7/4	8:19 A.M.	2.0
220	8/7	1:10 A.M.	4.1
221	8/7	10:46 P.M.	3.6
⋮	⋮	⋮	⋮

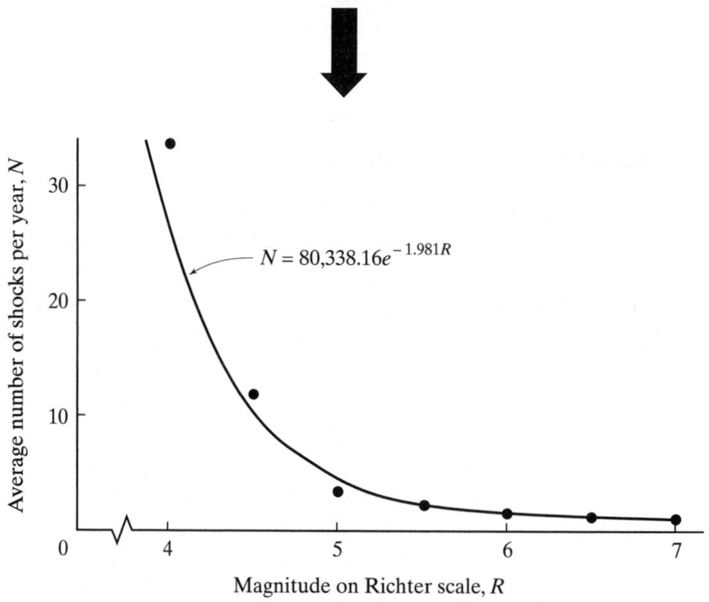

$$N = 80{,}338.16e^{-1.981R}$$

FIGURE 1.1.1

By way of contrast, the bottom of Figure 1.1.1 shows a statistical summary (using some of the regression techniques we will learn later) of a set of seismograph data recorded in southern California (59). Plotted above the Richter (R) value of 4.0, for example, is the average number (N) of earthquakes occurring per year in that region having magnitudes in the range 3.75 to 4.25. Similar points are included for R-values centered at 4.5, 5.0, 5.5, 6.0, 6.5, and 7.0. Now we can see that the two variables *are* related: Describing the (N, R)'s exceptionally well is the equation $N = 80{,}338.16e^{-1.981R}$.

In general, statistical techniques are employed either to (1) describe what *did* happen or (2) predict what *might* happen. The graph at the bottom of Figure 1.1.1 does both. Having "fit" the model $N = \beta_0 e^{-\beta_1 R}$ to the observed set of minor tremors (and finding that $\beta_0 = 80{,}338.16$ and $\beta_1 = -1.981$), we can then use that same equation to predict the likelihood of events *not* represented in the data set. If $R = 8.0$, for example, we would expect N to equal 0.01:

$$N = 80{,}338.16e^{-1.981(8.0)}$$

$$= 0.01$$

(which implies that Californians can expect catastrophic earthquakes registering on the order of 8.0 on the Richter scale to occur, on the average, once every 100 years).

It is unarguably true that the interplay between description and prediction—similar to what we see in Figure 1.1.1—is the single most important theme in statistics. Additional examples highlighting other aspects of that connection will be discussed in Section 1.2. To set the stage for the rest of the text, though, we will conclude Section 1.1 with brief histories of probability and statistics. Both are interesting stories, replete with large casts of unusual characters and plots that have more than a few unexpected twists and turns.

Probability: The Early Years (Optional)

No one knows where or when the notion of chance first arose; it fades into our prehistory. Nevertheless, evidence linking early humans with devices for generating random events is plentiful: Archaeological digs, for example, throughout the ancient world consistently turn up a curious overabundance of *astragali*, the heel bones of sheep and other vertebrates. Why should the frequencies of these bones be so disproportionately high? One could hypothesize that our forbears were fanatical foot fetishists, but two other explanations seem more plausible: The bones were used for religious ceremonies *and for gambling*.

Astragali have six sides but are not symmetrical (see Figure 1.1.2). Those found in excavations typically have their sides numbered or engraved. For many ancient civilizations, astragali were the primary mechanism through which oracles solicited the opinions of their gods. In Asia Minor, for example, it was customary in divination rites to roll, or *cast*, five astragali. Each possible configuration was associated with the name of a god and carried with it the sought-after advice. An outcome of

FIGURE 1.1.2

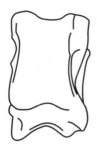

Sheep astragalus

(1, 3, 3, 4, 4), for instance, was said to be the throw of the savior Zeus, and its appearance was taken as a sign of encouragement (34):

> One one, two threes, two fours
> The deed which thou meditatest, go do it boldly.
> Put thy hand to it. The gods have given thee
>   favorable omens
> Shrink not from it in thy mind, for no evil
>   shall befall thee.

A (4, 4, 4, 6, 6), on the other hand, the throw of the child-eating Cronos, would send everyone scurrying for cover:

> Three fours and two sixes. God speaks as follows.
> Abide in thy house, nor go elsewhere,
> Lest a ravening and destroying beast come nigh thee.
> For I see not that this business is safe. But bide
>   thy time.

Gradually, over thousands of years, astragali were replaced by dice, and the latter became the most common means for generating random events. Pottery dice have been found in Egyptian tombs built before 2000 B.C.; by the time the Greek civilization was in full flower, dice were everywhere. (*Loaded* dice have also been found. Mastering the mathematics of probability would prove to be a formidable task for our ancestors, but they quickly learned how to cheat!)

The lack of historical records blurs the distinction initially drawn between divination ceremonies and recreational gaming. Among more recent societies, though, gambling emerged as a distinct entity, and its popularity was irrefutable. The Greeks and Romans were consummate gamblers, as were the early Christians (82).

Rules for many of the Greek and Roman games have been lost, but we can recognize the lineage of certain modern diversions in what was played during the Middle Ages. The most popular dice game of that period was called *hazard*, the name deriving from the Arabic *al zhar*, which means "a die." Hazard is thought to have been brought to Europe by soldiers returning from the Crusades; its rules are much like those of our modern-day craps. Cards were first introduced in the fourteenth century and immediately gave rise to a game known as *Primero*, an early form of poker. Board games, such as backgammon, were also popular during this period.

Given this rich tapestry of games and the obsession with gambling that characterized so much of the Western world, it may seem more than a little puzzling that a formal study of probability was not undertaken sooner than it was. As we will see shortly, the first instance of anyone *conceptualizing* probability, in terms of a mathematical model, occurred in the sixteenth century. That means that more than 2000 years of dice games, card games, and board games passed by before someone finally had the insight to write down even the simplest of probabilistic abstractions.

Historians generally agree that, as a subject, probability got off to a rocky start because of its incompatibility with two of the most dominant forces in the evolution of our Western culture, Greek philosophy and early Christian theology. The Greeks were comfortable with the notion of chance (something the Christians were not), but it went against their nature to suppose that random events could be quantified in any useful fashion. They believed that any attempt to reconcile mathematically what *did* happen with what *should have* happened was, in their phraseology, an improper juxtaposition of the "earthly plane" with the "heavenly plane."

Making matters worse was the antiempiricism that permeated Greek thinking. Knowledge, to them, was not something that should be derived by experimentation. It was better to reason out a question logically than to search for its explanation in a set of numerical observations. Together, these two attitudes had a deadening effect: The Greeks had no motivation to think about probability in any abstract sense, nor were they faced with the problems of interpreting data that might have pointed them in the direction of a probability calculus.

If the prospects for the study of probability were dim under the Greeks, they became even worse when Christianity broadened its sphere of influence. The Greeks and Romans at least accepted the *existence* of chance. They believed their gods to be either unable or unwilling to get involved in matters so mundane as the outcome of the roll of a die. Cicero writes:

> Nothing is so uncertain as a cast of dice, and yet there is no one who plays often who does not make a Venus-throw[1] and occasionally twice and thrice in succession. Then are we, like fools, to prefer to say that it happened by the direction of Venus rather than by chance?

For the early Christians, though, there was no such thing as chance: Every event that happened, no matter how trivial, was perceived to be a direct manifestation of God's deliberate intervention. In the words of St. Augustine:

> Nos eas causas quae dicuntur fortuitae ... non dicimus
>   nullas, sed latentes; easque tribuimus vel veri Dei ...
> (We say that those causes that are said to be by chance
>   are not non-existent but are hidden, and we attribute
>   them to the will of the true God ...)

Taking Augustine's position makes the study of probability moot, and it makes a probabilist a heretic. Not surprisingly, nothing of significance was accomplished in the subject for the next fifteen hundred years.

---

[1] When rolling four astragali, each of which is numbered on *four* sides, a Venus-throw was having each of the four numbers appear.

It was in the sixteenth century that probability, like a mathematical Lazarus, arose from the dead. Orchestrating its resurrection was one of the most eccentric figures in the entire history of mathematics, Gerolamo Cardano. By his own admission, Cardano personified the worst and the best—the Jekyll and the Hyde—of the Renaissance man. He was born in 1501 in Pavia. Facts about his personal life are difficult to verify. He wrote an autobiography, but his penchant for lying raises doubts about much of what he says. Whether true or not, though, his "one-sentence" self-assessment paints an interesting portrait (117):

> Nature has made me capable in all manual work, it has given me the spirit of a philosopher and ability in the sciences, taste and good manners, voluptuousness, gaiety, it has made me pious, faithful, fond of wisdom, meditative, inventive, courageous, fond of learning and teaching, eager to equal the best, to discover new things and make independent progress, of modest character, a student of medicine, interested in curiosities and discoveries, cunning, crafty, sarcastic, an initiate in the mysterious lore, industrious, diligent, ingenious, living only from day to day, impertinent, contemptuous of religion, grudging, envious, sad, treacherous, magician and sorcerer, miserable, hateful, lascivious, obscene, lying, obsequious, fond of the prattle of old men, changeable, irresolute, indecent, fond of women, quarrelsome, and because of the conflicts between my nature and soul I am not understood even by those with whom I associate most frequently.

Formally trained in medicine, Cardano's interest in probability derived from his addiction to gambling. His love of dice and cards was so all-consuming that he is said to have once sold all his wife's possessions just to get table stakes! Fortunately, something positive came out of Cardano's obsession. He began looking for a mathematical model that would describe, in some abstract way, the outcome of a random event. What he eventually formalized is now called the *classical definition of probability*: If the total number of possible outcomes, all equally likely, associated with some action is n and if m of those n result in the occurrence of some given event, then the probability of that event is m/n. If a fair die is rolled, there are $n = 6$ possible outcomes. If the event "outcome is greater than or equal to 5" is the one in which we are interested, then $m = 2$ (the outcomes 5 and 6) and the probability of the event is 2/6, or 1/3 (see Figure 1.1.3).

Cardano had tapped into the most basic principle in probability. The model he discovered may seem trivial in retrospect, but it represented a giant step forward: His was the first recorded instance of anyone computing a *theoretical*, as opposed to an empirical, probability. Still, the actual impact of Cardano's work was minimal. He

FIGURE 1.1.3

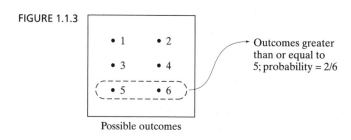

Possible outcomes

wrote a book in 1525, but its publication was delayed until 1663. By then, the focus of the Renaissance, as well as interest in probability, had shifted from Italy to France.

The date cited by many historians (those who are not Cardano supporters) as the "beginning" of probability is 1654. In Paris a well-to-do gambler, the Chevalier de Méré, asked several prominent mathematicians, including Blaise Pascal, a series of questions, the best-known of which was the *problem of points*:

> Two people, A and B, agree to play a series of fair games until one person has won six games. They each have wagered the same amount of money, the intention being that the winner will be awarded the entire pot. But suppose, for whatever reason, the series is prematurely terminated, at which point A has won five games and B three. How should the stakes be divided?

[The correct answer is that A should receive seven-eighths of the total amount wagered. (Hint: Suppose the contest were resumed. What scenarios would lead to A's being the first person to win six games?)]

Pascal was intrigued by de Méré's questions and shared his thoughts with Pierre Fermat, a Toulouse civil servant and probably the most brilliant mathematician in Europe. Fermat graciously replied, and from the now famous Pascal-Fermat correspondence came not only the solution to the problem of points but the foundation for more general results. More significantly, news of what Pascal and Fermat were working on spread quickly. Others got involved, of whom the best known was the Dutch scientist and mathematician Christiaan Huygens. The delays and the indifference that plagued Cardano a century earlier were not going to happen again.

Best remembered for his work in optics and astronomy, Huygens, early in his career, was intrigued by the problem of points. In 1657 he published *De Ratiociniis in Aleae Ludo* (Calculations in Games of Chance), a very significant work, far more comprehensive than anything Pascal and Fermat had done. For almost 50 years it was the standard "textbook" in the theory of probability. Huygens, of course, has supporters who feel that *he* should be credited as the founder of probability.

Almost all the mathematics of probability was still waiting to be discovered. What Huygens wrote was only the humblest of beginnings, a set of 14 propositions bearing little resemblance to the topics we teach today. But the foundation was there. The mathematics of probability was finally on firm footing.

Statistics: From Aristotle to Quetelet (Optional)

Historians generally agree that the subject of statistics began to take definite shape in the middle of the nineteenth century. What triggered its emergence was the union of three different "sciences," each of which had been developing along more or less independent lines (184).

The first of these sciences, what the Germans called *Staatenkunde*, involved the collection of comparative information on the history, resources, and military prowess of nations. Although efforts in this direction peaked in the seventeenth and eighteenth centuries, the concept was hardly new: Aristotle had done something similar in the fourth century B.C. Of the three movements, this one had the least influence on the development of modern statistics, but it did contribute some terminology: The word *statistics*, itself, first arose in connection with studies of this type.

The second movement, known as *political arithmetic*, was defined by one of its early proponents as "the art of reasoning by figures, upon things relating to government." Of more recent vintage than Staatenkunde, political arithmetic's roots were in seventeenth-century England. Making population estimates and constructing mortality tables were two of the problems it frequently dealt with. In spirit, political arithmetic was similar to what is now called *demography*.

The third component was the development of a *calculus of probability*. As we saw earlier, this was a movement that essentially started in seventeenth-century France in response to certain gambling questions, but it quickly became the "engine" for analyzing all kinds of data.

Staatenkunde: The Comparative Description of States

The need for gathering information on the customs and resources of nations has been obvious since antiquity. Aristotle is credited with the first major effort toward that objective: His *Politeiai*, written in the fourth century B.C., contained detailed descriptions of some 158 different city-states. Unfortunately, the thirst for knowledge that led to the *Politeiai* fell victim to the intellectual drought of the Dark Ages, and almost 2000 years elapsed before any similar projects of like magnitude were undertaken.

The subject resurfaced during the Renaissance, and the Germans showed the most interest. They not only gave it a name, *Staatenkunde*, meaning the comparative description of states, but they were also the first (in 1660) to incorporate the subject into a university curriculum. A leading figure in the German movement was Gottfried Achenwall, who taught at the University of Göttingen during the middle of the eighteenth century. Among Achenwall's claims to fame is that he was the first to use the word *statistics* in print. It appeared in the preface of his 1749 book *Abriss der Statswissenschaft der heutigen vornehmsten europaishen Reiche und Republiken*. (The word comes from the Italian root *stato*, meaning "state", implying that a statistician is someone concerned with government affairs.) As terminology, it seems to have been well received: For almost 100 years the word *statistics* continued to be associated with the comparative description of states. In the middle of the nineteenth century, though, the term was redefined, and statistics became the new name for what had previously been called political arithmetic.

How important was the work of Achenwall and his predecessors to the development of statistics? That would be difficult to say. To be sure, their contributions were more indirect than direct. They left no methodology and no general theory. But they did point out the need for collecting accurate data and, perhaps more importantly, reinforced the notion that something complex—even as complex as an entire nation—can be effectively studied by gathering information on its component parts. Thus, they were lending important support to the then growing belief that *induction*, rather than *deduction*, was a more sure-footed path to scientific truth.

Political Arithmetic

In the sixteenth century the English government began to compile records, called *bills of mortality*, on a parish-to-parish basis, showing numbers of deaths and their underlying causes. Their motivation largely stemmed from the plague epidemics that had periodically ravaged Europe in the not-too-distant past and were threatening to become a problem in England. Certain government officials, including the very influential Thomas Cromwell, felt that these bills would prove invaluable in helping to control the spread of an epidemic. At first, the bills were published only occasionally, but by the early seventeenth century they had become a weekly institution.[2]

Figure 1.1.4 (139) shows a portion of a bill that appeared in London in 1665. The gravity of the plague epidemic is strikingly apparent when we look at the numbers at the top: Out of 97,306 deaths, 68,596 (over 70%) were caused by the plague. The breakdown of certain other afflictions, though they caused fewer deaths, raises some interesting questions. What happened, for example, to the 23 people who were "frighted" or to the 397 who suffered from "rising of the lights"?

Among the faithful readers of the bills was John Graunt, a London merchant. Graunt not only read the bills, he studied them intently. He looked for patterns, computed death rates, devised ways of estimating population sizes, and even set up a primitive life table. His results were published in the 1662 treatise *Natural and Political Observations upon the Bills of Mortality*. This work was a landmark: Graunt had launched the twin sciences of vital statistics and demography and, although the name came later, it also signaled the beginning of political arithmetic. (Graunt did not have to wait long for accolades; in the year his book was published, he was elected to the prestigious Royal Society of London.)

High on the list of innovations that made Graunt's work unique were his objectives. Not content simply to describe a situation, although he was adept at doing so, Graunt often sought to go beyond his data and make generalizations (or, in current statistical terminology, draw *inferences*). Having been blessed with this particular turn of mind, he almost certainly qualifies as the world's first statistician. All Graunt really lacked was the probability theory that would have enabled him to frame his inferences more mathematically. That theory, though, was just beginning to unfold several hundred miles away in France.

Other seventeenth-century writers were quick to follow through on Graunt's ideas. William Petty's *Political Arithmetick* was published in 1690, although it was probably written some 15 years earlier. (It was Petty who gave the movement its name.) Perhaps even more significant were the contributions of Edmund Halley (of "Halley's comet" fame). Principally an astronomer, he also dabbled in political arithmetic, and in 1693 wrote *An Estimate of the Degrees of the Mortality of Mankind, drawn from Curious Tables of the Births and Funerals at the city of Breslaw; with an attempt to ascertain the Price of Annuities upon Lives*. (Book titles were longer then!)

---

[2] An interesting account of the bills of mortality is given in Daniel Defoe's *A Journal of the Plague Year*, which purportedly chronicles the London plague outbreak of 1665.

The bill for the year—A General Bill for this present year, ending the 19 of December, 1665, according to the Report made to the King's most excellent Majesty, by the Co. of Parish Clerks of Lond., & c.—gives the following summary of the results; the details of the several parishes we omit, they being made as in 1625, except that the out-parishes were now 12:—

Buried in the 27 Parishes within the walls	15,207
Whereof of the plague	9,887
Buried in the 16 Parishes without the walls	41,351
Whereof of the plague	28,838
At the Pesthouse, total buried	159
Of the plague	156
Buried in the 12 out-Parishes in Middlesex and surrey	18,554
Whereof of the plague	21,420
Buried in the 5 Parishes in the City and Liberties of Westminster	12,194
Whereof the plague	8,403
The total of all the christenings	9,967
The total of all the burials this year	97,306
Whereof of the plague	68,596

Abortive and Stillborne	617	Griping in the Guts	1,288	Palsie	30
Aged	1,545	Hang'd & made away themselves	7	Plague	68,596
Ague & Feaver	5,257	Headmould shot and mould fallen	14	Plannet	6
Appolex and Suddenly	116	Jaundice	110	Plurisie	15
Bedrid	10	Imposthume	227	Poysoned	1
Blasted	5	Kill by several accidents	46	Quinsie	35
Bleeding	16	King's Evill	86	Rickets	535
Cold & Cough	68	Leprosie	2	Rising of the Lights	397
Collick & Winde	134	Lethargy	14	Rupture	34
Comsumption & Tissick	4,808	Livergrown	20	Scurvy	105
Convulsion & Mother	2,036	Bloody Flux, Scowring & Flux	18	Shingles & Swine Pox	2
Distracted	5	Burnt and Scalded	8	Sores, Ulcers, Broken and	
Dropsie & Timpany	1,478	Calenture	3	Bruised Limbs	82
Drowned	50	Cancer, Cangrene & Fistula	56	Spleen	14
Executed	21	Canker and Thrush	111	Spotted Feaver & Purples	1,929
Flox & Smallpox	655	Childbed	625	Stopping of the Stomach	332
Found Dead in streets, fields, &c.	20	Chrisomes and Infants	1,258	Stone and Stranguary	98
French Pox	86	Meagrom and Headach	12	Surfe	1,251
Frighted	23	Measles	7	Teeth & Worms	2,614
Gout & Sciatica	27	Murthered & Shot	9	Vomiting	51
Grief	46	Overlaid & Starved	45	Wenn	8

Christened-Males	5,114	Females	4,853	In all	9,967
Buried-Males	58,569	Females	48,737	In all	97,306

Of the Plague	68,596
Increase in the Burials in the 130 Parishes and the Pesthouse this year	79,009
Increase of the Plague in the 130 Parishes and the Pesthouse this year	68,590

FIGURE 1.1.4

Halley shored up, mathematically, the efforts of Graunt and others to construct an accurate mortality table. In doing so, he laid the foundation for the important theory of annuities. Today, all life insurance companies base their premium schedules on methods similar to Halley's. (The first company to follow his lead was The Equitable, founded in 1765.)

For all its initial flurry of activity, political arithmetic did not fare particularly well in the eighteenth century, at least in terms of having its methodology fine-tuned. Still, the second half of the century did see some notable achievements for improving the quality of the databases: Several countries, including the United States in

1790, established a periodic census. To some extent, answers to the questions that interested Graunt and his followers had to be deferred until the theory of probability could develop just a little bit more.

Quetelet: The Catalyst

With political arithmetic furnishing the data and many of the questions, and the theory of probability holding out the promise of rigorous answers, the birth of statistics was at hand. All that was needed was a catalyst—someone to bring the two together. Several individuals served with distinction in that capacity. Karl Friedrich Gauss, the superb German mathematician and astronomer, was especially helpful in showing how statistical concepts could be useful in the physical sciences. Similar efforts in France were made by Laplace. But the man who perhaps best deserves the title of "matchmaker" was a Belgian, Adolphe Quetelet.

Quetelet was a mathematician, astronomer, physicist, sociologist, anthropologist, and poet. One of his passions was collecting data, and he was fascinated by the apparent regularity and predictability of social phenomena. In commenting on the nature of criminal tendencies, he once wrote the following (62):

> Thus we pass from one year to another with the sad perspective of seeing the same crimes reproduced in the same order and calling down the same punishments in the same proportions. Sad condition of humanity! ... We might enumerate in advance how many individuals will stain their hands in the blood of their fellows, how many will be forgers, how many will be poisoners, almost we can enumerate in advance the births and deaths that should occur. There is a budget which we pay with a frightful regularity; it is that of prisons, chains and the scaffold.

Given such an orientation, it was not surprising that Quetelet would see in probability theory an elegant means for expressing human behavior. For much of the nineteenth century he vigorously championed the cause of statistics, and as a member of more than 100 learned societies his influence was enormous. When he died in 1874, statistics had been brought to the brink of its modern era.

1.2 SOME EXAMPLES

Do stock markets rise and fall randomly? Is there a common element in the aesthetic standards of the ancient Greeks and the Shoshoni Indians? Can external forces, such as phases of the moon, affect admissions to mental hospitals? What kind of relationship exists between exposure to radiation and cancer mortality?

These questions are quite diverse in content, but they have some important traits in common. They are all difficult or impossible to study in a laboratory, and none of them admit any self-evident axioms from which one may reason deductively. Indeed, such questions are usually answered by collecting data, making guesses about the process generating those data, and then testing the guesses. As it turns out, this approach leads to still another similarity—the element of chance or uncertainty that affects each data point recorded.

The goal of this text is to develop the mathematical tools and concepts necessary for incorporating the chance element into the methodology for describing or making predictions about real-world phenomena. The examples that follow are cases in point.

CASE STUDY 1.2.1

Each evening, radio and TV reporters offer a bewildering array of averages and indices that presumably indicate the state of the stock market. But do they? Are these numbers conveying any really useful information? Some financial analysts would say "No," arguing that speculative markets tend to rise and fall randomly, much as though some hidden roulette wheel were spinning out the figures. In this example we attempt to examine quantitatively the reasonableness of this *random-movement* hypothesis.

We begin by formulating a theoretical construct, or *model*, that should describe the behavior of the market *if the (random) hypothesis were true*. To this end, we translate the term "random movement" into two assumptions:

(a) The chances of the market's rising or falling on a given day are unaffected by its actions on any previous days.

(b) The market is equally likely to go up or down.

Measuring the day-to-day randomness, or its absence, in the market's movements can be accomplished by looking at the length of *runs*. We define a *run of downturns of length k* to be a sequence of days starting with a rise, followed by k consecutive declines, then followed by a rise. So, for example, a daily sequence of the form (rise, fall, fall, rise) is a run of length two.

If the actual behavior of the market's run lengths differs markedly from the predictions of assumptions (a) and (b), we can reject the random-movement hypothesis as being unrealistic. To make such a comparison, we must deduce the model's implications as to run lengths. This deduction is not too difficult, even without the benefit of any formal training in probability.

Suppose a rise has occurred followed by a fall. For a run of length one, the market must next rise. By assumptions (a) and (b), this happens half the time, so we assign a probability of 1/2 to a run of length one. Our notation for this will be $P(1) = 1/2$. The other half of the time the market falls, giving the sequence (rise, fall, fall). A run of length two occurs if there is now a rise. Again, this happens half the time, making its probability half of the half represented by the (rise, fall, fall) sequence. Thus, the probability of a run of length two is $P(2) = (1/2) \cdot (1/2) = 1/4$. Continuing in this manner, we can see that, in general, a run of length k has probability $(1/2)^k$. Furthermore, if there are T total runs, it seems reasonable to expect $T \cdot (1/2)^k$ of them to be of length k.

Table 1.2.1 gives the distribution of 120 runs of downturns observed in daily closing prices of the Standard and Poor's 500 stock index between February 17, 1994 and February 9, 1996. The third column gives the corresponding expected numbers, as calculated from the expression $T \cdot (1/2)^k$, where $T = 120$.

Notice that the agreement between actual and predicted run frequencies seems good enough to lend some credence to assumptions (a) and (b). However, the longer runs do not fit the distribution very well. We should investigate modifying the model so that it fits the data better. One way to do that is to allow for the possibility that the market's rising or

TABLE 1.2.1   Runs in the Closing Prices for the S&P 500 Stock Index

Run Length, k	Observed	Expected
1	67	60.00
2	28	30.00
3	18	15.00
4	3	7.50
5	2	3.875
6+	2	3.75
	120	120.0

falling on any given day might not be a 50-50 proposition. This suggests that assumption (b) should be replaced with

(c) The likelihood of a fall in the market is some number p, where $0 \le p \le 1$.

The quantity p is known as the *parameter* of the model. Of course, (b) is a special case of (c), where $p = 1/2$.

Invoking the new assumptions, we can recalculate the probabilities of various run lengths. For example, following a (rise, fall) sequence, a rise would be expected $100(1 - p)\%$ of the time, so $P(1) = 1 - p$. Another fall, of course, would occur the remaining $p\%$ of the time. Since the chance of the next change being a rise is $1 - p$, the probability of the sequence (rise, fall, fall, rise)—that is, a run of length two—is $P(2) = p(1 - p)$. In general, $P(k) = p^{k-1}(1 - p)$.

Two questions now arise. Whichever of the two is more important for further study depends on the needs and interests of the model maker.

1. Is the initial assumption $p = 1/2$ justified?
2. Given the observed data, what is the best choice (or *estimate*) for p?

To answer Question 1, we must decide whether the discrepancies between observed and expected run lengths are small enough to be attributed to chance or large enough to render the model invalid. One way to answer Question 2 is to seek the value of p that best "explains" the observations, in terms of maximizing their likelihood of occurring. For the data from which Table 1.2.1 was derived, this type of estimate turns out to be $p = 0.43$. The corresponding expected values, based on $P(k) = p^{k-1}(1 - p) = (0.43)^{k-1}(0.57)$, are given in column 3 of Table 1.2.2.

TABLE 1.2.2   Runs in the Closing Prices for the S&P 500 Stock Index

Run Length, n	Observed	Expected [$p = 0.43$]
1	67	68.4
2	28	29.4
3	18	12.6
4	3	5.4
5	2	2.3
6+	2	1.9
	120	120.0

(continued on next page)

(Case Study 1.2.1 continued)

Except for the 3-runs, the fit of the model improves with this choice for the parameter. Based on what we have seen thus far, we would have to conclude that the data and either choice for the parameter do not offer any serious refutation of the hypothesis that speculative markets rise and fall randomly.

Comment.   The two questions raised at the conclusion of Case Study 1.2.1 touch on the dual themes of statistical inference: hypothesis testing and estimation. While it is necessary to be vague now about the mathematical techniques these two will require, it should be clear from the example that the notions of probability and expected value will play prominent roles.

Among the useful criteria for classifying experiments into statistical "types" is the nature of the set of possible outcomes. Case Study 1.2.1, for example, described an experiment with a *finite* number of outcomes. A simple extension of that idea leads to experiments with outcomes that are *countably infinite*. Such an outcome set would have been appropriate had we idealized the stock market model to allow for runs of *any* length. In either case, though, probabilities are calculated as *sums*. The probability that a run will be of either length 1 or length 2, for instance, is

$$P(1) + P(2) = p^0(1 - p)^1 + p^1(1 - p)^1 = 1 - p^2$$

There are many circumstances, however, where the possible outcomes are so numerous and so close together that it becomes convenient to define the outcome set as an interval of real numbers (that is, as an *uncountably infinite set*). Probabilities are then represented as integrals, the continuous analogs of sums. The next case study is based on data that would be considered "continuous."

CASE STUDY 1.2.2

Not all rectangles are created equal. Since antiquity, societies have expressed aesthetic preferences for rectangles having certain width (w) to length (l) ratios. Plato, for example, wrote that rectangles whose sides were in a $1:\sqrt{3}$ ratio were especially pleasing. (These are the rectangles formed from the two halves of an equilateral triangle.)

Another "standard" calls for the width-to-length ratio to be equal to the ratio of the length to the sum of the width and the length. That is,

$$\frac{w}{l} = \frac{l}{w + l} \tag{1.2.1}$$

Equation 1.2.1 implies that the width is $\frac{1}{2}(\sqrt{5} - 1)$, or approximately 0.618, times as long as the length. The Greeks called this the golden rectangle and used it often in their architecture (see Figure 1.2.1). Many other cultures were similarly inclined. The Egyptians, for example, built their pyramids out of stones whose faces were golden rectangles. Today, in our society, the golden rectangle remains an architectural and artistic standard, and even items such as drivers' licenses, business cards, and picture frames often have w/l ratios close to 0.618.

FIGURE 1.2.1
A golden rectangle

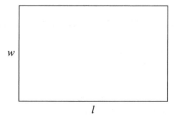

The study described here is an example from a field known as experimental aesthetics. The data are width-to-length ratios of beaded rectangles used by the Shoshoni Indians to decorate their leather goods. The question at issue is whether the golden rectangle can be considered an aesthetic standard for the Shoshonis, just as it was for the Greeks and the Egyptians.

It must be realized, of course, that even if the 0.618 ratio is adopted by a society as an aesthetic standard, there might still be considerable variability in the width-to-length ratios of individual rectangles. What should be close to 0.618, though, is the *average w/l* ratio. This suggests that the hypothesis (H) to be tested might be written as follows:

H: The "true" average width-to-length ratio characteristic of Shoshoni artistic work is 0.618.

Table 1.2.3 presents the w/l ratios for 20 rectangles found on Shoshoni handicraft (36). The average of these observed ratios is 0.661. The decision to be made, then, is whether H is true and the difference between 0.618 and 0.661 is solely the result of chance fluctuations, or whether H is false and the two societies do have different aesthetic standards. Ultimately, the choice will depend on how likely it is to obtain a sample average of 0.661 if, in fact, the true average is 0.618. Computing that likelihood, however, is not a simple task, so our final decision will have to be deferred. We return to the problem in Chapter 7.

TABLE 1.2.3   Width-To-Length Ratios of Shoshoni Rectangles

0.693	0.749	0.654	0.670
0.662	0.672	0.615	0.606
0.690	0.628	0.668	0.611
0.606	0.609	0.601	0.553
0.570	0.844	0.576	0.933

Case Study 1.2.2 asked whether a given set of observations (coming from a single population) conformed to a theoretically determined standard ($w/l = 0.618$). Another common type of question asks if *several* populations differ among themselves in some particular aspect. For the latter situation, the data will consist of several sets of observations, one set from each of the populations being compared. The next case study is a typical "k-sample" problem.

CASE STUDY 1.2.3

In folklore, the full moon is often portrayed as something sinister, a kind of evil force possessing the power to control our behavior. Over the centuries, many prominent writers and philosophers have shared this belief (116). Milton, in *Paradise Lost*, refers to

> Demoniac frenzy, moping melancholy
> And moon-struck madness.

And Othello, after the murder of Desdemona, laments:

> It is the very error of the moon,
> She comes more near the earth than she was wont
> And makes men mad.

On a more scholarly level, Sir William Blackstone, the renowned eighteenth-century English barrister, defined a "lunatic" as

> one who hath ... lost the use of his reason and who hath lucid intervals, sometimes enjoying his senses and sometimes not, and that frequently depending upon changes of the moon.

The possibility of lunar phases influencing human affairs is a theory not without supporters among the scientific community. Studies by reputable medical researchers have attempted to link the "Transylvania effect," as it has come to be known, with higher suicide rates, pyromania, and even epilepsy. In this example, we look at still another context in which this phenomenon might be expected to occur. Table 1.2.4 shows the admission rates to the emergency room of a Virginia mental health clinic *before*, *during*, and *after* the 12 full moons from August 1971 to July 1972 (12). Notice that for this particular set of data, the average admission rate *is* higher during the full moon than during the rest of the month.

TABLE 1.2.4   Admission Rates (Patients/Day)

Month	Before Full Moon	During Full Moon	After Full Moon
Aug.	6.4	5.0	5.8
Sept.	7.1	13.0	9.2
Oct.	6.5	14.0	7.9
Nov.	8.6	12.0	7.7
Dec.	8.1	6.0	11.0
Jan.	10.4	9.0	12.9
Feb.	11.5	13.0	13.5
Mar.	13.8	16.0	13.1
Apr.	15.4	25.0	15.8
May	15.7	13.0	13.3
June	11.7	14.0	12.8
July	15.8	20.0	14.5
Averages	10.9	13.3	11.5

For reasons that we will discuss in Chapter 6, hypothesis tests are always set up so that what is being tested is the absence or negation of any differences from population to population. Following that principle here leads us to state the hypothesis as follows:

> H: On the average, there is no difference in mental-hospital admission rates before, during, and after the full moon.
>
> The decision to reject H will be made only if it can be demonstrated that averages as different as 10.9, 13.3, and 11.4 are extremely unlikely to arise by chance alone. An analysis done in Chapter 13 suggests that these averages *are* considerably different, implying that the data could be used as evidence in support of the existence of a Transylvania effect.

Many scientific laws are, from a mathematical viewpoint, discoveries of functional relationships between variable quantities. A familiar example is the formula $s(t) = 16t^2$, where $s(t)$ is the distance in feet an object initially at rest falls in t seconds (neglecting air resistance). The final case study in this section applies an empirical curve-fitting procedure to the problem of estimating the relationship between radiation exposure and cancer mortality rates.

CASE STUDY 1.2.4

The oil embargo of 1973 raised some very serious questions about energy policies in the United States. One of the most controversial is whether nuclear reactors should assume a more central role in the production of electric power. Those in favor point to their efficiency and to the availability of nuclear material; those against warn of nuclear "incidents" and emphasize the health hazards posed by low-level radiation.

A cautionary case in point was the government's nuclear facility located in Hanford, Washington. What happened there is what environmentalists fear will be a recurrent problem if nuclear reactors are proliferated.

Until recently, Hanford was responsible for producing plutonium for atomic weapons. One of the major safety problems encountered there was the storage of radioactive wastes. Over the years, significant quantities of strontium 90 and cesium 137 leaked from their open-pit storage areas into the nearby Columbia River, which flows along the Washington-Oregon border and eventually empties into the Pacific Ocean.

To measure the health consequences of this contamination, an index of exposure was calculated for each of the nine Oregon counties having frontage on either the Columbia River or the Pacific Ocean. This particular index was based on several factors, including the county's stream distance from Hanford and the average distance of its population from any water frontage. As a covariate, the cancer mortality rate was determined for each of these same counties.

Table 1.2.5 shows the index of exposure and the cancer mortality rate (deaths per 100,000) for the nine Oregon counties affected (38). Higher index values represent higher levels of contamination.

A simple graph of the data (see Figure 1.2.2) suggests that the cancer mortality rate (y) and the index of exposure (x) vary *linearly*—that is, $y = a + bx$. Finding the numerical values for a and b that position the line so it best fits the data is an important problem in an area of statistics known as regression analysis. Here, the optimal line, based on methods derived in Chapter 11, has the equation $y = 114.72 + 9.23x$.

(continued on next page)

(Case Study 1.2.4 continued)

TABLE 1.2.5   Radioactive Contamination and Cancer Mortality in Oregon

County	Index of Exposure	Cancer Mortality per 100,000
Umatilla	2.49	147.1
Morrow	2.57	130.1
Gilliam	3.41	129.9
Sherman	1.25	113.5
Wasco	1.62	137.5
Hood River	3.83	162.3
Portland	11.64	207.5
Columbia	6.41	177.9
Clatsop	8.34	210.3

FIGURE 1.2.2

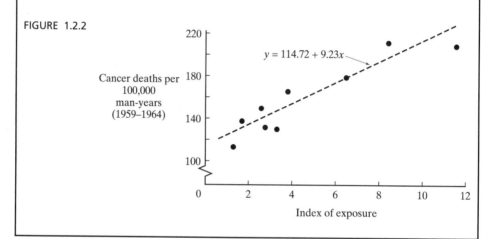

1.3   A CHAPTER SUMMARY

The concepts of probability lie at the very heart of all statistical problems, the case studies of Section 1.2 being typical examples. Acknowledging that fact, the next two chapters take a close look at some of those concepts. Chapter 2 states the axioms of probability and investigates their consequences. It also covers the basic skills for algebraically manipulating probabilities and gives an introduction to combinatorics, the mathematics of counting. Chapter 3 reformulates much of the material in Chapter 2 in terms of *random variables*, the latter being a concept of great convenience in applying probability to statistics. Over the years, particular measures of probability have emerged as being especially useful: The most prominent of these are profiled in Chapter 4.

    Our study of statistics proper begins with Chapter 5, which is a first look at the theory of parameter estimation. Chapter 6 introduces the notion of hypothesis testing, a procedure that, in one form or another, commands a major share of the remainder of the book. From a conceptual standpoint, these are very important chapters: Most formal applications of statistical methodology will involve either parameter estimation or hypothesis testing, or both.

Among the probability functions featured in Chapter 4, the *normal distribution*—more familiarly known as the bell-shaped curve—is sufficiently important to merit even further scrutiny. Chapter 7 derives in some detail many of the properties and applications of the normal distribution as well as those of several related probability functions. Much of the theory that supports the methodology appearing in Chapters 9 through 13 comes from Chapter 7.

Chapter 8 is new to the third edition and describes some of the basic principles of experimental "design." Its purpose is to provide a framework for comparing and contrasting the various statistical procedures profiled in Chapters 9 through 14.

Chapters 9, 12, and 13 continue the work of Chapter 7, but with the emphasis being on the comparison of several populations, similar to what was done in Case Study 1.2.3. Chapter 10 looks at the important problem of assessing the level of agreement between a set of data and the values predicted by the probability model from which those data presumably came (recall Case Study 1.2.1). Linear relationships, such as the one between radiation exposure and cancer mortality in Case Study 1.2.4, are examined in Chapter 11. (If desired, the material in Section 11.4, dealing with the relationship between a pair of random variables, can be taken up immediately after Chapter 3.)

Chapter 14 is an introduction to nonparametric statistics. The objective there is to develop procedures for answering some of the same sorts of questions raised in Chapters 8, 9, 11, and 12, but with fewer initial assumptions.

As a general format, each chapter contains numerous examples and case studies, the latter being actual experimental data taken from a variety of recent sources, primarily newspapers, magazines, and technical journals. We hope that these applications will make it abundantly clear that, while the general orientation of this text is theoretical, the consequences of that theory are never too far from having direct relevance to the "real world".

CHAPTER 2

Probability

Pierre de Fermat (1601–1665)

One of the most influential of seventeenth-century mathematicians, Fermat earned his living as a lawyer and administrator in Toulouse. He shares with Descartes credit for the invention of analytic geometry, but his most important work may have been in number theory. Fermat did not write for publication, preferring instead to send letters and papers to friends. His correspondence with Pascal was the starting point for the development of a mathematical theory of probability.

Blaise Pascal (1623–1662)

Pascal was the son of a nobleman. A prodigy of sorts, he had already published a treatise on conic sections by the age of 16. He also invented one of the early calculating machines to help his father with accounting work. Pascal's contributions to probability were stimulated by his correspondence, in 1654, with Fermat. Later that year he retired to a life of religious meditation.

2.1   INTRODUCTION

NASA officials recently estimated that the odds of a *Challenger*-type catastrophic accident during a shuttle flight are roughly 1 in 78. If 20 launches are scheduled over the next five years, what is the likelihood that at least one will end in disaster? If a polygraph test says that a criminal suspect is guilty, what are the chances that he or she actually is guilty? How likely is your favorite baseball player to hit safely in his next 30 games? If males and females mate randomly with respect to their genetic makeup, what proportion of the time will a recessive trait appear in the next generation? What are the odds that a poker player is dealt a full house or that a craps shooter makes his or her point? If a woman lives to be 70, how likely is she to die in her eighties? What are the chances that intelligent life capable of interstellar communication currently exists elsewhere in our galaxy?

All of these questions can be addressed by applying the probability theorems that we will learn in Chapter 2. Historically, a good portion of our modern "calculus" of probability dates back to the early work of Pascal and Fermat that was mentioned in Chapter 1. By the middle of the seventeenth century, the two Frenchmen had discovered many of the rules for computing probabilities that arise in simple, gambling-type situations. It was not until the twentieth century, though, that a rigorous and formal development of the mathematics of probability finally appeared. The breakthrough came in 1933 when the great Russian mathematician Andrei Kolmogorov published *Foundations of the Theory of Probability* and succeeded in reducing the fundamental properties of probability to four simple axioms.

We begin Chapter 2 with a review of some basic concepts from set theory. These will ultimately provide the necessary context for defining and manipulating probabilities. Sections 2.3, 2.4, and 2.5 introduce Kolmogorov's axioms and draw the important distinction between discrete probability functions and continuous probability functions. The remainder of Chapter 2 has a very practical orientation and uses a variety of examples to illustrate the application of probability to real-world problems.

2.2   SAMPLE SPACES AND THE ALGEBRA OF SETS

We begin our development of probability by defining four key words: *experiment, sample outcome, sample space*, and *event*. The latter three, all carryovers from classical set theory, give us a familiar mathematical framework within which to work; the former is "new" and provides the conceptual mechanism for casting real-world phenomena into probabilistic terms.

By an *experiment* we will mean any procedure that (1) can be repeated, theoretically, an infinite number of times; and (2) has a well-defined set of possible outcomes. Thus, rolling a pair of dice qualifies as an experiment; so does measuring a hypertensive's blood pressure or doing a spectrographic analysis to determine the carbon content of moon rocks. Each of the potential eventualities of an experiment is referred to as a *sample outcome, s*, and their totality is called the *sample space, S*. To signify the membership of s in S, we write $s \in S$. Any designated collection of sample outcomes, including individual outcomes, the entire sample space, and the null set, constitutes an *event*. The latter is said to *occur* if the outcome of the experiment is one of the members of that event.

EXAMPLE 2.2.1

Consider the experiment of flipping a coin three times. What is the sample space? Which sample outcomes make up the event A: Majority of coins show heads?

Think of each sample outcome here as an ordered triple, its components representing the outcomes of the first, second, and third tosses, respectively. Altogether, there are eight different triples, so those eight comprise the sample space:

$$S = \{\text{HHH}, \text{HHT}, \text{HTH}, \text{THH}, \text{HTT}, \text{THT}, \text{TTH}, \text{TTT}\}$$

By inspection, we see that four of the sample outcomes in S constitute the event A:

$$A = \{\text{HHH}, \text{HHT}, \text{HTH}, \text{THH}\}$$

EXAMPLE 2.2.2

Imagine rolling two dice, the first one red, the second one green. Each sample outcome is an ordered pair (face showing on red die, face showing on green die), and the entire sample space can be represented as a 6×6 matrix (see Figure 2.2.1).

Face showing on green die

Face showing on red die	1	2	3	4	5	6
1	(1, 1)	(1, 2)	(1, 3)	(1, 4)	(1, 5)	(1, 6)
2	(2, 1)	(2, 2)	(2, 3)	(2, 4)	(2, 5)	(2, 6)
3	(3, 1)	(3, 2)	(3, 3)	(3, 4)	(3, 5)	(3, 6)
4	(4, 1)	(4, 2)	(4, 3)	(4, 4)	(4, 5)	(4, 6)
5	(5, 1)	(5, 2)	(5, 3)	(5, 4)	(5, 5)	(5, 6)
6	(6, 1)	(6, 2)	(6, 3)	(6, 4)	(6, 5)	(6, 6)

A

FIGURE 2.2.1

Gamblers are often interested in the event A that the sum of the faces showing is a 7. Notice in Figure 2.2.1 that the sample outcomes contained in A are the six diagonal entries, $(1, 6)$, $(2, 5)$, $(3, 4)$, $(4, 3)$, $(5, 2)$, and $(6, 1)$.

EXAMPLE 2.2.3

A local TV station advertises two newscasting positions. If three women (W_1, W_2, W_3) and two men (M_1, M_2) apply, the "experiment" of hiring two coanchors generates a sample space of 10 outcomes:

$$S = \{(W_1, W_2), (W_1, W_3), (W_2, W_3), (W_1, M_1), (W_1, M_2), (W_2, M_1), (W_2, M_2), (W_3, M_1), (W_3, M_2), (M_1, M_2)\}$$

Does it matter here that the two positions being filled are equivalent? Yes. If the station were seeking to hire, say, a sports announcer and a weather forecaster, the number of possible outcomes would be 20: (W_2, M_1), for example, would represent a different staffing assignment than (M_1, W_2).

EXAMPLE 2.2.4

The number of sample outcomes associated with an experiment need not be finite. Suppose that a coin is tossed until the first tail appears. If the first toss is itself a tail, the outcome of the experiment is T; if the first tail occurs on the second toss, the outcome is HT; and so on. Theoretically, of course, the first tail may *never* occur, and the infinite nature of S is readily apparent:

$$S = \{\text{T, HT, HHT, HHHT}, \dots\}$$

EXAMPLE 2.2.5

There are three ways to indicate an experiment's sample space. If the number of possible outcomes is small, we can simply list them, as we did in Examples 2.2.1 through 2.2.3. In some cases it may be possible to *characterize* a sample space by showing the structure its outcomes necessarily possess. This is what we did in Example 2.2.4. A third option is to state a mathematical formula that the sample outcomes must satisfy.

A computer programmer is running a subroutine that solves a general quadratic equation, $ax^2 + bx + c = 0$. Her "experiment" consists of choosing values for the three coefficients a, b, and c. Define (1) S and (2) the event A: Equation has two equal roots.

First, the sample space. Since presumably no combinations of finite a, b, and c are inadmissible, we can characterize S by writing a series of inequalities:

$$S = \{(a, b, c): -\infty < a < \infty, -\infty < b < \infty, -\infty < c < \infty\}$$

Defining A requires the well-known result from algebra that a quadratic equation has equal roots if and only if its discriminant, $b^2 - 4ac$, vanishes. Membership in A, then, is contingent on a, b, and c satisfying an equation:

$$A = \{(a, b, c): b^2 - 4ac = 0\}$$

QUESTIONS

2.2.1 A graduating engineer has signed up for three job interviews. She intends to categorize each one as being either a "success" or a "failure" depending on whether it leads to a plant trip. Write out the appropriate sample space. What outcomes are in the event A: Second success occurs on third interview? In B: First success never occurs? (*Hint:* Notice the similarity between this situation and the coin-tossing experiment described in Example 2.2.1.)

2.2.2 Three dice are tossed, one red, one blue, and one green. What outcomes make up the event A that the sum of the three faces showing equals 5?

2.2.3 An urn contains six chips numbered 1 through 6. Three are drawn out. What outcomes are in the event "Second smallest chip is a 3"? Assume that the order of the chips is irrelevant.

2.2.4 Suppose that two cards are dealt from a standard 52-card poker deck. Let A be the event that the sum of the two cards is 8 (assume that aces have a numerical value of 1). How many outcomes are in A?

2.2.5 A woman has her purse snatched by two teenagers. She is subsequently shown a police line-up consisting of five suspects, including the two perpetrators. What is the sample space associated with the experiment "Woman picks two suspects out of lineup"? Which outcomes are in the event, A, that she makes at least one incorrect identification?

2.2.6 Consider the experiment of choosing coefficients for the quadratic equation $ax^2 + bx + c = 0$. Characterize the values of a, b, and c associated with the event A: Equation has imaginary roots.

2.2.7 In the game of craps, the person rolling the dice (the *shooter*) wins outright if his first toss is a 7 or an 11. If his first toss is a 2, 3, or 12, he loses outright. If his first roll is something else, say, a 9, that number becomes his "point" and he keeps rolling the dice until he either rolls another 9, in which case he wins, or a 7, in which case he loses. Characterize the sample outcomes contained in the event "Shooter wins with a point of 9."

2.2.8 A probability-minded despot offers a convicted murderer a final chance to gain his release. The prisoner is given 20 chips, 10 white and 10 black. All 20 are to be placed into two urns, according to any allocation scheme the prisoner wishes, with the one proviso being that each urn contain at least one chip. The executioner will then pick one of the two urns at random and from that urn, one chip at random. If the chip selected is white, the prisoner will be set free; if it is black, he "buys the farm." Characterize the sample space describing the prisoner's possible allocation options. (Intuitively, which allocation affords the prisoner the greatest chance of survival?)

Unions, Intersections, and Complements

Associated with events defined on a sample space are several operations collectively referred to as the *algebra of sets*. These are the rules that govern the ways in which one event can be combined with another. Consider, for example, the game of craps described in Question 2.2.7. The shooter wins on his initial roll if he throws either a 7 *or* an 11. In the language of the algebra of sets, the event "shooter rolls a 7 or an 11" is the *union* of two simpler events, "shooter rolls a 7" and "shooter rolls an 11." If E denotes the union and if A and B denote the two events making up the union, we write $E = A \cup B$. The next several definitions and examples illustrate those portions of the algebra of sets that we will find particularly useful in the chapters ahead.

DEFINITION 2.2.1. Let A and B be any two events defined over the same sample space S. Then

(a) The *intersection* of A and B, written $A \cap B$, is the event whose outcomes belong to both A and B.

(b) The *union* of A and B, written $A \cup B$, is the event whose outcomes belong to either A or B or both.

EXAMPLE 2.2.6

A single card is drawn from a poker deck. Let A be the event that an ace is selected:

$$A = \{\text{ace of hearts, ace of diamonds, ace of clubs, ace of spades}\}$$

Let B be the event "Heart is drawn":

$$B = \{2 \text{ of hearts}, 3 \text{ of hearts}, \ldots, \text{ace of hearts}\}$$

Then

$$A \cap B = \{\text{ace of hearts}\}$$

and

$$A \cup B = \{2 \text{ of hearts}, 3 \text{ of hearts}, \ldots, \text{ace of hearts}, \text{ace of diamonds}, \text{ace of clubs}, \text{ace of spades}\}$$

(Let C be the event "Club is drawn." Which cards are in $B \cup C$? In $B \cap C$?)

EXAMPLE 2.2.7

Let A be the set of x's for which $x^2 + 2x = 8$; let B be the set for which $x^2 + x = 6$. Find $A \cap B$ and $A \cup B$.

Since the first equation factors into $(x + 4)(x - 2) = 0$, its solution set is $A = \{-4, 2\}$. Similarly, the second equation can be written $(x + 3)(x - 2) = 0$, making $B = \{-3, 2\}$. Therefore,

$$A \cap B = \{2\}$$

and

$$A \cup B = \{-4, -3, 2\}$$

EXAMPLE 2.2.8

Consider the electrical circuit pictured in Figure 2.2.2. Let A_i denote the event that switch i fails to close, $i = 1, 2, 3, 4$. Let A be the event "Circuit is not completed." Express A in terms of the A_i's.

FIGURE 2.2.2

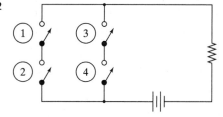

Call the ① and ② switches, line a; call the ③ and ④ switches, line b. By inspection, the circuit fails only if *both* line a and line b fail. But line a fails only if *either* ① *or* ② (or both) fail. That is, the event that line a fails is the union $A_1 \cup A_2$. Similarly, the failure of line b is the union $A_3 \cup A_4$. The event that the circuit fails, then, is an intersection:

$$A = (A_1 \cup A_2) \cap (A_3 \cup A_4)$$

DEFINITION 2.2.2.   Events A and B defined over the same sample space are said to be *mutually exclusive* if they have no outcomes in common—that is, if $A \cap B = \varnothing$, where $\varnothing$ is the null set.

EXAMPLE 2.2.9

Consider a single throw of two dice. Define A to be the event that the *sum* of the faces showing is odd. Let B be the event that the two faces themselves are odd. Then clearly the intersection is empty, the sum of two odd numbers necessarily being even. In symbols, $A \cap B = \varnothing$. (Recall the event $B \cap C$ asked for in Example 2.2.6.)

DEFINITION 2.2.3.   Let A be any event defined on a sample space S. The *complement* of A, written A^C, is the event consisting of all the outcomes in S other than those contained in A.

EXAMPLE 2.2.10

Let A be the set of (x, y)'s for which $x^2 + y^2 < 1$. Sketch the region in the xy-plane corresponding to A^C.

From analytic geometry, we recognize that $x^2 + y^2 < 1$ describes the interior of a circle of radius 1 centered at the origin. Figure 2.2.3 shows the obvious complement.

FIGURE 2.2.3

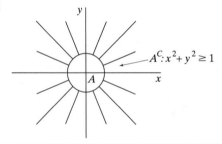

QUESTIONS

2.2.9 Sketch the regions in the xy-plane corresponding to $A \cup B$ and $A \cap B$ if

$$A = \{(x, y): 0 < x < 3, 0 < y < 3\}$$

and

$$B = \{(x, y): 2 < x < 4, 2 < y < 4\}$$

2.2.10 Referring to Example 2.2.7, find $A \cap B$ and $A \cup B$ if the two equations were replaced by inequalities: $x^2 + 2x \leq 8$ and $x^2 + x \leq 6$.

2.2.11 Find $A \cap B \cap C$ if $A = \{x: 0 \leq x \leq 4\}, B = \{x: 2 \leq x \leq 6\}$, and $C = \{x: x = 0, 1, 2, \ldots\}$.

2.2.12 An electronic system has four components divided into two pairs. The two components of each pair are wired in parallel; the two pairs are wired in series. Let A_{ij}, denote the event "ith component in jth pair fails," $i = 1, 2; j = 1, 2$. Let A be the event "System fails." Write A in terms of the A_{ij}'s.

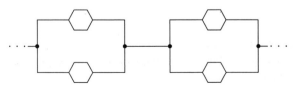

2.2.13 Let $A_i = \{x: 0 \le x < 1/i\}, i = 1, 2, \ldots, k$. Describe the sets

(a) $\displaystyle\bigcup_{i=1}^{k} A_i$

(b) $\displaystyle\bigcap_{i=1}^{k} A_i$

Note: The symbols $\displaystyle\bigcup_{i=1}^{k} A_i$ and $\displaystyle\bigcap_{i=1}^{k} A_i$ are shorthand for $A_1 \cup A_2 \cup \cdots \cup A_k$ and $A_1 \cap A_2 \cap \cdots \cap A_k$, respectively.

2.2.14 Define $A = \{x: 0 \le x \le 1\}, B = \{x: 0 \le x \le 3\}$ and $C = \{x: -1 \le x \le 2\}$. Draw diagrams showing each of the following sets of points:

(a) $A^C \cap B \cap C$

(b) $A^C \cup (B \cap C)$

(c) $A \cap B \cap C^C$

(d) $((A \cup B) \cap C^C)^C$

2.2.15 In poker, a five-card hand is called a *straight* if its denominations are consecutive—for example, a 4 of hearts, 5 of spades, 6 of spades, 7 of hearts, and 8 of clubs. A hand is called a *flush* if all five cards are in the same suit. If A denotes the set of straights and B, the set of flushes, how many outcomes are in the intersection $A \cap B$? (*Hint:* Picture the deck of 52 cards as a 4×13 matrix where the rows correspond to the four suits and the columns represent the 13 denominations.) *Note:* Aces can count "high" or "low"—that is, ace, 2, 3, 4, 5 qualifies as a straight, as does 10, jack, queen, king, ace.

Expressing Events Graphically: Venn Diagrams

Relationships based on two or more events can sometimes be difficult to express using only equations or verbal descriptions. An alternative approach that can be highly effective is to represent the underlying events graphically in a format known as a *Venn diagram*. Figure 2.2.4 shows Venn diagrams for an intersection, a union, a complement, and for two events that are mutually exclusive. In each case, the shaded interior of a region corresponds to the desired event.

FIGURE 2.2.4   Venn diagrams

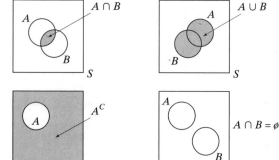

EXAMPLE 2.2.11

When two events A and B are defined on a sample space, we will frequently need to consider either

(a) the event that *exactly one* (of the two) occurs

or

(b) the event that at *most one* (of the two) occurs

Getting expressions for each of these is easy if we visualize the corresponding Venn diagrams.

The shaded area in Figure 2.2.5 represents the event E that either A or B, but not both, occurs (that is, exactly one occurs).

FIGURE 2.2.5

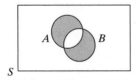

Just by looking at the diagram we can formulate an expression for E. The portion of A, for example, included in E is $A \cap B^C$. Similarly, the portion of B included in E is $B \cap A^C$. It follows, also by inspection, that E can be written as a union:

$$E = (A \cap B^C) \cup (B \cap A^C)$$

[Convince yourself that an equivalent expression for E is $(A \cap B)^C \cap (A \cup B)$.]

Figure 2.2.6 shows the event F that at *most one* (of the two events) occurs. Here a formal expression is obvious:

$$F = (A \cap B)^C$$

FIGURE 2.2.6

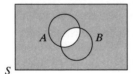

EXAMPLE 2.2.12

When Swampwater Tech's Class of '55 held its Fortieth Reunion, 100 graduates attended. Fifteen of those alumni were lawyers and rumor had it that 30 of the 100 were psychopaths. If 10 alumni were both lawyers and psychopaths, how many suffered from neither of those afflictions?

Let L be the set of lawyers and H, the set of psychopaths. If the symbol $N(Q)$ is defined to be the number of members in set Q, then

$$N(S) = 100$$
$$N(L) = 15$$
$$N(H) = 30$$
$$N(L \cap H) = 10$$

Summarizing all this information is the Venn diagram in Figure 2.2.7. Notice that

FIGURE 2.2.7

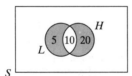

$$N(L \cup H) = \text{number of alumni suffering from at least one affliction}$$

$$= 5 + 10 + 20$$

$$= 35$$

which implies that $100 - 35$, or 65 were neither lawyers nor psychopaths. In effect,

$$N(L \cup H) = N(L) + N(H) - N(L \cap H)$$

QUESTIONS

2.2.16 During orientation week, the latest Batman movie was shown twice at State University. Among the entering class of 6000 freshmen, 850 went to see it the first time, 690 the second time, while 4700 failed to see it either time. How many saw it twice?

2.2.17 Let A and B be any two events. Use Venn diagrams to show that
  (a) the complement of their intersection is the union of their complements:

$$(A \cap B)^C = A^C \cup B^C$$

  (b) the complement of their union is the intersection of their complements:

$$(A \cup B)^C = A^C \cap B^C$$

(These two results are known as *DeMorgan's laws*.)

2.2.18 Let A, B, and C be any three events. Use Venn diagrams to show that
  (a) $A \cap (B \cup C) = (A \cap B) \cup (A \cap C)$ **(b)** $A \cup (B \cap C) = (A \cup B) \cap (A \cup C)$

2.2.19 Verify the associative laws for unions and intersections:
  (a) $A \cup (B \cup C) = (A \cup B) \cup C$ **(b)** $A \cap (B \cap C) = (A \cap B) \cap C$

2.2.20 Use a Venn diagram to suggest a formula for $N(A \cup B \cup C)$, the number of outcomes in the union of three events.

2.3   THE PROBABILITY FUNCTION

Having introduced in Section 2.2 the twin concepts of experiment and sample space, we are now ready to pursue in a formal way the all-important problem of assigning a "probability" to an experiment's outcome—and, more generally, to an event. The backdrop for our discussion will be the unions, intersections, and complements of set theory.

Over the years, the mathematical definition of probability has undergone a considerable metamorphosis, but the most recent formulations have not invalidated their predecessors. As a consequence, there are, today, four very different ways of defining what is to be meant by the probability of an event.

Classical Probability

Historically, the first definition evolved quite naturally out of the gambling context in which so many of the early problems studied by Pascal, Fermat, and others were posed. Imagine an experiment, or game, having n possible outcomes—*and suppose that those outcomes are all equally likely*. If some event A were satisfied by m of those n, it reasonably follows that the "probability of A" [written $P(A)$] should be set equal to m/n. This is called the *classical*, or *a priori*, definition of probability. Recall Example 2.2.2. If two fair dice are tossed, there are $n = 36$ possible outcomes (all equally likely); of those 36, a total of $m = 6$ satisfy the event A: Sum of the faces showing is a 7, so we would write $P(A) = \frac{6}{36}$, or $\frac{1}{6}$.

There are many situations where the classical definition of probability is entirely appropriate. We will see quite a few later in this chapter. Still, it has obvious limitations. What if the outcomes of the experiment are not equally likely? Or the number of outcomes is not finite? Questions such as these provided the impetus for the formation of a more general and more experimentally oriented definition of probability. The first formal statement of what became known as the *empirical*, or *a posteriori*, definition of probability is often credited to the twentieth-century German mathematician Richard von Mises, but the basic notion was implicit in the work of many other probabilists at least a century earlier.

Empirical Probability

Consider a sample space, S, and any event, A, defined on S. If our experiment were performed *one* time, either A or A^C would be the outcome. If it were performed n times, the resulting set of sample outcomes would be members of A on m occasions, m being some integer between 0 and n, inclusive. Hypothetically, we could continue this process an infinite number of times. As n gets large, the ratio m/n will fluctuate less and less. The number that m/n converges to is called the *empirical probability* of A; that is, $P(A) = \lim_{n \to \infty} m/n$ (see Figure 2.3.1).

While the von Mises approach does shore up some of the inadequacies seen in the classical definition of probability, it is not without shortcomings of its own. The limit it focuses on is not the usual one in standard analysis. For example, if a fair coin were to be tossed repeatedly with A being the event "Head appears," it seems reasonable to expect that $P(A) = \lim_{n \to \infty} m/n$ would equal $\frac{1}{2}$. The possibility exists, though, for the coin to come up tails every time, in which case $m/n = 0$, for all n. Also, there is a bit of an inconsistency in extolling $\lim_{n \to \infty} m/n$ as a way of defining a probability

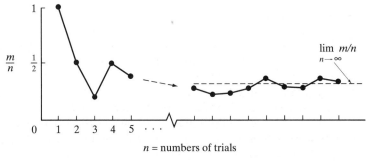

n = numbers of trials

FIGURE 2.3.1

experimentally when the very act of repeating an experiment under identical conditions an infinite number of times is physically impossible. And left unanswered is the question of how large n must be to give a good approximation for $\lim_{n \to \infty} m/n$.

Axiomatic Probability

The next attempt at defining probability was entirely a product of the twentieth century. Modern mathematicians have shown a keen interest in developing subjects axiomatically. It was to be expected, then, that probability would come under such scrutiny and be defined not as a ratio or as the limit of a ratio but simply as a function that behaved in accordance with a prescribed set of axioms. The major breakthrough on this front came in 1933 when Andrei Kolmogorov published *Grundbegriffe der Wahrscheinlichkeitsrechnung (Foundations of the Theory of Probability)*. Kolmogorov's work was a masterpiece of mathematical elegance—it reduced the behavior of the probability function to a set of just three or four simple postulates, three if the sample space is limited to a finite number of outcomes and four if S is infinite.

If S has a finite number of members, Kolmogorov showed that as few as three axioms are necessary and sufficient for characterizing the probability function P:

Axiom 1 Let A be any event defined over S. Then $P(A) \geq 0$.
Axiom 2 $P(S) = 1$.
Axiom 3 Let A and B be any two mutually exclusive events defined over S. Then

$$P(A \cup B) = P(A) + P(B)$$

When S has an infinite number of members, a fourth axiom is needed:

Axiom 4 Let $A_1, A_2, \ldots$, be events defined over S. If $A_i \cap A_j = \varnothing$ for each $i \neq j$, then

$$P\left(\bigcup_{i=1}^{\infty} A_i\right) = \sum_{i=1}^{\infty} P(A_i)$$

From these simple statements, all the other properties of the probability function can be derived.

Subjective Probability

Even more recent than the construction of an axiom system have been the efforts to define P in *subjective* terms, as a person's measure of belief that some given event will occur. For example, suppose that we ask "What is the probability that nuclear war will break out in the Mideast sometime in the next five years?" It is impossible to cast such a question meaningfully in a strictly empirical framework. Any number that we might come up with would necessarily be our own personal (subjective) assessment of the situation, based on the various countries' past histories, extrapolations of their current policies, and so on.

Some Basic Properties of *P*

Regardless of which definition is invoked, the basic properties of the probability function remain the same. In the next set of theorems are six results that we will find particularly useful.

THEOREM 2.3.1. $P(A^C) = 1 - P(A)$.

Proof.   By Axiom 2 and Definition 2.2.3,

$$P(S) = 1 = P(A \cup A^C)$$

But A and A^C are mutually exclusive, so

$$P(A \cup A^C) = P(A) + P(A^C)$$

and the result follows.

THEOREM 2.3.2. $P(\varnothing) = 0$.

Proof.   Since $\varnothing = S^C$, $P(\varnothing) = P(S^C) = 1 - P(S) = 0$.

THEOREM 2.3.3.   If $A \subset B$, then $P(A) \leq P(B)$.

Proof.   Note that the event B may be written in the form

$$B = A \cup (B \cap A^C)$$

where A and $(B \cap A^C)$ are mutually exclusive. Therefore,

$$P(B) = P(A) + P(B \cap A^C)$$

which implies that $P(B) \geq P(A)$ since $P(B \cap A^C) \geq 0$.

THEOREM 2.3.4.   For any event A, $P(A) \leq 1$.

Proof.   The proof follows immediately from Theorem 2.3.3 because $A \subset S$ and $P(S) = 1$.

THEOREM 2.3.5.   Let $A_1, A_2, \ldots, A_n$ be events defined over S. If $A_i \cap A_j = \varnothing$ for $i \neq j$, then

$$P\left(\bigcup_{i=1}^{n} A_i\right) = \sum_{i=1}^{n} P(A_i)$$

Proof.   The proof is a straightforward induction argument with Axiom 3 being the starting point.

THEOREM 2.3.6. $P(A \cup B) = P(A) + P(B) - P(A \cap B)$.

Proof.   The Venn diagram for $A \cup B$ certainly suggests that the statement of the theorem is true (recall Figure 2.2.4). More formally, we have from Axiom 3 that

$$P(A) = P(A \cap B^C) + P(A \cap B)$$

and

$$P(B) = P(B \cap A^C) + P(A \cap B)$$

Adding these two equations gives

$$P(A) + P(B) = \left[P(A \cap B^C) + P(B \cap A^C) + P(A \cap B)\right] + P(A \cap B)$$

By Theorem 2.3.5, the sum in the brackets is $P(A \cup B)$. If we subtract $P(A \cap B)$ from both sides of the equation, the result follows.

EXAMPLE 2.3.1

Let A and B be two events defined on a sample space S such that $P(A) = 0.3$, $P(B) = 0.5$, and $P(A \cup B) = 0.7$. Find (a) $P(A \cap B)$, (b) $P(A^C \cup B^C)$, and (c) $P(A^C \cap B)$.

(a) Transposing the terms in Theorem 2.3.6 yields a general formula for the probability of an intersection:

$$P(A \cap B) = P(A) + P(B) - P(A \cup B)$$

Here

$$P(A \cap B) = 0.3 + 0.5 - 0.7$$

$$= 0.1$$

(b) The two cross-hatched regions in Figure 2.3.2 correspond to A^C and B^C. The union of A^C and B^C consists of those regions that have cross-hatching in either or both directions. By inspection, the only portion of S *not* included in $A^C \cup B^C$ is the intersection, $A \cap B$. By Theorem 2.3.1, then,

$$P(A^C \cup B^C) = 1 - P(A \cap B)$$

$$= 1 - 0.1$$

$$= 0.9$$

(c) By definition, the event $A^C \cap B$ corresponds to the region in Figure 2.3.3 where the cross-hatching extends in *both* directions—that is, everywhere in B except the intersection with A. Therefore,

$$P(A^C \cap B) = P(B) - P(A \cap B)$$

$$= 0.5 - 0.1$$

$$= 0.4$$

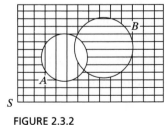

FIGURE 2.3.2

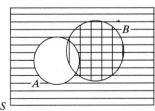

FIGURE 2.3.3

EXAMPLE 2.3.2

Show that

$$P(A \cap B) \geq 1 - P(A^C) - P(B^C)$$

for any two events A and B defined on a sample space S.

From Example 2.3.1a and Theorem 2.3.1,

$$P(A \cap B) = P(A) + P(B) - P(A \cup B)$$

$$= 1 - P(A^C) + 1 - P(B^C) - P(A \cup B)$$

But $P(A \cup B) \leq 1$ from Theorem 2.3.4, so

$$P(A \cap B) \geq 1 - P(A^C) - P(B^C)$$

EXAMPLE 2.3.3

Two cards are drawn from a poker deck without replacement. What is the probability that the second is higher in rank than the first?

Let A_1, A_2, and A_3 be the events "First card is lower in rank," "First card is higher in rank," and "Both cards have same rank," respectively. Clearly, the three A_i's are mutually exclusive and they account for all possible outcomes, so from Theorem 2.3.5,

$$P(A_1 \cup A_2 \cup A_3) = P(A_1) + P(A_2) + P(A_3) = P(S) = 1$$

Once the first card is drawn, there are three choices for the second that would have the same rank—that is, $P(A_3) = 3/51$. Symmetry, of course, demands that $P(A_1) = P(A_2)$. Therefore,

$$2P(A_2) + \frac{3}{51} = 1$$

implying that $P(A_2) = \frac{8}{17}$.

EXAMPLE 2.3.4

In a newly released martial arts film, the actress playing the lead role has a stunt double who handles all of the physically dangerous action scenes. According to the script, the actress appears in 40% of the film's scenes, her double appears in 30%, and the two of them are together 5% of the time. What is the probability that in a given scene (a) only the stunt double appears and (b) neither the lead actress nor the double appears?

(a) If L is the event "Lead actress appears in scene" and D is the event "Double appears in scene," we are given that $P(L) = 0.40$, $P(D) = 0.30$, and $P(L \cap D) = 0.05$. It follows that

$$P(\text{Only double appears}) = P(D) - P(L \cap D)$$

$$= 0.30 - 0.05$$

$$= 0.25$$

(recall Example 2.3.1c).

(b) The event "Neither appears" is the complement of the event "At least one appears." But $P(\text{At least one appears}) = P(L \cup D)$. From Theorems 2.3.1 and 2.3.6, then,

$$P(\text{Neither appears}) = 1 - P(L \cup D)$$
$$= 1 - \left[P(L) + P(D) - P(L \cap D)\right]$$
$$= 1 - [0.40 + 0.30 - 0.05]$$
$$= 0.35$$

EXAMPLE 2.3.5

Having endured (and survived) the mental trauma that comes from taking two years of chemistry, a year of physics, and a year of biology, Biff decides to test the medical school waters and sends his MCATs to two colleges, X and Y. Based on how his friends have fared, he estimates that his probability of being accepted at X is 0.7, and at Y is 0.4. He also suspects there is a 75% chance that at least one of his applications will be rejected. What is the probability that he gets at least one acceptance?

Let A be the event "School X accepts him" and B, the event "school Y accepts him." We are given that $P(A) = 0.7$, $P(B) = 0.4$, and $P(A^C \cup B^C) = 0.75$. What we are looking for is $P(A \cup B)$.

From Theorem 2.3.6,

$$P(A \cup B) = P(A) + P(B) - P(A \cap B)$$

Recall from Question 2.2.17 that $A^C \cup B^C = (A \cap B)^C$, so

$$P(A \cap B) = 1 - P\left[(A \cap B)^C\right] = 1 - 0.75 = 0.25$$

It follows that Biff's prospects are not all that bleak—he has an 85% chance of getting in somewhere:

$$P(A \cup B) = 0.7 + 0.4 - 0.25$$
$$= 0.85$$

Comment.   Notice that $P(A \cup B)$ varies directly with $P(A^C \cup B^C)$:

$$P(A \cup B) = P(A) + P(B) - \left(1 - P(A^C \cup B^C)\right)$$
$$= P(A) + P(B) - 1 + P(A^C \cup B^C)$$

If $P(A)$ and $P(B)$, then, are fixed, we get the curious result that Biff's chances of getting at least one acceptance increase if his chances of at least one rejection increase.

QUESTIONS

2.3.1 According to a family-oriented lobbying group, there is too much crude language and violence on television. Forty-two percent of the programs they screened had language they found offensive, 27% were too violent, and 10% were considered excessive in both language and violence. What percentage of programs did comply with the group's standards?

2.3.2 Let A and B be any two events defined on S. Suppose that $P(A) = 0.4$, $P(B) = 0.5$, and $P(A \cap B) = 0.1$. What is the probability that A or B but not both occur?

2.3.3 Express the following probabilities in terms of $P(A), P(B)$, and $P(A \cap B)$.
   (a) $P(A^C \cup B^C)$ **(b)** $P(A^C \cap (A \cup B))$

2.3.4 Let A and B be two events defined on S. If the probability that at least one of them occurs is 0.3 and the probability that A occurs but B does not occur is 0.1, what is $P(B)$?

2.3.5 Suppose that three fair dice are tossed. Let A_i be the event that a 6 shows on the ith die, $i = 1, 2, 3$. Does $P(A_1 \cup A_2 \cup A_3) = \frac{1}{2}$? Explain.

2.3.6 Events A and B are defined on a sample space S such that $P((A \cup B)^C) = 0.6$ and $P(A \cap B) = 0.2$. What is the probability that either A or B but not both will occur?

2.3.7 Let $A_1, A_2, \ldots, A_n$ be a series of events for which $A_i \cap A_j = \varnothing$ if $i \neq j$ and $A_1 \cup A_2 \cup \cdots \cup A_n = S$. Let B be any event defined on S. Express B as a union of intersections.

2.3.8 Draw the Venn diagrams that would correspond to the equations (a) $P(A \cap B) = P(B)$ and (b) $P(A \cup B) = P(B)$.

2.3.9 In the game of "odd man out" each player tosses a fair coin. If all the coins turn up the same except for one, the player tossing the different coin is declared the odd man out and is eliminated from the contest. Suppose that three people are playing. What is the probability that someone will be eliminated on the first toss? (*Hint:* Use Theorem 2.3.1.)

2.3.10 An urn contains 24 chips, numbered 1 through 24. One is drawn at random. Let A be the event that the number is divisible by 2 and let B be the event that the number is divisible by 3. Find $P(A \cup B)$.

2.3.11 If State's football team has a 10% chance of winning Saturday's game, a 30% chance of winning two weeks from now, and a 65% chance of losing both games, what are their chances of winning exactly once?

2.3.12 Events A_1 and A_2 are such that $A_1 \cup A_2 = S$ and $A_1 \cap A_2 = \varnothing$. Find p_2 if $P(A_1) = p_1$, $P(A_2) = p_2$, and $3p_1 - p_2 = \frac{1}{2}$.

2.3.13 Consolidated Industries has come under considerable pressure to eliminate its seemingly discriminatory hiring practices. Company officials have agreed that during the next five years, 60% of their new employees will be females and 30% will be minorities. One out of four new employees, though, will be white males. What percentage of their new hires will be minority females?

2.4 DISCRETE PROBABILITY FUNCTIONS

The six theorems proved in Section 2.3 address the problem of "manipulating" probabilities: If $P(A)$ is given, then $P(A^C) = 1 - P(A)$; for any two events A and B, $P(A \cup B) = P(A) + P(B) - P(A \cap B)$; and so on. Before we can put those results to much practical use, though, we need to become more familiar with the probability function itself.

There are two general types of probability functions, *discrete* and *continuous*, the distinction reflecting the nature of the sample space. Some experiments generate sample spaces containing either a finite or a countably infinite number of outcomes (recall Examples 2.2.1 through 2.2.4). Any probability function defined on such a sample space is said to be *discrete*. Any probability function defined on a sample space having an uncountably infinite number of outcomes (recall Example 2.2.5) is said to be *continuous*.

More is at issue here than just terminology: Discrete and continuous probability functions have fundamentally different interpretations and they are treated mathematically in very different ways. In point of fact, the distinction between the two underscores much of what we do from this point on.

Suppose that the sample space for a given experiment is either finite or countably infinite.[1] Then any P such that

(a) $0 \leq P(s)$ for each $s \in S$

(b) $\sum\limits_{\text{all } s \in S} P(s) = 1$

is said to be a *discrete probability function*. An immediate consequence of (a) and (b) is that the probability of any event A is the sum of the probabilities associated with the outcomes in A:

$$P(A) = \sum\limits_{\text{all } s \in A} P(s)$$

EXAMPLE 2.4.1

Suppose an experiment has only two possible outcomes, s_1 and s_2, where $P(s_1) = p$ and $P(s_2) = p^2$. What is p?
    By property (b),

$$p + p^2 = 1$$

since s_1 and s_2 comprise the entire sample space S. Solving the quadratic equation $p^2 + p - 1 = 0$ gives

$$p = \frac{-1 \pm \sqrt{1 + 4}}{2}$$

as solutions. But $p = (-1 - \sqrt{5})/2$ is inadmissible because of property (a). Therefore,

$$p = \frac{-1 + \sqrt{5}}{2}$$

EXAMPLE 2.4.2

A die is loaded in such a way that the probability associated with a given face is directly proportional to the number on that face. What is the probability of the event A, that an even number appears?
    To answer this question we make use of the fact that the sum of $P(s)$ over S necessarily equals 1. The experiment—tossing a die—generates a sample space containing six outcomes. But the six are not equally likely: by assumption,

$$P(\text{“}i\text{” face appears}) = P(i) = ki, \quad i = 1, 2, \ldots, 6$$

where k is a constant. From property (b),

$$\sum\limits_{\text{all } s \in S} P(s) = \sum\limits_{i=1}^{6} P(i) = \sum\limits_{i=1}^{6} ki = \frac{6(6 + 1)}{2} \cdot k = 21k = 1$$

---

[1] A set of outcomes is *countably infinite* if it can be put into a one-to-one correspondence with the positive integers.

which implies that $k = 1/21$ [and $P(i) = i/21$]. It follows, then, that the probability of A is $12/21$:

$$P(A) = P(\text{even number}) = \sum_{\text{all } s \in A} P(s) = P(2) + P(4) + P(6)$$

$$= \frac{2}{21} + \frac{4}{21} + \frac{6}{21}$$

$$= \frac{12}{21}$$

EXAMPLE 2.4.3

A fair coin is to be tossed until a head comes up for the first time. What are the chances of that happening on an odd-numbered toss?

Note that the sample space here is countably infinite—and so is the set of outcomes making up the event whose probability we are trying to find. Nevertheless, our approach is basically no different from the steps we followed in Example 2.4.2, except that the analysis requires the evaluation of sums whose indices go from 1 to infinity.

Suppose we let $P(k)$ denote the probability that the first head appears on the kth toss. Since the coin was presumed to be fair, $P(1) = \frac{1}{2}$. Furthermore, we would expect half the coins that showed a tail on the first toss to come up heads on the second, so, intuitively, $P(2) = \frac{1}{4}$. In general, $P(k) = \left(\frac{1}{2}\right)^k$, $k = 1, 2, \ldots$.

Let A be the event "First head appears on an odd-numbered toss." Then

$$P(A) = P(1) + P(3) + P(5) + \cdots$$

$$= \sum_{i=0}^{\infty} \left(\frac{1}{2}\right)^{2i+1}$$

$$= \frac{1}{2} \sum_{i=0}^{\infty} \left(\frac{1}{4}\right)^{i}$$

Recall the formula for the sum of a geometric series: If $0 < x < 1$,

$$\sum_{k=0}^{\infty} x^k = \frac{1}{1-x}$$

Applying that result here shows that $P(A) = \frac{2}{3}$:

$$P(A) = \frac{1}{2} \cdot \left(\frac{1}{1 - 1/4}\right)$$

$$= \frac{2}{3}$$

CASE STUDY 2.4.1

For good pedagogical reasons, the principles of probability are always taught by considering events defined on sample spaces generated by the simplest possible experiments. We toss coins, we roll dice, we draw chips from urns. It would be a serious error, though, to infer that the importance of probability extends no further than the nearest gambling table. In its infancy, probability and gambling *were* intimately related. But more than 340 years have passed since Huygens published *De Ratiociniis*. Today, the application of probability to gambling is totally inconsequential compared to the uses it finds in other areas of mathematics, business, medicine, engineering, and science.

Specifically, probability functions—properly chosen—can "model" complex real-world phenomena in much that same way that $P(\text{heads}) = \frac{1}{2}$ describes the behavior of a fair coin. A set of actuarial data provides us with a case in point. Over a period of 3 years (= 1096 days) in London, records showed that a total of 903 deaths occurred among males 85 years of age and older (168). Columns 1 and 2 of Table 2.4.1 give the breakdown of those 903 deaths according to the number occurring on a given day. Column 3 gives the *proportion* of days for which exactly s elderly men died.

TABLE 2.4.1

(1) Number of deaths, s	(2) Number of days	(3) Proportion [= Col.(2)/1096]	(4) $P(s)$
0	484	0.442	0.440
1	391	0.357	0.361
2	164	0.150	0.148
3	45	0.041	0.040
4	11	0.010	0.008
5	1	0.001	0.003
6+	0	0.000	0.000
	1096	1	1

For reasons that will be gone into at length in Chapter 4, the probability function that describes the behavior of this particular phenomenon is

$$P(s) = P(s \text{ elderly men die on a given day})$$

$$= \frac{e^{-0.82}(0.82)^s}{s!}, \qquad s = 0, 1, 2, \ldots \tag{2.4.1}$$

How do we know that the $P(s)$ in Equation 2.4.1 is an appropriate way to assign probabilities to the "experiment" of elderly men dying? Because it accurately predicts what happened. Column 4 of Table 2.4.1 shows $P(s)$ evaluated for $s = 0, 1, 2, \ldots$. To two decimal places, the agreement between entries in column 3 and entries in column 4 is perfect.

Choosing the probability function best suited to a given phenomenon is one of the most common—and most difficult—tasks faced by a statistician. In gambling situations, the selection of $P(s)$ is usually obvious, as has been the case in the examples seen thus far. In more elaborate contexts, such as the data described in Table 2.4.1, identifying $P(s)$ becomes increasingly difficult. Still, if we know where to look there are clues that can help us make the right choice. How to find probability functions and apply them appropriately are recurring themes in Chapters 3, 4, and 5.

CASE STUDY 2.4.2

Consider the following experiment: Every day for the next month you copy down each number that appears in the stories on the front pages of your hometown newspaper. Those numbers would necessarily be extremely diverse: One might be the age of a celebrity who just died, another might report the interest rate currently paid on government Treasury bills, and still another might give the number of square feet of retail space recently added to a local shopping mall.

Suppose you then calculated the proportion of those numbers whose leading digit was a 1, the proportion whose leading digit was a 2, and so on. What relationship would you expect those proportions to have? Would numbers starting with a 2, for example, occur as often as numbers starting with a 6?

Let $P(s)$ denote the probability that the first digit of a newspaper "random" number is s, $s = 1, 2, \ldots, 9$. Our intuition would tell us that each first digit should be equally likely—that is, $P(1) = P(2) = \ldots = P(9)$. Given the diversity of the nature of the numbers, there is no obvious reason why one digit should be more common than another. Our intuition, though, would be wrong—first digits are *not* equally likely!

Credit for making this rather remarkable discovery goes to Simon Newcomb, a mathematician who observed more than a hundred years ago that some portions of log tables are used more than others (71). Specifically, pages at the beginning of a table are invariably more dog-eared than pages at the end of a table, suggesting that users had more occasions to look up logs of numbers starting with small digits than they did numbers starting with large digits.

Almost 50 years later, a physicist, Frank Benford, reexamined Newcomb's claim in more detail and looked for a mathematical explanation. What is now known as *Benford's law* asserts that the first digits of many different types of measurements, or combinations of measurements, often follow the discrete probability model:

$$P(s) = P(\text{1st significant digit is } s) = \log\left(1 + \frac{1}{s}\right), s = 1, 2, \ldots, 9$$

Table 2.4.2 compares Benford's law to the uniform assumption that $P(s) = 1/9$, for all s. The differences are striking. According to Benford's law, for example, 1's are the most frequently occurring first digit, appearing 6.5 times (= 0.301/0.046) as often as 9's.

TABLE 2.4.2

s	"Uniform" Law	Benford's Law
1	0.111	0.301
2	0.111	0.176
3	0.111	0.125
4	0.111	0.097
5	0.111	0.079
6	0.111	0.067
7	0.111	0.058
8	0.111	0.051
9	0.111	0.046

Comment. A key to *why* Benford's law is true are the differences in proportional changes associated with each leading digit. To go from 1000 to 2000, for example, represents a 100% increase; to go from 8000 to 9000, on the other hand, is only a 12.5% increase. That would suggest that evolutionary phenomena such as stock prices would be more likely to start with 1's and 2's than with 8's and 9's—and they are. Still, the precise conditions under which

$$P(s) = \log\left(1 + \frac{1}{s}\right), \quad s = 1, 2, \ldots, 9$$ are not fully understood and remain a topic of research.

QUESTIONS

2.4.1 Ace–six flats are a type of crooked dice where the cube is foreshortened in the one–six direction, the effect being that 1's and 6's are more likely than 2's, 3's, 4's, and 5's. Let $P(i) = P(\text{"}i\text{"}$ face appears). Suppose that $P(1) = P(6) = \frac{1}{4}$ and $P(2) = P(3) = P(4) = P(5) = \frac{1}{8}$. If two such dice are rolled, what is the probability the sum of the faces will equal 7? [Assume that the probability of rolling an i on the first die and a j on the second is the *product* $P(i) \cdot P(j)$.] Compare your answer with the probability of rolling a 7 with two fair dice. How would a cheater playing craps use ace–six flats?

2.4.2 Three passengers (A, B, and C), each going to a different city, check their luggage at an airport terminal. The redcaps, feeling in a playful mood, shuffle the three destination tags and attach them to the bags at random (one to a bag). List the six outcomes in the sample space. What is the probability of the event A, that at least one set of luggage gets sent to the wrong city?

2.4.3 Recall Example 2.2.3. If the station management did not discriminate when filling the two positions, what is the probability that both coanchors would be women?

2.4.4 Show that

$$P(s) = \frac{1}{1 + \lambda}\left(\frac{\lambda}{1 + \lambda}\right)^s, \quad s = 0, 1, 2, \ldots; \quad \lambda > 0$$

qualifies as a discrete probability function.

2.4.5 An urn contains five chips, numbered 1 through 5. Three chips are drawn out at random. What is the probability the largest chip in the sample is a 4? Assume that the order in which the chips are drawn is irrelevant.

2.4.6 For any outcome in the sample space $S = \{s: s = 2, 3, 4, \ldots\}$, let $P(s) = k \cdot \left(\frac{2}{3}\right)^s$. Find the value of k that makes $P(s)$ a probability function.

2.4.7 Three fair dice are rolled, one red, one green, and one blue. What is the probability that the three faces are all different and that the blue die equals the sum of the red and the green?

2.4.8 Jean D'Alembert, a renowned eighteenth-century French mathematician, was once asked the following question: What is the probability of getting at least one head in two tosses of a fair coin? D'Alembert answered $\frac{2}{3}$, his argument being that there are three possible outcomes, H, TH, and TT, two of which—H and TH—satisfy the event "at least one head." Discuss his answer and his method of solution.

2.4.9 Suppose the outcomes in S are the positive integers and $P(s) = \frac{2}{3^s}$, $s = 1, 2, \ldots$. What is the probability that a number chosen at random from S will be even?

2.4.10 A loaded tetrahedral die has a probability equal to kj^3 of showing face j, where k is a constant and $j = 1, 2, 3, 4$. What proportion of the time will the face that comes up exceed 2?

2.5 CONTINUOUS PROBABILITY FUNCTIONS

Discrete probability functions, $P(s)$, concentrate all the probability associated with a sample space at either a finite or a countably infinite number of points. Tossing a fair die, for example, leads to a probability function that assigns positive values to just six points:

$$P(\text{face } i \text{ appears}) = \begin{cases} \frac{1}{6}, & i = 1, 2, 3, 4, 5, 6 \\ 0, & \text{elsewhere} \end{cases}$$

In contrast, *continuous probability functions* apply to situations where the number of outcomes in S is uncountably infinite, in which case the sample space probability is essentially "smeared" over the real line (or over some interval of the real line).

To emphasize the distinction between these two types of probability functions, we will use different notation in describing the continuous model. Outcomes will be denoted y (instead of s) and the probability function will be written $f(y)$ [instead of $P(s)$].

The properties listed on page 37 that define $P(s)$ carry over analogously for continuous probability functions. That is, if S is a sample space with an uncountable number of outcomes and if f is a real-valued function defined on S, then f is said to be a *continuous probability function* if

(a) $0 \leq f(y)$ for all $y \in S$

(b) $\displaystyle\int_S f(y)\,dy = 1$

Furthermore, if A is any event defined on S, it must be true that

$$P(A) = \int_A f(y)\,dy \tag{2.5.1}$$

(see Figure 2.5.1).

Equation 2.5.1 is the key to understanding the distinction between discrete and continuous probability functions. If f is a continuous probability function, $f(y)$ is *not* the probability that the outcome of the experiment is y. Rather, f is that particular function having the property that, for any event A, $P(A)$ is the integral of f over A. Indeed, it follows from Equation 2.5.1 that the probability of any single point, say y', is necessarily 0, even though $f(y')$ may very well be positive:

FIGURE 2.5.1

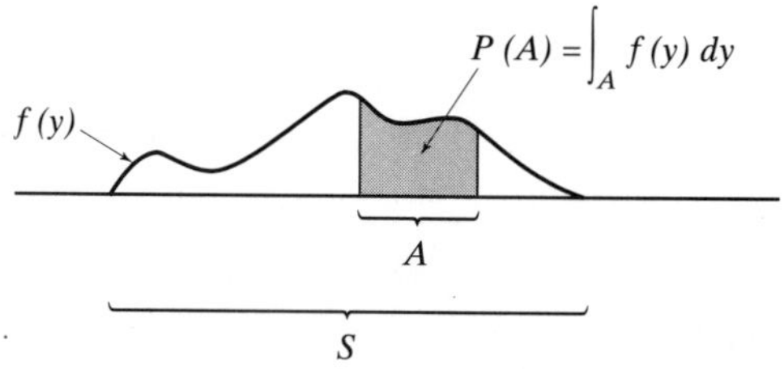

$$P(\text{outcome is } y') = P(A) = \int_A f(y)\,dy$$

$$= \int_{y'}^{y'} f(y)\,dy$$

$$= 0$$

EXAMPLE 2.5.1

The simplest f that can be defined over a (bounded) uncountably infinite sample space is the *uniform probability function*,

$$f(y) = \begin{cases} 1/(b-a), & \text{for } y \in [a,b] \\ 0, & \text{elsewhere} \end{cases}$$

(see Figure 2.5.2). Notice that $f(y)$ "qualifies" as a potential continuous probability function because it satisfies properties (a) and (b) on page 42:

(a)   Given that $b > a$, $f(y) \geq 0$ for all $-\infty < y < \infty$

(b) $\displaystyle \int_S f(y)\,dy = \int_a^b \frac{1}{b-a}\,dy = \frac{y}{b-a}\Big|_a^b = \frac{b}{b-a} - \frac{a}{b-a} = 1$

If $a = 0$ and $b = 1$,

$$f(y) = \begin{cases} 1, & \text{for } y \in [0,1] \\ 0, & \text{elsewhere} \end{cases}$$

and f is referred to as the *uniform distribution over the unit interval*.

The uniform probability model is important for two reasons. First, its simplicity makes it easy to work with mathematically. Theorems and definitions that may hold true for any continuous probability function $f(y)$ can sometimes best be illustrated by considering the uniform model as a special (and simple) case.

The second reason has to do with the familiar phrase "at random." To say that a number y has been chosen *at random* from the interval $[a, b]$ means that the probability function describing the sampling variability in y is the uniform model, $f(y) = 1/(b-a), a \leq y \leq b$. For example, suppose a computer is programmed to generate a sequence of, say, five random digits and it prints out the numbers 36620. The associated decimal, 0.36620, can be considered a value y representing the uniform distribution over the unit interval.

FIGURE 2.5.2

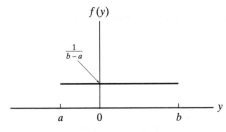

EXAMPLE 2.5.2

Associated with every continuous probability function is a *median*, which represents the halfway point in the accumulation of probability as we move along the real line from left to right ($-\infty$ to $+\infty$). By definition, the median of the probability function f is the value m for which $P(y \le m) = P(y \ge m) = \frac{1}{2}$. Find m if $f(y) = ky^2, 0 \le y \le 1$.

First, we need to calculate k so that $f(y)$ contains no unknown constants. By property (b) on page 42,

$$\int_0^1 ky^2\,dy = 1 = k \cdot \frac{y^3}{3}\bigg|_0^1 = \frac{k}{3}$$

which implies that $k = 3$. From the definition, then, for m,

$$P(y \le m) = \frac{1}{2} = \int_0^m 3y^2\,dy = \frac{3y^3}{3}\bigg|_0^m = m^3$$

so $m = \sqrt[3]{1/2} = 0.79$ (see Figure 2.5.3)

FIGURE 2.5.3 $f(y)$

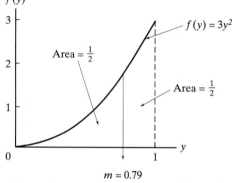

$m = 0.79$

EXAMPLE 2.5.3

In actuarial calculations, one of the simpler probability functions used for describing mortality in the general population is the quartic polynomial

$$f(y) = 3 \times 10^{-9} \cdot y^2(100 - y)^2, \qquad 0 \le y \le 100$$

where y denotes a person's age at death (in years). Based on that model, is it more likely that a person will (1) die between the ages of 50 and 60 or (2) live past 70?

Figure 2.5.4 shows the two areas under $f(y)$ that correspond to the probabilities of the events A: person dies between the ages of 50 and 60 and B: person lives past 70. Integrating $f(y)$ shows that $P(A)$ is slightly larger than $P(B)$:

$$P(A) = \int_{50}^{60} 3 \times 10^{-9} \cdot y^2(100 - y)^2\,dy$$

$$= 3 \times 10^{-9} \int_{50}^{60} (10000y^2 - 200y^3 + y^4)\,dy$$

$$= 3 \times 10^{-9} \left[\frac{10000y^3}{3} - \frac{200y^4}{4} + \frac{y^5}{5} \right]\bigg|_{50}^{60}$$

$$= 0.18$$

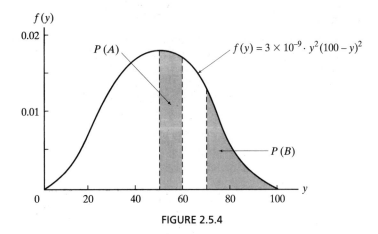

FIGURE 2.5.4

$$P(B) = \int_{70}^{100} 3 \times 10^{-9} \cdot y^2 (100 - y)^2 \, dy$$

$$= \int_{0}^{30} 3 \times 10^{-9} \cdot y^2 (100 - y)^2 \, dy \qquad \text{(by symmetry)}$$

$$= 3 \times 10^{-9} \left[\frac{10000 y^3}{3} - \frac{200 y^4}{4} + \frac{y^5}{5} \right]_{0}^{30}$$

$$= 0.16$$

EXAMPLE 2.5.4

A disgruntled Anchorage bush pilot, upset because his gasoline credit card was canceled, fires a single air-to-surface missile at the Alaskan pipeline. If the missile lands anywhere within 20 yards of the pipeline, major structural damage will be sustained and the flow of oil will be disrupted. Assume that the probability function reflecting the pilot's expertise as a bombardier is the expression

$$f(y) = \begin{cases} \dfrac{60 + y}{3600}, & -60 < y < 0 \\[2mm] \dfrac{60 - y}{3600}, & 0 \le y < 60 \\[2mm] 0, & \text{elsewhere} \end{cases}$$

where y denotes the perpendicular distance (in yards) from the pipeline to the point of impact. Does the pilot have at least a 60% chance of accomplishing his objective?

No. Let A be the event "Flow is disrupted." The probability of A is the area under $f(y)$ above the interval $(-20, +20)$. According to the integration, though, the chances are just 55 in 100 that the missile will land close enough to cause any serious damage:

FIGURE 2.5.5

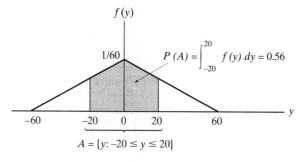

$$A = \{y: -20 \le y \le 20\}$$

$$P(A) = \int_{-20}^{20} f(y)\, dy = \int_{-20}^{0} \frac{60 + y}{3600}\, dy + \int_{0}^{20} \frac{60 - y}{3600}\, dy$$

$$= \left[\frac{60y}{3600} + \frac{y^2}{7200} \right]_{-20}^{0} + \left[\frac{60y}{3600} - \frac{y^2}{7200} \right]_{0}^{20}$$

$$= \frac{1200}{3600} - \frac{400}{7200} + \frac{1200}{3600} - \frac{400}{7200}$$

$$= 0.56$$

Figure 2.5.5 is a graph of $f(y)$ and shows the area representing $P(A)$.

EXAMPLE 2.5.5

For reasons we will learn in Chapter 4, the distance, y, that a molecule in a gas travels before colliding with another molecule is modeled probabilistically by the *exponential* function,

$$f(y) = \frac{1}{\mu} e^{-y/\mu}, \qquad y > 0$$

where μ is a positive constant known as the *mean free path* (i.e., the average distance traveled between collisions). For nitrogen (N_2) at room temperature and standard atmospheric pressure, $\mu = 0.00005$ cm. What is the probability that a nitrogen molecule, having just sustained a collision, travels at least 0.00010 cm before striking another molecule?

Figure 2.5.6 shows a graph of $f(y)$. The area under $f(y)$ to the right of 0.00010 is the probability in question:

FIGURE 2.5.6

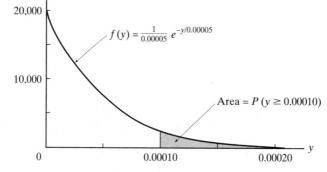

$$P(y \geq 0.00010) = \int_{0.00010}^{\infty} \frac{1}{0.00005} e^{-y/0.00005y} \, dy$$

$$= \int_{2}^{\infty} e^{-t} \, dt \quad (\text{where } t = y/0.00005)$$

$$= -e^{-t} \Big|_{2}^{\infty}$$

$$= e^{-2}$$

$$= 0.135$$

CASE STUDY 2.5.1

By far the most important of all continuous probability functions is the so-called bell-shaped curve, known more formally as the *normal* (or *Gaussian*) *distribution*. The sample space for the normal distribution is the entire real line; its probability function is given by

$$f(y) = \frac{1}{\sqrt{2\pi} \, \sigma} \exp\left[-\frac{1}{2}\left(\frac{y - \mu}{\sigma}\right)^2\right],$$

$$-\infty < y < \infty, \quad -\infty < \mu < \infty, \quad \sigma > 0$$

Depending on the values assigned to the parameters μ and σ, $f(y)$ can take on a variety of shapes and locations; three are illustrated in Figure 2.5.7.

The data in Table 2.5.1 are an example of a real-world phenomenon that can be modeled very nicely by a normal curve. Listed is a set of traffic fatality rates recently reported by each of our 50 states (102).

Grouping the data into classes ($2.0 \leq y < 3.0, 3.0 \leq y < 4.0, \ldots, 8.0 \leq y < 9.0$) and then representing the frequency of a class by the height of a bar yields the *histogram* pictured in Figure 2.5.8. If the vertical axis is changed from "frequency" to "density," where

$$\text{Density} = \frac{\text{Frequency}}{\text{Class width} \times \text{Total number of observations}}$$

the total area under the bars will necessarily equal 1 (why?), making it comparable in scale to a probability function. Figure 2.5.9 shows the particular normal curve having $\mu = 5.3$

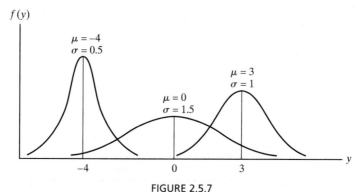

FIGURE 2.5.7

(continued on next page)

(Case Study 2.5.1 continued)

TABLE 2.5.1   Traffic Deaths per 100 Million MVM[1]

Ala.	6.4	La.	7.1	Ohio	4.5
Alaska	8.8	Maine	4.6	Okla.	5.0
Ariz.	6.2	Mass.	3.5	Oreg.	5.3
Ark.	5.6	Md.	3.9	Pa.	4.1
Calif	4.4	Mich.	4.2	R.I.	3.0
Colo.	5.3	Minn.	4.6	S.C.	6.5
Conn.	2.8	Miss.	5.6	S.Dak.	5.4
Del.	5.2	Mo.	5.6	Tenn.	7.1
Fla.	5.5	Mont.	7.0	Tex.	5.2
Ga.	6.1	N.C.	6.2	Utah	5.5
Hawaii	4.7	N.Dak.	4.8	Va.	4.5
Idaho	7.1	Nebr.	4.4	Vt.	4.7
Ill.	4.3	Nev.	8.0	W.Va.	6.2
Ind.	5.1	N.H.	4.6	Wash.	4.3
Iowa	5.9	N.J.	3.2	Wis.	4.7
Kans.	5.0	N.Mex.	8.0	Wyo.	6.5
Ky.	5.6	N.Y.	4.7		

[1] motor vehicle miles

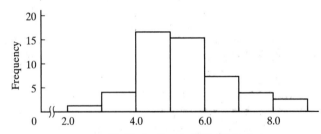

FIGURE 2.5.8

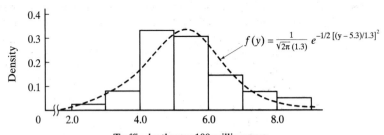

$$f(y) = \frac{1}{\sqrt{2\pi}\,(1.3)}\, e^{-1/2\,[(y-5.3)/1.3]^2}$$

FIGURE 2.5.9

and $\sigma = 1.3$ superimposed over the *density-scaled* histogram. Clearly, the normal curve is describing the state-to-state variability in traffic fatality rates very well. (We will have much more to say about this singularly important probability model—and how the values of μ and σ are estimated—in Chapter 7.)

QUESTIONS

2.5.1 What value for k allows the following $f(y)$ to qualify as a continuous probability function?

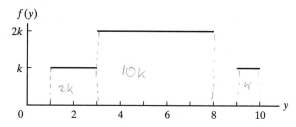

2.5.2 Suppose that the variability in a measurment y is modeled by the continuous probability function pictured below. What is the probability that y exceeds 4? Do not leave your answer as a function of c.

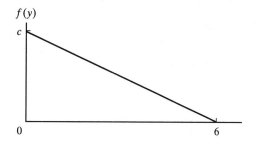

2.5.3 The length of a cotter pin that is part of a wheel assembly is supposed to be 6 cm. The machine that stamps out the parts, though, makes them $6 + y$ cm long, where y varies from pin to pin according to the probability function

$$f(y) = k(y + y^2), \qquad 0 \le y \le 2$$

where k is a constant. If a pin is longer than 7 cm, it is unusable. What proportion of cotter pins produced by this machine will be unusable?

2.5.4 A criminal court judge has heard many cases where the defendant was charged with grand theft auto and the jury returned a guilty verdict. But the final disposition was not always the same. Mitigating circumstances of various kinds led the judge over the years to impose unequal jail terms for what was basically the same offense. Looking back over court transcripts, he sees that y, the imposed sentence length (in years) has a distribution that can be described quite well by a continuous probability function having the form

$$f(y) = \frac{1}{9} y^2, \qquad 0 < y < 3$$

What proportion of those found guilty spent less than a year in jail?

2.5.5 A batch of small-caliber ammunition is accepted as satisfactory if one shell selected at random is fired and lands within 2 feet of the center of a target. Assume that for a given batch, the probability function describing y, the distance from the target center to a shell's point of impact, is

$$f(y) = \frac{2ye^{-y^2}}{1 - e^{-9}}, \qquad 0 \le y \le 3$$

Find the probability that the batch will be accepted.

2.5.6 Suppose a number y is to be chosen at random from the interval $[-2.5, 8.5]$. What is the probability that y will lie between 3.1 and 4.6?

2.5.7 Which of the following two sets of data is more likely to be a sample representing the probability function, $f(y) = 6y(1 - y)$, $0 \le y \le 1$? Explain. *Hint*: Start by grouping each set of data into the classes $0 \le y < 0.2$, $0.2 \le y < 0.4, \ldots, 0.8 \le y < 1.0$.

a	0.26	0.68	0.58	0.62	0.51
	0.75	0.33	0.71	0.42	0.83
	0.43	0.47	0.37	0.70	0.17
	0.53	0.21	0.24	0.58	0.57
	0.08	0.04	0.94	0.44	0.43
b	0.19	0.26	0.14	0.50	0.30
	0.72	0.09	0.43	0.37	0.06
	0.13	0.98	0.63	0.18	0.63
	0.86	0.51	0.81	0.47	0.11
	0.34	0.76	0.29	0.90	0.41

2.5.8 Mauna Loa is one of the most active volcanoes in the world: From 1832 to 1950, the Hawaiian landmark erupted 37 times. Furthermore, researchers have shown that the time between consecutive eruptions follows the probability function

$$f(y) = 0.027e^{-0.027y}, \quad y > 0$$

where y is measured in months. What are the chances that the next two Mauna Loa eruptions will occur within 5 months of one another?

2.5.9 The pth percentile of a continuous probability distribution is the value y_p for which $P(y \le y_p) = p/100$ (which makes a distribution's fiftieth percentile equal to the median defined in Example 2.5.2). Find the thirtieth percentile of the probability function

$$f_Y(y) = ky^3, \quad 1 \le y \le 2$$

2.5.10 Recall the definition in Question 2.5.9. For a bell-shaped distribution, will the numerical value of $y_5 - y_3$ be less than, equal to, or greater than the numerical value of $y_{51} - y_{49}$? Explain.

2.5.11 Assume that the reaction time of motorists over the age of 70 to a certain visual stimulus is described by a continuous probability function of the form

$$f(y) = ye^{-y}, \quad y > 0$$

where y is measured in seconds. Let A be the event "Motorist requires longer than 1.5 seconds to react." Find $P(A)$.

2.5.12 Given that

$$f(y) = \frac{1}{\sqrt{2\pi}\,\sigma} \exp\left[-\frac{1}{2}\left(\frac{y - \mu}{\sigma}\right)^2\right], \quad -\infty < y < \infty$$

is a probability function for any number μ and any positive number σ, evaluate

$$\int_0^\infty e^{-4y^2}\, dy$$

2.6 CONDITIONAL PROBABILITY

The probability of an event A may have to be recomputed if we know for certain that some other event, B, has already occurred. That probabilities *should* change in the light of additional information is certainly not unreasonable. Consider a fair die being tossed, with A defined as the event "6 appears." Clearly, $P(A) = \frac{1}{6}$. But suppose that the die has already been tossed—by someone who refuses to tell us whether or not A occurred but does enlighten us to the point of confirming that B occurred, where B is the event "Even number appears." What are the chances of A now? The answer, of course, is obvious: There are three equally likely even numbers making up the event B—one of them satisfies the event A, so the "updated" probability is $\frac{1}{3}$.

Notice that the effect of additional information, such as the knowledge that B has occurred, is to revise—indeed, to *shrink*—the original sample space S to a new set of outcomes S'. Here, the original S contained six outcomes, the conditional sample space, three (see Figure 2.6.1).

The symbol $P(A|B)$—read "the probability of A given B"—is used to denote a conditional probability. Specifically, $P(A|B)$ refers to the probability that A *will occur* given that B *has already occurred*.

It will be convenient to have a formula for $P(A|B)$ that can be evaluated in terms of the original S, rather than the revised S'. Suppose that S is a finite sample space with n outcomes and P is the equally likely probability function. Assume that A and B are two events containing a and b outcomes, respectively, and let c denote the number of outcomes in the intersection of A and B (see Figure 2.6.2). Based on the argument suggested in Figure 2.6.1, the *conditional probability of A given B is the ratio of c to b.* But c/b can be written as the quotient of two other ratios,

$$\frac{c}{b} = \frac{c/n}{b/n}$$

so, for this particular case,

$$P(A|B) = \frac{P(A \cap B)}{P(B)} \tag{2.6.1}$$

The same underlying reasoning that leads to Equation 2.6.1, though, holds true even when the outcomes are not equally likely or when S is uncountably infinite.

P (6, relative to S) = 1/6

P (6, relative to S') = 1/3

FIGURE 2.6.1

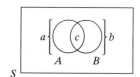

FIGURE 2.6.2

DEFINITION 2.6.1. Let A and B be any two events defined on S such that $P(B) > 0$. The conditional probability of A, assuming that B has already occured, is written $P(A|B)$ and, is given by

$$P(A|B) = \frac{P(A \cap B)}{P(B)}$$

Comment. Definition 2.6.1 can be cross-multiplied to give a frequently useful expression for the probability of an intersection. If $P(A|B) = P(A \cap B)/P(B)$, then

$$P(A \cap B) = P(A|B)P(B) \tag{2.6.2}$$

EXAMPLE 2.6.1

A card is drawn from a poker deck. What is the probability that the card is a club, given that the card is a king?

Intuitively, the answer is $\frac{1}{4}$: The king is equally likely to be a heart, diamond, club, or spade. More formally, let C be the event "Card is a club"; let K be the event "Card is a king." By Definition 2.6.1,

$$P(C|K) = \frac{P(C \cap K)}{P(K)}$$

But $P(K) = \frac{4}{52}$ and $P(C \cap K) = P(\text{card is a king of clubs}) = \frac{1}{52}$. Therefore, confirming our suspicion,

$$P(C|K) = \frac{1/52}{4/52} = \frac{1}{4}$$

[Notice in this example that the conditional probability $P(C|K)$ is numerically the same as the unconditional probability $P(C)$—they both equal $\frac{1}{4}$. This means that our knowledge that K has occurred gives us no additional insight about the chances of C occurring. Two events having this property are said to be *independent*. We will examine the consequences of independence in Section 2.7.]

EXAMPLE 2.6.2

The number of barefaced lies, s, that a certain politician tells during a news conference is described by the probability function

$$P(s) = \frac{8}{15}\left(\frac{1}{2}\right)^s, \qquad s = 0, 1, 2, 3$$

What is the probability that he tells at least two lies given that he tells at least one?

Let A be the event "Tells at least two lies" and let B be the event "Tells at least one lie." Notice that A is a proper subset of B, so $P(A \cap B) = P(A)$. Substituting into Definition 2.6.1, we get that $P(A|B) = 3/7$:

$$P(A|B) = \frac{P(A \cap B)}{P(B)} = \frac{P(A)}{P(B)}$$

$$= \frac{P(2) + P(3)}{P(1) + P(2) + P(3)}$$

$$= \frac{(8/15)(\frac{1}{2})^2 + (8/15)(\frac{1}{2})^3}{(8/15)(\frac{1}{2})^1 + (8/15)(\frac{1}{2})^2 + (8/15)(\frac{1}{2})^3}$$

$$= \frac{3}{7}$$

EXAMPLE 2.6.3

Two events A and B are defined such that (1) the probability that A occurs but B does not occur is 0.2 (2) the probability that B occurs but A does not occur is 0.1 and (3) the probability that neither occurs is 0.6. What is $P(A|B)$?

The three events whose probabilities are given are indicated on the Venn diagram shown in Figure 2.6.3. Since

$$P(\text{neither occurs}) = 0.6 = P((A \cup B)^C)$$

it follows that

$$P(A \cup B) = 1 - 0.6 = 0.4 = P(A \cap B^C) + P(A \cap B) + P(B \cap A^C)$$

so

$$P(A \cap B) = 0.4 - 0.2 - 0.1$$

$$= 0.1$$

From Definition 2.6.1, then,

$$P(A|B) = \frac{P(A \cap B)}{P(B)} = \frac{P(A \cap B)}{P(A \cap B) + P(B \cap A^C)}$$

$$= \frac{0.1}{0.1 + 0.1}$$

$$= 0.5$$

FIGURE 2.6.3

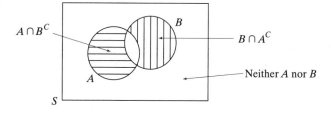

EXAMPLE 2.6.4

The possibility of importing liquified natural gas (LNG) from Algeria has been suggested as one way of coping with a future energy crunch. Complicating matters, though, is the fact that

LNG is highly volatile and poses an enormous safety hazard. Any major spill occurring near a U.S. port could result in a fire of catastrophic proportions. The question, therefore, of the *likelihood* of a spill becomes critical input for future policymakers who may have to decide whether or not to implement the proposal.

Two numbers need to be taken into account: (1) the probability that a tanker will have an accident near a port, and (2) the probability that a major spill will develop *given* that an accident has happened. Although no significant spills of LNG have yet occurred anywhere in the world, these probabilities can be approximated from records kept on similar tankers transporting less dangerous cargo. On the basis of such data, it has been estimated (40) that the probability is 8/50,000 that an LNG tanker will have an accident on any one trip. Given that an accident *has* occurred, it is suspected that only 3 times in 15,000 will the damage be sufficiently severe that a major spill would develop. What are the chances that a given LNG shipment would precipitate a catastrophic disaster?

Let A denote the event "Spill develops" and let B denote the event "Accident occurs." Past experience is suggesting that $P(B) = 8/50,000$ and $P(A|B) = 3/15,000$. Of primary concern is the probability that an accident will occur *and* a spill will ensue—that is, $P(A \cap B)$. Using Equation 2.6.2, we find that the chances of a catastrophic accident are on the order of 3 in 100 million:

$$P(\text{accident occurs and spill develops}) = P(A \cap B)$$
$$= P(A|B)P(B)$$
$$= (3/15,000) \cdot (8/50,000)$$
$$= 0.000000032$$

EXAMPLE 2.6.5

A sample space consists of the integers 1 through n. Each has a probability proportional to its magnitude. One integer is chosen at random. What are the chances that the 1 is chosen given that the number selected is between 1 and m?

By assumption,

$$P(\text{integer } s \text{ is chosen}) = P(s) = ks, \qquad s = 1, 2, \ldots, n$$

Since $\displaystyle\sum_{s=1}^{n} P(s) = k \sum_{s=1}^{n} s = k \cdot \frac{n(n + 1)}{2} = 1$, it follows that $k = \dfrac{2}{n(n + 1)}$ and $P(s) = \dfrac{2s}{n(n + 1)}$, $s = 1, 2, \ldots, n$.

Let A be the event that $s = 1$ and let B be the event that $s \leq m$. Then

$$P(A|B) = \frac{P(A \cap B)}{P(B)} = \frac{P(A)}{P(B)} = \frac{P(1)}{\displaystyle\sum_{s=1}^{m} P(s)}$$

From the same result that was used to find k,

$$\sum_{s=1}^{m} P(s) = \sum_{s=1}^{m} \frac{2s}{n(n + 1)} = \frac{2}{n(n + 1)} \sum_{s=1}^{m} s = \frac{2}{n(n + 1)} \cdot \frac{m(m + 1)}{2}$$
$$= \frac{m(m + 1)}{n(n + 1)}$$

Therefore,

$$P(s = 1 | s \leq m) = P(A|B) = \frac{2/[n(n+1)]}{[m(m+1)]/[n(n+1)]} = \frac{2}{m(m+1)}$$

Comment. Notice that the expression just derived for $P(A|B)$ checks out in a simple case where we already know the answer: If $m = 1$, $P(S = 1 | s \leq 1)$ *must* equal 1, but $\dfrac{2}{m(m+1)}$ does equal 1 when $m = 1$.

CASE STUDY 2.6.1

There once was a brainy baboon
Who always breathed down a bassoon
   For he said, "It appears
   That in billions of years
I shall certainly hit on a tune."
                   Eddington

The image of a monkey sitting at a typewriter, pecking away at random until he gets lucky and types out a perfect copy of the complete works of William Shakespeare, has long been a favorite model of statisticians and philosophers to illustrate the distinction between something that is theoretically possible but for all practical purposes, impossible. But if that monkey and his typewriter are replaced by a high-technology computer and if we program in the right sorts of conditional probabilities, the prospects for generating *something* intelligible become a little less far-fetched—maybe even disturbingly less far-fetched (10).

Simulating nonnumerical English text requires that 28 characters be dealt with: the 26 letters, the space, and the apostrophe. The simplest approach would be to assign each of those characters a number from 1 to 28. Then a random number in that range would be generated and the character corresponding to that number would be printed. A second random number would be generated, a corresponding second character would be printed, and so on.

Would that be a reasonable model? Of course not. Why should, say, X's have the same chance of being selected as E's when we know that the latter are much more common? At the very least, weights should be assigned to all the characters proportional to their relative probabilities. Table 2.6.1 shows the empirical distribution of the 26 letters, the space, and the apostrophe in the 35,224 characters making up Act III of *Hamlet*. Ranges of random numbers corresponding to each character's frequency are listed in the last column. If two random numbers were generated, say, 27351 and 11616, the computer would print the characters D and O. Doing that, of course, is equivalent to printing a D with probability $0.0312 = [(28425 - 27327 + 1)/35244 = 1099/35244]$ and an O with probability $0.0732 = [(12789 - 10212 + 1)/35244 = 2578/35244]$.

Extending this idea to *sequences* of letters requires an application of Definition 2.6.1. What is the probability, for example, that a T follows an E? By definition,

$$P(\text{T follows an E}) = P(\text{T}|\text{E}) = \frac{\text{number of ET's}}{\text{number of E's}}$$

(continued on next page)

(Case Study 2.6.1 continued)

TABLE 2.6.1

Character	Frequency	Probability	Random number range
Space	6934	0.1968	00001–06934
E	3277	0.0930	06935–10211
O	2578	0.0732	10212–12789
T	2557	0.0726	12790–15346
A	2043	0.0580	15347–17389
S	1856	0.0527	17390–19245
H	1773	0.0503	19246–21018
N	1741	0.0494	21019–22759
I	1736	0.0493	22760–24495
R	1593	0.0452	24496–26088
L	1238	0.0351	26089–27326
D	1099	0.0312	27327–28425
U	1014	0.0288	28426–29439
M	889	0.0252	29440–30328
Y	783	0.0222	30329–31111
W	716	0.0203	31112–31827
F	629	0.0178	31828–32456
C	584	0.0166	32457–33040
G	478	0.0136	33041–33518
P	433	0.0123	33519–33951
B	410	0.0116	33952–34361
V	309	0.0088	34362–34670
K	255	0.0072	34671–34925
'	203	0.0058	34926–35128
J	34	0.0010	35129–35162
Q	27	0.0008	35163–35189
X	21	0.0006	35190–35210
Z	14	0.0004	35211–35224

The analog of Table 2.6.1, then, would be an array having 28 rows and 28 columns. The entry in the ith row and jth column would be $P(i|j)$, the probability that letter i follows letter j.

In a similar fashion, conditional probabilities for longer sequences could also be estimated. For example, the probability that an A follows the sequence QU would be the ratio of QUA's to QU's:

$$P(\text{A follows QU}) = P(\text{A}|\text{QU}) = \frac{\text{number of QUA's}}{\text{number of QU's}}$$

What does our monkey gain by having a typewriter programmed with probabilities of sequences? Quite a bit. Figure 2.6.4 shows three lines of computer text generated by a program knowing only single-letter frequencies (Table 2.6.1). Nowhere does even a single correctly spelled word appear. Contrast that with Figure 2.6.5, showing computer text generated by a program that had been given estimates for conditional probabilities corresponding to all 614,656 ($= 28^4$) *four*-letter sequences. What we get is still garble, but the improvement is astounding—more than 80% of the letter combinations are at least words.

One can only wonder how "human" computer-generated text might be if conditional probabilities for, say, seven- or eight-letter sequences were available. Right now they are not, but given the rate our computer technology is developing, they soon will be. When that

```
AOOAAORH ONNNDGELC TEFSISO VTALIDMA POESDHEMHIESWON
PJTOMJ FTL FIM TAOFERLMT O NORDEERH HMFIOMRETWOVRCA
OSRIE IEOBOTOGIM NUDSEEWU WHHS AWUA HIDNEVE NL SELTS
```

FIGURE 2.6.4

```
A GO THIS BABE AND JUDGEMENT OF TIMEDIOUS RETCH AND NOT LORD
WHAL IF THE EASELVES AND DO AND MAKE AND BASE GATHEM I AY
BEATELLOUS WE PLAY MEANS HOLY FOOL MOUR WORK FROM INMOST
BED BE CONFOULD HAVE MANY JUDGEMENT WAS IT YOU MASSURE'S TO
LADY WOULD HAT PRIME THAT'S OUR THROWN AND DID WIFE FATHER'ST
LIVENGTH SLEEP TITH I AMBITION TO THIN HIM AND FORCE AND LAW'S
MAY BUT SMELL SO AND SPURSELY SIGNOR GENT MUCH CHIEF MIXTURN
```

FIGURE 2.6.5

day comes, our monkey will probably still never come up with text as creative as Hamlet's soliloquy but something profoundly simple-minded, like a political speech, might not be out of the question.

QUESTIONS

2.6.1 Suppose that two fair dice are tossed. What is the probability that the sum equals 10 given that it exceeds 8?

2.6.2 Suppose that $f(y) = ky^2, 0 \leq y \leq 1$. What is the probability that y is between 0 and $\frac{1}{2}$ given that y is between $\frac{1}{4}$ and 1?

2.6.3 Find $P(A \cap B)$ if $P(A) = 0.2, P(B) = 0.4$, and $P(A|B) + P(B|A) = 0.75$.

2.6.4 Recall the actuarial function discussed in Example 2.5.3, $f(y) = 3 \times 10^{-9} \cdot y^2(100 - y)^2$, $0 \leq y \leq 100$, where y denotes a person's age at death (in years). Which is larger, the conditional probability, $P(80 \leq y \leq 85 | y \geq 70)$, or the unconditional probability, $P(80 \leq y \leq 85)$? Does your answer seem intuitively reasonable? Explain.

2.6.5 Consider families with two children and assume that the four possible outcomes—(younger is a boy, older is a boy), (younger is a boy, older is a girl), and so on—are all equally likely. What is the probability that both children are boys given that at least one is a boy?

2.6.6 If $P(A|B) < P(A)$, show that $P(B|A) < P(B)$.

2.6.7 Let A and B be two events such that $P((A \cup B)^C) = 0.6$ and $P(A \cap B) = 0.1$. Let E be the event that either A or B but not both will occur. Find $P(E|A \cup B)$.

2.6.8 Suppose that in Question 2.6.5 we ignored the age of the children and distinguished only *three* family types; (boy, boy), (girl, boy), and (girl, girl). Would the conditional probability of both children being boys given that at least one is a boy be different from the answer found in Question 2.6.5? Explain.

2.6.9 Two events, A and B, are defined on a sample space S such that $P(A|B) = 0.6$, P(at least one of the events occurs) $= 0.8$, and P(exactly one of the events occurs) $= 0.6$. Find $P(A)$ and $P(B)$.

2.6.10 An urn contains one red chip and one white chip. One is drawn at random. If the chip selected is red, that chip together with two additional red chips are put back into the urn. If a white is drawn, the chip is returned to the urn. Then a second chip is drawn. What is the probability that both selections are red?

2.6.11 Given that $P(A) = a$ and $P(B) = b$, show that

$$P(A \mid B) \geq \frac{a + b - 1}{b}$$

2.6.12 An urn contains one white chip and a second chip that is equally likely to be white or black. A chip is drawn at random and returned to the urn. Then a second chip is drawn. What is the probability that a white appears on the second draw given that a white appeared on the first draw?

2.6.13 The operating lifetimes of light bulbs can often be modeled effectively by the family of exponential distributions introduced in Example 2.5.5,

$$f(y) = \lambda e^{-\lambda y}, \qquad y > 0$$

where y is the bulb's lifetime (in hours) and λ is a positive constant. Show that $P(y \geq r + t \mid y \geq t) = P(y \geq r)$. What does this relationship imply about the bulb wearing out as it gets older?

Applying Conditional Probability to Higher-Order Intersections

We have seen that conditional probabilities can be useful in evaluating intersection probabilities—that is, $P(A \cap B) = P(A \mid B)P(B) = P(B \mid A)P(A)$. A similar result holds for higher-order intersections. Consider $P(A \cap B \cap C)$. By thinking of $A \cap B$ as a single event—say, D—we can write

$$
\begin{aligned}
P(A \cap B \cap C) &= P(D \cap C) \\
&= P(C \mid D)P(D) \\
&= P(C \mid A \cap B)P(A \cap B) \\
&= P(C \mid A \cap B)P(B \mid A)P(A)
\end{aligned}
$$

Repeating this same argument for n events, $A_1, A_2, \ldots, A_n$, gives a formula for the general case:

$$P(A_1 \cap A_2 \cap \cdots \cap A_n) = P(A_n \mid A_1 \cap A_2 \cap \cdots \cap A_{n-1})$$
$$\cdot P(A_{n-1} \mid A_1 \cap A_2 \cap \cdots \cap A_{n-2}) \cdot \ldots \cdot P(A_2 \mid A_1) \cdot P(A_1) \qquad (2.6.3)$$

EXAMPLE 2.6.6

An urn contains five white chips, four black chips, and three red chips. Four chips are drawn sequentially and without replacement. What is the probability of obtaining the sequence (white, red, white, black)?

Figure 2.6.6. shows the evolution of the urn's composition as the desired sequence is assembled. Define the following four events:

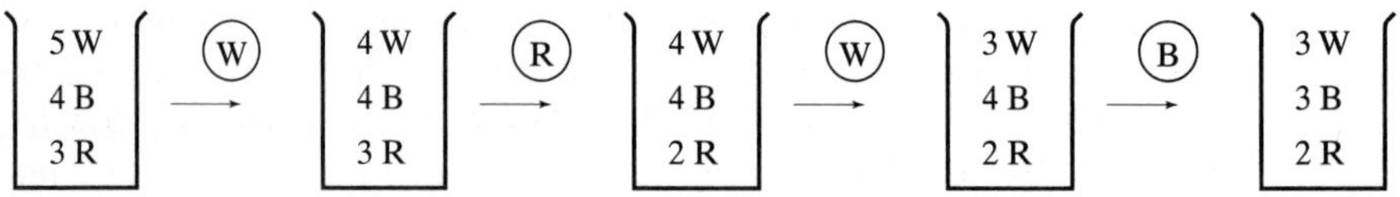

FIGURE 2.6.6

A: white chip is drawn on 1st selection

B: red chip is drawn on 2nd selection

C: white chip is drawn on 3rd selection

D: black chip is drawn on 4th selection

Our objective is to find $P(A \cap B \cap C \cap D)$.

From Equation 2.6.3,

$$P(A \cap B \cap C \cap D) = P(D|A \cap B \cap C) \cdot P(C|A \cap B) \cdot P(B|A) \cdot P(A)$$

Each of the probabilities on the right-hand side of the equation here can be gotten by just looking at the urns pictured in Figure 2.6.6: $P(D|A \cap B \cap C) = \frac{4}{9}$, $P(C|A \cap B) = \frac{4}{10}$, $P(B|A) = \frac{3}{11}$, and $P(A) = \frac{5}{12}$. Therefore, the probability of drawing a (white, red, white, black) sequence is 0.02:

$$P(A \cap B \cap C \cap D) = \frac{4}{9} \cdot \frac{4}{10} \cdot \frac{3}{11} \cdot \frac{5}{12}$$

$$= \frac{240}{11,880}$$

$$= 0.02$$

CASE STUDY 2.6.2

Since the late 1940s, tens of thousands of eyewitness accounts of strange lights in the skies, unidentified flying objects, even alleged abductions by little green men, have made headlines. None of these incidents, though, has produced any hard evidence, any irrefutable *proof* that Earth has been visited by a race of extraterrestrials. Still, the haunting question remains—are we alone in the universe? Or are there other civilizations, more advanced than ours, waiting for the right moment to make contact?

Until, or unless, a flying saucer plops down on the White House lawn and a strange-looking creature emerges demanding, "Take me to your leader," we may never know whether we have any cosmic neighbors. We can use Equation 2.6.3, though, to speculate on the *probability* of our not being alone.

Recent discoveries suggest that planetary systems much like our own may be quite common. If so, there are likely to be many planets whose chemical makeups, temperatures, pressures, and so on, are suitable for life. Let those planets be the points in our sample space. Relative to them, we can define three events:

A: life arises

B: technical civilization arises (one capable of interstellar communication)

C: technical civilization is flourishing *now*

In terms of A, B, and C, the probability a habitable planet is presently supporting a technical civilization is the probability of an intersection—specifically, $P(A \cap B \cap C)$. Associating a number with $P(A \cap B \cap C)$ is highly speculative at best, but the task is simplified considerably if we work instead with the equivalent conditional formula, $P(C|B \cap A) \cdot P(B|A) \cdot P(A)$.

(continued on next page)

(Case Study 2.6.2 continued)

Scientists speculate (141) that life of some kind may arise on one-third of all planets having a suitable environment and that life on maybe 1% of all those planets will evolve into a technical civilization. In our notation, $P(A) = \frac{1}{3}$ and $P(B \mid A) = 1/100$.

More difficult to estimate is $P(C \mid A \cap B)$. On Earth, we have had the capability of interstellar communication (that is, radio astronomy) for only a few decades, so $P(C \mid A \cap B)$, *empirically*, is on the order of 1×10^{-8}. But that may be an overly pessimistic estimate of a technical civilization's ability to endure. It may be true that if a civilization can avoid annihilating itself when it first develops nuclear weapons, its prospects for longevity are fairly good. If that were the case, $P(C \mid A \cap B)$ might be as large as 1×10^{-2}.

Putting these estimates into the computing formula for $P(A \cap B \cap C)$ gives us a range for the probability of a habitable planet currently supporting a technical civilization. The chances may be as small as 3.3×10^{-11} or as "large" as 3.3×10^{-5}:

$$(1 \times 10^{-8})\left(\frac{1}{100}\right)\left(\frac{1}{3}\right) < P(A \cap B \cap C) < (1 \times 10^{-2})\left(\frac{1}{100}\right)\left(\frac{1}{3}\right)$$

or

$$0.000000000033 < P(A \cap B \cap C) < 0.000033$$

A better way to put these figures in some kind of perspective is to think in terms of *numbers* rather than probabilities. Astronomers estimate there are 3×10^{11} habitable planets in our Milky Way galaxy. Multiplying that total by the two limits for $P(A \cap B \cap C)$ gives an indication of *how many* cosmic neighbors we are likely to have. Specifically, $3 \times 10^{11} \cdot 0.000000000033 \doteq 10$, while $3 \times 10^{11} \cdot 0.000033 \doteq 10,000,000$. So, on the one hand, we may be a galactic rarity. At the same time, the probabilities do not preclude the very real possibility that the heavens are abuzz with activity and that our neighbors number in the millions.

QUESTIONS

2.6.14 An urn contains six white chips, four black chips, and five red chips. Five chips are drawn out, one at a time and without replacement. What is the probability of getting the sequence (black, black, red, white, white)? Suppose that the chips are numbered 1 through 15. What is the probability of getting a specific sequence—say, $(2, 6, 4, 9, 13)$?

2.6.15 A man has n keys on a key ring, one of which opens the door to his apartment. Having celebrated a bit too much one evening, he returns home only to find himself unable to distinguish one key from another. Resourceful, he works out a fiendishly clever plan: He will choose a key at random and try it. If it fails to open the door, he will discard it and choose at random one of the remaining $n - 1$ keys, and so on. Clearly, the probability that he gains entrance with the first key he selects is $1/n$. Show that the probability the door opens with the *third* key he tries is also $1/n$. (*Hint:* What has to happen before he even gets to the third key?)

Calculating "Unconditional" Probabilities

We conclude this section with two very useful theorems that apply to *partitioned* sample spaces. By definition, a set of events $A_1, A_2, \ldots, A_n$ "partition" S if every outcome in the sample space belongs to one and only one of the A_i's—that is, the A_i's are mutually exclusive and their union is S (see Figure 2.6.7).

FIGURE 2.6.7

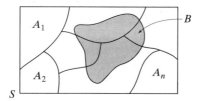

As pictured, B is any arbitrary event defined on S. Theorem 2.6.1 gives a formula for the "unconditional" probability of B; Theorem 2.6.2 develops a formula for the set of conditional probabilities, $P(A_j|B)$, $j = 1, 2, \ldots, n$.

THEOREM 2.6.1. Let $\{A_i\}_{i=1}^n$ be a set of events defined over S such that $S = \bigcup_{i=1}^n A_i$, $A_i \cap A_j = \varnothing$ for $i \neq j$, and $P(A_i) > 0$ for $i = 1, 2, \ldots, n$. For any event B,

$$P(B) = \sum_{i=1}^n P(B|A_i)P(A_i)$$

Proof. By the conditions imposed on the A_i's,

$$B = (B \cap A_1) \cup (B \cap A_2) \cup \cdots \cup (B \cap A_n)$$

and

$$P(B) = P(B \cap A_1) + P(B \cap A_2) + \ldots + P(B \cap A_n)$$

But each $P(B \cap A_i)$ can be written as the product $P(B|A_i)P(A_i)$, and the result follows.

EXAMPLE 2.6.7

Urn I contains two red chips and four white chips; urn II, three red and one white. A chip is drawn at random from urn I and transferred to urn II. Then a chip is drawn from urn II. What is the probability that the chip drawn from urn II is red?

Let B be the event "Chip drawn from urn II is red"; let A_1 and A_2 be the events "Chip transferred from urn I is red" and "Chip transferred from urn I is white," respectively. By inspection (see Figure 2.6.8), we can deduce all the probabilities appearing in the right-hand side of the formula in Theorem 2.6.1:

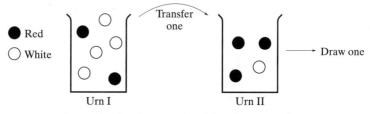

FIGURE 2.6.8

$$P(B\,|\,A_1) = \frac{4}{5} \qquad P(B\,|\,A_2) = \frac{3}{5}$$

$$P(A_1) = \frac{2}{6} \qquad P(A_2) = \frac{4}{6}$$

Putting all this information together, we see that the chances are 2 out of 3 that a red chip will be drawn from urn II:

$$P(B) = P(B\,|\,A_1)P(A_1) + P(B\,|\,A_2)P(A_2)$$

$$= \frac{4}{5} \cdot \frac{2}{6} + \frac{3}{5} \cdot \frac{4}{6}$$

$$= \frac{2}{3}$$

EXAMPLE 2.6.8

A standard poker deck is shuffled and the card on top is removed. What is the probability that the *second* card is an ace?

Define the following events:

B: second card is an ace

A_1:   top card was an ace

A_2:   top card was not an ace

Then $P(B\,|\,A_1) = \frac{3}{51}$, $P(B\,|\,A_2) = \frac{4}{51}$, $P(A_1) = \frac{4}{52}$, and $P(A_2) = \frac{48}{52}$. Since the A_i's partition the sample space of two-card selections, Theorem 2.6.1 applies. Substituting into the expression for $P(B)$ shows that $\frac{4}{52}$ is the probability that the second card is an ace:

$$P(B) = P(B\,|\,A_1)P(A_1) + P(B\,|\,A_2)P(A_2)$$

$$= \frac{3}{51} \cdot \frac{4}{52} + \frac{4}{51} \cdot \frac{48}{52}$$

$$= \frac{4}{52}$$

Comment. Notice that $P(B) = P(\text{2nd card is an ace})$ is numerically the same as $P(A_1) = P(\text{1st card is an ace})$. The analysis in Example 2.6.8 illustrates a basic principle in probability that says, in effect, "what you don't know, doesn't matter." Here, removal of the top card is irrelevant to any subsequent probability calculations *if the identity of that card remains unknown.*

EXAMPLE 2.6.9

Based on pretrial speculation, the probability that a jury returns a guilty verdict in a certain high-profile murder case is thought to be 15% if the defense can discredit the police department and 80% if they cannot. Veteran court observers believe that the skilled defense attorneys have a 70% chance of convincing the jury that the police either contaminated or planted some of the key evidence. What is the probability that the jury returns a guilty verdict?

Let B be the event "Jury returns a guilty verdict," let A_1 be the event "Jury believes that police acted improperly," and let A_2 be the event "Jury does not believe that police acted improperly." By assumption,

$$P(B|A_1) = 0.15 \qquad P(B|A_2) = 0.80$$
$$P(A_1) = 0.70 \qquad P(A_2) = 1 - P(A_1) = 1 - 0.70 = 0.30$$

According to Theorem 2.6.1, the jury has an "unconditional" *34.5%* chance of returning a guilty verdict:

$$P(B) = P(B|A_1)P(A_1) + P(B|A_2)P(A_2)$$
$$= (0.15)(0.70) + (0.80)(0.30)$$
$$= 0.345$$

EXAMPLE 2.6.10

A toy manufacturer buys ball bearings from three different suppliers—50% of her total order comes from supplier 1, 30% from supplier 2, and the rest from supplier 3. Past experience has shown that the quality control standards of the three suppliers are not all the same. Two percent of the ball bearings produced by supplier 1 are defective, while suppliers 2 and 3 produce defective bearings 3% and 4% of the time, respectively. What proportion of the ball bearings in the toy manufacturer's inventory are defective?

Let A_i be the event "Bearing came from supplier i," $i = 1, 2, 3$. Let B be the event "Bearing in toy manufacturer's inventory is defective." Then

$$P(A_1) = 0.5, \qquad P(A_2) = 0.3, \qquad P(A_3) = 0.2$$

and

$$P(B|A_1) = 0.02, \qquad P(B|A_2) = 0.03, \qquad P(B|A_3) = 0.04$$

Combining these probabilities according to Theorem 2.6.1 gives

$$P(B) = (0.02)(0.5) + (0.03)(0.3) + (0.04)(0.2)$$
$$= 0.027$$

meaning that the manufacturer can expect 2.7% of her ball-bearing stock to be defective.

EXAMPLE 2.6.11

Three chips are placed in an urn. One is red on both sides, a second is blue on both sides, and the third is red on one side and blue on the other. One chip is selected at random and placed on a table. Suppose that the color showing on that chip is red. What is the probability that the color underneath is also red (see Figure 2.6.9)?

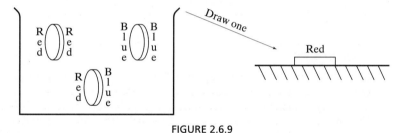

FIGURE 2.6.9

At first glance, it may seem that the answer is $\frac{1}{2}$: We know that the blue/blue chip has not been drawn, and only one of the remaining two—the red/red chip—satisfies the event that the color underneath is red. If this game were played over and over, though, and records were kept of the outcomes, it would be found that the proportion of times that a red top has a red bottom is $\frac{2}{3}$, not $\frac{1}{2}$. The reason has to do with both of the key results introduced in this section: Definition 2.6.1 and Theorem 2.6.1.

Define the following events:

A:	bottom side of chip drawn is red
B:	top side of chip drawn is red
A_1:	red/red chip is drawn
A_2:	blue/blue chip is drawn
A_3:	red/blue chip is drawn

From the definition of conditional probability,

$$P(A|B) = \frac{P(A \cap B)}{P(B)}$$

But $P(A \cap B) = P(\text{both sides are red}) = P(\text{red/red chip}) = \frac{1}{3}$. Theorem 2.6.1 can be used to find the denominator, $P(B)$:

$$P(B) = P(B|A_1)P(A_1) + P(B|A_2)P(A_2) + P(B|A_3)P(A_3)$$

$$= 1 \cdot \frac{1}{3} + 0 \cdot \frac{1}{3} + \frac{1}{2} \cdot \frac{1}{3}$$

$$= \frac{1}{2}$$

Therefore,

$$P(A|B) = \frac{1/3}{1/2} = \frac{2}{3}$$

Comment. The question posed in Example 2.6.11 gives rise to a simple but effective con game. The trick is to convince a "mark" that the initial analysis given on page 64 is correct, meaning that the bottom has a 50/50 chance of being the same color as the top. Under that incorrect presumption that the game is "fair," both participants put up the same amount of money, but the gambler (knowing the correct analysis) always bets that the bottom is the same color as the top. In the long run, then, the con artist will be winning an even-money bet two-thirds of the time!

QUESTIONS

2.6.16 In an upstate congressional race, the incumbent Republican (R) is running against a field of three Democrats (D_1, D_2, D_3) seeking the nomination. Political pundits estimate that the probabilities of $D_1, D_2,$ and D_3 winning the primary are 0.35, 0.40, and 0.25, respectively. Furthermore, results from a variety of polls are suggesting that R would have a 40% chance of defeating D_1 in the general election, a 35% chance of defeating D_2, and a 60% chance of defeating D_3. Assuming all these estimates to be accurate, what are the chances that the Republican will retain his seat?

2.6.17 A fair coin is tossed. If a head turns up, a fair die is tossed; if a tail turns up, two fair dice are tossed. What is the probability that the face (or the sum of the faces) showing on the die (or dice) is equal to 6?

2.6.18 Foreign policy experts estimate that the probability is 0.65 that war will break out next year between two Middle East countries if either side significantly escalates its terrorist activities: Otherwise, the likelihood of war is estimated to be 0.05. Based on what has happened this year, the chances of terrorism reaching a critical level in the next twelve months are thought to be 3 in 10. What is the probability that the two countries will go to war?

2.6.19 A telephone solicitor is responsible for canvassing three suburbs. In the past, 60% of the completed calls to Belle Meade have resulted in contributions, compared to 55% for Oak Hill and 35% for Antioch. Her list of telephone numbers includes 1000 households from Belle Meade, 1000 from Oak Hill, and 2000 from Antioch. Suppose that she picks a number at random from the list and places the call. What is the probability that she gets a donation?

2.6.20 If men constitute 47% of the population and tell the truth 78% of the time, while women tell the truth 63% of the time, what is the probability that a person selected at random will answer a question truthfully?

2.6.21 Urn I contains three red chips and one white chip. Urn II contains two red chips and two white chips. One chip is drawn from each urn and transferred to the other urn. Then a chip is drawn from the first urn. What is the probability that the chip ultimately drawn from urn I is red?

2.6.22 The crew of the Starship *Enterprise* is considering launching a surprise attack against the Borg in a neutral quadrant. Possible interference by the Klingons, though, is causing Captain Picard and Data to reassess their strategy. According to Data's calculations, the probability of the Klingons joining forces with the Borg is 0.2384. Captain Picard feels that the probability of the attack being successful is 0.8 if the *Enterprise* can catch the Borg alone, but only 0.3 if they have to engage both adversaries. Data claims that the mission would be a tactical misadventure if its probability of success were not at least 0.7306. Should the *Enterprise* attack?

2.6.23 Recall the "survival" lottery described in Question 2.2.8. What is the probability of release associated with the prisoner's optimal strategy?

2.6.24 State College is playing Backwater A&M for the conference football championship. If Backwater's first-string quarterback is healthy, A&M has a 75% chance of winning. If they have to start their backup quarterback, their chances of winning drop to 40%. The team physician says that there is a 70% chance that the first-string quarterback will play. What is the probability that Backwater wins the game?

2.6.25 An urn contains 40 red chips and 60 white chips. Six chips are drawn out and discarded, and a seventh chip is drawn. What is the probability that the seventh chip is red?

2.6.26 A study has shown that 7 out of 10 people will say "heads" if asked to call a coin toss. Given that the coin is fair, though, a head occurs, on the average, only 5 times out of 10. Does it follow that you have the advantage if you let the other person call the toss? Explain.

Bayes's Theorem

The next theorem has an interesting history. Its first explicit statement, coming in 1812, was due to Laplace, but its name derives from the Reverend Thomas Bayes, whose 1763 paper (published posthumously) had already outlined the result. On one level, the theorem is a relatively minor extension of the definition of conditional probability. When viewed from a loftier perspective, though, it takes on some rather profound philosophical implications. These implications, in fact, have precipitated a schism among practicing statisticians: "Bayesians" analyze data one way; "non-Bayesians," another [see (124) or (90)].

Our concern with the result will have nothing to do with its statistical interpretation. We will use it simply as the Reverend Bayes originally intended, as a formula for evaluating a certain kind of "inverse" probability. If we know $P(B|A_i)$ for all i, the theorem enables us to compute conditional probabilities "in the other direction"—that is, we can use the $P(B|A_i)$'s to find $P(A_j|B)$.

THEOREM 2.6.2.   (*Bayes*) Let $\{A_i\}_{i=1}^{n}$ be a set of n events, each with positive probability, that partition S in such a way that $\bigcup_{i=1}^{n} A_i = S$ and $A_i \cap A_j = \varnothing$ for $i \neq j$. For any event B (also defined on S), where $P(B) > 0$,

$$P(A_j|B) = \frac{P(B|A_j)P(A_j)}{\sum_{i=1}^{n} P(B|A_i)P(A_i)}$$

for any $1 \leq j \leq n$.

Proof.   From Definition 2.6.1,

$$P(A_j|B) = \frac{P(A_j \cap B)}{P(B)} = \frac{P(B|A_j)P(A_j)}{P(B)}$$

But Theorem 2.6.1 allows the denominator to be written as $\sum_{i=1}^{n} P(B|A_i)P(A_i)$ and the result follows.

EXAMPLE 2.6.12

A biased coin, twice as likely to come up heads as tails, is tossed once. If it shows heads, a chip is drawn from urn I, which contains three white chips and four red chips; if it shows tails, a chip is drawn from urn II, which contains six white chips and three red chips. Given that a white chip was drawn, what is the probability that the coin came up tails (see Figure 2.6.10)?

Since $P(\text{Heads}) = 2P(\text{Tails})$, it must be true that $P(\text{Heads}) = \frac{2}{3}$ and $P(\text{Tails}) = \frac{1}{3}$. Define the events

  B: white chip is drawn

  A_1:   coin came up heads (i.e., chip came from urn I)

  A_2:   coin came up tails (i.e., chip came from urn II)

FIGURE 2.6.10

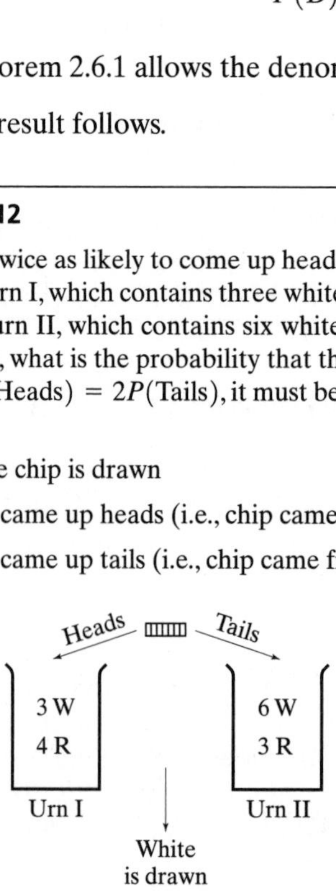

We are trying to find $P(A_2|B)$. From Figure 2.6.10,

$$P(B|A_1) = \frac{3}{7} \qquad P(B|A_2) = \frac{6}{9}$$

$$P(A_1) = \frac{2}{3} \qquad P(A_2) = \frac{1}{3}$$

so

$$P(A_2|B) = \frac{P(B|A_2)P(A_2)}{P(B|A_1)P(A_1) + P(B|A_2)P(A_2)}$$

$$= \frac{(6/9)(1/3)}{(3/7)(2/3) + (6/9)(1/3)}$$

$$= \frac{7}{16}$$

EXAMPLE 2.6.13

During a power blackout, 100 persons are arrested on suspicion of looting. Each is given a polygraph test. From past experience it is known that the polygraph is 90% reliable when administered to a guilty suspect and 98% reliable when given to someone who is innocent. Suppose that of the 100 persons taken into custody, only 12 were actually involved in any wrongdoing. What is the probability that a given suspect is innocent given that the polygraph says he is guilty?

Let B be the event "Polygraph says suspect is guilty" and let A_1 and A_2 be the events "Suspect is guilty" and "Suspect is not guilty," respectively. To say that the polygraph is "90% reliable when administered to a guilty suspect" means that $P(B|A_1) = 0.90$. Similarly, the 98% reliability for innocent suspects implies that $P(B^C|A_2) = 0.98$, or, equivalently, $P(B|A_2) = 0.02$.

We also know that $P(A_1) = 12/100$ and $P(A_2) = 88/100$. Substituting into Theorem 2.6.2, then, shows that the probability a suspect is innocent given that the polygraph says he is guilty is 0.14:

$$P(A_2|B) = \frac{P(B|A_2)P(A_2)}{P(B|A_1)P(A_1) + P(B|A_2)P(A_2)}$$

$$= \frac{(0.02)(88/100)}{(0.90)(12/100) + (0.02)(88/100)}$$

$$= 0.14$$

CASE STUDY 2.6.3

Bayes's theorem has been applied with considerable success to the problem of diagnosing medical conditions—specifically, to estimating the probability that a patient has a certain disease given that a particular diagnostic procedure *says* the patient does. The situation we

(continued on next page)

(Case Study 2.6.3 continued)

look at here is one such application and it makes a significant point: that when the disease being checked for is very rare, the number of incorrect diagnoses can be alarmingly high.

Consider the problem of "screening" for cervical cancer (135). Let A_1 be the event of a woman having the disease and B, the event of a positive biopsy—that is, B occurs when the diagnostic procedure indicates that she *does* have cervical cancer. We will assume that $P(A_1) = 0.0001$, $P(B|A_1) = 0.90$ (the test correctly identifies 90% of all the women who do have the disease), and $P(B|A_1^C) = 0.001$ (the test gives one false positive, on the average, out of every 1000 patients). Find $P(A_1|B)$, the probability a woman actually does have cervical cancer given that the biopsy says she does.

Although the method of solution here is straightforward, the actual numerical answer is not at all what we would expect. From Theorem 2.6.2,

$$P(A_1|B) = \frac{P(B|A_1)P(A_1)}{P(B|A_1)P(A_1) + P(B|A_1^C)P(A_1^C)}$$

$$= \frac{(0.9)(0.0001)}{(0.9)(0.0001) + (0.001)(0.9999)}$$

$$= 0.08$$

That is, only 8% of those women identified as having the disease actually do! Table 2.6.2 shows the strong dependence of $P(A_1|B)$ on $P(A_1)$ and $P(B|A_1^C)$. In light of these figures, the practicality of large-scale screening programs directed at diseases with low prevalence is open to question, particularly when the diagnostic procedure itself may be a health hazard, as would be the case in using annual chest X-rays to look for tuberculosis.

TABLE 2.6.2

$P(A_1)$	$P(B|A_1^C)$	$P(A_1|B)$
0.0001	0.001	0.08
	0.0001	0.47
0.001	0.001	0.47
	0.0001	0.90
0.01	0.001	0.90
	0.0001	0.99

QUESTIONS

2.6.27 Urn I contains two white chips and one red chip; urn II has one white chip and two red chips. One chip is drawn at random from urn I and transferred to urn II. Then one chip is drawn from urn II. Suppose that a red chip is selected from urn II. What is the probability that the chip transferred was white?

2.6.28 Suppose that 0.5% of all the students seeking treatment at a school infirmary are eventually diagnosed as having mononucleosis. Of those who do have mono, 90% complain of a sore throat. But 30% of those not having mono also have sore throats. If a student comes to the infirmary and says that he has a sore throat, what is the probability that he has mono?

2.6.29 A dashboard warning light is supposed to flash red if a car's oil pressure is too low. On a certain model, the probability of the light flashing when it should is 0.99; 2% of the time, though, it flashes for no apparent reason. If there is a 10% chance that the oil pressure really is low, what is the probability that a driver needs to be concerned if the warning light goes on?

2.6.30 Building permits were issued last year to three contractors starting up a new subdivision: Tara Construction built two houses; Westview, three houses; and Hearthstone, six houses. Tara's houses have a 60% probability of developing leaky basements; homes built by Westview and Hearthstone have that same problem 50% of the time and 40% of the time, respectively. Yesterday, the Better Business Bureau received a complaint from one of the new homeowners that his basement is leaking. Who is most likely to have been the contractor?

2.6.31 Two sections of a senior probability course are being taught. From what she has heard about the two instructors listed, Francesca estimates that her chances of passing the course are 0.85 if she gets professor X and 0.60 if she gets professor Y. The section into which she is put is determined by the registrar. Suppose that her chances of being assigned to professor X are 4 out of 10. Fifteen weeks later we learn that Francesca did, indeed, pass the course. What is the probability she was enrolled in professor X's section?

2.6.32 A liquor store owner is willing to cash personal checks for amounts up to $50, but she has become wary of customers who wear sunglasses. Fifty percent of checks written by persons wearing sunglasses bounce. In contrast, 98% of the checks written by persons not wearing sunglasses clear the bank. She estimates that 10% of her customers wear sunglasses. If the bank returns a check and marks it "insufficient funds," what is the probability it was written by someone wearing sunglasses?

2.6.33 Your next-door neighbor has a rather old and tempermental burglar alarm. If someone breaks into his house, the probability of the alarm sounding is 0.95. In the last 2 years, though, it has gone off on five different nights, each time for no apparent reason. Police records show that the chances of a home being burglarized in your community on any given night are 2 in 10,000. If your neighbor's alarm goes off tomorrow night, what is the probability his house is being burglarized?

2.6.34 Brett and Margo have each thought about murdering their rich Uncle Basil in hopes of claiming their inheritance a bit early. Hoping to take advantage of Basil's predilection for immoderate desserts, Brett has put rat poison in the cherries flambe; Margo, unaware of Brett's activities, has laced the chocolate mousse with cyanide. Given the amounts likely to be eaten, the probability of the rat poison being fatal is 0.60; the cyanide, 0.90. Based on other dinners where Basil was presented with the same dessert options, we can assume that he has a 50% chance of asking for the cherries flambe, a 40% chance of ordering the chocolate mousse, and a 10% chance of skipping dessert altogether. No sooner are the dishes cleared away when Basil drops dead. In the absence of any other evidence, who should be considered the prime suspect?

2.6.35 Josh takes a 20-question multiple-choice exam where each question has five answers. Some of the answers he knows, while others he gets right just by making lucky guesses. Suppose that the conditional probability of his knowing the answer to a randomly selected question given that he got it right is 0.92. How many of the 20 questions was he prepared for?

2.6.36 Recently the U.S. Senate Committee on Labor and Public Welfare investigated the feasibility of setting up a national screening program to detect child abuse. A team of consultants estimated the following probabilities: (1) 1 child in 90 is abused, (2) a physician can detect an abused child 90% of the time, and (3) a screening program would incorrectly label 3% of all nonabused children as abused. What is the probability that a child is actually abused given that the screening program diagnoses him as such? How does this probability change if the incidence of abuse is 1 in 1000? 1 in 50?

2.7 INDEPENDENCE

Section 2.6 dealt with the problem of reevaluating the probability of a given event in light of the additional information that some other event has already occurred. It often is the case, though, that the probability of the given event remains unchanged, regardless of the outcome of the second event—that is, $P(A|B) = P(A) = P(A|B^C)$. Events sharing this property are said to be *independent*. Definition 2.7.1 gives a necessary and sufficient condition for two events to be independent.

DEFINITION 2.7.1. Two events A and B are said to be *independent* if $P(A \cap B) = P(A) \cdot P(B)$.

Comment. The fact that the probability of the intersection of two independent events is equal to the product of their individual probabilities follows immediately from our first definition of independence, that $P(A|B) = P(A)$. Recall that the definition of conditional probability holds true for *any* two events A and B [provided that $P(B > 0)$]:

$$P(A|B) = \frac{P(A \cap B)}{P(B)}$$

But $P(A|B)$ can equal $P(A)$ only if $P(A \cap B)$ factors into $P(A)$ times $P(B)$.

EXAMPLE 2.7.1

Let A be the event of drawing a king from a standard poker deck and B, the event of drawing a diamond. Then, by Definition 2.7.1, A and B are independent because the probability of their intersection—drawing a king of diamonds—is equal to $P(A) \cdot P(B)$:

$$P(A \cap B) = \frac{1}{52} = \frac{1}{13} \cdot \frac{1}{4} = P(A) \cdot P(B)$$

EXAMPLE 2.7.2

Suppose that A and B are independent events. Does it follow that A^C and B^C are also independent? That is, does $P(A \cap B) = P(A) \cdot P(B)$ guarantee that $P(A^C \cap B^C) = P(A^C) \cdot P(B^C)$?

Yes. The proof is accomplished by equating two different expressions for $P(A^C \cup B^C)$. First, by Theorem 2.3.6,

$$P(A^C \cup B^C) = P(A^C) + P(B^C) - P(A^C \cap B^C) \tag{2.7.1}$$

But the union of two complements is the complement of their intersection (recall Question 2.2.17). Therefore,

$$P(A^C \cup B^C) = 1 - P(A \cap B) \tag{2.7.2}$$

Combining Equations 2.7.1 and 2.7.2, we get

$$1 - P(A \cap B) = 1 - P(A) + 1 - P(B) - P(A^C \cap B^C)$$

Since A and B are independent, $P(A \cap B) = P(A) \cdot P(B)$, so

$$P(A^C \cap B^C) = 1 - P(A) + 1 - P(B) - [1 - P(A) \cdot P(B)]$$
$$= [1 - P(A)][1 - P(B)]$$
$$= P(A^C) \cdot P(B^C)$$

the latter factorization implying that A^C and B^C are, themselves, independent. (If A and B are independent, are A and B^C independent?)

Defining the Independence of More Than Two Events

It is not immediately obvious how to extend Definition 2.7.1 to, say, *three* events. To call $A, B,$ and C independent, should we require that the probability of the three-way intersection factors into the product of the three original probabilities,

$$P(A \cap B \cap C) = P(A) \cdot P(B) \cdot P(C) \tag{2.7.3}$$

or should we impose the definition we already have on the three *pairs* of events:

$$P(A \cap B) = P(A) \cdot P(B)$$
$$P(B \cap C) = P(B) \cdot P(C) \tag{2.7.4}$$
$$P(A \cap C) = P(A) \cdot P(C)$$

As the next two examples show, neither condition by itself is sufficient. If three events satisfy Equations 2.7.3 *and* 2.7.4, we will call them independent (or *mutually independent*), but Equation 2.7.3 does not imply Equation 2.7.4, nor does Equation 2.7.4 imply Equation 2.7.3.

EXAMPLE 2.7.3

Suppose that two fair dice (one red and one green) are thrown, with events $A, B,$ and C defined as follows:

- A: a 1 or a 2 shows on the red die
- B: a 3, 4, or 5 shows on the green die
- C: the dice total is 4, 11, or 12

By direct summation, it is a simple matter to show that $P(A) = \frac{1}{3}$, $P(B) = \frac{1}{2}$, $P(C) = \frac{1}{6}$, $P(A \cap B) = \frac{1}{6}$, $P(A \cap C) = \frac{1}{18}$, $P(B \cap C) = \frac{1}{18}$, and $P(A \cap B \cap C) = \frac{1}{36}$. Note that Equation 2.7.3 is satisfied,

$$P(A \cap B \cap C) = \frac{1}{36} = P(A) \cdot P(B) \cdot P(C) = \left(\frac{1}{3}\right)\left(\frac{1}{2}\right)\left(\frac{1}{6}\right)$$

but Equation 2.7.4 is not:

$$P(B \cap C) = \frac{1}{18} \neq P(B) \cdot P(C) = \left(\frac{1}{2}\right)\left(\frac{1}{6}\right) = \frac{1}{12}$$

EXAMPLE 2.7.4

A roulette wheel has 36 numbers colored red or black according to the pattern indicated in Figure 2.7.1. Let A be the event "Red number appears"; B, the event "Even number appears"; and C, the event "Total is ≤ 18." Then $P(A) = P(B) = P(C) = \frac{1}{2}, P(A \cap B) = \frac{1}{4}, P(B \cap C) = \frac{1}{4}$, and $P(A \cap C) = \frac{1}{4}$. Clearly, A, B, and C are all "pairwise" independent (that is, Equation 2.7.4 holds), yet the probability of the three-way intersection does not factor in accordance with Equation 2.7.3:

$$P(A \cap B \cap C) = \frac{4}{36} = \frac{1}{9} \neq P(A) \cdot P(B) \cdot P(C) = \left(\frac{1}{2}\right)^3 = \frac{1}{8}$$

Roulette wheel pattern																	
1	2	3	4	5	6	·7	8	9	10	11	12	13	14	15	16	17	18
R	R	R	R	R	B	B	B	B	R	R	R	R	B	B	B	B	B
36	35	34	33	32	31	30	29	28	27	26	25	24	23	22	21	20	19

FIGURE 2.7.1

The upshot of Examples 2.7.3 and 2.7.4 is that for n events to be independent, the probabilities of *all* possible intersections must factor into the product of the probabilities of the component events.

DEFINITION 2.7.2. Events $A_1, A_2, \ldots, A_n$ are said to be *independent* if for every set of indices $i_1, i_2, \ldots, i_k$ between 1 and n, inclusive,

$$P(A_{i_1} \cap A_{i_2} \cap \cdots \cap A_{i_k}) = P(A_{i_1}) \cdot P(A_{i_2}) \cdot \ldots \cdot P(A_{i_k})$$

EXAMPLE 2.7.5

Suppose that a fair coin is flipped three times. Let A_1 be the event of a head on the first flip; A_2, a tail on the second flip; and A_3, a head on the third flip. Are A_1, A_2, and A_3 independent? Note, first of all, that

$$P(A_1) = P(A_2) = P(A_3) = \frac{1}{2}$$

Also,

$$P(A_1 \cap A_2) = P(\text{HTH, HTT}) = \frac{2}{8} = \left(\frac{1}{2}\right)\left(\frac{1}{2}\right) = P(A_1) \cdot P(A_2)$$

Similarly,

$$P(A_1 \cap A_3) = \frac{2}{8} = \left(\frac{1}{2}\right)\left(\frac{1}{2}\right) = P(A_1) \cdot P(A_3)$$

and

$$P(A_2 \cap A_3) = \frac{2}{8} = \left(\frac{1}{2}\right)\left(\frac{1}{2}\right) = P(A_2) \cdot P(A_3)$$

Finally,

$$P(A_1 \cap A_2 \cap A_3) = P(\text{HTH}) = \frac{1}{8} = \left(\frac{1}{2}\right)^3 = P(A_1) \cdot P(A_2) \cdot P(A_3)$$

By Definition 2.7.2, then, events A_1, A_2, and A_3, *are* independent.

QUESTIONS

2.7.1 Suppose that two events A and B, each having nonzero probability, are mutually exclusive. Are they also independent?

2.7.2 Suppose that $P(A \cap B) = 0.2$, $P(A) = 0.6$, and $P(B) = 0.5$.
(a) Are A and B mutually exclusive?
(b) Are A and B independent?
(c) Find $P(A^C \cup B^C)$.

2.7.3 A large company is responding to an affirmative-action commitment by setting up hiring quotas by race and sex for office personnel. So far they have agreed to employ the 120 people indicated in the following table. How many black women must they include if they want to be able to claim that the race and sex of the people on their staff are independent?

	White	Black
Male	50	30
Female	40	

2.7.4 Spike is not a terribly bright student. His chances of passing chemistry are 0.35; mathematics, 0.40; and both, 0.12. Are the events "Spike passes chemistry" and "Spike passes mathematics" independent? What is the probability that he fails both subjects?

2.7.5 How many probability equations need to be verified to establish the mutual independence of *four* events?

2.7.6 In a roll of a pair of fair dice (one red and one green), let A be the event the red die shows a 3, 4, or 5; let B be the event the green die shows a 1 or a 2; and let C be the event the dice total is 7. Show that A, B, and C are independent.

2.7.7 In a roll of a pair of fair dice (one red and one green), let A be the event of an odd number on the red die, let B be the event of an odd number on the green die, and let C be the event that the sum is odd. Show that any pair of these events are independent but that A, B, and C are not mutually independent.

2.7.8 If $A_1, A_2, \ldots, A_n$ are independent events, show that

$$P(A_1 \cup A_2 \cup \cdots \cup A_n) = 1 - [1 - P(A_1)] \cdot [1 - P(A_2)] \cdot \ldots \cdot [1 - P(A_n)]$$

Using Independence To Simplify Probability Calculations

While the previous examples in this section have focused on the problem of investigating whether or not a set of events are independent (by examining the conditions spelled out in Definition 2.7.2), there are many situations where the independence of $A_1, A_2, \ldots, A_n$ follows immediately from physical considerations. In these cases we can turn the definition around and use it to provide us with an easy method for evaluating probabilities of intersections.

EXAMPLE 2.7.6

An insurance company has three clients—one in Alaska, one in Missouri, and one in Vermont—whose estimated chances of living to the year 2010 are 0.7, 0.9, and 0.3, respectively. What is the probability that by the end of 2009 the company will have had to pay death benefits to exactly one of the three?

Let A_1 be the event "Alaska client survives through 2009." Define A_2 and A_3 analogously for the Missouri client and Vermont client, respectively. Then the event E: "Exactly one dies" can be written as the union of three intersections:

$$E = (A_1 \cap A_2 \cap A_3^C) \cup (A_1 \cap A_2^C \cap A_3) \cup (A_1^C \cap A_2 \cap A_3)$$

Since each of the intersections is mutually exclusive of the other two,

$$P(E) = P(A_1 \cap A_2 \cap A_3^C) + P(A_1 \cap A_2^C \cap A_3) + P(A_1^C \cap A_2 \cap A_3)$$

Furthermore, there is no reason to believe that for all practical purposes the fates of the three are not independent. That being the case, each of the intersection probabilities reduces to a product, and we can write

$$P(E) = P(A_1) \cdot P(A_2) \cdot P(A_3^C) + P(A_1) \cdot P(A_2^C) \cdot P(A_3) + P(A_1^C) \cdot P(A_2) \cdot P(A_3)$$

$$= (0.7)(0.9)(0.7) + (0.7)(0.1)(0.3) + (0.3)(0.9)(0.3)$$

$$= 0.543$$

Comment.   "Declaring" events independent for reasons other than those prescribed in Definition 2.7.2 is a necessarily subjective endeavor. Here we might feel fairly certain that a "random" person dying in Alaska will not affect the survival chances of a "random" person residing in Missouri (or Vermont). But there may be special circumstances that invalidate that sort of argument. For example, what if the three individuals in question were mercenaries fighting in an African border war and were all crew members assigned to the same helicopter? In practice, all we can do is look at each situation on an individual basis and try to make a reasonable judgment as to whether the occurrence of one event is likely to influence the outcome of another.

EXAMPLE 2.7.7

Audrey has registered for four courses in the upcoming fall term, one each in physics, English, economics, and sociology. Based on what has happened in the recent past, it would be reasonable to assume that she has a 20% chance of being bumped from the physics class, a 10% chance of being bumped from the English class, a 30% chance of being bumped from the economics class, and no chance of being bumped from the sociology class. What is the probability that she fails to get into at least one class?

For the events

A_1: Audrey is bumped from physics

A_2: Audrey is bumped from English

A_3: Audrey is bumped from economics

A_4: Audrey is bumped from sociology

$P(A_1) = 0.20$, $P(A_2) = 0.10$, $P(A_3) = 0.30$, and $P(A_4) = 0$. The chance that Audrey gets bumped from at least one class can be written as the probability of a union,

$$P\left(\begin{array}{c}\text{Audrey is bumped from}\\\text{at least one class}\end{array}\right) = P(A_1 \cup A_2 \cup A_3 \cup A_4) \qquad (2.7.5)$$

but evaluating Equation 2.7.5 is somewhat involved because the A_i's are not mutually exclusive. A much simpler solution is to express the complement of "bumped from at least one" as an intersection:

$$P\left(\begin{array}{c}\text{Audrey is bumped from}\\\text{at least one class}\end{array}\right) = 1 - P\left(\begin{array}{c}\text{Audrey is not bumped}\\\text{from any classes}\end{array}\right)$$

$$= 1 - P(A_1^C \cap A_2^C \cap A_3^C \cap A_4^C)$$

Since different departments are involved, the A_i's are likely to be independent events, so the intersection "factors" and we can write

$$P\left(\begin{array}{c}\text{Audrey is bumped from}\\\text{at least one class}\end{array}\right) = 1 - P(A_1^C)P(A_2^C)P(A_3^C)P(A_4^C)$$

$$= 1 - (0.80)(0.90)(0.70)(1.00)$$

$$= 0.496$$

EXAMPLE 2.7.8

Suppose that one of the genes associated with the control of carbohydrate metabolism exhibits two alleles—a dominant W and a recessive w. If the probabilities of the WW, Ww, and ww genotypes in the present generation are p, q, and r, respectively, for both males and females, what are the chances that an individual in the *next* generation will be a ww?

Let A denote the event that an offspring receives a w allele from its father; let B denote the event that it receives the recessive allele from its mother. What we are looking for is $P(A \cap B)$.

According to the information given,

$$p = P(\text{parent has genotype WW}) = P(\text{WW})$$

$$q = P(\text{parent has genotype Ww}) = P(\text{Ww})$$

$$r = P(\text{parent has genotype ww}) = P(\text{ww})$$

If an offspring is equally likely to receive either of its parent's alleles, the probabilities of A and B can be computed using Theorem 2.6.1:

$$P(A) = P(A|\text{WW})P(\text{WW}) + P(A|\text{Ww})P(\text{Ww}) + P(A|\text{ww})P(\text{ww})$$

$$= 0 \cdot p + \frac{1}{2} \cdot q + 1 \cdot r$$

$$= r + \frac{q}{2} = P(B)$$

Lacking any evidence to the contrary, there is every reason here to assume that A and B are independent events, in which case

$$P(A \cap B) = P(\text{offspring has genotype ww})$$

$$= P(A) \cdot P(B)$$

$$= \left(r + \frac{q}{2} \right)^2$$

(This particular model for allele segregation, together with the independence assumption, is called *random Mendelian mating*.)

EXAMPLE 2.7.9

Protocol for making financial decisions in a certain corporation follows the "circuit" pictured in Figure 2.7.2. Any budget is first screened by 1. If he approves it, the plan is forwarded to 2, 3, and 5. If either 2 or 3 concurs, it goes to 4. If either 4 or 5 say "yes," it moves on to 6 for a final reading. Only if 6 is also in agreement does the proposal pass. Suppose that 1, 5, and 6 each has a 50% chance of saying "yes," whereas 2, 3, and 4 will each concur with a probability of 0.70. If everyone comes to a decision independently, what is the probability that a budget will pass?

Probabilities of this sort are calculated by reducing the circuit to its component unions and intersections. Moreover, if all decisions are made independently, which is the case here, then every intersection becomes a product.

Let A_i be the event that person i approves the budget, $i = 1, 2, \ldots, 6$. Looking at Figure 2.7.2. we see that

$$P(\text{budget passes}) = P\big(A_1 \cap \{[(A_2 \cup A_3) \cap A_4] \cup A_5\} \cap A_6 \big)$$

$$= P(A_1) P\{[(A_2 \cup A_3) \cap A_4] \cup A_5\} P(A_6)$$

By assumption, $P(A_1) = 0.5$, $P(A_2) = 0.7$, $P(A_3) = 0.7$, $P(A_4) = 0.7$, $P(A_5) = 0.5$, and $P(A_6) = 0.5$, so

$$P([(A_2 \cup A_3) \cap A_4]) = [P(A_2) + P(A_3) - P(A_2)P(A_3)]P(A_4)$$

$$= [0.7 + 0.7 - (0.7)(0.7)](0.7)$$

$$= 0.637$$

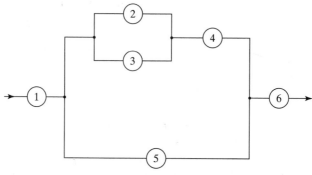

FIGURE 2.7.2

Therefore,

$$P(\text{budget passes}) = (0.5)\{0.637 + 0.5 - (0.637)(0.5)\}(0.5)$$

$$= 0.205$$

CASE STUDY 2.7.1

In 1964, a woman shopping in Los Angeles had her purse snatched by a young, blond female wearing a ponytail. The thief fled on foot but was seen shortly thereafter getting into a yellow automobile driven by a black male who had a mustache and a beard. A police investigation subsequently turned up a suspect, one Janet Collins, who was blond, wore a ponytail, and associated with a black male who drove a yellow car and had a mustache. An arrest was made.

Not having any tangible evidence, and no reliable witnesses, the prosecutor sought to build his case on the unlikelihood of Ms. Collins and her companion sharing these characteristics and not being the guilty parties. First, the bits of evidence that were available were assigned probabilities. It was estimated, for example, that the probability of a female wearing a ponytail in Los Angeles was $\frac{1}{10}$. Table 2.7.1 lists the probabilities quoted for the six "facts" agreed on by the victim and the eyewitnesses (41).

TABLE 2.7.1

Characteristic	Probability
Yellow automobile	$\frac{1}{10}$
Man with a mustache	$\frac{1}{4}$
Woman with a ponytail	$\frac{1}{10}$
Woman with blond hair	$\frac{1}{3}$
Black man with beard	$\frac{1}{10}$
Interracial couple in car	$\frac{1}{1000}$

The prosecutor multiplied these six numbers together and claimed that the product, $\left(\frac{1}{10}\right)\left(\frac{1}{4}\right)\cdots\left(\frac{1}{1000}\right)$, or 1 in 12 million, was the probability of the intersection—that is, the probability that a random couple would fit this description. A probability of 1 in 12 million is so small, he argued, that the only reasonable decision is to find the defendants guilty. The jury agreed and handed down a verdict of second-degree robbery. Later, though, the Supreme Court of California disagreed. Ruling on an appeal, the higher court reversed the decision, claiming that the probability argument was incorrect and misleading. (We will look at the defense counsel's counterargument in Chapter 3.)

QUESTIONS

2.7.9 Two fair dice are rolled. What is the probability that the number showing on one will be twice the number appearing on the other?

2.7.10 Urn I has three red chips, two black chips, and five white chips; urn II has two red, four black, and three white. One chip is drawn at random from each urn. What is the probability that both chips are the same color?

2.7.11 Suppose that for both men and women the distribution of blood types in the general population can be summarized by the following figures:

Blood type	Probability
A	0.40
B	0.10
AB	0.05
O	0.45

What is the probability that a man and woman getting married will have different blood types? What assumption are you making? Is it reasonable?

2.7.12 Dana and Cathy are playing tennis. The probability that Dana wins at least 1 out of 2 games is 0.3. What is the probability that Dana wins at least 1 out of 4?

2.7.13 Two proofreaders are responsible for finding punctuation errors in the editorial section of a newspaper. Jim has an 80% chance of spotting a hyphenation error, while Sally picks up on that same kind of mistake 50% of the time. If the probability is 0.40 that both will see a problem, what is the probability that a hyphenation error will go undetected? Are the events that Jim and Sally recognize a given error independent?

2.7.14 On her way to work, a commuter encounters four traffic signals. Assume that the distance between each of the four is sufficiently great that her probability of getting a green light at any intersection is independent of what happened at any previous intersection. The first two lights are green for 40 seconds of each minute; the last two, for 30 seconds of each minute. What is the probability that the commuter has to stop at least three times?

2.7.15 School board officials are debating whether to require all high school seniors to take a proficiency exam before graduating. A student passing all three parts (mathematics, language skills, and general knowledge) would be awarded a diploma; otherwise, he would receive only a certificate of attendance. A practice test given to this year's 9500 seniors resulted in the following numbers of failures:

Subject area	Number of students failing
Mathematics	3325
Language skills	1900
General knowledge	1425

If "Student fails mathematics," "Student fails language skills," and "Student fails general knowledge" are independent events, what proportion of next year's seniors can be expected to fail to qualify for a diploma? Does independence seem a reasonable assumption in this situation?

2.7.16 Consider the following four-switch circuit:

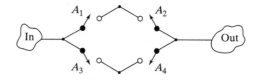

If all switches operate independently and $P(\text{switch closes}) = p$, what is the probability the circuit is completed?

2.7.17 Three points, X_1, X_2, and X_3, are chosen at random in the interval $(0, a)$. A second set of three points, Y_1, Y_2, and Y_3, are chosen at random in the interval $(0, b)$. Let A be the event that X_2 is between X_1 and X_3. Let B be the event that $Y_1 < Y_2 < Y_3$. Find $P(A \cap B)$.

2.7.18 Let A_1, A_2, and A_3 be any set of events that satisfy Definition 2.7.2. Find an expression for $P(A_1 \cup A_2 \cup A_3)$ that does not use complements. *Hint:* Look at the Venn diagram for $A_1 \cup A_2 \cup A_3$ and generalize the two-event formula for a union, $P(A_1 \cup A_2) = P(A_1) + P(A_2) - P(A_1 \cap A_2)$.

2.7.19 Use your answer to Question 2.7.18 to deduce a formula for $P(A_1 \cup A_2 \cup \cdots \cup A_n)$, where the A_i's are independent. What is an easier way to calculate the probability of a union if complements can be used (and independence holds)?

2.7.20 Two myopic deer hunters fire rifles simultaneously and independently at a nearby rooster. The probability of hunter A's shot killing the rooster is 0.2; hunter B's probability is 0.3. Suppose the rooster is hit and killed by only one bullet. What is the probability that hunter B fired the fatal shot?

2.8 REPEATED INDEPENDENT TRIALS

It is not uncommon for an experiment to be the composite of a finite or countably infinite number of "subexperiments," each of the latter being performed under essentially the same conditions. We have already seen simple examples of this sort of structure—for instance, tossing a coin twice. In this section we show how useful this model can be by applying it to several more complicated situations.

In general, the subexperiments comprising an experiment are referred to as *trials*. We will restrict our attention here to problems where the trials are independent—that is, for all j, the probability of any given outcome occurring on the jth trial is unaffected by what happened on the preceding $j - 1$ trials. For outcomes $A_1, A_2, \ldots$ defined on a set of such trials,

$$P(A_1 \cap A_2 \cap \cdots) = P(A_1) \cdot P(A_2) \cdot \ldots$$

EXAMPLE 2.8.1

In the wake of the *Challenger* disaster, NASA officials estimated that the chances of a similar catastrophic accident during a shuttle flight are roughly 1 in 78. If that assessment is correct, what is the probability that there will be at least one crash among the next 20 launches? Assume that the outcome of any flight has no effect on the success of any other flights.

Let A_i be the event that the ith shuttle crashes, $i = 1, 2, \ldots, 20$. By assumption, $P(A_i) = \frac{1}{78}$ and the A_i's are independent. An application of Definition 2.7.2 (on the complements of the A_i's) shows that the probability of at least one crash is a disturbingly large 0.23:

$$P(\text{at least one crash in 20 launches}) = P(A_1 \cup A_2 \cup \cdots \cup A_{20})$$

$$= 1 - P(\text{no crashes in 20 launches})$$

$$= 1 - P(A_1^C \cap A_2^C \cap \cdots \cap A_{20}^C)$$

$$= 1 - P(A_1^C)P(A_2^C) \cdots P(A_{20}^C)$$

$$= 1 - \left(\frac{77}{78}\right)^{20}$$

$$= 0.23$$

(see Question 2.8.8).

EXAMPLE 2.8.2

During the 1978 baseball season, Pete Rose of the Cincinnati Reds set a National League record by hitting safely in 44 consecutive games. Assume that Rose is a .300 hitter and that he comes to bat four times each game. If each at-bat is assumed to be an independent event, what probability might reasonably be associated with a hitting streak of that length?

For this problem we need to invoke the repeated independent trials model *twice*—once for the four at-bats making up a game and a second time for the 44 games making up the streak. Let A_i denote the event "Rose hits safely in ith game," $i = 1, 2, \ldots, 44$. Then

$$P(\text{Rose hits safely in 44 consecutive games}) = P(A_1 \cap A_2 \cap \cdots \cap A_{44})$$

$$= P(A_1) \cdot P(A_2) \cdot \ldots \cdot P(A_{44}) \qquad (2.8.1)$$

Since all the $P(A_i)$'s are equal, we can further simplify Equation 2.8.1 by writing

$$P(\text{Rose hits safely in 44 consecutive games}) = [P(A_1)]^{44}$$

To calculate $P(A_1)$ we should focus on the *complement* of A_1. Specifically,

$$P(A_1) = 1 - P(A_1^C)$$

$$= 1 - P(\text{Rose does } not \text{ hit safely in Game 1})$$

$$= 1 - P(\text{Rose makes four outs})$$

$$= 1 - (0.700)^4 \qquad (\text{why?})$$

$$= 0.76$$

Therefore, the probability of a .300 hitter putting together a 44-game streak (during a given set of 44 games) is 0.0000057:

$$P(\text{Rose hits safely in 44 consecutive games}) = (0.76)^{44}$$

$$= 0.0000057$$

EXAMPLE 2.8.3

A box contains one two-headed coin and eight fair coins. One is drawn at random and tossed seven times. Suppose that all seven tosses come up heads. What is the probability that the coin is fair?

This is basically a Bayes's problem, but the conditional probabilities on the right-hand-side of Theorem 2.6.2 appeal to the notion of independence as well. Define the events

B: seven heads occurred in seven tosses

A_1: coin tossed has two heads

A_2: coin tossed was fair

The question is asking for $P(A_2 | B)$.

By virtue of the composition of the box, $P(A_1) = \frac{1}{9}$ and $P(A_2) = \frac{8}{9}$. Also,

$$P(B | A_1) = P(\text{Head on 1st toss} \cap \cdots \cap \text{Head on 7th toss} | \text{Coin has 2 heads})$$

$$= 1^7 = 1$$

Similarly, $P(B | A_2) = \left(\frac{1}{2}\right)^7$. Substituting into Bayes's formula shows that the probability is 0.06 that the coin is fair:

$$P(A_2 | B) = \frac{P(B | A_2)P(A_2)}{P(B | A_1)P(A_1) + P(B | A_2)P(A_2)}$$

$$= \frac{\left(\frac{1}{2}\right)^7(8/9)}{1(1/9) + \left(\frac{1}{2}\right)^7(8/9)}$$

$$= 0.06$$

Comment.   Suppose the coin is flipped n times, and let B_n be the event that heads appear on all n tosses. Notice that

$$\lim_{n \to \infty} P(A_2 | B_n) = \lim_{n \to \infty} \frac{8\left(\frac{1}{2}\right)^n}{1 + 8\left(\frac{1}{2}\right)^n} = 0$$

which is the asymptotic result that is intuitively reasonable.

EXAMPLE 2.8.4

A computer is instructed to generate a random sequence using the digits 0 through 9; repetitions are permissible. What is the shortest length the sequence can be and still have at least a 70% probability of containing at least one 4?

Here, as in so many probability problems, the phrase *at least one* is an unmistakable verbal clue, pointing us toward the complement. Suppose the length of a sequence is n, and A_i is the event that the ith digit in that sequence is a 4, $i = 1, 2, \ldots, n$. Then

$$P(\text{at least one 4 appears in } n \text{ digits}) = P(A_1 \cup A_2 \cup \cdots \cup A_n)$$

$$= 1 - P(\text{no digit is a 4}) = 1 - P(A_1^C \cap A_2^C \cap \cdots \cap A_n^C)$$

Given that the digits are random, the A_i's are independent. Therefore,

$$P(\text{at least one 4 appears in } n \text{ digits}) = 1 - P(A_1^C)P(A_2^C) \cdots P(A_n^C)$$

$$= 1 - \left(\frac{9}{10}\right)^n$$

Table 2.8.1 shows the magnitude of $1 - \left(\frac{9}{10}\right)^n$ for various values of n. By inspection, the smallest n for which the sequence has at least a 70% probability of containing at least one 4 is 12.

TABLE 2.8.1

n	$1 - \left(\dfrac{9}{10}\right)^n$	≥ 0.70?
5	0.41	no
10	0.65	no
11	0.69	no
$\longrightarrow$ 12	0.72	yes

EXAMPLE 2.8.5

Repeated independent trials problems sometimes involve experiments consisting of a count-ably infinite number of subexperiments. Conceptually, such problems are approached no dif-ferently than the ones we have just seen. Their solutions, though, typically require an application of the formula for the sum of a geometric series. Recall that for $0 < t < 1$,

$$\sum_{k=0}^{\infty} t^k = \frac{1}{1-t} \tag{2.8.2}$$

Probabilities associated with games of chance often make use of Equation 2.8.2, a case in point being the familiar game of craps (recall Question 2.2.7). In this example the rules of craps are translated into sums of countably infinite intersections for the purpose of calculating the prob-ability that the *shooter* (the person rolling the dice) wins.

There are two basic ways the shooter can win: (1) by throwing either a 7 or an 11 on his first roll (this is called a *natural*); or (2) by throwing either a 4, 5, 6, 8, 9, or 10 on his first roll and then throwing that number again *before* he rolls a 7 (this is called *making his point*). Let A_1 be the event that the shooter throws a natural, and let A_4, A_5, A_6, A_8, A_9, and A_{10} be the events that the shooter eventually wins when his point is a 4, 5, 6, 8, 9, or 10, respectively. The A_i's are mutually exclusive, so

$$P(\text{shooter wins}) = P(A_1) + P(A_4) + P(A_5) + P(A_6) + P(A_8) + P(A_9) + P(A_{10})$$

The probability of throwing a natural is a simple finite sum:

$$P(A_1) = P(7 \text{ or } 11) = P(7) + P(11) = \frac{6}{36} + \frac{2}{36} = \frac{8}{36}$$

To determine the remaining $P(A_i)$'s, we need to think of the game as a series of repeated in-dependent trials. For example, the shooter will win with a point of 4 if he rolls a 4 on the first throw and a 4 on the second *or* a 4 on the first, something other than a 4 or a 7 on the second, and a 4 on the third *or* a 4 on the first, something other than a 4 or a 7 on the second and third, and a 4 on the fourth, and so on. Let B be the event that something other than a 4 or a 7 oc-curs. Then, appealing again to the fact that these events are all mutually exclusive, we can write

$$P(A_4) = P(4 \text{ on 1st} \cap 4 \text{ on 2nd}) + P(4 \text{ on 1st} \cap B \text{ on 2nd} \cap 4 \text{ on 3rd})$$

$$+ P(4 \text{ on 1st} \cap B \text{ on 2nd} \cap B \text{ on 3rd} \cap 4 \text{ on 4th}) + \cdots$$

If no one is cheating and the dice are fair, $P(4) = \frac{3}{36}$ and $P(B) = \frac{27}{36}$. Since each roll is an in-dependent trial,

$$P(A_4) = \left(\frac{3}{36}\right)\left(\frac{3}{36}\right) + \left(\frac{3}{36}\right)\left(\frac{27}{36}\right)\left(\frac{3}{36}\right) + \left(\frac{3}{36}\right)\left(\frac{27}{36}\right)\left(\frac{27}{36}\right)\left(\frac{3}{36}\right) + \cdots$$

$$= \left(\frac{3}{36}\right)^2 \sum_{k=0}^{\infty} \left(\frac{27}{36}\right)^k = \left(\frac{3}{36}\right)^2 \left[\frac{1}{1-(27/36)}\right]$$

$$= \frac{1}{36}$$

The other $P(A_i)$'s are calculated similarly. Because of symmetry we need only to determine $P(A_4), P(A_5)$, and $P(A_6)$: since the probability of throwing a 4 is the same as the probability of throwing a 10, $P(A_4) = P(A_{10})$—also, $P(A_5) = P(A_9)$ and $P(A_6) = P(A_8)$.

TABLE 2.8.2

Winning event, A_i	$P(A_i)$
A_1	$\frac{8}{36}$
A_4	$\frac{1}{36}$
A_5	$\frac{16}{360}$
A_6	$\frac{25}{396}$
A_8	$\frac{25}{396}$
A_9	$\frac{16}{360}$
A_{10}	$\frac{1}{36}$

Table 2.8.2 summarizes the results. Adding the seven entries in the second column gives the probability that we set out to find:

$$P(\text{shooter wins}) = \frac{8}{36} + \frac{1}{36} + \cdots + \frac{1}{36}$$

$$= 0.493$$

As even-money games of chance go, craps is relatively "fair"—the probability of the shooter winning is not much less than 0.500. On the other hand, the game goes very quickly so a player can still manage to lose a lot of money in a short period of time.

Comment.   Money can also be *won* very quickly playing craps. In 1980, a man walked into the Horseshoe Club in downtown Las Vegas carrying two suitcases—one empty, the other stuffed with $777,000 worth of $100 bills. Strolling over to a craps table, he bet the full amount against the shooter. The woman rolling the dice at the table first threw a six, then a nine, *then a seven*. She lost, he won! Moments later, after making a little stop at the cashier's window, he left the casino with *two* suitcases full of money. It was the largest recorded single bet in the history of Las Vegas.

We conclude this section with a "fun" problem that leads to an unusual and unexpected survival tip. The setting is a three-cornered pistol duel, where the participants fire sequentially at whomever they choose. In question is the strategy that should be followed by the person who is allowed to go first. What the analysis shows is that that individual's prospects for a long life are best served if he deliberately fires his first shot into the ground! At first glance it might seem that such a strategy is hopelessly suicidal, but the proof of its optimality is a relatively straightforward application of Definition 2.7.2 and Equation 2.8.2.

EXAMPLE 2.8.6

Andy, Bob, and Charley have gotten into a disagreement over a female acquaintance and decide to settle their dispute with a three-cornered pistol duel. Of the three, Andy is the worst shot, hitting his target only 30% of the time. Charley, a little better, is on-target 50% of the time, while Bob never misses (see Figure 2.8.1). The rules they agree to are simple: They are to fire at the targets of their choice in succession, and cyclically, in the order Andy, Bob, Charley, Andy, Bob, Charley, and so on until only one of them is left standing. (On each "turn," they get only one shot. If a combatant is hit, he no longer participates, either as a shooter or as a target.)

FIGURE 2.8.1

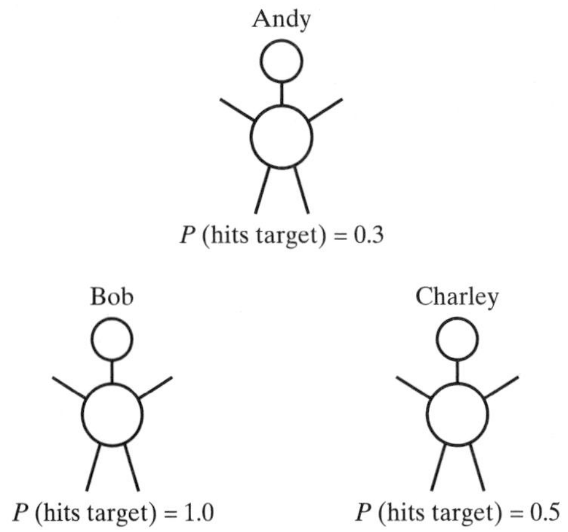

Andy

P (hits target) $= 0.3$

Bob

P (hits target) $= 1.0$

Charley

P (hits target) $= 0.5$

As Andy loads his revolver he mulls over his options (his objective, of course, is clear—to maximize his probability of survival). According to the rules, he has his choice of shooting at either Bob or Charley, but he quickly rules out the latter as being counterproductive to his future well-being. If he shot at Charley and had the misfortune of hitting him, it would then be Bob's turn, and Bob would have no recourse but to shoot at Andy. From Andy's point of view, this would be a decidedly grim turn of events, since Bob never misses. It seems clear, then, that Andy's only viable option is to shoot at Bob. This leaves two scenarios: (1) He might shoot at Bob and hit him, or (2) he might shoot at Bob and miss.

Consider the first possibility. If Andy hits Bob, Charley will proceed to shoot at Andy, Andy will shoot back at Charley, and so on, until one of them hits the other. Let CH_i and CM_i denote the events "Charley hits Andy with ith shot" and "Charley misses Andy with ith shot," respectively. Define AH_i and AM_i analogously. Then Andy's chances of survival (given that he has killed Bob) reduce to a countably infinite union of intersections:

$$P(\text{Andy survives}) = P\big((CM_1 \cap AH_1) \cup (CM_1 \cap AM_1 \cap CM_2 \cap AH_2)$$
$$\cup (CM_1 \cap AM_1 \cap CM_2 \cap AM_2 \cap CM_3 \cap AH_3) \cup \cdots\big)$$

Note that each intersection is mutually exclusive of all the others and its component events are independent. Therefore,

$$P(\text{Andy survives}) = P(CM_1)P(AH_1) + P(CM_1)P(AM_1)P(CM_2)P(AH_2)$$
$$+ P(CM_1)P(AM_1)P(CM_2)P(AM_2)P(CM_3)P(AH_3) + \cdots$$
$$= (0.5)(0.3) + (0.5)(0.7)(0.5)(0.3)$$
$$+ (0.5)(0.7)(0.5)(0.7)(0.5)(0.3) + \cdots$$
$$= (0.5)(0.3) \sum_{k=0}^{\infty} (0.35)^k$$
$$= (0.15)\left(\frac{1}{1 - 0.35}\right)$$
$$= \frac{3}{13}$$

Now consider the second scenario. If Andy shoots at Bob and misses, Bob will undoubtedly shoot at (and hit) Charley, since Charley is the more dangerous adversary. Then it will be Andy's turn again. Whether or not he sees another tomorrow will depend on his ability to make that very next shot count. Specifically,

$$P(\text{Andy survives}) = P(\text{Andy hits Bob on second turn})$$

$$= \frac{3}{10}$$

But $\frac{3}{10} > \frac{3}{13}$, so Andy is better off *not* hitting Bob with his first shot. And because we have already argued it would be foolhardy for Andy to shoot at Charley, Andy's optimal strategy is clear—deliberately miss everyone with the first shot.

QUESTIONS

2.8.1 A string of eight Christmas tree lights is wired in series. If the probability of any particular bulb being broken is 0.05, what is the probability that the string will not work? Assume that defective bulbs are independent events.

2.8.2 According to an advertising study, 15% of television viewers who have seen a certain automobile commercial can correctly identify the actor who does the voiceover. Suppose that 10 such people are watching TV and the commercial comes on. What is the probability that at least one of them can name the actor? What is the probability that exactly one can name the actor?

2.8.3 A fair die is rolled and then n fair coins are tossed, where n is the number showing on the die. What is the probability that no heads appear?

2.8.4 A fast-food chain is running a new promotion. For each purchase, a customer is given a game card that may win $10. The company claims that the probability of a person winning at least once in five tries is 0.32. What is the probability that a customer wins $10 on his or her first purchase?

2.8.5 Each of m urns contains three red chips and four white chips. A total of r samples with replacement are taken from each urn. What is the probability that at least one red chip is drawn from at least one urn?

2.8.6 In a certain Third World nation, statistics show that only 2000 out of 10,000 children born in the early 1960s reached the age of 21. If the same mortality rate is operative over the next generation, how many children should a couple plan to have if they want to be at least 75% certain that at least one of their offspring survives to adulthood?

2.8.7 If two fair dice are tossed, what is the smallest number of throws, n, for which the probability of getting at least one double six exceeds 0.5? (*Note:* This was one of the first problems that de Méré communicated to Pascal in 1654.)

2.8.8 Recall Example 2.8.1. Is it reasonable to assume that the 20 launches would, in fact, be independent trials, each having the same probability, $\frac{1}{78}$, of ending in disaster? What would happen, for example, if the first two flights crashed?

2.8.9 Players A, B, and C toss a fair coin in order. The first to throw a head wins. What are their respective chances of winning?

2.8.10 In rolling a pair of fair dice, what is the probability that a sum of 8 will appear before a sum of 7?

2.8.11 You are playing for the Monopoly Championship of the World. Your opponent is on Go. It is your turn and you have enough money to put a house on either Oriental Avenue or Vermont Avenue. The two properties are 6 and 8 spaces away from Go, respectively. Where should you put the house?

2.8.12 An urn contains w white chips, b black chips, and r red chips. The chips are drawn out at random, one at a time, with replacement. What is the probability that a white appears before a red?

2.8.13 A Coast Guard dispatcher receives an SOS from a ship that has run aground off the shore of a small island. Before the captain can relay her exact position, though, her radio goes dead. The dispatcher has n helicopter crews he can send out to conduct a search. He suspects the ship is somewhere either south in area I (with probability p) or north in area II (with probability $1 - p$). Each of the n rescue parties is equally competent and has probability r of locating the ship given it has run aground in the sector being searched. How should the dispatcher deploy the helicopter crews to maximize the probability that one of them will find the missing ship? *Hint*: Assume that m search crews are sent to area I and $n - m$ are sent to area II. Let B denote the event that the ship is found, let A_1 be the event that the ship is in area I, and let A_2 be the event that the ship is in area II. Use Theorem 2.6.1 to get an expression for $P(B)$; then differentiate with respect to m.

2.9 COMBINATORICS

Combinatorics is a time-honored branch of mathematics concerned with counting, arranging, and ordering. While blessed with a wealth of early contributors (there are references to combinatorial problems in the Old Testament), its emergence as a separate discipline is often credited to the German mathematician and philosopher Gottfried Wilhelm Leibniz (1646–1716), whose 1666 treatise, *Dissertatio de arte combinatoria*, was perhaps the first monograph written on the subject (98).

Applications of combinatorics are rich in both diversity and number. Users range from the molecular biologist trying to determine how many ways genes can be positioned along a chromosome, to a computer scientist studying queueing priorities, to a psychologist modeling the way we learn, to a weekend poker player wondering whether he should draw to a straight, or a flush, or a full house. Surprisingly enough, solutions to all of these questions are rooted in the same set of four basic theorems and rules, despite the considerable differences that seem to distinguish one question from another.

Counting Ordered Sequences: The Multiplication Rule

More often than not, the relevant "outcomes" in a combinatorial problem are ordered sequences. If two dice are rolled, for example, the outcome (4,5)—that is, the first die comes up 4 and the second die comes up 5—is an ordered sequence of length two. The number of such sequences is calculated by using the most fundamental result in combinatorics, the *multiplication rule*.

> **MULTIPLICATION RULE.** If operation A can be performed in m different ways and operation B in n different ways, the sequence (operation A, operation B) can be performed in $m \cdot n$ different ways.

Proof.   At the risk of belaboring the obvious, we can verify the multiplication rule by considering a *tree* diagram (see Figure 2.9.1). Since each version of A can be followed by any of n versions of B, and there are m of the former, the total number of "A, B" sequences that can be pieced together is obviously the product $m \cdot n$.

FIGURE 2.9.1   Operation A Operation B

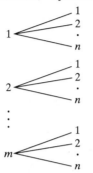

COROLLARY.   If operation A_i, $i = 1, 2, \ldots, k$, can be performed in n_i ways, $i = 1, 2, \ldots, k$, respectively, then the ordered sequence (operation A_1, operation $A_2, \ldots$, operation A_k) can be performed in $n_1 \cdot n_2 \cdot \ldots \cdot n_k$ ways.

EXAMPLE 2.9.1

The combination lock on a briefcase has two dials, each marked off with 16 notches (see Figure 2.9.2). To open the case, a person first turns the left dial in a certain direction for two revolutions and then stops on a particular mark. The right dial is set in a similar fashion, after having been turned in a certain direction for two revolutions. How many different settings are possible?

In the terminology of the multiplication rule, opening the briefcase corresponds to the four-step sequence (A_1, A_2, A_3, A_4) detailed in Table 2.9.1. Applying the previous corollary, we see that 1024 different settings are possible:

$$\text{Number of different settings} = n_1 \cdot n_2 \cdot n_3 \cdot n_4$$

$$= 2 \cdot 16 \cdot 2 \cdot 16$$

$$= 1024$$

FIGURE 2.9.2

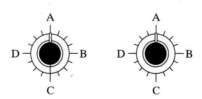

TABLE 2.9.1

Operation	Purpose	Number of options
A_1	Rotating the left dial in a particular direction	2
A_2	Choosing an endpoint for the left dial	16
A_3	Rotating the right dial in a particular direction	2
A_4	Choosing an endpoint for the right dial	16

Comment. Designers of locks should be aware that the number of dials, as opposed to the number of notches on each dial, is the critical factor in determining how many different settings are possible. A two-dial lock, for example, where each dial has 20 notches, gives rise to only $2 \cdot 20 \cdot 2 \cdot 20 = 1600$ settings. If those 40 notches, though, are distributed among *four* dials (10 to each dial), the number of different settings increases a hundredfold to *160,000* $(= 2 \cdot 10 \cdot 2 \cdot 10 \cdot 2 \cdot 10 \cdot 2 \cdot 10)$.

EXAMPLE 2.9.2

Alphonse Bertillon, a nineteenth-century French criminologist, developed an identification system based on 11 anatomical variables (height, head width, ear length, etc.) that presumably remained essentially unchanged during an individual's adult life. The range of each variable was divided into three subintervals: small, medium, and large. A person's *Bertillon configuration* was an ordered sequence of 11 letters, say

$$s, s, m, m, l, s, l, s, s, m, s$$

where a letter indicated the individual's "size" relative to a particular variable. How populated does a city have to be before it can be guaranteed that at least two citizens will have the same Bertillon configuration?

Viewed as an ordered sequence, a Bertillon configuration is an 11-step classification system, where three options are available at each step. By the multiplication rule, a total of 3^{11}, or 177,147, distinct sequences are possible. Therefore, any city with at least 177,148 adults would necessarily have at least two residents with the same pattern. (The limited number of possibilities generated by Bertillon's variables proved to be one of its major weaknesses. Still, it was widely used in Europe for criminal identification before the development of fingerprinting.)

EXAMPLE 2.9.3

In 1824 Louis Braille invented what would eventually become the standard alphabet for the blind. Based on an earlier form of "night writing" used by the French army for reading battlefield communiques in the dark, Braille's system replaced each written character with a six-dot matrix:

where certain dots were raised, the choice depending on the character being transcribed. The letter e, for example, has two raised dots and is written

Punctuation marks, common words, suffixes, and so on also have specified dot patterns. In all, how many different characters can be enciphered in Braille?

  Think of the dots as six distinct operations, numbered 1 to 6 (see Figure 2.9.3). In forming a Braille letter, we have two options for each dot: We can raise it or *not* raise it. The letter e, for example, corresponds to the six-step sequence (raise, do not raise, do not raise, do not raise, raise, do not raise). The number of such sequences, with $k = 6$ and $n_1 = n_2 = \ldots = n_6 = 2$, is 2^6, or 64. One of those 64 configurations, though, has *no* raised dots, making it of no use to a blind person. Figure 2.9.4 shows the entire 63-character Braille alphabet.

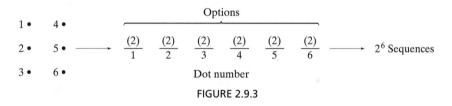

FIGURE 2.9.3

EXAMPLE 2.9.4

The annual NCAA ("March Madness") basketball tournament starts with a field of 64 teams. After six rounds of play, the squad that remains unbeaten is declared the national champion. How many different configurations of winners and losers are possible, starting with the first round? Assume that the initial pairing of the 64 invited teams into 32 first-round matches has already been done.

  Counting the number of ways a tournament of this sort can play out is an exercise in applying the multiplication rule twice. Notice, first, that the 32 first-round games can be decided in 2^{32} ways. Similarly, the resulting 16 second-round games can generate 2^{16} different winners, and so on. Overall, the tournament can be pictured as a six-step sequence, where the number of possible outcomes at the six steps are 2^{32}, 2^{16}, 2^8, 2^4, 2^2, and 2^1, respectively. It follows that the number of possible tournaments (not all of which, of course, would be equally likely!) is the product $2^{32} \cdot 2^{16} \cdot 2^8 \cdot 2^4 \cdot 2^2 \cdot 2^1$, or 2^{63}.

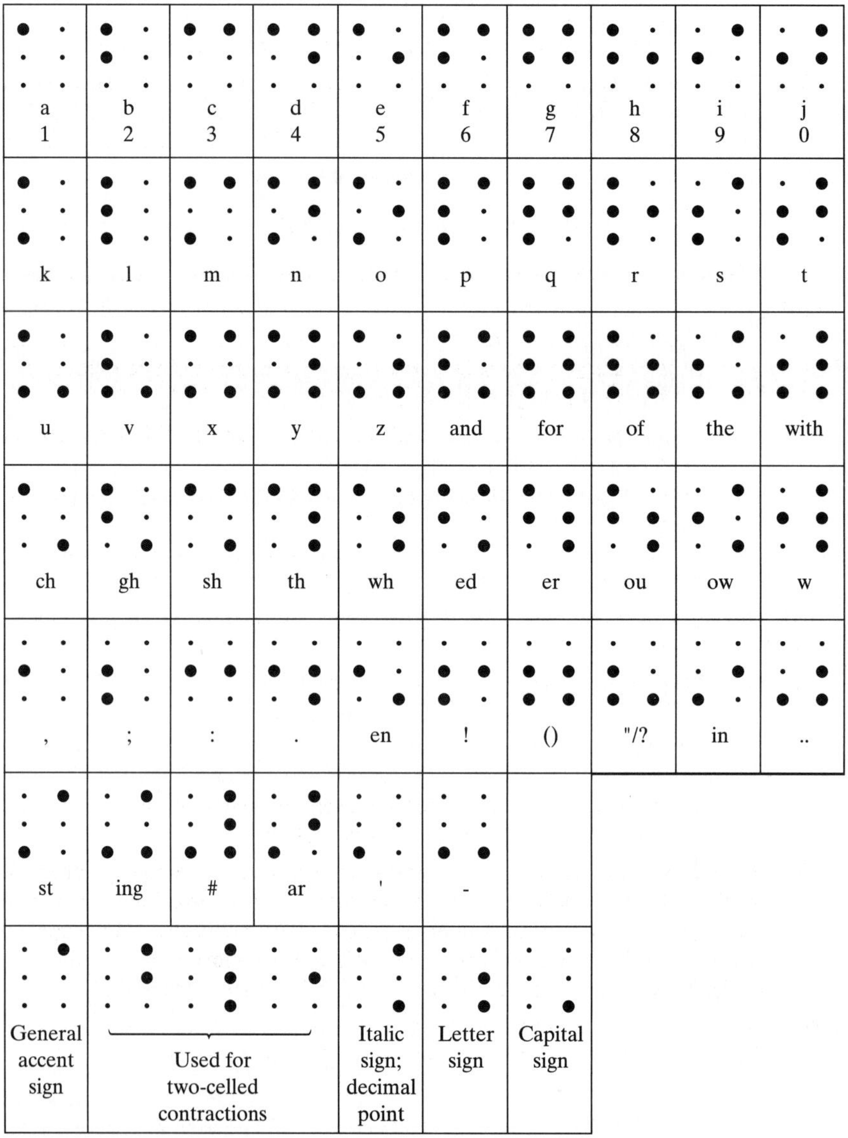
a 1
b 2
c 3
d 4
e 5
f 6
g 7
h 8
i 9
j 0
k
l
m
n
o
p
q
r
s
t
u
v
x
y
z
and
for
of
the
with
ch
gh
sh
th
wh
ed
er
ou
ow
w
,
;
:
.
en
!
()
"/?
in
..
st
ing
#
ar
'
-
General accent sign
Used for two-celled contractions
Italic sign; decimal point
Letter sign
Capital sign

FIGURE 2.9.4

QUESTIONS

2.9.1 A chemical engineer wishes to observe the effects of temperature, pressure, and catalyst concentration on the yield resulting from a certain reaction. If she intends to include two different temperatures, three pressures, and two levels of catalyst, how many different runs must she make in order to observe each temperature-pressure-catalyst combination exactly twice?

2.9.2 A coded message from a CIA operative to his Russian KGB counterpart is to be sent in the form Q4ET, where the first and last entries must be consonants; the second, an integer 1 through 9; and the third, one of the six vowels. How many different ciphers can be transmitted?

2.9.3 How many terms will be included in the expansion of

$$(a + b + c)(d + e + f)(x + y + u + v + w)$$

Which of the following will be included in that number: *aeu, cdx, bef, xvw*?

2.9.4 An octave contains 12 distinct notes (on a piano, five black keys and seven white keys). How many different eight-note melodies within a single octave can be written using the white keys only? How many different eight-note melodies within a single octave can be written if the black keys and white keys need to alternate?

2.9.5 Suppose that the format for license plates in a certain state is two letters followed by four numbers.
 (a) How many different plates can be made?
 (b) How many different plates are there if the letters can be repeated but no two numbers can be the same?
 (c) How many different plates can be made if repetitions of numbers and letters is allowed except that no plate can have four zeros?

2.9.6 How many integers between 100 and 999 have distinct digits, and how many of those are odd numbers?

2.9.7 A fast-food restaurant offers customers a choice of eight toppings that can be added to a hamburger. How many different hamburgers can be ordered?

2.9.8 In baseball there are 24 different "base-out" configurations (runner on first—two outs, bases loaded—none out, and so on). Suppose that a new game, sleazeball, is played where there are seven bases (excluding home plate) and each team gets five outs an inning. How many base-out configurations would be possible in sleazeball?

2.9.9 When they were first introduced, postal zip codes were five-digit numbers, theoretically ranging from 00000 to 99999. (In reality, the lowest zip code was 00601 for San Juan, Puerto Rico; the highest was 99950 for Ketchikan, Alaska.) An additional four digits have recently been added, so each zip code is now a nine-digit number. How many zip codes are at least as large as 60000–0000, are even numbers, and have a 7 as their third digit?

2.9.10 A restaurant offers a choice of 4 appetizers, 14 entrees, 6 desserts, and 5 beverages. How many different meals are possible if a diner intends to order only three courses? (Consider the beverage to be a "course".)

2.9.11 Proteins are chains of molecules chosen (with repetition) from some 20 different amino acids. In a living cell, proteins are synthesized through the *genetic code*, a mechanism whereby ordered sequences of nucleotides in the messenger RNA dictate the formation of a particular amino acid. The four key nucleotides are adenine, guanine, cytosine, and uracil (A, G, C, and U). Assuming A, G, C, or U can appear any number of times in a nucleotide chain and that all sequences are physically possible, what is the minimum length the chains must attain to have the capability of encoding the entire set of amino acids? *Note:* Each sequence in the genetic code must have the same number of nucleotides.

2.9.12 Residents of a condominium have an automatic garage door opener that has a row of eight buttons. Each garage door has been programmed to respond to a particular set of buttons being pushed. If the condominium houses 250 families, can residents be assured that no two garage doors will open on the same signal? If so, how many additional families can be added before the eight-button code becomes inadequate? *Note:* The order in which the buttons are pushed is irrelevant.

2.9.13 In international Morse code, each letter in the alphabet is symbolized by a series of dots and dashes: the letter "a," for example, is encoded as "·—". What is the maximum number of dots and/or dashes needed to represent any letter in the English alphabet?

2.9.14 The decimal number corresponding to a sequence of n binary digits $a_0, a_1 \ldots, a_{n-1}$, where each a_i is either 0 or 1, is defined to be

$$a_0 2^0 + a_1 2^1 + \ldots + a_{n-1} 2^{n-1}$$

For example, the sequence 0 1 1 0 is equal to 6 $(= 0 \cdot 2^0 + 1 \cdot 2^1 + 1 \cdot 2^2 + 0 \cdot 2^3)$. Suppose a fair coin is tossed nine times. Replace the resulting sequence of H's and T's with a binary sequence of 1's and 0's (1 for H, 0 for T). For how many sequences of tosses will the decimal corresponding to the observed set of heads and tails exceed 256?

Counting Permutations (when the objects are all distinct)

Ordered sequences arise in two fundamentally different ways. The first is the scenario addressed by the multiplication rule—a process is comprised of k operations, each allowing n_i options, $i = 1, 2, \ldots, k$; choosing one version of each operation leads to $n_1 n_2 \ldots n_k$ possibilities.

The second occurs when an ordered arrangement of some specified length k is formed from a finite collection of objects. Any such arrangement is referred to as a *permutation of length* k. For example, given the three objects A, B, and C, there are six different permutations of length 2 that can be formed if the objects cannot be repeated: AB, AC, BC, BA, CA, and CB.

> **THEOREM 2.9.1.** The number of permutations of length k that can be formed from a set of n distinct elements, repetitions not allowed, is denoted by the symbol $_nP_k$, where
>
> $$_nP_k = n(n-1)(n-2)\cdots(n-k+1) = \frac{n!}{(n-k)!}$$
>
> **Proof.** Any of the n objects may occupy the first position in the arrangement, any of $n-1$ the second, and so on—the number of choices available for filling the kth position will be $n - k + 1$ (see Figure 2.9.5). The theorem follows, then, from the multiplication rule: There will be $n(n-1)\cdots(n-k+1)$ ordered arrangements.
>
> **COROLLARY.** The number of ways to permute an entire set of n distinct objects is $_nP_n = n(n-1)(n-2)\cdots 1 = n!$.

FIGURE 2.9.5

$$\text{Choices:} \quad \underbrace{\frac{n}{1} \quad \frac{n-1}{2} \quad \cdots \quad \frac{n-(k-2)}{k-1} \quad \frac{n-(k-1)}{k}}_{\text{Permutations of length } k}$$

EXAMPLE 2.9.5

How many permutations of length $k = 3$ can be formed from the set of $n = 4$ distinct elements, A, B, C, and D?

According to Theorem 2.9.1, the number should be 24:

$$\frac{n!}{(n-k)!} = \frac{4!}{(4-3)!} = \frac{4 \cdot 3 \cdot 2 \cdot 1}{1} = 24$$

Confirming that figure, Table 2.9.2 lists the entire set of 24 permutations and illustrates the argument used in the proof of the theorem.

TABLE 2.9.2

1.	(ABC)
2.	(ABD)
3.	(ACB)
4.	(ACD)
5.	(ADB)
6.	(ADC)
7.	(BAC)
8.	(BAD)
9.	(BCA)
10.	(BCD)
11.	(BDA)
12.	(BDC)
13.	(CAB)
14.	(CAD)
15.	(CBA)
16.	(CBD)
17.	(CDA)
18.	(CDB)
19.	(DAB)
20.	(DAC)
21.	(DBA)
22.	(DBC)
23.	(DCA)
24.	(DCB)

EXAMPLE 2.9.6

In her sonnet with the famous first line, "How do I love thee? Let me count the ways," Elizabeth Barrett Browning listed eight. Suppose Ms. Browning had decided that writing greeting cards afforded her a better format for expressing her feelings. For how many years could she have corresponded with her favorite beau on a daily basis and never sent the same card twice? Assume that each card contains exactly four of the eight "ways" and that order matters.

In selecting the verse for a card, Ms. Browning would be creating a permutation of length $k = 4$ from a set of $n = 8$ distinct objects. According to Theorem 2.9.1, pushed. If the condominium houses 250 families, can residents be assured that no two garage doors will open on the same signal? If so, how many additional families can be added before the eight-button code becomes inadequate? *Note:* The order in which the buttons are pushed is irrelevant.

2.9.13 In international Morse code, each letter in the alphabet is symbolized by a series of dots and dashes: the letter "a," for example, is encoded as "·—". What is the maximum number of dots and/or dashes needed to represent any letter in the English alphabet?

2.9.14 The decimal number corresponding to a sequence of n binary digits $a_0, a_1 \ldots, a_{n-1}$, where each a_i is either 0 or 1, is defined to be

$$a_0 2^0 + a_1 2^1 + \ldots + a_{n-1} 2^{n-1}$$

For example, the sequence 0 1 1 0 is equal to $6 \left(= 0 \cdot 2^0 + 1 \cdot 2^1 + 1 \cdot 2^2 + 0 \cdot 2^3\right)$. Suppose a fair coin is tossed nine times. Replace the resulting sequence of H's and T's with a binary sequence of 1's and 0's (1 for H, 0 for T). For how many sequences of tosses will the decimal corresponding to the observed set of heads and tails exceed 256?

Counting Permutations (when the objects are all distinct)

Ordered sequences arise in two fundamentally different ways. The first is the scenario addressed by the multiplication rule—a process is comprised of k operations,

FIGURE 2.9.6

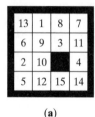 

(a)   (b)

each allowing n_i options, $i = 1, 2, \ldots, k$; choosing one version of each operation leads to $n_1 n_2 \ldots n_k$ possibilities.

The second occurs when an ordered arrangement of some specified length k is formed from a finite collection of objects. Any such arrangement is referred to as a *permutation of length k.* For example, given the three objects A, B, and C, there are six different permutations of length 2 that can be formed if the objects cannot be repeated: $AB, AC, BC, BA, CA,$ and CB.

THEOREM 2.9.1. The number of permutations of length k that can be formed

FIGURE 2.9.7

Theorem 2.9.1, once the four aces are assigned to one of those 49 positions, they can still be permuted in $_4P_4 = 4!$ ways. Similarly, the 48 non-aces can be arranged in $_{48}P_{48} = 48!$ ways. It follows from the multiplication rule, then, that the number of arrangements having consecutive aces is the product, $49 \cdot 4! \cdot 48!$, or, approximately, 1.46×10^{64}.

Comment.   Computing $n!$ can be quite cumbersome, even for n's that are fairly small: We saw in Example 2.9.7, for instance, that 16! is already in the trillions. Fortunately, an easy-to-use approximation is available. According to *Stirling's formula*,

$$n! \doteq \sqrt{2\pi} \, n^{n+1/2} e^{-n}$$

In practice, we apply Stirling's formula by writing

$$\log_{10}(n!) \doteq \log_{10}(\sqrt{2\pi}) + \left(n + \frac{1}{2}\right)\log_{10}(n) - n\log_{10}(e)$$

and then exponentiating the right-hand side.

Recall Example 2.9.8, where the number of arrangements was calculated to be $49 \cdot 4! \cdot 48!$, or $24 \cdot 49!$. Substituting into Stirling's formula, we can write

$$\log_{10}(49!) \doteq \log_{10}(\sqrt{2\pi}) + \left(49 + \frac{1}{2}\right)\log_{10}(49) - 49\log_{10}(e)$$

$$\approx 62.783366$$

Therefore,

$$24 \cdot 49! \doteq 24 \cdot 10^{62.78337}$$

$$= 1.46 \times 10^{64}$$

EXAMPLE 2.9.9

In chess a rook can move vertically and horizontally (see Figure 2.9.8). It can capture any unobstructed piece located anywhere in its own row or column. In how many ways can eight distinct rooks be placed on a chessboard (having eight rows and eight columns) so that no two can capture one another?

To start with a simpler problem, suppose that the eight rooks are all identical. Since no two rooks can be in the same row or same column (why?), it follows that each row must contain exactly one. The rook in the first row, however, can be in any of eight columns; the rook

FIGURE 2.9.8

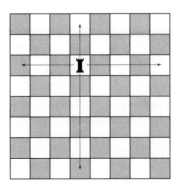

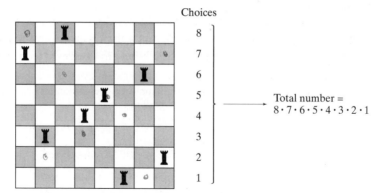

Total number =
$8 \cdot 7 \cdot 6 \cdot 5 \cdot 4 \cdot 3 \cdot 2 \cdot 1$

FIGURE 2.9.9

in the second row is then limited to being in one of seven columns, and so on. By the multiplication rule, then, the number of noncapturing configurations for eight identical rooks is $_8P_8$, or 8! (see Figure 2.9.9).

Now imagine the eight rooks to be distinct—they might be numbered, for example, 1 through 8. The rook in the first row could be marked with any of eight numbers; the rook in the second row with any of the remaining seven numbers; and so on. Altogether, there would be 8! numbering patterns *for each configuration*. The total number of ways to position eight distinct, noncapturing rooks, then, is 8! · 8!, or 1,625,702,400.

EXAMPLE 2.9.10

Consider the set of nine-digit numbers that can be formed by rearranging without repetition the integers 1 through 9. For how many of those permutations will the 1 and the 2 precede the 3 and the 4? That is, we want to count sequences like 7 2 5 1 3 6 9 4 8 but not like 6 8 1 5 4 2 7 3 9.

At first glance, this seems to be a problem well beyond the scope of Theorem 2.9.1. With the help of a symmetry argument, though, its solution is surprisingly simple.

Think of just the digits 1 through 4. By the Corollary on page 92, those four numbers give rise to 4! (= 24) permutations. Of those 24, only 4—(1, 2, 3, 4), (2, 1, 3, 4), (1, 2, 4, 3), and (2, 1, 4, 3)—have the property that the 1 and the 2 come before the 3 and the 4. It follows that 4/24 of the total number of 9-digit permutations should satisfy the condition being imposed on 1, 2, 3, and 4. Therefore,

$$\text{Number of permutations where } 1 \text{ and } 2 \text{ precede } 3 \text{ and } 4 = \frac{4}{24} \cdot 9!$$

$$= 60{,}480$$

QUESTIONS

2.9.15 The board of a large corporation has six members willing to be nominated for office. How many different "president/vice-president/treasurer" slates could be submitted to the stockholders?

2.9.16 How many ways can a set of four tires be put on a car if all the tires are interchangeable? How many ways are possible if two of the four are snow tires?

2.9.17 Use Stirling's formula to approximate 30!.
(*Note*: The exact answer is 265,252,859,812,268,935,315,188,480,000,000.)

2.9.18 The nine members of the music faculty baseball team, the Mahler Maulers, are all incompetent and each can play any position equally poorly. In how many different ways can the Maulers take the field?

2.9.19 A three-digit number is to be formed from the digits 1 through 7, with no digit being used more than once. How many such numbers would be less than 289?

2.9.20 Four men and four women are to be seated in a row of chairs numbered 1 through 8.
(a) How many total arrangements are possible?
(b) How many arrangements are possible if the men are required to sit in alternate chairs?

2.9.21 An engineer needs to take three technical electives sometime during his final four semesters. The three are to be selected from a list of 10. In how many ways can he schedule those classes, assuming that he never wants to take more than one technical elective in any given term?

2.9.22 How many ways can a 12-member cheerleading squad (6 men and 6 women) pair up to form 6 male-female teams? How many ways can 6 male-female teams be positioned along a sideline? What does the number $6!6!2^6$ represent? What does the number $6!6!2^6 2^{12}$ represent?

2.9.23 A new horror movie *Friday the 13th, Part X*, stars Jason's great-grandson as a psychotic trying to dismember eight camp counselors (four men and four women.)
(a) How many scenarios can the scriptwriters devise, assuming they intend for Jason to dispatch all the men before going after any of the women?
(b) How many scripts are possible if the only restriction put on Jason is that he save Muffy for last?

2.9.24 Suppose that a seemingly interminable German opera is recorded on all six sides of a three-record album. In how many ways can the six sides be played so that at least one is out of order?

2.9.25 A group of n families, each with m members, are to be lined up for a photograph. In how many ways can the nm people be arranged if members of a family must stay together?

2.9.26 Suppose that 10 people, including you and a friend, line up for a group picture. How many ways can the photographer rearrange the line if she wants to keep exactly three people between you and your friend?

2.9.27 Theorem 2.9.1 was the first mathematical result known to have been proved by induction, that feat being accomplished in 1321 by Levi ben Gerson. Assume that we do not know the multiplication rule. Prove the theorem the way Levi ben Gerson did.

2.9.28 In how many ways can a pack of 52 cards be dealt to 13 players, 4 to each, so that every player has one card of each suit?

2.9.29 If the definition of $n!$ is to hold for all nonnegative integers n, show that it follows that 0! must equal 1.

Counting Permutations (when the objects are not all distinct)

The corollary to Theorem 2.9.1 gives a formula for the number of ways an entire set of n objects can be permuted *if the objects are all distinct*. Fewer than those $n!$ permutations are possible, though, if some of the objects are identical. For example, there are $3! = 6$ ways to permute the three distinct objects A, B, and C:

$$ABC$$

$$ACB$$

$$BAC$$

$$BCA$$

$$CAB$$

$$CBA$$

If the three objects to permute, though, are A, A, and B—that is, if two of the three are identical—the number of permutations decreases to 3:

$$AAB$$

$$ABA$$

$$BAA$$

As we will see, there are many real-world applications where the n objects to be permuted belong to r different categories, each category containing 1 or more identical objects.

THEOREM 2.9.2. The number of ways to arrange n objects, n_1 being of one kind, n_2 of a second kind, ..., and n_r of an rth kind, is

$$\frac{n!}{n_1!n_2! \cdots n_r!}$$

where $\sum_{i=1}^{r} n_i = n$.

Proof. Let N denote the total number of such arrangements. For any one of those N, the similar objects (if they were actually different) could be arranged in $n_1!n_2! \cdots n_r!$ ways. (Why?) It follows that $N \cdot n_1!n_2! \cdots n_r!$ is the total number of ways to arrange n (distinct) objects. But $n!$ equals that same number. Setting $N \cdot n_1!n_2! \cdots n_r!$ equal to $n!$ gives the result.

Comment. Ratios like $n!/(n_1!n_2! \cdots n_r!)$ are called *multinomial coefficients* because the general term in the expansion of

$$\left(x_1 + x_2 + \cdots + x_r\right)^n$$

is

$$\frac{n!}{n_1!n_2! \cdots n_r!} x_1^{n_1} x_2^{n_2} \cdots x_r^{n_r}$$

EXAMPLE 2.9.11

A pastry in a vending machine costs 85¢. In how many ways can a customer put in two quarters, three dimes, and one nickel?

$$\overline{\quad1\quad}\quad\overline{\quad2\quad}\quad\overline{\quad3\quad}\quad\overline{\quad4\quad}\quad\overline{\quad5\quad}\quad\overline{\quad6\quad}$$

Order in which coins are deposited

FIGURE 2.9.10

If all coins of a given value are considered identical, then a typical deposit sequence, say *QDDQND* (see Figure 2.9.10), can be thought of as a permutation of $n = 6$ objects belonging to $r = 3$ categories, where

$$n_1 = \text{number of nickels} = 1$$

$$n_2 = \text{number of dimes} = 3$$

$$n_3 = \text{number of quarters} = 2$$

By Theorem 2.9.2, there are 60 such sequences:

$$\frac{n!}{n_1!\,n_2!\,n_3!} = \frac{6!}{1!\,3!\,2!} = 60$$

Of course, had we assumed the coins were distinct (having been minted at different places and different times), the number of distinct permutations would be 6!, or 720.

EXAMPLE 2.9.12

Prior to the seventeenth century there were no scientific journals, a state of affairs that made it difficult for researchers to document discoveries. If a scientist sent a copy of his work to a colleague, there was always a risk that the colleague might claim it as his own. The obvious alternative—wait to get enough material to publish a book—invariably resulted in lengthy delays. So, as a sort of interim documentation, scientists would sometimes send each other anagrams—letter puzzles that, when properly unscrambled, summarized in a sentence or two what had been discovered.

When Christiaan Huygens (1629–1695) looked through his telescope and saw the ring around Saturn, he composed the following anagram (181):

$$aaaaaaa, ccccc, d, eeeee, g, h, iiiiiii, llll, mm,$$

$$nnnnnnnnn, oooo, pp, q, rr, s, ttttt, uuuuu$$

How many ways can the 62 letters in Huygens's anagram be arranged?

Let $n_1(= 7)$ denote the number of a's, $n_2(= 5)$ the number of c's, and so on. Substituting into the appropriate multinomial coefficient, we find

$$N = \frac{62!}{7!\,5!\,1!\,5!\,1!\,1!\,7!\,4!\,2!\,9!\,4!\,2!\,1!\,2!\,1!\,5!\,5!}$$

as the total number of arrangements. To get a feeling for the magnitude of N, we need to apply Stirling's formula to the numerator. Since

$$62! \doteq \sqrt{2\pi}\, e^{-62} 62^{62.5}$$

then

$$\log(62!) \doteq \log(\sqrt{2\pi}) - 62 \cdot \log(e) + 62.5 \cdot \log(62)$$

$$\doteq 85.49731$$

The antilog of 85.49731 is 3.143×10^{85}, so

$$N \doteq \frac{3.143 \times 10^{85}}{7!5!1!5!1!1!7!4!2!9!4!2!1!2!1!5!5!}$$

is a number on the order of 3.6×10^{60}. Huygens was clearly taking no chances! (*Note:* When appropriately rearranged, the anagram becomes "Annulo cingitur tenui, plano, nusquam cohaerente, ad eclipticam inclinato," which translates to "Surrounded by a thin ring, flat, suspended nowhere, inclined to the ecliptic.")

EXAMPLE 2.9.13

What is the coefficient of x^{23} in the expansion of $(1 + x^5 + x^9)^{100}$?

To understand how this question relates to permutations, consider the simpler problem of expanding $(a + b)^2$:

$$(a + b)^2 = (a + b)(a + b)$$

$$= a \cdot a + a \cdot b + b \cdot a + b \cdot b$$

$$= a^2 + 2ab + b^2$$

Notice that each term in the first $(a + b)$ is multiplied by each term in the second $(a + b)$. Moreover, the coefficient that appears in front of each term in the expansion corresponds to the number of ways that that term can be formed. For example, the 2 in the term $2ab$ reflects the fact that the product ab can result from two different multiplications:

$$\underbrace{(a + b)(a + b)}_{ab} \qquad \text{or} \qquad \underbrace{(a + b)(a + b)}_{ab}$$

By analogy, the coefficient of x^{23} in the expansion of $(1 + x^5 + x^9)^{100}$ will be the number of ways that one term from each of the 100 factors $(1 + x^5 + x^9)$ can be multiplied together to form x^{23}. The only factors that will produce x^{23}, though, is the set of two x^9's, one x^5, and ninety-seven 1's:

$$x^{23} = x^9 \cdot x^9 \cdot x^5 \cdot 1 \cdot 1 \cdots 1$$

It follows that the *coefficient* of x^{23} is the number of ways to permute two x^9's, one x^5, and ninety-seven 1's. So, from Theorem 2.9.2,

$$\text{coefficient of } x^{23} = \frac{100!}{2!1!97!}$$

$$= 485{,}100$$

EXAMPLE 2.9.14

In how many ways can the word ABRACADABRA be formed in the array pictured in Figure 2.9.11? Assume that the word must begin with the top A and progress diagonally downward to the bottom A.

FIGURE 2.9.11

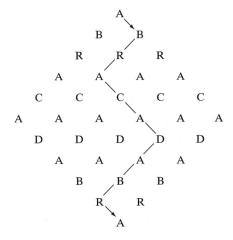

Notice that each admissible spelling of ABRACADABRA can be viewed as a path consisting of 10 steps, five to the right (R) and five to the left (L). Drawn in Figure 2.9.11 is the path

$$R \quad L \quad L \quad R \quad R \quad R \quad L \quad L \quad L \quad R$$
$$1 \quad 2 \quad 3 \quad 4 \quad 5 \quad 6 \quad 7 \quad 8 \quad 9 \quad 10$$
Steps

Clearly, there will be a one-to-one correspondence between the set of ABRACADABRA spellings and the set of permutations of 5 R's and 5 L's. By Theorem 2.9.2, then,

$$\text{Number of ABRACADABRA's} = \frac{10!}{5!5!}$$

$$= 252$$

EXAMPLE 2.9.15

In how many ways can the letters of the word

BROBDINGNAGIAN

be arranged without changing the order of the vowels?

The key here is to follow an argument similar to the one we used in Example 2.9.10. Table 2.9.3 shows a breakdown of the word's letter and vowel frequencies. By Theorem 2.9.2, the vowels can be permuted in 30 ways:

$$\frac{5!}{2!2!1!} = 30$$

TABLE 2.9.3

All letters	Vowels
$A - 2$	$A - 2$
$B - 2$	$I - 2$
$D - 1$	$O - 1$
$G - 2$	5
$I - 2$	
$N - 3$	
$O - 1$	
$R - 1$	
14	

One of those permutations (O, I, A, I, A) keeps the vowels in their original positions, imply-ing that $\frac{1}{30}$ of *all* the word's permutations should have the vowels in that same order. The num-ber of admissible arrangements, then, is

$$\frac{1}{30} \cdot \frac{14!}{2!2!1!2!2!3!1!1!}$$

or $30, 270, 240$.

QUESTIONS

2.9.30 Which state name can generate more permutations, TENNESSEE or FLORIDA?

2.9.31 How many numbers greater than 4,000,000 can be formed from the digits 2, 3, 4, 4, 5, 5, 5?

2.9.32 An interior decorator is trying to arrange a shelf containing eight books, three with red cov-ers, three with blue covers, and two with brown covers.
   (a) Assuming the titles and the sizes of the books are irrelevant, in how many ways can she arrange the eight books?
   (b) In how many ways could the books be arranged if they were all considered distinct?
   (c) In how many ways could the books be arranged if the red books were considered indis-tinguishable, but the other five were considered distinct?

2.9.33 Four Nigerians (A, B, C, D), three Chinese $(\#, *, \&)$, and three Greeks (α, β, γ) are lined up at the box office, waiting to buy tickets for the World's Fair.
   (a) How many ways can they position themselves if the Nigerians are to hold the first four places in line; the Chinese, the next three; and the Greeks, the last three?
   (b) How many arrangements are possible if members of the same nationality must stay together?
   (c) How many different queues can be formed?
   (d) Suppose a vacationing Martian strolls by and wants to photograph the ten for her scrap-book. A bit myopic, the Martian is quite capable of discerning the more obvious differences in human anatomy but is unable to distinguish one Nigerian (N) from another, one Chi-nese (C) from another, or one Greek (G) from another. Instead of perceiving a line to be $B*\beta AD\#\&C\alpha\gamma$, for example, she would see $NCGNNCCNGG$. From the Martian's per-spective, in how many different ways can the three nationalities of Earthlings line them-selves up?

2.9.34 Suppose a pitcher faces a batter who never swings. For how many different ball/strike sequences will the batter be called out on the fifth pitch?

2.9.35 What is the coefficient of $w^2x^3yz^3$ in the expansion of $(w + x + y + z)^9$?

2.9.36 Imagine six points in a plane, no three being collinear. How many ways can two triangles be drawn using the six points as vertices?

2.9.37 A delivery truck has to go from point X to point Y and make a stop at point 0. How many different routes are possible, assuming the driver never wants to go out of her way?

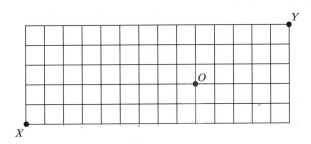

2.9.38 How many ways can the letters in the word

$$S\,L\,U\,M\,G\,U\,L\,L\,I\,O\,N$$

be arranged so that the three L's precede all the other consonants?

2.9.39 A tennis tournament has a field of $2n$ entrants, all of whom need to be scheduled to play in the first round. How many different pairings are possible?

2.9.40 What is the coefficient of x^{12} in the expansion of $\left(1 + x^3 + x^6\right)^{18}$?

2.9.41 In how many ways can the letters of the word

$$E\,L\,E\,E\,M\,O\,S\,Y\,N\,A\,R\,Y$$

be arranged so that the S is always immediately followed by a Y?

2.9.42 A palindrome is a phrase whose letters are in the same order whether they are read backward or forward, such as Napoleon's lament

Able was I ere I saw Elba

or the often cited

Madam, I'm Adam.

Words themselves can become the units in a palindrome, as in the sentence

Girl, bathing on Bikini, eyeing boy,
finds boy eyeing bikini on bathing girl.

Suppose the members of a set consisting of four objects of one type, six of a second type, and two of a third type are to be lined up in a row. How many of those permutations are palindromes?

2.9.43 Show that $(k!)!$ is divisible by $k!^{(k-1)!}$. (*Hint:* Think of a related permutation problem.)

Counting Combinations

Order is not always a meaningful characteristic of a collection of elements. Consider a poker player being dealt a five-card hand. Whether he receives a 2 of hearts, 4 of clubs, 9 of clubs, jack of hearts, and ace of diamonds *in that order,* or in any one of the other $5! - 1$ permutations of those particular five cards is irrelevant—the hand is still the same. As the last set of examples in this section bear out, there are many such situations—problems where our only legitimate concern is with the composition of a set of elements, not with any particular arrangement.

We call a collection of k *unordered* elements a *combination of size k.* For example, given a set of $n = 4$ distinct elements—A, B, C, and D—there are *six* ways to form combinations of size 2:

A and B B and C

A and C B and D

A and D C and D

A general formula for counting combinations can be derived quite easily from what we already know about counting permutations.

THEOREM 2.9.3. The number of ways to form combinations of size k from a set of n distinct objects, repetitions not allowed, is denoted by the symbols $\binom{n}{k}$ or $_nC_k$, where

$$\binom{n}{k} = {}_nC_k = \frac{n!}{k!(n-k)!}$$

Proof. Let the symbol $\binom{n}{k}$ denote the number of combinations satisfying the conditions of the theorem. Since each of those combinations can be ordered in $k!$ ways, the product $k!\binom{n}{k}$ must equal the number of *permutations* of length k that can be formed from n distinct elements. But n distinct elements can be formed into permutations of length k in $n(n-1)\cdots(n-k+1) = n!/(n-k)!$ ways. Therefore,

$$k!\binom{n}{k} = \frac{n!}{(n-k)!}$$

Solving for $\binom{n}{k}$ gives the result.

Comment. It often helps to think of combinations in the context of drawing objects out of an urn. If an urn contains n chips labeled 1 through n, the number of ways we can reach in and draw out different samples of size k is $\binom{n}{k}$. In deference to this sampling interpretation for the formation of combinations, $\binom{n}{k}$ is usually read "n things taken k at a time" or "n choose k."

Comment. The symbol $\binom{n}{k}$ appears in the statement of a familiar theorem from algebra,

$$(x + y)^n = \sum_{k=0}^{n} \binom{n}{k} x^k y^{n-k}$$

Since the expression being raised to a power involves two terms, x and y, the constants $\binom{n}{k}$, $k = 0, 1, \ldots, n$, are commonly referred to as *binomial coefficients*.

EXAMPLE 2.9.16

Eight politicians meet at a fund-raising dinner. How many greetings can be exchanged if each politician shakes hands with every other politician exactly once?

     Imagine the politicians to be eight chips—1 through 8—in an urn. A handshake corresponds to an unordered sample of size 2 chosen from that urn. Since repetitions are not allowed (even the most obsequious and overzealous of campaigners would not shake hands with himself!), Theorem 2.9.3 applies, and the total number of handshakes is

$$\binom{8}{2} = \frac{8!}{2!6!}$$

or 28.

EXAMPLE 2.9.17

The basketball recruiter for Swampwater Tech has scouted 16 former NBA starters that he thinks he can pass off as JUCO transfers—six are guards, seven are forwards, and three are centers. Unfortunately, his slush fund of illegal alumni donations is at an all-time low and he can afford to buy new Corvettes for only nine of the players. If he wants to keep three guards, four forwards, and two centers, how many ways can he parcel out the cars?

     This is a combination problem that also requires an application of the multiplication rule. First, note there are $\binom{6}{3}$ *sets* of three guards that could be chosen to receive Corvettes (think of drawing a set of three names out of an urn containing six names). Similarly, the forwards and centers can be bribed in $\binom{7}{4}$ and $\binom{3}{2}$ ways, respectively. It follows from the multiplication rule, then, that the total number of ways to divvy up the cars is the product

$$\binom{6}{3} \cdot \binom{7}{4} \cdot \binom{3}{2}$$

or *2100*(= $20 \cdot 35 \cdot 3$).

EXAMPLE 2.9.18

Your statistics teacher announces a 20-page reading assignment on Monday that is to be finished by Thursday morning. You intend to read the first x_1 pages Monday, the next x_2 pages Tuesday, and the final x_3 pages Wednesday, where $x_1 + x_2 + x_3 = 20$ and each $x_i \geq 1$. In how many ways can you complete the assignment? That is, how many different sets of values can be chosen for x_1, x_2, and x_3?

Imagine the 19 spaces *between* the 20 pages (see Figure 2.9.12). Choosing any two of those spaces automatically partitions the 20 pages into three nonempty sets. Spaces 3 and 7, for example, would correspond to reading three pages on Monday, four pages on Tuesday, and thirteen pages on Wednesday. The number of different values for the set (x_1, x_2, x_3), then, must equal the number of ways to select two "markers"—namely, $\binom{19}{2}$, or *171*.

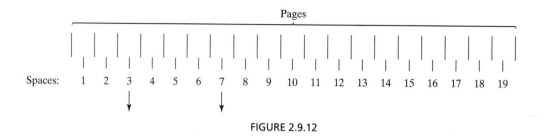

FIGURE 2.9.12

EXAMPLE 2.9.19

Mitch is trying to put a little zing into his cabaret act by telling four jokes at the beginning of each show. His current engagement is booked to run four months. If he gives one performance a night and never wants to repeat the same set of jokes on any two nights, what is the minimum number of jokes he needs in his repertoire?

Four months of performances create a demand for roughly 120 different sets of jokes. Let n denote the number of jokes that Mitch can tell. The question is asking for the smallest n for which $\binom{n}{4} \geq 120$. Trial-and-error calculations summarized in Table 2.9.4 show that the optimal n is surprisingly small: A set of only *9* jokes is sufficient to keep Mitch from having to repeat his opening monologue.

TABLE 2.9.4

n	$\binom{n}{4}$	≥ 120?
7	35	No
8	70	No
$\longrightarrow$ 9	126	Yes

EXAMPLE 2.9.20

Binomial coefficients have many interesting properties. Perhaps the most familiar is Pascal's triangle,[2] a numerical array where each entry is equal to the sum of the two numbers appearing diagonally above it (see Figure 2.9.13). Notice that each entry in Pascal's triangle can be expressed as a binomial coefficient, and the relationship just described appears to reduce to a simple equation involving those coefficients:

$$\binom{n+1}{k} = \binom{n}{k} + \binom{n}{k-1} \tag{2.9.1}$$

Prove that Equation 2.9.1 holds for all positive integers n and k.

Row

					Row					
			1		0			$\binom{0}{0}$		
		1		1	1		$\binom{1}{0}$		$\binom{1}{1}$	
	1		2		1	2	$\binom{2}{0}$	$\binom{2}{1}$	$\binom{2}{2}$	

$$\begin{array}{ccccccccc}
 & & & & 1 & & & & \\
 & & & 1 & & 1 & & & \\
 & & 1 & & 2 & & 1 & & \\
 & 1 & & 3 & & 3 & & 1 & \\
1 & & 4 & & 6 & & 4 & & 1
\end{array}$$

Row
0
1
2
3
4

$$\begin{array}{ccccccccc}
 & & & & \binom{0}{0} & & & & \\
 & & & \binom{1}{0} & & \binom{1}{1} & & & \\
 & & \binom{2}{0} & & \binom{2}{1} & & \binom{2}{2} & & \\
 & \binom{3}{0} & & \binom{3}{1} & & \binom{3}{2} & & \binom{3}{3} & \\
\binom{4}{0} & & \binom{4}{1} & & \binom{4}{2} & & \binom{4}{3} & & \binom{4}{4}
\end{array}$$

FIGURE 2.9.13

Consider a set of $n + 1$ distinct objects $A_1, A_2, \ldots, A_{n+1}$. We can obviously draw samples of size k from that set in $\binom{n+1}{k}$ different ways. Now, consider any particular object—for example, A_1. Relative to A_1, each of those $\binom{n+1}{k}$ samples belongs to one of two categories: those containing A_1 and those not containing A_1. To form samples containing A_1, we need to select $k - 1$ additional objects from the remaining n. This can be done in $\binom{n}{k-1}$ ways. Similarly, there are $\binom{n}{k}$ ways to form samples not containing A_1. Therefore, $\binom{n+1}{k}$ must equal $\binom{n}{k} + \binom{n}{k-1}$.

QUESTIONS

2.9.44 The crew of *Apollo 17* consisted of two pilots and one geologist. Suppose that NASA had actually trained a total of nine pilots and four geologists. How many possible *Apollo 17* crews could have been formed?

---

[2] Despite its name, Pascal's triangle was not discovered by Pascal. Its basic structure was known hundreds of years before the French mathematician was born. It was Pascal, though, who first made extensive use of its properties.

(a) Assume that the two pilot positions have identical duties.

(b) Assume that the two pilot positions are really a pilot and a copilot.

2.9.45 How many straight lines can be drawn between five points $(A, B, C, D,$ and $E)$, no three of which are collinear?

2.9.46 The Alpha Beta Zeta sorority is trying to fill a pledge class of nine new members during fall rush. Among the 25 available candidates, 15 have been judged marginally acceptable and 10 highly desirable. How many ways can the pledge class be chosen to give a two-to-one ratio of highly desirable to marginally acceptable candidates?

2.9.47 A boat has a crew of eight: Two of those eight can row only on the stroke side, while three can row only on the bow side. In how many ways can the two sides of the boat be manned?

2.9.48 Nine students, five men and four women, interview for four summer internships sponsored by a city newspaper.

(a) In how many ways can the newspaper choose a set of four interns?

(b) In how many ways can the newspaper choose a set of four interns if it must include two men and two women in each set?

(c) How many sets of four can be picked such that not everyone in a set is of the same sex?

2.9.49 The final exam in History 101 consists of five essay questions that the professor chooses from a pool of seven that are given to the students a week in advance. For how many possible sets of questions does a student need to be prepared? In this situation does order matter?

2.9.50 Ten basketball players meet in the school gym for a pickup game. How many ways can they form two teams of five each?

2.9.51 A chemist is trying to synthesize part of a straight-chain aliphatic hydrocarbon polymer that consists of 21 radicals—10 ethyls (E), 6 methyls (M), and 5 propyls (P). Assuming all arrangements of radicals are physically possible, how many different polymers can be formed if no two of the methyl radicals are to be adjacent?

2.9.52 In how many ways can the letters in

MISSISSIPPI

be arranged so that no two I's are adjacent?

2.9.53 Prove that $\sum_{k=0}^{n} \binom{n}{k} = 2^n$. Hint: Use the binomial expansion mentioned on page 105. How does this identity apply to the hamburger problem in Question 2.9.7?

2.9.54 Prove that

$$\binom{n}{0}^2 + \binom{n}{1}^2 + \cdots + \binom{n}{n}^2 = \binom{2n}{n}$$

(*Hint*: Rewrite the left-hand side as

$$\binom{n}{0}\binom{n}{n} + \binom{n}{1}\binom{n}{n-1} + \binom{n}{2}\binom{n}{n-2} + \cdots$$

and consider the problem of selecting a sample of n objects from an original set of $2n$ objects.)

2.9.55 Show that

$$\binom{n}{1} + \binom{n}{3} + \cdots = \binom{n}{0} + \binom{n}{2} + \cdots$$

[*Hint*: Consider the expansion of $(x - y)^n$.]

2.9.56 Prove that successive terms in the sequence $\binom{n}{0}, \binom{n}{1}, \ldots, \binom{n}{n}$ first increase and then decrease. [*Hint*: Examine the ratio of two successive terms, $\binom{n}{j+1} \Big/ \binom{n}{j}$.]

2.9.57 Imagine n molecules of a gas confined to a rigid container divided into two chambers by a semipermeable membrane. If i molecules are in the left chamber, the *entropy* of the system is defined by the equation

$$\text{Entropy} = \log\binom{n}{i}$$

If n is even, for what configuration of molecules will the entropy be maximized? (Entropy is a concept physicists find useful in characterizing heat exchanges, particularly those involving gases. In general terms, the entropy of a system is a measure of its disorder: As the "randomness" of the position and velocity vectors of a system of particles increases, so does its entropy.) *Hint*: See Question 2.9.56.

2.9.58 Compare the coefficients of t^k in $(1 + t)^d (1 + t)^e = (1 + t)^{d+e}$ to prove that

$$\sum_{j=0}^{k} \binom{d}{j}\binom{e}{k-j} = \binom{d+e}{k}$$

2.9.59 In how many ways can a five-horse race end, allowing for the possibility that two horses tie?

2.10   COMBINATORIAL PROBABILITY

In Section 2.9 our concern focused on counting the number of ways a given operation, or sequence of operations, could be performed. In Section 2.10 we want to couple those enumeration results with the notion of probability. Putting the two together makes a lot of sense—there are many combinatorial problems where an enumeration, by itself, is not particularly relevant. A poker player, for example, is not interested in knowing the total *number* of ways he can draw to a straight; he *is* interested, though, in his *probability* of drawing to a straight.

In a combinatorial setting, making the transition from an enumeration to a probability is easy. If there are n ways to perform a certain operation and a total of m of those satisfy some stated condition—call it A—then $P(A)$ is defined to be the ratio, m/n. This assumes, of course, that all possible outcomes are equally likely.

Historically, the "m over n" idea is what motivated the early work of Pascal, Fermat, and Huygens (recall Section 1.1). Today we recognize that not all probabilities are so easily characterized. Nevertheless, the m/n model—the so-called *classical* definition of probability—is entirely appropriate for describing a wide variety of phenomena.

EXAMPLE 2.10.1

An urn contains eight chips, numbered 1 through 8. A sample of three is drawn without replacement. What is the probability that the largest chip in the sample is a 5?

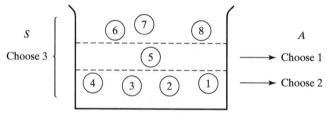

FIGURE 2.10.1

Let A be the event "Largest chip in sample is a 5." Figure 2.10.1 shows what must happen in order for A to occur: (1) the 5 chip must be selected, and (2) two chips must be drawn from the subpopulation of chips numbered 1 through 4. By the multiplication rule, the number of samples satisfying event A is the product $\binom{1}{1} \cdot \binom{4}{2}$.

The sample space S for the experiment of drawing three chips from the urn contains $\binom{8}{3}$ outcomes, all equally likely. In this situation, then, $m = \binom{1}{1} \cdot \binom{4}{2}$, $n = \binom{8}{3}$, and

$$P(A) = \frac{\binom{1}{1} \cdot \binom{4}{2}}{\binom{8}{3}}$$

$$= 0.11$$

EXAMPLE 2.10.2

In the Illinois state lottery six numbers are drawn from an urn containing 44 numbers. A $1 ticket buys two sets of six numbers. For a ticket to win, all six numbers drawn must match one of the two sets of six numbers showing on the ticket. What is the probability that a $1 investment will win you the Illinois lottery?

Figure 2.10.2 shows the sample space created by the selection process: all possible $\binom{44}{6}$ unordered sets of size 6, repetitions not allowed. Printed on a $1 ticket are two of those $\binom{44}{6}$ sets of six. The probability that one of the two is chosen is simply the ratio

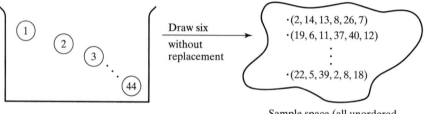

Sample space (all unordered
sets of six numbers from 1
through 44)

FIGURE 2.10.2

$$\frac{2}{\dbinom{44}{6}} = \frac{2}{7,059,052}$$

or about 1 in $3\frac{1}{2}$ million.

EXAMPLE 2.10.3

An urn contains n red chips numbered 1 through n, n white chips numbered 1 through n, and n blue chips numbered 1 through n (see Figure 2.10.3). Two chips are drawn at random and without replacement. What is the probability that the two drawn are either the same color or the same number?

FIGURE 2.10.3

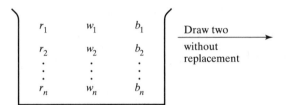

    Let A be the event that the two chips drawn are the same color; let B be the event that they have the same number. We are looking for $P(A \cup B)$.

    Since A and B here are mutually exclusive,

$$P(A \cup B) = P(A) + P(B)$$

With $3n$ chips in the urn, the total number of ways to draw an unordered sample of size two is $\dbinom{3n}{2}$. Moreover,

$$P(A) = P(2 \text{ reds} \cup 2 \text{ whites} \cup 2 \text{ blues})$$

$$= P(2 \text{ reds}) + P(2 \text{ whites}) + P(2 \text{ blues})$$

$$= 3\dbinom{n}{2} \Big/ \dbinom{3n}{2}$$

and

$$P(B) = P(\text{two 1's} \cup \text{two 2's} \cup \cdots \cup \text{two } n\text{'s})$$

$$= n\dbinom{3}{2} \Big/ \dbinom{3n}{2}$$

Therefore,

$$P(A \cup B) = \frac{3\dbinom{n}{2} + n\dbinom{3}{2}}{\dbinom{3n}{2}}$$

$$= \frac{n + 1}{3n - 1}$$

EXAMPLE 2.10.4

A fair die is tossed n times. What is the probability that the sum of the faces showing is $n + 2$?

The sample space associated with rolling a die n times has 6^n outcomes, all of which in this case are equally likely because the die is presumed fair. There are two "types" of outcomes that will produce a sum of $n + 2$—(a) $n - 1$ 1's and one 3 and (b) $n - 2$ 1's and two 2's (see Figure 2.10.4). By Theorem 2.9.2 the number of sequences having $n - 1$ 1's and one 3 is

$$\frac{n!}{1!(n - 1)!} = n;$$ likewise, there are $\dfrac{n!}{2!(n - 2)!} = \dbinom{n}{2}$ outcomes having $n - 2$ 2's and two 2's.

Therefore,

$$P(\text{sum} = n + 2) = \frac{n + \dbinom{n}{2}}{6^n}$$

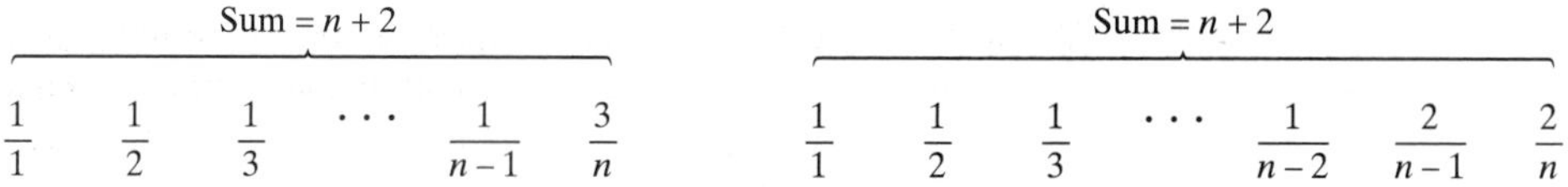

Sum = $n + 2$						Sum = $n + 2$					
$\frac{1}{1}$	$\frac{1}{2}$	$\frac{1}{3}$	$\cdots$	$\frac{1}{n-1}$	$\frac{3}{n}$	$\frac{1}{1}$	$\frac{1}{2}$	$\frac{1}{3}$	$\cdots$	$\frac{1}{n-2}$	$\frac{2}{n-1}$ $\frac{2}{n}$

FIGURE 2.10.4

EXAMPLE 2.10.5

To keep the monkey entertained, Tarzan gives Cheetah the following letters from a Scrabble set to play with:

$$A\ A\ A \quad E\ E \quad I \quad J \quad K\ L \quad N\ N \quad R \quad T \quad Z$$

What is the probability that Cheetah (who can't spell) rearranges the letters at random and forms the following sequence:

TARZAN LIKE JANE

(Ignore the spaces between the words).

If similar letters are considered indistinguishable, Theorem 2.9.2 applies, and the total number of ways to arrange the 14 letters is $14!/(3!2!1!1!1!1!2!1!1!1!)$, or 3,632,428,800. Only one of those sequences is the desired arrangement, so

$$P(\text{"TARZAN LIKE JANE"}) = \frac{1}{3,632,428,800}$$

Notice that the same answer is obtained if the 14 tiles are considered distinct. Under that scenario, the total number of permutations is $14!$, but the number of ways to spell TARZAN LIKE JANE increases to $3!2!2!$, because all the A's, E's, and N's can be permuted. Therefore,

$$P(\text{"TARZAN LIKE JANE"}) = \frac{3!2!2!}{14!} = \frac{1}{3,632,428,800}$$

EXAMPLE 2.10.6

Suppose that k people are selected at random from the general population. What are the chances that at least two of those k were born on the same day? Known as the *birthday problem*, this is a particularly intriguing example of combinatorial probability because its statement is so simple, its analysis is straightforward, yet its solution as we will see, goes strongly contrary to our intuition.

   Picture the k individuals lined up in a row to form an ordered sequence. If leap year is omitted, each person might have any of 365 birthdays. By the multiplication rule, the group as a whole generates a sample space of 365^k birthday sequences (see Figure 2.10.5).

   Define A to be the event "at least two people have the same birthday." If each person is assumed to have the same chance of being born on any given day, the 365^k sequences in Figure 2.10.5 are equally likely, and

$$P(A) = \frac{\text{Number of sequences in } A}{365^k}$$

   Counting the number of sequences in the numerator here is prohibitively difficult because of the complexity of the event A; fortunately, counting the number of sequences in A^C is quite easy. Notice that each birthday sequence in the sample space belongs to exactly one of two categories (see Figure 2.10.6):

1. At least two people have the same birthday.

2. All k people have different birthdays.

It follows that

$$\text{Number of sequences in } A = 365^k - \text{number of sequences where all } k \text{ people}$$
$$\text{have different birthdays}$$

Possible birthdays: $\underset{1}{\underline{(365)}}$ $\underset{2}{\underline{(365)}}$ $\cdots$ $\underset{k}{\underline{(365)}}$ $\longrightarrow$ 365^k different sequences

$\underbrace{\hspace{3cm}}$
Person

FIGURE 2.10.5

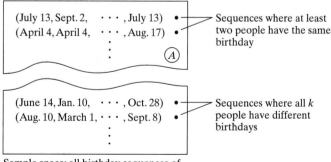

Sample space: all birthday sequences of length k (contains 365^k outcomes).

FIGURE 2.10.6

The number of ways to form birthday sequences for k people subject to the restriction that all k birthdays must be different is simply the number of ways to form permutations of length k from a set of 365 distinct objects:

$$_{365}P_k = 365(364) \cdots (365 - k + 1)$$

Therefore,

$$P(A) = P \text{ (at least two people have the same birthday)}$$

$$= \frac{365^k - 365(364) \cdots (365 - k + 1)}{365^k}$$

Table 2.10.1 shows $P(A)$ for k values of 15, 22, 23, 40, 50, and 70. Notice how the $P(A)$'s greatly exceed what our intuition would suggest.

TABLE 2.10.1

k	$P(A) = P$ (at least two have same birthday)
15	0.253
22	0.476
23	0.507
40	0.891
50	0.970
70	0.999

Comment. Presidential biographies offer one opportunity to "confirm" the unexpectedly large values that Table 2.10.1 gives for $P(A)$. Among our first $k = 40$ presidents, two did have the same birthday: Harding and Polk were both born on November 2. More surprising, though, are the death dates of the presidents: Adams, Jefferson, and Monroe all died on July 4, and Fillmore and Taft both died on March 8.

Comment. The values for $P(A)$ in Table 2.10.1 are actually slight *underestimates* for the true probabilities that at least two of k people will be born on the same day. The assumption made earlier that all 365^k birthday sequences are equally likely is not entirely true: Births are somewhat more common during the summer than they are during the winter. It has been proven, though, that any sort of deviation from the equally-likely model will only serve to *increase* the chances that two or more people will share the same birthday (106). So, if $k = 40$, for example, the probability is slightly greater than 0.891 that at least two were born on the same day.

EXAMPLE 2.10.7

One of the more instructive—and to some, one of the more useful—applications of combinatorics is the calculation of probabilities associated with various poker hands. It will be assumed in what follows that five cards are dealt from a poker deck and that no other cards are showing, although some may already have been dealt. The sample space is the set of $\binom{52}{5} = 2,598,960$ different hands, each having probability 1/2,598,960. What are the chances of being dealt (a) a

	2	3	4	5	6	7	8	9	10	J	Q	K	A
D													
H						×					×		
C						×							
S						×					×		

FIGURE 2.10.7

full house, (b) *one pair,* and (c) a *straight*? [Probabilities for the various other kinds of poker hands (two pairs, three-of-a-kind, flush, and so on) are gotten in much the same way.]

(a) *Full house.* A full house consists of three cards of one denomination and two of another. Figure 2.10.7 shows a full house consisting of three 7's and two Queens. Denominations for the three-of-a-kind can be chosen in $\binom{13}{1}$ ways. Then, given that a denomination has been decided on, the three requisite suits can be selected in $\binom{4}{3}$ ways. Applying the same reasoning to the pair gives $\binom{12}{1}$ available denominations, each having $\binom{4}{2}$ possible choices of suits. Thus, by the multiplication rule,

$$P(\text{full house}) = \frac{\binom{13}{1}\binom{4}{3}\binom{12}{1}\binom{4}{2}}{\binom{52}{5}} = 0.00144$$

(b) *One pair.* To qualify as a one-pair hand, the five cards must include two of the same denomination and three "single" cards—cards whose denominations match neither the pair nor each other. Figure 2.10.8 shows a pair of 6's. For the pair, there are $\binom{13}{1}$ possible denominations and, once selected, $\binom{4}{2}$ possible suits. Denominations for the three single cards can be chosen $\binom{12}{3}$ ways (see Question 2.10.16), and each card can have any of $\binom{4}{1}$ suits. Multiplying these factors together and dividing by $\binom{52}{2}$ gives a probability of 0.42:

	2	3	4	5	6	7	8	9	10	J	Q	K	A
D			×										×
H					×		×						
C					×								
S													

FIGURE 2.10.8

$$P(\text{one pair}) = \frac{\binom{13}{1}\binom{4}{2}\binom{12}{3}\binom{4}{1}\binom{4}{1}\binom{4}{1}}{\binom{52}{5}} = 0.42$$

(c) *Straight.* A straight is five cards having consecutive denominations *but not all in the same suit*—for example, a 4 of diamonds, 5 of hearts, 6 of hearts, 7 of clubs, and 8 of diamonds (see Figure 2.10.9). An ace may be counted "high" or "low," which means that (10, jack, queen, king, ace) is a straight and so is (ace, 2, 3, 4, 5). (If five consecutive cards are all in the same suit, the hand is called a *straight flush.* The latter is considered a fundamentally different type of hand in the sense that a straight flush "beats" a straight.) To get the numerator for $P(\text{straight})$, we will first ignore the condition that all five cards not be in the same suit and simply count the number of hands having consecutive denominations. Note there are 10 sets of consecutive denominations of length 5: (ace, 2, 3, 4, 5), $(2, 3, 4, 5, 6), \ldots, (10, \text{jack}, \text{queen}, \text{king}, \text{ace})$. With no restrictions on the suits, each card can be either a diamond, heart, club, or spade. It follows, then, that the number of five-card hands having consecutive denominations is $10 \cdot \binom{4}{1}^5$. But $40 \ (= 10 \cdot 4)$ of those hands are straight flushes. Therefore,

$$P(\text{straight}) = \frac{10 \cdot \binom{4}{1}^5 - 40}{\binom{52}{5}} = 0.00392$$

Table 2.10.2 shows the probabilities associated with all the different poker hands. Hand i beats hand j if $P(\text{hand } i) < P(\text{hand } j)$.

	2	3	4	5	6	7	8	9	10	J	Q	K	A
D		×					×						
H				×	×								
C						×							
S													

FIGURE 2.10.9

TABLE 2.10.2

Hand	Probability
One pair	0.42
Two pairs	0.048
Three-of-a-kind	0.021
Straight	0.0039
Flush	0.0020
Full house	0.0014
Four-of-a-kind	0.00024
Straight flush	0.000014
Royal flush	0.0000015

QUESTIONS

2.10.1 Ten equally qualified marketing assistants are candidates for promotion to associate buyer; seven are men and three are women. If the company intends to promote four of the ten at random, what is the probability that exactly two of the four are women?

2.10.2 An urn contains six chips, numbered 1 through 6. Two are chosen at random and their numbers are added together. What is the probability that the resulting sum is equal to 5?

2.10.3 An urn contains 20 chips, numbered 1 through 20. Two are drawn simultaneously. What is the probability that the numbers on the two chips will differ by more than 2?

2.10.4 A bridge hand (13 cards) is dealt from a standard 52-card deck. Let A be the event that the hand contains four aces; let B be the event that the hand contains four kings. Find $P(A \cup B)$.

2.10.5 Consider a set of 10 urns, 9 of which each contains three white chips and three red chips. The tenth contains five white chips and one red chip. An urn is picked at random. Then a sample of size 3 is drawn without replacement from that urn. If all three chips drawn are white, what is the probability the urn being sampled is the one with five white chips?

2.10.6 A committee of 50 politicians is to be chosen from among our 100 U.S. Senators. If the selection is done at random, what is the probability that each state will be represented?

2.10.7 Suppose that n fair dice are rolled. What are the chances that all n faces will be the same?

2.10.8 Five fair dice are rolled. What is the probability that the faces showing constitute a "full house"—that is, three faces show one number and two faces show a second number?

2.10.9 Imagine that the test tube pictured contains $2n$ grains of sand, n white and n black. Suppose the tube is vigorously shaken. What is the probability that the two colors of sand will completely separate; that is, all of one color fall to the bottom, and all of the other color lie on top? (*Hint*: Consider the $2n$ grains to be aligned in a row. In how many ways can the n white and the n black grains be permuted?)

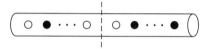

2.10.10 Does a monkey have a better chance of rearranging

$$A\,C\,C\,L\,L\,U\,U\,S \quad \text{to spell} \quad C\,A\,L\,C\,U\,L\,U\,S$$

or

$$A\,A\,B\,E\,G\,L\,R \quad \text{to spell} \quad A\,L\,G\,E\,B\,R\,A?$$

2.10.11 An apartment building has eight floors. If seven people get on the elevator on the first floor, what is the probability they all want to get off on different floors? On the same floor? What assumption are you making? Does it seem reasonable? Explain.

2.10.12 If the letters in the familiar phrase

$$S\,T\,A\,T\,I\,S\,T\,I\,C\,S \quad I\,S \quad F\,U\,N$$

are arranged at random, what are the chances that not all the S's will be adjacent?

2.10.13 Suppose each of 10 sticks is broken into a long part and a short part. The 20 parts are arranged into 10 pairs and glued back together, so that again there are 10 sticks. What is the probability that each long part will be paired with a short part? (*Note*: This problem is a model for the effects of radiation on a living cell. Each chromosome, as a result of being struck by ionizing radiation, breaks into two parts, one part containing the centromere. The cell will die unless the fragment containing the centromere recombines with one not containing a centromere.)

2.10.14 Six dice are rolled one time. What is the probability that each of the six faces appears?

2.10.15 Suppose that a randomly selected group of k people are brought together. What is the probability that exactly one pair has the same birthday?

2.10.16 For one-pair poker hands, why is the number of denominations for the three single cards $\binom{12}{3}$ rather than $\binom{12}{1}\binom{11}{1}\binom{10}{1}$?

2.10.17 Dana is not the world's best poker player. Dealt a 2 of diamonds, an 8 of diamonds, an ace of hearts, an ace of clubs, and an ace of spades, she discards the three aces. What are her chances of drawing to a flush?

2.10.18 A poker player is dealt a 7 of diamonds, a queen of diamonds, a queen of hearts, a queen of clubs, and an ace of hearts. He discards the 7. What is his probability of drawing to either a full house or four-of-a-kind?

2.10.19 Tim is dealt a 4 of clubs, a 6 of hearts, an 8 of hearts, a 9 of hearts, and a king of diamonds. He discards the 4 and the king. What are his chances of drawing to a straight flush? to a flush?

2.10.20 Five cards are dealt from a standard 52-card deck. What is the probability that the sum of the faces on the five cards is 48 or more?

2.10.21 Nine cards are dealt from a 52-card deck. Write a formula for the probability that three of the five even numerical denominations are represented twice, one of the three face cards appears twice, and a second face card appears once. *Note:* Face cards are the jacks, queens, and kings; 2, 4, 6, 8, and 10 are the even numerical denominations.

2.10.22 A coke hand in bridge is one where none of the 13 cards is an ace or is higher than a 9. What is the probability of being dealt such a hand?

2.10.23 A pinochle deck has 48 cards, two of each of six denominations (9, J, Q, K, 10, A) and the usual four suits. Among the many hands that count for meld is a *roundhouse*, which occurs when a player has a king and queen of each suit. In a hand of 12 cards, what is the probability of getting a "bare" roundhouse (a king and queen of each suit and no other kings or queens)?

2.10.24 A somewhat inebriated conventioneer finds himself in the embarrassing predicament of being unable to predetermine whether his next step will be forward or backward. What is the probability that after hazarding n such maneuvers he will have stumbled forward a distance of r steps? (*Hint:* Let x denote the number of steps he takes forward and y, the number backward. Then $x + y = n$ and $x - y = r$.)

CHAPTER 3

Random Variables

Jakob (Jacques) Bernoulli (1654–1705)

One of a Swiss family producing eight distinguished scientists, Jakob was forced by his father to pursue theological studies, but his love of mathematics eventually led him to a university career. He and his brother, Johann, were the most prominent champions of Leibniz's calculus on continental Europe, the two using the new theory to solve numerous problems in physics and mathematics. Bernoulli's main work in probability, Ars Conjectandi, was published after his death by his nephew, Nikolaus, in 1713.

3.1   INTRODUCTION

Throughout most of Chapter 2, probability functions were defined in terms of the elementary outcomes making up an experiment's sample space. Thus, if two fair dice were tossed, a P-value was assigned to each of the 36 possible pairs of upturned faces: $P((3, 2)) = \frac{1}{36}$, $P((2, 3)) = \frac{1}{36}$, $P((4, 6)) = \frac{1}{36}$, and so on. We have already seen, though, that in certain situations some attribute of an outcome may hold more interest for the experimenter than the outcome itself. A craps player, for example, may be concerned only that he throws a 7, not whether the 7 was the result of a 5 and a 2, a 4 and a 3, or a 6 and a 1. If so, it makes sense to replace the original sample space of 36 possible pairs with the more relevant (and simpler) 11-member set of all possible sums.

In this chapter, we investigate the consequences of redefining an experiment's sample space. More is at stake than simply the number of outcomes in S—the probability structure also changes. Consider, again, the craps player. The original sample space contains 36 outcomes, *all equally likely*. The revised sample space contains 11 outcomes, but the latter are *not* equally likely. The probability of getting a sum equal to 2, for example, is $1/36 [= P((1, 1))]$; but the probability of getting a sum equal to 3 is $2/36 [= P((1, 2)) + P((2, 1))]$. Other values for the "sum" probabilities are obtained similarly (see Figure 3.1.1).

In general, rules for redefining sample spaces—like going from (i, j)'s to $(i + j)$'s—are called *random variables*. As a conceptual framework, random variables are of fundamental importance: They provide a single rubric under which *all* probability problems may be brought. Even in cases where the original sample space needs no redefinition—that is, where the measurement recorded is the measurement of interest—the concept still applies: We simply take the random variable to be the identity mapping.

The primary purpose of Chapter 3 is to introduce the important definitions, concepts, and techniques associated with random variables. Taken together, these ideas comprise the mathematical foundation of modern probability and statistics.

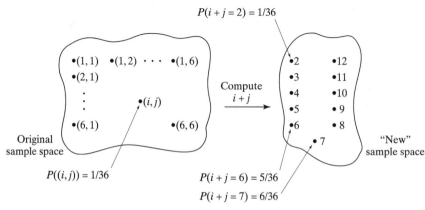

FIGURE 3.1.1

3.2   THE PROBABILITY DENSITY FUNCTION

The place to begin a discussion of random variables is by formalizing the general notion introduced in Section 3.1. We start with a definition.

DEFINITION 3.2.1.   A real-valued function whose domain is the sample space S is called a *random variable*. We denote random variables by uppercase letters, often X or Y.

Figure 3.2.1 is a "picture" of Definition 3.2.1. Any random variable—say, X—is simply a mapping from the sample space S to the real line. If the range of the mapping contains either a finite or a countably infinite number of values, the random variable is said to be *discrete*; if the range includes an interval of real numbers, bounded or unbounded, the random variable is said to be *continuous*. To parallel the notation introduced for probability functions in Chapter 2, discrete random variables will usually be denoted by the letter X; continuous random variables, by the letter Y.

FIGURE 3.2.1

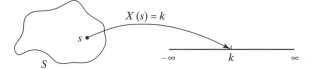

Describing the Variation of a Discrete Random Variable

Associated with each discrete random variable X is a *probability density function* (or *pdf*), $p_X(k)$. By definition $p_X(k)$ is the sum of all the probabilities associated with outcomes in S that get mapped into k by the random variable X. That is,

$$p_X(k) = P(\{s \in S \,|\, X(s) = k\})$$

Conceptually, $p_X(k)$ describes the probability structure induced on the real line by the random variable X.

For instance, in the dice example described in Section 3.1, $X(s) = X((i, j)) = i + j$, from which it follows that

$$
\begin{aligned}
p_X(3) &= P(\text{dice sum equals 3}) \\
&= P(\{s \in S \,|\, X(s) = 3\}) \\
&= P((1, 2), (2, 1)) \\
&= \frac{1}{36} + \frac{1}{36} = \frac{2}{36}
\end{aligned}
$$

Figure 3.2.2 shows $p_X(k)$ for all k.

For notational simplicity, we will usually delete all references to s and S and write

$$p_X(k) = P(X = k)$$

In words, $p_X(k)$ is the "probability that the random variable X takes on the value k."

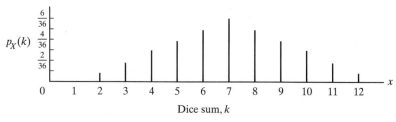

Dice sum, k

FIGURE 3.2.2

EXAMPLE 3.2.1

A not very skillful player throws two darts at the board pictured in Figure 3.2.3. Assume that his throws are independent and that the probability of a dart landing in any particular region is proportional to the area of that region. Furthermore, suppose that his final score is defined to be the *product* of the points assigned to the regions where the two darts land. What is the probability that he earns a score of 4?

FIGURE 3.2.3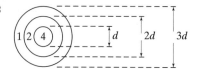

If (a, b) denotes the event of getting a points with the first dart and b with the second, then S contains a total of 9 outcomes:

$$S = \{(1, 1), (1, 2), (1, 4), (2, 1), (2, 2), (2, 4), (1, 4), (2, 4), (4, 4)\}$$

Let X be the random variable that computes the player's score:

$$X(s) = X\big((a, b)\big) = ab$$

By inspection, the outcomes in S that get mapped by X into a score of 4 are $(1, 4), (4, 1)$, and $(2, 2)$. Therefore,

$$
\begin{aligned}
p_X(4) = P(X = 4) &= P(\{s \in S \mid X(s) = 4\}) \\
&= P((1, 4), (4, 1), (2, 2)) \\
&= P\big((1, 4)\big) + P\big((4, 1)\big) + P\big((2, 2)\big)
\end{aligned}
$$

Given that the throws are independent, $P\big((a, b)\big) = P(a) \cdot P(b)$, so

$$P(X = 4) = P(1) \cdot P(4) + P(4) \cdot P(1) + P(2) \cdot P(2) \qquad (3.2.1)$$

To find $P(1)$, $P(2)$, and $P(4)$ we need to compute the areas of the three regions shown in Figure 3.2.3. By simple geometry,

$$\text{area of ``4'' region} = \frac{\pi d^2}{4}$$

$$\text{area of ``2'' region} = \pi d^2 - \frac{\pi d^2}{4} = \frac{3\pi d^2}{4}$$

$$\text{area of ``1'' region} = \frac{9\pi d^2}{4} - \pi d^2 = \frac{5\pi d^2}{4}$$

Using the proportionality assumption, we get

$$P(4) = \frac{\pi d^2/4}{9\pi d^2/4} = \frac{1}{9}$$

$$P(2) = \frac{3\pi d^2/4}{9\pi d^2/4} = \frac{3}{9}$$

$$P(1) = \frac{5\pi d^2/4}{9\pi d^2/4} = \frac{5}{9}$$

A final substitution into Equation 3.2.1 gives $\frac{19}{81}$ as the probability of the player scoring a total of 4:

$$P(X = 4) = \left(\frac{5}{9}\right)\left(\frac{1}{9}\right) + \left(\frac{1}{9}\right)\left(\frac{5}{9}\right) + \left(\frac{3}{9}\right)\left(\frac{3}{9}\right)$$

$$= \frac{19}{81}$$

In general, the random variable defined here can take on any of five values: 1, 2, 4, 8, and 16. Table 3.2.1 shows the entire probability distribution of the random variable X. The same information is shown graphically in Figure 3.2.4.

TABLE 3.2.1

k	$P(X = k)$
1	$\frac{25}{81}$
2	$\frac{30}{81}$
4	$\frac{19}{81}$
8	$\frac{6}{81}$
16	$\frac{1}{81}$

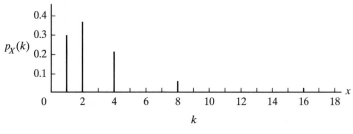

FIGURE 3.2.4

EXAMPLE 3.2.2

As part of her warm-up drill, each player on State's basketball team is required to shoot free throws until two baskets are made. If Rhonda has a 65% success rate at the foul line, what is the pdf of the random variable X that describes the number of throws it takes her to complete the drill? Assume that individual throws constitute independent events.

Figure 3.2.5 illustrates what must occur if the drill is to end on the kth toss, $k = 2, 3, 4, \ldots$: First, Rhonda needs to make exactly one basket sometime during the first $k - 1$ attempts, and, second, she needs to make a basket on the kth toss. Written formally,

$$p_X(k) = P(X = k) = P(\text{drill ends on } k\text{th throw})$$

$$= P((1 \text{ basket and } k - 2 \text{ misses in first } k - 1 \text{ throws}) \cap (\text{basket on } k\text{th throw}))$$

$$= P(1 \text{ basket and } k - 2 \text{ misses}) \cdot P(\text{basket})$$

FIGURE 3.2.5

Exactly one basket

Miss	Basket	Miss		Miss	Basket
1	2	3	...	$k-1$	k

Attempts

Notice that $k - 1$ different sequences have the property that exactly one of the first $k - 1$ throws results in a basket:

$$k - 1 \text{ sequences} \begin{cases} \dfrac{B}{1} \quad \dfrac{M}{2} \quad \dfrac{M}{3} \quad \dfrac{M}{4} \cdots \dfrac{M}{k-1} \\[2mm] \dfrac{M}{1} \quad \dfrac{B}{2} \quad \dfrac{M}{3} \quad \dfrac{M}{4} \cdots \dfrac{M}{k-1} \\[2mm] \qquad\qquad \vdots \\[2mm] \dfrac{M}{1} \quad \dfrac{M}{2} \quad \dfrac{M}{3} \quad \dfrac{M}{4} \cdots \dfrac{B}{k-1} \end{cases}$$

Since each sequence has probability $(0.35)^{k-2}(0.65)$,

$$P(1 \text{ basket and } k - 2 \text{ misses}) = (k - 1)(0.35)^{k-2}(0.65)$$

Therefore,

$$p_X(k) = (k - 1)(0.35)^{k-2}(0.65) \cdot (0.65)$$

$$= (k - 1)(0.35)^{k-2}(0.65)^2, \quad k = 2, 3, 4, \ldots \tag{3.2.2}$$

Table 3.2.2 shows the pdf evaluated for specific values of k. Although the range of k is infinite, the bulk of the probability associated with X is concentrated in the values 2 through 7: It is highly unlikely, for example, that Rhonda would need more than seven shots to complete the drill.

TABLE 3.2.2

k	$p_X(k)$
2	0.4225
3	0.2958
4	0.1553
5	0.0725
6	0.0317
7	0.0133
8+	0.0089

EXAMPLE 3.2.3

Imagine a series of repeated trials, where each trial results in one of two possible outcomes. Any sequence of consecutive similar outcomes is called a *run*. The series ssfsssff, for example, contains four runs: ss, f, sss, and ff. Suppose a coin with a 2/3 probability of coming up heads is tossed three times. Let the random variable X denote the number of runs that are produced. Find $p_X(k)$.

The first two columns of Table 3.2.3 list the experiment's $8(= 2^3)$ possible outcomes together with each outcome's probability. In the third column are the corresponding values of the random variable. We need to calculate $P(X = k)$ for all k.

TABLE 3.2.3

Outcome	Probability	X = number of runs
HHH	$(2/3)^3$	1
HHT	$(2/3)^2(1/3)$	2
HTH	$(2/3)^2(1/3)$	3
THH	$(2/3)^2(1/3)$	2
HTT	$(2/3)(1/3)^2$	2
THT	$(2/3)(1/3)^2$	3
TTH	$(2/3)(1/3)^2$	2
TTT	$(1/3)^3$	1

Notice that $X = 1$, for example, if the outcome is either HHH or TTT. Therefore, $P(X = 1) = p_X(1) = P(\text{HHH or TTT}) = P(\text{HHH}) + P(\text{TTT}) = (2/3)^3 + (1/3)^3 = 3/9$. Collecting terms in a similar fashion produces the entire pdf, as shown in Table 3.2.4.

TABLE 3.2.4

k	$p_X(k)$
1	$(2/3)^3 + (1/3)^3 = 3/9$
2	$2(2/3)^2(1/3) + 2(2/3)(1/3)^2 = 4/9$
3	$(2/3)^2(1/3) + (2/3)(1/3)^2 = 2/9$

Comment. *Summing $p_X(k)$ provides a partial check that the analysis followed in finding a pdf was correct:* For any discrete random variable, $\sum\limits_{\text{all } k} p_X(k)$ must equal 1. Here, the "check" holds—$p_X(1) + p_X(2) + p_X(3) = \dfrac{3}{9} + \dfrac{4}{9} + \dfrac{2}{9} = 1.$

Comment. The pdf associated with a discrete random variable can be expressed in any of three ways: (1) as a formula, (2) in a table, or (3) as a graph where the value of $p_X(k)$ is denoted by the height of a spike. Examples of these three formats are Equation 3.2.2, Table 3.2.4, and Figure 3.2.4, respectively.

Describing the Variation of a Continuous Random Variable

Associated with each continuous random variable Y is also a pdf, $f_Y(y)$, but $f_Y(y)$ in this case is *not* the probability that the random variable Y takes on the value y. Rather, $f_Y(y)$ is a function having the property that for all a and b,

$$P(a \le Y \le b) = P(\{s \in S \mid a \le Y(s) \le b\}) = \int_a^b f_Y(y)\, dy$$

(see Figure 3.2.6). For any continuous random variable, of course, the probability associated with any given point y is 0:

$$P(Y = y) = \int_y^y f_Y(t)\, dt = 0$$

FIGURE 3.2.6

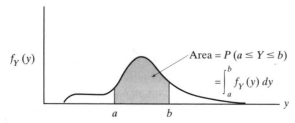

EXAMPLE 3.2.4

Continuous random variables often involve the identity mapping, $Y(s) = s$. When they do, the questions they seek to answer and the techniques that are used are no different than the approaches taken with continuous probability functions in Section 2.5.

Consider a manufacturer of electrical equipment marketing a light bulb that has an average life expectancy of 3000 hours. A moneyback guarantee is offered on bulbs that fail to last at least 300 hours. For what proportion of the company's sales will a refund need to be made?

The sample space appropriate for bulb lifetimes is the set of nonnegative real numbers, $S = \{y : y \ge 0\}$. If the random variable Y is defined to be the length of time a bulb remains operable, then our objective is to find $P(Y < 300)$. Viewed as a random variable, Y here is simply the mapping $Y(y) = y$.

Experience has shown that lifetimes of electrical equipment often follow an exponential probability model (recall Example 2.5.5). In random variable notation,

$$f_Y(y) = \lambda e^{-\lambda y}, \quad y \geq 0$$

where $1/\lambda$ is equal to the item's average life expectancy. Here, $1/\lambda = 3000$, so $f_Y(y) = \frac{1}{3000} e^{-y/3000}$ and

$$P(\text{manufacturer makes refund}) = P(Y < 300)$$

$$= \int_0^{300} \left(\frac{1}{3000}\right) e^{-y/3000} \, dy$$

$$= \int_0^{0.1} e^{-u} \, du = -e^{-u} \Big|_0^{0.1} = -0.90 + 1$$

$$= 0.10$$

(see Figure 3.2.7).

FIGURE 3.2.7

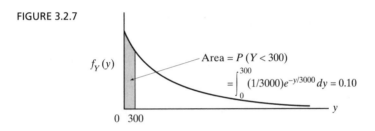

QUESTIONS

3.2.1 An urn contains five chips, numbered 1 through 5. Two are drawn without replacement. Tabulate the pdf for X, the larger of the two.

3.2.2 A fair coin is tossed three times. Let the random variable X denote the number of heads in the tosses times the number of tails. Use a listing of the eight possible outcomes for the three tosses to tabulate the pdf for X.

3.2.3 Let X denote the number of letters in a word chosen at random from the quotation

> The Bird of Time has but a little way
> to flutter—and the Bird is on the wing.

Tabulate $p_X(k)$.

3.2.4 Hemophilia is a recessive sex-linked disease. If a woman who is a carrier—that is, who has the recessive hemophilia gene but not the symptoms of the disease—has a child with a man who is normal, the probability is $\frac{1}{4}$ that that child will be hemophilic. Suppose such a couple intend to have three children. Let the random variable X denote the number of those children who will be hemophilic. Tabulate $p_X(k)$, the pdf for X.

3.2.5 Suppose that five people, including you and a friend, line up at random. Let the random variable X denote the number of people standing between you and your friend. Graph $p_X(k)$.

3.2.6 A fair die is tossed three times. Let X denote the number of different faces that appear (so $X = 1, 2,$ or 3). Graph the pdf for X.

3.2.7 Let the random variable X denote the number of aces in a five-card hand dealt from a standard 52-card poker deck. Find a formula for $p_X(k) = P(X = k)$.

3.2.8 A fair die is tossed repeatedly. Let the random variable X denote the toss at which the 5 face appears for the rth time.
(a) Find a formula for $p_X(k)$.
(b) Use the answer to Part (a) to calculate the probability that the third 5 comes sometime before the seventh toss.
Hint: Generalize the argument in Example 3.2.2 by using Theorem 2.9.2.

3.2.9 Urn I and Urn II each has two red chips and two white chips. Two chips are drawn from each urn without replacement. Let X_1 be the number of red chips in the first sample and X_2 the number of red chips in the second sample. Find $p_{X_3}(k)$, where $X_3 = X_1 + X_2$.

3.2.10 For persons infected with a certain form of malaria, the length of time Y spent in remission is described by the continuous pdf $f_Y(y) = (1/9)y^2$, $0 \le y \le 3$, where Y is measured in years. What is the probability that a malaria patient's remission lasts longer than one year?

3.2.11 Let Y be a continuous random variable described by the pdf

$$f_Y(y) = 3(1 - y)^2, \quad 0 \le y \le 1$$

Find $P(|Y - \frac{1}{2}| > \frac{1}{4})$. Draw a graph of $f_Y(y)$ and show the area representing the desired probability.

3.2.12 The length of time, Y, that a customer stands in line in front of a bank teller's window before being served is described by the exponential pdf $f_Y(y) = 0.2e^{-0.2y}$, $y \ge 0$, where Y is measured in minutes. However, the customer will leave if the wait would be longer than 10 minutes. Suppose the customer goes to the bank twice in the next month. Let the random variable X denote the number of times the customer leaves because the line is too long. Calculate $p_X(1)$.

3.3 THE HYPERGEOMETRIC AND BINOMIAL DISTRIBUTIONS

We saw in Section 3.2 that random variables can reasonably be defined in many different ways even if the structure of the underlying sample space S is much the same. The outcomes in Example 3.2.3 and Question 3.2.2, 3.2.4, and 3.2.6, for instance, are exactly the same but the random variable X is different in each case. Still, not all random variables are equally useful, and some find many more applications than others. This section looks at two specific discrete random variables that are exceptionally important, both for their theoretical implications as well as for their ability to solve real-world problems.

The Hypergeometric Distribution

In Chapter 2, we encountered numerous examples of the *urn model*—that is, events that were equivalent to drawing samples without replacement from an urn containing two different types of chips. The *hypergeometric distribution* is the pdf that covers all of those situations.

THEOREM 3.3.1. Suppose that an urn contains r red chips and w white chips $(r + w = N)$. If n chips are drawn out at random, without replacement, and X

denotes the total number of red chips selected, then X is said to have a *hypergeometric distribution*, and

$$p_X(k) = P(X = k) = \frac{\binom{r}{k}\binom{w}{n-k}}{\binom{N}{n}}$$

where k varies over all the integers for which $\binom{r}{k}$ and $\binom{w}{n-k}$ are defined.

Proof. The proof follows the same rationale as that used in finding the probabilities of poker hands in Section 2.10. Consider the chips to be distinguishable. From Theorem 2.9.3, the total number of ways to select a sample of size n is $\binom{N}{n}$. Similarly, there are $\binom{r}{k}$ ways to select a sample of k red chips, and, for each of those, $\binom{w}{n-k}$ ways to select enough white chips $(n-k)$ to fill out the sample. By the multiplication rule, then, the number of ways to form samples having exactly k red chips is $\binom{r}{k}\binom{w}{n-k}$. Since each of the $\binom{N}{n}$ possible samples is assumed to be equally likely, it follows that the probability of getting exactly k red chips is the ratio $\binom{r}{k}\binom{w}{n-k}\Big/\binom{N}{n}$.

Comment. The name *hypergeometric* derives from a series introduced by the Swiss mathematician and physicist, Leonhard Euler, in 1769:

$$1 + \frac{ab}{c}x + \frac{a(a+1)b(b+1)}{2!c(c+1)}x^2 + \frac{a(a+1)(a+2)b(b+1)(b+2)}{3!c(c+1)(c+2)}x^3 + \cdots$$

This is an expansion of considerable flexibility: Given appropriate values for a, b, and c, it reduces to many of the standard infinite series used in analysis. In particular, if a is set equal to 1, and b and c are set equal to each other, it reduces to the familiar *geometric* series,

$$1 + x + x^2 + x^3 + \cdots$$

hence the name *hypergeometric*. The relationship of the probability function in Theorem 3.3.1 to Euler's series becomes apparent if we set $a = -n$, $b = -r$, $c = w - n + 1$, and multiply the series by $\binom{w}{n}\Big/\binom{N}{n}$. Then the coefficient of x^k will be

$$\frac{\binom{r}{k}\binom{w}{n-k}}{\binom{N}{n}}$$

the value the theorem gives for $P(X = k)$.

EXAMPLE 3.3.1

Keno is among the most popular games played in Las Vegas even though it ranks as one of the least "fair" in the sense that the odds are overwhelmingly in favor of the house. (Betting on keno is only a little less foolish than playing a slot machine!) A keno card has 80 numbers, 1 through 80, from which the player selects a sample of size k, where k can be anything from 1 to 15 (see Figure 3.3.1). The "caller" then announces 20 winning numbers, chosen at random from the 80. If—and how much—the player wins depends on how many of his numbers match the 20 identified by the caller. Suppose that a player bets on a 10–spot ticket. What is his probability of "catching" five numbers?

FIGURE 3.3.1

KENO

First Game	No. Of Games	Price
Last Game		

1	2	3	4	5	6	7	8	9	10
11	12	13	14	15	16	17	18	19	20
21	22	23	24	25	26	27	28	29	30
31	32	33	34	35	36	37	38	39	40

Winning Ticket Must Be Cashed Before Start Of Next Game

41	42	43	44	45	46	47	48	49	50
51	52	53	54	55	56	57	58	59	60
61	62	63	64	65	66	67	68	69	70
71	72	73	74	75	76	77	78	79	80

Consider an urn containing 80 numbers, 20 of which are winners, and 60 losers (see Figure 3.3.2). By betting on a 10–spot ticket, the player, in effect, is drawing a sample of size 10 from that urn. Let X denote the number of winning numbers included among the player's 10 selections. What we are trying to find is $P(X = 5)$.

FIGURE 3.3.2

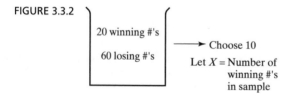

20 winning #'s

60 losing #'s

Choose 10

Let X = Number of winning #'s in sample

By Theorem 3.3.1 (with $r = 20$, $w = 60$, $n = 10$, $N = 80$, and $k = 5$), the player has approximately a 5% chance of guessing exactly five winning numbers:

$$p_X(5) = P(X = 5) = \frac{\binom{20}{5}\binom{60}{5}}{\binom{80}{10}} = 0.05$$

EXAMPLE 3.3.2

Urn I contains five red chips and four white chips; urn II contains four red and five white. Two chips are to be transferred from urn I to urn II. Then a single chip is to be drawn from urn II (see Figure 3.3.3). What is the probability that the chip drawn from the second urn will be white?

FIGURE 3.3.3

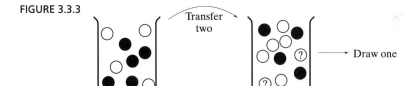

Urn I   Urn II

Let B be the event "White chip is drawn from urn II." Let A_i, $i = 0, 1, 2$, denote the event "i white chips are transferred from urn I to urn II." Then, by Theorem 2.6.1,

$$P(B) = P(B|A_0)P(A_0) + P(B|A_1)P(A_1) + P(B|A_2)P(A_2)$$

Note that $P(B|A_i) = (5 + i)/11$ and that $P(A_i)$ is gotten directly from Theorem 3.3.1. Therefore,

$$P(B) = \left(\frac{5}{11}\right)\frac{\binom{4}{0}\binom{5}{2}}{\binom{9}{2}} + \left(\frac{6}{11}\right)\frac{\binom{4}{1}\binom{5}{1}}{\binom{9}{2}} + \left(\frac{7}{11}\right)\frac{\binom{4}{2}\binom{5}{0}}{\binom{9}{2}}$$

$$= \left(\frac{5}{11}\right)\left(\frac{10}{36}\right) + \left(\frac{6}{11}\right)\left(\frac{20}{36}\right) + \left(\frac{7}{11}\right)\left(\frac{6}{36}\right)$$

$$= \frac{53}{99}$$

EXAMPLE 3.3.3

A carpet cleaning company is trying to establish name recognition in a community consisting of 60,000 households. The company's management team estimates that 5000 of those families would do business with the firm if they were contacted and informed of the services available. With that in mind, the company has hired a staff of telemarketers to place 1000 calls. Write a formula for the probability that at least 100 new customers will be identified.

There is no physical "urn" in this problem, but the statistical structure of the telephone calls is exactly the same as the chip selection in Example 3.3.2. In the terminology of Theorem 3.3.1, X = number of new customers identified, $N = 60,000$, $r = 5,000$, and

$$p_X(k) = \frac{\binom{5000}{k}\binom{55,000}{1000-k}}{\binom{60,000}{1000}}, \quad k = 0, 1, \ldots, 1000$$

The probability that at least 100 new customers are found can be calculated by summing values of $p_X(k)$:

$$P(X \geq 100) = 1 - P(X \leq 99)$$

$$= 1 - \sum_{k=0}^{99} \frac{\binom{5000}{k}\binom{55,000}{1000-k}}{\binom{60,000}{1000}} \qquad (3.3.1)$$

Comment. Getting an exact answer for the summation in Equation 3.3.1 is difficult because of the large factorials in both the numerator and denominator. Fortunately, a quick and easy-to-use approximation is available; we will learn the details in Chapter 4.

EXAMPLE 3.3.4

The hypergeometric distribution figures prominently in an important area of statistics known as *acceptance sampling*. Consider the problem faced by a manufacturer who orders a supply of parts from an outside contractor. When the shipment arrives, the manufacturer would like to have some assurance that the parts meet the agreed-to specifications. Every item, of course, could be inspected, but that would be costly, time-consuming, and maybe unreasonable (what if the part were a flashbulb?). A better approach is to inspect a sample of size n and accept the shipment only if the sample is of sufficiently high quality.

Suppose, for example, a shipment contains 100 items and a sample of size $n = 2$ is inspected. Let the random variable X denote the number of defectives in the sample. If the manufacturer decides to return all 100 items if $X \geq 1$, what is the probability that a 10% defective shipment will be accepted?

Viewed as an "urn" problem, a 10% defective shipment (of $N = 100$ items) contains $r = 10$ bad items and $w = 90$ good items (see Figure 3.3.4). If the "decision rule" calls for the shipment to be sent back if $X \geq 1$, then

$$P(\text{shipment is accepted}) = P(X = 0) = \frac{\binom{10}{0}\binom{90}{2}}{\binom{100}{2}}$$

$$= 0.81$$

Similar acceptance probabilities can be computed for other presumed levels of incoming quality as well. If the shipment were *20%* defective, for instance, it would be accepted *64%* of the time:

$$P(\text{shipment is accepted}) = P(X = 0) = \frac{\binom{20}{0}\binom{80}{2}}{\binom{100}{2}} = 0.64$$

FIGURE 3.3.4 $r = 10$ bad
$w = 90$ good

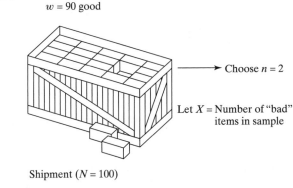

Choose $n = 2$

Let X = Number of "bad" items in sample

Shipment ($N = 100$)

Figure 3.3.5 shows $P(X = 0)$ plotted against the percentage of defectives in the shipment. Graphs of this sort are called *operating characteristic curves*: They summarize how a sampling plan will respond to all possible levels of incoming quality.

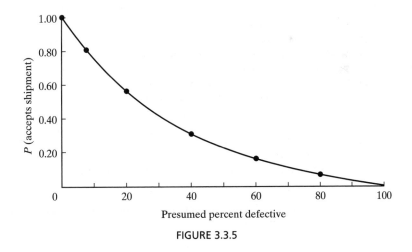

FIGURE 3.3.5

QUESTIONS

3.3.1 Acme Manufacturing recently announced three job openings in its accounting department. From an initial list of 24 applicants, a search committee identified nine candidates—five men and four women—who seemed equally qualified. Priding itself on a long history as an equal opportunity employer, Acme would like to continue that tradition and make the three appointments *at random*. The company's legal department, though, has cautioned the personnel office that that may not be a good idea. If the three chosen happen to be the same gender, the selection process will seem to be sexist and Acme may become embroiled in expensive litigation. What is the probability that a "random" selection will appear to be discriminatory?

3.3.2 A hung jury is one that is unable to reach a unanimous decision. Suppose that a pool of 25 potential jurors are assigned to a murder case where the evidence is so overwhelmingly against the defendant that 23 of the 25 would return a guilty verdict. The other two potential jurors would vote to acquit regardless of the facts. What is the probability that a 12–member panel chosen at random from the pool of 25 will be unable to reach a unanimous decision?

3.3.3 A city has 4050 children under the age of 10, including 514 who have not been vaccinated for measles. Sixty-five of the city's children are enrolled in the ABC Day Care Center. Suppose the municipal health department sends a doctor and a nurse to ABC to immunize any child who has not already been vaccinated. Find a formula for the pdf $p_X(k)$, where the random variable X denotes the number of children at ABC who have not been vaccinated.

3.3.4 Country A inadvertently launches 10 guided missiles—6 armed with nuclear warheads—at Country B. In response, Country B fires 7 antiballistic missiles, each of which will destroy exactly one of the incoming rockets. The antiballistic missiles have no way of detecting, though, which of the 10 rockets are carrying nuclear warheads. What are the chances that Country B will be hit by at least one nuclear missile?

3.3.5 Anne is studying for a history exam covering the French Revolution that will consist of five essay questions selected at random from a list of 10 the professor has handed out to the class in advance. Not exactly a Napoleon buff, Anne would like to avoid researching all 10 questions but still be reasonably assured of getting a fairly good grade. Specifically, she wants to have at least an 85% chance of getting at least four of the five questions right. Will it be sufficient if she studies eight of the 10 questions?

3.3.6 Each year a college awards five merit-based scholarships to members of the entering freshmen class who have exceptional high school records. The initial pool of applicants for the upcoming academic year has been reduced to a "short list" of eight men and ten women, all of whom seem equally deserving. If the awards are made at random from among the 18 finalists, what are the chances that both men and women will be represented?

3.3.7 A local lottery is conducted weekly by choosing five chips at random and without replacement from a population of 40 chips, numbered 1 through 40; order does not matter. The winning numbers are announced on five successive commercials during the Monday night broadcast of a televised movie. Suppose the first three winning numbers match three of yours. What are your chances at that point of winning the lottery?

3.3.8 A display case contains 35 gems, of which 10 are real diamonds and 25 are fake diamonds. A burglar removes four gems at random, one at a time and without replacement. What is the probability that the last gem she steals is the second real diamond in the set of four?

3.3.9 A bleary-eyed student awakens one morning, late for an 8:00 class, and pulls two socks out of a drawer that contains two black, six brown, and two blue socks, all randomly arranged. What is the probability that the two he draws are a matched pair?

3.3.10 Show directly that the set of probabilities associated with the hypergeometric distribution sum to 1. *Hint*: Expand the identity

$$(1 + \mu)^N = (1 + \mu)^r (1 + \mu)^{N-r}$$

and equate coefficients.

3.3.11 Suppose a population contains n_1 objects of one kind, n_2 objects of a second kind, ..., and n_t objects of a tth kind, where $n_1 + n_2 + \cdots + n_t = N$. A sample of size n is drawn at random and without replacement. Let X_i denote the number of objects in the sample of the ith kind, $i = 1, 2, \ldots, t$. Deduce an expression for

$$P(X_1 = k_1, X_2 = k_2, \ldots, X_t = k_t)$$

by generalizing Theorem 3.3.1.

3.3.12 Sixteen students—five freshmen, four sophomores, four juniors, and three seniors—have applied for membership in their school's Communications Board, a group that oversees the college's newspaper, literary magazine, and radio show. Eight positions are open. If the selection is done at random, what is the probability that each class gets two representatives? (*Hint:* Use the generalized hypergeometric model asked for in Question 3.3.11.)

3.3.13 As the owner of a chain of sporting goods stores, you have just been offered a "deal" on a shipment of 100 robot table tennis machines. The price is right, but the prospect of picking up the merchandise at midnight from an unmarked van parked on the side of the New Jersey Turnpike is a bit disconcerting. Being of low repute yourself, you do not consider the legality of the transaction to be an issue, but you do have concerns about being cheated. If too many of the machines are in poor working order, the offer ceases to be a bargain. Suppose you decide to close the deal only if a sample of 10 machines contains no more than one defective. Construct the corresponding operating characteristic curve. For approximately what incoming quality will you accept a shipment 50% of the time?

The Binomial Distribution

By any criterion, the most important of all the discrete pdfs is the *binomial distribution*. Like the hypergeometric, the binomial "model" is one that appeared frequently in Chapter 2. In general, it applies to situations involving a series of independent and identical trials, where each trial can have only one of two possible outcomes.

Imagine three distinguishable coins being tossed, each having a probability p of coming up heads. The set of possible outcomes are the eight listed in Table 3.3.1. If the probability of any of the coins coming up heads is p, then the probability of the *sequence* (H, H, H) is p^3, since the coin tosses qualify as independent trials. Similarly, the probability of (T, H, H) is $(1 - p)p^2$. The fourth column of Table 3.3.1 shows the probabilities associated with each of the three-coin sequences.

TABLE 3.3.1

1st coin	2nd coin	3rd coin	Probability	X = number of heads
H	H	H	p^3	3
H	H	T	$p^2(1 - p)$	2
H	T	H	$p^2(1 - p)$	2
T	H	H	$p^2(1 - p)$	2
H	T	T	$p(1 - p)^2$	1
T	H	T	$p(1 - p)^2$	1
T	T	H	$p(1 - p)^2$	1
T	T	T	$(1 - p)^3$	0

Suppose that our main interest in the coin tosses, though, is only in the *number* of heads that occurred: Whether the actual sequence was, say, (H, H, T) or (H, T, H) is immaterial. That being the case, it makes sense to define a variable X equal to the number of heads observed in a sequence of three tosses. The last column of Table 3.3.1 lists the value of X associated with each outcome in the sample space. Notice that *three* outcomes, each having an individual probability of $p^2(1 - p)$, yield the value $X = 2$, so $p_X(2) = P(X = 2) = 3p^2(1 - p)$. Table 3.3.2 lists all the values for $p_X(k)$.

TABLE 3.3.2

X = number of heads	$P(X = k) = p_X(k)$
0	$(1 - p)^3$
1	$3p(1 - p)^2$
2	$3p^2(1 - p)$
3	p^3

Now, more generally, suppose that n coins are tossed, in which case X can equal any integer from 0 through n. By analogy,

$$P(X = k) = p_X(k) = \begin{pmatrix} \text{number of ways} \\ \text{to arrange } k \\ \text{heads and } n - k \text{ tails} \end{pmatrix} \cdot \begin{pmatrix} \text{probability of any} \\ \text{particular sequence} \\ \text{having } k \text{ heads} \\ \text{and } n - k \text{ tails} \end{pmatrix}$$

$$= \begin{pmatrix} \text{number of ways} \\ \text{to arrange } k \\ \text{heads and } n - k \text{ tails} \end{pmatrix} \cdot p^k(1 - p)^{n-k}$$

The number of ways to arrange k H's and $n - k$ T's, though, is $\dfrac{n!}{k!(n - k)!}$, or $\dbinom{n}{k}$ (recall Theorem 2.9.2).

THEOREM 3.3.2. Consider a series of n independent trials, each resulting in one of two possible outcomes, "success" or "failure." Let $p = P$ (success occurs at any given trial) and assume that p remains constant from trial to trial. Let the variable X denote the total number of successes in the n trials. Then X is said to have a *binomial distribution* and

$$p_X(k) = P(X = k) = \binom{n}{k} p^k(1 - p)^{n-k}, \quad k = 0, 1, \ldots, n$$

EXAMPLE 3.3.5

As the lawyer for a client accused of murder, you are looking for ways to establish "reasonable doubt" in the minds of the jurors. Central to the prosecutor's case is testimony from a forensics expert who claims that a blood sample taken from the scene of the crime matches the DNA of your client. One-tenth of 1% of the time, though, such tests are in error.

Suppose your client is actually guilty. If six other laboratories in the country are capable of doing this kind of DNA analysis (and you hire them all), what are the chances that at least one will make a mistake and conclude that your client is innocent?

Each of the six analyses constitutes an independent trial, where $p = P(\text{lab makes mistake}) = 0.001$. Let $X =$ number of labs that make mistake (and call client innocent). Substituting into Theorem 3.3.2 shows that the lawyer's strategy is not likely to work:

$$P(\text{at least one lab says client is innocent}) = P(X \geq 1)$$

$$= 1 - P(X = 0)$$

$$= 1 - \binom{6}{0}(0.001)^0(0.999)^6$$

$$= 0.006$$

For the defendant, the calculated 0.006 is hardly reassuring. With such small values for n and p, though, getting contradictory forensic results would be a longshot at best.

EXAMPLE 3.3.6

Kingwest Pharmaceuticals is experimenting with a new affordable AIDS medication, PM-17, that may have the ability to strengthen a victim's immune system. Thirty monkeys infected with the HIV complex have been given the drug. Researchers intend to wait 6 weeks and then count the number of animals whose immunological responses show a marked improvement. Any inexpensive drug capable of being effective 60% of the time would be considered a major breakthrough; medications whose chances of success are 50% or less are not likely to have any commercial potential.

Yet to be finalized are guidelines for interpreting results. Kingwest hopes to avoid making either of two errors: (1) rejecting a drug that would ultimately prove to be marketable and (2) spending additional development dollars on a drug whose effectiveness, in the long run, would be 50% or less. As a tentative "decision rule," the project manager suggests that unless *16 or more* of the monkeys show improvement, research on PM-17 should be discontinued.

(a) What are the chances that the "16 or more" rule will cause the company to reject PM-17, *even if the drug is 60% effective?*

(b) How often will the "16 or more" rule allow a 50%-effective drug to be perceived as a major breakthrough?

Solution (a): Each of the monkeys is one of $n = 30$ independent trials, where the outcome is either a "success" (monkey's immune system is strengthened) or a "failure" (monkey's immune system is not strengthened). By assumption, the probability that PM-17 produces an immunological improvement in any given monkey is $p = P(\text{success}) = 0.60$.

Let the random variable X denote the number of monkeys (out of 30) that show improvement after 6 weeks. The probability that the "16 or more" rule will cause a 60%-effective drug to be discarded is the sum of $p_X(k)$ from 0 to 15:

$$P(X < 16) = P(X \leq 15) = \sum_{k=0}^{15} \binom{30}{k}(0.60)^k(0.40)^{30-k}$$

$$= 0.1754$$

Roughly 18% of the time, in other words, a "breakthrough" drug such as PM-17 will produce test results so mediocre (as measured by the "16 or more" rule) that the company will be misled into thinking it has no potential.

*Solution **(b)**:* The other error Kingwest can make is to conclude that PM-17 warrants further study when, in fact, its value for p is below a marketable level. The chance that that particular incorrect inference will be drawn here is the probability that X will be greater than or equal to 16 when $p = 0.5$. That is,

$$P(\text{PM-17 is overestimated}) = P(X \geq 16 \text{ when } p = 0.5)$$

$$= \sum_{k=16}^{30} \binom{30}{k}(0.5)^k(0.5)^{30-k}$$

$$= 0.43$$

Thus, even if PM-17's success rate is an unacceptably low 50%, it has a 43% chance of performing sufficiently well in 30 trials to satisfy the "16 or more" criterion.

Comment.   Evaluating binomial summations when n is either moderate sized or large, which is the case in Example 3.3.6, is tedious, even with a calculator. In practice, a much better approach is to use a statistical software package. The most widely used of these packages, a program known as MINITAB, will be introduced in Appendix 3.A.1.

EXAMPLE 3.3.7

Baseball teams A and B have won their respective league pennants and will face each other in the next World Series. The first team to win four games will be declared the world champion. Oddsmakers believe that A is the better team and has a 55% chance of defeating B on any given day. What is the probability that A will win the World Series?

Notice, first, that the event "A wins the World Series" is the union of four simpler events, all mutually exclusive: "A wins in 4 games," "A wins in 5 games," "A wins in 6 games," and "A wins in 7 games." That is,

$$P(A \text{ wins}) = P\big((A \text{ wins in 4}) \cup (A \text{ wins in 5}) \cup (A \text{ wins in 6}) \cup (A \text{ wins in 7})\big)$$

$$= P(A \text{ wins in 4}) + P(A \text{ wins in 5}) + P(A \text{ wins in 6}) + P(A \text{ wins in 7})$$

Consider the case "A wins in 6." For the latter to happen, A must win exactly three of the first five games *and* win the sixth game (see Figure 3.3.6). Let the random variable X denote the number of times A wins *in the first 5 games*. Given that $p = P(A \text{ wins any given game}) = 0.55$, and assuming the games are independent, X is binomial and we can write

$$P(A \text{ wins in 6}) = P\big((A \text{ wins 3 of first 5}) \cap (A \text{ wins 6th})\big)$$

$$= P(A \text{ wins 3 of first 5}) \cdot P(A \text{ wins 6th})$$

$$= \binom{5}{3}(0.55)^3(0.45)^2 \cdot (0.55)$$

$$= 0.185$$

FIGURE 3.3.6

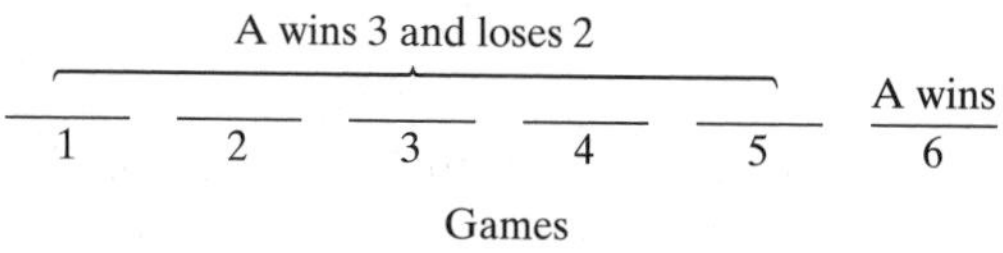

Similar reasoning shows that $P(A$ wins in 4$) = 0.092$, $P(A$ wins in 5$) = 0.165$, and $P(A$ wins in 7$) = 0.167$. Summing all these probabilities, we find that A has almost a 61% chance of winning the World Series:

$$P(A \text{ wins Series}) = 0.092 + 0.165 + 0.185 + 0.167$$

$$= 0.609$$

EXAMPLE 3.3.8

For reasons not entirely clear, Doomsday Airlines books a daily shuttle service from Altoona to Hoboken. They offer two round-trip flights, one on a two-engine prop plane, the other on a four-engine prop plane. Suppose that each engine on each plane will fail independently with the same probability p and that each plane will arrive safely at its destination only if at least half its engines remain in working order. Assuming that you want to continue living, for what values of p would you prefer to fly in the two-engine plane?

Let X denote the number of engines on each plane that remain operable. For the two-engine plane,

$$P(\text{flight lands safely}) = P(X \geq 1) = \sum_{k=1}^{2} \binom{2}{k}(1-p)^k p^{2-k} \tag{3.3.2}$$

For the four-engine plane,

$$P(\text{flight lands safely}) = P(X \geq 2) = \sum_{k=2}^{4} \binom{4}{k}(1-p)^k p^{4-k} \tag{3.3.3}$$

When to opt for the two-engine plane, then, reduces to an algebra problem: We look for the values of p for which

$$\sum_{k=1}^{2} \binom{2}{k}(1-p)^k p^{2-k} > \sum_{k=2}^{4} \binom{4}{k}(1-p)^k p^{4-k} \tag{3.3.4}$$

To minimize the number of terms that need to be dealt with, it will prove expedient to rephrase the problem using the complements of Equations 3.3.2 and 3.3.3. The set of p values for which Inequality 3.3.4 is true is equivalent to the set for which

$$\sum_{k=0}^{1} \binom{4}{k}(1-p)^k p^{4-k} > \binom{2}{0}(1-p)^0 p^2$$

Simplifying the inequality

$$\binom{4}{0}(1-p)^0 p^4 + \binom{4}{1}(1-p)^1 p^3 > \binom{2}{0}(1-p)^0 p^2$$

gives

$$(3p - 1)(p - 1) < 0 \tag{3.3.5}$$

But $(p - 1)$ is never positive, so Inequality 3.3.5 will be true only when $(3p - 1) > 0$, which gives $p > \frac{1}{3}$ as the desired solution set. Figure 3.3.7 is a graph of the two "safe return" probabilities, $P(X \geq 1 | n = 2)$ and $P(X \geq 2 | n = 4)$, as a function of p.

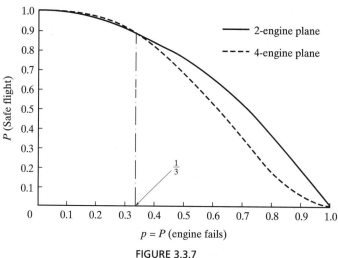

FIGURE 3.3.7

CASE STUDY 3.3.1

Consider again the evidence presented in *People* v. *Collins*, as outlined in Case Study 2.7.1. The prosecution's case rested on the unlikelihood of a given couple's matching up with the six characteristics reported by the several eyewitnesses of the crime. It was estimated that the joint occurrence of a white female with blond hair combed in a ponytail riding in a yellow car with a black male having a beard and a mustache was on the order of 1 in 12 million—a number so small, the prosecution contended, that Ms. Collins and her male friend were clearly guilty, a classic open-and-shut case. Not so, argued the counsel for the defense. By approaching the same data from a slightly different perspective, they were able to show that "reasonable doubt" had not really been eliminated, despite the apparent 12-million-to-1 odds.

Suppose that n is taken to be the total number of couples who could conceivably have been in the area and perpetrated the crime, and p is the probability that any such couple would share the six characteristics introduced by the prosecution as evidence. Define X to be the number of couples matching up with the eyewitness accounts. It is not unreasonable to assume that X is binomial, in which case

$$P(X = k) = \binom{n}{k} p^k (1 - p)^{n-k}, \quad k = 0, 1, \ldots, n$$

Therefore,

$$P(X = 1) = np(1 - p)^{n-1}$$

and

$$P(X \geq 1) = 1 - P(X = 0) = 1 - (1 - p)^n$$

from which it follows that

$$P(X > 1) = 1 - (1 - p)^n - np(1 - p)^{n-1}$$

Now, consider the ratio

$$\frac{P(X > 1)}{P(X \geq 1)} = \frac{1 - (1 - p)^n - np(1 - p)^{n-1}}{1 - (1 - p)^n}$$ (3.3.6)

= P(more than one of the n couples fit the description given that at least one does)

= P(there is at least one other couple who could have committed the crime)

If $P(X > 1)/P(X \geq 1)$ is anything other than a very small number, we would have to accept the possibility that Ms. Collins and her friend have a pair of lookalikes and that perhaps *they* were the culprits.

Table 3.3.3 shows the value of the probability ratio (Equation 3.3.6) for various values of n befitting a large metropolitan area and for the prosecutor's estimate of $p(= 1/12,000,000)$. What the last column makes clear is that $P(X > 1)/P(X \geq 1)$ is *not* a particularly small number.

TABLE 3.3.3

p	n	$P(X > 1)/P(X \geq 1)$
1/12,000,000	1,000,000	0.0410
1/12,000,000	2,000,000	0.0810
1/12,000,000	5,000,000	0.1939
1/12,000,000	10,000,000	0.3595

Looked at in this way, the evidence is certainly not as incriminating as the "1-in-12,000,000" argument would have us believe. At least that was the opinion of the California Supreme Court: Based on the probability argument just presented, they overturned the initial verdict of "guilty" that had been handed down by the Superior Court of Los Angeles County.

QUESTIONS

3.3.14 An investment analyst has tracked a certain blue-chip stock for the past six months and found that on any given day it either goes up a point or down a point. Furthermore, it went up on 25% of the days and down on 75%. What is the probability that at the close of trading four days from now the price of the stock will be the same as it is today? Assume that the daily fluctuations are independent events.

3.3.15 In a nuclear reactor, the fission process is controlled by inserting special rods into the radioactive core to absorb neutrons and slow down the nuclear chain reaction. When functioning properly, these rods serve as a first-line defense against a core meltdown. Suppose a reactor has 10 control rods, each operating independently and each having a 0.80 probability of being properly inserted in the event of an "incident." Furthermore, suppose that a meltdown will be prevented if at least half the rods perform satisfactorily. What is the probability that, upon demand, the system will fail?

3.3.16 Suppose that since the early 1950s some 10,000 independent UFO sightings have been reported to civil authorities. If the probability that any sighting is genuine is on the order of 1 in 100,000, what is the probability that at least 1 of the 10,000 was genuine?

3.3.17 Two lighting systems are being proposed for an employee work area. One requires 50 bulbs, each having a probability of 0.05 of burning out within a month's time. The second has 100 bulbs, each with a 0.02 burnout probability. Whichever system is installed will be inspected once a month for the purpose of replacing burned-out bulbs. Which system is likely to require less maintenance? Answer the question by comparing the probabilities that each will require at least one bulb to be replaced at the end of 30 days.

3.3.18 The great English diarist Samuel Pepys asked his friend Sir Isaac Newton the following question: Is it more likely to get at least one 6 when 6 dice are rolled, at least two 6's when 12 dice are rolled, or at least three 6's when 18 dice are rolled? After considerable correspondence (see (145)), Newton convinced the skeptical Pepys that the first event is the most likely. Compute the three probabilities.

3.3.19 The gunner on a small assault boat fires six missiles at an attacking plane. Each has a 20% chance of being on target. If two or more of the shells find their mark, the plane will crash. At the same time, the pilot of the plane fires 10 air-to-surface rockets, each of which has a 0.05 chance of critically disabling the boat. Would you rather be on the plane or the boat?

3.3.20 In his 1889 publication *Natural Inheritance*, the renowned British scientist Sir Francis Galton described a pinball-type board that he called a *quincunx*. As pictured, the quincunx has five rows of pegs, the pegs in each row being the same distance apart. At the bottom of the board are five cells, numbered 0 through 4. A ball pushed between the pegs in the first row will hit the middle peg in the second row, veer to the right or to the left, strike a peg in the third row, veer to the right or to the left, and so on. If the ball has a 50–50 chance of going in either direction each time it hits a peg, what is the probability that it ends up in cell 3?

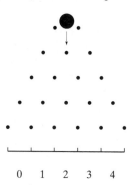

3.3.21 If a family has four children, is it more likely they will have two boys and two girls or three of one sex and one of the other? Assume that the probability of a child being a boy is $\frac{1}{2}$ and that the births are independent events.

3.3.22 Experience has shown that only $\frac{1}{3}$ of all patients having a certain disease will recover if given the standard treatment. A new drug is to be tested on a group of 12 volunteers. If the FDA requires that at least seven of these patients recover before it will license the new drug, what is the probability that the treatment will be discredited even if it has the potential to increase an individual's recovery rate to $\frac{1}{2}$?

3.3.23 Transportation to school for a rural county's 76 children is provided by a fleet of four buses. Drivers are chosen on a day-to-day basis and come from a pool of local farmers who have agreed to be "on call." What is the smallest number of drivers that need to be in the pool if the county wants to have at least a 95% probability on any given day that all the buses will run? Assume that each driver has an 80% chance of being available if contacted.

3.3.24 Recall Example 3.3.7. Make a graph of $P(A$ wins Series$)$ as a function of p, where $p = P(A$ wins any given game$)$. Assume that A is the better team and $p > 0.50$. For what value of p will A have an 80% chance of winning the World Series?

3.3.25 The captain of a Navy gunboat orders a volley of 25 missiles to be fired at random along a 500-foot stretch of shoreline that he hopes to establish as a beachhead. Dug into the beach is a 30-foot-long bunker serving as the enemy's first line of defense. The captain has reason to believe that the bunker will be destroyed if at least three of the missiles are on target. What is the probability of that happening?

3.3.26 Suppose that the variation in a measurement Y is described by the continuous pdf $f_Y(y) = 6y(1 - y), 0 \le y \le 1$. If five independent values of Y are observed, what is the probability that exactly three will lie between $\frac{1}{4}$ and $\frac{1}{2}$?

3.3.27 A computer has generated seven random numbers over the interval 0 to 1. Is it more likely that (1) exactly three will be in the interval $\frac{1}{2}$ to 1 or (2) fewer than three will be greater than $\frac{3}{4}$?

3.3.28 Use the expansion of $(x + y)^n$ (recall page 105) to verify that the formula given for $p_X(k)$ in Theorem 3.3.2 sums to 1 as k goes from 0 to n.

3.3.29 Suppose a series of n independent trials can each end in one of *three* possible outcomes. Let the random variables X_1 and X_2 denote the numbers of trials that result in outcomes 1 and 2, respectively. Let p_1 and p_2 denote the probabilities associated with outcomes 1 and 2. Generalize Theorem 3.3.2 to deduce a formula for $P(X_1 = k_1$ and $X_2 = k_2)$.

3.3.30 Repair calls for central air conditioners fall into three general categories: coolant leakage, compressor failure, and electrical malfunction. Experience has shown that the probabilities associated with the three are 0.5, 0.3, and 0.2, respectively. Suppose that a dispatcher has logged in 10 service requests for tomorrow morning. Use the answer to Question 3.3.29 to calculate the probability that 3 of those 10 will involve coolant leakage and 5 will be compressor failures.

3.3.31 Suppose n batteries are put into n toy robots, and the robots are left on for five hours. If the battery life, Y, is described by the pdf $f_Y(y) = (1/\theta)e^{-y/\theta}$, $y > 0$, find an expression for the probability that exactly r robots are still working after the five hours have elapsed.

3.3.32 Listed in the following table is the length distribution of World Series competition for the 50 years from 1926 to 1975.

World Series lengths

Number of Games, X	Number of Years
4	9
5	11
6	8
7	22
	50

If it is assumed that each World Series game is an independent event and that the probability of either team's winning any particular contest is 0.5, find the probability model describing the series length, X—that is, find $f_X(x)$, $x = 4, 5, 6, 7$. How well does the model fit the data? (Compute the "expected" frequencies.)

3.4 THE CUMULATIVE DISTRIBUTION FUNCTION

There are several ways to characterize the variation associated with a random variable. The most direct is the *pdf*, as typified by the functions $p_X(k)$ and $f_Y(y)$ introduced in Sections 3.2 and 3.3. Another is the *cdf*, or cumulative distribution function.

Unlike that for the pdf, the definition of the cdf is the same, regardless of whether the underlying random variable is discrete or continuous. As a general policy, we will use the letter W in theorems and definitions where the nature of the random variable is irrelevant.

> **DEFINITION 3.4.1.** Let W be a random variable defined on a sample space S. For any real number w, the *cumulative distribution function of W* [abbreviated *cdf* and written $F_W(w)$] is the probability associated with the set of sample points in S that get mapped by W into values on the real line *less than or equal to w*. Formally,
>
> $$F_W(w) = P(\{s \in S \,|\, W(s) \leq w\})$$

As we did with pdf's, references to s and S will usually be deleted and we will write

$$F_W(w) = P(W \leq w)$$

If the random variable is discrete, $F_X(x)$ is a step function, with jumps occurring at the values of $x = k$ for which $p_X(k) > 0$. If the random variable is continuous, $F_Y(y)$ is continuous (in the calculus sense) and monotonically nondecreasing.

EXAMPLE 3.4.1

A fair die is rolled four times. Let the random variable X denote the number of sixes that appear. Find $F_X(x)$, the cdf for X.

Note, first, that X has a binomial distribution with $n = 4$ and $p = \frac{1}{6}$. From Theorem 3.3.2,

$$p_X(k) = P(X = k) = \binom{4}{k}\left(\frac{1}{6}\right)^k\left(\frac{5}{6}\right)^{4-k}, \quad k = 0, 1, 2, 3, 4$$

(see Figure 3.4.1).

FIGURE 3.4.1

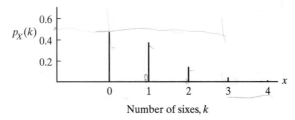

Number of sixes, k

To find $F_X(x)$, we look at Figure 3.4.1 and see which ranges of x values give the same value for $P(X \leq x)$. For example, if x is any number less than 0, $F_X(x) = P(X \leq x) = 0$; for any x in the semiopen interval $[0, 1)$,

$$F_X(x) = P(X \le x) = P(X = 0) = \binom{4}{0}\left(\frac{1}{6}\right)^0\left(\frac{5}{6}\right)^4 = \left(\frac{5}{6}\right)^4 = 0.482$$

for $1 \le x < 2$,

$$F_X(x) = P(X \le x) = P(X = 0) + P(X = 1)$$

$$= \binom{4}{0}\left(\frac{1}{6}\right)^0\left(\frac{5}{6}\right)^4 + \binom{4}{1}\left(\frac{1}{6}\right)^1\left(\frac{5}{6}\right)^3 = \left(\frac{5}{6}\right)^4 + 4\left(\frac{1}{6}\right)\left(\frac{5}{6}\right)^3 = 0.868$$

Continuing this argument establishes $F_X(x)$ to be a step function with jumps at the points $x = 0, 1, 2, 3$, and 4:

$$F_X(x) = \begin{cases} 0 & x < 0 \\[2mm] \left(\frac{5}{6}\right)^4 = 0.482 & 0 \le x < 1 \\[2mm] \left(\frac{5}{6}\right)^4 + 4\left(\frac{1}{6}\right)\left(\frac{5}{6}\right)^3 = 0.868 & 1 \le x < 2 \\[2mm] \left(\frac{5}{6}\right)^4 + 4\left(\frac{1}{6}\right)\left(\frac{5}{6}\right)^3 + 6\left(\frac{1}{6}\right)^2\left(\frac{5}{6}\right)^2 = 0.984 & 2 \le x < 3 \\[2mm] \left(\frac{5}{6}\right)^4 + 4\left(\frac{1}{6}\right)\left(\frac{5}{6}\right)^3 + 6\left(\frac{1}{6}\right)^2\left(\frac{5}{6}\right)^2 + 4\left(\frac{1}{6}\right)^3\left(\frac{5}{6}\right) = 0.999 & 3 \le x < 4 \\[2mm] 1 & 4 \le x \end{cases}$$

Figure 3.4.2 is a graph of $F_X(x)$.

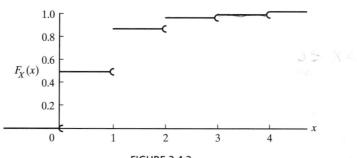

FIGURE 3.4.2

EXAMPLE 3.4.2

Time intervals between consecutively occurring events are frequently modeled using an exponential pdf, $f_Y(y) = \lambda e^{-\lambda y}$, $y > 0$, where the constant λ reflects the rate at which the events are occurring (recall Question 2.5.8). Find the cdf, $F_Y(y)$, of an exponential random variable for which $\lambda = 0.4$.

A graph of the pdf for Y (see Figure 3.4.3) shows that only two cases (i.e., ranges of y) need to be considered in calculating $F_Y(y)$: $y < 0$ and $y \ge 0$. The first is trivial: If $y < 0$, $F_Y(y) = P(Y \le y) = 0$. That is, there is no accumulated probability to the left of any value y, where y is less than 0. For $y \ge 0$,

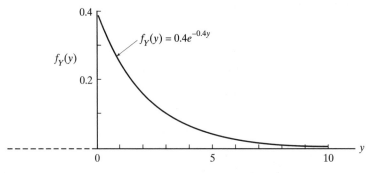

FIGURE 3.4.3

$$F_Y(y) = P(Y \le y) = \int_{-\infty}^{0} 0\, dt + \int_{0}^{y} 0.4e^{-0.4t}\, dt$$

$$= 0 + \int_{0}^{0.4y} e^{-u}\, du$$

$$= -e^{-u}\Big|_{0}^{0.4y} = 1 - e^{-0.4y}$$

Illustrating the claim made on page 144, $F_Y(y)$ is continuous (in the calculus sense) and monotonically nondecreasing (see Figure 3.4.4).

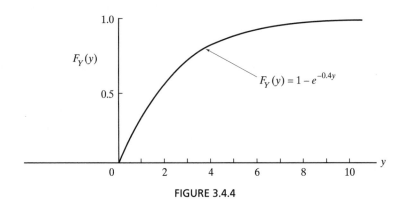

FIGURE 3.4.4

EXAMPLE 3.4.3

If a pdf is piecewise continuous and has discontinuities at a finite number of points, its cdf will still be continuous. Figure 3.4.5 shows the pdf for a continuous random variable Y, where

$$f_Y(y) = \begin{cases} 0, & y < 0 \\ 2y, & 0 \le y \le \tfrac{1}{2} \\ 6 - 6y, & \tfrac{1}{2} < y \le 1 \\ 0, & y > 1 \end{cases}$$

FIGURE 3.4.5

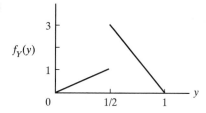

Find the corresponding cdf.

Looking at the form of $f_Y(y)$, we see that $F_Y(y)$ will have four different functional expressions, depending on whether $y < 0$, $0 \le y \le \frac{1}{2}$, $\frac{1}{2} < y \le 1$, or $y > 1$. For $y < 0$, $F_Y(y) = P(Y \le y) = 0$. For $0 \le y \le \frac{1}{2}$,

$$F_Y(y) = P(Y \le y) = \int_{-\infty}^{0} 0 \, dt + \int_{0}^{y} 2t \, dt$$

$$= y^2$$

(see Figure 3.4.6). For $\frac{1}{2} < y \le 1$,

$$F_Y(y) = P(Y \le y) = \int_{-\infty}^{0} 0 \, dt + \int_{0}^{1/2} 2t \, dt + \int_{1/2}^{y} (6 - 6t) \, dt$$

$$= \frac{1}{4} + \left(6t - 3t^2 \right) \Big|_{1/2}^{y}$$

$$= 6y - 3y^2 - 2$$

(see Figure 3.4.7). Of course, for $y > 1$, $F_Y(y) = 1$. Putting all these cases together gives

$$F_Y(y) = \begin{cases} 0 & y < 0 \\ y^2 & 0 \le y \le \frac{1}{2} \\ 6y - 3y^2 - 2 & \frac{1}{2} < y \le 1 \\ 1 & y > 1 \end{cases}$$

Graphed, the cdf is S-shaped, as shown in Figure 3.4.8.

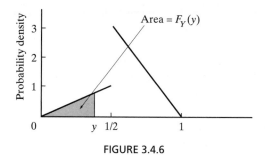

FIGURE 3.4.6

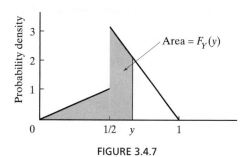

FIGURE 3.4.7

FIGURE 3.4.8

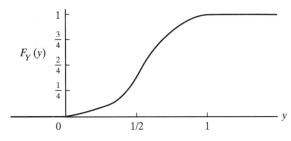

QUESTIONS

3.4.1 Graph the cdf corresponding to a random variable whose pdf is given by

$$p_X(k) = \frac{1}{3}, \quad k = 1, 2, 3$$

3.4.2 Let Y be a continuous random variable with pdf

$$f_Y(y) = \begin{cases} \dfrac{3}{4}, & 0 \le y \le 1 \\ \dfrac{1}{4}, & 2 \le y \le 3 \\ 0, & \text{elsewhere} \end{cases}$$

   (a) Graph $f_Y(y)$.   **(b)** Find and graph $F_Y(y)$.

3.4.3 Find and graph the cdf, $F_Y(y)$, of the random variable Y whose pdf is the function

$$f_Y(y) = \begin{cases} 3y(1 - y), & 0 \le y \le 1 \\ \frac{1}{2}, & 2 \le y \le 3 \\ 0, & \text{elsewhere} \end{cases}$$

3.4.4 Find and graph the cdf associated with a random variable distributed *uniformly* over the interval $[a, b]$ (recall Example 2.5.1).

3.4.5 Suppose that a random variable's pdf is given by

$$f_Y(y) = 1/10, \quad -5 \le y \le 5$$

For what value of y does the cdf equal 0.60?

3.4.6 Let the random variable X denote the number of aces a player receives in a five-card poker hand. Graph the cdf of X.

3.4.7 An urn contains four chips, numbered 1 through 4, where the probability associated with a chip is proportional to its magnitude. Find and graph the cdf corresponding to the number showing on a chip drawn at random.

3.4.8 If the pdf for Y is

$$f_Y(y) = \begin{cases} 0, & |y| > 1 \\ 1 - |y|, & |y| \le 1 \end{cases}$$

find and graph $F_Y(y)$.

3.4.9 Suppose that Y is a random variable for which $F_Y(3) = 0.82$ and $F_Y(2) = 0.25$. What does $F_Y(3) - F_Y(2) = 0.82 - 0.25 = 0.57$ represent?

Relating cdf's to Probabilities

Applications of cdf's are found in many areas of mathematical statistics, as we will see in the chapters ahead. At this point, their most obvious connection is with the pdf, and they provide an alternative method for calculating probabilities. Because $F_W(w) = P(W \le w)$, it follows that

(a) $$P(W > w) = 1 - F_W(w)$$
(b) $$P(a < W \le b) = F_W(b) - F_W(a)$$
(c) $$P(W = w) = F_W(w) - \lim_{t \to w^-} F_W(t)$$

Properties (a) and (b) follow immediately, but (c) needs a word of explanation. If the random variable is continuous, its cdf is continuous, and $\lim_{t \to y^-} F_Y(t) = F_Y(y)$. Property (c), then, confirms the fact that the probability associated with any specific value of a continuous random variable is 0:

$$P(Y = y) = F_Y(y) - \lim_{t \to y^-} F_Y(t)$$
$$= F_Y(y) - F_Y(y)$$
$$= 0$$

If the random variable is discrete,

$$P(X = x) = F_X(x) - \lim_{t \to x^-} F_X(t)$$

will be 0 everywhere *except at the points for which $p_X(x) > 0$* [in which case $F_X(x) > \lim_{t \to x^-} F_X(t)$]. Figure 3.4.9 shows the cdf of the (discrete) random variable discussed in Example 3.4.1. Notice that for a point such as $x = 1.5$,

$$P(X = 1.5) = F_X(1.5) - \lim_{t \to 1.5^-} F_X(t)$$
$$= P(X = 0) + P(X = 1) - \left[P(X = 0) + P(X = 1) \right]$$
$$= 0$$

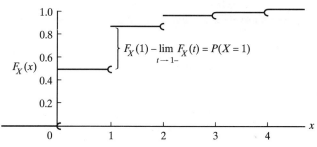

FIGURE 3.4.9

On the other hand, Property (c) gives the correct nonzero value for $P(X = x)$ when $p_X(x) > 0$. Consider the jump-point $x = 1.0$:

$$P(X = 1.0) = F_X(1.0) - \lim_{t \to 1.0^-} F_X(t)$$

$$= P(X = 0) + P(X = 1) - P(X = 0)$$

$$= P(X = 1)$$

(see Figure 3.4.9).

> **THEOREM 3.4.1.** If Y is a continuous random variable with pdf $f_Y(y)$ and cdf $F_Y(y)$, then
>
> $$f_Y(y) = F'_Y(y)$$
>
> provided $F'_Y(y)$ exists at all but a finite number of points.
>
> **Proof.** The statement of the theorem follows immediately from the fundamental theorem of calculus and the intermediate value theorem.

EXAMPLE 3.4.4

Suppose that a random variable has the cdf shown in Figure 3.4.10. In functional form,

$$F_Y(y) = \begin{cases} 0 & y < 0 \\ \dfrac{3y}{4} & 0 \le y \le 1 \\ \dfrac{3}{4} & 1 < y \le 2 \\ \dfrac{y}{4} + \dfrac{1}{4} & 2 < y \le 3 \\ 1 & y > 3 \end{cases}$$

Find the corresponding pdf.

Since $F_Y(y)$ is everywhere continuous and $F'_Y(y)$ exists at all but four points, we can use Theorem 3.4.1 to find $f_Y(y)$. Differentiating $F_Y(y)$ gives

FIGURE 3.4.10

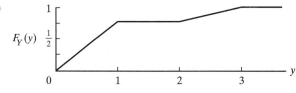

$$f_Y(y) = F_Y'(y) = \begin{cases} 0 & y < 0 \\ \dfrac{3}{4} & 0 \le y \le 1 \\ 0 & 1 < y \le 2 \\ \dfrac{1}{4} & 2 < y \le 3 \\ 0 & y > 3 \end{cases}$$

which shows that $f_Y(y)$ is a simple step-type function (see Figure 3.4.11).

FIGURE 3.4.11

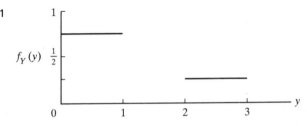

QUESTIONS

3.4.10 A continuous random variable Y has a cdf given by

$$F_Y(y) = \begin{cases} 0 & y < 0 \\ y^2 & 0 \le y < 1 \\ 1 & y \ge 1 \end{cases}$$

Find $P(\frac{1}{2} < Y \le \frac{3}{4})$ two ways—first, by using the cdf and second, by using the pdf.

3.4.11 Suppose that $f_Y(y)$ is a symmetric and continuous pdf: $f_Y(y) = f_Y(-y)$, for $y > 0$. Show that

$$P(-a < Y < a) = 2 \cdot F_Y(a) - 1$$

for $a > 0$.

3.4.12 A random variable Y has cdf

$$F_Y(y) = \begin{cases} 0 & y < 1 \\ \ln y & 1 \le y \le e \\ 1 & e < y \end{cases}$$

Find

(a) $P(Y < 2)$

(b) $P(2 < Y \le 2\frac{1}{2})$

(c) $P(2 < Y < 2\frac{1}{2})$

(d) $f_Y(y)$

3.4.13 Suppose that Y is a continuous random variable defined over the closed interval A. Describe an event, B, having the property that the probability of B is 1, but B is not the entire sample space. Describe an event, C, for which $P(C) = 0$, yet C is not the empty set.

3.4.14 The cdf for a random variable Y is defined by $F_Y(y) = 0$ for $y < 0$; $F_Y(y) = 4y^3 - 3y^4$ for $0 \le y \le 1$; and $F_Y(y) = 1$ for $y > 1$. Find $P(\frac{1}{4} \le Y \le \frac{3}{4})$ by integrating $f_Y(y)$.

3.4.15 Let Y be a random variable denoting the age at which a piece of equipment fails. In reliability theory, the probability that an item fails at time y given that it has survived until time y is called the *hazard rate*, $h(y)$. In terms of pdf's and cdf's,

$$h(y) = \frac{f_Y(y)}{1 - F_Y(y)}$$

Find $h(y)$ if Y is described by an exponential pdf, $f_Y(y) = (1/\lambda)e^{-y/\lambda}, y > 0$. Interpret your answer.

3.4.16 Draw pictures of the pdf's that produced the following cdf's:

(a)

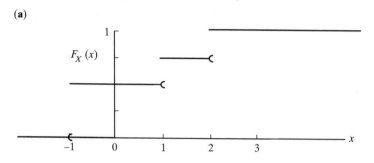

(b)

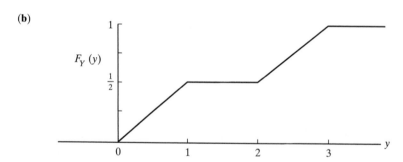

3.4.17 Suppose that Y is a continuous random variable for which $F_Y(y) = 1 - e^{-y}, y \geq 0$ (and 0 elsewhere). Calculate $P(1 \leq e^Y \leq 2)$.

3.4.18 Suppose that in a certain Third World nation the distribution of per family disposable income, Y, is described by the pdf

$$f_Y(y) = ye^{-y}, y > 0$$

where y is measured in thousands of dollars. Find the first, second, and third quartiles of the income distribution. That is, approximate the values of y for which $F_Y(y) = 0.25, F_Y(y) = 0.50$, and $F_Y(y) = 0.75$.

3.4.19 In the past, persons afflicted with a certain neurological disease have had a 30% chance of complete recovery. A radically different therapy has been tested recently on ten patients, and eight have recovered. Let the random variable X denote the number who recover when given the new therapy. Find $1 - F_X(7)$ under the assumption that the new therapy is no better than the old. In very general terms, how would the magnitude of $1 - F_X(7)$ be used to draw an inference about the efficacy of the new treatment?

3.5   JOINT DENSITIES

Sections 3.2 and 3.4 introduced the basic terminology for describing the probabilistic behavior of a *single* random variable. Such information, while adequate for many problems, is insufficient in situations where more than one random variable has a major influence on the outcome of an experiment. Consider an electronic system that contains two components, one for backup, but both under load. Suppose that the only way the system will fail is if both components fail. The *system's* life, Z, will then depend "jointly" on the distributions of the *component* lives, X and Y. Knowing only $f_X(x)$ and $f_Y(y)$, though, will not necessarily provide us with enough information to determine $f_Z(z)$. What is needed is a probability function describing the "simultaneous" behavior of X and Y^1.

> **DEFINITION 3.5.1.**
>
> **(a)** Suppose that X and Y are two discrete random variables defined on the same sample space S. The *joint probability density function of X and Y* (or *joint pdf*) is denoted $p_{X,Y}(x, y)$, where
>
> $$p_{X,Y}(x, y) = P(\{s \in S \,|\, X(s) = x, Y(s) = y\})$$
> $$= P(X = x, Y = y)$$
>
> **(b)** Suppose that X and Y are two continuous random variables defined over the same sample space S. The joint pdf of X and Y, $f_{X,Y}(x, y)$, is the surface having the property that for any region R in the xy-plane,
>
> $$P((X, Y) \in R) = P(\{s \in S \,|\, (X(s), Y(s)) \in R\})$$
> $$= \int_R \int f_{X,Y}(x, y)\, dx\, dy$$

EXAMPLE 3.5.1

A supermarket has two express lines. Let X and Y denote the number of customers in the first and in the second, respectively, at any given time. During nonrush hours, the joint pdf of X and Y is summarized by the following table:

		X			
		0	1	2	3
	0	0.1	0.2	0	0
	1	0.2	0.25	0.05	0
Y	2	0	0.05	0.05	0.025
	3	0	0	0.025	0.05

---

[1] For the next several sections we will suspend our earlier practice of using X to denote discrete random variables and Y to denote continuous random variables. To which category a random variable belongs will need to be determined from the context of the problem. Typically, though, X and Y will either both be discrete or both be continuous.

Find $P(|X - Y| = 1)$, the probability that X and Y differ by exactly 1. By definition,

$$P(|X - Y| = 1) = \sum_{|x-y|=1}\sum p_{X,Y}(x, y)$$

$$= p_{X,Y}(0, 1) + p_{X,Y}(1, 0) + p_{X,Y}(1, 2)$$

$$+ p_{X,Y}(2, 1) + p_{X,Y}(2, 3) + p_{X,Y}(3, 2)$$

$$= 0.2 + 0.2 + 0.05 + 0.05 + 0.025 + 0.025$$

$$= 0.55$$

[Would you expect $p_{X,Y}(x, y)$ to be symmetric? Would you expect the event $|X - Y| \geq 2$ to have zero probability?]

EXAMPLE 3.5.2

A study claims that the daily number of hours, X, a teenager watches television and the daily number of hours, Y, he works on his homework are approximated by the joint pdf,

$$f_{X,Y}(x, y) = xye^{-(x+y)}, \qquad x > 0, \quad y > 0$$

What is the probability a teenager chosen at random spends at least twice as much time watching television as he does working on his homework?

The region, R, in the xy-plane corresponding to the event "$X \geq 2Y$" is shown in Figure 3.5.1. It follows that $P(X \geq 2Y)$ is the volume under $f_{X,Y}(x, y)$ above the region R:

$$P(X \geq 2Y) = \int_0^\infty \int_0^{x/2} xye^{-(x+y)} \, dy \, dx$$

FIGURE 3.5.1

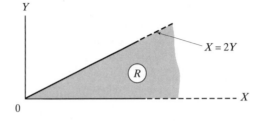

Separating variables, we can write

$$P(X \geq 2Y) = \int_0^\infty xe^{-x}\left[\int_0^{x/2} ye^{-y} \, dy\right] dx$$

and the double integral reduces to $\frac{7}{27}$:

$$P(X \geq 2Y) = \int_0^\infty xe^{-x}\left[1 - \left(\frac{x}{2} + 1\right)e^{-x/2}\right]dx$$

$$= \int_0^\infty xe^{-x}\,dx - \int_0^\infty \frac{x^2}{2}e^{-3x/2}\,dx - \int_0^\infty xe^{-3x/2}\,dx$$

$$= 1 - \frac{16}{54} - \frac{4}{9}$$

$$= \frac{7}{27}$$

EXAMPLE 3.5.3

Consider the electronic system mentioned in the beginning of this section. Suppose that the two components operate independently and have identical performance characteristics. Let X and Y be random variables denoting their life spans. Experience with wear-out times suggests that in certain cases a good choice for $f_{X,Y}(x, y)$ would be

$$f_{X,Y}(x, y) = \begin{cases} \lambda^2 e^{-\lambda(x+y)}, & x \geq 0, \quad y \geq 0 \\ 0, & \text{otherwise} \end{cases}$$

where λ is some constant greater than 0.

   Suppose that the manufacturer advertises a money-back guarantee if the system fails to last for more than 1000 hours. What proportion of the systems sold is likely to be returned for refunds?

   Since the system fails only if both components fail,

$$P(\text{refund}) = P(X \leq 1000, \quad Y \leq 1000)$$

$$= \int_0^{1000} \int_0^{1000} \lambda^2 e^{-\lambda(x+y)}\,dy\,dx$$

$$= \int_0^{1000} \left(\int_0^{1000} \lambda^2 e^{-\lambda x}e^{-\lambda y}\,dy\right)dx$$

The integration in parentheses is done with respect to y, with x being treated as a constant. The expression $\lambda e^{-\lambda x}$ can therefore be factored out of the y integration, so

$$\int_0^{1000} \left(\int_0^{1000} \lambda^2 e^{-\lambda x}e^{-\lambda y}\,dy\right)dx = \int_0^{1000} \lambda e^{-\lambda x}\left(\int_0^{1000} \lambda e^{-\lambda x}\,dy\right)dx$$

$$= \int_0^{1000} \lambda e^{-\lambda x}\left(1 - e^{-\lambda \cdot 1000}\right)dx$$

$$= \left(1 - e^{-\lambda \cdot 1000}\right)\int_0^{1000} \lambda e^{-\lambda x}\,dx$$

which implies that

$$P(\text{refund}) = \left(1 - e^{-1000\lambda}\right)^2$$

EXAMPLE 3.5.4

Let X, Y, and $f_{X,Y}(x, y)$ be defined as they were in Example 3.5.3. However, suppose the system itself is modified so that one component is kept on reserve—and activated only when the other needs replacing. As before, the system fails only when both components burn out, but now the component lives are cumulative. Again we seek the probability that the system fails in 1000 hours or less. Translated into a statement about X and Y, the probability of a refund now reduces to

$$P(\text{refund}) = P(X + Y \le 1000) = \int_R \int \lambda^2 e^{-\lambda(x+y)} \, dy \, dx$$

where R is the shaded region shown in Figure 3.5.2.

As in the preceding example, the double integral is evaluated by first holding x constant. Here, though, the upper limit of the integration for y depends on x: For x fixed, y varies between 0 and $1000 - x$ (see Figure 3.5.3).

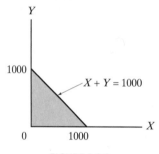

FIGURE 3.5.2

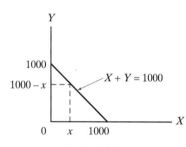

FIGURE 3.5.3

Therefore,

$$\int_R \int f_{X,Y}(x, y) \, dy \, dx = \int_0^{1000} \left(\int_0^{1000-x} \lambda^2 e^{-\lambda x} e^{-\lambda y} \, dy \right) dx$$

$$= \int_0^{1000} \lambda e^{-\lambda x} \left(\int_0^{1000-x} \lambda e^{-\lambda y} \, dy \right) dx$$

$$= \int_0^{1000} \lambda e^{-\lambda x} \left(1 - e^{-\lambda(1000-x)} \right) dx$$

$$= \int_0^{1000} \left(\lambda e^{-\lambda x} - \lambda e^{-\lambda \cdot 1000} \right) dx$$

$$= 1 - e^{-\lambda \cdot 1000} - 1000 \lambda e^{-\lambda \cdot 1000}$$

so

$$P(\text{refund}) = 1 - (1 + 1000\lambda)e^{-1000\lambda}$$

Comment. Note that with a bit more effort we can get the pdf for the sum of the component lives. Let $Z = X + Y$. The argument that was just used to find $P(Z \le 1000)$ obviously holds for any $z > 0$. Therefore,

$$P(\text{system fails in } z \text{ hours or less}) = P(Z \le z)$$

$$= F_Z(z) = 1 - (1 + \lambda z)e^{-\lambda z}$$

Differentiating gives $f_Z(z)$ (recall Theorem 3.4.1),

$$f_Z(z) = F_Z'(z) = \lambda^2 z e^{-\lambda z}, \quad z > 0$$

EXAMPLE 3.5.5

The binomial assumptions given in Section 3.3 can be easily generalized to form a *trinomial* model having a joint pdf. Imagine a series of n independent trials, each ending in one of three possible outcomes, where $p_1 = P(\text{Outcome 1})$, $p_2 = P(\text{Outcome 2})$, and $1 - p_1 - p_2 = P(\text{Outcome 3})$ (see Figure 3.5.4). Let X and Y denote the numbers of trials ending in Outcome 1 and Outcome 2, respectively. Find $p_{X,Y}(x, y)$.

$$\text{Possible outcomes} \begin{cases} 1 \\ 2 \\ 3 \end{cases} \quad \begin{cases} 1 \\ 2 \\ 3 \end{cases} \cdots \begin{cases} 1 \\ 2 \\ 3 \end{cases} \quad \begin{matrix} p_1 = P(\text{Outcome 1}) \\ p_2 = P(\text{Outcome 2}) \end{matrix}$$

$$\begin{matrix} 1 & 2 & n \end{matrix} \quad 1 - p_1 - p_2 = P(\text{Outcome 3})$$

Independent trials

FIGURE 3.5.4

Following the approach taken on page 136, we can write

$$p_{X,Y}(x, y) = P(X = x, Y = y)$$

$$= \left\{ \begin{matrix} \text{Number of sequences} \\ \text{for which Outcome 1} \\ \text{occurs } x \text{ times and} \\ \text{Outcome 2 occurs } y \\ \text{times} \end{matrix} \right\} \cdot \left\{ \begin{matrix} \text{Probability of any} \\ \text{particular sequence} \\ \text{having } x \text{ "1's" and } y \\ \text{"2's" (and } n - x - y \text{ "3's")} \end{matrix} \right\}$$

$$= \frac{n!}{x! y! (n - x - y)!} p_1^x p_2^y (1 - p_1 - p_2)^{n-x-y}$$

where the combinatorial term is an application of Theorem 2.9.2.

Suppose a marksmanship competition requires that four shots be fired at a target divided into three regions (see Table 3.5.1). To advance to the next level, a contestant must score at least 16 points. How likely is that to happen if the probabilities of the shooter hitting the three regions are the numbers listed in the third column?

TABLE 3.5.1

Region	Points	Probability
A	5	1/10
B	3	3/10
C	1	6/10

Notice that four different groupings of shots will yield totals greater than or equal to 16: $(5, 5, 5, 5)$, $(5, 5, 5, 3)$, $(5, 5, 5, 1)$, and $(5, 5, 3, 3)$. The probability of each grouping is calculated by substituting into the trinomial pdf. Here, X = number of 5's and Y = number of 3's. Table 3.5.2 summarizes the results. Adding the entries in the last column shows that the chances of the shooter advancing are a little less than 1 in 100:

$$P(\text{shooter advances}) = 0.0001 + 0.0012 + 0.0024 + 0.0054$$

$$= 0.0091$$

TABLE 3.5.2

Grouping	Sum	(x, y)	$f_{X,Y}(x, y)$	
$(5, 5, 5, 5)$	20	$(4, 0)$	$\dfrac{4!}{4!0!0!} \left(\dfrac{1}{10}\right)^4 \left(\dfrac{3}{10}\right)^0 \left(\dfrac{6}{10}\right)^0$	$= 0.0001$
$(5, 5, 5, 3)$	18	$(3, 1)$	$\dfrac{4!}{3!1!0!} \left(\dfrac{1}{10}\right)^3 \left(\dfrac{3}{10}\right)^1 \left(\dfrac{6}{10}\right)^0$	$= 0.0012$
$(5, 5, 5, 1)$	16	$(3, 0)$	$\dfrac{4!}{3!0!1!} \left(\dfrac{1}{10}\right)^3 \left(\dfrac{3}{10}\right)^0 \left(\dfrac{6}{10}\right)^1$	$= 0.0024$
$(5, 5, 3, 3)$	16	$(2, 2)$	$\dfrac{4!}{2!2!0!} \left(\dfrac{1}{10}\right)^2 \left(\dfrac{3}{10}\right)^2 \left(\dfrac{6}{10}\right)^0$	$= 0.0054$

Geometric Probability

One particularly important special case of Definition 3.5.1 is the *joint uniform pdf*, which is represented by a surface having a constant height everywhere above a specified rectangle in the xy-plane. That is,

$$f_{X,Y}(x, y) = \frac{1}{(b - a)(d - c)}, \quad a \le x \le b, c \le y \le d$$

If R is some region in the rectangle where X and Y are defined, $P((X, Y) \in R)$ reduces to a simple ratio of areas:

$$P((X, Y) \in R) = \frac{\text{area of } R}{(b - a)(d - c)} \tag{3.5.1}$$

Calculations based on Equation 3.5.1 are referred to as *geometric probabilities*.

EXAMPLE 3.5.6

Two friends agree to meet on the University Commons "sometime around 12:30." But neither of them is particularly punctual—or patient. What will actually happen is that each will arrive at random sometime in the interval from 12:00 to 1:00. If one arrives and the other is not there, the first person will wait 15 min or until 1:00, whichever comes first, and then leave. What is the probability the two will get together?

To simplify notation, we can represent the time period from 12:00 to 1:00 as the interval from 0 to 60 min. Then if x and y denote the two arrival times, the sample space is the 60×60 square shown in Figure 3.5.5. Furthermore, the event M, "the two friends meet," will occur if and only if $|x - y| \leq 15$ or, equivalently, if and only if $-15 \leq x - y \leq 15$. These inequalities appear as the shaded region in Figure 3.5.5.

FIGURE 3.5.5

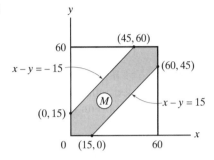

Notice that the areas of the two triangles above and below M are each equal to $\frac{1}{2}(45)(45)$. It follows that the two friends have a 44% chance of meeting:

$$P(M) = \frac{\text{area of } M}{\text{area of } S}$$

$$= \frac{(60)^2 - 2\left[\frac{1}{2}(45)(45)\right]}{(60)^2}$$

$$= 0.44$$

EXAMPLE 3.5.7

A carnival operator wants to set up a ringtoss game. Players will throw a ring of diameter d onto a grid of squares, the side of each square being of length s (see Figure 3.5.6). If the ring lands entirely inside a square, the player wins a prize. To ensure a profit, the operator must keep the player's chances of winning down to something less than one in five. How small can the operator make the ratio d/s?

First, it will be assumed that the player is required to stand far enough away so that no skill is involved and the ring is falling at random on the grid. From Figure 3.5.7, we see that in order for the ring not to touch any side of the square, the ring's center must be somewhere in the interior of a smaller square, each side of which is a distance $d/2$ from one of the grid lines. Since the area of a grid square is s^2 and the area of an interior square is $(s - d)^2$, the probability of a winning toss can be written as the ratio:

$$P(\text{ring touches no lines}) = \frac{(s - d)^2}{s^2}$$

But the operator requires that

$$\frac{(s - d)^2}{s^2} \leq 0.20$$

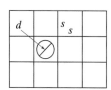

FIGURE 3.5.6

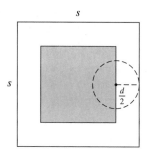

FIGURE 3.5.7

Solving for d/s gives

$$\frac{d}{s} \geq 1 - \sqrt{0.20} = 0.55$$

That is, if the diameter of the ring is at least 55% as long as the side of one of the squares, the player will have no more than a 20% chance of winning.

QUESTIONS

3.5.1 If $p_{X,Y}(x, y) = cxy$ at the points $(1, 1), (2, 1), (2, 2)$, and $(3, 1)$, and equals 0 elsewhere, find c.

3.5.2 Let X and Y be two continuous random variables defined over the unit square. What does c equal if $f_{X,Y}(x, y) = c(x^2 + y^2)$?

3.5.3 Suppose that random variables X and Y vary in accordance with the joint pdf, $f_{X,Y}(x, y) = c(x + y), 0 < x < y < 1$. Find c.

3.5.4 Find c if $f_{X,Y}(x, y) = cxy$ for X and Y defined over the triangle whose vertices are the points $(0, 0), (0, 1)$, and $(1, 1)$.

3.5.5 An urn contains four red chips, three white chips, and two blue chips. A random sample of size 3 is drawn without replacement. Let X denote the number of white chips in the sample and Y the number of blue. Write a formula for the joint pdf of X and Y.

3.5.6 Four cards are drawn from a standard poker deck. Let X be the number of kings drawn and Y the number of queens. Find $p_{X,Y}(x, y)$.

3.5.7 An advisor looks over the schedules of his 50 students to see how many math and science courses each has registered for in the coming semester. He summarizes his results in a table. What is the probability that a student selected at random will have signed up for more math courses than science courses?

		\multicolumn{3}{c}{Number of math courses, X}		
		0	1	2
Number or science courses, Y	0	11	6	4
	1	9	10	3
	2	5	0	2

3.5.8 Suppose that two fair dice are tossed one time. Let X denote the number of 2's that appear, and Y the number of 3's. Write the matrix giving the joint probability density function for X and Y. Suppose a third random variable, Z, is defined, where $Z = X + Y$. Use $p_{X,Y}(x, y)$ to find $p_Z(z)$.

3.5.9 Suppose that X and Y have a bivariate uniform density over the unit square:

$$f_{X,Y}(x, y) = \begin{cases} c, & 0 < x < 1, 0 < y < 1 \\ 0, & \text{elsewhere} \end{cases}$$

(a) Find c.   **(b)** Find $P\left(0 < X < \frac{1}{2}, 0 < Y < \frac{1}{4}\right)$.

3.5.10 Let X and Y have the joint pdf

$$f_{X,Y}(x, y) = 2e^{-(x+y)}, \quad 0 < x < y, \quad 0 < y$$

Find $P(Y < 3X)$.

3.5.11 A point is chosen at random from the interior of a circle whose equation is $x^2 + y^2 \leq 4$. Let the random variables X and Y denote the x- and y-coordinates of the sampled point. Find $f_{X,Y}(x, y)$.

3.5.12 Find $P(X < 2Y)$ if $f_{X,Y}(x, y) = x + y$ for X and Y each defined over the unit interval.

3.5.13 Suppose that five independent observations are drawn from the continuous pdf, $f_T(t) = 2t$, $0 \leq t \leq 1$. Let X denote the number of t's that fall in the interval $0 \leq t < \frac{1}{3}$ and let Y denote the number of t's that fall in the interval $\frac{1}{3} \leq t < \frac{2}{3}$. Find $p_{X,Y}(1, 2)$.

3.5.14 A point is chosen at random from the interior of a right triangle with base b and height h. What is the probability that the y value is between 0 and $h/2$?

Joint cdf's

Not surprisingly, the applications cited for joint *pdf's* suggest that we might also find a use for joint *cdf's*. The latter are defined in a way that is entirely consistent with their univariate counterparts.

> **DEFINITION 3.5.2.**   Let X and Y be two random variables defined on the same sample space S. The *joint cumulative distribution function* (or *joint cdf*) of X and Y is denoted $F_{X,Y}(x, y)$, where
>
> $$F_{X,Y}(x, y) = P(\{s \in S \mid X(s) \leq x \quad \text{and} \quad Y(s) \leq y\})$$
> $$= P(X \leq x, \ Y \leq y)$$
>
> The domain of $F_{X,Y}(x, y)$ is the set of all pairs of real numbers.

Given the joint pdf of two random variables X and Y, we can easily find the variables' joint cdf. If X and Y are discrete,

$$F_{X,Y}(x, y) = \sum_{u \leq x, \, v \leq y} \sum p_{X,Y}(u, v)$$

If X and Y are continuous,

$$F_{X,Y}(x, y) = \int_{-\infty}^{y} \int_{-\infty}^{x} f_{X,Y}(u, v) \, du \, dv$$

We will also find it useful later to go in the other direction—that is, to find the pdf given the cdf. Recall in the univariate case that when Y is continuous, $f_Y(y)$ is the derivative of $F_Y(y)$. Here we have to differentiate *twice*.

THEOREM 3.5.1.   Let X and Y be continuous random variables defined over the same sample space S and let $F_{X,Y}(x, y)$ be their joint cdf. Then

$$f_{X,Y}(x, y) = \frac{\partial^2}{\partial x\, \partial y} F_{X,Y}(x, y)$$

Proof.   See 93.

QUESTIONS

3.5.15   Consider the experiment of simultaneously tossing a fair coin and rolling a fair die. Let X denote the number of heads showing on the coin and Y the number of spots showing on the die.
   (a) List the outcomes in S.
   (b) Find $F_{X,Y}(1, 2)$.
   (c) What would the graph of $F_{X,Y}(x, y)$ look like?

3.5.16   An urn contains 12 chips—4 red, 3 black, and 5 white. A sample of size 4 is to be drawn without replacement. Let X denote the number of white chips in the sample; Y the number of red. Find $F_{X,Y}(1, 2)$.

3.5.17   Let the random variables X and Y denote the number of letters and the number of vowels, respectively, in each word of the following quotation:

Saepe creat molles aspera spina rosas.

   Tabulate $F_{X,Y}(x, y)$.

3.5.18   Prove that

$$P(a < X \le b, c < Y \le d) = F_{X,Y}(b, d) - F_{X,Y}(a, d) - F_{X,Y}(b, c) + F_{X,Y}(a, c)$$

3.5.19   Find and graph $f_{X,Y}(x, y)$ if the joint cdf for random variables X and Y is

$$F_{X,Y}(x, y) = xy, \qquad 0 < x < 1, \quad 0 < y < 1$$

3.5.20   Find the joint pdf associated with two random variables X and Y whose joint cdf is

$$F_{X,Y}(x, y) = \left(1 - e^{-\lambda y}\right)\left(1 - e^{-\lambda x}\right), \qquad x > 0, \quad y > 0$$

3.5.21   Given that $F_{X,Y}(x, y) = k(4x^2y^2 + 5xy^4), 0 < x < 1, 0 < y < 1$, find the corresponding pdf and use it to calculate $P(0 < X < \frac{1}{2}, \frac{1}{2} < Y < 1)$.

Marginal Densities

Joint pdf's and single-variable pdf's are, themselves, intimately related: Given an $f_{X,Y}(x, y)$, [or $p_{X,Y}(x, y)$] we can "recover" the individual pdf's for X and Y by integrating out (or summing over) the unwanted variable.

THEOREM 3.5.2.   Let X and Y be discrete random variables with joint pdf $p_{X,Y}(x, y)$. The *individual* pdf's for X and Y—$p_X(x)$ and $p_Y(y)$, respectively— can be derived from the joint pdf by an appropriate summation:

(a) $p_X(x) = \sum_{\text{all } y} p_{X,Y}(x, y)$ **(b)** $p_Y(y) = \sum_{\text{all } x} p_{X,Y}(x, y)$

Integrating $f_{X,Y}(x, y)$ gives $f_X(x)$ and $f_Y(y)$ if X and Y are both continuous:

(a) $f_X(x) = \displaystyle\int_{-\infty}^{\infty} f_{X,Y}(x, y)\, dy$ **(b)** $f_Y(y) = \displaystyle\int_{-\infty}^{\infty} f_{X,Y}(x, y)\, dx$

Proof.   The proof will be given for the discrete case only. The continuous case is handled in much the same way.

By definition,

$$p_X(x) = P(X = x) = P\left\{ \bigcup_{\text{all } y}(X = x, Y = y) \right\}$$

But the events $(X = x, Y = y_i)$ and $(X = x, Y = y_j)$ are mutually exclusive for $i \neq j$, implying that

$$P\left\{ \bigcup_{\text{all } y}(X = x, Y = y) \right\} = \sum_{\text{all } y} P(X = x, Y = y)$$

Therefore,

$$p_X(x) = \sum_{\text{all } y} P(X = x, Y = y) = \sum_{\text{all } y} p_{X,Y}(x, y)$$

EXAMPLE 3.5.8

Consider an experiment consisting of three flips of a fair coin. Let X denote the number of heads on the last flip and Y the total number of heads for the three tosses. Table 3.5.3 shows the (x, y) value associated with each of the eight possible outcomes. Find $p_X(x)$ and $p_Y(y)$.

TABLE 3.5.3

Outcome	(x, y)	$P(X = x, Y = y)$
(H, H, H)	(1, 3)	$\frac{1}{8}$
(T, H, H)	(1, 2)	$\frac{1}{8}$
(H, T, H)	(1, 2)	$\frac{1}{8}$
(H, H, T)	(0, 2)	$\frac{1}{8}$
(T, T, H)	(1, 1)	$\frac{1}{8}$
(T, H, T)	(0, 1)	$\frac{1}{8}$
(H, T, T)	(0, 1)	$\frac{1}{8}$
(T, T, T)	(0, 0)	$\frac{1}{8}$

By combining the second and third columns of Table 3.5.3, we can write the joint pdf of X and Y as the 2×4 matrix in Table 3.5.4. Note that summing across the rows gives $p_X(x)$, while summing down the columns yields $p_Y(y)$.

Comment. When $p_{X,Y}(x, y)$ is written as a matrix, the individual densities will appear, as they do in Table 3.5.4, as "margins." For that reason, $p_X(x)$ and $p_Y(y)$, in the context of a joint pdf, are often referred to as *marginal densities*. The word *marginal*, though, is nothing but a reminder that a second variable was originally involved—there is no difference between a pdf and a marginal pdf.

TABLE 3.5.4

		Y				
		0	1	2	3	$p_X(x)$
X	0	$\frac{1}{8}$	$\frac{1}{4}$	$\frac{1}{8}$	0	$\frac{1}{2}$
	1	0	$\frac{1}{8}$	$\frac{1}{4}$	$\frac{1}{8}$	$\frac{1}{2}$
$p_Y(y)$		$\frac{1}{8}$	$\frac{3}{8}$	$\frac{3}{8}$	$\frac{1}{8}$	

EXAMPLE 3.5.9

Suppose that X and Y are two random variables jointly distributed over the first quadrant of the xy-plane according to the pdf,

$$f_{X,Y}(x, y) = \begin{cases} y^2 e^{-y(x+1)}, & x \geq 0, \quad y \geq 0 \\ 0, & \text{elsewhere} \end{cases}$$

Find the two marginal pdf's.

First, consider $f_X(x)$. By Theorem 3.5.2,

$$f_X(x) = \int_{-\infty}^{\infty} f_{X,Y}(x, y)\, dy = \int_0^{\infty} y^2 e^{-y(x+1)}\, dy$$

In the integrand, substitute

$$u = y(x + 1)$$

making $du = (x + 1)\, dy$. This gives

$$f_X(x) = \frac{1}{x + 1} \int_0^{\infty} \frac{u^2}{(x + 1)^2} e^{-u}\, du = \frac{1}{(x + 1)^3} \int_0^{\infty} u^2 e^{-u}\, du$$

After applying integration by parts (twice) to $\int_0^{\infty} u^2 e^{-u}\, du$, we get

$$f_X(x) = \frac{1}{(x + 1)^3} \left[-u^2 e^{-u} - 2u e^{-u} - 2e^{-u} \right]_0^{\infty}$$

$$= \frac{1}{(x + 1)^3} \left[2 - \lim_{u \to \infty} \left(\frac{u^2}{e^u} + \frac{2u}{e^u} + \frac{2}{e^u} \right) \right]$$

$$= \frac{2}{(x + 1)^3}$$

Finding $f_Y(y)$ is a bit easier:

$$f_Y(y) = \int_{-\infty}^{\infty} f_{X,Y}(x, y)\, dx = \int_0^{\infty} y^2 e^{-y(x+1)}\, dx$$

$$= y^2 e^{-y} \int_0^{\infty} e^{-yx}\, dx = y^2 e^{-y} \left(\frac{1}{y}\right)\left(-e^{-yx}\Big|_0^{\infty}\right)$$

$$= ye^{-y}$$

QUESTIONS

3.5.22 Find $f_X(x)$ and $f_Y(y)$ if the joint pdf for X and Y is

$$f_{X,Y}(x, y) = \frac{1}{x}, \quad 0 < y < x, \ 0 < x < 1$$

3.5.23 Suppose X and Y have a joint pdf given by

$$f_{X,Y}(x, y) = 6x, \quad 0 < x < 1, \ 0 < y < 1 - x$$

Find $f_X(x)$ and $f_Y(y)$. Also, sketch the two marginals.

3.5.24 The campus recruiter for an international conglomerate classifies the large number of students she interviews into three categories—the lower quarter, the middle half, and the upper quarter. If she meets six students on a given morning, what is the probability that they will be evenly divided among the three categories? What is the marginal probability that exactly two will belong to the middle half?

3.5.25 Find $f_X(x)$ if $f_{X,Y}(x, y) = \frac{1}{2}$, $0 \le x < y \le 2$.

3.5.26 Suppose that $f_{X,Y}(x, y) = 6(1 - x - y)$ for x and y defined over the unit square, subject to the restriction that $0 \le x + y \le 1$. Find the marginal pdf for X.

3.5.27 Find $f_Y(y)$ if $f_{X,Y}(x, y) = 2e^{-x}e^{-y}$ for X and Y defined over the shaded region pictured.

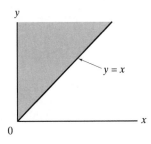

3.5.28 For each of the following joint pdf's, find $f_X(x)$ and $f_Y(y)$.

(a) $f_{X,Y}(x, y) = \frac{1}{2}$, $\quad 0 < x < 2, \ 0 < y < 1$

(b) $f_{X,Y}(x, y) = xye^{-(x+y)}$, $\quad x > 0, \ y > 0$

(c) $f_{X,Y}(x, y) = \frac{3}{2} \cdot y^2$, $\quad 0 \le x \le 2, \ 0 \le y \le 1$

(d) $f_{X,Y}(x, y) = c(x + y)$, $\quad 0 < x < 1, \ 0 < y < 1$

(e) $f_{X,Y}(x, y) = 2$, $\quad 0 < x < y < 1$

(f) $f_{X,Y}(x, y) = ye^{-xy-y}$, $\quad x > 0, \ y > 0$

(g) $f_{X,Y}(x, y) = 4xy$, $\quad 0 < x < 1, \ 0 < y < 1$

(h) $f_{X,Y}(x, y) = \frac{2}{3} \cdot (x + 2y)$, $\quad 0 < x < 1, \ 0 < y < 1$

Multivariate Densities

The definitions and theorems in this section extend in a very straightforward way to situations involving more than two variables. The joint pdf for n discrete random variables, for example, is denoted $p_{X_1,\ldots,X_n}(x_1,\ldots,x_n)$ where

$$p_{X_1,\ldots,X_n}(x_1,\ldots,x_n) = P(X_1 = x_1, \ldots, X_n = x_n)$$

For n continuous random variables, the joint pdf is that function $f_{X_1,\ldots,X_n}(x_1,\ldots,x_n)$ having the property that for any region R in n-space,

$$P((X_1,\ldots,X_n) \in R) = \iint_R \cdots \int f_{X_1,\ldots,X_n}(x_1,\ldots,x_n)\,dx_1 \cdots dx_n$$

And if $F_{X_1,\ldots,X_n}(x_1,\ldots,x_n)$ is the joint *cdf* of continuous random variables $X_1,\ldots,X_n$—that is, $F_{X_1,\ldots,X_n}(x_1,\ldots,x_n) = P(X_1 \le x_1, \ldots, X_n \le x_n)$—then

$$f_{X_1,\ldots,X_n}(x_1,\ldots,x_n) = \frac{\partial^n}{\partial X_1 \cdots \partial X_n} F_{X_1,\ldots,X_n}(x_1,\ldots,x_n)$$

The notion of a marginal pdf also extends readily, although in the n-variate case, a marginal pdf can, itself, be a joint pdf. Given $X_1,\ldots,X_n$, the marginal pdf of any subset of r of those variables $(X_{i_1}, X_{i_2}, \ldots, X_{i_r})$ is derived by integrating (or summing) the joint pdf with respect to the remaining $n - r$ variables $(X_{j_1}, X_{j_2}, \ldots, X_{j_{n-r}})$. If the X_i's are all continuous, for example,

$$f_{X_{i_1},\ldots,X_{i_r}}(x_{i_1},\ldots,x_{i_r}) = \int_{-\infty}^{\infty} \int_{-\infty}^{\infty} \cdots \int_{-\infty}^{\infty} f_{X_1,\ldots,X_n}(x_1,\ldots,x_n)\,dX_{j_1} \cdots dX_{j_{n-r}}$$

QUESTIONS

3.5.29 A certain brand of fluorescent bulbs will last, on the average, 1000 hours. Suppose that four of these bulbs are installed in an office. What is the probability that all four are still functioning after 1050 hours? If X_i denotes the ith bulb's life, assume that

$$f_{X_1, X_2, X_3, X_4}(x_1, x_2, x_3, x_4) = \prod_{i=1}^{4}\left(\frac{1}{1000}\right)e^{-x_i/1000}$$

for $x_i > 0, i = 1, 2, 3, 4$.

3.5.30 A hand of six cards is dealt from a standard poker deck. Let X denote the number of aces, Y the number of kings, and Z the number of queens.
(a) Write a formula for $p_{X,Y,Z}(x, y, z)$.
(b) Find $p_{X,Y}(x, y)$ and $p_{X,Z}(x, z)$.

3.5.31 Calculate $p_{X,Y}(0, 1)$ if $p_{X,Y,Z}(x, y, z) = \dfrac{3!}{x!\,y!\,z!\,(3 - x - y - z)!}\left(\frac{1}{2}\right)^x\left(\frac{1}{12}\right)^y\left(\frac{1}{6}\right)^z\left(\frac{1}{4}\right)^{3-x-y-z}$
for $x, y, z = 0, 1, 2, 3$ and $0 \le x + y + z \le 3$.

3.5.32 Suppose that the random variables X, Y, and Z have the multivariate pdf

$$f_{X,Y,Z}(x, y, z) = (x + y)e^{-z}$$

for $0 < x < 1, 0 < y < 1$, and $z > 0$. Find (a) $f_{X,Y}(x, y)$, (b) $f_{Y,Z}(y, z)$, and (c) $f_Z(z)$.

3.5.33 The four random variables W, X, Y, and Z have the multivariate pdf

$$f_{W,X,Y,Z}(w, x, y, z) = 16wxyz$$

for $0 < w < 1, 0 < x < 1, 0 < y < 1$, and $0 < z < 1$. Find the marginal pdf, $f_{W,X}(w, x)$, and use it to compute $P(0 < W < \frac{1}{2}, \frac{1}{2} < X < 1)$.

3.6   INDEPENDENT RANDOM VARIABLES

The concept of independent events that was introduced in Section 2.7 leads quite naturally to a similar definition for independent random variables.

DEFINITION 3.6.1. Random variables X and Y are said to be *independent* if for any intervals A and B,

$$P(X \in A, Y \in B) = P(X \in A) \cdot P(Y \in B)$$

Although it *defines* independence, Definition 3.6.1 is of little value in *establishing* independence. Given a continuous X and a continuous Y, it would be impossible to check all intervals A and B to verify the relationship between $P(X \in A, Y \in B)$ and $P(X \in A) \cdot P(Y \in B)$. A more workable characterization is provided in Theorem 3.6.1.

THEOREM 3.6.1. Two random variables X and Y are independent if and only if

$$f_{X,Y}(x, y) = f_X(x) \cdot f_Y(y) \quad \left[\text{or } p_{X,Y}(x, y) = p_X(x) \cdot p_Y(y) \right]$$

for all x and y.

Proof. We will show that independence implies that the joint pdf factors into a product of the marginals. The converse is left as an exercise.

Suppose that X and Y are discrete and independent; let a and b be any two numbers. Then

$$p_{X,Y}(a, b) = P(X = a, Y = b) = P(X = a) \cdot P(Y = b) = p_X(a) \cdot p_Y(b)$$

Suppose, instead, that X and Y are both continuous (and independent), and take A and B to be two arbitrary intervals. We can write

$$\int_A \left(\int_B f_{X,Y}(x, y)\, dy \right) dx = \int_A \int_B f_{X,Y}(x, y)\, dy\, dx = P(X \in A, Y \in B)$$

$$= P(X \in A) \cdot P(Y \in B)$$

$$= \int_A f_X(x)\, dx \cdot \int_B f_Y(y)\, dy$$

$$= \int_A \left(\int_B f_X(x) \cdot f_Y(y)\, dy \right) dx$$

Note that the functions

$$\int_B f_{X,Y}(x, y)\, dy \quad \text{and} \quad \int_B f_X(x) f_Y(y)\, dy$$

have equal integrals over every interval A; therefore, by a theorem of calculus, the two are equal. But then it follows that $f_{X,Y}(x, y)$ and $f_X(x) \cdot f_Y(y)$ have equal integrals over every interval B, so by the same theorem, *they* are equal.

EXAMPLE 3.6.1

The joint pdf for two random variables X and Y is given by

$$f_{X,Y}(x, y) = 12xy(1 - y)$$

for $0 \le x \le 1$ and $0 \le y \le 1$. Are X and Y independent?

To answer that question using Theorem 3.6.1 requires that we first find the marginal pdfs for X and Y. Here

$$f_X(x) = \int_{y=0}^{1} 12xy(1 - y)\, dy$$

$$= 12x \left[\frac{y^2}{2} - \frac{y^3}{3} \right]\Big|_0^1$$

$$= 2x$$

and

$$f_Y(y) = \int_{x=0}^{1} 12xy(1 - y)\, dx$$

$$= 12y(1 - y) \left[\frac{x^2}{2} \right]\Big|_0^1$$

$$= 6y(1 - y)$$

Since $f_{X,Y}(x, y) = 12xy(1 - y) = 2x \cdot 6y(1 - y) = f_X(x) \cdot f_Y(y)$, it follows from the factorization criterion in Theorem 3.6.1 that X and Y *are* independent.

QUESTIONS

3.6.1 Two fair dice are tossed. Let X denote the number appearing on the first die and Y the number on the second. Show that X and Y are independent.

3.6.2 Recall the joint pdf used in Example 3.5.3—$f_{X,Y}(x, y) = \lambda^2 e^{-\lambda(x+y)}$, $x \ge 0$, $y \ge 0$. Are the random variables X and Y independent? Does your answer agree with the expression we found for $P(\text{refund})$? Explain.

3.6.3 Let X and Y be random variables with joint pdf

$$f_{X,Y}(x, y) = k, \quad 0 \le x \le 1, \quad 0 \le y \le 1, \quad 0 \le x + y \le 1$$

Give a geometric argument to show that X and Y are not independent.

3.6.4 Are the random variables X and Y independent if $f_{X,Y}(x, y) = \frac{2}{3}(x + 2y)$, $0 \le x \le 1$, $0 \le y \le 1$?

3.6.5 Suppose that random variables X and Y are independent with marginal pdfs, $f_X(x) = 2x$, $0 \le x \le 1$ and $f_Y(y) = 3y^2, 0 \le y \le 1$. Find $P(Y < X)$.

3.6.6 Find the joint cdf of the independent random variables X and Y, where $f_X(x) = \dfrac{x}{2}, 0 \le x \le 2$

and $f_Y(y) = 2y, \quad 0 \le y \le 1$.

3.6.7 If two random variables X and Y are independent with marginal pdf's $f_X(x) = 2x, 0 \le x \le 1$

and $f_Y(y) = 1, 0 \le y \le 1$, calculate $P\left(\dfrac{Y}{X} > 2\right)$.

3.6.8 Suppose $f_{X,Y}(x, y) = xye^{-(x+y)}$, $x > 0$, $y > 0$. Prove for any real numbers a, b, c, and d that

$$P(a < X < b, c < Y < d) = P(a < X < b) \cdot P(c < Y < d)$$

thereby establishing the independence of X and Y.

3.6.9 Given the joint pdf $f_{X,Y}(x, y) = 2x + y - 2xy, 0 < x < 1, 0 < y < 1$, find numbers a, b, c, and d such that

$$P(a < X < b, c < Y < d) \ne P(a < X < b) \cdot P(c < Y < d)$$

thus demonstrating that X and Y are not independent.

3.6.10 Prove that if X and Y are two independent random variables, then $U = g(X)$ and $V = h(Y)$ are also independent.

3.6.11 If two random variables X and Y are defined over a region in the XY-plane that is *not* a rectangle (possibly infinite) with sides parallel to the coordinate axes, can X and Y be independent?

Establishing the Independence of n Random Variables

In Chapter 2, extending the notion of independence from *two* events to n events proved to be something of a problem: The independence of each subset of the n events had to be checked separately (recall Definition 2.7.2). This is not necessary in the case of random variables: To generalize Theorem 3.6.1 we need only establish that the joint pdf factors into a product of the n marginals.

> **DEFINITION 3.6.2.**   The n random variables $X_1, X_2, \ldots, X_n$ are said to be *independent* if, for all $x_1, x_2, \ldots, x_n$,
>
> $$f_{X_1, X_2, \ldots, X_n}(x_1, x_2, \ldots, x_n) = f_{X_1}(x_1) \cdot f_{X_2}(x_2) \cdots f_{X_n}(x_n)$$
>
> $$\left[\text{or } p_{X_1, X_2, \ldots, X_n}(x_1, x_2, \ldots, x_n) = p_{X_1}(x_1) \cdot p_{X_2}(x_2) \cdots p_{X_n}(x_n)\right]$$

> **DEFINITION 3.6.3.**   Let $X_1, X_2, \ldots, X_n$ be a set of n independent random variables, all having the same pdf. Then $X_1, X_2, \ldots, X_n$ are said to be a *random sample of size n*.

EXAMPLE 3.6.2

Consider k urns, each holding n chips, numbered 1 through n. A chip is to be drawn at random from each urn. What is the probability that all k chips will bear the same number?

If $X_1, X_2, \ldots, X_k$ denote the numbers on the 1st, 2nd, $\ldots$, and kth chips, respectively, we are looking for the probability that $X_1 = X_2 = \cdots = X_k$. In terms of the joint pdf,

$$P(X_1 = X_2 = \cdots = X_k) = \sum_{x_1 = x_2 = \cdots = x_k} p_{X_1, X_2, \ldots, X_k}(x_1, x_2, \ldots, x_k)$$

Each of the selections here is obviously independent of all the others so the joint pdf factors according to Definition 3.6.2, and we can write

$$P(X_1 = X_2 = \cdots = X_k) = \sum_{i=1}^{n} p_{X_1}(x_i) \cdot p_{X_2}(x_i) \cdots p_{X_k}(x_i)$$

$$= n \cdot \left(\frac{1}{n} \cdot \frac{1}{n} \cdot \ldots \cdot \frac{1}{n} \right)$$

$$= \frac{1}{n^{k-1}}$$

QUESTIONS

3.6.12 Write down the joint probability density function for a random sample of size n drawn from the exponential pdf, $f_X(x) = (1/\lambda)e^{-x/\lambda}$, $x > 0$.

3.6.13 Suppose that X_1, X_2, X_3, and X_4 are independent random variables, each with pdf $f_X(x_i) = 4x_i^3$, $0 \le x_i \le 1$. Find

(a) $P\left(X_1 < \frac{1}{2}\right)$

(b) $P\left(\text{exactly one } X_i < \frac{1}{2}\right)$

(c) $f_{X_1, X_2, X_3, X_4}(x_1, x_2, x_3, x_4)$

(d) $F_{X_2, X_3}(x_2, x_3)$

3.6.14 A random sample of size $n = 2k$ is taken from a uniform pdf defined over the unit interval. Calculate $P\left(X_1 < \frac{1}{2}, X_2 > \frac{1}{2}, X_3 < \frac{1}{2}, X_4 > \frac{1}{2}, \ldots, X_{2k} > \frac{1}{2}\right)$.

3.7 COMBINING AND TRANSFORMING RANDOM VARIABLES

Frequently, the random variables being measured in an experiment are not, themselves, the researcher's ultimate objective. What *is* of primary interest is some function of those variables. Example 3.5.4 is a case in point: There the life, Z, of an electronic system depended on the *sum*, $X + Y$, of two component lives. At issue was $f_Z(z)$. Other situations may require a change in the *scale* of a random variable. For example, suppose that X is originally calibrated in degrees Fahrenheit but the forces of metric conversion demand its reexpression in degrees Celsius. How does the pdf of Y, the Celsius random variable, compare to that of X?

In cases such as these, it is inefficient (and perhaps very difficult) to compute the pdf's of the "new" random variables directly. Easier methods are available. If $Y = u(X)$ and $f_X(x)$ is known, we can find $f_Y(y)$ by writing the cdf for X in terms of y and then differentiating (recall Theorem 3.4.1). A similar technique works well in bivariate problems where $Z = u(X, Y)$ and we seek $f_Z(z)$.

EXAMPLE 3.7.1

Suppose that a random variable X has pdf

$$f_X(x) = \begin{cases} 6x(1 - x), & 0 < x < 1 \\ 0, & \text{elsewhere} \end{cases}$$

Let Y be a second random variable, where

$$Y = 2X + 1 \tag{3.7.1}$$

What is the pdf for Y?

We begin by finding the *cdf* for Y. Note that Y maps the range of X-values—$0 < x < 1$—onto the interval $(1, 3)$ (see Figure 3.7.1). As a result, the functional form for $F_Y(y)$ will be comprised of three cases, two of which are trivial. If $y \le 1$, $F_Y(y) = P(Y \le y) = 0$; likewise, if $y \ge 3$, $F_Y(y) = P(Y \le y) = 1$.

FIGURE 3.7.1

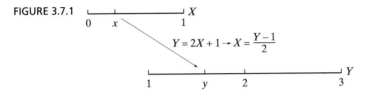

The nontrivial case occurs when $1 < y < 3$. Then

$$F_Y(y) = P(Y \le y) = P(Y \le 1) + P(1 < Y \le y)$$
$$= 0 + P(1 < 2X + 1 \le y)$$
$$= P\left(0 < X \le \frac{y-1}{2}\right) = \int_0^{(y-1)/2} 6x(1-x)\,dx$$
$$= (3x^2 - 2x^3)\Big|_0^{\frac{y-1}{2}}$$
$$= -y^3/4 + 3y^2/2 - 9y/4 + 1$$

Differentiating $F_Y(y)$ gives $f_Y(y)$:

$$f_Y(y) = \begin{cases} 0, & y \le 1 \\ -\dfrac{3y^2}{4} + 3y - \dfrac{9}{4}, & 1 < y < 3 \\ 0, & y \ge 3 \end{cases}$$

EXAMPLE 3.7.2

With the help of appropriately defined transformations, random variables from uniform pdf's can be used to "simulate" random variables from other, more complicated distributions. For instance, suppose X has the particular uniform pdf, $f_X(x) = 1, 0 < x < 1$. Let $Y = -\ln X/\lambda$. Show that Y has an exponential pdf, $f_Y(y) = \lambda e^{-\lambda y}, y > 0$.

By definition,

$$F_Y(y) = P(Y \le y) = P\left(\frac{-\ln X}{\lambda} \le y\right)$$
$$= P(\ln X > -\lambda y) = P(X > e^{-\lambda y})$$
$$= \int_{e^{-\lambda y}}^1 1\,dx = 1 - e^{-\lambda y}$$

Therefore,

$$f_Y(y) = F'_Y(y) = \lambda e^{-\lambda y}, \quad y > 0$$

Figure 3.7.2 illustrates the uniform-to-exponential transformation. Listed at the top is a random sample of 50 x_i's drawn from the uniform pdf, $f_X(x) = 1, 0 < x < 1$. Shown at bottom is the corresponding set of 50 y_i's, where

$$y_i = -\frac{1}{4}\ln x_i$$

x

0.079314	0.547541	0.162005	0.617252	0.067823	0.721707	0.667332
0.126818	0.593661	0.721408	0.957336	0.730714	0.228548	0.726847
0.260272	0.457467	0.251776	0.941628	0.950140	0.443904	0.432315
0.709331	0.277033	0.597627	0.699589	0.370324	0.158024	0.734098
0.921673	0.702557	0.997364	0.782082	0.509667	0.290098	0.004718
0.151204	0.066982	0.663140	0.980192	0.855357	0.802308	0.553256
0.034927	0.485729	0.924998	0.107632	0.215962	0.627184	0.741630
0.406028						

y

0.63358	0.15058	0.45503	0.12062	0.67271	0.08153	0.10112
0.51625	0.13036	0.08164	0.01090	0.07843	0.36900	0.07976
0.33651	0.19551	0.34480	0.01504	0.01279	0.20304	0.20965
0.08586	0.32090	0.12870	0.08932	0.24834	0.46125	0.07728
0.02039	0.08826	0.00066	0.06145	0.16850	0.30938	1.33911
0.47228	0.67583	0.10269	0.00500	0.03906	0.05507	0.14798
0.83862	0.18053	0.01949	0.55726	0.38316	0.11663	0.07473
0.22533						

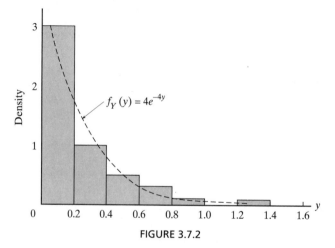

FIGURE 3.7.2

The first x-value that appears, for example, is 0.079314; the first y-value is $-\frac{1}{4}\ln(0.079314)$, or 0.63359. Graphed, the histogram of the y_i's (scaled to make the combined area of its bars equal to 1) has a shape entirely consistent with the predicted exponential pdf, $f_Y(y) = 4e^{-4y}$, $y > 0$.

EXAMPLE 3.7.3

The velocity of a gas molecule of mass m is a random variable X with pdf $f_X(x) = ax^2 e^{-bx^2}$, $x > 0$, where a and b are constants depending on the gas. Find the pdf for the kinetic energy, Y, of such a molecule, where $Y = (m/2)X^2$.

Let $F_Y(y)$ be the cdf for Y. Then

$$F_Y(y) = P(Y \le y) = P\left(\frac{m}{2} \cdot X^2 \le y\right)$$

$$= P\left(X^2 \le \frac{2y}{m}\right)$$

Figure 3.7.3 is a diagram of the transformation. Because of the way $f_X(x)$ is defined, x-values less than 0 (i.e., negative velocities) have zero probability, so the event $X^2 \le 2y/m$ is equivalent to $X \le \sqrt{2y/m}$. That is,

FIGURE 3.7.3

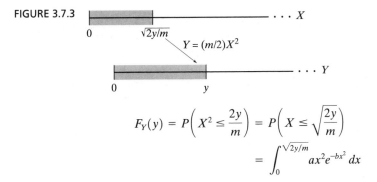

$$F_Y(y) = P\left(X^2 \le \frac{2y}{m}\right) = P\left(X \le \sqrt{\frac{2y}{m}}\right)$$

$$= \int_0^{\sqrt{2y/m}} ax^2 e^{-bx^2}\, dx$$

Finally, from a theorem in calculus,

$$f_Y(y) = F_Y'(y) = a\left(\sqrt{\frac{2y}{m}}\right)^2 e^{-b(\sqrt{2y/m})^2} \cdot \frac{d}{dy}\left(\sqrt{\frac{2y}{m}}\right)$$

$$= a \cdot \frac{2y}{m} \cdot e^{-b(2y/m)} \cdot \sqrt{\frac{2}{m}} \cdot \frac{1}{2} \cdot y^{-1/2}$$

$$= \frac{a\sqrt{2}}{m^{3/2}} \cdot \sqrt{y}\, e^{-2by/m}, \quad y > 0$$

QUESTIONS

3.7.1 An urn contains four red chips and three white chips. Two are drawn out at random without replacement. Let X denote the number of red chips in the sample. Find the pdf for Y, where $Y = 2X - 1$.

3.7.2 Suppose that the random variable X takes on the values -1, 1, and 4, each with probability $\frac{1}{3}$, and is 0 elsewhere. Find the pdf of $Y = 3X + 2$.

3.7.3 Let X have the uniform pdf over the unit interval. Find $f_Y(y)$, where $Y = -3X - 4$.

3.7.4 If X has the exponential pdf,

$$f_X(x) = 2e^{-2x}, \quad x > 0$$

find the *cdf* for $Y = 2X + 4$.

3.7.5 If $f_X(x) = 6x(1 - x)$, $0 < x < 1$, find $f_Y(y)$, where $Y = 2X - 3$.

3.7.6 Suppose that X has the uniform pdf over the interval (a, b). What linear transformation of X represents a random variable having the uniform pdf over $(0, 1)$?

3.7.7 Suppose that X has pdf $f_X(x) = e^{-x}$, $x > 0$.
(a) Find the pdf for $Y = 1/X$.   (b) Find the pdf for $Y = \ln X$.

3.7.8 Find the pdf $f_Y(y)$ of the random variable $Y = \ln X$, where $f_X(x) = xe^{-x^2/2}$, $x \ge 0$.

3.7.9 If the random variable X has pdf $f_X(x) = 3x^2$, $0 < x < 1$, and if $Y = 4X^2$, what is $f_Y(y)$?

3.7.10 A random variable X has density function $f_X(x) = \frac{3}{8}x^2$ over the interval $0 \le x \le 2$ (and 0, elsewhere). Suppose that a circle is generated by a radius whose length is the value of X. Find the density function for Y, the *area* of the circle.

3.7.11 The temperature, X, achieved in a certain chemical reaction varies considerably from experiment to experiment but appears to be described quite well by a pdf of the form

$$f_X(x) = xe^{-x^2/2}, \quad x > 0$$

where x is measured in degrees Fahrenheit. The conversion formula for going from degrees Fahrenheit (X) to degrees Celsius (Y) is

$$Y = \frac{5}{9} \cdot (X - 32)$$

Describe the distribution of temperatures in terms of degrees Celsius. That is, find $f_Y(y)$.

3.7.12 Find the pdf of $R = A \cdot \sin\theta$, where A is a constant and θ is uniformly distributed on $(-\pi/2, \pi/2)$. Variables like R arise quite often in the theory of ballistics. If a projectile is fired at an angle α with a velocity ν, the distance R that it travels can be expressed as $R = (\nu^2/g) \cdot \sin 2\alpha$, where g is the gravitational constant.

Some More Difficult Transformations

In doing transformation problems, caution must be exercised in identifying the set of x's that get mapped into the event $Y \leq y$. The best approach is to sketch diagrams like the ones in Figure 3.7.1 and 3.7.2. The next two examples show some of the complications that can arise.

EXAMPLE 3.7.4

Suppose X has the uniform pdf over the interval $(-1, 2)$:

$$f_X(x) = \begin{cases} \dfrac{1}{3}, & -1 < x < 2 \\ 0, & \text{elsewhere} \end{cases}$$

Find the pdf for Y, where $Y = X^2$.

Here, the set of the x's that get mapped into the interval $Y \leq y$ has a different form depending on whether $0 \leq y < 1$ or $1 \leq y < 4$. To see this, suppose, first of all, that $0 \leq y < 1$. Then the set of x's that get mapped into $0 \leq Y \leq y$ are those from $-\sqrt{y}$ to $+\sqrt{y}$ (see Figure 3.7.4). Therefore,

$$F_Y(y) = P(Y \leq y) = P\left(-\sqrt{y} \leq X \leq +\sqrt{y}\right)$$
$$= \int_{-\sqrt{y}}^{\sqrt{y}} \left(\frac{1}{3}\right) dx = \frac{2\sqrt{y}}{3} \qquad (3.7.2)$$

FIGURE 3.7.4

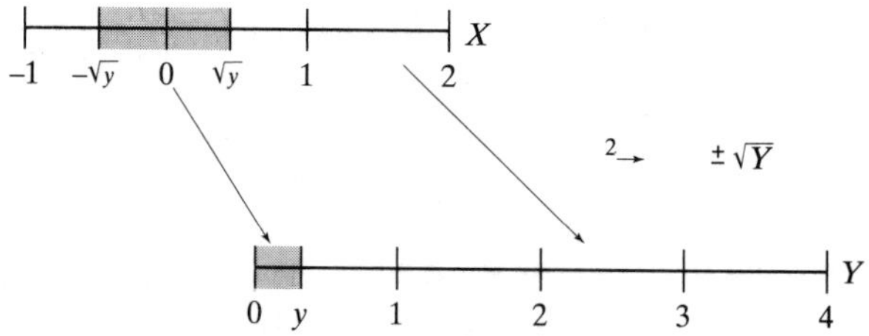

On the other hand, suppose $1 \leq y < 4$. Now, from Figure 3.7.4, the corresponding x's range from -1 to $\sqrt{y}$, and

$$F_Y(y) = P(Y \leq y) = P\left(-1 < X \leq \sqrt{y}\right)$$
$$= \int_{-1}^{\sqrt{y}} \left(\frac{1}{3}\right) dx = \frac{\sqrt{y} + 1}{3} \qquad (3.7.3)$$

Equations 3.7.2 and 3.7.3, together with the obvious "boundary" cases (when $y < 0$ and $y \geq 4$), define $F_Y(y)$:

$$F_Y(y) = \begin{cases} 0, & y < 0 \\ \dfrac{2\sqrt{y}}{3}, & 0 \leq y < 1 \\ \dfrac{\sqrt{y} + 1}{3}, & 1 \leq y < 4 \\ 1, & y \geq 4 \end{cases}$$

Differentiating gives the pdf:

$$f_Y(y) = \begin{cases} \dfrac{1}{3\sqrt{y}}, & 0 \leq y < 1 \\ \dfrac{1}{6\sqrt{y}}, & 1 \leq y < 4 \\ 0, & \text{elsewhere} \end{cases}$$

EXAMPLE 3.7.5

Suppose that X and Y have a joint uniform density over the unit square:

$$f_{X,Y}(x, y) = \begin{cases} 1, & 0 < x < 1, 0 < y < 1 \\ 0, & \text{elsewhere} \end{cases}$$

Find the pdf for their product—that is, find $f_Z(z)$, where $Z = XY$.

For $0 < z < 1$, $F_Z(z)$ is the volume above the shaded region in Figure 3.7.5 Specifically,

$$F_Z(z) = P(Z \leq z) = P(XY \leq z) = \iint_R f_{X,Y}(x, y)\, dy\, dx$$

FIGURE 3.7.5

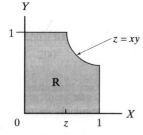

By inspection, we see that the double integral over R can be split up into *two* double integrals—one letting x range from 0 to z, the other having x-values extending from z to 1:

$$F_Z(z) = \int_0^z \left(\int_0^1 1\, dy \right) dx + \int_z^1 \left(\int_0^{z/x} 1\, dy \right) dx$$

But

$$\int_0^z \left(\int_0^1 1\, dy \right) dx = \int_0^z 1\, dx = z$$

and

$$\int_z^1 \left(\int_0^{z/x} 1 \, dy \right) dx = \int_z^1 \left(\frac{z}{x} \right) dx = z \ln x \Big|_z^1 = -z \ln z$$

It follows that

$$F_Z(z) = \begin{cases} 0, & z \le 0 \\ z - z \ln z, & 0 < z < 1 \\ 1, & z \ge 1 \end{cases}$$

in which case

$$f_Z(z) = \begin{cases} -\ln z, & 0 < z < 1 \\ 0, & \text{elsewhere} \end{cases}$$

QUESTIONS

3.7.13 Let X and Y have the bivariate uniform pdf over the unit square. Define $Z = X + Y$. Find $F_Z(z)$. (*Hint:* Consider two cases, $0 < z \le 1$ and $1 < z < 2$. For each case, draw a diagram showing the appropriate region of integration.)

3.7.14 Let X and Y be continuous random variables for which $f_{X,Y}(x, y) = x + y$, $0 < x < 1$, $0 < y < 1$. Find $f_Z(z)$, where $Z = XY$.

3.7.15 Suppose that the random variables X and Y have the joint uniform density over the unit square. Find (a) the cdf and (b) the pdf for $Z = X/Y$.

3.7.16 A number is chosen at random from the interval $(0, 3)$. A second number is chosen independently and at random from the interval $(0, 4)$. What is the eightieth percentile of the sum of the two numbers? [By definition, the 80th percentile, z_{80}, is that number for which $P(X + Y \le z_{80}) = 0.80$.]

Finding the pdf of X + Y

For reasons that will become apparent a little later, we frequently have to deal with the problem of finding the pdf of the *sum* of two or more identically distributed and independent random variables. Examples 3.7.6 and 3.7.7 illustrate the simplest of such problems, situations where only two variables are to be added. Notice that in the discrete case we work directly with the pdf, $P(X + Y = z)$. When X and Y are continuous we first find the *cdf* for the sum—then differentiate.

EXAMPLE 3.7.6

Suppose that X and Y are two independent binomial random variables, each with the same success probability but defined on m and n trials, respectively. Specifically,

$$p_X(k) = \binom{m}{k} p^k q^{m-k}, \quad k = 0, 1, \ldots, m$$

and

$$p_Y(k) = \binom{n}{k}p^k q^{n-k}, \quad k = 0, 1, \ldots, n$$

Let $Z = X + Y$. Find $p_Z(z)$.

Being a sum of x- and y-values, any given z can come about in a number of different ways, all mutually exclusive: $z = 0 + z = 1 + (z - 1)$, and so on. Therefore,

$$P(Z = z) = P\{(X = 0, Y = z) \cup (X = 1, Y = z - 1) \cup \cdots \cup (X = z, Y = 0)\}$$

$$= \sum_{k=0}^{z} P(X = k, Y = z - k)$$

and, since X and Y are independent,

$$P(Z = z) = \sum_{k=0}^{z} P(X = k) \cdot P(Y = z - k)$$

$$= \sum_{k=0}^{z} \binom{m}{k}p^k q^{m-k} \binom{n}{z-k}p^{z-k}q^{n-z+k}$$

$$= \sum_{k=0}^{z} \binom{m}{k}\binom{n}{z-k}p^z q^{m+n-z}$$

Recall the statement of Question 2.9.58:

$$\sum_{k=0}^{z} \binom{m}{k}\binom{n}{z-k} = \binom{m+n}{z}$$

It follows that

$$P(Z = z) = p_Z(z) = \binom{m+n}{z}p^z q^{m+n-z}, \quad z = 0, 1, \ldots, m + n$$

Notice that the binomial distribution "reproduces" itself—that is, X and Y were binomial and their sum, $Z = X + Y$, also proves to be binomial. Not all random variables share this property. The sum of two independent *uniform* random variables, for example, is not itself uniform (recall Question 3.7.13).

EXAMPLE 3.7.7

Let X and Y be two independent random variables with pdf's

$$f_X(x) = e^{-x}, \quad x > 0$$

and

$$f_Y(y) = e^{-y}, \quad y > 0$$

Find the pdf for Z, where $Z = X + Y$. Since

$$F_Z(z) = P(Z \leq z) = P(X + Y \leq z),$$

the cdf for Z is the volume above the shaded region, R, pictured in Figure 3.7.6.

FIGURE 3.7.6

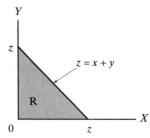

For $z > 0$

$$F_Z(z) = \iint_R f_{X,Y}(x, y)\, dy\, dx = \int_0^z e^{-x} \left(\int_0^{z-x} e^{-y}\, dy \right) dx$$

$$= \int_0^z e^{-x}(1 - e^{x-z})\, dx = \int_0^z (e^{-x} - e^{-z})\, dx$$

$$= -e^{-x} \Big|_0^z - xe^{-z} \Big|_0^z$$

$$= 1 - e^{-z} - ze^{-z}$$

and the pdf for the sum readily follows:

$$f_Z(z) = F_Z'(z) = \begin{cases} ze^{-z}, & z > 0 \\ 0, & \text{elsewhere} \end{cases}$$

QUESTIONS

3.7.17 Let X and Y be two independent random variables with probability density functions

$$p_X(x) = \frac{e^{-r} r^x}{x!}, \quad x = 0, 1, 2, \ldots$$

and

$$p_Y(y) = \frac{e^{-s} s^y}{y!}, \quad y = 0, 1, 2, \ldots$$

Let $Z = X + Y$. Find $f_Z(z)$. Do X and Y reproduce themselves?

3.7.18 If X and Y have the joint pdf

$$f_{X,Y}(x, y) = 2(x + y), \quad 0 \le x \le y \le 1$$

find $f_Z(z)$, where $Z = X + Y$.

3.7.19 Let X and Y have the joint pdf

$$f_{X,Y}(x, y) = xe^{-x} \cdot e^{-y}, \quad x > 0, \quad y > 0$$

Find $f_Z(z)$ for $Z = X + Y$.

3.7.20 If a random variable X is independent of two random variables Y and Z, prove that X is also independent of the *sum* of Y and Z.

Some Frequently Encountered Transformations

The cdf method we have used in this section for finding the pdf's of functions of random variables is extremely powerful and its generality makes it very useful. For certain kinds of problems, though, a more direct application of the technique is available. Theorems 3.7.1 and 3.7.2 give formulas for $f_Y(y)$ if (1) $Y = aX + b$ or (2) $Y = X^2$. Theorem 3.7.3 shows the general formula for $f_Z(z)$ when $Z = X + Y$, and X and Y are independent. Theorem 3.7.4 gives a general expression for $Z = X/Y$ when the random variables X and Y are independent and continuous.

THEOREM 3.7.1. Let X and Y be random variables such that $Y = aX + b$, where $a \neq 0$ and b are constants.

(a) If X is discrete,

$$p_Y(y) = p_X\left(\frac{y - b}{a}\right)$$

(b) If X is continuous,

$$f_Y(y) = \frac{1}{|a|} f_X\left(\frac{y - b}{a}\right)$$

THEOREM 3.7.2. Let X be a continuous random variable with pdf $f_X(x)$. Let $Y = X^2$. For $y > 0$,

$$f_Y(y) = \frac{1}{2\sqrt{y}}\left(f_X(\sqrt{y}) + f_X(-\sqrt{y})\right)$$

THEOREM 3.7.3. Let X and Y be independent random variables and let $Z = X + Y$.

(a) If X and Y are discrete,

$$p_Z(z) = \sum_{\text{all } x} p_X(x)p_Y(z - x)$$

(b) If X and Y are continuous,

$$f_Z(z) = \int_{-\infty}^{\infty} f_X(x)f_Y(z - x)\, dx$$

THEOREM 3.7.4. Let $Z = X/Y$, where the random variables X and Y are continuous and independent. Then

$$f_Z(z) = \int_{-\infty}^{\infty} f_X(yz)f_Y(y)|y|\, dy$$

Comment. An integral of the form

$$\int_{-\infty}^{\infty} f_X(x)f_Y(z - x)\, dx$$

is referred to as the *convolution* of the functions f_X and f_Y. Besides their frequent appearances in random-variable problems, convolutions turn up in many areas of mathematics and engineering.

QUESTIONS

3.7.21 Use Theorem 3.7.3 to rederive the pdf worked out in Example 3.7.7.

3.7.22 Find $f_Y(y)$ if $Y = X^2$ and $f_X(x) = 6x(1 - x), 0 < x < 1$.

3.7.23 Let X be a random variable with pdf

$$f_X(x) = 2x, \qquad 0 < x < 1$$

Let $Y = 3X - 1$. Find $f_Y(y)$.

3.7.24 Let X and Y have the joint pdf

$$f_{X,Y}(x, y) = 4e^{-x-4y}$$

for $x > 0$ and $y > 0$. Define $Z = X + Y$. Find $f_Z(z)$.

3.7.25 Let X_1, X_2, and X_3 be independent random variables with pdf

$$f_{X_i}(x) = e^{-x}, \qquad x > 0, \quad i = 1, 2, 3$$

Let $Z = X_1 + X_2 + X_3$. Find $f_Z(z)$.

3.8   ORDER STATISTICS

The single-variable transformations taken up in Section 3.7 all involved some standard mathematical operation, such as $Y = aX + b$ or $Y = X^2$. The bivariate transformations were similarly arithmetic, typically being concerned with either sums or products. In this section we will consider a different sort of transformation, one involving the *ordering* of an entire *set* of random variables. This particular transformation has wide applicability in many areas of statistics, and we will see some of its consequences in later chapters. Here, though, we will limit our discussion to one basic result: a derivation of the marginal pdf for the ith largest observation, $i = 1, 2, \ldots, n$, in a random sample of size n.

DEFINITION 3.8.1. Let Y be continuous random variable for which $y_1, y_2, \ldots, y_n$ are the values of a random sample of size n. Reorder the y_i's from smallest to largest:

$$y_1' < y_2' < \cdots < y_n'$$

(No two of the y_i's are equal, except with probability zero, since Y is continuous.) Define the random variable Y_i' to have the value $y_i', 1 \le i \le n$. Then Y_i' is called the ith *order statistic*. Sometimes Y_n' and Y_1' are denoted $Y_{\max}$ and $Y_{\min}$, respectively.

EXAMPLE 3.8.1

Suppose that four measurements are made on the random variable Y: $y_1 = 3.4$, $y_2 = 4.6$, $y_3 = 2.6$, and $y_4 = 3.2$. The corresponding ordered sample would be

$$2.6 \leq 3.2 \leq 3.4 \leq 4.6$$

The random variable representing the smallest observation would be denoted Y_1', with its value for this particular sample being 2.6. Similarly, the value for the second-order statistic, Y_2', is 3.2, and so on.

THEOREM 3.8.1.   Let Y be a continuous random variable with probability density function $f_Y(y)$. If a random sample of size n is drawn from $f_Y(y)$, the marginal pdf for the ith order statistic is given by

$$f_{Y_i'}(y) = \frac{n!}{(i-1)!(n-i)!}\left[F_Y(y)\right]^{i-1}\left[1-F_Y(y)\right]^{n-i}f_Y(y)$$

for $1 \leq i \leq n$.

Proof.   A standard way to verify a theorem of this sort is to take advantage of the fact that we already know the correct answer and give an induction argument on i; here, it should be noted, the induction is slightly unusual in that it proceeds from n to 1 rather than from 1 to n.

The first step is to find $f_{Y_n'}(y)$. This can be done by differentiating the corresponding cdf. Note that

$$F_{Y_n'}(y) = P(Y_n' \leq y) = P(Y_1, Y_2, \ldots, Y_n \leq y)$$

$$= P(Y_1 \leq y) \cdot P(Y_2 \leq y) \cdot \cdots \cdot P(Y_n \leq y) \qquad \text{(why?)}$$

$$= \left[F_Y(y)\right]^n$$

Therefore, $f_{Y_n'}(y) = F_{Y_n'}'(y) = n\left[F_Y(y)\right]^{n-1}f_Y(y)$, which, according to Theorem 3.8.1, is the appropriate form for $i = n$.

Next comes the induction step: We assume the theorem to be correct for $f_{Y_{i+1}'}(y)$ and seek an expression for $f_{Y_i'}(y)$. By definition,

$$F_{Y_i'}(y) = P(Y_i' \leq y) = P(Y_i' \leq y, Y_{i+1}' \leq y) + P(Y_i' \leq y, Y_{i+1}' > y)$$

$$= P(Y_{i+1}' \leq y) + P(Y_i' \leq y, Y_{i+1}' > y)$$

The first summand on the right is just $F_{Y_{i+1}'}(y)$; the second is obtained by noticing that exactly i of the Y_i's must be less than or equal to y, and this can occur in $\binom{n}{i}$ ways. Thus, appealing to the binomial distribution,

$$F_{Y_i'}(y) = F_{Y_{i+1}'}(y) + \binom{n}{i}\left[F_Y(y)\right]^i\left[1-F_Y(y)\right]^{n-1} \qquad (3.8.1)$$

We then take the derivative of Equation 3.8.1 to get the pdf for Y_i':

$$f_{Y_i}(y) = \frac{n!}{i!(n-i-1)!} [F_Y(y)]^i [1 - F_Y(y)]^{n-i-1} f_Y(y) + \frac{n!}{i!(n-i)!}$$
$$\cdot \{i[F_Y(y)]^{i-1}[1 - F_Y(y)]^{n-i} - (n-i)[F_Y(y)]^i[1 - F_Y(y)]^{n-i-1}\} f_Y(y)$$

$$= \frac{n!}{i!(n-i)!} [F_Y(y)]^{i-1}[1 - F_Y(y)]^{n-i-1} f_Y(y)$$
$$\cdot \{(n-1)F_Y(y) + i[1 - F_Y(y)] - (n-i)F_Y(y)\}$$

$$= \frac{n!}{i!(n-i)!} [F_Y(y)]^{i-1}[1 - F_Y(y)]^{n-i-1} f_Y(y)[i(1 - F_Y(y))]$$

$$= \frac{n!}{(i-1)!(n-i)!} [F_Y(y)]^{i-1}[1 - F_Y(y)]^{n-i} f_Y(y)$$

Comparing the latter expression with the statement of Theorem 3.8.1 completes the induction.

COROLLARY. Let $Y_1, Y_2, \ldots, Y_n$ be a random sample of size n from the continuous pdf $f_Y(y)$. Let $Y_{\min}$ and $Y_{\max}$ denote the smallest and largest order statistics, respectively. Then

(a) $f_{Y_{\min}}(y) = n \cdot f_Y(y) \cdot [1 - F_Y(y)]^{n-1}$

(b) $f_{Y_{\max}}(y) = n \cdot f_Y(y) \cdot [F_Y(y)]^{n-1}$

EXAMPLE 3.8.2

Suppose that three observations are taken from an exponential pdf, $f_Y(y) = e^{-y}, y > 0$. Intuitively, how does the pdf for Y_1', the first order statistic, compare with the pdf for Y_1, the first recorded observation? Illustrate the difference by calculating $P(Y_1' < 1.0)$ and $P(Y_1 < 1.0)$.

The pdf for any random observation—say, Y_1—is simply the probability model being sampled. In this case, $f_{Y_1}(y) = e^{-y}, y > 0$. On the other hand, Y_1' is the smallest of the three observations in the sample, so we would expect its pdf to have relatively more area associated with small values of y and relatively less area associated with large values of y. Figure 3.8.1 shows that the two pdf's do have precisely that relationship.

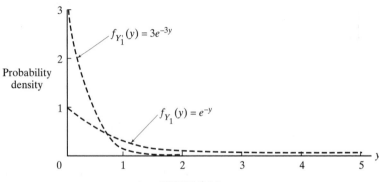

FIGURE 3.8.1

To use Theorem 3.8.1 to find $f_{Y_i'}(y)$, we first note that

$$F_Y(y) = \int_0^y e^{-t}\, dt = -e^{-t}\Big|_0^y = 1 - e^{-y}$$

Given, then, that $n = 3$ and $i = 1$,

$$f_{Y_1'}(y) = \frac{3!}{0!2!}\,(1 - e^{-y})^0(1 - [1 - e^{-y}])^2 e^{-y}$$

$$= 3e^{-3y}$$

As predicted, $P(Y_1' < 1) > P(Y_1 < 1)$:

$$P(Y_1' < 1) = \int_0^1 3e^{-3y}\, dy = \int_0^3 e^{-u}\, du = -e^{-u}\Big|_0^3 = 1 - e^{-3}$$

$$= 0.95$$

$$P(Y_1 < 1) = \int_0^1 e^{-y}\, dy = -e^{-y}\Big|_0^1 = 1 - e^{-1}$$

$$= 0.63$$

EXAMPLE 3.8.3

A random sample of size 10 is drawn from a continuous pdf, $f_Y(y)$. What are the chances that the largest observation, Y_{10}', is less than the pdf's median, m?

According to the Corollary following Theorem 3.8.1,

$$P(Y_{10}' < m) = \int_{-\infty}^m 10 f_Y(y)[F_Y(y)]^9\, dy \tag{3.8.2}$$

Depending on the complexity of $f_Y(y)$ and $F_Y(y)$, the integral in Equation 3.8.2 might be very difficult to evaluate directly. However, because the question is asking for the probability that the *largest* order statistic is *less than* some number, an indirect solution is available that requires no integration whatsoever. Notice that $Y_{10}' < m$ if and only if *all* the observations are less than m. That is,

$$P(Y_{10}' < m) = P(Y_1 < m, Y_2 < m, \dots, Y_{10} < m) \tag{3.8.3}$$

But the 10 observations here are independent, so the intersection probability on the right-hand side of Equation 3.8.3 factors into a product of 10 terms. Moreover, each of those terms equals $\frac{1}{2}$, so

$$P(Y_{10}' < m) = P(Y_1 < m) \cdot P(Y_2 < m) \cdots P(Y_{10} < m)$$

$$= \left(\tfrac{1}{2}\right)^{10}$$

$$= 0.00098$$

EXAMPLE 3.8.4

Suppose that many years of observation have confirmed that the annual maximum flood tide Y (in feet) for a certain river can be modeled by the pdf

$$f_Y(y) = \frac{1}{20}, \quad 20 < y < 40$$

(*Note*: It is unlikely that flood tides would be described by anything as simple as a uniform pdf. We are making that choice here solely to facilitate the mathematics.) The Army Corps of Engineers are planning to build a levee along a certain portion of the river, and they want to make it high enough so that there is only a 30% chance that the second worst flood in the next 33 years will overflow the embankment. How high should the levee be? (We assume that there will be only one potential flood per year.)

Let h be the desired height. If $Y_1, Y_2, \ldots, Y_{33}$ denote the flood tides for the next $n = 33$ years, what we require of h is that

$$P(Y'_{32} > h) = 0.30$$

As a starting point, notice that for $20 < y < 40$,

$$F_Y(y) = \int_{20}^{y} \frac{1}{20} \, dy = \frac{y}{20} - 1$$

Therefore,

$$f_{Y'_{32}}(y) = \frac{33!}{31!1!} \left(\frac{y}{20} - 1 \right)^{31} \left(2 - \frac{y}{20} \right)^{1} \cdot \frac{1}{20}$$

and h is the solution of the integral equation

$$\int_{h}^{40} (33)(32) \left(\frac{y}{20} - 1 \right)^{31} \left(2 - \frac{y}{20} \right)^{1} \cdot \frac{dy}{20} = 0.30 \tag{3.8.4}$$

If we make the substitution

$$u = \frac{y}{20} - 1$$

Equation 3.8.4 simplifies to

$$P(Y'_{32} > h) = 33(32) \int_{(h/20)-1}^{1} u^{31}(1 - u) \, du$$

$$= 1 - 33 \left(\frac{h}{20} - 1 \right)^{32} + 32 \left(\frac{h}{20} - 1 \right)^{33} \tag{3.8.5}$$

Setting the right-hand side of Equation 3.8.5 equal to 0.30 and solving for h by trial and error gives

$$h = 39.3 \text{ feet}$$

QUESTIONS

3.8.1 Suppose the length of time, in minutes, that you have to wait at a bank teller's window is uniformly distributed over the interval $(0, 10)$. If you go to the bank four times during the next month, what is the probability that your second longest wait will be less than 5 minutes?

3.8.2 A random sample of size $n = 6$ is taken from the pdf $f_Y(y) = 3y^2, 0 \le y \le 1$. Find $P(Y'_5 > 0.75)$.

3.8.3 What is the probability that the larger of two random observations drawn from any continuous pdf will exceed the sixtieth percentile?

3.8.4 A random sample of size 5 is drawn from the pdf $f_Y(y) = 2y$, $0 \leq y \leq 1$. Calculate $P(Y'_1 < 0.6 < Y'_5)$. *Hint:* Consider the complement.

3.8.5 Suppose that $Y_1, Y_2, \ldots, Y_n$ is a random sample of size n drawn from a continuous pdf, $f_Y(y)$, whose median is m. Is $P(Y'_1 > m)$ less than, equal to, or greater than $P(Y'_n > m)$?

3.8.6 Let $Y_1, Y_2, \ldots, Y_n$ be a random sample from the exponential pdf $f_y(y) = e^{-y}$, $y > 0$. What is the smallest n for which $P(Y_{\min} < 0.2) > 0.9$?

3.8.7 Calculate $P(0.6 < Y'_4 < 0.7)$ if a random sample of size 6 is drawn from the uniform pdf defined over the interval $(0, 1)$.

3.8.8 A random sample of size $n = 5$ is drawn from the pdf $f_Y(y) = 2y, 0 < y < 1$. On the same set of axes, graph the pdfs for Y_2, Y'_1, and Y'_5.

3.8.9 Suppose that n observations are taken at random from the pdf

$$f_Y(y) = \frac{1}{\sqrt{2\pi}\,(6)} e^{-\frac{1}{2}\left(\frac{y-20}{6}\right)^2}, \quad -\infty < y < \infty$$

What is the probability that the smallest observation is larger than 20?

3.8.10 Suppose that n observations are chosen at random from a continuous pdf $f_Y(y)$. What is the probability that the last observation recorded will be the smallest number in the entire sample?

3.8.11 In a certain large metropolitan area the proportion, Y, of students bused varies widely from school to school. The distribution of proportions is roughly described by the following pdf:

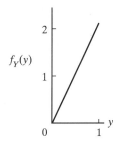

Suppose the enrollment figures for five schools selected at random are examined. What is the probability that the school with the fourth highest proportion of bused children will have a Y-value in excess of 0.75? What is the probability that none of the schools will have fewer than 10% of their students bused?

3.9 CONDITIONAL DENSITIES

We have already seen that many of the concepts defined in Chapter 2 relating to the probabilities of *events*—for example, independence—have their random-variable counterparts. Another of these carryovers is the notion of a conditional probability, or, in what will be our present terminology, a *conditional probability density function*. Applications of conditional pdf's are not uncommon. The height and girth of a tree, for instance, can be considered a pair of random variables. While it is easy to measure girth, it can be difficult to determine height; thus it might be of interest to a lumberman to know the probabilities of a Ponderosa pine's attaining certain heights given

a known value for its girth. Or consider the plight of a school board member ago-
nizing over which way to vote on a proposed budget increase. Her task would be that
much easier if she knew the conditional probability that x additional tax dollars would
stimulate an average increase of y points among twelfth-graders taking a standardized proficiency exam.

Finding Conditional pdfs for Discrete Random Variables

In the case of discrete random variables, a conditional pdf can be treated in the
same way as a conditional probability. Note the similarity between Definitions 3.9.1
and 2.6. 1.

> **DEFINITION 3.9.1.** Let X and Y be discrete random variables. The *condition-
> al probability density function of Y given x*—that is, the probability that Y takes
> on the value y given that X is equal to x—is denoted $p_{Y|x}(y)$ and given by
>
> $$p_{Y|x}(y) = P(Y = y \mid X = x) = \frac{p_{X,Y}(x, y)}{p_X(x)}$$
>
> for $p_X(x) \neq 0$.

EXAMPLE 3.9.1

Recall the coin-tossing experiment in Example 3.5.6; Table 3.9.1 reproduces the joint pdf,
$p_{X,Y}(x, y)$. A simple application of Definition 3.9.1 gives

$$p_{Y|0}(0) = \frac{1/8}{1/2} = \frac{1}{4} \qquad p_{Y|1}(0) = \frac{0}{1/2} = 0$$

$$p_{Y|0}(1) = \frac{1/4}{1/2} = \frac{1}{2} \qquad p_{Y|1}(1) = \frac{1/8}{1/2} = \frac{1}{4}$$

and so on.

TABLE 3.9.1

		\(Y\) 0	1	2	3	$p_X(x)$
X	0	$\frac{1}{8}$	$\frac{1}{4}$	$\frac{1}{8}$	0	$\frac{1}{2}$
	1	0	$\frac{1}{8}$	$\frac{1}{4}$	$\frac{1}{8}$	$\frac{1}{2}$
$p_Y(y)$		$\frac{1}{8}$	$\frac{3}{8}$	$\frac{3}{8}$	$\frac{1}{8}$	

Comment.   The notion of a conditional pdf generalizes easily to situations involving more
than two discrete random variables. For example, if X, Y, and Z have the joint pdf
$p_{X,Y,Z}(x, y, z)$, the *joint conditional pdf* of, say, X and Y given that $Z = z$ is the ratio

$$p_{X,Y|z}(x, y) = \frac{p_{X,Y,Z}(x, y, z)}{p_Z(z)}$$

QUESTIONS

3.9.1 Five cards are dealt from a standard poker deck. Let X be the number of aces received, and Y, the number of kings. Compute $P(X = 2|Y = 2)$.

3.9.2 Suppose that X and Y have the joint pdf

$$p_{X,Y}(x, y) = \frac{xy^2}{39}$$

for the points $(1, 2)$, $(1, 3)$, $(2, 2)$, and $(2, 3)$, and is 0, otherwise. Find the conditional probability that X is 1 given that Y is 2.

3.9.3 An urn contains eight red chips, six white chips, and four blue chips. A sample of size 3 is drawn without replacement. Let X denote the number of red chips in the sample and Y, the number of white chips. Find an expression for $p_{Y|x}(y)$.

3.9.4 A fair coin is tossed five times. Let Y denote the total number of heads occurring in the five tosses and let X denote the number of heads occurring in the last two tosses. Find the conditional pdf $p_{Y|x}(y)$.

3.9.5 Suppose that the random variables X, Y, and Z have a trivariate distribution described by the joint pdf

$$p_{X,Y,Z}(x, y, z) = \frac{xy}{9z}$$

defined for the points $(1, 1, 1)$, $(2, 1, 2)$, $(1, 2, 2)$, $(2, 2, 2)$, and $(2, 2, 1)$. Tabulate the joint conditional pdf of X and Y given each of the possible values for z.

3.9.6 Given that the two discrete random variables X and Y follow the joint pdf $p_{X,Y}(x, y) = k(x + y)$, for $x = 1, 2, 3$ and $y = 1, 2, 3$,
(a) Find k.
(b) Evaluate $p_{Y|x}(1)$ for all values of x for which $p_X(x) > 0$.

3.9.7 Let X have the pdf

$$p_X(x) = \binom{n}{x} p^x (1 - p)^{n-x}, \qquad x = 0, 1, \ldots, n$$

and let Y have the pdf

$$p_Y(y) = \binom{n}{y} p^y (1 - p)^{n-y}, \qquad y = 0, 1, \ldots, n$$

Define $Z = X + Y$. Show that the conditional pdf $p_{X|z}(x)$ is hypergeometric.

Finding Conditional pdfs for Continuous Random Variables

If the variables X and Y are continuous, we can still appeal to the quotient $f_{X,Y}(x, y)/f_X(x)$ as the definition of $f_{Y|x}(y)$ and argue its propriety by analogy. A more satisfying approach, though, is to arrive at the same conclusion by taking the limit of Y's "conditional" *cdf*.

If X is continuous, a direct evaluation of $F_{Y|x}(y) = P(Y \le y|X = x)$, via Definition 2.6.1, is impossible, since the denominator would be 0. Alternatively, we can think of $P(Y \le y|X = x)$ as a limit:

$$P(Y \le y \mid X = x) = \lim_{h \to 0} P(Y \le y \mid x \le X \le x + h)$$

$$= \lim_{h \to 0} \frac{\displaystyle\int_x^{x+h} \int_{-\infty}^y f_{X,Y}(t, u)\, du\, dt}{\displaystyle\int_x^{x+h} f_X(t)\, dt}$$

Evaluating the quotient of the limits gives $0/0$, so l'Hôpital's rule is indicated:

$$P(Y \le y \mid X = x) = \lim_{h \to 0} \frac{\dfrac{d}{dh} \displaystyle\int_x^{x+h} \int_{-\infty}^y f_{X,Y}(t, u)\, du\, dt}{\dfrac{d}{dh} \displaystyle\int_x^{x+h} f_X(t)\, dt} \qquad (3.9.1)$$

By the fundamental theorem of calculus,

$$\frac{d}{dh} \int_x^{x+h} g(t)\, dt = g(x + h)$$

which simplifies Equation 3.9.1 to

$$P(Y \le y \mid X = x) = \lim_{h \to 0} \frac{\displaystyle\int_{-\infty}^y f_{X,Y}\big[(x + h), u\big]\, du}{f_X(x + h)}$$

$$= \frac{\displaystyle\int_{-\infty}^y \lim_{h \to 0} f_{X,Y}(x + h, u)\, du}{\lim_{h \to 0} f_X(x + h)} = \int_{-\infty}^y \frac{f_{X,Y}(x, u)}{f_X(x)}\, du$$

provided that the limit operation and the integration can be interchanged [see (8) for a discussion of when such an interchange is valid]. It follows from this last expression that $f_{X,Y}(x, y)/f_X(x)$ behaves as a conditional probability density function should, and we are justified in extending Definition 3.9.1 to the continuous case.

EXAMPLE 3.9.2

Let X and Y be continuous random variables with joint pdf

$$f_{X,Y}(x, y) = \begin{cases} \left(\dfrac{1}{8}\right)(6 - x - y), & 0 < x < 2, \; 2 < y < 4 \\ 0, & \text{elsewhere} \end{cases}$$

Find (a) $f_X(x)$, (b) $f_{Y\mid x}(y)$, and (c) $P(2 < Y < 3 \mid x = 1)$.

(a) From Theorem 3.5.2,

$$f_X(x) = \int_{-\infty}^\infty f_{X,Y}(x, y)\, dy = \int_2^4 \left(\frac{1}{8}\right)(6 - x - y)\, dy$$

$$= \left(\frac{1}{8}\right)(6 - 2x), \qquad 0 < x < 2$$

(b) Substituting into the "continuous" statement of Definition 3.9.1, we can write

$$f_{Y|x}(y) = \frac{f_{X,Y}(x, y)}{f_X(x)} = \frac{(1/8)(6 - x - y)}{(1/8)(6 - 2x)}$$

$$= \frac{6 - x - y}{6 - 2x}, \qquad 0 < x < 2, \ 2 < y < 4$$

(c) To find $P(2 < Y < 3 | x = 1)$ we simply integrate $f_{Y|1}(y)$ over the interval $2 < Y < 3$:

$$P(2 < Y < 3 | x = 1) = \int_2^3 f_{Y|1}(y)\, dy$$

$$= \int_2^3 \frac{5 - y}{4}\, dy$$

$$= \frac{5}{8}$$

[A partial check that the derivation of a conditional pdf is correct can be gotten by integrating $f_{Y|x}(y)$ over the entire range of Y. That integral should be 1. Here, $\int_{-\infty}^{\infty} f_{Y|x}(y)\, dy = \int_2^4 [(5 - y)/4]\, dy$ *does* equal 1.]

QUESTIONS

3.9.8 Let X be a nonnegative random variable. We say that X *is memoryless* if

$$P(X > s + t | X > t) = P(X > s) \qquad \text{for all } s, t \geq 0$$

Show that a random variable with pdf $f_X(x) = (1/\lambda)e^{-x/\lambda}$, $x > 0$, is memoryless.

3.9.9 Given the joint pdf

$$f_{X,Y}(x, y) = 2e^{-(x+y)}, \qquad 0 < x < y, \ y > 0$$

find

(a) $P(Y < 1 | X < 1)$ **(b)** $P(Y < 1 | X = 1)$ **(c)** $f_{Y|x}(y)$

3.9.10 Find the conditional pdf of Y given x if

$$f_{X,Y}(x, y) = x + y$$

for $0 \leq x \leq 1$ and $0 \leq y \leq 1$.

3.9.11 If

$$f_{X,Y}(x, y) = 2, \qquad x \geq 0, \ y \geq 0, \ x + y \leq 1$$

show that the conditional pdf of Y given x is uniform.

3.9.12 Suppose that

$$f_{Y|x}(y) = \frac{2y + 4x}{1 + 4x} \qquad \text{and} \qquad f_X(x) = \frac{1}{3} \cdot (1 + 4x)$$

for $0 < x < 1$ and $0 < y < 1$. Find the marginal pdf for Y.

3.9.13 Suppose that X and Y are jointly distributed according to the joint pdf

$$f_{X,Y}(x, y) = \frac{2}{5} \cdot (2x + 3y), \qquad 0 \le x \le 1, \quad 0 \le y \le 1$$

Find (a) $f_X(x)$, (b) $f_{Y|x}(y)$, and (c) $P(\frac{1}{4} \le Y \le \frac{3}{4} | X = \frac{1}{2})$.

3.9.14 If X and Y have the joint pdf

$$f_{X,Y}(x, y) = 2, \qquad 0 < x < y < 1$$

find $P(0 < X < \frac{1}{2} | Y = \frac{3}{4})$.

3.9.15 Find $P(X < 1 | Y = 1\frac{1}{2})$ if X and Y have the joint pdf

$$f_{X,Y}(x, y) = xy/2, \qquad 0 < x < y < 2$$

3.9.16 Suppose that X_1, X_2, X_3, X_4, and X_5 have the joint pdf

$$f_{X_1, X_2, X_3, X_4, X_5}(x_1, x_2, x_3, x_4, x_5) = 32x_1 x_2 x_3 x_4 x_5$$

for $0 < x_i < 1$, $i = 1, 2, \ldots, 5$. Find the joint conditional pdf of X_1, X_2, and X_3 given that $X_4 = x_4$ and $X_5 = x_5$.

3.9.17 Suppose the random variables X and Y are jointly distributed according to the pdf

$$f_{X,Y}(x, y) = \frac{6}{7} \left(x^2 + \frac{xy}{2} \right), \qquad 0 < x < 1, \quad 0 < y < 2$$

Find
(a) $f_X(x)$ **(b)** $P(X > 2Y)$ **(c)** $P(Y > 1 | X > \frac{1}{2})$

3.10 EXPECTED VALUES

Probability density functions, as we have already seen, provide a global overview of a random variable's behavior. If X is discrete, $p_X(k)$ gives $P(X = k)$ for all k; if Y is continuous, and A is any interval, or countable union of intervals, $P(Y \in A) = \int_A f_Y(y)\, dy$. Detail that explicit, though, is not always necessary—or even helpful. There are times when a more prudent strategy is to focus the information contained in a pdf by summarizing certain of its features with single numbers.

The first such feature that we will examine is *central tendency*, a term referring to the "average" value of a random variable. Consider the pdf's $p_X(k)$ and $f_Y(y)$ pictured in Figure 3.10.1. Although we obviously cannot predict with certainty what values any future X's and Y's will take on, it seems clear that X values will tend to lie somewhere near, μ_X, and Y values, somewhere near μ_Y. In some sense, then, we can characterize $p_X(k)$ by μ_X, and $f_Y(y)$ by μ_Y.

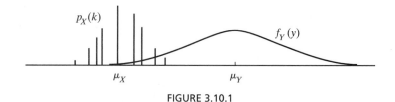

FIGURE 3.10.1

The most frequently used measure for describing central tendency—that is, for quantifying μ_X and μ_Y—is the *expected value*. Discussed at some length in this section and in Section 3.11, the expected value of a random variable is a slightly more abstract formulation of what we are already familiar with in simple discrete settings as the arithmetic average. Here, though, the values included in the average are "weighted" by the pdf.

Gambling affords a familiar illustration of the notion of an expected value. Consider the game of roulette. After bets are placed, the croupier spins the wheel and declares one of 38 numbers, $00, 0, 1, 2, \ldots, 36$, to be the winner. Disregarding what seems to be a perverse tendency of many roulette wheels to land on numbers for which no money has been wagered, we will assume that each of these 38 numbers is equally likely. Suppose that our particular bet is $1 on "odds." If X denotes our winnings, then X takes on the value 1 if an odd number occurs, and -1 otherwise. By the uniformity assumption,

$$p_X(1) = P(X = 1) = \frac{18}{38} = \frac{9}{19}$$

and

$$p_X(-1) = P(X = -1) = \frac{20}{38} = \frac{10}{19}$$

It follows that we will win $\$1\frac{9}{19}$ of the time and lose $\$1\frac{10}{19}$ of the time. Intuitively, then, if we persist in this foolishness, we stand to *lose,* on the average, a little more than 5 cents each time we play the game:

$$\text{"expected" winnings} = \$1 \cdot \frac{9}{19} + (-\$1) \cdot \frac{10}{19}$$

$$= -\$0.053 \doteq -5¢$$

The number -0.053 is called the *expected value of* X.

Physically, an expected value can be thought of as a center of gravity. Here, for example, imagine two bars of height $\frac{10}{19}$ and $\frac{9}{19}$ positioned along a weightless X-axis at the points -1 and $+1$, respectively (see Figure 3.10.2). If a fulcrum were placed at the point -0.053, the system would be in balance, implying that we can think of that point as marking off the "center" of the random variable's distribution.

If X is a discrete random variable taking on each of its values with the same probability, the expected value of X is simply the everyday notion of an arithmetic average or mean:

FIGURE 3.10.2

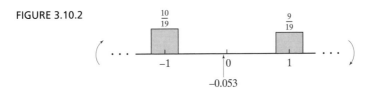

$$\text{expected value of } X = \sum_{\text{all } k} k \cdot \frac{1}{n} = \frac{1}{n} \sum_{\text{all } k} k$$

Extending this idea to a discrete X described by an arbitrary pdf, $p_X(k)$, gives

$$\text{expected value of } X = \sum_{\text{all } k} k \cdot p_X(k) \tag{3.10.1}$$

For a continuous random variable, Y, the summation in Equation 3.10.1 is replaced by an integration and $k \cdot p_X(k)$ becomes $y \cdot f_Y(y)$.

DEFINITION 3.10.1. Let X be a discrete random variable with probability function $p_X(k)$. The *expected value of X* is denoted $E(X)$ (or sometimes μ or μ_X) and is given by

$$E(X) = \mu = \mu_X = \sum_{\text{all } k} k \cdot p_X(k)$$

Similarly, if Y is a continuous random variable with pdf $f_Y(Y)$,

$$E(Y) = \mu = \mu_Y = \int_{-\infty}^{\infty} y \cdot f_Y(y)\, dy$$

Comment. It is assumed that both the sum and the integral in Definition 3.10.1 converge absolutely:

$$\sum_{\text{all } k} |k| p_X(k) < \infty \qquad \int_{-\infty}^{\infty} |y| f_Y(y)\, dy < \infty$$

If not, we say that the random variable has no finite expected value. One immediate reason for requiring *absolute* convergence is that a convergent sum that is not absolutely convergent depends on the order in which the terms are added, and order should not be a consideration when defining a mean.

EXAMPLE 3.10.1

An urn contains nine chips, five red and four white. Three are drawn out at random without replacement. Let X denote the number of red chips in the sample. Find $E(X)$.

From Section 3.3, we recognize X to be a hypergeometric random variable, where

$$P(X = k) = p_X(k) = \frac{\binom{5}{k}\binom{4}{3-k}}{\binom{9}{3}}, \qquad k = 0, 1, 2, 3$$

Therefore,

$$E(X) = \sum_{k=0}^{3} k \cdot \frac{\binom{5}{k}\binom{4}{3-k}}{\binom{9}{3}}$$

$$= (0)\left(\frac{4}{84}\right) + (1)\left(\frac{30}{84}\right) + (2)\left(\frac{40}{84}\right) + (3)\left(\frac{10}{84}\right)$$

$$= \frac{5}{3}$$

Comment.   A general formula for the expected value of a hypergeometric random variable can be derived using the technique illustrated in Example 3.10.5. That is, suppose an urn contains r red chips and w white chips, and let X denote the number of red chips in a sample of size n. It can be shown that $E(X) = \frac{rn}{r + w}$ (see Question 3.10.24). In Example 3.10.1, $r = 5, w = 4$, and $n = 3$. As predicted, the formula gives the same answer as $\sum_{\text{all } k} k \cdot p_X(k)$—namely, $E(X) = \frac{5 \cdot 3}{5 + 4} = \frac{5}{3}$.

EXAMPLE 3.10.2

Records show that 642 students recently entered a Florida public school district that serves migrant workers. Of those 642, a total of 125 have not received their vaccinations. The district's physician is scheduled to go from school to school next Tuesday to give shots to those who need them. If we know that approximately 12% of the district's students are absent on any given day, how many unvaccinated students are likely to miss the doctor's visit?

This is a hypergeometric problem where r = number of students needing vaccinations = 125 and w = number of students already vaccinated = 642 − 125 = 517. An absenteeism rate of 12% corresponds to a sample of $n = (0.12)(642) \doteq 77$ missing students (see Figure 3.10.3). Define the random variable X to be the number of unvaccinated students who are absent when the physician visits. By the general formula, that number will be 15, *on the average*:

$$E(X) = \frac{125 \cdot 77}{125 + 517} \doteq 15$$

FIGURE 3.10.3

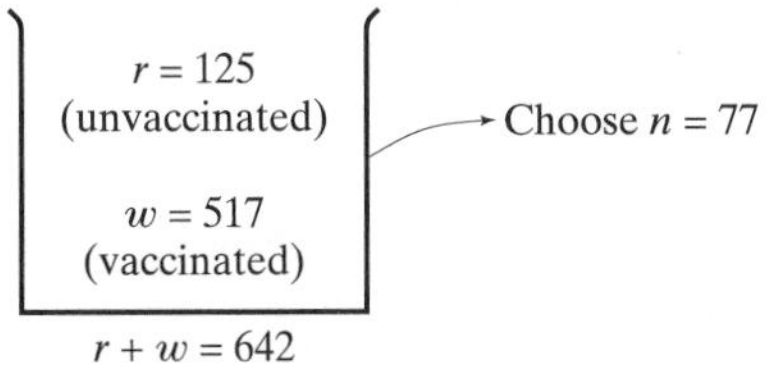

$r = 125$
(unvaccinated)

→ Choose $n = 77$

$w = 517$
(vaccinated)

$r + w = 642$

EXAMPLE 3.10.3

Recall Question 3.2.10, where the length of time Y (in years) that a malaria patient spends in remission is presumed to follow the pdf

$$f_Y(y) = \frac{1}{9} \cdot y^2, \qquad 0 < y < 3 \tag{3.10.2}$$

What is the *average* length of time such a patient spends in remission?

Here Y is continuous, so by part (b) of Definition 3.10.1,

$$E(Y) = \int_{-\infty}^{\infty} y \cdot f_Y(y)\, dy = \int_0^3 y \cdot \left(\frac{1}{9}\right) y^2\, dy$$

$$= \frac{y^4}{36}\Big|_0^3$$

$$= 2.25 \text{ years}$$

Comment. Note that the *median* of a distribution is not necessarily the same as its expected value. Let m denote the median for the pdf of Equation 3.10.2. Then

$$P(Y < m) = \int_0^m \frac{1}{9} \cdot y^2\, dy$$

$$= \frac{m^3}{27}$$

which *must* equal $\frac{1}{2}$, implying that

$$m = \sqrt[3]{\frac{27}{2}}$$

$$= 2.38 \text{ years}$$

In general, a random variable's expected value and median are equal only if $f_Y(y)$ [or $p_X(k)$] is symmetric. Unless the pdf is markedly skewed, though, μ and m will be quite similar.

EXAMPLE 3.10.4

Among the more common versions of the "numbers" racket is a game called D.J., its name deriving from the fact that the winning ticket is determined from Dow Jones averages. Three sets of stocks are used: Industrials, Transportations, and Utilities. Traditionally, the three are quoted at two different times, 11 A.M. and noon. The last digits of the earlier quotation are arranged to form a three-digit number; the noon quotation generates a second three-digit number, formed the same way. Those two numbers are then added together and the last three digits of that sum become the winning pick. Figure 3.10.4 shows a set of quotations for which *906* would be declared the winner.

The payoff in D.J. is 700 to 1. Suppose that we bet $5. How much do we stand to win, or lose, *on the average*?

Let p denote the probability of our number being the winner and let X denote our earnings. Then

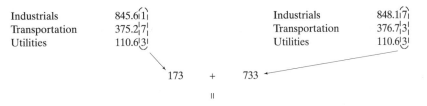

FIGURE 3.10.4

$$X = \begin{cases} \$3500 & \text{with probability } p \\ -\$5 & \text{with probability } 1 - p \end{cases}$$

and

$$E(X) = \$3500 \cdot p - \$5 \cdot (1 - p)$$

Our intuition would suggest (and this time it would be correct!) that each of the possible winning numbers, 000 through 999, is equally likely. That being the case, $p = 1/1000$ and

$$E(X) = \$3500 \cdot \left(\frac{1}{1000}\right) - \$5 \cdot \left(\frac{999}{1000}\right) = -\$1.50$$

On the average, then, we lose $1.50 on a $5 bet.

EXAMPLE 3.10.5

Let X be a binomial random variable defined on n trials, where $p = P(\text{success})$. Find $E(X)$.
    Applying Definition 3.10.1 to the pdf for a binomial, we can write

$$E(X) = \sum_{k=0}^{n} k \cdot p_X(k) = \sum_{k=0}^{n} k \binom{n}{k} p^k (1 - p)^{n-k}$$

$$= \sum_{k=0}^{n} \frac{k \cdot n!}{k!(n - k)!} p^k (1 - p)^{n-k}$$

$$= \sum_{k=1}^{n} \frac{n!}{(k - 1)!(n - k)!} p^k (1 - p)^{n-k} \qquad (3.10.3)$$

At this point, a "trick" is called for. If $E(X) = \sum_{\text{all } k} g(k)$ can be factored in such a way that

$E(X) = h \sum_{\text{all } k} p_{X^*}(k)$, where $p_{X^*}(k)$ is the pdf for some random variable X^*, then $E(X) = h$,

since the sum of a pdf over its entire range is 1. Here, suppose that np is factored out of Equation 3.10.3. Then

$$E(X) = np \sum_{k=1}^{n} \frac{(n - 1)!}{(k - 1)!(n - k)!} p^{k-1} (1 - p)^{n-k}$$

$$= np \sum_{k=1}^{n} \binom{n - 1}{k - 1} p^{k-1} (1 - p)^{n-k}$$

Now, let $j = k - 1$. It follows that

$$E(X) = np \sum_{j=0}^{n-1} \binom{n-1}{j} p^j (1-p)^{n-j-1}$$

Finally, letting $m = n - 1$ gives

$$E(X) = np \sum_{j=0}^{m} \binom{m}{j} p^j (1-p)^{m-j}$$

and, since the value of the sum is 1 (why?),

$$E(X) = np \tag{3.10.4}$$

Equation 3.10.4 should come as no surprise. If a multiple-choice test, for example, has 100 questions, each with five possible answers, we would "expect" to get 20 correct if we were just guessing. But $20 = E(X) = 100(\frac{1}{5}) = np$.

EXAMPLE 3.10.6

Consider the following game. A fair coin is flipped until the first tail appears; we win \$2 if it appears on the first toss, \$4 if it appears on the second toss, and, in general, $\$2^k$ if it first occurs on the kth toss. Let the random variable X denote our winnings. How much should we have to pay in order for this to be a fair game? [*Note*: A fair game is one where the difference between the ante and $E(X)$ is 0.]

Known as the St. Petersburg paradox, this problem has a rather unusual answer. First, note that

$$p_X(2^k) = P(X = 2^k) = \frac{1}{2^k}, \qquad k = 1, 2, \ldots$$

Therefore,

$$E(X) = \sum_{\text{all } k} 2^k p_X(2^k) = \sum_{k=1}^{\infty} 2^k \cdot \frac{1}{2^k} = 1 + 1 + 1 + \cdots$$

which is a divergent sum. That is, X does not have a finite expected value, so in order for this game to be fair, our ante would have to be an infinite amount of money!

Comment. Mathematicians have been trying to "explain" the St. Petersburg paradox for almost 200 years. The answer seems clearly absurd—no gambler would consider paying even \$25 to play such a game, much less an infinite amount—yet the computations involved in showing that X has no finite expected value are unassailably correct. Where the difficulty lies, according to one common theory, is with our inability to put in perspective the very small probabilities of winning very large payoffs. Furthermore, the problem assumes that our opponent has infinite capital, which is an impossible state of affairs. We get a much more reasonable answer for $E(X)$ if the stipulation is added that our winnings can be at most, say, \$1000 (see Question 3.10.18) or if the payoffs are assigned according to some formula other than 2^k (see Question 3.10.19).

Comment. There are two important lessons to be learned from the St. Petersburg paradox. First is the realization that $E(X)$ is not necessarily a meaningful characterization of the "location" of a distribution. Question 3.10.23 shows another situation where the formal computation of $E(X)$ gives a similarly inappropriate answer. Second, we need to be aware that the notion of expected value is not necessarily synonymous with the concept of "worth." Just because a game, for example, has a positive expected value—even a very *large* positive expected value—does not imply that someone would want to play it. Suppose, for example, that you had the opportunity to spend your last $10,000 on a sweepstakes ticket where the prize was a billion dollars but the probability of winning was only 1 in 10,000. The expected value of such a bet would be over $90,000,

$$E(X) = \$1{,}000{,}000{,}000\left(\frac{1}{10{,}000}\right) + (-\$10{,}000)\left(\frac{9{,}999}{10{,}000}\right)$$

$$= \$90{,}001$$

but it is doubtful that many people would rush out to buy a ticket. (Economists have long recognized the distinction between a payoff's numerical value and its perceived desirability. They refer to the latter as *utility*.)

EXAMPLE 3.10.7

Suppose that 50 people are to be given a blood test to see who has a certain disease. The obvious laboratory procedure is to examine each person's blood individually, meaning that 50 tests would eventually be run. An alternative strategy is to divide each person's blood sample into two parts—say, A and B. All of the A's would then be mixed together and treated as one sample. If that "pooled" sample proved to be negative for the disease, all 50 individuals must necessarily be free of the infection, and no further testing would need to be done. If the pooled sample gave a positive reading, of course, all 50 B samples would have to be analyzed separately. Under what conditions would it make sense for a laboratory to consider pooling the 50 samples?

   In principle, the pooling strategy is preferable (i.e., more economical) if it can substantially reduce the number of tests that need to be performed. Whether or not it can depends ultimately on the probability p that a person is infected with the disease.

   Let the random variable X denote the number of tests that will have to be performed if the samples are pooled. Clearly,

$$X = \begin{cases} 1 & \text{if none of the 50 is infected} \\ 51 & \text{if at least one of the 50 is infected} \end{cases}$$

But

$$P(X = 1) = p_X(1) = P(\text{none of the 50 is infected})$$

$$= (1 - p)^{50}$$

(assuming independence), and

$$P(X = 51) = p_X(51) = 1 - P(X = 1) = 1 - (1 - p)^{50}$$

Therefore,

$$E(X) = 1 \cdot (1 - p)^{50} + 51 \cdot \left[1 - (1 - p)^{50}\right]$$

   Table 3.10.1 shows $E(X)$ as a function of p. As our intuition would suggest, the pooling strategy becomes increasingly feasible as the prevalence of the disease diminishes. If the chance of a person being infected is 1 in 1000, for example, the pooling strategy requires an average of only 3.4 tests, a dramatic improvement over the 50 tests that would be needed if the samples were tested one by one. On the other hand, if 1 in 10 individuals is infected, pooling would be clearly inappropriate, requiring *more* than 50 tests $[E(X) = 50.7]$.

TABLE 3.10.1

p	$E(X)$
0.5	51.0
0.1	50.7
0.01	20.8
0.001	3.4
0.0001	1.2

EXAMPLE 3.10.8

Among continuous pdf's, one that finds especially many applications in physics is the Rayleigh distribution,

$$f_Y(y) = \frac{y}{a^2} e^{-y^2/2a^2}, \qquad a > 0; \quad 0 < y < \infty \tag{3.10.5}$$

Find $E(Y)$.

From Definition 3.10.1,

$$E(Y) = \int_0^\infty y \cdot \frac{y}{a^2} e^{-y^2/2a^2} \, dy$$

Let $v = y/(\sqrt{2}\, a)$. Then

$$E(Y) = 2\sqrt{2}a \int_0^\infty v^2 e^{-v^2} \, dv \tag{3.10.6}$$

The integrand in Equation 3.10.6 is a special case of the general form $v^{2k}e^{-v^2}$. For $k = 1$,

$$\int_0^\infty v^{2k} e^{-v^2} \, dv = \int_0^\infty v^2 e^{-v^2} \, dv = \tfrac{1}{4}\sqrt{\pi}$$

Therefore,

$$E(Y) = 2\sqrt{2}\, a \cdot \tfrac{1}{4}\sqrt{\pi}$$
$$= a\sqrt{\pi/2}$$

Comment. The distribution in Example 3.10.8 is named for John William Strutt, Baron Rayleigh, the nineteenth- and twentieth-century British physicist who showed that Equation 3.10.5 is the solution to a problem arising in the study of wave motion. If two waves are superimposed, it is well known that the height of the resultant at any time t is simply the algebraic sum of the corresponding heights of the waves being added (see Figure 3.10.5). Seeking to extend that notion, Rayleigh posed the following question: If n waves, each having the same amplitude h and the same wavelength, are superimposed randomly with respect to phase, what can we say about the amplitude R of the resultant? Clearly, R is a random variable, its value depending on the particular collection of phase angles represented by the sample. What

Rayleigh was able to show in his 1880 paper (156) is that when n is large, the probabilistic behavior of R is described by the pdf

$$f_R(r) = \frac{2r}{nh^2} \cdot e^{-r^2/nh^2}, \qquad r > 0$$

which is just a special case of Equation 3.10.5 with $a = \sqrt{2/nh^2}$.

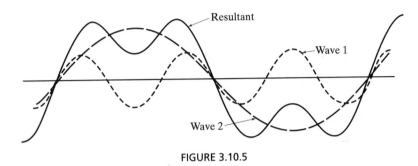

FIGURE 3.10.5

QUESTIONS

3.10.1 Recall the game of Keno described in Example 3.3.1. The following are all the payoffs on a $1 wager where the player has bet on 10 numbers. Calculate $E(X)$, where the random variable X denotes the amount of money won.

Number of correct guesses	Payoff	Probability
< 5	−$1	.935
5	2	.0514
6	18	.0115
7	180	.0016
8	1,300	1.35×10^{-4}
9	2,600	6.12×10^{-6}
10	10,000	1.12×10^{-7}

3.10.2 Cracker Jack first appeared in 1893 at the Chicago World's Fair. Enormously popular ever since (250 million boxes are sold each year), the snack owes more than a little of its success, especially with children, to the toy included in each box. When a new Nutty Deluxe flavor was introduced in the mid–1990s, that familiar marketing gimmick was raised to a new level. Placed in one box was a certificate redeemable for a $10,000 ring; in 50 other boxes were certificates for a *Breakfast at Tiffany's* video (a movie in which the leading character, Holly Golightly, finds her engagement ring in a Cracker Jack box); the usual toys and puzzles were put in all the other boxes. Calculate the expected value of the prize in a box of Nutty Deluxe Cracker Jack. Assume that 5 million boxes were distributed during that first year. Also, assume that each video was worth $30 and each other prize 1.2¢.

3.10.3 In the game of redball, two drawings are made without replacement from a bowl that has four white ping-pong balls and two red ping-pong balls. The amount won is determined by how many of the red balls are selected. For a $5 bet, a player can opt to be paid under either Rule A or Rule B, as shown. If you were playing the game, which would you choose? Why?

A		B	
No. of red balls drawn	Payoff	No. of red balls drawn	Payoff
0	0	0	0
1	$2	1	$1
2	$10	2	$20

3.10.4 A carpet cleaning company is trying to establish its presence in a community consisting of 60,000 households. The company estimates that 5000 of those families would do business with the firm if they were contacted by telephone and made aware of the services that were available. Suppose a staff of telemarketers is hired to place 1000 calls. On the average, how many new customers would such an effort identify?

3.10.5 The working age population of Moore County consists of 3015 whites and 575 minorities. A women's clothing manufacturer is building a plant in the area and intends to employ 250 local residents. If the hiring is done at random, how many minorities are likely to be included among the 250?

3.10.6 Calculate $E(Y)$ for the random variable whose pdf is graphed below.

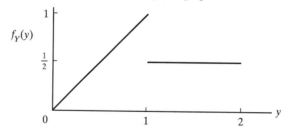

3.10.7 Calculate $E(Y)$ for the following pdf's:

(a) $f_Y(y) = 3(1 - y)^2, \quad 0 \le y \le 1$

(b) $f_Y(y) = 4ye^{-2y}, \quad y > 0$

(c) $f_Y(y) = \begin{cases} 3/4, & 0 \le y \le 1 \\ 1/4, & 2 \le y \le 3 \\ 0, & \text{elsewhere} \end{cases}$

(d) $f_Y(y) = \sin y, \quad 0 \le y \le \pi/2$

3.10.8 Show that

$$f_Y(y) = \frac{1}{y^2}, \quad y \ge 1$$

is a valid pdf but that Y does not have a finite expected value.

3.10.9 Let the random variable Y have the uniform distribution over the interval $[a, b]$ (recall Example 2.5.1). Find $E(Y)$ using Definition 3.10.1. Also, deduce the value of $E(Y)$, knowing that the expected value is the center of gravity of $f_Y(y)$.

3.10.10 Show that the expected value associated with the exponential distribution, $f_Y(y) = \lambda e^{-\lambda y}, y > 0$, is $1/\lambda$, where λ is a positive constant.

3.10.11 Based on recent experience, 10-year-old passenger cars going through a motor vehicle inspection station have an 80% chance of passing the emissions test. Suppose that 200 such cars will be checked out next week. Write two formulas that show the number of cars that are expected to pass.

3.10.12 Suppose that 15 observations are chosen at random from the pdf $f_Y(y) = 3y^2$, $0 \le y \le 1$. Let X denote the number that lie in the interval $\left(\frac{1}{2}, 1\right)$. Find $E(X)$.

3.10.13 A city has 74,806 registered automobiles. Each is required to display a bumper decal showing that the owner paid an annual wheel tax of $50. By law, new decals need to be purchased during the month of the owner's birthday. How much wheel tax revenue can the city expect to receive in November?

3.10.14 Regulators have found that 23 of the 68 investment companies that filed for bankruptcy in the past five years failed because of fraud, not for reasons related to the economy. Suppose that nine additional firms will be added to the bankruptcy rolls during the next quarter. How many of those failures are likely to be attributed to fraud?

3.10.15 Let X denote the number of letters in a word chosen at random from the quotation

The Bird of Time has but a little way
to flutter—and the Bird is on the Wing.

Tabulate $p_X(k)$, and use it to calculate the expected value of X.

3.10.16 An urn contains four chips numbered 1 through 4. Two are drawn without replacement. Let the random variable X denote the larger of the two. Find $E(X)$.

3.10.17 A fair coin is tossed until a head appears. The payoff is $\left(\frac{1}{2}\right)^k$ dollars if the 1st head occurs on the kth toss, $k = 1, 2, 3, \dots$. If the bet is $1, what is $E(X)$, where X denotes the amount won?

3.10.18 How much would you have to ante to make the St. Petersburg game "fair" (recall Example 3.10.6) if the most you could win was $1000? That is, the payoffs are 2^k for $1 \le k \le 9$, and $1000 for $k \ge 10$.

3.10.19 For the St. Petersburg problem (Example 3.10.6) find the expected payoff if
 (a) the amounts won are c^k instead of 2^k, where $0 < c < 2$.
 (b) the amounts won are $\log 2^k$. [This was a modification suggested by D. Bernoulli (a nephew of James Bernoulli) to take into account the decreasing marginal utility of money—the more you have, the less useful a bit more is.]

3.10.20 A fair die is rolled 3 times. Let X denote the number of different faces showing, $X = 1, 2, 3$. Find $E(X)$.

3.10.21 Two distinct integers are chosen at random from the first five positive integers. Compute the expected value of the absolute value of the difference of the two numbers.

3.10.22 Suppose that two evenly matched teams are playing in the World Series. On the average, how many games will be played? (The winner is the first team to get four victories.) Assume that each game is an independent event.

3.10.23 An urn contains one white chip and one black chip. A chip is drawn at random. If it is white, the "game" is over; if it is black, that chip and another black one are put into the urn. Then another chip is drawn at random from the "new" urn and the same rules for ending or continuing the game are followed (if the chip is white, the game is over; if the chip is black, it is replaced in the urn, together with another chip of the same color). The drawings continue until a white chip is selected. Show that the expected number of drawings necessary to get a white chip is not finite.

3.10.24 A random sample of size n is drawn without replacement from an urn containing r red chips and w white chips. Define the random variable X to be the number of red chips in the sample. Use the summation technique described in Example 3.10.5 to prove that $E(X) = rn/(r + w)$.

3.10.25 Given that X is a nonnegative, integer-valued random variable, show that

$$E(X) = \sum_{k=1}^{\infty} P(X \geq k)$$

3.10.26 For two continuous random variables, X and Y, the conditional expectation of Y given $X = x$ is written $E(Y|x)$ and given by the integral over y of the conditional pdf:

$$E(Y|x) = \int_{-\infty}^{\infty} y \cdot f_{Y|x}(y)\, dy$$

The definition for discrete X and Y is analogous. Let

$$f_{X,Y}(x, y) = \frac{6}{7}\left(x^2 + \frac{xy}{2}\right), \qquad 0 < x < 1, \quad 0 < y < 2$$

Find $E(Y|1)$.

3.10.27 Let X and Y have the joint pdf

$$f_{X,Y}(x, y) = \begin{cases} x + y, & 0 \leq x \leq 1, \quad 0 \leq y \leq 1 \\ 0, & \text{elsewhere} \end{cases}$$

Find $E(Y|x)$ and graph it as a function of x (see Question 3.10.26).

3.11 PROPERTIES OF EXPECTED VALUES

We defined the expected value of a random variable in Section 3.10—the obvious next step is to investigate some of its mathematical properties. Three of the most important will be taken up in this section.

Calculating the Expected Value of a Linear Combination

We begin by investigating the expected value of the simplest *function* of a random variable, a linear transformation.

THEOREM 3.11.1. For any random variables X and Y (discrete or continuous) and any constants a and b,

$$E(aX + bY) = aE(X) + bE(Y)$$

provided both $E(X)$ and $E(Y)$ exist.

Proof. We will prove the theorem by establishing that $E(aX) = aE(X)$ and $E(X + Y) = E(X) + E(Y)$. Only the continuous case will be considered.

Let $f_{aX}(t)$ be the probability density function for aX. Then

$$E(aX) = \int_{-\infty}^{\infty} t \cdot f_{aX}(t)\, dt = \int_{-\infty}^{\infty} t \cdot \frac{1}{|a|} \cdot f_X\left(\frac{t}{a}\right) dt$$

the last equality being a consequence of Theorem 3.7.1. Assume that $a > 0$, so $a = |a|$. Making the substitutions $x = t/a$ and $dx = (1/a)\,dt$, we can write

$$E(aX) = \int_{-\infty}^{\infty} ax\left(\frac{1}{a}\right)f_X(x)a\,dx = a\int_{-\infty}^{\infty} x \cdot f_X(x)\,dx = aE(X)$$

The derivation for $a < 0$ follows similarly.

The crux of the second part of the proof is to find an expression for $E(X + Y)$. One approach would be to derive a general formula for $f_{X+Y}(t)$ and then apply Definition 3.10.1. A simpler and more illuminating mode of attack, though, is to return to the basic concept of an expected value. The random variable $X + Y$ takes on values of the form $x + y$, with the "likelihood" of such a value being $f_{X,Y}(x, y)$. It follows that $E(X + Y)$ should equal

$$\int_{-\infty}^{\infty}\int_{-\infty}^{\infty} (x + y)f_{X,Y}(x, y)\,dy\,dx$$

Once we have written $E(X + Y)$ in terms of $f_{X,Y}(x, y)$, verifying that $E(X + Y) = E(X) + E(Y)$ is an exercise in using the definition of marginal distributions. By splitting the integrand into two parts, we find that

$$\begin{aligned} E(X + Y) &= \int_{-\infty}^{\infty}\int_{-\infty}^{\infty} (x + y)f_{X,Y}(x, y)\,dy\,dx \\ &= \int_{-\infty}^{\infty}\int_{-\infty}^{\infty} x \cdot f_{X,Y}(x, y)\,dy\,dx + \int_{-\infty}^{\infty}\int_{-\infty}^{\infty} y \cdot f_{X,Y}(x, y)\,dy\,dx \\ &= \int_{-\infty}^{\infty} x\left(\int_{-\infty}^{\infty} f_{X,Y}(x, y)\,dy\right)dx + \int_{-\infty}^{\infty} y\left(\int_{-\infty}^{\infty} f_{X,Y}(x, y)\,dx\right)dy \\ &= \int_{-\infty}^{\infty} x \cdot f_X(x)\,dx + \int_{-\infty}^{\infty} y \cdot f_Y(y)\,dy \end{aligned}$$

But the latter two integrals are simply $E(X)$ and $E(Y)$, respectively, so the result is proved.

A straightforward induction argument extends Theorem 3.11.1 to the case of n random variables.

COROLLARY. Let $W_1,\ W_2,\ \ldots,\ W_n$ be any random variables for which $E(W_i) < \infty$, $i = 1, 2, \ldots, n$, and let $a_1, a_2, \ldots, a_n$ be any set of constants. Then

$$E(a_1 W_1 + a_2 W_2 + \cdots + a_n W_n) = a_1 E(W_1) + a_2 E(W_2) + \cdots + a_n E(W_n)$$

Comment. The problem-solving implications of Theorem 3.11.1 and its corollary should not be underestimated. There are many real-world events that can be modeled as a linear combination $a_1 W_1 + a_2 W_2 + \cdots + a_n W_n$, where the W_i's are relatively simple random variables. Finding $E(a_1 W_1 + a_2 W_2 + \cdots + a_n W_n)$ *directly* may be prohibitively difficult because of the inherent complexity of the linear combination. It may very well be the case, though, that calculating the individual $E(W_i)$'s is easy. Compare, for instance, Example 3.11.1 with Example 3.10.5. Both derive the formula that $E(X) = np$, when X is a binomial random variable. The approach taken in Example 3.11.1 (i.e., using Theorem 3.11.1) is *much* easier.

EXAMPLE 3.11.1

Let X be a binomial random variable defined on n independent trials, each trial resulting in success with probability p. Find $E(X)$.

Note, first, that X can be thought of as a sum, $X = X_1 + X_2 + \cdots + X_n$, where X_i represents the number of successes occurring at the ith trial:

$$X_i = \begin{cases} 1 & \text{if the } i\text{th trial produces a success} \\ 0 & \text{if the } i\text{th trial produces a failure} \end{cases}$$

(Any X_i defined in this way on an individual trial is called a *Bernoulli* random variable. Every binomial, then, can be thought of as the sum of n independent Bernoullis.) By assumption, $p_{X_i}(1) = p$ and $p_{X_i}(0) = 1 - p, i = 1, 2, \ldots, n$. Using the corollary,

$$E(X) = E(X_1) + E(X_2) + \cdots + E(X_n)$$
$$= n \cdot E(X_1)$$

the last step being a consequence of the X_i's having identical distributions. But

$$E(X_1) = 1 \cdot p + 0 \cdot (1 - p) = p$$

so $E(X) = np$, which is what we found before (recall Equation 3.10.4).

EXAMPLE 3.11.2

A disgruntled secretary is upset about having to stuff envelopes. Handed a box of n letters and n envelopes, she vents her frustration by putting the letters into the envelopes *at random*. How many people, on the average, will receive their correct mail?

If X denotes the number of envelopes properly stuffed, what we want is $E(X)$. However, applying Definition 3.10.1 here would prove formidable because of the difficulty in getting a workable expression for $p_X(k)$ [see (87)]. By using the corollary to Theorem 3.11.1, though, we can solve the problem quite easily.

Let X_i denote a random variable equal to the number of correct letters put into the ith envelope, $i = 1, 2, \ldots, n$. Then X_i equals 0 or 1, and

$$p_{X_i}(k) = P(X_i = k) = \begin{cases} \dfrac{1}{n} & \text{for } k = 1 \\ \dfrac{n-1}{n} & \text{for } k = 0 \end{cases}$$

But $X = X_1 + X_2 + \cdots + X_n$ and $E(X) = E(X_1) + E(X_2) + \cdots + E(X_n)$.) Furthermore, each of the X_i's has the same expected value, $1/n$:

$$E(X_i) = \sum_{k=0}^{1} k \cdot P(X_i = k) = 0 \cdot \frac{n-1}{n} + 1 \cdot \frac{1}{n} = \frac{1}{n}$$

It follows that

$$E(X) = \sum_{i=1}^{n} E(X_i) = n \cdot \left(\frac{1}{n}\right)$$

$$= 1$$

showing that, *regardless of n,* the expected number of properly stuffed envelopes is 1. (Are the X_i's independent? Does it matter?)

EXAMPLE 3.11.3

Ten fair dice are rolled. Calculate the expected value of the sum of the faces showing.
    If the random variable X denotes the sum of the faces showing on the 10 dice, then

$$X = X_1 + X_2 + \cdots + X_{10}$$

where X_i is the number showing on the ith die, $i = 1, 2, \ldots, 10$. By assumption, $p_{X_i}(k) = \dfrac{1}{6}$ for

$k = 1, 2, 3, 4, 5, 6$, so $E(X_i) = \displaystyle\sum_{k=1}^{6} k \cdot \frac{1}{6} = \frac{1}{6} \sum_{k=1}^{6} k = \frac{1}{6} \cdot \frac{6(7)}{2} = 3.5$. By the corollary to

Theorem 3.11.1,

$$E(X) = E(X_1) + E(X_2) + \cdots + E(X_{10})$$

$$= 10(3.5)$$

$$= 35$$

    Notice that $E(X)$ can also be deduced here by appealing to the notion that expected values are centers of gravity. It should be clear from our work with combinatorics that $P(X = 10) = P(X = 60), P(X = 11) = P(X = 59), P(X = 12) = P(X = 58)$, and so on. The probability function $p_X(k)$ is symmetric, in other words, which implies that its center of gravity is the midpoint of the range of its X-values. It must be the case, then, that $E(X)$ equals $\dfrac{10 + 60}{2}$ or 35.

EXAMPLE 3.11.4

The honor count in a (13–card) bridge hand can vary from 0 to 37 according to the formula

honor count $= 4 \cdot$ (number of aces) $+ 3 \cdot$ (number of kings)

$$+ 2 \cdot \text{(number of queens)} + 1 \cdot \text{(number of jacks)}$$

What is the expected honor count of North's hand?
    The solution here is a bit unusual in that we use the corollary *backwards.* If X_i, $i = 1, 2, 3, 4$, denotes the honor count for North, South, East, and West, respectively, and if X denotes the analogous sum for the entire deck, we can write

$$X = X_1 + X_2 + X_3 + X_4$$

But

$$X = E(X) = 4 \cdot 4 + 3 \cdot 4 + 2 \cdot 4 + 1 \cdot 4 = 40$$

By symmetry, $E(X_i) = E(X_j), i \neq j$, so it follows that $40 = 4 \cdot E(X_1)$, which implies that 10 is the expected honor count of North's hand. (Try doing this problem directly, without making use of the fact that the deck's honor count is 40.)

EXAMPLE 3.11.5 (Optional)

A friend proposes the following game. She will select at random some number between 0 and 100 and offer you that amount in cash. You may accept the money or reject it. If you reject it, she will choose another number at random from the same interval (0 to 100) and now offer you *that* amount. As before, you may either accept this second offer or reject it. If you reject it, she will make a third and final offer (again choosing a number at random from 0 to 100); you must accept this one. Should you play the game if your friend insists the ante be \$65, and if you *do* elect to play, what should your strategy be?

Let X denote the amount we ultimately receive playing the game. We need to find $E(X)$ *under the optimal strategy* and compare that figure to \$65. If the former exceeds the latter, it would make sense mathematically to play the game.

Intuitively, the *form* of the optimal strategy seems clear: We should accept any initial offer exceeding some cutoff c_1 and any second offer exceeding a cutoff c_2. (Will c_1 be less than, greater than, or equal to c_2?) Let X_i denote the amount received from the ith offer (after we decide whether or not to accept it) and let X denote the amount we ultimately receive at the game's conclusion. Then $X = X_1 + X_2 + X_3$ and $E(X) = E(X_1) + E(X_2) + E(X_3)$. Let Y_i, $i = 1, 2, 3$, denote the random number chosen on each occasion. Then

$$X_1 = \begin{cases} 0 & \text{if } 0 \le Y_1 < c_1 \\ Y_1 & \text{if } Y_1 \ge c_1 \end{cases}$$

and

$$E(X_1) = \int_0^{c_1} 0 \cdot \frac{1}{100}\, dy_1 + \int_{c_1}^{100} y_1 \cdot \frac{1}{100}\, dy_1$$
$$= \frac{(100 - c_1)(100 + c_1)}{2 \cdot 100}$$

Similarly,

$$X_2 = \begin{cases} 0 & \text{if } 0 \le Y_2 \le c_2 \text{ and } Y_1 < c_1 \text{ or } Y_1 \ge c_1 \\ Y_2 & \text{if } Y_2 \ge c_2 \text{ and } Y_1 < c_1 \end{cases}$$

and

$$E(X_2) = \int_0^{c_2}\int_0^{c_1} 0 \cdot f_{Y_1, Y_2}(y_1, y_2)\, dy_1\, dy_2 + \int_{c_2}^{100}\int_0^{c_1} y_2 \cdot f_{Y_1, Y_2}(y_1, y_2)\, dy_1\, dy_2$$
$$= 0 + \int_{c_2}^{100}\int_0^{c_1} y_2 \cdot \frac{1}{100} \cdot \frac{1}{100}\, dy_1\, dy_2 \qquad \text{(Why?)}$$
$$= \frac{c_1(100 - c_2)(100 + c_2)}{2(100)^2}$$

Finally,

$$X_3 = \begin{cases} 0 & \text{if } Y_1 \ge c_1 \text{ or } Y_1 < c_1 \text{ and } Y_2 \ge c_2 \\ Y_3 & \text{if } Y_1 \le c_1 \text{ and } Y_2 \le c_2 \end{cases}$$

which gives

$$E(X_3) = \int_0^{100} \int_0^{c_2} \int_0^{c_1} y_3 \cdot f_{Y_1, Y_2, Y_3}(y_1, y_2, y_3) \, dy_1 \, dy_2 \, dy_3$$

$$= \frac{1}{(100)^3} c_1 c_2 \cdot \frac{y_3^2}{2}\Big|_0^{100} = \frac{c_1 c_2}{2 \cdot 100}$$

Thus our expression for $E(X)$—in terms of c_1 and c_2—becomes

$$E(X) = \frac{(100 - c_1)(100 + c_1)}{200} + \frac{c_1(100 - c_2)(100 + c_2)}{2(100)^2} + \frac{c_1 c_2}{200}$$

$$= 50 - \frac{c_1^2}{200} + \frac{c_1}{2} - \frac{c_1 c_2^2}{20,000} + \frac{c_1 c_2}{200}$$

To determine the optimal strategy, we need to solve

$$\frac{\partial E(X)}{\partial c_1} = 0$$

and

$$\frac{\partial E(X)}{\partial c_2} = 0$$

simultaneously. But

$$\frac{\partial E(X)}{\partial c_1} = -\frac{c_1}{100} + \frac{1}{2} - \frac{c_2^2}{20,000} + \frac{c_2}{200}$$

and

$$\frac{\partial E(X)}{\partial c_2} = -\frac{c_1 c_2}{10,000} + \frac{c_1}{200}$$

Setting these two equations equal to 0 gives

$$c_1 = \$62.50 \text{ and } c_2 = \$50.00$$

When the c's are put back into the expression for $E(X)$, we find that

$$E(X) = \frac{(100 - 62.50)(100 + 62.50)}{200} + \frac{62.50(100 - 50.00)(100 + 50.00)}{2(100)^2} + \frac{(62.50)(50.00)}{200}$$

$$= \$69.53$$

Our optimal strategy, then, is to take the first offer if it exceeds (or equals) \$62.50; if it happens to be less than that, we decline it and take the second offer if *it* exceeds (or equals) \$50.00. Should we proceed in that fashion, our expected value is \$69.53. Therefore, if our decision to play hinges on the relative sizes of $E(X)$ and the \$65 ante, we should go ahead and put up the money—we stand to make a profit of \$4.53 per game, on the average.

QUESTIONS

3.11.1 Eight cards are drawn from a poker deck. What is the expected number of clubs included among the eight? *Hint*: Let $X_i, i = 1, 2, \ldots, 8$, denote the number of clubs (1 or 0) showing on the ith card.

3.11.2 Suppose that X_i is a random variable for which $E(X_i) = \mu, i = 1, 2, \ldots, n$. Under what conditions will the following be true?

$$E\left(\sum_{i=1}^{n} a_i X_i\right) = \mu$$

3.11.3 Suppose that the daily closing price of a stock goes up an eighth of a point with probability p and down an eighth of a point with probability q, where $p > q$. After n days how much gain can we expect the stock to have achieved? Assume that the daily price fluctuations are independent events.

3.11.4 Let $X_1, X_2, \ldots, X_n$ be a random sample of size n drawn from a population with expected value $E(X)$. The *sample mean*, denoted $\bar{X}$, is the arithmetic average of the X_i's:

$$\bar{X} = \frac{1}{n} \sum_{i=1}^{n} X_i$$

Find $E(\bar{X})$.

3.11.5 Marksmanship competition at a certain level requires each contestant to take 10 shots with each of two different hand guns. Final scores are computed by taking a weighted average of four times the number of bull's-eyes made with the first gun plus six times the number gotten with the second. If Cathie has a 30% chance of hitting the bull's-eye with each shot from the first gun and a 40% chance with each shot from the second gun, what is her expected score?

3.11.6 An urn contains n chips numbered 1 through n. A sample of size r ($< n$) is drawn. What is the expected value of the sum of the chips in the sample? Does it matter if the selections are made with replacement or without replacement?

Calculating the Expected Value of a Nonlinear Function

The utility of linear combinations notwithstanding, there are many situations that call for the expected value of a *nonlinear* function of one or more random variables. Extending what we have already done to cover this more general case is not particularly difficult: The technique introduced in the proof of Theorem 3.11.1 for finding the expected value of $X + Y$ also works for arbitrary functions.

THEOREM 3.11.2. If X is a discrete random variable with pdf $p_X(k)$ and if $g(X)$ is any function of X, then

$$E[g(X)] = \sum_{\text{all } k} g(k) \cdot p_X(k)$$

provided that

$$\sum_{\text{all } k} |g(k)| p_X(k) < \infty$$

If Y is a continuous random variable, with pdf $f_Y(y)$,

$$E[g(Y)] = \int_{-\infty}^{\infty} g(y) \cdot f_Y(y) \, dy$$

provided that

$$\int_{-\infty}^{\infty} |g(y)| f_Y(y) \, dy < \infty$$

Proof.   We will prove the result for the discrete case. See (136) for details showing how the argument is modified when the pdf is continuous.

Let $W = g(X)$. The set of all possible k-values, $k_1, k_2, \ldots$, will give rise to
a set of w-values, $w_1, w_2, \ldots$, where, in general, more than one k may be associated with a given w. Let S_j be the set of k's for which $g(k) = w_j$ [so $\bigcup_j S_j$ is
the entire set of k-values for which $p_X(k)$ is defined]. We obviously have that
$P(W = w_j) = P(X \in S_j)$, and we can write

$$E(W) = \sum_j w_j \cdot P(W = w_j) = \sum_j w_j \cdot P(X \in S_j)$$

$$= \sum_j w_j \sum_{k \in S_j} p_X(k)$$

$$= \sum_j \sum_{k \in S_j} w_j \cdot p_X(k)$$

$$= \sum_j \sum_{k \in S_j} g(k) p_X(k) \qquad \text{(why?)}$$

$$= \sum_{\text{all } k} g(k) p_X(k)$$

Since it is being assumed that $\sum_{\text{all } k} |g(k)| p_X(k) < \infty$, the statement of the the-
orem holds.

EXAMPLE 3.11.6

Suppose that X is a random variable whose pdf is nonzero only for the three values $-2, 1$,
and $+2$:

k	$p_X(k)$
-2	$\frac{5}{8}$
1	$\frac{1}{8}$
2	$\frac{2}{8}$
	1

Let $W = g(X) = X^2$. Verify the statement of Theorem 3.11.2 by computing $E(W)$ two
ways—first, by finding $p_W(w)$ and summing $w \cdot p_W(w)$ over w and, second, by summing
$g(k) \cdot p_X(k)$ over k.

By inspection, the pdf for W is defined for only two values, 1 and 4:

$w(=k^2)$	$p_W(w)$
1	$\frac{1}{8}$
4	$\frac{7}{8}$
	$\overline{1}$

Taking the first approach to find $E(W)$ gives

$$E(W) = \sum_w w \cdot p_W(w) = 1 \cdot \left(\frac{1}{8}\right) + 4 \cdot \left(\frac{7}{8}\right)$$

$$= \frac{29}{8}$$

To find the expected value via Theorem 3.11.2, we take

$$E[g(X)] = \sum_k k^2 \cdot p_X(k) = (-2)^2 \cdot \frac{5}{8} + (1)^2 \cdot \frac{1}{8} + (2)^2 \cdot \frac{2}{8}$$

with the sum here reducing to the answer we already found, $29/8$.

For this particular situation, neither approach was easier than the other. In general, that will not be the case. Finding $p_W(w)$ is often quite difficult, and on those occasions Theorem 3.11.2 can be of great benefit.

EXAMPLE 3.11.7

Suppose the amount of propellant, Y, put into a can of spray paint is a random variable with pdf

$$f_Y(y) = 3y^2, \qquad 0 < y < 1$$

Experience has shown that the largest surface area that can be painted by a can having Y amount of propellant is 20 times the area of a circle generated by a radius of Y ft. If the Purple Dominoes, a newly formed urban gang, have just stolen their first can of spray paint, can they expect to have enough to cover a 5′ × 8′ subway panel with grafitti?

No. By assumption, the maximum area (in ft²) that can be covered by a can of paint is described by the function

$$g(Y) = 20\pi Y^2$$

According to the second statement in Theorem 3.11.2, though, the average value for $g(Y)$ is slightly less than the desired 40 ft²:

$$E[g(Y)] = \int_0^1 20\pi y^2 \cdot 3y^2 \, dy$$

$$= \frac{60\pi y^5}{5} \Big|_0^1$$

$$= 12\pi$$

$$\doteq 37.7 \text{ ft}^2$$

EXAMPLE 3.11.8

A fair coin is tossed until a head appears. You will be given $\left(\frac{1}{2}\right)^k$ dollars if that first head occurs on the kth toss. How much money can you expect to be paid?

Let the random variable X denote the toss at which the first head appears. Then

$$p_X(k) = P(X = k) = P(\text{1st } k - 1 \text{ tosses are tails and } k\text{th toss is a head})$$
$$= \left(\tfrac{1}{2}\right)^{k-1} \cdot \tfrac{1}{2}$$
$$= \left(\tfrac{1}{2}\right)^k, \qquad k = 1, 2, \ldots$$

Moreover,

$$E(\text{amount won}) = E\left[\left(\tfrac{1}{2}\right)^X\right] = E[g(X)] = \sum_{\text{all } k} g(k) \cdot p_X(k)$$

$$= \sum_{k=1}^{\infty} \left(\tfrac{1}{2}\right)^k \cdot \left(\tfrac{1}{2}\right)^k$$

$$= \sum_{k=1}^{\infty} \left(\tfrac{1}{2}\right)^{2k} = \sum_{k=1}^{\infty} \left(\tfrac{1}{4}\right)^k$$

$$= \sum_{k=0}^{\infty} \left(\tfrac{1}{4}\right)^k - \left(\tfrac{1}{4}\right)^0$$

$$= \frac{1}{1 - \frac{1}{4}} - 1$$

$$= \$\frac{1}{3}$$

EXAMPLE 3.11.9

In one of the early applications of probability to physics, James Clerk Maxwell (1831–1879) showed that the speed S of a molecule in a perfect gas has a density function given by

$$f_S(s) = 4\sqrt{\frac{a^3}{\pi}} s^2 e^{-as^2}, \qquad s > 0$$

where a is a constant depending on the temperature of the gas and the mass of the particle. What is the average *energy* of a molecule in a perfect gas?

Let m denote the molecule's mass. Recall from physics that energy (W), mass (m), and speed (S) are related through the equation

$$W = \frac{1}{2} mS^2 = g(S)$$

To find $E(W)$ we appeal to the second part of Theorem 3.11.2:

$$E(W) = \int_0^\infty g(s) f_S(s)\, ds$$

$$= \int_0^\infty \frac{1}{2} ms^2 \cdot 4\sqrt{\frac{a^3}{\pi}} s^2 e^{-as^2}\, ds$$

$$= 2m\sqrt{\frac{a^3}{\pi}} \int_0^\infty s^4 e^{-as^2}\, ds$$

Make the substitution $t = as^2$. Then

$$E(W) = \frac{m}{a\sqrt{\pi}} \int_0^\infty t^{3/2} e^{-t} \, dt$$

But

$$\int_0^\infty t^{3/2} e^{-t} \, dt = \left(\frac{3}{2}\right)\left(\frac{1}{2}\right)\sqrt{\pi} \quad \text{(see Question 4.6.7),}$$

so

$$E(\text{energy}) = E(W) = \frac{m}{a\sqrt{\pi}} \left(\frac{3}{2}\right)\left(\frac{1}{2}\right)\sqrt{\pi}$$

$$= \frac{3m}{4a}$$

EXAMPLE 3.11.10

Consolidated Industries is planning to market a new product and they are trying to decide how many to manufacture. They estimate that each item sold will return a profit of m dollars; each one not sold represents an n dollar loss. Furthermore, they suspect the demand for the product, V, will have an exponential distribution,

$$f_V(v) = \left(\frac{1}{\lambda}\right)e^{-v/\lambda}, \quad v > 0$$

How many items should the company produce if they want to maximize their expected profit? (Assume that n, m, and λ are known.)

If a total of x items are made, the company's profit can be expressed as a function $Q(v)$, where

$$Q(v) = \begin{cases} mv - n(x - v) & \text{if } v < x \\ mx & \text{if } v \geq x \end{cases}$$

and v is the number of items sold. It follows that their *expected* profit is

$$E[Q(V)] = \int_0^\infty Q(v) \cdot f_V(v) \, dv$$

$$= \int_0^x [(m + n)v - nx]\left(\frac{1}{\lambda}\right)e^{-v/\lambda} \, dv + \int_x^\infty mx \cdot \left(\frac{1}{\lambda}\right)e^{-v/\lambda} \, dv \qquad (3.11.1)$$

The integration here is straightforward, though a bit tedious. Equation 3.11.1 eventually simplifies to

$$E[Q(V)] = \lambda \cdot (m + n) - \lambda \cdot (m + n)e^{-x/\lambda} - nx$$

To find the optimal production level, we need to solve $dE[Q(V)]/dx = 0$ for x. But

$$\frac{dE[Q(V)]}{dx} = (m + n)e^{-x/\lambda} - n$$

and the latter equals 0 when

$$x = -\lambda \cdot \ln\left(\frac{n}{m+n}\right)$$

(How many items should the company manufacture if the demand function is

$$f_V(v) = 0.0001e^{-0.0001v}, \qquad v > 0$$

and m and n are fixed at 50 cents and \$2, respectively?)

QUESTIONS

3.11.7 Let X have the probability density function

$$f_X(x) = \begin{cases} 2(1-x), & 0 < x < 1 \\ 0, & \text{elsewhere} \end{cases}$$

Suppose that $Y = g(X) = X^3$. Find $E(Y)$ two different ways.

3.11.8 A tool and die company makes castings for steel stress-monitoring gauges. Their annual profit, Q, in hundreds of thousands of dollars, can be expressed as a function of product demand, y:

$$Q(y) = 2(1 - e^{-2y})$$

Suppose that the demand (in thousands) for their castings follows an exponential pdf, $f_Y(y) = 6e^{-6y}$, $y > 0$. Find the company's expected profit.

3.11.9 A box is to be constructed so that its height is 5 inches and its base is Y inches by Y inches, where Y is a random variable described by the pdf, $f_Y(y) = 6y(1 - y), 0 < y < 1$. Find the expected volume of the box.

3.11.10 Grades on the last Economics 301 exam were not very good. Graphed, their distribution had a shape similar to the pdf

$$f_Y(y) = \frac{1}{5000}(100 - y), \qquad 0 \le y \le 100$$

As a way of "curving" the results, the professor announces that he will replace each person's grade, Y, with a new grade, $g(Y)$, where $g(Y) = 10\sqrt{Y}$. Has the professor's strategy been successful in raising the class average above 60?

3.11.11 Find $E(Y^2)$ if the random variable Y has the pdf pictured below:

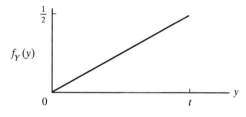

3.11.12 The hypotenuse, Y, of the isosceles right triangle shown is a random variable having a uniform pdf over the interval $[6, 10]$. Calculate the expected value of the triangle's area. Do not leave the answer as a function of a.

3.11.13 An urn contains n chips numbered 1 through n. Assume that the probability of choosing chip i is equal to $ki, i = 1, 2, \ldots, n$. If one chip is drawn, calculate $E\left(\dfrac{1}{X}\right)$, where the random variable X denotes the number showing on the chip selected. *Hint*: Recall that the sum of the first n integers is $n(n+1)/2$.

Calculating Expected Values for Functions of Several Variables

Theorem 3.9.2 can be extended to include functions of any number of random variables. We formally state the generalization only for the bivariate case, but the examples that follow involve functions of two, three, and four random variables. For a proof of Theorem 3.11.3, see (118).

THEOREM 3.11.3. Suppose that X and Y are discrete random variables with joint density function $f_{X,Y}(x, y)$. Let $g(X, Y)$ be any function of X and Y. Then

$$E[g(X, Y)] = \sum_{\text{all } x} \sum_{\text{all } y} g(x, y) \cdot f_{X,Y}(x, y)$$

provided that

$$\sum_{\text{all } x} \sum_{\text{all } y} |g(x, y)| \cdot f_{X,Y}(x, y) < \infty$$

If X and Y are continuous random variables,

$$E[g(X, Y)] = \int_{-\infty}^{\infty} \int_{-\infty}^{\infty} g(x, y) \cdot f_{X,Y}(x, y)\, dx\, dy$$

provided that

$$\int_{-\infty}^{\infty} \int_{-\infty}^{\infty} |g(x, y)| \cdot f_{X,Y}(x, y)\, dx\, dy < \infty$$

EXAMPLE 3.11.11

In Example 3.5.6 we considered two random variables whose joint pdf was given by the 2×4 matrix shown in Table 3.11.1

TABLE 3.11.1

		Y 0	1	2	3
X	0	$\frac{1}{8}$	$\frac{1}{4}$	$\frac{1}{8}$	0
	1	0	$\frac{1}{8}$	$\frac{1}{4}$	$\frac{1}{8}$

Define

$$g(X, Y) = 3X - 2XY + Y$$

Find $E[g(X, Y)]$ directly, and then by using Theorem 3.11.3.

Let $Z = 3X - 2XY + Y$. By inspection, Z can take on the values $0, 1, 2$, and 3 with pdf $f_Z(z)$ as shown in Table 3.11.2.

TABLE 3.11.2

z	0	1	2	3
$f_Z(z)$	$\frac{1}{4}$	$\frac{1}{2}$	$\frac{1}{4}$	0

From Definition 3.10.1, $E[g(X, Y)]$ is equal to 1:

$$E[g(X, Y)] = E(Z) = \sum_{\text{all } z} z \cdot f_Z(z)$$

$$= 0 \cdot \frac{1}{4} + 1 \cdot \frac{1}{2} + 2 \cdot \frac{1}{4} + 3 \cdot 0$$

$$= 1$$

We get the same answer for $E[g(X, Y)]$ by applying Theorem 3.11.3 to the joint pdf given in Table 3.11.1:

$$E[g(X, Y)] = 0 \cdot \frac{1}{8} + 1 \cdot \frac{1}{4} + 2 \cdot \frac{1}{8} + 3 \cdot 0 + 3 \cdot 0 + 2 \cdot \frac{1}{8} + 1 \cdot \frac{1}{4} + 0 \cdot \frac{1}{8}$$

$$= 1$$

The advantage, of course, enjoyed by the latter solution is that we avoid the intermediate step of having to determine $f_Z(z)$.

EXAMPLE 3.11.12

An electrical circuit has three resistors, R_X, R_Y, and R_Z, wired in parallel (see Figure 3.11.1). The nominal resistance of each is 15 ohms, but their *actual* resistances, X, Y, and Z, vary between 10 and 20 according to the joint pdf,

$$f_{X, Y, X}(x, y, z) = \frac{1}{675,000}(xy + xz + yz), \qquad \begin{matrix} 10 \le x \le 20 \\ 10 \le y \le 20 \\ 10 \le z \le 20 \end{matrix}$$

FIGURE 3.11.1

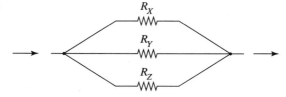

What is the expected resistance for the circuit?

Let R denote the circuit's resistance. A well-known result in physics holds that

$$\frac{1}{R} = \frac{1}{X} + \frac{1}{Y} + \frac{1}{Z}$$

or, equivalently,

$$R = \frac{XYZ}{XY + XZ + YZ} = R(X, Y, Z)$$

Integrating $R(x, y, z) \cdot f_{X,Y,Z}(x, y, z)$ shows that the expected resistance is 5.0:

$$E(R) = \int_{10}^{20} \int_{10}^{20} \int_{10}^{20} \frac{xyz}{xy + xz + yz} \cdot \frac{1}{675{,}000} (xy + xz + yz) \, dx \, dy \, dz$$

$$= \frac{1}{675{,}000} \int_{10}^{20} \int_{10}^{20} \int_{10}^{20} xyz \, dx \, dy \, dz$$

$$= 5.0$$

EXAMPLE 3.11.13

Two points, $Q = (x, y)$ and $Q' = (x', y')$, are chosen at random inside a square having sides of length s. What is the expected value of D^2, the square of the distance between Q and Q'? (See Figure 3.11.2.)

FIGURE 3.11.2

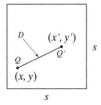

Written in terms of the coordinates of Q and Q', D^2 is a function of *four* random variables,

$$D^2 = g(X, X', Y, Y') = (X' - X)^2 + (Y' - Y)^2$$

Therefore,

$$E(D^2) = \int_0^s \int_0^s \int_0^s \int_0^s [(x' - x)^2 + (y' - y)^2] \cdot f_{X, X', Y, Y'}(x, x', y, y') \, dx \, dx' \, dy \, dy'$$

Since X, X', Y, and Y' are all to be chosen at random over the interval $(0, s)$,

$$f_{X, X', Y, Y'}(x, x', y, y') = f_X(x) \cdot f_{X'}(x') \cdot f_Y(y) \cdot f_{Y'}(y')$$

$$= \frac{1}{s^4}$$

so the expression for $E(D^2)$ simplifies to

$$E(D^2) = \frac{1}{s^4} \int_0^s \int_0^s \int_0^s \int_0^s \left[(x' - x)^2 + (y' - y)^2 \right] dx\, dx'\, dy\, dy'$$

The integrations here are lengthy, but straightforward; they simplify to

$$E(D^2) = \frac{s^2}{3}$$

QUESTIONS

3.11.14 Two fair dice are tossed one time. Let X denote the number of 2's that appear and Y the number of 3's. Let $Z = X\, Y^2$. Find $E\left[g(X, Y) \right]$ two ways.

3.11.15 Suppose that $f_{X,Y}(x, y) = e^{-x-y}$, $x > 0, y > 0$. Find $E(X + Y)$.

3.11.16 Find $E(R)$ for a two-resistor circuit similar to the one described in Example 3.11.12 where $f_{X,Y}(x, y) = k(x + y)$, $10 \leq x \leq 20$, $10 \leq y \leq 20$.

3.11.17 Two points, X and Y, are chosen at random along perpendicular sides of the unit square. What is the expected value of the area of the rectangle whose sides are of length X and Y?

3.11.18 An urn contains n chips numbered 1 through n. A sample of size 2 is drawn without replacement. Show that the expected value of the product of the two drawn is

$$\frac{1}{12}(n + 1)(3n + 2)$$

Hint: Recall that $\displaystyle\sum_{k=1}^n k^2 = \frac{n(n + 1)(2n + 1)}{6}$.

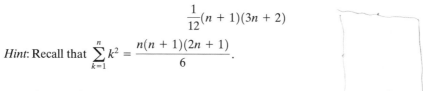

Calculating the Expected Value of a Product

The final result in this section is a special case of Theorem 3.11.3 dealing with the expected value of a *product* of random variables. Note that unlike the opening theorem in this section that addressed the expected values of sums, the statement we are about to make for products is true *only if the variables are independent*.

THEOREM 3.11.4.   If X and Y are independent random variables,

$$E(X\, Y) = E(X) \cdot E(Y)$$

provided both $E(X)$ and $E(Y)$ exist.

Proof.   Let X and Y both be discrete. Using Theorems 3.6.1 and 3.11.3, we can easily establish the desired factorization:

$$
\begin{aligned}
E(X\, Y) &= \sum_{\text{all } x} \sum_{\text{all } y} xy \cdot p_{X,Y}(x, y) \\
&= \sum_{\text{all } x} \sum_{\text{all } y} xy \cdot p_X(x) \cdot p_Y(y) \\
&= \sum_{\text{all } x} x \cdot p_X(x) \cdot \left[\sum_{\text{all } y} y \cdot p_Y(y) \right] \\
&= E(X) \cdot E(Y)
\end{aligned}
$$

The proof for continuous X and Y is left as an exercise.

Comment. Theorem 3.11.4 is not an if and only if statement: Just because $E(X \ Y)$ equals $E(X) \cdot E(Y)$, it does not follow that X and Y are independent. See (87) for a counterexample.

QUESTIONS

3.11.19 Two fair dice are tossed. What is the expected value of the product of the faces showing?

3.11.20 Let $X_1, X_2, \ldots, X_n$ be a set of mutually independent and continuous random variables. Show that

$$E(X_1 X_2 \cdots X_n) = E(X_1) \cdot E(X_2) \cdots E(X_n)$$

3.12 THE VARIANCE

The expected value is an effective measure of central tendency but it tells us nothing about the *dispersion* of a pdf—that is, the extent to which a random variable's values are spread out. The two discrete probability functions in the following table have the same expected value (namely, 0), but their configurations are clearly quite different:

k	$f_{X_1}(k)$	k	$f_{X_2}(k)$
-1	$\frac{1}{2}$	$-1{,}000{,}000$	$\frac{1}{2}$
1	$\frac{1}{2}$	$1{,}000{,}000$	$\frac{1}{2}$

It is not immediately obvious, though, how the dispersion in a pdf should be quantified. Suppose that X is any discrete random variable. One seemingly reasonable approach would be to average the deviations of X from their mean—that is, calculate the expected value of $X - \mu$. As it happens, that strategy will not work because the negative deviations will exactly cancel the positive deviations, making the numerical value of such an average always 0, regardless of the amount of spread present in $p_X(k)$:

$$E(X - \mu) = E(X) - \mu = \mu - \mu = 0 \tag{3.12.1}$$

Another possibility would be to modify Equation 3.12.1 by making all the deviations positive—that is, replace $E(X - \mu)$ with $E(|X - \mu|)$. This does work, and it *is* sometimes used to measure dispersion, but the absolute value is somewhat troublesome mathematically: It does not have a simple arithmetic formula, nor is it a differentiable function. *Squaring* the deviations proves to be a much better approach.

DEFINITION 3.12.1. The *variance* of a random variable is the expected value of its squared deviations from μ. If X is discrete with pdf $p_X(k)$,

$$\mathrm{Var}(X) = \sigma^2 = E\big[(X - \mu)^2\big] = \sum_{\text{all } k} (k - \mu)^2 \cdot p_X(k)$$

If Y is continuous with pdf $f_Y(y)$,

$$\text{Var}(Y) = \sigma^2 = E\big[(Y - \mu)^2\big] = \int_{-\infty}^{\infty} (y - \mu)^2 \cdot f_Y(y)\, dy$$

[If $E(X^2)$ or $E(Y^2)$ is not finite, the variance is not defined.]

Comment. One unfortunate consequence of Definition 3.12.1 is that the units for the variance are the square of the units for the random variable: If Y is measured in inches, for example, the units for $\text{Var}(Y)$ are inches^2. This causes obvious problems in relating the variance back to the sample values. For that reason, in applied statistics, where unit compatibility is especially important, dispersion is measured not by the variance but by the *standard deviation*, which is defined to be the square root of the variance. That is,

$$\sigma = \text{standard deviation} = \begin{cases} \sqrt{\displaystyle\sum_{\text{all } k} (k - \mu)^2 \cdot p_X(k)} & \text{if } X \text{ is discrete} \\[2em] \sqrt{\displaystyle\int_{-\infty}^{\infty} (y - \mu)^2 \cdot f_Y(y)\, dy} & \text{if } Y \text{ is continuous} \end{cases}$$

Comment. The analogy between the expected value of a random variable and the center of gravity of a physical system was pointed out in Section 3.10. A similar equivalency holds between the variance and what engineers call a *moment of inertia*. If a set of weights having masses $m_1, m_2, \ldots$ are positioned along a (weightless) rigid bar at distances $r_1, r_2, \ldots$ from an axis of rotation (see Figure 3.12.1), the moment of inertia of the system is defined to be value $\sum_i m_i r_i^2$. Notice, though, that if the masses were the probabilities associated with a discrete random variable and if the axis of rotation were actually μ, then $r_1, r_2, \ldots$ could be written $(k_1 - \mu), (k_2 - \mu), \ldots$ and $\sum_i m_i r_i^2$ would be the same as the variance, $\sum_{\text{all } k} (k - \mu)^2 \cdot p_X(k)$.

THEOREM 3.12.1. Let W be any random variable, discrete or continuous, having mean μ and for which $E(W^2)$ is finite. Then

$$\text{Var}(W) = \sigma^2 = E(W^2) - \mu^2$$

FIGURE 3.12.1

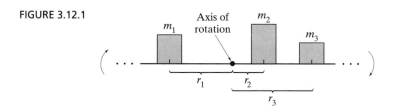

Proof. The proof is a simple application of the distributive property of expected values:

$$\begin{aligned}
\mathrm{Var}(W) &= E\big((W - \mu)^2\big) \\
&= E\big(W^2 - 2\mu W + \mu^2\big) \\
&= E(W^2) - 2\mu E(W) + \mu^2 \\
&= E(W^2) - 2\mu^2 + \mu^2 \\
&= E(W^2) - \mu^2
\end{aligned}$$

EXAMPLE 3.12.1

An urn contains five chips, two red and three white. Suppose that two are drawn out at random, *without replacement*. Let X denote the number of red chips in the sample. Find $\mathrm{Var}(X)$.

Regardless of which formula we elect to use, Definition 3.12.1 or Theorem 3.12.1, we first need to find μ. Here, since X is hypergeometric,

$$\mu = E(X) = \sum_{x=0}^{2} x \cdot \frac{\binom{2}{x}\binom{3}{2-x}}{\binom{5}{2}} = 0.8$$

The variance via Definition 3.12.1, then, becomes

$$\mathrm{Var}(X) = E\big[(X - \mu)^2\big] = \sum_{\text{all } x} (x - \mu)^2 \cdot f_X(x)$$

$$= (0 - 0.8)^2 \cdot \frac{\binom{2}{0}\binom{3}{2}}{\binom{5}{2}} + (1 - 0.8)^2 \cdot \frac{\binom{2}{1}\binom{3}{1}}{\binom{5}{2}} + (2 - 0.8)^2 \cdot \frac{\binom{2}{2}\binom{3}{0}}{\binom{5}{2}}$$

$$= 0.36$$

To find $\mathrm{Var}(X)$ using Theorem 3.12.1, we begin by computing $E(X^2)$. From Theorem 3.11.2,

$$E(X^2) = \sum_{\text{all } x} x^2 \cdot f_X(x) = 0^2 \cdot \frac{\binom{2}{0}\binom{3}{2}}{\binom{5}{2}} + 1^2 \cdot \frac{\binom{2}{1}\binom{3}{1}}{\binom{5}{2}} + 2^2 \cdot \frac{\binom{2}{2}\binom{3}{0}}{\binom{5}{2}}$$

$$= 1.00$$

Therefore, according to our second formula,

$$\mathrm{Var}(X) = E(X^2) - \mu^2 = 1.00 - (0.8)^2$$

$$= 0.36$$

confirming what we calculated earlier.

QUESTIONS

3.12.1 Find $\text{Var}(X)$ for the urn problem of Example 3.12.1 if the sampling is done *with* replacement.

3.12.2 Find the variance of Y if

$$f_Y(y) = \begin{cases} \dfrac{3}{4}, & 0 \le y \le 1 \\[2mm] \dfrac{1}{4}, & 2 \le y \le 3 \\[2mm] 0, & \text{elsewhere} \end{cases}$$

3.12.3 Ten equally qualified applicants, six men and four women, apply for three lab technician positions. Unable to justify choosing any of the applicants over all the others, the personnel director decides to select the three at random. Let X denote the number of men hired. Compute the standard deviation of X.

3.12.4 Compute the variance for a uniform random variable defined on the unit interval.

3.12.5 Use Theorem 3.12.1 to find the variance of the random variable Y, where

$$f_Y(y) = 3(1 - y)^2, \quad 0 < y < 1$$

3.12.6 If

$$f_Y(y) = \frac{2y}{k^2}, \quad 0 \le y \le k$$

for what value of k does $\text{Var}(Y) = 2$?

3.12.7 Calculate the standard deviation, σ, for the random variable Y whose pdf is graphed:

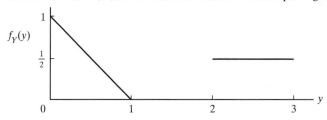

3.12.8 Consider the pdf defined by

$$f_Y(y) = \frac{2}{y^3}, \quad y \ge 1$$

Show that (a) $\int_1^\infty f_Y(y)\, dy = 1$, (b) $E(Y) = 2$, and (c) $\text{Var}(Y)$ is not finite.

3.12.9 Frankie and Johnny play the following game. Frankie selects a number at random from the interval $[a, b]$. Johnny, not knowing Frankie's number, is to pick a second number from that same interval and pay Frankie an amount, W, equal to the squared difference between the two [so $0 \le W \le (b - a)^2$]. What should be Johnny's strategy if he wants to minimize his expected loss?

3.12.10 Let Y_1, Y_2, Y_3, Y_4 be a random sample from $f_Y(y) = 2y, 0 \le y \le 1$. Find the mean and the variance of the second-order statistic.

3.12.11 Let X be a random variable with finite mean μ. Define for every real number a, $g(a) = E\big[(X - a)^2\big]$. Show that

$$g(a) = E\big[(X - \mu)^2\big] + (\mu - a)^2.$$

What is another name for $\min_a g(a)$?

3.13   PROPERTIES OF VARIANCES

When applied to sums of random variances, the variance has properties that are similar, *but not identical*, to those derived for the expected value in Section 3.11.

Calculating the Variance of a Linear Combination

If W is a random variable and a and b are constants, we know that $E(aW + b) = aE(W) + b$. Here we begin by deriving a formula for the *variance* of $aW + b$.

THEOREM 3.13.1.   Let W be any random variable, discrete or continuous, and let a and b be any two constants. Then

$$\text{Var}(aW + b) = a^2\,\text{Var}(W)$$

Proof.   Since $E(aW + b) = a\mu + b$,

$$\begin{aligned}
\text{Var}(aW + b) &= E\big([(aW + b) - (a\mu + b)]^2\big) \\
&= E\big(a^2(W - \mu)^2\big) \\
&= a^2 E\big((W - \mu)^2\big) \\
&= a^2\,\text{Var}(W)
\end{aligned}$$

EXAMPLE 3.13.1

A random variable Y is described by the pdf

$$f_Y(y) = 2y, \quad 0 < y < 1$$

What is the standard deviation of $3Y + 2$?

First, we need to find the variance of Y. But

$$E(Y) = \int_0^1 y \cdot 2y \, dy = \frac{2}{3}$$

and

$$E(Y^2) = \int_0^1 y^2 \cdot 2y \, dy = \frac{1}{2}$$

so

$$\text{Var}(Y) = E(Y^2) - \mu^2 = \frac{1}{2} - \left(\frac{2}{3}\right)^2$$

$$= \frac{1}{18}$$

Then, by Theorem 3.13.1,

$$\text{Var}(3Y + 2) = (3)^2 \cdot \text{Var}(Y) = 9 \cdot \frac{1}{18}$$

$$= \frac{1}{2}$$

which makes the standard deviation of $3Y + 2$ equal to $\sqrt{\frac{1}{2}}$, or *0.71*.

QUESTIONS

3.13.1   If $E(W) = \mu$ and $\text{Var}(W) = \sigma^2$, show that

$$E\left(\frac{W - \mu}{\sigma}\right) = 0 \quad \text{and} \quad \text{Var}\left(\frac{W - \mu}{\sigma}\right) = 1$$

3.13.2 If Y denotes a temperature recorded in degrees Fahrenheit, then $\frac{5}{9}(Y - 32)$ is the corresponding temperature in degrees Celsius. If the standard deviation for a set of temperatures is 15.7°F, what is the standard deviation of the equivalent Celsius temperatures?

3.13.3 Let Y be a uniform random variable defined on the interval $(1000, 3000)$. Use Theorem 3.13.1 to find the variance of Y by considering the transformation $(Y - 2000)/1000$.

Calculating the Variance of a Sum of Random Variables

For *any* random variables $W_1, W_2, \ldots, W_n$, discrete or continuous, dependent or independent, we saw in Section 3.11 that $E(W_1 + W_2 + \cdots + W_n) = E(W_1) + E(W_2) + \cdots + E(W_n)$ [provided the $E(W_i)$'s are finite]. There is a similar result for variances, but it does not hold with the same degree of generality—the variables must be independent.

> **THEOREM 3.13.2.** Let $W_1, W_2, \ldots, W_n$ be a set of independent random variables for which $E(W_i^2)$ is finite for all i. Then
>
> $$\mathrm{Var}(W_1 + W_2 + \cdots + W_n) = \mathrm{Var}(W_1) + \mathrm{Var}(W_2) + \cdots + \mathrm{Var}(W_n)$$
>
> **Proof.** We give a proof for $W_1 + W_2$; an induction completes the argument for general n. From Theorems 3.11.1 and 3.12.1,
>
> $$\mathrm{Var}(W_1 + W_2) = E((W_1 + W_2)^2) - [E(W_1) + E(W_2)]^2$$
>
> Writing out the squares gives
>
> $$\begin{aligned} \mathrm{Var}(W_1 + W_2) &= E(W_1^2 + 2W_1 W_2 + W_2^2) - [E(W_1)]^2 \\ &\quad - 2E(W_1)E(W_2) - [E(W_2)]^2 \\ &= E(W_1^2) - [E(W_1)]^2 + E(W_2^2) - [E(W_2)]^2 \\ &\quad + 2[E(W_1 W_2) - E(W_1)E(W_2)] \end{aligned} \qquad (3.13.1)$$
>
> By the independence of W_1 and W_2, $E(W_1 W_2) = E(W_1)E(W_2)$, making the last term in Equation 3.13.1 vanish. The remaining terms combine to give the desired result: $\mathrm{Var}(W_1 + W_2) = \mathrm{Var}(W_1) + \mathrm{Var}(W_2)$.

EXAMPLE 3.13.2

The binomial random variable, being a sum of n independent Bernoullis, is an obvious candidate for Theorem 3.13.2. Let X_i denote the number of successes occurring on the ith trial. Then

$$X_i = \begin{cases} 1 & \text{with probability } p \\ 0 & \text{with probability } 1 - p \end{cases}$$

and

$$X = X_1 + X_2 + \cdots + X_n = \text{total number of successes in } n \text{ trials.}$$

Find $\mathrm{Var}(X)$.

Note that

$$E(X_i) = 1 \cdot p + 0 \cdot (1 - p)$$

and

$$E(X_i^2) = (1)^2 \cdot p + (0)^2 \cdot (1 - p) = p$$

so

$$\text{Var}(X_i) = E(X_i^2) - [E(X_i)]^2 = p - p^2$$
$$= p(1 - p)$$

It follows, then, that the *variance of a binomial random variable is* $np(1 - p)$:

$$\text{Var}(X) = \sum_{i=1}^{n} \text{Var}(X_i) = np(1 - p)$$

EXAMPLE 3.13.3

In statistics, we often have to draw inferences based on $\bar{W}$, the average computed from a random sample of n observations. Two properties of $\bar{W}$ are especially important. First, if the W_i's come from a population whose mean is μ, then $E(\bar{W}) = \mu$ (recall Question 3.11.4). Second, if the W_i's come from a population whose variance is σ^2, then $\text{Var}(\bar{W}) = \sigma^2/n$.

To see the latter, we can appeal to Theorems 3.13.1 and 3.13.2. Let

$$\bar{W} = \frac{1}{n} \sum_{i=1}^{n} W_i = \frac{1}{n} \cdot W_1 + \frac{1}{n} \cdot W_2 + \cdots + \frac{1}{n} \cdot W_n$$

Then

$$\text{Var}(\bar{W}) = \left(\frac{1}{n}\right)^2 \cdot \text{Var}(W_1) + \left(\frac{1}{n}\right)^2 \cdot \text{Var}(W_2) + \cdots + \left(\frac{1}{n}\right)^2 \cdot \text{Var}(W_n)$$
$$= \left(\frac{1}{n}\right)^2 \sigma^2 + \left(\frac{1}{n}\right)^2 \sigma^2 + \cdots + \left(\frac{1}{n}\right)^2 \sigma^2$$
$$= \frac{\sigma^2}{n}$$

QUESTIONS

3.13.4 A mason is contracted to build a patio retaining wall. Plans call for the base of the wall to be a row of 50 10-inch bricks, each separated by $\frac{1}{2}$-inch-thick mortar. Suppose that the bricks used are randomly chosen from a population of bricks whose mean length is 10 inches and whose standard deviation is $\frac{1}{32}$ inch. Also, suppose that the mason, on the average, will make the mortar $\frac{1}{2}$ inch thick, but the actual dimension varies from brick to brick, the standard deviation of the thicknesses being $\frac{1}{16}$ inch. What is the standard deviation of L, the length of the first row of the wall? What assumption are you making?

3.13.5 Let X be a binomial random variable based on n trials and a success probability of p_X; let Y be an independent binomial random variable based on m trials and a success probability of p_Y. Find $E(W)$ and $\text{Var}(W)$, where $W = 4X + 6Y$.

3.13.6 An electric circuit has six resistors wired in series, each nominally being 5 ohms. What is the maximum standard deviation that can be allowed in the manufacture of these resistors if the combined circuit resistance is to have a standard deviation no greater than 0.4 ohm?

3.13.7 Carry out the induction argument to complete the proof of Theorem 3.13.2.

3.13.8 A gambler plays n hands of poker. If he wins the kth hand, he collects k dollars; if he loses the kth hand, he collects nothing. Let T denote his total winnings in n hands. Assuming that his chances of winning each hand are constant and are independent of his success or failure at any other hand, find $E(T)$ and $\text{Var}(T)$.

Approximating the Variance of a Function of Random Variables

It is not an uncommon problem for a laboratory scientist to have to measure several quantities, each subject to a certain amount of "error," in order to calculate a final desired result. For example, a physics student trying to determine the acceleration due to gravity, G, knows that the distance, D, traveled by a freely falling body in time, T, is related to G by the equation

$$D = \tfrac{1}{2}GT^2$$

(assuming the body is initially at rest) or, equivalently,

$$G = \frac{2D}{T^2}.$$

Suppose distance and time are to be measured directly with a yardstick and a stopwatch. The values obtained, D and T, will not be exactly correct; rather, we can think of them as being realizations of random variables, with those variables having "true" values μ_D and μ_T and variances $\text{Var}(D)$ and $\text{Var}(T)$, the latter two numbers reflecting the lack of precision in the measuring process. Suppose we know from past experience the precisions characteristic of the distance and time measurements—what can we then conclude about the precision in the calculated value for G? That is, knowing $\text{Var}(D)$ and $\text{Var}(T)$, can we find $\text{Var}(G)$?

By way of background, we have already seen one result that bears directly on this sort of "error-propagation" problem. If the quantity to be calculated, W, is the *sum* of n independently measured quantities, $W_1, W_2, \ldots, W_n$, and if the variance associated with each of the W_i's is known, we can appeal to Theorem 3.13.2 and say that

$$\text{Var}(W) = \text{Var}(W_1) + \text{Var}(W_2) + \cdots + \text{Var}(W_n) \qquad (3.13.2)$$

In general, extending Equation 3.13.2 in any *exact* way to situations where W is some arbitrary function of a set of W_i's—say, $W = g(W_1, W_2, \ldots, W_n)$—is extremely difficult. It is a relatively simple matter, though, to get an approximation for the variance of W by considering a Taylor expansion of the function $g(W_1, W_2, \ldots, W_n)$. We will look at a specific example of this technique before taking up the general formulation.

EXAMPLE 3.13.4

Suppose X and Y are independent random variables with means μ_X and μ_Y and variances $\text{Var}(X)$ and $\text{Var}(Y)$. Let $Z = XY$. We wish to find an approximation for $\text{Var}(Z)$.

Using the first-order terms in a Taylor expansion of the function $g(X, Y) = XY$ around the point (μ_X, μ_Y) gives

$$Z = g(X, Y) \doteq \mu_X \mu_Y + (X - \mu_X)\left[\frac{\partial g}{\partial X}\bigg|_{(\mu_X, \mu_Y)}\right] + (Y - \mu_Y)\left[\frac{\partial g}{\partial Y}\bigg|_{(\mu_X, \mu_Y)}\right]$$

$$= \mu_X \mu_Y + (X - \mu_X)\left[Y\bigg|_{(\mu_X, \mu_Y)}\right] + (Y - \mu_Y)\left[X\bigg|_{(\mu_X, \mu_Y)}\right]$$

$$= \mu_X \mu_Y + (X - \mu_X)\mu_Y + (Y - \mu_Y)\mu_X.$$

It follows, then, by an application of Theorems 3.13.1 and 3.13.2 that

$$\text{Var}(Z) \doteq \mu_Y^2 \, \text{Var}(X) + \mu_X^2 \, \text{Var}(Y) \tag{3.13.3}$$

(In situations where μ_X and μ_Y are unknown, they would be replaced by the actual x- and y-values recorded.)

A physics application of this particular functional relationship would be the familiar equation relating distance, D, rate, R, and time, T:

$$D = RT$$

Suppose an experiment were performed where both R and T were measured, with the values obtained being $R = 2.1$ feet/second and $T = 6.0$ seconds. Furthermore, suppose it were known that the standard deviations associated with R and T are 0.1 feet/second and 0.2 seconds, respectively. Then the calculated value for the distance would be

$$D = (2.1 \text{ ft/sec})(6.0 \text{ sec}) = 12.6 \text{ feet}$$

and it would have an approximate standard deviation, from Equation 3.13.3, of 0.7 feet:

$$\text{standard deviation of } D = \sqrt{\text{Var}(D)}$$

$$\doteq \sqrt{(6.0)^2(0.1)^2 + (2.1)^2(0.2)^2}$$

$$= 0.7 \text{ feet}$$

Consider, now, the general case where W is a function of n independent random variables, $W = g(W_1, W_2, \ldots, W_n)$. Assume that each W_i has mean μ_i and variance $\text{Var}(W_i)$. By expanding $g(W_1, W_2, \ldots, W_n)$ around the point $(\mu_1, \mu_2, \ldots, \mu_n)$—and ignoring higher-order terms—we have that

$$W \doteq g(\mu_1, \mu_2, \ldots, \mu_n) + (W_1 - \mu_1)\left[\frac{\partial g}{\partial W_1}\bigg|_{(\mu_1, \ldots, \mu_n)}\right]$$

$$+ (W_2 - \mu_2)\left[\frac{\partial g}{\partial W_2}\bigg|_{(\mu_1, \ldots, \mu_n)}\right] + \cdots + (W_n - \mu_n)\left[\frac{\partial g}{\partial W_n}\bigg|_{(\mu_1, \ldots, \mu_n)}\right].$$

Therefore,

$$\text{Var}(W) \doteq \left[\frac{\partial g}{\partial W_1}\bigg|_{(\mu_1, \mu_2, \ldots, \mu_n)}\right]^2 \text{Var}(W_1) + \left[\frac{\partial g}{\partial W_2}\bigg|_{(\mu_1, \mu_2, \ldots, \mu_n)}\right]^2 \text{Var}(W_2)$$

$$+ \cdots + \left[\frac{\partial g}{\partial W_n}\bigg|_{(\mu_1, \mu_2, \ldots, \mu_n)}\right]^2 \text{Var}(W_n). \tag{3.13.4}$$

CASE STUDY 3.13.1

In a typical dental X-ray unit, electrons from the cathode of the Xray tube are decelerated by nuclei in the anode, thereby producing Bremsstrahlung radiation (X rays). These emissions, when collimated by a lead-lined tube, effect the desired image on a sheet of film.

Tennessee state regulations (153) require that the distance, Q, from the focal spot on the anode of an X-ray tube to the patient's skin be at least 18 cm. On some equipment, particularly older units, that distance cannot be measured directly because the exact location of the focal spot cannot be determined just by looking at the tube's outer housing. When this is the case, state inspectors resort to an indirect measuring procedure. Two films are exposed, one at the unknown distance Q and a second at a distance $Q + Z$. The two diameters, X and Y, of the resulting circular images are then measured (see Figure 3.13.1).

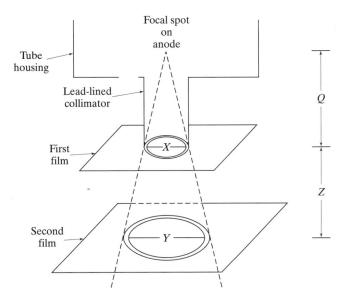

FIGURE 3.13.1   Indirect measuring procedure.

By similar triangles,

$$\frac{X}{Q} = \frac{Y}{Q + Z} \quad \text{or} \quad Q = \frac{XZ}{Y - X} \tag{3.13.5}$$

Phrased in the context of our previous notation,

$$Q = g(X, Y, Z) = XZ(Y - X)^{-1}$$

During the course of one such inspection (86), values measured for the two diameters X and Y and the backoff distance Z were 6.4 cm, 9.7 cm, and 10.2 cm, respectively. From Equation 3.13.5, then, the anode-to-patient distance is estimated to be

$$Q = \frac{(6.4)(10.2)}{9.7 - 6.4} = 19.8 \text{ cm}$$

(continued on next page)

(Case Study 3.13.1 continued)

indicating that the unit is in compliance. If the error in Q, though, were sufficiently large, there might still be a sizable probability that the *true* Q was less than 18 cm, meaning the unit was, in fact, out of compliance. It is not unreasonable, therefore, to inquire about the magnitude of $\text{Var}(Q)$.

To apply Equation 3.13.4, we first need to compute the partial derivatives of $g(X, Y, Z)$. In this case,

$$\frac{\partial g}{\partial X} = \frac{XZ}{(Y-X)^2} + \frac{Z}{(Y-X)}$$

$$\frac{\partial g}{\partial Y} = \frac{-XZ}{(Y-X)^2}$$

and

$$\frac{\partial g}{\partial Z} = \frac{X}{(Y-X)}$$

Inspectors feel that the standard deviation in any of their measurements is on the order of 0.08 cm, so $\text{Var}(X) = \text{Var}(Y) = \text{Var}(Z) = (0.08)^2$. Substituting the variance estimates and the partial derivatives, evaluated at the point $(\mu_X, \mu_Y, \mu_Z) \doteq (6.4, 9.7, 10.2)$ into Equation 3.13.4 gives

$$\text{Var}(Q) \doteq \left[\frac{(6.4)(10.2)}{(9.7-6.4)^2} + \frac{10.2}{(9.7-6.4)}\right]^2 (0.08)^2$$

$$+ \left[\frac{-(6.4)(10.2)}{(9.7-6.4)^2}\right]^2 (0.08)^2 + \left[\frac{6.4}{(9.7-6.4)}\right]^2 (0.08)^2$$

$$= 0.782$$

Therefore, the estimated standard deviation associated with the calculated value of Q is $\sqrt{0.782}$, or 0.88 cm. (See Question 3.13.12.)

QUESTIONS

3.13.9 A physics student is trying to determine the gravitational constant, G, using the expression

$$G = \frac{2D}{T^2}$$

where both distance (D) and time (T) are to be measured. Suppose that the standard deviation of the measurement errors in D is 0.0025 feet and in T, 0.045 seconds. If the experimental apparatus is set up so that D will be 4 feet, then T will be approximately $\frac{1}{2}$ second. If D is set at 16 feet, T will be close to 1 second. Which of these two sets of values for D and T will give a smaller variance for the calculated G?

3.13.10 Suppose that $W_1, W_2, \ldots,$ and W_n are independent random variables with variances $\sigma_1^2, \sigma_2^2, \ldots,$ and σ_n^2, respectively, and let $W = W_1 + W_2 + \cdots + W_n$. Compare $\text{Var}(W)$ using Theorem 3.13.2 and Equation 3.13.4.

3.13.11 If h is its height and a and b are the lengths of its two parallel sides, the area of a trapezoid is given by

$$A = \tfrac{1}{2}(a + b)h$$

Find an expression that approximates σ_A if a, b, and h are measured independently with standard deviations σ_a, σ_b, and σ_h, respectively.

3.13.12 In Case Study 3.13.1, notice that the difference between 19.8 cm (the calculated distance) and 18 cm (the state regulation minimum distance) is slightly more than two standard deviations. What does that imply about the probability that this particular X-ray machine is operating safely?

3.14   CHEBYSHEV'S INEQUALITY

If Y is a continuous random variable with pdf $f_Y(y)$—and if we *know* $f_Y(y)$—then

$$P(a \le Y \le b) = \int_a^b f_Y(y)\,dy \tag{3.14.1}$$

for any interval (a, b). If, on the other hand, Y is a random variable and we know nothing about its pdf, then obviously the only probability statement we can make about Y lying between a and b is the trivial one,

$$0 \le P(a \le Y \le b) \le 1 \tag{3.14.2}$$

Equation 3.14.1 and Inequality 3.14.2 represent the extremes in making pronouncements about a random variable's behavior; in this section we look at a famous result that strikes a compromise.

Suppose that $f_Y(y)$ is unknown *but we do have a value for the variance of Y.* Intuitively, that should "buy" us something, and it does. An upper bound can be derived for the probability that Y lies outside an ε-neighborhood of μ. That is, we can find a nontrivial c, where $c = c(\sigma^2, \varepsilon)$, such that

$$P(|Y - \mu| \ge \varepsilon) \le c(\sigma^2, \varepsilon)$$

for *any* random variable Y having mean μ and variance σ^2. (The same result holds if the random variable is discrete.)

THEOREM 3.14.1.   (Chebyshev's inequality.) Let W be any random variable with mean μ and variance σ^2. For any $\varepsilon > 0$,

$$P(|W - \mu| < \varepsilon) \ge 1 - \frac{\sigma^2}{\varepsilon^2}$$

or, equivalently,

$$P(|W - \mu| \ge \varepsilon) \le \frac{\sigma^2}{\varepsilon^2}$$

Proof. In the continuous case,

$$\text{Var}(Y) = \int_{-\infty}^{\infty} (y - \mu)^2 f_Y(y)\, dy$$

$$= \int_{-\infty}^{\mu - \varepsilon} (y - \mu)^2 f_Y(y)\, dy + \int_{\mu - \varepsilon}^{\mu + \varepsilon} (y - \mu)^2 f_Y(y)\, dy$$

$$+ \int_{\mu + \varepsilon}^{\infty} (y - \mu)^2 f_Y(y)\, dy$$

Omitting the nonnegative middle integral gives an inequality:

$$\text{Var}(Y) \geq \int_{-\infty}^{\mu - \varepsilon} (y - \mu)^2 f_Y(y)\, dy + \int_{\mu + \varepsilon}^{\infty} (y - \mu)^2 f_Y(y)\, dy$$

$$\geq \int_{|y - \mu| \geq \varepsilon} (y - \mu)^2 f_Y(y)\, dy$$

$$\geq \int_{|y - \mu| \geq \varepsilon} \varepsilon^2 f_Y(y)\, dy$$

$$= \varepsilon^2 P(|Y - \mu| \geq \varepsilon)$$

Division by ε^2 completes the proof. (If the random variabale is discrete, replace the integrals with summations.)

EXAMPLE 3.14.1

A student makes 100 check transactions between receiving his January and February bank statements. Rather than subtract the amounts he spends exactly, he rounds off each check-book entry to the nearest dollar. Use Chebyshev's inequality to get an upper bound for the probability that the student's accumulated error (either positive or negative) after his 100 transactions is $5 or more.

Let Y_i denote the round-off error associated with the ith transaction, $i = 1, 2, \dots, 100$. It can be assumed (why?) that the Y_i's are independent random variables and follow a uniform pdf over the interval $\left(-\$\frac{1}{2},\ +\$\frac{1}{2}\right)$. Therefore,

$$E(Y_i) = 0$$

and

$$\text{Var}(Y_i) = \frac{1}{12}$$

(see Question 3.12.4).

Let $Y = Y_1 + Y_2 + \cdots + Y_{100}$ denote the student's total accumulated error. There is no simple way to find the pdf for Y but its expected value and variance can be derived easily: By the corollary to Theorem 3.11.1,

$$E(Y) = \mu = 0$$

and by Theorem 3.13.2,

$$\text{Var}(Y) = \frac{100}{12} = 8.3$$

Substituting $E(Y)$ and $\text{Var}(Y)$ into Theorem 3.14.1, we can write

$$P(|Y| \geq \$5) = P(|Y - \mu| \geq \varepsilon) \leq \frac{8.3}{25} = 0.33$$

There is at *most* a 33% chance, then, that the student's total will be off by as much as $5.

EXAMPLE 3.14.2

Suppose that W is a random variable with $\mu = 150$ and $\sigma = 20$. Is the following equation possible?

$$P(110 < W < 190) = 0.65$$

No. If $\mu = 150$ and $\sigma = 20$, then

$$P(110 < W < 190) = P(\mu - 2\sigma < W < \mu + 2\sigma) \tag{3.14.3}$$

According to Chebyshev's inequality, the probability in Equation 3.14.3 *must* be greater than $1 - (1/2^2) = 0.75$. Therefore, no matter what $f_W(w)$ might be, it cannot be true that $P(110 < W < 190)$ is only 0.65.

EXAMPLE 3.14.3

The relationship between the *sample* mean of a random sample of n observations, $\bar{W} = (1/n) \sum_{i=1}^{n} W_i$, and the (unknown) *true* mean, μ, of the pdf from which the W_i's are taken is a problem of pivotal importance in statistics. Typically, our only source of information about μ is what we can glean from $\bar{W}$. Any attempt, then, to draw an inference about μ will necessarily be predicated on the probabilistic behavior of $\bar{W}$.

Historically, one of the earliest results relating the behavior of the random variable $\bar{W}$ to the constant μ was the *weak law of large numbers*, which says that $\bar{W}$ "converges" to μ as n gets large. More formally, if $W_1, W_2, \ldots, W_n$ are random variables with the same mean μ and the same variance σ^2, then for every $\varepsilon > 0$ and $\delta > 0$ there is an N such that

$$P(|\bar{W} - \mu| > \varepsilon) < \delta$$

if $n > N$. Equivalently,

$$\lim_{n \to \infty} P(|\bar{W} - \mu| > \varepsilon) = 0 \tag{3.14.4}$$

That Equation 3.14.4 is true follows almost immediately from Theorem 3.14.1. Since $\bar{W} = (1/n)(W_1 + W_2 + \cdots + W_n)$,

$$\text{Var}(\bar{W}) = \frac{1}{n^2} \sum_{i=1}^{n} \text{Var}(W_i) = \frac{1}{n^2} n\sigma^2$$

$$= \frac{\sigma^2}{n}$$

and, of course, $E(\bar{W}) = \mu$. By Chebyshev's inequality,

$$P(|\bar{W} - \mu| > \varepsilon) \leq \frac{\text{Var}(\bar{W})}{\varepsilon^2}$$

But $\text{Var}(\bar{W})/\varepsilon^2 = \sigma^2/n\varepsilon^2$ and the latter goes to 0 as $n \to \infty$.

QUESTIONS

3.14.1 Suppose that Y is an exponential random variable with pdf $f_Y(y) = e^{-y}$, $y > 0$.
   (a) Compute the *exact* probability that Y takes on a value more than two standard deviations away from its mean.
   (b) Use Chebyshev's inequality to get an upper bound for the probability asked for in part (a).

3.14.2 A fair die is tossed 100 times. Let X_k denote the outcome on the kth roll. Use Theorem 3.14.1 to get a lower bound for the probability that $X = X_1 + X_2 + \cdots + X_{100}$ is between 300 and 400.

3.14.3 Suppose that the distribution of scores on an IQ test has mean 100 and standard deviation 16. Show that the probability of a student having an IQ above 148 or below 52 is at most $\frac{1}{9}$.

3.14.4 Use Chebyshev's inequality to get a lower bound for the number of times a fair coin must be tossed in order for the probability to be at least 0.90 that the ratio of the observed number of heads to the total number of tosses be between 0.4 and 0.6.

3.15   HIGHER MOMENTS

The quantities we have identified as the mean and the variance are actually special cases of what are referred to more generally as the *moments* of a random variable. More precisely, $E(W)$ is the *first moment about the origin* and σ^2 is the *second moment about the mean*. As the terminology suggests, we will have occasion to define higher moments of W. Just as $E(W)$ and σ^2 reflect a random variable's location and dispersion, so is it possible to characterize other aspects of a distribution in terms of other moments. We will see, for example, that the skewness of a distribution—that is, the extent to which it is not symmetric around μ—can be effectively measured in terms of a *third* moment. Likewise, there are issues that arise in certain applied statistics problems that require a knowledge of the "flatness" of a pdf, a property that can be quantified by the *fourth* moment.

> **DEFINITION 3.15.1.** Let W be any random variable with pdf $f_W(w)$. For any positive integer r,
>
> **1.** The *rth moment of W about the origin*, μ_r, is given by
>
> $$\mu_r = E(W^r)$$
>
> provided $\int_{-\infty}^{\infty} |w|^r \cdot f_W(w)\, dw < \infty$ (or provided the analogous condition on the *summation* of $|w|^r$ holds, if W is discrete). When $r = 1$, we usually delete the subscript and write $E(W)$ as μ rather than μ_1.

2. The *rth moment of W about the mean*, μ'_r, is given by

$$\mu'_r = E\big[(W - \mu)^r\big]$$

provided the finiteness conditions of part 1 hold.

Comment. We can express μ'_r in terms of $\mu_j,\, j = 1, 2, \ldots, r$, by simply writing out the binomial expansion of $(W - \mu)^r$:

$$\mu'_r = E\big[(W - \mu)^r\big] = \sum_{j=0}^{r} \binom{r}{j} E(W^j)(-\mu)^{r-j}$$

Thus,

$$\mu'_2 = E\big[(W - \mu)^2\big] = \sigma^2 = \mu_2 - \mu_1^2$$

$$\mu'_3 = E\big[(W - \mu)^3\big] = \mu_3 - 3\mu_1\mu_2 + 2\mu_1^3$$

$$\mu'_4 = E\big[(W - \mu)^4\big] = \mu_4 - 4\mu_1\mu_3 + 6\mu_1^2\mu_2 - 3\mu_1^4$$

and so on.

EXAMPLE 3.15.1

The *skewness* of a pdf can be measured in terms of its third moment about the mean. If a pdf is symmetric, $E\big[(W - \mu)^3\big]$ will obviously be 0; for pdf's not symmetric, $E\big[(W - \mu)^3\big]$ will not be zero. In practice, the symmetry (or lack of symmetry) of a pdf is often measured by the *coefficient of skewness*, γ_1, where

$$\gamma_1 = \frac{E\big[(W - \mu)^3\big]}{\sigma^3}$$

Dividing μ'_3 by σ^3 makes γ_1 dimensionless.

A second "shape" parameter in common use is the *coefficient of kurtosis*, γ_2, which involves the *fourth* moment about the mean. Specifically,

$$\gamma_2 = \frac{E\big[(W - \mu)^4\big]}{\sigma^4} - 3$$

For certain pdf's, γ_2 is a useful measure of peakedness: relatively "flat" pdf's are said to be *platykurtic*; more peaked pdf's are called *leptokurtic* [see (87)].

QUESTIONS

3.15.1 Let Y be a uniform random variable defined over the interval $(0, 2)$. Find an expression for the rth moment of Y about the origin. Also, use the binomial expansion as described in the comment to find $E\big[(Y - \mu)^6\big]$.

3.15.2 Find the coefficient of skewness for an exponential random variable having the pdf

$$f_Y(y) = e^{-y}, \quad y > 0$$

Use the fact that if k is a positive integer,

$$\int_0^\infty y^k e^{-y}\, dy = k!$$

3.15.3 Suppose that W is a random variable for which $E\big[(W - \mu)^3\big] = 10$ and $E(W^3) = 4$. Is it possible that $\mu = 2$?

3.15.4 If $Y = aX + b$, show that Y has the same coefficients of skewness and kurtosis as X.

An Existence Theorem for Higher Moments

Earlier in this chapter we encountered random variables whose means did not exist—recall, for example, the St. Petersburg paradox. More generally, there are random variables having certain of their higher moments finite and certain others, not finite. Addressing the question of whether or not a given $E(W^j)$ is finite is the following existence theorem.

> **THEOREM 3.15.1.** If the kth moment of a random variable exists, all moments of order less than k exist.

> **Proof.** Let $f_Y(y)$ be the pdf of a continuous random variable Y. By Definition 3.15.1, $E(Y^k)$ exists if and only if
>
> $$\int_{-\infty}^\infty |y|^k \cdot f_Y(y)\, dy < \infty \qquad (3.15.1)$$
>
> Let $1 \le j < k$. To prove the theorem we must show that
>
> $$\int_{-\infty}^\infty |y|^j \cdot f_Y(y)\, dy < \infty$$
>
> is implied by Inequality 3.15.1. But
>
> $$\int_{-\infty}^\infty |y|^j \cdot f_Y(y)\, dy = \int_{|y|\le 1} |y|^j \cdot f_Y(y)\, dy + \int_{|y|>1} |y|^j \cdot f_Y(y)\, dy$$
>
> $$\le \int_{|y|\le 1} f_Y(y)\, dy + \int_{|y|>1} |y|^j \cdot f_Y(y)\, dy$$
>
> $$\le 1 + \int_{|y|>1} |y|^j \cdot f_Y(y)\, dy$$
>
> $$\le 1 + \int_{|y|>1} |y|^k \cdot f_Y(y)\, dy < \infty$$
>
> Therefore, $E(Y^j)$ exists, $j = 1, 2, \ldots, k - 1$. The proof for discrete random variables is similar.

EXAMPLE 3.15.2

Many of the random variables that play a major role in statistics have moments existing for *all* k, as does, for instance, the normal distribution introduced in Case Study 2.5.1. Still, it is not difficult to find well-known models for which this is *not* true. A case in point is the *Student t distribution*, a probability function widely used in inference procedures.

The pdf for a Student t random variable is given by

$$f_Y(y) = \frac{c(n)}{\left(1 + \dfrac{y^2}{n}\right)^{(n+1)/2}}, \qquad -\infty < y < \infty, \quad n \geq 1$$

where n is referred to as the distribution's "degrees of freedom" and $c(n)$ is a constant. By definition, the $(2k)$th moment is the integral

$$E(Y^{2k}) = c(n) \cdot \int_{-\infty}^{\infty} \frac{y^{2k}}{\left(1 + \dfrac{y^2}{n}\right)^{(n+1)/2}} \, dy$$

Is $E(Y^{2k})$ finite?

Not necessarily. Recall from calculus that an integral of the form

$$\int_{-\infty}^{\infty} \frac{1}{y^\alpha} \, dy$$

will converge only if $\alpha > 1$. Also, the convergence properties for integrals of

$$\frac{y^{2k}}{\left(1 + \dfrac{y^2}{n}\right)^{(n+1)/2}}$$

are the same as those for

$$\frac{y^{2k}}{\left(y^2\right)^{(n+1)/2}} = \frac{1}{y^{n+1-2k}}$$

Therefore, if $E(Y^{2k})$ is to be finite, we must have

$$n + 1 - 2k > 1$$

or, equivalently, $2k < n$. Thus a Student t random variable with, say, $n = 9$ degrees of freedom has $E(X^8) < \infty$, but no moment of order higher than eight exists.

QUESTIONS

3.15.5 Suppose that the random variable Y is described by the pdf

$$f_Y(y) = c \cdot y^{-6}, \quad y > 1$$

(a) Find c.
(b) What is the highest moment of Y that exists?

3.15.6 If $r > 0$ and $E|X_i|^r < \infty$ for all i, show that $E|X_1 + \cdots + X_n|^r < \infty$.

3.16   MOMENT-GENERATING FUNCTIONS

Finding moments of random variables directly, particularly the higher moments defined in Section 3.15, is conceptually straightforward but can be quite problematic: Depending on the nature of the pdf, integrals and sums of the form $\int_{-\infty}^{\infty} y^r f_Y(y)\, dy$ and $\sum_{\text{all } k} k^r p_X(k)$ can be very difficult to evaluate. Fortunately, an alternative method is available. For many pdf's, we can find a *moment-generating function* (or *mgf*), $M_W(t)$, one of whose properties is that the rth derivative of $M_W(t)$ evaluated at 0 is equal to $E(W^r)$.

Calculating a Random Variable's Moment-Generating Function

In principle, what we call a moment-generating function is a direct application of Theorem 3.11.2.

DEFINITION 3.16.1.   Let W be a random variable. The *moment-generating function (mgf) for* W is denoted $M_W(t)$ and given by

$$M_W(t) = E(e^{tW}) = \begin{cases} \sum_{\text{all } k} e^{tk} p_W(k) & \text{if } W \text{ is discrete} \\[2mm] \int_{-\infty}^{\infty} e^{tw} f_W(w)\, dw & \text{if } W \text{ is continuous} \end{cases}$$

at all values of t for which the expected value exists.

EXAMPLE 3.16.1

Let X be a binomial random variable for which

$$p_X(k) = \binom{n}{k} p^k (1 - p)^{n-k}, \quad k = 0, 1, \ldots, n$$

Derive the moment-generating function for X.
   Recall Newton's binomial expansion formula:

$$(x + y)^n = \sum_{k=0}^{n} \binom{n}{k} x^k y^{n-k} \tag{3.16.1}$$

Applying Equation 3.16.1 to Definition 3.16.1 shows that $(1 - p + pe^t)^n$ is the moment-generating function for a binomial random variable:

$$M_X(t) = E(e^{tX}) = \sum_{k=0}^{n} e^{tk} \cdot \binom{n}{k} p^k (1 - p)^{n-k}$$

$$= \sum_{k=0}^{n} \binom{n}{k} (pe^t)^k (1 - p)^{n-k}$$

$$= (1 - p + pe^t)^n$$

In this case $M_X(t)$ is defined for all values of t.

EXAMPLE 3.16.2

Suppose that Y has an exponential pdf, where $f_Y(y) = \lambda e^{-\lambda y}$, $y > 0$. Find $M_Y(t)$.

Since the exponential pdf describes a continuous random variable, $M_Y(t)$ is an integral:

$$M_Y(t) = E(e^{tY}) = \int_0^\infty e^{ty} \cdot \lambda e^{-\lambda y} \, dy$$

$$= \int_0^\infty \lambda e^{-(\lambda - t)y} \, dy$$

After making the substitution $u = (\lambda - t)y$, we can write

$$M_Y(t) = \int_{\mu=0}^\infty \lambda e^{-u} \frac{du}{\lambda - t}$$

$$= \frac{\lambda}{\lambda - t} \left[-e^{-u} \Big|_{\mu=0}^\infty \right]$$

$$= \frac{\lambda}{\lambda - t} \left[1 - \lim_{\mu \to \infty} e^{-u} \right] = \frac{\lambda}{\lambda - t} = \frac{1}{1 - t/\lambda}$$

Notice that $M_Y(t)$ exists and is nonzero only when $u = (\lambda - t)y > 0$, which implies that t must be less than λ. For $t \geq \lambda$, $M_Y(t)$ fails to exist.

QUESTIONS

3.16.1 Let X be a discrete random variable with

$$p_X(k) = \begin{cases} p(1 - p)^{k-1}, & k = 1, 2, \ldots \\ 0, & \text{elsewhere} \end{cases}$$

Show that $M_X(t) = (pe^t)/(1 - qe^t)$, where $q = 1 - p$. *Hint*: Recall the formula for the sum of a geometric series,

$$\sum_{k=0}^\infty r^k = \frac{1}{1 - r} \qquad \text{for} \quad 0 < r < 1$$

3.16.2 Two chips are drawn at random and without replacement from an urn that contains five chips, numbered 1 through 5. If the sum of the chips drawn is even, the random variable X equals 5; if the sum of the chips drawn is odd, $X = -3$. Find the moment-generating function for X.

3.16.3 Find the expected value of e^{3X} if X is a binomial random variable with $n = 10$ and $p = \frac{1}{3}$.

3.16.4 Find the moment-generating function for the discrete random variable X whose probability function is given by

$$p_X(k) = \left(\frac{3}{4}\right)^k \left(\frac{1}{4}\right), \quad k = 0, 1, 2, \ldots$$

3.16.5 Show that the moment-generating function of the random variable Y having pdf $f_Y(y) = \frac{1}{3}, -1 < x < 2$, is

$$M_Y(t) = \begin{cases} \dfrac{e^{2t} - e^{-t}}{3t}, & t \neq 0 \\ 1, & t = 0 \end{cases}$$

3.16.6 Let X have pdf

$$f_Y(y) = \begin{cases} y, & 0 \leq y \leq 1 \\ 2 - y, & 1 \leq y \leq 2 \\ 0, & \text{elsewhere} \end{cases}$$

Find $M_Y(t)$.

3.16.7 A random variable X is said to have a *Poisson distribution* if $p_X(k) = P(X = k) = e^{-\lambda}\lambda^k/k!$, $k = 0, 1, 2, \ldots$. Find the moment-generating function for a Poisson random variable. *Hint*: Use the fact that

$$e^r = \sum_{k=0}^{\infty} \frac{r^k}{k!}$$

3.16.8 In Case Study 2.5.1, the pdf for a *normal random variable* is given as

$$f_Y(y) = \frac{1}{\sqrt{2\pi}\sigma} \exp\left[-\frac{1}{2}\left(\frac{y - \mu}{\sigma}\right)^2\right], \quad -\infty < y < \infty$$

Show that the corresponding moment-generating function is given by

$$M_Y(t) = e^{\mu t + \sigma^2 t^2/2}$$

Hint: Complete the square of the exponent in the integral defining $M_Y(t)$.

Using Moment-Generating Functions to Find Moments

Having practiced *finding* the functions $M_X(t)$ and $M_Y(t)$, we now turn to the theorem that spells out their relationship to X^r and Y^r.

> **THEOREM 3.16.1.** Let W be a random variable with probability density function $f_W(w)$. [If W is continuous, $f_W(w)$ must be sufficiently smooth to allow the order of differentiation and integration to be interchanged.] Let $M_W(t)$ be the moment-generating function for W. Then, provided the rth moment exists,
> $$M_W^{(r)}(0) = E(W^r)$$
>
> **Proof.** We will verify the theorem for the continuous case where r is either 1 or 2. The extensions to discrete random variables and to an arbitrary positive integer r are straightforward.
> For $r = 1$,
> $$M_Y^{(1)}(0) = \frac{d}{dt}\int_{-\infty}^{\infty} e^{ty}f_Y(y)\,dy\bigg|_{t=0} = \int_{-\infty}^{\infty} \frac{d}{dt}e^{ty}f_Y(y)\,dy\bigg|_{t=0}$$
> $$= \int_{-\infty}^{\infty} ye^{ty}f_Y(y)\,dy\bigg|_{t=0} = \int_{-\infty}^{\infty} ye^{0\cdot y}f_Y(y)\,dy$$
> $$= \int_{-\infty}^{\infty} yf_Y(y)\,dy = E(Y)$$

For $r = 2$,

$$M_Y^{(2)}(0) = \frac{d^2}{dt^2} \int_{-\infty}^{\infty} e^{ty} f_Y(y) \, dy \bigg|_{t=0} = \int_{-\infty}^{\infty} \frac{d^2}{dt^2} e^{ty} f_Y(y) \, dy \bigg|_{t=0}$$

$$= \int_{-\infty}^{\infty} y^2 e^{ty} f_Y(y) \, dy \bigg|_{t=0} = \int_{-\infty}^{\infty} y^2 e^{0 \cdot y} f_Y(y) \, dy \bigg|_{t=0}$$

$$= \int_{-\infty}^{\infty} y^2 f_Y(y) \, dy = E(Y^2)$$

EXAMPLE 3.16.3

Find the expected value of the exponential random variable, where $f_Y(y) = \lambda e^{-\lambda y}$, $y > 0$, by differentiating its moment-generating function.

As derived in Example 3.16.2,

$$M_Y(t) = \frac{1}{1 - t/\lambda} = (1 - t/\lambda)^{-1}$$

But

$$M_Y^{(1)}(t) = (-1)(1 - t/\lambda)^{-2}(-1/\lambda) = \frac{\lambda}{(\lambda - t)^2}$$

so, by Theorem 3.16.1,

$$E(Y) = M_Y^{(1)}(0) = \frac{\lambda}{(\lambda - 0)^2} = \frac{1}{\lambda}$$

EXAMPLE 3.16.4

For the geometric distribution, defined by $p_X(k) = pq^{k-1}$, $k = 1, 2, \ldots$, we saw in Question 3.16.1 that $M_X(t) = pe^t/(1 - qe^t)$. Find $E(X)$ by differentiating $M_X(t)$.

To simplify the calculus, we start by reexpressing $M_X(t)$ as a product:

$$M_X(t) = pe^t(1 - qe^t)^{-1}$$

Then, using the product rule, we can write

$$M_X^{(1)}(t) = pe^t(-1)(1 - qe^t)^{-2}(-qe^t) + (1 - qe^t)^{-1} pe^t$$

$$= \frac{pqe^{2t}}{(1 - qe^t)^2} + \frac{pe^t}{1 - qe^t}$$

Setting $t = 0$ gives

$$M_X^{(1)}(0) = E(X) = \frac{pqe^{2 \cdot 0}}{(1 - qe^0)^2} + \frac{pe^0}{1 - qe^0}$$

$$= \frac{1}{p}$$

EXAMPLE 3.16.5

Moment-generating functions can also be helpful in finding variances. Recall from Theorem 3.12.1 that for any random variable W, $\text{Var}(W) = E(W^2) - [E(W)]^2$. Equivalently,

$$\text{Var}(W) = M_W^{(2)}(0) - [M_W^{(1)}(0)]^2 \tag{3.16.2}$$

Use Equation 3.16.2 to find the variance of a binomial random variable.

We know from Example 3.16.1 that if X is a binomial random variable defined on n independent trials, where $p = P(\text{success})$, then $M_X(t) = (1 - p + pe^t)^n$. Therefore,

$$M_X^{(1)}(t) = n(1 - p + pe^t)^{n-1} \cdot pe^t$$

and

$$M_X^{(2)}(t) = pe^t \cdot n(n-1)(1 - p + pe^t)^{n-2} \cdot pe^t + n(1 - p + pe^t)^{n-1} \cdot pe^t$$

Setting $t = 0$ gives

$$M_X^{(1)}(0) = np = E(X)$$

and

$$M_X^{(2)}(0) = n(n-1)p^2 + np = E(X^2)$$

From Equation 3.16.2, then,

$$\text{Var}(X) = n(n-1)p^2 + np - (np)^2$$
$$= np(1-p)$$

(the same answer we found in Example 3.13.2).

QUESTIONS

3.16.9 For a Poisson random variable, $M_X(t) = e^{-\lambda + \lambda e^t}$ (see Question 3.16.7). Differentiate $M_X(t)$ to verify that $E(X) = \lambda$ and $\text{Var}(X) = \lambda$.

3.16.10 Find $E(Y^4)$ if Y is an exponential random variable with $f_Y(y) = \lambda e^{-\lambda y}, y > 0$.

3.16.11 The form of the moment-generating function for a normal random variable is $M_Y(t) = e^{at + b^2 t^2/2}$ (recall Question 3.16.8). Differentiate $M_Y(t)$ to verify that $a = E(Y)$ and $b^2 = \text{Var}(Y)$.

3.16.12 What is $E(Y^4)$ if the random variable Y has moment-generating function $M_Y(t) = (1 - \alpha t)^{-k}$?

3.16.13 Find $E(Y^2)$ if the moment-generating function for Y is given by $M_Y(t) = e^{-t + 4t^2}$. Use Question 3.16.8 to find $E(Y^2)$ without taking any derivatives. *Hint*: Recall Theorem 3.12.1.

3.16.14 Find an expression for $E(X^k)$ if

$$M_X(t) = (1 - p_1 - p_2) + p_1 e^t + p_2 e^{2t}$$

Hint: Start by finding $E(X)$ and $E(X^2)$.

3.16.15 Find the variance of Y if $M_Y(t) = e^{2t}/(1 - t^2)$.

Using Moment-Generating Functions to Identify pdf's

Finding moments is not the only application of moment-generating functions. They are also used to identify the pdf of *sums* of random variables—that is, finding $f_W(w)$, where $W = W_1 + W_2 + \cdots + W_n$. Their assistance in the latter is particularly important for two reasons: (1) Many statistical procedures are defined in terms of sums, and (2) alternative methods for deriving $f_{W_1 + W_2 + \cdots W_n}(w)$ are extremely cumbersome.

The next two theorems give the background results necessary for deriving $f_W(w)$. Theorem 3.16.2 states a key uniqueness property of moment-generating functions: If W_1 and W_2 are random variables with the same mgfs, they must necessarily have the same pdfs. In practice, applications of Theorem 3.16.2 typically rely on one or both of the algebraic properties cited in Theorem 3.16.3.

> **THEOREM 3.16.2.**   Suppose that W_1 and W_2 are random variables for which $M_{W_1}(t) = M_{W_2}(t)$ for some interval of t's containing 0. Then $f_{W_1}(w) = f_{W_2}(w)$.

> **THEOREM 3.16.3.**
>
> **(a)** Let W be a random variable with moment-generating function $M_W(t)$. Let $V = aW + b$. Then
>
> $$M_V(t) = e^{bt} M_W(at)$$
>
> **(b)** Let $W_1, W_2, \ldots, W_n$ be independent random variables with moment-generating functions $M_{W_1}(t), M_{W_2}(t), \ldots$, and $M_{W_n}(t)$, respectively. Let $W = W_1 + W_2 + \cdots + W_n$. Then
>
> $$M_W(t) = M_{W_1}(t) \cdot M_{W_2}(t) \cdots M_{W_n}(t)$$

EXAMPLE 3.16.6

Suppose that X_1 and X_2 are independent binomial random variables with $p_{X_1}(k) = \binom{n}{k} p^k (1-p)^{n-k}$, $k = 0, 1, \ldots, n$ and $p_{X_2}(k) = \binom{m}{k} p^k (1-p)^{m-k}$, $k = 0, 1, \ldots, m$. Find $p_X(k)$, the probability function for the sum $X = X_1 + X_2$.

We know from Example 3.16.1 that $M_{X_1}(t) = \left(1 - p + pe^t\right)^n$ and $M_{X_2}(t) = \left(1 - p + pe^t\right)^m$. Moreover, from Theorem 3.16.3,

$$M_X(t) = \left(1 - p + pe^t\right)^n \cdot \left(1 - p + pe^t\right)^m$$
$$= \left(1 - p + pe^t\right)^{n+m}$$

Notice that $M_X(t)$ has the *form* of the moment-generating function for a binomial random variable defined on $n + m$ trials. By the uniqueness property in Theorem 3.16.2, then,

$$p_X(k) = \binom{n+m}{k} p^k (1-p)^{n+m-k}, \quad k = 0, 1, \ldots, n + m$$

EXAMPLE 3.16.7

For a normal curve having mean μ and standard deviation σ, $f_Y(y) = (1/\sqrt{2\pi}\sigma) \exp\left[-\frac{1}{2}\left(\frac{y-\mu}{\sigma}\right)^2\right]$, $-\infty < y < \infty$ and $M_Y(t) = e^{\mu t + \sigma^2 t^2 / 2}$. By definition, a *standard normal curve* is one for which $\mu = 0$ and $\sigma = 1$. Denoted Z, standard normal curves have pdf $f_Z(z) = (1/\sqrt{2\pi}) e^{-z^2/2}$, $-\infty < z < \infty$, and mgf $M_Z(t) = e^{t^2/2}$. Suppose Y is a normal random variable with mean μ and standard deviation σ. Show that the ratio $\dfrac{Y - \mu}{\sigma}$ is a standard normal random variable, Z.

Write $\dfrac{Y - \mu}{\sigma}$ as $\dfrac{1}{\sigma} Y - \dfrac{\mu}{\sigma}$. By Part (a) of Theorem 3.16.3,

$$M_{(Y-\mu)/\sigma}(t) = e^{-\mu t/\sigma} M_Y\left(\frac{t}{\sigma}\right)$$

$$= e^{-\mu t/\sigma} e^{(\mu t/\sigma + \sigma^2 (t/\sigma)^2/2)}$$

$$= e^{t^2/2}$$

But $M_Z(t) = e^{t^2/2}$ so it follows from Theorem 3.16.2 that the pdf for $\dfrac{Y - \mu}{\sigma}$ is the same as $f_Z(z)$. (We call $\dfrac{Y - \mu}{\sigma}$ a *Z-transformation*. Its importance will become evident in Chapter 4.)

EXAMPLE 3.16.8

Suppose the random variable W has moment-generating function

$$M_W(t) = \frac{1}{1 - t/2} \cdot \left(\frac{1}{3} + \frac{2}{3} e^t\right)^4$$

Calculate $P(W > 1.5)$.

Notice, first, that $M_W(t)$ is the product of $\dfrac{1}{1 - t/2}$ and $\left(\dfrac{1}{3} + \dfrac{2}{3} e^t\right)^4$, which are the moment-generating functions corresponding to

$$f_Y(y) = 2e^{-2y}, \quad y > 0$$

and

$$p_X(k) = \binom{4}{k}\left(\frac{2}{3}\right)^k\left(\frac{1}{3}\right)^{4-k}, \quad k = 0, 1, 2, 3, 4$$

respectively. Therefore, $W = X + Y$, and

$P(W > 1.5) = 1 - P(W \le 1.5)$

$\qquad = 1 - \left[P(X = 0 \cap Y \le 1.5) + P(X = 1 \cap Y \le 0.5)\right]$

$\qquad = 1 - \left[\binom{4}{0}\left(\frac{2}{3}\right)^0\left(\frac{1}{3}\right)^4 \cdot \int_0^{1.5} 2e^{-2y}\, dy + \binom{4}{1}\left(\frac{2}{3}\right)^1\left(\frac{1}{3}\right)^3 \cdot \int_0^{0.5} 2e^{-2y}\, dy\right]$

$\qquad = 1 - 0.0741$

$\qquad = 0.93$

QUESTIONS

3.16.16 Use Theorems 3.16.2 and 3.16.3 to determine which of the following statements is true:
  (a) The sum of two independent Poisson random variables has a Poisson distribution.
  (b) The sum of two independent exponential random variables has an exponential distribution.
  (c) The sum of two independent normal random variables has a normal distribution.

3.16.17 Calculate $P(X \le 2)$ if $M_X(t) = \left(\dfrac{1}{4} + \dfrac{3}{4}e^t\right)^5$.

3.16.18 Suppose that $Y_1, Y_2, \ldots, Y_n$ is a random sample of size n from a normal distribution with mean μ and standard deviation σ. Use moment-generating functions to deduce the pdf of $\bar{Y} = \dfrac{1}{n}\sum_{i=1}^{n} Y_i$.

3.16.19 Suppose the moment-generating function for a random variable W is given by

$$M_W(t) = e^{-3+3e^t} \cdot \left(\frac{2}{3} + \frac{1}{3}e^t\right)^4$$

Calculate $P(W \le 1)$. *Hint*: See Question 3.16.9.

3.16.20 Suppose that X is a Poisson random variable, where $p_X(k) = e^{-\lambda}\lambda^k/k!, k = 0, 1, \ldots$.
   (a) Does the random variable $W = 3X$ have a Poisson distribution?
   (b) Does the random variable $W = 3X + 1$ have a Poisson distribution?

3.16.21 Suppose that Y is a normal random variable, where $f_Y(y) = (1/\sqrt{2\pi}\sigma)\exp\left[-\dfrac{1}{2}\left(\dfrac{y-\mu}{\sigma}\right)^2\right]$, $-\infty < y < \infty$.
   (a) Does the random variable $W = 3Y$ have a normal distribution?
   (b) Does the random variable $W = 3Y + 1$ have a normal distribution?

APPENDIX 3.A.1   MINITAB APPLICATIONS

Numerous software packages are available for doing a variety of probability and statistical calculations. Among the first to be developed and one that continues to be very popular is MINITAB. Beginning here, we will include at the ends of certain chapters a short discussion of MINITAB solutions to some of the problems that were discussed in that chapter. What other software packages can do and the ways their outputs are formatted are likely to be quite similar.

Contained in MINITAB are subroutines that can do some of the more important pdf and cdf computations described in Sections 3.3 and 3.4. In the case of binomial random variables, for instance, the statements

```
MTB  > pdf k;
SUBC > binomial n p.
```

and

```
MTB  > cdf k;
SUBC > binomial n p.
```

will calculate $\binom{n}{k}p^k(1-p)^{n-k}$ and $\sum_{r=0}^{k}\binom{n}{r}p^r(1-p)^{n-r}$, respectively. Figure 3.A.1.1 shows the MINITAB program for doing the cdf calculation $(= P(X \le 15))$ asked for in Part (a) of Example 3.3.6.

The commands pdf k and cdf k can be run on many of the probability models most likely to be encountered in real-world problems. Those on the list that we have already seen are the binomial, Poisson, normal, uniform, and exponential distributions.

FIGURE 3.A.1.1   MTB > cdf 15;
                  SUBC> binomial 30 0.60.

Cumulative Distribution Function

Binomial with n = 30 and p = 0.600000

x	P(X <= x)
15.00	0.1754

FIGURE 3.A.1.2   MTB > cdf;
                  SUBC> binomial 4 0.167.

Cumulative Distribution Function

Binomial with n = 4 and p = 0.167000

x	P(X <= x)
0	0.4815
1	0.8676
2	0.9837
3	0.9992
4	1.0000

For discrete random variables, the cdf can be printed out in its entirety (that is, for every integer) by deleting the argument k and using the command MTB < cdf;. Typical is the output in Figure 3.A.1.2, corresponding to the cdf evaluated in Example 3.4.1.

Also available is an *inverse cdf* command, which in the case of a continuous random variable Y and a specified probability p identifies the value y having the property that $P(Y \le y) = F_Y(Y) = p$. For example, if $p = 0.60$ and Y is an exponential random variable with pdf $f_Y(y) = e^{-y}$, $y > 0$, the value $y = 0.9163$ has the property that $P(Y \le 0.9163) = F_Y(0.9163) = 0.60$. That is,

$$F_Y(0.9163) = \int_0^{0.9163} e^{-y}\, dy = 0.60$$

With MINITAB the number 0.9163 is found by using the command MTB > invcdf 0.60 (see Figure 3.A.1.3).

FIGURE 3.A.1.3   MTB > invcdf 0.60;
                  SUBC> exponential 1.

Inverse Cumulative Distribution Function

Exponential with mean = 1.00000

P(X <= x)	x
0.6000	0.9163

Special Distributions

Lambert Adolphe Jacques Quetelet (1796–1874)

Although he maintained lifelong literary and artistic interests, Quetelet's mathematical talents led him to a doctorate from the University of Ghent and from there to a college teaching position in Brussels. In 1833 he was appointed astronomer at the Brussels Royal Observatory, after having been largely responsible for its founding. His work with the Belgian census marked the beginning of his pioneering efforts in what today would be called mathematical sociology. Quetelet was well known throughout Europe in scientific and literary circles: At the time of his death he was a member of more than 100 learned societies.

4.1 INTRODUCTION

To "qualify" as a probability model, a function defined over a sample space S needs to satisfy only two criteria: (1) It must be nonnegative for all outcomes in S, and (2) it must sum or integrate to 1. That means, for example, that $f_Y(y) = \dfrac{y}{4} + \dfrac{7y^3}{2}$, $0 \le y \le 1$ can be considered a pdf because $f_Y(y) \ge 0$ for all $0 \le y \le 1$ and $\displaystyle\int_0^1 \left(\frac{y}{4} + \frac{7y^3}{2} \right) dy = 1$.

It certainly does not follow, though, that every $f_Y(y)$ and $p_X(k)$ that satisfy these two criteria would actually be used as probability models. A pdf has practical significance only if it does, indeed, model the probabilistic behavior of real-world phenomena. In point of fact, only a handful of functions do [and $f_Y(y) = \dfrac{y}{4} + \dfrac{7y^3}{2}$, $0 \le y \le 1$ is not one of them!].

Whether a probability function—say, $f_Y(y)$—adequately models a given phenomenon ultimately depends on whether the physical factors that influence the value of Y parallel the mathematical assumptions implicit in $f_Y(y)$. Surprisingly, many measurements (i.e., random variables) that seem to be very different are actually the consequence of the same set of assumptions (and will, therefore, be modeled by the same pdf). That said, it makes sense to single out these "real-world" pdf's and investigate their properties in more detail. This, of course, is not an idea we are seeing for the first time—recall the attention given to the binomial and hypergeometric distributions in Section 3.4.

Chapter 4 continues in the spirit of Section 3.4 by examining five other widely used models. Three of the five are discrete; the other two are continuous. One of the continuous pdf's is the normal (or Gaussian) distribution, which, by far, is the most important of all probability models. As we will see, the normal "curve" figures prominently in every chapter from this point on.

Examples play a major role in Chapter 4. The only way to appreciate fully the generality of a probability model is to look at some of its specific applications. Included in this chapter are case studies ranging from the discovery of alpha-particle radiation to an early ESP experiment to an analysis of pregnancy durations to counting bug parts in peanut butter.

4.2 THE POISSON DISTRIBUTION

The binomial distribution problems that appeared in Section 3.4 all had relatively small values for n, so evaluating $p_X(k) = P(X = k) = \dbinom{n}{k} p^k (1 - p)^{n-k}$ was not particularly difficult. But suppose n were 1000 and k, 500. Evaluating $p_X(500)$ would be a formidable task for many hand-held calculators, even today. Two hundred years ago, the prospect of doing cumbersome binomial calculations *by hand* was a catalyst for mathematicians to develop some easy-to-use approximations. One of the first such approximations was the *Poisson limit*, which eventually gave rise to the *Poisson distribution*. Both are described in Section 4.2.

Simeon Denis Poisson (1781–1840) was an eminent French mathematician and physicist, an academic administrator of some note, and, according to an 1826 letter from the mathematician Abel to a friend, a man who knew "how to behave with a great deal of dignity." One of Poisson's many interests was the application of probability to the law, and in 1837 he wrote *Recherches sur la Probabilite de Jugements*. Included in the latter is a limit for $p_X(k) = \binom{n}{k} p^k (1 - p)^{n-k}$ that holds when n approaches ∞, p approaches 0, and np remains constant. In practice, Poisson's limit is used to approximate hard-to-calculate binomial probabilities where the values of n and p reflect the conditions of the limit—that is, when n is large and p is small.

The Poisson Limit

Deriving an asymptotic expression for the binomial probability model is a straightforward exercise in calculus, given that np is to remain fixed as n increases.

THEOREM 4.2.1. If $n \to \infty$ and $p \to 0$ in such a way that $\lambda = np$ remains constant, then for any nonnegative integer k,

$$\lim_{n \to \infty} \binom{n}{k} p^k (1 - p)^{n-k} = \frac{e^{-np}(np)^k}{k!}$$

Proof. We begin by rewriting the binomial probability in terms of λ:

$$\lim_{n \to \infty} \binom{n}{k} p^k (1 - p)^{n-k} = \lim_{n \to \infty} \binom{n}{k} \left(\frac{\lambda}{n}\right)^k \left(1 - \frac{\lambda}{n}\right)^{n-k}$$

$$= \lim_{n \to \infty} \frac{n!}{k!(n - k)!} \lambda^k \left(\frac{1}{n^k}\right) \left(1 - \frac{\lambda}{n}\right)^{-k} \left(1 - \frac{\lambda}{n}\right)^n$$

$$= \frac{\lambda^k}{k!} \lim_{n \to \infty} \frac{n!}{(n - k)!} \frac{1}{(n - \lambda)^k} \left(1 - \frac{\lambda}{n}\right)^n$$

But since $\left[1 - (\lambda/n)\right]^n \to e^{-\lambda}$ as $n \to \infty$, we need only show that

$$\frac{n!}{(n - k)!(n - \lambda)^k} \to 1$$

to prove the theorem. However, note that

$$\frac{n!}{(n - k)!(n - \lambda)^k} = \frac{n(n - 1) \cdots (n - k + 1)}{(n - \lambda)(n - \lambda) \cdots (n - \lambda)}$$

a quantity that, indeed, tends to 1 as $n \to \infty$.

EXAMPLE 4.2.1

Tables 4.2.1 and 4.2.2 give an indication of the *rate* at which

$$\binom{n}{k} p^k (1 - p)^{n-k}$$

converges to

$$\frac{e^{-np}(np)^k}{k!}$$

In both cases $\lambda = np$ is equal to 1, but in the former, n is set equal to 5—in the latter, to 100. We see in Table 4.2.1 ($n = 5$) that for some k the agreement between the binomial probability and Poisson's limit is not very good. If n is as large as 100, though (Table 4.2.2), the agreement is remarkably good for all k.

TABLE 4.2.1 Binomial Probabilities and Poisson Limits; $n = 5$ and $p = \frac{1}{5}(\lambda = 1)$

k	$\binom{5}{k}(0.2)^k(0.8)^{5-k}$	$\dfrac{e^{-1}(1)^k}{k!}$
0	0.328	0.368
1	0.410	0.368
2	0.205	0.184
3	0.051	0.061
4	0.006	0.015
5	0.000	0.003
6+	0	0.001
	1.000	1.000

TABLE 4.2.2 Binomial Probabilities and Poisson Limits; $n = 100$ and $p = \frac{1}{100}(\lambda = 1)$

k	$\binom{100}{k}(0.01)^k(0.99)^{100-k}$	$\dfrac{e^{-1}(1)^k}{k!}$
0	0.366032	0.367879
1	0.369730	0.367879
2	0.184865	0.183940
3	0.060999	0.061313
4	0.014942	0.015328
5	0.002898	0.003066
6	0.000463	0.000511
7	0.000063	0.000073
8	0.000007	0.000009
9	0.000001	0.000001
10	0.000000	0.000000
	1.000000	0.999999

EXAMPLE 4.2.2

Shadyrest Hospital draws its patients from a rural area that has 12,000 elderly residents. The probability that any one of the 12,000 will have a heart attack on any given day and will need to be connected to a special cardiac monitoring machine has been estimated to be 1 in 8000. Currently, the hospital has three such machines. What is the probability that that equipment will be inadequate to meet tomorrow's emergencies?

Let X denote the number of residents who will need the cardiac machine tomorrow. Note that X is a binomial random variable based on a large $n(= 12,000)$ and a small $p(= 1/8000)$. As such, Poisson's limit can be used to approximate $p_X(k)$ for any k. In particular,

$P(\text{Shadyrest's cardiac facilities are inadequate}) = P(X > 3)$

$$= 1 - P(X \leq 3)$$

$$= 1 - \sum_{k=0}^{3} \binom{12,000}{k}\left(\frac{1}{8000}\right)^k\left(\frac{7999}{8000}\right)^{12,000-k}$$

$$\doteq 1 - \sum_{k=0}^{3} \frac{e^{-1.5}(1.5)^k}{k!}$$

$$= 0.0656$$

where $\lambda = np = 12,000(1/8000) = 1.5$. On the average, then, Shadyrest will not be able to meet all the cardiac needs of its clientele once every 15 or 16 days. (Based on the binomial and Poisson limit comparisons shown on page 248, we would expect the approximation here to be excellent—$n(= 12{,}000)$ is much larger and $p(= \frac{1}{8000})$ is much smaller than their counterparts in Table 4.2.2, so the conditions of Theorem 4.2.1 are more nearly satisfied.)

CASE STUDY 4.2.1

Leukemia is a rare form of cancer whose cause and mode of transmission remain largely unknown. While evidence abounds that excessive exposure to radiation can increase a person's risk of contracting the disease, it is at the same time true that most cases occur among persons whose history contains no such overexposure. A related issue, one maybe even more basic than the causality question, concerns the *spread* of the disease. It is safe to say that the prevailing medical opinion is that most forms of leukemia are not contagious— still, the hypothesis persists that some forms of the disease, particularly the childhood variety, may be. What continues to fuel this speculation are the discoveries of so-called "leukemia clusters," aggregations in time and space of unusually large numbers of cases.

To date, one of the most frequently cited leukemia clusters in the medical literature occurred during the late 1950s and early 1960s in Niles, Illinois, a suburb of Chicago (68). In the $5\frac{1}{3}$-year period from 1956 to the first four months of 1961, physicians in Niles reported a total of eight cases of leukemia among children less than 15 years of age. The number at risk (that is, the number of residents in that age range) was 7076. To assess the likelihood of that many cases occurring in such a small population, it is necessary to look first at the leukemia incidence in neighboring towns. For all of Cook county, excluding Niles, there were 1,152,695 children less than 15 years of age—and among those, 286 diagnosed cases of leukemia. That gives an average $5\frac{1}{3}$-year leukemia rate of 24.8 cases per 100,000:

$$\frac{286 \text{ cases for } 5\frac{1}{3} \text{ years}}{1{,}152{,}695 \text{ children}} \times \frac{100{,}000}{100{,}000} = 24.8 \text{ cases}/100{,}000 \text{ children in } 5\frac{1}{3} \text{ years}$$

Now, imagine the 7076 children in Niles to be a series of $n = 7076$ (independent) Bernoulli trials, each having a probability of $p = 24.8/100{,}000 = 0.000248$ of contracting leukemia. The question then becomes, given an n of 7076 and a p of 0.000248, how likely is it that eight "successes" would occur? (The expected number, of course, would be $7076 \times 0.000248 = 1.75$.) Actually, for reasons that will be elaborated on in Chapter 6, it will prove more meaningful to consider the related event, eight *or more* cases occurring in a $5\frac{1}{3}$-year span. If the probability associated with the latter is very small, it could be argued that leukemia did not occur randomly in Niles and that, perhaps, contagion was a factor.

Using the binomial distribution, we can express the probability of eight or more cases as

$$P(8 \text{ or more cases}) = \sum_{k=8}^{7076} \binom{7076}{k} (0.000248)^k (0.999752)^{7076-k} \tag{4.2.1}$$

Much of the computational unpleasantness implicit in Equation 4.2.1 can be avoided by appealing to Theorem 4.2.1. Given that $np = 7076 \times 0.000248 = 1.75$,

$$P(X \geq 8) = 1 - P(X \leq 7)$$

$$\doteq 1 - \sum_{k=0}^{7} \frac{e^{-1.75}(1.75)^k}{k!}$$

$$= 1 - 0.99951$$

$$= 0.00049$$

(continued on next page)

(Case Study 4.2.1 continued)

How close can we expect 0.00049 to be to the "true" binomial sum? Very close. Considering the accuracy of the Poisson limit when n is as small as 100 (recall Table 4.2.2), we should feel very confident here, where n is 7076.

Interpreting the 0.00049 probability is not nearly as easy as assessing its accuracy. The fact that the probability is so very small tends to denigrate the hypothesis that leukemia in Niles occurred at random. On the other hand, rare events, such as clusters, *do* happen by chance. The basic difficulty in putting the probability associated with a given cluster in any meaningful perspective is not knowing in how many similar communities leukemia did *not* exhibit a tendency to cluster. That there is no obvious way to do this is one reason the leukemia controversy is still with us.

QUESTIONS

4.2.1 If a typist averages one misspelling in every 3250 words, what are the chances that a 6000-word report is free of all such errors? Answer the question two ways—first, by using an exact binomial analysis, and second, by using a Poisson approximation. Does the similarity (or dissimilarity) of the two answers surprise you? Explain.

4.2.2 A medical study recently documented that 905 mistakes were made among the 289,411 prescriptions written during one year at a large metropolitan teaching hospital. Suppose a patient is admitted with a condition serious enough to warrant 10 different prescriptions. Approximate the probability that at least one will contain an error.

4.2.3 Five hundred people are attending the first annual "I was Hit by Lightning" Club. Approximate the probability that at most one of the 500 was born on Poisson's birthday.

4.2.4 A chromosome mutation linked with colorblindness is known to occur, on the average, once in every 10,000 births.
   (a) Approximate the probability that exactly 3 of the next 20,000 babies born will have the mutation.
   (b) How many babies out of the next 20,000 would have to be born with the mutation to convince you that the "1 in 10,000" estimate is too low? *Hint*: Calculate $P(X \geq k) = 1 - P(X \leq k - 1)$ for various k. (Recall Case Study 4.2.1.)

4.2.5 Suppose that 1% of all items in a supermarket are not priced properly. A customer buys 10 items. What is the probability that she will be delayed by the cashier because one or more of her items requires a price check? Calculate both a binomial answer and a Poisson answer. Is the binomial model "exact" in this case? Explain.

4.2.6 A newly formed life insurance company has underwritten term policies on 120 women between the ages of 40 and 44. Suppose that each woman has a 1/150 probability of dying during the next calendar year, and each death requires the company to pay out $50,000 in benefits. Approximate the probability that the company will have to pay at least $150,000 in benefits next year.

4.2.7 According to an airline industry report, roughly 1 piece of luggage out of every 200 that are checked is lost. Suppose that a frequent-flying businesswoman will be checking 120 bags over the course of the next year. Approximate the probability that she will lose 2 or more pieces of luggage.

4.2.8 Electromagnetic fields generated by power transmission lines are suspected by some researchers to be a cause of cancer. Especially at risk would be telephone linemen because of their frequent proximity to high-voltage wires. According to one study, two cases of a rare form of cancer were detected among a group of 9500 linemen (164). In the general population, the incidence of that particular condition is on the order of one in a million. What would you conclude? *Hint*: Recall the approach taken in Case Study 4.2.1.

4.2.9 Astronomers estimate that as many as 100 billion stars in the Milky Way galaxy are encircled by planets. If so, we may have a plethora of cosmic neighbors. Let p denote the probability that any such solar system contains intelligent life. How small can p be and still give a 50-50 chance that we are not alone?

The Poisson Distribution

The real significance of Poisson's limit theorem went unrecognized for more than 50 years. For most of the latter part of the nineteenth century, Theorem 4.2.1 was taken strictly at face value: It provided a convenient approximation for $p_X(k)$ when X is binomial, n is large, and p is small. But then in 1898 a German professor, Ladislaus von Bortkiewicz, published a monograph entitled *Das Gesetz der Kleinen Zahlen (The Law of Small Numbers)* that would quickly transform Poisson's "limit" into Poisson's "distribution."

What is best remembered about Bortkiewicz's monograph is the curious set of data described in Question 4.2.10. The measurements recorded were the numbers of Prussian cavalry soldiers who were kicked to death by their horses. In analyzing those figures, Bortkiewicz was able to show that the function $e^{-\lambda}\lambda^k/k!$ is a useful probability model in its own right, even when (1) no explicit binomial random variable is present and (2) values for n and p are unavailable. Other researchers were quick to follow Bortkiewicz's lead, and a steady stream of Poisson distribution applications began showing up in technical journals. Today the function $p_X(k) = e^{-\lambda}\lambda^k/k!$ is universally recognized as being among the three or four most important data models in all of statistics.

THEOREM 4.2.2.   The random variable X is said to have a *Poisson distribution* if

$$p_X(k) = P(X = k) = \frac{e^{-\lambda}\lambda^k}{k!}, \quad k = 0, 1, 2, \ldots$$

where λ is a positive constant. Also, for any Poisson random variable, $E(X) = \lambda$ and $\text{Var}(X) = \lambda$.

Proof.   To show that $p_X(k)$ qualifies as a probability function, note, first of all, that $p_X(k) \geq 0$ for all nonnegative integers k. Also, $p_X(k)$ sums to 1:

$$p_X(k) = \sum_{k=0}^{\infty} \frac{e^{-\lambda}\lambda^k}{k!} = e^{-\lambda}\sum_{k=0}^{\infty} \frac{\lambda^k}{k!} = e^{-\lambda} \cdot e^{\lambda} = 1$$

since $\sum_{k=0}^{\infty} \dfrac{\lambda^k}{k!}$ is the Taylor series expansion of e^{λ}.

The expected value for X can be obtained by direct summation:

$$E(X) = \sum_{k=0}^{\infty} k \cdot p_X(k)$$

$$= \sum_{k=0}^{\infty} k \cdot \frac{e^{-\lambda}\lambda^k}{k!}$$

$$= \lambda \sum_{k=1}^{\infty} \frac{e^{-\lambda}\lambda^{k-1}}{(k-1)!}$$

$$= \lambda \sum_{j=0}^{\infty} \frac{e^{-\lambda}\lambda^j}{j!} = \lambda \cdot 1 = \lambda$$

where $j = k - 1$. The proof that $\text{Var}(X) = \lambda$ is done in a similar fashion. (Recall that both of these results were established using moment-generating functions in Chapter 3—see Question 3.16.9.)

Fitting the Poisson Distribution to Data

Poisson data invariably refer to the numbers of times a predefined event occurs during a series of specified "units" (often time or space). For example, X_i might be the number of traffic accidents reported at a given intersection during Week i. If such records are kept for an entire year, the resulting data set would be the sample $X_1, X_2, \ldots, X_{52}$, where each X_i is a nonnegative integer.

Whether or not a set of X_i's can be viewed as Poisson data depends on whether the proportions of 0's, 1's, 2's, and so on *in the sample* are numerically similar to the probabilities that $X = 0, 1, 2$, and so on, as predicted by $p_X(k) = e^{-\lambda}\lambda^k/k!$. The next two case studies show data sets where the variability in the observed X_i's *is* consistent with the probabilities predicted by the Poisson distribution. Notice in each case that the parameter λ in $p_X(k)$ is replaced by the average value of the X_i's—that is, by $\frac{1}{n}\sum_{i=1}^{n} x_i$. The justification for making that substitution will be explored in Chapter 5.

CASE STUDY 4.2.2

Among the early research projects investigating the nature of radiation was a 1910 study of α-particle emission by Ernest Rutherford and Hans Geiger (140). For each of 2608 eighth-minute intervals, the two physicists recorded the number of α-particles emitted from a polonium source (as detected by what would eventually be called a Geiger counter). The numbers and proportions of times that k such particles were detected in a given eighth-minute ($k = 0, 1, 2, \ldots$) are detailed in the first three columns of Table 4.2.3. Two α particles, for example, were detected in each of 383 eighth-minute intervals, meaning that $X = 2$ was the observation recorded 15% ($= 383/2608 \times 100$) of the time.

To see whether a probability function of the form $p_X(k) = e^{-\lambda}\lambda^k/k!$ can adequately model the observed proportions in the third column, we first need to replace λ with the sample's average value for X. Suppose the six observations comprising the "11+" category are each assigned the value 11. Then

TABLE 4.2.3

No. Detected, k	Frequency	Proportion	$p_X(k) = e^{-3.87}(3.87)^k/k!$
0	57	0.02	0.02
1	203	0.08	0.08
2	383	0.15	0.16
3	525	0.20	0.20
4	532	0.20	0.20
5	408	0.16	0.15
6	273	0.10	0.10
7	139	0.05	0.05
8	45	0.02	0.03
9	27	0.01	0.01
10	10	0.00	0.00
11+	6	0.00	0.00
	2608	1.0	1.0

$$\bar{x} = \frac{57(0) + 200(1) + 383(2) + \cdots + 6(11)}{2608} = \frac{10,097}{2608}$$

$$= 3.87$$

and the presumed model is $p_X(k) = e^{-3.87}(3.87)^k/k!$, $k = 0, 1, 2, \ldots$. Notice how closely the entries in the fourth column [i.e., $p_X(0)$, $p_X(1)$, $p_X(2),\ldots$] agree with the sample proportions appearing in the third column. The conclusion here is inescapable: The phenomenon of radiation can be modeled very effectively by the Poisson distribution.

CASE STUDY 4.2.3

Table 4.2.4 gives the numbers of fumbles made by 110 Division IA football teams during a recent weekend's slate of 55 games (95). Do the data support the contention that the number of fumbles, X, that a team makes during a game is a Poisson random variable?

TABLE 4.2.4

2	1	2	2	3	1	3	4	3	4	5
5	2	1	3	2	5	2	4	1	2	2
1	0	4	2	4	1	2	0	2	0	3
0	1	2	0	1	2	2	3	5	1	3
2	3	4	5	4	3	6	0	3	1	2
1	2	2	1	2	1	3	2	4	2	4
4	2	0	5	4	3	6	5	3	5	1
3	1	1	3	1	4	3	1	5	1	2
1	3	4	4	4	2	7	4	2	5	3
1	3	6	2	1	1	4	1	2	3	0

The first step in summarizing these data is to tally the frequencies and calculate the sample proportions associated with each value of X (see Columns 1–3 of Table 4.2.5). Notice, also, that the average number of fumbles per team is 2.55:

(continued on next page)

(Case Study 4.2.3 continued)

TABLE 4.2.5

No. of Fumbles, k	Frequency	Proportion	$p_X(k) = e^{-2.55}(2.55)^k/k!$
0	8	0.07	0.08
1	24	0.22	0.20
2	27	0.25	0.25
3	20	0.18	0.22
4	17	0.16	0.14
5	10	0.09	0.07
6	3	0.03	0.03
7+	1	0.01	0.01
	110	1.0	1.0

$$\bar{x} = \frac{8(0) + 24(1) + 27(2) + \cdots + 1(7)}{110}$$

$$= 2.55$$

Substituting 2.55 for λ, then, gives $p_X(k) = e^{-2.55}(2.55)^k/k!$ as the particular Poisson model most likely to fit the data.

The fourth column of Table 4.2.5 shows $p_X(k)$ evaluated for each of the eight values listed for k: $p_X(0) = e^{-2.55}(2.55)^0/0! = 0.08$, and so on. Once again, the row-by-row agreement is quite strong. There appears to be nothing in these data that would refute the presumption that the number of fumbles a team makes is a Poisson random variable.

The Poisson Model: The Law of Small Numbers

Given that the expression $e^{-\lambda}\lambda^k/k!$ models phenomena as diverse as α-radiation and football fumbles raises an obvious question: *Why* is that same $p_X(k)$ describing such different random variables? The answer, of course, is that the underlying physical conditions that produce those two sets of measurements are actually much the same, despite how superficially different the resulting data may seem to be. Both phenomena are examples of a set of mathematical assumptions known as the *Poisson model*. Any measurements that are derived from conditions that mirror those assumptions will necessarily vary in accordance with the Poisson distribution.

Consider, for example, the number of fumbles that a football team makes during the course of a game. Imagine dividing a time interval of length T into n non-overlapping subintervals, each of length $\dfrac{T}{n}$, where n is large (see Figure 4.2.1).

Suppose that

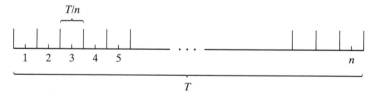

FIGURE 4.2.1

1. The probability that two or more fumbles occur in any given subinterval is essentially 0.

2. Fumbles are independent events.

3. The probability that a fumble occurs during a given subinterval is constant over the entire interval from 0 to T.

The n subintervals, then, are analogous to the n independent trials that form the backdrop for the "binomial model": In each subinterval there will be either 0 fumbles or 1 fumble, where

$$p_n = P(\text{fumble occurs in a given subinterval})$$

remains constant from subinterval to subinterval.

Let the random variable X denote the total number of fumbles a team makes during time T, and let λ denote the *rate* at which a team fumbles (e.g., λ might be expressed as 0.10 fumbles per minute). Then

$$E(X) = \lambda T = np_n \quad \text{(why?)}$$

which implies that $p_n = \dfrac{\lambda T}{n}$. From Theorem 4.2.1, then,

$$
\begin{aligned}
p_x(k) = P(X = k) &= \binom{n}{k}\left(\frac{\lambda T}{n}\right)^k\left(1 - \frac{\lambda T}{n}\right)^{n-k} \\
&\doteq \frac{e^{-n(\lambda T/n)}\left[n(\lambda T/n)\right]^k}{k!} \\
&= \frac{e^{-\lambda T}(\lambda T)^k}{k!}
\end{aligned}
\tag{4.2.2}
$$

So, if a team fumbles at the rate of, say, 0.10 times per minute and they have the ball for 30 minutes during a game, $\lambda T = (0.1)(30) = 3.0$, and the probability that they fumble exactly k times is approximated by the pdf, $p_X(k) = e^{-3.0}(3.0)^k/k!, k = 0, 1, 2 \ldots$.

Now we can see more clearly why Poisson's "limit," as given in Theorem 4.2.1, is so important. The three Poisson model assumptions listed at the top of the page for football fumbles are so unexceptional that they apply to countless real-world phenomena. Each time they do, the pdf $P_X(k) = e^{-\lambda T}(\lambda T)^k/k!$ finds another application.

Calculating Poisson Probabilities

In practice, calculating Poisson probabilities is an exercise in choosing T so that λT represents the expected number of occurrences in whatever "unit" is associated with the random variable X. They look different, but the pdf's $p_X(k) = e^{-\lambda}\lambda^k/k!$ and $p_X(k) = e^{-\lambda T}(\lambda T)^k/k!$ are exactly the same and will give identical values for $P(X = k)$ once λ and T are properly defined.

EXAMPLE 4.2.3

Suppose that typographical errors are made at the rate of 0.4 per page in State Tech's campus newspaper. If next Tuesday's edition is 16 pages long, what is the probability that fewer than 3 typos will appear?

We start by defining X to be the number of errors that will appear *in 16 pages*. The assumptions of independence and constant probability are not unreasonable in this setting, so X is likely to be a Poisson random variable. To answer the question using the formula in Theorem 4.2.2, we need to set λ equal to $E(X)$. But if the error rate is 0.4 errors/page, the expected number of typos in 16 pages will be *6.4*:

$$0.4 \frac{\text{errors}}{\text{page}} \times 16 \text{ pages} = 6.4 \text{ errors}$$

It follows, then, that

$$P(X < 3) = P(X \le 2) = \sum_{k=0}^{2} \frac{e^{-6.4}(6.4)^k}{k!}$$

$$= \frac{e^{-6.4}(6.4)^0}{0!} + \frac{e^{-6.4}(6.4)^1}{1!} + \frac{e^{-6.4}(6.4)^2}{2!}$$

$$= 0.046$$

If Equation 4.2.2 is used, we would define

$$\lambda = 0.4 \text{ errors/page}$$

and

$$T = 16 \text{ pages}$$

Then $\lambda T = E(X) = 6.4$ and $(X < 3)$ would be $\sum_{k=0}^{2} e^{-6.4}(6.4)^k/k!$, the same numerical value found from Theorem 4.2.2.

EXAMPLE 4.2.4

Entomologists estimate that an average person consumes almost a pound of bug parts each year (163). There are that many insect eggs, larvae, and miscellaneous body pieces in the foods we eat and the liquids we drink. The Food and Drug Administration (FDA) sets a Food Defect Action Level (FDAL) for each product: Bug-part concentrations below the FDAL are considered acceptable. The legal limit for peanut butter, for example, is 30 insect fragments per 100 grams. Suppose the crackers you just bought from a vending machine are spread with 20 g of peanut butter. What are the chances that that snack will include at least 5 crunchy critters?

Let X denote the number of bug parts in 20 g of peanut butter. Assuming the worst, we will set the contamination level equal to the FDA limit—that is, 30 fragments/100 g (or 0.30 fragments/g). Notice that $E(X) = 6.0$:

$$\frac{0.30 \text{ fragments}}{\text{g}} \times 20 \text{ g} = 6.0 \text{ fragments}$$

It follows, then, that the probability that your snack contains 5 or more bug parts is a disgusting *0.71*:

$$P(X \geq 5) = 1 - P(X \leq 4) = 1 - \sum_{k=0}^{4} \frac{e^{-6.0}(6.0)^k}{k!}$$

$$= 1 - 0.2851$$

$$= 0.71$$

Bon appetit!

EXAMPLE 4.2.5

Suppose that X_1 and X_2 are independent Poisson random variables such that $E(X_1) = \lambda_1$ and $E(X_2) = \lambda_2$. Let $X = X_1 + X_2$. Show that X is a Poisson random variable with $E(X) = \lambda_1 + \lambda_2$.

We begin by writing the pdf for X as a convolution of X_1 and X_2:

$$p_X(k) = P(X = k) = P(X_1 + X_2 = k)$$

$$= \sum_{r=0}^{k} P(X_1 = r) \cdot P(X_2 = k - r)$$

$$= \sum_{r=0}^{k} \frac{e^{-\lambda_1}\lambda_1^r}{r!} \cdot \frac{e^{-\lambda_2}\lambda_2^{k-r}}{(k-r)!}$$

$$= e^{-(\lambda_1+\lambda_2)} \sum_{r=0}^{k} \frac{\lambda_1^r \lambda_2^{k-r}}{r!(k-r)!} \qquad (4.2.3)$$

Earlier we had occasion to mention Newton's binomial expansion (recall the comment after Theorem 2.9.3). Applying that result here enables us to evaluate a sum similar to the one that appears in Equation 4.2.3:

$$(\lambda_1 + \lambda_2)^k = \sum_{r=0}^{k} \frac{k!}{r!(k-r)!} \lambda_1^r \lambda_2^{k-r}$$

It follows, then, that

$$p_X(k) = \frac{e^{-(\lambda_1+\lambda_2)}(\lambda_1 + \lambda_2)^k}{k!}, \quad k = 0, 1, 2, \ldots$$

which implies that (1) X is Poisson and (2) $E(X) = \lambda_1 + \lambda_2$.

Comment. The fact that the sum of two independent Poissons is Poisson can also be established using moment-generating functions. If X is a Poisson random variable for which $E(X) = \lambda$,

$$M_X(t) = E(e^{tX}) = \sum_{k=0}^{\infty} e^{tk} \cdot \frac{e^{-\lambda}\lambda^k}{k!}$$

$$= e^{-\lambda} \sum_{k=0}^{\infty} \frac{(\lambda e^t)^k}{k!} = e^{-\lambda} \cdot e^{-\lambda} \cdot e^{\lambda e^t}$$

$$= e^{-\lambda + \lambda e^t}$$

Furthermore, if X_1 and X_2 are two independent Poisson random variables with parameters λ_1 and λ_2, respectively, and if $X = X_1 + X_2$, then

$$M_X(t) = M_{X_1}(t) \cdot M_{X_2}(t) \qquad \text{(from Theorem 3.16.3)}$$

$$= e^{-\lambda_1 + \lambda_1 e^t} \cdot e^{-\lambda_2 + \lambda_2 e^t}$$

$$= e^{-(\lambda_1 + \lambda_2) + (\lambda_1 + \lambda_2)e^t}$$

and we recognize the latter to be the moment-generating function for a Poisson random variable whose expected value is $\lambda_1 + \lambda_2$.

QUESTIONS

4.2.10 During the latter part of the nineteenth century, Prussian officials gathered information relating to the hazards that horses posed to cavalry soldiers. A total of 10 cavalry corps were monitored over a period of 20 years. Recorded for each year and each corps was X, the annual number of fatalities due to kicks. Summarized in the following table are the 200 values recorded for X (13). Show that these data can be modeled by a Poisson pdf. Follow the procedure illustrated in Case Studies 4.2.2 and 4.2.3.

No. of Deaths, k	Observed Number of Corps-Years in Which k Fatalities Occurred
0	109 —
1	65 —
2	22 —
3	3
4	1
	200

4.2.11 A random sample of 356 seniors enrolled at the University of West Florida was categorized according to X, the number of times they had changed majors (100). Based on the summary of that information shown in the following table, would you conclude that X can be treated as a Poisson random variable?

Number of Major Changes	Frequency
0	237
1	90
2	22
3	7

4.2.12 Midwestern Skies books 10 commuter flights each week. Passenger totals are much the same from week to week, as are the numbers of pieces of luggage that are checked. Listed in the following table are the numbers of bags that were lost during each of the first 40 weeks in 1997. Do these figures support the presumption that the number of bags lost by Midwestern during a typical week is a Poisson random variable?

Week	Bags Lost	Week	Bags Lost	Week	Bags Lost
1	1	14	2	27	1
2	0	15	1	28	2
3	0	16	3	29	0
4	3	17	0	30	0
5	4	18	2	31	1
6	1	19	5	32	3
7	0	20	2	33	1
8	2	21	1	34	2
9	0	22	1	35	0
10	2	23	1	36	1
11	3	24	2	37	4
12	1	25	1	38	2
13	2	26	3	39	1
				40	0

4.2.13 The following are the daily numbers of death notices for women over the age of 80 that appeared in the London *Times* over a three-year period (66).

Number of Deaths	Observed Frequency
0	162
1	267
2	271
3	185
4	111
5	61
6	27
7	8
8	3
9	1
	1096

(a) Does the Poisson pdf provide a good description of the variability pattern evident in these data?

(b) If your answer to Part (a) is "no," which of the Poisson model assumptions do you think might not be holding?

4.2.14 A certain species of European mite is capable of damaging the bark on orange trees. The following are the results of inspections done on 100 saplings chosen at random from a large orchard. The measurement recorded, X, is the number of mite infestations found on the trunk of each tree. Is it reasonable to assume that X is a Poisson random variable? If not, which of the Poisson model assumptions is likely not to be true?

No. of Infestations, k	No. of Trees
0	55
1	20
2	21
3	1
4	1
5	1
6	0
7	1

4.2.15 A tool and die press that stamps out cams used in small gasoline engines tends to break down once every five hours. The machine can be repaired and put back on line quickly, but each such incident costs $50. What is the probability that maintenance expenses for the press will be no more than $100 on a typical eight-hour workday?

4.2.16 In a new fiber optic communication system, transmission errors occur at the rate of 1.5 per 10 seconds. What is the probability that more than two errors will occur during the next half-minute?

4.2.17 Assume that the number of hits, X, that a baseball team makes in a nine-inning game has a Poisson distribution. If the probability that a team makes zero hits is 1/3, what are their chances of getting two or more hits?

4.2.18 Flaws in metal sheeting produced by a high-temperature roller occur at the rate of one per 10 square feet. What is the probability that three or more flaws will appear in a 5-by-8-foot panel?

4.2.19 Suppose a radioactive source is metered for two hours, during which time the total number of alpha particles counted is 482. What is the probability that exactly three particles will be counted in the next two minutes? Answer the question two ways—first, by defining X to be the number of particles counted in two minutes, and second, by defining X to be the number of particles counted in one minute.

4.2.20 Suppose that on-the-job injuries in a textile mill occur at the rate of 0.1 per day.
   (a) What is the probability that two accidents will occur during the next (five-day) work week?
   (b) Is the probability that four accidents will occur over the next two work weeks the square of your answer to Part (a)? Explain.

4.2.21 Find $P(X = 4)$ if the random variable X has a Poisson distribution such that $P(X = 1) = P(X = 2)$.

4.2.22 Let X be a Poisson random variable with parameter λ. Show that the probability that X is even is $\frac{1}{2}(1 + e^{-2\lambda})$.

4.2.23 Let X_1 and X_2 be two independent Poisson random variables, each with expected value equal to 2. Let $X = X_1 + X_2$. Show that the conditional pdf of X_1 given that $X = x$ is binomial.

4.2.24 If X_1 is a Poisson random variable for which $E(X_1) = \lambda$ and if the conditional pdf of X_2 given that $X_1 = x_1$ is binomial with parameters x_1 and p, show that the marginal pdf of X_2 is Poisson with $E(X_2) = \lambda p$.

Intervals Between Events: The Poisson/Exponential Relationship

Situations sometimes arise where the time interval between consecutively occurring events is an important random variable. Imagine being responsible for the maintenance on a network of computers. Clearly, the number of technicians you would need to employ in order to be capable of responding to service calls in a timely fashion would be a function of the "waiting time" from one breakdown to another.

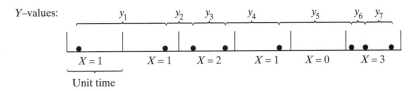

FIGURE 4.2.2

Figure 4.2.2 shows the relationship between the random variables X and Y, where X denotes the number of occurrences in a unit of time and Y denotes the interval between consecutive occurrences. Pictured are six intervals: $X = 0$ on one occasion, $X = 1$ on three occasions, $X = 2$ once, and $X = 3$ once. Resulting from those eight occurrences are seven measurements on the random variable Y. Obviously, the pdf for Y will depend on the pdf for X. One particularly important special case of that dependence is the Poisson/exponential relationship outlined in Theorem 4.2.3.

THEOREM 4.2.3.   Suppose a series of events satisfying the Poisson model are occurring at the rate of λ per unit time. Let the random variable Y denote the interval between consecutive events. Then Y has the exponential distribution

$$f_Y(y) = \lambda e^{-\lambda y}, \quad y > 0$$

Proof.   Suppose an event has occurred at time a. Consider the interval that extends from a to $a + y$. Since the (Poisson) events are occurring at the rate of λ per unit time, the probability that no outcomes will occur in the interval $(a, a + y)$ is $\dfrac{e^{-\lambda y}(\lambda y)^0}{0!} = e^{-\lambda y}$. Define the random variable Y to denote the interval between consecutive occurrences. Notice that there will be no occurrences in the interval $(a, a + y)$ only if $Y > y$. Therefore,

$$P(Y > y) = e^{-\lambda y}$$

or, equivalently,

$$P(Y \le y) = 1 - P(Y > y) = 1 - e^{-\lambda y}$$

Let $f_Y(y)$ be the (unknown) pdf for Y. It must be true that

$$P(Y \le y) = \int_0^y f_Y(t)\, dt$$

Taking derivatives of the two expressions for $P(Y \le y)$, we can write

$$\frac{d}{dy} \int_0^y f_Y(t)\, dt = \frac{d}{dy}(1 - e^{-\lambda y})$$

which implies that

$$f_Y(y) = \lambda e^{-\lambda y}, \quad y > 0$$

CASE STUDY 4.2.4

Over "short" geological periods, a volcano's eruptions are believed to be Poisson events—that is, they are thought to occur independently and at a constant rate. If so, the pdf describing the intervals between eruptions should have the form $f_Y(y) = \lambda e^{-\lambda y}$. Collected for the purpose of testing that presumption are the data in Table 4.2.6, showing the intervals (in months) that elapsed between 37 consecutive eruptions of Mauna Loa, a 14,000-foot volcano in Hawaii (97). During the period covered—1832 to 1950—eruptions were occurring at the rate of $\lambda = 0.027$ per month (or once every 3.1 years). Is the variability in these 36 y_i's consistent with the statement of Theorem 4.2.3?

TABLE 4.2.6

126	73	3	6	37	23
73	23	2	65	94	51
26	21	6	68	16	20
6	18	6	41	40	18
41	11	12	38	77	61
26	3	38	50	91	12

To answer that question requires that the data be reduced to a density-scaled histogram and superimposed on a graph of the predicted exponential pdf (recall Case Study 2.5.1). Table 4.2.7 details the construction of the histogram. Notice in Figure 4.2.3 that the shape of that histogram *is* entirely consistent with the theoretical model—$f_Y(y) = 0.027e^{-0.027y}$—stated in Theorem 4.2.3.

TABLE 4.2.7

Interval (mos), y	Frequency	Density
$0 \le y < 20$	13	0.0181
$20 \le y < 40$	9	0.0125
$40 \le y < 60$	5	0.0069
$60 \le y < 80$	6	0.0083
$80 \le y < 100$	2	0.0028
$100 \le y < 120$	0	0.0000
$120 \le y < 140$	1	0.0014
	36	

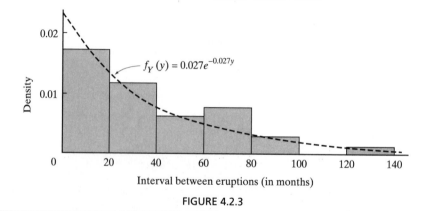

FIGURE 4.2.3

EXAMPLE 4.2.6

Among the most famous of all meteor showers are the Perseids, which occur each year in early August. In some areas the frequency of visible Perseids can be as high as 40 per hour. Given that such sightings are Poisson events, calculate the probability that an observer who has just seen a meteor will have to wait at least five minutes before seeing another.

Let the random variable Y denote the interval (in minutes) between consecutive sightings. Expressed in the units of Y, the *40 per hour* rate of visible Perseids becomes *0.67 per minute*. A straightforward integration, then, shows that the probability is *0.036* that an observer will have to wait five minutes or more to see another meteor:

$$
\begin{aligned}
P(Y > 5) &= \int_5^\infty 0.67 e^{-0.67y}\, dy \\
&= \int_{3.33}^\infty e^{-u}\, du \quad \text{(where } u = 0.67y) \\
&= -e^{-u}\Big|_{3.33}^\infty = e^{-3.33} \\
&= 0.036
\end{aligned}
$$

QUESTIONS

4.2.25 Suppose that commercial airplane crashes in a certain country occur at the rate of 2.5 per year.
(a) Is it reasonable to assume that such crashes are Poisson events? Explain.
(b) What is the probability that four or more crashes will occur next year?
(c) What is the probability that the next two crashes will occur within three months of one another?

4.2.26 Records show that deaths occur at the rate of 0.1 per day among patients residing in a large nursing home. If someone dies today, what are the chances that a week or more will elapse before another death occurs?

4.2.27 Suppose that Y_1 and Y_2 are independent exponential random variables, each having pdf $f_Y(y)=\lambda e^{-\lambda y}$, $y > 0$. If $Y = Y_1 + Y_2$, it can be shown that

$$
f_{Y_1+Y_2}(y) = \lambda^2 y e^{-\lambda y}, \quad y > 0
$$

Recall Case Study 4.2.4. What is the probability that the next three eruptions of Mauna Loa will be less than 40 months apart?

4.2.28 Fifty spotlights have just been installed in an outdoor security system. According to the manufacturer's specifications, these particular lights are expected to burn out at the rate of 1.1 per 100 hours. What is the expected number of bulbs that will fail to last for at least 75 hours?

4.3   THE NORMAL DISTRIBUTION

The Poisson limit described in Section 4.2 was not the only, or even the first, approximation developed for the purpose of facilitating the calculation of binomial probabilities. Early in the eighteenth century, Abraham DeMoivre proved that areas under the curve $f_Z(z) = \dfrac{1}{\sqrt{2\pi}} e^{-z^2/2}$, $-\infty < z < \infty$ can be used to estimate

$$P\left(a \le \frac{X - np}{\sqrt{np(1-p)}} \le b\right),$$ where X is a binomial random variable and n is large.

Figure 4.3.1 illustrates the central idea in DeMoivre's discovery. Listed in Figure 4.3.1a is a random sample of 50 observations representing a binomial random variable for which $n = 60$ and $p = P(\text{success}) = 0.40$ (the MINITAB syntax for generating these numbers is outlined in Appendix 4.A.1). In Figure 4.3.1b are the corresponding values of $Z = \dfrac{X - np}{\sqrt{np(1-p)}}$; in this case, $Z = \dfrac{X - 24}{\sqrt{14.4}}$. A density-scaled histogram (recall Case Study 2.5.1) summarizing the latter is shown in Figure 4.3.1c. Superimposed over the histogram is the function $f_Z(z) = \dfrac{1}{\sqrt{2\pi}} e^{-z^2/2}$,

(a)

27	29	23	22	21	21	22
26	26	20	26	25	27	32
22	27	22	20	19	19	21
23	28	23	27	29	13	24
22	25	25	20	25	26	15
24	17	28	21	16	24	22
25	25	21	23	23	20	25
30						

(b) Z-ratio

0.79057	1.31762	−0.26352	−0.52705	−0.79057	−0.79057	−0.52705
0.52705	0.52705	−1.05409	0.52705	0.26352	0.79057	2.10819
−0.52705	0.79057	−0.52705	−1.05409	−1.31762	−1.31762	−0.79057
−0.26352	1.05409	−0.26352	0.79057	1.31762	−2.89875	0.00000
−0.52705	0.26352	0.26352	−1.05409	0.26352	0.52705	−2.37171
0.00000	−1.84466	1.05409	−0.79057	−2.10819	0.00000	−0.52705
0.26352	0.26352	−0.79057	−0.26352	−0.26352	−1.05409	0.26352
1.58114						

(c)

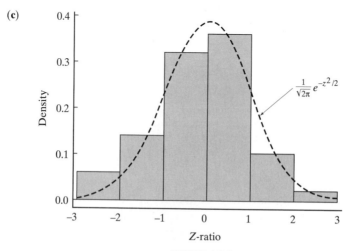

FIGURE 4.3.1

$-\infty < z < \infty$. Clearly, the curve is modeling quite well the variation associated with the ratio $\dfrac{X - 24}{\sqrt{14.4}}$.

The formal statement of the approximation suggested in Figure 4.3.1 is known as the *DeMoivre-Laplace limit theorem*. Laplace is credited with generalizing DeMoivre's original idea and bringing it to the full attention of the mathematics community by including it in his influential 1812 book, *Theorie Analytique des Probabilites*.

THEOREM 4.3.1. Let X be a binomial random variable defined on n independent trials for which $p = P(\text{success})$. For any numbers a and b,

$$\lim_{n \to \infty} P\left(a \le \frac{X - np}{\sqrt{np(1 - p)}} \le b \right) = \frac{1}{\sqrt{2\pi}} \int_a^b e^{-z^2/2} \, dz$$

Proof. One of the ways to verify Theorem 4.3.1 is to show that the limit of the moment-generating function for $\dfrac{X - np}{\sqrt{np(1 - p)}}$ as $n \to \infty$ is $e^{t^2/2}$ and that $e^{t^2/2}$

is also the value of $\displaystyle\int_{-\infty}^{\infty} e^{tz} \cdot \frac{1}{\sqrt{2\pi}} e^{-z^2/2} \, dz$. By Theorem 3.16.2, then, the limiting

pdf of $Z = \dfrac{X - np}{\sqrt{np(1 - p)}}$ is the function $f_Z(z) = \dfrac{1}{\sqrt{2\pi}} e^{-z^2/2}$, $-\infty < z < \infty$.

We will omit the details here but prove a more general result in Chapter 7.

Comment. We saw in Section 4.2 that Poisson's *limit* is actually a special case of Poisson's *distribution*, $p_X(k) = \dfrac{e^{-\lambda} \lambda^k}{k!}$, $k = 0, 1, 2, \ldots$. Similarly, the DeMoivre-Laplace limit is a pdf in its own right. Justifying that assertion, of course, requires proving that $f_Z(z) = \dfrac{1}{\sqrt{2\pi}} e^{-z^2/2}$ integrates to 1 for $-\infty < z < \infty$.

Curiously, there is no algebraic or trigonometric substitution that can be used to demonstrate that the area under $f_Z(z)$ is 1. However, by using polar coordinates, we can verify a necessary and sufficient alternative—namely, that the *square* of

$$\int_{-\infty}^{\infty} \frac{1}{\sqrt{2\pi}} e^{-z^2/2} \, dz \text{ equals 1.}$$

To begin, note that

$$\frac{1}{\sqrt{2\pi}} \int_{-\infty}^{\infty} e^{-x^2/2} \, dx \cdot \frac{1}{\sqrt{2\pi}} \int_{-\infty}^{\infty} e^{-y^2/2} \, dy = \frac{1}{2\pi} \int_{-\infty}^{\infty} \int_{-\infty}^{\infty} e^{-\frac{1}{2}(x^2 + y^2)} \, dx \, dy$$

Let $x = r \cos\theta$ and $y = r \sin\theta$, so $dx \, dy = r \, dr \, d\theta$. Then

$$\frac{1}{2\pi} \int_{-\infty}^{\infty} \int_{-\infty}^{\infty} e^{-\frac{1}{2}(x^2 + y^2)} \, dx \, dy = \frac{1}{2\pi} \int_0^{2\pi} \int_0^{\infty} e^{-r^2/2} \, r \, dr \, d\theta$$

$$= \frac{1}{2\pi} \int_0^{\infty} r e^{-r^2/2} \, dr \cdot \int_0^{2\pi} d\theta$$

$$= 1$$

Comment. The function $f_Z(z) = \dfrac{1}{\sqrt{2\pi}} e^{-z^2/2}$ is referred to as the *standard normal* (or *Gaussian*) *curve*. By convention, any random variable whose probabilistic behavior is described by a standard normal curve is denoted by Z (rather than X, Y, or W). Since $M_Z(t) = e^{t^2/2}$, it follows readily that $E(Z) = 0$ and $\text{Var}(Z) = 1$ (see Question 4.3.35). Without question, the standard normal curve is the single most important probability model in all of statistics because of both its theoretical implications as well as its many practical applications.

Finding Areas Under the Standard Normal Curve

In order to use Theorem 4.3.1, we need to be able to find the area under $f_Z(z)$ above an arbitrary interval $[a, b]$. In practice, such values are obtained in one of two ways—either by using a *normal table*, a copy of which appears at the back of every statistics book, or by running a computer software package. Typically, both approaches give the cdf, $F_Z(z) = P(Z \le z)$, associated with Z (and from the cdf we can deduce the desired area).

Table 4.3.1 shows a portion of the normal table that appears in Appendix A.1. Each row under the Z heading represents a number along the horizontal axis of $f_Z(z)$ rounded off to the nearest tenth; columns 0 through 9 allow that number to be written to the hundredths place. Entries in the body of the table are areas under $f_Z(z)$ to

TABLE 4.3.1

Z	0	1	2	3	4	5	6	7	8	9
−3.	0.0013	0.0010	0.0007	0.0005	0.0003	0.0002	0.0002	0.0001	0.0001	0.0000
⋮					⋮					
−0.4	0.3446	0.3409	0.3372	0.3336	0.3300	0.3264	0.3228	0.3192	0.3156	0.3121
−0.3	0.3821	0.3783	0.3745	0.3707	0.3669	0.3632	0.3594	0.3557	0.3520	0.3483
−0.2	0.4207	0.4168	0.4129	0.4090	0.4052	0.4013	0.3974	0.3936	0.3897	0.3859
−0.1	0.4602	0.4562	0.4522	0.4483	0.4443	0.4404	0.4364	0.4325	0.4286	0.4247
−0.0	0.5000	0.4960	0.4920	0.4880	0.4840	0.4801	0.4761	0.4721	0.4681	0.4641
0.0	0.5000	0.5040	0.5080	0.5120	0.5160	0.5199	0.5239	0.5279	0.5319	0.5359
0.1	0.5398	0.5438	0.5478	0.5517	0.5557	0.5596	0.5636	0.5675	0.5714	0.5753
0.2	0.5793	0.5832	0.5871	0.5910	0.5948	0.5987	0.6026	0.6064	0.6103	0.6141
0.3	0.6179	0.6217	0.6255	0.6293	0.6331	0.6368	0.6406	0.6443	0.6480	0.6517
0.4	0.6554	0.6591	0.6628	0.6664	0.6700	0.6736	0.6772	0.6808	0.6844	0.6879
0.5	0.6915	0.6950	0.6985	0.7019	0.7054	0.7088	0.7123	0.7157	0.7190	0.7224
0.6	0.7257	0.7291	0.7324	0.7357	0.7389	0.7422	0.7454	0.7486	0.7517	0.7549
0.7	0.7580	0.7611	0.7642	0.7673	0.7703	0.7734	0.7764	0.7794	0.7823	0.7852
0.8	0.7881	0.7910	0.7939	0.7967	0.7995	0.8023	0.8051	0.8078	0.8106	0.8133
0.9	0.8159	0.8186	0.8212	0.8238	0.8264	0.8289	0.8315	0.8340	0.8365	0.8389
1.0	0.8413	0.8438	0.8461	0.8485	0.8508	0.8531	0.8554	0.8577	0.8599	0.8621
1.1	0.8643	0.8665	0.8686	0.8708	0.8729	0.8749	0.8770	0.8790	0.8810	0.8830
1.2	0.8849	0.8869	0.8888	0.8907	0.8925	0.8944	0.8962	0.8980	0.8997	0.9015
1.3	0.9032	0.9049	0.9066	0.9082	0.9099	0.9115	0.9131	0.9147	0.9162	0.9177
1.4	0.9192	0.9207	0.9222	0.9236	0.9251	0.9265	0.9278	0.9292	0.9306	0.9319
⋮						⋮				
3.	0.9987	0.9990	0.9993	0.9995	0.9997	0.9998	0.9998	0.9999	0.9999	1.0000

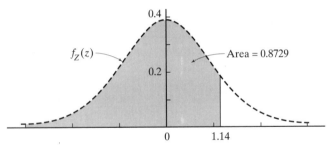

FIGURE 4.3.2

the left of the number indicated by the entry's row and column. For example, the number listed at the intersection of the "1.1" row and the "4" column is 0.8729, which means that the area under $f_Z(z)$ from $-\infty$ to 1.14 is 0.8729. That is,

$$\int_{-\infty}^{1.14} \frac{1}{\sqrt{2\pi}} e^{-z^2/2} \, dz = 0.8729 = P(-\infty < Z \le 1.14) = F_Z(1.14)$$

(see Figure 4.3.2).

Areas under $f_z(z)$ *to the right of a number* or *between two numbers* can also be calculated from the information given in normal tables. Since the total area under $f_Z(z)$ is 1,

$$P(b < Z < +\infty) = \text{area under } f_Z(z) \text{ to the right of } b$$
$$= 1 - \text{ area under } f_Z(z) \text{ to the left of } b$$
$$= 1 - P(-\infty < Z \le b)$$
$$= 1 - F_Z(b)$$

Similarly, the area under $f_z(z)$ *between* two numbers a and b is necessarily the area under $f_Z(z)$ to the left of b *minus* the area under $f_Z(z)$ to the left of a:

$$P(a \le Z \le b) = \text{area under } f_Z(z) \text{ between } a \text{ and } b$$
$$= \text{area under } f_Z(z) \text{ to the left of } b - \text{area under } f_Z(z) \text{ to the left of } a$$
$$= P(-\infty < Z \le b) - P(-\infty < Z < a)$$
$$= F_Z(b) - F_Z(a)$$

The Continuity Correction

Figure 4.3.3 shows a familiar-looking calculus scenario—a continuous curve, $f_Y(y)$, is being used to approximate the area under a set of histograms. Suppose the areas of those rectangles represent probabilities associated with a discrete random variable. While

$$P(c \le X \le d) \doteq \int_c^d f_Y(y) \, dy$$

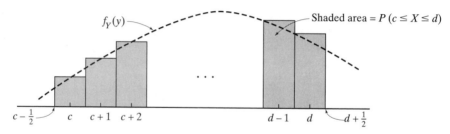

FIGURE 4.3.3

it seems clear from the diagram that the approximation would be better if the integration extended from $c - \frac{1}{2}$ (where the histogram areas actually begin) to $d + \frac{1}{2}$ (where the histogram areas actually end). That is, we should write

$$P(c \leq X \leq d) \doteq \int_{c-\frac{1}{2}}^{d+\frac{1}{2}} f_Y(y)\,dy$$

Replacing the limits c and d with $c - \frac{1}{2}$ and $d + \frac{1}{2}$ is referred to as the *continuity correction*. Such an adjustment is appropriate in the application of Theorem 4.3.1 because the discreteness of the binomial random variable X necessarily implies that

$$P\left(a \leq \frac{X - np}{\sqrt{np(1-p)}} \leq b\right) = P(c \leq X \leq d)$$

where c and d are integers.

Comment. Even with the continuity correction refinement, normal curve approximations to binomial probabilities can be inadequate if n is too small, especially if p is too close to either 0 or 1. As a rule of thumb, the DeMoivre-Laplace limit should be used only if the magnitudes of n and p are such that (1) $np - 3\sqrt{np(1-p)} > 0$ and (2) $np + 3\sqrt{np(1-p)} < n$.

EXAMPLE 4.3.1

Oak Hill has 74,806 registered automobiles. A city ordinance requires each to display a bumper decal showing that the owner paid an annual wheel tax of $50. By law, new decals need to be purchased during the month of the owner's birthday. This year's budget assumes that at least $306,000 in decal revenue will be collected in November. What is the probability that taxes reported in that month will be less than anticipated and produce a budget shortfall?

Let the (binomial) random variable X denote the number of cars (out of 74,806) whose fees will be paid in November. Since we can reasonably assume that roughly 1/12 of all birthdays will come in November,

$$P(\text{wheel tax revenue} < \$306{,}000) = P(50X < \$306{,}000)$$
$$= P(X < 6120)$$
$$= P(X \leq 6119)$$
$$= \sum_{k=0}^{6119} \binom{74{,}806}{k} \left(\frac{1}{12}\right)^k \left(\frac{11}{12}\right)^{74{,}806-k}$$

At this point we turn to Theorem 4.3.1. Notice first that the continuity correction modifies the target event to be $X \leq 6119.5$ rather than $X \leq 6119$. Also,

$$np = 74{,}806(1/12) = 6233.8$$

and

$$np(1 - p) = 74{,}806(1/12)(11/12) = 5714.3$$

Therefore,

$$P(\text{budget shortfall}) = P(X \leq 6119.5) = P\left(\frac{X - 6233.8}{\sqrt{5714.3}} \leq \frac{6119.5 - 6233.8}{\sqrt{5714.3}} \right)$$

$$= P\left(\frac{X - np}{\sqrt{np(1 - p)}} \leq -1.51 \right)$$

$$\doteq \frac{1}{\sqrt{2\pi}} \int_{-\infty}^{-1.51} e^{-z^2/2} \, dz$$

$$= P(Z \leq -1.51)$$

From Appendix A.1, though, $F_Z(-1.51)$—that is, the area under a standard normal curve to the left of -1.51—is *0.0655*. The probability, then, is about 1 in 16 that Oak Hill's November wheel tax revenue will be less than what the budget projected.

CASE STUDY 4.3.1

Research in extrasensory perception has ranged from the slightly unconventional to the downright bizarre. Toward the latter part of the nineteenth century and even well into the twentieth century, much of what was done involved spiritualists and mediums. But beginning around 1910, experimenters moved out of the seance parlors and into the laboratory, where they began setting up controlled studies that could be analyzed statistically. In 1938, Pratt and Woodruff, working out of Duke University, did an experiment that became a prototype for an entire generation of ESP research (63).

The investigator and a subject sat at opposite ends of a table. Between them was a screen with a large gap at the bottom. Five blank cards, visible to both participants, were placed side by side on the table beneath the screen. On the subject's side of the screen one of the standard ESP symbols (see Figure 4.3.4) was hung over each of the blank cards.

FIGURE 4.3.4

The experimenter shuffled a deck of ESP cards, picked up the top one, and concentrated on it. The subject tried to guess its identity: If he thought it was a *circle*, he would point to the blank card on the table that was beneath the circle card hanging on his side of the

(continued on next page)

(Case Study 4.3.1 continued)

screen. The procedure was then repeated. Altogether, a total of 32 subjects, all students, took part in the experiment. They made a total of 60,000 guesses—and were correct 12,489 times.

With five denominations involved, the probability of a subject's making a correct identification just by chance was $\frac{1}{5}$. Assuming a binomial model, the expected number of correct guesses would be $60,000 \times \frac{1}{5}$, or 12,000. The question is, how "near" to 12,000 is 12,489? Should we write off the observed excess of 489 as nothing more than luck, or can we conclude that ESP has been demonstrated?

To effect a resolution between the conflicting "luck" and "ESP" hypotheses, we need to compute the probability of the students' getting 12,489 or more correct answers *under the presumption that* $p = \frac{1}{5}$. Only if that probability is very small can 12,489 be construed as evidence in support of ESP.

Let the random variable X denote the number of correct responses in 60,000 tries. Then

$$P(X \geq 12,489) = \sum_{k=12,489}^{60,000} \binom{60,000}{k} \left(\frac{1}{5}\right)^k \left(\frac{4}{5}\right)^{60,000-k} \tag{4.3.1}$$

At this point the DeMoivre-Laplace limit theorem becomes a welcome alternative to computing the 47,512 binomial probabilities implicit in Equation 4.3.1. First we apply the continuity correction and rewrite $P(X \geq 12,489)$ as $P(X \geq 12,488.5)$. Then

$$P(X \geq 12,489) = P\left(\frac{X - np}{\sqrt{np(1-p)}} \geq \frac{12,488.5 - 60,000(1/5)}{\sqrt{60,000(1/5)(4/5)}}\right)$$

$$= P\left(\frac{X - np}{\sqrt{np(1-p)}} \geq 4.99\right)$$

$$\doteq \frac{1}{\sqrt{2\pi}} \int_{4.99}^{\infty} e^{-x^2/2}\, dx$$

$$= 0.0000003$$

this last value being obtained from a more extensive version of Table A.1 in the Appendix.

Here, the fact that $P(X \geq 12,489)$ is so extremely small makes the "luck" hypothesis $\left(p = \frac{1}{5}\right)$ untenable. It would appear that something other than chance had to be responsible for the occurrence of so many correct guesses. Still, it does not follow that ESP has necessarily been demonstrated. Flaws in the experimental setup as well as errors in reporting the scores could have inadvertently produced what appears to be a statistically significant result. Suffice it to say that a great many scientists remain highly skeptical of ESP research in general and of the Pratt-Woodruff experiment in particular. [For a more thorough critique of the data we have just described, see (42).]

Comment. This is a good set of data for illustrating why we need formal mathematical methods for interpreting data. The fact is, our intuitions, when left unsupported by probability calculations, can often be deceived. A typical first reaction to the Pratt–Woodruff results is to dismiss as inconsequential the 489 additional correct answers. To many, it seems entirely believable that 60,000 guesses could produce, by chance, an extra 489 correct responses. Only after making the $P(X \geq 12,489)$ computation do we see the utter implausibility of that conclusion. What statistics is doing here is what we would like it to do in general—rule out hypotheses that are not supported by the data and point us in the direction of inferences that are more likely to be true.

QUESTIONS

4.3.1 Use Appendix Table A.1 to evaluate the following integrals. In each case, draw a diagram of $f_Z(z)$ and shade the area that corresponds to the integral.

(a) $\int_{-0.44}^{1.33} \frac{1}{\sqrt{2\pi}} e^{-z^2/2} \, dz$

(b) $\int_{-\infty}^{0.94} \frac{1}{\sqrt{2\pi}} e^{-z^2/2} \, dz$

(c) $\int_{-1.48}^{\infty} \frac{1}{\sqrt{2\pi}} e^{-z^2/2} \, dz$

(d) $\int_{-\infty}^{-4.32} \frac{1}{\sqrt{2\pi}} e^{-z^2/2} \, dz$

4.3.2 Let Z be a standard normal random variable. Use Appendix Table A.1 to find the numerical value for each of the following probabilities. Show each of your answers as an area under $f_Z(z)$.

(a) $P(0 \leq Z \leq 2.07)$
(c) $P(Z > -1.06)$
(e) $P(Z \geq 4.61)$
(b) $P(-0.64 \leq Z < -0.11)$
(d) $P(Z < -2.33)$

4.3.3 **(a)** Let $0 < a < b$. Which number is larger?

$$\int_a^b \frac{1}{\sqrt{2\pi}} e^{-z^2/2} \, dz \quad \text{or} \quad \int_{-b}^{-a} \frac{1}{\sqrt{2\pi}} e^{-z^2/2} \, dz$$

(b) Let $a > 0$. Which number is larger?

$$\int_a^{a+1} \frac{1}{\sqrt{2\pi}} e^{-z^2/2} \, dz \quad \text{or} \quad \int_{a-1/2}^{a+1/2} \frac{1}{\sqrt{2\pi}} e^{-z^2/2} \, dz$$

4.3.4 **(a)** Evaluate $\int_0^{1.24} e^{-z^2/2} \, dz$.

(b) Evaluate $\int_{-\infty}^{\infty} 6e^{-z^2/2} \, dz$.

4.3.5 Assume that the random variable Z is described by a standard normal curve $f_Z(z)$. For what values of z are the following statements true?

(a) $P(Z \leq z) = 0.33$
(c) $P(-1.00 \leq Z \leq z) = 0.5004$
(e) $P(z < Z \leq 2.03) = 0.15$
(b) $P(Z \geq z) = 0.2236$
(d) $P(-z < Z < z) = 0.80$

4.3.6 Let z_α denote the value of Z for which $P(Z \geq z_\alpha) = \alpha$. By definition, the *interquartile range*, Q, for the standard normal curve is the difference

$$Q = z_{.25} - z_{.75}$$

Find Q.

4.3.7 Nailbiter Airlines knows that, on average, only 90% of the ticket-holders for the Thursday night Washington-to-Nashville flight will show up at the gate in time to board the plane. For that reason, the company routinely sells more tickets than their aircraft has seats. Suppose they have just booked 260 passengers for next week's flight (and the plane has 240 seats).

(a) Write a formula for the exact probability that not all the ticket-holders who show up next Thursday can be accommodated.

(b) Use the normal curve to approximate the probability asked for in Part (a).

4.3.8 Hertz Brothers, a small, family-owned radio manufacturer, produces electronic components domestically but subcontracts the cabinets to a foreign supplier. Although inexpensive, the foreign supplier has a quality control program that leaves much to be desired. On the average, only 80% of the standard 1600-unit shipment that Hertz receives is usable. Currently, Hertz has back orders for 1260 radios but storage space for no more than 1310 cabinets. What are the chances that the number of usable units in Hertz's latest shipment will be large enough to allow Hertz to fill all the orders already on hand, yet small enough to avoid causing any inventory problems?

4.3.9 Fifty-five percent of the registered voters in Sheridanville favor their incumbent mayor in her bid for reelection. If 400 voters go to the polls, approximate the probability that
(a) the race ends in a tie
(b) the challenger scores an upset victory

4.3.10 State Tech's basketball team, the Fighting Logarithms, have a 70% foul-shooting percentage.
(a) Write a formula for the exact probability that out of their next 100 free throws they will make between 75 and 80, inclusive.
(b) Approximate the probability asked for in Part (a).

4.3.11 A random sample of 747 obituaries published recently in Salt Lake City newspapers revealed that 344 (or 46%) of the decedents died in the three-month period following their birthdays (114). Assess the statistical significance of that finding by approximating the probability that 46% or more would die in that particular interval if deaths occurred randomly throughout the year. What would you conclude on the basis of your answer?

4.3.12 There is a theory embraced by certain parapsychologists that hypnosis can enhance a person's ESP ability. To test that hypothesis, an experiment was set up with 15 hypnotized subjects (22). Each was asked to make 100 guesses using the same sort of ESP cards and protocol that were described in Case Study 4.3.1. A total of 326 correct identifications were made. Can it be argued on the basis of those results that hypnosis does have an effect on a person's ESP ability? Explain.

4.3.13 If $p_X(k) = \binom{10}{k}(0.7)^k(0.3)^{10-k}, k = 0, 1, \ldots, 10$, is it appropriate to approximate $P(4 \le X \le 8)$ by computing

$$P\left(\frac{3.5 - 10(0.7)}{\sqrt{10(0.7)(0.3)}} \le Z \le \frac{8.5 - 10(0.7)}{\sqrt{10(0.7)(0.3)}}\right)$$

Explain.

4.3.14 A sell-out crowd of 42,200 is expected at Cleveland's Jacobs Field for next Tuesday's game with the Baltimore Orioles, the last before a long road trip. The ballpark's concession manager is trying to decide how much food to have on hand. Looking at records from games played earlier in the season, she knows that, on the average, 38% of all those in attendance will buy a hot dog. How large an order should she place if she wants to have no more than a 20% chance of demand exceeding supply?

Central Limit Theorem

It was pointed out in Example 3.11.1 that every binomial random variable X can be written as the sum of n independent Bernoulli random variables $X_1, X_2, \ldots, X_n$, where

$$X_i = \begin{cases} 1 & \text{with probability } p \\ 0 & \text{with probability } 1 - p \end{cases}$$

But if $X = X_1 + X_2 + \cdots + X_n$, Theorem 4.3.1 can be reexpressed as

$$\lim_{n \to \infty} P\left(a \le \frac{X_1 + X_2 + \cdots + X_n - np}{\sqrt{np(1-p)}} \le b\right) = \frac{1}{\sqrt{2\pi}} \int_a^b e^{-z^2/2} \, dz \qquad (4.3.2)$$

Implicit in Equation 4.3.2 is an obvious question: Does the DeMoivre-Laplace limit apply to sums of other types of random variables as well? Remarkably, the answer is "yes." Efforts to extend Equation 4.3.2 have continued for more than 150 years. Russian probabilists—A. M. Lyapunov, in particular—made many of the key advances (98). In 1920, George Polya gave these new generalizations a name that has been associated with the result ever since: He called it the *central limit theorem* ("Uber den zentralen Grenzwertsatz der Wahrscheinlichkeitsrechnung und das Momenten-problem," *Mathematische Zeitschrift*, vol. 8, 1920, pp. 171–181).

THEOREM 4.3.2.   *Central Limit Theorem*   Let $W_1, W_2, \ldots$ be an infinite sequence of independent random variables, each with the same distribution. Suppose that the mean μ and the variance σ^2 of $f_W(w)$ are both finite. For any numbers a and b,

$$\lim_{n \to \infty} P\left(a \le \frac{W_1 + \cdots + W_n - n\mu}{\sqrt{n}\sigma} \le b\right) = \frac{1}{\sqrt{2\pi}} \int_a^b e^{-z^2/2}\, dz$$

Proof.   See Appendix 4.A.2.

Comment.   The central limit theorem is often stated in terms of the *average* of $W_1, W_2, \ldots,$ and W_n, rather than their sum. Since

$$E\left[\frac{1}{n}(W_1 + \cdots + W_n)\right] = E(\bar{W}) = \mu \quad \text{and} \quad \text{Var}\left[\frac{1}{n}(W_1 + \cdots + W_n)\right] = \sigma^2/n,$$

Theorem 4.3.2 can be stated in the equivalent form

$$\lim_{n \to \infty} P\left(a \le \frac{\bar{W} - \mu}{\sigma/\sqrt{n}} \le b\right) = \frac{1}{\sqrt{2\pi}} \int_a^b e^{-z^2/2}\, dz$$

We will use both formulations, the choice depending on which is more convenient for the problem at hand.

EXAMPLE 4.3.2

The top of Table 4.3.2 shows a MINITAB simulation where 40 random samples of size 5 were drawn from a uniform pdf defined over the interval $[0, 1]$. Each row corresponds to a different sample. The sum of the five numbers appearing in a given sample is denoted "y" and is listed in column C6. For this particular uniform pdf, $\mu = 1/2$ and $\sigma^2 = 1/12$ (recall Question 3.12.4), so

$$\frac{W_1 + \cdots + W_n - n\mu}{\sqrt{n}\sigma} = \frac{Y - 5/2}{\sqrt{5/12}}$$

At the bottom of Table 4.3.2 is a density-scaled histogram of the 40 "Z ratios," $\dfrac{y - 5/2}{\sqrt{5/12}}$ (as listed in column C7). Notice the close agreement between the distribution of those ratios and $f_Z(z)$: What we see there is entirely consistent with the statement of Theorem 4.3.2.

Comment.   Theorem 4.3.2 is an asymptotic result, yet it can provide surprisingly good approximations *even when n is very small*. Example 4.3.2 is a typical case in point: The uniform pdf over $[0, 1]$ looks nothing like a bell-shaped curve, yet random samples as small as $n = 5$ yield sums that behave probabilistically much like the theoretical limit.

TABLE 4.3.2

	C1	C2	C3	C4	C5	C6	C7
	y1	y2	y3	y4	y5	y	Z ratio
1	0.556099	0.646873	0.354373	0.673821	0.233126	2.46429	-0.05532
2	0.497846	0.588979	0.272095	0.956614	0.819901	3.13544	0.98441
3	0.284027	0.209458	0.414743	0.614309	0.439456	1.96199	-0.83348
4	0.599286	0.667891	0.194460	0.839481	0.694474	2.99559	0.76777
5	0.280689	0.692159	0.036593	0.728826	0.314434	2.05270	-0.69295
6	0.462741	0.349264	0.471254	0.613070	0.489125	2.38545	-0.17745
7	0.556940	0.246789	0.719907	0.711414	0.918221	3.15327	1.01204
8	0.102855	0.679119	0.559210	0.014393	0.518450	1.87403	-0.96975
9	0.642859	0.004636	0.728131	0.299165	0.801093	2.47588	-0.03736
10	0.017770	0.568188	0.416351	0.908079	0.075108	1.98550	-0.79707
11	0.331291	0.410705	0.118571	0.979254	0.242582	2.08240	-0.64694
12	0.355047	0.961126	0.920597	0.575467	0.585492	3.39773	1.39076
13	0.626197	0.304754	0.530345	0.933018	0.675899	3.07021	0.88337
14	0.211714	0.404505	0.045544	0.213012	0.520614	1.39539	-1.71125
15	0.535199	0.130715	0.603642	0.333023	0.405782	2.00836	-0.76164
16	0.810374	0.153955	0.082226	0.827269	0.897901	2.77172	0.42095
17	0.687550	0.185393	0.620878	0.013395	0.819712	2.32693	-0.26812
18	0.424193	0.529199	0.201554	0.157073	0.090455	1.40248	-1.70028
19	0.397373	0.143507	0.973991	0.234845	0.681147	2.43086	-0.10711
20	0.413788	0.653468	0.017335	0.556255	0.900568	2.54141	0.06416
21	0.602607	0.094162	0.247676	0.638875	0.653910	2.23723	-0.40708
22	0.963678	0.375850	0.909377	0.307358	0.828882	3.38515	1.37126
23	0.967499	0.868809	0.940770	0.405564	0.814348	3.99699	2.31913
24	0.439913	0.446679	0.075227	0.983295	0.554581	2.49970	-0.00047
25	0.215774	0.407494	0.002307	0.971140	0.437144	2.03386	-0.72214
26	0.108881	0.271860	0.972351	0.604762	0.210347	2.16820	-0.51402
27	0.337798	0.173911	0.309916	0.300208	0.666831	1.78866	-1.10200
28	0.635017	0.187311	0.365419	0.831417	0.463567	2.48273	-0.02675
29	0.563097	0.065293	0.841320	0.518055	0.685137	2.67290	0.26786
30	0.687242	0.544286	0.980337	0.649507	0.077364	2.93874	0.67969
31	0.784501	0.745614	0.459559	0.565875	0.529171	3.08472	0.90584
32	0.505460	0.355340	0.163285	0.352540	0.896521	2.27315	-0.35144
33	0.336992	0.734869	0.824409	0.321047	0.682283	2.89960	0.61906
34	0.784279	0.194038	0.323756	0.430020	0.459238	2.19133	-0.47819
35	0.548008	0.788351	0.831117	0.200790	0.823102	3.19137	1.07106
36	0.096383	0.844281	0.680927	0.656946	0.050867	2.32940	-0.26429
37	0.161502	0.972933	0.038113	0.515530	0.553788	2.24187	-0.39990
38	0.677552	0.232181	0.307234	0.588927	0.365403	2.17130	-0.50922
39	0.470454	0.267230	0.652802	0.633286	0.410964	2.43474	-0.10111
40	0.104377	0.819950	0.047036	0.189226	0.399502	1.56009	-1.45610

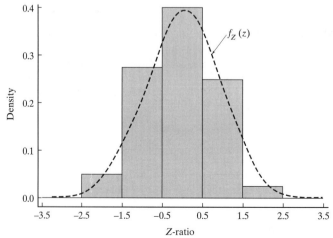

In general, samples from symmetric pdfs will produce sums that "converge" quickly to the theoretical limit. On the other hand, if the underlying pdf is sharply skewed—for example, $f_Y(y) = 10e^{-10y}$, $y > 0$—it would take a larger n to achieve the level of agreement present in Figure 4.3.2.

EXAMPLE 4.3.3

A random sample of size $n = 15$ is drawn from the pdf $f_Y(y) = 3(1 - y)^2$, $0 \le y \le 1$. Let $\bar{Y} = (1/15) \sum_{i=1}^{15} Y_i$. Use the central limit theorem to approximate $P\left(\frac{1}{8} \le \bar{Y} \le \frac{3}{8}\right)$.

Note, first of all, that

$$E(Y) = \int_0^1 y \cdot 3(1 - y)^2 \, dy = \frac{1}{4}$$

and

$$\sigma^2 = \text{Var}(Y) = E(Y^2) - \mu^2 = \int_0^1 y^2 \cdot 3(1 - y)^2 \, dy - \left(\frac{1}{4}\right)^2 = \frac{3}{80}$$

According, then, to the central limit theorem formulation that appears in the comment on page 273, the probability that $\bar{Y}$ will lie between $\frac{1}{8}$ and $\frac{3}{8}$ is approximately 0.99:

$$P\left(\frac{1}{8} \le \bar{Y} \le \frac{3}{8}\right) = P\left(\frac{1/8 - 1/4}{\sqrt{3/80}/\sqrt{15}} \le \frac{\bar{Y} - 1/4}{\sqrt{3/80}/\sqrt{15}} \le \frac{3/8 - 1/4}{\sqrt{3/80}/\sqrt{15}}\right)$$

$$= P(-2.50 \le Z \le 2.50)$$

$$= 0.9876$$

EXAMPLE 4.3.4

In Example 3.14.1, Chebyshev's inequality was used to get an upper bound for the probability that the accumulated rounding errors made on 100 check transactions (each recorded to the nearest dollar) will be \$5 or more. Assuming that each roundoff error, Y_i, is a uniform random variable defined over the interval $(-\$\frac{1}{2}, +\$\frac{1}{2})$, it followed from Theorem 3.14.1 that

$$P(|Y_1 + Y_2 + \cdots + Y_{100}| \ge \$5) \le 0.33$$

What is the approximate value for $P(|Y_1 + Y_2 + \cdots + Y_{100}| \ge \$5)$ based on the central limit theorem?

Since $E(Y_i) = 0$ and $\text{Var}(Y_i) = 1/12$ (see Question 3.12.4), $E(Y_1 + Y_2 + \cdots + Y_{100}) = 100\mu = 0$ and $\text{Var}(Y_1 + Y_2 + \cdots + Y_{100}) = 100\sigma^2 = 100/12$. Applying the transformation given in Theorem 4.3.2, we find that the approximate probability that $|Y_1 + Y_2 + \cdots + Y_{100}| \ge \$5$ is quite a bit less than the Chebyshev upper bound:

$$P(|Y_1 + Y_2 + \cdots + Y_{100}| \ge \$5) = 1 - P(-5 < Y_1 + Y_2 + \cdots + Y_{100} < 5)$$

$$= 1 - P\left(\frac{-5 - 0}{10/\sqrt{12}} < \frac{Y_1 + Y_2 + \cdots + Y_{100} - 0}{10/\sqrt{12}} < \frac{5 - 0}{10/\sqrt{12}}\right)$$

$$\doteq 1 - P(-1.73 < Z < 1.73)$$

$$= 0.0836$$

(see Question 4.3.16).

EXAMPLE 4.3.5

The annual number of earthquakes registering 2.5 or higher on the Richter scale and having an epicenter within 40 miles of downtown Memphis follows a Poisson distribution with $\lambda = 6.5$. Calculate the exact probability that nine or more such earthquakes will strike next year, and compare that value to an approximation based on the central limit theorem.

If X denotes the number of earthquakes of that magnitude that will hit Memphis next year, the exact probability that $X \geq 9$ is a Poisson sum:

$$P(X \geq 9) = 1 - P(X \leq 8) = 1 - \sum_{x=0}^{8} \frac{e^{-6.5}(6.5)^x}{x!}$$

$$= 1 - 0.7916$$

$$= 0.2084$$

For Poisson random variables, the ratio $\dfrac{W_1 + \cdots + W_n - n\mu}{\sqrt{n}\,\sigma}$ that appears in the central limit theorem reduces to $\dfrac{X - \lambda}{\sqrt{\lambda}}$ (see Question 4.3.18). Therefore,

$$P(X \geq 9) = 1 - P(X \leq 8) = 1 - P(X \leq 8.5)$$

$$= 1 - P\left(\frac{X - 6.5}{\sqrt{6.5}} \leq \frac{8.5 - 6.5}{\sqrt{6.5}}\right)$$

$$\doteq 1 - P(Z \leq 0.78)$$

$$= 0.2170$$

(Notice that the event "$X \leq 8$" is replaced with "$X \leq 8.5$" before applying the central limit theorem transformation. As always, the *continuity correction* is appropriate whenever a discrete probability model is being approximated by the area under a curve.)

Comment.   No one articulated the role played by the normal curve in the sweeping generality of the central limit theorem more eloquently than did Sir Francis Galton. Writing in the flowery style that was characteristic of his day and time, the renowned British scientist could hardly restrain his enthusiasm for a probability model that he realized had such truly extraordinary implications (52):

> I know of scarcely anything so apt to impress the imagination as the wonderful form of cosmic order expressed by the "Law of Frequency of Error" [the normal curve]. The law would have been personified by the Greeks and deified, if they had known of it. It reigns with serenity and in complete self effacement amidst the wildest confusion. The huger the mob, and the greater the anarchy, the more perfect is its sway. It is the supreme law of Unreason.

QUESTIONS

4.3.15 A fair coin is tossed 200 times. Let $X_i = 1$ if the ith toss comes up heads and $X_i = 0$, otherwise, $i = 1, 2, \ldots, 200$. Calculate
  (a) the Chebyshev lower bound for the probability that $X = X_1 + X_2 + \cdots + X_{200}$ is within 5 of $E(X)$.
  (b) the central limit theorem approximation for $P(|X - E(X)| \leq 5)$.

4.3.16 Why is the probability calculated in Example 4.3.4, 0.0836, so much smaller than the upper bound derived from the Chebyshev inequality?

4.3.17 Suppose that 100 fair dice are tossed. Estimate the probability that the sum of the faces showing exceeds 370. Include a continuity correction in your analysis.

4.3.18 If $X_1, X_2, \ldots, X_n$ are independent Poisson random variables with parameters $\lambda_1, \lambda_2, \ldots, \lambda_n$, respectively, and if $X = X_1 + X_2 + \cdots + X_n$, then X is a Poisson random variable with parameter $\lambda = \sum_{i=1}^{n} \lambda_i$ (recall Example 4.2.5). What specific form does the ratio in Theorem 4.3.2 take if the X_i's are Poisson random variables?

4.3.19 An electronics firm receives, on the average, 50 orders per week for a particular silicon chip. If the company has 60 chips on hand, use the central limit theorem to approximate the probability that they will be unable to fill all their orders for the upcoming week. Assume that weekly demands follow a Poisson distribution. *Hint*: See Question 4.3.18.

4.3.20 Considerable controversy has arisen over the possible aftereffects of a nuclear weapons test conducted in Nevada in 1957. Included as part of the test were some 3000 military and civilian "observers." Now, more than 40 years later, eight cases of leukemia have been diagnosed among those 3000. The expected number of cases, based on the demographic characteristics of the observers, was three. Assess the statistical significance of those findings. Calculate both an exact answer using the Poisson distribution as well as an approximation based on the central limit theorem.

The Normal Curve as a Model for Individual Measurements

Because of the central limit theorem, we know that sums (or averages) of virtually any set of random variables, when suitably scaled, have distributions that can be approximated by a standard normal curve. Perhaps even more surprising is the fact that many *individual* measurements, when suitably scaled, also have a standard normal distribution. Why should the latter be true? What do single observations have in common with samples of size n?

Astronomers in the early nineteenth century were among the first to understand the connection. Imagine looking through a telescope for the purpose of determining the location of a star. Conceptually, the data point, Y, eventually recorded is the sum of two components: (1) the star's *true* location μ^* (which remains unknown) and (2) measurement error. By definition, measurement error is the net effect of all those factors that cause the random variable Y to have a different value than μ^*. Typically, these effects will be additive, in which case the random variable can be written as a sum:

$$Y = \mu^* + W_1 + W_2 + \cdots + W_t \tag{4.3.3}$$

where W_1, for example, might represent the effect of atmospheric irregularities, W_2 the effect of seismic vibrations, W_3 the effect of parallax distortions, and so on.

If Equation 4.3.3 is a valid representation of the random variable Y, then it would follow that the central limit theorem applies to the *individual* Y_i's. Moreover, if

$$E(Y) = E(\mu^* + W_1 + W_2 + \cdots + W_t) = \mu$$

and

$$\text{Var}(Y) = \text{Var}(\mu^* + W_1 + W_2 + \cdots + W_t) = \sigma^2$$

the ratio in Theorem 4.3.2 takes the form $\dfrac{Y - \mu}{\sigma}$. Furthermore, t is likely to be very large, so the approximation implied by the central limit theorem is essentially an equality—that is, *we take the pdf of* $\dfrac{Y - \mu}{\sigma}$ *to be* $f_Z(z)$.

Finding an actual formula for $f_Y(y)$, then, becomes an exercise in applying Theorem 3.7.1. Given that $\dfrac{Y - \mu}{\sigma} = Z$,

$$Y = \mu + \sigma Z$$

and

$$
\begin{aligned}
f_Y(y) &= \frac{1}{\sigma} f_Z\left(\frac{y - \mu}{\sigma}\right) \\
&= \frac{1}{\sqrt{2\pi}\sigma} e^{-\frac{1}{2}\left(\frac{y-\mu}{\sigma}\right)^2}, \quad -\infty < y < \infty
\end{aligned}
$$

DEFINITION 4.3.1. A random variable Y is said to be normally distributed with mean μ and variance σ^2 if

$$f_Y(y) = \frac{1}{\sqrt{2\pi}\sigma} e^{-\frac{1}{2}\left(\frac{y-\mu}{\sigma}\right)^2}, \quad -\infty < y < \infty$$

The symbol $Y \sim N(\mu, \sigma^2)$ will sometimes be used to denote the fact that Y has a normal distribution with mean μ and variance σ^2.

Comment. Areas under an "arbitrary" normal distribution, $f_Y(y)$, are calculated by finding the equivalent area under the standard normal distribution, $f_Z(z)$:

$$P(a \le Y \le b) = P\left(\frac{a - \mu}{\sigma} \le \frac{Y - \mu}{\sigma} \le \frac{b - \mu}{\sigma}\right) = P\left(\frac{a - \mu}{\sigma} \le Z \le \frac{b - \mu}{\sigma}\right)$$

The ratio $\dfrac{Y - \mu}{\sigma}$ is often referred to as either a *Z transformation* or a *Z score*.

EXAMPLE 4.3.6

In many states a motorist is legally drunk or driving under the influence (DUI), if his or her blood alcohol concentration, Y, is 0.10% or higher. When a suspected DUI offender is pulled over, police often request a sobriety test. Although the breath analyzers used for that purpose are remarkably precise, the machines do exhibit a certain amount of measurement error. Because of that variability, the possibility exists that a driver's *true* blood alcohol concentration may be *under* 0.10% even though the analyzer gives a reading *over* 0.10%.

Experience has shown that repeated breath analyzer measurements taken on the same person produce a distribution of responses that can be described by a normal pdf with μ equal to the person's true blood alcohol concentration and σ equal to 0.004%. Suppose a driver is stopped at a roadblock on his way home from a party. Having celebrated a bit more than he should have, he has a true blood alcohol concentration of 0.095%, just barely under the legal limit. If he takes the breath analyzer test, what are the chances that he will be incorrectly booked on a DUI charge?

Since a DUI arrest occurs when $Y \geq 0.10\%$, we need to find $P(Y \geq 0.10)$ when $\mu = 0.095$ and $\sigma = 0.004$ (the percentage is irrelevant to any probability calculation and can be ignored). An application of the Z transformation shows that the driver has almost an 11% chance of being falsely accused:

$$P(Y \geq 0.10) = P\left(\frac{Y - 0.095}{0.004} \geq \frac{0.10 - 0.095}{0.004}\right)$$

$$= P(Z \geq 1.25) = 1 - P(Z < 1.25)$$

$$= 1 - 0.8944 = 0.1056$$

Figure 4.3.5 shows $f_Y(y), f_Z(z)$, and the two areas that are equivalent.

FIGURE 4.3.5

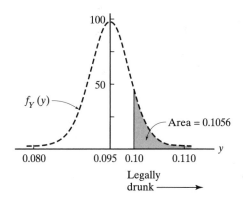

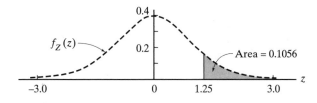

EXAMPLE 4.3.7

Mensa (from the Latin word for "mind") is an international society devoted to intellectual pursuits. Any person who has an IQ in the upper 2% of the general population is eligible to join. What is the *lowest* IQ that will qualify a person for membership? Assume that IQs are normally distributed with $\mu = 100$ and $\sigma = 16$.

Let the random variable Y denote a person's IQ, and let the constant y_L be the lowest IQ that qualifies someone to be a card-carrying Mensan. The two are related by a probability equation:

$$P(Y \geq y_L) = 0.02$$

or, equivalently,

$$P(Y < y_L) = 1 - 0.02 = 0.98 \qquad (4.3.4)$$

(see Figure 4.3.6).

FIGURE 4.3.6

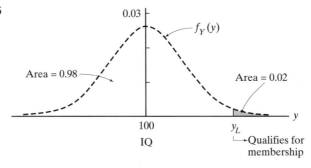

Applying the Z transformation to Equation 4.3.4 gives

$$P(Y < y_L) = P\left(\frac{Y - 100}{16} < \frac{Y_L - 100}{16}\right) = P\left(Z < \frac{y_L - 100}{16}\right) = 0.98$$

From the standard normal table in Appendix Table A.1, though,

$$P(Z < 2.05) = 0.9798 \doteq 0.98$$

Since $\dfrac{y_L - 100}{16}$ and 2.05 are both cutting off the same area of 0.02 under $f_Z(z)$, they must be equal, which implies that *133* is the lowest acceptable IQ for Mensa:

$$y_L = 100 + 16(2.05) = 133$$

EXAMPLE 4.3.8

The Army is soliciting proposals for the development of a truck-launched antitank missile. Pentagon officials are requiring that the automatic sighting mechanism be sufficiently reliable to guarantee that 95% of the missiles will fall no more than 50 ft short of their target or no more than 50 ft beyond. What is the largest σ compatible with that degree of precision? Assume that Y, the horizontal distance a missile travels, is normally distributed with its mean (μ) equal to the length of the separation between the truck and the target.

The requirement that a missile has a 95% probability of landing within 50 ft of its target can be expressed by the equation

$$P(\mu - 50 \leq Y \leq \mu + 50) = 0.95$$

(see Figure 4.3.7). Equivalently,

$$P\left(\frac{\mu - 50 - \mu}{\sigma} \leq \frac{Y - \mu}{\sigma} \leq \frac{\mu + 50 - \mu}{\sigma}\right) = P\left(\frac{-50}{\sigma} \leq Z \leq \frac{50}{\sigma}\right) = 0.95 \qquad (4.3.5)$$

Following the approach taken in Example 4.3.6, we can "match" Equation 4.3.5 using the information provided in Appendix Table A.1. Specifically,

$$P(-1.96 \le Z \le 1.96) = 0.95$$

It must be true, then, that

$$1.96 = \frac{50}{\sigma}$$

which implies that $\sigma = 25.5$.

FIGURE 4.3.7

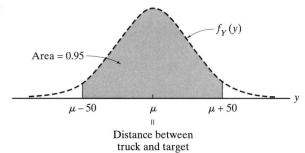

Area = 0.95

$f_Y(y)$

$\mu - 50$ μ $\mu + 50$ y

||

Distance between
truck and target

Any value of σ *larger* than 25.5 will result in $f_Y(y)$ being flatter, and that would have the consequence that fewer than 95% of the missiles would land within 50 ft of their targets. Conversely, if the sighting mechanism produces a σ *smaller* than 25.5, it will be performing at a level that exceeds the contract specifications (and perhaps costing an amount that makes the proposal noncompetitive).

THEOREM 4.3.3.   Let Y be a normally distributed random variable with mean μ and variance σ^2. The moment-generating function for Y is

$$M_Y(t) = e^{\mu t + (\sigma^2 t^2)/2}$$

Proof.   By definition,

$$M_Y(t) = E(e^{tY}) = \int_{-\infty}^{\infty} e^{ty} \cdot \frac{1}{\sqrt{2\pi}\,\sigma} e^{-\frac{1}{2}\left(\frac{y-\mu}{\sigma}\right)^2} dy$$

$$= \frac{1}{\sqrt{2\pi}\,\sigma} \int_{-\infty}^{\infty} e^{-(y^2 - 2\mu y - 2\sigma^2 t y + \mu^2)/2\sigma^2} dy$$

After completing the square of the exponent of e, we can express the mgf in the form

$$M_Y(t) = \frac{1}{\sqrt{2\pi}\,\sigma} \int_{-\infty}^{\infty} e^{-[(y - \mu - \sigma^2 t)^2 - (\mu + \sigma^2 t)^2 + \mu^2]/2\sigma^2} dy$$

$$= e^{(\sigma^4 t^2 + 2t\mu\sigma^2)/2\sigma^2} \cdot \frac{1}{\sqrt{2\pi}\,\sigma} \int_{-\infty}^{\infty} e^{-\frac{1}{2}\left[\frac{y - (\mu + t\sigma^2)}{\sigma}\right]^2} dy$$

Notice that the second factor in the expression for $M_Y(t)$ is equal to 1, because it represents the integral of a normal pdf over its entire range. Therefore,

$$M_Y(t) = e^{\mu t + (\sigma^2 t^2 / 2)}$$

EXAMPLE 4.3.9

Suppose a random variable Y has the moment-generating function $M_Y(t) = e^{3t+8t^2}$. Calculate $P(-1 \le Y \le 9)$.

To begin, notice that $M_Y(t)$ has the same *form* as the moment-generating function for a normal random variable. That is,

$$e^{3t+8t^2} = e^{\mu t + (\sigma^2 t^2)/2}$$

where $\mu = 3$ and $\sigma^2 = 16$. To evaluate $P(-1 \le Y \le 9)$, then, requires an application of the Z transformation:

$$P(-1 \le Y \le 9) = P\left(\frac{-1-3}{4} \le \frac{Y-3}{4} \le \frac{9-3}{4}\right) = P(-1.00 \le Z \le 1.50)$$

$$= 0.9332 - 0.1587$$

$$= 0.7745$$

THEOREM 4.3.4. Let Y_1 be a normally distributed random variable with mean μ_1 and variance σ_1^2, and let Y_2 be a normally distributed random variable with mean μ_2 and variance σ_2^2. Define $Y = Y_1 + Y_2$. If Y_1 and Y_2 are independent, Y is normally distributed with mean $\mu_1 + \mu_2$ and variance $\sigma_1^2 + \sigma_2^2$.

Proof. Let $M_{Y_i}(t)$ denote the moment-generating function for Y_i, $i = 1, 2$, and let $M_Y(t)$ be the moment-generating function for Y. Since $Y = Y_1 + Y_2$, and the Y_i's are independent,

$$M_Y(t) = M_{Y_1}(t) \cdot M_{Y_2}(t)$$
$$= e^{\mu_1 t + (\sigma_1^2 t^2)/2} \cdot e^{\mu_2 t + (\sigma_2^2 t^2)/2}$$
$$= e^{(\mu_1 + \mu_2)t + (\sigma_1^2 + \sigma_2^2)t^2/2}$$

We recognize the latter, though, to be the moment-generating function for a normal random variable with mean $\mu_1 + \mu_2$ and variance $\sigma_1^2 + \sigma_2^2$. The result follows by virtue of the uniqueness property stated in Theorem 3.16.2.

COROLLARY. Let $Y_1, Y_2, \ldots, Y_n$ be a random sample of size n from a normal distribution with mean μ and variance σ^2. Then the sample mean, $\bar{Y} = \frac{1}{n} \sum_{i=1}^{n} Y_i$, is also normally distributed with mean μ but with variance equal to σ^2/n (which implies that $\dfrac{\bar{Y} - \mu}{\sigma/\sqrt{n}}$ is a standard normal random variable, Z).

COROLLARY. Let $Y_1, Y_2, \ldots, Y_n$ be any set of independent normal random variables with means $\mu_1, \mu_2, \ldots, \mu_n$ and variances $\sigma_1^2, \sigma_2^2, \ldots, \sigma_n^2$, respectively. Let $a_1, a_2, \ldots, a_n$ be any set of constants. Then $Y = a_1 Y_1 + a_2 Y_2 + \cdots + a_n Y_n$ is normally distributed with mean $\mu = \sum_{i=1}^{n} a_i \mu_i$ and variance $\sigma^2 = \sum_{i=1}^{n} a_i^2 \sigma_i^2$.

EXAMPLE 4.3.10

The elevator in the athletic dorm at Swampwater Tech has a maximum capacity of 2400 lb. Suppose that 10 football players get on at the twentieth floor. If the weights of Tech's players are normally distributed with a mean of 220 lb and a standard deviation of 20 lb, what is the probability that there will be 10 fewer Muskrats at tomorrow's practice?

Let the random variables $Y_1, Y_2, \ldots, Y_{10}$ denote the weights of the 10 players. At issue is the probability that $Y = \sum_{i=1}^{10} Y_i$ exceeds 2400 lb. But

$$P\left(\sum_{i=1}^{10} Y_i > 2400\right) = P\left(\frac{1}{10} \sum_{i=1}^{10} Y_i > \frac{1}{10} \cdot 2400\right) = P(\bar{Y} > 240.0)$$

A Z transformation can be applied to the latter expression using the corollary on page 282:

$$P(\bar{Y} > 240.0) = P\left(\frac{\bar{Y} - 220}{20/\sqrt{10}} > \frac{240.0 - 220}{20/\sqrt{10}}\right) = P(Z > 3.16)$$

$$= 0.0008$$

Clearly, the chances of a Muskrat splat are minimal. (How much would the probability change if *11* players boarded the elevator?)

EXAMPLE 4.3.11

The personnel department of a large corporation gives two aptitude tests to job applicants. One measures verbal ability; the other, quantitative ability. From many years' experience, the company has found that a person's verbal score, Y_1, is normally distributed with $\mu_1 = 50$ and $\sigma_1 = 10$. The quantitative scores, Y_2, are normally distributed with $\mu_2 = 100$ and $\sigma_2 = 20$, and Y_1 and Y_2 appear to be independent. A composite score, Y, is assigned to each applicant, where

$$Y = 3Y_1 + 2Y_2$$

To avoid unnecessary paperwork, the company automatically rejects any applicant whose composite score is below 375. If six individuals submit résumés, what are the chances that fewer than half will fail the screening test?

First we need to calculate the probability that any given candidate will score below the composite cutoff. Since Y is a linear combination of independent normal random variables, Y itself is normally distributed with

$$E(Y) = 3E(Y_1) + 2E(Y_2) = 3(50) + 2(100) = 350$$

and

$$\mathrm{Var}(Y) = 3^2 \mathrm{Var}(Y_1) + 2^2 \mathrm{Var}(Y_2) = 9(100) + 4(400) = 2500$$

A Z transformation, then, shows that the probability of a random applicant being summarily rejected is *0.6915*:

$$P(Y < 357) = P\left(\frac{Y - 350}{\sqrt{2500}} < \frac{375 - 350}{\sqrt{2500}}\right) = P(Z < 0.50)$$

$$= 0.6915$$

Now, let the random variable X denote the number of applicants (out of six) whose Y-values would be less than 375. By its structure, X is binomial with $n = 6$ and $p = P(Y < 375) = 0.6915$. Therefore,

P(fewer than half of the applicants will fail the test)

$$= P(X < 3) = P(X \le 2) = \sum_{k=0}^{2} \binom{6}{k}(0.6915)^k(0.3085)^{6-k}$$

$$= 0.0774$$

EXAMPLE 4.3.12

Let $Y_1, Y_2, \ldots, Y_9$ be a random sample of size 9 from a normal distribution where $\mu = 2$ and $\sigma = 2$. Let $Y_1^*, Y_2^*, Y_3^*, Y_4^*$ be an independent random sample from a normal distribution for which $\mu = 1$ and $\sigma = 1$. Find $P(\bar{Y} \ge \bar{Y}*)$.

The corollary on page 282 can be applied here because the event $\bar{Y} \ge \bar{Y}*$ can be written in terms of a linear combination—specifically, $\bar{Y} - \bar{Y}* \ge 0$. Moreover,

$$E(\bar{Y} - \bar{Y}*) = E(\bar{Y}) - E(\bar{Y}*) = E(Y) - E(Y^*) = 2 - 1 = 1$$

and

$$\mathrm{Var}(\bar{Y} - \bar{Y}*) = \mathrm{Var}(\bar{Y}) + \mathrm{Var}(\bar{Y}*) \qquad \text{(why?)}$$

$$= \frac{\mathrm{Var}(Y)}{9} + \frac{\mathrm{Var}(Y^*)}{4} = \frac{2^2}{9} + \frac{1^2}{4} = \frac{25}{36}$$

so

$$P(\bar{Y} \ge \bar{Y}*) = P(\bar{Y} - \bar{Y}* \ge 0) = P\left(\frac{\bar{Y} - \bar{Y}* - 1}{\sqrt{25/36}} \ge \frac{0 - 1}{\sqrt{25/36}} \right) = P(Z \ge -1.20)$$

$$= 0.8849$$

QUESTIONS

4.3.21 Econo-Tire is planning an advertising campaign for its newest product, an inexpensive radial. Preliminary road tests conducted by the firm's quality control department have suggested that the lifetimes of these tires will be normally distributed with an average of 30,000 miles and a standard deviation of 5000 miles. The marketing division would like to run a commercial that makes the claim that at least nine out of ten drivers will get at least 25,000 miles on a set of Econo-Tires. Based on the road test data, is the company justified in making that assertion?

4.3.22 A large computer chip manufacturing plant under construction in Westbank is expected to add 1400 children to the county's public school system once the permanent work force arrives. Any child with an IQ under 80 or over 135 will require individualized instruction that will cost the city an additional $1750 per year. How much money should Westbank anticipate spending next year to meet the needs of its new special ed students? Assume that IQ scores are normally distributed with a mean (μ) of 100 and a standard deviation (σ) of 16.

4.3.23 Records for the past several years show that the amount of money collected daily by a prominent televangelist is normally distributed with a mean (μ) of $20,000 and a standard deviation (σ) of $5000. What are the chances that tomorrow's donations will exceed $30,000?

4.3.24 The following letter was written to a well-known dispenser of advice to the lovelorn (161):

> Dear Abby: You wrote in your column that a woman is pregnant for 266 days. Who said so? I carried my baby for ten months and five days, and there is no doubt about it because I know the exact date my baby was conceived. My husband is in the Navy and it

couldn't have possibly been conceived any other time because I saw him only once for an hour, and I didn't see him again until the day before the baby was born.

I don't drink or run around, and there is no way this baby isn't his, so please print a retraction about the 266-day carrying time because otherwise I am in a lot of trouble.

San Diego Reader

Whether or not San Diego Reader is telling the truth is a judgment that lies beyond the scope of any statistical analysis, but quantifying the plausibility of her story does not. According to the collective experience of generations of pediatricians, pregnancy durations, Y, tend to be normally distributed with $\mu = 266$ days and $\sigma = 16$ days. Do a probability calculation that addresses San Diego Reader's credibility. What would you conclude?

4.3.25 A criminologist has developed a questionnaire for predicting whether a teenager will become a delinquent. Scores on the questionnaire can range from 0 to 100, with higher values reflecting a presumably greater criminal tendency. As a rule of thumb, the criminologist decides to classify a teenager as a potential delinquent if his or her score exceeds 75. The questionnaire has already been tested on a large sample of teenagers, both delinquent and nondelinquent. Among those considered nondelinquent, scores were normally distributed with a mean (μ) of 60 and a standard deviation (σ) of 10. Among those considered delinquent, scores were normally distributed with a mean of 80 and a standard deviation of 5.

   (a) What proportion of the time will the criminologist misclassify a nondelinquent as a delinquent? A delinquent as a nondelinquent?

   (b) On the same set of axes, draw the normal curves that represent the distributions of scores made by delinquents and nondelinquents. Shade the two areas that correspond to the probabilities asked for in Part (a).

4.3.26 The cross-sectional area of plastic tubing for use in pulmonary resuscitators is normally distributed with $\mu = 12.5$ mm^2 and $\sigma = 0.2$ mm^2. When the area is less than 12.0 mm^2 or greater than 13.0 mm^2, the tube does not fit properly. If the tubes are shipped in boxes of 1000, how many wrong-sized tubes per box can doctors expect to find?

4.3.27 At State University, the average score of the entering class on the verbal portion of the SAT is 565, with a standard deviation of 75. Marian scored a 660. How many of State's other 4250 freshmen did better? Assume that the scores are normally distributed.

4.3.28 A college professor teaches Chemistry 101 each fall to a large class of freshmen. For tests, she uses standardized exams that she knows from past experience produce bell-shaped grade distributions with a mean of 70 and a standard deviation of 12. Her philosophy of grading is to impose standards that will yield, in the long run, 20% A's, 26% B's, 38% C's, 12% D's, and 4% F's. Where should the cutoff be between the A's and the B's? Between the B's and the C's?

4.3.29 Suppose the random variable Y can be described by a normal curve with $\mu = 40$. For what value of σ is

$$P(20 \leq Y \leq 60) = 0.50$$

4.3.30 It is estimated that 80% of all 18-year-old women have weights ranging from 103.5 to 144.5 lb. Assuming the weight distribution can be adequately modeled by a normal curve and assuming that 103.5 and 144.5 are equidistant from the average weight μ, calculate σ.

4.3.31 Recall the breath analyzer problem described in Example 4.3.6. Suppose the driver's blood alcohol concentration is actually 0.11% rather than 0.095%. What is the probability that the breath analyzer will make an error in his favor and indicate that he is *not* legally drunk? Suppose the police offer the driver a choice—either take the sobriety test once or take it twice and average the readings. Which option should a "0.095%" driver take? Which option should a "0.11%" driver take? Explain.

4.3.32 If a random variable Y is normally distributed with mean μ and standard deviation σ, the Z ratio $\dfrac{Y - \mu}{\sigma}$ is often referred to as a *normed* score: It indicates the magnitude of y *relative to the distribution from which it came.* "Norming" is sometimes used as an affirmative action mechanism in hiring decisions. Suppose a cosmetics company is seeking a new sales manager. The aptitude test they have traditionally given for that position shows a distinct gender bias: Scores for men are normally distributed with $\mu = 62.0$ and $\sigma = 7.6$, while scores for women are normally distributed with $\mu = 76.3$ and $\sigma = 10.8$. Laura and Michael are the two candidates vying for the position: Laura has scored 92 on the test and Michael 75. If the company agrees to norm the scores for gender bias, whom should they hire?

4.3.33 Given that

$$E\big(e^{tZ}\big) = \int_{-\infty}^{\infty} e^{tz} \cdot \frac{1}{\sqrt{2\pi}}\, e^{-z^2/2}\, dz = e^{t^2/2}$$

use Theorem 3.16.3 to deduce that

$$M_Y(t) = e^{\mu t + (\sigma^2 t^2)/2}$$

when Y is normally distributed with mean μ and variance σ^2.

4.3.34 Use moment-generating functions to prove the two corollaries on page 282.

4.3.35 Suppose the random variable Y has moment-generating function $M_Y(t) = e^{\mu t + (\sigma^2 t^2)/2}$. Differentiate $M_Y(t)$ to verify that $E(Y) = \mu$ and $\text{Var}(Y) = \sigma^2$.

4.3.36 The IQs of nine randomly selected people are recorded. Let $\bar{Y}$ denote their average. Assuming the distribution from which the Y_i's were drawn is normal with a mean of 100 and a standard deviation of 16, what is the probability that $\bar{Y}$ will exceed 103? What is the probability that any arbitrary Y_i will exceed 103? What is the probability that exactly three of the Y_i's will exceed 103?

4.3.37 Let $Y_1, Y_2, \ldots, Y_n$ be a random sample from a normal distribution where the mean is 2 and the variance is 4. How large must n be in order that

$$P\big(1.9 \le \bar{Y} \le 2.1\big) \ge 0.99$$

4.3.38 A circuit contains three resistors wired in series. Each is rated at 6 ohms. Suppose, however, that the true resistance of each one is a normally distributed random variable with a mean of 6 ohms and a standard deviation of 0.3 ohm. What is the probability that the combined resistance will exceed 19 ohms? How "precise" would the manufacturing process have to be to make the probability less than 0.005 that the combined resistance of the circuit would exceed 19 ohms?

4.3.39 The cylinders and pistons for a certain internal combustion engine are manufactured by a process that gives a normal distribution of cylinder diameters with a mean of 41.5 cm and a standard deviation of 0.4 cm. Similarly, the distribution of piston diameters is normal with a mean of 40.5 cm and a standard deviation of 0.3 cm. If the piston diameter is greater than the cylinder diameter, the former can be reworked until the two "fit". What proportion of cylinder–piston pairs will need to be reworked?

4.4 THE GEOMETRIC DISTRIBUTION

Consider a series of independent trials, each having one of two possible outcomes, success or failure. Let $p = P(\text{trial ends in success})$. Define the random variable X to be the trial *at which the first success occurs*. Figure 4.4.1 suggests a formula for the pdf of X:

FIGURE 4.4.1

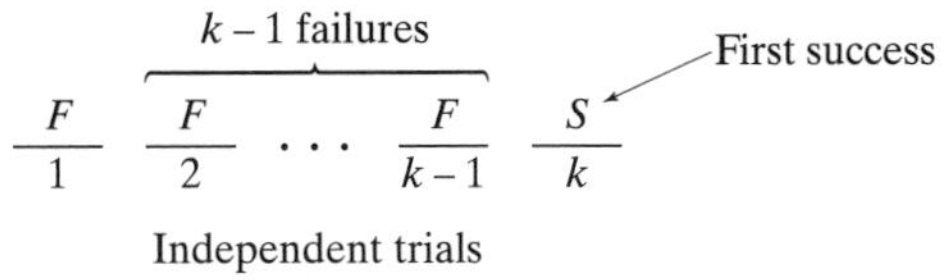

$$p_X(k) = P(X = k) = P(\text{first success occurs on } k\text{th trial})$$

$$= P(\text{first } k - 1 \text{ trials end in failure and } k\text{th trial ends in success})$$

$$= P(\text{first } k - 1 \text{ trials end in failure}) \cdot P(k\text{th trial ends in success})$$

$$= (1 - p)^{k-1}p, \quad k = 1, 2, \ldots \qquad (4.4.1)$$

We call the probability model in Equation 4.4.1 a *geometric distribution* (with parameter p).

   Comment. Even without its association with independent trials and Figure 4.4.1, the function $p_X(k) = (1 - p)^{k-1}p$, $k = 1, 2, \ldots$ qualifies as a discrete pdf because (1) $p_X(k) \geq 0$ for all k and (2) $\sum\limits_{\text{all } k} p_X(k) = 1$:

$$\sum_{k=1}^{\infty} (1 - p)^{k-1}p = p \sum_{j=0}^{\infty} (1 - p)^j$$

$$= p \cdot \left(\frac{1}{1 - (1 - p)} \right)$$

$$= 1$$

EXAMPLE 4.4.1

A pair of fair dice are tossed until a sum of 7 appears for the first time. What is the probability that more than four rolls will be required for that to happen?
   Each throw of the dice here is an independent trial for which

$$p = P(\text{sum} = 7) = \frac{6}{36} = \frac{1}{6}$$

Let X denote the roll at which the first sum of 7 appears. Clearly, X has the structure of a geometric random variable, and

$$P(X > 4) = 1 - P(X \leq 4) = 1 - \sum_{k=1}^{4} \left(\frac{5}{6} \right)^{k-1} \left(\frac{1}{6} \right)$$

$$= 1 - \frac{671}{1296}$$

$$= 0.48$$

THEOREM 4.4.1. Let X have a geometric distribution with $p_X(k) = (1 - p)^{k-1}p$, $k = 1, 2, \ldots$ Then

(1) $M_X(t) = \dfrac{pe^t}{1 - (1 - p)e^t}$

(2) $E(X) = \dfrac{1}{p}$

(3) $\mathrm{Var}(X) = \dfrac{1 - p}{p^2}$

Proof.   By definition,

$$M_X(t) = E\big(e^{tX}\big) = \sum_{k=1}^{\infty} e^{tk} \cdot (1 - p)^{k-1}p$$

$$= \frac{p}{1 - p} \sum_{k=1}^{\infty} \big[(1 - p)e^t\big]^k$$

$$= \frac{p}{1 - p} \sum_{k=0}^{\infty} \big[(1 - p)e^t\big]^k - \frac{p}{1 - p}\big[(1 - p)e^t\big]^0$$

For t sufficiently close to 0, $(1 - p)e^t < 1$. Using the formula for the sum of a geometric series, then, we can write

$$M_X(t) = \frac{p}{1 - p} \cdot \frac{1}{1 - (1 - p)e^t} - \frac{p}{1 - p}$$

$$= \frac{pe^t}{1 - (1 - p)e^t}$$

[Formulas for $E(X)$ and $\mathrm{Var}(X)$ are derived by differentiating $M_X(t)$; the details will be left as an exercise.]

EXAMPLE 4.4.2

A grocery store is sponsoring a sales promotion where the cashiers give away one of the letters A, E, L, S, U, and V for each purchase. If a customer collects all six (spelling VALUES), he or she gets \$10 worth of groceries free. What is the expected number of trips to the store a customer needs to make in order to get a complete set? Assume the different letters are given away randomly.

Let X_i denote the number of purchases necessary to get the ith different letter, $i = 1, 2, \ldots, 6$, and let X denote the number of purchases necessary to qualify for the \$10. Then $X = X_1 + X_2 + \cdots + X_6$ (see Figure 4.4.2). Clearly, X_1 equals 1 with probability 1, so $E(X_1) = 1$. Having received the first letter, the chances of getting a different one are $\frac{5}{6}$ for each subsequent trip to the store. Therefore,

$$f_{x_2}(k) = P\big(X_2 = k\big) = \left(\frac{1}{6}\right)^{k-1}\frac{5}{6}, \quad k = 1, 2 \ldots$$

That is, X_2 is a geometric random variable with parameter $p = \frac{5}{6}$. By Theorem 4.4.1, $E(X_2) = \frac{6}{5}$. Similarly, the chances of getting a *third* different letter are $\frac{4}{6}$ (for each purchase), so

$$f_{X_3}(k) = P\big(X_3 = k\big) = \left(\frac{2}{6}\right)^{k-1}\left(\frac{4}{6}\right), \quad k = 1, 2, \ldots$$

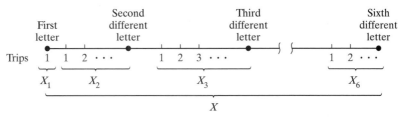

FIGURE 4.4.2

and $E(X_3) = \frac{6}{4}$. Continuing in this fashion, we can find the remaining $E(X_i)$'s. It follows that a customer will have to make *14.7* trips to the store, on the average, to collect a complete set of six letters:

$$E(X) = \sum_{i=1}^{6} E(X_i)$$

$$= 1 + \frac{6}{5} + \frac{6}{4} + \frac{6}{3} + \frac{6}{2} + \frac{6}{1}$$

$$= 14.7$$

EXAMPLE 4.4.3

Geometric random variables have a curious *memoryless* property: The probability that it takes an additional $X = k$ trials to obtain the first success is unaffected by however many failures have already been observed. That is,

$$P(X = n - 1 + k \mid X > n - 1) = P(X = k) \qquad (4.4.2)$$

Prove Equation 4.4.2.

We know from the definition of conditional probability that

$$P(X = n - 1 + k \mid X > n - 1) = \frac{P\big((X = n - 1 + k) \cap (X > n - 1)\big)}{P(X > n - 1)}$$

$$= \frac{P(X = n - 1 + k)}{1 - P(X \le n - 1)}$$

Moreover,

$$P(X \le n - 1) = \sum_{k=1}^{n-1} (1 - p)^{k-1} p = p \sum_{j=0}^{n-2} (1 - p)^j$$

showing that the cdf, $F_X(n - 1)$, for a geometric random variable is p times the partial sum of a geometric series $\big(= 1 + (1 - p) + \cdots + (1 - p)^{n-2}\big)$. Formulas for many partial sums are well known.

Here,

$$p \sum_{j=0}^{n-2} (1 - p)^j = p \frac{\big[(1 - p)^{n-1} - 1\big]}{1 - p - 1} = 1 - (1 - p)^{n-1}$$

Therefore,

$$P(X = n - 1 + k \mid X > n - 1) = \frac{p(1 - p)^{n-1+k-1}}{1 - [1 - (1 - p)^{n-1}]}$$

$$= p(1 - p)^{k-1}$$

and the latter equals $P(X = k)$.

Comment.   Radioactive decay is a physical process for which the memoryless property described in Example 4.4.3 applies. If "time" is divided into consecutive intervals of equal duration, the period in which a nucleus decays is modeled by the geometric distribution, where p is a function of the atom's half-life.

EXAMPLE 4.4.4

One of the "can't miss" schemes that every would-be gambler sooner or later reinvents is the *double-your-bet* strategy. Imagine playing a series of evenly matched games. You bet \$1 on the first game; if you lose, you bet \$2 on the second game; if you lose that one, too, you bet \$4 on the third game; and so on.

Suppose you win for the first time on the kth game. At that point you receive $\$2^k$ and *your net winnings will be \$1*:

$$\begin{array}{l} \text{net amount won after} \\ \text{winning } k\text{th game} \end{array} = \begin{array}{l} \text{money won} \\ \text{on } k\text{th game} \end{array} - \begin{array}{l} \text{money lost on} \\ \text{previous } k - 1 \text{ games} \end{array}$$

$$= 2^k - \left(1 + 2 + 4 + \cdots + 2^{k-1}\right)$$

$$= 2^k - \left(2^k - 1\right)$$

$$= \$1$$

It would appear that doubling our bets guarantees a profit. Where is the catch (or should we all book the next flight to Las Vegas)?

The devil in this case is in the expected value. In order to bankroll the strategy just described, a player needs to have $\$2^k - 1$ in order to be eligible to play the kth game (to win for the first time on the third try, for example, a player would have lost \$1 on the first game, \$2 on the second game, and would have wagered \$4 on the third game, so the money spent at that point is $1 + 2 + 4 = \$7$, or $\$2^3 - 1$). Now, if it takes \$3 to be eligible to win on the second game, and \$7 to be eligible to win on the third game, how much capital does a player need to have *on the average*?

Let X denote the game where the player wins for the first time. Clearly, X is a geometric random variable for which $p_X(k) = \frac{1}{2}^{k-1} \cdot \frac{1}{2}, k = 1, 2, \ldots$. Moreover, to win on the kth game requires an investment of $g(k) = \$2^k - 1$, so the *expected* amount of money needed is $E[g(X)]$, where

$$E[g(X)] = E[2^X - 1] = \sum_{k=1}^{\infty} (2^k - 1)(\tfrac{1}{2})^{k-1}\tfrac{1}{2}$$

$$= \sum_{k=1}^{\infty} \left(1 - (\tfrac{1}{2})^k\right)$$

$$= \frac{1}{2} + \frac{3}{4} + \frac{7}{8} + \cdots$$

Since every term in the infinite series that defines $E[g(X)]$ is larger than the one that precedes it, the gambler would need to have an infinite amount of money in order to implement a double-your-bet strategy! (On a more practical note, casinos always have house limits, so players would not be allowed to double their bets indefinitely anyway. Recall that a similar analysis played a role in the St. Petersburg analysis introduced in Example 3.10.6.)

QUESTIONS

4.4.1 Because of her past convictions for mail fraud and forgery, Jody has a 30% chance each year of having her tax returns audited. What is the probability that she will escape detection for at least three years? Assume that she exaggerates, distorts, misrepresents, lies, and cheats every year.

4.4.2 A teenager is trying to get a driver's license. Write out the formula for the pdf $p_X(k)$, where the random variable X is the number of tries that he needs to pass the road test. Assume that his probability of passing the exam on any given attempt is 0.10. On the average, how many attempts is he likely to require before he gets his license?

4.4.3 Is the following set of data likely to have come from the geometric pdf $p_X(k) = \left(\frac{3}{4}\right)^{k-1} \cdot \left(\frac{1}{4}\right)$, $k = 1, 2, \ldots$? Explain.

2	8	1	2	2	5	1	2	8	3
5	4	2	4	7	2	2	8	4	7
2	6	2	3	5	1	3	3	2	5
4	2	2	3	6	3	6	4	9	3
3	7	5	1	3	4	3	4	6	2

4.4.4 Differentiate the moment-generating function for a geometric random variable and verify the expressions given for $E(X)$ and $\text{Var}(X)$ in Theorem 4.4.1.

4.4.5 Show that the cdf for a geometric random variable is given by $F_X(t) = P(X \le t) = 1 - (1 - p)^{[t]}$, where $[t]$ denotes the greatest integer in t.

4.4.6 Suppose three fair dice are tossed repeatedly. Let the random variable X denote the roll on which a sum of 4 appears for the first time. Use the expression for $F_X(t)$ given in Question 4.4.5 to evaluate $P(65 \le X \le 75)$.

4.4.7 Suppose that the random variables X_1 and X_2 have mgfs $M_{X_1}(t) = \dfrac{\frac{1}{2}e^t}{1 - \left(1 - \frac{1}{2}\right)e^t}$ and

$M_{X_2}(t) = \dfrac{\frac{1}{4}e^t}{1 - \left(1 - \frac{1}{4}\right)e^t}$, respectively. Let $X = X_1 + X_2$. Does X have a geometric distribution? Assume that X_1 and X_2 are independent.

4.4.8 Recently married, a young couple plans to continue having children until they have their first girl. Suppose the probability that a child is a girl is $\frac{1}{2}$, the outcome of each birth is an independent event, and the birth at which the first girl appears has a geometric distribution. What is the couple's expected family size? Is the geometric pdf a reasonable model here? Discuss.

4.4.9 Sometimes the geometric random variable is defined to be the number of trials, X, *preceding* the first success. Write down the corresponding pdf and derive the moment-generating function for X two ways—(1) by evaluating $E(e^{tX})$ directly and (2) by using Theorem 3.16.3.

4.4.10 The *factorial moment-generating function* for any random variable W is the expected value of t^W. Moreover, $\dfrac{d^r}{dt^r} E(t^W)\Big|_{t=1} = E[W(W - 1) \cdots (W - r + 1)]$. Find the factorial moment-generating function for a geometric random variable and use it to verify the expected value and variance formulas given in Theorem 4.4.1.

4.5   THE NEGATIVE BINOMIAL DISTRIBUTION

The geometric distribution introduced in Section 4.4 can be generalized in a very straightforward fashion. Imagine waiting for the rth (instead of the first) success in a series of independent trials, where each trial has a probability of p of ending in success (see Figure 4.5.1).

FIGURE 4.5.1

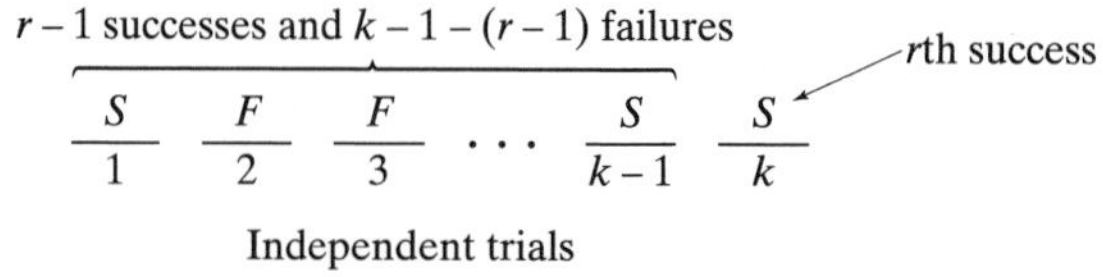

$r - 1$ successes and $k - 1 - (r - 1)$ failures

rth success

$$
\begin{array}{ccccc}
S & F & F & \cdots & S & S \\
1 & 2 & 3 & & k-1 & k
\end{array}
$$

Independent trials

Let the random variable X denote the trial at which the rth success occurs. Then

$$p_X(k) = P(X = k) = P(r\text{th success occurs on }k\text{th trial})$$

$$= P(r - 1 \text{ successes occur in first } k - 1 \text{ trials} \\ \text{and success occurs on } k\text{th trial})$$

$$= P(r - 1 \text{ successes occur in first } k - 1 \text{ trials}) \cdot \\ P(\text{success occurs on } k\text{th trial})$$

$$= \binom{k - 1}{r - 1} p^{r-1}(1 - p^{k-1-(r-1)}) \cdot p$$

$$= \binom{k - 1}{r - 1} p^{r}(1 - p)^{k-r}, \quad k = r, r + 1, \ldots \qquad (4.5.1)$$

Any random variable whose pdf has the form given in Equation 4.5.1 is said to have a *negative binomial distribution* (with parameter p).

Comment.   Two equivalent formulations of the negative binomial structure are widely used. Sometimes X is defined to be the number of trials *preceding* the rth success; other times, X is taken to be the number of trials in *excess of r* that are necessary to achieve the rth success. The underlying probability structure is the same, however X is defined. We will primarily use Equation 4.5.1; properties of the other two definitions for X will be covered in the exercises.

THEOREM 4.5.1.   Let X have a negative binomial distribution with $p_X(k) = \binom{k - 1}{r - 1} p^{r}(1 - p)^{k-r}, k = r, r + 1 \ldots$. Then

$$\textbf{(1) } M_X(t) = \left[\frac{pe^t}{1 - (1 - p)e^t} \right]^{r}$$

$$\textbf{(2) } E(X) = \frac{r}{p}$$

$$\textbf{(3) } \text{Var}(X) = \frac{r(1 - p)}{p^2}$$

Proof.   All of these results follow immediately from the fact that X can be written as the sum of r independent geometric random variables, $X_1, X_2, \ldots, X_r$, each with parameter p. That is,

$$X = \text{total number of trials to achieve } r\text{th success}$$

$$= \text{number of trials to achieve 1st success} + \text{number of additional trials to achieve 2nd success} + \cdots + \text{number of additional trials to achieve } r\text{th success}$$

$$= X_1 + X_2 + \cdots + X_r$$

where

$$p_{X_i}(k) = (1 - p)^{k-1}p, \quad k = 1, 2, \ldots, i = 1, 2, \ldots, r.$$

Therefore,

$$M_X(t) = M_{X_1}(t)M_{X_2}(t) \ldots M_{X_r}(t)$$

$$= \left[\frac{pe^t}{1 - (1 - p)e^t} \right]^r$$

Also, from Theorem 4.4.1,

$$E(X) = E(X_1) + E(X_2) + \cdots + E(X_r)$$

$$= \frac{1}{p} + \frac{1}{p} + \cdots + \frac{1}{p}$$

$$= \frac{r}{p}$$

and

$$\text{Var}(X) = \text{Var}(X_1) + \text{Var}(X_2) + \cdots + \text{Var}(X_r)$$

$$= \frac{1 - p}{p^2} + \frac{1 - p}{p^2} + \cdots + \frac{1 - p}{p^2}$$

$$= \frac{r(1 - p)}{p^2}$$

EXAMPLE 4.5.1

The California Mellows are a semipro baseball team. Eschewing all forms of violence, the laid-back Mellow batters never swing at a pitch, and should they be fortunate enough to reach base on a walk, they never try to steal. On the average, how many runs will the Mellows score in a nine-inning road game, assuming the opposing pitcher has a 50% probability of throwing a strike on any given pitch?

The solution to this problem illustrates very nicely the interplay between the physical constraints imposed by a question (in this case, by the rules of baseball) and the mathematical characteristics of the underlying probability model. The negative binomial distribution appears *twice* in this analysis, along with several of the properties associated with expected values and linear combinations.

To begin, we calculate the probability of a Mellow batter striking out. Let the random variable X denote the number of pitches necessary for that to happen. Clearly, $X = 3, 4, 5,$ or 6 (why can X not be larger than 6?), and

$$p_X(k) = P(X = k) = P(2 \text{ strikes are called in the first } k - 1$$
$$\text{pitches and the } k\text{th pitch is the 3rd strike})$$

$$= \binom{k-1}{2}(\tfrac{1}{2})^3(\tfrac{1}{2})^{k-3}, \quad k = 3, 4, 5, 6$$

Therefore,

$$P(\text{batter strikes out}) = \sum_{k=3}^{6} p_X(k) = (\tfrac{1}{2})^3 + \binom{3}{2}(\tfrac{1}{2})^4 + \binom{4}{2}(\tfrac{1}{2})^5 + \binom{5}{2}(\tfrac{1}{2})^6$$

$$= \frac{21}{32}$$

Now, let the random variable W denote the number of walks the Mellows get in a given inning. In order for W to take on the value w, exactly two of the first $w + 2$ batters must strike out, as must the $(w + 3)$rd (see Figure 4.5.2). The pdf for W, then, is a negative binomial with $p = P(\text{batter strikes out}) = \frac{21}{32}$:

$$p_W(w) = P(W = w) = \binom{w + 2}{2}\left(\frac{21}{32}\right)^3\left(\frac{11}{32}\right)^w, \quad w = 0, 1, 2, \ldots$$

FIGURE 4.5.2

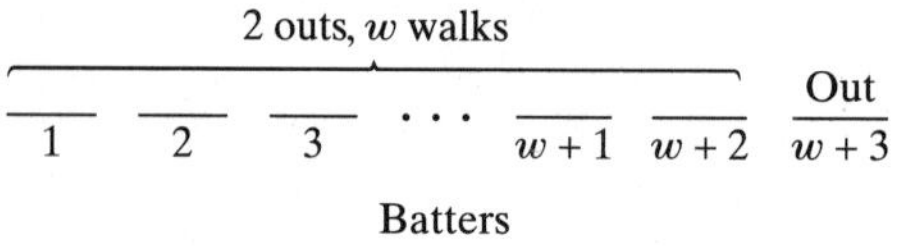

In order for a run to score, the pitcher must walk a Mellows batter with the bases loaded. Let the random variable R denote the total number of runs walked in during a given inning. Then

$$R = \begin{cases} 0 & \text{if } w \le 3 \\ w - 3 & \text{if } w > 3 \end{cases}$$

and

$$E(R) = \; = \sum_{w=4}^{w} (w - 3)\binom{w + 2}{2}\left(\frac{21}{32}\right)^3\left(\frac{11}{32}\right)^w$$

$$= \sum_{w=0}^{w} (w - 3) \cdot P(W = w) - \sum_{w=0}^{3} (w - 3) \cdot P(W = w)$$

$$= E(W) - 3 + \sum_{w=0}^{\infty} (3 - w) \cdot \binom{w + 2}{2}\left(\frac{21}{32}\right)^3\left(\frac{11}{32}\right)^w \tag{4.5.2}$$

To evaluate $E(W)$ using the statement of Theorem 4.5.1 requires a linear transformation to rescale W to the format of Equation 4.5.1. Let

$$T = W + 3 = \text{total number of Mellow batters appearing in a given inning}$$

Then

$$p_T(t) = p_W(t - 3) = \binom{t-1}{2}\left(\frac{21}{32}\right)^3\left(\frac{11}{32}\right)^{t-3}, \quad t = 3, 4, \ldots$$

which we recognize as a negative binomial pdf with $r = 3$ and $p = \frac{21}{32}$. Therefore,

$$E(T) = \frac{3}{21/32} = \frac{32}{7}$$

which makes $E(W) = E(T) - 3 = \frac{32}{7} - 3 = \frac{11}{7}$.

From Equation 4.5.2, then, the expected number of runs scored by the Mellows in a given inning is *0.202*:

$$E(R) = \frac{11}{7} - 3 + 3 \cdot \binom{2}{2}\left(\frac{21}{32}\right)^3\left(\frac{11}{32}\right)^0 + 2 \cdot \binom{3}{2}\left(\frac{21}{32}\right)^3\left(\frac{11}{32}\right)^1 + 1 \cdot \binom{4}{2}\left(\frac{21}{32}\right)^3\left(\frac{11}{32}\right)^2$$

$$= 0.202$$

Each of the nine innings, of course, would have the same value for $E(R)$, so the expected number of runs in a *game* is the sum $0.202 + 0.202 + \cdots + 0.202 = 9(0.202)$, or *1.82*.

QUESTIONS

4.5.1 A door-to-door encyclopedia salesperson is required to document five in-home visits each day. Suppose that she has a 30% chance of being invited into any given home, with each address representing an independent trial. What is the probability that she requires fewer than eight houses to achieve her fifth success?

4.5.2 An underground military installation is fortified to the extent that it can withstand up to three direct hits from air-to-surface missiles and still function. Suppose an enemy aircraft is armed with missiles, each having a 30% chance of scoring a direct hit. What is the probability that the installation will be destroyed with the seventh missile fired?

4.5.3 Darryl's statistics homework last night was to flip a fair coin and record the toss, X, where heads appears for the second time. The experiment was to be repeated a total of 100 times. The following are the 100 values for X that Darryl turned in this morning. Do you think that he actually did the assignment? Explain.

3	7	3	2	9	3	4	3	3	2
7	3	8	4	3	3	3	4	3	3
4	3	2	2	4	5	2	2	2	4
2	5	6	4	2	6	2	8	3	2
8	2	3	2	4	3	2	6	3	3
3	2	5	3	6	4	5	6	5	6
3	5	2	7	2	10	4	3	2	2
4	2	4	5	5	5	6	2	4	3
3	4	4	6	3	4	2	5	5	2
5	7	5	3	2	7	4	4	4	3

4.5.4 Let X_1, X_2, and X_3 be three independent negative binomial random variables with pdf's

$$p_{X_i}(k) = \binom{k-1}{2} \left(\frac{4}{5}\right)^3 \left(\frac{1}{5}\right)^{k-3}, \quad k = 3, 4, 5, \ldots$$

for $i = 1, 2, 3$. Define $X = X_1 + X_2 + X_3$. Find $P(10 \le X \le 12)$. *Hint*: Use the moment-generating functions of X_1, X_2, and X_3 to deduce the pdf of X.

4.5.5 Let the random variable X denote the number of trials *in excess of r* that are required to achieve the rth success in a series of independent trials, where p is the probability of success at any given trial. Show that

$$p_X(k) = \binom{k+r-1}{k} p^r (1-p)^k, \quad k = 0, 1, 2, \ldots$$

[*Note*: This particular formula for $p_X(k)$ is often used in place of Equation 4.5.1 as the definition of the pdf for a negative binomial random variable.]

4.5.6 Calculate the mean, variance, and moment-generating function for a negative binomial random variable X whose pdf is given by the expression

$$p_X(k) = \binom{k+r-1}{k} p^r (1-p)^k, \quad k = 0, 1, 2, \ldots$$

(see Question 4.5.5).

4.5.7 Differentiate the moment-generating function $M_X(t) = \left[\dfrac{pe^t}{1 - (1-p)e^t}\right]^r$ to verify the formula given in Theorem 4.5.1 for $E(X)$.

4.5.8 Suppose that $X_1, X_2, \ldots, X_k$ are independent negative binomial random variables with parameters r_1 and p, r_2 and $p, \ldots$, and r_k and p, respectively. Let $X = X_1 + X_2 + \cdots + X_k$. Find $M_X(t), p_X(t), E(X)$, and $\mathrm{Var}(X)$.

4.5.9 For a negative binomial random variable whose pdf is given by Equation 4.5.1, find $E(X)$ directly by evaluating $\displaystyle\sum_{k=r}^{\infty} k \binom{k-1}{r-1} p^r (1-p)^{k-r}$. *Hint*: Reduce the sum to one involving negative binomial probabilities with parameters $r+1$ and p.

4.5.10 When a machine is improperly adjusted, it has probability 0.15 of producing a defective item. Each day the machine is run until three defective items are produced. If this occurs, it is stopped and checked for adjustment. What is the probability that an improperly adjusted machine will produce five or more items before being stopped? What is the average number of items an improperly adjusted machine will produce before being stopped?

4.6 THE GAMMA DISTRIBUTION

Suppose a series of independent events are occurring at the constant rate of λ per unit time. If the random variable Y denotes the interval between consecutive occurrences, we know from Theorem 4.2.3 that $f_Y(y) = \lambda e^{-\lambda y}$, $y > 0$. Equivalently, Y can be interpreted as the "waiting time" for the first occurrence. This section generalizes the Poisson/exponential relationship and focuses on the interval, or waiting time, required for the rth event to occur (see Figure 4.6.1).

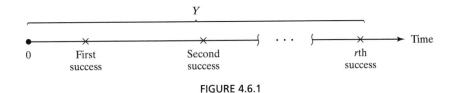

FIGURE 4.6.1

THEOREM 4.6.1. Suppose that Poisson events are occurring at the constant rate of λ per unit time. Let the random variable Y denote the waiting time for the rth event. Then Y has a *gamma distribution with parameters r and* λ, where

$$f_Y(y) = \frac{\lambda^r}{(r-1)!}\, y^{r-1} e^{-\lambda y}, \quad y > 0$$

Proof. We will establish the formula for the gamma pdf $f_Y(y)$ by deriving and differentiating its cdf, $F_Y(y)$. Let Y denote the waiting time to the rth occurrence. Then

$$F_Y(y) = P(Y \le y) = 1 - P(Y > y)$$

$$= 1 - P(\text{fewer than } r \text{ events occur in } [0, y])$$

$$= 1 - \sum_{k=0}^{r-1} e^{-\lambda y} \frac{(\lambda y)^k}{k!}$$

since the number of events that occur in the interval $[0, y]$ is a Poisson random variable with parameter λy.

From Theorem 3.4.1,

$$f_Y(y) = F_Y'(y) = \frac{d}{dy}\left[1 - \sum_{k=0}^{r-1} e^{-\lambda y} \frac{(\lambda y)^k}{k!}\right]$$

$$= \sum_{k=0}^{r-1} \lambda e^{-\lambda y} \frac{(\lambda y)^k}{k!} - \sum_{k=1}^{r-1} \lambda e^{-\lambda y} \frac{(\lambda y)^{k-1}}{(k-1)!}$$

$$= \sum_{k=0}^{r-1} \lambda e^{-\lambda y} \frac{(\lambda y)^k}{k!} - \sum_{k=0}^{r-2} \lambda e^{-\lambda y} \frac{(\lambda y)^k}{k!}$$

$$= \frac{\lambda^r}{(r-1)!}\, y^{r-1} e^{-\lambda y}, \quad y > 0$$

EXAMPLE 4.6.1

Engineers designing the next generation of space shuttles plan to include two fuel pumps—one active, the other in reserve. If the primary pump malfunctions, the second is automatically brought on line.

Suppose a typical mission is expected to require that fuel be pumped for at most 50 hours. According to the manufacturer's specifications, pumps are expected to fail once every 100 hours (so $\lambda = 0.01$). What are the chances that such a fuel pump system would not remain functioning for the full 50 hours?

Let Y denote the time that will elapse before the second pump breaks down. In the notation of Theorem 4.6.1, Y is a gamma random variable with parameters $r = 2$ and $\lambda = 0.01$. Therefore,

$$f_Y(y) = \frac{(0.01)^2}{1!} ye^{-0.01y}, \quad y > 0$$

and

$$P(\text{system fails to last for 50 hours}) = \int_0^{50} 0.0001ye^{-0.01y}\, dy$$

$$= \int_0^{0.50} ue^{-u}\, du$$

where $u = 0.01y$. The probability, then, that the primary pump and its backup would not remain operable for the targeted 50 hours is *0.09*:

$$\int_0^{0.50} ue^{-u}\, du = (-u - 1)e^{-u}\Big|_{\mu=0}^{0.50}$$

$$= 0.09$$

THEOREM 4.6.2. Suppose that Y is a gamma random variable with pdf
$$f_Y(y) = \frac{\lambda^r}{(r-1)!} y^{r-1}e^{-\lambda y}, \quad y > 0. \text{ Then}$$

(1) $M_Y(t) = \left(\dfrac{1}{1 - t/\lambda}\right)^r$

(2) $E(Y) = \dfrac{r}{\lambda}$

(3) $\text{Var}(Y) = \dfrac{r}{\lambda^2}$

Proof. If the gamma random variable Y denotes the waiting time for the rth occurrence, then $Y = Y_1 + Y_2 + \cdots + Y_r$, where Y_i = waiting time for each individual occurrence, $i = 1, 2, \ldots, r$ (recall Figure 4.6.1). But each Y_i is an independent exponential random variable with parameter λ and moment-generating function $M_{Y_i}(t) = (1 - t/\lambda)^{-1}$. Therefore,

$$M_Y(t) = M_{Y_1}(t) \cdot M_{Y_2}(t) \cdots M_{Y_r}(t)$$

$$= (1 - t/\lambda)^{-1} \cdot (1 - t/\lambda)^{-1} \cdots (1 - t/\lambda)^{-1}$$

$$= (1 - t/\lambda)^{-r}$$

The formulas for $E(Y)$ and $\text{Var}(Y)$ follow immediately from the fact that $E(Y_i) = 1/\lambda$ and $\text{Var}(Y_i) = 1/\lambda^2$ if Y_i is exponential with parameter λ.

EXAMPLE 4.6.2

In a certain large industrial plant, on-the-job accidents and illnesses that require a worker to be confined to a bed occur at the rate of 0.7 per hour. The company's infirmary has 10 beds. Use the central limit theorem and the properties of the gamma distribution to approximate the probability that the infirmary will be inadequate to meet the health emergencies that arise during tomorrow's eight-hour workday.

Let Y_i denote the waiting time for the ith patient. Then $Y = Y_1 + Y_2 + \cdots + Y_{11}$ denotes the length of time from the start of the workday to when the *eleventh* person needs a bed. Clearly, $P(Y < 8) = P$(infirmary is unable to provide enough beds).

Here Y is a gamma random variable with parameters $r = 11$ and $\lambda = 0.7$, so $E(Y) = 11/0.7 = 15.7$ and $\text{Var}(Y) = 11/(0.7)^2 = 22.45$. Using the central limit theorem, then, we find that the probability of the infirmary having too few beds to accommodate tomorrow's demand is approximately *0.05*:

$$P(Y < 8) = P\left(\frac{Y - 15.7}{\sqrt{22.45}} < \frac{8 - 15.7}{\sqrt{22.45}}\right)$$

$$\doteq P(Z < -1.63)$$

$$= 0.05$$

Comment.   With the help of computer software, the exact answer to the question posed in Example 4.6.2 can be readily obtained. According to MINITAB,

$$P(Y < 8) = \int_0^8 \frac{(0.7)^{11}}{10!} y^{10} e^{-0.7y} \, dy$$

$$= 0.03$$

EXAMPLE 4.6.3

Suppose that Y_1 and Y_2 are independent random variables with pdf's

$$f_{Y_1}(y) = \frac{3^6}{5!} y^5 e^{-3y}, \quad y > 0$$

and

$$f_{Y_2}(y) = \frac{3^7}{6!} y^6 e^{-3y}, \quad y > 0$$

respectively. Let $Y = Y_1 + Y_2$. Graph $f_Y(y)$, the pdf for Y.

By inspection, Y_1 is a gamma random variable with parameters $r = 6$ and $\lambda = 3$; similarly, Y_2 is gamma with $r = 7$ and $\lambda = 3$. As we have seen before, moment-generating functions often provide an easy route for finding pdf's of sums. Here, with the help of Theorem 4.6.2,

$$M_Y(t) = M_{Y_1}(t) \cdot M_{Y_2}(t)$$

$$= \left(\frac{1}{1 - t/3}\right)^6 \cdot \left(\frac{1}{1 - t/3}\right)^7$$

$$= \left(\frac{1}{1 - t/3}\right)^{13}$$

But $\left(\dfrac{1}{1-t/3}\right)^{13}$ has the form of the moment-generating function of a gamma random variable with $r = 13$ and $\lambda = 3$, so

$$f_Y(y) = \frac{3^{13}}{12!}\, y^{12} e^{-3y}, \quad y > 0$$

(see Figure 4.6.2).

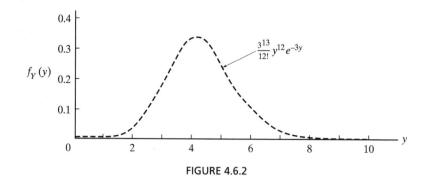

FIGURE 4.6.2

Comment. The gamma pdf can be extended to include noninteger values of r. For any $r > 0$, let

$$\Gamma(r) = \int_0^\infty y^{r-1} e^{-y}\, dy$$

We can then define Y to be a gamma random variable with parameters $r (> 0)$ and $\lambda (> 0)$ if

$$f_Y(y) = \frac{\lambda^r}{\Gamma(r)}\, y^{r-1} e^{-\lambda y}, \quad y > 0 \tag{4.6.1}$$

When r is an integer, $\Gamma(r) = (r - 1)!$, and Equation 4.6.1 reduces to the special case of the gamma pdf that appears in Theorem 4.6.1. The formulas given earlier in this section for $M_Y(t)$, $E(Y)$, and $\text{Var}(Y)$ remain the same whether or not r is an integer.

QUESTIONS

4.6.1 Use the fact that $\Gamma(r) = (r - 1)!$ when r is an integer to verify that

$$\int_0^\infty \frac{\lambda^r}{(r-1)!}\, y^{r-1} e^{-\lambda y}\, dy = 1$$

(recall the previous comment).

4.6.2 An Arctic weather station has three electronic wind gauges. Only one is used at any given time. The lifetime of each gauge is exponentially distributed with a mean of 1000 hours. What is the pdf of Y, the random variable measuring the time until the last gauge wears out?

4.6.3 In Example 4.6.2, what might account for the sizeable discrepancy between the exact value for $P(Y < 8)$ and its central limit theorem approximation?

4.6.4 Differentiate the gamma moment-generating function to verify the formulas for $E(Y)$ and $\text{Var}(Y)$ given in Theorem 4.6.2.

4.6.5 If the random variable Y has the gamma pdf given in Theorem 4.6.1, show that

$$E(Y^m) = \frac{(m + r - 1)!}{(r - 1)!\lambda^m}$$

Hint: Use the fact that $\int_0^\infty y^{r-1}e^{-y} = (r - 1)!$ when r is a positive integer.

4.6.6 Suppose a set of measurements $Y_1, Y_2, \ldots, Y_{100}$ is taken from a gamma pdf for which $E(Y) = 1.5$ and $\text{Var}(Y) = 0.75$. How many Y_i's would you expect to find in the interval $(1.0, 2.5)$?

4.6.7 Given that $\Gamma(r) = \int_0^\infty y^{r-1}e^{-y}\,dy$ for $r > 0$, prove that

    (a) $\Gamma(1) = 1$ **(b)** $\Gamma(r + 1) = r\Gamma(r)$ **(c)** $\Gamma(\frac{1}{2}) = \sqrt{\pi}$

Hint: Consider $E(Z^2)$, where Z is a standard normal random variable.

APPENDIX 4.A.1   MINITAB APPLICATIONS

Calculations involving Poisson, exponential, normal, and gamma random variables can be readily handled with MINITAB's PDF and CDF commands (recall Appendix 3.A.1). Figure 4.A.1.1(a) shows the syntax for doing the Poisson calculation in Example 4.2.2. Values of $p_X(k) = e^{-1.5}(1.5)^k/k!$ for all k can be printed out by using the PDF command without specifying a particular k [see Figure 4.A.1.1(b)].

(a)

```
MTB > cdf 3;
SUBC> poisson 1.5.
```

Cumulative Distribution Function

Poisson with mu = 1.50000

x	P(X <= x)
3.00	0.9344

```
MTB > let k1 = 1 - 0.9344
MTB > print k1
```

Data Display

K1   0.0656000

(b)

```
MTB > pdf;
SUBC> poisson 1.5.
```

Probability Density Function

Poisson with mu = 1.50000

x	P(X = x)
0	0.2231
1	0.3347
2	0.2510
3	0.1255
4	0.0471
5	0.0141
6	0.0035
7	0.0008
8	0.0001
9	0.0000

$P(X > 3) = 0.0656$

FIGURE 4.A.1.1

Areas under normal curves between points *a* and *b* are calculated by subtracting $F_Y(a)$ from $F_Y(b)$, just as we did in Section 4.3 (recall the comment after Definition 4.3.1). There is no need, however, to reexpress the probability as an area under the *standard* normal curve. Figure 4.A.1.2 shows the MINITAB calculation for the probability that the random variable *Y* lies between 48 and 51, where *Y* is normally distributed with $\mu = 50$ and $\sigma = 4$. According to the computer,

$$P(48 < Y < 51) = F_Y(51) - F_Y(48) = 0.5987 - 0.3085$$

$$= 0.2902$$

```
MTB > cdf 51;
SUBC> normal 50 4.
```

Cumulative Distribution Function

```
Normal with mean = 50.0000 and standard deviation = 4.00000

          x       P( X <= x)
    51.0000         0.5987
```

```
MTB > cdf 48;
SUBC> normal 50 4.
```

Cumulative Distribution Function

```
Normal with mean = 50.0000 and standard deviation = 4.00000

          x       P( X <= x)
    48.0000         0.3085
```

```
MTB > let k1 = 0.5987 - 0.3085
MTB > print k1
```

Data Display

```
K1            0.290200
```

FIGURE 4.A.1.2

Exponential and gamma integrations can also be done on MINITAB, but the computer expresses those two pdf's as $f_Y(y) = (1/\lambda)e^{-y/\lambda}$ [instead of $f_Y(y) = \lambda e^{-\lambda y}$] and $f_Y(y) = \dfrac{1}{\lambda^r(r-1)!}y^{r-1}e^{-y/\lambda}$ [instead of $f_Y(y) = \dfrac{\lambda^r}{(r-1)!}y^{r-1}e^{-\lambda y}$]. Therefore, to evaluate $\int_0^1 0.50e^{-0.50y}\,dy$, for example, we would write

```
MTB  > cdf 1;
SUBC > exponential 2.
```

(rather than SUBC > exponential 0.50).

Recall Example 4.6.1. In the notation of Theorem 4.6.1, $P(Y < 50)$ is the cdf evaluated at 50 for a gamma random variable having $r = 2$ and $\lambda = 0.01$. In MINITAB's notation, the second parameter is entered as *100* ($= 1/0.01$) (see Figure 4.A.1.3).

FIGURE 4.A.1.3   MTB > cdf 50;
SUBC> gamma 2 100.

Cumulative Distribution Function

Gamma with a = 2.00000 and b = 100.000

x	P(X <= x)
50.0000	0.0902

On several occasions in Chapter 4 we made use of MINITAB's RANDOM command, a subroutine that generates samples from a specific pdf. Simulations of that sort can be very helpful in illustrating a variety of statistical concepts. Shown in Figure 4.3.1(a), for example, is a random sample of 50 X_i's representing a binomial distribution for which $n = 60$ and $p = 0.40$. The entries that follow in Figure 4.3.1(b) are the corresponding approximate Z-ratios,

$$Z\text{-ratio} = \frac{X - E(X)}{\sqrt{\text{Var}(X)}} = \frac{X - 60(0.40)}{\sqrt{60(0.40)(0.60)}} = \frac{X - 24}{\sqrt{14.4}}$$

Figure 4.A.1.4 shows the syntax that was used to generate those two outputs. (In addition to the binomial distribution, the RANDOM command can also be used to generate samples from the uniform, Poisson, normal, exponential, and gamma pdf's.)

```
MTB > random 50 c1;
SUBC> binomial 60 0.40.
```

Data Display

```
C1
    27    29    23    22    21    21    22    26    26    20    26    25    27
    32    22    27    22    20    19    19    21    23    28    23    27    29
    13    24    22    25    25    20    25    26    15    24    17    28    21
    16    24    22    25    25    21    23    23    20    25    30
```

```
MTB > let c2 = (c1 - 24)/sqrt(14.4)
MTB > name c2 'Z-ratio'
MTB > print c2
```

Data Display

```
Z-ratio
    0.79057    1.31762   -0.26352   -0.52705   -0.79057   -0.79057   -0.52705
    0.52705    0.52705   -1.05409    0.52705    0.26352    0.79057    2.10819
   -0.52705    0.79057   -0.52705   -1.05409   -1.31762   -1.31762   -0.79057
   -0.26352    1.05409   -0.26352    0.79057    1.31762   -2.89875    0.00000
   -0.52705    0.26352    0.26352   -1.05409    0.26352    0.52705   -2.37171
    0.00000   -1.84466    1.05409   -0.79057   -2.10819    0.00000   -0.52705
    0.26352    0.26352   -0.79057   -0.26352   -0.26352   -1.05409    0.26352
    1.58114
```

FIGURE 4.A.1.4

Often the first step in summarizing a large set of measurements is the construction of their *histogram*, a graphical format especially effective at highlighting the shape of a distribution. A *density-scaled histogram* is one whose vertical axis is calibrated in such a way that the total area under the histogram's bars is equal to 1. The latter version allows for a direct comparison between the sample distribution and the theoretical pdf from which the data presumably came (recall Case Study 4.2.4). Figure 4.A.1.5 shows the MINITAB syntax that produces the density-scaled histogram pictured in Figure 4.2.3.

```
MTB > set c1
DATA> 126 73 26 6 41 26 73 23 21 18 11 3 3 2 6 6 12 38
DATA> 6 65 68 41 38 50 37 94 16 40 77 91 23 51 20 18 61 12
DATA> end
MTB > set c2
DATA> 0 20 40 60 80 100 120 140
DATA> end
MTB > Histogram c1;
SUBC>    Density
SUBC>    CutPoint c2;
SUBC>    Bar;
SUBC>      Type 1;
SUBC>      Color 1.
```

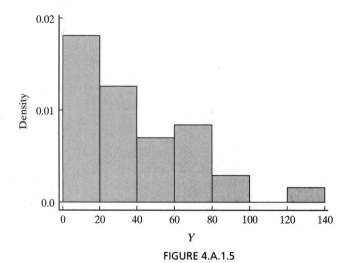

FIGURE 4.A.1.5

MINITAB Windows

There is a Windows version of MINITAB that is very convenient for doing many of the data applications that will be discussed in these end-of-chapter appendices. The necessary point-and-click steps will be set off in boxes like the following:

Constructing Histograms Using MINITAB Windows

1. Enter the data in C1.
2. Click on GRAPH, then on HISTOGRAM.
3. Type C1 in the GRAPH VARIABLES box.
4. Click on OK.

APPENDIX 4.A.2   A PROOF OF THE CENTRAL LIMIT THEOREM

Proving Theorem 4.3.2 in its full generality is beyond the level of this text. However, we can establish a slightly weaker version of the result by assuming that the moment-generating function of each W_i exists. Motivating that derivation is the following lemma.

LEMMA.   Let $W_1, W_2, \ldots$ be a set of random variables such that $\lim_{n \to \infty} M_{W_n}(t) = M_W(t)$ for all t in some interval about 0. Then $\lim_{n \to \infty} F_{W_n}(w) = F_W(w)$ for all $-\infty < w < \infty$.

To prove the central limit theorem using moment-generating functions requires showing that

$$\lim_{n \to \infty} M_{(W_1 + \cdots + W_n - n\mu)/(\sqrt{n}\sigma)}(t) = M_Z(t) = e^{t^2/2}$$

For notational simplicity, let

$$\frac{W_1 + \cdots + W_n - n\mu}{\sqrt{n}\sigma} = \frac{S_1 + \cdots + S_n}{\sqrt{n}}$$

where $S_i = (W_i - \mu)/\sigma$. Notice that $E(S_i) = 0$ and $\text{Var}(S_i) = 1$. Moreover, from Theorem 3.16.3,

$$M_{(S_1 + \cdots + S_n)/\sqrt{n}}(t) = \left[M\left(\frac{t}{\sqrt{n}} \right) \right]^n$$

where $M(t)$ denotes the moment-generating function common to each of the S_i's.

By virtue of the way the S_i's are defined, $M(0) = 1$, $M^{(1)}(0) = E(S_i) = 0$, and $M^{(2)}(0) = \text{Var}(S_i) = 1$. Applying Taylor's theorem, then, to $M(t)$, we can write

$$M(t) = 1 + M^{(1)}(0)t + \tfrac{1}{2}M^{(2)}(r)t^2 = 1 + \tfrac{1}{2}t^2 M^{(2)}(r)$$

for some number r, $|r| < |t|$. Thus

$$\lim_{n \to \infty} \left[M\left(\frac{t}{\sqrt{n}} \right) \right]^n = \lim_{n \to \infty} \left[1 + \frac{t^2}{2n} M^{(2)}(s) \right]^n, \quad |s| < \frac{|t|}{\sqrt{n}}$$

$$= \exp \lim_{n \to \infty} n \ln \left[1 + \frac{t^2}{2n} M^{(2)}(s) \right]$$

$$= \exp \lim_{n \to \infty} \frac{t^2}{2} \cdot M^{(2)}(s) \cdot \frac{\ln\left[1 + \dfrac{t^2}{2n} M^{(2)}(s) \right] - \ln(1)}{\dfrac{t^2}{2n} M^{(2)}(s)}$$

The existence of $M(t)$ implies the existence of all its derivatives. In particular, $M^{(3)}(t)$ exists, so $M^{(2)}(t)$ is continuous. Therefore, $\lim_{t \to 0} M^{(2)}(t) = M^{(2)}(0) = 1$. Since $|s| < |t|/\sqrt{n}$, $s \to 0$ as $n \to \infty$, so

$$\lim_{n \to \infty} M^{(2)}(s) = M^{(2)}(0) = 1$$

Also, as $n \to \infty$, the quantity $(t^2/2n)M^{(2)}(s) \to 0 \cdot 1 = 0$, so it plays the role of "Δx" in the definition of the derivative. Hence we obtain

$$\lim_{n \to \infty} \left[M\left(\frac{t}{\sqrt{n}} \right) \right]^n = \exp \frac{t^2}{2} \cdot 1 \cdot \ln^{(1)}(1) = e^{(1/2)t^2}$$

Since this last expression is the moment-generating function for a standard normal random variable, the theorem is proved.

CHAPTER 5

Estimation

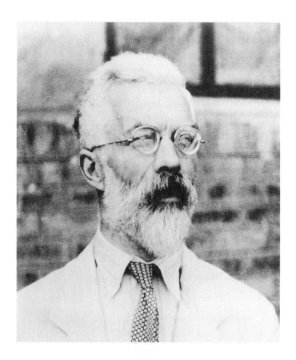

Ronald Aylmer Fisher (1890–1962)

A towering figure in the development of both applied and mathematical statistics, Fisher took formal training in mathematics and theoretical physics (he graduated from Cambridge in 1912). After a brief career as a teacher, he accepted a post in 1919 as statistician at the Rothamsted Experimental Station. There the day-to-day problems encountered in collecting and interpreting agricultural data led directly to much of his most important work in the theory of estimation and experimental design. Fisher was also a prominent geneticist and devoted considerable time to the development of a quantitative argument that would support Darwin's theory of natural selection. He returned to academia in 1933, succeeding Karl Pearson as the Galton Professor of Eugenics at the University of London. Fisher was knighted in 1952.

5.1 INTRODUCTION

The ability of probability functions to describe, or *model*, experimental data was demonstrated in numerous examples in Chapter 4. In Section 4.2, for example, the Poisson distribution was shown to predict very well the number of alpha emissions from a radioactive source as well as the number of fumbles made by a college football team. In Section 4.3 another probability model, the normal curve, was applied to phenomena as diverse as breath analyzer readings and IQ scores. Other models illustrated in Chapter 4 included the exponential, negative binomial, and gamma distributions.

All of these probability functions, of course, are actually *families* of models in the sense that each includes one or more *parameters*. The Poisson model, for instance, is indexed by the occurrence rate, λ. Changing λ changes the probabilities associated with $p_X(k)$ [see Figure 5.1.1, which compares $p_X(k) = e^{-\lambda}\lambda^k/k!$, $k = 0, 1, 2, \ldots$ for $\lambda = 1$ and $\lambda = 4$]. Similarly, the binomial model is defined in terms of the success probability p; the normal distribution, by the two parameters μ and σ.

Before any of these models can be applied, values need to be assigned to their parameters. Typically, this is done by taking a random sample (of n observations) and using those measurements to *estimate* the unknown parameter(s).

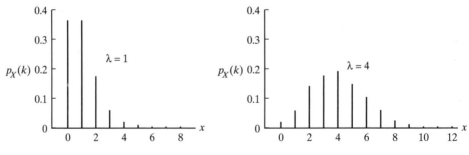

FIGURE 5.1.1

EXAMPLE 5.1.1

Imagine being handed a coin whose probability, p, of coming up heads is unknown. Your assignment is to toss the coin three times and use the resulting sequence of H's and T's to suggest a value for p. Suppose the sequence of three tosses turns out to be HHT. Based on those outcomes, what can be reasonably inferred about p?

Start by defining the random variable X to be the number of heads in a given toss. Then

$$X = \begin{cases} 1 & \text{if a toss comes up heads} \\ 0 & \text{if a toss comes up tails} \end{cases}$$

and the theoretical probability model for X is the function

$$p_X(k) = p^k(1-p)^{1-k} = \begin{cases} p & \text{for } k = 1 \\ 1-p & \text{for } k = 0 \end{cases}$$

Expressed in terms of X, the sequence HHT corresponds to a sample of size $n = 3$, where $X_1 = 1, X_2 = 1,$ and $X_3 = 0$.

Since the X_i's are independent random variables, the probability associated with the sample is $p^2(1 - p)$:

$$P(X_1 = 1 \cap X_2 = 1 \cap X_3 = 0) = P(X_1 = 1) \cdot P(X_2 = 1) \cdot P(X_3 = 0) = p^2(1 - p)$$

Knowing that our objective is to identify a plausible value (i.e., an "estimate") for p, it could be argued that a reasonable choice for that parameter would be the value that maximizes the probability of the sample. Figure 5.1.2 shows $P(X_1 = 1, X_2 = 1, X_3 = 0)$ *as a function of p*. By inspection, we see that the value that maximizes the probability of HHT is $p = \frac{2}{3}$.

FIGURE 5.1.2

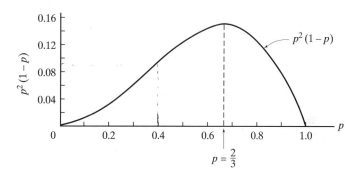

More generally, suppose we toss the coin n times and record the set of outcomes X_1, $X_2, \ldots, X_n$. Then

$$P(X_1 = k_1, X_2 = k_2, \ldots, X_n = k_n) = p^{k_1}(1 - p)^{1-k_1} \ldots p^{k_n}(1 - p)^{1-k_n}$$

$$= p^{\sum_{i=1}^{n} k_i}(1 - p)^{n - \sum_{i=1}^{n} k_i}$$

$$= p^k(1 - p)^{n-k}$$

where $k = \sum_{i=1}^{n} k_i$. The value of p that maximizes $P(X_1 = k_1, \ldots, X_n = k_n)$, of course, is the value for which the derivative of $p^k(1 - p)^{n-k}$ *with respect to p* is 0. But

$$\frac{d}{dp}\left[p^k(1 - p)^{n-k}\right] = k\left[p^{k-1}(1 - p)^{n-k}\right] + \left[k - n\right]p^k(1 - p)^{n-k-1} \qquad (5.1.1)$$

If the derivative is set equal to 0, Equation 5.1.1 reduces to

$$k(1 - p) + (k - n)p = 0$$

Solving for p identifies

$$\frac{k}{n}$$

as the value of the parameter that is most consistent with the n observations $k_1, k_2, \ldots, k_n$.

Comment.   Any function of a random sample whose objective is to approximate a parameter is called a *statistic*, or an *estimator*. If θ is the parameter being approximated, its estimator will be denoted $\hat{\theta}$. When an estimator is evaluated (by substituting the actual measurements recorded), the resulting number is called an *estimate*. In Example 5.1.1, the function $\frac{1}{n} \sum_{i=1}^{n} X_i$ is an estimator for p; the value $\frac{2}{3}$ that is calculated when the $n = 3$ observations are $X_1 = 1$, $X_2 = 1$, and $X_3 = 0$ is an estimate of p.

In this chapter, we look at some of the practical, as well as the mathematical, issues involved in the problem of estimating parameters. How is the functional form of an estimator determined? What statistical properties does a given estimator have? What properties would we *like* an estimator to have? As we answer these questions, our focus will begin to shift away from the study of probability and toward the study of statistics.

5.2 ESTIMATING PARAMETERS: THE METHOD OF MAXIMUM LIKELIHOOD AND THE METHOD OF MOMENTS

Suppose $Y_1, Y_2, \ldots, Y_n$ is a random sample from a continuous pdf $f_Y(y)$, whose unknown parameter is θ. [Note: To emphasize that our focus is on the parameter, we will identify continuous pdf's in this chapter as $f_Y(y; \theta)$; similarly, discrete probability models with an unknown parameter θ will be denoted $p_X(k; \theta)$]. The question is, how should we use the data to approximate θ?

In Example 5.1.1, we saw that the parameter p in the discrete probability model $f_X(k; p) = p^k(1 - p)^{1-k}$, $k = 0, 1$ could reasonably be estimated by the function $\frac{1}{n} \sum_{i=1}^{n} X_i$. How would the form of our estimator change if the data came from an exponential distribution? Or a Poisson distribution?

In this section we introduce two techniques for finding estimators—the method of maximum likelihood and the method of moments. Others are available, but these are the two that are the most widely used. Often, but not always, they give the same answer.

The Method of Maximum Likelihood

The basic idea behind maximum likelihood estimation is the rationale that was appealed to in Example 5.1.1. That is, it seems plausible to choose as the estimate for θ that value of the parameter that maximizes the "likelihood" of the sample. The latter is measured by a *likelihood function*, which is simply the product of the underlying pdf evaluated for each of the data points. In Example 5.1.1, the likelihood function for the sample HHT (i.e, for $X_1 = 1$, $X_2 = 1$, and $X_3 = 0$) is the product $p^2(1 - p)$.

DEFINITION 5.2.1. Let $W_1, W_2, \ldots, W_n$ be a random sample from $f_W(w; \theta)$, where θ is an unknown parameter. The *likelihood function*, $L(\theta)$, is the product of the pdf $f_W(w; \theta)$ evaluated at the n data points. That is,

$$L(\theta) = \prod_{i=1}^{n} f_W(w_i; \theta)$$

Comment. Joint pdf's and likelihood functions look the same, but the two are interpreted differently. A joint pdf defined for a set of n random variables is a multivariate function *of those n random variables*. In contrast, L is a function *of θ*; it should not be considered a function of the w_i's.

DEFINITION 5.2.2.   Let $W_1, W_2, \ldots, W_n$ be a random sample from $f_W(w; \theta)$ and let $L(\theta)$ be the corresponding likelihood function. Suppose $L(\hat{\theta}) \geq L(\theta)$ for all possible values of θ. Then $\hat{\theta}$ is called the *maximum-likelihood estimate* (or MLE) for θ.

Finding the $\hat{\theta}$ that maximizes a likelihood function is basically an exercise in calculus. Instead of setting the derivative of $L(\theta)$ equal to 0, though, and solving for θ, it is often easier to set the derivative of $\ln L(\theta)$ equal to 0. Since $\ln L(\theta)$ increases with $L(\theta)$, the same $\hat{\theta}$ that maximizes the ln of the likelihood function maximizes the likelihood function.

EXAMPLE 5.2.1

Suppose $k_1, k_2, \ldots, k_n$ is a set of n observations representing the geometric probability model, $p_X(k_i) = (1 - p)^{k_i-1}p, k_i = 1, 2, \ldots$ [recall that $p = P(\text{any given trial ends in success})$ and the random variable X denotes the trial at which the first success occurs]. Find the MLE for p.

We begin by writing the sample's likelihood function. According to Definition 5.2.1,

$$L(p) = \prod_{i=1}^{n}(1 - p)^{k_i-1}p$$

$$= (1 - p)^{\sum_{i=1}^{n} k_i - n} p^n$$

Let $k = \sum_{i=1}^{n} k_i$. Taking the ln of $L(p)$ and differentiating with respect to p gives

$$\ln L(p) = (k - n)\ln(1 - p) + n\ln p$$

and

$$\frac{d \ln L(p)}{dp} = \frac{k - n}{1 - p}(-1) + \frac{n}{p}$$

Now, to find the p that maximizes $\ln L(p)$ [and $L(p)$], we set the derivative equal to 0. But

$$\frac{k - n}{1 - p}(-1) + \frac{n}{p} = 0$$

implies that

$$p(n - k) + n(1 - p) = 0$$

and solving the latter gives

$$\hat{p} = \text{MLE for } p = \frac{n}{k}$$

[*Note*: The second derivative of $\ln L(p)$ is negative, which guarantees that p produces a maximum value for $L(p)$ and not a minimum.]

EXAMPLE 5.2.2

An experimenter has reason to believe that the pdf describing the variability in a certain type of measurement is the continuous model

$$f_Y(y; \theta) = \frac{1}{\theta^2} y e^{-y/\theta}, \quad 0 < y < \infty; 0 < \theta < \infty$$

If five data points have been determined—$Y_1 = 9.2$, $Y_2 = 5.6$, $Y_3 = 18.4$, $Y_4 = 12.1$, and $Y_5 = 10.7$—what would be a reasonable estimate for the unknown parameter θ?

Having actual data, as we do here, does not change the procedure for finding maximum likelihood estimates. We should still derive a general formula for $\hat{\theta}$ first; only as the very last step should the given y_i's be substituted into the expression for the MLE.

Here,

$$L(\theta) = \prod_{i=1}^{n} \frac{1}{\theta^2} y_i e^{-y_i/\theta}$$

$$= \theta^{-2n} \prod_{i=1}^{n} y_i e^{-(1/\theta) \sum_{i=1}^{n} y_i}$$

and

$$\ln L(\theta) = -2n \ln \theta + \ln \prod_{i=1}^{n} y_i - \frac{1}{\theta} \sum_{i=1}^{n} y_i$$

Setting the derivative of $\ln L(\theta)$ equal to 0 gives

$$\frac{d \ln L(\theta)}{d\theta} = \frac{-2n}{\theta} + \frac{1}{\theta^2} \sum_{i=1}^{n} y_i = 0$$

which implies that

$$\hat{\theta} = \frac{1}{2n} \sum_{i=1}^{n} y_i$$

For these particular observations, $n = 5$ and

$$\sum_{i=1}^{5} y_i = 9.2 + 5.6 + 18.4 + 12.1 + 10.7 = 56.0$$

so

$$\hat{\theta} = \frac{1}{2(5)} (56.0) = 5.6$$

There are a few situations where the equations $\dfrac{dL(\theta)}{d\theta} = 0$ or $\dfrac{d \ln L(\theta)}{d\theta} = 0$ are not meaningful and do not yield solutions for $\hat{\theta}$. In those cases, the MLE often turns out to be an order statistic, for reasons having to do with the *range* of the random variable.

EXAMPLE 5.2.3

Suppose $y_1, y_2, \ldots, y_n$ is a set of measurements representing an exponential pdf with $\lambda = 1$ but with an unknown "threshold" parameter, θ. That is,

$$f_Y(y; \theta) = e^{-(y-\theta)}, \quad y \geq \theta; \quad \theta > 0$$

(see Figure 5.2.1). Find the MLE for θ.

FIGURE 5.2.1

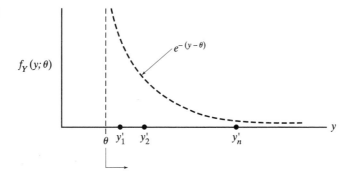

Proceeding in the usual fashion, we start by deriving an expression for the likelihood function:

$$L(\theta) = \prod_{i=1}^{n} e^{-(y_i - \theta)}$$

$$= e^{-\sum_{i=1}^{n} y_i + n\theta}$$

Here, finding $\hat{\theta}$ by solving the equation $\dfrac{d \ln L(\theta)}{d\theta} = 0$ will not work because

$\dfrac{d \ln L(\theta)}{d\theta} = \dfrac{d}{d\theta}\left(-\sum_{i=1}^{n} y_i + n\theta\right) = n$. Instead, we need to look at the likelihood function directly.

Notice that $L(\theta) = e^{-\sum_{i=1}^{n} y_i + n\theta}$ is maximized when the exponent of e is maximized. But for given $y_1, y_2, \ldots, y_n$ (and n), making $-\sum_{i=1}^{n} y_i + n\theta$ as large as possible requires that θ be as large as possible. Figure 5.2.1 shows how large θ can be: It can be moved to the right *only as far as the smallest order statistic.* Any value of θ larger than $y_{\min}$ would violate the condition on $f_Y(y; \theta)$ that $y \geq \theta$. Therefore, $\hat{\theta} = y_{\min}$.

CASE STUDY 5.2.1

"What are you majoring in?" may be the most common question asked of a college student. For some, the answer is simple: Having decided on a field of study, they doggedly stay with it all the way to graduation. For many, though, the path is not so straight. Pre-meds losing the battle with Organic Chemistry and engineers unable to appreciate the Joy of Secants may find their roads to commencement taking a few detours.

Listed in the first two columns of Table 5.2.1 are the results of a "major" poll conducted in the fall of 1993 at the University of West Florida (100). Recorded for each of 356 upperclassmen was the number of times, X, that he or she had switched majors.

Based on the nature of these data, it would not be unreasonable to hypothesize that X has a Poisson distribution (recall the discussion on pages 254–255). Do the actual frequencies support that contention?

(continued on next page)

(Case Study 5.2.1 continued)

TABLE 5.2.1

Number of major changes	Observed Frequency	Expected Frequency
0	237	230.4
1	90	100.2
2	22	21.8
3	7	3.6
	356	356.0

To see if $p_X(k) = \dfrac{e^{-\lambda}\lambda^k}{k!}$ can provide an adequate fit to these 356 observations requires that we first find an estimate for λ. Given that $X_1 = k_1, X_2 = k_2, \ldots,$ and $X_n = k_n$,

$$L(\lambda) = \prod_{i=1}^{n} \frac{e^{-\lambda}\lambda^{k_i}}{k_i!}$$

$$= \frac{e^{-n\lambda}\lambda^{\sum_{i=1}^{n} k_i}}{\prod_{i=1}^{n} k_i!}$$

$$\ln L(\lambda) = -n\lambda + \left(\sum_{i=1}^{n} k_i\right)\ln\lambda - \ln\prod_{i=1}^{n} k_i!$$

and

$$\left.\frac{d\ln L(\lambda)}{d\lambda}\right| = -n + \frac{\sum_{i=1}^{n} k_i}{\lambda}$$

Setting the derivative equal to 0 shows that the MLE for λ is the sample mean:

$$\hat{\lambda} = \frac{1}{n}\sum_{i=1}^{n} k_i \tag{5.2.1}$$

According to the information appearing in Table 5.2.1, 237 of the k_i's were equal to 0, 90 were equal to 1, and so on. Substituting into Equation 5.2.1, then, gives

$$\hat{\lambda} = \frac{1}{356}[237 \cdot 0 + 90 \cdot 1 + 22 \cdot 2 + 7 \cdot 3]$$

$$= 0.435$$

so the specific model being proposed is

$$p_X(k) = \frac{e^{-0.435}(0.435)^k}{k!}, \quad k = 0, 1, 2, \ldots$$

The corresponding expected frequencies $\left[= 356 \cdot p_X(k)\right]$ for each value of X are listed in column 3 of Table 5.2.1. Agreement with the observed frequencies appears to be quite good. Our conclusion would be that nothing in these data rules out using the Poisson as a "major-change" model. [Formal procedures, known as *goodness-of-fit tests*, have been developed for assessing the agreement (or lack of agreement) between a set of observed and expected frequencies. These will be taken up in Chapter 10.]

Finding MLEs When More Than One Parameter Is Unknown

If a family of probability models is indexed by two or more unknown parameters—say, $\theta_1, \theta_2, \ldots, \theta_k$—finding MLEs for the θ_i's requires the solution of a set of k simultaneous equations. If $k = 2$, for example, we would typically need to solve the system

$$\frac{\partial \ln L(\theta_1, \theta_2)}{\partial \theta_1} = 0$$

$$\frac{\partial \ln L(\theta_1, \theta_2)}{\partial \theta_2} = 0$$

EXAMPLE 5.2.4

Suppose a random sample of size n is drawn from the two parameter normal pdf,

$$f_Y(y; \mu, \sigma^2) = \frac{1}{\sqrt{2\pi}\sigma} e^{-\frac{1}{2}\left(\frac{y-\mu}{\sigma}\right)^2}, \quad -\infty < y < \infty; -\infty < \mu < \infty; \sigma^2 > 0$$

Use the method of maximum likelihood to find formulas for $\hat{\mu}$ and $\hat{\sigma}^2$.

We start by finding $L(\mu, \sigma^2)$ and $\ln L(\mu, \sigma^2)$:

$$L(\mu, \sigma^2) = \prod_{i=1}^{n} \frac{1}{\sqrt{2\pi}\sigma} e^{-\frac{1}{2}\left(\frac{y_i-\mu}{\sigma}\right)^2}$$

$$= (2\pi\sigma^2)^{-n/2} e^{-\frac{1}{2}\sum_{i=1}^{n}\left(\frac{y_i-\mu}{\sigma}\right)^2}$$

and

$$\ln L(\mu, \sigma^2) = -\frac{n}{2}\ln(2\pi\sigma^2) - \frac{1}{2}\sum_{i=1}^{n}\left(\frac{y_i-\mu}{\sigma}\right)^2$$

Moreover,

$$\frac{\partial \ln L(\mu, \sigma^2)}{\partial \mu} = -\sum_{i=1}^{n}\left(\frac{y_i-\mu}{\sigma}\right)\left(-\frac{1}{\sigma}\right)$$

and

$$\frac{\partial \ln L(\mu, \sigma^2)}{\partial \sigma^2} = -\frac{n}{2} \cdot \frac{1}{2\pi\sigma^2} \cdot 2\pi - \frac{1}{2}\sum_{i=1}^{n}(y_i-\mu)^2\left(\frac{-1}{\sigma^4}\right)$$

Setting the two derivatives equal to 0 gives the equations

$$\sum_{i=1}^{n}(y_i - \mu) = 0 \tag{5.2.2}$$

and

$$-n\sigma^2 + \sum_{i=1}^{n}(y_i - \mu)^2 = 0 \tag{5.2.3}$$

Equation 5.2.2 simplifies to

$$\sum_{i=1}^{n} y_i = n\mu$$

which implies that $\hat{\mu} = \dfrac{1}{n} \displaystyle\sum_{i=1}^{n} y_i = \bar{y}$. Substituting $\hat{\mu}$, then, into Equation 5.2.3 gives

$$-n\sigma^2 + \sum_{i=1}^{n}(y_i - \bar{y})^2 = 0$$

or

$$\hat{\sigma}^2 = \frac{1}{n}\sum_{i=1}^{n}(y_i - \bar{y})^2$$

Comment. The method of maximum likelihood has a long history: Daniel Bernoulli was using it as early as 1777 (120). It was Ronald Fisher, though, in the early years of the twentieth century, who first studied the mathematical properties of likelihood estimation in any detail, and the procedure is often credited to him.

QUESTIONS

5.2.1 A random sample of size 8—$X_1 = 1$, $X_2 = 0$, $X_3 = 1$, $X_4 = 1$, $X_5 = 0$, $X_6 = 1$, $X_7 = 1$, and $X_8 = 0$—is taken from the probability function

$$p_X(k; \theta) = \theta^k(1 - \theta)^{1-k}, k = 0, 1; \quad 0 < \theta < 1$$

Find the MLE for θ.

5.2.2 The number of red chips and white chips in an urn is unknown, but the *proportion, p,* of reds is either $\frac{1}{3}$ or $\frac{1}{2}$. A sample of size 5, drawn with replacement, yields the sequence red, white, white, red, and white. What is the MLE for p?

5.2.3 Use the sample $Y_1 = 8.2$, $Y_2 = 9.1$, $Y_3 = 10.6$, and $Y_4 = 4.9$ to calculate the MLE for λ in the exponential pdf

$$f_Y(y; \lambda) = \lambda e^{-\lambda y}, \quad y \geq 0$$

5.2.4 Suppose a random sample of size n is drawn from the probability model

$$p_X(k; \theta) = \frac{\theta^{2k}e^{-\theta^2}}{k!}, \quad k = 0, 1, 2, \dots$$

Find a formula for the MLE, $\hat{\theta}$.

5.2.5 Given that $Y_1 = 2.3$, $Y_2 = 1.9$, and $Y_3 = 4.6$ is a random sample from

$$f_Y(y; \theta) = \frac{y^3 e^{-y/\theta}}{6\theta^4}, \quad y \geq 0$$

calculate the MLE for θ.

5.2.6 Use the method of maximum likelihood to estimate θ in the pdf

$$f_Y(y; \theta) = \frac{\theta}{2\sqrt{y}}e^{-\theta\sqrt{y}}, \quad y > 0$$

Evaluate $\hat{\theta}$ for the following random sample of size 4: $Y_1 = 6.2$, $Y_2 = 7.0$, $Y_3 = 2.5$, and $Y_4 = 4.2$.

5.2.7 Experience has shown that in a certain state the distribution of voters supporting Democratic candidates for local offices is described quite well by the pdf

$$f_Y(y; \theta) = \theta y^{\theta-1}, \quad 0 < y < 1; \quad 0 < \theta < \infty$$

where Y is the proportion of registrants in a precinct who vote Democratic. Suppose that voters in five randomly selected precincts are polled prior to an election and the proportions intending to vote for Democratic candidates are 0.45, 0.68, 0.87, 0.36, and 0.54, respectively. Estimate θ.

5.2.8 The following data show the number of occupants in passenger cars observed during one hour at a busy intersection in Los Angeles (61). Suppose it can be assumed that these data follow a geometric distribution, $p_X(k; p) = (1 - p)^{k-1}p, k = 1, 2, \ldots$. Estimate p and compare the observed and expected frequencies for each value of X.

Number of Occupants	Frequency
1	678
2	227
3	56
4	28
5	8
6+	14
	1011

5.2.9 (a) Based on the random sample $Y_1 = 6.3$, $Y_2 = 1.8$, $Y_3 = 14.2$, and $Y_4 = 7.6$, use the method of maximum likelihood to estimate the parameter θ in the uniform pdf

$$f_Y(y; \theta) = \frac{1}{\theta}, \quad 0 \le y \le \theta$$

(b) Suppose the random sample in Part (a) represents the two-parameter uniform pdf

$$f_Y(y; \theta_1, \theta_2) = \frac{1}{\theta_2 - \theta_1}, \quad \theta_1 \le y \le \theta_2$$

Find the MLEs for θ_1 and θ_2.

5.2.10 Find the MLE for θ in the pdf

$$f_Y(y; \theta) = \frac{2y}{1 - \theta^2}, \quad \theta \le y \le 1$$

if a random sample of size 6 yielded the measurements 0.70, 0.63, 0.92, 0.86, 0.43, and 0.21.

5.2.11 A random sample of size n is taken from the pdf

$$f_Y(y; \theta) = 2y\theta^2, \quad 0 \le y \le \frac{1}{\theta}$$

Find an expression for $\hat{\theta}$, the MLE for θ.

5.2.12 If the random variable Y denotes an individual's income, Pareto's law claims that $P(Y \ge y) = \left(\frac{k}{y}\right)^\theta$, where k is the entire population's minimum income. It follows that $F_Y(y) = 1 - \left(\frac{k}{y}\right)^\theta$, and, by differentiation,

$$f_Y(y; \theta) = \theta k^{\theta} \left(\frac{1}{y}\right)^{\theta+1}, \quad y \geq k; \quad \theta \geq 1$$

Assume k is known. Find the MLE for θ if income information has been collected on a random sample of 25 individuals.

5.2.13 Suppose a random sample of size n is drawn from a normal pdf where the mean μ is known but the variance σ^2 is unknown. Use the method of maximum likelihood to find a formula for $\hat{\sigma}^2$. Compare your answer to the MLE found in Example 5.2.4.

The Method of Moments

A second procedure for estimating parameters is the *method of moments*. Proposed near the turn of the twentieth century by the great British statistician, Karl Pearson, the method of moments is often more tractable than the method of maximum likelihood in situations where the underlying probability model has multiple parameters.

Suppose that Y is a continuous random variable and its pdf is a function of k unknown parameters, $\theta_1, \theta_2, \ldots, \theta_k$. The first k moments of Y, if they exist, are given by the integrals

$$E(Y^j) = \int_{-\infty}^{\infty} y^j \cdot f_Y(y; \theta_1, \theta_2, \ldots, \theta_k) \, dy, \quad j = 1, 2, \ldots, k$$

In general, each $E(Y^j)$ will be a different function of the k parameters. That is,

$$E(Y^1) = g_1(\theta_1, \theta_2, \ldots, \theta_k)$$
$$E(Y^2) = g_2(\theta_1, \theta_2, \ldots, \theta_k)$$
$$\vdots \qquad \vdots$$
$$E(Y^k) = g_k(\theta_1, \theta_2, \ldots, \theta_k)$$

Corresponding to each *theoretical* moment, $E(Y^j)$, is a *sample* moment, $\frac{1}{n} \sum_{i=1}^{n} y_i^j$.

Intuitively, the jth sample moment is an approximation to the jth theoretical moment. Setting the two equal *for each* j produces a system of k simultaneous equations, the solutions to which are a set of estimates, $\hat{\theta}_1, \hat{\theta}_2, \ldots, \hat{\theta}_k$.

DEFINITION 5.2.3. Let W_1, W_2, $\ldots$, W_n be a random sample from $f_W(w; \theta_1, \theta_2, \ldots, \theta_k)$. The *method of moments* estimates $\hat{\theta}_1, \hat{\theta}_2, \ldots, \hat{\theta}_k$ for the model's unknown parameters are the solutions of the k simultaneous equations

$$\int_{-\infty}^{\infty} w \cdot f_W(w; \theta_1, \theta_2, \ldots, \theta_k) \, dw = \frac{1}{n} \sum_{i=1}^{n} w_i$$

$$\int_{-\infty}^{\infty} w^2 f_W(w; \theta_1, \theta_2, \ldots, \theta_k) \, dw = \frac{1}{n} \sum_{i=1}^{n} w_i^2$$

$$\vdots$$

$$\int_{-\infty}^{\infty} w^k f_W(w; \theta_1, \theta_2, \ldots, \theta_k) \, dw = \frac{1}{n} \sum_{i=1}^{n} w_i^k$$

EXAMPLE 5.2.5

Suppose that $Y_1 = 0.42, Y_2 = 0.10, Y_3 = 0.65,$ and $Y_4 = 0.23$ is a random sample of size 4 from the pdf

$$f_Y(y; \theta) = \theta y^{\theta-1}, \quad 0 \leq y \leq 1$$

Find the method of moments estimate for θ.

Taking the same approach that was followed in finding maximum likelihood estimates, we will derive a general expression for the method of moments estimate before making any use of the four data points. Notice that only one equation needs to be solved because the pdf is indexed by just a single parameter.

The first theoretical moment of Y is $\dfrac{\theta}{\theta + 1}$:

$$E(Y) = \int_0^1 y \cdot \theta y^{\theta-1} \, dy$$

$$= \theta \cdot \left. \frac{y^{\theta+1}}{\theta + 1} \right|_0^1$$

$$= \frac{\theta}{\theta + 1}$$

Setting $E(Y)$ equal to $\dfrac{1}{n} \sum_{i=1}^{n} y_i (= \bar{y})$, the first sample moment, gives

$$\frac{\theta}{\theta + 1} = \bar{y}$$

which implies that the method of moments estimate for θ is

$$\hat{\theta} = \frac{\bar{y}}{1 - \bar{y}}$$

Here, $\bar{y} = \frac{1}{4}(0.42 + 0.10 + 0.65 + 0.23) = 0.35$, so

$$\hat{\theta} = \frac{0.35}{1 - 0.35} = 0.54$$

CASE STUDY 5.2.2

Although hurricanes generally strike only the eastern and southern coastal regions of the United States, they do occasionally sweep inland before completely dissipating. The U.S. Weather Bureau confirms that in the period from 1900 to 1969 a total of 36 hurricanes moved as far as the Appalachians. In Table 5.2.2 are listed the maximum 24-hour precipitation levels recorded for those 36 storms during the time they were over the mountains (60).

Figure 5.2.2 shows the data's density-scaled histogram. Its skewed shape suggests that Y, the maximum 24-hour precipitation associated with inland hurricanes, can be modeled by the "general" two-parameter gamma pdf,

(continued on next page)

(Case Study 5.2.2 continued)

$$f_Y(y; r, \lambda) = \frac{\lambda^r}{\Gamma(r)} y^{r-1} e^{-\lambda y}, \quad y > 0$$

(recall the comment on page 300). Use the method of moments to estimate r and λ and then fit $f_Y(y; \hat{r}, \hat{\lambda})$ to the 36 y_i's in Table 5.2.2.

From Theorem 4.6.2,

$$E(Y) = \frac{r}{\lambda}$$

TABLE 5.2.2   Maximum 24-Hour Precipitation Recorded for 36 Inland Hurricanes (1900–1969)

Year	Name	Location	Maximum Precipitation (inches)
1969	Camille	Tye River, Va.	31.00
1968	Candy	Hickley, N.Y.	2.82
1965	Betsy	Haywood Gap, N.C.	3.98
1960	Brenda	Cairo, N.Y.	4.02
1959	Gracie	Big Meadows, Va.	9.50
1957	Audrey	Russels Point, Ohio	4.50
1955	Connie	Slide Mt., N.Y.	11.40
1954	Hazel	Big Meadows, Va.	10.71
1954	Carol	Eagles Mere, Pa.	6.31
1952	Able	Bloserville 1–N, Pa.	4.95
1949		North Ford # 1, N.C.	5.64
1945		Crossnore, N.C.	5.51
1942		Big Meadows, Va.	13.40
1940		Rhodhiss Dam, N.C.	9.72
1939		Caesars Head, S.C.	6.47
1938		Hubbardston, Mass.	10.16
1934		Balcony Falls, Va.	4.21
1933		Peekamoose, N.Y.	11.60
1932		Caesars Head, S.C.	4.75
1932		Rockhouse, N.C.	6.85
1929		Rockhouse, N.C.	6.25
1928		Roanoke, Va.	3.42
1928		Caesars Head, S.C.	11.80
1923		Mohonk Lake, N.Y.	0.80
1923		Wappingers Falls, N.Y.	3.69
1920		Landrum, S.C.	3.10
1916		Altapass, N.C.	22.22
1916		Highlands, N.C.	7.43
1915		Lookout Mt., Tenn.	5.00
1915		Highlands, N.C.	4.58
1912		Norcross, Ga.	4.46
1906		Horse Cove, N.C.	8.00
1902		Sewanee, Tenn.	3.73
1901		Linville, N.C.	3.50
1900		Marrobone, Ky.	6.20
1900		St. Johnsbury, Vt.	0.67

FIGURE 5.2.2

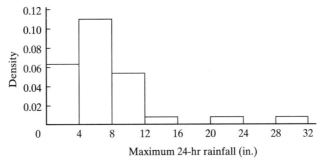

Maximum 24-hr rainfall (in.)

and

$$\text{Var}(Y) = \frac{r}{\lambda^2} = E(Y^2) - \left[E(Y)\right]^2$$

so

$$E(Y^2) = \frac{r}{\lambda^2} + \frac{r^2}{\lambda^2} = \frac{r(r+1)}{\lambda^2}$$

Also, according to the figures in Table 5.2.2,

$$\frac{1}{36} \sum_{i=1}^{36} y_i = 7.29$$

and

$$\frac{1}{36} \sum_{i=1}^{36} y_i^2 = 85.59$$

To find $\hat{r}$ and $\hat{\lambda}$, then, we need to solve the two equations

$$\frac{r}{\lambda} = 7.29$$

and

$$\frac{r(r+1)}{\lambda^2} = 85.59$$

Substituting $r = 7.29\lambda$ into the second equation gives

$$\frac{(7.29\lambda)(7.29\lambda + 1)}{\lambda^2} = 85.59$$

or $\lambda = 0.22$. Then, from the first equation, $r = 1.60 \left[= 7.29(0.22)\right]$.
The estimated model,

$$f_Y(y; 1.60, 0.22) = \frac{(0.22)^{1.60}}{\Gamma(1.60)} y^{1.60-1} e^{-0.22y}$$

(Case Study 5.2.2 continued)

FIGURE 5.2.3

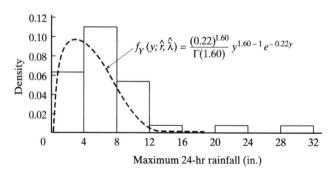

$$f_Y(y; \hat{r}, \hat{\lambda}) = \frac{(0.22)^{1.60}}{\Gamma(1.60)} y^{1.60-1} e^{-0.22y}$$

Maximum 24-hr rainfall (in.)

is superimposed on the data's density-scaled histogram in Figure 5.2.3.[1] Considering the relatively small number of observations in the sample, the agreement is quite good. (The adequacy of the approximation here would come as no surprise to a meteorologist: The gamma distribution is frequently used to describe the variation in precipitation levels.)

QUESTIONS

5.2.14 Let $y_1, y_2, \ldots, y_n$ be a random sample of size n from the uniform pdf, $f_Y(y; \theta) = \frac{1}{\theta}, 0 \le y \le \theta$.

Find a formula for the method of moments estimate for θ. Compare the values of the method of moments estimate and the maximum likelihood estimate if a random sample of size 5 consists of the numbers 17, 92, 46, 39, and 56 (recall Question 5.2.9).

5.2.15 Use the method of moments to estimate θ in the pdf

$$f_Y(y; \theta) = (\theta^2 + \theta)y^{\theta-1}(1 - y), \quad 0 < y < 1$$

Assume that a random sample of size n has been collected.

5.2.16 A criminologist is searching through FBI files to document the prevalence of a rare double-whorl fingerprint. Among six consecutive sets of 100,000 prints scanned by a computer, the numbers of persons having the abnormality are 3, 0, 3, 4, 2, and 1, respectively. Assume that double whorls are Poisson events. Use the method of moments to estimate their occurrence rate, λ. How would your answer change if λ were estimated using the method of maximum likelihood?

5.2.17 Find the method of moments estimate for λ if a random sample of size n is taken from the exponential pdf, $f_Y(y; \lambda) = \lambda e^{-\lambda y}$, $y \ge 0$.

5.2.18 Suppose that $Y_1 = 8.3$, $Y_2 = 4.9$, $Y_3 = 2.6$, and $Y_4 = 6.5$ is a random sample of size 4 from the two-parameter uniform pdf,

$$f_Y(y; \theta_1, \theta_2) = \frac{1}{2\theta_2}, \quad \theta_1 - \theta_2 \le y \le \theta_1 + \theta_2$$

Use the method of moments to calculate $\hat{\theta}_1$ and $\hat{\theta}_2$.

---

[1] From tables of the gamma function (33), $\Gamma(1.60) = 0.89352$.

5.2.19 Find a formula for the method of moments estimate for the parameter θ in the Pareto pdf,

$$f_Y(y; \theta) = \theta k^{\theta} \left(\frac{1}{y}\right)^{\theta+1}, \quad y \geq k; \quad \theta \geq 1$$

Assume that k is known and the data consist of a random sample of size n. Compare your answer to the MLE found in Question 5.2.12.

5.2.20 Calculate the method of moments estimate for the parameter θ in the probability function

$$p_X(k; \theta) = \theta^k (1 - \theta)^{1-k}, \quad k = 0, 1$$

if a sample of size 5 is the set of numbers $0, 0, 1, 0, 1$.

5.2.21 Find $\hat{\mu}$ and $\hat{\sigma}^2$, the method of moments estimates for μ and σ^2, based on a random sample of size n drawn from a normal pdf, where $\mu = E(Y)$ and $\sigma^2 = \text{Var}(Y)$. Compare your answers with the MLE formulas derived in Example 5.2.4.

5.2.22 Use the method of moments to derive formulas for estimating the parameters r and p in the negative binomial pdf,

$$p_X(k; r, p) = \binom{k - 1}{r - 1} p^r (1 - p)^{k-r}, \quad k = r, r + 1, \dots$$

5.2.23 Bird songs can be characterized by the number of clusters of "syllables" that are strung together in rapid succession. If the last cluster is defined as a "success," it may be reasonable to treat the *number* of clusters in a song as a geometric random variable. Does the model $p_X(k) = (1 - p)^{k-1} p, k = 1, 2, \dots$ adequately describe the following distribution of 250 song lengths (91)? Begin by finding the method of moments estimate for p. Then calculate the set of "expected" frequencies.

No. of clusters/song, X	Frequency
1	132
2	52
3	34
4	9
5	7
6	5
7	5
8	6
	250

5.3 INTERVAL ESTIMATION

Point estimates, no matter how they are determined, share the same fundamental weakness: They provide no indication of their inherent precision. We know, for instance, that $\hat{\lambda} = \bar{X}$ is both the maximum likelihood and the method of moments estimator for the Poisson parameter, λ. But suppose a sample of size 6 is taken from the probability model $p_X(k) = e^{-\lambda} \lambda^k / k!$ and we find that $\hat{\lambda} = 6.8$. Does it follow that the true λ is likely to be close to $\hat{\lambda}$—say, in the interval from 6.7 to 6.9—or is the estimation process so imprecise that λ might actually be as small as 1.0, or as large as 12.0? Unfortunately, point estimates, by themselves, do not allow us to make those kinds of extrapolations. Any such statements require that the *variation* of the estimator be taken into account.

The usual way to quantify the amount of uncertainty in an estimator is to construct a *confidence interval*. In principle, confidence intervals are ranges of numbers that have a high probability of "containing" the unknown parameter as an interior point. By looking at the *width* of a confidence interval, we can get a good sense of the estimator's precision.

EXAMPLE 5.3.1

Suppose $Y_1 = 6.5, Y_2 = 9.2, Y_3 = 9.9,$ and $Y_4 = 12.4$ constitute a random sample of size 4 from

$$f_Y(y; \mu) = \frac{1}{\sqrt{2\pi}\,(0.8)}\, e^{-\frac{1}{2}\left(\frac{y-\mu}{0.8}\right)^2}, \quad -\infty < y < \infty$$

that is, from a normal distribution where σ is equal to 0.8 but the mean, μ, is unknown. What values of μ are believable in light of the four data points?

First of all, we can say from Example 5.2.4 that the MLE for μ is 9.5 $\left(= \bar{Y} = \frac{1}{n} \sum_{i=1}^{n} Y_i = \frac{1}{4}(38.0) \right)$. More important, though, we already know how the MLE is likely to vary from sample to sample: According to the corollary following Theorem 4.3.4, $\dfrac{\bar{Y} - \mu}{\sigma/\sqrt{n}} = \dfrac{\bar{Y} - \mu}{0.8/\sqrt{4}}$ has a standard normal pdf, $f_Z(z)$. The probability, then, that $\dfrac{\bar{Y} - \mu}{0.8/\sqrt{4}}$ will fall between two specified values can be deduced from Appendix Table A.1. For example,

$$P(-1.96 \le Z \le 1.96) = 0.95 = P\left(-1.96 \le \frac{\bar{Y} - \mu}{0.8/\sqrt{4}} \le 1.96\right) \tag{5.3.1}$$

(see Figure 5.3.1).

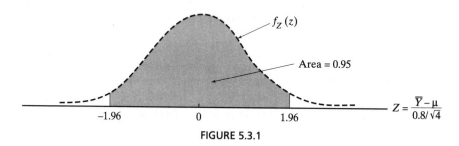

FIGURE 5.3.1

"Inverting" probability statements of the sort illustrated in Equation 5.3.1 is the mechanism by which we can identify a set of parameter values compatible with the sample data. If

$$P\left(-1.96 \le \frac{\bar{Y} - \mu}{0.8/\sqrt{4}} \le 1.96\right) = 0.95$$

then

$$P\left(\bar{Y} - 1.96\,\frac{0.8}{\sqrt{4}} \le \mu \le \bar{Y} + 1.96\,\frac{0.8}{\sqrt{4}}\right) = 0.95$$

which implies that the random interval

$$\left(\bar{Y} - 1.96 \frac{0.8}{\sqrt{4}}, \bar{Y} + 1.96 \frac{0.8}{\sqrt{4}} \right)$$

has a 95% chance of containing μ as an interior point.

After substituting for $\bar{Y}$, the random interval in this case reduces to

$$\left(9.50 - 1.96 \frac{0.8}{\sqrt{4}}, 9.50 + 1.96 \frac{0.8}{\sqrt{4}} \right) = (8.72, 10.28)$$

We call $(8.72, 10.28)$ a *95% confidence interval for* μ. In the long run, 95% of the intervals constructed in this fashion will contain the unknown μ; the remaining 5% will lie either entirely to the left of μ or entirely to the right. For a given set of data, of course, we have no way of knowing whether the calculated $\left(\bar{y} - 1.96 \cdot \frac{0.8}{\sqrt{4}}, \bar{y} + 1.96 \cdot \frac{0.8}{\sqrt{4}} \right)$ is one of the 95% that contains μ or one of the 5% that does not (see Figure 5.3.2).

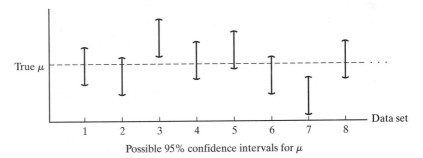

Possible 95% confidence intervals for μ

FIGURE 5.3.2

Appendix 5.A.1 outlines a MINITAB simulation of Figure 5.3.2. Listed are the endpoints of 50 different 95% confidence intervals and whether or not each contains the unknown μ (*94% do!*).

CASE STUDY 5.3.1

In the eighth century B.C., the Etruscan civilization was the most advanced in all of Italy. Its art forms and political innovations were destined to leave indelible marks on the entire Western world. Originally located along the western coast between the Arno and Tiber rivers (the region now known as Tuscany), it spread quickly across the Apennines and eventually overran much of Italy. But as quickly as it came, it faded. Militarily it was to prove no match for the burgeoning Roman legions, and by the dawn of Christianity it was all but gone.

No chronicles of the Etruscan empire have ever been found, and to this day its origins remain shrouded in mystery. Were the Etruscans native Italians, or were they immigrants? And if they were immigrants, where did they come from? Much of what *is* known has come from anthropometric studies—that is, investigations that use body measurements to determine racial characteristics and ethnic origins.

A case in point is the set of data given in Table 5.3.1, showing the sizes of 84 Etruscan skulls unearthed in various archeological digs throughout Italy (6). The sample mean, $\bar{y}$, of

(continued on next page)

(Case Study 5.3.1 continued)

TABLE 5.3.1

Maximum Head Breadths (mm) of 84 Etruscan Males

141	148	132	138	154	142	150
146	155	158	150	140	147	148
144	150	149	145	149	158	143
141	144	144	126	140	144	142
141	140	145	135	147	146	141
136	140	146	142	137	148	154
137	139	143	140	131	143	141
149	148	135	148	152	143	144
141	143	147	146	150	132	142
142	143	153	149	146	149	138
142	149	142	137	134	144	146
147	140	142	140	137	152	145

those measurements is 143.8 mm. Researchers believe that skull widths of present-day Italian males are normally distributed with a mean (μ) of 132.4 mm and a standard deviation (σ) of 6.0 mm. What does the difference between $\bar{y} = 143.8$ and $\mu = 132.4$ imply about the likelihood that Etruscans and Italians share the same ethnic origin?

One way to answer that question is to construct a 95% confidence interval for the true mean of the population represented by the 84 y_i's in Table 5.3.1. If that confidence interval fails to contain $\mu = 132.4$, it could be argued that the Etruscans were not the forebears of modern Italians. (Of course, it would also be necessary to factor in whatever evolutionary trends in skull sizes have occurred for *Homo sapiens*, in general, over the past 3000 years.)

It follows from the discussion in Example 5.3.1 that the endpoints for a 95% confidence interval for μ are given by the general formula

$$\left(\bar{y} - 1.96 \cdot \frac{\sigma}{\sqrt{n}}, \bar{y} + 1.96 \cdot \frac{\sigma}{\sqrt{n}} \right)$$

Here, that expression reduces to

$$\left(143.8 - 1.96 \cdot \frac{6.0}{\sqrt{84}}, 143.8 + 1.96 \cdot \frac{6.0}{\sqrt{84}} \right) = (142.5 \text{ mm}, 145.1 \text{ mm})$$

Since the value $\mu = 132.4$ is not contained in the 95% confidence interval (or even close to being contained), we would conclude that a sample mean of 143.8 (based on a sample of size 84) is not likely to come from a population where $\mu = 132.4$. It would appear, in other words, that Italians are not direct descendants of Etruscans.

Comment. Random intervals can be constructed to have whatever "confidence" we choose. Suppose $z_{\alpha/2}$ is defined to be the value for which $P(Z \geq z_{\alpha/2}) = \alpha/2$. If $\alpha = 0.05$, for example, $z_{\alpha/2} = z_{.025} = 1.96$. A $100(1 - \alpha)\%$ *confidence inter-*

val for μ, then, is the range of numbers

$$\left(\bar{y} - z_{\alpha/2} \cdot \frac{\sigma}{\sqrt{n}}, \bar{y} + z_{\alpha/2} \cdot \frac{\sigma}{\sqrt{n}} \right)$$

In practice, α is typically set at either $0.10, 0.05,$ or $0.01,$ although in some fields *50%* confidence intervals are frequently used.

Confidence Intervals for the Binomial Parameter, *p*

Perhaps the most frequently encountered applications of confidence intervals are those involving the binomial parameter, p. Opinion surveys are often the context: When polls are released, it has become standard practice to issue a disclaimer by saying that the findings have a certain *margin of error*. As we will see later in this section, margins of error are related to 95% confidence intervals.

The inversion technique followed in Example 5.3.1 can be applied to large-sample binomial random variables as well. We know from Theorem 4.3.1 that $(X - np)/\sqrt{np(1 - p)} = (X/n - p)/\sqrt{p(1 - p)/n}$ has approximately a standard normal distribution when X is binomial and n is large. It is also true that the pdf describing

$$\frac{X/n - p}{\sqrt{\dfrac{(X/n)(1 - X/n)}{n}}}$$

can be approximated by $f_Z(z)$, a result that seems plausible given that X/n is the MLE for p.

Therefore,

$$P\left(-z_{\alpha/2} \leq \frac{X/n - p}{\sqrt{\dfrac{(X/n)(1 - X/n)}{n}}} \leq z_{\alpha/2} \right) \doteq 1 - \alpha \qquad (5.3.2)$$

Rewriting Equation 5.3.2 by isolating p in the center of the inequalities leads to the formula given in Theorem 5.3.1.

THEOREM 5.3.1. Let the random variable X denote the number of successes in n independent trials, where n is large and $p = P(\text{success})$ is unknown. An approximate *100(1 − α)% confidence interval for p* is the set of numbers

$$\left(\frac{x}{n} - z_{\alpha/2}\sqrt{\frac{(x/n)(1 - x/n)}{n}}, \ \frac{x}{n} + z_{\alpha/2}\sqrt{\frac{(x/n)(1 - x/n)}{n}} \right)$$

CASE STUDY 5.3.2

Intelligent life on other planets is a cinematic theme that continues to be box office magic. Theatergoers seem equally enthralled by intergalactic brethren portrayed as hostile aggressors, like the faceless machines in H. G. Wells's *War of the Worlds*, or benign free spirits, like the Reese's-eating nebbish in Stephen Spielberg's *E.T.*

(continued on next page)

(Case Study 5.3.2 continued)

What is not so clear is the extent to which people actually believe that such creatures exist. In a close encounter of the statistical kind, a recent Media-General-Associated Press poll found that 713 of 1517 respondents accepted the idea of intelligent life existing on other worlds. Based on those results, what might we reasonably conclude about the proportion of *all* Americans who believe we are not alone?

Given that $n = 1517$ and $x = 713$, the "believable" values for p according to Theorem 5.3.1 are the numbers from *0.44* to *0.50*:

$$\left(\frac{713}{1517} - 1.96\sqrt{\frac{(713/1517)(1 - 713/1517)}{1517}}, \quad \frac{713}{1517} + 1.96\sqrt{\frac{(713/1517)(1 - 713/1517)}{1517}} \right)$$

$$= (0.44, 0.50)$$

If the *true proportion* of Americans, in other words, who believe in extraterrestrial life is less than 0.44 or greater than 0.50, it would be highly unlikely that a *sample proportion* (based on 1517 responses) would be 0.47.

Comment. We call $(0.44, 0.50)$ a 95% confidence interval for p, but it does not follow that p has a 95% chance of lying between 0.44 and 0.50. The parameter p is a constant, so it falls between 0.44 and 0.50 either 0% of the time or 100% of the time. The "95%" refers to the *procedure* by which the interval is constructed, not to any particular interval.

Comment. Robert Frost was certainly more familiar with iambic pentameters than he was with estimated parameters, but in 1942 he wrote a couplet that sounded very much like a poet's perception of a confidence interval (88):

> We dance round in a ring and suppose,
> But the Secret sits in the middle and knows.

EXAMPLE 5.3.2

Central to every statistical software package is a random number generator. Two or three simple commands are typically all that are required to output a sample of size n representing any of the standard probability models. But how can we be certain that numbers purporting to be random observations from, say, a normal distribution with $\mu = 50$ and $\sigma = 10$ actually *do* represent that particular pdf?

The answer is, we cannot; however, a number of "tests" are available to check whether the simulated measurements appear to be random *with respect to a given criterion*. One such procedure is the *median test*.

Suppose $Y_1, Y_2, \ldots, Y_n$ denote measurements presumed to have come from a continuous pdf $f_Y(y)$. Let X denote the number of Y_i's that are less than the median of $f_Y(y)$. If the sample *is* random, we would expect the difference between $\frac{x}{n}$ and $\frac{1}{2}$ to be small. More specifically, a 95% confidence interval based on $\frac{x}{n}$ should contain the value 0.5.

Listed in Table 5.3.2 is a set of 60 y_i's generated by MINITAB to represent the exponential pdf, $f_Y(y) = e^{-y}$, $y \geq 0$. Does this sample pass the median test?

The median here is $m = 0.69315$:

$$\int_0^m e^{-y}\, dy = -e^{-y}\Big|_0^m = 1 - e^{-m} = 0.5$$

TABLE 5.3.2

0.00940*	0.75095	2.32466	0.66715*	3.38765	3.01784	0.05509*
0.93661	1.39603	0.50795*	0.11041*	2.89577	1.20041	1.44422
0.46474*	0.48272*	0.48223*	3.59149	1.38016	0.41382*	0.31684*
0.58175*	0.86681	0.55491*	0.07451*	1.88641	2.40564	1.07111
5.05936	0.04804*	0.07498*	1.52084	1.06972	0.62928*	0.09433*
1.83196	1.91987	1.92874	1.93181	0.78811	2.16919	1.16045
0.81223	1.84549	1.20752	0.11387*	0.38966*	0.42250*	0.77279
1.31728	0.81077	0.59111*	0.36793*	0.16938*	2.41135	0.21528*
0.54938*	0.73217	0.52019*	0.73169			

*number $\leq 0.69315 \left[= \text{median of } f_Y(y) = e^{-y}, y > 0\right]$

which implies that $m = -\ln(0.5) = 0.69315$. Notice that of the 60 entries in Table 5.3.2, a total of $X = 26$ (those marked with an asterisk, *) fall to the left of the median. For these particular y_i's, then, $\dfrac{x}{n} = \dfrac{26}{60} = 0.433$.

Let p denote the (unknown) probability that a random observation produced by MINITAB's generator will lie to the left of the pdf's median. Based on these 60 observations, the 95% confidence interval for p is the range of numbers extending from *0.308* to *0.558*:

$$\left(\frac{26}{30} - 1.96\sqrt{\frac{(26/60)(1 - 26/60)}{60}}, \quad \frac{26}{60} + 1.96\sqrt{\frac{(26/60)(1 - 26/60)}{60}}\right)$$

$$= (0.308, 0.558)$$

The fact that the value $p = 0.50$ is contained in the confidence interval implies that these data *do* pass the median test. It is entirely believable, in other words, that a bona fide exponential random sample of size 60 would have 26 observations falling below the pdf's median, and 34 above.

Margin of Error

In the popular press, estimates for p $\left(\text{i.e., values of } \dfrac{x}{n}\right)$ are typically accompanied by a *margin of error*, as opposed to a confidence interval. The two are related: A margin of error is half the maximum width of a 95% confidence interval. (The number actually quoted is usually expressed as a percentage.)

Let w denote the width of a 95% confidence interval for p. From Theorem 5.3.1,

$$w = \frac{x}{n} + 1.96\sqrt{\frac{(x/n)(1 - x/n)}{n}} - \left(\frac{x}{n} - 1.96\sqrt{\frac{(x/n)(1 - x/n)}{n}}\right)$$

$$= 3.92\sqrt{\frac{(x/n)(1 - x/n)}{n}}$$

Notice that for fixed n, w is a function of the product $\left(\dfrac{x}{n}\right)\left(1 - \dfrac{x}{n}\right)$. But given that $0 \le \dfrac{x}{n} \le 1$, the largest value that $\left(\dfrac{x}{n}\right)\left(1 - \dfrac{x}{n}\right)$ can achieve is $\frac{1}{2} \cdot \frac{1}{2}$, or $\frac{1}{4}$ (see Question 5.3.16). Therefore,

$$\max w = 3.92\sqrt{\frac{1}{4n}}$$

DEFINITION 5.3.1. The *margin of error* associated with an estimate $\dfrac{x}{n}$, where x is the number of successes in n independent trials, is $100d\%$, where

$$d = \frac{1.96}{2\sqrt{n}}$$

EXAMPLE 5.3.3

A *USA Today* poll taken immediately after the liberation of Kuwait reported that 91% of the respondents approved of George Bush's performance as president (172). Inherent in that figure, the article said, is a "4% margin of error." Approximately how many people were interviewed?

The answer is six hundred. From Definition 5.3.1,

$$0.04 = \frac{1.96}{2\sqrt{n}}$$

which implies that $n = \left(\dfrac{1.96}{0.08}\right)^2 = 600$.

Comment. The phrase "margin of error" must not be taken too literally. The 4% cited in the *USA Today* story reflects the variability of $\dfrac{X}{600}$ *under the presumptions that the 600 respondents constitute a random sample from the target population and that no biases are influencing their answers.* As every pollster knows all too well, though, satisfying those conditions can be very difficult. How the subjects are selected, the context in which the survey is conducted, even the wording and placement of a question can dramatically alter the nature of the responses.

Ultimately, what is called the "margin of error" quantifies only one facet of the imprecision of $\dfrac{X}{n}$ in estimating p. Any of a host of factors other than the inherent variability of $\hat{p}$ may prove to have a much greater effect.

Choosing Sample Sizes

Related to confidence intervals and margins of error is an important experimental design question. Suppose a researcher wishes to estimate the binomial parameter p based on results from a series of n independent trials, *but n has yet to be determined.* Larger values of n will, of course, yield estimates having greater precision, but more observations also demand greater expenditures of time and money. How can those two concerns best be reconciled?

If the experimenter can articulate the minimal degree of precision that would be considered acceptable, a Z transformation can be used to calculate the smallest (i.e., the cheapest) sample size capable of achieving that objective. For example, suppose we want $\frac{X}{n}$ to have at least a $100(1 - \alpha)\%$ probability of lying within a distance d of p. The problem is solved, then, if we can find the smallest n for which

$$P\left(-d \le \frac{X}{n} - p \le d\right) = 1 - \alpha \tag{5.3.3}$$

THEOREM 5.3.2. Let $\frac{X}{n}$ be the estimator for the parameter p in a binomial distribution. In order for $\frac{X}{n}$ to have at least a $100(1 - \alpha)\%$ probability of being within a distance d of p, the sample size should be no smaller than

$$n = \frac{z_{\alpha/2}^2}{4d^2}$$

where $z_{\alpha/2}$ is the value for which $P(Z \ge z_{\alpha/2}) = \alpha/2$.

Proof. Start by dividing the terms in the probability portion of Equation 5.3.3 by the standard deviation of $\frac{X}{n}$ to form an approximate Z ratio:

$$P\left(-d \le \frac{X}{n} - p \le d\right) = P\left(\frac{-d}{\sqrt{p(1-p)/n}} \le \frac{X/n - p}{\sqrt{p(1-p)/n}} \le \frac{d}{\sqrt{p(1-p)/n}}\right)$$

$$\doteq P\left(\frac{-d}{\sqrt{p(1-p)/n}} \le Z \le \frac{d}{\sqrt{p(1-p)/n}}\right) = 1 - \alpha$$

But $P(-z_{\alpha/2} \le Z \le z_{\alpha/2}) = 1 - \alpha$, so

$$\frac{d}{\sqrt{p(1-p)/n}} = z_{\alpha/2}$$

which implies that

$$n = \frac{z_{\alpha/2}^2 p(1-p)}{d^2} \tag{5.3.4}$$

Equation 5.3.4 is not an acceptable final answer, though, because the right-hand side is a function of p, the unknown parameter. But $p(1 - p) \le \frac{1}{4}$ for $0 \le p \le 1$, so the sample size

$$n = \frac{z_{\alpha/2}^2}{4d^2}$$

would necessarily cause $\dfrac{X}{n}$ to satisfy Equation 5.3.3, regardless of the actual value of p. (Notice the connection between the statements of Theorem 5.3.2 and Definition 5.3.1.)

EXAMPLE 5.3.3

A public health survey is being planned in a large metropolitan area for the purpose of estimating the proportion of children, ages 0 to 14, who are lacking adequate polio immunization. Organizers of the project would like the sample proportion of inadequately immunized children, $\dfrac{X}{n}$, to have at least a 98% probability of being within 0.05 of the true proportion, p. How large should the sample be?

Here $100(1 - \alpha) = 98$, so $\alpha = 0.02$ and $z_{\alpha/2} = 2.33$. By Theorem 5.3.2, then, the smallest acceptable sample size is *543*:

$$n = \frac{(2.33)^2}{4(0.05)^2}$$

$$= 543$$

Comment. Occasionally, there may be reason to believe that p is necessarily less than some number r_1, where $r_1 < \frac{1}{2}$, or greater than some number r_2, where $r_2 > \frac{1}{2}$. If so, the factors $p(1 - p)$ in Equation 5.3.4 can be replaced by either $r_1(1 - r_1)$ or $r_2(1 - r_2)$, and the sample size required to estimate p with a specified precision will be reduced, perhaps by a considerable amount.

Suppose, for example, that previous immunization studies suggest that no more than 20% of children between the ages of 0 and 14 are inadequately immunized. The smallest sample size, then, for which

$$P\left(-0.05 \le \frac{X}{n} - p \le 0.05\right) = 0.98$$

is *348*, an n that represents almost a 36% reduction $\left(= \dfrac{543 - 348}{543} \times 100\right)$ from the original 543:

$$n = \frac{(2.33)^2}{(0.05)^2}(0.20)(0.80)$$

$$= 348$$

Comment. Theorems 5.3.1 and 5.3.2 are both based on the assumption that the X in X/n varies according to a binomial model. What we learned in Section 3.3, though, seems to contradict that assumption: Samples used in opinion surveys are invariably drawn *without replacement*, in which case X is hypergeometric, not binomial. The consequences of that particular "error," however, are easily corrected and frequently negligible.

It can be shown mathematically that the expected value of X/n is the same regardless of whether X is binomial or hypergeometric; its variance, though, is different. If X is binomial,

$$\text{Var}\left(\frac{X}{n}\right) = \frac{p(1 - p)}{n}$$

If X is hypergeometric,

$$\text{Var}\left(\frac{X}{n}\right) = \frac{p(1-p)}{n}\left(\frac{N-n}{N-1}\right)$$

where N is the total number of subjects in the population.

Since $(N-n)/(N-1) < 1$, the actual variance of X/n is somewhat smaller than the (binomial) variance we have been assuming, $p(1-p)/n$. The ratio $(N-n)/(N-1)$ is called the *finite correction factor*. If N is much larger than n, which is typically the case, then the magnitude of $(N-n)/(N-1)$ will be so close to 1 that the variance of X/n is equal to $p(1-p)/n$ for all practical purposes. The "binomial" assumption in those situations is more than adequate. Only when the sample is a sizable fraction of the population do we need to include the finite correction factor in any calculations that involve the variance of X/n.

QUESTIONS

5.3.1 The production of a nationally marketed detergent results in certain workers receiving prolonged exposures to a *Bacillus subtilis* enzyme. Nineteen workers were tested to determine the effects of those exposures, if any, on various respiratory functions. One such function, airflow rate, is measured by computing the ratio of a person's forced expiratory volume (FEV_1) to his or her vital capacity (VC). (Vital capacity is the maximum volume of air a person can exhale after taking as deep a breath as possible; FEV_1 is the maximum volume of air a person can exhale in one second.) In persons with no lung dysfunction, the "norm" for FEV_1/VC ratios is 0.80. Based on the following data (151), is it believable that exposure to the *Bacillus subtilis* enzyme has no effect on the FEV_1/VC ratio? Answer the question by constructing a 95% confidence interval. Assume that FEV_1/VC ratios are normally distributed with $\sigma = 0.09$.

Subject	FEV$_1$/VC	Subject	FEV$_1$/VC
RH	0.61	WS	0.78
RB	0.70	RV	0.84
MB	0.63	EN	0.83
DM	0.76	WD	0.82
WB	0.67	FR	0.74
RB	0.72	PD	0.85
BF	0.64	EB	0.73
JT	0.82	PC	0.85
PS	0.88	RW	0.87
RB	0.82		

5.3.2 Mercury pollution is widely recognized as a serious ecological problem. Much of the mercury released into the environment originates as a byproduct of coal burning and other industrial processes. It does not become dangerous until it falls into large bodies of water where microorganisms convert it to methylmercury (CH_3^{203}), an organic form that is particularly toxic. Fish are the intermediaries: They ingest and absorb the methylmercury and are then eaten by humans. Men and women, however, may not metabolize CH_3^{203} at the same rate. In one study investigating that question, six women were given a known amount of protein-bound methylmercury. Shown in the following table are the half-lives of the methylmercury in their systems (103). For men, the average CH_3^{203} half-life is believed to be 80 days. Assume that for both genders, CH_3^{203} half-lives are normally distributed with a standard deviation (σ) of eight days. Construct a 95% confidence interval for the true female CH_3^{203} half-life. Based on these data, is it believable that males and females metabolize methylmercury at the same rate? Explain.

Females	CH_3^{203} half-life
AE	52
EH	69
LJ	73
AN	88
KR	87
LU	56

5.3.3 Suppose a sample of size n is to be drawn from a normal distribution where σ is known to be 14.3. How large does n have to be to guarantee that the length of the 95% confidence interval for μ will be less than 3.06?

5.3.4 What "confidence" would be associated with each of the following intervals? Assume that the random variable Y is normally distributed and that σ is known.

(a) $\left(\bar{y} - 1.64 \cdot \dfrac{\sigma}{\sqrt{n}}, \bar{y} + 2.33 \cdot \dfrac{\sigma}{\sqrt{n}} \right)$ **(b)** $\left(-\infty, \bar{y} + 2.58 \cdot \dfrac{\sigma}{\sqrt{n}} \right)$

(c) $\left(\bar{y} - 1.64 \cdot \dfrac{\sigma}{\sqrt{n}}, 0 \right)$

5.3.5 Five independent samples, each of size n, are to be drawn from a normal distribution where σ is known. For each sample, the interval $\left(\bar{y} - 0.96 \cdot \dfrac{\sigma}{\sqrt{n}}, \bar{y} + 1.06 \cdot \dfrac{\sigma}{\sqrt{n}} \right)$ will be constructed. What is the probability that at least four of the intervals will contain the unknown μ?

5.3.6 Suppose that $y_1, y_2, \ldots, y_n$ is a random sample of size n from a normal distribution where σ is known. Depending on how the tail area probabilities are split up, an infinite number of random intervals having a 95% probability of containing μ can be constructed. What is unique about the particular interval $\left(\bar{y} - 1.96 \cdot \dfrac{\sigma}{\sqrt{n}}, \bar{y} + 1.96 \cdot \dfrac{\sigma}{\sqrt{n}} \right)$?

5.3.7 If the standard deviation (σ) associated with the pdf that produced the following sample is 3.6, would it be correct to claim that

$$\left(2.61 - 1.96 \cdot \dfrac{3.6}{\sqrt{20}}, 2.61 + 1.96 \cdot \dfrac{3.6}{\sqrt{20}} \right) = (1.03, 4.19)$$

is a 95% confidence interval for μ? Explain.

2.5	0.1	0.2	1.3
3.2	0.1	0.1	1.4
0.5	0.2	0.4	11.2
0.4	7.4	1.8	2.1
0.3	8.6	0.3	10.1

5.3.8 Food-poisoning outbreaks are often the result of contaminated salads. In one study carried out to assess the magnitude of that problem, the New York City Department of Health examined 220 tuna salads marketed by various retail and wholesale outlets. A total of 179 were found to be unsatisfactory for health reasons (149). Find a 90% confidence interval for p, the true proportion of contaminated tuna salads marketed in New York City.

5.3.9 In 1927, the year he hit 60 home runs, Babe Ruth batted .356, having collected 192 hits in 540 official at-bats (130). Based on his performance that season, construct a 95% confidence interval for Ruth's probability of getting a hit in a future at-bat.

5.3.10 To buy a 30-second commercial break during the telecast of Super Bowl XXIX cost approximately $1,000,000. Not surprisingly, potential sponsors wanted to know how many people might be watching. In a survey of 1015 potential viewers, 281 said they expected to see less than a quarter of the advertisements aired during the game. Define the relevant parameter, calculate its MLE, and estimate it using a 90% confidence interval.

5.3.11 During one of the first "beer wars" in the early 1980s, a taste test between Schlitz and Budweiser was the focus of a nationally broadcast TV commercial. One hundred people agreed to drink from two unmarked mugs and indicate which of the two beers they liked better; fifty-four said "Bud." Construct and interpret the corresponding 95% confidence interval for p, the true proportion of beer-drinkers who prefer Budweiser to Schlitz. How would Budweiser and Schlitz executives each put these results in the best possible light for their respective companies?

5.3.12 If $(0.57, 0.63)$ is a 50% confidence interval for p, what does $\dfrac{x}{n}$ equal and how many observations were taken?

5.3.13 Suppose a coin is to be tossed n times for the purpose of estimating p, where $p = P(\text{heads})$. How large must n be to guarantee that the length of the 99% confidence interval for p will be less than 0.02?

5.3.14 On the morning of November 9, 1994—the day after the electoral landslide that returned Republicans to power in both branches of Congress—several key races were still in doubt. The most prominent was the Washington contest involving Democrat Tom Foley, the reigning speaker of the house. An Associated Press story showed how narrow the margin had become (110):

> With 99 percent of precincts reporting, Foley trailed Republican challenger George Nethercutt by just 2,174 votes, or 50.6 percent to 49.4 percent. About 14,000 absentee ballots remained uncounted, making the race too close to call.

Let $p = P(\text{absentee voter prefers Foley})$. How small could p have been and still have given Foley a 20% chance of overcoming Nethercutt's lead and winning the election?

5.3.15 Which of the following two intervals has the greater probability of containing the binomial parameter p?

$$\left(\frac{X}{n} - 0.67\sqrt{\frac{(X/n)(1 - X/n)}{n}}, \quad \frac{X}{n} + 0.67\sqrt{\frac{(X/n)(1 - X/n)}{n}} \right)$$

$$\text{or} \quad \left(\frac{X}{n}, \infty \right)$$

5.3.16 Examine the first two derivatives of the function $g(p) = p(1 - p)$ to verify the claim on page 330 that $p(1 - p) \leq \frac{1}{4}$ for $0 < p < 1$.

5.3.17 *Money* magazine reported that 30% of 1013 adults telephoned at random could not correctly define any of the four main types of life insurance. Built into that figure, the article cautioned, is a "3.1% margin of error." Verify that computation and explain in a short paragraph what the 3.1% implies.

5.3.18 Viral infections contracted early during a woman's pregnancy can be very harmful to the fetus. One study found a total of 86 deaths and birth defects among 202 pregnancies complicated by a first-trimester German measles infection (44). Is it believable that the true proportion of abnormal births under similar circumstances could be as high as 50%? Answer the question by calculating the margin of error for the sample proportion, 86/202.

5.3.19 Rewrite Definition 5.3.1 to cover the case where a finite correction factor needs to be included (i.e., situations where the sample size n is not negligible relative to the population size N).

5.3.20 A Forbes-Gallop poll in the summer of 1994 questioned 304 chief executives chosen from a list of 865 of the nation's largest companies. To the question "Over the next 6 months do you expect the overall U.S. business climate to get better, worse, or remain about the same?" 70 of the 304 said "better" (47). What margin of error is associated with their claim that 23% of CEOs $\left(= \frac{70}{304} \times 100 \right)$ are bullish on the economy? Include a finite correction factor in your calculation (see Question 5.3.19).

5.3.21 Given that n observations will produce a binomial parameter estimator, $\frac{X}{n}$, having a margin of error equal to 0.06, how many observations are required for the proportion to have a margin of error half that size?

5.3.22 Given that a political poll shows that 52% of the sample favors candidate A, whereas 48% would vote for candidate B, and given that the margin of error associated with the survey is 0.05, does it make sense to claim that the two candidates are tied? Explain.

5.3.23 Assume that the binomial parameter p is to be estimated with the function $\frac{X}{n}$, where X is the number of successes in n independent trials. Which demands the larger sample size: requiring that $\frac{X}{n}$ have a 96% probability of being within 0.05 of p, or requiring that $\frac{X}{n}$ have a 92% probability of being within 0.04 of p?

5.3.24 Suppose that p is to be estimated by $\frac{X}{n}$ and we are willing to assume that the true p will not be greater than 0.4. What is the smallest n for which $\frac{X}{n}$ will have a 99% probability of being within 0.05 of p?

5.3.25 Let p denote the true proportion of college students who support the movement to colorize classic films. Let the random variable X denote the number of students (out of n) who prefer colorized versions to black and white. What is the smallest sample size for which the probability is 80% that the difference between $\frac{X}{n}$ and p is less than 0.02?

5.3.26 University officials are planning to audit 1586 new appointments to estimate the proportion p who have been incorrectly processed by the Payroll Department.

   (a) How large does the sample size need to be in order for $\frac{X}{n}$, the sample proportion, to have an 85% chance of lying within 0.03 of p?
   (b) Past audits suggest that p will not be larger than 0.10. Using that information, recalculate the sample size asked for in Part (a).

5.4 PROPERTIES OF ESTIMATORS

The method of maximum likelihood and the method of moments described in Section 5.2 both use very reasonable criteria to identify estimators for unknown parameters, yet the two do not always yield the same answer. For example, given that Y_1, $Y_2, \ldots, Y_n$ is a random sample from the uniform pdf, $f_Y(y; \theta) = 1/\theta, 0 \le y \le \theta$, the MLE for θ is $\hat{\theta} = Y_{\max}$ while the method of moments estimator is $\hat{\theta} = \dfrac{2}{n} \sum_{i=1}^{n} Y_i$. Implicit in those two formulas is an obvious question—which should we use?

More generally, the fact that parameters have multiple estimators (actually, an infinite number of $\hat{\theta}$'s can be found for any given θ) requires that we investigate the statistical properties associated with the estimation process. What qualities should a "good" estimator have? Is it possible to find a "best" $\hat{\theta}$? These and other questions relating to the theory of estimation will be addressed in the next several sections.

To understand the *mathematics* of estimation, we must first keep in mind that every estimator is a function of a set of random variables—that is, $\hat{\theta} = h(Y_1, Y_2, \ldots, Y_n)$. As such, any $\hat{\theta}$, itself, is a random variable: It has a pdf, an expected value, and a variance, all three of which play key roles in evaluating its capabilities.

We will denote the pdf of an estimator (at some point u) with the symbol $f_{\hat{\theta}}(u)$ or $p_{\hat{\theta}}(u)$, depending on whether $\hat{\theta}$ is a continuous or a discrete random variable. Probability calculations involving θ will reduce to integrals of $f_{\hat{\theta}}(u)$ (if $\hat{\theta}$ is continuous) or sums of $p_{\hat{\theta}}(u)$ (if $\hat{\theta}$ is discrete).

EXAMPLE 5.4.1

(a) Suppose a coin for which $p = P(\text{heads})$ is unknown is to be tossed 10 times for the purpose of estimating p with the function $\hat{p} = \dfrac{X}{10}$, where X is the observed number of heads. If $p = 0.60$, what is the probability that $\left| \dfrac{X}{10} - 0.60 \right| \le 0.10$? That is, what are the chances that the estimator will fall within 0.10 of the true value of the parameter? Here $\hat{p}$ is discrete—the only values $\dfrac{X}{10}$ can take on are $0/10, 1/10, \ldots, 10/10$. Moreover, when $p = 0.60$,

$$p_{\hat{p}}\left(\frac{k}{10} \right) = P\left(\hat{p} = \frac{k}{10} \right) = P(X = k) = \binom{10}{k}(0.60)^k(0.40)^{10-k}, \quad k = 0, 1, \ldots, 10$$

Therefore,

$$P\left(\left| \frac{X}{10} - 0.60 \right| \le 0.10 \right) = P\left(0.60 - 0.10 \le \frac{X}{10} \le 0.60 + 0.10 \right)$$

$$= P(5 \le X \le 7)$$

$$= \sum_{k=5}^{7} \binom{10}{k}(0.60)^k(0.40)^{10-k}$$

$$= 0.6665$$

(b) How likely is the estimator $\dfrac{X}{n}$ to lie within 0.10 of p if the coin in Part (a) is tossed *100* times?

Given that n is so large, a Z transformation can be used to approximate the variation in $\dfrac{X}{100}$. Since $E\left(\dfrac{X}{n}\right) = p$ and $\mathrm{Var}\left(\dfrac{X}{n}\right) = p(1 - p)/n$, we can write

$$P\left(\left|\frac{X}{100} - 0.60\right| \le 0.10\right) = P\left(0.50 \le \frac{X}{100} \le 0.70\right)$$

$$= P\left(\frac{0.50 - 0.60}{\sqrt{\dfrac{(0.60)(0.40)}{100}}} \le \frac{X/100 - 0.60}{\sqrt{\dfrac{(0.60)(0.40)}{100}}} \le \frac{0.70 - 0.60}{\sqrt{\dfrac{(0.60)(0.40)}{100}}}\right)$$

$$\doteq P(-2.04 \le Z \le 2.04)$$

$$= 0.9586$$

Figure 5.4.1 shows the two probabilities just calculated as areas under the probability functions describing $\dfrac{X}{10}$ and $\dfrac{X}{100}$. As we would expect, the larger sample size produces a more precise estimator—with $n = 10$, $\dfrac{X}{10}$ has only a 67% chance of lying in the range from 0.50 to 0.70; for $n = 100$, though, the probability of $\dfrac{X}{100}$ falling within 0.10 of the true p $(= 0.60)$ increases to 96%.

FIGURE 5.4.1

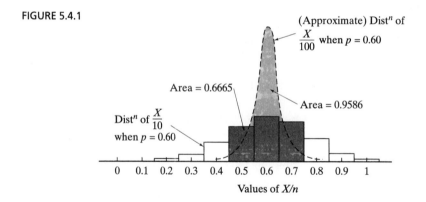

(Approximate) Dist^n of $\dfrac{X}{100}$ when $p = 0.60$

Area = 0.6665

Dist^n of $\dfrac{X}{10}$ when $p = 0.60$

Area = 0.9586

Values of *X/n*

Are the additional 90 observations worth the gain in precision that we see in Figure 5.4.1? Maybe yes and maybe no. In general, the answer to that sort of question depends on two factors: (1) the cost of taking additional measurements, and (2) the cost of making bad decisions or inappropriate inferences because of inaccurate estimates. In practice, both costs—especially the latter—can be very difficult to quantify.

Unbiasedness

Because they are random variables, estimators will take on different values from sample to sample. Typically, some samples will yield $\hat{\theta}$'s that underestimate θ while others will lead to $\hat{\theta}$'s that are numerically too large. Intuitively, we would like the under-

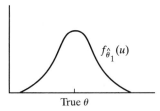
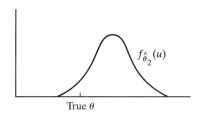

FIGURE 5.4.2

estimates to somehow "balance out" the overestimates—that is, $\hat{\theta}$ should not systematically err in any one particular direction.

Figure 5.4.2 shows the pdfs for two estimators, $\hat{\theta}_1$ and $\hat{\theta}_2$. Common sense tells us that $\hat{\theta}_1$ is the better of the two because $f_{\hat{\theta}_1}(u)$ is centered with respect to the true θ; $\hat{\theta}_2$, on the other hand, will tend to give estimates that are too large because the bulk of $f_{\hat{\theta}_2}(u)$ lies to the right of the true θ.

> **DEFINITION 5.4.1.**   Let $W_1, W_2, \ldots, W_n$ be a random sample from $f_W(w; \theta)$. An estimator $\hat{\theta} = h(W_1, W_2, \ldots, W_n)$ is said to be *unbiased for θ* if $E(\hat{\theta}) = \theta$ for all θ.

EXAMPLE 5.4.2

It was mentioned at the outset of this section that $\hat{\theta}_1 = \dfrac{2}{n} \sum_{i=1}^{n} Y_i$ and $\hat{\theta}_2 = Y_{\max}$ are two estimates for θ in the uniform pdf, $f_Y(y; \theta) = 1/\theta, 0 \le y \le \theta$. Are either or both unbiased?

An application of the corollary to Theorem 3.11.1, together with the fact that $E(Y_i) = \theta/2$ for all i, proves that $\hat{\theta}_1$ is unbiased for θ:

$$E(\hat{\theta}_1) = E\left(\frac{2}{n} \sum_{i=1}^{n} Y_i\right)$$

$$= \frac{2}{n} \sum_{i=1}^{n} E(Y_i)$$

$$= \frac{2}{n} \sum_{i=1}^{n} \frac{\theta}{2}$$

$$= \frac{2}{n} \cdot \frac{n\theta}{2}$$

$$= \theta$$

The maximum likelihood estimator, on the other hand, is obviously biased—since $Y_{\max}$ is necessarily less than or equal to θ, $f_{\hat{\theta}_2}(u)$ will not be centered with respect to θ and $E(\hat{\theta}_2)$ will be *less than* θ. The exact extent to which $\hat{\theta}_2$ tends to underestimate θ is easily calculated. Recall from the corollary to Theorem 3.8.1 that

$$f_{\hat{\theta}_2}(u) = f_{Y_{\max}}(u) = n \cdot \frac{1}{\theta} \cdot \left(\frac{u}{\theta}\right)^{n-1}, \quad 0 \le u \le \theta$$

Therefore,

$$E(\hat{\theta}_2) = \int_0^\theta u \cdot \frac{n}{\theta} \left(\frac{u}{\theta}\right)^{n-1} du$$

$$= \frac{n}{\theta^n} \cdot \frac{u^{n+1}}{n+1}\Big|_0^\theta$$

$$= \frac{n}{n+1}\theta$$

If $n = 3$, in other words, Y_{max} will be only $\frac{3}{4}$ as large as θ, on the average. As n increases, though, the "bias" in $\hat{\theta}_2$ decreases [which makes sense because $f_{\hat{\theta}_2}(u)$ will become increasingly concentrated around θ as the sample size gets large].

Comment.   For any finite n, we can construct an estimator based on Y_{max} that *is* unbiased. Let $\hat{\theta}_3 = \dfrac{n+1}{n} \cdot Y_{max}$. Then

$$E(\hat{\theta}_3) = E\left(\frac{n+1}{n} \cdot Y_{max}\right)$$

$$= \frac{n+1}{n} \cdot E(Y_{max})$$

$$= \frac{n+1}{n} \cdot \frac{n}{n+1}\theta$$

$$= \theta$$

EXAMPLE 5.4.3

Let $W_1, W_2, \ldots, W_n$ be a random sample from a probability model whose mean is μ. Let

$$\hat{\mu} = h(W_1, W_2, \ldots, W_n) = \sum_{i=1}^n a_i W_i$$

where the a_i's are constants. For what values of $a_1, a_2, \ldots, a_n$ will $\hat{\mu}$ be unbiased?

If the mean of $f_W(w; \mu)$ is μ, then $E(W_i) = \mu$ for all i. By assumption, $E(\hat{\mu})$ is to equal μ, so

$$E\left(\sum_{i=1}^n a_i W_i\right) = \mu = \sum_{i=1}^n a_i E(W_i)$$

$$= \sum_{i=1}^n a_i \mu$$

$$= \mu \sum_{i=1}^n a_i$$

which implies that $a_1 + a_2 + \ldots + a_n$ *must equal 1* if $\hat{\mu}$ is to be unbiased for μ.

EXAMPLE 5.4.4

Given a random sample $Y_1, Y_2, \ldots, Y_n$ from a normal distribution where both μ and σ^2 are unknown, the MLE for σ^2 is

$$\hat{\sigma}^2 = \frac{1}{n} \sum_{i=1}^{n} (Y_i - \bar{Y})^2$$

(recall Example 5.2.4). Is $\hat{\sigma}^2$ unbiased for σ^2? If not, what function of $\hat{\sigma}^2$ does have an expected value equal to σ^2?

Recall, first, from Chapter 3 that for any random variable W, $\text{Var}(W) = E(W^2) - [E(W)]^2$ and for any average, $\bar{W}$, of a sample of n random variables, $W_1, W_2, \ldots, W_n$, $E(\bar{W}) = E(W_i)$ and $\text{Var}(\bar{W}) = \dfrac{\text{Var}(W_i)}{n}$. Using those results, we can write

$$E(\hat{\sigma}^2) = E\left[\frac{1}{n} \sum_{i=1}^{n} (Y_i - \bar{Y})^2\right]$$

$$= E\left[\frac{1}{n} \sum_{i=1}^{n} (Y_i^2 - 2Y_i\bar{Y} + \bar{Y}^2)\right]$$

$$= E\left[\frac{1}{n}\left(\sum_{i=1}^{n} Y_i^2 - n\bar{Y}^2\right)\right]$$

$$= \frac{1}{n}\left[\sum_{i=1}^{n} E(Y_i^2) - nE(\bar{Y}^2)\right]$$

$$= \frac{1}{n}\left[\sum_{i=1}^{n} (\sigma^2 + \mu^2) - n\left(\frac{\sigma^2}{n} + \mu^2\right)\right]$$

$$= \frac{n-1}{n} \sigma^2$$

Since the latter is not equal to σ^2, $\hat{\sigma}^2$ is biased.

To "unbias" the MLE in this case, we need simply multiply $\hat{\sigma}^2$ by $\dfrac{n}{n-1}$. By convention, the unbiased version of the MLE for σ^2 in a normal distribution is denoted S^2 and is referred to as the *sample variance*:

$$S^2 = \text{sample variance} = \frac{n}{n-1} \cdot \frac{1}{n} \sum_{i=1}^{n} (Y_i - \bar{Y})^2$$

$$= \frac{1}{n-1} \sum_{i=1}^{n} (Y_i - \bar{Y})^2$$

Comment.   The square root of the sample variance is called the *sample standard deviation*:

$$S = \text{sample standard deviation} = \sqrt{\frac{1}{n-1} \sum_{i=1}^{n} (Y_i - \bar{Y})^2}$$

In practice, S is the most commonly used estimator for σ *even though* $E(S) \neq \sigma$ [despite the fact that $E(S^2) = \sigma^2$].

EXAMPLE 5.4.5

By definition, the *geometric mean* of a set of n numbers is the nth root of their product. Let Y_1 and Y_2 be a random sample of size 2 from the pdf $f_Y(y; \theta) = \dfrac{1}{\theta} e^{-y/\theta}$, $y > 0$, where θ is an unknown parameter. Find an unbiased estimator for θ based on the sample's geometric mean, $\sqrt{Y_1 Y_2}$.

By Theorem 3.11.3,

$$E\left(\sqrt{Y_1 Y_2}\right) = \int_0^\infty \int_0^\infty (y_1 y_2)^{\frac{1}{2}} \cdot \frac{1}{\theta} e^{-y_1/\theta} \cdot \frac{1}{\theta} e^{-y_2/\theta} \, dy_1 \, dy_2$$

$$= \left[\int_0^\infty y^{\frac{1}{2}} \cdot \frac{1}{\theta} e^{-y/\theta} \, dy \right]^2$$

Let $t = y/\theta$. Then $dt = dy/\theta$ and

$$E\left(\sqrt{Y_1 Y_2}\right) = \left[\int_0^\infty (\theta t)^{\frac{1}{2}} \cdot e^{-t} \, dt \right]^2$$

$$= \theta \left[\int_0^\infty t^{\frac{1}{2}} e^{-t} \, dt \right]^2$$

But $\int_0^\infty t^{\frac{1}{2}} e^{-t} \, dt = \Gamma\left(\dfrac{3}{2}\right) = \frac{1}{2}\sqrt{\pi}$ (recall the comment following Example 4.6.3). Therefore,

$$E\left(\sqrt{Y_1 Y_2}\right) = \theta\left(\tfrac{1}{2}\sqrt{\pi}\right)^2 = \frac{\theta \pi}{4}$$

which implies that

$$\hat{\theta} = \frac{4\sqrt{Y_1 Y_2}}{\pi}$$

is unbiased for θ.

Table 5.4.1 is a computer simulation showing the performance of the estimator $\hat{\theta} = 4\sqrt{Y_1 Y_2}/\pi$ when $\theta = 1$. In columns C1 and C2 are 40 random samples drawn from the pdf $f_Y(y; 1) = e^{-y}$, $y > 0$. The corresponding geometric means $\sqrt{y_1 y_2}$ are listed in column C3 and the 40 simulated $\hat{\theta}$'s appear in column C4.

Sample 28 yielded the smallest estimate ($\hat{\theta} = 0.13792$), while Sample 29 erred the most in the other direction ($\hat{\theta} = 3.97022$). Notice that the *average* of the 40 $\hat{\theta}$'s (= 1.02) is very close to the parameter's *true* value ($\theta = 1.00$). That the two agree so well, of course, is not surprising, given that $\hat{\theta}$ is unbiased for θ.

TABLE 5.4.1

	C1 y1	C2 y2	C3 sqrt	C4 Est.	
1	0.70495	1.01324	0.84515	1.07608	
2	3.96959	0.58870	1.52869	1.94639	
3	0.26150	2.92107	0.87399	1.11280	
4	0.44146	0.31922	0.37540	0.47797	
5	1.55721	1.86945	1.70620	2.17241	
6	1.68906	0.41461	0.83684	1.06550	
7	0.36449	0.33562	0.34976	0.44532	
8	1.12210	0.23355	0.51193	0.65180	
9	1.54124	0.45424	0.83671	1.06534	
10	0.12599	1.73641	0.46773	0.59554	
11	0.20148	0.07541	0.12326	0.15694	
12	0.53266	0.29699	0.39774	0.50641	
13	0.20425	1.49059	0.55177	0.70254	
14	4.49631	0.48274	1.47327	1.87583	
15	0.07196	2.43756	0.41882	0.53326	
16	0.50555	1.45129	0.85656	1.09061	
17	2.00492	0.61484	1.11027	1.41364	
18	4.40562	0.37557	1.28632	1.63780	
19	0.07702	0.46802	0.18986	0.24174	
20	0.13929	0.17789	0.15741	0.20043	average $\hat{\theta} = 1.02$
21	0.09732	0.47298	0.21455	0.27317	
22	0.24751	0.15451	0.19556	0.24899	
23	0.20255	1.43477	0.53909	0.68639	
24	0.04071	0.48771	0.14091	0.17941	
25	0.23687	0.72270	0.41375	0.52680	
26	0.85065	1.06104	0.95004	1.20963	
27	0.33847	0.97953	0.57580	0.73313	
28	0.67740	0.01732	0.10832	0.13792	
29	1.62282	5.99154	3.11820	3.97022	
30	1.28070	0.09598	0.35060	0.44640	
31	3.40310	1.22856	2.04473	2.60343	
32	2.53520	0.64045	1.27423	1.62240	
33	1.53845	0.38732	0.77193	0.98285	
34	3.60054	1.10229	1.99220	2.53655	
35	0.30786	0.86581	0.51628	0.65735	
36	2.50065	0.09313	0.48259	0.61445	
37	0.52834	1.12503	0.77098	0.98164	
38	0.80602	2.84524	1.51437	1.92816	
39	0.17185	1.04371	0.42351	0.53923	
40	0.98211	0.58988	0.76114	0.96911	

QUESTIONS

5.4.1 Two chips are drawn without replacement from an urn containing five chips, numbered 1 through 5. The average of the two drawn is to be used as an estimator, $\hat{\theta}$, for the true average of all the chips ($\theta = 3$). Calculate $P(|\hat{\theta} - 3| > 1.0)$.

5.4.2 Suppose a random sample of size $n = 6$ is drawn from the uniform pdf $f_Y(y; \theta) = 1/\theta$, $0 \leq y \leq \theta$ for the purpose of using $\hat{\theta} = Y_{max}$ to estimate θ.

(a) Calculate the probability that $\hat{\theta}$ falls within 0.2 of θ given that the parameter's true value is 3.0.

(b) Calculate the probability of the event asked for in Part (a) assuming the sample size is 3 instead of 6.

5.4.3 Five hundred adults are asked whether they favor a bipartisan campaign finance reform bill. If the true proportion of the electorate in favor of the legislation is 52%, what are the chances that fewer than half of those in the sample support the proposal? Use a Z transformation to approximate the answer.

5.4.4 A sample of size $n = 16$ is drawn from a normal distribution where $\sigma = 10$ but μ is unknown. If $\mu = 20$, what is the probability that the estimator $\hat{\mu} = \bar{Y}$ will lie between 19.0 and 21.0?

5.4.5 Suppose $X_1, X_2, \ldots, X_n$ is a random sample of size n drawn from a Poisson pdf, where λ is an unknown parameter. Show that $\hat{\lambda} = \bar{X}$ is unbiased for λ. For what type of parameter, in general, will the sample mean necessarily be an unbiased estimator? *Hint:* The answer is implicit in the derivation showing that $\bar{X}$ is unbiased for the Poisson λ.

5.4.6 Let $Y_{\min}$ be the smallest order statistic in a random sample of size n drawn from the uniform pdf, $f_Y(y; \theta) = 1/\theta, 0 \le y \le \theta$. Find an unbiased estimator for θ based on $Y_{\min}$.

5.4.7 Suppose that 14, 10, 18, and 21 constitute a random sample of size 4 drawn from a uniform pdf defined over the interval $[0, \theta]$, where θ is unknown. Find an unbiased estimator for θ based on Y_3', the third order statistic. What numerical value does the estimator have for these particular observations? Is it possible that we would know that an estimate for θ based on Y_3' was incorrect, even if we had no idea what the true value of θ might be? Explain.

5.4.8 A random sample of size 2, Y_1 and Y_2, is drawn from the pdf,

$$f_Y(y; \theta) = 2y\theta^2, \quad 0 < y < \frac{1}{\theta}$$

What must c equal if the statistic $c(Y_1 + 2Y_2)$ is to be an unbiased estimator for $\frac{1}{\theta}$?

5.4.9 A sample of size 1 is drawn from the uniform pdf defined over the interval $[0, \theta]$. Find an unbiased estimator for θ^2. *Hint:* Is $\hat{\theta} = Y^2$ unbiased?

5.4.10 We showed in Example 5.4.4 that $\hat{\sigma}^2 = \frac{1}{n} \sum_{i=1}^{n} (Y_i - \bar{Y})^2$ is biased for σ^2. Suppose μ is known and does not have to be estimated by $\bar{Y}$. Show that $\hat{\sigma}^2 = \frac{1}{n} \sum_{i=1}^{n} (Y_i - \mu)^2$ is unbiased for σ^2.

5.4.11 As an alternative to imposing unbiasedness, an estimator's distribution can be "centered" by requiring that its median be equal to the unknown parameter θ. If it is, $\hat{\theta}$ is said to be *median unbiased*. Let $Y_1, Y_2, \ldots, Y_n$ be a random sample of size n from the uniform pdf, $f_Y(y; \theta) = 1/\theta, 0 \le y \le \theta$. For arbitrary n, is $\hat{\theta} = \frac{n+1}{n} \cdot Y_{\max}$ median unbiased? Is it median unbiased for any value of n?

5.4.12 Let $Y_1, Y_2, \ldots, Y_n$ be a random sample of size n from the pdf $f_Y(y; \theta) = \frac{1}{\theta} e^{-y/\theta}, y > 0$. Let $\hat{\theta} = n \cdot Y_{\min}$. Is $\hat{\theta}$ unbiased for θ? Is $\hat{\theta} = \frac{1}{n} \sum_{i=1}^{n} Y_i$ unbiased for θ?

5.4.13 An estimator $\hat{\theta}_n = h(W_1, W_2, \ldots, W_n)$ is said to be *asymptotically unbiased for* θ if $\lim_{n \to \infty} E(\hat{\theta}_n) = \theta$. Is the MLE for σ^2 in a normal pdf, where both μ and σ^2 are unknown, asymptotically unbiased?

Efficiency

As we have seen, unknown parameters can have a multiplicity of unbiased estimators. For samples drawn from the uniform pdf, $f_Y(y; \theta) = 1/\theta, 0 \le y \le \theta$, for example, both $\hat{\theta} = \dfrac{n+1}{n} \cdot Y_{\max}$ and $\hat{\theta} = \dfrac{2}{n} \sum\limits_{i=1}^{n} Y_i$ have expected values equal to θ. Does it matter which we choose?

Yes. Unbiasedness is not the only property we would like an estimator to have; also important is its *precision*. Figure 5.4.3 shows the pdf's associated with two hypothetical estimators, $\hat{\theta}_1$ and $\hat{\theta}_2$. Both are unbiased for θ, but $\hat{\theta}_2$ is clearly the better of the two because of its smaller variance. For any value r,

$$P\big(\theta - r \le \hat{\theta}_2 \le \theta + r\big) > P\big(\theta - r \le \hat{\theta}_1 \le \theta + r\big)$$

That is, $\hat{\theta}_2$ has a greater chance of being within a distance r of the unknown θ than does $\hat{\theta}_1$.

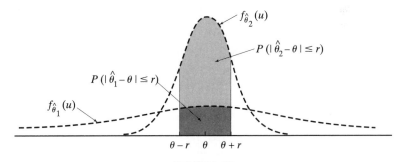

FIGURE 5.4.3

DEFINITION 5.4.2. Let $\hat{\theta}_1$ and $\hat{\theta}_2$ be two unbiased estimators for a parameter θ. If

$$\text{Var}\big(\hat{\theta}_1\big) < \text{Var}\big(\hat{\theta}_2\big)$$

we say that $\hat{\theta}_1$ is *more efficient* than $\hat{\theta}_2$. Also, the *relative efficiency of $\hat{\theta}_1$ with respect to $\hat{\theta}_2$* is the ratio $\text{Var}\big(\hat{\theta}_2\big)/\text{Var}\big(\hat{\theta}_1\big)$.

EXAMPLE 5.4.6

Let Y_1, Y_2, and Y_3 be a random sample from a normal distribution where both μ and σ are unknown. Which is a more efficient estimator for μ,

$$\hat{\mu}_1 = \frac{1}{4}Y_1 + \frac{1}{2}Y_2 + \frac{1}{4}Y_3$$

or

$$\hat{\mu}_2 = \frac{1}{3}Y_1 + \frac{1}{3}Y_2 + \frac{1}{3}Y_3$$

Notice, first, that both $\hat{\mu}_1$ and $\hat{\mu}_2$ are unbiased for μ:

$$E(\hat{\mu}_1) = E\left(\frac{1}{4}Y_1 + \frac{1}{2}Y_2 + \frac{1}{4}Y_3\right)$$

$$= \frac{1}{4}E(Y_1) + \frac{1}{2}E(Y_2) + \frac{1}{4}E(Y_3)$$

$$= \frac{1}{4}\mu + \frac{1}{2}\mu + \frac{1}{4}\mu$$

$$= \mu$$

and

$$E(\hat{\mu}_2) = E\left(\frac{1}{3}Y_1 + \frac{1}{3}Y_2 + \frac{1}{3}Y_3\right)$$

$$= \frac{1}{3}E(Y_1) + \frac{1}{3}E(Y_2) + \frac{1}{3}E(Y_3)$$

$$= \frac{1}{3}\mu + \frac{1}{3}\mu + \frac{1}{3}\mu$$

$$= \mu$$

But $\text{Var}(\hat{\mu}_2) < \text{Var}(\hat{\mu}_1)$ so $\hat{\mu}_2$ is the more efficient of the two:

$$\text{Var}(\hat{\mu}_1) = \text{Var}\left(\frac{1}{4}Y_1 + \frac{1}{2}Y_2 + \frac{1}{4}Y_3\right)$$

$$= \frac{1}{16}\text{Var}(Y_1) + \frac{1}{4}\text{Var}(Y_2) + \frac{1}{16}\text{Var}(Y_3)$$

$$= \frac{3\sigma^2}{8}$$

$$\text{Var}(\hat{\mu}_2) = \text{Var}\left(\frac{1}{3}Y_1 + \frac{1}{3}Y_2 + \frac{1}{3}Y_3\right)$$

$$= \frac{1}{9}\text{Var}(Y_1) + \frac{1}{9}\text{Var}(Y_2) + \frac{1}{9}\text{Var}(Y_3)$$

$$= \frac{3\sigma^2}{9}$$

(The relative efficiency of $\hat{\mu}_2$ to $\hat{\mu}_1$ is

$$\frac{3\sigma^2}{8} \bigg/ \frac{3\sigma^2}{9}$$

or *1.125*.)

EXAMPLE 5.4.7

Let $Y_1, Y_2, \ldots, Y_n$ be a random sample from the uniform pdf defined over the interval $[0, \theta]$. We know from Example 5.4.2 that $\hat{\theta}_1 = \frac{2}{n}\sum_{i=1}^{n} Y_i$ and $\hat{\theta}_2 = \frac{n+1}{n} \cdot Y_{\max}$ are both unbiased for θ. Which estimator is more efficient?

Recall from Theorem 3.12.1 that $\text{Var}(W) = E(W^2) - [E(W)]^2$ for any random variable W. Therefore,

$$\text{Var}(\hat{\theta}_1) = \text{Var}\left(\frac{2}{n}\sum_{i=1}^{n}Y_i\right)$$

$$= \frac{4}{n^2}\sum_{i=1}^{n}\text{Var}(Y_i)$$

$$= \frac{4}{n^2}\sum_{i=1}^{n}\left[E(Y_i^2) - \left[E(Y_i)\right]^2\right]$$

But $E(Y_i) = \dfrac{\theta}{2}$ (by symmetry) and $E(Y_i^2) = \displaystyle\int_0^\theta y^2 \cdot \frac{1}{\theta}\,dy = \frac{\theta^2}{3}$, so

$$\text{Var}(\hat{\theta}_1) = \frac{4}{n^2}\sum_{i=1}^{n}\left(\frac{\theta^2}{3} - \frac{\theta^2}{4}\right)$$

$$= \frac{4}{n^2}\cdot\frac{n\theta^2}{12}$$

$$= \frac{\theta^2}{3n}$$

Similarly,

$$\text{Var}(\hat{\theta}_2) = \text{Var}\left(\frac{n+1}{n}\cdot Y_{\max}\right)$$

$$= \left(\frac{n+1}{n}\right)^2\cdot\text{Var}(Y_{\max})$$

$$= \left(\frac{n+1}{n}\right)^2\left[E(Y_{\max}^2) - \left[E(Y_{\max})\right]^2\right]$$

From the corollary to Theorem 3.8.1,

$$f_{Y_{\max}}(y) = \frac{n}{\theta}\left(\frac{y}{\theta}\right)^{n-1}$$

so

$$E(Y_{\max}^2) = \int_0^\theta y^2 \cdot \frac{n}{\theta}\left(\frac{y}{\theta}\right)^{n-1}dy$$

$$= \frac{n}{\theta^n}\int_0^\theta y^{n+1}\,dy = \left(\frac{n}{\theta^n}\right)\frac{y^{n+2}}{n+2}\Big|_0^\theta = \frac{n}{n+2}\theta^2$$

We already know that $E(Y_{\max}) = \dfrac{n}{n+1}\theta$, so

$$\text{Var}(\hat{\theta}_2) = \left(\frac{n+1}{n}\right)^2\left[\frac{n\theta^2}{n+2} - \left(\frac{n}{n+1}\right)^2\theta^2\right]$$

$$= \frac{\theta^2}{n(n+2)}$$

Notice that $n(n+2)/3n > 1$ for $n > 1$, which implies that $\hat{\theta}_2 = \dfrac{n+1}{n}\cdot Y_{\max}$ has a smaller variance (and is more efficient) than $\hat{\theta}_1 = \dfrac{2}{n}\sum_{i=1}^{n}Y_i$.

CASE STUDY 5.4.1

During World War II, a very simple statistical procedure was developed for estimating German war production. It was based on *serial numbers* and proved to be incredibly reliable. When the war ended and the Third Reich's "true" production figures were revealed, it was found that serial number estimates were far more accurate in every instance than all the information gleaned from the more traditional espionage operations, spies, and informants.

Every piece of German equipment, whether it was a V-2 rocket, a tank, or just an automobile tire, was stamped with a serial number that indicated the order in which it was manufactured. If the total number of, say, Mark I tanks produced by a certain date was N, each would bear one of the integers 1 to N. As the war progressed, some of these numbers became known to the Allies—either by the direct capture of a piece of equipment or from records seized when a command post was overrun. For the War Department's statisticians, the problem was to estimate N using the sample of "captured" serial numbers, $1 \leq Y'_1 < Y'_2 < \ldots < Y'_n \leq N$.

Several approaches were proposed. One model assumed that the n serial numbers were one of the $\binom{N}{n}$ possible sets of n ordered integers from 1 to N and that each set was equally likely. That is,

$$P\left(Y'_1 = y'_1 < Y'_2 = y'_2 < \ldots < Y'_n = y'_n\right) = \binom{N}{n}^{-1}$$

The parameter N was then estimated by adding the average "gap" in the serial numbers to the largest serial number:

$$\hat{N}_1 = Y_{\max} + \frac{1}{n-1} \sum_{i>j} \left(Y'_i - Y'_j - 1\right)$$

So, if five tanks were captured and they bore the numbers 14, 28, 92, 146, and 298, the estimate for the total number of tanks produced would be *368*:

$$\hat{N}_1 = 298 + \frac{1}{4}\left[(298 - 146 - 1) + \ldots (28 - 14 - 1)\right]$$

$$= 368$$

A second estimator used was a discrete version of the modified MLE referred to as $\hat{\theta}_2$ in Example 5.4.7:

$$\hat{N}_2 = \left(\frac{n+1}{n}\right) \cdot Y_{\max} - 1$$

Both $\hat{N}_1$ and $\hat{N}_2$ are very good estimators, but $\hat{N}_2$ has a slightly smaller variance: It can be shown that

$$\frac{\text{Var}(N_2)}{\text{Var}(N_1)} = 1 - \frac{1}{n^2}$$

[see (56) for details].

The difference in the accuracy of $\hat{N}_1$ and $\hat{N}_2$ compared with estimates obtained from intelligence reports and covert activities was astounding. The serial number estimate for German tank production in 1942, for example, was 3400, a figure very close to the actual output. The "official" estimate, based on information gathered through more conventional wartime channels, was a grossly inflated 18,000.

Discrepancies of that magnitude were not uncommon. The sophisticated Nazi propaganda machine may have been the root cause of the "normal" estimates consistently erring on the high side. Germany sought to intimidate her enemies by exaggerating the country's industrial prowess. On people, the carefully orchestrated dissembling worked exactly as planned; on $\hat{N}_1$ and $\hat{N}_2$, though, it had no effect whatsoever!

QUESTIONS

5.4.14 Let $X_1, X_2, \ldots, X_n$ denote the outcomes of a series of n independent trials, where

$$X_i = \begin{cases} 1 & \text{with probability } p \\ 0 & \text{with probability } 1 - p \end{cases}$$

for $i = 1, 2, \ldots, n$. Let $X = X_1 + X_2 + \ldots + X_n$.

(a) Show that $\hat{p}_1 = X_1$ and $\hat{p}_2 = \dfrac{X}{n}$ are unbiased estimators for p.

(b) Intuitively, $\hat{p}_2$ is a better estimator than $\hat{p}_1$ because $\hat{p}_1$ fails to include any or all of the information about the parameter contained in trials 2 through n. Verify that speculation by comparing the variances of $\hat{p}_1$ and $\hat{p}_2$.

5.4.15 Suppose that $n = 5$ observations are taken from the uniform pdf, $f_Y(y; \theta) = 1/\theta$, $0 \le y \le \theta$, where θ is unknown. Two unbiased estimators for θ are

$$\hat{\theta}_1 = \frac{6}{5} \cdot Y_{\max} \quad \text{and} \quad \hat{\theta}_2 = 6 \cdot Y_{\min}$$

Which estimator would be better to use? *Hint*: What must be true of $\text{Var}(Y_{\max})$ and $\text{Var}(Y_{\min})$ given that $f_Y(y; \theta)$ is symmetric? Does your answer as to which estimator is better make sense on intuitive grounds? Explain.

5.4.16 Let $Y_1, Y_2, \ldots, Y_n$ be a random sample of size n from the pdf $f_Y(y; \theta) = \dfrac{1}{\theta} e^{-y/\theta}$, $y > 0$.

(a) Show that $\hat{\theta}_1 = Y_1$, $\hat{\theta}_2 = \bar{Y}$, and $\hat{\theta}_3 = n \cdot Y_{\min}$ are all unbiased estimators for θ.

(b) Find the variances of $\hat{\theta}_1$, $\hat{\theta}_2$, and $\hat{\theta}_3$.

(c) Calculate the relative efficiencies of $\hat{\theta}_1$ to $\hat{\theta}_3$ and $\hat{\theta}_2$ to $\hat{\theta}_3$.

5.4.17 Given a random sample of size n from a Poisson distribution, $\hat{\lambda}_1 = X_1$ and $\hat{\lambda}_2 = \bar{X}$ are two unbiased estimators for λ. Calculate the relative efficiency of $\hat{\lambda}_1$ to $\hat{\lambda}_2$.

5.4.18 If $Y_1, Y_2, \ldots, Y_n$ are random observations from a uniform pdf over $[0, \theta]$, both

$$\hat{\theta}_1 = \left(\frac{n+1}{n}\right) \cdot Y_{\max} \quad \text{and} \quad \hat{\theta}_2 = (n+1) \cdot Y_{\min}$$ are unbiased estimators for θ. Show that $\text{Var}(\hat{\theta}_2)/\text{Var}(\hat{\theta}_1) = n^2$.

5.5   MINIMUM-VARIANCE ESTIMATORS: THE CRAMÉR-RAO LOWER BOUND

Given two estimators, $\hat{\theta}_1$ and $\hat{\theta}_2$, each unbiased for the parameter θ, we know from Section 5.4 which is "better"—the one with the smaller variance. But nothing in that section speaks to the more fundamental question of how good $\hat{\theta}_1$ and $\hat{\theta}_2$ are *relative to the infinitely many other unbiased estimators for θ*. Is there a $\hat{\theta}_3$, for example, that has a smaller variance than does either $\hat{\theta}_1$ or $\hat{\theta}_2$? Can we identify the unbiased estimator having the *smallest* variance? Addressing those concerns is one of the most elegant, yet practical, theorems in all of mathematical statistics, a result known as the *Cramér-Rao lower bound*.

Suppose a random sample of size n is taken from a probability distribution $f_W(w; \theta)$, where θ is an unknown parameter. Associated with $f_W(w; \theta)$ is a theoretical limit below which the variance of any unbiased estimator for θ cannot fall. That limit is the Cramér-Rao lower bound. If the variance of a given $\hat{\theta}$ is *equal* to the Cramér-Rao lower bound, we know that that estimator is *optimal* in the sense that no unbiased $\hat{\theta}$ can estimate θ with greater precision.

THEOREM 5.5.1.   *Cramér-Rao Inequality*   Let $W_1, W_2, \ldots, W_n$ be a random sample from $f_W(w; \theta)$, where $f_W(w; \theta)$ has continuous first-order and second-order partial derivatives at all but a finite set of points. Suppose the set of w's for which $f_W(w; \theta) \neq 0$ does not depend on θ. Let $\hat{\theta} = h(W_1, W_2, \ldots, W_n)$ be any unbiased estimator for θ. Then

$$\text{Var}(\hat{\theta}) \geq \left\{ nE\left[\left(\frac{\partial \ln f_W(W; \theta)}{\partial \theta} \right)^2 \right] \right\}^{-1} = \left\{ -nE\left[\frac{\partial^2 \ln f_W(W; \theta)}{\partial \theta^2} \right] \right\}^{-1}$$

Proof.   See (8.3).

EXAMPLE 5.5.1

Suppose the random variables $X_1, X_2, \ldots, X_n$ denote the number of successes in each of n independent trials, where $p = P$ (success occurs at any given trial) is an unknown parameter. Then

$$p_{X_i}(k; p) = p^k(1 - p)^{1-k}, \quad k = 0, 1; \quad 0 < p < 1$$

Let $X = X_1 + X_2 + \cdots + X_n =$ total number of successes and define $\hat{p} = \dfrac{X}{n}$. Clearly, $\hat{p}$ is unbiased for $p(E(\hat{p}) = E\left(\dfrac{X}{n}\right) = \dfrac{E(X)}{n} = \dfrac{np}{n} = p)$. How does $\text{Var}(\hat{p})$ compare with the Cramér-Rao lower bound for $p_{X_i}(k; p)$?

Note, first, that

$$\text{Var}(\hat{p}) = \text{Var}\left(\frac{X}{n}\right) = \frac{1}{n^2}\text{Var}(X) = \frac{1}{n^2}np(1 - p) = \frac{p(1 - p)}{n}$$

(since X is a binomial random variable). To evaluate, say, the *second* form of the Cramér-Rao lower bound, we begin by writing

$$\ln p_{X_i}(X_i; p) = X_i \ln p + (1 - X_i)\ln(1 - p)$$

Then

$$\frac{\partial \ln p_{X_i}(X_i; p)}{\partial p} = \frac{X_i}{p} - \frac{1 - X_i}{1 - p}$$

and

$$\frac{\partial^2 \ln p_{X_i}(X_i; p)}{\partial p^2} = -\frac{X_i}{p^2} - \frac{1 - X_i}{(1 - p)^2}$$

Taking the expected value of the second derivative gives

$$E\left[\frac{\partial^2 \ln p_{X_i}(X_i; p)}{\partial p^2}\right] = -\frac{p}{p^2} - \frac{(1 - p)}{(1 - p)^2} = -\frac{1}{p(1 - p)}$$

The Cramér-Rao lower bound, then, reduces to

$$\frac{1}{-n\left[-\dfrac{1}{p(1 - p)}\right]} = \frac{p(1 - p)}{n}$$

which *equals* the variance of $\hat{p} = \dfrac{X}{n}$. It follows that $\dfrac{X}{n}$ is the preferred statistic for estimating the binomial parameter p: No unbiased estimator can possibly be more precise.

DEFINITION 5.5.1.   Let Θ denote the set of all estimators $\hat{\theta} = h(W_1, W_2, \ldots, W_n)$ that are unbiased for the parameter θ in the pdf $f_W(w; \theta)$. We say that $\hat{\theta}^*$ is a *best* (or *minimum-variance*) estimator if $\hat{\theta}^* \in \Theta$ and

$$\text{Var}(\hat{\theta}^*) \le \text{Var}(\hat{\theta}) \quad \text{for all } \hat{\theta} \in \Theta$$

DEFINITION 5.5.2.
   (a) An unbiased estimator $\hat{\theta} = h(W_1, W_2, \ldots, W_n)$ is said to be *efficient* if the variance of $\hat{\theta}$ equals the Cramér-Rao lower bound for $f_W(w; \theta)$.
   (b) The *efficiency* of an unbiased estimator $\hat{\theta}$ is the ratio of the Cramér-Rao lower bound for $f_W(w; \theta)$ to the variance of $\hat{\theta}$.

Comment.   The designations "efficient" and "best" are not synonymous. If the variance of an unbiased estimator is equal to the Cramér-Rao lower bound, then that estimator by definition is a best estimator. The converse, though, is not always true. There are situations for which the variances of *no* unbiased estimators achieve the Cramér-Rao lower bound. None of those, then, is *efficient*, but one (or more) could still be termed *best*. For the independent trials described in Example 5.5.1, $\hat{p} = \dfrac{X}{n}$ is both efficient *and* best.

EXAMPLE 5.5.2

If $Y_1, Y_2, \ldots, Y_n$ is a random sample from $f_Y(y; \theta) = 2y/\theta^2, 0 < y < \theta, \hat{\theta} = \frac{3}{2} \cdot \bar{Y}$ is an unbiased estimator for θ (see Question 5.5.1). Show that the variance of $\hat{\theta}$ is *less than* the Cramér-Rao lower bound for $f_Y(y; \theta)$.

Applying Theorems 3.12.1 and 3.13.1 to the proposed estimator, we can write

$$\text{Var}(\hat{\theta}) = \text{Var}\left(\frac{3}{2} \cdot \bar{Y}\right) = \text{Var}\left(\frac{3}{2} \cdot \frac{1}{n} \sum_{i=1}^{n} Y_i\right)$$

$$= \frac{9}{4n^2} \sum_{i=1}^{n} \text{Var}(Y_i)$$

where

$$\text{Var}(Y_i) = E(Y_i^2) - \left[E(Y_i)\right]^2$$

$$= \int_0^\theta y^2 \cdot \frac{2y}{\theta^2} \, dy - \left[\int_0^\theta y \cdot \frac{2y}{\theta^2} \, dy\right]^2$$

$$= \frac{\theta^2}{18}$$

Therefore,

$$\text{Var}(\hat{\theta}) = \frac{9}{4n^2} \sum_{i=1}^{n} \frac{\theta^2}{18} = \frac{9}{4n^2} \cdot \frac{n\theta^2}{18}$$

$$= \frac{\theta^2}{8n}$$

To calculate the Cramér-Rao lower bound for $f_Y(y; \theta)$, we first note that

$$\ln f_Y(y; \theta) = \ln[2y\theta^{-2}] = \ln 2y - 2\ln \theta$$

and

$$\frac{\partial \ln f_Y(y; \theta)}{\partial \theta} = \frac{-2}{\theta}$$

Therefore,

$$E\left[\left(\frac{\partial \ln f_Y(Y; \theta)}{\partial \theta}\right)^2\right] = E\left(\frac{4}{\theta^2}\right) = \int_0^\theta \frac{4}{\theta^2} \cdot \frac{2y}{\theta^2} \, dy$$

$$= \frac{4}{\theta^2}$$

and

$$\left\{nE\left[\left(\frac{\partial \ln f_Y(Y; \theta)}{\partial \theta}\right)^2\right]\right\}^{-1} = \frac{\theta^2}{4n}$$

Is the variance of $\hat{\theta}$ less than the Cramér-Rao lower bound? Yes, $\frac{\theta^2}{8n} < \frac{\theta^2}{4n}$. Is the statement of Theorem 5.5.1 contradicted? No, because the theorem does not apply in this situation: The range of $f_Y(y; \theta)$ is a function of θ, a condition that violates one of the Cramér-Rao assumptions.

QUESTIONS

5.5.1 Verify the claim made in Example 5.5.2 that $\hat{\theta} = \frac{3}{2} \cdot \bar{Y}$ is an unbiased estimator for the parameter θ in $f_Y(y; \theta) = 2y/\theta^2, 0 < y < \theta$.

5.5.2 Let $Y_1, Y_2, \ldots, Y_n$ be a random sample from $f_Y(y; \theta) = \dfrac{1}{\theta} e^{-y/\theta}, y > 0$. Compare the Cramér-Rao lower bound for $f_Y(y; \theta)$ to the variance of the MLE for $\theta, \hat{\theta} = \dfrac{1}{n} \sum_{i=1}^{n} Y_i$. Is $\bar{Y}$ a best estimator for θ?

5.5.3 Let $X_1, X_2, \ldots, X_n$ be a random sample of size n from the Poisson distribution, $p_X(k; \lambda) = \dfrac{e^{-\lambda}\lambda^k}{k!}, k = 0, 1, \ldots$. Show that $\hat{\lambda} = \dfrac{1}{n} \sum_{i=1}^{n} X_i$ is an efficient estimator for λ.

5.5.4 Suppose a random sample of size n is taken from a normal distribution with mean μ and variance σ^2, where σ^2 is known. Compare the Cramér-Rao lower bound for $f_Y(y; \mu)$ with the variance of $\hat{\mu} = \bar{Y} = \dfrac{1}{n} \sum_{i=1}^{n} Y_i$. Is $\bar{Y}$ an efficient estimator for μ?

5.5.5 Let $Y_1, Y_2, \ldots, Y_n$ be a random sample from the uniform pdf $f_Y(y; \theta) = 1/\theta, 0 \le y \le \theta$. Compare the Cramér-Rao lower bound for $f_Y(y; \theta)$ with the variance of the unbiased estimator $\hat{\theta} = \dfrac{n+1}{n} \cdot Y_{\max}$. Discuss.

5.5.6 Let $Y_1, Y_2, \ldots, Y_n$ be a random sample of size n from the pdf

$$f_Y(y; \theta) = \frac{1}{(r-1)!\theta^r} y^{r-1} e^{-y/\theta}, \quad y > 0$$

(a) Show that $\hat{\theta} = \dfrac{1}{nr} \sum_{i=1}^{n} Y_i$ is an unbiased estimator for θ.

(b) Show that $\dfrac{1}{nr} \sum_{i=1}^{n} Y_i$ is a minimum-variance estimator for θ.

5.5.7 Prove the equivalence of the two forms given for the Cramér-Rao lower bound in Theorem 5.5.1.

5.6 SUFFICIENCY

Sufficiency is a property of an estimator that relates to the amount of "information" it contains. To develop the concept fully requires more theoretical background than the previous chapters have provided. That being the case, our objective in Section 5.6 is limited to providing an intuitive explanation of the property and stating a few key theorems.

   If n observations are drawn from some probability distribution, $f_W(w; \theta)$, we know that the accompanying sample space is a set of n-tuples, $(w_1, w_2, \ldots, w_n)$. Moreover, any estimator $\hat{\theta}$ has the effect of partitioning that sample space into a set of mutually exclusive and exhaustive subsets. For example, suppose two observations are drawn from a Poisson distribution, $p_X(k; \lambda) = e^{-\lambda}\lambda^k/k!$, for the purpose of estimating λ with $\hat{\lambda} = \bar{X} = \frac{1}{2}(X_1 + X_2)$. Notice that $\hat{\lambda}$ will equal, say, 3 if any of the following 2-tuples occurs: $(0, 6), (1, 5), (2, 4), (3, 3), (4, 2), (5, 1)$, or $(6, 0)$. Likewise, $\hat{\lambda}$ will equal 2.5 if either $(0, 5), (1, 4), (2, 3), (3, 2), (4, 1)$, or $(5, 0)$ is the sample drawn. Clearly, each possible outcome can be assigned to a unique subset of 2-tuples according to the value of $\hat{\lambda}$ it produces.

Whether or not $\hat{\lambda}$ is "sufficient" for λ depends on whether the particular 2-tuple observed—say, $(1, 5)$—conveys any more information about λ than what is already contained in the statement "$\hat{\lambda} = 3$." If knowing which partition set an outcome belongs to reveals as much information about the unknown parameter as does the particular outcome, itself, then the method of partitioning—that is, $\hat{\lambda}$—is said to be *sufficient* (for λ).

Imagine a set of four independent trials where two successes and two failures—in that order—are observed. The sample outcome might be written (s, s, f, f) or, in terms of the usual Bernoulli random variable, $(1, 1, 0, 0)$. The estimate for $p = P(\text{success})$ would be the familiar ratio

$$\hat{p} = \frac{\text{number of successes}}{\text{number of trials}} = \frac{2}{4} = 0.5$$

Notice the structure of the conditional probability of $(1, 1, 0, 0)$ *given that* $\hat{p} = 0.5$:

$$P\big((1, 1, 0, 0)\,|\,\hat{p} = 0.5\big) = \frac{P\big((1, 1, 0, 0) \text{ and } \hat{p} = 0.5\big)}{P(\hat{p} = 0.5)}$$

$$= \frac{P(1, 1, 0, 0)}{P(\text{exactly 2 successes in 4 trials})}$$

$$= \frac{p^2(1 - p)^2}{\binom{4}{2}p^2(1 - p)^2} = \binom{4}{2}^{-1}$$

But $P\big((1, 0, 1, 0)\,|\,\hat{p} = 0.5\big)$ will also equal $\binom{4}{2}^{-1}$, as will $P\big((0, 0, 1, 1)\,|\,\hat{p} = 0.5\big)$, and so on. All of these conditional probabilities are independent of p. So, knowing that the particular outcome is, say, $(1, 1, 0, 0)$ adds nothing to what we already know about p (once we have been informed that $\hat{p} = 0.5$). Just as we did for $\hat{\lambda}$ in the previous Poisson discussion, we say that the estimator here, $\hat{p} = \dfrac{\text{number of successes}}{\text{number of trials}}$, is sufficient for p.

DEFINITION 5.6.1. Let $W_1, W_2, \ldots, W_n$ be a random sample from $f_W(w; \theta)$. The estimator $\hat{\theta} = h(W_1, W_2, \ldots, W_n)$ is said to be *sufficient* for θ if for all θ and all possible sample points, the conditional pdf of $W_1, W_2, \ldots, W_n$, given $\hat{\theta}$, does not depend on θ.

Comment. If $\hat{\theta}$ is sufficient for θ, then any one-to-one function of $\hat{\theta}$—say, $k\hat{\theta}$ or $\hat{\theta} + k$—will also be sufficient for θ.

In practice, sufficiency is not usually established by using Definition 5.6.1 directly. Several factorization techniques have been developed that accomplish that objective with much less effort. Among the most widely used is the *Fisher-Neyman criterion*.

THEOREM 5.6.1. *Fisher-Neyman* Let $W_1, W_2, \ldots, W_n$ be a random sample from $f_W(w; \theta)$. The estimator $\hat{\theta} = h(W_1, W_2, \ldots, W_n)$ is sufficient for θ if and only if the joint pdf of the W_i's factors into a product of the pdf for $\hat{\theta}$ times a second function that does not depend on θ. That is, $\hat{\theta}$ is sufficient for θ if and only if

$$\prod_{i=1}^{n} f_W(w_i; \theta) = f_{\hat{\theta}}(\hat{\theta}; \theta) \cdot s(w_1, w_2, \ldots, w_n)$$

Proof.   See (188).

EXAMPLE 5.6.1

Let $X_1, X_2, \ldots, X_n$ be a sample of n independent Bernoulli random variables with unknown parameter p:

$$p_{X_i}(k; p) = p^k (1 - p)^{1-k}, \quad k = 0, 1; \quad 0 \leq p \leq 1$$

Show that $\hat{p} = \sum_{i=1}^{n} X_i$ is sufficient for p.

Multiplying $p_{X_i}(k; p)$ for all n X_i's gives the sample's joint pdf:

$$p_{X_1}(k_1; p) \ldots p_{X_n}(k_n; p) = p^{\sum_{i=1}^{n} k_i} (1 - p)^{n - \sum_{i=1}^{n} k_i}$$

Moreover, $\hat{p}$ is a binomial random variable since it represents the number of successes in n independent Bernoulli trials. In the notation of Theorem 5.6.1,

$$f_{\hat{p}}(\hat{p}; p) = \left(\begin{array}{c} n \\ \sum_{i=1}^{n} k_i \end{array} \right) p^{\sum_{i=1}^{n} k_i} (1 - p)^{n - \sum_{i=1}^{n} k_i}$$

Now, suppose we choose

$$s(k_1, k_2, \ldots, k_n) = \left(\begin{array}{c} n \\ \sum_{i=1}^{n} k_i \end{array} \right)^{-1}$$

Then

$$\prod_{i=1}^{n} p_{X_i}(k_i; p) = f_{\hat{p}}(\hat{p}; p) \cdot s(k_1, k_2, \ldots, k_n)$$

proving that $\hat{p} = \sum_{i=1}^{n} X_i$ is sufficient for p. [Here, of course, $\hat{p}$ is *biased* for p— $E(\hat{p}) = E\left(\sum_{i=1}^{n} X_i \right) = np$—so the estimator that would actually be used is $\sum_{i=1}^{n} X_i/n$, which, by the comment following Definition 5.6.1, is also sufficient for p].

EXAMPLE 5.6.2

If $Y_1, Y_2, \ldots, Y_n$ is a random sample from the uniform pdf, $f_Y(y; \theta) = 1/\theta, 0 \leq y \leq \theta$, we know that $\hat{\theta} = Y_{max}$ is the MLE for θ (recall Question 5.2.9). Show that Y_{max} is also sufficient for θ.

To begin, we note that the joint pdf for $Y_1, Y_2, \ldots, Y_n$ is simply $(1/\theta)^n$. Also, we saw in Example 5.4.2 that

$$f_{Y_{\max}}(y_{\max}; \theta) = \frac{n y_{\max}^{n-1}}{\theta^n}, \quad 0 \leq y \leq \theta$$

If $s(y_1, y_2, \ldots, y_n)$ is set equal to $1/n y_{\max}^{n-1}$, then

$$\prod_{i=1}^{n} f_{Y_i}(y_i; \theta) = f_{\hat{\theta}}(\hat{\theta}; \theta) \cdot s(y_1, y_2, \ldots, y_n)$$

and we can use the Fisher-Neyman criterion to establish the fact that $\hat{\theta} = Y_{\max}$ is sufficient for θ.

QUESTIONS

5.6.1 Let $X_1, X_2, \ldots, X_n$ be a random sample from the Poisson distribution, $p_{X_i}(k; \lambda) = e^{-\lambda} \lambda^k / k!$, $k = 0, 1, 2, \ldots$. Show that $\hat{\lambda} = \bar{X}$ is sufficient for λ.

5.6.2 Suppose a random sample of size n is drawn from the pdf,

$$f_Y(y; \theta) = e^{-(y-\theta)}, \quad \theta \leq y$$

Show that $\hat{\theta} = Y_{\min}$ is sufficient for the threshold parameter θ.

5.6.3 Let $X_1, X_2,$ and X_3 be a set of three independent Bernoulli random variables with unknown parameter $p = P(X_i = 1)$. It was shown in Example 5.6.1 that $\hat{p} = X_1 + X_2 + X_3$ is sufficient for p. Show that the linear combination $\hat{p}* = X_1 + 2X_2 + 3X_3$ is *not* sufficient for p.

5.6.4 If $\hat{\theta}$ is sufficient for θ, show that any one-to-one function of θ is also sufficient for θ.

Using the Fisher-Neyman criterion requires that $f_{\hat{\theta}}(\hat{\theta}; \theta)$ be explicitly identified as one of the two factors that multiply together to give the sample's joint pdf. Depending on the complexity of $\hat{\theta}$, though, it may be quite difficult to get an expression for $f_{\hat{\theta}}(\hat{\theta}; \theta)$. An easier-to-use criterion for establishing sufficiency is posed in Theorem 5.6.2.

> **THEOREM 5.6.2.** *Factorization Theorem* Let $W_1, W_2, \ldots, W_n$ be a random sample from $f_W(w; \theta)$. The estimator $\hat{\theta} = h(W_1, W_2, \ldots, W_n)$ is sufficient for θ if and only if there are functions $g(\hat{\theta}; \theta)$ and $u(w_1, w_2, \ldots, w_n)$ such that
>
> $$\prod_{i=1}^{n} f_W(w_i; \theta) = g(\hat{\theta}; \theta) \cdot u(w_1, w_2, \ldots, w_n)$$
>
> ***Proof.***   See (72).

EXAMPLE 5.6.3

A random sample of size n is drawn from the pdf $f_Y(y; \theta) = \theta y^{\theta-1}, 0 < y < 1, \theta > 0$. Use the factorization theorem to find an estimator that would be sufficient for θ.

Notice, first, that the objective here is quite different than it was in Examples 5.6.1 and 5.6.2. In those previous discussions, we already had an estimator and the question was whether or not $\hat{\theta}$ was sufficient. Here we intend to use a factorization criterion *backward*, as a mechanism for suggesting the functional form that the estimator should have.

As always, multiplying the n individual pdf's gives the sample's joint pdf:

$$\prod_{i=1}^{n} f_{Y_i}(y_i; \theta) = \theta y_1^{\theta-1} \cdot \theta y_2^{\theta-1} \ldots \theta y_n^{\theta-1}$$

$$= \theta^n \left(\prod_{i=1}^{n} y_i \right)^{\theta-1}$$

Now, suppose we define $\hat{\theta} = \prod_{i=1}^{n} y_i$ and $u(y_1, y_2, \ldots, y_n) = 1$. Then

$$\theta^n \left(\prod_{i=1}^{n} y_i \right)^{\theta-1} = g(\hat{\theta}; \theta) \cdot u(y_1, y_2, \ldots, y_n)$$

which implies that $\hat{\theta} = \prod_{i=1}^{n} Y_i$ is sufficient for θ.

EXAMPLE 5.6.4

Suppose that $\hat{\theta}_{\text{MLE}}$ is the maximum likelihood estimator for θ based on a random sample of size n drawn from the pdf $f_W(w; \theta)$. Show that $\hat{\theta}_{\text{MLE}}$ is necessarily a function of $\hat{\theta}_S$, where $\hat{\theta}_S$ is sufficient for θ.

Let $L(\theta) = \prod_{i=1}^{n} f_{W_i}(w_i; \theta)$ be the likelihood function of the n data points. We know from Theorem 5.6.2 that

$$L(\theta) = g(\hat{\theta}_S; \theta) \cdot u(w_1, w_2, \ldots, w_n)$$

Obviously, any θ that maximizes $L(\theta)$ must maximize $g(\hat{\theta}_S; \theta)$. But any θ that maximizes $g(\hat{\theta}_S; \theta)$ will necessarily be a function of $\hat{\theta}_S$. (This is the primary theoretical justification for why maximum likelihood estimators are preferred to method of moments estimators.)

Sufficiency as it relates to efficiency

In the set Θ of all unbiased estimators for the parameter θ based on a random sample $W_1, W_2, \ldots, W_n$ drawn from $f_W(w; \theta)$, there will be a subset Θ_S whose members are sufficient for θ. It can be proved that every $\hat{\theta} \in \Theta_S$ has a smaller variance than any $\hat{\theta} \in \Theta_S^C$. In looking for minimum-variance unbiased estimators, then, we need only focus on $\hat{\theta}$'s that are sufficient for θ.

Moreover, it will be true for many pdf's that Θ_S has only *one* member. Therefore, to construct a minimum-variance estimator, we typically need simply to find the $\hat{\theta}$ sufficient for θ and then perform whatever transformations are necessary to make it unbiased.

Comment. Explicit consideration of point estimation can be traced back to the time of Galileo, perhaps even earlier. Much of the structure that we now associate with the subject, though, was formulated in the early years of the twentieth century by Sir Ronald A. Fisher. It was Fisher who introduced the notions of unbiasedness, efficiency, and sufficiency.

QUESTIONS

5.6.5 Let X_1, X_2, ..., X_n be a random sample of size n from the geometric distribution, $p_X(k; p) = (1 - p)^{k-1}p$, $k = 1, 2, \ldots$. Show that $\hat{p} = \sum_{i=1}^{n} X_i$ is sufficient for p.

5.6.6 Show that $\hat{\sigma}^2 = \sum_{i=1}^{n} Y_i^2$ is sufficient for σ^2 if Y_1, Y_2, ..., Y_n is a random sample from a normal pdf with $\mu = 0$.

5.6.7 Illustrate the claim made in Example 5.6.4 by finding the MLE for θ in the pdf $f_Y(y; \theta) = \theta y^{\theta-1}$, $0 < y < 1$, and showing that $\hat{\theta}$ is a function of $\prod_{i=1}^{n} y_i$ (see Example 5.6.3).

5.6.8 A probability model $f_W(w; \theta)$ is said to be expressed in *exponential form* if it can be written as

$$f_W(w; \theta) = e^{K(y)p(\theta)+S(y)+q(\theta)}$$

where the range of W is independent of θ. Show that $\hat{\theta} = \sum_{i=1}^{n} K(Y_i)$ is sufficient for θ.

5.6.9 Write the pdf $f_Y(y; \lambda) = \lambda e^{-\lambda y}$, $y > 0$, in exponential form and deduce a sufficient statistic for λ (see Question 5.6.8). Assume that the data consist of a random sample of size n.

5.6.10 Let Y_1, Y_2, ..., Y_n be a random sample from a Pareto pdf,

$$f_Y(y; \theta) = \theta/(1 + y)^{\theta+1}, \quad 0 < y < \infty; 0 < \theta < \infty$$

Write $f_Y(y; \theta)$ in exponential form and deduce a sufficient statistic for θ (see Question 5.6.8).

5.7 CONSISTENCY

The properties of estimators that we have examined thus far—for instance, unbiasedness and sufficiency—have assumed that the data consist of a *fixed* sample size n. It sometimes makes sense, though, to consider the *asymptotic* behavior of estimators: We may find, for example, that an estimator possesses a desirable property *in the limit* that it fails to exhibit for any finite n.

Recall Example 5.4.4, which focused on the MLE for σ^2 in a sample of size n drawn from a normal pdf [that is, on $\hat{\sigma}^2 = \dfrac{1}{n}\sum_{i=1}^{n}(Y_i - \bar{Y})^2$]. For any finite n, $\hat{\sigma}^2$ is biased:

$$E\left(\frac{1}{n}\sum_{i=1}^{n}(Y_i - \bar{Y})^2\right) = \frac{n-1}{n}\sigma^2 \neq \sigma^2$$

As n goes to infinity, though, the limit of $E(\hat{\sigma}^2)$ does equal σ^2, and we say that σ^2 is *asymptotically unbiased*.

Introduced in this section is a second asymptotic characteristic of an estimator, a property known as *consistency*. Unlike asymptotic unbiasedness, consistency refers to the shape of the pdf for $\hat{\theta}_n$ and how that shape changes as a function of n. (To emphasize the fact that the estimator for a parameter is now being viewed as a *sequence* of estimators, we will write $\hat{\theta}_n$ instead of $\hat{\theta}$.)

DEFINITION 5.7.1.   An estimator $\hat{\theta}_n = h(W_1, W_2, \ldots, W_n)$ is said to be *consistent* for θ if it converges in probability to θ—that is, if for all $\varepsilon > 0$,

$$\lim_{n \to \infty} \left(P|\hat{\theta}_n - \theta| < \varepsilon \right) = 1$$

Comment.   To solve certain kinds of sample size problems, it can be helpful to think of Definition 5.7.1 in an epsilon/delta context; that is, $\hat{\theta}_n$ is consistent for θ if for all $\varepsilon > 0$ and $\delta > 0$, there exists an $n(\varepsilon, \delta)$ such that

$$P(|\hat{\theta}_n - \theta| < \varepsilon) > 1 - \delta \quad \text{for} \quad n > n(\varepsilon, \delta)$$

EXAMPLE 5.7.1

Let $Y_1, Y_2, \ldots, Y_n$ be a random sample from the uniform pdf

$$f_Y(y; \theta) = \frac{1}{\theta}, \quad 0 \le y \le \theta$$

and let $\hat{\theta}_n = Y_{max}$. We already know that Y_{max} is biased for θ, but is it consistent? Recall from Example 5.4.7 that

$$f_{Y_{max}}(y) = \frac{n y^{n-1}}{\theta^n}, \quad 0 \le y \le \theta$$

Therefore,

$$P(|\hat{\theta}_n - \theta| < \varepsilon) = P(\theta - \varepsilon < \hat{\theta}_n < \theta) = \int_{\theta - \varepsilon}^{\theta} \frac{n y^{n-1}}{\theta^n} \, dy = \frac{y^n}{\theta^n} \Big|_{\theta - \varepsilon}^{\theta}$$

$$= 1 - \left(\frac{\theta - \varepsilon}{\theta} \right)^n$$

Since $[(\theta - \varepsilon)/\theta] < 1$, it follows that $[(\theta - \varepsilon)/\theta]^n \to 0$ as $n \to \infty$. Therefore, $\lim_{n \to \infty} P(|\hat{\theta}_n - \theta| < \varepsilon) = 1$, proving that $\hat{\theta}_n = Y_{max}$ is consistent for θ.

Figure 5.7.1 illustrates the convergence of $\hat{\theta}_n$. As n increases, the shape of $f_{Y_{max}}(y)$ changes in such a way that the pdf becomes increasingly concentrated in an ε-neighborhood of θ. For any $n > n(\varepsilon, \delta), P(|\hat{\theta}_n - \theta| < \varepsilon) > 1 - \delta$.

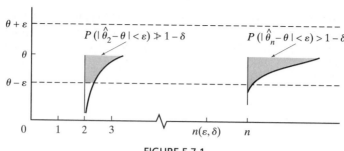

FIGURE 5.7.1

If θ, ε, and δ are specified, we can calculate $n(\varepsilon, \delta)$, the smallest sample size that will enable $\hat{\theta}_n$ to achieve a given precision. For example, suppose $\theta = 4$. How large a sample is required to give $\hat{\theta}_n$ an 80% chance of lying within 0.10 of θ?

In the terminology of the comment on page 359, $\varepsilon = 0.10$, $\delta = 0.20$, and

$$P(|\hat{\theta} - 4| < 0.10) = 1 - \left(\frac{4 - 0.10}{4}\right)^n \geq 1 - 0.20$$

Therefore,

$$(0.975)^{n(\varepsilon,\delta)} = 0.20$$

which implies that $n(\varepsilon, \delta) = 64$.

Comment. Notice the similarity between the definition of consistency and Chebyshev's inequality (Theorem 3.14.1). It follows that we should be able to use the inequality to establish whether an estimator $\hat{\theta}_n$ is consistent.

Suppose $W_1, W_2, \ldots, W_n$ is a random sample from any probability distribution $f_W(w; \mu)$, where $E(W) = \mu$ and $Var(W) = \sigma^2 < \infty$. Let $\hat{\mu}_n = \frac{1}{n} \sum_{i=1}^{n} W_i$. Is $\hat{\mu}_n$ consistent for μ?

According to Chebyshev's inequality,

$$P(|\hat{\mu}_n - \mu| < \varepsilon) > 1 - \frac{Var(\hat{\mu}_n)}{\varepsilon^2}$$

But $Var(\hat{\mu}_n) = Var\left(\frac{1}{n} \sum_{i=1}^{n} W_i\right) = \frac{1}{n^2} \sum_{i=1}^{n} Var(W_i) = (1/n^2) \cdot n\sigma^2 = \sigma^2/n$, so

$$P(|\hat{\mu}_n - \mu| < \varepsilon) > 1 - \frac{\sigma^2}{n\varepsilon^2}$$

For any ε, δ, and σ^2, an n can be found that makes $\frac{\sigma^2}{n\varepsilon^2} < \delta$. Therefore,

$\lim_{n \to \infty} P(|\hat{\mu}_n - \mu| < \varepsilon) = 1$ (i.e., $\hat{\mu}_n$ is consistent for μ). (The fact that $\hat{\mu}_n = \frac{1}{n} \sum_{i=1}^{n} W_i$ is consistent for μ is sometimes referred to as the *weak law of large numbers*; it was first proved by Chebyshev in 1866.)

Comment. We saw in Example 5.6.4 that one of the theoretical properties supporting the method of maximum likelihood as a reasonable mechanism for identifying estimators is the fact that MLEs are necessarily functions of sufficient statistics. As an additional justification for using maximum likelihood estimators, it can be proved that under very general conditions, MLEs are also consistent [see (83)].

QUESTIONS

5.7.1 How large a sample must be taken from a normal pdf where $E(Y) = 18$ in order to guarantee

that $\hat{\mu}_n = \bar{Y}_n = \dfrac{1}{n} \displaystyle\sum_{i=1}^{n} Y_i$ has a 90% probability of lying somewhere in the interval $[16, 20]$?

Assume that $\sigma = 5.0$.

5.7.2 Let $Y_1, Y_2, \ldots, Y_n$ be a random sample of size n from a normal pdf having $\mu = 0$. Show that

$S_n^2 = \dfrac{1}{n} \displaystyle\sum_{i=1}^{n} Y_i^2$ is a consistent estimator for $\sigma^2 = \text{Var}(Y)$.

5.7.3 Suppose $Y_1, Y_2, \ldots, Y_n$ is a random sample from the exponential pdf, $f_Y(y; \lambda) = \lambda e^{-\lambda y}$, $y > 0$.
  (a) Show that $\hat{\lambda}_n = Y_1$ is not consistent for λ.

  (b) Show that $\hat{\lambda}_n = \displaystyle\sum_{i=1}^{n} Y_i$ is not consistent for λ.

5.7.4 An estimator $\hat{\theta}_n$ is said to be *squared-error consistent* for θ if $\displaystyle\lim_{n \to \infty} E\big[(\hat{\theta}_n - \theta)^2\big] = 0$.
  (a) Show that any squared-error consistent $\hat{\theta}_n$ is asymptotically unbiased (see Question 5.4.13).
  (b) Show that any squared-error consistent $\hat{\theta}_n$ is consistent in the sense of Definition 5.7.1.

5.7.5 Suppose $\hat{\theta}_n = Y_{\max}$ is to be used as an estimator for the parameter θ in the uniform pdf, $f_Y(y; \theta) = 1/\theta$, $0 \le y \le \theta$. Show that $\hat{\theta}_n$ is squared-error consistent (see Question 5.7.4).

5.7.6 If $2n + 1$ random observations are drawn from a continuous and symmetric pdf with mean μ and if $f_Y(\mu; \mu) \neq 0$, then the *sample median*, Y'_{n+1}, is unbiased for μ, and $\text{Var}(Y'_{n+1}) \doteq 1/(8[f_Y(\mu; \mu)]^2 n)$ [see (49)]. Show that $\hat{\mu}_n = Y'_{n+1}$ is consistent for μ.

APPENDIX 5.A.1   MINITAB APPLICATIONS

Because of their ability to generate random observations from many of the standard probability distributions, computers can be very effective in illustrating estimation properties and procedures. Recall Figure 5.4.3, showing a simulation consisting of 40

samples of size two drawn from the pdf $f_Y(y; \theta) = \dfrac{1}{\theta} e^{-y/\theta}$, $y > 0$. Computed for each

(in column C4) is the estimate $\hat{\theta} = 4\sqrt{y_1 y_2}/\pi$. As a demonstration of the concept of unbiasedness, it was pointed out that the average of those 40 $\hat{\theta}$'s is *1.02*, a number very close to *1.00*, the theoretical expected value of $\hat{\theta}$.

The behavior of confidence intervals can also be modeled by using MINITAB's RANDOM command. Figure 5.A.1.1 gives the syntax and output that would

```
MTB > random 50 c1–c4;
SUBC > normal 10 0.8.
MTB > rmean c1–c4 c5
MTB > let c6 = c5 - 1.96* (0.8)/sqrt(4)
MTB > let c7 = c5 + 1.96* (0.8)/sqrt(4)
MTB > name c6 'Low.Lim.' c7 'Upp.Lim.'
MTB > print c6 c7
```

Data Display

Row	Low.Lim.	Upp.Lim.	Contains μ = 10?	
1	8.7596	10.3276	Yes	
2	8.8763	10.4443	Yes	
3	8.8337	10.4017	Yes	
4	9.5800	11.1480	Yes	
5	8.5106	10.0786	Yes	
6	9.6946	11.2626	Yes	
7	8.7079	10.2759	Yes	
8	10.0014	11.5694	NO	
9	9.3408	10.9088	Yes	
10	9.5428	11.1108	Yes	
11	8.4650	10.0330	Yes	
12	9.6346	11.2026	Yes	
13	9.2076	10.7756	Yes	
14	9.2517	10.8197	Yes	
15	8.7568	10.3248	Yes	
16	9.8439	11.4119	Yes	
17	9.3297	10.8977	Yes	
18	9.5685	11.1365	Yes	
19	8.9728	10.5408	Yes	
20	8.5775	10.1455	Yes	
21	9.3979	10.9659	Yes	
22	9.2115	10.7795	Yes	
23	9.6277	11.1957	Yes	
24	9.4252	10.9932	Yes	47 of the 50
25	9.6868	11.2548	Yes	95% confidence intervals
26	8.8779	10.4459	Yes	contain the true μ (= 10)
27	9.1570	10.7250	Yes	
28	9.3277	10.8957	Yes	
29	9.1606	10.7286	Yes	
30	8.8919	10.4599	Yes	
31	9.3838	10.9518	Yes	
32	8.7575	10.3255	Yes	
33	10.4602	12.0282	NO	
34	8.9437	10.5117	Yes	
35	9.0049	10.5729	Yes	
36	9.0148	10.5828	Yes	
37	8.8110	10.3790	Yes	
38	9.1981	10.7661	Yes	
39	9.0042	10.5722	Yes	
40	9.7019	11.2699	Yes	
41	9.2167	10.7847	Yes	
42	8.3901	9.9581	NO	
43	8.6337	10.2017	Yes	
44	9.4606	11.0286	Yes	
45	9.3278	10.8958	Yes	
46	8.5843	10.1523	Yes	
47	9.0541	10.6221	Yes	
48	9.2042	10.7722	Yes	
49	9.2710	10.8390	Yes	
50	9.5697	11.1377	Yes	

FIGURE 5.A.1.1

correspond to the confidence interval calculation described in Example 5.3.1. Fifty samples of size 4 have been drawn from a normal pdf for which $\mu = 10$ and $\sigma = 0.8$. The columns labeled "Low.Lim." and "Upp.Lim." are the endpoints for a 95% confidence interval for μ:

$$\text{Low.Lim.} = \bar{y} - 1.96\,\frac{0.8}{\sqrt{4}}$$

$$\text{Upp.Lim.} = \bar{y} + 1.96\,\frac{0.8}{\sqrt{4}}$$

As the last column in the DATA DISPLAY indicates, only three of the 50 confidence intervals fail to contain $\mu = 10$: Samples 8 and 33 yield intervals that lie entirely to the right of the parameter, while sample 42 produces a range of values that lies entirely to the left. The remaining 47 intervals, though, or $94\% \left(= \dfrac{47}{50} \times 100 \right)$ do contain the true value of μ as an interior point.

Hypothesis Testing

Pierre-Simon, Marquis de Laplace (1749–1827)

As a young man, Laplace went to Paris to seek his fortune as a mathematician, disregarding his father's wishes that he enter the clergy. He soon became a protégé of d'Alembert and at the age of 24 was elected to the Academy of Sciences. Laplace was recognized as one of the leading figures of that group for his work in physics, celestial mechanics, and pure mathematics. He also enjoyed some political prestige, and his friend, Napoleon Bonaparte, made him Minister of the Interior for a brief period. With the restoration of the Bourbon monarchy, Laplace renounced Napoleon for Louis XVIII, who later made him a marquis.

6.1   INTRODUCTION

Inferences, as we saw in Chapter 5, often reduce to numerical estimates of parameters, either in the form of single points or as confidence intervals, but not always. In many experimental situations, the conclusion to be drawn is *not* numerical and is more aptly phrased as a choice between two conflicting theories, or *hypotheses*. A court psychiatrist, for example, may be called upon to pronounce an accused murderer either "sane" or "insane"; the FDA must decide whether a new flu vaccine is "effective" or "ineffective"; a geneticist concludes that the inheritance of eye color in a certain strain of *Drosophila melanogaster* either "does" or "does not" follow classical Mendelian principles. In this chapter we examine the statistical methodology, and the attendant consequences, involved in making decisions of this sort.

The process of dichotomizing the possible conclusions of an experiment and then using the theory of probability to choose one option over the other is known as *hypothesis testing*. The two competing propositions are called the *null hypothesis* (written H_0) and the *alternative hypothesis* (written H_1). How we go about choosing between H_0 and H_1 is conceptually similar to the way a jury deliberates in a court trial. The null hypothesis is analogous to the defendant: Just as the latter is presumed innocent until "proven" guilty, so is the null hypothesis "accepted" unless the data argue overwhelmingly to the contrary. Mathematically, choosing between H_0 and H_1 is an exercise in applying the basic rules that are followed in making legal arguments to "evidence" that consists of measurements made on random variables.

Chapter 6 focuses on basic principles—in particular, on the probabilistic structure that underlies the decision-making process. Specific applications will be taken up later, beginning in Chapter 7.

6.2   THE DECISION RULE

We will introduce the basic concepts of hypothesis testing with an example. Imagine a petroleum company searching for additives that might increase gas mileage. As a pilot study, they send 30 cars fueled with a new additive on a road trip from Boston to Los Angeles. Without the additive, those same cars are known to average 25.0 mpg with a standard deviation (σ) of 2.4 mpg.

Suppose it turns out that the 30 cars averaged $\bar{y} = 26.3$ mpg *with* the additive. What should the company conclude? If the additive *is* effective but the position is taken that the increase from 25.0 to 26.3 is due solely to chance, the company will have mistakenly passed up a potentially lucrative product. On the other hand, if the additive is *not* effective but the firm interprets the mileage increase as "proof" that the additive works, time and money will ultimately be wasted developing a product that has no intrinsic value.

The correct way to view the increase from 25.0 mpg to 26.3 mpg is to picture the company's choices in the context of the courtroom analogy mentioned in Section 6.1. Here, the null hypothesis, which is typically a statement reflecting the status quo, would be the assertion that the additive has no effect; the alternative hypothesis would claim that the additive does work. By agreement, we give H_0 (like the defendant) the benefit of the doubt. If the road trip average, then, is "close" to 25.0

in some probabilistic sense still to be determined, we must conclude that the new additive has not demonstrated its superiority. To get any more specific requires that we define what *close* means.

At this point, rephrasing the question in random variable terminology will prove helpful. Let $Y_1, Y_2, \ldots, Y_{30}$ denote the mileages recorded by each of the cars during the cross-country test run. We will assume that the Y_i's are normally distributed with an unknown mean μ. Furthermore, suppose that prior experience with road tests of this type suggest that σ will equal *2.4*.[1] That is,

$$f_Y(y;\mu) = \frac{1}{\sqrt{2\pi}\,(2.4)}\, e^{-\frac{1}{2}\left(\frac{y-\mu}{2.4}\right)^2}, \quad -\infty < y < \infty$$

The two competing hypotheses, then, can be expressed as statements about μ. In effect, we are *testing*

$$H_0: \mu = 25.0 \quad \text{(additive is } not \text{ effective)}$$

versus

$$H_1: \mu > 25.0 \quad \text{(additive } is \text{ effective)}$$

Values of the sample mean, $\bar{y}$, less than or equal to 25.0 are certainly grounds for *accepting* the null hypothesis; averages a bit larger than 25.0 would also lead to that conclusion (because of the commitment to give H_0 the benefit of the doubt). On the other hand, we would probably view a cross-country average of, say, 35.0 mpg as exceptionally strong evidence *against* the null hypothesis, and our decision would be "reject H_0." It follows that somewhere between 25.0 and 35.0 there is a point—call it $\bar{y}^*$—where for all practical purposes the credibility of H_0 ends (see Figure 6.2.1).

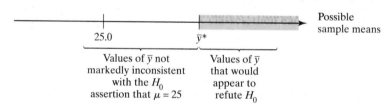

FIGURE 6.2.1

Finding an appropriate numerical value for $\bar{y}^*$ is accomplished by combining the courtroom analogy with what we know about the probabilistic behavior of $\bar{Y}$. Suppose, for the sake of argument, we set $\bar{y}^*$ equal to *25.25* mpg. Doing so would result in the null hypothesis being rejected 28% of the time *even if it were true*. That is,

$$P(\text{we reject } H_0 \mid H_0 \text{ is true}) = P(\bar{Y} \geq 25.25 \mid \mu = 25.0)$$

$$= P\left(\frac{\bar{Y} - 25.0}{2.4/\sqrt{30}} \geq \frac{25.25 - 25.0}{2.4/\sqrt{30}}\right)$$

$$= P(Z \geq 0.57)$$

$$= 0.2843$$

---

[1] In practice, the value of σ usually needs to be estimated; we will return to that more frequently encountered scenario in Chapter 7.

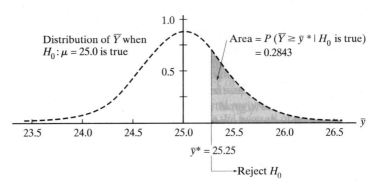

FIGURE 6.2.2

(see Figure 6.2.2). Is 28% an inappropriately large probability for making this kind of incorrect inference? Yes. No jury would convict a defendant knowing it had a 28% chance of sending an innocent person to jail.

Clearly, we need to make $\bar{y}^*$ larger. Would it be reasonable to set $\bar{y}^*$ equal to, say, 26.25? No, because that value would give the null hypothesis *too* much benefit of the doubt. If $\bar{y}^* = 26.25$, the probability of rejecting H_0 *if H_0 were true* is only 0.0022:

$$P\left(\text{we reject } H_0 \,|\, H_0 \text{ is true}\right) = P(\bar{Y} \geq 26.25 \,|\, \mu = 25.0)$$

$$= P\left(\frac{\bar{Y} - 25.0}{2.4/\sqrt{30}} \geq \frac{26.25 - 25.0}{2.4/\sqrt{30}}\right)$$

$$= P(Z \geq 2.85)$$

$$= 0.0022$$

(see Figure 6.2.3). Requiring that much evidence before rejecting H_0 would be analogous to a jury not returning a guilty verdict unless the prosecutor could produce a

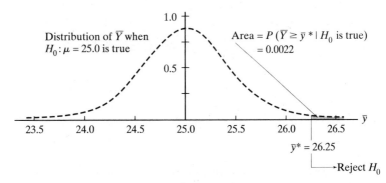

FIGURE 6.2.3

roomful of eyewitnesses, an obvious motive, a signed confession, and a dead body in the trunk of the defendant's car!

If a probability of 0.28 represents too little benefit of the doubt being accorded to H_0 and 0.0022 represents too much, what value *should* we choose for $P(\bar{Y} \geq \bar{y}^* \mid H_0$ is true)? While there is no way to answer that question definitively or mathematically, researchers who use hypothesis testing have come to a consensus that the probability of rejecting H_0 when H_0 is true should be somewhere in the neighborhood of *0.05*. Experience seems to suggest that when a 0.05 probability is used, null hypotheses are neither dismissed too capriciously nor embraced too wholeheartedly. (More will be said about this particular probability, and its consequences, in Section 6.3.)

Suppose the 0.05 "criterion" is applied here. Finding the corresponding $\bar{y}^*$ is a calculation identical to what we did in Example 4.3.6. Given that

$$P(\bar{Y} \geq \bar{y}^* \mid H_0 \text{ is true}) = 0.05$$

it follows that

$$P\left(\frac{\bar{Y} - 25.0}{2.4/\sqrt{30}} \geq \frac{\bar{y}^* - 25.0}{2.4/\sqrt{30}}\right) = P\left(Z \geq \frac{\bar{y}^* - 25.0}{2.4/\sqrt{30}}\right) = 0.05$$

But we know from Appendix A.1 that $P(Z \geq 1.64) = 0.05$. Therefore,

$$\frac{\bar{y}^* - 25.0}{2.4/\sqrt{30}} = 1.64 \tag{6.2.1}$$

which implies that $\bar{y}^* = 25.718$.

The company's statistical strategy is now completely determined: They should reject the null hypothesis that the additive has no effect if $\bar{y} \geq 25.718$. The actual sample mean, though, is reported to be 26.3 mpg, implying that H_0 should be rejected. It appears that the additive *does* increase mileage.

Comment.   It must be remembered that rejecting H_0 does not *prove* that H_0 is false, any more than a jury's decision to convict guarantees that the defendant is guilty. The 0.05 decision rule is simply saying that *if* the *true* mean (μ) is 25.0, sample means ($\bar{y}$) as large or larger than 25.718 are expected to occur only 5% of the time. Because of that small probability, a reasonable conclusion when $\bar{y} \geq 25.718$ is that μ is *not* 25.0. Usually that inference will, in fact, be correct; 5% of the time, though, we will make the mistake of rejecting H_0 when H_0 is actually true.

Table 6.2.1 is a computer simulation of this particular 0.05 decision rule. A total of 75 random samples, each of size 30, have been drawn from a normal distribution having $\mu = 25.0$ and $\sigma = 2.4$. The corresponding $\bar{y}$ for each sample is then compared with $\bar{y}^* = 25.718$. As the entries in the table indicate, 5 of the samples lead to the erroneous conclusion that $H_0: \mu = 25.0$ should be rejected.

Since each sample mean has a 0.05 probability of exceeding 25.718 (when $\mu = 25.0$), we would expect that 75(0.05), or *3.75*, of the data sets to result in a "reject H_0" conclusion. Reassuringly, the observed number of incorrect inferences (= 5) is quite close to that expected value.

TABLE 6.2.1

$\bar{y}$	$\geq 25.718?$	$\bar{y}$	$\geq 25.718?$	$\bar{y}$	$\geq 25.718?$
25.133	no	25.259	no	25.200	no
24.602	no	25.866	yes	25.653	no
24.587	no	25.623	no	25.198	no
24.945	no	24.550	no	24.758	no
24.761	no	24.919	no	24.842	no
24.177	no	24.770	no	25.383	no
25.306	no	25.080	no	24.793	no
25.601	no	25.307	no	24.874	no
24.121	no	24.004	no	25.513	no
25.516	no	24.772	no	24.862	no
24.547	no	24.843	no	25.034	no
24.235	no	25.771	yes	25.150	no
25.809	yes	24.233	no	24.639	no
25.719	yes	24.853	no	24.314	no
25.307	no	25.018	no	25.045	no
25.011	no	25.176	no	24.803	no
24.783	no	24.750	no	24.780	no
25.196	no	25.578	no	25.691	no
24.577	no	24.807	no	24.207	no
24.762	no	24.298	no	24.743	no
25.805	yes	24.807	no	24.618	no
24.380	no	24.346	no	25.401	no
25.224	no	25.261	no	24.958	no
24.371	no	25.062	no	25.678	no
25.033	no	25.391	no	24.795	no

Expressing Decision Rules in Terms of Z Ratios

In general, decision rules are statements that spell out the conditions under which the null hypothesis is to be rejected. There will always be a variety of equivalent ways to express the same guidelines. Depending on the context, though, one version may be much easier to work with than another.

Recall Equation 6.2.1. Rejecting $H_0: \mu = 25.0$ when

$$\bar{y} \geq \bar{y}^* = 25.0 + 1.64 \cdot \frac{2.4}{\sqrt{30}} = 25.718$$

is clearly equivalent to rejecting H_0 when

$$\frac{\bar{y} - 25.0}{2.4/\sqrt{30}} \geq 1.64 \tag{6.2.2}$$

(if one rejects the null hypothesis, the other will necessarily do the same).

We know from Chapter 4 that the random variable $\dfrac{\bar{Y} - 25.0}{2.4/\sqrt{30}}$ has a standard normal distribution (if $\mu = 25.0$). When a particular $\bar{y}$ is substituted for $\bar{Y}$ (as in Inequality 6.2.2), we call $\dfrac{\bar{y} - 25.0}{2.4/\sqrt{30}}$ the *observed z*. In this case and in many other frequently encountered hypothesis testing situations, we will find that decision rules are easier to interpret if the "ratio" format is used (as opposed to the "$\bar{y}$*" format).

> **DEFINITION 6.2.1.**   Any function of the observed data whose numerical value dictates whether H_0 is accepted or rejected is called a *test statistic*. The set of values for the test statistic that result in the null hypothesis being rejected is called the *critical region* and is denoted C. The particular point in C that separates the rejection region from the acceptance region is called the *critical value*.

Comment.   For the gas mileage example, both $\bar{Y}$ and $\dfrac{\bar{Y} - 25.0}{2.4/\sqrt{30}}$ qualify as test statistics. If the sample mean is used, the associated critical region would be written

$$C = \{\bar{y}; \bar{y} \geq 25.718\}$$

(and 25.718 is the critical value). If the decision rule is framed in terms of a Z ratio,

$$C = \left\{z; z = \frac{\bar{y} - 25.0}{2.4/\sqrt{30}} \geq 1.64\right\}$$

In this latter case, the critical value is 1.64.

> **DEFINITION 6.2.2.**   The probability that the test statistic lies in the critical region *when H_0 is true* is called the *level of significance* and is denoted α.

Comment.   In principle, the value chosen for α should reflect the consequences of making the mistake of rejecting H_0 when H_0 is true. As those consequences get more severe, the critical region C should be defined so that α gets smaller. In practice, though, efforts to quantify the costs of making incorrect inferences are arbitrary at best. In most situations, experimenters abandon any such attempts and routinely set the level of significance equal to 0.05. If another α is used, it is likely to be either 0.001, 0.01, or 0.10.

One-Sided Versus Two-Sided Alternatives

In most hypothesis tests, H_0 consists of a single number, typically the value of the parameter that represents the status quo. The "25.0" in H_0: $\mu = 25.0$, for example, is the mileage that would be expected when the additive has no effect. If the mean of a normal distribution is the parameter being tested, our general notation for the null hypothesis will be H_0: $\mu = \mu_o$, where μ_o is the status quo value of μ.

Alternative hypotheses, by way of contrast, invariably embrace entire ranges of parameter values. If there is reason to believe *before any data are collected* that the parameter being tested is necessarily restricted to one particular "side" of H_0, then H_1 is defined to reflect that limitation and we say that the alternative hypothesis is *one sided.* Two variations are possible: H_1 can be one sided *to the left* $(H_1: \mu < \mu_o)$ or it can be one sided *to the right* $(H_1: \mu > \mu_o)$. If no such a priori information is available, the alternative hypothesis needs to accommodate the possibility that the true parameter value might lie on either side of μ_0. Any such alternative is said to be *two sided.* For testing $H_0: \mu = \mu_o$, the two-sided alternative is written $H_1: \mu \neq \mu_o$.

In the gasoline example, it was tacitly assumed that the additive would either have *no* effect (in which case $\mu = 25.0$ and H_0 would be true) or it would *increase* mileage (implying that the true mean would lie somewhere "to the right" of H_0). Accordingly, we wrote the alternative hypothesis as $H_1: \mu > 25.0$. Had we been interested, though, in the possibility that the additive might interfere with the gasoline's combustibility and actually *decrease* mileage, it would have been more appropriate to use a two-sided alternative $(H_1: \mu \neq 25.0)$.

Whether the alternative hypothesis is defined to be one sided or two sided is important because the nature of H_1 plays a key role in determining the form of the critical region. We saw earlier that the 0.05 decision rule for testing

$$H_0: \mu = 25.0$$

versus

$$H_1: \mu > 25.0$$

calls for H_0 to be rejected if $\dfrac{\bar{y} - 25.0}{2.4/\sqrt{30}} \geq 1.64$. That is, only if the sample mean is substantially *larger* than 25.0 will we reject H_0.

If the alternative hypothesis had been two sided, sample means either much smaller than 25.0 *or* much larger than 25.0 would be evidence against H_0 (and in support of H_1). Moreover, the 0.05 probability associated with the critical region C would be split into two halves, with 0.025 being assigned to the left-most portion of C, and 0.025 to the right-most portion. From Appendix Table A.1, though, $P(Z \leq -1.96) = P(Z \geq 1.96) = 0.025$, so the two-sided 0.05 decision rule would call for $H_0: \mu = 25.0$ to be rejected if $\dfrac{\bar{y} - 25.0}{2.4/\sqrt{30}}$ is either (1) ≤ -1.96 or (2) ≥ 1.96.

Testing $H_0: \mu = \mu_o$ (σ known)

Let z_α be the number having the property that $P(Z \geq z_\alpha) = \alpha$. Values for z_α can be found from the standard normal cdf tabulated in Appendix A.1. If $\alpha = 0.05$, for example, $z_{.05} = 1.64$ (see Figure 6.2.4). Of course, by the symmetry of the normal curve, the value that Z is *less than* $100\alpha\%$ of the time is $-z_\alpha$.

FIGURE 6.2.4

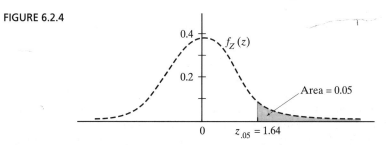

THEOREM 6.2.1. Let $Y_1, Y_2, \ldots, Y_n$ be a random sample of size n from a normal distribution where σ is known. Let $z = \dfrac{\bar{y} - \mu_o}{\sigma/\sqrt{n}}$.

(a) To test $H_0 : \mu = \mu_o$ versus $H_1 : \mu > \mu_o$ at the α level of significance, reject H_0 if $z \geq z_\alpha$.

(b) To test $H_0 : \mu = \mu_o$ versus $H_1 : \mu < \mu_o$ at the α level of significance, reject H_0 if $z \leq -z_\alpha$.

(c) To test $H_0 : \mu = \mu_o$ versus $H_1 : \mu \neq \mu_o$ at the α level of significance, reject H_0 if z is either $(1) \leq -z_{\alpha/2}$ or $(2) \geq z_{\alpha/2}$.

EXAMPLE 6.2.1

As part of a "Math for the Twenty-First Century" initiative, Bayview High was chosen to participate in the evaluation of a new algebra and geometry curriculum. In the recent past, Bayview's students would be considered "typical," having earned scores on standardized exams that are very consistent with national averages.

Two years ago, a cohort of 86 Bayview sophomores, all randomly selected, were assigned to a special set of classes that integrated algebra and geometry. According to test results that have just been released, those students averaged 502 on the SAT-I math exam; nationwide, seniors averaged 494 with a standard deviation of 124. Can it be claimed at the $\alpha = 0.05$ level of significance that the new curriculum had an effect?

To begin, we define the parameter μ to be the true average SAT-I math score that we could expect the new curriculum to produce. The obvious "status quo" value for μ is the current national average—that is, $\mu_o = 494$. The alternative hypothesis here should be two sided because the possibility certainly exists that a revised curriculum—however well intentioned—would actually *lower* a student's achievement.

According to Part (c) of Theorem 6.2.1, then, we should reject $H_0 : \mu = 494$ in favor of $H_1 : \mu \neq 494$ at the $\alpha = 0.05$ level of significance if the test statistic z is either $(1) \leq -z_{.025}(= -1.96)$ or $(2) \geq z_{.025}(= 1.96)$. But $\bar{y} = 502$, so

$$z = \frac{502 - 494}{124/\sqrt{86}} = 0.60$$

implying that our decision should be "Fail to reject H_0." Even though Bayview's 502 is 8 points above the national average, it does not follow that the improvement was due to the new curriculum: An increase of that magnitude could easily have occurred by chance, even if the new curriculum had no effect whatsoever (see Figure 6.2.5).

FIGURE 6.2.5

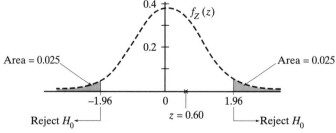

The *P*-Value

There are two general ways to quantify the amount of evidence against H_0 that is contained in a given set of data. The first involves the *level of significance* concept introduced in Definition 6.2.2. Using that format, the experimenter selects a value for α (usually 0.05 or 0.01) *before any data are collected*. Once α is specified, a corresponding critical region can be identified. If the test statistic falls in the critical region, we reject H_0 at the α level of significance. Another strategy is to calculate a *P-value*.

> **DEFINITION 6.2.3.** The *P-value* associated with an observed test statistic is the probability of getting a value for that test statistic as extreme or more extreme than what was actually observed (relative to H_1) *given that H_0 is true*.

Comment.   Test statistics that yield small *P*-values should be interpreted as evidence *against* H_0. More specifically, if the *P*-value calculated for a test statistic is less than or equal to α, the null hypothesis can be rejected at the α level of significance. Or, put another way, the *P*-value is the smallest α at which we can reject H_0.

EXAMPLE 6.2.2

Recall Example 6.2.1. Given that $H_0: \mu = 494$ is being tested against $H_1: \mu \neq 494$, what *P*-value is associated with the calculated test statistic, $z = 0.60$, and how should it be interpreted?

If $H_0: \mu = 494$ is true, the random variable $Z = \dfrac{\bar{Y} - 494}{124/\sqrt{86}}$ has a standard normal pdf.

Relative to the two-sided H_1, any value of Z greater than or equal to 0.60 *or* less than or equal to -0.60 qualifies as being "as extreme or more extreme" than the observed z. Therefore, by Definition 6.2.3,

$$P\text{-value} = P(Z \geq 0.60) + P(Z \leq -0.60)$$

$$= 0.2743 + 0.2743$$

$$= 0.5486$$

(see Figure 6.2.6).

FIGURE 6.2.6

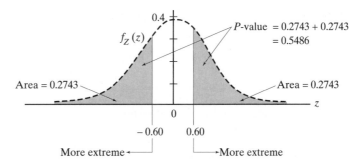

As noted in the preceding comment, P-values can be used as decision rules. In Example 6.2.1, 0.05 was the stated level of significance. Having determined here that the P-value associated with $z = 0.60$ is 0.5486, we know that $H_0: \mu = 494$ would *not* be rejected at the given α. Indeed, the null hypothesis would not be rejected for any value of α up to and including 0.5486.

Notice that the P-value would have been halved had H_1 been one sided. Suppose we were confident that the new algebra and geometry classes would not *lower* a student's math SAT. The appropriate hypothesis test in that case would be $H_0: \mu = 494$ versus $H_1: \mu > 494$. Moreover, only values in the right-hand tail of $f_Z(z)$ would be considered more extreme than the observed $z = 0.60$, so

$$P\text{-value} = P(Z \geq 0.60) = 0.2743$$

QUESTIONS

6.2.1 State the decision rule that would be used to test the following hypotheses. Evaluate the appropriate test statistic and state your conclusion.
  (a) $H_0: \mu = 120$ versus $H_1: \mu < 120$; $\bar{y} = 114.2$, $n = 25$, $\sigma = 18$, $\alpha = 0.08$
  (b) $H_0: \mu = 42.9$ versus $H_1: \mu \neq 42.9$; $\bar{y} = 45.1$, $n = 16$, $\sigma = 3.2$, $\alpha = 0.01$
  (c) $H_0: \mu = 14.2$ versus $H_1: \mu > 14.2$; $\bar{y} = 15.8$, $n = 9$, $\sigma = 4.1$, $\alpha = 0.13$

6.2.2 An herbalist is experimenting with juices extracted from berries and roots that may have the ability to affect the Stanford-Binet IQ scores of students afflicted with mild cases of attention deficit disorder (ADD). A random sample of 22 children diagnosed with the condition have been drinking Brain-Blaster daily for two months. Past experience suggests that children with ADD score an average of 95 on the IQ test with a standard deviation of 15. If the data are to be analyzed using the $\alpha = 0.06$ level of significance, what values of $\bar{y}$ would cause H_0 to be rejected? Assume that H_1 is two sided.

6.2.3 (a) Suppose $H_0: \mu = \mu_o$ is rejected in favor of $H_1: \mu \neq \mu_o$ at the $\alpha = 0.05$ level of significance. Would H_0 necessarily be rejected at the $\alpha = 0.01$ level of significance?
  (b) Suppose $H_0: \mu = \mu_o$ is rejected in favor of $H_1: \mu \neq \mu_o$ at the $\alpha = 0.01$ level of significance. Would H_0 necessarily be rejected at the $\alpha = 0.05$ level of significance?

6.2.4 Company records show that drivers get an average of 32,500 miles on a set of Road Hugger All-Weather radial tires. Hoping to improve that figure, the company has added a new polymer to the rubber that should help protect the tires from deterioration caused by extreme temperatures. Fifteen drivers who tested the new tires have reported getting an average of 33,800 miles. Can the company claim that the polymer has produced a statistically significant increase in tire mileage? Test $H_0: \mu = 32,500$ against a one-sided alternative at the $\alpha = 0.05$ level. Assume that the standard deviation (σ) of the tire mileages has not been affected by the addition of the polymer and is still 4000 miles.

6.2.5 If $H_0: \mu = \mu_o$ is rejected in favor of $H_1: \mu > \mu_o$, will it necessarily be rejected in favor of $H_1: \mu \neq \mu_o$? Assume that α remains the same.

6.2.6 A random sample of size 16 is drawn from a normal distribution having $\sigma = 6.0$ for the purpose of testing $H_0: \mu = 30$ versus $H_1: \mu \neq 30$. The experimenter chooses to define the critical region C to be the set of sample means lying in the interval (29.9, 30.1). What level of significance does the test have? Why is (29.9, 30.1) a poor choice for the critical region? What range of $\bar{y}$ values should comprise C, assuming the same α is to be used?

6.2.7 Recall the breath analyzers described in Example 4.3.5. The following are 30 blood alcohol determinations made by Analyzer GTE-10, a three-year-old unit that may be in need of recalibration. All 30 measurements were made using a test sample on which a properly adjusted machine would give a reading of 12.6%.

12.3	12.7	13.6	12.7	12.9	12.6
12.6	13.1	12.6	13.1	12.7	12.5
13.2	12.8	12.4	12.6	12.4	12.4
13.1	12.9	13.3	12.6	12.6	12.7
13.1	12.4	12.4	13.1	12.4	12.9

(a) If μ denotes the true average reading that Analyzer GTE-10 would make on a person whose blood alcohol concentration is 12.6%, test

$$H_0: \mu = 12.6$$

versus

$$H_1: \mu \neq 12.6$$

at the $\alpha = 0.05$ level of significance. Assume that $\sigma = 0.4$. Would you recommend that the machine be readjusted?

(b) What statistical assumptions are implicit in the hypothesis test done in Part (a)? Is there any reason to suspect that those assumptions may not be satisfied?

6.2.8 Calculate the P-values for the hypothesis tests indicated in Question 6.2.1. Do they agree with your decisions on whether or not to reject H_0?

6.2.9 Suppose $H_0: \mu = 120$ is tested against $H_1: \mu \neq 120$. If $\sigma = 10$ and $n = 16$, what P-value is associated with the sample mean $\bar{y} = 122.3$? Under what circumstances will H_0 be rejected?

6.2.10 As a class research project, Rosaura wants to see whether the stress of final exams elevates the blood pressures of freshmen women. When they are not under any untoward duress, 18-year-old women have systolic blood pressures that average 120 mm Hg with a standard deviation of 12 mm Hg. If Rosaura finds that the average blood pressure for the 50 women in Statistics 101 on the day of the final exam is 125.2, what should she conclude? Set up and test an appropriate hypothesis.

6.2.11 As input for a new inflation model, economists predicted that the average cost of a hypothetical "food basket" in east Tennessee in July would be $145.75. The standard deviation (σ) of basket prices was assumed to be $9.50, a figure that has held fairly constant over the years. To check their prediction, a sample of 25 baskets representing different parts of the region were checked in late July, and the average cost was $149.75. Let $\alpha = 0.05$. Is the difference between the economists' prediction and the sample mean statistically significant?

6.3 TESTING BINOMIAL DATA—$H_0: p = p_o$

Suppose $X_1, X_2, \ldots, X_n$ denote the outcomes in a series of n independent trials, where $P(X_i = 1) = p$ and $P(X_i = 0) = 1 - p$. If the parameter p is unknown, it will sometimes be appropriate to test the null hypothesis $H_0: p = p_o$, where p_o is some particularly relevant value of p. Any such procedure is called a *binomial hypothesis test* because the statistic used is a function of $X = X_1 + X_2 + \cdots + X_n$, and we know from Example 3.11.1 that the sum of a set of n independent and identically distributed Bernoulli random variables is described probabilistically by the binomial model,

$$p_X(k; p) = P(X = k) = \binom{n}{k} p^k (1 - p)^{n-k}, \ k = 0, 1, \ldots, n.$$

Two different procedures for testing $H_0: p = p_o$ need to be considered, the distinction resting on the magnitude of n. In general, if

$$0 < np_o - 3\sqrt{np_o(1 - p_o)} < np_o + 3\sqrt{np_o(1 - p_o)} < n \qquad (6.3.1)$$

we do a "large-sample" test of $H_0: p = p_o$ based on an approximate Z ratio. Otherwise, a "small-sample" decision rule is used, one where the critical region is defined in terms of the exact binomial distribution associated with X.

A Large-Sample Test for the Binomial Parameter *p*

Suppose the number of observations, n, making up a set of Bernoulli random variables is sufficiently large that Inequality 6.3.1 is satisfied. We know in that case from Section 4.3 that the ratio $\dfrac{X - np_o}{\sqrt{np_o(1 - p_o)}}$ has approximately a standard normal pdf, $f_Z(z)$ if $p = p_o$. Values of $\dfrac{X - np_o}{\sqrt{np_o(1 - p_o)}}$ close to 0, of course, would be evidence in favor of $H_0: p = p_o$ [since $E\left(\dfrac{X - np_o}{\sqrt{np_o(1 - p_o)}}\right) = 0$ when $p = p_o$]. Conversely, the credibility of $H_0: p = p_o$ clearly diminishes as $\dfrac{X - np_o}{\sqrt{np_o(1 - p_o)}}$ moves farther and farther away from 0. The large-sample test of $H_0: p = p_o$, then, takes the same basic form as the test of $H_0: \mu = \mu_o$ in Section 6.2.

THEOREM 6.3.1. Let $X_1, X_2, \ldots, X_n$ be a random sample of n Bernoulli random variables for which $0 < np_o - 3\sqrt{np_o(1 - p_o)} < np_o + 3\sqrt{np_o(1 - p_o)} < n$.

Let $X = X_1 + X_2 + \cdots + X_n$ and define $z = \dfrac{x - np_o}{\sqrt{np_o(1 - p_o)}}$.

   (a) To test $H_0: p = p_o$ versus $H_1: p > p_o$ at the α level of significance, reject H_0 if $z \geq z_\alpha$.

   (b) To test $H_0: p = p_o$ versus $H_1: p < p_o$ at the α level of significance, reject H_0 if $z \leq -z_\alpha$.

   (c) To test $H_0: p = p_o$ versus $H_1: p \neq p_o$ at the α level of significance, reject H_0 if z is either (1) $\leq -z_{\alpha/2}$ or (2) $\geq z_{\alpha/2}$.

CASE STUDY 6.3.1

In gambling parlance, a *point spread* is a hypothetical increment added to the score of the presumably weaker of two teams playing. By intention, its magnitude should have the effect of making the game a toss-up; that is, each team should have a 50% chance of beating the spread.

In practice, setting the "line" on a game is a highly subjective endeavor, which raises the question of whether or not the Las Vegas crowd actually gets it right. Addressing that issue, a recent study examined the records of 124 National Football League games; it was found that in 67 of the matchups (or *54%*) the favored team beat the spread. Is the difference between 54% and 50% small enough to be written off to chance, or did the study uncover convincing evidence that odds makers are *not* capable of accurately quantifying the competitive edge that one team holds over another?

Let $p = P$(favored team beats spread). If p is any value other than 0.50, the bookies are assigning point spreads incorrectly. To be tested, then, are the hypotheses

$$H_0: p = 0.50$$

versus

$$H_1: p \neq 0.50$$

We will take 0.05 to be the level of significance.

In the terminology of Theorem 6.3.1, $n = 124$, $p_o = 0.50$, and

$$X_i = \begin{cases} 1 & \text{if favored team beats spread in } i\text{th game} \\ 0 & \text{if favored team does not beat spread in } i\text{th game} \end{cases}$$

for $i = 1, 2, \ldots, 124$. Therefore, the binomial random variable $X = X_1 + X_2 + \ldots + X_{124}$ denotes the total number of times the favored team beat the spread.

According to the two-sided decision rule given in Part (c) of Theorem 6.3.1, the null hypothesis should be rejected if z is either less than or equal to $-1.96 \ (= -z_{.05/2})$ or greater than or equal to $1.96 \ (= z_{.05/2})$. But

$$z = \frac{67 - 124(0.50)}{\sqrt{124(0.50)(0.50)}} = 0.90$$

does *not* fall in the critical region, so $H_0: p = 0.50$ should not be rejected at the $\alpha = 0.05$ level of significance. The outcomes of these 124 games, in other words, are entirely consistent with the presumption that bookies know which of two teams is better, and by how much.

Comment. *P*-values can be used to summarize binomial hypothesis tests, just as they were in Section 6.2 when the null hypothesis was $H_0: \mu = \mu_o$. In Case Study 6.3.1, for example, the observed test statistic is 0.90 and H_1 is two sided, so

$$P\text{-value} = P(Z \leq -0.90) + P(Z \geq 0.90)$$

$$= 0.1841 + 0.1841$$

$$= 0.37$$

For any $\alpha < 0.37$, then, our conclusion that the bookies are competent would remain unchanged.

CASE STUDY 6.3.2

There is a theory that people may tend to "postpone" their deaths until after some event that has particular meaning to them has passed (123). Birthdays, a family reunion, or the return of a loved one have all been suggested as the sorts of personal milestones that might have such an effect. National elections may be another. Studies have shown that the

(continued on next page)

(Case Study 6.3.2 continued)

mortality rate in the United States drops noticeably during the Septembers and Octobers of presidential election years. If the postponement theory is to be believed, the reason for the decrease is that many of the elderly who would have died in those two months "hang on" until they see who wins.

Some years ago, a national periodical reported the findings of a study that looked at obituaries published in a Salt Lake City newspaper. Among the 747 decedents the paper identified, 60, or *8.0%*, had died in the three-month period preceding their birth months (114). If individuals are dying randomly with respect to their birthdays, we would expect 25% to die during any given three-month interval. What should we make, then, of the decrease from 25% to 8%? Has the study provided convincing evidence that the postponement theory is valid?

Imagine the 747 deaths being divided into two categories: those that occurred in the three-month period prior to a person's birthday and those that occurred at other times during the year. Let $X_i = 1$ if the ith person belongs to the first category and $X_i = 0$, otherwise. Then $X = X_1 + X_2 + \cdots + X_{747}$ denotes the total number of deaths in the first category. By its structure, X is a binomial random variable with parameter p, where

$$p = P(X_i = 1) = P(\text{person dies in 3 months prior to birth month})$$

If people do *not* postpone their deaths (to wait for a birthday), p should be 3/12, or 0.25; if they do, p will be something *less than* 0.25. Assessing the decrease from 25% to 8%, then, is done with a one-sided binomial hypothesis test:

$$H_0: p = 0.25$$

versus

$$H_1: p < 0.25$$

Let $\alpha = 0.05$. According to Part (b) of Theorem 6.3.1, H_0 should be rejected if

$$z = \frac{x - np_o}{\sqrt{np_o(1 - p_o)}} \leq -z_{.05} = -1.64$$

Substituting for $x, n,$ and p_o, we find that the test statistic falls far to the left of the critical value:

$$z = \frac{60 - 747(0.25)}{\sqrt{747(0.25)(0.75)}} = -10.7$$

The evidence is overwhelming, therefore, that the decrease from 25% to 8% is due to something other than chance. Explanations other than the postponement theory, of course, may be wholly or partially responsible for the nonrandom distribution of deaths. Still, the data show a pattern entirely consistent with the notion that we do have some control over when we die.

Comment. A similar conclusion was reached in a study conducted among the Chinese community living in California. The "significant event" in that case was not a birthday—it was the annual Harvest Moon festival, a celebration that holds particular meaning for elderly women. Based on census data tracked over a 24-year period, it was determined that 51 deaths among elderly Chinese women should have occurred during the week *before* the festivals, and 52 deaths *after* the festivals. In point of fact, *33* died the week before and *70* died the week after (23).

A Small-Sample Test for the Binomial Parameter *p*

Suppose $X_1, X_2, \ldots, X_n$ is a random sample of Bernoulli random variables where n is too small for Inequality 6.3.1 to hold. The decision rule, then, for testing $H_0: p = p_o$ that was given in Theorem 6.3.1 would not be appropriate. Instead, the critical region is defined by using the exact binomial distribution (rather than a normal approximation).

EXAMPLE 6.3.1

For $i = 1, 2, \ldots, 19$, suppose that

$$X_i = \begin{cases} 1 & \text{with probability } p \\ 0 & \text{with probability } 1 - p \end{cases}$$

Let $X = \sum_{i=1}^{19} X_i$. How should

$$H_0: p = 0.85$$

versus

$$H_1: p \neq 0.85$$

be tested if α is to be kept in the neighborhood of 0.10? [Note that Theorem 6.3.1 does not apply here because Inequality 6.3.1 is not satisfied—specifically, $np_o + 3\sqrt{np_o(1 - p_o)} = 19(0.85) + 3\sqrt{19(0.85)(0.15)} = 20.8$ is not less than $n(= 19)$.]

If the null hypothesis is true, the expected value of X is 19(0.85), or *16.2*. Intuitively, values of X to the extreme right or extreme left of 16.2 should constitute the critical region.

Figure 6.3.1 is a MINITAB printout of $p_X(k) = \binom{19}{k}(0.85)^k(0.15)^{19-k}$. By inspection, we can see that the critical region

$$C = \{x: x \leq 13 \quad \text{or} \quad x = 19\}$$

would produce an α close to the desired 0.10 (and would keep the probabilities associated with the two sides of the rejection region roughly the same):

$$P(X \in C \mid H_0 \text{ is true}) = P(X \leq 13 \mid p = 0.85) + P(X = 19 \mid p = 0.85)$$

$$= 0.0001 + 0.0007 + 0.0032 + 0.0122 + 0.0374 + 0.0456$$

$$= 0.0992$$

FIGURE 6.3.1   MTB > pdf;
                  SUBC> binomial 19 0.85.

Probability Density Function

Binomial with n = 19 and p = 0.850000

X	P(X = x)	
8	0.0000	
9	0.0001	
10	0.0007	
11	0.0032	$\rightarrow P(X \leq 13) = 0.0536$
12	0.0122	
13	0.0374	
14	0.0907	
15	0.1714	
16	0.2428	
17	0.2428	
18	0.1529	
19	0.0456	$\rightarrow P(X = 19) = 0.0456$

QUESTIONS

6.3.1 Commercial fishermen working certain parts of the Atlantic Ocean sometimes find their efforts being hindered by the presence of whales. Ideally, they would like to scare away the whales without frightening the fish. One of the strategies being experimented with is to transmit underwater the sounds of a killer whale. On the 52 occasions that that technique has been tried, it worked 24 times (that is, the whales immediately left the area). Experience has shown, though, that 40% of all whales sighted near fishing boats leave of their own accord, anyway, probably just to get away from the noise of the boat.

     (a) Let $p = P$ (whale leaves area after hearing sounds of killer whale). Test $H_0: p = 0.40$ versus $H_1: p > 0.40$ at the $\alpha = 0.05$ level of significance. Can it be argued on the basis of these data that transmitting underwater predator sounds is an effective technique for clearing fishing waters of unwanted whales?

     (b) Calculate the P-value for these data. For what values of α would H_0 be rejected?

6.3.2 Efforts to find a genetic explanation for why certain people are right-handed and others left-handed have been largely unsuccessful. Reliable data are difficult to find because of environmental factors that also influence a child's "handedness." To avoid that complication, researchers often study the analogous problem of "pawedness" in animals, where both genotypes and the environment can be partially controlled. In one such experiment (28), mice were put into a cage having a feeding tube that was equally accessible from the right or the left. Each mouse was then carefully watched over a number of feedings. If it used its right paw more than half the time to activate the tube, it was defined to be "right-pawed." Observations of this sort showed that 67% of mice belonging to strain A/J are right-pawed. A similar protocol was followed on a sample of 35 mice belonging to strain A/HeJ. Of those 35, a total of 18 were eventually classified as right-pawed. Test whether the proportion of right-pawed mice found in the A/HeJ sample was significantly different from what was known about the A/J strain. Use a two-sided alternative and let 0.05 be the probability associated with the critical region.

6.3.3 Defeated in his most recent attempt to win a congressional seat because of a sizeable gender gap, a politician has spent the last two years speaking out in favor of women's-rights issues. A newly released poll claims to have contacted a random sample of 120 of the politician's current supporters and found that 72 were men. In the election that he lost, exit polls indicated that 65% of those who voted for him were men. Using an $\alpha = 0.05$ level of significance, test the null hypothesis that his proportion of male supporters has remained the same. Make the alternative hypothesis one sided.

6.3.4 Suppose $H_0: p = 0.45$ is to be tested against $H_1: p > 0.45$ at the $\alpha = 0.14$ level of significance, where $p = P(i\text{th trial ends in success})$. If the sample size is 200, what is the smallest number of successes that will cause H_0 to be rejected?

6.3.5 Recall the median test described in Example 5.3.2. Reformulate that analysis as a hypothesis test rather than a confidence interval. What P-value is associated with the outcomes listed in Table 5.3.2?

6.3.6 Among the early attempts to validate the postponement theory introduced in Case Study 6.3.2 was an examination of the birth dates and death dates of 348 U.S. celebrities (123). It was found that 16 of those individuals had died in the month preceding their birth month. Set up and test the appropriate H_0 against a one-sided H_1. Use the 0.05 level of significance.

6.3.7 What α levels are possible with a decision rule of the form "Reject H_0 if $x \geq k$" when $H_0: p = 0.5$ is to be tested against $H_1: p > 0.5$ using a random sample of size $n = 7$?

6.3.8 The following is a MINITAB printout of the binomial pdf $p_X(k) = \binom{9}{k}(0.6)^k(0.4)^{9-k}$, $k = 0, 1, \ldots, 9$. Suppose $H_0: p = 0.6$ is to be tested against $H_1: p > 0.6$ and we wish the level of significance to be *exactly* 0.05. Use Theorem 2.6.1 to combine two different critical regions into a single *randomized decision rule* for which $\alpha = 0.05$.

```
MTB > pdf;
SUBC> binomial 9 0.6.
```

Probability Density Function

```
Binomial with n = 9 and p = 0.600000

     X          P(X = x)
     0          0.0003
     1          0.0035
     2          0.0212
     3          0.0743
     4          0.1672
     5          0.2508
     6          0.2508
     7          0.1612
     8          0.0605
     9          0.0101
```

6.3.9 Suppose $H_0: p = 0.75$ is to be tested against $H_1: p < 0.75$ using a random sample of size $n = 7$ and the decision rule "Reject H_0 if $x \leq 3$."
(a) What is the test's level of significance?
(b) Graph the probability that H_0 will be rejected *as a function of p*.

6.4   TYPE I AND TYPE II ERRORS

Errors are an inevitable by-product of hypothesis testing. No matter what sort of mathematical facade is laid atop the decision making process, there is no way to avoid the possibility of drawing an incorrect inference. One kind of error—rejecting H_0 when H_0 is true—figured prominently in Section 6.3: It was argued that critical regions should be defined so as to keep the probability of making such errors small, say, on the order of 0.05. In this section we want to examine in more detail the structure of hypothesis testing from the standpoint of controlling and interpreting the probability of making errors.

In any hypothesis test there are two different kinds of errors that can be committed: We can reject H_0 when H_0 is true or we can accept H_0 when H_0 is false. These are called *Type I* and *Type II* errors, respectively. Similarly, there are two kinds of correct decisions: We can accept a true H_0 or reject a false one. Figure 6.4.1 shows the four possible "decision–state of nature" combinations.

Once an inference is made, there is no way to know whether an error, in fact, was committed. It is possible, though, to calculate the *probability* of having made an error, under each hypothesis.

FIGURE 6.4.1

		True State of Nature	
		H_0 is true	H_1 is true
Our Decision	Accept H_0	Correct decision	Type II error
	Reject H_0	Type I error	Correct decision

Computing the Probability of Committing a Type I Error

Recall the fuel additive example developed in Section 6.2: $H_0: \mu = 25.0$ was to be tested against $H_1: \mu > 25.0$ using a sample of size $n = 30$. The decision rule stated that H_0 should be rejected if $\bar{y}$, the average mpg with the new additive, equalled or exceeded 25.718. In that case, the probability of committing a Type I error is *0.05*:

$$P(\text{Type I error}) = P(\text{reject } H_0 \mid H_0 \text{ is true})$$
$$= P(\bar{Y} \geq 25.718 \mid \mu = 25.0)$$
$$= P\left(\frac{\bar{Y} - 25.0}{2.4/\sqrt{30}} \geq \frac{25.718 - 25.0}{2.4/\sqrt{30}}\right)$$
$$= P(Z \geq 1.64) = 0.05$$

Of course, the fact that the probability of committing a Type I error equals 0.05 should come as no surprise. In our earlier discussion of how "beyond reasonable doubt" should be interpreted numerically, we specifically chose the critical region so that the probability of the decision rule rejecting H_0 when H_0 is true *would* be 0.05.

In general, the probability of committing a Type I error is referred to as a test's *level of significance* and is denoted α (recall Definition 6.2.2). The concept is a crucial one: The level of significance is a single-number summary of the "rules" by which the decision process is being conducted. In essence, α reflects the amount of evidence the experimenter is demanding to see before abandoning the null hypothesis.

Computing the Probability of Committing a Type II Error

We just saw that calculating the probability of a Type I error is a nonproblem: There are no computations necessary, since the probability equals whatever value the experimenter sets *a priori* for α. A similar situation does not hold for Type II errors. First, Type II error probabilities are not specified explicitly by the experimenter; second, each hypothesis test has an infinite number of Type II error probabilities, one for each value of the parameter admissible under H_1.

As an example, suppose we want to find the probability of committing a Type II error in the gasoline experiment if the true μ (*with the additive*) were 25.750. By definition,

$$P(\text{Type II error} \mid \mu = 25.750) = P(\text{we accept } H_0 \mid \mu = 25.750)$$

$$= P(\bar{Y} < 25.718 \mid \mu = 25.750)$$

$$= P\left(\frac{\bar{Y} - 25.75}{2.4/\sqrt{30}} < \frac{25.718 - 25.75}{2.4/\sqrt{30}}\right)$$

$$= P(Z < -0.07) = 0.4721$$

So, even if the new additive increased the fuel economy to 25.750 mpg (from 25 mpg), our decision rule would be "tricked" 47% of the time: that is, it would tell us on those occasions *not* to reject H_0.

The symbol for the probability of committing a Type II error is β. Figure 6.4.2 shows the sampling distribution of $\bar{Y}$ when $\mu = 25.0$ (i.e., when H_0 is true) and when $\mu = 25.750$ (H_1 is true); the areas corresponding to α and β are shaded.

Clearly, the magnitude of β is a function of the presumed value for μ. If, for example, the gasoline additive is so effective as to raise fuel efficiency to 26.8 mpg, the

FIGURE 6.4.2

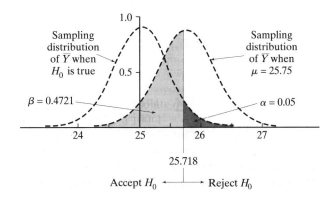

Sampling distribution of $\bar{Y}$ when H_0 is true

Sampling distribution of $\bar{Y}$ when $\mu = 25.75$

$\beta = 0.4721$

$\alpha = 0.05$

25.718

Accept H_0 ⟷ Reject H_0

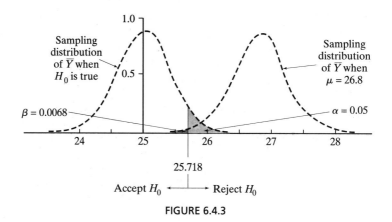

FIGURE 6.4.3

probability that our decision rule would lead us to make a Type II error is a much smaller *0.0068*:

$$P(\text{Type II error}\,|\,\mu = 26.8) = P(\text{we accept } H_0\,|\,\mu = 26.8)$$

$$= P(\bar{Y} < 25.718\,|\,\mu = 26.8) = P\left(\frac{\bar{Y} - 25.0}{2.4/\sqrt{30}} < \frac{25.718 - 26.8}{2.4/\sqrt{30}}\right)$$

$$= P(Z < -2.47) = 0.0068$$

(see Figure 6.4.3).

Power Curves

If β is the probability that we *accept* H_0 when H_1 is true, then $1 - \beta$ is the probability of the complement, that we *reject* H_0 when H_1 is true. We call $1 - \beta$ the *power* of the test; it represents the ability of the decision rule to "recognize" (correctly) that H_0 is false.

The alternative hypothesis H_1 usually depends on a parameter, which makes $1 - \beta$ a function of that parameter. The relationship they share can be pictured by drawing a *power curve*, which is simply a graph of $1 - \beta$ versus the set of all possible parameter values.

Figure 6.4.4 shows the power curve for testing

$$H_0: \mu = 25.0$$

versus

$$H_1: \mu > 25.0$$

where μ is the mean of a normal distribution with $\sigma = 2.4$, and the decision rule is "Reject H_0 if $\bar{y} \geq 25.718$." The two marked points on the curve represent the $(\mu, 1 - \beta)$ pairs just determined, $(25.75, 0.5297)$ and $(26.8, 0.9932)$. One other point can be gotten for every power curve, without doing any calculations: When $\mu = \mu_0$ (the value specified by H_0), $1 - \beta = \alpha$. Of course, as the true mean gets farther and farther away from the H_0 mean, the power will converge to 1.

FIGURE 6.4.4

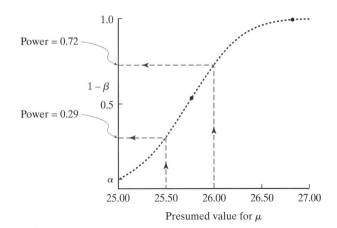

Power curves serve two different purposes. On the one hand, they completely characterize the "performance" that can be expected from a hypothesis test. In Figure 6.4.4, for example, the two arrows show that the probability of rejecting $H_0: \mu = 25$ in favor of $H_1: \mu > 25$ when $\mu = 26.0$ is approximately 0.72. (Or, equivalently, Type II errors will be committed roughly 28% of the time when $\mu = 26.0$.) As the true mean moves closer to μ_o (and becomes more difficult to distinguish) the power of the test understandably diminishes. If $\mu = 25.5$, for example, the graph shows that $1 - \beta$ falls to 0.29.

Power curves are also useful for *comparing* one inference procedure with another. For every conceivable hypothesis testing situation, a variety of procedures for choosing between H_0 and H_1 will be available. How do we know which to use?

The answer to that question is not always simple. Some procedures will be computationally more convenient or easier to explain than others; some will make slightly different assumptions about the pdf being sampled. Associated with each of them, though, is a power curve. If the selection of a hypothesis test is to hinge solely on its ability to distinguish H_0 from H_1, then the procedure to choose is the one having the *steepest* power curve.

Figure 6.4.5 shows the power curves for two hypothetical methods A and B, each of which is testing $H_0: \theta = \theta_o$ versus $H_1: \theta \neq \theta_o$ at the α level of significance. From the standpoint of power, Method B is clearly the better of the two—it always has a higher probability of correctly rejecting H_0 when the parameter θ is not equal to θ_o.

FIGURE 6.4.5

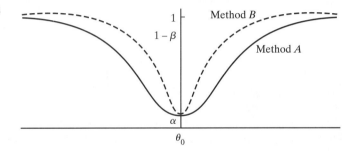

Factors That Influence the Power of a Test

The ability of a test procedure to reject H_0 when H_0 is false is clearly of prime importance, a fact that raises an obvious question: What can an experimenter do to influence the value of $1 - \beta$? In the case of the Z test described in Theorem 6.2.1, $1 - \beta$ is a function of α, σ, and n. By appropriately raising or lowering the values of those parameters, the power of the test against any given μ can be made to equal any desired level.

The Effect of α on $1 - \beta$

Consider again the test of

$$H_0: \mu = 25.0$$

versus

$$H_1: \mu > 25.0$$

discussed earlier in this section. In its original form, $\alpha = 0.05, \sigma = 2.4, n = 30$, and the decision rule called for H_0 to be rejected if $\bar{y} \geq 25.718$.

Figure 6.4.6 shows what happens to $1 - \beta$ (when $\mu = 25.75$) if σ, n, and μ are held constant but α is increased to 0.10. The top pair of distributions shows the con-

FIGURE 6.4.6

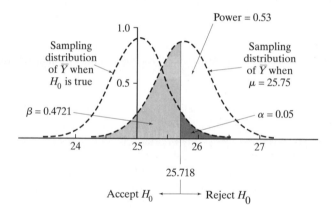

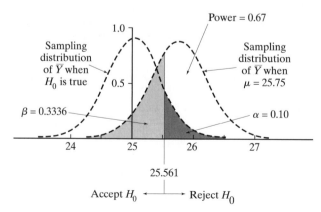

figuration that appears in Figure 6.4.2; the power in this case is $1 - 0.4721$, or *0.53*. The bottom portion of the graph illustrates what happens when α is set at 0.10 instead of 0.05—the decision rule changes from "Reject H_0 if $\bar{y} \geq 25.718$" to "Reject $\bar{H}_0$ if $y \geq 25.561$" (see Question 6.4.2) and the power increases from 0.53 to *0.67*:

$$1 - \beta = P(\text{reject } H_0 \mid H_1 \text{ is true})$$

$$= P(\bar{Y} \geq 25.561 \mid \mu = 25.75)$$

$$= P\left(\frac{\bar{Y} - 25.75}{2.4/\sqrt{30}} \geq \frac{25.561 - 25.75}{2.4/\sqrt{30}}\right)$$

$$= P(Z \geq -0.43)$$

$$= 0.6664$$

The specifics of Figure 6.4.6 accurately reflect what is true in general: *Increasing α decreases β and increases the power.* That said, it does not follow *in practice* that experimenters should manipulate α to achieve a desired $1 - \beta$. For all the reasons cited in Section 6.2, α should typically be set equal to a number somewhere in the neighborhood of 0.05. If the corresponding $1 - \beta$ against a particular μ is deemed to be inappropriate, adjustments should be made in the values of σ and/or n.

The Effects of σ and n on $1 - \beta$

Although it may not always be feasible (or even possible), *decreasing σ will necessarily increase $1 - \beta$.* In the gasoline additive example, σ is assumed to be 2.4 mpg, the latter being a measure of the variation in gas mileages from driver to driver achieved in a cross-country road trip from Boston to Los Angeles (recall page 365). Intuitively, the environmental differences inherent in a trip of that magnitude would be considerable. Different drivers would encounter different weather conditions, varying amounts of traffic, and perhaps take alternate routes.

Suppose, instead, the drivers simply did laps around a test track rather than drive on actual highways. Conditions from driver to driver would then be much more uniform and the value of σ would surely be smaller. What would be the effect on $1 - \beta$ when $\mu = 25.75$ (and $\alpha = 0.05$) if σ could be reduced from 2.4 mpg to 1.2 mpg?

As Figure 6.4.7 shows, reducing σ has the effect of making the H_0 distribution of $\bar{Y}$ more concentrated around $\mu_o (= 25)$ and the H_1 distribution of $\bar{Y}$ more concentrated around $\mu (= 25.75)$. Substituting into Equation 6.2.1 (with 1.2 for σ in place of 2.4), we find that the critical value $\bar{y}^*$ moves closer to μ_o (from 25.718 to *25.359* $\left(= 25 + 1.64 \cdot \dfrac{1.2}{\sqrt{30}}\right)$) and the proportion of the H_1 distribution above the rejection region (i.e., the power) *increases* from 0.53 to *0.96*:

$$1 - \beta = P(\bar{Y} \geq 25.359 \mid \mu = 25.75)$$

$$= P\left(Z \geq \frac{25.359 - 25.75}{1.2/\sqrt{30}}\right) = P(Z \geq -1.78)$$

$$= 0.9625$$

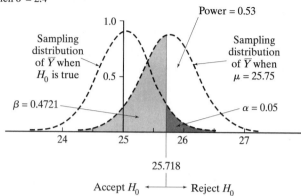

FIGURE 6.4.7   When $\sigma = 2.4$

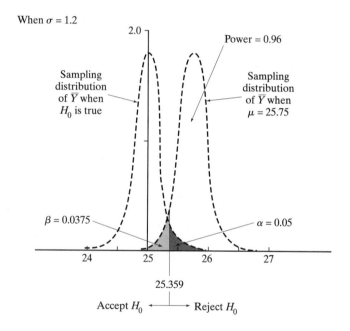

When $\sigma = 1.2$

In theory, reducing σ can be a very effective way of increasing the power of a test, as Figure 6.4.7 makes abundantly clear. In practice, though, refinements in the way data are collected that would have a substantial impact on the magnitude of σ are often either difficult to identify or prohibitively expensive. More typically, experimenters achieve the same effect by simply increasing the sample size.

Look again at the two sets of distributions in Figure 6.4.7. The increase in $1 - \beta$ from 0.53 to 0.96 was accomplished by cutting the denominator of the test statistic $\left[z = (\bar{y} - 25)/(\sigma/\sqrt{30})\right]$ in half by reducing the standard deviation from 2.4 to 1.2. The same numerical effect would be produced if σ were left unchanged but n was increased from 30 to 120—that is, $1.2/\sqrt{30} = 2.4/\sqrt{120}$. Because it can easily be increased or decreased, the sample size is the parameter that researchers almost invariably turn to as the mechanism for ensuring that a hypothesis test will have a sufficiently high power against a given alternative.

EXAMPLE 6.4.1

Suppose an experimenter wishes to test

$$H_0: \mu = 100$$

versus

$$H_1: \mu > 100$$

at the $\alpha = 0.05$ level of significance and wants $1 - \beta$ to equal 0.60 when $\mu = 103$. What is the smallest (i.e., cheapest) sample size that will achieve that objective? Assume that the variable being measured is normally distributed with $\sigma = 14$.

Finding n, given values for $\alpha, 1 - \beta, \sigma$, and μ, requires that two simultaneous equations be written for the critical value $\bar{y}*$, one in terms of the H_0 distribution and the other in terms of the H_1 distribution. Setting the two equal will yield the minimum sample size that achieves the desired α and $1 - \beta$.

Consider, first, the consequences of the level of significance being equal to 0.05. By definition,

$$\alpha = P(\text{we reject } H_0 \,|\, H_0 \text{ is true})$$

$$= P(\bar{Y} \geq \bar{y}* \,|\, \mu = 100)$$

$$= P\left(\frac{\bar{Y} - 100}{14/\sqrt{n}} \geq \frac{\bar{y}* - 100}{14/\sqrt{n}}\right)$$

$$= P\left(Z \geq \frac{\bar{y}* - 100}{14/\sqrt{n}}\right)$$

$$= 0.05$$

But $P(Z \geq 1.64) = 0.05$, so

$$\frac{\bar{y}* - 100}{14/\sqrt{n}} = 1.64$$

or, equivalently,

$$\bar{y}* = 100 + 1.64 \cdot \frac{14}{\sqrt{n}} \tag{6.4.1}$$

Similarly,

$$1 - \beta = P(\text{we reject } H_0 \,|\, H_1 \text{ is true})$$

$$= P(\bar{Y} \geq \bar{y}* \,|\, \mu = 103)$$

$$= P\left(\frac{\bar{Y} - 103}{14/\sqrt{n}} \geq \frac{\bar{y}* - 103}{14/\sqrt{n}}\right)$$

$$= 0.60$$

From Appendix Table A.1, though, $P(Z \geq -0.25) = 0.5987 \doteq 0.60$, so

$$\frac{\bar{y}* - 103}{14/\sqrt{n}} = -0.25$$

which implies that

$$\bar{y}* = 103 - 0.25 \cdot \frac{14}{\sqrt{n}} \qquad (6.4.2)$$

It follows, then, from Equations 6.4.1 and 6.4.2 that

$$100 + 1.64 \cdot \frac{14}{\sqrt{n}} = 103 - 0.25 \cdot \frac{14}{\sqrt{n}}$$

Solving for n shows that a minimum of *78* observations must be taken to guarantee that the hypothesis test will have the desired precision.

Decision Rules for Non-Normal Data

Our discussion of hypothesis testing thus far has been confined to inferences involving either binomial data or normal data. Decision rules for other types of probability functions are rooted in the same basic principles.

In general, to test $H_0: \theta = \theta_o$, where θ is the unknown parameter in a pdf $f_y(y; \theta)$, we initially define the decision rule in terms of $\hat{\theta}$, where the latter is a sufficient statistic for θ. The corresponding critical region is the set of values of $\hat{\theta}$ least compatible with θ_o (but admissible under H_1) whose total probability when H_0 is true is α. In the case of testing $H_0: \mu = \mu_o$ versus $H_1: \mu > \mu_o$, for example, where the data are normally distributed, $\bar{Y}$ is a sufficient statistic for μ, and the least likely values for the sample mean that are admissible under H_1 are those for which $\bar{y} \geq \bar{y}*$, where $P(\bar{Y} \geq \bar{y}* \mid H_0 \text{ is true}) = \alpha$.

EXAMPLE 6.4.2

A random sample of size $n = 8$ is drawn from the uniform pdf, $f_y(y; \theta) = 1/\theta, 0 \leq y \leq \theta$ for the purpose of testing

$$H_0: \theta = 2.0$$

versus

$$H_1: \theta < 2.0$$

at the $\alpha = 0.10$ level of significance. Suppose the decision rule is to be based on Y_8', the largest order statistic. What would be the probability of committing a Type II error when $\theta = 1.7$?

If H_0 is true, Y_8' should be close to 2.0, and values of the largest order statistic that are much *smaller* than 2.0 would be evidence in favor of $H_1: \theta < 2.0$. It follows, then, that the form of the decision rule should be

"Reject $H_0: \theta = 2.0$ if $y_8' \leq c$"

where $P(Y_8' \leq c \mid H_0 \text{ is true}) = 0.10$.

From the Corollary to Theorem 3.8.1,

$$f_{Y_8'}(y; \theta = 2) = 8\left(\frac{y}{2}\right)^7 \cdot \frac{1}{2}, \quad 0 \le y \le 2$$

Therefore, the constant c that appears in the $\alpha = 0.10$ decision rule must satisfy the equation

$$\int_0^c 8\left(\frac{y}{2}\right)^7 \cdot \frac{1}{2} dy = 0.10$$

or, equivalently,

$$\left(\frac{c}{2}\right)^8 = 0.10$$

implying that $c = 1.50$.

Now, β when $\theta = 1.7$ is, by definition, the probability that Y_8' falls in the acceptance region when $H_1: \theta = 1.7$ is true. That is,

$$\beta = P(Y_8' > 1.50 | \theta = 1.7)$$

$$= \int_{1.50}^{1.7} 8\left(\frac{y}{1.7}\right)^7 \cdot \frac{1}{1.7} dy = 1 - \left(\frac{1.5}{1.7}\right)^8$$

$$= 0.63$$

(see Figure 6.4.8).

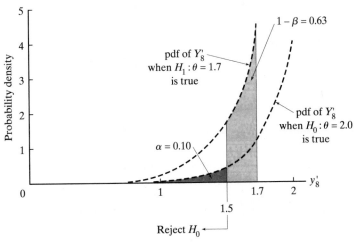

FIGURE 6.4.8

EXAMPLE 6.4.3

Four measurements are taken on a Poisson random variable, where $p_X(k; \lambda) = e^{-\lambda}\lambda^k/k!$, $k = 0, 1, 2, \ldots$, for the purpose of testing

$$H_0: \lambda = 0.8$$

versus

$$H_1: \lambda > 0.8$$

What decision rule should be used if the level of significance is to be 0.10, and what will be the power of the test when $\lambda = 1.2$?

From Question 5.6.1, we know that $\bar{X}$ is a sufficient statistic for λ; the same would be true, of course, for $\sum_{i=1}^{4} X_i$. It will be more convenient to state the decision rule in terms of the latter because we already know the probability model that describes its behavior: If the X_i's are Poisson with parameter λ, $\sum_{i=1}^{4} X_i$ is Poisson with parameter 4λ (recall Question 3.16.16).

Figure 6.4.9 is a MINITAB printout of the Poisson probability function having $\lambda = 3.2$, which would be the sampling distribution of $\sum_{i=1}^{4} X_i$ when $H_0: \lambda = 0.8$ is true. By inspection, the decision rule "Reject $H_0: \lambda = 0.8$ if $\sum_{i=1}^{4} x_i \geq 6$" gives an α close to the desired 0.10.

If H_1 is true and $\lambda = 1.2$, $\sum_{i=1}^{4} X_i$ will have a Poisson distribution with a parameter equal to 4.8. According to Figure 6.4.10, the probability that the sum of a random sample of size four from such a distribution would equal or exceed 6 (i.e., $1 - \beta$ when $\lambda = 1.2$) is *0.3489.*

FIGURE 6.4.9   MTB > pdf;
                     SUBC> poisson 3.2.

Probability Density Function

Poisson with mu = 3.20000

	X	P(X = x)
	0	0.0408
	1	0.1304
	2	0.2087
	3	0.2226
	4	0.1781
	5	0.1140
critical region	6	0.0608
	7	0.0278
	8	0.0111
	9	0.0040
	10	0.0013
	11	0.0004
	12	0.0001
	13	0.0000

$\alpha = P(\text{reject } H_0 | H_0 \text{ is true})$
$= 0.1055$

FIGURE 6.4.10   MTB > pdf;
             SUBC> poisson 4.8.

Probability Density Function

Poisson with mu = 4.80000

X	P(X = x)
0	0.0082
1	0.0395
2	0.0948
3	0.1517
4	0.1820
5	0.1747
6	0.1398
7	0.0959
8	0.0575
9	0.0307
10	0.0147
11	0.0064
12	0.0026
13	0.0009
14	0.0003
15	0.0001
16	0.0000

$1 - \beta = P(\text{reject } H_0 | H_1, \text{is true})$
$= 0.3489$

EXAMPLE 6.4.4

Suppose a random sample of seven observations is taken from the pdf $f_Y(y; \theta) = (\theta + 1)y^\theta$, $0 \leq y \leq 1$, to test

$$H_0: \theta = 2$$

versus

$$H_1: \theta > 2$$

As a decision rule, the experimenter plans to record X, the number of y_i's that exceed 0.9, and reject H_0 if $X \geq 4$. What proportion of the time would such a decision rule lead to a Type I error?

To evaluate $\alpha = P(\text{reject } H_0 | H_0 \text{ is true})$, we first need to recognize that X is a binomial random variable where $n = 7$ and the parameter p is an area under $f_Y(y; \theta = 2)$:

$$p = P(Y \geq 0.9 \,|\, H_0 \text{ is true}) = P(Y \geq 0.9 \,|\, f_Y(y; 2) = 3y^2)$$

$$= \int_{0.9}^{1} 3y^2 \, dy$$

$$= 0.271$$

It follows, then, that H_0 will be incorrectly rejected 9.2% of the time:

$$\alpha = P(X \geq 4 \,|\, \theta = 2) = \sum_{k=4}^{7} \binom{7}{k}(0.271)^k(0.729)^{7-k}$$

$$= 0.092$$

Comment.   The basic notions of Type I and Type II errors first arose in a quality control context. The pioneering work was done at the Bell Telephone Laboratories: There the terms *producer's risk* and *consumer's risk* were introduced for what we now call α and β. Eventually, these ideas were generalized by Neyman and Pearson in the 1930s and evolved into the theory of hypothesis testing as we know it today.

QUESTIONS

6.4.1 Recall the "Math for the Twenty-First Century" hypothesis test done in Example 6.2.1. Calculate the power of that test when the true mean is 500.

6.4.2 Carry out the details to verify the decision rule change cited on page 387 in connection with Figure 6.4.6.

6.4.3 For the decision rule found in Question 6.2.2 to test $H_0: \mu = 95$ versus $H_1: \mu \neq 95$ at the $\alpha = 0.06$ level of significance, calculate $1 - \beta$ when $\mu = 90$.

6.4.4 Construct a power curve for the $\alpha = 0.05$ test of $H_0: \mu = 60$ versus $H_1: \mu \neq 60$ if the data consist of a random sample of size 16 from a normal distribution having $\sigma = 4$.

6.4.5 If $H_0: \mu = 240$ is tested against $H_1: \mu < 240$ at the $\alpha = 0.01$ level of significance with a random sample of 25 normally distributed observations, what proportion of the time will the procedure fail to recognize when μ has dropped to 220? Assume that $\sigma = 50$.

6.4.6 Suppose $n = 36$ observations are taken from a normal distribution where $\sigma = 8.0$ for the purpose of testing $H_0: \mu = 60$ versus $H_1: \mu \neq 60$ at the $\alpha = 0.07$ level of significance. The lead investigator skipped statistics class the day decision rules were being discussed and intends to reject H_0 if $\bar{y}$ falls in the region $(60 - \bar{y}^*, 60 + \bar{y}^*)$.
(a) Find $\bar{y}^*$.
(b) What is the power of the test when $\mu = 62$?
(c) What would the power of the test be when $\mu = 62$ if the critical region had been defined the correct way?

6.4.7 If $H_0: \mu = 200$ is to be tested against $H_1: \mu < 200$ at the $\alpha = 0.10$ level of significance based on a random sample of size n from a normal distribution where $\sigma = 15.0$, what is the smallest value for n that will make the power equal to at least 0.75 when $\mu = 197$?

6.4.8 Will $n = 45$ be a sufficiently large sample to test $H_0: \mu = 10$ versus $H_1: \mu \neq 10$ at the $\alpha = 0.05$ level of significance if the experimenter wants the Type II error probability to be no greater than 0.20 when $\mu = 12$? Assume that $\sigma = 4$.

6.4.9 If $H_0: \mu = 30$ is tested against $H_1: \mu > 30$ using $n = 16$ observations (normally distributed) and if $1 - \beta = 0.85$ when $\mu = 34$, what does α equal? Assume that $\sigma = 9$.

6.4.10 Suppose a sample of size 1 is taken from the pdf $f_Y(y) = (1/\lambda)e^{-y/\lambda}$, $y > 0$, for the purpose of testing

$$H_0: \lambda = 1$$

versus

$$H_1: \lambda > 1$$

The null hypothesis will be rejected if $y \geq 3.20$.
(a) Calculate the probability of committing a Type I error.
(b) Calculate the probability of committing a Type II error when $\lambda = \frac{4}{3}$.
(c) Draw a diagram that shows the α and β calculated in Parts (a) and (b) as areas.

6.4.11 Polygraphs used in criminal investigations typically measure five bodily functions: (1) thoracic respiration, (2) abdominal respiration, (3) blood pressure and pulse rate, (4) muscular movement and pressure, and (5) galvanic skin response. In principle, the magnitude of these responses when the subject is asked a relevant question ("Did you murder your wife?") indicate whether he is lying or telling the truth. The procedure, of course, is not infallible, as a recent study bore out (73). Seven experienced polygraph examiners were given a set of 40 records—20 were from innocent suspects and 20 from guilty suspects. The subjects had been asked 11 questions, on the basis of which each examiner was to make an overall judgment: "Innocent" or "Guilty." The results are as follows:

		Suspect's True Status	
		Innocent	Guilty
Examiner's	"Innocent"	131	15
Decision	"Guilty"	9	125

What would be the numerical values of α and β in this context? In a judicial setting, should Type I and Type II errors carry equal weight? Explain.

6.4.12 An urn contains 10 chips. An unknown number of the chips are white; the others are red. We wish to test

$$H_0: \text{ exactly half the chips are white}$$

$$\text{versus}$$

$$H_1: \text{ more than half the chips are white}$$

We will draw, without replacement, three chips and reject H_0 if two or more are white. Find α. Also, find β when the urn is (a) 60% white and (b) 70% white.

6.4.13 Suppose that a random sample of size 5 is drawn from a uniform pdf

$$f_Y(y; \theta) = \begin{cases} \dfrac{1}{\theta}, & 0 < y < \theta \\ 0, & \text{elsewhere} \end{cases}$$

We wish to test

$$H_0: \theta = 2$$

$$\text{versus}$$

$$H_1: \theta > 2$$

by rejecting the null hypothesis if $y_{\max} \geq k$. Find the value of k that makes the probability of committing a Type I error equal to 0.05.

6.4.14 A sample of size 1 is taken from the pdf

$$f_Y(y) = (\theta + 1)y^\theta, \quad 0 \leq y \leq 1$$

The hypothesis $H_0: \theta = 1$ is to be rejected in favor of $H_1: \theta > 1$ if $y \geq 0.90$. What is the test's level of significance?

6.4.15 A series of n Bernoulli trials is to be observed as data for testing

$$H_0: p = \tfrac{1}{2}$$

$$\text{versus}$$

$$H_1: p > \tfrac{1}{2}$$

The null hypothesis will be rejected if x, the observed number of successes, equals n. For what value of p will the probability of committing a Type II error equal 0.05?

6.4.16 Let X_1 be a binomial random variable with $n = 2$ and $p_{X_1} = P(\text{success})$. Let X_2 be an independent binomial random variable with $n = 4$ and $p_{X_2} = P(\text{success})$. Let $X = X_1 + X_2$. Calculate α if

$$H_0: p_{X_1} = p_{X_2} = \tfrac{1}{2}$$

versus

$$H_1: p_{X_1} = p_{X_2} > \tfrac{1}{2}$$

is to be tested by rejecting the null hypothesis when $x \geq 5$.

6.4.17 A sample of size 1 from the pdf $f_Y(y) = (1 + \theta)y^\theta, 0 \leq y \leq 1$, is to be the basis for testing

$$H_0: \theta = 1$$

versus

$$H_1: \theta < 1$$

The critical region will be the interval $y \leq \tfrac{1}{2}$. Find an expression for $1 - \beta$ as a function of θ.

6.4.18 An experimenter takes a sample of size 1 from the Poisson probability model, $p_X(k) = e^{-\lambda}\lambda^k/k!$, $k = 0, 1, 2, \ldots$, and wishes to test

$$H_0: \lambda = 6$$

versus

$$H_1: \lambda < 6$$

by rejecting H_0 if $x \leq 2$.

(a) Calculate the probability of committing a Type I error.
(b) Calculate the probability of committing a Type II error when $\lambda = 4$.

6.4.19 A sample of size 1 is taken from the geometric probability model, $p_X(k) = (1 - p)^{k-1}p$, $k = 1, 2, 3, \ldots$, to test $H_0: p = 1/3$ versus $H_1: p > 1/3$. The null hypothesis is to be rejected if $x \geq 4$. What is the probability that a Type II error will be committed when $p = \tfrac{1}{2}$?

6.4.20 Suppose that one observation from the exponential pdf, $f_Y(y) = \lambda e^{-\lambda y}$, $y > 0$, is to be used to test $H_0: \lambda = 1$ versus $H_1: \lambda < 1$. The decision rule calls for the null hypothesis to be rejected if $y \geq \ln 10$. Find β as a function of λ.

6.4.21 A random sample of size 2 is drawn from a uniform pdf defined over the interval $[0, \theta]$. We wish to test

$$H_0: \theta = 2$$

versus

$$H_1: \theta < 2$$

by rejecting H_0 when $y_1 + y_2 \leq k$. Find the value for k that gives a level of significance of 0.05.

6.4.22 Suppose that the hypotheses of Question 6.4.21 are to be tested with a decision rule of the form, "Reject $H_0: \theta = 2$ if $y_1 y_2 \leq k^*$." Find the value of k^* that gives a level of significance of 0.05 (see Example 3.7.5).

6.5   A NOTION OF OPTIMALITY: THE GENERALIZED LIKELIHOOD RATIO

In the next several chapters we will be looking closely at some of the particular hypothesis tests that statisticians most often need to use in dealing with real-world problems. All of these have the same conceptual heritage—a very fundamental notion known as the *generalized likelihood ratio*, or *GLR*. More than just a principle, the generalized likelihood ratio is a working criterion for actually *suggesting* test procedures. In a sense, the GLR does for hypothesis testing what the principle of maximum likelihood does for estimation.

As a first look at this important idea, we will conclude Chapter 6 with an application of the generalized likelihood ratio to the problem of testing the parameter θ in a uniform pdf. Notice the relationship here between the likelihood ratio and the definition of an "optimal" hypothesis test.

Suppose $Y_1, Y_2, \ldots, Y_n$ is a random sample from a uniform pdf over the interval $[0, \theta]$, where θ is unknown, and our objective is to test

$$H_0 : \theta = \theta_o$$

versus

$$H_1 : \theta < \theta_o$$

at a specified level of significance α. Is there a "best" decision rule for choosing between H_0 and H_1? And, if so, according to what criterion is it best?

As a starting point in answering those questions, it will be necessary to define two parameter spaces, ω and Ω. In general, ω is the set of unknown parameter values admissible under H_0. In the case of the uniform, the only parameter is θ, and the null hypothesis restricts it to a single point:

$$\omega = \{\theta : \theta = \theta_o\}$$

The second parameter space, Ω, is the set of all possible values of all unknown parameters. Here,

$$\Omega = \{\theta : 0 < \theta \le \theta_o\}$$

Now, recall the definition of the likelihood function, L, from Definition 5.3.1. Given a sample of size n from a uniform pdf,

$$L = L(\theta) = \prod_{i=1}^{n} f_Y(y_i; \theta) = \begin{cases} \left(\dfrac{1}{\theta}\right)^n, & 0 \le y_i \le \theta \\ 0, & \text{otherwise} \end{cases}$$

For reasons the following will make clear, we will want to maximize $L(\theta)$ twice, once under ω and again under Ω. Since θ can take on only one value—θ_o—under ω,

$$\max_{\omega} L(\theta) = L(\theta_o) = \begin{cases} \left(\dfrac{1}{\theta_o}\right)^n, & 0 \le y_i \le \theta_o \\ 0, & \text{otherwise} \end{cases}$$

Maximizing $L(\theta)$ under Ω—that is, with *no* restrictions—is accomplished by simply substituting the MLE for θ into $L(\theta)$. For the uniform parameter, $Y_{\max}$ is the maximum likelihood estimator (recall Example 5.3.1). Therefore,

$$\max_{\Omega} L(\theta) = \left(\frac{1}{Y_{\max}} \right)^n$$

For notational simplicity, we denote $\max_{\omega} L(\theta)$ and $\max_{\Omega} L(\theta)$ by $L(\hat{\omega})$ and $L(\hat{\Omega})$, respectively.

DEFINITION 6.5.1.   Let $Y_1, Y_2, \ldots, Y_n$ be a random sample from $f_Y(y; \theta_1, \ldots, \theta_k)$. The generalized likelihood ratio, λ, is defined to be

$$\lambda = \frac{\max_{\omega} L(\theta_1, \ldots, \theta_k)}{\max_{\Omega} L(\theta_1, \ldots, \theta_k)} = \frac{L(\hat{\omega})}{L(\hat{\Omega})}$$

For the uniform distribution,

$$\lambda = \frac{(1/\theta_0)^n}{(1/y_{\max})^n} = \left(\frac{y_{\max}}{\theta_0} \right)^n$$

Note that, in general, λ will always be positive but never greater than 1 (why?). Furthermore, values of the likelihood ratio close to 1 suggest that the data are very compatible with H_0. That is, the observations are "explained" almost as well by the H_0 parameters as by *any* parameters [as measured by $L(\hat{\omega})$ and $L(\hat{\Omega})$]. For these values of λ we should *accept* H_0. Conversely, if $L(\hat{\omega})/L(\hat{\Omega})$ were close to 0, the data would not be very compatible with the parameter values in ω and it would make sense to *reject* H_0.

DEFINITION 6.5.2.   A generalized-likelihood-ratio test (GLRT) is one that rejects H_0 whenever

$$0 < \lambda \leq \lambda*$$

where $\lambda*$ is chosen so that

$$P(0 < \lambda \leq \lambda* \,|\, H_0 \text{ is true}) = \alpha$$

Let $f(\lambda \,|\, H_0)$ denote the pdf of the generalized likelihood ratio when H_0 is true. If $f(\lambda \,|\, H_0)$ were known, $\lambda*$ (and, therefore, the decision rule) could be determined by solving the equation

$$\alpha = \int_0^{\lambda*} f(\lambda \,|\, H_0) \, d\lambda$$

(see Figure 6.5.1). In most situations, though, $f(\lambda \,|\, H_0)$ is *not* known, and it becomes necessary to show that λ is a monotonic function of some quantity W, where the distribution of W is known. Once we have found such a statistic, any test based on W will be equivalent to one based on λ.

FIGURE 6.5.1

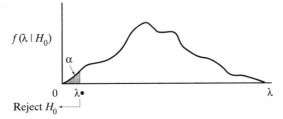

Here, a suitable W is easy to find. Note that

$$P\left(\lambda \le \lambda^* \mid H_0\right) = \alpha = P\left[\left(\frac{Y_{\max}}{\theta_0}\right)^n \le \lambda^* \mid H_0\right]$$

$$= P\left(\frac{Y_{\max}}{\theta_0} \le \sqrt[n]{\lambda^*} \mid H_0\right)$$

Let $W = Y_{\max}/\theta_0$ and $w^* = \sqrt[n]{\lambda^*}$. Then

$$P\left(\lambda \le \lambda^* \mid H_0\right) = P\left(W \le w^* \mid H_0\right) \tag{6.5.1}$$

Here the right-hand side of Equation 6.5.1 can be evaluated from what we already know about the density function for the largest order statistic from a uniform distribution. Let $f_{Y_{\max}}(y; \theta_0)$ be the density function for $Y_{\max}$. Then

$$f_W(w; \theta_0) = \theta_0 f_{Y_{\max}}(\theta_0 w; \theta_0) \qquad \text{(recall Theorem}$$
$$\text{3.7.1)}$$

which, from Example 5.3.3, reduces to

$$\frac{\theta_0 n(\theta_0 w)^{n-1}}{\theta_0^n} = nw^{n-1}, \qquad 0 \le w \le 1$$

Therefore,

$$P\left(W \le w^* \mid H_0\right) = \int_0^{w^*} nw^{n-1}\, dw = (w^*)^n = \alpha$$

implying that the critical value for W is

$$w^* = \sqrt[n]{\alpha}$$

That is, the GLRT calls for H_0 to be rejected if

$$w = \frac{y_{\max}}{\theta_0} \le \sqrt[n]{\alpha}$$

Comment.   The GLR is applied to other hypothesis-testing situations in a manner very similar to what was described here: First we find $L(\hat{\omega})$ and $L(\hat{\Omega})$, then λ, and finally W. The algebra involved, though, usually becomes considerably more formidable. For example, in the "normal" model taken up in Chapters 7 and 8, both parameter spaces are two-dimensional and the likelihood function is a product of densities of the form

$$f_Y(y; \mu, \sigma^2) = \frac{1}{\sqrt{2\pi}\sigma} e^{-(1/2)[(y-\mu)/\sigma]^2}, \quad -\infty < y < \infty$$

QUESTIONS

6.5.1 Let $X_1, X_2, \ldots, X_n$ be a random sample from the geometric probability function

$$p_X(k; p) = (1 - p)^{k-1}p, \quad k = 1, 2, \ldots$$

Find λ, the generalized likelihood ratio for testing $H_0: p = p_0$ versus $H_1: p \neq p_0$.

6.5.2 Let $Y_1, Y_2, \ldots, Y_{10}$ be a random sample from an exponential pdf with unknown parameter λ. Find the form of the GLRT for $H_0: \lambda = \lambda_0$ versus $H_1: \lambda \neq \lambda_0$. What integral would have to be evaluated to determine the critical value if α were equal to 0.05?

6.5.3 Let $Y_1, Y_2, \ldots, Y_n$ be a random sample from a normal pdf with unknown mean μ and variance 1. Find the form of the GLRT for $H_0: \mu = \mu_0$ versus $H_1: \mu \neq \mu_0$.

6.5.4 In the scenario of Question 6.5.3, suppose the alternative hypothesis is $H_1: \mu = \mu_1$, for some particular value of μ_1. How does the likelihood ratio test change in this case? In what way does the critical region depend on the particular value of μ_1?

6.5.5 Let x denote the number of successes observed in a sequence of n independent Bernoulli trials, where $p = P(\text{success})$.
  (a) Show that the critical region of the likelihood ratio test of $H_0: p = \frac{1}{2}$ versus $H_1: p \neq \frac{1}{2}$ can be written in the form

$$x \cdot \ln(x) + (n - x) \cdot \ln(n - x) \geq \lambda^{**}$$

  (b) Use the symmetry of the graph of

$$f(x) = x \cdot \ln(x) + (n - x) \cdot \ln(n - x)$$

  to show that the critical region can be written in the form

$$\left| \bar{x} - \frac{1}{2} \right| \geq k$$

  where k is a constant determined by α.

6.5.6 Suppose a sufficient statistic exists for the parameter θ. Use Theorem 5.9.2 to show that the critical region of a likelihood ratio test will depend on the sufficient statistic.

CHAPTER 7

The Normal Distribution

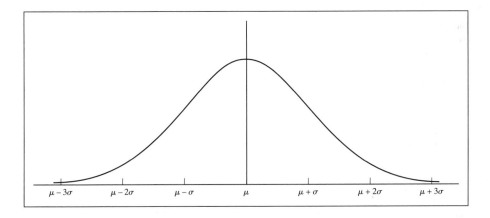

Francis Galton

I know of scarcely anything so apt to impress the imagination as the wonderful form of cosmic order expressed by the "law of frequency of error" (the normal distribution). The law would have been personified by the Greeks and deified, if they had known of it. It reigns with serenity and in complete self effacement amidst the wildest confusion. The huger the mob, and the greater the anarchy, the more perfect is its sway. It is the supreme law of Unreason.

7.1   INTRODUCTION

Finding probability distributions to describe—and, ultimately, to predict—empirical data is one of the most important contributions a statistician can make to the research scientist. Already we have seen a number of functions playing that role. The binomial is an obvious model for the number of correct responses in the Pratt-Woodruff ESP experiment (Case Study 4.3.1); the probability of holding a winning ticket in a game of Keno is given by the hypergeometric (Example 3.3.1); and applications of the Poisson have run the gamut from radioactive decay (Case Study 4.2.2) to Saturday afternoon football fumbles (Case Study 4.2.3). Those examples notwithstanding, by far the most widely used probability model in statistics is the *normal* (or *Gaussian*) distribution,

$$f_Y(y) = \frac{1}{\sqrt{2\pi}\,\sigma} e^{-(1/2)[(y-\mu)/\sigma]^2}, \qquad -\infty < y < \infty \qquad (7.1.1)$$

Some of the history surrounding the normal curve has already been discussed in Chapter 4—how it first appeared as a limiting form of the binomial, but then soon found itself used most often in non-binomial situations. We also learned how to find areas under normal curves and did some problems involving sums and averages. In this chapter, we will take a second look at the properties and applications of this singularly important pdf, this time paying particular attention to the part it plays in estimation and hypothesis testing.

7.2   POINT ESTIMATES FOR μ AND σ^2

We saw in Chapter 4 that the normal distribution is a two-parameter family—μ being a measure of location and σ^2 a measure of dispersion. Maximum-likelihood estimates for those two parameters were derived in Example 5.2.4: Given a random sample of size n,

$$\hat{\mu} = \bar{y} = \frac{1}{n}\sum_{i=1}^{n} y_i$$

and

$$\hat{\sigma}^2 = \frac{1}{n}\sum_{i=1}^{n}(y_i - \bar{y})^2$$

Properties of $\hat{\mu}$

The important statistical properties of $\hat{\mu}$ follow immediately from the definitions and theorems introduced in Chapter 5.

THEOREM 7.2.1.   Let $Y_1, Y_2, \ldots, Y_n$ be a random sample from a normal distribution with mean μ and variance σ^2. Then $\bar{Y}$, the maximum-likelihood estimator for μ, is unbiased, efficient, and consistent. Moreover, if σ^2 is known, $\bar{Y}$ is sufficient.

Proof.   The unbiasedness of $\bar{Y}$ is a special case of Example 5.6.2. To show that $\bar{Y}$ is efficient, note that

$$\frac{\partial \ln f_Y(y; \mu, \sigma^2)}{\partial \mu} = \frac{y - \mu}{\sigma^2}$$

and

$$\frac{\partial^2 \ln f_Y(y; \mu, \sigma^2)}{\partial \mu^2} = -\frac{1}{\sigma^2}$$

From Theorem 5.8.1, then, the Cramer-Rao lower bound for the variance of an unbiased estimator for μ is

$$\frac{1}{-n\left(-\dfrac{1}{\sigma^2}\right)} = \frac{\sigma^2}{n}$$

But the variance of the maximum-likelihood estimator *does* achieve that bound: Var $(\bar{Y}) = \sigma^2/n$, so the efficiency of $\bar{Y}$ is established.

Chebyshev's inequality can be used to prove that $\bar{Y}$ is consistent. Substituting into Theorem 3.14.1, we can write

$$P(|\bar{Y} - \mu| < \varepsilon) \geq 1 - \frac{\text{Var}(\bar{Y})}{\varepsilon^2}$$

or, equivalently,

$$P(|\bar{Y} - \mu| < \varepsilon) \geq 1 - \frac{\sigma^2}{n\varepsilon^2}$$

from which it follows that $\bar{Y}$ converges in probability to μ (i.e., is consistent): For any $\delta > 0$, $\bar{Y}$ will be in an ε-neighborhood of μ at least $100(1 - \delta)\%$ of the time, provided $n = n(\varepsilon, \delta) \geq \sigma^2/\varepsilon^2\delta$.

The sufficiency of $\bar{Y}$ follows from the Fisher-Neyman criterion (Theorem 5.9.1). (See Question 7.2.9.)

Estimating σ^2

In practice, the variance of a normal distribution is not usually estimated by its MLE because $\hat{\sigma}^2$ is biased—$E(\hat{\sigma}^2) = \left(\dfrac{n - 1}{n}\right)\sigma^2$ (recall Example 5.4.4). Instead, we use the *sample variance*, S^2. The latter is an estimator calculated from $\hat{\sigma}^2$ in such a way that it *is* unbiased:

$$S^2 = \frac{n}{n - 1}\hat{\sigma}^2 = \frac{1}{n - 1}\sum_{i=1}^{n}(Y_i - \bar{Y})^2$$

For small n, the numerical difference between S^2 and $\hat{\sigma}^2$ can obviously be considerable. As the sample size increases, though, the "bias" in $\hat{\sigma}^2$ gets smaller and smaller; asymptotically, it goes to 0 (recall Question 5.4.13).

Fitting a Normal Distribution to Data

The rudiments of fitting a normal curve to a set of bell-shaped data have already been touched on in Case Study 2.5.1. First, the ny_i's are grouped into k equal-width classes; the number of observations falling into the ith class is the class frequency, f_i. Then the *density* of each class is calculated according to the formula

$$\text{class density} = \frac{\text{class frequency}}{\text{class width} \times n}$$

(see Figure 2.5.9).

When data are grouped, values for the individual y_i's are no longer available, and the formulas given earlier for $\hat{\mu}$ and S^2 cannot be used. Instead, we estimate μ and σ^2 with the *grouped sample mean* $(\bar{y}_g)$ and the *grouped sample variance* (S_g^2), respectively. By definition,

$$\bar{y}_g = \frac{1}{n} \sum_{i=1}^{k} f_i m_i$$

and

$$s_g^2 = \frac{1}{n-1} \sum_{i=1}^{k} f_i (m_i - \bar{y}_g)^2 = \frac{n \sum_{i=1}^{k} f_i m_i^2 - \left(\sum_{i=1}^{k} f_i m_i \right)^2}{n(n-1)}$$

where m_i is the midpoint of the ith class and f_i is the frequency of the ith class, $i = 1, 2, \ldots, k$. In effect, the "grouped" estimators are simply approximating each y_i by the midpoint of the class to which that observation belongs.

CASE STUDY 7.2.1

Victorian England produced a flowering of statistical thinking, stimulated in large measure by the remarkable Francis Galton. His ground-breaking research in anthropology, psychology, and biology was the product of a restless intelligence abetted by the opportunities that leisure afforded him as an English gentleman. (Having Charles Darwin as a cousin was no small advantage, either!)

Galton's 1889 treatise on heredity, *Natural Inheritance*, had a profound influence on an entire generation of scientists seeking to express statistical ideas in more rigorous formats. Among those who took Galton's approach to heart was Karl Pearson. Destined to become one of the founders of modern statistics, Pearson pioneered much of the early work in biometry and in 1901 started *Biometrika*, a prestigious journal that has remained at the forefront of its field for the entire twentieth century.

Early work in biometry was often characterized by the analysis of large sets of data. Some of Pearson's first efforts in *Biometrika*, for example, dealt with studies involving 999 breadths of crabs, 8689 hospital admissions of enteric fever victims, and 25,878 heights of United States Army recruits. The latter are summarized in Table 7.2.1. Is it reasonable to assert that "height" is a normally distributed random variable?

Judging from Figure 7.2.1, the answer is yes. Shown there is a normal curve superimposed over the data's density-scaled histogram. The estimates used for μ and σ^2 are $\bar{y}_g$ and s_g^2, respectively. More specifically,

TABLE 7.2.1

Height (in.)	Midpoint, m_i	Frequency, f_i	Density
$54.0 \leq y < 55.0$	54.5	5	0.00019
$55.0 \leq y < 56.0$	55.5	3	0.00012
$56.0 \leq y < 57.0$	56.5	7	0.00027
$57.0 \leq y < 58.0$	57.5	6	0.00023
$58.0 \leq y < 59.0$	58.5	10	0.00039
$59.0 \leq y < 60.0$	59.5	15	0.00058
$60.0 \leq y < 61.0$	60.5	50	0.00193
$61.0 \leq y < 62.0$	61.5	526	0.02033
$62.0 \leq y < 63.0$	62.5	1237	0.04780
$63.0 \leq y < 64.0$	63.5	1947	0.07524
$64.0 \leq y < 65.0$	64.5	3019	0.11666
$65.0 \leq y < 66.0$	65.5	3475	0.13428
$66.0 \leq y < 67.0$	66.5	4054	0.15666
$67.0 \leq y < 68.0$	67.5	3631	0.14031
$68.0 \leq y < 69.0$	68.5	3133	0.12107
$69.0 \leq y < 70.0$	69.5	2075	0.08018
$70.0 \leq y < 71.0$	70.5	1485	0.05738
$71.0 \leq y < 72.0$	71.5	680	0.02628
$72.0 \leq y < 73.0$	72.5	343	0.01325
$73.0 \leq y < 74.0$	73.5	118	0.00456
$74.0 \leq y < 75.0$	74.5	42	0.00162
$75.0 \leq y < 76.0$	75.5	9	0.00035
$76.0 \leq y < 77.0$	76.5	6	0.00023
$77.0 \leq y < 78.0$	77.5	2	0.00008
		25878	

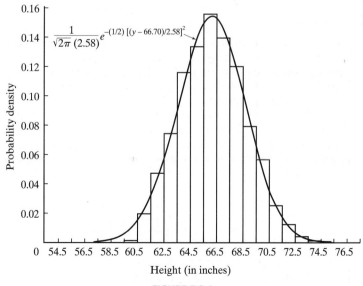

$$\frac{1}{\sqrt{2\pi}\,(2.58)}e^{-(1/2)\,[(y-66.70)/2.58]^2}$$

FIGURE 7.2.1

(continued on next page)

(Case Study 7.2.1 continued)

$$\bar{y}_g = \frac{1}{25{,}878} \{(5)(54.5) + \cdots + (2)(77.5)\}$$

$$= 67.60 \text{ in.}$$

and

$$s_g^2 = \frac{1}{(25{,}878)(25{,}877)}$$

$$\cdot \left(\left[25{,}878\{(5)(54.5)^2 + \cdots + (2)(77.5)^2\} \right] - \{(5)(54.5) + \cdots + (2)(77.5)\}^2 \right)$$

$$= 6.656 \text{ in.}^2$$

Clearly, the agreement between the data and the normal curve is excellent.

Drawing Inferences About μ

Suppose a random sample of n measurements, $Y_1, Y_2, \ldots, Y_n$, is to be taken on a trait that is thought to be normally distributed, the objective being to draw an inference about the underlying pdf's true mean (μ). If σ is *known*, we already know how to proceed: A decision rule for testing $H_0: \mu = \mu_0$ is given in Theorem 6.2.1 and the construction of a confidence interval for μ is discussed on page 324. Recall that both of those procedures are based on the fact that the ratio $\dfrac{\bar{Y} - \mu}{\sigma/\sqrt{n}}$ has a standard normal distribution, $f_Z(z)$.

In practice, though, the parameter σ^2 is seldom known. Typically, the only information the experimenter has about either parameter is what can be gleaned from the Y_i's themselves. The variance can be estimated, of course, using S^2, but what effect does that have on the "Z" ratio—are $\dfrac{\bar{Y} - \mu}{\sigma/\sqrt{n}}$ and $\dfrac{\bar{Y} - \mu}{S/\sqrt{n}}$ probabilistically equivalent?

Historically, many early practitioners of statistics felt that replacing σ with S had no effect on the distribution of the ratio. Sometimes they were right. If the sample size is anywhere near the magnitudes that Pearson frequently dealt with, the calculated S is essentially a constant and for all practical purposes equal to the true σ. Under those conditions, the ratio $\dfrac{\bar{Y} - \mu}{S/\sqrt{n}}$ *will* behave much like a standard normal random variable, Z. When n is *small*, though, replacing σ with S *does* matter, and it changes the way we draw inferences about μ. Indeed, deriving the exact distribution of $\dfrac{\bar{Y} - \mu}{S/\sqrt{n}}$ was one of the major statistical accomplishments of the early twentieth century.

CASE STUDY 7.2.2

Credit for recognizing that $\dfrac{\bar{Y} - \mu}{\sigma/\sqrt{n}}$ and $\dfrac{\bar{Y} - \mu}{S/\sqrt{n}}$ do not have the same distribution goes to William Sealy Gossett. After graduating in 1899 from Oxford with a First Class degree in Chemistry, Gossett took a position at Arthur Guinness, Son & Co., Ltd., a firm that brewed a thick dark ale known as stout. Given the task of making the art of brewing more scientific, Gossett quickly realized that any experimental studies that might be undertaken would necessarily face two obstacles. First, sample sizes would invariably be small because the company was unable to control the quality of its raw materials. And second, there would never be any way to know the value of the true variance, σ^2, associated with any given set of measurements.

So, when the objective of a study was to draw an inference about μ, Gossett found himself working with the ratio $\dfrac{\bar{Y}-\mu}{S/\sqrt{n}}$, where n was often on the order of 4 or 5. The more he encountered that situation, the more he became convinced that ratios of that sort are *not* adequately described by the standard normal pdf. In particular, the distribution of $\dfrac{\bar{Y}-\mu}{S/\sqrt{n}}$ seemed to have the same general bell-shaped configuration as $f_Z(z)$, but the tails were "thicker"—that is, ratios much smaller than 0 or much greater than 0 were not as rare as the standard normal pdf would predict.

Figure 7.2.2 illustrates the distinction between the distributions of $\dfrac{\bar{Y}-\mu}{\sigma/\sqrt{n}}$ and $\dfrac{\bar{Y}-\mu}{S/\sqrt{n}}$ that caught Gossett's attention. In Figure 7.2.2a, 200 samples of size $n=4$ have been drawn from a normal distribution where the value of σ is known. For each sample, the ratio $\dfrac{\bar{Y}-\mu}{\sigma/\sqrt{4}}$ has been computed. Superimposed over the shaded histogram of those 200 ratios is the standard normal curve, $f_Z(z)$. Clearly, the probabilistic behavior of the random variable $\dfrac{\bar{Y}-\mu}{\sigma/\sqrt{4}}$ is entirely consistent with $f_Z(z)$.

The histogram pictured in Figure 7.2.2b is also based on 200 samples of size $n=4$ drawn from a normal distribution. Here, though, S has been calculated for each sample, so

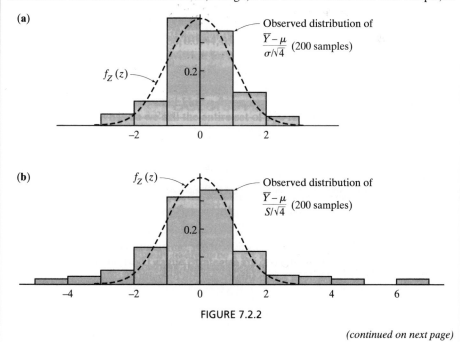

(a)

$f_Z(z)$

Observed distribution of $\dfrac{\bar{Y}-\mu}{\sigma/\sqrt{4}}$ (200 samples)

(b)

$f_Z(z)$

Observed distribution of $\dfrac{\bar{Y}-\mu}{S/\sqrt{4}}$ (200 samples)

FIGURE 7.2.2

(continued on next page)

(Case Study 7.2.2 continued)

the ratios comprising the histogram are $\dfrac{\bar{Y} - \mu}{S/\sqrt{4}}$ rather than $\dfrac{\bar{Y} - \mu}{\sigma/\sqrt{4}}$. In this case, the super-imposed standard normal pdf does *not* adequately describe the histogram—specifically, it underestimates the number of ratios much smaller than 0 as well as the number much larger than 0 (which is exactly what Gossett had noted!).

Gossett called the quotient $\dfrac{\bar{Y} - \mu}{S/\sqrt{n}}$ a *t ratio* and derived the formula for $f_T(t)$. Eventually, a host of other ratios, all addressing related, but different, inference questions, were shown to follow the same pdf. We will have much more to say about the mathematical properties and the applications of this very important *t distribution* in Section 7.4.

QUESTIONS

7.2.1 In the home, the amount of radiation emitted by a color television set does not pose a health problem of any consequence. The same may not be true in department stores, where as many as 15 or 20 sets may be turned on at the same time and in a relatively confined area. The following readings (in milliroentgens per hour) were taken at 10 different department stores, each having at least five TV sets in their sales areas (81). (The recommended safety limit set by the National Council on Radiation Protection is 0.5 mr/h.)

Store	Radiation level (mr/h)
1	0.40
2	0.48
3	0.60
4	0.15
5	0.50
6	0.80
7	0.50
8	0.36
9	0.16
10	0.89

(a) Let the random variable Y denote the radiation level in a department store's television sales area. If Y is assumed to be normally distributed, what values would you assign to μ and σ^2 based on these data?

(b) According to your answer to Part (a), what proportion of department stores would be expected to have radiation levels exceeding the NCRP's recommended safety limit?

7.2.2 In a nongeriatric population, platelet counts ranging from 140 to 440 (1000s per mm³ of blood) are considered "normal." The following are the platelet counts recorded for 24 female nursing-home residents (159). Based on these data, what proportion of the female geriatric population would be expected to have "abnormal" platelet counts? *Note*: If y_i denotes the platelet count of the *i*th subject,

$$\sum_{i=1}^{24} y_i = 4645 \quad \text{and} \quad \sum_{i=1}^{24} y_i^2 = 959{,}265$$

Subject	Count	Subject	Count
1	125	13	180
2	170	14	180
3	250	15	280
4	270	16	240
5	144	17	270
6	184	18	220
7	176	19	110
8	100	20	176
9	220	21	280
10	200	22	176
11	170	23	188
12	160	24	176

7.2.3 Given that the appropriate model for the data in Case Study 7.2.1 is

$$f_Y(y) = \frac{1}{\sqrt{2\pi}\,(2.58)}\,e^{-(1/2)[(y-67.6)/2.58]^2}$$

compute the expected number of recruits whose height would be somewhere in the interval [60.0 in., 61.0 in.].

7.2.4 In 1994, scores on the Mathematics portion of the SAT exam averaged 479 with a standard deviation of 124. Assuming the scores are normally distributed, fill in the missing entries in the breakdown given in the following table (127). Does the normality assumption seem reasonable? *Note*: For the purpose of calculating probabilities, ranges have been expanded to be contiguous. The interval 350–390, for example, is treated as the set of values $345 \le y < 395$. Also, 200–240 and 750–800 become "<245" and "≥745," respectively.

Range	Frequency (in 1000s)	Probability	Expected Frequency
200–240	15.7	0.0294	
250–290	50.0	0.0400	42.0
300–340	97.2	0.0707	
350–390	120.8	0.1082	113.7
400–440	145.6	0.1453	
450–490	153.9		
500–540	149.9		
550–590	118.8		
600–640	87.5	0.0848	89.1
650–690	60.1		
700–740	36.0		
750–800	14.9	0.0160	
	1,050.4		

7.2.5 If a normal curve were superimposed over a density-scaled histogram of the SAT scores given in Question 7.2.4, what would be the height of the curve and the height of the histogram at the point $y = 570$?

7.2.6 The following is a histogram of 100 observations generated by MINITAB that presumably represent a random sample from a normal distribution having $\mu = 50$ and $\sigma = 10$. How well do the location and dispersion of the sample reflect the location and dispersion of the underlying pdf? Answer the question by calculating $\bar{y}_g$ and s_g.

Range	Frequency
$20 \le y < 30$	1
$30 \le y < 40$	13
$40 \le y < 50$	48
$50 \le y < 60$	26
$60 \le y < 70$	10
$70 \le y < 80$	2

7.2.7 One of the many statistically related biological topics that interested Francis Galton was the classification of fingerprints. He and Edward Henry of Scotland Yard devised the system that is still being used by the FBI today. Among the fingerprint characteristics singled out in their approach is a person's *ridge count*, a number that can range from 0 to several hundred. The following is a summary of ridge counts measured on a random sample of 825 males (21). If "ridge count" is a normally distributed random variable, what proportion of males would be expected to have ridge counts of 100 or more? Answer the question by first calculating $\bar{y}_g$ and s_g and then finding an appropriate area under the corresponding normal curve.

Ridge Count	Frequency
$0 \le y < 40$	22
$40 \le y < 80$	64
$80 \le y < 120$	173
$120 \le y < 160$	207
$160 \le y < 200$	239
$200 \le y < 240$	103
$240 \le y < 280$	14
$280 \le y < 320$	3
	825

7.2.8 Let $f_Y(y; \mu)$ denote a normal pdf where σ^2 is known. Show that $f_Y(y; \mu)$ can be written in exponential form (see Question 5.6.8). Does it follow that $\bar{Y}$ is a sufficient statistic for μ?

7.2.9 Let $f_Y(y; \sigma^2)$ denote a normal pdf where μ is known. Show that $f_Y(y; \sigma^2)$ can be written in exponential form and use that fact to suggest a sufficient statistic for σ^2.

7.3 THE χ^2 DISTRIBUTION; INFERENCES ABOUT σ^2

The MLE for the scale parameter of a normal pdf (σ^2) was derived in Section 5.4. An unbiased estimator for σ^2 based on the MLE, was introduced in Section 7.2:

$S^2 = \dfrac{1}{n-1} \sum_{i=1}^{n} (Y_i - \bar{Y})^2$. The next logical step is to develop inference procedures

for σ^2—that is, hypothesis tests and confidence intervals. To do so requires the introduction of a new family of pdf's, the *chi-square distribution*.

DEFINITION 7.3.1. A random variable Y is said to have a *chi-square distribution with n degrees of freedom*, where n is a positive integer, if

$$f_Y(y) = \frac{1}{2^{n/2}\Gamma(n/2)} y^{(n/2)-1} e^{-y/2}, \qquad y > 0$$

The symbol χ_n^2 will often be used in place of Y.

Comment.   The chi-square distribution is a special case of the gamma distribution defined in Theorem 4.6.1. Specifically, $f_{\chi_n^2}(y)$ is a gamma pdf for which

$$r = \frac{n}{2} \text{ and } \lambda = \tfrac{1}{2}.$$

All chi-square distributions are skewed to the right, but the nature of their shape depends on whether n is either (1) 1 or 2 or (2) greater than or equal to 3. Figure 7.3.1 shows $f_{\chi_n^2}(y)$ for $n = 1, 2, 3,$ and 4.

Because of the complexity of the chi-square pdf, finding areas under $f_{\chi_n^2}(y)$ by direct integration is cumbersome. Fortunately, tables of certain lower and upper percentiles of $f_{\chi_n^2}(y)$ are widely available.

Figure 7.3.2 shows the top portion of the *chi-square table* that appears in Appendix A.3. Successive rows refer to different chi-square distributions (each having a different number of degrees of freedom). The column headings denote the areas *to the left* of the numbers listed in the body of the table.

We will use the symbol $\chi_{p,n}^2$ to denote the number along the horizontal axis that cuts off to its left an area of p under the chi-square distribution with n degrees of freedom. For example, from the fifth row of the chi-square table, we see the numbers *1.145* and *15.086* under the column headings *.05* and *.99*, respectively. It follows that

$$P\left(\chi_5^2 \leq 1.145\right) = 0.05$$

and

$$P\left(\chi_5^2 \leq 15.086\right) = 0.99$$

(see Figure 7.3.3). In terms of the $\chi_{p,n}^2$ notation, $1.145 = \chi_{.05,5}^2$ and $15.086 = \chi_{.99,5}^2$. (The area *to the right* of 15.086, of course, must be 0.01.)

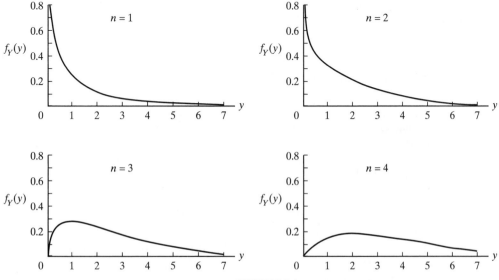

FIGURE 7.3.1

df	.01	.025	.05	p .10	.90	.95	.975	.99
1	0.000157	0.000982	0.00393	0.0158	2.706	3.841	5.024	6.635
2	0.0201	0.0506	0.103	0.211	4.605	5.991	7.378	9.210
3	0.115	0.216	0.352	0.584	6.251	7.815	9.348	11.345
4	0.297	0.484	0.711	1.064	7.779	9.488	11.143	13.277
5	0.554	0.831	1.145	1.610	9.236	11.070	12.832	15.086
6	0.872	1.237	1.635	2.204	10.645	12.592	14.449	16.812
7	1.239	1.690	2.167	2.833	12.017	14.067	16.013	18.475
8	1.646	2.180	2.733	3.490	13.362	15.507	17.535	20.090
9	2.088	2.700	3.325	4.168	14.684	16.919	19.023	21.666
10	2.558	3.247	3.940	4.865	15.987	18.307	20.483	23.209
11	3.053	3.816	4.575	5.578	17.275	19.675	21.920	24.725
12	3.571	4.404	5.226	6.304	18.549	21.026	23.336	26.217

FIGURE 7.3.2

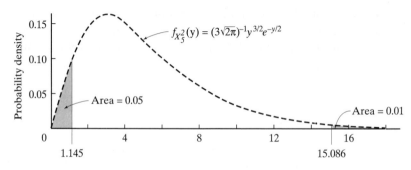

FIGURE 7.3.3

QUESTIONS

7.3.1 Use Appendix Table A.3 to find the following cutoffs and indicate their location on the graph of the appropriate chi-square distribution.

(a) $\chi^2_{.95,14}$ (b) $\chi^2_{.90,2}$ (c) $\chi^2_{.025,9}$

7.3.2 Evaluate the following probabilities:

(a) $P(\chi^2_{17} \geq 8.672)$ (b) $P(\chi^2_6 < 10.645)$

(c) $P(9.591 \leq \chi^2_{20} \leq 34.170)$ (d) $P(\chi^2_2 < 9.210)$

7.3.3 Find the value y that satisfies each of the following equations:

(a) $P(\chi^2_9 \geq y) = 0.99$ (b) $P(\chi^2_{15} \leq y) = 0.05$

(c) $P(9.542 \leq \chi^2_{22} \leq y) = 0.09$ (d) $P(y \leq \chi^2_{31} \leq 48.232) = 0.95$

7.3.4 For what value of n is each of the following statements true?

(a) $P(\chi^2_n \geq 5.009) = 0.975$ (b) $P(27.204 \leq \chi^2_n \leq 30.144) = 0.05$

(c) $P(\chi^2_n \leq 19.281) = 0.05$ (d) $P(10.085 \leq \chi^2_n \leq 24.769) = 0.80$

7.3.5 For df values beyond the range of Appendix Table A.3, chi-square cutoffs can be approximated by using a formula based on cutoffs from the standard normal pdf, $f_Z(z)$. Define $\chi^2_{p,n}$ and z_p^* so that $P(\chi^2_n \leq \chi^2_{p,n}) = p$ and $P(Z \leq z_p^*) = p$, respectively. Then

$$\chi^2_{p,n} \doteq n\left(1 - \frac{2}{9n} + z_p^*\sqrt{\frac{2}{9n}}\right)^3$$

Approximate the 95th percentile of the chi-square distribution with 200 df. That is, find the value of y for which

$$P(\chi^2_{200} \leq y) \doteq 0.95$$

7.3.6 Show directly—without appealing to the fact that χ^2_n is a gamma random variable—that $f_Y(y)$ as stated in Definition 7.3.1 is a true probability density function.

7.3.7 From the comment following Definition 7.3.1, deduce the moment-generating function for a chi-square random variable and use it to show that $E(\chi^2_n) = n$ and $Var(\chi^2_n) = 2n$.

Properties of χ^2_n

Like certain other probability models we have encountered—notably, the binomial, Poisson, and normal—the chi-square distribution reproduces itself. That is, the sum of independent chi-square random variables is, itself, a chi-square random variable.

> **THEOREM 7.3.1.** Suppose Y_1 and Y_2 are independent chi-square random variables with n and m degrees of freedom, respectively. Let $Y = Y_1 + Y_2$. Then Y has a chi-square distribution with $n + m$ degrees of freedom.
>
> **Proof.** See Example 4.6.3.

The next two theorems are the key results connecting the chi-square distribution to inference procedures involving σ^2. Theorem 7.3.2 is a general statement that the sum of the squares of independent standard normal random variables has a chi-square distribution. Theorem 7.3.3 then points out that S^2, the sample variance, is actually a special case of Theorem 7.3.2.

> **THEOREM 7.3.2.** Let $Z_1, Z_2, \ldots, Z_n$ be a set of n independent standard normal random variables. Then $\sum\limits_{i=1}^{n} Z_i^2$ has a chi-square distribution with n degrees of freedom.
>
> **Proof.** The proof follows by induction. First, suppose that $n = 1$. Then
>
> $$F_{Z_1^2}(t) = P(Z_1^2 \leq t) = P(-\sqrt{t} \leq Z_1 \leq \sqrt{t})$$
> $$= 2P(0 \leq Z_1 \leq \sqrt{t})$$
> $$= \frac{2}{\sqrt{2\pi}} \int_0^{\sqrt{t}} e^{-z^2/2}\, dz$$
>
> Differentiation gives the density function for Z_1^2:
>
> $$f_{Z_1^2}(t) = F'_{Z_1^2}(t) = \frac{2}{\sqrt{2\pi}} \frac{1}{2\sqrt{t}} e^{-t/2} = \frac{1}{2^{1/2}\Gamma(1/2)} t^{(1/2)-1} e^{-t/2}$$

Therefore, by inspection, Z_1^2 has a χ_1^2 pdf.

Now, suppose that the theorem is true for the first $n - 1$ random variables. We can write the sum of the first n Z_i^2's as

$$Z_1^2 + \cdots + Z_n^2 = Z_1^2 + \left(Z_2^2 + \cdots + Z_n^2 \right)$$

By what we have just proved, Z_1^2 is χ_1^2; moreover, by the induction hypothesis, $\sum_{i=2}^{n} Z_i^2$ has a chi-square distribution with $n - 1$ degrees of freedom. The statement, then, that $\sum_{i=1}^{n} Z_i^2 = \chi_n^2$ follows from Theorem 7.3.1.

EXAMPLE 7.3.1

The assertion made in Theorem 7.3.2 can easily be examined by simulating the distribution of the sum of squared standard normals. Tables have been published and computer software is available that will give random samples from the standard normal pdf, $f_Z(z)$. One such set of $n = 4$ Z_i's are the numbers $(1.026, -0.315, -0.586, 1.522)$. For that particular sample,

$$\sum_{i=1}^{4} Z_i^2 = (1.026)^2 + (-0.315)^2 + (-0.586)^2 + (1.522)^2$$

$$= 3.812$$

The entries in Table 7.3.1 are the values of $\sum_{i=1}^{4} Z_i^2$ for 100 random samples of four independent standard normal random variables, including the set just mentioned. Figure 7.3.4 shows the density-scaled histogram of these 100 sums. Superimposed is the pdf that Theorem 7.3.2 claims the $\sum_{i=1}^{4} Z_i^2$'s are representing—namely, $f_{\chi_4^2}(y)$. Clearly, the histogram *does* have a configuration much like the chi-square pdf.

TABLE 7.3.1

3.812	4.608	3.876	2.194	4.786	0.583
10.095	2.455	5.413	2.291	10.413	5.302
2.513	1.056	0.226	2.559	1.351	6.637
2.031	4.589	2.427	3.257	1.744	1.309
3.566	1.443	5.728	2.508	3.581	6.982
4.829	2.851	3.880	1.188	0.962	1.914
5.643	7.594	3.063	0.638	8.065	1.531
3.969	4.458	0.444	2.006	3.892	2.431
2.286	2.809	2.160	5.834	5.652	10.019
2.153	1.530	5.829	4.025	4.540	5.731
2.924	2.173	5.979	5.535	1.367	2.054
7.083	0.306	1.405	8.169	1.679	6.348
9.265	3.836	6.843	3.975	1.223	8.020
3.896	1.375	4.942	1.127	8.274	4.438
6.753	1.046	5.487	1.059	7.090	1.869
1.474	5.066	3.917	0.959	1.206	2.487
9.192	8.195	3.051	1.207		

FIGURE 7.3.4

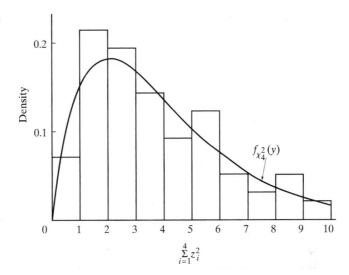

THEOREM 7.3.3.   Let $Y_1, Y_2, \ldots, Y_n$ be a random sample from a normal distribution with mean μ and variance σ^2. Define

$$S^2 = \frac{1}{n-1} \sum_{i=1}^{n} (Y_i - \bar{Y})^2$$

Then the ratio

$$\frac{(n-1)S^2}{\sigma^2}$$

has a chi-square distribution with $n-1$ degrees of freedom.

Proof.   See Appendix 7.A.2.

Constructing Confidence Intervals for σ^2

Since $\dfrac{(n-1)S^2}{\sigma^2}$ has a chi-square distribution with $n-1$ degrees of freedom, we can write

$$P\left(\chi^2_{\alpha/2,\, n-1} \leq \frac{(n-1)S^2}{\sigma^2} \leq \chi^2_{1-\alpha/2,\, n-1} \right) = 1 - \alpha \qquad (7.3.1)$$

If Equation 7.3.1 is then inverted to isolate σ^2 in the center of the inequalities, the two endpoints will necessarily define a $100(1 - \alpha)\%$ confidence interval for the population variance. The algebraic details will be left as an exercise.

THEOREM 7.3.4.   Let s^2 denote the sample variance calculated from a random sample of n observations drawn from a normal distribution with mean μ and variance σ^2. Then

(a) a $100(1 - \alpha)\%$ confidence interval for σ^2 is the set of values

$$\left(\frac{(n - 1)s^2}{\chi^2_{1-\alpha/2, n-1}}, \frac{(n - 1)s^2}{\chi^2_{\alpha/2, n-1}} \right)$$

(b) a $100(1 - \alpha)\%$ confidence interval for σ is the set of values

$$\left(\sqrt{\frac{(n - 1)s^2}{\chi^2_{1-\alpha/2, n-1}}}, \sqrt{\frac{(n - 1)s^2}{\chi^2_{\alpha/2, n-1}}} \right)$$

CASE STUDY 7.3.1

The chain of events that define the geological evolution of the Earth began hundreds of millions of years ago. Fossils play a key role in documenting the *relative* times those events occurred, but to establish an *absolute* chronology, scientists rely primarily on radioactive decay.

One of the newest dating techniques uses a rock's potassium-argon ratio. Almost all minerals contain potassium (K) as well as certain of its isotopes, including ^{40}K. The latter, though, is unstable and decays into isotopes of argon and calcium, ^{40}Ar and ^{40}Ca. By knowing the rates at which the various daughter products are formed and by measuring the amounts of ^{40}Ar and ^{40}K present in a specimen, geologists can estimate the object's age.

Critical to the interpretation of any such dates, of course, is the precision of the underlying procedure. One obvious way to estimate that precision is to use the technique on a sample of rocks known to have the same age. Whatever variation occurs, then, from rock to rock is reflecting the inherent precision (or lack of precision) of the procedure.

Table 7.3.2 lists the potassium-argon estimated ages of 19 mineral samples, all taken from the Black Forest in southeastern Germany (101). Assume that the procedure's estimated ages are normally distributed with (unknown) mean μ and (unknown) variance σ^2. Construct a 95% confidence interval for σ.

TABLE 7.3.2

Specimen	Estimated Age (millions of years)
1	$y_1 = 249$
2	$y_2 = 254$
3	$y_3 = 243$
4	$y_4 = 268$
5	$y_5 = 253$
6	$y_6 = 269$
7	$y_7 = 287$
8	$y_8 = 241$
9	$y_9 = 273$
10	$y_{10} = 306$
11	$y_{11} = 303$
12	$y_{12} = 280$
13	$y_{13} = 260$
14	$y_{14} = 256$
15	$y_{15} = 278$
16	$y_{16} = 344$
17	$y_{17} = 304$
18	$y_{18} = 283$
19	$y_{19} = 310$

Here

$$\sum_{i=1}^{19} y_i = 5261$$

$$\sum_{i=1}^{19} y_i^2 = 1,469,945$$

so the sample variance is *733.4*:

$$s^2 = \frac{19(1,469,945) - (5261)^2}{19(18)} = 733.4$$

Since $n = 19$, the critical values appearing in the left-hand and right-hand limits of the σ confidence interval come from the chi-square pdf with *18* df. According to Appendix Table A.3,

$$P\left(8.23 < \chi_{18}^2 < 31.53\right) = 0.95$$

so the 95% confidence interval for the potassium-argon method's precision is the set of values

$$\left(\sqrt{\frac{(19-1)(733.4)}{31.53}}, \sqrt{\frac{(19-1)(733.4)}{8.23}}\right)$$

$$= (20.5 \text{ million years}, 40.0 \text{ million years})$$

EXAMPLE 7.3.2

The width of a confidence interval for σ^2 is a function of both n and S^2:

$$\text{Width} = \text{upper limit} - \text{lower limit}$$

$$= \frac{(n-1)S^2}{\chi_{\alpha/2, n-1}^2} - \frac{(n-1)S^2}{\chi_{1-\alpha/2, n-1}^2} \tag{7.3.2}$$

$$= (n-1)S^2\left(\frac{1}{\chi_{\alpha/2, n-1}^2} - \frac{1}{\chi_{1-\alpha/2, n-1}^2}\right)$$

As n gets larger, the interval will tend to get narrower because the unknown σ^2 is being estimated more precisely. What is the smallest number of observations that will guarantee that the average width of a 95% confidence interval for σ^2 is no greater than σ^2?

Since S^2 is an unbiased estimator for σ^2, Equation 7.3.2 implies that the expected width of a 95% confidence interval for the variance is the expression

$$E(\text{width}) = (n-1)\sigma^2\left(\frac{1}{\chi_{.025, n-1}^2} - \frac{1}{\chi_{.975, n-1}^2}\right)$$

Clearly, then, for the expected width to be less than or equal to σ^2, n must be chosen so that

$$(n-1)\left(\frac{1}{\chi_{.025, n-1}^2} - \frac{1}{\chi_{.975, n-1}^2}\right) \leq 1$$

Trial and error can be used to identify the desired n. The first three columns in Figure 7.3.5 come from the chi-square distribution in Appendix Table A.3. As the computation in the last column indicates, $n = 39$ is the smallest sample size that will yield 95% confidence intervals for σ^2 whose average width is less than σ^2.

n	$\chi^2_{.025,\,n-1}$	$\chi^2_{.975,\,n-1}$	$(n-1)\left(\dfrac{1}{\chi^2_{.025,\,n-1}} - \dfrac{1}{\chi^2_{.975,\,n-1}}\right)$
15	5.629	26.119	1.95
20	8.907	32.852	1.55
30	16.047	45.722	1.17
38	22.106	55.668	1.01
39	22.878	56.895	0.99

FIGURE 7.3.5

Testing $H_0: \sigma^2 = \sigma_o^2$

The generalized-likelihood-ratio criterion introduced in Section 6.5 can be used to set up hypothesis tests for σ^2. The complete derivation appears in Appendix 7.A.3. Theorem 7.3.5 states the resulting decision rule. Playing a key role—just as it did in the construction of confidence intervals for σ^2—is the chi-square ratio from Theorem 7.3.3.

> **THEOREM 7.3.5.** Let s^2 denote the sample variance calculated from a random sample of n observations drawn from a normal distribution with mean μ and variance σ^2. Let $\chi^2 = (n-1)s^2/\sigma_o^2$.
>
> **(a)** To test $H_0: \sigma^2 = \sigma_o^2$ versus $H_1: \sigma^2 > \sigma_o^2$ at the α level of significance, reject H_0 if $\chi^2 \geq \chi^2_{1-\alpha,\,n-1}$.
>
> **(b)** To test $H_0: \sigma^2 = \sigma_o^2$ versus $H_1: \sigma^2 < \sigma_o^2$ at the α level of significance, reject H_0 if $\chi^2 \leq \chi^2_{\alpha,\,n-1}$.
>
> **(c)** To test $H_0: \sigma^2 = \sigma_o^2$ versus $H_1: \sigma^2 \neq \sigma_o^2$ at the α level of significance, reject H_0 if χ^2 is either $(1) \leq \chi^2_{\alpha/2,\,n-1}$ or $(2) \geq \chi^2_{1-\alpha/2,\,n-1}$.

CASE STUDY 7.3.2

Home buyers can choose a variety of ways to finance mortgages, ranging from fixed-rate 30-year notes to 1-year adjustables, where interest rates can move up or down from year to year. During the first quarter of 1994, Tennessee lenders were charging an average rate of 8.84% on a $100,000 loan amortized over 30 years; the standard deviation from bank to bank was 0.10%.

Since 1-year adjustables give banks considerable flexibility in responding quickly to changing economic climates, we might reasonably expect those rates to have a greater standard deviation than the 0.10% that characterizes 30-year fixed notes. Lenders should be more willing to incur higher risks to compete for potential clients if they know they can make adjustments as time goes by.

Table 7.3.3 lists rates quoted by $n = 9$ lenders for 1-year adjustables (167). The sample standard deviation for those nine y_i's is $s = 0.22$. Do these data lend credence to the speculation that rates for 1-year adjustables are more variable than rates for conventional mortgages?

TABLE 7.3.3

Lender	Initial rate on 1-year adjustables, y_i
AmSouth Mortgage	6.38%
Boatmen's National Mortgage	6.63
Cavalry Bank	6.88
First American National Bank	6.75
First Investment	6.13
First Republic	6.50
NationsBanc Mortgage	6.63
Union Planters	6.38
MortgageSouth Corp.	6.50

Let σ^2 denote the variance of the population represented by the y_i's in Table 7.3.3. To judge whether a standard-deviation increase from 0.10% to 0.22% is statistically significant requires that we test

$$H_0: \quad \sigma^2 = (0.10)^2$$

versus

$$H_1: \quad \sigma^2 > (0.10)^2$$

Let $\alpha = 0.05$. With $n = 9$, the rejection region for the chi-square ratio [from Part (a) of Theorem 7.3.5] starts at $\chi^2_{1-\alpha,\,n-1} = \chi^2_{.95,8} = 15.507$ (see Figure 7.3.6). But

$$\chi^2 = \frac{(n-1)s^2}{\sigma^2} = \frac{(9-1)(0.22)^2}{(0.10)^2} = 38.72$$

so our decision is clear: Reject H_0.

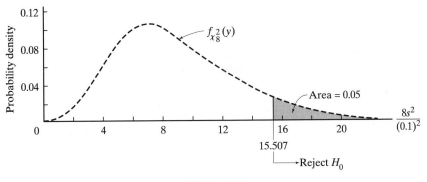

FIGURE 7.3.6

QUESTIONS

7.3.8 Is it believable that the numbers $65, 30$, and 55 are a random sample of size 3 from a normal distribution with $\mu = 50$ and $\sigma = 10$? Answer the question by using a chi-square distribution. *Hint*: Let $Z_i = (Y_i - 50)/10$ and use Theorem 7.3.2.

7.3.9 If Y is a chi-square random variable with n degrees of freedom, the pdf of $(Y - n)/\sqrt{2n}$ converges to $f_Z(z)$ as n goes to infinity (recall Question 7.3.7). Use the asymptotic normality of $(Y - n)/\sqrt{2n}$ to approximate the fortieth percentile of a chi-square random variable with 200 degrees of freedom.

7.3.10 Use the fact that $(n - 1)S^2/\sigma^2$ is a chi-square random variable with $n - 1$ df to prove that

$$\text{Var}(S^2) = \frac{2\sigma^4}{n - 1}$$

Hint: Use the fact that the variance of a chi-square random variable with k df is $2k$.

7.3.11 Let $Y_1, Y_2, \ldots, Y_n$ be a random sample of size n from a normal distribution having mean μ and variance σ^2. What is the smallest value of n for which

$$P\left(\frac{S^2}{\sigma^2} < 2\right) \geq 0.95$$

Hint: Use a trial-and-error method similar to the approach taken in Example 7.3.2.

7.3.12 **(a)** Use the asymptotic normality of chi-square random variables (see Question 7.3.9) to derive large-sample confidence interval formulas for σ and σ^2.
(b) Use your answer to Part (a) to construct an approximate 95% confidence interval for the standard deviation of estimated potassium-argon ages based on the 19 y_i's in Table 7.3.2.

7.3.13 Let $Y_1, Y_2, \ldots, Y_n$ be a random sample from a normal distribution. Use the statement of Question 7.3.10 to prove that S^2 is consistent for σ^2.

7.3.14 Start with the fact that $(n - 1)S^2/\sigma^2$ has a chi-square distribution with $n - 1$ df (if the Y_i's are normally distributed) and derive the confidence interval formulas given in Theorem 7.3.4.

7.3.15 A random sample of size $n = 19$ is drawn from a normal distribution for which $\sigma^2 = 12.0$. In what range are we likely to find the sample variance, s^2? Answer the question by finding two numbers a and b such that

$$P(a \leq S^2 \leq b) = 0.95$$

7.3.16 One of the occupational hazards of being an airplane pilot is the hearing loss that results from being exposed to high noise levels. To document the magnitude of the problem, a team of researchers measured the cockpit noise levels in 18 commercial aircraft. The results (in decibels) are as follows (84).

Plane	Noise Level (dB)	Plane	Noise Level (dB)
1	74	10	72
2	77	11	90
3	80	12	87
4	82	13	73
5	82	14	83
6	85	15	86
7	80	16	83
8	75	17	83
9	75	18	80

(a) Assume that cockpit noise levels are normally distributed. Use Theorem 7.3.4 to construct a 95% confidence interval for the standard deviation of noise levels from plane to plane.

(b) Use these same data to construct two *one-sided* 95% confidence intervals for σ.

7.3.17 In Case Study 7.3.1, the 95% confidence interval was constructed for σ rather than for σ^2. In practice, is an experimenter more likely to focus on the standard deviation or on the variance, or do you think that both formulas in Theorem 7.3.4 are likely to be used equally often? Explain.

7.3.18 According to many investment counselors, foreign stocks have the potential for a high yield, but the variability in their dividends may be greater than what is typical for American companies. According to one broker's report, the standard deviation of dividends earned by domestic service-industry stocks is roughly 3.0%. If the standard deviation of the dividends earned by a random sample of 14 foreign stocks is 5.6%, can we conclude at the 0.05 level of significance that foreign stocks, in general, are more volatile?

7.3.19 The A above middle C is the note given to an orchestra, usually by the oboe, for tuning purposes. Its pitch is defined to be the sound of a tuning fork vibrating at 440 cycles per second (cps). No tuning fork, of course, will always vibrate at exactly 440 cps; rather, the pitch, Y, is a random variable. Suppose that Y is normally distributed with $\mu = 440$ and variance σ^2. With the standard manufacturing process, $\sigma^2 = 1.1$. A new production technique has just been suggested, and its proponents claim it will yield values of σ^2 less than 1.1. To test that assertion, six tuning forks have been made according to the new procedure. The resulting vibration frequencies are found to be 440.8, 440.3, 439.2, 439.8, 440.6, and 441.1 cps. Do an appropriate hypothesis test. State your conclusion in terms of the 0.05 level of significance.

7.3.20 If a 90% confidence interval for σ^2 is reported to be (51.47, 261.90), what is the value of the sample standard deviation?

7.3.21 Let $Y_1, Y_2, \ldots, Y_n$ be a random sample of size n from the pdf

$$f_Y(y) = \left(\frac{1}{\theta}\right) e^{-y/\theta}, \qquad y > 0; \theta > 0$$

(a) Use moment-generating functions to show that the ratio $2n\bar{Y}/\theta$ has a chi-square distribution with $2n$ df.

(b) Use the result in Part (a) to derive a $100(1 - \alpha)\%$ confidence interval for θ.

7.4   THE *F* AND *t* DISTRIBUTIONS

There are three especially important "sampling distributions" related to the normal pdf. These are the distributions involved in testing hypotheses and constructing confidence intervals. We have already seen in Section 7.3 that inferences about σ^2 derive from $\dfrac{(n-1)S^2}{\sigma^2}$, a ratio whose probabilistic behavior is described by the *chi-square distribution*. Introduced in this section are the *F* and *t* probability functions. These are the sampling distributions that allow us to make inferences about μ.

The *F* Distribution

Named for the great British statistician Sir Ronald A. Fisher, the *F* distribution is defined as a quotient of independent chi-square random variables.

THEOREM 7.4.1. Suppose that U and V are independent chi-square random variables with m and n degrees of freedom, respectively. Let

$$F = \frac{U/m}{V/n}$$

Then the pdf for F is given by

$$f_{F_{m,n}}(r) = \frac{\Gamma\left(\dfrac{m+n}{2}\right)}{\Gamma\left(\dfrac{m}{2}\right)\Gamma\left(\dfrac{n}{2}\right)} \frac{m^{m/2}n^{n/2}r^{(m/2)-1}}{(n+mr)^{(m+n)/2}}, \quad r > 0$$

and we say that the ratio $\dfrac{U/m}{V/n}$ has an *F distribution with m and n degrees of freedom*.

Proof. We begin by finding the pdf for U/V. For notational simplicity, let $c = m/2$ and $d = n/2$. From Definition 7.3.1, then,

$$f_U(u) = \frac{1}{\Gamma(c)2^c} u^{c-1}e^{-u/2}, \quad u > 0$$

and

$$f_V(v) = \frac{1}{\Gamma(d)2^d} v^{d-1}e^{-v/2}, \quad v > 0$$

Figure 7.4.1 shows the region of integration to find the cdf of the quotient U/V. That is,

$$F_{U/V}(r) = P(U/V \le r) = P(U/r \le V)$$

Therefore,

$$F_{U/V}(r) = \frac{1}{\Gamma(c)\Gamma(d)2^{c+d}} \int_0^\infty \left(\int_0^{rv} u^{c-1}e^{-u/2}\,du \right) v^{d-1}e^{-v/2}\,dv$$

Thus

$$f_{U/V}(r) = \frac{1}{\Gamma(c)\Gamma(d)2^{c+d}} \int_0^\infty \left[(rv)^{c-1}e^{-rv/2}v \right]v^{d-1}e^{-v/2}\,dv \qquad (7.4.1)$$

FIGURE 7.4.1

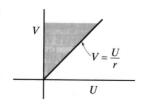

Note that to obtain the preceding, we have interchanged the outer integral and d/dr, then used the fundamental theorem of calculus (where does the extra v come from?). Simplifying the integral in Equation 7.4.1 gives

$$f_{U/V}(r) = \frac{1}{\Gamma(c)\Gamma(d)2^{c+d}} r^{c-1} \int_0^\infty v^{c+d-1} e^{-[(1+r)/2]v} \, dv$$

We recognize the integrand as the variable part of a gamma density with $r = c + d$ and $\gamma = (1 + r)/2$, so the integral has value $2^{c+d}\Gamma(c + d)/(1 + r)^{c+d}$. Therefore,

$$f_{U/V}(r) = \frac{\Gamma(c + d)}{\Gamma(c)\Gamma(d)} \cdot \frac{r^{c-1}}{(1 + r)^{c+d}} \tag{7.4.2}$$

The statement of the theorem, then, follows from the fact that

$$f_{(n/m)(U/V)}(r) = f_{F_{m,n}}(r) = \frac{m}{n} f_{U/V}\left(\frac{m}{n} r\right)$$

F Tables

When graphed, an F distribution looks very much like a typical chi-square distribution—values of $\dfrac{U/m}{V/n}$ can never be negative and the F pdf is skewed sharply to the right. Clearly, the complexity of $f_{F_{m,n}}(r)$ makes the function difficult to work with directly. Tables, though, are widely available that give various percentiles of F distributions for different values of m and n.

Figure 7.4.2 shows $f_{F_{3,5}}(r)$. In general, the symbol $F_{p,m,n}$ will be used to denote the $100p$th percentile of the F distribution with m and n degrees of freedom. Here, the 95th percentile of $f_{F_{3,5}}(r)$—that is, $F_{.95,3,5}$—is *5.41* (see page 726 of Appendix Table A.4).

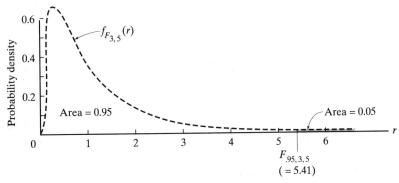

FIGURE 7.4.2

QUESTIONS

7.4.1 Use Appendix Table A.4 to find
  (a) $F_{.50,6,7}$ (b) $F_{.001,15,5}$ (c) $F_{.90,2,2}$

7.4.2 Let U and V be independent chi-square random variables with 7 and 9 degrees of freedom, respectively. Is it more likely that $\dfrac{U/7}{V/9}$ will be between (1) 2.51 and 3.29 or (2) 3.29 and 4.20?

7.4.3 Use Appendix Table A.4 to find the values of x that satisfy the following equations:
  (a) $P(0.109 < F_{4,6} < x) = 0.95$ (b) $P(0.427 < F_{11,7} < 1.69) = x$
  (c) $P(F_{x,x} > 5.35) = 0.01$ (d) $P(0.115 < F_{3,x} < 3.29) = 0.90$
  (e) $P\left(x < \dfrac{U/2}{V/3}\right) = 0.25$, where U is a chi-square random variable with 2 df and V is an independent chi-square random variable with 3 df.

7.4.4 Suppose that two independent samples of size n are drawn from a normal distribution with variance σ^2. Let S_1^2 and S_2^2 denote the two sample variances. Use the fact that $\dfrac{(n-1)S^2}{\sigma^2}$ has a chi-square distribution with $n-1$ df to explain why

$$\lim_{\substack{n \to \infty \\ m \to \infty}} F_{m,n} = 1$$

(see Appendix Table A.4).

7.4.5 If the random variable F has an F distribution with m and n degrees of freedom, show that $1/F$ has an F distribution with n and m degrees of freedom.

7.4.6 Use the result claimed in Question 7.4.5 to express percentiles of $f_{F_{n,m}}(r)$ in terms of percentiles from $f_{F_{m,n}}(r)$. That is, if we know the values a and b for which $P(a \le F_{m,n} \le b) = q$, what values of c and d will satisfy the equation $P(c \le F_{n,m} \le d) = q$? "Check" your answer with Appendix Table A.4 by comparing the values of $F_{.05,2,8}$, $F_{.95,2,8}$, $F_{.05,8,2}$, and $F_{.95,8,2}$.

7.4.7 The entries in Table 7.3.1 represent 100 independent chi-square random variables, each with 4 df. Divide them into 50 consecutive groups of two and calculate the corresponding ratios—for example $\dfrac{3.812}{10.095} = 0.38$, $\dfrac{2.513}{2.031} = 1.24$ and so on. Compare the tenth, fiftieth, and nintieth percentiles of the sample with those same percentiles from the particular F distribution that the ratios are representing.

7.4.8 A random variable Y is said to have a *beta distribution* with parameters t and s if

$$f_Y(y) = \frac{\Gamma(t+s)}{\Gamma(t)\Gamma(s)}\, y^{t-1}(1-y)^{s-1}, \quad 0 < y < 1, \quad t > 0, \quad s > 0$$

Use the fact that $\displaystyle\int_0^1 f_Y(y)\,dy = 1$ to find $E(U/V)$, where U and V are independent chi-square random variables with m and n degrees of freedom, respectively. *Hint*: Use Equation 7.4.2, and in the integral defining $E(U/V)$, make the substitution $r = \dfrac{w}{1-w}$.

7.4.9 Use the expression for $E(U/V)$ derived in Question 7.4.8 to show that $E(F_{m,n}) = \dfrac{n}{n-2}$, for $n > 2$.

The Student *t* distribution

Earlier in this chapter, it was pointed out that if $y_1, y_2, \ldots, y_n$ is a random sample from a normal distribution with mean μ and standard deviation σ, the ratio $\dfrac{\bar{Y} - \mu}{\sigma/\sqrt{n}}$ has a standard normal distribution but $\dfrac{\bar{Y} - \mu}{S/\sqrt{n}}$ does not (recall Figure 7.2.2). Credit for recognizing the latter and for deriving the pdf of $\dfrac{\bar{Y} - \mu}{S/\sqrt{n}}$ is given to W. S. Gosset, who—writing under the pseudonym "Student"—called $\dfrac{\bar{Y} - \mu}{S/\sqrt{n}}$ a *t ratio*.

Derived in this section are some of the important mathematical properties and relationships associated with Gosset's *Student t distribution*. As we will see, this distribution plays a fundamental role in a host of procedures designed to draw inferences about the mean (μ) of a normal distribution.

DEFINITION 7.4.1. Let Z be a standard normal random variable and V an independent chi-square random variable with n df. The *Student t ratio with n degrees of freedom* is denoted T_n, where

$$T_n = \frac{Z}{\sqrt{V/n}}$$

LEMMA. The pdf for T_n is symmetric: $f_{T_n}(t) = f_{T_n}(-t)$, for all t.

Proof. Since

$$-T_n = \frac{-Z}{\sqrt{V/n}}$$

is the ratio of a standard normal random variable to an independent chi-square random variable, it must have a Student t distribution, $f_{T_n}(n)$. But the pdf of $-T_n$ is $f_{T_n}(-t)$ at the point t. Therefore, $f_{T_n}(-t) = f_{T_n}(t)$, for all t.

THEOREM 7.4.2. The pdf for a Student t random variable with n degrees of freedom is given by

$$f_{T_n}(n) = \frac{\Gamma\left(\dfrac{n+1}{2}\right)}{\sqrt{n\pi}\,\Gamma\left(\dfrac{n}{2}\right)\left(1 + \dfrac{t^2}{n}\right)^{(n+1)/2}}, \qquad -\infty < t < \infty$$

Proof. Note that $T_n^2 = \dfrac{Z^2}{V/n}$ has an F distribution with 1 and n df. Therefore,

$$f_{T_n^2}(t) = \frac{n^{n/2}\Gamma\left(\dfrac{n+1}{2}\right)}{\Gamma\left(\dfrac{1}{2}\right)\Gamma\left(\dfrac{n}{2}\right)}\, t^{-1/2}\,\frac{1}{(n+t)^{(n+1)/2}}, \qquad t > 0$$

Suppose that $t > 0$. By the symmetry of $f_{T_n}(t)$,

$$F_{T_n}(t) = P(T_n \leq t) = \frac{1}{2} + P(0 \leq T_n \leq t)$$

$$= \frac{1}{2} + \frac{1}{2} P(-t \leq T_n \leq t)$$

$$= \frac{1}{2} + \frac{1}{2} P(0 \leq T_n^2 \leq t^2)$$

$$= \frac{1}{2} + \frac{1}{2} F_{T_n^2}(t^2)$$

Differentiating $F_{T_n}(t)$ gives the stated result:

$$f_{T_n}(t) = F'_{T_n}(t) = t \cdot f_{T_n^2}(t^2)$$

$$= t \frac{n^{n/2} \Gamma\left(\dfrac{n+1}{2}\right)}{\Gamma\left(\dfrac{1}{2}\right) \Gamma\left(\dfrac{n}{2}\right)} (t^2)^{-(1/2)} \frac{1}{(n + t^2)^{(n+1)/2}}$$

$$= \frac{\Gamma\left(\dfrac{n+1}{2}\right)}{\sqrt{n\pi}\, \Gamma\left(\dfrac{n}{2}\right)} \cdot \frac{1}{\left[1 + \left(\dfrac{t^2}{n}\right)\right]^{(n+1)/2}}$$

Comment.   Over the years, the lower-case t has come to be the accepted symbol for the random variable of Definition 7.4.1. We will follow that convention when the context allows some flexibility. In mathematical statements about distributions, though, we will be consistent with random-variable notation and denote the Student t ratio as T_n.

$f_{T_n}(n)$ and $f_Z(z)$: How the Two pdf's Are Related

Despite the considerable disparity in the appearance of the formulas for $f_{T_n}(t)$ and $f_Z(z)$, Student t distributions and the standard normal distribution have much in common. Both are bell shaped, symmetric, and centered around 0. Student t curves, though, are flatter.

Figure 7.4.3 is a graph of two Student t distributions—one with 2 df and the other with 10 df. Also pictured is the standard normal pdf, $f_Z(z)$. Notice that as n increases, $f_{T_n}(t)$ becomes more and more like $f_Z(z)$.

The convergence of $f_{T_n}(t)$ to $f_Z(z)$ is a consequence of two of the estimation properties we have already studied: (1) The sample standard deviation S is asymptotically unbiased for σ, and (2) the standard deviation of S goes to 0 as n goes to infinity (recall Question 7.3.10). Therefore, as n gets large, the probabilistic behavior of

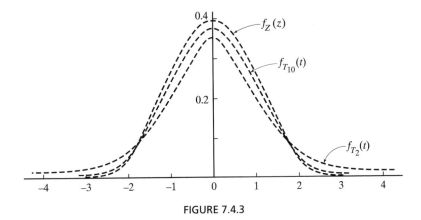

FIGURE 7.4.3

$\dfrac{\bar{Y} - \mu}{S/\sqrt{n}}$ will become increasingly similar to the distribution of $\dfrac{\bar{Y} - \mu}{\sigma/\sqrt{n}}$—that is, to $f_Z(z)$.

t Tables

We have already seen that doing hypothesis tests and constructing confidence intervals requires knowing lower and upper percentiles of certain distributions—for example, $\chi^2_{.10, 6}$, $z_{.025}$. There will be a similar need to identify appropriate "cutoffs" from Student t distributions.

Figure 7.4.4 shows a portion of the t table that appears in the back of every statistics book. Each row corresponds to a different Student t pdf. The column headings give the area *to the right* of the number appearing in the body of the table.

For example, the entry *4.541* listed in the $\alpha = .01$ column and the df = 3 row has the property that $P(T_3 \geq 4.541) = 0.01$.

More generally, we will use the symbol $t_{\alpha, n}$ to denote the $100(1 - \alpha)$th percentile of $f_{T_n}(t)$. That is, $P(T_n \geq t_{\alpha, n}) = \alpha$ (see Figure 7.4.5). No lower percentiles of

df	.20	.15	.10	.05	.025	.01	.005
1	1.376	1.963	3.078	6.3138	12.706	31.821	63.657
2	1.061	1.386	1.886	2.9200	4.3027	6.965	9.9248
3	0.978	1.250	1.638	2.3534	3.1825	4.541	5.8409
4	0.941	1.190	1.533	2.1318	2.7764	3.747	4.6041
5	0.920	1.156	1.476	2.0150	2.5706	3.365	4.0321
6	0.906	1.134	1.440	1.9432	2.4469	3.143	3.7074
⋮			⋮				
30	0.854	1.055	1.310	1.6973	2.0423	2.457	2.7500
∞	0.84	1.04	1.28	1.64	1.96	2.33	2.58

α

FIGURE 7.4.4

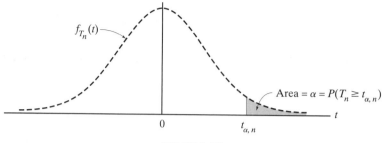

FIGURE 7.4.5

Student t curves need to be tabulated because the symmetry of $f_{T_n}(t)$ implies that $P(T_n \le -t_{\alpha, n}) = \alpha$.

The number of different Student t pdf's summarized in a t table varies considerably. Many tables will provide cutoffs for degrees of freedom ranging only from 1 to 30; others will include df values from 1 to 50, or even from 1 to 100. The last row in any t table, though, is always labeled "∞": Those entries, of course, correspond to z_α.

A Special Case of the Student t Ratio

The Student t ratio was cast in the most general of terms in Definition 7.4.1. Different inference objectives will require that the ratio be reformulated in different ways before it can be applied. We conclude this chapter by introducing one such special case of $Z/\sqrt{V/n}$ that has already been alluded to—namely, that $\dfrac{\bar{Y} - \mu}{S/\sqrt{n}}$ is a T ratio. Applications of Theorem 7.4.3 will be the focus of Sections 7.5 and 7.6.

THEOREM 7.4.3. Let $Y_1, Y_2, \dots, Y_n$ be a random sample from a normal distribution with mean μ and standard deviation σ. Then

$$T_{n-1} = \frac{\bar{Y} - \mu}{S/\sqrt{n}}$$

has a Student t distribution with $n - 1$ degrees of freedom.

Proof. We can rewrite $\dfrac{\bar{Y} - \mu}{S/\sqrt{n}}$ in the form

$$\frac{\bar{Y} - \mu}{S/\sqrt{n}} = \frac{\dfrac{\bar{Y} - \mu}{\sigma/\sqrt{n}}}{\sqrt{\dfrac{(n-1)S^2}{\sigma^2(n-1)}}}$$

But $\dfrac{\bar{Y} - \mu}{\sigma/\sqrt{n}}$ is a standard normal random variable and $\dfrac{(n-1)S^2}{\sigma^2}$ has a chi-square distribution with $n - 1$ df. Moreover, it is shown in Appendix 7.A.2 that

$$\frac{\bar{Y} - \mu}{\sigma/\sqrt{n}} \quad \text{and} \quad \frac{(n-1)S^2}{\sigma^2}$$

are independent. The statement of the theorem follows immediately, then, from Definition 7.4.1.

QUESTIONS

7.4.10 Use Appendix Table A.2 to find the following probabilities:

    (a) $P(T_6 \geq 1.134)$ **(b)** $P(T_{15} \leq 0.866)$

    (c) $P(T_3 \geq -1.250)$ **(d)** $P(-1.055 < T_{29} < 2.462)$

7.4.11 What values of x satisfy the following equations?

    (a) $P(-x \leq T_{22} \leq x) = 0.98$ **(b)** $P(T_{13} \geq x) = 0.85$

    (c) $P(T_{26} < x) = 0.95$ **(d)** $P(T_2 \geq x) = 0.025$

7.4.12 Which of the following differences is larger? Explain.

$$t_{.05,n} - t_{.10,n} \text{ or } t_{.10,n} - t_{.15,n}$$

7.4.13 A random sample of size $n = 9$ is drawn from a normal distribution with $\mu = 27.6$. Within what interval $(-a, +a)$ can we expect to find $\dfrac{\bar{Y} - 27.6}{S/\sqrt{9}}$ *80% of the time? 90% of the time?*

7.4.14 Suppose a random sample of size $n = 11$ is drawn from a normal distribution with $\mu = 15.0$. For what value of k is

$$P\left(\left| \frac{\bar{Y} - 15.0}{S/\sqrt{11}} \right| \geq k \right) = 0.05$$

7.4.15 Let $\bar{Y}$ and S denote the sample mean and sample standard deviation, respectively, based on a set of $n = 20$ measurements taken from a normal distribution with $\mu = 90.6$. Find the function $k(S)$ for which

$$P(90.6 - k(S) \leq \bar{Y} \leq 90.6 + k(S)) = 0.99$$

7.4.16 Show that as $n \to \infty$, the pdf of a Student t random variable with n df converges to $f_Z(z)$. *Hint:* To show that the constant term in the pdf for T_n converges to $1/\sqrt{2\pi}$, use Stirling's formula,

$$n! \doteq \sqrt{2\pi n} \, n^n e^{-n}$$

Also, recall that $\lim\limits_{n \to \infty} \left(1 + \dfrac{a}{n}\right)^n = e^a$.

7.4.17 Evaluate the integral

$$\int_0^\infty \frac{1}{1 + x^2} \, dx$$

using the Student t distribution.

7.5 DRAWING INFERENCES ABOUT μ

One of the most common of all statistical objectives is to draw inferences about the *mean* of the population being represented by a set of data. Indeed, we have already taken a first look at that problem in Section 6.2. If the y_i's come from a normal distribution where σ is known, the null hypothesis $H_0: \mu = \mu_o$ can be tested by calculating a Z *ratio*, $\dfrac{\bar{Y} - \mu}{\sigma/\sqrt{n}}$ (recall Theorem 6.2.1).

Implicit in that solution, though, is an assumption not likely to be satisfied: Rarely does an experimenter "know" the value of σ. Much more typical is the situation where there is reason to believe that the data are normally distributed, but nothing is known about either μ or σ. Inferences, then, must necessarily be based on the T_{n-1} ratio, $\dfrac{\bar{Y} - \mu}{S/\sqrt{n}}$ and not on the Z ratio. In this section, we examine the two formats that those inferences take: (1) constructing a confidence interval for μ and (2) testing the null hypothesis that $\mu = \mu_o$.

Constructing a Confidence Interval for μ

The fact that $\dfrac{\bar{Y} - \mu}{S/\sqrt{n}}$ has a Student t distribution with $n - 1$ degrees of freedom justifies the statement that

$$P\left(-t_{\alpha/2,\, n-1} \le \frac{\bar{Y} - \mu}{S/\sqrt{n}} \le t_{\alpha/2,\, n-1}\right) = 1 - \alpha$$

or, equivalently, that

$$P\left(\bar{Y} - t_{\alpha/2,\, n-1} \cdot \frac{S}{\sqrt{n}} \le \mu \le \bar{Y} + t_{\alpha/2,\, n-1} \cdot \frac{S}{\sqrt{n}}\right) = 1 - \alpha \qquad (7.5.1)$$

(provided the Y_i's are a random sample from a normal distribution).

When the actual data values are then used to evaluate $\bar{Y}$ and S, the lower and upper endpoints identified in Equation 7.5.1 define a $100(1 - \alpha)\%$ confidence interval for μ.

THEOREM 7.5.1. Let $y_1\ y_2, \ldots, y_n$ be a random sample of size n from a normal distribution with (unknown) mean μ. A $100(1 - \alpha)\%$ confidence interval for μ is the set of values

$$\left(\bar{y} - t_{\alpha/2,\, n-1} \cdot \frac{s}{\sqrt{n}},\, \bar{y} + t_{\alpha/2,\, n-1} \cdot \frac{s}{\sqrt{n}}\right)$$

CASE STUDY 7.5.1

To hunt flying insects, bats emit high-frequency sounds and then listen for their echoes. Until an insect is located, these pulses are emitted at intervals of from 50 to 100 milliseconds. When an insect *is* detected, the pulse-to-pulse interval suddenly decreases—sometimes to as low as 10 milliseconds—thus enabling the bat to pinpoint its prey's position.

This raises an interesting question: How far apart are the bat and the insect when the bat first senses that the insect is there? Or, put another way, what is the effective range of a bat's echolocation system?

The technical problems that had to be overcome in measuring the bat-to-insect detection distance were far more complex than the statistical problems involved in analyzing the actual data. The procedure that finally evolved was to put a bat into an 11-by-16-foot room, along with an ample supply of fruit flies, and record the action with two synchronized 16 mm sound-on-film cameras. By examining the two sets of pictures frame by frame, scientists could follow the bat's flight pattern and, at the same time, monitor its pulse frequency. For each insect that was caught (57), it was therefore possible to estimate the distance between the bat and the insect at the precise moment the bat's pulse-to-pulse interval decreased (see Table 7.5.1).

TABLE 7.5.1

Catch Number	Detection Distance (cm)
1	62
2	52
3	68
4	23
5	34
6	45
7	27
8	42
9	83
10	56
11	40

Define μ to be a bat's true average detection distance. Use the 11 observations in Table 7.5.1 to construct a 95% confidence interval for μ.

Letting $y_1 = 62, y_2 = 52, \ldots, y_{11} = 40$, we have that

$$\sum_{i=1}^{11} y_i = 532 \quad \text{and} \quad \sum_{i=1}^{11} y_i^2 = 29{,}000$$

Therefore,

$$\bar{y} = \frac{532}{11} = 48.4 \text{ cm}$$

and

$$s = \sqrt{\frac{11(29{,}000) - (532)^2}{11(10)}} = 18.1 \text{ cm}$$

If the population from which the y_i's are being drawn is normal, the behavior of

$$\frac{\bar{Y} - \mu}{S/\sqrt{n}}$$

will be described by a Student t curve with 10 degrees of freedom. From Table A.2 in the Appendix,

$$P(-2.2281 < T_{10} < 2.2281) = 0.95$$

Accordingly, the 95% confidence interval for μ is

(continued on next page)

(Case Study 7.5.1 continued)

$$\left(\bar{y} - 2.2281\left(\frac{s}{\sqrt{11}}\right), \bar{y} + 2.2281\left(\frac{s}{\sqrt{11}}\right)\right)$$

$$= \left(48.4 - 2.2281\left(\frac{18.1}{\sqrt{11}}\right), 48.4 + 2.2281\left(\frac{18.1}{\sqrt{11}}\right)\right)$$

$$= (36.2 \text{ cm}, 60.6 \text{ cm}).$$

EXAMPLE 7.5.1

The sample mean and sample standard deviation for the random sample of size $n = 20$ given in the following list are 2.6 and 3.6, respectively. Let μ denote the true mean of the distribution being represented by these y_i's.

2.5	0.1	0.2	1.3
3.2	0.1	0.1	1.4
0.5	0.2	0.4	11.2
0.4	7.4	1.8	2.1
0.3	8.6	0.3	10.1

Is it correct to say that a 95% confidence interval for μ is the set of values

$$\left(\bar{y} - t_{.025, n-1} \cdot \frac{s}{\sqrt{n}}, \bar{y} + t_{.025, n-1} \cdot \frac{s}{\sqrt{n}}\right)$$

$$= \left(2.6 - 2.0930 \cdot \frac{3.6}{\sqrt{20}}, 2.6 + 2.0930 \cdot \frac{3.6}{\sqrt{20}}\right)$$

$$= (0.9, 4.3)$$

No. It *is* true that all the correct factors have been used in calculating $(0.9, 4.3)$, but Theorem 7.5.1 does not apply in this case because the normality assumption it makes is clearly being violated. Figure 7.5.1 is a histogram of the 20 y_i's. The extreme skewness that is so evident there is not consistent with the presumption that the data's underlying pdf is a normal distribution. As a result, the pdf describing the probabilistic behavior of $\dfrac{\bar{Y} - \mu}{S/\sqrt{20}}$ would *not* be $f_{T_{19}}(t)$.

FIGURE 7.5.1

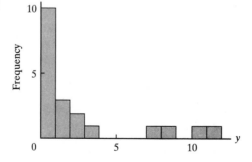

Comment. To say that $\dfrac{\bar{Y} - \mu}{S/\sqrt{20}}$ in this situation is not *exactly* a T_{19} random variable leaves unanswered a critical question: Is the ratio *approximately* a T_{19} random variable? We will revisit the normality assumption—and what happens when that assumption is not satisfied—later in this section when we discuss a critically important property known as *robustness*.

QUESTIONS

7.5.1 The following table lists the costs of repairing minivan bumpers damaged by a 5-mph collision (175). Use these seven observations to construct a 95% confidence interval for μ, the true average repair cost for the population of *all* minivan models that are similarly damaged. *Note*: The sample standard deviation for these data is *$719.43*.

Model	Cost of repairing bumper, y_i
Nissan Quest	$1154
Oldsmobile Silhouette	1106
Dodge Grand Caravan SE	1560
Chevrolet Lumina	1769
Toyota Previa LE	2299
Pontiac Trans Sport SE	1741
Mazda MPV	3179

7.5.2 Creativity, as any number of studies have shown, is very much a province of the young. Whether the focus is music, literature, science, or mathematics, an individual's best work seldom occurs late in life. Einstein, for example, made his most profound discoveries at the age of 26; Newton, at the age of 23. The following are 12 scientific breakthroughs dating from the middle of the sixteenth century to the early years of the twentieth century (192). All represented high-water marks in the careers of the scientists involved.

Discovery	Discoverer	Year	Age, y_i
Earth goes around sun	Copernicus	1543	40
Telescope, basic laws of astronomy	Galileo	1600	34
Principles of motion, gravitation, calculus	Newton	1665	23
Nature of electricity	Franklin	1746	40
Burning is uniting with oxygen	Lavoisier	1774	31
Earth evolved by gradual processes	Lyell	1830	33
Evidence for natural selection controlling evolution	Darwin	1858	49
Field equations for light	Maxwell	1864	33
Radioactivity	Curie	1896	34
Quantum theory	Planck	1901	43
Special theory of relativity, $E = mc^2$	Einstein	1905	26
Mathematical foundations for quantum theory	Schrödinger	1926	39

(a) What can be inferred from these data about the *true* average age at which scientists do their best work? Answer the question by constructing a 95% confidence interval.

(b) Before constructing a confidence interval for a set of observations extending over a long period of time, we should be convinced that the y_i's exhibit no biases or trends. If, for example, the age at which scientists made major discoveries decreased from century to century, then the parameter μ would no longer be a constant, and the confidence interval would be meaningless. Plot "date" versus "age" for these 12 discoveries. Put "date" on the abscissa. Does the variability in the y_i's appear to be random with respect to time?

7.5.3 Fueled by the popularity of low-fat diets, the 1990s saw a profusion of new food products claiming to be "no fat" or "low fat." To assess the impact of those products, measurements were taken on the daily fat intakes of 10 males, ages 25 to 34. What does μ represent in this context?

Use the data—128.1, 57.1, 117.0, 146.1, 84.3, 142.3, 107.8, 86.2, 103.7, and 128.7—to construct a 90% confidence interval for μ. *Note*:

$$\sum_{i=1}^{10} y_i = 1101.3 \quad \text{and} \quad \sum_{i=1}^{10} y_i^2 = 128,428.67$$

7.5.4 Construct a 99% confidence interval for the true average department-store radiation exposure level using the data from Question 7.2.1.

7.5.5 Small and nonprofessional investors would like to reap the benefits available from the stock market but often lack the expertise to select a safe, profitable, and balanced portfolio. For them, participating in a mutual fund can be a good strategy; there the investor relies on experts to do the decision making. *Forbes* magazine lists over 750 such funds. The following is a random sample of 30 of those plans; recorded for each is its annualized total return for the period from 7/31/84 to 7/16/96.

Acorn Fund	17.2
AIM Equity-Aggressive Growth	16.8
American National Growth	13.2
Babson Growth Fund	13.6
Berger Growth & Income	12.4
Composite Growth & Income-A	13.4
Davis Growth Opportunity-A	14.9
Dean Witter Dividend Growth	15.1
Dreyfus Special Growth-Investor	11.6
FBL-Growth Common Stock	11.4
Fidelity Destiny Portfolio I	18.7
Fidelity Retirement Growth	15.7
Fidelity Select-Health Care	22.4
Wayne Hummer Growth	12.9
IDS Discovery Fund-A	11.6
IDS Equity Select-A	14.5
Invesco Advisor-Equity	13.7
Lord Abbett Affiliated Fund	15.0
Mass Investors Growth Stock-A	13.7
Mutual Series-Beacon	16.1
Penn Square Mutual Fund-A	13.7
T Rowe Price Growth & Income	13.2
T Rowe Price New Era	12.9
Royce Fund-Value	11.5
SBSF Fund	13.4
Seligman Growth Fund-A	13.8
SIFE Trust-Class II	16.9
Stratton Monthly Dividend Shares	11.3
USAA Mutual-Aggressive Growth	12.9
Vanguard/Trustees Equity-US	13.3

Suppose an investor chooses a fund from the *Forbes* list at random. Based on the data given here, and assuming the general state of the economy remains the same, what would be a reasonable estimate for the *lowest* annual return that might be realized? The *highest* annual return? *Note*: $\bar{y} = 14.2$ and $s = 2.4$.

7.5.6 If a normally distributed sample of size $n = 16$ produces a 95% confidence interval for μ that ranges from 44.7 to 49.9, what are the values of $\bar{y}$ and s?

7.5.7 Two samples, each of size n, are taken from a normal distribution with unknown mean μ and unknown standard deviation σ. A 90% confidence interval for μ is constructed with the first sample, and a 95% confidence interval for μ is constructed with the second. Will the 95% confidence interval necessarily be longer than the 90% confidence interval? Explain.

7.5.8 Revenues reported last week from nine boutiques franchised by an international clothier averaged $59,540 with a standard deviation of $6,860. Based on those figures, in what range might the company expect to find the average revenue of all of its boutiques?

7.5.9 What "confidence" is associated with each of the following random intervals? Assume that the Y_i's are normally distributed.

(a) $\left(\bar{Y} - 2.0930\left(\dfrac{S}{\sqrt{20}}\right), \bar{Y} + 2.0930\left(\dfrac{S}{\sqrt{20}}\right) \right)$

(b) $\left(\bar{Y} - 1.345\left(\dfrac{S}{\sqrt{15}}\right), \bar{Y} + 1.345\left(\dfrac{S}{\sqrt{15}}\right) \right)$

(c) $\left(\bar{Y} - 1.7056\left(\dfrac{S}{\sqrt{27}}\right), \bar{Y} + 2.7787\left(\dfrac{S}{\sqrt{27}}\right) \right)$

(d) $\left(-\infty, \bar{Y} + 1.7247\left(\dfrac{S}{\sqrt{21}}\right) \right)$

7.5.10 The following are the median home resale prices reported in 17 U.S. cities for the fourth quarter of 1994 (178). Would it be reasonable to estimate the true U.S. median home resale price for that period by substituting these data into Theorem 7.5.1 to find a 95% confidence interval for μ? Explain.

City	Median Selling Price (in thousands)
Albuquerque	$114.5
Atlanta	93.4
Baton Rouge	77.1
Charlotte	104.6
Cleveland	98.1
Dallas	92.3
Denver	119.0
Fort Lauderdale	101.8
Indianapolis	89.2
Memphis	85.1
New Orleans	77.8
Peoria	66.6
Philadelphia	115.4
Richmond	99.2
Sacramento	121.5
Salt Lake City	102.2
Seattle	156.4

Testing H_0: $\mu = \mu_o$ (The one-sample t test)

Suppose a (normally distributed) random sample of size n is observed for the purpose of testing the null hypothesis that $\mu = \mu_o$. If σ is unknown—which is usually the case—the procedure we use is called a *one-sample t test*. Conceptually, the latter is much like the Z test of Theorem 6.2.1, except that the decision rule is defined in terms of $t = \dfrac{\bar{y} - \mu_o}{s/\sqrt{n}}$ rather than $z = \dfrac{\bar{y} - \mu_o}{\sigma/\sqrt{n}}$ [which requires that the critical values come from $f_{T_{n-1}}(t)$ rather than $f_Z(z)$].

THEOREM 7.5.2. Let $y_1, y_2, \ldots, y_n$ be a random sample of size n from a normal distribution where σ is unknown. Let $t = \dfrac{\bar{y} - \mu_o}{s/\sqrt{n}}$.

(a) To test $H_0: \mu = \mu_o$ versus $H_1: \mu > \mu_o$ at the α level of significance, reject H_0 if $t \geq t_{\alpha, n-1}$.

(b) To test $H_0: \mu = \mu_o$ versus $H_1: \mu < \mu_o$ at the α level of significance, reject H_0 if $t \leq -t_{\alpha, n-1}$.

(c) To test $H_0: \mu = \mu_o$ versus $H_1: \mu \neq \mu_o$ at the α level of significance, reject H_0 if t is either (1) $\leq -t_{\alpha/2, n-1}$ or (2) $\geq t_{\alpha/2, n-1}$.

Proof. Appendix 7.A.4 gives the complete derivation that justifies using the procedure described in Theorem 7.5.2. In short, the test statistic $t = \dfrac{\bar{y} - \mu_o}{s/\sqrt{n}}$ is a monotonic function of the λ that appears in Definition 6.5.2, which makes the one-sample t test a GLRT.

EXAMPLE 7.5.2

Pica is a children's disorder characterized by a craving for nonfood substances such as clay, plaster, and paint. Anyone affected runs the risk of ingesting high levels of lead, which can result in kidney damage and neurological dysfunction. Checking a child's blood lead level is a standard procedure for diagnosing the condition.

Among children between the ages of 6 months and 5 years, blood lead levels of 16.0 mg/l are considered "normal." Recently, a random sample of 12 children enrolled in Molly's Mighty Bear Nursery had their blood lead levels checked. The resulting sample mean and sample standard deviation were 18.65 and 5.049, respectively. Can it be concluded that children at this particular facility have a higher risk of pica? At the $\alpha = 0.05$ level, in other words, is the increase from 16.0 to 18.65 statistically significant?

Let μ denote the true average blood lead level for children enrolled at Mighty Bear. The hypotheses to be tested are

$$H_0: \quad \mu = 16.0$$

versus

$$H_1: \quad \mu > 16.0$$

Given that $\alpha = 0.05$, $n = 12$, and H_0 is one sided to the right, the critical value from Part (a) of Theorem 7.5.2 (and Appendix Table A.2) is $t_{.05, 11} = 1.7959$ (see Figure 7.5.2).

Substituting $\bar{y}$ and s into the t ratio gives a test statistic that lies just a little to the right of $t_{.05, 11}$:

$$t = \frac{\bar{y} - \mu_o}{s/\sqrt{n}} = \frac{18.65 - 16.0}{5.049/\sqrt{12}} = 1.82$$

It would be correct to claim, then, that the $\bar{y}$ of 18.65 *does* represent a statistically significant increase in blood lead levels.

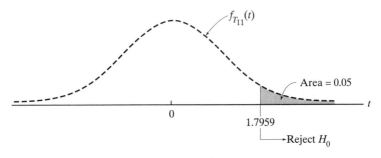

FIGURE 7.5.2

EXAMPLE 7.5.3

Three banks serve a metropolitan area's inner-city neighborhoods: Federal Trust, American United, and Third Union. The state banking commission is concerned that loan applications from inner-city residents are not being accorded the same consideration that comparable requests have received from individuals in rural areas. Both constituencies claim to have anecdotal evidence suggesting that the other group is being given preferential treatment.

Records show that last year these three banks approved 62% of all the home mortgage applications filed by rural residents. Listed in Table 7.5.2 are the approval rates posted over that same period by the 12 branch offices of Federal Trust (FT), American United (AU), and Third Union (TU) that work primarily with the inner-city community. Do these figures lend any credence to the contention that the banks are treating inner-city residents and rural residents differently? Analyze the data using an $\alpha = 0.05$ level of significance.

TABLE 7.5.2

Bank	Location	Affiliation	Percent Approved
1	3rd & Morgan	AU	59
2	Jefferson Pike	TU	65
3	East 150th & Clark	TU	69
4	Midway Mall	FT	53
5	N. Charter Highway	FT	60
6	Lewis & Abbot	AU	53
7	West 10th & Lorain	FT	58
8	Highway 70	FT	64
9	Parkway Northwest	AU	46
10	Lanier & Tower	TU	67
11	King & Tara Court	AU	51
12	Bluedot Corners	FT	59

As a starting point, we might want to test

$$H_0: \quad \mu = 62$$

versus

$$H_1: \quad \mu \neq 62$$

where μ is the true average approval rate for all inner-city banks. Table 7.5.3 summarizes the analysis. The two critical values are $\pm t_{.025, 11} = \pm 2.2010$, and the observed t ratio is $-1.66 \left(= \dfrac{58.667 - 62}{6.946/\sqrt{12}} \right)$, so our decision is "Fail to reject H_0."

TABLE 7.5.3

Banks	n	$\bar{y}$	s	t ratio	Critical value	Reject H_0?
All	12	58.667	6.946	-1.66	± 2.2010	No

The "overall" analysis of Table 7.5.3, though, may be too simplistic. Common sense would tell us to look also at the three banks separately. What emerges, then, is an entirely different picture (see Table 7.5.4). Now we can see why both groups felt discriminated against: American United ($t = -3.63$) and Third Union ($t = +4.33$) each had rates that differed significantly from 62%—*but in opposite directions!* Only Federal Trust seems to be dealing with inner-city residents and rural residents in an even-handed way.

TABLE 7.5.4

Banks	n	$\bar{y}$	s	t ratio	Critical value	Reject H_0?
American United	4	52.25	5.38	-3.63	± 3.1825	Yes
Federal Trust	5	58.80	3.96	-1.81	± 2.7764	No
Third Union	3	67.00	2.00	$+4.33$	± 4.3027	Yes

QUESTIONS

7.5.11 Recall the *Bacillus subtilis* data in Question 5.3.1. Test the null hypothesis that exposure to the enzyme does not affect a worker's respiratory capacity (as measured by the FEV_1/VC ratio). Use a one-sided H_1 and let $\alpha = 0.05$.

7.5.12 Recall Case Study 5.3.1. Assess the credibility of the theory that Etruscans were native Italians by testing an appropriate H_0 against a two-sided H_1. Set α equal to 0.05. Use 143.8 mm and 6.0 mm for $\bar{y}$ and s, respectively, and let $\mu_o = 132.4$. Do these data appear to satisfy the distribution assumption made by the t test? Explain.

7.5.13 MBAs 'R Us advertises that its program increases a person's score on the GMAT by an average of 40 points. As a way of checking the validity of that claim, a consumer watchdog group hires 15 students to take both the review course and the GMAT. Prior to starting the course, the 15 students were given a diagnostic test that predicted how well they would do on the GMAT in the absence of any special training. The following table gives each student's actual GMAT score minus his or her predicted score. Set up and carry out an appropriate hypothesis test. Use the 0.05 level of significance.

Subject	y_i = act. GMAT $-$ pre. GMAT	y_i^2
SA	35	1225
LG	37	1369
SH	33	1089
KN	34	1156
DF	38	1444
SH	40	1600
ML	35	1225
JG	36	1296
KH	38	1444
HS	33	1089
LL	28	784
CE	34	1156
KK	47	2209
CW	42	1764
DP	46	2116

7.5.14 Recall the Shoshoni rectangle data described in Case Study 1.2.2. Let μ denote the true average w/l ratio preferred by the Shoshonis. At the $\alpha = 0.05$ level, test H_0: $\mu = 0.618$ versus H_1: $\mu \neq 0.618$. What does your conclusion suggest about the "universality" of the Golden Rectangle? *Note*: $\bar{y}$ and s for these data are *0.661* and *0.093*, respectively.

7.5.15 A manufacturer of pipe for laying underground electrical cables is concerned about the pipe's rate of corrosion and whether a special coating may retard that rate. As a way of measuring corrosion, the manufacturer examines a short length of pipe and records the depth of the maximum pit. The manufacturer's tests have shown that in a year's time in the particular kind of soil the manufacturer must deal with, the average depth of the maximum pit in a foot of pipe is 0.0042 inches. To see whether that average can be reduced, 10 pipes are coated with a new plastic and buried in the same soil. After one year, the following maximum pit depths are recorded (in inches): 0.0039, 0.0041, 0.0038, 0.0044, 0.0040, 0.0036, 0.0034, 0.0036, 0.0046, and 0.0036. Given that the sample standard deviation for these 10 measurements is 0.00383 inches, can it be concluded at the $\alpha = 0.05$ level of significance that the plastic coating is beneficial?

7.5.16 The first analysis done in Example 7.5.3 (using all $n = 12$ banks with $\bar{y} = 58.667$) failed to reject H_0: $\mu = 62$ at the $\alpha = 0.05$ level. Had μ_o been, say, 61.7 or 58.6, the same conclusion would have been reached. What do we call the entire set of μ_o's for which H_0: $\mu = \mu_o$ would *not* be rejected at the $\alpha = 0.05$ level?

Testing H_0: $\mu = \mu_o$ When the Normality Assumption Is Not Met

Every t test makes the same explicit assumption—namely, that the set of n y_i's is normally distributed. But suppose the normality assumption is *not* true. What are the consequences? Is the validity of the t test compromised?

Figure 7.5.3 addresses the first question. We know that if the normality assumption *is* true, the pdf describing the variation of the t ratio, $\dfrac{\bar{Y} - \mu_o}{S/\sqrt{n}}$, is $f_{T_{n-1}}(t)$. The latter, of course, provides the decision rule's critical values. If H_0: $\mu = \mu_o$ is to be tested against $H_1: \mu \neq \mu_o$, for example, the null hypothesis is rejected if t is either (1) $\leq -t_{\alpha/2, n-1}$ or (2) $\geq t_{\alpha/2, n-1}$ (which makes the Type I error probability equal to α).

If the normality assumption is *not* true, the pdf of $\dfrac{\bar{Y} - \mu_o}{S/\sqrt{n}}$ will not be $f_{T_{n-1}}(t)$

and

$$P\left(\frac{\bar{Y} - \mu_o}{S/\sqrt{n}} \leq -t_{\alpha/2,\, n-1}\right) + P\left(\frac{\bar{Y} - \mu_o}{S/\sqrt{n}} \geq t_{\alpha/2,\, n-1}\right) \neq \alpha$$

In effect, violating the normality assumption creates *two* α's: The "nominal" α is the Type I error probability we specify at the outset—typically, 0.05 or 0.01. The "true" α is the actual probability that $\dfrac{\bar{Y} - \mu_o}{S/\sqrt{n}}$ falls in the rejection region (when H_0 is true). For the two-sided decision rule pictured in Figure 7.5.3,

$$\text{true } \alpha = \int_{-\infty}^{-t_{\alpha/2,\, n-1}} f_{T*}(t)\, dt + \int_{t_{\alpha/2,\, n-1}}^{\infty} f_{T*}(t)\, dt$$

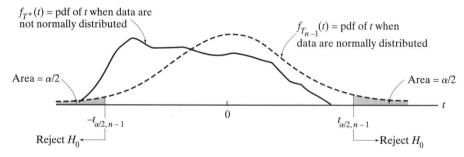

FIGURE 7.5.3

Whether or not the validity of the t test is "compromised" by the normality assumption being violated depends on the numerical difference between the two α's. If $f_{T*}(t)$ is, in fact, quite similar in shape and location to $f_{T_{n-1}}(t)$, then the true α will be approximately equal to the nominal α. In that case, the fact that the y_i's are not normally distributed would be essentially irrelevant. On the other hand, if $f_{T*}(t)$ and $f_{T_{n-1}}(t)$ are dramatically different (as they appear to be in Figure 7.5.3), it would follow that the normality assumption *is* critical, and establishing the "significance" of a t ratio becomes problematic.

Unfortunately, getting an exact expression for $f_{T*}(t)$ is essentially impossible, because the distribution depends on the pdf being sampled, and there is seldom any way of knowing precisely what that pdf might be. However, we can still meaningfully explore the sensitivity of the t ratio to violations of the normality assumption by simulating samples of size n from selected distributions and comparing the resulting histogram of t ratios to $f_{T_{n-1}}(t)$.

Figure 7.5.4 shows four such simulations, using MINITAB; the first three consist of 100 random samples of size $n = 6$. In Figure 7.5.4(a), the samples come from a uniform pdf defined over the interval $[0, 1]$; in Figure 7.5.4(b), the underlying pdf is the exponential with $\lambda = 1$; and in Figure 7.5.4(c), the data are coming from a Poisson pdf with $\lambda = 5$.

(a)

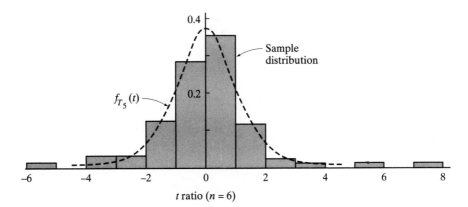

Probability density

1

$f_Y(y) = 1$

0 1 y

```
MTB > random 100 c1-c6;
SUBC> uniform 01.
MTB > rmean c1-c6 c7
MTB > rstdev c1-c6 c8
MTB > let c9 = sqrt(6)*(((c7) - 0.5)/(c8))
MTB > histogram c9;
SUBC> start -5.5;
SUBC> increment 1.
```

This command calculates

$$\frac{\bar{y} - \mu}{s/\sqrt{n}} = \frac{\bar{y} - 0.5}{s/\sqrt{6}}$$

```
Histogram of C9    N = 100

Midpoint   Count
 -5.500      1    *
 -4.500      0
 -3.500      3    ***
 -2.500      3    ***
 -1.500     12    ************
 -0.500     29    *****************************
  0.500     36    ************************************
  1.500     11    ***********
  2.500      2    **
  3.500      1    *
  4.500      0
  5.500      1    *
  6.500      0
  7.500      1    *
```

0.4

Sample
distribution

$f_{T_5}(t)$

0.2

-6 -4 -2 0 2 4 6 8

t ratio ($n = 6$)

FIGURE 7.5.4

(b)

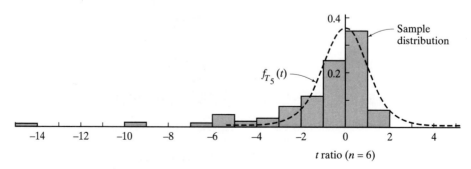

```
MTB > random 100 c1-c6;
SUBC> exponential 1.
MTB > rmean c1-c6 c7
MTB > rstdev c1-c6 c8
MTB > let c9 = sqrt(6)*(((c7) - 1.0)/(c8))
MTB > histogram c9;
SUBC> start -14.5;
SUBC> increment 1.
```

$$\left[= \frac{\bar{y} - \mu}{s/\sqrt{6}} \right]$$

```
Histogram of C9     N = 100

Midpoint    Count
 -14.500      1   *
 -13.500      0
 -12.500      0
 -11.500      0
 -10.500      0
  -9.500      1   *
  -8.500      0
  -7.500      0
  -6.500      1   *
  -5.500      4   ****
  -4.500      2   **
  -3.500      3   ***
  -2.500      8   ********
  -1.500     11   ***********
  -0.500     25   *************************
   0.500     37   *************************************
   1.500      7   *******
```

FIGURE 7.5.4   *(continued)*

(c)

```
MTB > random 100 c1-c6;
SUBC> poisson 5.
MTB > rmean c1-c6 c7
MTB > rstdev c1-c6 c8
MTB > let c9 = sqrt(6)*(((c7) - 5.0)/(c8))
MTB > histogram c9;
SUBC> start -4.500;
SUBC> increment 1.

Histogram of C9    N = 100

Midpoint   Count
 -4.500      1    *
 -3.500      3    ***
 -2.500      3    ***
 -1.500     11    ***********
 -0.500     32    ********************************
  0.500     37    *************************************
  1.500     10    **********
  2.500      2    **
  3.500      1    *
```

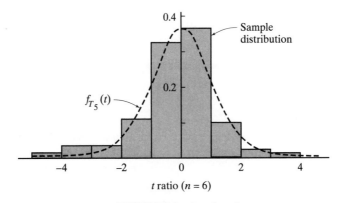

FIGURE 7.5.4   *(continued)*

(**d**)

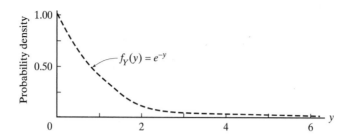

```
MTB > random 100 cl-cl5;
SUBC> exponential 1.
MTB > rmean cl-cl5 cl6
MTB > rstdev cl-cl5 cl7
MTB > let cl8 = sqrt(15)*(((cl6 1.0)/(cl7))
MTB > histogram cl8;
SUBC> start -3.5;
SUBC> increment 1.
```

Character Histogram

```
Histogram of C18     N = 100

Midpoint   Count
  -3.500       2   **
  -2.500       5   *****
  -1.500      15   ***************
  -0.500      25   *************************
   0.500      42   ******************************************
   1.500      10   **********
   2.500       1   *
```

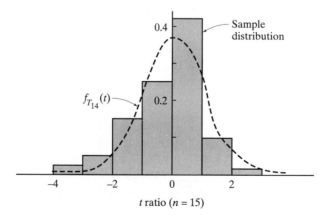

FIGURE 7.5.4   *(continued)*

If the normality assumption were true, t ratios based on samples of size 6 would vary in accordance with the Student t distribution with 5 df. At the bottom of pages 441–443, $f_{T_5}(t)$ has been superimposed over the histograms of the t ratios coming from the three different pdf's. What we see there is really quite remarkable. The t ratios based on y_i's coming from a uniform pdf, for example, are behaving much the same way as t ratios would vary if the y_i's were normally distributed—that is, $f_{T*}(t)$ in this case appears to be very similar to $f_{T_5}(t)$. The same is true for samples coming from a Poisson distribution (see page 443). For both of those underlying pdf's, in other words, the true α would not be much different than the nominal α.

Figure 7.5.4(b) tells a slightly different story. When samples of size 6 are drawn from an exponential pdf, the t ratios are *not* in particularly close agreement with $f_{T_5}(t)$. Specifically, very negative t ratios are occurring much more often than the Student t curve would predict, while large positive t ratios are occurring less often (see Question 7.5.17). But look at Figure 7.5.4(d). When the sample size is increased to $n = 15$, the skewness so prominent in Figure 7.5.4(b) is mostly gone.

Reflected in these specific simulations are some general properties of the t ratio:

1. The distribution of $t = \dfrac{\bar{Y} - \mu}{S/\sqrt{n}}$ is relatively unaffected by the pdf of the y_i's [provided $f_Y(y)$ is not too skewed and n is not too small].

2. As n increases, the pdf of $t = \dfrac{\bar{Y} - \mu}{S/\sqrt{n}}$ becomes increasingly similar to $f_{T_{n-1}}(t)$.

In mathematical statistics, the term *robust* is used to describe a procedure that is not heavily dependent on whatever assumptions it makes. Figure 7.5.4 shows that the *t test is robust with respect to departures from normality*.

From a practical standpoint, it would be difficult to overstate the importance of the t test being robust. If the pdf of $\dfrac{\bar{Y} - \mu}{S/\sqrt{n}}$ varied dramatically depending on the origin of the y_i's, we would never know if the true α associated with, say, a 0.05 decision rule was anywhere near 0.05. That degree of uncertainty would make the t test virtually worthless.

QUESTIONS

7.5.17 Explain why the distribution of t ratios calculated from small samples drawn from the exponential pdf, $f_Y(y) = e^{-y}$, $y \geq 0$, will be skewed to the left (recall Figure 7.5.4(b)). *Hint*: What does the shape of $f_Y(y)$ imply about the possibility of each y_i being close to 0? If the entire sample did consist of y_i's close to 0, what value would the t ratio have?

7.5.18 Suppose 100 samples of size $n = 3$ are taken from each of the pdf's

$$\textbf{(1)}\ \ f_Y(y) = 2y, \qquad 0 \leq y \leq 1$$

and

$$\textbf{(2)}\ \ f_Y(y) = 4y^3, \qquad 0 \leq y \leq 1$$

and for each set of three observations the ratio

$$\frac{\bar{Y} - \mu}{S/\sqrt{3}}$$

is calculated, where μ is the expected value of the particular pdf being sampled. How would you expect the distributions of the two sets of ratios to be different? How would they be similar? Be as specific as possible.

7.5.19 Suppose that random samples of size n are drawn from the uniform pdf, $f_Y(y) = 1, 0 \le y \le 1$. For each sample, the ratio $t = \dfrac{\bar{Y} - 0.5}{S/\sqrt{n}}$ is calculated. Parts (a) and (d) of Figure 7.5.4 suggest that the pdf of t will become increasingly similar to $f_{T_{n-1}}(t)$ as n increases. To which pdf is $f_{T_{n-1}}(t)$, itself, converging as n increases?

7.5.20 On which of the following sets of data would you be reluctant to do a t test? Explain.

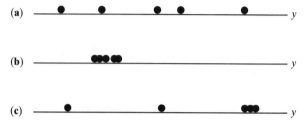

Power Calculations and Sample Size Determinations (Optional)

If the assumptions of Theorem 7.5.2 are satisfied, we know that the probability of committing a Type I error with a one-sample t test is α. But what about a Type II error? If $\mu = \mu_1$, where $\mu_1 \ne \mu_o$, what are the chances that the observed $\bar{y}$ and s will take on values that will "deceive" the decision maker into *accepting* H_0? To answer that question requires the following result, which gives the sampling distribution of the t ratio when H_1, rather than H_0, is true.

> **THEOREM 7.5.3.** Let $Y_1, Y_2, \ldots, Y_n$ be a random sample from a normal distribution with mean μ_1 and variance σ^2. Define
>
> $$T_\Delta = \frac{\bar{Y} - \mu_1 + \Delta}{S/\sqrt{n}} = \frac{\bar{Y} - \mu_o}{S/\sqrt{n}}$$
>
> where $\Delta = \mu_1 - \mu_o$. Then T_Δ is said to be a noncentral T variable with $n - 1$ degrees of freedom and noncentrality parameter γ, where
>
> $$\gamma = \frac{\sqrt{n}\,\Delta}{\sigma}$$
>
> Also,
>
> $$f_{T_\Delta}(t) = \frac{e^{-(1/2)\gamma^2} \Gamma\left(\dfrac{n}{2}\right)}{\sqrt{\pi(n-1)}\,\Gamma\left(\dfrac{n}{2} - \dfrac{1}{2}\right)} \left(1 + \frac{t^2}{n-1}\right)^{-n/2} g(t)$$

where

$$g(t) = \sum_{r=0}^{\infty} \left(\frac{\sqrt{2}\,\gamma t}{\sqrt{n-1}} \right)^r \left[1 + \left(\frac{t^2}{n-1} \right) \right]^{-r/2} \frac{\Gamma[(1/2)(n+r)]}{r!\,\Gamma(n/2)}$$

The probability of committing a Type II error, given that $\mu = \mu_1$, is the integral of $f_{T_\Delta}(t)$ between the two critical values defined by the original decision rule:

$$P(\text{accept } H_0 \mid H_1 \text{ is true and } \mu = \mu_1)$$

$$= P\left[-t_{\alpha/2,\,n-1} < \frac{\bar{Y} - \mu_0}{S/\sqrt{n}} < t_{\alpha/2,\,n-1} \,\middle|\, \mu = \mu_1 \right]$$

$$= P\left[-t_{\alpha/2,\,n-1} < \frac{\bar{Y} - \mu_1 + \Delta}{S/\sqrt{n}} < t_{\alpha/2,\,n-1} \,\middle|\, \mu = \mu_1 \right]$$

$$= \int_{-t_{\alpha/2,\,n-1}}^{t_{\alpha/2,\,n-1}} f_{T_\Delta}(t)\,dt = \beta$$

Therefore, the *power* of the test (at $\mu = \mu_1$ and for some specified noncentrality parameter γ) is the sum of two integrals:

$$1 - \beta = \int_{-\infty}^{-t_{\alpha/2,\,n-1}} f_{T_\Delta}(t)\,dt + \int_{t_{\alpha/2,\,n-1}}^{\infty} f_{T_\Delta}(t)\,dt \tag{7.5.2}$$

Figure 7.5.5 gives solutions to Equation 7.5.2 for a broad range of sample sizes and noncentrality parameters. The ordinate on the graph is simply $1 - \beta$; the abscissa is expressed in terms of ϕ, where $\phi = \gamma/\sqrt{2} = \sqrt{n/2}\,(\Delta/\sigma)$. Making up the body of the table are two sets of curves corresponding to two-sided tests at the $\alpha = 0.01$ and $\alpha = 0.05$ levels of significance. (If H_1 is one sided, these same two sets of curves give $1 - \beta$ for tests at levels 0.005 and 0.025, respectively.)

Problems requiring Figure 7.5.5 generally fall into one of two categories:

1. Find β (or $1 - \beta$) when the true mean has shifted a certain number of standard deviations away from the H_0 mean.
2. Find the smallest sample size that achieves a specified probability of rejecting H_0 when μ has shifted a given distance away from μ_o.

The second problem, which is the more important of the two, is the Student t version of the "sample size" question introduced in Example 6.4.1 for the simpler case where σ is known and the test statistic is a Z ratio.

EXAMPLE 7.5.4

Suppose an experimenter wishes to test

$$H_0: \quad \mu = \mu_o$$

$$\text{versus}$$

$$H_1: \quad \mu \neq \mu_o$$

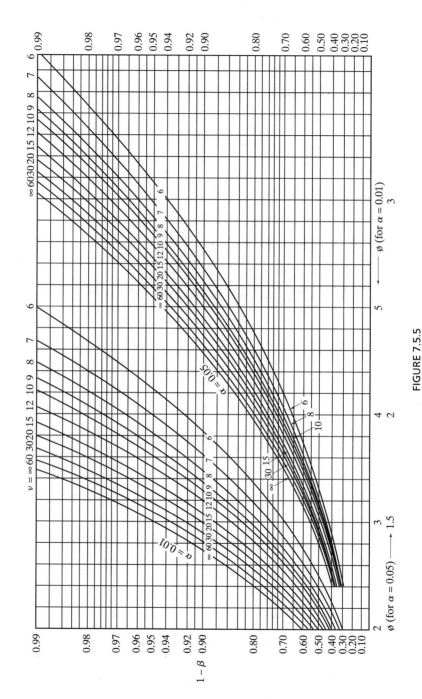

FIGURE 7.5.5

448

at the $\alpha = 0.05$ level of significance, using a sample of size $n = 20$. What is the probability of rejecting H_0 if the true μ has shifted 0.5 standard deviations to the right of μ_o—that is, what is $1 - \beta$ when $\dfrac{\Delta}{\sigma} = 0.5$?

Notice, first of all, that with H_1 being two sided and $n = 20$, the $\alpha = 0.05$ decision rule is

$$\text{``Reject } H_0\colon \mu = \mu_o \text{ if } \frac{\bar{y} - \mu_o}{s/\sqrt{20}} \text{ is either}$$

$$(1) \le -2.093 \quad \text{or} \quad (2) \ge 2.093\text{''} \quad \left(\text{where } \pm 2.093 = \pm t_{.025,19}\right).$$

Therefore,

$$P\left(\text{reject } H_0 \,\Big|\, \frac{\Delta}{\sigma} = 0.5\right) = 1 - \beta$$

$$= \int_{-\infty}^{-2.093} f_{T_\Delta}\left(t; \frac{\Delta}{\sigma} = 0.5\right) dt + \int_{2.093}^{\infty} f_{T_\Delta}\left(t; \frac{\Delta}{\sigma} = 0.5\right) dt \qquad (7.5.3)$$

To use Figure 7.5.5 to evaluate the integrals in Equation 7.5.3, we first must calculate ϕ. Here,

$$\phi = \sqrt{\frac{n}{2}} \cdot \frac{\Delta}{\sigma} = \sqrt{\frac{20}{2}} \cdot (0.5) = 1.58$$

A vertical line, then, should be drawn from the point $\phi = 1.58$ on the horizontal axis to the $19(= n - 1)$ df curve and extended horizontally to the vertical axis. The corresponding $1 - \beta$ is approximately 0.57.

Figure 7.5.6 shows the $\alpha = 0.05$ rejection region and both the H_0 and H_1 distributions of $\dfrac{\bar{Y} - \mu_o}{S/\sqrt{20}}$. The probability of rejecting H_0 when $\dfrac{\Delta}{\sigma} = 0.5$—which is the 0.57 that we found from Figure 7.5.5—is the *unshaded* area under the noncentral t distribution. The shaded area ($= 0.43$) is β, the probability of committing a Type II error.

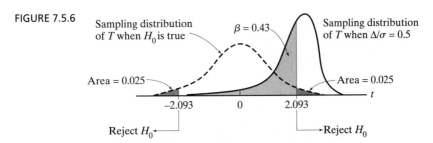

FIGURE 7.5.6

Sampling distribution of T when H_0 is true

$\beta = 0.43$

Sampling distribution of T when $\Delta/\sigma = 0.5$

Area = 0.025

Area = 0.025

t

-2.093 0 2.093

Reject H_0 Reject H_0

As μ gets farther and farther away from μ_o, it makes sense that $1 - \beta$ should *increase* because the H_1 distribution of $\dfrac{\bar{Y} - \mu_o}{S/\sqrt{n}}$ will have increasingly less overlap with the H_0 distribution of $\dfrac{\bar{Y} - \mu_o}{S/\sqrt{n}}$. Figure 7.5.7 shows the situation when $\dfrac{\Delta}{\sigma} = 0.75$. In this case, $\phi = \sqrt{\dfrac{20}{2}}\,(0.75) = 2.37$, and $1 - \beta$, according to Figure 7.5.5, is approximately 0.89.

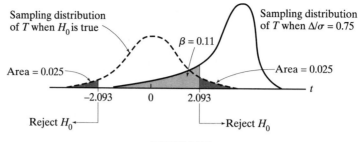

FIGURE 7.5.7

Figure 7.5.8 gives the complete power function for testing $H_0: \mu = \mu_o$ under these conditions. The two +'s on the curve correspond to Δ/σ values of 0.50 and 0.75.

FIGURE 7.5.8

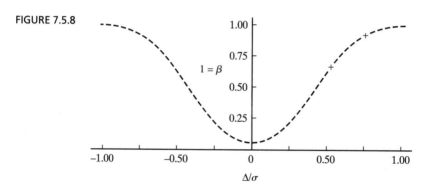

EXAMPLE 7.5.5

What is the smallest number of normally distributed observations that will allow us to test

$$H_0: \quad \mu = \mu_o$$

versus

$$H_1: \quad \mu \neq \mu_o$$

at the $\alpha = 0.05$ level of significance with a power equal to 0.90 when $\Delta/\sigma = 0.70$?

Answering sample size questions of this sort requires a trial-and-error approach. We choose an n, calculate the associated ϕ, and use the $n - 1$ df curve in Figure 7.5.5 to find the corresponding $1 - \beta$. If $1 - \beta$ is not as large as the targeted value, we choose a larger n and repeat the process.

Here,

$$\phi = \sqrt{\frac{n}{2} \cdot \frac{\Delta}{\sigma}} = \sqrt{\frac{n}{2}}(0.70)$$

As a first guess, suppose we let $n = 10$. Then $\phi = \sqrt{10/2} \cdot (0.70) = 1.57$. From Figure 7.5.5 the corresponding $1 - \beta$ (using the $10 - 1 = 9$ df curve) is *0.50*, which is less than the desired 0.90, implying that $n = 10$ is too small a sample size.

TABLE 7.5.5

n	$\phi = \sqrt{\dfrac{n}{2}} \cdot (0.70)$	df	$1 - \beta$
10	1.57	9	0.50
15	1.92	14	0.69
20	2.21	19	0.85
23	2.37	22	0.89
24	2.42	23	0.90

Table 7.5.5 shows a range of sample sizes, together with the value of $1 - \beta$ each would achieve when $\Delta/\sigma = 0.70$. The smallest n that meets the test's stated objectives is *24*.

QUESTIONS

7.5.21 Suppose an experimenter plans to test $H_0: \mu = 0.10$ versus $H_1: \mu \neq 0.10$ at the 0.05 level of significance. She wants the inference procedure to be sufficiently precise so that if $|\mu - 0.10|/\sigma$ is greater than 0. 60, H_0 will be rejected at least 90% of the time. How large should n be?

7.5.22 What is the probability of committing a Type II error when $\Delta/\sigma = 0.80$ if $H_0: \mu = 20$ is tested against $H_1: \mu \neq 20$ at the $\alpha = 0.01$ level of significance using a sample of size $n = 25$?

7.5.23 What is the smallest sample size that has at least a 70% chance of detecting that μ has shifted 1.2 standard deviations to the right of μ_o if $H_0: \mu = \mu_o$ is tested against $H_1: \mu \neq \mu_o$ at (a) the 0.05 level of significance and (b) the 0.01 level of significance?

7.5.24 For a given $\mu \neq \mu_o$, the probability that a t test rejects $H_0: \mu = \mu_o$ in favor of $H_1: \mu \neq \mu_o$ increases as n gets larger. Draw two sets of diagrams showing the central and noncentral t distributions when $n = n_1$ and $n = n_2$, where n_2 is greater than n_1. Show on the diagrams why $1 - \beta$ is larger when $n = n_2$. That is, what happens to $f_{T_{n-1}}(t)$ and $f_{T_\Delta}(t)$ when n increases from n_1 to n_2?

7.5.25 Seven observations have been collected for the purpose of testing $H_0: \mu = 5.0$ versus $H_1: \mu \neq 5.0$ at the $\alpha = 0.05$ level of significance. Suppose H_1 is true and the true mean has shifted two standard deviations to the left of 5.0 $(= \mu_o)$. How often will the test reject H_0?

APPENDIX 7.A.1   MINITAB APPLICATIONS

Many statistical procedures, including several featured in this chapter, require that the sample mean and sample standard deviation be calculated. MINITAB's DESCRIBE command gives $\bar{y}$ and s, along with several other useful numerical characteristics of a sample. Figure 7.A.1.1 shows the DESCRIBE input and output for the 20 observations cited in Example 7.5.1.

```
MTB > set c1
DATA> 2.5 3.2 0.5 0.4 0.3 0.1 0.1 0.2 7.4 8.6 0.2 0.1
DATA> 0.4 1.8 0.3 1.3 1.4 11.2 2.1 10.1
DATA> end
MTB > describe c1
```

Descriptive Statistics

Variable	N	Mean	Median	TrMean	StDev	SEMean
C1	20	2.610	0.900	2.272	3.617	0.809

Variable	Min	Max	Q1	Q3
C1	0.100	11.200	0.225	3.025

FIGURE 7.A.1.1

Here,

```
N = sample size
Mean = sample mean = ȳ
Median = middle observation (in terms of magnitude), or average of
         the middle two if n is even
TrMean = trimmed mean = average of the "middle" 90% of a sample; that
         is, the average of the yᵢ's that remain after the smallest 5%
         have been deleted and the largest 5% have been deleted
StDev = sample standard deviation = s
SEMean = standard error of the mean = s/√n
Min = smallest observation
Max = largest observation
Q1 = first quartile = 25th percentile
Q3 = third quartile = 75th percentile
```

If only the sample mean or the sample standard deviation is required, the commands

```
MTB > mean c1
```

and

```
MTB > standard deviation c1
```

will calculate $\bar{y}$ and s, respectively,

Describing Samples Using MINITAB Windows

1. Enter data in C1. Click on STAT, then on DISPLAY DESCRIPTIVE STATISTICS.
2. Type C1 in Variables box; click on OK.

Percentiles of chi-square, t, and F distributions can be obtained using the INVCDF command introduced in Appendix 3.A.1. Figure 7.A.1.2 shows the syntax for printing out $\chi^2_{.95,6}(= 12.592)$ and $F_{.01,4,7}(= 0.067)$.

To find Student t cutoffs, the $t_{\alpha,n-1}$ notation needs to be expressed as a percentile. We have defined $t_{.10,13}$, for example, to be the value for which

$$P(T_{13} \geq t_{.10,13}) = 0.10$$

In the terminology of the INVCDF command, though, $t_{.10,13}(= 1.350)$ is the *90th* percentile of the $f_{T_{13}}(t)$ pdf (see Figure 7.A.1.3).

```
MTB > invcdf 0.95;
SUBC> chisq 6.
```
Inverse Cumulative Distribution Function
```
Chisquare with 6 d.f.

P( X <= x)         x
   0.9500     12.5916

MTB > invcdf 0.01;
SUBC> f 4 7.
```
Inverse Cumulative Distribution Function
```
F distribution with 4 d.f. in numerator and 7 d.f. in denominator

P( X <= x)        x
   0.0100     0.0668
```

FIGURE 7.A.1.2

```
MTB > invcdf 0.90;
SUBC> t 13.
```
Inverse Cumulative Distribution Function
```
Student's t distribution with 13 d.f.
P( X <= x)         x
   0.9000     1.3502
```

FIGURE 7.A.1.3

The MINITAB command for constructing a confidence interval for μ (Theorem 7.5.1) is "TINTERVAL X Y", where X denotes the desired value for the confidence coefficient $100(1 - \alpha)$ and Y is the column where the data are stored. Figure 7.A.1.4 shows the TINTERVAL command applied to the bat data from Case Study 7.5.1; $100(1 - \alpha)$ is taken to be 0.95.

```
MTB > set c1
DATA> 62 52 68 23 34 45 27 42 83 56 40
DATA> end
MTB > tinterval 0.95 c1
```
Confidence Intervals
```
Variable    N     Mean    StDev    SE Mean      95.0 %  C.I.
C1         11    48.36    18.08       5.45    ( 36.21,     60.52)
```

FIGURE 7.A.1.4

Constructing Confidence Intervals Using MINITAB Windows

1. Enter data in c1.
2. Click on STAT, then on BASIC STATISTICS, then on 1-SAMPLE T.
3. Enter c1 in Variables box, click on CONFIDENCE INTERVAL, and enter the value of $100(1 - \alpha)$. Click on OK.

Figure 7.A.1.5 shows the input and output for doing a t test on the approval data given in Table 7.5.2. The basic command is "TTEST X Y", where X is the value of μ_o and Y is the column where the data are stored. If no other punctuation is used, the program automatically takes H_1 to be two sided. If a one-sided test, *to the right* is desired, we write

```
MTB  > ttest X Y;
SUBC > alternative +1.
```

For a one-sided test *to the left*, the subcommand becomes "alternative −1".

```
MTB > set c1
DATA> 59 65 69 53 60 53 58 64 46 67 51 59
DATA> end
MTB > ttest 62 c1
```

T-Test of the Mean

Test of mu = 62.00 vs mu not = 62.00

Variable	N	Mean	StDev	SE Mean	T	P-Value
C1	12	58.67	6.95	2.01	-1.66	0.12

FIGURE 7.A.1.5

Notice that no value for α is entered, and the conclusion is not phrased as either "Accept H_0" or "Reject H_0." Rather, the analysis ends with the calculation of the data's *P-value*.

Here,

$$P\text{-value} = P(T_{11} \leq -1.66) + P(T_{11} \geq 1.66)$$

$$= 0.06 + 0.06$$

$$= 0.12$$

(recall Definition 6.2.3). Since the *P-value* exceeds the intended $\alpha(= 0.05)$, the conclusion is "Fail to reject H_0."

Testing $H_0: \mu = \mu_0$ Using MINITAB Windows

1. Enter data in c1.
2. Click on STAT, then on BASIC STATISTICS, then on 1-SAMPLE T.
3. Type c1 in Variables box; click on TEST MEAN and enter value of μ_0.
4. Click on NOT EQUAL, then on whichever H_1 is desired. Click on OK.

APPENDIX 7.A.2   SOME DISTRIBUTION RESULTS FOR $\bar{Y}$ AND S^2

THEOREM 7.A.2.1.   Let $Y_1, Y_2, \ldots, Y_n$ be a random sample of size n from a normal distribution with mean μ and variance σ^2. Define

$$\bar{Y} = \frac{1}{n} \sum_{i=1}^{n} Y_i \quad \text{and} \quad S^2 = \frac{1}{n-1} \sum_{i=1}^{n} (Y_i - \bar{Y})^2$$

Then

(a) $\bar{Y}$ and S^2 are independent.

(b) $\dfrac{(n-1)S^2}{\sigma^2}$ has a chi-square distribution with $n-1$ degrees of freedom.

Proof.   The proof of this theorem relies on certain linear algebra techniques as well as a change-of-variables formula for multiple integrals. Definition 7.A.2.1 and the lemma that follows review the necessary background results. For further details, see (43) or (200).

DEFINITION 7.A.2.1.

(a) A matrix A is said to be *orthogonal* if $AA^T = I$.

(b) Let β be any n-dimensional vector over the real numbers. That is, $\beta = (c_1, c_2, \ldots, c_n)$, where each c_j is a real number. The *length* of β will be defined as

$$\|\beta\| = (c_1^2 + \cdots + c_n^2)^{1/2}$$

(Note that $\|\beta\|^2 = \beta\beta^T$.)

LEMMA.

(a) A matrix A is orthogonal if and only if

$$\|A\beta\| = \|\beta\| \quad \text{for each } \beta$$

(b) If a matrix A is orthogonal, then $\det A = 1$.

(c) Let g be a one-to-one continuous mapping on a subset, D, of n-space. Then

$$\int_{g(D)} f(x_1, \ldots, x_n) \, dx_1 \cdots dx_n = \int_D f(g(y_1, \ldots, y_n)) \det J(g) \, dy_1 \cdots dy_n$$

where $J(g)$ is the Jacobian of the transformation.

Set $X_i = (Y_i - \mu)/\sigma$ for $i = 1, 2, \ldots, n$. Then all the X_i's are $N(0, 1)$. Let A be an $n \times n$ orthogonal matrix whose last row is $(1/\sqrt{n}, 1/\sqrt{n}, \ldots, 1/\sqrt{n})$. Let $\vec{X} = (X_1, \ldots, X_n)^T$ and define $\vec{Z} = (Z_1, Z_2, \ldots, Z_n)^T$ by the transformation $\vec{Z} = A\vec{X}$. [Note that $Z_n = (1/\sqrt{n})X_1 + \cdots + (1/\sqrt{n})X_n = \sqrt{n}\,\bar{X}$.]

For any set D,

$$P(\vec{Z} \in D) = P(A\vec{X} \in D) = P(\vec{X} \in A^{-1}D)$$

$$= \int_{A^{-1}D} f_{X_1,\ldots,X_n}(x_1,\ldots,x_n)\,dx_1\cdots dx_n$$

$$= \int_D f_{X_1,\ldots,X_n}(g(\vec{z}))\det J(g)\,dz_1\cdots dz_n$$

$$= \int_D f_{X_1,\ldots,X_n}(A^{-1}\vec{z})\cdot 1 \cdot dz_1\cdots dz_n$$

where $g(\vec{z}) = A^{-1}\vec{z}$. But A^{-1} is orthogonal, so setting $(x_1,\ldots,x_n)^T = A^{-1}z$, we have that

$$x_1^2 + \cdots + x_n^2 = z_1^2 + \cdots + z_n^2$$

Thus

$$f_{X_1,\ldots,X_n}(\vec{x}) = (2\pi)^{-n/2}e^{-(1/2)(x_1^2+\cdots+x_n^2)}$$

$$= (2\pi)^{-n/2}e^{-(1/2)(z_1^2+\cdots+z_n^2)}$$

From this we conclude that

$$P(\vec{Z} \in D) = \int_D (2\pi)^{-n/2}e^{-(n/2)(z_1^2+\cdots+z_n^2)}\,dz_1\cdots dz_n$$

implying that the Z_j's are independent standard normals.

Finally,

$$\sum_{j=1}^n Z_j^2 = \sum_{j=1}^{n-1} Z_j^2 + n\bar{X}^2 = \sum_{j=1}^n X_j^2 = \sum_{j=1}^n (X_j - \bar{X})^2 + n\bar{X}^2$$

Therefore,

$$\sum_{j=1}^{n-1} Z_j^2 = \sum_{j=1}^n (X_j - \bar{X})^2$$

and the conclusion follows for standard normal variables. Also, since $\bar{Y} = \sigma\bar{X} + \mu$ and $\sum_{i=1}^n (Y_i - \bar{Y})^2 = \sigma^2 \sum_{i=1}^n (X_i - \bar{X})^2$, the conclusion follows for $N(\mu,\sigma^2)$ variables.

Comment. As part of the proof just presented, we established a version of *Fisher's lemma*:

Let $X_1, X_2,\ldots,X_n$ be independent standard normal random variables and let A be an orthogonal matrix. Define $(Z_1,\ldots,Z_n)^T = A(X_1,\ldots,X_n)^T$. Then the Z_j's are independent standard normal random variables.

APPENDIX 7.A.3   A PROOF OF THEOREM 7.3.5

We begin by considering the test of $H_0: \sigma^2 = \sigma_o^2$ against a two-sided H_1. The relevant parameter spaces are

$$\omega = \{(\mu, \sigma^2): \quad -\infty < \mu < \infty, \quad \sigma^2 = \sigma_0^2\}$$

and

$$\Omega = \{(\mu, \sigma^2): \quad -\infty < \mu < \infty, \quad 0 \le \sigma^2\}$$

In both, the MLE for μ is $\bar{y}$. In ω, the MLE for σ^2 is simply σ_0^2; in Ω, $\hat{\sigma}^2 = (1/n)\sum_{i=1}^{n}(y_i - \bar{y})^2$ (see Section 7.2). Therefore, the two likelihood functions, maximized over ω and over Ω, are

$$L(\hat{\omega}) = \left(\frac{1}{2\pi\sigma_0^2}\right)^{n/2} \exp\left[-\frac{1}{2}\sum_{i=1}^{n}\left(\frac{y_i - \bar{y}}{\sigma_0}\right)^2\right]$$

and

$$L(\hat{\Omega}) = \left[\frac{n}{2\pi\sum_{i=1}^{n}(y_i - \bar{y})^2}\right]^{n/2} \exp\left\{-\frac{n}{2}\sum_{i=1}^{n}\left[\frac{y_i - \bar{y}}{\sqrt{\sum_{i=1}^{n}(y_i - \bar{y})^2}}\right]^2\right\}$$

$$= \left[\frac{n}{2\pi\sum_{i=1}^{n}(y_i - \bar{y})^2}\right]^{n/2} e^{-n/2}$$

It follows that the generalized-likelihood-ratio criterion is given by

$$\lambda = \frac{L(\hat{\omega})}{L(\hat{\Omega})}$$

$$= \left[\frac{\sum_{i=1}^{n}(y_i - \bar{y})^2}{n\sigma_0^2}\right]^{n/2} \exp\left[-\frac{1}{2}\sum_{i=1}^{n}\left(\frac{y_i - \bar{y}}{\sigma_0}\right)^2 + \frac{n}{2}\right]$$

$$= \left(\frac{\hat{\sigma}^2}{\sigma_0^2}\right)^{n/2} e^{-(n/2)(\hat{\sigma}^2/\sigma_0^2)+(n/2)}$$

We need to know the behavior of λ, considered as a function of $(\hat{\sigma}^2/\sigma_0^2)$. For simplicity, let $x = (\hat{\sigma}^2/\sigma_0^2)$. Then $\lambda = x^{n/2}e^{-(n/2)x+n/2}$ and the inequality $\lambda \le \lambda^*$ is equivalent to $xe^{-x} \le e^{-1}(\lambda^*)^{2/n}$. The right-hand side is again an arbitrary constant, say k^*. Figure 7.A.3.1 is a graph of $y = xe^{-x}$. Notice that the values of $x = (\hat{\sigma}^2/\sigma_0^2)$ for which $xe^{-x} \le k^*$, and equivalently $\lambda \le \lambda^*$, fall into two regions, one for values of $\hat{\sigma}^2/\sigma_0^2$

FIGURE 7.A.3.1

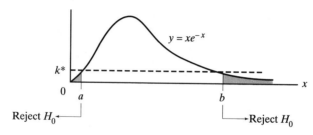

close to 0 and the other for values of $\hat{\sigma}^2/\sigma_0^2$ much larger than 1 (why 1?). According to the likelihood-ratio principle, we should reject H_0 for any $\lambda \le \lambda^*$, where $P(\Lambda \le \lambda^* | H_0) = \alpha$. But λ^* determines (via k^*) numbers a and b so that the critical region is $C = \{(\hat{\sigma}^2/\sigma_0^2): (\hat{\sigma}^2/\sigma_0^2) \le a$ or $(\hat{\sigma}^2/\sigma_0^2) \ge b\}$.

Comment.   At this point it is necessary to make a slight approximation. Just because $P(\Lambda \le \lambda^* | H_0) = \alpha$, it does not follow that

$$P\left[\frac{(1/n)\sum_{i=1}^{n}(Y_i - \bar{Y})^2}{\sigma_0^2} \le a\right] = \frac{\alpha}{2} = P\left[\frac{(1/n)\sum_{i=1}^{n}(Y_i - \bar{Y})^2}{\sigma_0^2} \ge b\right]$$

and, in fact, the two tails of the critical regions will *not* have exactly the same probability. Nevertheless, the two are numerically close enough so that we will not substantially compromise the likelihood-ratio criterion by setting each one equal to $\alpha/2$.
    Note that

$$P\left[\frac{(1/n)\sum_{i=1}^{n}(Y_i - \bar{Y})^2}{\sigma_0^2} \le a\right] = P\left[\frac{\sum_{i=1}^{n}(Y_i - \bar{Y})^2}{\sigma_0^2} \le na\right]$$

$$= P\left[\frac{(n-1)S^2}{\sigma_0^2} \le na\right]$$

$$= P(\chi_{n-1}^2 \le na)$$

and, similarly,

$$P\left[\frac{(1/n)\sum_{i=1}^{n}(Y_i - \bar{Y})^2}{\sigma_0^2} \ge b\right] = P(\chi_{n-1}^2 \ge nb)$$

Thus we will choose as critical values $\chi_{\alpha/2, n-1}^2$ and $\chi_{1-\alpha/2, n-1}^2$ and reject H_0 if either

$$\frac{(n-1)s^2}{\sigma_0^2} \le \chi_{\alpha/2, n-1}^2$$

FIGURE 7.A.3.2

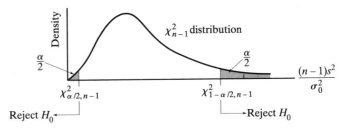

or

$$\frac{(n-1)s^2}{\sigma_0^2} \geq \chi^2_{1-\alpha/2,\, n-1}$$

(see Figure 7.A.3.2).

   Comment.   One-sided tests for dispersion are set up in a similar fashion. In the case of

$$H_0: \quad \sigma^2 = \sigma_0^2$$

versus

$$H_1: \quad \sigma^2 < \sigma_0^2$$

H_0 is rejected if

$$\frac{(n-1)s^2}{\sigma_0^2} \leq \chi^2_{\alpha,\, n-1}$$

For

$$H_0: \quad \sigma^2 = \sigma_0^2$$

versus

$$H_1: \quad \sigma^2 > \sigma_0^2$$

H_0 is rejected if

$$\frac{(n-1)s^2}{\sigma_0^2} \geq \chi^2_{1-\alpha,\, n-1}$$

APPENDIX 7.A.4   A PROOF THAT THE ONE-SAMPLE t TEST IS A GLRT

THEOREM 7.A.4.1.   The one-sample t test, as outlined in Theorem 7.5.2, is a GLRT.

Proof.   Consider the test of $H_0: \mu = \mu_o$ versus $H_1: \mu \neq \mu_o$. The two parameter spaces restricted to H_0 and $H_0 \cup H_1$—that is, ω and Ω, respectively—are given by

$$\omega = \{(\mu, \sigma^2): \mu = \mu_0; 0 \leq \sigma^2 < \infty\}$$

and

$$\Omega = \{(\mu, \sigma^2): \quad -\infty < \mu < \infty; \quad 0 \le \sigma^2 < \infty\}$$

Without elaborating the details (see Section 7.2 for a very similar problem), it can be readily shown that, under ω,

$$\hat{\mu} = \mu_0 \text{ and } \hat{\sigma}^2 = \frac{1}{n} \sum_{i=1}^{n} (y_i - \mu_0)^2$$

Under Ω,

$$\hat{\mu} = \bar{y} \text{ and } \hat{\sigma}^2 = \frac{1}{n} \sum_{i=1}^{n} (y_i - \bar{y})^2$$

Therefore, since

$$L(\mu, \sigma^2) = \left(\frac{1}{\sqrt{2\pi}\,\sigma} \right)^n \exp\left[-\frac{1}{2} \sum_{i=1}^{n} \left(\frac{y_i - \mu}{\sigma} \right)^2 \right]$$

direct substitution gives

$$L(\hat{\omega}) = \left[\frac{\sqrt{n}}{\sqrt{2\pi}\sqrt{\sum_{i=1}^{n} (y_i - \mu_0)^2}} \right]^n e^{-n/2}$$

$$= \left[\frac{ne^{-1}}{2\pi \sum_{i=1}^{n} (y_i - \mu_0)^2} \right]^{n/2}$$

and

$$L(\hat{\Omega}) = \left[\frac{ne^{-1}}{2\pi \sum_{i=1}^{n} (y_i - \bar{y})^2} \right]^{n/2}$$

From $L(\hat{\omega})$ and $L(\hat{\Omega})$ we get the likelihood ratio:

$$\lambda = \frac{L(\hat{\omega})}{L(\hat{\Omega})} = \left[\frac{\sum_{i=1}^{n} (y_i - \bar{y})^2}{\sum_{i=1}^{n} (y_i - \mu_0)^2} \right]^{n/2}, \quad 0 < \lambda \le 1$$

As is often the case, it will prove to be more convenient to base a test on a monotonic function of λ, rather than on λ itself. We begin by rewriting the ratio's denominator:

$$\sum_{i=1}^{n} (y_i - \mu_0)^2 = \sum_{i=1}^{n} [(y_i - \bar{y}) + (\bar{y} - \mu_0)]^2$$

$$= \sum_{i=1}^{n} (y_i - \bar{y})^2 + n(\bar{y} - \mu_0)^2$$

Therefore,

$$\lambda = \left[1 + \frac{n(\bar{y} - \mu_0)^2}{\sum\limits_{i=1}^{n} (y_i - \bar{y})^2} \right]^{-n/2}$$

$$= \left(1 + \frac{t^2}{n - 1} \right)^{-n/2}$$

where

$$t = \frac{\bar{y} - \mu_0}{s/\sqrt{n}}$$

Observe that as t^2 increases, λ decreases. This implies that the original GLRT—which, by definition, would have rejected H_0 for any λ that was too small, say, less than λ^*—is equivalent to a test that rejects H_0 whenever t^2 is too large. But t is an observation of the random variable

$$T = \frac{\bar{Y} - \mu_0}{S/\sqrt{n}} \qquad (= T_{n-1} \text{ by Theorem 7.4.3})$$

Thus "too large" translates numerically into $t_{\alpha/2, n-1}$:

$$0 < \lambda \leq \lambda^* \Leftrightarrow t^2 \geq \left(t_{\alpha/2, n-1} \right)^2$$

But

$$t^2 \geq \left(t_{\alpha/2, n-1} \right)^2 \Leftrightarrow t \leq -t_{\alpha/2, n-1} \text{ or } t \geq t_{\alpha/2, n-1}$$

and the theorem is proved.

CHAPTER 8

Types of Data: A Brief Overview

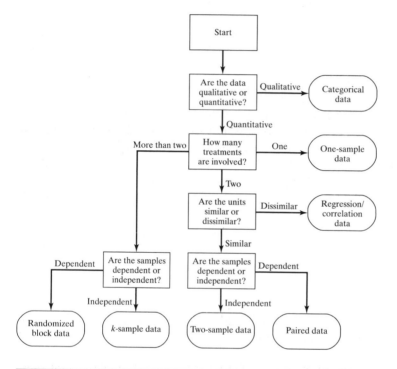

The practice of statistics is typically conducted on two distinct levels. Analyzing data requires first and foremost an understanding of random variables. Which pdfs are modeling the observations? What parameters are involved, and how should they be estimated? Broader issues, though, need to be addressed as well. How is the entire set of measurements configured? Which factors are being investigated; in what ways are they related? Altogether, seven different types of data are profiled in Chapter 8. Collectively, they represent a sizeable fraction of the "experimental designs" any researcher is likely to encounter.

8.1   INTRODUCTION

Chapters 6 and 7 have introduced the basic principles of statistical inference. The typical objective in that material was either to construct a confidence interval or to test the credibility of a null hypothesis. A variety of formulas and decision rules were derived to accommodate distinctions in the nature of the data and the parameter being investigated. It should not go unnoticed, though, that every set of data in those two chapters, despite their superficial differences, shares a critically important common denominator—each represents the exact same *experimental design*.

In a very real sense, a working knowledge of statistics requires that the subject be pursued at two different levels. On the one hand, attention needs to be paid to the mathematical properties inherent *in the individual measurements*. These are what might be thought of as the "micro" structure of statistics. What is the pdf of the Y_i's? Do we know $E(Y_i)$ or $\text{Var}(Y_i)$? Are the Y_i's independent?

Viewed collectively, though, every set of measurements also has a certain overall structure, or *design*. It will be those "macro" features that we focus on in this chapter. A number of issues need to be addressed. How is one design different from another? Under what circumstances is a given design desirable? Or undesirable? How does the design of an experiment influence the analysis of that experiment?

The answers to some of these questions will need to be deferred until each design is taken up individually and in detail later in the text. For now our objective is much more limited—Chapter 8 is meant to be a brief introduction to some of the important ideas involved in the classification of data. What we learn here will serve as a backdrop and a frame of reference for the multiplicity of statistical procedures derived in Chapters 9 through 14.

Definitions

To describe an experimental design, and to distinguish one from another, requires that we understand several key definitions.

Treatments and Treatment Levels.   The word *treatment* is used to denote any condition or trait that is "applied to" or "characteristic of" the subjects being measured. Different versions, extents, or aspects of a treatment are referred to as *levels*. Illustrating that distinction is the breakdown in Table 8.1.1, which shows consumer

TABLE 8.1.1

Age of Subject	Sports Coupe		Four-Door Sedan	
	Male	Female	Male	Female
21–44	8	7	6	7
	7	6	8	5
45–64	7	6	6	8
	7	5	7	8
65+	4	3	7	9
	6	5	9	8

reactions (on a scale of 1 to 10) to two new automobile models. Listed are the opinions given by a total of 24 subjects. *Age*, *gender*, and *model of car* are all considered treatments. The three levels of age are the ranges 21–44, 45–64, and 65+. Similarly, male and female are the two levels of gender, and sports coupe and four-door sedan are the model levels.

Blocks.   Sometimes groups of subjects share certain characteristics that affect the way they respond to treatments, yet those characteristics are of no intrinsic interest to the experimenter. We call any such group of related subjects a *block*.

Table 8.1.2 gives the yields of corn (in bushels) that were harvested from three fields: A, B, and C. Equal acreages in each field were treated with one of three fertilizers: Gro-Fast, King's Formula 6, or Greenway. The objective was to compare the effectiveness of the three fertilizers.

TABLE 8.1.2

Field	Gro-Fast	Fertilizer King's Formula 6	Greenway
A	126	137	119
B	84	89	87
C	113	121	124

Even city slickers can readily appreciate that no three fields will be entirely identical in their ability to grow corn. Variations in drainage, soil composition, and sunlight will inevitably have effects on fertility. The precise nature of those field-to-field differences, though, is not being quantified, nor is it the experiment's focus. In the lingo of experimental design, fields A, B, and C are *blocks*. (Gro-Fast, King's Formula 6, and Greenway, on the other hand, are treatment levels because they represent specific formulations and their comparison is the study's stated objective.)

Independent and Dependent Samples.   Whatever the context, data collected for the purpose of comparing two or more treatment levels are necessarily either *dependent* or *independent*. Table 8.1.3 is an example of the former. Listed are interest rates on home mortgage loans offered by three competing banks. The 9.6, 10.1, and 9.8 reported on January 15 are considered dependent samples because of what they have in common: All three reflect, probably to no small degree, the particular economic conditions that prevailed on January 15. By the same argument, entries 9.4, 9.9,

TABLE 8.1.3

Date	Second Union	Bankers Trust	Commerce Mutual
Jan. 15	9.6%	10.1%	9.8%
March 10	9.4	9.9	9.8
July 8	9.3	9.6	9.5
Sept. 1	10.6	11.0	10.4

TABLE 8.1.4

Brand A	Brand B
852	810
829	801
864	835
843	807
832	819

and 9.8 are also related—in their case, by virtue of whatever special circumstances were present on March 10. Without exception, measurements that belong to the same block are considered to be dependent. In practice, there are many different ways to make measurements dependent; "place" and "time" (as in Tables 8.1.2 and 8.1.3) are two of the most common.

Contrast the structure of Table 8.1.3 with the two sets of measurements in Table 8.1.4, showing the lengths of time (in hours) that it took 10 light bulbs to burn out. Five of the bulbs were brand A; the other five were brand B. Here there is no row-by-row common denominator analogous to "date" in Table 8.1.3. The *852* recorded for the first brand A bulb has no special link to the *810* recorded for the first brand B bulb. Similarly, the *829* and *801* in the second row are unrelated. Because of the absence of any direct connections between these two sets of observations, row-by-row, we say that brand A and brand B measurements are independent samples.

Similar and Dissimilar Units.   Units must also be taken into account when we classify a data set's macrostructure. Two measurements are said to be *similar* if their units are the same and *dissimilar* otherwise. Tables 8.1.1, 8.1.2, 8.1.3, and 8.1.4 have all been examples of data that are unit compatible. The information displayed in Table 8.1.5 does not follow that pattern. It shows (1) the amount of living area and (2) the asking price for five properties listed by a local realtor. Since the first measurement is recorded in square feet and the second is in dollars, the two are considered *dissimilar*.

TABLE 8.1.5

Property	Living Area (in square feet)	Asking price
1049 Ridgeview	2860	$210,500
2878 Tyne	3210	219,900
6086 Harding	2350	146,000
4111 Franklin	5340	359,500

Quantitative Measurements and Qualitative Measurements.   Finally, a distinction needs to be drawn between measurements that are *quantitative* and those that are *qualitative*. By definition, quantitative data are observations where the possible values are numerical. "Values" for qualitative data are either categories or traits.

TABLE 8.1.6

Borrower	Type	Classification
Olden Properties	Real estate	Loss
High Builders	Construction	Doubtful
Maverick CDs	Commercial	Loss
Adam East	Commercial	Substandard
Bayou Construction	Construction	Marginal

Table 8.1.6 illustrates qualitative data on the status of a bank's five largest loans in trouble. Here, one measurement has three possible (nonnumerical) values; the other has four:

$$\text{Type of loan} = \begin{cases} \text{Commercial} \\ \text{Construction} \\ \text{Real estate} \end{cases}$$

$$\text{Loan classification} = \begin{cases} \text{Marginal} \\ \text{Substandard} \\ \text{Doubtful} \\ \text{Loss} \end{cases}$$

(By way of comparison, all the data in Tables 8.1.1–8.1.5 are quantitative.)

CASE STUDY 8.1.1

Table 8.1.7 tracks the recent history of U.S. postage rates (166). On May 16, 1971, the cost of sending a letter first class was 8¢; by January 1, 1995 (nine price hikes later), a stamp cost 32¢.

TABLE 8.1.7

Date	Years after Jan 1, 1971	Cost (¢)
May 16, 1971	0.37	8
March 2, 1974	3.17	10
Dec. 31, 1975	5.00	13
May 29, 1978	7.41	15
March 22, 1981	10.22	18
Nov. 1, 1981	10.83	20
Feb. 17, 1985	14.13	22
April 3, 1988	17.25	25
Feb. 3, 1991	20.09	29
Jan. 1, 1995	24.00	32

The figures in Table 8.1.8 give the numbers of passenger boardings by month for fiscal years 1991 and 1992, as reported by the Pensacola Regional Airport. Relative to the definitions just introduced, how are these two sets of data comparable? How are they different?

In both cases, the information recorded is *quantitative* and *dependent*, with the source of the dependency being "time." For the stamp data, there are two treatments, "Years after

TABLE 8.1.8

Month	Passenger Boardings (Fiscal 1991)	Passenger Boardings (Fiscal 1992)
July	41,388	44,148
Aug.	44,880	42,038
Sept.	33,556	35,157
Oct.	34,805	39,568
Nov.	33,025	34,185
Dec.	34,873	37,604
Jan.	31,330	28,231
Feb.	30,954	29,109
March	32,402	38,080
April	38,020	34,184
May	42,828	39,842
June	41,204	46,727

Jan. 1, 1971" and "Cost (¢)." For the airport data, there is one treatment—"Passenger board-ings"—but it appears at two levels, "Fiscal 1991" and "Fiscal 1992." Moreover, the units in Table 8.1.7 are *dissimilar*, while those in Table 8.1.8 are *similar*.

Possible Designs

Clearly, the definitions cited on pages 463–465 can give rise to an enormous number of different experimental designs, far more than can be covered in this text. Still, the number of designs *that are widely used* is quite small. The vast majority of data like-ly to be encountered fall into one of the following seven designs:

One-sample data

Two-sample data

k-sample data

Paired data

Randomized block data

Regression data

Categorical data

The postage figures in Table 8.1.7, for example, qualify as *regression data*; the pas-senger boardings in Table 8.1.8 are *paired data*. (The ratings in Table 8.1.1, on the other hand, have a more complicated experimental structure and cannot be described by any of these seven basic designs.)

In Section 8.2, each design will be profiled and illustrated and reduced to a mathematical model. Special attention will be given to each design's objectives—that is, for what type of inference is it likely to be used?

8.2 CLASSIFYING DATA

The answers to no more than four questions are needed to classify a set of data into one of the seven basic models listed in the preceding section:

1. Are the observations quantitative or qualitative?
2. Are the units similar or dissimilar?
3. How many treatment levels are involved?
4. Are the observations dependent or independent?

In Section 8.2, we use these four questions as the starting point in distinguishing one experimental design from another.

One-Sample Data

The simplest of all experimental designs, *one-sample data* consist of a single random sample of size n. Necessarily, the n observations are measurements reflecting one particular set of conditions or one specific treatment. They could be either qualitative or quantitative. Typical is Table 8.2.1, showing for a sample of 10 airlines the percentages of flights that landed within 15 minutes of their scheduled arrival times (177).

TABLE 8.2.1

Carrier	Flights on Time
United	82.0%
America West	88.0
Delta	76.1
USAir	83.5
TWA	78.1
Continental	77.3
Southwest	92.1
Alaska	87.4
American	79.3
Northwest	82.7

By far, the two most frequently encountered examples of one-sample data are (1) a random sample of n normally distributed observations and (2) a random sample of "successes" and "failures" occurring in a series of n independent Bernoulli trials. For samples from a normal distribution, the objective is often to construct confidence intervals or test hypotheses about μ (using the Student t distribution) or to draw inferences about σ^2 (using the χ^2 distribution). Theorems 7.5.1 and 7.5.2 detail the procedures for drawing conclusions about μ; Theorems 7.3.4 and 7.3.5 deal with confidence intervals and hypothesis tests for σ^2.

Data recorded as "success" or "failure" are typically modeled by the binomial distribution, and inference procedures focus on the unknown success probability, p. Theorem 6.3.1 gives the large-sample decision rule for testing $H_0: p = p_o$; confidence intervals for p are taken up in Theorem 5.3.1.

FIGURE 8.2.1

Treatment	Model equation
Y_1	
Y_2	
$\vdots$	$Y_i = \mu + \varepsilon_i, \quad i = 1, 2, \ldots, n$
Y_n	

Mathematical Model

Figure 8.2.1 illustrates the structure of one-sample data. For the purpose of comparing experimental designs, it often helps to represent data points as sums of fixed and variable components. These expressions are known as *model equations*. For one-sample data, the model equation for an arbitrary Y_i is written

$$Y_i = \mu + \varepsilon_i$$

where μ denotes the (fixed) mean of the probability distribution being represented by the data and ε_i is a random variable that reflects the "error" in the measurement—that is, the deviation in the measurement from its mean, μ.

If the Y_i's are quantitative measurements, the assumption often made is that ε_i is a *normal* random variable with mean 0 and standard deviation σ. The latter is equivalent to assuming that Y_i is normally distributed with mean μ and standard deviation σ.

Two-Sample Data

The one-sample design typically requires that a set of measurements be compared to a fixed standard—for example, testing the null hypothesis $H_0: \mu = \mu_o$. More likely to be encountered, though, are situations where an appropriate standard fails to exist or cannot be identified. In those cases, measurements need to be taken on each of the treatment levels being compared. The simplest such design occurs when only two treatment levels are involved and the two samples are independent.

Consider the data in Table 8.2.2, showing the caffeine content in two types of instant coffee (170). "Spray-dried" and "Freeze-dried" are the *two* treatment levels,

TABLE 8.2.2

	Spray-dried (x_i)	Freeze-dried (y_i)
	4.8	3.7
	4.0	3.4
	3.8	2.8
	4.3	3.7
	3.9	
	4.6	
	3.1	
	3.1	
	3.7	
Sample mean:	3.92	3.40

the units are *similar* (caffeine grams per 100 grams of dry matter), the observations are *quantitative*, and the two samples are *independent*. Those are the conditions that define *two-sample data*.

Two-sample inferences tend to be hypothesis tests rather than confidence intervals, although both techniques will be developed in Chapter 9. In Table 8.2.2., for example, the two sample means are $\bar{x} = 3.92$ (for the Spray-dried method) and $\bar{y} = 3.40$ (for the Freeze-dried). Suppose μ_X and μ_Y denote the true means associated with the Spray-dried and Freeze-dried methods, respectively. Is the null hypothesis $H_0: \mu_X = \mu_Y$ credible in light of the difference between $\bar{x}$ and $\bar{y}$? As we will see in Section 9.2, the answer to that question takes the form of a *two-sample t test*.

Mathematical Model.   Let X_i and Y_j denote the *i*th and *j*th observations in the X and Y samples, respectively. The assumptions implicit in the two-sample format imply that the X's and Y's are independent and that

$$X_i = \mu_X + \varepsilon_i, \qquad i = 1, 2, \ldots, n$$

and

$$Y_j = \mu_Y + \varepsilon_j, \qquad j = 1, 2, \ldots, m$$

In many situations, the error terms, ε_i and ε_j, are assumed to be normally distributed with mean 0 and the same standard deviation σ (see Figure 8.2.2).

FIGURE 8.2.2

Treatments		Model equation
X	Y	
X_1	Y_1	$X_i = \mu_X + \varepsilon_i, \quad i = 1, 2, \ldots, n$
X_2	Y_2	
$\vdots$	$\vdots$	$Y_j = \mu_Y + \varepsilon_j, \quad j = 1, 2, \ldots, m$
X_n	Y_m	

k-Sample Data

When more than two treatment levels are being compared, and when the samples representing those levels are independent, the observations are said to be *k-sample data*. Although their assumptions are comparable, two-sample data and *k*-sample data are treated as distinct experimental designs because the methods for analyzing them are totally different.

Table 8.2.3 summarizes a set of *k*-sample data where $k = 3$. The same strain of bacteria was grown in each of nine Petri dishes, and the latter were divided into three groups. Each group was treated with a different antibacterial agent. Two days later the diameters of the areas showing no bacterial growth were measured (in centimeters).

Typically, the objective with *k*-sample data is to test $H_0: \mu_1 = \mu_2 = \ldots = \mu_k$, where μ_j represents the true mean associated with the *j*th treatment level. For the data in Table 8.2.3, for example, the issue to be resolved is whether the differences among

TABLE 8.2.3

	M21z	ATC3	B169
	3.8	2.9	5.0
	3.5	3.1	4.8
	4.3	2.8	4.6
Sample means:	3.87	2.93	4.80

the sample means (3.87, 2.93, and 4.80) are sufficiently large to reject the hypothesis that $\mu_1 = \mu_2 = \mu_3$.

The *t* test format that figures so prominently in the interpretation of one-sample and two-sample data cannot be extended to accommodate *k*-sample data. A more powerful technique, known as the *analysis of variance*, is needed. The latter will be developed in Chapters 12 and 13.

Mathematical Model.   The only structural difference between the mathematical models for two-sample and *k*-sample data is the number of treatment levels compared (see Figure 8.2.3). However, with $k > 2$, using different letters to represent different treatment levels is unwieldy. Double-subscript notation is much more convenient—Y_{ij} will denote the *i*th observation in the *j*th sample. Likewise, the error terms will be written ε_{ij}. As before, the latter are usually assumed to be normally distributed with mean 0 and the same standard deviation σ for all *i* and *j*. Moreover, all the samples must be independent.

FIGURE 8.2.3

Treatment levels				Model equation
1	2	$\cdots$	k	
Y_{11}	Y_{12}	$\cdots$	Y_{1k}	$Y_{ij} = \mu_j + \varepsilon_{ij},$
Y_{21}	Y_{22}	$\cdots$	Y_{2k}	$i = 1, 2, \ldots, n_j,$
$\vdots$	$\vdots$	$\cdots$	$\vdots$	$j = 1, 2, \ldots, k$
$Y_{n_1 1}$	$Y_{n_2 2}$	$\cdots$	$Y_{n_k k}$	

Paired Data

In two-sample and *k*-sample designs, treatment levels are compared using *independent* samples. An alternative is to use *dependent* samples by grouping subjects into *blocks*. If only two treatment levels are involved, dependent measurements are classified as *paired data*. A typical scenario is the application of two treatments or conditions to the same subject—for example, blood pressure measurements taken "before" and "after" a patient has received medication.

Table 8.2.4 shows a paired-data comparison of a baseball team's batting averages. The two treatment levels are *when* a game was played ("Nighttime" or "Daytime"). The two entries in a given row—for example, the .310 and .320 for HA—are clearly dependent: A player with a high average during night games is likely to have

TABLE 8.2.4

Player	Nighttime Ave.	Daytime Ave.
HA, rf	.310	.320
EM, 3b	.286	.290
WC, 1f	.302	.298
JA, 1b	.280	.287
DC, c	.214	.226
RS, 2b	.302	.300
JL, ss	.276	.290
BB, cf	.285	.295

a high average during day games as well. Likewise, poor-hitting players will probably have low batting averages regardless of when games are scheduled.

The statistical objective of two-sample data and paired data is often the same. Both seek to examine the plausibility of the null hypothesis that the true averages (μ_X and μ_Y) associated with the two treatment levels are equal.

Mathematical Model. The responses to treatment levels X and Y *for the ith pair* are denoted X_i and Y_i, respectively. Both measurements necessarily reflect the particular conditions that characterize the ith pair. We will denote the "pair effect" by the symbol B_i. That is, $X_i = \mu_X + B_i + \varepsilon_i$ and $Y_i = \mu_Y + B_i + \varepsilon'_i$. The fact that B_i is the same for both X_i and Y_i is precisely what makes the samples dependent (see Figure 8.2.4).

FIGURE 8.2.4

Treatments			Model equation
	X	Y	
1	X_1	Y_1	$X_i = \mu_X + B_i + \varepsilon_i,$
Pair 2	X_2	Y_2	$Y_i = \mu_Y + B_i + \varepsilon'_i,$
$\vdots$	$\vdots$	$\vdots$	$i = 1, 2, \ldots, n$
n	X_n	Y_n	

Randomized Block Data

When dependent samples are used to compare *more than two* treatment levels, the measurements are referred to as *randomized block data*. Despite being an obvious generalization of paired data, the randomized block design is treated separately because the methods required for its analysis are entirely different (recall the similar justification for keeping two-sample data and k-sample data as two separate designs).

Table 8.2.5 summarizes the results of a randomized block experiment set up to investigate the possible effects of "blood doping," a controversial procedure whereby athletes are injected with additional red blood cells for the purpose of enhancing performance (16). Seven runners were the subjects (and, thus, the blocks). Each was timed in three 10,000-meter races: once after receiving extra red blood cells, once

TABLE 8.2.5

Subject	No injection	Placebo	Blood doping
1	34.03	34.53	33.03
2	32.85	32.70	31.55
3	33.50	33.62	32.33
4	32.52	31.23	31.20
5	34.15	32.85	32.80
6	33.77	33.05	33.07

after being injected with a placebo, and once after receiving no treatment whatsoever. Listed are the times (in minutes) to complete the race.

Clearly, the times in a given row are dependent—all three depend to some extent on the inherent speed of the subject, regardless of whichever treatment level might also be operative. Documenting differences from subject to subject, though, would not be the objective for doing this sort of study. If μ_1, μ_2, and μ_3 denote the true average times characteristic of the "No injection," "Placebo," and "Blood doping" treatment levels, respectively, the experimenter's first priority would be to test $H_0\colon \mu_1 = \mu_2 = \mu_3$. As we will see in Chapter 13, the decision as to whether or not a null hypothesis of this sort should be rejected turns out to be another application of the analysis of variance.

Mathematical Model.   Randomized block data have the same basic structure as do paired data. As we saw with k-sample data, though, the multiplicity of treatment levels dictates that double subscript notation be used (see Figure 8.2.5). As before, the B_i component is the term that makes the observations in a given row—$Y_{i1}, Y_{i2}, \ldots$, and Y_{ik}—dependent.

FIGURE 8.2.5

	Treatments levels				Model equations
	1	2	$\cdots$	k	
1	Y_{11}	Y_{12}	$\cdots$	Y_{1k}	$Y_{ij} = \mu_j + B_i + \varepsilon_{ij},$
2	Y_{21}	Y_{22}	$\cdots$	Y_{2k}	$i = 1, 2, \ldots, n,$
Block ⋮	⋮	⋮	$\cdots$	⋮	$j = 1, 2, \ldots, k$
n	Y_{n1}	Y_{n2}	$\cdots$	Y_{nk}	

Regression Data

All the experimental designs introduced up to this point share the property that their measurements have the same units. Moreover, each has had the same basic objective: to quantify or to compare the effects of one or more treatment levels. In contrast, *regression data* typically consist of measurements with dissimilar units, and their objective is to study the functional relationship between the variables rather than test the null hypothesis that a set of means are all equal.

Table 8.2.6, showing the increase in the cost of a first class postage stamp from 1971 to 1995, is an example of regression data (recall Case Study 8.1.1). Any direct

TABLE 8.2.6

Date	Years after Jan. 1, 1971	Cost (in cents)
5/16/71	0.37	8
3/2/74	3.17	10
12/31/75	5.00	13
5/29/78	7.41	15
3/22/81	10.22	18
11/1/81	10.83	20
2/17/85	14.13	22
4/3/88	17.25	25
2/3/91	20.09	29
1/1/95	24.00	32

comparison of the information in the second and third columns is impossible because the units are incompatible. It makes sense, instead, to focus on the *relationship* between "Years after Jan. 1, 1971" and "Cost."

Graphing is especially helpful with regression data. Figure 8.2.6 shows a plot of "Cost" (= y) versus "Years after Jan. 1, 1971" (= x). Superimposed is a straight line— $y = 7.50 + 1.04x$—that "best" fits the 10 (x_i, y_i)'s (using a technique we will learn in Chapter 10).

Mathematical Model.   Regression data often have the form (x_i, Y_i), where x_i is a number and Y_i is a random variable (having different units from x_i). A particularly important special case is the so-called *linear model*, where the mean of Y_i is linearly related to x_i. That is, $Y_i = \beta_0 + \beta_1 x_i + \varepsilon_i$, where ε_i is normally distributed with mean 0 and standard deviation σ. More generally, $E(Y_i)$ can be any function, $g(x_i, \beta_0, \beta_1, \dots)$, of x_i—for example, $E(Y_i) = \beta_0 x_i^{\beta_1}$ or $E(Y_i) = \beta_0 e^{\beta_1 x_i}$ (see Figure 8.2.7).

FIGURE 8.2.6

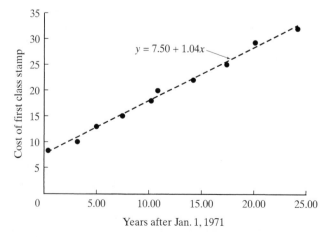

$y = 7.50 + 1.04x$

Cost of first class stamp

Years after Jan. 1, 1971

FIGURE 8.2.7

		Independent variable	Dependent variable	Model equation
	1	x_1	Y_1	
Subject	2	x_2	Y_2	$Y_i = g(x_i, \beta_0, \beta_1, \ldots) + \varepsilon_i,$
	$\vdots$	$\vdots$	$\vdots$	$i = 1, 2, \ldots, n$
	n	x_n	Y_n	

Categorical Data

If the information recorded for each of two dissimilar variables is qualitative rather than quantitative, we call the measurements *categorical data*. Typical is a recent study undertaken to investigate the relationship—if one exists—between a physician's Specialty (X) and his or her Malpractice history (Y). The range of each variable was reduced to three (non-numerical) classes:

$$\text{Specialty} = \begin{cases} \text{orthopedic surgery (OS)} \\ \text{obstetrics-gynecology (OB)} \\ \text{internal medicine (IM)} \end{cases}$$

$$\text{Malpractice history} = \begin{cases} \text{A:} & \text{no claim} \\ \text{B:} & \text{one or more claims ending} \\ & \text{in nonzero indemnity} \\ \text{C:} & \text{one or more claims but} \\ & \text{none requiring compensation} \end{cases}$$

In its original form, the information collected on the 1942 physicians interviewed looked like the listing in Figure 8.2.8 (31). Data of this sort are usually summarized by tallying the number of times each (X, Y) "combination" occurs and displaying those frequencies in a *contingency table* (see Figure 8.2.9).

The inference procedure that typically accompanies the construction of a contingency table is a hypothesis test, where H_0 states that the random variables X and Y are independent. This is a very frequently encountered experimental design, especially in the social sciences. The statistical technique for analyzing categorical data is the *chi-square test*, a procedure that will be described in Chapter 11.

FIGURE 8.2.8

Case	Physician	Specialty	Malpractice history
1	SB	IM	B
2	LL	OB	B
3	ML	OS	C
4	EM	IM	A
$\vdots$	$\vdots$	$\vdots$	$\vdots$
1942	MS	OB	C

	Orthopedic surgery	Obstetrics-gynecology	Internal medicine	Totals
No claims	147	349	709	1205
At least one claim lost	106	14	62	317
At least one claim, but no damages awarded	156	149	115	420
Totals	409	647	886	1942

FIGURE 8.2.9

Mathematical Model. The assumptions associated with categorical data are far less specific than those we have seen in the six previous experimental designs. There is no requirement of normality, for example, and no particular model equation. In effect, X and Y can be any discrete random variables whatsoever (see Figure 8.2.10).

FIGURE 8.2.10

	First variable	Second variable	Model equation
	X_1	Y_1	
Observation	X_2	Y_2	X and Y are discrete random variables
	$\vdots$	$\vdots$	
	X_n	Y_n	

A Flowchart for Classifying Data

It was mentioned at the outset of this section that classifying data into the seven models we have described requires that a maximum of four questions be answered (recall page 468). Figure 8.2.11 is a flowchart that summarizes the model-identification process.

EXAMPLE 8.2.1

The federal Community Reinvestment Act of 1977 was enacted out of concern that banks were reluctant to make loans in low and moderate-income areas, even when applicants seemed otherwise acceptable. The figures in Table 8.2.7 show one particular bank's credit penetration in 10 low-income census tracts (A through J) and 10 high-income census tracts (K through T). To which of the seven models do these data belong?

Note, first, that the measurements (1) are quantitative and (2) have similar units. "Low income" and "High income" correspond to *two* treatment levels, and the two samples are clearly independent (the *4.6* recorded in tract A, for example, has nothing specific in common with the *11.6* recorded in tract K). From the flowchart, then, the answers "quantitative/similar/two/independent" imply that these are *two-sample data*.

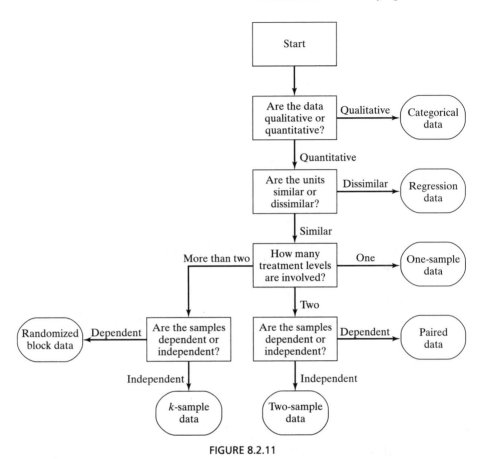

FIGURE 8.2.11

TABLE 8.2.7

Low income census tract	Percent of households with credit	High income census tract	Percent of households with credit
A	4.6	K	11.6
B	6.6	L	8.5
C	3.3	M	8.2
D	9.8	N	15.1
E	6.9	O	12.6
F	11.0	P	11.3
G	6.0	Q	9.1
H	4.6	R	4.2
I	4.2	S	6.4
J	5.1	T	5.9

EXAMPLE 8.2.2

Beginning in 1991, a rule change in college football narrowed the distance between the goalposts from 23′4″ to 18′6″. The consequences of that legislation on the probability of players successfully kicking points after touchdowns (PATs) are reflected in Table 8.2.8. The numbers in the first column are based on all college games played through September of the 1990 season; those in the second column come from the 1991 season (174). What experimental design is represented?

TABLE 8.2.8

PATs	"Wide" goalposts (1990 season)	"Narrow" goalposts (1991 season)
Successful	959	829
Unsuccessful	46	82
Total	1005	911
Percent successful	95.4	91.0

Despite the numerical appearance of the information in Table 8.2.8, the actual data here are qualitative, not quantitative. Entries 959, 829, 46, and 82 are not measurements; they are *summaries* of measurements. What was recorded for each attempted conversion were two pieces of *qualitative* information:

$$\text{Type of goalpost} = \begin{cases} \text{wide} \\ \text{narrow} \end{cases}$$

$$\text{Outcome of kick} = \begin{cases} \text{successful} \\ \text{unsuccessful} \end{cases}$$

Only later were the 1916 data points summed up, cross-classified, and reduced to the four frequencies appearing in Table 8.2.8. By the answer to the first question posed in Figure 8.2.11, then, these are *categorical data*.

EXAMPLE 8.2.3

People looking at the vertical lines in Figure 8.2.12 will tend to perceive the rightmost one as shorter, even though the two are equal. Moreover, the perceived difference in those lengths—what psychologists call the "strength" of the illusion—has been shown to be a function of age.

Recently, a study was done to see whether individuals who are hypnotized and regressed to different ages also perceive the illusion differently. Table 8.2.9 shows the illusion strengths measured for eight subjects while they were (1) awake, (2) regressed to age 9, and (3) regressed to age 5 (126). Which of the seven experimental designs do these data represent?

Look again at the sequence of questions posed by the flowchart in Figure 8.2.11:

1. Are the data qualitative or quantitative? *Quantitative*
2. Are the units similar or dissimilar? *Similar*
3. How many treatment levels are involved? *More than two*
4. Are the observations dependent or independent? *Dependent*

According to the flowchart, then, these measurements qualify as *randomized block data*.

FIGURE 8.2.12

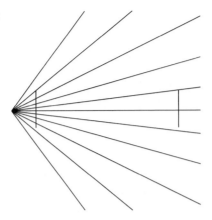

TABLE 8.2.9

Subject	(1) Awake	(2) Regressed to Age 9	(3) Regressed to Age 5
1	0.81	0.69	0.56
2	0.44	0.31	0.44
3	0.44	0.44	0.44
4	0.56	0.44	0.44
5	0.19	0.19	0.31
6	0.94	0.44	0.69
7	0.44	0.44	0.44
8	0.06	0.19	0.19

QUESTIONS

Identify the experimental design (one-sample, two-sample, etc.) that each of the following data sets represents.

8.2.1 To see whether low-priced homes are easier to sell than moderately priced homes, a national realty company collected the following information on the lengths of times homes were on the market before being sold.

City	Number of Days on Market	
	Low-priced	Moderately priced
Buffalo	55	70
Charlotte	40	30
Newark	70	110

8.2.2 In a survey conducted by State University's Learning Center, a sample of three freshmen said they studied 6, 4, and 10 hours, respectively, over the weekend. The same question was posed to three sophomores, who reported study times of 4, 5, and 7 hours. For three juniors, the responses were 2, 8, and 6 hours.

8.2.3 A public relations firm hired by a would-be presidential candidate has conducted a poll to see whether their client faces a gender gap. Out of 800 men interviewed, 325 strongly supported the candidate, 151 were strongly opposed, and 324 were undecided. Among the 750 women included in the sample, 258 were strong supporters, 241 were strong opponents, and 251 were undecided.

8.2.4 A company claims to have produced a blended gasoline that can improve a car's fuel consumption. They decide to compare their product with the leading gas currently on the market. Three different cars were used for the test: a Porsche, a Buick, and a VW. The Porsche got 13.6 mpg with the new gas and 12.2 mpg with the "standard" gas; the Buick got 18.7 mpg with the new gas and 18.5 with the standard; the figures for the VW were 34.5 and 32.6, respectively.

8.2.5 Two methods (A and B) are available for removing dangerous heavy metals from public water supplies. Eight water samples collected from various parts of the United States were used to compare the two methods. Four were treated with Method A and four were treated with Method B. After the processes were completed, each sample was rated for purity on a scale of 1 to 100.

Method A	Method B
88.6	81.4
92.1	84.6
90.7	91.4
93.6	78.6

8.2.6 As part of a study investigating the effects of television on academic performance, four seventh graders were asked to keep a log of the number of hours of TV they watched each day. After six weeks, two pieces of information were recorded for each subject: (1) average daily TV watching time (in hours) and (2) GPA earned during that grading period. For Mike, Donna, Lisa, and Charles, the data reported were (2.50, 3.10), (1.00, 3.32), (1.50, 3.49), and (4.50, 2.36), respectively.

8.2.7 To see if any geographical pricing differences exist, the cost of a basic cable TV package was determined for a random sample of six cities; three in the southeast and three in the northwest. Monthly charges for the southeastern cities were $13.20, $11.55, and $16.75; residents in the three northwestern cities paid $14.80, $17.65, and $19.20.

8.2.8 Out of 120 senior citizens polled, 65 favored a complete overhaul of the health care system while 55 preferred more modest changes. When the same choice was put to 85 first-time voters, 40 said they were in favor of major reform while 45 opted for minor revisions.

8.2.9 To evaluate the effectiveness of an SAT review course, four students were asked to take the exam twice—the first time without any special preparation and the second time after having had the review course.

Student	SAT (no review)	SAT (with review)
DF	1040	1120
ML	1110	1140
AS	1020	1200
SH	1200	1250

8.2.10 Health officials tracking the spread of AIDS reported that the number of cases confirmed in a certain midwestern city increased from 19 in 1994 to 21, 30, 39, and 57 during the next four years.

8.2.11 A consumer advocacy group, investigating the prices of steel-belted radial tires produced by three major manufacturers, collects the following data.

Year	Company A	Company B	Company C
1985	$62.00	$68.00	$65.00
1990	$70.00	$72.00	$69.00
1995	$78.00	$75.00	$75.00

8.2.12 A small fourth-grade class is randomly split into two groups. Each group is taught fractions using a different method. After three weeks, both groups are given the same 100-point test. The scores of students in the first group are 82, 86, 91, 72, and 68; the scores reported for the second group are 76, 63, 80, 72, and 67.

8.2.13 To estimate the drop in barometric pressure that precedes stormy weather, a meteorologist identifies a random sample of five tornadoes that occurred locally over the last 15 years. Barometric pressures recorded an hour before each storm hit were 27.5, 28.6, 27.9, 28.9, and 28.5.

8.2.14 The following is a breakdown of what 120 college freshmen intend to do next summer.

	Work	School	Play
Male	22	14	19
Female	14	31	20

8.2.15 An efficiency study was done on the delivery of first-class mail originating from the four cities listed in the following table. Recorded for each city was the average length of time (in days) that it took a letter to reach a destination in that same city. Samples were taken on two occasions, Sept. 1, 1997 and Sept. 1, 1999.

City	Sept. 1, 1997	Sept. 1, 1999
Wooster	1.8	1.7
Midland	2.0	2.0
Beaumont	2.2	2.5
Manchester	1.9	1.7

8.2.16 As part of a review of its rate structure, an automobile insurance company has compiled the following data on claims filed by five male policyholders and five female policyholders.

Client (male)	Claims filed in 1998	Client (female)	Claims filed in 1998
MK	$2750	SB	0
JM	0	ML	0
AK	0	MS	0
KT	$1500	BM	$2150
JT	0	LL	0

8.2.17 To illustrate the complexity and arbitrariness of IRS regulations, a tax-reform lobbying group has sent the same five clients to each of two professional tax preparers. The following are the estimated tax liabilities quoted by each of the preparers.

Client	Preparer A	Preparer B
GS	$31,281	$26,850
MB	14,256	13,958
AA	26,197	25,520
DP	8,283	9,107
SB	47,825	43,192

8.2.18 An investigation was conducted of 107 fatal poisonings of children. Each death was caused by one of three drugs. In each instance it was determined how the child received the fatal overdose. Responsibility for the 107 accidents was assessed according to the following breakdown.

	Drug A	Drug B	Drug C
Child Responsible	10	10	18
Parent Responsible	10	14	10
Another Person Responsible	4	18	13

8.2.19 The production of a certain organic chemical requires ammonium chloride. The manufacturer can obtain the ammonium chloride in one of three forms: powdered, moderately ground, and coarse. To see if the consistency of the NH_4Cl is itself a factor that needs to be considered, the manufacturer decides to run the reaction seven times with each form of ammonium chloride. The following are the resulting yields (in pounds).

Powdered NH_4Cl	Moderately Ground NH_4Cl	Coarse NH_4Cl
146	150	141
152	144	138
149	148	142
161	155	146
158	154	139
154	148	137
149	150	145

8.2.20 In Eastern Europe a study was done on 50 people bitten by rabid animals. Twenty victims were given the standard Pasteur treatment, while the other 30 were given the Pasteur treatment in addition to one or more doses of antirabies gamma globulin. Nine of those given the standard treatment survived; twenty survived in the gamma globulin group.

8.2.21 As part of an affirmative-action litigation, records were produced showing the average salaries earned by White, Black, and Hispanic workers in a large manufacturing plant. Three different departments were selected at random for the comparison. The entries shown are average annual salaries, in thousands of dollars.

	White	Black	Hispanic
Department 1	20.2	19.8	19.9
Department 2	20.6	19.0	19.2
Department 3	19.7	20.0	18.4

8.2.22 A pharmaceutical company is testing two new drugs designed to improve the blood-clotting ability of hemophiliacs. Six subjects volunteering for the study are randomly divided into two groups of size three. The first group is given drug A; the second group, drug B. The response variable in each case is the subject's prothrombin time, a number that reflects the time it takes for a clot to form. The results (in seconds) for group A are 32.6, 46.7, and 81.2; for group B, 25.9, 33.6, and 35.1.

8.2.23 A developmental psychologist is studying the relationship between a child's age (x) and his or her score (y) on a manual dexterity test. The (x_i, y_i)'s recorded for a sample of five children are $(6, 82)$, $(7, 85)$, $(6, 76)$, $(5, 62)$, and $(8, 92)$.

8.2.24 Roughly 360,000 bankruptcies were filed in U.S. Federal Court during 1981; by 1990 the annual number was more than twice that figure. The following are the numbers of business failures reported year by year through the 1980s (165).

Year	Bankruptcies filed
1981	360,329
1982	367,866
1983	374,734
1984	344,275
1985	364,536
1986	477,856
1987	561,274
1988	594,567
1989	642,993
1990	726,484

8.2.25 Male cockroaches can be very antagonistic toward other male cockroaches. Encounters may be fleeting or quite spirited, the latter often resulting in missing antennae and broken wings. A study was done to see whether cockroach density has any effect on the frequency of serious altercations. Ten groups of four male cockroaches (*Byrsotria fumigata*) were each subjected to three levels of density: high, intermediate, and low. The following are the numbers of "serious" encounters per minute that were observed (15).

Group	High	Intermediate	Low
1	0.30	0.11	0.12
2	0.20	0.24	0.28
3	0.17	0.13	0.20
4	0.25	0.36	0.15
5	0.27	0.20	0.31
6	0.19	0.12	0.16
7	0.27	0.19	0.20
8	0.23	0.08	0.17
9	0.37	0.18	0.18
10	0.29	0.20	0.20
Averages:	0.25	0.18	0.20

CHAPTER 9

Two-Sample Problems

William Sealy Gosset ("Student") (1876–1937)

After earning an Oxford degree in mathematics and chemistry, Gosset began working in 1899 for Messrs. Guinness, a Dublin brewery. Fluctuations in materials and temperature and the necessarily small-scale experiments inherent in brewing convinced him of the necessity for a new small-sample theory of statistics. Writing under the pseudonym "Student," he published work with the t ratio that was destined to become a cornerstone of modern statistical methodology.

9.1 INTRODUCTION

The simplicity of the one-sample model makes it the logical starting point for any discussion of statistical inference, but it also limits its applicability to the real world. Very few experiments involve just a single treatment or a single set of conditions. On the contrary, researchers almost invariably design experiments to compare responses to *several* treatment levels—or, at the very least, to compare a single treatment with a control.

In this chapter we examine the simplest of these multilevel designs, the *two-sample problem*. Structurally, the two-sample problem always falls into one of two different formats: Either two (presumably) different treatment levels are applied to two independent sets of similar subjects or the same treatment is applied to two (presumably) different kinds of subjects. Comparing the effectiveness of germicide A relative to that of germicide B by measuring the zones of inhibition each one produces in two sets of similarly cultured Petri dishes would be an example of the first type. Another would be testing whether monkeys raised by themselves (treatment X) react differently in a stress situation from monkeys raised with siblings (treatment Y). On the other hand, examining the bones of 60-year-old men and 60-year-old women, all life-long residents of the same city, to see whether both sexes absorb environmental strontium-90 at the same rate would be an example of the second type.

Inference in two-sample problems usually reduces to a comparison of *location* parameters. We might assume, for example, that the population of responses associated with, say, treatment X is normally distributed with mean μ_X and standard deviation σ_X while the Y distribution is normal with mean μ_Y and standard deviation σ_Y. Comparing location parameters, then, reduces to testing $H_0: \mu_X = \mu_Y$. As always, the alternative may be either one sided, $H_1: \mu_X < \mu_Y$ or $H_1: \mu_X > \mu_Y$, or two sided, $H_1: \mu_X \neq \mu_Y$. (If the data are binomial, the location parameters are p_X and p_Y, the true "success" probabilities for treatments X and Y, and the null hypothesis takes the form $H_0: p_X = p_Y$.)

Sometimes, although much less frequently, it becomes more relevant to compare the *variabilities* of two treatments, rather than their locations. A food company, for example, trying to decide which of two types of machines to buy for filling cereal boxes would naturally be concerned about the *average* weights of the boxes filled by each type, but they would also want to know something about the *variabilities* of the weights. Obviously, a machine that produced high proportions of "underfills" and "overfills" would be a distinct liability. In a situation of this sort, the appropriate null hypothesis is $H_0: \sigma_X^2 = \sigma_Y^2$.

For comparing the means of two normal populations, the standard procedure is the *two-sample t test*. As described in Section 9.2, this is a relatively straightforward extension of Chapter 7's one-sample *t* test. For comparing variances, though, it will be necessary to introduce a completely new test—this one based on the *F* distribution of Section 7.6. The binomial version of the two-sample problem, testing $H_0: p_X = p_Y$, is taken up in Section 9.4.

It was mentioned in connection with one-sample problems that certain inferences, for various reasons, are more aptly phrased in terms of confidence intervals rather than hypothesis tests. The same is true of two-sample problems. In Section 9.5, confidence intervals are constructed for the location *difference* of two populations, $\mu_X - \mu_Y$ (or $p_X - p_Y$), and the variability *quotient*, σ_X^2/σ_Y^2.

9.2   TESTING H_0: $\mu_X = \mu_Y$—THE TWO-SAMPLE t TEST

We will suppose the data for a given experiment consist of two independent random samples, $X_1, X_2, \ldots, X_n$ and $Y_1, Y_2, \ldots, Y_m$, representing either of the models referred to in Section 9.1. Furthermore, the two populations from which the X's and Y's are drawn will be presumed normal. Let μ_X and μ_Y denote their means. Our problem will be to derive a procedure for testing H_0: $\mu_X = \mu_Y$. Of course, to accept H_0 is to accept the equivalence of the two treatments (or the two sets of subjects), at least in terms of the average effects they elicit.

As it turns out, the precise form of the test we are looking for depends on the variances of the X and Y populations. If it can be assumed that σ_X^2 and σ_Y^2 are equal, it is a relatively straightforward task to produce the GLRT for H_0: $\mu_X = \mu_Y$. (This is, in fact, what we will do in Theorem 9.2.2.) But if the variances of the two populations are *not* equal, the problem becomes much more complex. This second case, known as the Behrens-Fisher problem, is more than 70 years old and remains one of the more famous "unsolved" problems in statistics. What headway investigators *have* made has been confined to approximate solutions [see, for example, Sukhatme (157) or Cochran (25)]. These however, will not be discussed here; we will restrict our attention to testing H_0: $\mu_X = \mu_Y$ when it can be assumed that $\sigma_X^2 = \sigma_Y^2$.

For the one-sample test that $\mu = \mu_0$, the GLRT was shown to be a function of a special case of the t ratio introduced in Definition 7.4.1 (recall Theorem 7.4.3). We begin this section with a theorem that gives still another special case of Definition 7.4.1. This one will do for the two-sample GLRT what $\sqrt{n}(\bar{Y} - \mu_0)/S$ did for the one-sample GLRT.

THEOREM 9.2.1.   Let $X_1, X_2, \ldots, X_n$ be a random sample of size n from a normal distribution with mean μ_X and standard deviation σ and let $Y_1, Y_2, \ldots, Y_m$ be an independent random sample of size m from a normal distribution with mean μ_Y and standard deviation σ. Let S_X^2 and S_Y^2 be the two corresponding sample variances, and S_p^2, the *pooled variance*, where

$$S_p^2 = \frac{(n-1)S_X^2 + (m-1)S_Y^2}{n+m-2} = \frac{\sum\limits_{i=1}^{n}(X_i - \bar{X})^2 + \sum\limits_{i=1}^{m}(Y_i - \bar{Y})^2}{n+m-2}$$

Then

$$T_{n+m-2} = \frac{\bar{X} - \bar{Y} - (\mu_X - \mu_Y)}{S_p\sqrt{\dfrac{1}{n} + \dfrac{1}{m}}}$$

has a Student t distribution with $n + m - 2$ degrees of freedom.

Proof.   The method of proof here is very similar to what was used for Theorem 7.4.3. Note that an equivalent formulation of T_{n+m-2} is

$$T_{n+m-2} = \cfrac{\cfrac{\bar{X} - \bar{Y} - (\mu_X - \mu_Y)}{\sigma\sqrt{\dfrac{1}{n} + \dfrac{1}{m}}}}{\sqrt{S_p^2/\sigma^2}}$$

$$= \cfrac{\cfrac{\bar{X} - \bar{Y} - (\mu_X - \mu_Y)}{\sigma\sqrt{\dfrac{1}{n} + \dfrac{1}{m}}}}{\sqrt{\dfrac{1}{n+m-2}\left[\displaystyle\sum_{i=1}^{n}\left(\dfrac{X_i - \bar{X}}{\sigma}\right)^2 + \sum_{i=1}^{m}\left(\dfrac{Y_i - \bar{Y}}{\sigma}\right)^2\right]}}$$

But $E(\bar{X} - \bar{Y}) = \mu_X - \mu_Y$ and $\text{Var}(\bar{X} - \bar{Y}) = \sigma^2/n + \sigma^2/m$, so the numerator of the ratio has a standard normal distribution, $f_Z(z)$.

In the denominator,

$$\sum_{i=1}^{n}\left(\frac{X_i - \bar{X}}{\sigma}\right)^2 = \frac{(n-1)S_X^2}{\sigma^2}$$

and

$$\sum_{i=1}^{m}\left(\frac{Y_i - \bar{Y}}{\sigma}\right)^2 = \frac{(m-1)S_Y^2}{\sigma^2}$$

are independent χ^2 random variables with $n - 1$ and $m - 1$ df, respectively, so

$$\sum_{i=1}^{n}\left(\frac{X_i - \bar{X}}{\sigma}\right)^2 + \sum_{i=1}^{m}\left(\frac{Y_i - \bar{Y}}{\sigma}\right)^2$$

has a χ^2 distribution with $n + m - 2$ df (recall Theorem 7.3.1). Also, by Appendix 7.A.2, the numerator and denominator are independent. It follows from Definition 7.4.1, then, that

$$\frac{\bar{X} - \bar{Y} - (\mu_X - \mu_Y)}{S_p\sqrt{\dfrac{1}{n} + \dfrac{1}{m}}}$$

has a Student t distribution with $n + m - 2$ df.

THEOREM 9.2.2.   Let $X_1, X_2, \ldots, X_n$ and $Y_1, Y_2, \ldots, Y_m$ be independent random samples from normal distributions with means μ_X and μ_Y, respectively, and with the same standard deviation σ. Let

$$t = \frac{\bar{x} - \bar{y}}{s_p\sqrt{\dfrac{1}{n} + \dfrac{1}{m}}}$$

(a) To test $H_0: \mu_X = \mu_Y$ versus $H_1: \mu_X > \mu_Y$ at the α level of significance, reject H_0 if $t \geq t_{\alpha,n+m-2}$.

(b) To test $H_0: \mu_X = \mu_Y$ versus $H_1: \mu_X < \mu_Y$ at the α level of significance, reject H_0 if $t \leq -t_{\alpha, n+m-2}$.

(c) To test $H_0: \mu_X = \mu_Y$ versus $H_1: \mu_X \neq \mu_Y$ at the α level of significance, reject H_0 if t is either (1) $\leq -t_{\alpha/2, n+m-2}$ or (2) $\geq t_{\alpha/2, n+m-2}$.

Proof. See Appendix 9.A.1.

CASE STUDY 9.2.1

Cases of disputed authorship are not very common, but when they do occur they can be very difficult to resolve. Speculation has persisted for several hundred years that some of Shakespeare's works were written by Sir Francis Bacon. And whether it was Alexander Hamilton or James Madison who wrote certain of the Federalist Papers is still an open question. A similar, though more recent, dispute centers around Mark Twain (17).

In 1861, a series of 10 essays appeared in the *New Orleans Daily Crescent*. Signed "Quintus Curtius Snodgrass," the essays purported to chronicle the author's adventures as a member of the Louisiana militia. While historians generally agree that the accounts referred to actually did happen, there seems to be no record of anyone named Quintus Curtius Snodgrass. Adding to the mystery is the fact that the style of the pieces bears unmistakable traces—at least to some critics—of the humor and irony that made Mark Twain so famous.

Most typically, efforts to unravel these sorts of "yes, he did—no, he didn't" controversies rely heavily on literary and historical clues. But not always. There is also a statistical approach to the problem. Studies have shown that authors are remarkably consistent in the extent to which they use words of a certain length. That is, a given author will use roughly the same proportion of, say, three-letter words in something he writes this year as he did in whatever he wrote last year. The same holds true for words of any length. *But*, the proportion of three-letter words that author A consistently uses will very likely be different from the proportion of three-letter words that author B uses. It follows that by comparing the proportions of words of a certain length in essays known to be the work of Mark Twain to the proportions found in the 10 Snodgrass essays, we should be able to assess the likelihood of the two authors' being one and the same.

Table 9.2.1 shows the proportions of three-letter words found in eight Twain essays and in the 10 Snodgrass essays. (Each of the Twain works was written at approximately the same time the Snodgrass essays appeared.)

TABLE 9.2.1   Proportion of Three-Letter Words

Twain	Proportion	QCS	Proportion
Sergeant Fathom letter	0.225	Letter I	0.209
Madame Caprell letter	0.262	Letter II	0.205
Mark Twain letters in		Letter III	0.196
Territorial Enterprise		Letter IV	0.210
First letter	0.217	Letter V	0.202
Second letter	0.240	Letter VI	0.207
Third letter	0.230	Letter VII	0.224
Fourth letter	0.229	Letter VIII	0.223
First *Innocents Abroad* letter		Letter IX	0.220
First half	0.235	Letter X	0.201
Second half	0.217		

If $x_1 = 0.225, x_2 = 0.262,\ldots, x_8 = 0.217$, and $y_1 = 0.209, y_2 = 0.205,\ldots, y_{10} = 0.201$, then

$$\bar{x} = \frac{1.855}{8} = 0.2319 \quad \text{and} \quad \bar{y} = \frac{2.097}{10} = 0.2097$$

To analyze these data, we need to decide what the magnitude of the difference between the sample means, $\bar{x} - \bar{y} = 0.2319 - 0.2097 = 0.0222$, actually tells us. Let μ_X and μ_Y denote the proportions of three-letter words in *all* essays written by Twain and by Snodgrass, respectively. Of course, not having examined the complete works of the two authors, we have no way of evaluating either μ_X or μ_Y, so they become the unknown parameters of the problem. What needs to be decided, then, is whether an observed *sample* difference (in the proportions of three-letter words) as large as 0.0222 implies that the two *true* proportions, μ_X and μ_Y, are themselves not the same. Or is 0.0222 small enough to still be compatible with the hypothesis that they are? Put more formally, we must choose between

$$H_0: \quad \mu_X = \mu_Y$$

and

$$H_1: \quad \mu_X \neq \mu_Y$$

Since

$$\sum_{i=1}^{8} x_i^2 = 0.4316 \quad \text{and} \quad \sum_{i=1}^{10} y_i^2 = 0.4406$$

the two sample variances are

$$s_X^2 = \frac{8(0.4316) - (1.855)^2}{8(7)}$$

$$= 0.0002103$$

and

$$s_Y^2 = \frac{10(0.4406) - (2.097)^2}{10(9)}$$

$$= 0.0000955$$

Combined, they give a pooled standard deviation of 0.0121:

$$s_p = \sqrt{\frac{\sum_{i=1}^{8}(x_i - 0.2319)^2 + \sum_{i=1}^{10}(y_i - 0.2097)^2}{n + m - 2}}$$

$$= \sqrt{\frac{(n - 1)s_X^2 + (m - 1)s_Y^2}{n + m - 2}}$$

$$= \sqrt{\frac{7(0.0002103) + 9(0.0000955)}{8 + 10 - 2}}$$

$$= \sqrt{0.0001457}$$

$$= 0.0121$$

(*continued on next page*)

(Case Study 9.2.1 continued)

According to Theorem 9.2.1, if $H_0 : \mu_X = \mu_Y$ is true, the sampling distribution of

$$T = \frac{\bar{X} - \bar{Y}}{S_p \sqrt{\frac{1}{8} + \frac{1}{10}}}$$

is described by a Student t curve with $16 (= 8 + 10 - 2)$ degrees of freedom.

Suppose we let $\alpha = 0.01$. By Part (c) of Theorem 9.2.2, H_0 should be rejected in favor of a two-sided H_1 if either (1) $t \le -t_{\alpha/2, n+m-2} = -t_{.005, 16} = -2.9208$ or (2) $t \ge t_{\alpha/2, n+m-2} = t_{.005, 16} = 2.9208$ (see Figure 9.2.1). But

$$t = \frac{0.2319 - 0.2097}{0.0121 \sqrt{1/8 + 1/10}}$$

$$= 3.88$$

a value falling considerably to the right of $t_{.005, 16}$. Therefore, we *reject* H_0—it would appear that Twain and Snodgrass were not the same person.

FIGURE 9.2.1

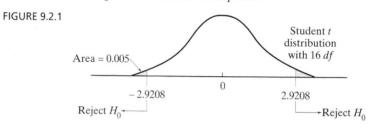

Comment. The X_i's and Y_i's in Table 9.2.1, being proportions, are necessarily *not* normally distributed random variables, so the basic assumption of Theorem 9.2.2 is not met. Fortunately, the consequences of non-normality on the probabilistic behavior of T_{n+m-2} are frequently minimal. The robustness property of the *one-sample t ratio* that we investigated in Chapter 7 (recall Figure 7.5.4) also holds true for the *two-sample t ratio*.

CASE STUDY 9.2.2

Dislike your statistics instructor? Retaliation time will come at the end of the semester, when you pepper the student course evaluation form with 1's. Were you pleased? Then send a signal with a load of 5's. Either way, students' evaluations of their instructors do matter. These instruments are commonly used for promotion, tenure, and merit raise decisions.

Studies of student course evaluations show that they do have value. They tend to show reliability and consistency. Yet questions remain as to the ability of these questionnaires to identify good teachers and courses.

A veteran instructor of developmental psychology decided to do a study (189) on how a single changed factor might affect his student course evaluations. He had attended a workshop extolling the virtue of an enthusiastic style in the classroom—more hand gestures, increased voice pitch variability, and the like. The vehicle for the study was the large-lecture undergraduate developmental psychology course he had taught in the fall semester. He set about to teach the spring semester offering in the same way, with the exception of a more enthusiastic style.

The professor fully understood the difficulty of controlling for the many variables. He selected the spring class to have the same demographics as the one in the fall. He used the same textbook, syllabus, and tests. He listened to audio tapes of the fall lectures and reproduced them as closely as possible, covering the same topics in the same order.

The first step in examining the effect of enthusiasm on course evaluations is to establish that students have, in fact, perceived an increase in enthusiasm. Table 9.2.2 summarizes the ratings the instructor received on the "enthusiasm" question for the two semesters. Unless the increase in sample means (2.14 to 4.21) is statistically significant, there is no point in trying to compare fall and spring responses to other questions.

TABLE 9.2.2

Fall, x_i	Spring, y_i
$n = 229$	$m = 243$
$\bar{x} = 2.14$	$\bar{y} = 4.21$
$s_X = 0.94$	$s_Y = 0.83$

Let μ_X and μ_Y denote the true means associated with the two different teaching styles. There is no reason to think that increased enthusiasm on the part of the instructor would *decrease* the students' perception of enthusiasm, so it can be argued here that H_1 should be one sided. That is, we want to test

$$H_0: \quad \mu_X = \mu_Y$$

versus

$$H_1: \quad \mu_X < \mu_Y$$

Let $\alpha = 0.05$.

Since $n = 229$ and $m = 243$, the t statistic has $229 + 243 - 2 = 470$ degrees of freedom. Thus, the decision rule calls for the rejection of H_0 if

$$t = \frac{\bar{x} - \bar{y}}{s_P \sqrt{\dfrac{1}{229} + \dfrac{1}{243}}} \leq -t_{\alpha,\,n+m-2} = -t_{.05,\,470}$$

A glance at Table A.2 shows that for any value $n > 100$, z_α is a good approximation of $t_{\alpha,n}$. That is, $-t_{.05,470} \doteq -z_{.05} = -1.64$.

The pooled standard deviation for these data is *0.885*:

$$s_P = \sqrt{\frac{228(0.94)^2 + 242(0.83)^2}{229 + 243 - 2}} = 0.885$$

Therefore,

$$t = \frac{2.14 - 4.21}{0.885\sqrt{\dfrac{1}{229} + \dfrac{1}{243}}} = -25.42$$

and our conclusion is a resounding rejection of H_0—the increased enthusiasm was, indeed, noticed.

The real question of interest is whether the change in enthusiasm produced a *perceived* change in some other aspect of teaching that we know did *not* change. For example,

(continued on next page)

(Case Study 9.2.2 continued)

the instructor did not become more knowledgeable about the material over the course of the two semesters. The student ratings, though, disagree.

Table 9.2.3 shows the instructor's fall and spring ratings on the "knowledgeable" question. Is the increase from $\bar{x} = 3.61$ to $\bar{y} = 4.05$ statistically significant? Yes. For these data, $s_P = 0.898$ and

$$t = \frac{3.61 - 4.05}{0.898\sqrt{\dfrac{1}{229} + \dfrac{1}{243}}} = -5.33$$

which falls far to the left of the 0.05 critical value ($= -1.64$).

TABLE 9.2.3

Fall, x_i	Spring, y_i
$n = 229$	$m = 243$
$\bar{x} = 3.61$	$\bar{y} = 4.05$
$s_X = 0.84$	$s_Y = 0.95$

What we can glean from these data is both reassuring yet a bit disturbing. Table 9.2.2 appears to confirm the widely held belief that enthusiasm is an important factor in effective teaching. Table 9.2.3, on the other hand, strikes a more cautionary note. It speaks to another widely held belief—that student evaluations can sometimes be difficult to interpret. Questions that purport to be measuring one trait may, in fact, be reflecting something entirely different.

Comment. It occasionally happens that an experimenter wants to test $H_0: \mu_X = \mu_Y$ and *knows* the values of σ_X^2 and σ_Y^2. For those situations, the t test of Theorem 9.2.2 is inappropriate. If the n X_i's and m Y_i's are normally distributed, it follows from Theorem 7.3.1 that

$$Z = \frac{\bar{X} - \bar{Y} - (\mu_X - \mu_Y)}{\sqrt{\dfrac{\sigma_X^2}{n} + \dfrac{\sigma_Y^2}{m}}} \tag{9.2.1}$$

has a standard normal distribution. Any such test of $H_0: \mu_X = \mu_Y$, then, should be based on an observed Z ratio rather than an observed t ratio.

QUESTIONS

9.2.1 Ring Lardner was one of this country's most popular writers during the 1920s and 1930s. He was also a chronic alcoholic who died prematurely at the age of 48. The following table lists the life spans of some of Lardner's contemporaries (35). Those in the sample on the left were all problem drinkers; they died, on the average, at age 65. The 12 (sober) writers on the right tended to live a full 10 years longer. Can it be argued that an increase of that magnitude is statistically significant? Test an appropriate null hypothesis against a one-sided H_1. Use the 0.05 level of significance. *Note*: The pooled sample standard deviation for these two samples is *13.9*.

Authors Noted for Alchohol Abuse		Authors Not Noted for Alchohol Abuse	
Name	Age at death	Name	Age at death
Ring Lardner	48	Carl Van Doren	65
Sinclair Lewis	66	Ezra Pound	87
Raymond Chandler	71	Randolph Bourne	32
Eugene O'Neill	65	Van Wyck Brooks	77
Robert Benchley	56	Samuel Eliot Morrison	89
J.P. Marquand	67	John Crowe Ransom	86
Dashiell Hammett	67	T.S. Eliot	77
e.e. cummings	70	Conrad Aiken	84
Edmund Wilson	77	Ben Ames Williams	64
Average:	65.2	Henry Miller	88
		Archibald MacLeish	90
		James Thurber	67
		Average:	75.5

9.2.2 Poverty Point is the name given to a number of widely scattered archaeological sites throughout Louisiana, Mississippi, and Arkansas. These are the remains of a society thought to have flourished during the period from 1700 to 500 B.C. Among their characteristic artifacts are ornaments that were fashioned out of clay and then baked. The following table shows the dates (in years B.C.) associated with four of these baked clay ornaments found in two different Poverty Point sites, Terral Lewis and Jaketown (77). The averages for the two samples are 1133.0 and 1013.5, respectively. Is it believable that these two settlements developed the technology to manufacture baked clay ornaments at the same time? Set up and test an appropriate H_0 against a two-sided H_1 at the $\alpha = 0.05$ level of significance. *Note*: $s_X = 266.9$ and $s_Y = 224.3$.

Terral Lewis Estimates, x_i	Jaketown Estimates, y_i
1492	1346
1169	942
883	908
988	858

9.2.3 *Nod-swimming* in male ducks is a highly ritualized behavioral trait. The term refers to a rapid back-and-forth movement of a duck's head. It frequently occurs during courtship displays and occasionally occurs when the duck is approached by another male perceived to have higher status. It *may* depend on the duck's "race." In an experiment investigating the latter (89), two sets of green-winged teals, American and European, were photographed for several days. The following table gives the frequencies (per 10,000 frames of film) with which each bird initiated the nod-swimming motion. At the 0.01 level of significance, test the null hypothesis that the true average nod-swimming frequencies characteristic of American and European ducks are the same.

Amer. male	Freq., x_i	Eur. male	Freq., y_i
A	14.6	G	3.6
B	28.8	H	8.2
C	19.1	I	7.8
D	23.1	J	27.5
E	50.3	K	7.0
F	35.7	L	19.7
		M	17.0
		N	3.5
		O	13.3
		P	12.4
		Q	19.0
		R	14.1

Note: For these two samples,

$$\sum_{i=1}^{6} x_i = 171.6 \qquad \sum_{i=1}^{6} x_i^2 = 5745.60$$

$$\sum_{i=1}^{12} y_i = 153.1 \qquad \sum_{i=1}^{12} y_i^2 = 2526.09$$

9.2.4 A major source of "mercury poisoning" comes from the ingestion of methylmercury (CH_3^{203}), which is found in contaminated fish (recall Question 5.3.2). Among the questions pursued by medical investigators trying to understand the nature of this particular health problem is whether methylmercury is equally hazardous to men and women. The following are the half-lives of methylmercury in the systems of six women and nine men who volunteered for a study where each subject was given an oral administration of CH_3^{203}. Is there evidence here that women metabolize methylmercury at a different rate than men do? Do an appropriate two-sample t test at the $\alpha = 0.01$ level of significance. *Note:* The two sample standard deviations for these data are $s_X = 15.1$ and $s_Y = 8.1$.

Methylmercury (CH_3^{203}) Females, x_i	Half-Lives (in Days) Males, y_i
52	72
69	88
73	87
88	74
87	78
56	70
	78
	93
	74

9.2.5 The use of carpeting in hospitals, while having definite esthetic merits, raises an obvious question: Are carpeted floors sanitary? One way to get at an answer is to compare bacterial levels in carpeted and uncarpeted rooms. Airborne bacteria can be counted by passing room air at a known rate over a growth medium, incubating that medium, and then counting the number of bacterial colonies that form. In one such study done in a Montana hospital (186), room air was pumped over a Petri dish at the rate of 1 cubic foot per minute. This procedure was repeated in 16 patient rooms, 8 carpeted and 8 uncarpeted. The results, expressed in terms of "bacteria per cubic foot of air," are listed in the following table.

Carpeted Rooms	Bacteria/ft^3	Uncarpeted Rooms	Bacteria/ft^3
212	11.8	210	12.1
216	8.2	214	8.3
220	7.1	215	3.8
223	13.0	217	7.2
225	10.8	221	12.0
226	10.1	222	11.1
227	14.6	224	10.1
228	14.0	229	13.7

For the carpeted rooms,

$$\sum_{i=1}^{8} x_i = 89.6 \quad \text{and} \quad \sum_{i=1}^{8} x_i^2 = 1053.70$$

For the uncarpeted rooms,

$$\sum_{i=1}^{8} y_i = 78.3 \quad \text{and} \quad \sum_{i=1}^{8} y_i^2 = 838.49$$

Test whether carpeting has any effect on the level of airborne bacteria in patient rooms. Let $\alpha = 0.05$.

9.2.6 In addition to marketing tea, Lipton also sells packaged dinner entrees. The company was interested in knowing whether the buying habits for such products differed between singles and married couples. In particular, in a poll of consumers, they were asked to respond to the question "Do you use coupons regularly?" by a numerical scale, where 1 stands for agree strongly, 2 for agree, 3 for neutral, 4 for disagree, and 5 for disagree strongly. The results of the poll are given in the following table (20).

Use Coupons Regularly	
Single (X)	Married (Y)
$n = 31$	$n = 57$
$\bar{x} = 3.10$	$\bar{y} = 2.43$
$s_X = 1.469$	$s_Y = 1.350$

Is the observed difference significant at the $\alpha = 0.05$ level?

9.2.7 Accidents R Us and Roadkill specialize in writing insurance policies for high-risk drivers. Last year, Accidents R Us processed 100 claims. Settlements averaged $2000 and had a sample standard deviation of $600. A smaller firm, Roadkill resolved only 50 claims, but the payouts averaged $2500 with a sample standard deviation of $700. Can we conclude from last year's experience that the average awards paid by the two companies tend not to be the same? Set up and carry out an appropriate analysis.

9.2.8 A company markets two brands of latex paint—regular and a more expensive brand that claims to dry an hour faster. A consumer magazine decides to test this claim by painting 10 panels with each product. The average drying time of the regular brand is 2.1 hours with a sample standard deviation of 12 minutes. The fast-drying version has an average of 1.6 hours with a sample standard deviation of 16 minutes. Test the null hypothesis that the more expensive brand dries an hour quicker. Use a one-sided H_1. Let $\alpha = 0.05$.

9.2.9 (a) Suppose $H_0: \mu_X = \mu_Y$ is to be tested against $H_1: \mu_X \neq \mu_Y$. The two sample sizes are 6 and 11. If $s_p = 15.3$, what is the smallest value for $|\bar{x} - \bar{y}|$ that will result in H_0 being rejected at the $\alpha = 0.01$ level of significance?

   (b) What is the smallest value for $\bar{x} - \bar{y}$ that will lead to the rejection of $H_0: \mu_X = \mu_Y$ in favor of $H_1: \mu_X > \mu_Y$ if $\alpha = 0.05$, $s_p = 214.9$, $n = 13$, and $m = 8$?

9.2.10 Suppose that $H_0: \mu_X = \mu_Y$ is being tested against $H_1: \mu_X \neq \mu_Y$, where σ_X^2 and σ_Y^2 are known to be 17.6 and 22.9, respectively. If $n = 10$, $m = 20$, $\bar{x} = 81.6$, and $\bar{y} = 79.9$, what P-value would be associated with the observed Z ratio?

9.2.11 An executive has two routes that she can take to and from work each day. The first is by interstate; the second requires driving through town. On the average it takes her 33 minutes to get to work by the interstate and 35 minutes by going through town. The standard deviations for the two routes are 6 and 5 minutes, respectively. Assume the distributions of the times for the two routes are approximately normally distributed.

   (a) What is the probability that on a given day driving through town would be the quicker of her choices?

   (b) What is the probability that driving through town for an entire week (10 trips) would yield a lower average time than taking the interstate for the entire week?

9.2.12 Prove that the Z ratio given in Equation 9.2.1 has a standard normal distribution.

9.2.13 If $X_1, X_2, \ldots, X_n$ and $Y_1, Y_2, \ldots, Y_m$ are independent random samples from normal distributions with the same σ^2, prove that their pooled sample variance, s_p^2, is an unbiased estimator for σ^2.

9.2.14 Let $X_1, X_2, \ldots, X_n$ and $Y_1, Y_2, \ldots, Y_m$ be independent random samples drawn from normal distributions with means μ_X and μ_Y, respectively, and with the same known variance σ^2. Use the generalized-likelihood-ratio criterion to derive a test procedure for choosing between $H_0: \mu_X = \mu_Y$ and $H_1: \mu_X \neq \mu_Y$.

9.2.15 When $\sigma_X^2 \neq \sigma_Y^2$, $H_0: \mu_X = \mu_Y$ can be tested by using the statistic

$$t = \frac{\bar{x} - \bar{y}}{\sqrt{s_X^2/n + s_Y^2/m}}$$

which has an approximate t distribution with v degrees of freedom, where v is the greatest integer in

$$\frac{\left(s_X^2/n + s_Y^2/m\right)^2}{\left(s_X^2/n\right)^2/(n-1) + \left(s_Y^2/m\right)^2/(m-1)}$$

A person exposed to an infectious agent, either by contact or by vaccination, normally develops antibodies to that agent. Presumably, the severity of an infection is related to the number of antibodies produced. The degree of antibody response is indicated by saying that the person's blood serum has a certain *titer*, with higher titers indicating greater concentrations of antibodies. The following table gives the titers of 22 persons involved in a tularemia epidemic in Vermont (18). Eleven were quite ill; the other 11 were asymptomatic. Use an approximate t ratio to test $H_0: \mu_X = \mu_Y$ against a one-sided H_1 at the 0.05 level of significance.

Note: The sample standard deviations for the "Severely ill" and "Asymptomatic" groups are 428 and 183, respectively.

Severely Ill		Asymptomatic	
Subject	Titer	Subject	Titer
1	640	12	10
2	80	13	320
3	1280	14	320
4	160	15	320
5	640	16	320
6	640	17	80
7	1280	18	160
8	640	19	10
9	160	20	640
10	320	21	160
11	160	22	320

9.2.16 For the approximate two-sample t test described in Question 9.2.15, it will be true that

$$v < n + m - 2$$

Why is that a disadvantage for the approximate test? That is, why is it better to use the Theorem 9.2.1 version of the t test if, in fact, $\sigma_X^2 = \sigma_Y^2$?

9.3   TESTING H_0: $\sigma_X^2 = \sigma_Y^2$—THE F TEST

Although by far the majority of two-sample problems are set up to detect possible shifts in location parameters, situations sometimes arise where it is equally important—perhaps even more important—to compare variability parameters. Two machines on an assembly line, for example, may be producing items whose *average* dimensions (μ_X and μ_Y) of some sort—say, thickness—are not significantly different but whose variabilities (as measured by σ_X^2 and σ_Y^2) are. This becomes a critical piece of information if the increased variability results in an unacceptable proportion of items from one of the machines falling outside the engineering specifications (see Figure 9.3.1).

In this section we will examine the generalized-likelihood-ratio test of H_0: $\sigma_X^2 = \sigma_Y^2$ versus H_1: $\sigma_X^2 \neq \sigma_Y^2$. The data will consist of two independent random samples of sizes n and m: The first—$X_1, X_2, \ldots, X_n$—is assumed to have come from a normal distribution having mean μ_X and variance σ_X^2; the second—$Y_1, Y_2, \ldots, Y_m$—from a normal distribution having mean μ_Y and variance σ_Y^2. (All four parameters are assumed to be unknown.) Theorem 9.3.1 gives the test procedure that will be used. The proof will not be given, but it follows the same basic pattern we have seen in other GLRTs; the important step is showing that the likelihood ratio is a monotonic function of the F distribution defined in Theorem 7.4.1.

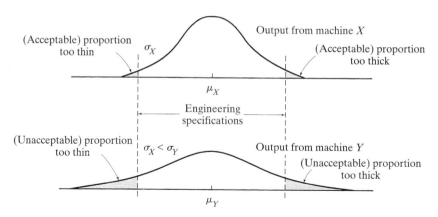

FIGURE 9.3.1   Variability of machine outputs.

Comment.   Tests of $H_0: \sigma_X^2 = \sigma_Y^2$ arise in another, more routine, context. Recall that the procedure for testing the equality of μ_X and μ_Y depended on whether or not the two population variances were equal. This implies that a test of $H_0: \sigma_X^2 = \sigma_Y^2$ should precede every test of $H_0: \mu_X = \mu_Y$. If the former is accepted, the t test on μ_X and μ_Y is done according to Theorem 9.2.2; but if $H_0: \sigma_X^2 = \sigma_Y^2$ is rejected, Theorem 9.2.2 is not entirely appropriate. A frequently used alternative in that case is the approximate t test described in Question 9.2.15.

THEOREM 9.3.1.   Let $X_1, X_2, \ldots, X_n$ and $Y_1, Y_2, \ldots, Y_m$ be independent random samples from normal distributions with means μ_X and μ_Y and standard deviations σ_X and σ_Y, respectively.

(a) To test $H_0: \sigma_X^2 = \sigma_Y^2$ versus $H_1: \sigma_X^2 > \sigma_Y^2$ at the α level of significance, reject H_0 if $s_Y^2/s_X^2 \leq F_{\alpha, m-1, n-1}$.

(b) To test $H_0: \sigma_X^2 = \sigma_Y^2$ versus $H_1: \sigma_X^2 < \sigma_Y^2$ at the α level of significance, reject H_0 if $s_Y^2/s_X^2 \geq F_{1-\alpha, m-1, n-1}$.

(c) To test $H_0: \sigma_X^2 = \sigma_Y^2$ versus $H_1: \sigma_X^2 \neq \sigma_Y^2$ at the α level of significance, reject H_0 if s_Y^2/s_X^2 is either (1) $\leq F_{\alpha/2, m-1, n-1}$ or (2) $\geq F_{1-\alpha/2, m-1, n-1}$.

Comment.   The GLRT described in Theorem 9.3.1 is *approximate* for the same sort of reason the GLRT for $H_0: \sigma^2 = \sigma_0^2$ was approximate (see Theorem 7.3.5). The distribution of the test statistic, S_Y^2/S_X^2, is not symmetric, and the two ranges of variance ratios yielding λ's less than or equal to λ^* (i.e., the left tail and right tail of the critical region) have slightly different areas. For the sake of convenience, though, it is customary to choose the two critical values so that each cuts off the same area, $\alpha/2$.

CASE STUDY 9.3.1

Electroencephalograms are records showing fluctuations of electrical activity in the brain. Among the several different kinds of brain "waves" produced, the dominant ones are usually *alpha* waves. These have a characteristic frequency of anywhere from 8 to 13 cycles per second.

    The objective of the experiment described in this example was to see whether sensory deprivation over an extended period of time has any effect on the alpha-wave pattern. The subjects were 20 inmates in a Canadian prison. They were randomly split into two equal-sized groups. Members of one group were placed in solitary confinement; those in the other group were allowed to remain in their own cells. Seven days later, alpha-wave frequencies were measured for all 20 subjects (53), as shown in Table 9.3.1.

TABLE 9.3.1   Alpha-Wave Frequencies (CPS)

Nonconfined, x_i	Solitary Confinement, y_i
10.7	9.6
10.7	10.4
10.4	9.7
10.9	10.3
10.5	9.2
10.3	9.3
9.6	9.9
11.1	9.5
11.2	9.0
10.4	10.9

    Judging from Figure 9.3.2, there was an apparent *decrease* in alpha-wave frequency for persons in solitary confinement. There also appears to have been an *increase* in the variability for that group. We will use the F test to determine whether the observed difference in variability ($s_X^2 = 0.21$ versus $s_Y^2 = 0.36$) is statistically significant.

FIGURE 9.3.2   Alpha-wave frequencies (cps).

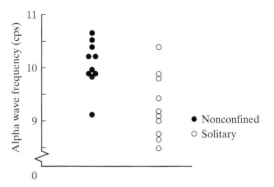

(continued on next page)

(Case Study 9.3.1 continued)

Let σ_X^2 and σ_Y^2 denote the true variances of alpha-wave frequencies for nonconfined and solitary-confined prisoners, respectively. The hypotheses to be tested are

$$H_0: \quad \sigma_X^2 = \sigma_Y^2$$

versus

$$H_1: \quad \sigma_X^2 \neq \sigma_Y^2$$

Let $\alpha = 0.05$ be the level of significance. Given that

$$\sum_{i=1}^{10} x_i = 105.8 \qquad \sum_{i=1}^{10} x_i^2 = 1121.26$$

$$\sum_{i=1}^{10} y_i = 97.8 \qquad \sum_{i=1}^{10} y_i^2 = 959.70$$

the sample variances become

$$s_X^2 = \frac{10(1121.26) - (105.8)^2}{10(9)} = 0.21$$

and

$$s_Y^2 = \frac{10(959.70) - (97.8)^2}{10(9)} = 0.36$$

Dividing the sample variances gives an observed F ratio of *1.71*:

$$F = \frac{s_Y^2}{s_X^2} = \frac{0.36}{0.21} = 1.71$$

Both n and m are 10, so we would expect S_Y^2/S_X^2 to behave like an F random variable with 9 and 9 degrees of freedom (assuming $H_0: \sigma_X^2 = \sigma_Y^2$ is true). From Table A.4 in the Appendix, we see that the values cutting off areas of 0.025 in either tail of that distribution are 0.248 and 4.03 (see Figure 9.3.3).

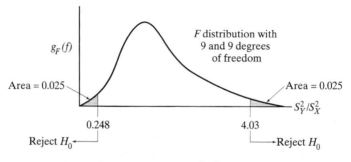

FIGURE 9.3.3   Distribution of S_Y^2/S_X^2 when H_0 is true.

Our conclusion, then, is to *accept* H_0. (In light of the comment preceding Theorem 9.3.1, it would now be appropriate to test H_0: $\mu_X = \mu_Y$ using the two-sample t test of Section 9.2.)

QUESTIONS

9.3.1 Short people tend to live longer than tall people, according to a theory held by certain medical researchers. Reasons for the disparity remain unclear, but studies have shown that short baseball players enjoy a longer life expectancy than tall baseball players. A similar finding has been documented for professional boxers. The following table (143) is a breakdown of the life spans of 31 former presidents, grouped into two categories—"Short" ($\leq 5'7''$) and "Tall" ($\geq 5'8''$). The sample variance for the short presidents is 73.6 years^2; for the tall presidents, 86.9 years^2.

Short Presidents ($\leq 5'7''$)			Tall Presidents ($\geq 5'8''$)		
President	Height	Age	President	Height	Age
Madison	5'4"	85	W. Harrison	5'8"	68
Van Buren	5'6"	79	Polk	5'8"	53
B. Harrison	5'6"	67	Taylor	5'8"	65
J. Adams	5'7"	90	Grant	$5'8\frac{1}{2}''$	63
J.Q. Adams	5'7"	80	Hayes	$5'8\frac{1}{2}''$	70
			Truman	5'9"	88
			Fillmore	5'9"	74
			Pierce	5'10"	64
			A. Johnson	5'10"	66
			T. Roosevelt	5'10"	60
			Coolidge	5'10"	60
			Eisenhower	5'10"	78
			Cleveland	5'11"	71
			Wilson	5'11"	67
			Hoover	5'11"	90
			Monroe	6'	73
			Tyler	6'	71
			Buchanan	6'	77
			Taft	6'	72
			Harding	6'	57
			Jackson	6'1"	78
			Washington	6'2"	67
			Arthur	6'2"	56
			F. Roosevelt	6'2"	63
			L. Johnson	6'2"	64
			Jefferson	$6'2\frac{1}{2}''$	83

(a) Test H_0: $\sigma_X^2 = \sigma_Y^2$ against a two-sided H_1 at the $\alpha = 0.05$ level of significance.
(b) Based on your conclusion in Part (a), would it be appropriate to test H_0: $\mu_X = \mu_Y$ using the two-sample t test of Theorem 9.2.2?

9.3.2 A safe investment for the nonexpert is the certificate of deposit (CD) issued by many banks and other financial institutions. Typically, the larger the term of the investment, the higher the interest rate paid. The following table gives samples of 6-month CD rates and 12-month rates for a $10,000 investment. Is there a difference in the variability of the rates paid, at the $\alpha = 0.05$ level?

$10,000 CD rates	
6 month	12 month
5.10	5.20
5.10	5.40
5.31	5.28
5.00	5.20
5.26	5.59
5.10	5.83
5.26	5.21
5.02	5.40
5.15	5.25
5.35	5.21

Note: For the 6-month rates, $s_X = 0.122$; for the 12-month rates, $s_Y = 0.209$.

9.3.3 Among the standard personality inventories used by psychologists is the thematic apperception test (TAT). A subject is shown a series of pictures and is asked to make up a story about each one. Interpreted properly, the content of the stories can provide valuable insights into the subject's mental well-being. The following data show the TAT results for 40 women, 20 of whom were the mothers of normal children and 20 the mothers of schizophrenic children. In each case the subject was shown the same set of 10 pictures. The figures recorded were the numbers of stories (out of 10) that revealed a *positive* parent–child relationship, one where the mother was clearly capable of interacting with her child in a flexible, open-minded way (187).

TAT Scores

Mothers of Normal Children					Mothers of Schizophrenic Children				
8	4	6	3	1	2	1	1	3	2
4	4	6	4	2	7	2	1	3	1
2	1	1	4	3	0	2	4	2	3
3	2	6	3	4	3	0	1	2	2

(a) Test $H_0: \sigma_X^2 = \sigma_Y^2$ versus $H_1: \sigma_X^2 \neq \sigma_Y^2$, where σ_X^2 and σ_Y^2 are the variances of the scores of mothers of normal children and scores of mothers of schizophrenic children, respectively. Let $\alpha = 0.05$.

(b) If $H_0: \sigma_X^2 = \sigma_Y^2$ is accepted in part (a), test $H_0: \mu_X = \mu_Y$ versus $H_1: \mu_X \neq \mu_Y$. Set α equal to 0.05.

9.3.4 In a study designed to investigate the effects of a strong magnetic field on the early development of mice (7), 10 cages, each containing three 30-day-old albino female mice, were subjected for a period of 12 days to a magnetic field having an average strength of 80 Oe/cm. Thirty other mice, housed in 10 similar cages, were not put in the magnetic field and served as controls. Listed in the table are the weight gains, in grams, for each of the 20 sets of mice.

| | In magnetic field | | Not in magnetic field | |
Cage	Weight gain (g)	Cage	Weight gain (g)
1	22.8	11	23.5
2	10.2	12	31.0
3	20.8	13	19.5
4	27.0	14	26.2
5	19.2	15	26.5
6	9.0	16	25.2
7	14.2	17	24.5
8	19.8	18	23.8
9	14.5	19	27.8
10	14.8	20	22.0

Test whether the variances of the two sets of weight gains are significantly different. Let $\alpha = 0.05$. *Note*: For the mice in the magnetic field, $s_X = 5.67$; for the other mice, $s_Y = 3.18$.

9.3.5 Raynaud's syndrome is characterized by the sudden impairment of blood circulation in the fingers, a condition that results in discoloration and heat loss. The magnitude of the problem is evidenced in the following data, where 20 subjects (10 "normals" and 10 with Raynaud's syndrome) immersed their right forefingers in water kept at 19°C. The heat output (in cal/cm^2/minute) of the forefinger was then measured with a calorimeter (96).

| | Normal Subjects | | Subjects with Raynaud's Syndrome | |
Patient	Heat Output (cal/cm^2/min)	Patient	Heat Output (cal/cm^2/min)
W.K.	2.43	R.A.	0.81
M.N.	1.83	R.M.	0.70
S.A.	2.43	F.M.	0.74
Z.K.	2.70	K.A.	0.36
J.H.	1.88	H.M.	0.75
J.G.	1.96	S.M.	0.56
G.K.	1.53	R.M.	0.65
A.S.	2.08	G.E.	0.87
T.E.	1.85	B.W.	0.40
L.F.	2.44	N.E.	0.31
	$\bar{x} = 2.11$		$\bar{y} = 0.62$
	$s_X = 0.37$		$s_Y = 0.20$

Test that the heat-output variances for normal subjects and those with Raynaud's syndrome are the same. Use a two-sided alternative and the 0.05 level of significance.

9.3.6 Because of the designated hitter rule, baseball is not played the same way in the American League as it is in the National League. Strategies are different, and the scores of the games are different. What may also be affected are the *lengths* of the games. The following table gives a recent year's average completion times for American League home games and National League home games. Is there any evidence here that the variation in game times may not be the same for the two leagues? Set up and carry out an appropriate hypothesis test at the $\alpha = 0.05$ level of significance.

American League		National League	
Team	Average home game (in minutes)	Team	Average home game (in minutes)
Baltimore	177	Atlanta	166
Boston	177	Chicago	154
California	165	Cincinnati	159
Chicago	172	Houston	168
Cleveland	172	Los Angeles	174
Detroit	179	Montreal	174
Kansas City	163	New York	177
Milwaukee	175	Philadelphia	167
Minnesota	166	Pittsburgh	165
New York	182	San Diego	161
Oakland	177	San Francisco	164
Seattle	168	St. Louis	161
Texas	179		
Toronto	177	Sample average:	165.8
Sample average:	173.5	Sample std. dev.:	6.8
Sample std. dev.:	5.9	Sample size:	12
Sample size:	14		

9.3.7 For the data in Question 9.2.4, the sample variances for the methylmercury half-lives are 227.77 for the females and 65.25 for the males. Does the magnitude of that difference invalidate using Theorem 9.2.2 to test $H_0: \mu_X = \mu_Y$? Explain.

9.3.8 Crosstown busing to compensate for de facto segregation was begun on a fairly large scale in Nashville during the 1960s. Progress was made, but critics argued that too many racial imbalances were left unaddressed. Among the data cited in the early 1970s are the following figures, showing the percentages of African-American students enrolled in a random sample of 18 public schools (155). Nine of the schools were located in predominantly African-American neighborhoods; the other nine, in predominantly white neighborhoods. Which version of the two-sample t test, Theorem 9.2.2 or the approximation in Question 9.2.15, would be more appropriate for deciding whether the difference between 35.9% and 19.7% is statistically significant? Justify your answer.

Schools in African-American neighborhoods	Schools in white neighborhoods
36%	21%
28	14
41	11
32	30
46	29
39	6
24	18
32	25
45	23
Average: 35.9%	Average: 19.7%

9.3.9 Show that the generalized likelihood ratio for testing H_0: $\sigma_X^2 = \sigma_Y^2$ versus H_1: $\sigma_X^2 \neq \sigma_Y^2$ as described in Theorem 9.3.1 is given by

$$\lambda = \frac{L(\hat{\omega})}{L(\hat{\Omega})} = \frac{(m+n)^{(n+m)/2}}{n^{n/2} m^{m/2}} \frac{\left[\sum\limits_{i=1}^{n}(x_i - \bar{x})^2\right]^{n/2} \left[\sum\limits_{j=1}^{m}(y_j - \bar{y})^2\right]^{m/2}}{\left[\sum\limits_{i=1}^{n}(x_i - \bar{x})^2 + \sum\limits_{j=1}^{m}(y_j - \bar{y})^2\right]^{(m+n)/2}}$$

9.3.10 Let $X_1, X_2, \ldots, X_n$ and $Y_1, Y_2, \ldots, Y_m$ be independent random samples from normal distributions with means μ_X and μ_Y and standard deviations σ_X and σ_Y, respectively, where μ_X and μ_Y are known. Derive the GLRT for H_0: $\sigma_X^2 = \sigma_Y^2$ versus H_1: $\sigma_X^2 > \sigma_Y^2$.

9.4 BINOMIAL DATA: TESTING H_0: $p_X = p_Y$

Up to this point, the data considered in Chapter 9 have been independent random samples of sizes n and m drawn from two *continuous* distributions—in fact, from two *normal* distributions. Obviously, many other sorts of data might have to be dealt with. The X's and Y's might represent continuous random variables, for example, but have density functions other than the normal. Or they might be *discrete*. In this section we consider the most common example of this latter type: situations where the two sets of data are *binomial*.

Suppose that n Bernoulli trials related to treatment X have resulted in x successes, and m (independent) Bernoulli trials related to treatment Y in y successes. We wish to test whether p_X and p_Y, the *true* probabilities of success for treatment X and treatment Y, are equal:

$$H_0: \quad p_X = p_Y \quad (= p)$$

versus

$$H_1: \quad p_X \neq p_Y$$

The level of significance will be α.

Here the two parameter spaces are given by

$$\omega = \{(p_X, p_Y): 0 \leq p_X = p_Y \leq 1\}$$

and

$$\Omega = \{(p_X, p_Y): 0 \leq p_X \leq 1, 0 \leq p_Y \leq 1\}$$

Furthermore, the likelihood function can be written

$$L = p_X^x (1 - p_X)^{n-x} \cdot p_Y^y (1 - p_Y)^{m-y}$$

Setting the derivative of $\ln L$ with respect to $p(= p_X = p_Y)$ equal to 0 and solving for p gives a not too surprising result—namely,

$$\hat{p} = \frac{x + y}{n + m}$$

That is, the MLE for p under H_0 is the pooled success proportion. Similarly, solving $\partial \ln L / \partial p_X = 0$ and $\partial \ln L / \partial p_Y = 0$ gives the two original sample proportions as the unrestricted MLEs for p_X and p_Y:

$$\hat{p}_X = \frac{x}{n}, \quad \hat{p}_Y = \frac{y}{m}$$

Putting $\hat{p}$, $\hat{p}_X$, and $\hat{p}_Y$ back into L gives the generalized likelihood ratio:

$$\lambda = \frac{L(\hat{\omega})}{L(\hat{\Omega})} = \frac{[(x+y)/(n+m)]^{x+y}[1-(x+y)/(n+m)]^{n+m-x-y}}{(x/n)^x[1-(x/n)]^{n-x}(y/m)^y[1-(y/m)]^{m-y}} \qquad (9.4.1)$$

Equation 9.4.1 is such a difficult function to work with that it is necessary to find an approximation to the usual generalized-likelihood-ratio test. There are several available. It can be shown, for example, that $-2\ln\lambda$ for this problem has an asymptotic χ^2 distribution with 1 degree of freedom (188). Thus, an approximate two-sided, $\alpha = 0.05$ test is to reject H_0 if $-2\ln\lambda \geq 3.84$.

Another approach, and the one most often used, is to appeal to the central limit theorem and make the observation that

$$\frac{\dfrac{X}{n} - \dfrac{Y}{m} - E\left(\dfrac{X}{n} - \dfrac{Y}{m}\right)}{\sqrt{\mathrm{Var}\left(\dfrac{X}{n} - \dfrac{Y}{m}\right)}}$$

has an approximate standard normal distribution. Under H_0, of course

$$E\left(\frac{X}{n} - \frac{Y}{m}\right) = 0$$

and

$$\mathrm{Var}\left(\frac{X}{n} - \frac{Y}{m}\right) = \frac{p(1-p)}{n} + \frac{p(1-p)}{m}$$

$$= \frac{(n+m)p(1-p)}{nm}$$

If p is now replaced by $(x+y)/(n+m)$, its MLE under ω, we get the statement of Theorem 9.4.1. Details of the proof will be omitted.

THEOREM 9.4.1.   Let x and y denote the numbers of successes observed in two independent sets of n and m Bernoulli trials, respectively, where p_X and p_Y are the true success probabilities associated with each set of trials. Let

$$\hat{p} = \frac{x+y}{n+m} \text{ and define}$$

$$z = \frac{\dfrac{x}{n} - \dfrac{y}{m}}{\sqrt{\dfrac{\hat{p}(1-\hat{p})}{n} + \dfrac{\hat{p}(1-\hat{p})}{m}}}$$

(a) To test $H_0: p_X = p_Y$ versus $H_1: p_X > p_Y$ at the α level of significance, reject H_0 if $z \geq z_\alpha$.

(b) To test $H_0: p_X = p_Y$ versus $H_1: p_X < p_Y$ at the α level of significance, reject H_0 if $z \leq -z_\alpha$.

(c) To test $H_0: p_X = p_Y$ versus $H_1: p_X \neq p_Y$ at the α level of significance, reject H_0 if z is either (1) $\leq -z_{\alpha/2}$ or (2) $\geq z_{\alpha/2}$.

Comment.   The utility of Theorem 9.4.1 actually extends beyond the scope we have just described. Any continuous variable can always be dichotomized and "transformed" into a Bernoulli variable. For example, blood pressure can be recorded in terms of "mm Hg," a continuous variable, or simply as "normal" or "abnormal," a Bernoulli variable. The next two case studies illustrate these two sources of binomial data. In the first, the variables begin and end as Bernoulli, while in the second, the initial measurement of "number of nightmares per month" is dichotomized into "often" and "seldom."

CASE STUDY 9.4.1

Local judges have a little discretion in the disposition of criminal cases that appear before their court. For some cases, the judge and the defendant's lawyer will enter into a plea bargain, where the accused pleads guilty to a lesser charge. How often this happens is measured by the *mitigation rate*, the proportion of criminal cases where the defendant qualifies for prison time but receives a greatly shortened term or no prison time at all.

A recent Florida Corrections Department study showed that the mitigation rate in Escambia County from January 1994 through March 1996 was *61.7%* (1033 out of 1675 cases), making it the state's fourth highest. Not happy with that distinction, the area's State Attorney instituted some new policies designed to limit the number of plea bargains. A follow-up study (122) revealed that the July 1996 through June 1997 mitigation rate decreased to *52.1%* (344 out of 660 cases). Is it fair to attribute that decline to the State Attorney's efforts, or can the drop from 61.7% to 52.1% be written off to chance?

Let p_X be the true probability that mitigation would have occurred during the period January 1994 through March 1996, and let p_Y denote the analogous probability for July 1996 through June 1997. The hypotheses to be tested are

$$H_0: \quad p_X = p_Y \quad (= p)$$

versus

$$H_1: \quad p_X > p_Y$$

Let $\alpha = 0.01$.

If H_0 is true, the pooled estimate of p would be the overall mitigation rate. That is,

$$\hat{p} = \frac{1033 + 344}{1675 + 660} = \frac{1377}{2335} = 0.590$$

The sample proportions of the mitigation rate for the first period and second period are $1033/1675 = 0.617$ and $344/660 = 0.521$, respectively. According to Theorem 9.4.1, then, the test statistic is equal to 4.25:

$$z = \frac{0.617 - 0.521}{\sqrt{\dfrac{(0.590)(0.410)}{1675} + \dfrac{(0.590)(0.410)}{660}}} = 4.25$$

Since z exceeds the $\alpha = 0.01$ critical value $(z_{.01} = 2.33)$, we should reject the null hypothesis and conclude that the more stringent policies laid down by the State Attorney did have the desired effect of lowering the county's mitigation rate.

CASE STUDY 9.4.2

Over the years, numerous studies have sought to characterize the nightmare sufferer. Out of these has emerged the stereotype of someone with high anxiety, low ego strength, feelings of inadequacy, and poorer-than-average physical health. What is not so well known, though, is whether men fall into this pattern with the same frequency as women. To this end, a recent investigation (70) looked at nightmare frequencies for a sample of 160 men and 192 women. Each subject was asked whether he (or she) experienced nightmares "often" (at least once a month) or "seldom" (less than once a month). Is the difference between 34.4% and 31.3% (see Table 9.4.1) statistically significant?

TABLE 9.4.1   Frequency of Nightmares

	Men	Women	Total
Nightmares often	55	60	115
Nightmares seldom	105	132	237
Totals	160	192	
% often:	34.4	31.3	

Let p_M and p_W denote the true proportions of men having nightmares often and women having nightmares often, respectively. The hypotheses to be tested are

$$H_0: \quad p_M = p_W$$

versus

$$H_1: \quad p_M \neq p_W$$

Let $\alpha = 0.05$. Then $\pm z_{.025} = \pm 1.96$ become the two critical values. Moreover,

$$\hat{p} = \frac{55 + 60}{160 + 192} = 0.327, \text{ so}$$

$$z = \frac{0.344 - 0.313}{\sqrt{\dfrac{(0.327)(0.673)}{160} + \dfrac{(0.327)(0.673)}{192}}}$$

$$= 0.62$$

The conclusion, then, is clear: We fail to reject the null hypothesis—these data provide no convincing evidence that the frequency of nightmares is different for men than for women.

QUESTIONS

9.4.1 The phenomenon of handedness has been extensively studied in human populations. The percentages of adults who are right-handed, left-handed, and ambidextrous are well documented. What is not so well known is that a similar phenomenon is present in lower animals. Dogs, for example, can be either right-pawed or left-pawed. Suppose that in a random sample of 200 beagles it is found that 55 are left-pawed and that in a random sample of 200 collies 40 are left-pawed. Can we conclude that the true proportion of collies that are left-pawed is significantly different from the true proportion of beagles that are left-pawed? Let $\alpha = 0.05$.

9.4.2 In a study designed to see whether a controlled diet could retard the process of arteriosclerosis, a total of 846 randomly chosen persons were followed over an eight-year period. Half were instructed to eat only certain foods; the other half could eat whatever they wanted. At the end of eight years, 66 persons in the diet group were found to have died of either myocardial infarction or cerebral infarction, as compared to 93 deaths of a similar nature in the control group (191). Do the appropriate analysis. Let $\alpha = 0.05$.

9.4.3 Water witching, the practice of using the movements of a forked twig to locate underground water (or minerals), dates back over 400 years. Its first detailed description appears in Agricola's *De re Metallica*, published in 1556. That water witching works remains a belief widely held among rural people in Europe and throughout the Americas. [In 1960 the number of "active" water witches in the United States was estimated to be more than 20,000 (183).] Reliable evidence supporting or refuting water witching is hard to find. Personal accounts of isolated successes or failures tend to be strongly biased by the attitude of the observer. The following data show the outcomes of all the wells dug in Fence Lake, New Mexico, where 29 "witched" wells and 32 "nonwitched" wells were sunk. Recorded for each well was whether it proved to be successful (S) or unsuccessful (U). What would you conclude?

Witched Wells					Nonwitched Wells				
S	S	S	S	U	U	S	S	S	S
U	S	S	S	S	S	S	S	S	S
S	U	S	U	S	S	U	S	S	S
S	S	S	S	S	S	U	S	S	S
S	S	S	S	S	S	S	S	U	S
U	S	S	S		U	S	S	S	S
					S	S			

9.4.4 If flying saucers are a genuine phenomenon, it would follow that the nature of sightings (that is, their physical characteristics) should be similar in different parts of the world. A prominent UFO investigator compiled a listing of 91 sightings reported in Spain and 1117 reported elsewhere. Among the information recorded was whether the saucer was on the ground or hovering. His data are summarized in the following table (78). Let p_S and p_{NS} denote the true probabilities of "Saucer on ground" in Spain and Not in Spain, respectively. Test H_0: $p_S = p_{NS}$ against a two-sided H_1. Let $\alpha = 0.01$.

	In Spain	Not in Spain
Saucer on ground	53	705
Saucer hovering	38	412

9.4.5 Suppose H_0: $p_X = p_Y$ is being tested against H_1: $p_X \neq p_Y$ on the basis of two independent sets of 100 Bernoulli trials. If x, the number of successes in the first set, is 60 and y, the number of successes in the second set, is 48, what P-value would be associated with the data?

9.4.6 A total of 8605 students are enrolled full-time at State University this semester, 4134 of whom are women. Of the 6001 students who live on campus, 2915 are women. Can it be argued that the difference in the proportion of men and women living on campus is statistically significant? Carry out an appropriate analysis. Let $\alpha = 0.05$.

9.4.7 The kittiwake is a seagull whose mating behavior is basically monogamous. Normally, the birds separate for several months after the completion of one breeding season and reunite at the beginning of the next. Whether or not the birds actually do reunite, though, may be affected by the success of their "relationship" the season before. A total of 769 kittiwake pair-bonds were studied (32) over the course of two breeding seasons; of those 769, some 609 successfully bred during the first season; the remaining 160 were unsuccessful. The following season, 175 of the previously successful pair-bonds "divorced," as did 100 of the 160 whose prior relationship left something to be desired. Can we conclude that the two divorce rates (29% and 63%) are significantly different at the 0.05 level?

	Breeding in previous year	
	Successful	Unsuccessful
Number divorced	175	100
Number not divorced	434	60
Total	609	160
Percent divorced	29	63

9.4.8 A utility infielder for a National League club batted .260 last season in 300 trips to the plate. This year he hit .250 in 200 at-bats. The owners are trying to cut his pay for next year on the grounds that his output has deteriorated. The player argues, though, that his performances the last two seasons have not been significantly different, so his salary should not be reduced. Who is right?

9.4.9 Compute $-2 \ln \lambda$ (see Equation 9.4.1) for the nightmare data of Case Study 9.4.2, and use it to test the equality of $p_X = p_Y$. Let $\alpha = 0.01$.

9.5 CONFIDENCE INTERVALS FOR THE TWO-SAMPLE PROBLEM

Two-sample data lend themselves nicely to the hypothesis-testing format because a meaningful H_0 can always be defined (which was not the case for every set of *one-sample* data). The same inferences, though, can just as easily be phrased in terms of confidence intervals. Simple inversions similar to the derivation of Equation 7.5.1 will yield confidence intervals for $\mu_X - \mu_Y, \sigma_X^2/\sigma_Y^2$, and $p_X - p_Y$.

> **THEOREM 9.5.1.** Let $X_1, X_2, \ldots, X_n$ and $Y_1, Y_2, \ldots, Y_m$ be independent random samples drawn from normal distributions with means μ_X and μ_Y, respectively, and with the same standard deviation, σ. Let s_p denote the data's pooled standard deviation. A $100(1 - \alpha)\%$ confidence interval for $\mu_X - \mu_Y$ is given by
>
> $$\left(\bar{x} - \bar{y} - t_{\alpha/2, n+m-2} s_p \sqrt{\frac{1}{n} + \frac{1}{m}}, \bar{x} - \bar{y} + t_{\alpha/2, n+m-2} s_p \sqrt{\frac{1}{n} + \frac{1}{m}} \right)$$

Proof. We know from Theorem 9.2.1 that

$$\frac{\bar{X} - \bar{Y} - (\mu_X - \mu_Y)}{S_p\sqrt{\dfrac{1}{n} + \dfrac{1}{m}}}$$

has a Student t distribution with $n + m - 2$ df. Therefore,

$$P\left(-t_{\alpha/2,\,n+m-2} \leq \frac{\bar{X} - \bar{Y} - (\mu_X - \mu_Y)}{S_p\sqrt{\dfrac{1}{n} + \dfrac{1}{m}}} \leq t_{\alpha/2,\,n+m-2}\right) = 1 - \alpha \qquad (9.5.1)$$

Rewriting Equation 9.5.1 by isolating $\mu_X - \mu_Y$ in the center of the inequalities gives the endpoints stated in the theorem.

CASE STUDY 9.5.1

Occasionally in forensic medicine, or in the aftermath of a bad accident, identifying the sex of a victim can be a very difficult task. In some of these cases, dental structure provides a useful criterion, since individual teeth will remain in good condition long after other tissues have deteriorated. Furthermore, studies have shown that female teeth and male teeth have different physical and chemical characteristics.

    The extent to which X-rays can penetrate tooth enamel, for instance, is different for men than it is for women. Listed in Table 9.5.1 are "spectropenetration gradients" for eight female teeth and eight male teeth (51). These numbers are measures of the rate of change in the amount of X-ray penetration through a 500-micron section of tooth enamel at a wavelength of 600 nm as opposed to 400 nm.

TABLE 9.5.1   Enamel Spectropenetration Gradients

Male, x_i	Female, y_i
4.9	4.8
5.4	5.3
5.0	3.7
5.5	4.1
5.4	5.6
6.6	4.0
6.3	3.6
4.3	5.0

    Let μ_X and μ_Y be the population means of the spectropenetration gradients associated with male teeth and with female teeth, respectively. Note that

$$\sum_{i=1}^{8} x_i = 43.4 \qquad \sum_{i=1}^{8} x_i^2 = 239.32$$

from which

$$\bar{x} = \frac{43.4}{8} = 5.4$$

(continued on next page)

(Case Study 9.5.1 continued)

and

$$s_X^2 = \frac{8(239.32) - (43.4)^2}{8(7)} = 0.55$$

Similarly,

$$\sum_{i=1}^{8} y_i = 36.1 \qquad \sum_{i=1}^{8} y_i^2 = 166.95$$

so that

$$\bar{y} = \frac{36.1}{8} = 4.5$$

and

$$s_Y^2 = \frac{8(166.95) - (36.1)^2}{8(7)} = 0.58$$

Therefore, the pooled standard deviation is equal to 0.75:

$$s_p = \sqrt{\frac{7(0.55) + 7(0.58)}{8 + 8 - 2}} = \sqrt{0.565} = 0.75$$

We know that the ratio

$$\frac{\bar{X} - \bar{Y} - (\mu_X - \mu_Y)}{S_p\sqrt{\frac{1}{8} + \frac{1}{8}}}$$

will be approximated by a Student t curve with 14 degrees of freedom. Since $t_{.025,14} = 2.1448$, the 95% confidence interval for $\mu_X - \mu_Y$ is given by

$$\left(\bar{x} - \bar{y} - 2.1448 s_p\sqrt{\tfrac{1}{8} + \tfrac{1}{8}}, \bar{x} - \bar{y} + 2.1448 s_p\sqrt{\tfrac{1}{8} + \tfrac{1}{8}}\right)$$
$$= \left(5.4 - 4.5 - 2.1448(0.75)\sqrt{0.25}, 5.4 - 4.5 + 2.1448(0.75)\sqrt{0.25}\right)$$
$$= (0.1, 1.7)$$

Comment. Here the 95% confidence interval does not include the value 0. This means that had we tested

$$H_0: \quad \mu_X = \mu_Y$$

versus

$$H_1: \quad \mu_X \neq \mu_Y$$

at the $\alpha = 0.05$ level of significance, H_0 would have been rejected.

THEOREM 9.5.2. Let $X_1, X_2, \ldots, X_n$ and $Y_1, Y_2, \ldots, Y_m$ be independent random samples drawn from normal distributions with standard deviations σ_X and σ_Y, respectively. A $100(1 - \alpha)\%$ confidence interval for the variance ratio, σ_X^2/σ_Y^2, is given by

$$\left(\frac{s_X^2}{s_Y^2} F_{\alpha/2,\, m-1,\, n-1}, \frac{s_X^2}{s_Y^2} F_{1-\alpha/2,\, m-1,\, n-1}\right)$$

Proof.   Start with the fact that $\dfrac{S_Y^2/\sigma_Y^2}{S_X^2/\sigma_X^2}$ has an F distribution with $m-1$ and $n-1$ df, and follow that strategy used in the proof of Theorem 9.5.1—that is, isolate σ_X^2/σ_Y^2 in the center of the analogous inequalities.

CASE STUDY 9.5.2

The easiest way to measure the movement, or flow, of a glacier is with a camera. First a set of reference points is marked off at various sites near the glacier's edge. Then these points, along with the glacier, are photographed from an airplane. The problem is this: How long should the time interval be between photographs? If too *short* a period has elapsed, the glacier will not have moved very far and the errors associated with the photographic technique will be relatively large. If too *long* a period has elapsed, parts of the glacier might be deformed by the surrounding terrain, an eventuality that could introduce substantial variability into the point-to-point velocity estimates.

    Two sets of flow rates for the Antarctic's Hoseason Glacier have been calculated (104), one based on photographs taken *three* years apart, the other, *five* years apart (see Table 9.5.2). On the basis of other considerations, it can be assumed that the "true" flow rate was constant for the eight years in question.

TABLE 9.5.2   Flow Rates Estimated for the Hoseason Glacier
(Meters Per Day)

Three-Year Span, x_i	Five-Year Span, y_i
0.73	0.72
0.76	0.74
0.75	0.74
0.77	0.72
0.73	0.72
0.75	
0.74	

    The objective here is to assess the relative variabilities associated with the three- and five-year time periods. One way to do this—assuming the data to be normal—is to construct, say, a 95% confidence interval for the variance ratio. If that interval does not contain the value "1", we infer that the two time periods lead to flow rate estimates of significantly different precision.

    From Table 9.5.2,

$$\sum_{i=1}^{7} x_i = 5.23 \quad \text{and} \quad \sum_{i=1}^{7} x_i^2 = 3.9089$$

so that

$$s_X^2 = \frac{7(3.9089) - (5.23)^2}{7(6)} = 0.000224$$

Similarly,

(continued on next page)

(Case Study 9.5.2 continued)

$$\sum_{i=1}^{5} y_i = 3.64 \quad \text{and} \quad \sum_{i=1}^{5} y_i^2 = 2.6504$$

making

$$s_Y^2 = \frac{5(2.6504) - (3.64)^2}{5(4)} = 0.000120$$

The two critical values come from Table A.4 in the Appendix:

$$F_{.025,4,6} = 0.109 \quad \text{and} \quad F_{.975,4,6} = 6.23$$

When all of these quantities are substituted into the statement of Theorem 9.5.2, we get a 95% confidence interval for σ_X^2/σ_Y^2:

$$\left(\frac{0.000224}{0.000120} 0.109, \frac{0.000224}{0.000120} 6.23 \right) = (0.203, 11.629)$$

Thus, although the three-year data had a larger *sample* variance than the five-year data, no conclusions can be drawn about the *true* variances being different, because the ratio $\sigma_X^2/\sigma_Y^2 = 1$ is contained in the confidence interval.

THEOREM 9.5.3. Let x and y denote the numbers of successes observed in two independent sets of n and m Bernoulli trials, respectively. If p_X and p_Y denote the true success probabilities, an approximate $100(1 - \alpha)\%$ confidence interval for $p_X - p_Y$ is given by

$$\left(\frac{x}{n} - \frac{y}{m} - z_{\alpha/2} \sqrt{ \frac{\left(\frac{x}{n}\right)\left(1 - \frac{x}{n}\right)}{n} + \frac{\left(\frac{y}{m}\right)\left(1 - \frac{y}{m}\right)}{m} }, \right.$$

$$\left. \frac{x}{n} - \frac{y}{m} + z_{\alpha/2} \sqrt{ \frac{\left(\frac{x}{n}\right)\left(1 - \frac{x}{n}\right)}{n} + \frac{\left(\frac{y}{m}\right)\left(1 - \frac{y}{m}\right)}{m} } \right)$$

Proof. See Question 9.5.5.

CASE STUDY 9.5.3

Until almost the end of the nineteenth century the mortality associated with surgical operations—even minor ones—was extremely high. The major problem was infection. The germ theory as a model for disease transmission was still unknown, so there was no concept of sterilization. As a result, many patients died from postoperative complications.

The major breakthrough that was so desperately needed finally came when Joseph Lister, a British physician, began reading about some of the work done by Louis Pasteur.

In a series of classic experiments, Pasteur had succeeded in demonstrating the part that yeasts and bacteria play in fermentation. What Lister conjectured was that human infections might have a similar organic origin. To test his theory he began using carbolic acid as an operating-room disinfectant. The data in Table 9.5.3 show the outcomes of 75 amputations performed by Lister, 35 without the aid of carbolic acid and 40 with it (190).

TABLE 9.5.3   Mortality Rates—Lister's Amputations

		Carbolic acid used?		
		No	Yes	Total
Patient	Yes	19	34	53
lived?	No	16	6	22
	Total	35	40	

Let p_W (estimated by $\frac{34}{40}$) and $p_{W/O}$ (estimated by $\frac{19}{35}$) denote the true survival probabilities for patients amputated "with" and "without" the use of carbolic acid, respectively. To construct a 95% confidence interval for $p_W - p_{W/O}$ we note that $z_{\alpha/2} = 1.96$; then Theorem 9.5.3 reduces to

$$\left(\frac{34}{40} - \frac{19}{35} - 1.96\sqrt{\frac{\left(\frac{34}{40}\right)\left(1 - \frac{34}{40}\right)}{40} + \frac{\left(\frac{19}{35}\right)\left(1 - \frac{19}{35}\right)}{35}},\right.$$

$$\left.\frac{34}{40} - \frac{19}{35} + 1.96\sqrt{\frac{\left(\frac{34}{40}\right)\left(1 - \frac{34}{40}\right)}{40} + \frac{\left(\frac{19}{35}\right)\left(1 - \frac{19}{35}\right)}{35}}\right)$$

$$= \left(0.31 - 1.96\sqrt{0.0103}, 0.31 + 1.96\sqrt{0.0103}\right)$$

$$= (0.11, 0.51)$$

Since $p_W - p_{W/O} = 0$ is not included in the interval, we would conclude that the presence or absence of carbolic acid *does* constitute a significant effect. Specifically, patients on whom carbolic acid is used appear to have a *better* chance of recovery.

QUESTIONS

9.5.1 During the 1990s, computer and communications industries were the glamour businesses. Were their high profiles, though, reflected in the compensation paid to their CEOs (48)? The following table lists samples of 1995 salary plus bonuses (in $1000s) for chief executive officers from (1) the computer and communications industry and (2) the more traditional financial services industry. Construct a 95% confidence interval for the difference in the average compensation received by the two groups. *Note*: The pooled standard deviation for these data is 411.

1995 CEO Salary + Bonuses (1,000s)			
Computers & Communications		Financial Services	
Company	Comp.	Company	Comp.
Adobe Systems	668	Boatmen's Bancshs	1150
Alltel	1235	CCB Financial	491
America Online	200	Commercial Federal	566
Applied Materials	1688	First Chicago NBD	1296
BMC Software	752	First of America Bk	498
Frontier	1235	Great Western Finl	953
Nynex	1485	Huntington Bancshs	1208
Read-Rite	1020	Magna Group	504
Solectron	788	MBIA	750
		National City	799
		Old National Bncp	292
		OnBancorp	500
		PNC Bank	1557
		RCSB Financial	647
		Summit Bancorp	1267

9.5.2 In 1965 a silver shortage in the United States prompted Congress to authorize the minting of silverless dimes and quarters. They also recommended that the silver content of half-dollars be reduced from 90% to 40%. Historically, fluctuations in the amount of rare metals found in coins are not uncommon (69). The following data may be a case in point. Listed are the silver percentages found in samples of a Byzantine coin minted on two separate occasions during the reign of Manuel I (1143–1180). Construct a 90% confidence interval for $\mu_X - \mu_Y$, the true average difference in the coin's silver content (= "early" − "late"). What does the interval imply about the outcome of testing $H_0: \mu_X = \mu_Y$? *Note:* $s_X = 0.54$ and $s_Y = 0.36$.

Early Coinage, x_i (% Ag)	Late Coinage, y_i (% Ag)
5.9	5.3
6.8	5.6
6.4	5.5
7.0	5.1
6.6	6.2
7.7	5.8
7.2	5.8
6.9	
6.2	
Average: 6.7	Average: 5.6

9.5.3 Male fiddler crabs solicit attention from the opposite sex by standing in front of their burrows and waving their claws at the females who walk by. If a female likes what she sees, she pays the male a brief visit in his burrow. If everything goes well and the crustacean chemistry clicks, she will stay a little longer and mate. In what may be a ploy to lessen the risk of spending the night alone, some of the males build elaborate mud domes over their burrows. Do the following data (202) suggest that a male's time spent waving to females is influenced by whether his burrow has a dome? Answer the question by constructing and interpreting a 95% confidence interval for $\mu_X - \mu_Y$. *Note:* $s_p = 11.2$.

% of Time Spent Waving to Females	
Males with Domes, x_i	Males without Domes, y_i
100.0	76.4
58.6	84.2
93.5	96.5
83.6	88.8
84.1	85.3
	79.1
	83.6

9.5.4 Recall the caffeine content data in Table 8.2.2. Let μ_X be the average caffeine content of spray-dried instant coffee, and μ_Y the average for freeze-dried coffee. Construct a 99% confidence interval for $\mu_X - \mu_Y$. What do the endpoints of your interval imply about the outcome of testing $H_1: \mu_X = \mu_Y$ versus $H_1: \mu_X \neq \mu_Y$ at the $\alpha = 0.01$ level of significance?

9.5.5 Carry out the details to complete the proof of Theorem 9.5.1.

9.5.6 Suppose that $X_1, X_2, \ldots, X_n$ and $Y_1, Y_2, \ldots, Y_m$ are independent random samples from normal distributions with means μ_X and μ_Y and *known* standard deviations σ_X and σ_Y, respectively. Derive a $100(1 - \alpha)\%$ confidence interval for $\mu_X - \mu_Y$.

9.5.7 Construct a 95% confidence interval for σ_X^2/σ_Y^2 based on the presidential life span data in Question 9.3.1. The hypothesis test referred to in Part (a) of that question leads to a "fail to reject H_0" conclusion. Does that agree with your confidence interval? Explain.

9.5.8 One of the parameters used in evaluating myocardial function is the end diastolic volume (EDV). The following table shows EDVs recorded for eight persons considered to have normal cardiac function and for six with constrictive pericarditis (182). Would it be correct to use Theorem 9.2.1 to test $H_0: \mu_X = \mu_Y$? Answer the question by constructing a 95% confidence interval for σ_X^2/σ_Y^2.

Normal, x_i	Constrictive pericarditis, y_i
62	24
60	56
78	42
62	74
49	44
67	28
80	
48	

9.5.9 Complete the proof of Theorem 9.5.2.

9.5.10 Construct an 80% confidence interval for the difference $p_M - p_W$ in the nightmare frequency data summarized in Case Study 9.4.2.

9.5.11 If p_X and p_Y denote the true success probabilities associated with two sets of n and m independent Bernoulli trials, respectively, the ratio

$$\frac{\frac{X}{n} - \frac{Y}{m} - (p_X - p_Y)}{\sqrt{\frac{(X/n)(1 - X/n)}{n} + \frac{(Y/m)(1 - Y/m)}{m}}}$$

has approximately a standard normal distribution. Use that fact to prove Theorem 9.5.3.

9.5.12 Suicide rates in the United States tend to be much higher for men than for women, at all ages. That pattern may not extend to all professions, though. Death certificates obtained for the 3637 members of the American Chemical Society who died over a 20-year period revealed that 106 of the 3522 male deaths were suicides, as compared to 13 of the 115 female deaths (92). Construct a 95% confidence interval for the difference in suicide rates. What would you conclude?

APPENDIX 9.A.1   A DERIVATION OF THE TWO-SAMPLE t TEST (A PROOF OF THEOREM 9.2.2)

To begin, we note that both the restricted and unrestricted parameter spaces, ω and Ω, are three dimensional:

$$\omega = \{(\mu_X, \mu_Y, \sigma): -\infty < \mu_X = \mu_Y < \infty, 0 < \sigma < \infty\}$$

and

$$\Omega = \{(\mu_X, \mu_Y, \sigma): -\infty < \mu_X < \infty, -\infty < \mu_Y < \infty, 0 < \sigma < \infty\}$$

Since the X's and Y's are independent (and normal),

$$L(\omega) = \prod_{i=1}^{n} f_X(x_i) \prod_{j=1}^{m} f_Y(y_j)$$

$$= \left(\frac{1}{\sqrt{2\pi}\sigma}\right)^{n+m} \exp\left\{-\frac{1}{2\sigma^2}\left[\sum_{i=1}^{n}(x_i - \mu)^2 + \sum_{j=1}^{m}(y_j - \mu)^2\right]\right\} \quad (9.A.1.1)$$

where $\mu = \mu_X = \mu_Y$. If we take $\ln L(\omega)$ and solve $\partial \ln L(\omega)/\partial \mu = 0$ and $\partial \ln L(\omega)/\partial \sigma^2 = 0$ simultaneously, the solutions will be the restricted maximum-likelihood estimates:

$$\hat{\mu} = \frac{\sum_{i=1}^{n} x_i + \sum_{j=1}^{m} y_j}{n + m} \quad (9.A.1.2)$$

and

$$\hat{\sigma}^2 = \frac{\sum_{i=1}^{n}(x_i - \hat{\mu})^2 + \sum_{j=1}^{m}(y_j - \hat{\mu})^2}{n + m} \quad (9.A.1.3)$$

Substituting Equations 9.A.1.2 and 9.A.1.3 into Equation 9.A.1.1 gives the numerator of the generalized likelihood ratio:

$$L(\hat{\omega}) = \left(\frac{e^{-1}}{2\pi\hat{\sigma}^2}\right)^{(n+m)/2}$$

Similarly, the likelihood function unrestricted by the null hypothesis is

$$L(\Omega) = \left(\frac{1}{\sqrt{2\pi}\sigma}\right)^{n+m} \exp\left\{-\frac{1}{2\sigma^2}\left[\sum_{i=1}^{n}(x_i - \mu_X)^2 + \sum_{j=1}^{m}(y_j - \mu_Y)^2\right]\right\} \quad (9.A.1.4)$$

Here, solving

$$\frac{\partial \ln L(\Omega)}{\partial \mu_X} = 0 \qquad \frac{\partial \ln L(\Omega)}{\partial \mu_Y} = 0 \qquad \frac{\partial \ln L(\Omega)}{\partial \sigma^2} = 0$$

gives

$$\hat{\mu}_X = \bar{x} \qquad \hat{\mu}_Y = \bar{y}$$

$$\hat{\sigma}_\Omega^2 = \frac{\sum_{i=1}^{n}(x_i - \bar{x})^2 + \sum_{j=1}^{m}(y_j - \bar{y})^2}{n + m}$$

If these estimates are substituted into Equation 9.A.1.4, the maximum value for $L(\Omega)$ simplifies to

$$L(\hat{\Omega}) = \left(e^{-1}/2\pi\hat{\sigma}_\Omega^2\right)^{(n+m)/2}$$

It follows, then, that the generalized likelihood ratio, λ, is equal to

$$\lambda = \frac{L(\hat{\omega})}{L(\hat{\Omega})} = \left(\frac{\hat{\sigma}_\Omega^2}{\hat{\sigma}^2}\right)^{(n+m)/2}$$

or, equivalently,

$$\lambda^{2/(n+m)} = \frac{\sum_{i=1}^{n}(x_i - \bar{x})^2 + \sum_{j=1}^{m}(y_j - \bar{y})^2}{\sum_{i=1}^{n}\left[x_i - \left(\frac{n\bar{x} + m\bar{y}}{n + m}\right)\right]^2 + \sum_{j=1}^{m}\left[y_j - \left(\frac{n\bar{x} + m\bar{y}}{n + m}\right)\right]^2}$$

Using the identity

$$\sum_{i=1}^{n}\left(x_i - \frac{n\bar{x} + m\bar{y}}{n + m}\right)^2 = \sum_{i=1}^{n}(x_i - \bar{x})^2 + \frac{m^2 n}{(n + m)^2}(\bar{x} - \bar{y})^2$$

we can write $\lambda^{2/(n+m)}$ as

$$\lambda^{2/(n+m)} = \frac{\sum_{i=1}^{n}(x_i - \bar{x})^2 + \sum_{j=1}^{m}(y_j - \bar{y})^2}{\sum_{i=1}^{n}(x_i - \bar{x})^2 + \sum_{j=1}^{m}(y_j - \bar{y})^2 + \frac{nm}{n + m}(\bar{x} - \bar{y})^2}$$

$$= \frac{1}{1 + \dfrac{(\bar{x} - \bar{y})^2}{\left[\sum_{i=1}^{n}(x_i - \bar{x})^2 + \sum_{j=1}^{m}(y_j - \bar{y})^2\right]\left(\dfrac{1}{n} + \dfrac{1}{m}\right)}}$$

$$= \frac{n + m - 2}{n + m - 2 + \dfrac{(\bar{x} - \bar{y})^2}{s_p^2\left[(1/n) + (1/m)\right]}}$$

where s_p^2 is the pooled variance:

$$s_p^2 = \frac{1}{n + m - 2}\left[\sum_{i=1}^{n}(x_i - \bar{x})^2 + \sum_{j=1}^{m}(y_j - \bar{y})^2\right]$$

Therefore, in terms of the observed t ratio, $\lambda^{2/(n+m)}$ simplifies to

$$\lambda^{2/(n+m)} = \frac{n + m - 2}{n + m - 2 + t^2} \tag{9.A.1.5}$$

At this point the proof is almost complete. The generalized-likelihood-ratio criterion, rejecting $H_0: \mu_X = \mu_Y$ when $0 < \lambda \leq \lambda^*$, is clearly equivalent to rejecting the null hypothesis when $0 < \lambda^{2/(n+m)} \leq \lambda^{**}$. But both of these, from Equation 9.A.1.5, are the same as rejecting H_0 when t^2 is too large. Thus the decision rule in terms of t^2 is

$$\text{Reject } H_0: \mu_X = \mu_Y \text{ in favor of } H_1: \mu_X \neq \mu_Y \text{ if } t^2 \geq t^{*2}$$

Or, phrasing this in still another way, we should reject H_0 if either $t \geq t^*$ or $t \leq -t^*$, where

$$P(-t^* < T < t^* \mid H_0: \mu_X = \mu_Y \text{ is true}) = 1 - \alpha$$

By Theorem 9.2.1, though, T has a Student t distribution with $n + m - 2$ df, which makes $\pm t^* = \pm t_{\alpha/2, n+m-2}$, and the theorem is proved.

APPENDIX 9.A.2 POWER CALCULATIONS FOR A TWO-SAMPLE t TEST

Power calculations for a two-sample t test proceed along the same lines established for the one-sample t test and described in Section 7.5. Basically, there are two different questions that can be answered: (1) Given n, m, and α, what is the probability that $H_0: \mu_X = \mu_Y$ will be rejected if, in fact, the X and Y distributions have shifted apart a distance Δ? (2) Given α, what are the smallest values of n and m for which the probability of making a Type II error is no larger than β—for some fixed $\mu_X - \mu_Y$? [In both these questions the location shift $(\Delta = \mu_X - \mu_Y)$ is usually expressed in terms of standard deviations (Δ/σ).] Figure 7.5.5 can be used to approximate both answers.

As an example of the first situation, imagine testing

$$H_0: \quad \mu_X = \mu_Y$$

versus

$$H_1: \quad \mu_X \neq \mu_Y$$

with $n = 13$, $m = 9$, and $\alpha = 0.01$. We might have reason to ask the following: If μ_X has shifted 1.5 standard deviations to the right of μ_Y $[\Delta/\sigma = (\mu_X - \mu_Y)/\sigma = 1.5]$, what is the probability that H_0 will be rejected? Recall that the abscissa in Figure 7.5.5 is scaled in terms of ϕ, where

$$\phi = \frac{\Delta}{\sigma_{\hat{\Delta}}}\left(\frac{1}{\sqrt{2}}\right)$$

and $\sigma_{\hat{\Delta}}$ is the standard deviation of the sample estimator for Δ—namely, $\bar{X} - \bar{Y}$. Therefore,

$$\sigma_{\hat{\Delta}} = \sigma\sqrt{\frac{1}{n} + \frac{1}{m}} = \sigma\sqrt{\frac{1}{13} + \frac{1}{9}}$$

and

$$\phi = \frac{\Delta}{\sigma\sqrt{1/13 + 1/9}}\frac{1}{\sqrt{2}}$$

$$= \frac{\Delta}{\sigma}\frac{1}{\sqrt{1/13 + 1/9}}\frac{1}{\sqrt{2}}$$

$$= (1.5)\left(\frac{1}{0.434}\right)\left(\frac{1}{1.414}\right)$$

$$= 2.4$$

With the combined sample size totaling 22, the estimator for σ (that is, S_p) will have 20 degrees of freedom. The probability, then, of rejecting H_0 is gotten by entering Figure 7.5.5 with a ϕ of 2.4 and reading off $1 - \beta$ from the $\alpha = 0.01$ curve having $v = 20$ degrees of freedom:

$$1 - \beta = P\left(\text{reject } H_0 \middle| \frac{\Delta}{\sigma} = 1.5\right) = 0.71$$

The second problem, choosing n and m to satisfy requirements imposed on α and β, is likely to be much more relevant to an experimenter than the first procedure. As a numerical illustration of this second problem, suppose it has been decided that the hypotheses to be tested are

$$H_0: \quad \mu_X = \mu_Y$$

versus

$$H_1: \quad \mu_X \neq \mu_Y$$

and that the level of significance should be 0.05. The question is, how large should n and m be?

To simplify matters, we will assume that n and m are to be equal. Finally, as a precision requirement, we will insist that the sample size be large enough to enable the test to reject H_0 at least 80% of the time if $|\mu_X - \mu_Y|/\sigma \geq 1.75$. Accordingly, ϕ reduces to

$$\phi = \frac{\Delta}{\sigma_{\hat{\Delta}}} \times \left(\frac{1}{\sqrt{2}}\right) = \frac{\Delta}{\sigma\sqrt{(2/n)}} \times \frac{1}{\sqrt{2}} = \frac{\sqrt{n}}{2}\frac{\Delta}{\sigma} = \frac{\sqrt{n}}{2} \times 1.75$$

$$= 0.875\sqrt{n}$$

Now, suppose that n were 9. Then $\phi = 0.875\sqrt{9} = 2.625$ and $\nu = 9 + 9 - 2 = 16$. From Figure 7.5.5, the probability of rejecting H_0 under these circumstances (two samples of size 9 and $\Delta/\sigma = 1.75$) is approximately 0.94. This figure, however, considerably exceeds our power requirement of 0.80, implying that a smaller sample size would be adequate. So, suppose that n were 4. Then $\phi = 0.875\sqrt{4} = 1.75$, $\nu = 6$, and $1 - \beta = 0.55$. But now the test would not be precise enough. Table 9.A.2.1 lists $1 - \beta$ for sample sizes ranging from $n = 4$ to $n = 9$.

TABLE 9.A.2.1   Values of $1 - \beta$ as a Function of n

n	ϕ	ν	$1 - \beta$
4	1.75	6	0.55
5	1.96	8	0.67
6	2.14	10	0.78
7	2.31	12	0.85
8	2.47	14	0.90
9	2.62	16	0.94

Notice that $1 - \beta$ exceeds 0.80 for the first time when $n = 7$. This means that the experimenter should take two samples of size 7.

QUESTIONS

9.A.2.1 Suppose $H_0: \mu_X = \mu_Y$ is to be tested against $H_1: \mu_X \neq \mu_Y$ at the $\alpha = 0.05$ level of significance with independent random samples of sizes $n = 4$ and $m = 6$. What is the probability of committing a Type II error if $|\mu_X - \mu_Y|/\sigma = 1.5$?

9.A.2.2 Construct a power curve for the hypothesis test described in Question 9.A.2.1.

9.A.2.3 An experimenter intends to collect two independent normal random samples of sizes 8 and 14 for the purpose of testing $H_0: \mu_X = \mu_Y$ against a two-sided alternative at the $\alpha = 0.05$ level of significance. How often can such a test be expected to reject H_0 if μ_X shifts 1.8 standard deviations to the right of μ_Y?

9.A.2.4 Researchers planning to do a two-sample t test for the purpose of choosing between $H_0: \mu_X = \mu_Y$ and $H_1: \mu_X \neq \mu_Y$ have already decided that one sample size should be n, and the other, $2n$. Moreover, they want to have at least a 90% chance of rejecting H_0 if the means differ in absolute value by 1.5 standard deviations. If the intention is to set $\alpha = 0.05$, what is the smallest acceptable value for n?

9.A.2.5 An experiment is to be conducted to determine whether vampire bats prefer blood at room temperature or at body temperature. Equal numbers of bats are to be given access to drinking tubes attached to a supply of blood kept at one of the two temperatures. The response variable will be the amount of blood (in milliliters) that each bat drinks [see (19)]. The experimenter wants to test whether the average amounts of room-temperature and body-temperature blood consumed are equal (against a two-sided alternative that they are not). If α is going to be set at 0.05 and if the experimenter wants to have at least an 85% chance of rejecting H_0 when, in fact, $|\mu_X - \mu_Y|/\sigma \geq 1.50$, what is the minimum number of bats that should be put in each group?

APPENDIX 9.A.3   MINITAB APPLICATIONS

MINITAB has a simple command—TWOSAMPLE C1 C2—for doing a two-sample t test on a set of x_i's and y_i's stored in columns C1 and C2, respectively. The same command automatically constructs a 95% confidence interval for $\mu_X - \mu_Y$.

Figure 9.A.3.1 shows the syntax for analyzing the Quintus Curtius Snodgrass data in Table 9.2.1. Notice that a subcommand is included. If we write

```
MTB > twosample c1 c2
```

MINITAB will assume the two population variances are not equal, and it will perform the approximate t test described in Question 9.2.15. If the intention is to assume that $\sigma_X^2 = \sigma_Y^2$ (and do the t test as described in Theorem 9.2.1), the proper syntax is

```
MTB > twosample c1 c2;
SUBC > pooled.
```

As is typical, MINITAB associates the test statistic with a P-value rather than an "Accept H_0" or "Reject H_0" conclusion. Here, $P = 0.0013$, which is consistent with the decision reached in Case Study 9.2.1 to "reject H_0 at the $\alpha = 0.01$ level of significance."

Figure 9.A.3.2 shows the "unpooled" analysis of these same data. The conclusion is the same, although the P-value has almost tripled, because both the test statistic and its degrees of freedom have decreased (recall Question 9.2.16).

```
MTB > set c1
DATA> 0.225 0.262 0.217 0.240 0.230 0.229 0.235 0.217
DATA> end
MTB > set c2
DATA> 0.209 0.205 0.196 0.210 0.202 0.207 0.224 0.223
DATA> 0.220 0.201
DATA> end
MTB > name c1 'X' c2 'Y'
MTB > twosample c1 c2;
SUBC> pooled.
```

Two Sample T-Test and Confidence Interval

```
Twosample T for X vs Y
          N        Mean      StDev     SE Mean
X         8       0.2319    0.0146      0.0051
Y        10       0.20970   0.00966     0.0031

95% C.I. for mu X - mu Y: ( 0.0101,  0.0343)
T-Test mu X = mu Y (vs not =): T= 3.88 P=0.0013 DF= 16
Both use Pooled StDev = 0.0121
```

FIGURE 9.A.3.1

```
MTB > set c1
DATA> 0.225 0.262 0.217 0.240 0.230 0.229 0.235 0.217
DATA> end
MTB > set c2
DATA> 0.209 0.205 0.196 0.210 0.202 0.207 0.224 0.223
DATA> 0.220 0.201
DATA> end
MTB > name c1 'X' c2 'Y'
MTB > twosample c1 c2
```

Two Sample T-Test and Confidence Interval

```
Twosample T for X vs Y
          N      Mean     StDev    SE Mean
X         8     0.2319    0.0146    0.0051
Y        10     0.20970   0.00966   0.0031

95% C.I. for mu X - mu Y: (0.0090, 0.0354)
T-Test mu X = mu Y (vs not =): T= 3.70 P=0.0035 DF= 11
```

FIGURE 9.A.3.2

Testing H_0: $\mu_X = \mu_Y$ Using MINITAB Windows

1. Enter the two samples in C1 and C2, respectively.
2. Click on STAT, then on BASIC STATISTICS, then on 2-SAMPLE T.
3. Click on SAMPLES IN DIFFERENT COLUMNS, and type C1 in FIRST box and C2 in SECOND box.
4. Click on NOT EQUAL and then again on the desired H_1.
5. Enter CONFIDENCE LEVEL value for $100(1 - \alpha)$.
6. Click on ASSUME EQUAL VARIANCES if a pooled test is desired.
7. Click on OK.

CHAPTER 10

Goodness-of-Fit Tests

Karl Pearson (1857–1936)

Called by some the founder of twentieth-century statistics, Pearson received his university education at Cambridge, concentrating on physics, philosophy, and law. He was called to the bar in 1881 but never practiced. In 1911 Pearson resigned his chair of applied mathematics and mechanics at University College, London, and became the first Galton Professor of Eugenics, as was Galton's wish. Together with Weldon, Pearson founded the prestigious journal Biometrika and served as its principal editor from 1901 until his death.

10.1 INTRODUCTION

The give and take between the mathematics of probability and the empiricism of statistics should be, by now, a theme comfortably familiar. Time and time again we have seen repeated measurements, no matter what their source, exhibiting a regularity of pattern that can be well approximated by one or more of the handful of probability functions introduced in Chapter 4. Until now, all the inferences resulting from this interfacing have been parameter specific, a fact to which the many hypothesis tests about means, variances, and binomial proportions paraded forth in Chapters 6, 7, and 9 bear ample testimony. Still, there are other situations where the basic *form* of $f_Y(y)$, rather than the value of its parameters, is the most important question at issue. These situations are the focus of Chapter 10.

A geneticist, for example, might want to know whether the inheritance of a certain set of traits follows the same set of ratios as those prescribed by Mendelian theory. The objective of a psychologist, on the other hand, might be to confirm or refute a newly proposed model for cognitive serial learning. Probably the most habitual users of inference procedures directed at the entire $f_Y(y)$, though, are statisticians themselves: As a prelude to doing any sort of hypothesis test or confidence interval, an attempt should be made, sample size permitting, to verify that the data are, indeed, representative of whatever distribution that procedure presumes. Usually, this will mean testing to see whether or not the Y_i's are normal.

In general, any procedure that seeks to determine whether a set of data could reasonably have originated from some given probability distribution, or *class* of probability distributions, is called a *goodness-of-fit* test. The principle behind the particular goodness–of–fit test we will look at is very straightforward: First the observed Y_i's are grouped, more or less arbitrarily, into k classes; then each class's "expected" occupancy is calculated on the basis of the presumed model. If it should happen that the set of observed and expected frequencies show considerable disagreement (as measured by the appropriate statistic), our conclusion will be that the supposed $f_Y(y)$ was incorrect.

In practice, the method has two variants, depending on the specificity of the null hypothesis. Section 10.3 describes the version to use when both the form of the presumed $f_Y(y)$ and the values of all its parameters are given. The more typical situation occurs when $f_Y(y)$ is designated but its parameters need to be estimated; this is taken up in Section 10.4.

A somewhat different application of this same idea is the subject of Section 10.5. There the null hypothesis is that two random variables are *independent*—that is, $f_{X,Y}(x, y) = f_X(x) \cdot f_Y(y)$. In more than a few fields of endeavor, this is the particular inference procedure that is used the most often.

10.2 THE MULTINOMIAL DISTRIBUTION

Their diversity notwithstanding, many goodness-of-fit tests are based on essentially the same statistic, one whose asymptotic distribution is a chi square. The underlying structure of that statistic, though, derives from the *multinomial distribution*, a k-variate extension of the familiar binomial. In this section we define the multinomial and state those of its properties that bear directly on the problem of goodness-of-fit testing.

Given a series of n independent Bernoulli trials, each with success probability p, we know that the pdf for Y, the total number of successes, is

$$P(Y = y) = f_Y(y) = \binom{n}{y} p^y (1 - p)^{n-y}, \quad y = 0, 1, \ldots, n \qquad (10.2.1)$$

One of the obvious ways to generalize Equation 10.2.1 is to consider situations where at each trial k outcomes can occur, rather than just two. This means that Y will be allowed to take on any one of the values $y_1, y_2, \ldots, y_k$ with respective probabilities p_1, $p_2, \ldots, p_k$, the latter satisfying the constraint

$$\sum_{i=1}^{k} p_i = 1$$

(see Figure 10.2.1).

FIGURE 10.2.1

$$
\text{Possible outcomes} \left\{
\begin{array}{cccc}
y_1 & y_1 & & y_1 \\
y_2 & y_2 & p_i = p(Y = y_i), & y_2 \\
\vdots & \vdots & i = 1, 2, \ldots, k & \vdots \\
y_k & y_k & \cdots & y_k \\
\hline
1 & 2 & & n
\end{array}
\right.
$$

Independent trials

As a way of summarizing the outcomes pictured in Figure 10.2.1, a vector of random variables—$(X_1, X_2, \ldots, X_k)$—can be defined, where

$$X_i = \text{number of times } y_i \text{ occurs}, \quad i = 1, 2, \ldots, k$$

Of course, $\sum_{i=1}^{k} X_i = n$.

THEOREM 10.2.1. Let X_i denote the number of times the random variable Y equals $y_i, i = 1, 2, \ldots, k$, in a series of n independent trials, where $p_i = P(Y = y_i)$. The vector $(X_1, X_2, \ldots, X_k)$ is a *multinomial random variable*, and

$$P(X_1 = x_1, X_2 = x_2, \ldots, X_k = x_k) = f_{X_1, X_2, \ldots, X_k}(x_1, x_2, \ldots, x_k)$$

$$= \frac{n!}{x_1! \, x_2! \cdots x_k!} \, p_1^{x_1} p_2^{x_2} \cdots p_k^{x_k},$$

$$x_i = 0, \ldots, n; \quad i = 1, \ldots, k; \quad \sum_{i=1}^{k} x_i = n$$

Proof. The multinomial pdf can be justified by applying the same reasoning that is used in deriving the binomial pdf. Any particular sequence of x_1 y_1's, x_2 y_2's, $\ldots$, and x_k y_k's necessarily has probability $p_1^{x_1} p_2^{x_2} \ldots p_k^{x_k}$. Moreover, the total number of outcome sequences that will generate the values $(x_1, x_2, \ldots, x_k)$ is the number of ways to permute n objects, x_1 of one type, x_2 of a second type,..., and x_k of a kth type. But the latter is a direct application of Theorem 2.9.2—that is, $\dfrac{n!}{x_1! x_2! \ldots x_k!}$, and the statement of the theorem follows.

Comment. Depending on the context, the y_i's associated with the random variable in Figure 10.2.1 can be either *single* numerical values (or categories) or *ranges* of numerical values (or categories). Example 10.2.1 illustrates the first type; Example 10.2.2, the second. The only requirements imposed on the y_i's are (1) they must span all of Y's possible outcomes and (2) they must be mutually exclusive.

EXAMPLE 10.2.1

Suppose a loaded die is tossed 12 times, where

$$p_i = P(\text{face } i \text{ appears}) = ki, \quad i = 1, 2, \ldots, 6$$

What is the probability that each face will appear exactly twice?

Note, first, that the sum of the p_i's must equal 1, which makes $k = 1/21$ and $p_i = i/21$:

$$\sum_{i=1}^{6} p_i = 1 = \sum_{i=1}^{6} ki = k \cdot \frac{6(6+1)}{2}$$

implying that $k = 1/21$. In the terminology of Theorem 10.2.1, the random variable Y denotes the outcome on a given throw of the die, so $y_i = i, i = 1, 2, \ldots, 6$. It follows that X_i is the number of tosses for which $Y = y_i$.

The question is asking for the probability of the vector

$$(X_1, X_2, X_3, X_4, X_5, X_6) = (2, 2, 2, 2, 2, 2)$$

According to Theorem 10.2.1,

$$P(X_1 = 2, X_2 = 2, \ldots, X_6 = 2) = \frac{12!}{2! \, 2! \cdots 2!} \left(\frac{1}{21}\right)^2 \left(\frac{2}{21}\right)^2 \cdots \left(\frac{6}{21}\right)^2$$

$$= 0.0005$$

EXAMPLE 10.2.2

Five observations are drawn at random from the pdf

$$f_Y(y) = 6y(1 - y), \quad 0 \le y \le 1$$

What is the probability that one of the observations lies in the interval $[0, 0.25)$, none in the interval $[0.25, 0.50)$, three in the interval $[0.50, 0.75)$, and one in the interval $[0.75, 1.00)$?

Figure 10.2.2 shows the pdf being sampled, together with the ranges y_1, y_2, y_3, and y_4 and the disposition of the five data points. The p_i's of Theorem 10.2.1 are now areas. Integrating $f_Y(y)$ from 0 to 0.25, for example, gives p_1:

$$p_1 = \int_0^{0.25} 6y(1 - y)\,dy$$

$$= 3y^2 \Big|_0^{0.25} - 2y^3 \Big|_0^{0.25}$$

$$= 5/32$$

FIGURE 10.2.2

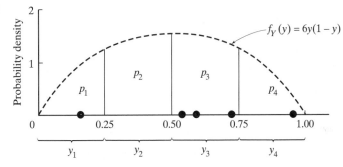

By symmetry, $p_4 = 5/32$. Moreover, since the area under $f_Y(y)$ equals 1,

$$p_2 = p_3 = \frac{1}{2}\left(1 - \frac{10}{32}\right) = \frac{11}{32}$$

Let X_i denote the number of observations that fall into the ith range, $i = 1, 2, 3, 4$. The probability, then, associated with the multinomial vector $(1, 0, 3, 1)$ is *0.0198*:

$$P(X_1 = 1, X_2 = 0, X_3 = 3, X_4 = 1) = \frac{5!}{1!\,0!\,3!\,1!}\left(\frac{5}{32}\right)^1 \left(\frac{11}{32}\right)^0 \left(\frac{11}{32}\right)^3 \left(\frac{5}{32}\right)^1$$

$$= 0.0198$$

A Multinomial/Binomial Relationship

Since the multinomial pdf is conceptually a straightforward generalization of the binomial pdf, it should come as no surprise that each X_i in a multinomial vector is, itself, a binomial random variable.

THEOREM 10.2.2. Suppose the vector $(X_1, X_2, \ldots, X_k)$ is a multinomial random variable with parameters n, p_1, p_2, $\ldots$, and p_k. Then the marginal pdf of X_i, $i = 1, 2, \ldots, k$, is the binomial with parameters n and p_i.

Proof.   To deduce the pdf for X_i we need simply to dichotomize the possible values of the random variable Y—y_1, y_2, $\ldots$, y_k—into "y_i" and "not y_i." Then X_i becomes, in effect, the number of "successes" in n independent Bernoulli trials, where the probability of success at any given trial is p_i. By Theorem 3.3.2, it follows that X_i is a binomial random variable with parameters n and p_i.

Comment. Theorem 10.2.2 gives the pdf for any given X_i in a multinomial vector. Since that pdf is the binomial, we also know the mean and variance of each X_i—specifically, $E(X_i) = np_i$ and $\text{Var}(X_i) = np_i(1 - p_i)$.

EXAMPLE 10.2.3

A physics professor has just given an exam to 50 students enrolled in a thermodynamics class. From past experience, she has reason to believe that the scores will be normally distributed with $\mu = 80.0$ and $\sigma = 5.0$. Students scoring 90 or above will receive A's, between 80 and 89, B's, and so on. What are the expected values and variances for the numbers of students receiving each of the five letter grades?

Let the random variable Y denote the score a student makes on the exam, and let y_1, y_2, y_3, y_4, and y_5 be the ranges corresponding to the letter grades A, B, C, D, and F, respectively. Then

$$p_1 = P(\text{student earns an } A)$$

$$= P(90 \leq Y \leq 100)$$

$$= P\left(\frac{90 - 80}{5} \leq \frac{Y - 80}{5} \leq \frac{100 - 80}{5}\right)$$

$$= P(2.00 \leq Z \leq 4.00)$$

$$= 0.0228$$

Now, if X_1 is the number of A's that are earned,

$$E(X_1) = np_1 = 50(0.0228) = 1.14$$

and

$$\text{Var}(X_1) = np_1(1 - p_1) = 50(0.0228)(0.9772) = 1.11$$

Table 10.2.1 lists the means and variances for all the X_i's. Each is an illustration of the comment following Theorem 10.2.2.

TABLE 10.2.1

Score	Grade	p_i	$E(X_i)$	$\text{Var}(X_i)$
$90 \leq Y \leq 100$	A	0.0228	1.14	1.11
$80 \leq Y < 90$	B	0.4772	23.86	12.47
$70 \leq Y < 80$	C	0.4772	23.86	12.47
$60 \leq Y < 70$	D	0.0228	1.14	1.11
$Y < 60$	F	0.0000	0.00	0.00

QUESTIONS

10.2.1 The Advanced Placement Program allows high school students to enroll in special classes in which a subject is studied at the college level. Proficiency is measured by a national examination. Universities typically grant course credit for a sufficiently strong performance. The possible scores are 1, 2, 3, 4, and 5, with 5 being the highest. The following table gives the probabilities associated with the scores recently made on the U.S. History test (1):

Score	Probability
1	0.116
2	0.325
3	0.236
4	0.211
5	0.112

Suppose six students from a class take the test. What is the probability they earn three 5's, two 4's, and a 3?

10.2.2 In Mendel's classical experiments with peas, he produced hybrids in such a way that the probabilities of observing the different phenotypes listed below were 9/16, 3/16, 3/16, and 1/16, respectively. Suppose that four such hybrid plants were selected at random. What is the probability that each of the four phenotypes would be represented?

Type	Probability
Round and yellow	9/16
Round and green	3/16
Angular and yellow	3/16
Angular and green	1/16

10.2.3 In classifying hypertension, three categories are used: individuals whose systolic blood pressures are less than 140, those with blood pressures between 140 and 160, and those with blood pressures over 160. For males between the ages of 18 and 24, systolic blood pressures are normally distributed with a mean equal to 124 and a standard deviation equal to 13.7. Suppose a random sample of 10 individuals from that particular demographic group are examined. What is the probability that six of their blood pressures will be in the first group, three in the second, and one in the third?

10.2.4 An army enlistment officer categorizes potential recruits by IQ into three groups—class I: < 90, class II: 90–110, and class III: >110. Given that the IQs in the population from which the recruits are drawn are normally distributed with $\mu = 100$ and $\sigma = 16$, calculate the probability that of seven enlistees, two will belong to class I, four to class II, and one to class III.

10.2.5 Recall the pipeline-missile problem described in Example 2.5.4. Suppose that six missiles are fired at the pipeline. What is the probability that two land within 20 feet to the left of the pipeline and four land within 20 feet to the right?

10.2.6 Based on his performance so far this season, a baseball player has the following probabilities associated with each official at-bat:

Outcome	Probability
Out	.713
Single	.270
Double	.010
Triple	.002
Home run	.005

If he has five official at-bats in tomorrow's game, what are the chances he makes two outs and hits two singles and a double?

10.2.7 Suppose that a random sample of 50 observations are taken from the pdf

$$f_Y(y) = 3y^2, \qquad 0 \le y \le 1$$

Let X_i be the number of observations lying in the interval $((i-1)/4, i/4)$, $i = 1, 2, 3, 4$.
(a) Write a formula for $f_{X_1, X_2, X_3, X_4}(3, 7, 15, 25)$.
(b) Find $\text{Var}(X_3)$.

10.2.8 Let the vector of random variables (X_1, X_2, X_3) have the trinomial pdf with parameters n, p_1, p_2, and $p_3 = 1 - p_1 - p_2$. That is,

$$P(X_1 = x_1, X_2 = x_2, X_3 = x_3) = \frac{n!}{x_1! \, x_2! x_3!} \, p_1^{x_1} p_2^{x_2} p_3^{x_3},$$

$$x_i = 0, 1, \dots, n; \quad i = 1, 2, 3; \quad x_1 + x_2 + x_3 = n$$

By definition, the moment-generating function for (X_1, X_2, X_3) is given by

$$M_{X_1, X_2, X_3}(t_1, t_2, t_3) = E\left(e^{t_1 X_1 + t_2 X_2 + t_3 X_3}\right)$$

Show that

$$M_{X_1, X_2, X_3}(t_1, t_2, t_3) = \left(p_1 e^{t_1} + p_2 e^{t_2} + p_3 e^{t_3}\right)^n$$

10.2.9 If $M_{X_1, X_2, X_3}(t_1, t_2, t_3)$ is the moment-generating function for (X_1, X_2, X_3), then $M_{X_1, X_2, X_3}(t_1, 0, 0)$, $M_{X_1, X_2, X_3}(0, t_2, 0)$, and $M_{X_1, X_2, X_3}(0, 0, t_3)$ are the moment-generating functions for the marginal pdf's of X_1, X_2, and X_3, respectively. Use this fact, together with the result of Question 10.2.8, to verify the statement of Theorem 10.2.2.

10.2.10 Let $(x_1, x_2, \dots, x_k)$ be the vector of sample observations representing a multinomial random variable with parameters n, p_1, p_2, $\dots$, and p_k. Show that the maximum likelihood estimate for p_i is x_i/n, $i = 1, 2, \dots, k$.

10.3 GOODNESS-OF-FIT TESTS: ALL PARAMETERS KNOWN

The simplest version of a goodness-of-fit test arises when an experimenter is able to specify completely the probability model from which the sample data are alleged to have come. It might be supposed, for example, that the Y_i's are being generated by a Poisson pdf with parameter λ equal to 6.3, or by a normal distribution with $\mu = 500$ and $\sigma = 100$. For cases such as these, the hypotheses to be tested will be written

$$H_0: \quad f_Y(y) = f_0(y)$$

versus

$$H_1: \quad f_Y(y) \ne f_0(y)$$

where $f_Y(y)$ and $f_0(y)$ are the true and the presumed pdf's, respectively. In some situations it will prove more convenient to characterize the model in terms of the probabilities associated with the k nonoverlapping intervals described in Section 10.2. Then the problem takes the form

$$H_0: \quad p_1 = \pi_1, \quad p_2 = \pi_2, \dots, p_k = \pi_k,$$

versus

$$H_1: \quad p_i \ne \pi_i \quad \text{for at least one } i$$

Karl Pearson proposed the first statistic for testing either of these sets of hypotheses in 1900. Couched in the language of the multinomial, Pearson's method requires that the n observations be grouped into k intervals (or k classes if Y is discrete) and that $\pi_1, \pi_2, \ldots, \pi_k$ [or $f_0(y)$] be specified. Theorem 10.3.1 defines Pearson's statistic, gives its asymptotic distribution, and locates its critical region.

THEOREM 10.3.1.   Let $(X_1, X_2, \ldots, X_k)$ be a multinomial random variable with parameters n, p_1, p_2, $\ldots$, and p_k. Then

(a) The random variable

$$C = \sum_{i=1}^{k} \frac{(X_i - np_i)^2}{np_i}$$

has approximately a χ^2 distribution with $k - 1$ degrees of freedom. For the approximation to be adequate, the k classes should be defined so that $np_i \geq 5$, for all i.

(b) At the α level of significance, $H_0: p_1 = \pi_1, p_2 = \pi_2, \ldots, p_k = \pi_k$ is rejected in favor of H_1: at least one $p_i \neq \pi_i$ if

$$c = \sum_{i=1}^{k} \frac{(x_i - n\pi_i)^2}{n\pi_i} \geq \chi^2_{1-\alpha, k-1}$$

Proof.   A formal proof lies beyond the scope of this text. We will present a heuristic argument for part (a) for the special case $k = 2$. That $c \geq \chi^2_{1-\alpha, k-1}$ is a reasonable critical region is evident by inspection. If agreement between the actual data and the presumed model were perfect, each x_i would equal its corresponding $n\pi_i$ (recall Theorem 10.2.2) and c would be 0 (and, of course, H_0 should be accepted). Conversely, as the discrepancies between the observed and expected frequencies proliferate, and c increases, the credibility of H_0 should surely diminish. On intuitive grounds, then, a test rejecting H_0 when c is large makes sense.

Now, returning to part (a), suppose $k = 2$. Then

$$C = \frac{(X_1 - np_1)^2}{np_1} + \frac{(X_2 - np_2)^2}{np_2}$$

$$= \frac{(X_1 - np_1)^2}{np_1} + \frac{[n - X_1 - n(1 - p_1)]^2}{n(1 - p_1)}$$

$$= \frac{(X_1 - np_1)^2(1 - p_1) + (-X_1 + np_1)^2 p_1}{np_1(1 - p_1)}$$

$$= \frac{(X_1 - np_1)^2}{np_1(1 - p_1)}$$

From Theorem 10.2.2, $E(X_1) = np_1$ and $\text{Var}(X_1) = np_1(1 - p_1)$, the two implying that C can be written

$$C = \left[\frac{X_1 - E(X_1)}{\sqrt{\text{Var}(X_1)}} \right]^2$$

By Theorem 4.3.1, then, C is the square of a variable that is asymptotically a standard normal, and the statement of part (a) follows (for $k = 2$) from Theorem 7.3.2. [A proof of the general statement can be accomplished by showing that the limit of the moment-generating function for C—as n goes to ∞—is the moment-generating function for a χ^2_{k-1} random variable. See (55) for details.]

Comment.   Although Pearson formulated his statistic before any general theories of hypothesis testing had been developed, it has since been shown that C is, in fact, asymptotically equivalent to the generalized-likelihood-ratio test of $H_0: p_1 = \pi_1$, $p_2 = \pi_2, \ldots, p_k = \pi_k$.

CASE STUDY 10.3.1

Inhabiting many tropical waters is a small (<1 mm) crustacean, *Ceriodaphnia cornuta*, that occurs in two distinct morphological forms: One has a series of "horns" protruding from its exoskeleton, while the other is more rounded (see Figure 10.3.1). An experiment was set up to test whether either variant is more conducive than the other to the survival of the species, in terms of its likelihood of being eaten (198).

FIGURE 10.3.1
Forms of *C. cornuta.*

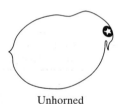
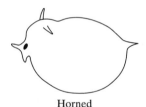

Unhorned   Horned

A large number of *C. cornuta* were introduced into a holding tank in a 3-to-1 ratio—three of the unhorned variety were added to every one with horns. Also present in the tank was a natural predator of *C. cornuta*, a small (6-cm) fish, *Melaniris chagresi*. After approximately one hour, long enough for the predator to have completed its feeding, the fish was sacrificed and the contents of its stomach examined. Among the 44 crustacean casualties, the unhorned-to-horned ratio was 40 to 4. Can it be concluded that there is a *true* differential predation rate between the two polymorphs?

Here, the two natural classes for the response variable are "unhorned" and "horned," and under the null hypothesis that morphology has no effect on survival, it would follow that the probability of either form's being eaten should be proportional to the numbers of each kind available. If $p_1 = P$ (unhorned *C. cornuta* is eaten) and $p_2 = P$ (horned *C. cornuta* is eaten), the experimenter's objective reduces to a test of

$$H_0: \quad p_1 = \frac{3}{4}, \quad p_2 = \frac{1}{4}$$

versus

$$H_1: \quad p_1 \neq \frac{3}{4}, \quad p_2 \neq \frac{1}{4}$$

Let $\alpha = 0.05$.

FIGURE 10.3.2
χ_1^2 distribution.

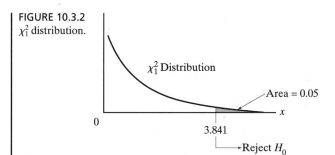

χ_1^2 Distribution

Area = 0.05

x

0

3.841

Reject H_0

Since $k = 2$, the behavior of C will be approximated by a χ_1^2 distribution, for which the 0.05 critical value is 3.841 (see Figure 10.3.2). Substituting the values for the x_i's and π_i's into the test statistic gives a c value of *5.93*:

$$c = \frac{\left[40 - 44(3/4)\right]^2}{44(3/4)} + \frac{\left[4 - 44(1/4)\right]^2}{44(1/4)}$$

$$= 5.93$$

Our conclusion, then, is to *reject H_0*—it would appear that morphology *does* have an effect on *C. cornuta*'s chances of being eaten, the presumption being that the unhorned variety is tastier.

Comment.   The final conclusion reached in this study was not what the preceding analysis suggested. Using similar goodness-of-fit arguments, the experimenter was able to show that the actual reason for the disparity in predation rates was not the presence of absence of horns but, rather, the enlarged eyespot. The latter renders the otherwise nearly transparent *C. cornuta* more visible—and, as a result, more edible!

CASE STUDY 10.3.2

Once upon a time, when there were no computers, or even calculators, people used books of tables to find trignometric and logarithmic functions. In the 1930s, an engineer, F. Benford, reexamined the claim made many years earlier by Simon Newcomb that the early pages in library logarithm books were dirtier than the last pages (recall Case Study 2.4.2). Why should students and researchers have more reason to look up logarithms beginning with 1 or 2, rather than 8 or 9? Benford began looking closely at a variety of data sets, including molecular weights of chemicals, surface areas of rivers, and baseball statistics.

What he confirmed to his surprise was the fact that the first nonzero digits in these various numbers are *not* equally likely to be 1's, 2's, ..., and 9's, as our intuition would almost certainly suggest. They tend to follow, instead, the probability function

$$p(k) = P(\text{1st nonzero digit is } k)$$

$$= \log_{10}(k + 1) - \log_{10}(k), \quad k = 1, 2, \ldots, 9 \qquad (10.3.1)$$

(continued on next page)

(Case Study 10.3.2 continued)

TABLE 10.3.1

Digit	Probability
1	0.301
2	0.176
3	0.125
4	0.097
5	0.079
6	0.067
7	0.058
8	0.051
9	0.046

[see (71) for an explanation as to why Equation 10.3.1 describes the occurrence of first digits]. Table 10.3.1 lists the values of $p(k)$, now known as *Benford's law*, for all k.

One particularly intriguing application of Benford's law occurs in auditing, where eagle-eyed examiners are ever on the lookout for budgets whose numbers have been fabricated to cover up falsified records. Bookkeepers are not likely to be aware of Equation 10.3.1 and would tend to "make up" entries in such a way that each first digit from 1 to 9 would occur roughly the same percentage of the time. A goodness-of-fit test, then, using $p(k)$ as the H_0 values for $\pi_1, \pi_2, \ldots,$ and π_9, would be one way to identify possible instances of "creative" accounting.

An example of a Benford accounting analysis is summarized in Table 10.3.2. The values in Column 2 are a breakdown of the 355 first digits appearing in the 1997–98 operating budget for the University of West Florida (100). The corresponding expected frequencies based on Benford's law are listed in Column 4, and the goodness-of-fit test statistic, c, is the sum of the entries in Column 5:

$$c = \frac{[111 - 355 \cdot (0.301)]^2}{355 \cdot (0.301)} + \cdots + \frac{[20 - 355 \cdot (0.046)]^2}{355 \cdot (0.046)}$$

$$= 2.49$$

TABLE 10.3.2

Digit	Observed	Benford p_i	Expected $(= 355 \cdot p_i)$	$(x_i - 355 p_i)^2 / 355 p_i$
1	111	0.301	106.9	0.16
2	60	0.176	62.5	0.10
3	46	0.125	44.4	0.06
4	29	0.097	34.4	0.86
5	26	0.079	28.0	0.15
6	22	0.067	23.8	0.13
7	21	0.058	20.6	0.01
8	20	0.051	18.1	0.20
9	20	0.046	16.3	0.82
	355	1.000	355.0	2.49

Here, with $k = 9$ classes, the critical value for the hypothesis test comes from the chi-square distribution with 8 df. If α is set equal to 0.05, $\chi^2_{.95,8} = 15.507$, so our conclusion is "fail to reject H_0." Relative to Benford's law, there is nothing suspicious about the first digits in the University's budget.

EXAMPLE 10.3.1

A new statistics software package claims to be able to generate random samples from any continuous pdf. Asked to produce 40 observations representing the pdf $f_Y(y) = 6y(1 - y)$, $0 \le y \le 1$, it printed out the numbers displayed in Table 10.3.3. Are these 40 y_i's a believable random sample from $f_Y(y)$? Do an appropriate goodness-of-fit test using the $\alpha = 0.05$ level of significance.

TABLE 10.3.3

0.18	0.06	0.27	0.58	0.98
0.55	0.24	0.58	0.97	0.36
0.48	0.11	0.59	0.15	0.53
0.29	0.46	0.21	0.39	0.89
0.34	0.09	0.64	0.52	0.64
0.71	0.56	0.48	0.44	0.40
0.80	0.83	0.02	0.10	0.51
0.43	0.14	0.74	0.75	0.22

To apply Theorem 10.3.1 to a continuous pdf requires that the data first be reduced to a set of classes. Table 10.3.4 shows one possible grouping. The π_i's in Column 3 are the areas under $f_Y(y)$ above each of the five classes. For example,

$$\pi_1 = \int_0^{0.20} 6y(1 - y)\, dy = 0.104$$

TABLE 10.3.4

Class	Observed frequency, x_i	π_i	$40\,\pi_i$
$0 \le y < 0.20$	8	0.104	4.16
$0.20 \le y < 0.40$	8	0.248	9.92
$0.40 \le y < 0.60$	14	0.296	11.84
$0.60 \le y < 0.80$	5	0.248	9.92
$0.80 \le y < 1.00$	5	0.104	4.16

Column 4 shows the expected frequencies for each of the classes. Notice that $40\,\pi_1$ and $40\,\pi_5$, though, are both less than 5, which fails to satisfy the "$np_i \le 5$" restriction cited in Part (a) of Theorem 10.3.1. That violation can be easily corrected, though—we need simply to combine the first two classes and the last two classes (see Table 10.3.5).

TABLE 10.3.5

Class	Observed frequency, x_i	π_i	$40\,\pi_i$
$0 \le y < 0.40$	16	0.352	14.08
$0.40 \le y < 0.60$	14	0.296	11.84
$0.60 \le y \le 1.00$	10	0.352	14.08

The test statistic c, then, is calculated from the entries in Table 10.3.5:

$$c = \frac{(16 - 14.08)^2}{14.08} + \frac{(14 - 11.84)^2}{11.84} + \frac{(10 - 14.08)^2}{14.08}$$

$$= 1.84$$

Since the number of classes ultimately being used is three, the number of degrees of freedom associated with c is 2, and we should reject the null hypothesis that the 40 y_i's are a random sample from $f_Y(y) = 6y(1 - y), 0 \leq y \leq 1$ if $c \geq \chi^2_{.95,2}$. But the latter is 5.991, so—based on these data—there is no compelling reason to doubt the software package's claim.

QUESTIONS

10.3.1 Verify the following identity concerning the statistic of Theorem 10.3.1. Note that the right-hand side is sometimes more convenient for calculations.

$$\sum_{i=1}^{k} \frac{(X_i - np_i)^2}{np_i} = \sum_{i=1}^{k} \frac{X_i^2}{np_i} - n$$

10.3.2 One hundred unordered samples of size 2 are drawn without replacement from an urn containing six red chips and four white chips. Test the adequacy of the hypergeometric model if zero whites were obtained 35 times; one white, 55 times; and two whites, 10 times. Use the 0.10 decision rule.

10.3.3 Consider again the previous question. Suppose, however, that we did not know whether the samples had been drawn with or without replacement. Test whether sampling *with* replacement is a reasonable model.

10.3.4 Show that the common belief in the propensity of babies to choose an inconvenient hour for birth has a basis in observation. A maternity hospital reported that out of one year's total of 2650 births, some 494 occurred between midnight and 4 A.M. (158). Use the goodness-of-fit test to show that the data are not what we should expect if births are assumed to occur uniformly in all time periods. Let $\alpha = 0.05$.

10.3.5 Analyze the data in the previous problem using the techniques of Section 6.3. What is the relationship between the two test statistics?

10.3.6 A number of reports in the medical literature suggest that the season of birth and the incidence of schizophrenia may be related, with a higher proportion of schizophrenics being born during the early months of the year. A study (64) following up on this hypothesis looked at 5139 persons born in England or Wales during the years 1921–1955 who were admitted to a psychiatric ward with a diagnosis of schizophrenia. Of these 5139, 1383 were born in the first quarter of the year. Based on census figures in the two countries, the expected number of persons, out of a random 5139, who would be born in the first quarter is 1292.1. Do an appropriate χ^2 test with $\alpha = 0.05$.

10.3.7 In a move that shocked candy traditionalists, the M&M/Mars Company recently replaced the tan M&M's with blue ones. More than 10 million people voted in an election to select the new color. On learning of the change, one concerned consumer counted the number of each color appearing in three pounds of M&M's (50). His tally, shown in the following table, suggests that not all the colors appear equally often—blues, in particular, are decidedly less common than browns. According to an M&M/Mars spokesperson, there are actually three frequencies associated with the six colors: 30% of M&M's are brown, yellow and red each account for 20%, and orange, blue, and green each occur 10% of the time. Test at the $\alpha = 0.05$ level of significance the hypothesis that the consumer's data are consistent with the companies stated intentions.

Color	Number
Brown	455
Yellow	343
Red	318
Orange	152
Blue	130
Green	129

10.3.8 Question 10.2.2 listed the probabilities associated with Mendel's study of inheritance in peas. In an experiment designed to test that earlier hypothesis, Mendel recorded the following results from 556 dihybrid crosses. Carry out the appropriate goodness-of-fit test. Let $\alpha = 0.01$.

Type	Number
Round and yellow	315
Round and green	108
Angular and yellow	101
Angular and green	32

10.3.9 The following table lists World Series lengths for the 50 years from 1926 to 1975. Test at the 0.10 level whether these data are compatible with the model that each World Series game is an independent Bernoulli trial with $p = P(\text{AL wins}) = P(\text{NL wins}) = 1/2$.

Number of games	Number of years
4	9
5	11
6	8
7	22

10.3.10 Records kept at an eastern racetrack showed the following distribution of winners as a function of their starting-post position. All 144 races were run with a full field of eight horses.

Starting post	1	2	3	4	5	6	7	8
Number of winners	32	21	19	20	16	11	14	11

Test an appropriate goodness-of-fit hypothesis. Let $\alpha = 0.05$.

10.3.11 It was noted in Question 4.3.24 that the mean (μ) and standard deviation (σ) of pregnancy durations are 266 days and 16 days, respectively. Accepting those as the true parameter values, test whether the additional assumption that pregnancy durations are normally distributed is supported by the following list of 70 pregnancy durations reported by County General Hospital. Let $\alpha = 0.10$ be the level of significance. Use "$220 \le y < 230$," "$230 \le y < 240$," and so on, as the classes.

251	264	234	283	226	244	269	241	276	274
263	243	254	276	241	232	260	248	284	253
265	235	259	279	256	256	254	256	250	269
240	261	263	262	259	230	268	284	259	261
268	268	264	271	263	259	294	259	263	278
267	293	247	244	250	266	286	263	274	253
281	286	266	249	255	233	245	266	265	264

10.3.12 Recall Example 2.5.1, where it was claimed that in a certain state the length of time, Y, that a person convicted of grand theft auto actually spends in jail is described by the pdf

$$f_Y(y) = \frac{1}{9} y^2, \quad 0 \le y \le 3$$

As part of a general investigation into the inequities of judicial sentences, a district attorney reviews the records of 50 persons convicted of grand theft auto. Of those 50, 8 served less than one year in prison, 16 served between one and two years, and 26 between two and three years. Are these data compatible with the presumed $f_Y(y)$? Let $\alpha = 0.05$.

10.4 GOODNESS-OF-FIT TESTS: PARAMETERS UNKNOWN

More common than the sort of problems described in Section 10.3 are situations where the experimenter has reason to believe that the response variable follows some particular *family* of pdf's—say the normal or the Poisson—but has little or no prior information to suggest what values should be assigned to the model's parameters. In cases such as these, we will carry out the goodness-of-fit test by first estimating all unknown parameters, preferably with the method of maximum likelihood. The appropriate test statistic, denoted c_1, is a modified version of Pearson's c:

$$c_1 = \sum_{i=1}^{k} \frac{(x_i - n\hat{p}_i)^2}{n\hat{p}_i}$$

Here, the sample estmate of p_i—that is, $\hat{p}_i$—is used, rather than its null hypothesis value, π_i.

We pay a price, though, for having to rely on the data to fill in details about the presumed model: Each parameter estimated reduces by one the number of degrees of freedom associated with the χ^2 distribution approximating the sampling distribution of C_1—and as the number of degrees of freedom decreases, so does the power of the test.

THEOREM 10.4.1. Suppose that $f_0(y)$ is a pdf having r unknown parameters. To test $H_0: f_Y(y) = f_0(y)$ versus $H_1: f_Y(y) \neq f_0(y)$, reject the null hypothesis if

$$c_1 = \sum_{i=1}^{k} \frac{(x_i - n\hat{p}_i)^2}{n\hat{p}_i} \ge \chi^2_{1-\alpha,\, k-1-r}$$

where $(n\hat{p}_1, \ldots, n\hat{p}_k)$ are the *estimated* expected values obtained by replacing the unknown parameters in $f_0(y)$ with their MLEs. To ensure that C_1 is adequately described by the χ^2 distribution with $k - 1 - r$ degrees of freedom, the classes should be defined so that $n\hat{p}_i \ge 5$ for all i.

CASE STUDY 10.4.1

Despite the fact that batters occasionally go on lengthy hitting streaks, there is reason to believe that the number of hits a baseball player gets in a game behaves much like a binomial random variable. Data demonstrating that claim has come from a study (121) of National League box scores from Opening Day through mid-July in 1996. Players had exactly four official at-bats a total of 4096 times during that period. The resulting distribution of their hits is summarized in Table 10.4.1. Are these numbers consistent with the hypothesis that Y, the number of hits in four at-bats, is binomially distributed? Let $\alpha = 0.05$.

TABLE 10.4.1

Number of Hits	Observed no., x_i	Expected no., $n\hat{p}_i$
0	1280	1289.1
1	1717	1728.0
2	915	868.6
3	167	194.0
4	17	16.3

Here

$$f_0(i) = \binom{4}{i} p^i (1 - p)^{4-i}, \quad i = 0, 1, 2, 3, 4 \tag{10.4.1}$$

where $p = P(\text{batter gets a hit})$ is an unknown parameter. Let

$$X_i = \text{number of times batter gets } i \text{ hits}, i = 0, 1, \dots, 4 \tag{10.4.2}$$

The expected values for the X_i's derive from Theorem 10.2.2:

$$E(X_i) = np_i = 4096 \cdot \binom{4}{i} p^i (1 - p)^{4-i}$$

The p in Equation 10.4.1 is unknown, though, so the $E(X_i)$'s in Equation 10.4.2 cannot be determined. Instead, we need to *estimate* the expected values by first estimating the parameter p. Recall that the MLE for the parameter in a binomial pdf is the sample average number of successes per trial—in this case,

$$\hat{p} = \frac{1280(0) + 1717(1) + 915(2) + 167(3) + 17(4)}{4096(4)} = \frac{4116}{16{,}384} = 0.251$$

Substituting the value 0.251 for p in Equation 10.4.2, then, gives the estimated expected value of X_i for each i. For example,

$$\widehat{E(X_0)} = 4096 \cdot \binom{4}{0} (0.251)^0 (1 - 0.251)^4 = 1289.1$$

The entire set of estimates for $E(X_i)$ appears in Column 3 of Table 10.4.1.

To assess the significance of the differences between the x_i's and their estimated expected values, we compute the test statistic, c_1. Here,

(continued on next page)

(Case Study 10.4.1 continued)

$$c_1 = \frac{(1280 - 1289.1)^2}{1289.1} + \frac{(1717 - 1728.0)^2}{1728.0} + \frac{(915 - 868.6)^2}{868.6}$$

$$+ \frac{(167 - 194.0)^2}{194.0} + \frac{(17 - 16.3)^2}{16.3}$$

$$= 6.401$$

By Theorem 10.4.1, we should reject the null hypothesis that Y is binomially distributed if

$$c_1 \geq \chi^2_{.95,\, 5-1-1} = \chi^2_{.95,\, 3} = 7.815 \tag{10.4.3}$$

Since Inequality 10.4.3 is *not* satisfied, the claim made at the outset is supported—the number of hits that players make in a game behaves much like a binomial random variable.

CASE STUDY 10.4.2

The Poisson probability function often models events that occur over time, which suggests that athletic contests are likely to be fertile sources of such data. Case Study 4.2.3, for example, argued that the number of fumbles made during a game by a college football team has a Poisson distribution. We are now in a position to examine that assertion more rigorously by carrying out a goodness-of-fit analysis.

The data in Table 10.4.2 show the numbers of fumbles, Y, made by 110 college teams during the course of 55 games (95). At the $\alpha = 0.01$ level of significance, test the null hypothesis that Y has a Poisson distribution.

TABLE 10.4.2

Number of Fumbles, k	Observed No., x_i	Expected No., $n\hat{p}_i$
0	8	8.6
1	24	21.9
2	27	27.9
3	20	23.7
4	17	15.1
5+	14	12.8
	110	110.0

Case Study 4.2.3 calculated the MLE for the rate parameter and found $\hat{\lambda}$ to be 2.55 fumbles per team. The particular model we are trying to fit to the data, then, has the pdf

$$f_0(y) = \frac{e^{-2.55}(2.55)^y}{y!}, \quad y = 0, 1, \ldots$$

Estimated expected frequencies based on $f_0(y)$ are calculated much like they were in Example 10.4.1. Let X_i denote the number of teams making i fumbles. Then

$$\widehat{E(X_i)} = n\hat{p}_i = 110 \cdot \frac{e^{-2.55}(2.55)^i}{i!}, \quad i = 0, 1, 2, \ldots$$

(see Column 3 of Table 10.4.2). Notice that the last class—"5+"—is open ended. This is necessary because the Poisson model is defined for all non-negative integers (even though the data will terminate at some finite k). To find $n\hat{p}_i$ for that last class, we simply subtract all the other estimated expected frequencies from the total sample size:

$$\widehat{E(X_{5+})} = 110 - 8.6 - 21.9 - 27.9 - 23.7 - 15.1$$

$$= 12.8$$

Now, substituting into the test statistic from Theorem 10.4.1 gives

$$c_1 = \sum_{i=1}^{5} \frac{(x_i - n\hat{p}_{i_0})^2}{n\hat{p}_{i_0}}$$

$$= \frac{(8 - 8.6)^2}{8.6} + \cdots + \frac{(14 - 12.8)^2}{12.8}$$

$$= 1.20$$

Since $k - 1 - r = 6 - 1 - 1 = 4$, the appropriate critical value is *13.277*, the 99th percentile of a χ_4^2 distribution. Our conclusion is clear cut—the data collected from these 110 teams are consistent with the hypothesis that the underlying probability model describing the occurrence of fumbles is the Poisson (see Figure 10.4.1).

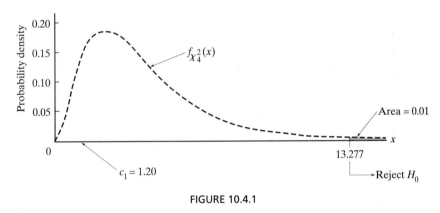

FIGURE 10.4.1

CASE STUDY 10.4.3

Certainly the most frequent assumption made in statistics, whether explicitly or implicitly, is that the random variable being measured is normally distributed. As we have already seen, this was the starting point for all the t, χ^2, and F tests covered in Chapters 7 and 9. In practice, tests for normality are typically based on Theorem 10.4.1 with $r = 2$, because both μ and σ will usually be unknown.

Recall the Etruscan skull data described in Question 7.5.12. The stated intention there was to use the one-sample t test to choose between $H_0: \mu = 132.4$ and $H_1: \mu \neq 132.4$. Do those data, though, satisfy the assumptions of that procedure? Specifically, can it be assumed that skull width is a normally distributed random variable?

(continued on next page)

(Case Study 10.4.3 continued)

TABLE 10.4.3

Skull Width (mm)	Observed Frequency, x_i
125–129	1
130–134	4
135–139	10
140–144	33
145–149	24
150–154	9
155–159	3
	84

Table 10.4.3 shows a frequency distribution constructed for the 84 y_i's listed. Estimated expected frequencies need to be calculated using a Z transformation, where the unknown μ and σ are replaced by the sample mean and sample standard deviation, respectively (in this case, $\bar{y} = 143.8$ and $s = 6.0$). For example, the null hypothesis probability that a skull width would fall into the "140–144" class is approximately *0.3120*:

$$P(140 \leq Y \leq 144) = P(139.5 < Y < 144.5)$$

$$\doteq P\left(\frac{139.5 - 143.8}{6.0} < Z < \frac{144.5 - 143.8}{6.0}\right)$$

$$= P(-0.72 < Z < 0.12)$$

$$= 0.3120$$

It follows that the estimated expected frequency for that range is 84(0.3120), or *26.2*.

Table 10.4.4 shows the entire set of observed and expected frequencies. Notice that the first and last classes have been made open ended to accommodate the infinite range of the normal curve. Moreover, the first two classes need to be combined, as do the last two, in order to comply with the "$n\hat{p}_i \geq 5$" restriction.

TABLE 10.4.4

Skull Width	x_i	$\hat{p}_i$	$84\hat{p}_i$
≤ 129	1	0.0087	0.7
130–134	4	0.0519	4.4
135–139	10	0.1752	14.7
140–144	33	0.3120	26.2
145–149	24	0.2811	23.6
150–154	9	0.1336	11.2
155+	3	0.0375	3.2
	84	1.0000	84.0

Table 10.4.5 shows the *final* set of classes. As indicated at the bottom of the last column, the value of the test statistic, c_1, is *3.61*.

TABLE 10.4.5

Skull Width (mm)	x_i	$\hat{p}_i$	$84\hat{p}_i$	$(x_i - 84\hat{p}_i)^2/84\hat{p}_i$
≤ 134	5	0.0606	5.1	0.00
135–139	10	0.1752	14.7	1.50
140–144	33	0.3120	26.2	1.76
145–149	24	0.2811	23.6	0.01
150+	12	0.1711	14.4	0.34
	84	1.0000	84.0	3.61

Since $r = 2$ parameters were estimated and the final calculations were based on $k = 5$ classes, the number of degrees of freedom associated with c_1 is $5 - 1 - 2$, or 2. Had we elected to carry out the test at the $\alpha = 0.05$ level of significance, the critical value would be 5.991 $(= \chi^2_{.95, 2})$, and our conclusion would be to "accept" the normality assumption.

QUESTIONS

10.4.1 A public policy polling group is investigating whether people living in the same household tend to make independent political choices. They select 200 homes where exactly three voters live. The residents are asked separately for their opinion ("yes" or "no") on a city charter amendment. If their opinions are formed independently, the number saying "yes" should be binomially distributed. Do an appropriate goodness-of-fit test on the data below. Let $\alpha = 0.05$.

No. Saying "yes"	Frequency
0	30
1	56
2	73
3	41

10.4.2 From 1837 to 1932, the United States Supreme Court had 48 vacancies. The table below shows the number of years in which exactly y of the vacancies occurred (185). At the $\alpha = 0.01$ level of significance, test the hypothesis that these data can be described by a Poisson pdf.

Number of Vacancies, y	Number of Years
0	59
1	27
2	9
3	1
4+	0

10.4.3 As a way of studying the spread of a plant disease known as creeping rot, a field of cabbage plants was divided into 270 *quadrats*, each quadrat containing the same number of plants. The following table lists the numbers of plants per quadrat showing signs of creeping rot infestation.

Number of Infected Plants/Quadrat	Number of Quadrats
0	38
1	57
2	68
3	47
4	23
5	9
6	10
7	7
8	3
9	4
10	2
11	1
12	1
13+	0

Can the number of plants infected with creeping rot per quadrat be described by a Poisson pdf? Let $\alpha = 0.05$. What might be a physical reason for the Poisson not being appropriate in this situation? Which assumption of the Poisson appears to be violated?

10.4.4 Carry out the details for a goodness-of-fit test on the horse kick data of Question 4.2.10. Use the 0.01 level of significance.

10.4.5 In rotogravure, a method of printing by rolling paper over engraved, chrome-plated cylinders, the printed paper can be flawed by undesirable lines called *bands*. Bands occur when grooves form on the cylinder's surface. When this happens, the presses must be stopped, and the cylinders repolished or replated. The following table gives the number of workdays a printing firm experienced between successive banding shutdowns (37). Fit these data with an exponential model and perform the appropriate goodness-of-fit test at the 0.05 level of significance.

Workdays between Shutdowns	Number Observed
0–1	130
1–2	41
2–3	25
3–4	8
4–5	2
5–6	3
6–7	1
7–8	1

10.4.6 Do a goodness-of-fit test for normality on the SAT data in Question 7.2.4, using the estimates given for μ and σ. Let $\alpha = 0.05$.

10.4.7 A sociologist is studying various aspects of the personal lives of preeminent nineteenth-century scholars. A total of 120 subjects in her sample had families consisting of two children. The distribution of the number of boys in those families is summarized in the following table. Can it be concluded that the number of boys in two-child families of preeminent scholars is binomially distributed? Let $\alpha = 0.05$.

Number of boys	0	1	2
Number of families	24	64	32

10.4.8 The percent return on a stock over a period of time is, by definition,

$$\frac{\text{new price} - \text{old price}}{\text{old price}} \times 100$$

The following table gives the monthly returns of IBM stock from January 1961 through December 1967. If stock prices tend to move somewhat randomly, the returns might follow a normal distribution. Test that assumption at the 0.10 level by performing the appropriate goodness-of-fit test.

7.2	6.2	3.0	2.7	2.8	−2.7	2.4
6.8	3.6	9.2	−1.2	−0.2	−6.4	−0.8
−0.8	−14.8	−13.4	−13.6	14.1	2.6	−10.8
−2.1	15.4	−2.1	8.6	−5.4	5.3	10.2
3.1	−8.6	−0.4	2.6	1.6	9.3	−1.5
4.5	6.9	5.2	4.4	−4.0	5.5	−0.6
−3.1	−4.4	−0.9	−3.8	−1.5	−0.7	9.5
2.0	−0.3	6.8	−1.1	−4.2	4.6	4.5
2.7	4.0	−1.2	−5.0	−0.6	4.1	0.2
8.0	−2.2	−3.0	−2.8	−5.6	−0.9	4.6
13.6	−1.2	7.5	7.9	4.9	10.1	−3.5
6.7	2.1	−1.4	9.7	8.2	3.3	2.4

Note: $\bar{y}$ and s for these data are 1.59 and 5.97, respectively.

10.4.9 Because it satisfies all the assumptions implicit in the Poisson model, radioactive decay should be described by a probability function of the form $p_X(k) = e^{-\lambda}\lambda^k/k!$, $k = 0, 1, 2, \ldots$, where the random variable X denotes the number of particles emitted (or counted) during a given time interval. Does that hold true for the Rutherford and Geiger data given in Case Study 4.2.2? Set up and carry out an appropriate analysis.

10.4.10 Does the distribution of deaths among women over the age of 80, as given in Question 4.2.13, follow a Poisson model? Do a goodness-of-fit test with $\alpha = 0.05$.

10.4.11 Is the following set of data likely to have come from the geometric pdf, $p_X(k) = (1 - p)^{k-1}p$, $k = 1, 2, \ldots$?

2	8	1	2	2	5	1	2	8	3
5	4	2	4	7	2	2	8	4	7
2	6	2	3	5	1	3	3	2	5
4	2	2	3	6	3	6	4	9	3
3	7	5	1	3	4	3	4	6	2

10.4.12 To raise money for a new rectory, the members of a church hold a raffle. A total of n tickets are sold (numbered 1 through n), out of which a total of 50 winners are to be drawn, presumably at random. The following are the 50 lucky numbers.

108	110	21	6	44
89	68	50	13	63
84	64	69	92	12
46	78	113	104	105
9	115	58	2	20
19	96	28	72	81
32	75	3	49	86
94	61	35	31	56
17	100	102	114	76
106	112	80	59	73

Set up a goodness-of-fit test that focuses on the randomness of the draw. Use the 0.05 level of significance.

10.5 CONTINGENCY TABLES

We have seen that inferences about parameters and about entire pdf's are two frequent objectives of statistical methodology. A third are questions related to *independence*: Does knowing the value of a first random variable provide us with any insight into the probable behavior of a second? Examples are commonplace. Are the incidence rates of cancer and other illnesses related to industrial pollution, high-fat diets, or poor mental health? Do a politician's approval ratings depend on the gender of the respondents? Are trends in juvenile delinquency linked to the latest fads in teen music?

The notion of independence, of course, has already turned up in a number of different contexts, both probabilistic and statistical. To recast it in an inference setting requires nothing new, conceptually, and we can even use the same notation that was introduced in Chapter 2. Let $A_1, A_2, \ldots, A_r$ be a partition of the sample space S,

$$\bigcup_{i=1}^{r} A_i = S, \quad A_i \cap A_j = \emptyset, \quad i \neq j$$

Suppose that $B_1, B_2, \ldots, B_c$ is another partition of S. Then the question of whether criteria A and criteria B are independent can be written

H_0: A_i and B_j are independent for $1 \leq i \leq r$, $1 \leq j \leq c$

versus

H_1: A_i and B_j are *not* independent for $1 \leq i \leq r$, $1 \leq j \leq c$

The methodology for choosing between H_0 and H_1 follows closely the pattern established by Theorems 10.3.1 and 10.4.1. First, we select a random sample, $Y_1, Y_2, \ldots, Y_n$, from S, and then we define the random variable X_{ij} to be the number of observations belonging to the intersection $A_i \cap B_j$. Under H_0,

$$P[Y_k \in (A_i \cap B_j)] = P(Y_k \in A_i) \cdot P(Y_k \in B_j) = p_i q_j, \quad k = 1, 2, \ldots, n$$

where $\sum_{i=1}^{r} p_i = 1$ and $\sum_{j=1}^{c} q_j = 1$. Therefore, $E(X_{ij}) = n p_i q_j$, and, by analogy with C and C_1, the goodness-of-fit statistic

$$C_2 = \sum_{i=1}^{r} \sum_{j=1}^{c} \frac{(X_{ij} - n\hat{p}_i\hat{q}_j)^2}{n\hat{p}_i\hat{q}_j}$$

has an asymptotic χ^2 distribution. Typically, the p_i's and the q_j's will both be estimated, the former with MLEs

$$\hat{p}_i = \frac{1}{n} \sum_{j=1}^{c} x_{ij}$$

and the latter by

$$\hat{q}_j = \frac{1}{n} \sum_{i=1}^{r} x_{ij}$$

However, since

$$\sum_{i=1}^{r} \hat{p}_i = 1 \quad \text{and} \quad \sum_{j=1}^{c} \hat{q}_j = 1$$

only $(r - 1) + (c - 1)$ parameters need to be estimated directly. Since the Y's are being categorized into a total of $r \cdot c$ classes, it follows from Theorem 10.4.1 that the number of degrees of freedom associated with C_2 is

$$rc - 1 - (r - 1) - (c - 1) = rc - r - c + 1 = (r - 1)(c - 1)$$

Data for a test of independence are generally presented in tabular form, with rows representing the categories of one criteria and columns the categories of the other. Such displays are called *contingency tables*—a name probably due to Karl Pearson (see Figure 10.5.1). Notice that

$$\hat{p}_i = \frac{R_i}{n}$$

$$\hat{q}_j = \frac{C_j}{n}$$

	B_1	B_2	$\ldots$	B_c	Row total
A_1	x_{11}	x_{12}	$\ldots$	x_{1c}	R_1
A_2	x_{21}	x_{22}		x_{2c}	R_2
$\vdots$	$\vdots$	$\vdots$	x_{ij}	$\vdots$	$\vdots$
A_r	x_{r1}	x_{r2}		x_{rc}	R_r
Column total	C_1	C_2	$\ldots$	C_c	n

FIGURE 10.5.1

and

$$\widehat{E(X_{ij})} = \text{estimated expected frequency for } i\text{th row and } j\text{th column}$$

$$= n\hat{p}_i\hat{q}_j$$

$$= n \cdot \frac{R_i}{n} \cdot \frac{C_j}{n} = \frac{R_i \cdot C_j}{n} \tag{10.5.1}$$

THEOREM 10.5.1.   Let $(x_i, y_i), i = 1, 2, \ldots, n$ be a set of categorical data reduced to a contingency table having r rows and c columns. Let the random variable X_{ij} denote the number of data points that belong to the ith row of X and the jth column of Y. Let $\hat{p}_i$ and $\hat{q}_j$ be the proportions of observations belonging to the ith row of X and the jth column of Y, respectively. Define

$$C_2 = \sum_{i=1}^{r} \sum_{j=1}^{c} \frac{(X_{ij} - n\hat{p}_i\hat{q}_j)^2}{n\hat{p}_i\hat{q}_j}$$

To test H_0: X and Y are independent versus H_1: X and Y are dependent at the α level of significance, reject H_0 if $c_2 \geq \chi^2_{1-\alpha,\,(r-1)(c-1)}$.

Comment.   The χ^2 distribution with $(r-1)(c-1)$ degrees of freedom provides an adequate approximation to the distribution of C_2 only if $n\hat{p}_i\hat{q}_j \geq 5$ for all i and j. If one or more cells in a contingency table have estimated expected frequencies that are substantially less than 5, the table should be "collapsed" and the rows and/or columns redefined.

CASE STUDY 10.5.1

The magazine rack at any bookstore, crammed with hundreds of issues, makes it abundantly clear that the periodical world has become highly competitive. Old favorites like *Time, Sports Illustrated*, and *Cosmopolitan* are still to be found, but they now must vie for the readers' attention with a proliferation of specialty publications like *Omni* and *PC World*.

More than ever, a magazine's survival depends on attractiveness and effective promotion, rather than just content. Surprisingly, price may or may not be an important factor. Some analysts believe that higher cover prices enhance a magazine's likelihood of success because advertisers are more willing to pay for space if they think the target audience is affluent; others are not so sure.

A recent study explored the pricing question by looking at 234 magazines (76). Two pieces of information were collected on each—its cover price and whether it continued to be published. Table 10.5.1 summarizes the data into a "4 × 2" contingency table—that is, a cross-classification consisting of 4 rows and 2 columns. Notice that the last two rows suggest

TABLE 10.5.4

		Ebert Ratings			
		Down	Sideways	Up	Total
Siskel ratings	Down	24 (11.8)	8 (8.4)	13 (24.8)	45
	Sideways	8 (8.4)	13 (6.0)	11 (17.6)	32
	Up	10 (21.8)	9 (15.6)	64 (45.6)	83
	Total	42	30	88	160

Table 10.5.4 displays the entire set of estimated expected frequencies, all calculated the same way.

Now, suppose we wish to test

H_0:   Siskel ratings and Ebert ratings are independent

versus

H_1:   Siskel ratings and Ebert ratings are dependent

at the $\alpha = 0.01$ level of significance. With $r = 3$ and $c = 3$, the number of degrees of freedom associated with the test statistic is $(3 - 1)(3 - 1) = 4$, and H_0 should be rejected if

$$c_2 \geq \chi^2_{.99, 4} = 13.277$$

But

$$c_2 = \frac{(24 - 11.8)^2}{11.8} + \frac{(8 - 8.4)^2}{8.4} + \cdots + \frac{(64 - 45.6)^2}{45.6}$$

$$= 45.37$$

so the evidence is overwhelming that Siskel and Ebert's judgments are not independent.

QUESTIONS

10.5.1 Market researchers often gather information by telephone, but calling only listed numbers may badly skew the responses, if listed and unlisted households are fundamentally different with respect to the question being asked. The following is the slightly modified summary of a survey done by Pacific Bell to see whether home ownership is related to telephone listing (132). At the $\alpha = 0.05$ and $\alpha = 0.10$ levels of significance, test whether those two "conditions" are independent.

	Listed	Unlisted
Own	628	146
Rent	172	54

10.5.2 Many factors influence a company's decision to relocate to another site. The State of Florida, hoping to attract such relocations, sponsored a study (46) on how different companies view various factors. One part of the study compared the importance of a high-quality work force to manufacturing firms and to nonmanufacturing firms. At the $\alpha = 0.05$ level of significance, do the following data suggest that the importance of a high-quality work force is not viewed the same by all types of businesses?

		Manufacturing	Other
Importance	Extremely or somewhat	168	73
	Not very	42	26

10.5.3 A total of 1154 girls attending a public high school were given a questionnaire that measured how much each had exhibited delinquent behavior (115). From an analysis of the results, the researchers categorized 111 of the girls as "delinquent." The following is a cross-classification of the delinquents and the nondelinquents according to their birth order. At the $\alpha = 0.01$ level of significance, is there evidence here to support the contention that birth order and delinquency are related?

	Delinquent	Not delinquent
Oldest	24	450
In Between	29	312
Youngest	35	211
Only Child	23	70

10.5.4 In a study (44) investigating the effect of rubella infections (German measles) on childbirth, a total of 578 pregnancies were classified in retrospect as having been either "normal" or "abnormal," the latter group including abortions, stillbirths, birth defects, and all infant deaths within two years. Altogether, there were 86 abnormal pregnancies. The second variable looked at was *when* the rubella infection occurred—during the first trimester or after the first trimester. It was found that 59 of the 86 abnormal births were among the 202 pregnancies complicated during the first trimester; the remaining 27 were born to mothers who contracted the virus after the first trimester. Can it be concluded that the risk of an abnormal birth is dependent on when during the pregnancy the virus is contracted? Let $\alpha = 0.01$.

10.5.5 A market research study has investigated the relationship between an adult's self-perception and his attitude toward small cars. A total of 299 persons living in a large metropolitan area were surveyed. On the basis of their responses to a questionnaire, each was "assigned" to one of three distinct personality types: (1) cautious conservative, (2) middle-of-the-roader, and (3) confident explorer. At the same time, each was solicited for his overall opinion of small cars. The results are summarized below (80). Test whether these two traits are independent. Use the 0.01 level of significance.

		Self-Perception		
		Cautious Conservative	Middle-of-the-Roader	Confident Explorer
Opinion of Small Cars	Favorable	79	58	49
	Neutral	10	8	9
	Unfavorable	10	34	42

10.5.6 High blood pressure is known to be one of the major contributors to coronary heart disease. A study was done to see whether or not there is a significant relationship between the blood pressures of children and those of their fathers (79). If such a relationship did exist, it might be possible to use one group to screen for high-risk individuals in the other group. The subjects were 92 eleventh graders, 47 males and 45 females, and their fathers. Blood pressures for both the children and the fathers were categorized as belonging to either the lower, middle, or upper third of their respective distributions. Test whether or not the blood pressures of children can be considered to be independent of the blood pressures of their fathers. Let $\alpha = 0.05$.

		Child's Blood Pressure		
		Lower Third	Middle Third	Upper Third
Father's	Lower third	14	11	8
blood	Middle third	11	11	9
pressure	Upper third	6	10	12

10.5.7 The following data were collected as part of a study to see whether a mouse's early upbringing has any effect on its aggressiveness later in life (74). A total of 307 mice were divided into two groups shortly after birth. Each of the 167 mice in the first group was raised by its natural mother; the remaining 140 in the second group were raised by "foster" mice. When each mouse was three months old, it was put into a small cage with another mouse it had not seen before. The two were then watched for a predetermined period of time (six minutes) to see whether they would start fighting. Set up and carry out an appropriate χ^2 test. Let $\alpha = 0.05$.

	Natural Mother	Foster Mother
Number fighting	27	47
Number not fighting	140	93
	167	140

10.5.8 The Hopwood Decision resulted from a 1996 U.S. Fifth Circuit Court of Appeals case that greatly limited the Texas universities' affirmative-action programs for admission of minority students. As a consequence, minority enrollment dropped significantly. One solution proposed was to accept all students in the top 10% of their graduating class. The success of such a plan in achieving diversity would hinge on the enrollment rates for the different racial groups. The following are the average numbers of freshmen in the top 10% of their classes admitted and enrolled, by race, at UT-Austin for the years 1990–1996. Are the enrollment rates dependent on the racial groups? Do the appropriate analysis using the $\alpha = 0.05$ level of significance.

	Admitted	Enrolled
White	2592	1481
African-American	159	78
Hispanic	800	375
Asian	667	399

10.5.9 Portfolio turnover expresses the past year's trading activity as a percentage of an account's average assets. The following table summarizes the performances of 100 mutual funds cross-classified according to portfolio turnover and annual return. Test the independence assumption. Let $\alpha = 0.05$.

		Annual Return	
		$\leq 10\%$	$>10\%$
Portfolio	$\geq 100\%$	11	10
Return	$<100\%$	55	24

10.5.10 Feelings of alienation can have very negative effects on a person's mental well-being. For that reason, sociologists have speculated that urban areas with especially transient populations are likely to have higher suicide rates than cities where neighborhoods are more stable. Test that hypothesis on the data given in the table, which show the suicide rates and mobility indexes for 25 American cities (197). Begin by reducing the data to a 2 × 2 contingency table. Use the two sample means, $\bar{x} = 56.0$ and $\bar{y} = 20.8$, to dichotomize the x_i's and y_i's into two categories, "high" and "low." (*Note:* The *x*-variable here is defined in such a way that a city with a high population transiency has a *low* mobility index, and vice versa.)

City	Suicides per 100,000, y_i	Mobility Index, x_i	City	Suicides per 100,000, y_i	Mobility Index, x_i
New York	19.3	54.3	Washington	22.5	37.1
Chicago	17.0	51.5	Minneapolis	23.8	56.3
Philadelphia	17.5	64.6	New Orleans	17.2	82.9
Detroit	16.5	42.5	Cincinnati	23.9	62.2
Los Angeles	23.8	20.3	Newark	21.4	51.9
Cleveland	20.1	52.2	Kansas City	24.5	49.4
St. Louis	24.8	62.4	Seattle	31.7	30.7
Baltimore	18.0	72.0	Indianapolis	21.0	66.1
Boston	14.8	59.4	Rochester	17.2	68.0
Pittsburgh	14.9	70.0	Jersey City	10.1	56.5
San Francisco	40.0	43.8	Louisville	16.6	78.7
Milwaukee	19.3	66.2	Portland	29.3	33.2
Buffalo	13.8	67.6			

APPENDIX 10.A.1 MINITAB APPLICATIONS

The MINITAB command CHISQUARE, followed by the columns in which the observed frequencies have been entered, performs the χ^2 test for independence described in Theorem 10.5.1. Figure 10.A.1.1 shows the input and output for the MINITAB analysis of the data in Case Study 10.5.2. In addition to the estimated expected frequencies and the value of the test statistic, the CHISQUARE routine also indicates the number of degrees of freedom associated with c_2 and its *P*-value. Here the *P*-value is so small there is no question that the null hypothesis of independence should be rejected.

FIGURE 10.A.1.1
```
MTB > set c1
DATA> 24 8 10
DATA> end
MTB > set c2
DATA> 8 13 9
DATA> end
MTB > set c3
DATA> 13 11 64
DATA> end
MTB > chisquare c1-c3
```

Chi-Square Test

Expected counts are printed below observed counts

	C1	C2	C3	Total
1	24	8	13	45
	11.81	8.44	24.75	
2	8	13	11	32
	8.40	6.00	17.60	
3	10	9	64	83
	21.79	15.56	45.65	
Total	42	30	88	160

```
ChiSq = 12.574 + 0.023 + 5.578 +
         0.019 + 8.167 + 2.475 +
         6.377 + 2.767 + 7.376 = 45.357
df = 4, p = 0.000
```

Testing for Independence Using MINITAB Windows

1. Enter each column of observed frequencies in a separate column.
2. Click on STAT, then on TABLES, then on CHISQUARE TEST.
3. Enter the COLUMNS CONTAINING THE TABLE; click on OK.

CHAPTER 11

Regression

Francis Galton (1822–1911)

Galton had earned a Cambridge mathematics degree and completed two years of medical school when his father died, leaving him with a substantial inheritance. Free to travel, he became an explorer of some note, but when The Origin of Species *was published in 1859, his interests began to shift from geography to statistics and anthropology (Charles Darwin was his cousin). It was Galton's work on fingerprints that made possible their use in human identification. He was knighted in 1909.*

11.1 INTRODUCTION

One of the major objectives of all analytical inquiry is the determination of the relationships that prevail among the various components of a complex system. If those relationships are sufficiently understood, the possibility exists that the system's output can be effectively predicted, or maybe even controlled.

Consider, for example, the formidable problem of relating the incidence of cancer to its many contributing causes—diet, genetic makeup, pollution, and cigarette smoking, to name only a few. Or think of the Wall Street financier, trying to anticipate trends in stock prices by tracking market indices and corporate performances, as well as the overall economic climate. In those situations, a host of variables are involved, and the analysis becomes very intricate. Fortunately, many of the fundamental ideas associated with the study of relationships can be nicely illustrated when only *two* variables are involved. The latter will be the focus of Chapter 11.

Section 11.2 gives a computational technique for determining the "best" equation describing a set of points, $(x_1, y_1), (x_2, y_2), \ldots$, and (x_n, y_n), where *best* is defined geometrically. Section 11.3 adds a probability distribution to the y-variable, which allows for a variety of inference procedures to be developed. The consequences of both measurements being random variables is the topic of Section 11.4. Then Section 11.5 takes up the special case of Section 11.4, where the variability in X and Y is described by the *bivariate normal pdf*.

11.2 THE METHOD OF LEAST SQUARES

We begin our study of the relationship between two variables by asking a simple geometry question. Given a set of n points—$(x_1, y_1), (x_2, y_2), \ldots, (x_n, y_n)$—and a positive integer m, which polynomial of degree m is "closest" to the given points?

Suppose that the desired polynomial, $p(x)$, is written

$$p(x) = \sum_{k=0}^{m} \beta_k x^k$$

where β_0, and $\beta_1, \ldots$, and β_m are to be determined. The *method of least squares* chooses as "solutions" those β_k's minimizing the sum of squares of the vertical distances from the data points to the presumed polynomial. That is, the polynomial $p(x)$ that we will call "best" is the one whose coefficients minimize the function L, where

$$L = \sum_{i=1}^{n} [y_i - p(x_i)]^2$$

Theorem 11.2.1 summarizes the method of least squares as it applies to the important special case where $p(x)$ is a linear polynomial.

THEOREM 11.2.1. Given n points $(x_1, y_1), (x_2, y_2), \ldots, (x_n, y_n)$, the straight line $y = \beta_0 + \beta_1 x$ minimizing

$$L = \sum_{i=1}^{n} [y_i - (\beta_0 + \beta_1 x_i)]^2$$

has slope

$$\beta_1 = \frac{n \sum_{i=1}^{n} x_i y_i - \left(\sum_{i=1}^{n} x_i \right)\left(\sum_{i=1}^{n} y_i \right)}{n \left(\sum_{i=1}^{n} x_i^2 \right) - \left(\sum_{i=1}^{n} x_i \right)^2}$$

and y-intercept

$$\beta_0 = \frac{\sum_{i=1}^{n} y_i - \beta_1 \sum_{i=1}^{n} x_i}{n} = \bar{y} - \beta_1 \bar{x}$$

Proof. The proof is accomplished by the usual device of taking the partial derivatives of L with respect to β_0 and β_1, setting the resulting expressions equal to 0, and solving. By the first step we get

$$\frac{\partial L}{\partial \beta_1} = \sum_{i=1}^{n} (-2)x_i [y_i - (\beta_0 + \beta_1 x_i)]$$

and

$$\frac{\partial L}{\partial \beta_0} = \sum_{i=1}^{n} (-2)[y_i - (\beta_0 + \beta_1 x_i)]$$

Now, set the right-hand sides of $\partial L / \partial \beta_0$ and $\partial L / \partial \beta_1$ equal to 0 and simplify. This gives

$$n\beta_0 + \left(\sum_{i=1}^{n} x_i \right)\beta_1 = \sum_{i=1}^{n} y_i$$

and

$$\left(\sum_{i=1}^{n} x_i \right)\beta_0 + \left(\sum_{i=1}^{n} x_i^2 \right)\beta_1 = \sum_{i=1}^{n} x_i y_i$$

An application of Cramer's rule gives the solution for β_1 stated in the theorem. The expression for β_0 follows immediately.

CASE STUDY 11.2.1

A manufacturer of air conditioning units is having assembly problems due to the failure of a connecting rod to meet finished-weight specifications. Too many rods are being completely tooled, then rejected as overweight. To reduce that cost, the company's quality control department wants to quantify the relationship between the weight of the finished rod, y, and that of the rough casting, x (129). Castings likely to produce rods that are too heavy can then be discarded before undergoing the final (and costly) tooling process.

As a first step in examining the xy-relationship, 25 (x_i, y_i) pairs are measured (see Table 11.2.1). Graphed, the points suggest that the weight of the finished rod is linearly re-

TABLE 11.2.1

Rod Number	Rough Weight, x	Finished Weight, y	Rod Number	Rough Weight, x	Finished Weight, y
1	2.745	2.080	14	2.635	1.990
2	2.700	2.045	15	2.630	1.990
3	2.690	2.050	16	2.625	1.995
4	2.680	2.005	17	2.625	1.985
5	2.675	2.035	18	2.620	1.970
6	2.670	2.035	19	2.615	1.985
7	2.665	2.020	20	2.615	1.990
8	2.660	2.005	21	2.615	1.995
9	2.655	2.010	22	2.610	1.990
10	2.655	2.000	23	2.590	1.975
11	2.650	2.000	24	2.590	1.995
12	2.650	2.005	25	2.565	1.955
13	2.645	2.015			

FIGURE 11.2.1

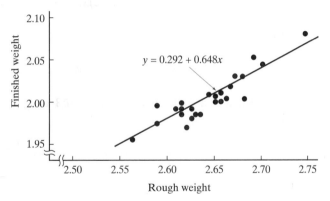

lated to the weight of the rough casting (see Figure 11.2.1). Use Theorem 11.2.1 to find the best straight line approximating the xy-relationship.

From Table 11.2.1, we find that

$$\sum_{i=1}^{25} x_i = 66.075 \quad \sum_{i=1}^{25} x_i^2 = 174.672925$$

$$\sum_{i=1}^{25} y_i = 50.12 \quad \sum_{i=1}^{25} y_i^2 = 100.49865$$

$$\sum_{i=1}^{25} x_i y_i = 132.490725$$

Therefore,

$$\beta_1 = \frac{25(132.490725) - (66.075)(50.12)}{25(174.672925) - (66.075)^2} = 0.642$$

and

(continued on next page)

(Case Study 11.2.1 continued)

$$\beta_0 = \frac{50.12 - 0.642(66.075)}{25} = 0.308$$

making the least-squares line

$$y = 0.308 + 0.642x$$

The manufacturer is now in a position to make some informed policy decisions. If the weight of a rough casting is, say, 2.71 oz., the least-squares line predicts that its finished weight will be *2.05 oz.*:

$$\text{estimated weight} = \beta_0 + \beta_1(2.71)$$

$$= 0.308 + 0.642(2.71)$$

$$= 2.05$$

In the event that finished weights of 2.05 oz. are considered to be too heavy, rough castings weighing 2.71 oz. (or more) should be discarded.

Residuals

The difference between an observed y_i and the value of the least-squares line when $x = x_i$ is called the *i*th *residual*. Its magnitude reflects the failure of the least-squares line to "model" that particular point. A *residual plot* is a graph of the *i*th residual versus x_i, for all *i*. Applied statisticians find residual plots to be very helpful in assessing the appropriateness of fitting a straight line through a set of points.

> **DEFINITION 11.2.1.** Let β_0 and β_1 be the least-squares coefficients associated with the sample $(x_1, y_1), (x_2, y_2), \ldots, (x_n, y_n)$. For any value of x, the quantity $\hat{y} = \beta_0 + \beta_1 x$ is known as the *predicted value* of y. For each $i, i = 1, \ldots, n$, the difference $y_i - \hat{y}_i = y_i - (\beta_0 + \beta_1 x_i)$ is called a *residual*.

EXAMPLE 11.2.1

Make the residual plot for the data in Case Study 11.2.1. What does its appearance imply about the suitability of fitting those points with a straight line?

We begin by calculating the residuals for each of the 25 data points. The first observation recorded, for example, was $(x_1, y_1) = (2.745, 2.080)$. The corresponding predicted value, $\hat{y}_1$, is *2.071*:

$$\hat{y}_1 = 0.308 + 0.642(2.745)$$

$$= 2.070$$

The first residual, then, is $y_1 - \hat{y}_1 = 2.080 - 2.070$, or *0.010*. The complete set of residuals appears in the last column of Table 11.2.2.

For a least-squares straight line to be a fully adequate representation of a set of points, none of the residuals should be exceptionally large, nor should the *set* of residuals exhibit any patterns or trends. Figure 11.2.2 is a plot of the residuals from Table 11.2.2—that is, a graph of

$y_i - \hat{y}_i$ versus x_i. To an applied statistician, there is nothing here that would raise any serious doubts about using a straight line to describe the xy-relationship—the magnitudes of the residuals are all comparable and, collectively, they appear to be distributed randomly.

TABLE 11.2.2

x_i	y_i	$\hat{y}_i$	$y_i - \hat{y}_i$
2.745	2.080	2.070	0.010
2.700	2.045	2.041	0.004
2.690	2.050	2.035	0.015
2.680	2.005	2.029	-0.024
2.675	2.035	2.025	0.010
2.670	2.035	2.022	0.013
2.665	2.020	2.019	0.001
2.660	2.005	2.016	-0.011
2.655	2.010	2.013	-0.003
2.655	2.000	2.013	-0.013
2.650	2.000	2.009	-0.009
2.650	2.005	2.009	-0.004
2.645	2.015	2.006	0.009
2.635	1.990	2.000	-0.010
2.630	1.990	1.996	-0.006
2.625	1.995	1.993	0.002
2.625	1.985	1.993	-0.008
2.620	1.970	1.990	-0.020
2.615	1.985	1.987	-0.002
2.615	1.990	1.987	0.003
2.615	1.995	1.987	0.008
2.610	1.990	1.984	0.006
2.590	1.975	1.971	0.004
2.590	1.995	1.971	0.024
2.565	1.955	1.955	0.000

FIGURE 11.2.2

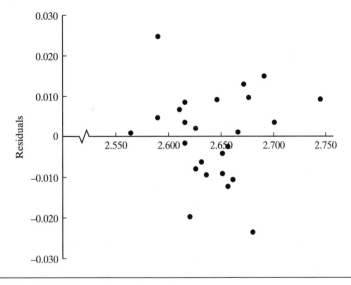

CASE STUDY 11.2.2

Table 11.2.3 lists Social Security costs for selected years from 1965 through 1992 (112). During that period, payouts rose from \$17.1 billion to \$285.1 billion. Substituting those seven (x_i, y_i)'s into the formulas in Theorem 11.2.1 gives

$$y = -66.2 + 10.3x$$

as the least-squares straight line describing the xy-relationship. Is it reasonable to predict that Social Security costs in the year 2000 (that is, when $x = 40$) will be *\$345.8* billion $[= -66.2 + 10.3(40)]$?

No! At first glance, the least-squares line does appear to fit the data quite well (see Figure 11.2.3). A closer look, though, suggests that the underlying xy-relationship may be curvilinear rather than linear. The residual plot (Figure 11.2.4) confirms that suspicion—there we see a distinctly nonrandom pattern.

TABLE 11.2.3

Year	Years After 1960, x	Social Security Cost (\$ Billion), y
1965	5	\$ 17.1
1970	10	29.6
1975	15	63.6
1980	20	117.1
1985	25	186.4
1990	30	346.5
1992	32	285.1

FIGURE 11.2.3

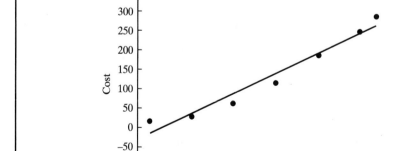

FIGURE 11.2.4

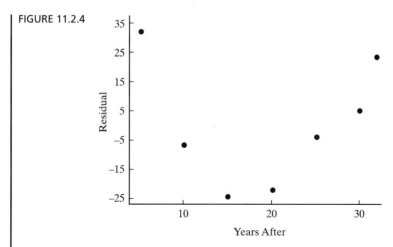

Years After

Clearly, extrapolating these data linearly would be foolish. Based on the information in Table 11.2.3, the $345.8 billion projection is likely to underestimate substantially the cost of Social Security at the start of the Third Millennium.

QUESTIONS

11.2.1 Crickets make their chirping sound by sliding one wing cover very rapidly back and forth over the other. Biologists have long been aware that there is a linear relationship between *temperature* and the frequency with which a cricket chirps, although the slope and y-intercept of the relationship varies from species to species. The following table lists 15 frequency-temperature observations recorded for the striped ground cricket, *Nemobius fasciatus fasciatus* (125). Plot these data and find the equation of the least-squares line, $y = \beta_0 + \beta_1 x$. Suppose a cricket of this species is observed to chirp 18 times per second. What would be the estimated temperature?

Observation Number	Chirps per Second, x_i	Temperature, y_i (°F)
1	20.0	88.6
2	16.0	71.6
3	19.8	93.3
4	18.4	84.3
5	17.1	80.6
6	15.5	75.2
7	14.7	69.7
8	17.1	82.0
9	15.4	69.4
10	16.2	83.3
11	15.0	79.6
12	17.2	82.6
13	16.0	80.6
14	17.0	83.5
15	14.4	76.3

Note:

$$\sum_{i=1}^{15} x_i = 249.8 \qquad \sum_{i=1}^{15} x_i^2 = 4{,}200.56$$

$$\sum_{i=1}^{15} y_i = 1{,}200.6 \qquad \sum_{i=1}^{15} x_i y_i = 20{,}127.47$$

11.2.2 The aging of whisky in charred oak barrels brings about a number of chemical changes that enhance its taste and darken its color. The following table shows the change in a whisky's proof as a function of the number of years it is stored (146).

Age, x (years)	Proof, y
0	104.6
0.5	104.1
1	104.4
2	105.0
3	106.0
4	106.8
5	107.7
6	108.7
7	110.6
8	112.1

(*Note:* The proof initially decreases because of dilution by moisture in the staves of the barrels.) Graph these data and draw in the least-squares line.

11.2.3 As water temperature increases, sodium nitrate ($NaNO_3$) becomes more soluble. The following table (94) gives the number of parts of sodium nitrate that dissolve in 100 parts of water.

Temperature (Degrees Celsius), x	Parts Dissolved, y
0	66.7
4	71.0
10	76.3
15	80.6
21	85.7
29	92.9
36	99.4
51	113.6
68	125.1

Calculate the residuals, $\hat{y}_1, \hat{y}_2, \ldots, \hat{y}_9$, and draw the residual plot. Does it suggest that fitting a straight line through these data would be appropriate? *Note:*

$$\sum_{i=1}^{9} x_i = 234 \qquad \sum_{i=1}^{9} y_i = 811.3$$

$$\sum_{i=1}^{9} x_i^2 = 10{,}144 \qquad \sum_{i=1}^{9} x_i y_i = 24{,}628.6$$

11.2.4 What, if anything, is unusual about the following residual plots?

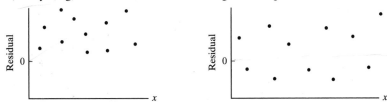

11.2.5 The following is the residual plot that results from fitting the equation $y = 6.0 + 2.0x$ to a set of $n = 10$ points. What, if anything, would be wrong with predicting that y will equal 30.0 when $x = 12$?

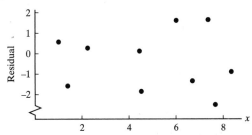

11.2.6 Would the following residual plot produced by fitting a least-squares straight line to a set of $n = 13$ points cause you to doubt that the underlying xy-relationship is linear? Explain.

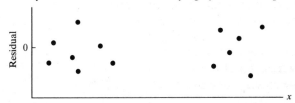

11.2.7 The relationship between school funding and student performance continues to be a hotly debated political and philosophical issue. Typical of the data available are the following figures, showing the 1991 per-pupil expenditures and average SAT scores for 13 randomly chosen districts in Virginia (27).

District	Spending per Pupil, x	Average SAT Score, y
Augusta	$3877	886
Chesapeake	3947	817
Chesterfield	3754	904
Dinwiddie	3864	754
Fairfax	5770	975
Hanover	3736	861
Henrico	4377	887
Loudoun	5107	922
Lynchburg	4002	905
Montgomery	4078	890
Newport News	4259	852
Pittsylvania	3591	869
Prince William	4613	909

Graph the data and superimpose the least-squares line, $y = \beta_0 + \beta_1 x$. What would you conclude about the xy-relationship? Does your graph suggest any obvious follow-up studies? *Note*:

$$\sum_{i=1}^{13} x_i = 54{,}975 \qquad \sum_{i=1}^{13} y_i = 11{,}431$$

$$\sum_{i=1}^{13} x_i^2 = 237{,}083{,}328 \quad \sum_{i=1}^{13} x_i y_i = 48{,}593{,}986$$

11.2.8 A new, presumably simpler laboratory procedure has been proposed for recovering calcium oxide (CaO) from solutions that contain magnesium. Critics of the method argue that the results are too dependent on the person who performs the analysis. To demonstrate their concern, they arrange for the procedure to be run on 10 samples, each containing a known amount of CaO. Nine of the ten tests are done by Chemist A; the other is run by Chemist B. Based on the results summarized in the following table, does their criticism seem justified? Answer the question by constructing a residual plot. *Note*: The least-squares straight line for these data has the equation $y = -0.228 + 0.995x$.

Chemist	CaO Present (in mg), x	CaO Recovered (in mg), y
A	4.0	3.7
A	8.0	7.8
A	12.5	12.1
A	16.0	15.6
A	20.0	19.8
A	25.0	24.5
B	31.0	31.1
A	36.0	35.5
A	40.0	39.4
A	40.0	39.5

11.2.9 Recall the radioactive contamination problem described in Case Study 1.2.4. For the nine (x_i, y_i)'s in Table 1.2.5,

$$\sum_{i=1}^{9} x_i = 41.56 \qquad \sum_{i=1}^{9} x_i^2 = 289.4222$$

$$\sum_{i=1}^{9} y_i = 1{,}416.1 \qquad \sum_{i=1}^{9} x_i y_i = 7{,}439.37$$

Verify that the least-squares straight line for these points has the equation $y = 114.72 + 9.23x$. Also, construct the corresponding residual plot. Does it seem reasonable to conclude that x and y are linearly related?

11.2.10 Would you have any reservations about fitting the following data with a straight line? Explain.

x	y
3	20
7	37
5	29
1	10
10	59
12	69
6	39
11	58
8	47
9	48
2	18
4	29

11.2.11 When two closely related species are crossed, the progeny will tend to have physical traits that lie somewhere between those of the two parents. Whether a similar mixing occurs with behavioral traits was the focus of an experiment where the subjects were mallard and pintail ducks (150). A total of 11 males were studied; all were second-generation crosses. A rating scale was devised that measured the extent to which the plumage of each of the ducks resembled the plumage of the first generation's parents. A score of 0 indicated that the hybrid had the same appearance (phenotype) as a pure mallard; a score of 20 meant that the hybrid looked like a pintail. Similarly, certain behavioral traits were quantified and a second scale was constructed that ranged from 0 (completely mallard-like) to 15 (completely pintail-like). Use Theorem 11.2.1 and the following data to summarize the relationship between the plumage and behavioral indices. Does a linear model seem adequate?

Male	Plumage Index, x	Behavioral Index, y
R	7	3
S	13	10
D	14	11
F	6	5
W	14	15
K	15	15
U	4	7
O	8	10
V	7	4
J	9	9
L	14	11

11.2.12 Verify that the coefficients β_0 and β_1 of the least-squares straight line are solutions of the matrix equation

$$\begin{pmatrix} n & \sum_{i=1}^{n} x_i \\ \sum_{i=1}^{n} x_i & \sum_{i=1}^{n} x_i^2 \end{pmatrix} \begin{pmatrix} \beta_0 \\ \beta_1 \end{pmatrix} = \begin{pmatrix} \sum_{i=1}^{n} y_i \\ \sum_{i=1}^{n} x_i y_i \end{pmatrix}$$

11.2.13 Prove that a least-squares straight line must necessarily pass through the point $(\bar{x}, \bar{y})$.

11.2.14 In some regression situations, there are *a priori* reasons for assuming that the xy-relationship being approximated passes through the origin. If so, the equation to be fit to the (x_i, y_i)'s has the form $y = \beta_1 x$. Use the least-squares criterion to show that the "best" slope in that case is given by

$$\beta_1 = \frac{\sum_{i=1}^{n} x_i y_i}{\sum_{i=1}^{n} x_i^2}$$

11.2.15 One of the most startling scientific discoveries of the twentieth century was the announcement in 1929 by the American astronomer Edwin Hubble that the universe is expanding. If v is a galaxy's recession velocity (relative to any other galaxy) and d is its distance (from that same galaxy), Hubble's law states that

$$v = Hd$$

where H is known as Hubble's constant. (To cosmologists, Hubble's constant is a critically important number—its reciprocal, after being properly scaled, is an estimate of the age of the universe.) The following are distance and velocity measurements made on 11 galactic clusters (24). Use the formula cited in Question 11.2.14 to estimate Hubble's constant.

Cluster	Distance (millions of light-years)	Velocity (thousands of miles/sec)
Virgo	22	0.75
Pegasus	68	2.4
Perseus	108	3.2
Coma Berenices	137	4.7
Ursa Major No. 1	255	9.3
Leo	315	12.0
Corona Borealis	390	13.4
Gemini	405	14.4
Bootes	685	24.5
Ursa Major No. 2	700	26.0
Hydra	1100	38.0

11.2.16 Given a set of n linearly related points, $(x_1, y_1), (x_2, y_2), \ldots,$ and (x_n, y_n), use the least-squares criterion to find formulas for
(a) β_0 if the slope of the xy-relationship is known to be β_1^*
(b) β_1 if the y-intercept of the xy-relationship is known to be β_0^*.

11.2.17 Among the problems faced by job seekers wanting to reenter the work force, eroded skills, and outdated backgrounds are two of the most difficult to overcome. Knowing that, employers are often wary of hiring individuals who have spent lengthy periods of time away from the job. The following table shows the percentages of hospitals willing to rehire medical technicians who have been away from that career for x years (134). It can be argued that the fitted line should necessarily have a y-intercept of 100 because no employer would refuse to hire someone (due to outdated skills) whose career had not been interrupted at all—that is, applicants for whom $x = 0$. Under that assumption, use the result from Question 11.2.16 to fit these data with the model $y = 100 + \beta_1 x$.

Years of Inactivity, x	Percent of Hospitals Willing to Hire, y
0.5	100
1.5	94
4	75
8	44
13	28
18	17

11.2.18 Set up (but do not solve) the equations necessary for determining the least-squares estimates for the trigonometric model,

$$y = \beta_0 + \beta_1 x + \beta_2 \sin x$$

Assume that the data consist of the random sample $(x_1, y_1), (x_2, y_2), \ldots,$ and (x_n, y_n).

Nonlinear Models

Obviously, not all xy-relationships can be adequately described by straight lines. Curvilinear relationships of all sorts can be found in every field of endeavor. Many of these nonlinear models, though, can still be fit using Theorem 11.2.1, provided the data have been "linearized" by a suitable transformation.

Exponential Regression. Suppose the relationship between two variables is best described by an exponential function of the form

$$y = \beta_0 e^{\beta_1 x} \tag{11.2.1}$$

Depending on the value of β_1, Equation 11.2.1 will look like one of the graphs pictured in Figure 11.2.5. Those curvilinear shapes notwithstanding, though, there is a *linear* model also related to Equation 11.2.1.

If $y = \beta_0 e^{\beta_1 x}$, it is necessarily true that

$$\ln y = \ln \beta_0 + \beta_1 x \tag{11.2.2}$$

which implies that *ln y and x have a linear relationship*. That being the case, the formulas of Theorem 11.2.1 *applied to x and ln y* should yield the slope and y-intercept of Equation 11.2.2.

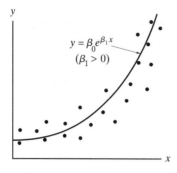

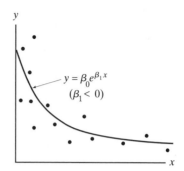

FIGURE 11.2.5

Specifically,

$$\beta_1 = \frac{n \sum_{i=1}^{n} x_i \ln y_i - \left(\sum_{i=1}^{n} x_i \right) \left(\sum_{i=1}^{n} \ln y_i \right)}{n \sum_{i=1}^{n} x_i^2 - \left(\sum_{i=1}^{n} x_i \right)^2}$$

and

$$\ln \beta_0 = \frac{\sum_{i=1}^{n} \ln y_i - \beta_1 \sum_{i=1}^{n} x_i}{n}$$

Comment. If the rate at which y changes is proportional to y—that is, if $\frac{dy}{dx} = \beta_1 y$ (or, equivalently, if $\frac{dy}{y} = \beta_1 \, dx$)—the xy-relationship will necessarily have the form given in Equation 11.2.1 (see Question 11.2.23).

CASE STUDY 11.2.3

Over the past 25 years computers have steadily decreased in size as they have grown in power. The ability to have more computing ability in a 4-pound laptop than in a mainframe of the 1970s is a result of engineers squeezing more and more transistors onto silicon chips. The rate at which this miniaturization occurs is known as Moore's law, after Gordon Moore, one of the founders of the Intel Corporation. His prediction, first articulated in 1965, was that the number of transistors per chip would double every 18 months.

Table 11.2.4 lists some of the growth benchmarks—namely, the number of transistors per chip—associated with the Intel chips marketed over the 20-year period from 1975 through 1995. Based on these figures, is it believable that chip capacity is, in fact, doubling at a fixed rate (meaning that Equation 11.2.1 applies)? And if so, how close is the actual doubling time to Moore's prediction of 18 months?

A plot of y versus x shows that their relationship is certainly not linear (see Figure 11.2.6). The scatterplot more closely resembles the graph of $y = \beta_0 e^{\beta_1 x}$ when $\beta_1 > 0$, as shown in Figure 11.2.5.

TABLE 11.2.4

Chip	Year	Years after 1975, x	Transistors per Chip, y
8080	1975	0	4,500
8086	1978	3	29,000
80286	1982	7	90,000
80386	1985	10	229,000
80486	1989	14	1,200,000
Pentium	1993	18	3,100,000
Pentium Pro	1995	20	5,500,000

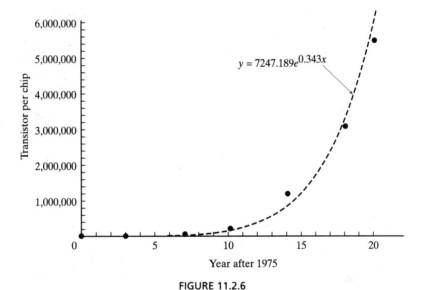

FIGURE 11.2.6

Table 11.2.5 shows the calculation of the sums required to evaluate the formulas for β_1 and $\ln \beta_0$ given on page 572. Here the slope and the y-intercept of the linearized model (Equation 11.2.2) are *0.342810* and *8.888369*, respectively:

TABLE 11.2.5

Years after 1975, x_i	x_i^2	Transistors per chip, y_i	$\ln y_i$	$x_i \cdot \ln y_i$
0	0	4,500	8.41183	0
3	9	29,000	10.27505	30.82515
7	49	90,000	11.40756	79.85292
10	100	229,000	12.34148	123.41480
14	196	1,200,000	13.99783	195.96962
18	324	3,100,000	14.94691	269.04438
20	400	5,500,000	15.52026	310.40520
72	1078		86.90093	1009.51207

(continued on next page)

(Case Study 11.2.3 continued)

$$\beta_1 = \frac{7(1009.51207) - 72(86.90093)}{7(1078) - (72)^2}$$

$$= 0.342810$$

and

$$\ln \beta_0 = \frac{86.9093 - (0.342810)(72)}{72}$$

$$= 8.888369$$

Therefore,

$$\beta_0 = e^{\ln \beta_0} = e^{8.888369} = 7247.189$$

which implies that the best-fitting exponential model describing Intel's technological advances in chip design has the equation

$$y = 7247.189e^{0.343x}$$

(see Figure 11.2.6).

To compare Equation 11.2.1 to Moore's "18-month doubling time" prediction requires that we write $y = 7247.189e^{0.343x}$ in the form $y = 7247.189(2)^x$. But

$$e^{0.343} = 2^{0.495}$$

so another way to express the fitted curve would be

$$y = 7247.189(2^{0.495x}) \tag{11.2.3}$$

In Equation 11.2.3, though, y doubles when $2^{0.495x} = 2$, or, equivalently, when $0.495x = 1$, which implies that *2.0 years* is the empirically determined technology doubling time, a pace not too much slower than Moore's prediction of 18 months.

Logarithmic Regression.   Another frequently encountered curvilinear model that can be easily linearized is the equation

$$y = \beta_0 x^{\beta_1} \tag{11.2.4}$$

Taking the common log of both sides of Equation 11.2.4 gives

$$\log y = \log \beta_0 + \beta_1 \log x$$

which implies that *log y is linear with log x*. Therefore,

$$\beta_1 = \frac{n \sum_{i=1}^{n} \log x_i \cdot \log y_i - \left(\sum_{i=1}^{n} \log x_i \right) \left(\sum_{i=1}^{n} \log y_i \right)}{n \sum_{i=1}^{n} (\log x_i)^2 - \left(\sum_{i=1}^{n} \log x_i \right)^2}$$

and

$$\log \beta_0 = \frac{\sum\limits_{i=1}^{n} \log y_i - \beta_1 \sum\limits_{i=1}^{n} \log x_i}{n}$$

Regressions of this type have slower growth rates than exponential models and are particularly useful in describing biological and engineering phenomena.

CASE STUDY 11.2.4

Among mammals, the relationship between the age at which an animal develops locomotion and the age at which it first begins to play has been widely studied. Table 11.2.6 lists "onset" times for locomotion and for play in 11 different species (31). Graphed, the data show a pattern that suggests that $y = \beta_0 x^{\beta_1}$ would be a good function for modeling the xy-relationship (see Figure 11.2.7).

TABLE 11.2.6

Species	Locomotion Begins, x_i (days)	Play Begins, y_i (days)
Homo sapiens	360	90
Gorilla gorilla	165	105
Felis catus	21	21
Canis familiaris	23	26
Rattus norvegicus	11	14
Turdus merula	18	28
Macaca mulatta	18	21
Pan troglodytes	150	105
Saimiri sciurens	45	68
Cercocebus alb.	45	75
Tamiasciureus hud.	18	46

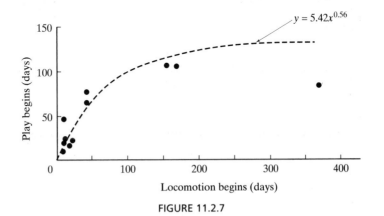

FIGURE 11.2.7

The sums and sums of squares necessary to find β_0 and β_1 are calculated in Table 11.2.7. Substituting into the formulas on pages 574–575 for the slope and y-intercept of the linearized model gives

(continued on next page)

(Case Study 11.2.4 continued)

$$\beta_1 = \frac{11(30.43743) - (17.74744)(18.01965)}{11(31.06763) - (17.74744)^2}$$

$$= 0.56$$

and

$$\log \beta_0 = \frac{18.01965 - (0.56)(17.74744)}{11}$$

$$= 0.73364$$

Therefore, $\beta_0 = 10^{0.73364} = 5.42$, and the equation describing the xy-relationship is $y = 5.42x^{0.56}$ (see Figure 11.2.7).

TABLE 11.2.7

x_i	$\log x_i$	y_i	$\log y_i$	$(\log x_i)^2$	$\log x_i \log y_i$
360	2.55630	90	1.95424	6.53467	4.99562
165	2.21748	105	2.02119	4.91722	4.48195
21	1.32222	21	1.32222	1.74827	1.74827
23	1.36173	26	1.41497	1.85431	1.92681
11	1.04139	14	1.14613	1.08449	1.19357
18	1.25527	28	1.44716	1.57570	1.81658
18	1.25527	21	1.32222	1.57570	1.65974
150	2.17609	105	2.02119	4.73537	4.39829
45	1.65321	68	1.83251	2.73310	3.02952
45	1.65321	75	1.87506	2.73310	3.09987
18	1.25527	46	1.66276	1.57570	2.08721
	17.74744		18.01965	31.06763	30.43743

Logistic Regression.   *Growth* is a fundamental characteristic of organisms, institutions, and ideas. In biology, it might refer to the change in size of a *Drosophila* population; in economics, to the proliferation of global markets; in political science, to the gradual acceptance of tax reform. Prominent among the many growth models capable of describing situations of this sort is the logistic equation

$$y = \frac{L}{1 + e^{\beta_0 + \beta_1 x}} \tag{11.2.5}$$

where β_0, β_1, and L are constants. For different values of β_0 and β_1, Equation 11.2.5 generates a variety of S-chaped curves.

To linearize Equation 11.2.5, we start with its reciprocal:

$$\frac{1}{y} = \frac{1 + e^{\beta_0 + \beta_1 x}}{L}$$

Therefore,

$$\frac{L}{y} = 1 + e^{\beta_0 + \beta_1 x}$$

and

$$\frac{L - y}{y} = e^{\beta_0 + \beta_1 x}$$

Equivalently,

$$\ln\left(\frac{L - y}{y}\right) = \beta_0 + \beta_1 x$$

which implies that $\ln\left(\dfrac{L - y}{y}\right)$ *is linear with x*.

Comment. The parameter L is interpreted as the limit to which y is converging as x increases. In practice, L is often estimated simply by plotting the data and "eye-balling" the y-asymptote.

CASE STUDY 11.2.5

Where to set college admission requirements for scholarship athletes has been a fiercely debated issue for several years. At the center of the controversy are SAT scores and how effective they are in predicting academic success. Addressing that issue, the National Collegiate Athletic Association (NCAA) recently compiled the data in Table 11.2.8 (173), showing the relationship between athletes' SAT scores (x) and their graduation rates (y).

The scatterplot for these six data points has a definite S-shaped appearance (see Figure 11.2.8), which makes Equation 11.2.5 a good candidate for modeling the xy-relationship. The limit to which the graduation rates are converging (as SAT scores increase) appears to be about *48*. Quantify the graduation rate/SAT score relationship by fitting a logistic equation to these data. Let $L = 48$.

TABLE 11.2.8

SAT Score, x	Graduation Rate (%), y
480	0.3
690	4.6
900	15.6
1100	33.4
1320	44.4
1530	45.7

(continued on next page)

(Case Study 11.2.5 continued)

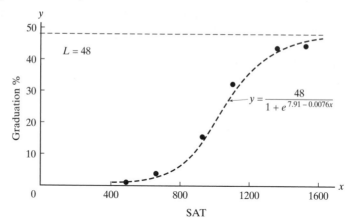

FIGURE 11.2.8

TABLE 11.2.9

x_i	y_i	$\ln\left(\dfrac{48 - y_i}{y_i}\right)$	x_i^2	$x_i \cdot \ln\left(\dfrac{48 - y_i}{y_i}\right)$
480	0.3	5.06890	230,400	2433.072
690	4.6	2.24440	476,100	1548.636
900	15.6	0.73089	810,000	657.801
1100	33.4	−0.82753	1,210,000	−910.283
1320	44.4	−2.51231	1,742,400	−3316.249
1530	45.7	−2.98919	2,340,900	−4573.461
6020		1.71516	6,809,800	−4160.484

The form of the linearized version of Equation 11.2.5 requires that we find the sums of x_i, $\ln\left(\dfrac{48 - y_i}{y_i}\right)$, x_i^2, and $x_i \cdot \ln\left(\dfrac{48 - y_i}{y_i}\right)$ (see Table 11.2.9). Substituting $\ln\left(\dfrac{48 - y_i}{y_i}\right)$ for y_i in the formulas for β_0 and β_1 in Theorem 11.2.1 gives

$$\beta_1 = \frac{6(-4160.484) - (6020)(1.71516)}{6(6,809,800) - (6020)^2}$$

$$= -0.0076$$

and

$$\beta_0 = \frac{1.71516 - (-0.0076)(6020)}{6}$$

$$= 7.91$$

so the best-fitting logistic curve has the equation

$$y = \frac{48}{1 + e^{7.91 - 0.00764}}$$

Other Curvilinear Models.   While the exponential, logarithmic, and logistic equations are three of the most common curvilinear models, there are several others that deserve mention as well. Table 11.2.10 lists a total of six nonlinear equations, including the three already described. Along with each is the particular transformation that reduces the equation to a linear form. Proofs for Parts (d), (e), and (f) will be left as exercises.

TABLE 11.2.10

(a) If $y = \beta_0 e^{\beta_1 x}$, then $\ln y$ is linear with x.

(b) If $y = \beta_0 x^{\beta_1}$, then $\log y$ is linear with $\log x$.

(c) If $y = L/(1 + e^{\beta_0 + \beta_1 x})$, then $\ln\left(\dfrac{L - y}{y}\right)$ is linear with x.

(d) If $y = \dfrac{1}{\beta_0 + \beta_1 x}$, then $\dfrac{1}{y}$ is linear with x.

(e) If $y = \dfrac{x}{\beta_0 + \beta_1 x}$, then $\dfrac{1}{y}$ is linear with $\dfrac{1}{x}$.

(f) If $y = 1 - e^{-x^{\beta_1}/\beta_0}$, then $\ln \ln\left(\dfrac{1}{1 - y}\right)$ is linear with $\ln x$.

QUESTIONS

11.2.19 Radioactive gold (^{195}Au-aurothiomalate) has an affinity for inflamed tissues and is sometimes used as a tracer to diagnose arthritis. The data in the following table (54) come from an experiment investigating the length of time and the concentrations that ^{195}Au-aurothiomalate is retained in a person's blood. Listed are the serum gold concentrations found in 10 blood samples taken from patients given an initial dose of 50 mg. Follow-up readings were made at various times, ranging from one to seven days after injection. In each case, the retention is expressed as a percentage of the patient's day-zero serum gold concentration.

Days after Injection, x	Serum Gold % Concentration, y
1	94.5
1	86.4
2	71.0
2	80.5
2	81.4
3	67.4
5	49.3
6	46.8
6	42.3
7	36.6

(a) Fit an exponential curve to these data.

(b) Estimate the half-life of ^{195}Au-aurothiomalate; that is, how long does it take for half the gold to disappear from a person's blood?

Note: If x denotes days after injection and y denotes serum gold % concentration, then

$$\sum_{i=1}^{10} x_i = 35, \quad \sum_{i=1}^{10} x_i^2 = 169, \quad \sum_{i=1}^{10} \ln y_i = 41.35720, \text{ and } \sum_{i=1}^{10} x_i \ln y_i = 137.97415.$$

11.2.20 The growth of the federal debt is one of the characterizing features of the U.S. economy during the 1980s. The increase in that obligation over the decade appears to follow an exponential model. For the following data (165), find the best such curve, using the method of least squares together with an appropriate linearizing transformation. Graph the data and superimpose the least squares curve. *Note:* $\sum_{i=1}^{11} \ln y_i = 6.19815$ and $\sum_{i=1}^{11} x_i \cdot \ln y_i = 51.6005$.

Year	Years after 1979, x	Federal Debt (in trillions), y
1980	1	0.908
1981	2	0.998
1982	3	1.142
1983	4	1.377
1984	5	1.572
1985	6	1.823
1986	7	2.125
1987	8	2.350
1988	9	2.602
1989	10	2.867
1990	11	3.233

11.2.21 The prices of used cars sold wholesale at auctions are helpful to banks for the purpose of establishing limits on car loans. The following table gives data from 1993 showing the average auction wholesale prices for the Toyota Corolla DLX four-door sedan (111).

Age (in years), x	Wholesale Price, y
1	$7250
2	6175
3	5200
4	4400
5	3825
6	3275

(a) Fit these data with a model of the form $y = \beta_0 e^{\beta_1 x}$. Graph the (x_i, y_i)'s and superimpose the least-squares curve.

(b) What would you predict the wholesale price of a seven-year-old Corolla DLX to be?

(c) In April 1993, the wholesale price of a *new* Corolla DLX was $9630. Is that figure consistent with the widely held belief that a new car depreciates substantially the moment the sales agreement is signed? Explain.

11.2.22 The following are the tuitions that were charged at Vanderbilt University from 1982 to 1991 (109).

Year	Years after 1981, x	Tuition (in thousands), y
1982	1	$6.1
1983	2	6.8
1984	3	7.5
1985	4	8.5
1986	5	9.3
1987	6	10.5
1988	7	11.5
1989	8	12.625
1990	9	13.975
1991	10	14.975

(a) Plot the data.

(b) Use the fact that $\sum_{i=1}^{10} \ln y_i = 22.78325$ and $\sum_{i=1}^{10} x_i \cdot \ln y_i = 133.68654$ to fit the data with an exponential model.

(c) Superimpose the answer to Part (b) on the graph in Part (a).

(d) Suppose a freshman entered Vanderbilt in 1991, graduated four years later, got married in three years, and had a daughter two years after that. Based solely on an extrapolation of the data from 1982 to 1991, what might he expect his daughter's tuition bill to be for four years at Vanderbilt? Assume that she enrolls at age 18.

11.2.23 Suppose a set of n (x_i, y_i)'s are measured on a phenomenon whose theoretical xy-relationship is of the form $y = \beta_0 e^{\beta_1 x}$.

(a) Recall the comment on page 572. Show that $\dfrac{dy}{dx} = \beta_1 y$ implies that $y = \beta_0 e^{\beta_1 x}$.

(b) On what kind of graph paper would the (x_i, y_i)'s show a linear relationship?

11.2.24 In 1959, the Ise Bay typhoon devastated parts of Japan. For seven metropolitan areas in the storm's path, the following table gives the number of homes damaged as a function of peak wind gust (107). Show that a model of the form $y = \beta_0 x^{\beta_1}$ provides a good model for the data.

City	Peak Wind Gust (hundred mph), x	Number of Damaged Homes (in thousands), y
A	0.98	25,000
B	0.74	0.950
C	1.12	200,000
D	1.34	150,000
E	0.87	0.940
F	0.65	0.090
G	1.39	260,000

Note: $\quad \sum_{i=1}^{7} \log x_i = -0.067772 \qquad\qquad \sum_{i=1}^{7} \log y_i = 19.9513$

$$\sum_{i=1}^{7} (\log x_i)^2 = 0.0948679 \qquad \sum_{i=1}^{7} (\log x_i)(\log y_i) = 1.85483$$

11.2.25 Studies have shown that certain ants in a colony are assigned foraging duties, which require them to come and go from the colony on a regular basis. Furthermore, if y is the colony size and x is the number of ants that forage, the relationship between y and x has the form $y = \beta_0 x^{\beta_1}$, where β_0 and β_1 vary from species to species. Once the parameter values have been estimated for a particular kind of ant, biologists can count the (relatively small) number of ants that forage and then use the regression equation to estimate the (much larger) number of ants living in the colony. The following table gives the results of a "calibration" study done on the red wood ant (*Formica polyctena*): Listed are the actual colony sizes, y, and the foraging sizes, x, recorded for 15 of their colonies (85).

Foraging Size, x	Colony Size, y
45	280
74	222
118	288
70	601
220	1,205
823	2,769
647	2,828
446	3,229
765	3,762
338	7,551
611	8,834
4,119	12,584
850	12,605
11,600	34,661
64,512	139,043

(a) Find β_0 and β_1.

(b) If the number of red wood ants seen foraging is 2500, what would be a reasonable estimate for the size of the colony from which they came?

Note:
$$\sum_{i=1}^{15} \log x_i = 41.77441 \qquad \sum_{i=1}^{15} \log y_i = 52.79857$$

$$\sum_{i=1}^{15} (\log x_i)^2 = 126.60450 \qquad \sum_{i=1}^{15} \log x_i \cdot \log y_i = 156.03811$$

11.2.26 Over the years, many efforts have been made to demonstrate that the human brain is appreciably different in structure from the brains of lower-order primates. In point of fact, such differences in gross anatomy are disconcertingly difficult to discern. The following are the average areas of the striate cortex (x) and the prestriate cortex (y) found for humans and for three species of chimpanzees (119).

	Area	
Primate	Striate Cortex, x (mm^2)	Prestriate Cortex, y (mm^2)
Homo	2613	7838
Pongo	1876	2864
Cercopithecus	933	1334
Galago	78.9	40.8

Plot the data and superimpose the least-squares curve, $y = \beta_0 x^{\beta_1}$.

11.2.27 Years of experience buying and selling commercial real estate have convinced many investors that the value of land zoned for business (y) is inversely related to its distance (x) from the center of town—that is, $y = \beta_0 + \beta_1 \cdot \dfrac{1}{x}$. If that suspicion is correct, what should be the appraised value of a piece of property located $\frac{1}{4}$ mile from the town square, based on the following recent sales?

Land Parcel	Distance from Center of City (in thousand feet), x	Value (in thousands), y
H1	1.00	$20.5
B6	0.50	42.7
Q4	0.25	80.4
L4	2.00	10.5
T7	4.00	6.1
D9	6.00	6.0
E4	10.00	3.5

11.2.28 Verify the claims made in Parts (d), (e), and (f) of Table 11.2.10—that is, prove that the transformations cited will linearize the original models.

11.2.29 During the 1960s, when the Cold War was fueling an arms race between the Soviet Union and the United States, the number of American intercontinental ballistic missiles (ICBMs) rose from 18 to 1054 (9). Moreover, the sizes of the ICBM stockpile during that decade had an S-shaped pattern, suggesting that the logistic curve would provide a good model. Graph the following data, and approximate the xy-relationship with the function $y = \dfrac{L}{1 + e^{\beta_0 + \beta_1 x}}$. Assume that $L = 1055$.

Years	Years after 1959, x	Number of ICBMS, y
1960	1	18
1961	2	63
1962	3	294
1963	4	424
1964	5	834
1965	6	854
1966	7	904
1967	8	1054
1968	9	1054
1969	10	1054

11.2.30 The following table shows a portion of the results from a clinical trial investigating the effectiveness of a monoamine oxidase inhibitor as a treatment for depression (194). The relationship between y, the percentage of subjects showing improvement, and x, the patient's age, appears to be S-shaped. Graph the data and superimpose a graph of the least-squares curve $y = \dfrac{L}{1 + e^{\beta_0 + \beta_1 x}}$. Take L to be 60.

Age Group	Age Mid-Point, x	% Improved, y	$\ln\left(\dfrac{60 - y}{y}\right)$
$[28, 32)$	30	11	1.49393
$[32, 36)$	34	14	1.18958
$[36, 40)$	38	19	0.76913
$[40, 44)$	42	32	-0.13353
$[44, 48)$	46	42	-0.84730
$[48, 52)$	50	48	-1.38629
$[52, 56)$	54	50	-1.60944
$[56, 60)$	58	52	-1.87180

11.3 THE LINEAR MODEL

Section 11.2 views the problem of "curve fitting" from a purely geometrical perspective. The observed (x_i, y_i)'s are assumed to be nothing more than points in the xy-plane, devoid of any statistical properties. It is more realistic, though, to think of each y as the value recorded for a random variable Y, meaning that a *distribution* of possible y-values is associated with every value of x.

Consider, for example, the connecting rod weights analyzed in Case Study 11.2.1. The first rod listed in Table 11.2.1 had an initial weight of $x = 2.745$ oz. and, after the tooling process was completed, a finished weight of $y = 2.080$ oz. It does not follow from that one observation, of course, that an initial weight of 2.745 oz. necessarily leads to a finished weight of 2.080 oz. Common sense tells us that the tooling process will not always have exactly the same effect, even on rods having the same initial weight. Associated with each x, then, there *will* be a range of possible y-values. The symbol $f_{Y|x}(y)$ is used to denote the pdf's of these "conditional" distributions.

> **DEFINITION 11.3.1.** Let $f_{Y|x}(y)$ denote the pdf of the random variable Y for a given value x, and let $E(Y|x)$ denote the expected value associated with $f_{Y|x}(y)$. The function
>
> $$y = E(Y|x)$$
>
> is called the *regression curve of Y on x*.

EXAMPLE 11.3.1

Suppose that corresponding to each value of x in the interval $0 \leq x \leq 1$ is a distribution of y-values having the pdf

$$f_{Y|x}(y) = \frac{x + y}{x + \frac{1}{2}}, \quad 0 \leq y \leq 1; \quad 0 \leq x \leq 1$$

Find and graph the regression curve of Y on x.

Notice, first of all, that for any x between 0 and 1, $f_{Y|x}(y)$ does qualify as a pdf:

(1) $f_{Y|x}(y) \geq 0$, for $0 \leq y \leq 1$ and any $0 \leq x \leq 1$

(2) $\displaystyle \int_0^1 f_{Y|x}(y)\, dy = \int_0^1 \left(\frac{x + y}{x + \frac{1}{2}}\right) dy = 1$

Moreover,

$$E(Y \mid x) = \int_0^1 y \cdot f_{Y\mid x}(y) \, dy = \int_0^1 y \cdot \frac{x + y}{x + \frac{1}{2}} \, dy$$

$$= \left(\frac{xy^2}{2(x + \frac{1}{2})} + \frac{y^3}{3(x + \frac{1}{2})} \right) \Big|_0^1$$

$$= \frac{3x + 2}{6x + 3}, \quad 0 \le x \le 1$$

Figure 11.3.1 shows the regression curve, $y = E(Y \mid x) = \dfrac{3x + 2}{6x + 3}$, together with three of

the conditional distributions—$f_{Y\mid 0}(y) = 2y$, $f_{Y\mid \frac{1}{2}}(y) = y + \frac{1}{2}$, and $f_{y\mid 1}(y) = \dfrac{2y + 2}{3}$. The

$f_{Y\mid x}(y)$'s, of course, should be visualized as coming out of the plane of the paper.

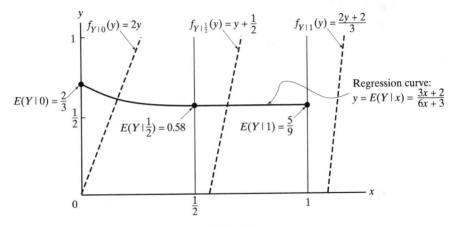

FIGURE 11.3.1

A Special Case

Definition 11.3.1 introduces the notion of a regression curve in the most general of contexts. In practice, there is one special case of the function $y = E(Y \mid x)$ that is particularly important. Known as the *simple linear model*, it makes four assumptions:

(1) $f_{Y\mid x}(y)$ is a normal pdf for all x.

(2) The standard deviation, σ, associated with $f_{Y\mid x}(y)$ is the same for all x.

(3) The means of all the conditional Y-distributions are collinear—that is,

$$y = E(Y \mid x) = \beta_0 + \beta_1 x$$

(4) All of the conditional distributions represent independent random variables.

(See Figure 11.3.2.)

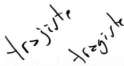

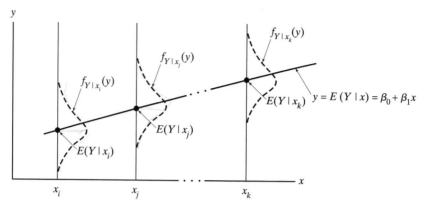

FIGURE 11.3.2

Estimating the Linear Model Parameters

Implicit in the simple linear model are three parameters—β_0, β_1, and σ^2. Typically, all three will be unknown and need to be estimated. Since the model assumes a probability structure for the Y-variable, estimates can be obtained using the method of maximum likelihood, as opposed to the method of least squares that we saw in Section 11.2. (Maximum-likelihood estimates are preferable to least-squares estimates because MLEs have probability distributions that can be used to set up hypothesis tests and confidence intervals.)

THEOREM 11.3.1. Let $(x_1, Y_1), (x_2, Y_2), \ldots,$ and (x_n, Y_n) be a set of points satisfying the simple linear model, $E(Y|x) = \beta_0 + \beta_1 x$. The maximum-likelihood estimators for β_0, β_1, and σ^2 are given by

$$\hat{\beta}_1 = \frac{n \sum_{i=1}^{n} x_i Y_i - \left(\sum_{i=1}^{n} x_i \right) \left(\sum_{i=1}^{n} Y_i \right)}{n \left(\sum_{i=1}^{n} x_i^2 \right) - \left(\sum_{i=1}^{n} x_i \right)^2}$$

$$\hat{\beta}_0 = \bar{Y} - \hat{\beta}_1 \bar{x}$$

and

$$\hat{\sigma}^2 = \frac{1}{n} \sum_{i=1}^{n} (Y_i - \hat{Y}_i)^2$$

where $\hat{Y}_i = \hat{\beta}_0 + \hat{\beta}_1 x_i, i = 1, \ldots, n.$

Proof. Since each Y_i is assumed to be normally distributed with mean equal to $\beta_0 + \beta_1 x_i$ and variance equal to σ^2, the sample's likelihood function, L, is the product

$$L = \prod_{i=1}^{n} f_{Y|x_i}(y_i)$$

$$= \prod_{i=1}^{n} \frac{1}{\sqrt{2\pi}\sigma} e^{-\frac{1}{2}\left(\frac{y_i - \beta_0 - \beta_1 x_i}{\sigma}\right)^2}$$

The maximum of L occurs when the partial derivatives with respect to β_0, and β_1, and σ^2 all vanish.

It will be a little easier, computationally, to differentiate $-2 \ln L$, and the latter will be maximized for the same parameter values that maximize L. Here,

$$-2 \ln L = n \cdot \ln(2\pi) + n \cdot \ln(\sigma^2) + \frac{1}{\sigma^2} \sum_{i=1}^{n} (y_i - \beta_0 - \beta_1 x_i)^2$$

Setting the three partial derivatives equal to 0 gives

$$\frac{\partial(-2 \ln L)}{\partial \beta_0} = \frac{2}{\sigma^2} \sum_{i=1}^{n} (y_i - \beta_0 - \beta_1 x_i)(-1) = 0$$

$$\frac{\partial(-2 \ln L)}{\partial \beta_1} = \frac{2}{\sigma^2} \sum_{i=1}^{n} (y_i - \beta_0 - \beta_1 x_i)(-x_i) = 0$$

$$\frac{\partial(-2 \ln L)}{\partial \sigma^2} = \frac{n}{\sigma^2} - \frac{2}{(\sigma^2)^2} \sum_{i=1}^{n} (y_i - \beta_0 - \beta_1 x_i)^2 = 0$$

The first two equations depend only on β_0 and β_1, and the resulting solutions for $\hat{\beta}_0$ and $\hat{\beta}_1$ have the same form as those found in the proof of Theorem 11.2.1. Substituting the solutions for the first two equations into the third gives the claimed $\hat{\sigma}^2$.

Comment.   Note the similarity in the formulas for the maximum-likelihood estimators and the least-squares estimators for $\hat{\beta}_0$ and $\hat{\beta}_1$. The least-squares estimates, of course, are numbers, while the MLEs are random variables.

Up to this point, random variables have been denoted with upper-case letters and their values with lower-case letters. In this section, bold-face $\hat{\boldsymbol{\beta}}_0$ and $\hat{\boldsymbol{\beta}}_1$ will represent the MLE *random variables*, and plain-text $\hat{\beta}_0$ and $\hat{\beta}_1$ refer to specific values taken on by those random variables.

Properties of Linear Model Estimators

By virtue of the assumptions that define the simple linear model, we know that the estimators $\hat{\boldsymbol{\beta}}_0$, $\hat{\boldsymbol{\beta}}_1$, and $\hat{\sigma}^2$ are random variables. Before those MLEs can be used to set up inference procedures, though, we need to establish their basic statistical properties—specifically, their means, variances, and pdf's.

THEOREM 11.3.2.   Let $(x_1, Y_1), (x_2, Y_2), \ldots,$ and (x_n, Y_n) be a set of points satisfying the simple linear model, $E(Y \mid x) = \beta_0 + \beta_1 x$. Let $\hat{\boldsymbol{\beta}}_0, \hat{\boldsymbol{\beta}}_1,$ and $\hat{\sigma}^2$ be the MLEs for $\beta_0, \beta_1,$ and σ^2, respectively. Then

(a) $\hat{\boldsymbol{\beta}}_0$ and $\hat{\boldsymbol{\beta}}_1$ are both normally distributed.

(b) $\hat{\boldsymbol{\beta}}_0$ and $\hat{\boldsymbol{\beta}}_1$ are both unbiased: $E(\hat{\boldsymbol{\beta}}_0) = \beta_0$ and $E(\hat{\boldsymbol{\beta}}_1) = \beta_1$.

(c) $\mathrm{Var}(\hat{\boldsymbol{\beta}}_1) = \dfrac{\sigma^2}{\sum\limits_{i=1}^{n} (x_i - \bar{x})^2}$

(d) $\mathrm{Var}(\hat{\boldsymbol{\beta}}_0) = \dfrac{\sigma^2 \displaystyle\sum_{i=1}^{n} x_i^2}{n \displaystyle\sum_{i=1}^{n} (x_i - \bar{x})^2} = \sigma^2 \left[\dfrac{1}{n} + \dfrac{\bar{x}^2}{\displaystyle\sum_{i=1}^{n} (x_i - \bar{x})^2} \right]$

Proof.   We will prove the statements for $\hat{\boldsymbol{\beta}}_1$; the results for $\hat{\boldsymbol{\beta}}_0$ follow similarly. Since

$$\sum_{i=1}^{n} (x_i - \bar{x})^2 = \sum_{i=1}^{n} (x_i^2 - 2x_i\bar{x} + \bar{x}^2)$$

$$= \sum_{i=1}^{n} x_i^2 - n\bar{x}^2$$

$$= \sum_{i=1}^{n} x_i^2 - \left(\frac{1}{n}\right)\left(\sum_{i=1}^{n} x_i\right)^2$$

and

$$\sum_{i=1}^{n} (x_i - \bar{x})(Y_i - \bar{Y}) = \sum_{i=1}^{n} x_i Y_i - \bar{x}\sum_{i=1}^{n} Y_i - \bar{Y}\sum_{i=1}^{n} x_i + n\bar{x}\bar{Y}$$

$$= \sum_{i=1}^{n} x_i Y_i - n\bar{x}\bar{Y}$$

$$= \sum_{i=1}^{n} x_i Y_i - \left(\frac{1}{n}\right)\left(\sum_{i=1}^{n} x_i\right)\left(\sum_{i=1}^{n} Y_i\right)$$

we can write

$$\hat{\boldsymbol{\beta}}_1 = \frac{n\displaystyle\sum_{i=1}^{n} x_i Y_i - \left(\displaystyle\sum_{i=1}^{n} x_i\right)\left(\displaystyle\sum_{i=1}^{n} Y_i\right)}{n\displaystyle\sum_{i=1}^{n} x_i^2 - \left(\displaystyle\sum_{i=1}^{n} x_i\right)^2} = \frac{\displaystyle\sum_{i=1}^{n} (x_i - \bar{x})(Y_i - \bar{Y})}{\displaystyle\sum_{i=1}^{n} (x_i - \bar{x})^2}$$

But

$$\sum_{i=1}^{n} (x_i - \bar{x}) = \sum_{i=1}^{n} x_i - n\bar{x} = \sum_{i=1}^{n} x_i - \sum_{i=1}^{n} x_i = 0,$$

so

$$\hat{\boldsymbol{\beta}}_1 = \frac{\displaystyle\sum_{i=1}^{n} (x_i - \bar{x})Y_i}{\displaystyle\sum_{i=1}^{n} (x_i - \bar{x})^2} - \frac{\bar{Y}\displaystyle\sum_{i=1}^{n} (x_i - \bar{x})^2}{\displaystyle\sum_{i=1}^{n} (x_i - \bar{x})^2}$$

$$= \frac{\displaystyle\sum_{i=1}^{n} (x_i - \bar{x})Y_i}{\displaystyle\sum_{i=1}^{n} (x_i - \bar{x})^2} \tag{11.3.1}$$

Equation 11.3.1 shows that the MLE for the slope is a linear combination of independent normal random variables. By the corollary to Theorem 4.3.4, then, $\hat{\beta}_1$ is normally distributed.

It also follows from Equation 11.3.1 that

$$E(\hat{\beta}_1) = \frac{1}{\sum\limits_{i=1}^{n}(x_i - \bar{x})^2} \sum\limits_{i=1}^{n}(x_i - \bar{x})E(Y_i)$$

$$= \frac{1}{\sum\limits_{i=1}^{n}(x_i - \bar{x})^2} \sum\limits_{i=1}^{n}(x_i - \bar{x})(\beta_0 + \beta_1 x_i)$$

$$= \frac{1}{\sum\limits_{i=1}^{n}(x_i - \bar{x})^2} \sum\limits_{i=1}^{n}(x_i - \bar{x})\beta_1 x_i \quad \text{(why?)}$$

$$= \frac{1}{\sum\limits_{i=1}^{n}(x_i - \bar{x})^2} \left[\sum\limits_{i=1}^{n}(x_i - \bar{x})\beta_1 x_i - \underbrace{\sum\limits_{i=1}^{n}(x_i - \bar{x})\beta_1 \bar{x}}_{0} \right]$$

$$= \frac{1}{\sum\limits_{i=1}^{n}(x_i - \bar{x})^2} \sum\limits_{i=1}^{n}(x_i - \bar{x})^2 \beta_1$$

$$= \beta_1$$

which verifies that $\hat{\beta}_1$ is unbiased for β_1.

Finally, from Theorems 3.13.1 and 3.13.2,

$$\text{Var}(\hat{\beta}_1) = \text{Var}\left(\frac{1}{\sum\limits_{i=1}^{n}(x_i - \bar{x})^2} \sum\limits_{i=1}^{n}(x_i - \bar{x})Y_i \right)$$

$$= \frac{1}{\left(\sum\limits_{i=1}^{n}(x_i - \bar{x})^2\right)^2} \sum\limits_{i=1}^{n}(x_i - \bar{x})^2 \sigma^2$$

$$= \frac{\sigma^2}{\sum\limits_{i=1}^{n}(x_i - \bar{x})^2}$$

THEOREM 11.3.3. Let $(x_1, Y_1), (x_2, Y_2), \ldots, (x_n, Y_n)$ satisfy the assumptions of the simple linear model. Then

(a) $\hat{\beta}_1, \bar{Y}$, and $\hat{\sigma}^2$ are mutually independent.

(b) $\dfrac{n\hat{\sigma}^2}{\sigma^2}$ has a chi-square distribution with $n - 2$ degrees of freedom.

Proof. See Appendix 11.A.2.

COROLLARY. Let $\hat{\sigma}^2$ be the MLE for σ^2 in a simple linear model. Then $\dfrac{n}{n-2} \cdot \hat{\sigma}^2$ is an unbiased estimator for σ^2.

Proof. Recall that the expected value of a χ_k^2 distribution is k (see Question 7.3.7). Therefore,

$$E\left(\frac{n}{n-2} \cdot \hat{\sigma}^2\right) = \frac{\sigma^2}{n-2} E\left(\frac{n\hat{\sigma}^2}{\sigma^2}\right)$$

$$= \frac{\sigma^2}{n-2} \cdot (n-2) \qquad \text{[by Part (b) of Theorem 11.3.3]}$$

$$= \sigma^2$$

COROLLARY. The random variables $\hat{Y}$ and $\hat{\sigma}^2$ are independent.

Proof. See Question 11.3.13.

Estimating σ^2

We know that the (biased) MLE for σ^2 in a simple linear model is

$$\hat{\sigma}^2 = \frac{1}{n} \sum_{i=1}^{n} \left(Y_i - \hat{\beta}_0 - \hat{\beta}_1 x_i\right)^2$$

The unbiased estimator for σ^2 based on $\hat{\sigma}^2$ is denoted S^2, where

$$S^2 = \frac{n}{n-2} \hat{\sigma}^2 = \frac{1}{n-2} \sum_{i=1}^{n} \left(Y_i - \hat{\beta}_0 - \hat{\beta}_1 x_i\right)^2$$

Statistical software packages—including MINITAB—typically print out s, rather than $\hat{\sigma}$, in summarizing the calculations associated with regression data. To accommodate that convention, we will use s^2 rather $\hat{\sigma}^2$ in writing the formulas for the test statistics and confidence intervals that arise in connection with the simple linear model.

Comment. Calculating $\displaystyle\sum_{i=1}^{n} \left(Y_i - \hat{\beta}_0 - \hat{\beta}_1 x_i\right)^2 = \sum_{i=1}^{n} \left(Y_i - \hat{Y}_i\right)^2$ can be cumbersome. Three (algebraically equivalent) computing formulas are available that may be easier to use, depending on the data:

$$\sum_{i=1}^{n} \left(Y_i - \hat{Y}_i\right)^2 = \sum_{i=1}^{n} \left(Y_i - \bar{Y}\right)^2 - \hat{\beta}_1^2 \sum_{i=1}^{n} \left(x_i - \bar{x}\right)^2 \qquad (11.3.2)$$

$$\sum_{i=1}^{n} \left(Y_i - \hat{Y}_i\right)^2 = \sum_{i=1}^{n} \left(Y_i - \bar{Y}\right)^2 - \hat{\beta}_1 \sum_{i=1}^{n} \left(x_i - \bar{x}\right)\left(Y_i - \bar{Y}\right) \qquad (11.3.3)$$

$$\sum_{i=1}^{n} \left(Y_i - \hat{Y}_i\right)^2 = \sum_{i=1}^{n} Y_i^2 - \hat{\beta}_0 \sum_{i=1}^{n} Y_i - \hat{\beta}_1 \sum_{i=1}^{n} x_i Y_i \qquad (11.3.4)$$

Drawing Inferences about β_1

Hypothesis tests and confidence intervals for β_1 can be carried out by defining a t statistic based on the properties that appear in Theorems 11.3.2 and 11.3.3.

THEOREM 11.3.4. Let $(x_1, Y_1), (x_2, Y_2), \ldots,$ and (x_n, Y_n) be a set of points that satisfy the assumptions of the simple linear model, and let $S^2 = \frac{1}{n-2} \sum_{i=1}^{n} (Y_i - \hat{\beta}_0 - \hat{\beta}_1 x_i)^2$. Then

$$T_{n-2} = \frac{\hat{\beta}_1 - \beta_1}{S \Big/ \sqrt{\sum_{i=1}^{n} (x_i - \bar{x})^2}} = \frac{\hat{\beta}_1 - \beta_1}{\sqrt{\widehat{\mathrm{Var}}(\hat{\beta}_1)}}$$

has a Student t distribution with $n - 2$ degrees of freedom.

Proof. We know from Theorem 11.3.2 that

$$Z = \frac{\hat{\beta}_1 - \beta_1}{\sigma \Big/ \sqrt{\sum_{i=1}^{n} (x_i - \bar{x})^2}}$$

has a standard normal pdf. Furthermore, $\dfrac{n\hat{\sigma}^2}{\sigma^2} = \dfrac{(n-2)S^2}{\sigma^2}$ has a χ^2 pdf with $n - 2$ degrees of freedom, and, by Theorem 11.3.3, Z and $\dfrac{(n-2)S^2}{\sigma^2}$ are independent. From Definition 7.4.1, then, it follows that

$$Z \Big/ \sqrt{\frac{(n-2)S^2}{\sigma^2} \Big/ (n-2)} = \frac{\hat{\beta}_1 - \beta_1}{S \Big/ \sqrt{\sum_{i=1}^{n} (x_i - \bar{x})^2}}$$

has a Student t distribution with $n - 2$ degrees of freedom.

THEOREM 11.3.5. Let $(x_1, Y_1), (x_2, Y_2), \ldots,$ and (x_n, Y_n) be a set of points that satisfy the assumptions of the simple linear model. Let

$$t = \frac{\hat{\beta}_1 - \beta_1^o}{S \Big/ \sqrt{\sum_{i=1}^{n} (x_i - \bar{x})^2}}$$

(a) To test $H_0: \beta_1 = \beta_1^o$ versus $H_1: \beta_1 > \beta_1^o$ at the α level of significance, reject H_0 if $t \geq t_{\alpha, n-2}$.

(b) To test $H_0: \beta_1 = \beta_1^o$ versus $H_1: \beta_1 < \beta_1^o$ at the α level of significance, reject H_0 if $t \leq -t_{\alpha, n-2}$.

(c) To test $H_0: \beta_1 = \beta_1^o$ versus $H_1: \beta_1 \neq \beta_1^o$ at the α level of significance, reject H_0 if t is either (1) $\leq -t_{\alpha/2, n-2}$ or (2) $\geq t_{\alpha/2, n-2}$.

Proof. The decision rule given here is, in fact, a GLRT. A formal proof proceeds along the lines followed in Appendix 7.A.4. We will omit the details.

Comment. A particularly common application of Theorem 11.3.5 is to test $H_0: \beta_1 = 0$. If the null hypothesis that the slope is 0 is rejected, it can be concluded (at the α level of significance) that Y *is dependent on* x. Conversely, if $H_0: \beta_1 = 0$ is *not* rejected, the data have not effectively ruled out the possibility that the variation in Y is independent of x.

CASE STUDY 11.3.1

By late 1971, all cigarette packs had to be labeled with the words, "Warning: The Surgeon General Has Determined That Smoking Is Dangerous To Your Health." The case against smoking rested heavily on statistical, rather than laboratory, evidence. Extensive surveys of smokers and nonsmokers had revealed the former to have much higher risks of dying from a variety of causes, including heart disease.

Typical of that research are the data in Table 11.3.1, showing the annual cigarette consumption, x, and the corresponding mortality rate, Y, due to coronary heart disease (CHD) for 21 countries (105). Do these data support the suspicion that smoking contributes to CHD mortality? Test $H_0: \beta_1 = 0$ versus $H_1: \beta_1 > 0$ at the $\alpha = 0.05$ level of significance.

TABLE 11.3.1

Country	Cigarette Consumption per Adult per Year, x	CHD Mortality per 100,000 (ages 35–64), Y
United States	3900	256.9
Canada	3350	211.6
Australia	3220	238.1
New Zealand	3220	211.8
United Kingdom	2790	194.1
Switzerland	2780	124.5
Ireland	2770	187.3
Iceland	2290	110.5
Finland	2160	233.1
West Germany	1890	150.3
Netherlands	1810	124.7
Greece	1800	41.2
Austria	1770	182.1
Belgium	1700	118.1
Mexico	1680	31.9
Italy	1510	114.3
Denmark	1500	144.9
France	1410	59.7
Sweden	1270	126.9
Spain	1200	43.9
Norway	1090	136.3

From Table 11.3.1,

$$\sum_{i=1}^{21} x_i = 45{,}110 \qquad\qquad \sum_{i=1}^{21} y_i = 3042.2$$

$$\sum_{i=1}^{21} x_i^2 = 109{,}957{,}100 \qquad \sum_{i=1}^{21} y_i^2 = 529{,}321.58$$

$$\sum_{i=1}^{21} x_i y_i = 7{,}319{,}602$$

and it follows that

$$\hat{\beta}_1 = \frac{n\sum_{i=1}^{n} x_i y_i - \left(\sum_{i=1}^{n} x_i\right)\left(\sum_{i=1}^{n} y_i\right)}{n\left(\sum_{i=1}^{n} x_i^2\right) - \left(\sum_{i=1}^{n} x_i\right)^2}$$

$$= \frac{21(7{,}319{,}602) - (45{,}110)(3042.2)}{21(109{,}957{,}100) - (45{,}110)^2} = 0.06$$

and

$$\hat{\beta}_0 = \frac{\sum_{i=1}^{n} y_i - \hat{\beta}_1 \sum_{i=1}^{n} x_i}{n}$$

$$= \frac{3042.2 - 0.06009767(45{,}110)}{21} = 15.77$$

The two other quantities needed for the test statistic are

$$\sum_{i=1}^{n}(x_i - \bar{x})^2 = \sum_{i=1}^{n} x_i^2 - (1/n)\left(\sum_{i=1}^{n} x_i\right)^2$$

$$= 109{,}957{,}100 - (1/21)(45{,}100)^2 = 13{,}056{,}523.81$$

and

$$s^2 = \frac{1}{21 - 2} \sum_{i=1}^{21}(y_i - 15.77 - 0.06x_i)^2$$

$$= 2181.66$$

To test

$$H_0: \quad \beta_1 = 0$$

versus

$$H_0: \quad \beta_1 > 0$$

at the $\alpha = 0.05$ level of significance, we should reject the null hypothesis if $t \geq t_{.05,19} = 1.7291$. But

$$t = \frac{\hat{\beta}_1 - \beta_1^o}{s\big/\sqrt{\sum_{i=1}^{n}(x_i - \bar{x})^2}} = \frac{0.06 - 0}{46.708/3613.38}$$

$$= 4.64$$

so our conclusion is clear cut—reject H_0. It would appear that the level of CHD mortality in a country *is* dependent on its citizens' smoking habits.

THEOREM 11.3.6. Let $(x_1, Y_1), (x_2, Y_2), \ldots,$ and (x_n, Y_n) be a set of points that satisfy the assumptions of the simple linear model, and let $S^2 = \dfrac{1}{n-2} \sum_{i=1}^{n} (y_i - \hat{\beta}_0 - \hat{\beta}_1 x_i)^2$. Then

$$\left(\hat{\beta}_1 - t_{\alpha/2,\, n-2} \cdot \frac{s}{\sqrt{\sum_{i=1}^{n} (x_i - \bar{x})^2}}, \ \hat{\beta}_1 + t_{\alpha/2,\, n-2} \cdot \frac{s}{\sqrt{\sum_{i=1}^{n} (x_i - \bar{x})^2}} \right)$$

is a $100(1 - \alpha)\%$ confidence interval for β_1.

Proof. Let T_{n-2} denote a Student t random variable with $n - 2$ degrees of freedom, in which case

$$P\left(-t_{\alpha/2, n-2} \leq T_{n-2} \leq t_{\alpha/2, n-2}\right) = 1 - \alpha$$

Substitute the expression for T_{n-2} given in Theorem 11.3.4 and isolate β_1 in the center of the inequalities. The resulting endpoints will be the expressions appearing in the statement of the theorem.

CASE STUDY 11.3.2

For many firms, expenses are linear functions of sales. That appears to be the case for Acme Manufacturing, a company that markets industrial gases (3). Table 11.3.2 shows Acme's annual sales (x) and expenses (y) for the years 1985 through 1992. Graphed, the xy-relationship is described nicely by the line $y = 24.61 + 0.22x$, where 24.61 and 0.22 are the values of $\hat{\beta}_0$ and $\hat{\beta}_1$ calculated from the formulas in Theorem 11.3.1 (see Figure 11.3.3).

The true slope in this situation—β_1—is particularly important from the company's perspective because it represents the amount that expenses are likely to increase when sales go up by one unit. That said, it makes sense to construct, say, a 95% confidence interval for β_1 based on the observed $\hat{\beta}_1$.

Here,

$$\sum_{i=1}^{8} (x_i - \bar{x})^2 = 1{,}867{,}559.88$$

$$s^2 = \frac{1}{8-2} \sum_{i=1}^{8} (y_i - 24.61 - 0.22x_i)^2$$

$$= 138.78$$

and

$$t_{.025,6} = 2.4469$$

so the expression given in Theorem 11.3.6 reduces to

$$\left(0.22 - 2.4469 \cdot \frac{11.78}{\sqrt{1,867,559.88}}, 0.22 + 2.4469 \cdot \frac{11.78}{\sqrt{1,867,559.88}}\right)$$

$$= (\$0.20, \$0.24)$$

Judging from these data, then, the company can anticipate that expenses will rise some-where between 20 and 24 cents for every \$1 increase in sales. So, if the company's annual sales were to grow by \$500,000, for example, it would not be unreasonable to expect that an additional \$100,000 to \$120,000 in expenses would be incurred.

TABLE 11.3.2

Year	Sales (in thousands), x	Expenses (in thousands), y
1985	1765	407
1986	1942	466
1987	2132	489
1988	2431	545
1989	2642	610
1990	2895	659
1991	2931	686
1992	3217	724

FIGURE 11.3.3

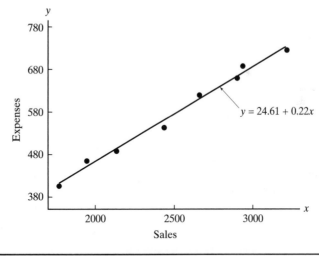

Drawing Inferences about β_0

In practice, the value of β_0 is not likely to be as important as the value of β_1. Slopes often quantify particularly important aspects of xy-relationships, which was true, for example, in Case Study 11.3.2. Nevertheless, hypothesis tests and confidence intervals for β_0 can be easily derived from the results given in Theorems 11.3.2 and 11.3.3.

The (GLRT) procedure for assessing the credibility of $H_0: \beta_0 = \beta_0^o$ is based on a Student t random variable with $n - 2$ degrees of freedom:

$$T_{n-2} = \frac{(\hat{\beta}_0 - \beta_0^o)\sqrt{n}\sqrt{\sum_{i=i}^{n}(x_i - \bar{x})^2}}{S\sqrt{\sum_{i=1}^{n}x_i^2}} = \frac{\hat{\beta}_0 - \beta_0^o}{\sqrt{\widehat{\text{Var}}(\hat{\beta}_0)}} \qquad (11.3.5)$$

"Inverting" Equation 11.3.5 (recall the proof of Theorem 11.3.6) yields

$$\left(\hat{\beta}_0 - t_{\alpha/2, n-2} \frac{S\sqrt{\sum_{i=1}^{n}x_i^2}}{\sqrt{n}\sqrt{\sum_{i=1}^{n}(x_i - \bar{x})^2}}, \quad \hat{\beta}_0 + t_{\alpha/2, n-2} \frac{S\sqrt{\sum_{i=1}^{n}x_i^2}}{n\sqrt{\sum_{i=1}^{n}(x_i - \bar{x})^2}} \right)$$

as the formula for a $100(1 - \alpha)\%$ confidence interval for β_0.

QUESTIONS

11.3.1 Insect flight ability can be measured in a laboratory by attaching the insect to a nearly fric-tionless rotating arm with a thin wire. The "tethered" insect then flies in circles until exhaust-ed. The nonstop distance flown can easily be calculated from the number of revolutions made by the arm. The following are measurements of this sort made on *Culex tarsalis* mosquitos of four different ages. The response variable is the average distance flown until exhaustion for 40 females of the species (138).

Age, x_i (weeks)	Distance Flown, y_i (thousand meters)
1	12.6
2	11.6
3	6.8
4	9.2

Fit a straight line to these data and test that the slope is zero. Use a two-sided alternative and the 0.05 level of significance.

11.3.2 The best straight line through the Virginia SAT/funding data described in Question 11.2.7 has the equation $y = 645.888 + 0.055x$, where $s = 42.745$.
(a) Construct a 95% confidence interval for β_1.
(b) What does your answer to Part (a) imply about the outcome of testing $H_0: \beta_1 = 0$ versus $H_1: \beta_1 \neq 0$ at the $\alpha = 0.05$ level of significance?
(c) Graph the data and superimpose the regression line. How would you summarize these data, and their implications, to a meeting of the School Board?

11.3.3 Based on the data in Question 11.2.1, the relationship between y, the ambient temperature, and x, the frequency of a cricket's chirping, is given by $y = 25.2 + 3.29x$, where $s = 3.83$. At the $\alpha = 0.01$ level of significance, can the hypothesis that chirping frequency is not related to tem-perature be rejected?

11.3.4 Suppose an experimenter intends to do a regression analysis by taking a total of $2n$ data points, where the x_i's are restricted to the interval $[0, 5]$. If the xy-relationship is assumed to be linear and if the objective is to estimate the slope with the greatest possible precision, what values should be assigned to the x_i's?

11.3.5 Suppose a total of $n = 9$ measurements are to be taken on a simple linear model, where the x_i's will be set equal to $1, 2, \ldots$, and 9. If the variance associated with the xy-relationship is known to be 45.0, what is the probability that the estimated slope will be within 1.5 units of the true slope?

11.3.6 Prove the useful computing formula that

$$\sum_{i=1}^{n}(Y_i - \hat{\beta}_0 - \hat{\beta}_1 x_i)^2 = \sum_{i=1}^{n} Y_i^2 - \hat{\beta}_0 \sum_{i=1}^{n} Y_i - \hat{\beta}_1 \sum_{i=1}^{n} x_i Y_i$$

11.3.7 The sodium nitrate ($NaNO_3$) solubility data in Question 11.2.3 is described nicely by the regression line $y = 67.508 + 0.871x$, where $s = 0.959$. Construct a 90% confidence interval for the y-intercept, β_0.

11.3.8 Set up and carry out an appropriate hypothesis test for the Hanford radioactive contamination data given in Question 11.2.9. Let $\alpha = 0.05$. Justify your choice of H_0 and H_1. What do you conclude?

11.3.9 Test $H_0: \beta_1 = 0$ versus $H_1: \beta_1 \neq 0$ for the plumage index/behavioral index data given in Question 11.2.11. Let $\alpha = 0.05$. Use the fact that $y = 0.61 + 0.84x$ is the best straight line describing the xy-relationship.

11.3.10 Let $(x_1, Y_1), (x_2, Y_2), \ldots$, and (x_n, Y_n) be a set of points satisfying the assumptions of the simple linear model. Prove that

$$E(\bar{Y}) = \beta_0 + \beta_1 \bar{x}$$

11.3.11 Derive a formula for a 95% confidence interval for β_0 if n (x_i, Y_i)'s are taken on a simple linear model where σ is known.

11.3.12 Which, if any, of the assumptions of the simple linear model appear to be violated in the following scatterplot? Which, if any, appear to be satisfied? Which, if any, cannot be assessed by looking at the scatterplot?

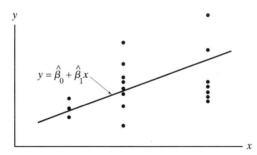

11.3.13 Use Theorem 11.3.3 to derive the formula for a $100(1 - \alpha)\%$ confidence interval for σ^2. Express the endpoints in terms of s^2, rather than $\hat{\sigma}^2$.

11.3.14 Use the expression found in Question 11.3.13 to construct a 90% confidence interval for σ^2 in the mallard/pintail data described in Question 11.2.11. *Note:* $s = 2.4$.

11.3.15 Determining small quantities of calcium in the presence of magnesium is a difficult problem for analytical chemists. Direct precipitation is not feasible. One alternative is to use alcohol as a solvent. The following data show the results of applying the latter method to 10 mixtures containing known quantities of CaO (67). A critical question to be answered is whether the discrepancies between what was present and what was found are random, or do they reflect an intrinsic weakness of the procedure? If the latter is true, we should be able to write y as a linear function of x and reject either $H_0: \beta_1 = 1$, $H_0: \beta_0 = 0$, or both. *Note:* The regression line has the equation $y = -0.2281 + 0.9948x$ and $s = 0.2067$.

(a) At the $\alpha = 0.05$ level of significance, test $H_0: \beta_0 = 0$ versus $H_1: \beta_0 \neq 0$.

(b) At the $\alpha = 0.05$ level of significance, test $H_0: \beta_1 = 1$ versus $H_1: \beta_1 \neq 1$.

CaO Present (mg), x	CaO Recovered (mg), y
4.0	3.7
8.0	7.8
12.5	12.1
16.0	15.6
20.0	19.8
25.0	24.5
31.0	31.1
36.0	35.5
40.0	39.4
40.0	39.5

Drawing Inferences about $E(Y|x)$

In addition to constructing confidence intervals for β_0, β_1, and σ^2, we will sometimes find it also helpful to draw a similar sort of inference about $E(Y|x)$. In Case Study 11.3.2, for example, the random variable Y represents the expenses incurred as a result of having x amount of sales. It would certainly be in the company's interest to have some idea of the range of costs likely to be encountered if x increased to, say, 3500.

Intuition tells us that a reasonable point estimator for $E(Y|x)$ is the height of the regression line at x—that is, $\hat{Y} = \hat{\beta}_0 + \hat{\beta}_1 x$. By Theorem 11.3.2, the latter is unbiased:

$$E(\hat{Y}) = E(\hat{\beta}_0 + \hat{\beta}_1 x) = E(\hat{\beta}_0) + xE(\hat{\beta}_1) = \beta_0 + \beta_1 x$$

Of course, to use $\hat{Y}$ in any inference procedure requires that we know its variance. But

$$\begin{aligned}
\text{Var}(\hat{Y}) &= \text{Var}(\hat{\beta}_0 + \hat{\beta}_1 x) = \text{Var}(\bar{Y} - \hat{\beta}_1 \bar{x} + \hat{\beta}_1 x) \\
&= \text{Var}\left[\bar{Y} + \hat{\beta}_1(x - \bar{x})\right] \\
&= \text{Var}(\bar{Y}) + (x - \bar{x})^2 \text{Var}(\hat{\beta}_1) \quad \text{(Why?)} \\
&= \frac{1}{n}\sigma^2 + \frac{(x - \bar{x})^2}{\displaystyle\sum_{i=1}^{n}(x_i - \bar{x})^2}\sigma^2 \\
&= \sigma^2\left[\frac{1}{n} + \frac{(x - \bar{x})^2}{\displaystyle\sum_{i=1}^{n}(x_i - \bar{x})^2}\right]
\end{aligned}$$

An application of Definition 7.4.1, then, allows us to construct a T random variable based on $\hat{Y}$. Specifically,

$$T_{n-2} = \frac{\hat{Y} - (\beta_0 + \beta_1 x)}{\sigma \sqrt{\dfrac{1}{n} + \dfrac{(x - \bar{x})^2}{\displaystyle\sum_{i=1}^{n}(x_i - \bar{x})^2}}} \Bigg/ \sqrt{\frac{(n-2)S^2}{\sigma^2} \cdot \frac{1}{n-2}} = \frac{\hat{Y} - (\beta_0 + \beta_1 x)}{S \sqrt{\dfrac{1}{n} + \dfrac{(x - \bar{x})^2}{\displaystyle\sum_{i=1}^{n}(x_i - \bar{x})^2}}}$$

has a Student t distribution with $n - 2$ degrees of freedom. Isolating $\beta_0 + \beta_1 x$ $[= E(Y|x)]$ in the center of the inequalities $P(-t_{\alpha/2, n-2} \le T_{n-2} \le t_{\alpha/2, n-2}) = 1 - \alpha$ produces a $100(1 - \alpha)\%$ confidence interval for $E(Y|x)$.

THEOREM 11.3.7.   Let $(x_1, Y_1), (x_2, Y_2), \ldots,$ and (x_n, Y_n) be a set of points that satisfy the assumptions of the simple linear model. A $100(1 - \alpha)\%$ confidence interval for $E(Y|x) = \beta_0 + \beta_1 x$ is given by $(\hat{y} - w, \hat{y} + w)$, where

$$w = t_{\alpha/2, n-2} \cdot s \sqrt{\frac{1}{n} + \frac{(x - \bar{x})^2}{\displaystyle\sum_{i=1}^{n}(x_i - \bar{x})^2}}$$

and $\hat{y} = \hat{\beta}_0 + \hat{\beta}_1 x$.

EXAMPLE 11.3.2

Look again at Case Study 11.3.2. Suppose the company's management believes that sales will stabilize over the next several years at the \$3,500,000 level. If that were to happen, what would be their average annual expenses? Answer the question by constructing a 95% confidence interval for $E(Y|3500)$.

Here, $n = 8$, $t_{.025, 6} = 2.4469$, $\displaystyle\sum_{i=1}^{8}(x_i - \bar{x})^2 = 1{,}867{,}559.88$, $s = 11.78$, $\hat{\beta}_0 = 24.61$, $\hat{\beta}_1 = 0.22$, and $\bar{x} = 2494.38$. From Theorem 11.3.7, then,

$$\hat{y} = 24.61 + (0.22)(3500) = 794.61$$

$$w = 2.4469(11.78)\sqrt{\frac{1}{8} + \frac{(3500 - 2494.38)^2}{1{,}867{,}559.88}}$$

$$= 23.53$$

and the 95% confidence interval for $E(Y|3500)$ is

$$(794.61 - 23.53, \ 794.61 + 23.53)$$

or

$$(\$770.9 \text{ (thousands)}, \$818.0 \text{ (thousands)})$$

Comment.   Notice from the formula in Theorem 11.3.7 that the width of a confidence interval for $E(Y|x)$ increases as the value of x becomes more extreme. That is, we are better able to predict the location of the regression line for an x-value close to $\bar{x}$ than we are for x-values that are either very small or very large.

Figure 11.3.4 shows the dependence of w on x for the data from Case Study 11.3.2. The lower and upper limits for the 95% confidence interval for $E(Y|x)$ have been calculated for all x. Pictured is the dotted curve (or 95% *confidence band*) connecting those endpoints. As the graph shows, the width of the band is smallest when $x = 2494.38 \ (= \bar{x})$.

FIGURE 11.3.4

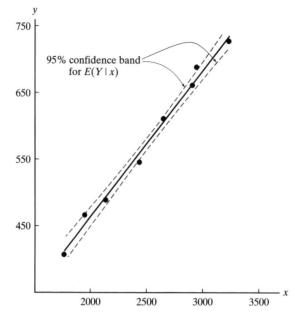

Drawing Inferences about Future Observations

A variation on Theorem 11.3.7 is the so-called *prediction problem*, where the objective is to estimate the future "single" outcome of a random variable, rather than the parameters of its pdf. In Case Study 11.3.2, for example, we can imagine the company wanting to predict the *actual* (not the *average*) expenses for next year that would result from a sales volume of, say, x.

Let $(x_1, Y_1), (x_2, Y_2), \ldots, (x_n, Y_n)$ be a set of n points that satisfy the assumptions of the simple linear model, and let (x, Y) be a hypothetical future observation, where Y is independent of the n Y_i's. A *prediction interval* is a range of numbers that contains Y with a specified probability.

Consider the difference, $\hat{Y} - Y$. Clearly,

$$E(\hat{Y} - Y) = E(\hat{Y}) - E(Y) = (\beta_0 + \beta_1 x) - (\beta_0 + \beta_1 x) = 0$$

and

$$\mathrm{Var}(\hat{Y} - Y) = \mathrm{Var}(\hat{Y}) + \mathrm{Var}(Y)$$

$$= \sigma^2 \left[\frac{1}{n} + \frac{(x - \bar{x})^2}{\sum_{i=1}^{n}(x_i - \bar{x})^2} \right] + \sigma^2$$

$$= \sigma^2 \left[1 + \frac{1}{n} + \frac{(x - \bar{x})^2}{\sum_{i=1}^{n}(x_i - \bar{x})^2} \right]$$

Following exactly the same steps that were taken in the derivation of Theorem 11.3.7, a Student t random variable with $n - 2$ degrees of freedom can be constructed from

$\hat{Y} - Y$ (using Definition 7.4.1). Inverting the equation $P\left(-t_{\alpha/2,n-2} \le T_{n-2} \le t_{\alpha/2,n-2}\right) = 1 - \alpha$ will then yield the prediction interval $(\hat{y} - w, \hat{y} + w)$ given in Theorem 11.3.8.

> **THEOREM 11.3.8.** Let $(x_1, Y_1), (x_2, Y_2), \dots,$ and (x_n, Y_n) be a set of n points that satisfy the assumptions of the simple linear model. A $100(1 - \alpha)\%$ prediction interval for Y at the fixed value x is given by $(\hat{y} - w, \hat{y} + w)$, where
>
> $$w = t_{\alpha/2,\, n-2} \cdot s \sqrt{1 + \frac{1}{n} + \frac{(x - \bar{x})^2}{\displaystyle\sum_{i=1}^{n}(x_i - \bar{x})^2}}$$
>
> and $\hat{y} = \hat{\beta}_0 + \hat{\beta}_1 x$.

EXAMPLE 11.3.3

Based on the data in Case Study 11.3.2, we calculated in Example 11.3.2 that a 95% confidence interval for $E(Y|3500)$ is $(770.9, 818.0)$. How does that compare to the corresponding 95% prediction interval for Y?

When $x = 3500$, $\hat{y} = 794.61$ for both intervals. From Theorem 11.3.8, the width of the 95% prediction interval for Y is 37.21:

$$w = 2.4469 \cdot 11.78\sqrt{1 + \frac{1}{8} + \frac{(3500 - 2494.38)^2}{1{,}867{,}559.88}}$$

$$= 37.21$$

The 95% prediction interval, then, is

$$(794.61 - 37.21, 794.61 + 37.21)$$

or $(757.2, 831.6)$, which makes it 58% wider than the 95% confidence interval for $E(Y|3500)$.

Testing the Equality of Two Slopes

We saw in Chapter 9 that the comparison of two treatments or two conditions often leads to a hypothesis test that the mean of one is equal to the mean of the other. Similarly, the comparison of two linear xy-relationships often requires that we test $H_0: \beta_1 = \beta_1^*$, where β_1 and β_1^* are the true slopes associated with the two regressions.

If the data points taken on the two regressions are all independent, a two-sample t test can be set up based on the properties in Theorems 11.3.2 and 11.3.3. Theorem 11.3.9 identifies the appropriate test statistic and summarizes the GLRT decision rule. Details of the proof will be omitted.

> **THEOREM 11.3.9.** Let $(x_1, Y_1), (x_2, Y_2), \dots, (x_n, Y_n)$ and $(x_1^*, Y_1^*), (x_2^*, Y_2^*), \dots, (x_m^*, Y_m^*)$ be two independent sets of points, each satisfying the assumptions of the simple linear model—that is, $E(Y|x) = \beta_0 + \beta_1 x$ and $E(Y^*|x^*) = \beta_0^* + \beta_1^* x^*$.

(a) Let

$$T_{n+m-4} = \frac{\hat{\beta}_1 - \hat{\beta}_1^* - (\beta_1 - \beta_1^*)}{S\sqrt{\dfrac{1}{\displaystyle\sum_{i=1}^{n}(x_i - \bar{x})^2} + \dfrac{1}{\displaystyle\sum_{i=1}^{m}(x_i^* - \bar{x}^*)^2}}}$$

where

$$S = \sqrt{\frac{\displaystyle\sum_{i=1}^{n}[Y_i - (\hat{\beta}_0 + \hat{\beta}_1 x_i)]^2 + \sum_{i=1}^{m}[Y_i^* - (\hat{\beta}_0^* + \beta_1^* x_i)]^2}{n + m - 4}}$$

Then T_{n+m-4} has a Student t distribution with $n + m - 4$ degrees of freedom.

(b) To test $H_0: \beta_1 = \beta_1^*$ versus $H_1: \beta_1 \neq \beta_1^*$ at the α level of significance, reject H_0 if t is either (1) $\leq -t_{\alpha/2, n+m-4}$ or (2) $\geq t_{\alpha/2, n+m-4}$, where

$$t = \frac{\hat{\beta}_1 - \hat{\beta}_1^*}{S\sqrt{\dfrac{1}{\displaystyle\sum_{i=1}^{n}(x_i - \bar{x})^2} + \dfrac{1}{\displaystyle\sum_{i=1}^{m}(x_i^* - \bar{x}^*)^2}}}$$

(One-sided tests are defined in the usual way by replacing $\pm t_{\alpha/2, n+m-4}$ with either $t_{\alpha, n+m-4}$ or $-t_{\alpha, n+m-4}$.)

EXAMPLE 11.3.4

Genetic variability is thought to be a key factor in the survival of a species, the idea being that "diverse" populations should have a better chance of coping with changing environments. Table 11.3.3 summarizes the results of a study designed to test that hypothesis experimentally [data slightly modified from (4)]. Two populations of fruit flies (*Drosophila serrata*)—one that was cross-bred (Strain *A*) and the other, in-bred (Strain *B*)—were put into sealed containers where food and space were kept to a minimum. Recorded every hundred days were the numbers of *Drosophila* alive in each population.

Figure 11.3.5 shows a graph of the two sets of population figures. For both strains, growth was approximately linear over the period covered. Strain *A*, though, with an estimated slope of 0.74, increased at a faster rate than did Strain *B*, where the estimated slope was 0.45. The question is, do we have enough evidence here to reject the null hypothesis that the two true slopes are equal? Is the difference between 0.74 and 0.45 statistically significant?

Let $\alpha = 0.05$ and let $(x_i, y_i), i = 1, 2, \ldots, 6$, and $(x_i^*, y_i^*), i = 1, 2, \ldots, 6$, denote the times and population sizes for Strain *A* and Strain *B*, respectively. Our objective is to test $H_0: \beta_1 = \beta_1^*$ versus $H_1: \beta_1 > \beta_1^*$. Rejecting H_0, of course, would support the contention that genetic variability benefits a species' chances of survival.

From Table 11.3.3, $\bar{x} = \bar{x}^* = 250$ and

$$\sum_{i=1}^{6}(x_i - \bar{x})^2 = \sum_{i=1}^{6}(x_i^* - \bar{x}^*)^2 = 175,000$$

TABLE 11.3.3

Date	Day no., $x(=x^*)$	Strain A pop^n, y	Strain B pop^n, y^*
Feb 2	0	100	100
May 13	100	250	203
Aug 21	200	304	214
Nov 29	300	403	295
Mar 8	400	446	330
Jun 16	500	482	324

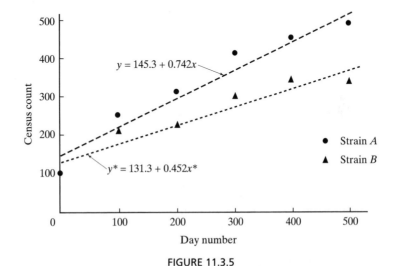

FIGURE 11.3.5

Also,

$$\sum_{i=1}^{6}\left[y_i-\left(145.3-0.742x_i\right)\right]^2=5512.14$$

and

$$\sum_{i=1}^{6}\left[y_i^*-\left(131.3+0.452x_i^*\right)\right]^2=3960.14$$

so

$$s=\sqrt{\frac{5512.14+3960.14}{6+6-4}}=34.41$$

Since H_1 is one sided to the right, we should reject H_0 if $t\geq t_{.05,8}=1.8595$. But

$$t=\frac{0.742-0.452}{34.41\sqrt{\dfrac{1}{175,000}+\dfrac{1}{175,000}}}$$

$$=2.50$$

These data, then, *do* support the theory that genetically mixed populations have a better chance of survival in hostile environments.

QUESTIONS

11.3.16 Regression techniques can be very useful in situations where one variable—say, y—is difficult to measure, but x is not. Once such an xy-relationship has been "calibrated," based on a set of (x_i, y_i)'s, future values of Y can be easily estimated using $\hat{\beta}_0 + \hat{\beta}_1 x$. Determining the volume of an irregularly shaped object, for example, is often difficult, but weighing that object is likely to be easy. The following table shows the weights (in kilograms) and the volumes (in cubic decimeters) of 18 children between the ages of 5 and 8 (19). The estimated regression line has the equation $y = -0.104 + 0.988x$, where $s = 0.202$.

Weight, x	Volume, y	Weight, x	Volume, y
17.1	16.7	15.8	15.2
10.5	10.4	15.1	14.8
13.8	13.5	12.1	11.9
15.7	15.7	18.4	18.3
11.9	11.6	17.1	16.7
10.4	10.2	16.7	16.6
15.0	14.5	16.5	15.9
16.0	15.8	15.1	15.1
17.8	17.6	15.1	14.5

(a) Construct a 95% confidence interval for $E(Y|14.0)$.

(b) Construct a 95% prediction interval for the volume of a child weighing 14.0 kilograms.

11.3.17 Construct a 95% confidence interval for $E(Y|2.750)$ using the connecting rod data given in Case Study 11.2.1.

11.3.18 For the CHD mortality data of Case Study 11.3.1, construct a 99% confidence interval for the expected death rate in a country where the cigarette consumption is 2500 per adult per year. Is a public health official more likely to be interested in a 99% confidence interval for $E(Y|2500)$ or a 99% prediction interval for Y when $x = 2500$?

11.3.19 Better technology has reduced the number of U.S. airliner near-collisions (defined to be planes passing within 500 feet of one another) from 91 in 1990 to 34 in 1995. Based on the following data (180), what would be a reasonable worst-case scenario for the number of near-collisions that might occur in 1996? *Note*: The regression line describing the xy-relationship is $y = 97.867 - 11.057x$ and $s = 6.987$.

Year	Years after 1989, x	No. of Near Collisions, y
1990	1	91
1991	2	78
1992	3	59
1993	4	44
1994	5	49
1995	6	34

11.3.20 In 1987, the average amount (calculated over all insured cars) paid by automobile insurance companies to settle bodily injury claims was $138.38; by 1993, the average had increased to $212.48. Based on the following data (179), calculate a 95% confidence interval for the average amount for such claims likely to be paid in 1994. *Note*: For these seven (x_i, y_i)'s, $y = 132.4 + 12.2x$ and the estimate for σ is $s = 6.13$.

Year	Years after 1986, x	Average Claim, y
1987	1	$138.38
1988	2	$155.33
1989	3	$173.94
1990	4	$185.85
1991	5	$200.83
1992	6	$201.42
1993	7	$212.48

11.3.21 Recall Question 11.3.15. A second method for recovering calcium from magnesium is available that requires less time and work than the alcohol technique. The following table shows the results from a set of runs done with the nonalcohol procedure. The data's estimated regression line is $y = -0.0748 + 1.0024x$, with $s = 0.1261$. Let β_1 and β_1^* denote the true slopes associated with the alcohol and nonalcohol procedures, respectively. Test $H_0: \beta_1 = \beta_1^*$ versus $H_1: \beta_1 \neq \beta_1^*$ at the $\alpha = 0.05$ level of significance. Which method, if either, would you recommend should be adopted? Explain.

CaO Present (mg), x	CaO Recovered (mg), y
4.0	3.9
8.0	8.1
12.5	12.4
16.0	16.0
20.0	19.8
25.0	25.0
31.0	31.1
36.0	35.8
40.0	40.1
40.0	40.1

11.3.22 Attorneys representing a group of male buyers employed by Flirty Fashions are filing a reverse discrimination suit against the female-owned company. Central to their case are the following data, showing the relationship between years of service and annual salary for the firm's

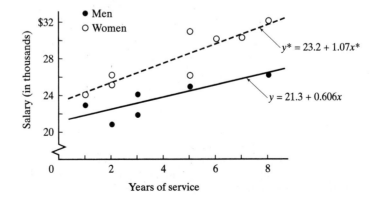

14 buyers, 6 of whom are men. The plaintiffs claim that the difference in slopes (0.606 for men versus 1.07 for women) is prima facie evidence that the company's salary policies discriminate against men. As the lawyer for Flirty Fashions, how would you respond? *Note*:

$$\sum_{i=1}^{6} (y_i - 21.3 - 0.606x_i)^2 = 5.983$$

and

$$\sum_{i=1}^{8} (y_i^* - 23.2 - 1.07x_i^*)^2 = 13.804$$

Also, $\sum_{i=1}^{6} (x_i - \bar{x})^2 = 31.33$ and $\sum_{i=1}^{8} (x_i^* - \bar{x}^*)^2 = 46$.

11.3.23 Polls taken during a city's last two administrations (one Democratic, one Republican) suggested that public support of the two mayors fell off linearly with years in office. Can it be concluded from the following data that the rates at which the two administrations lost favor were significantly different? Let $\alpha = 0.05$. *Note*: $y = 69.3077 - 3.4615x$ with an estimated standard deviation of 0.9058 and $y^* = 59.9407 - 2.7373x^*$ with an estimated standard deviation of 1.2368.

Democratic Mayor		Republican Mayor	
Years after Taking Office, x_i	Percent in Support, y_i	Years after Taking Office, x_i^*	Percent in Support, y_i^*
2	63	1	58
3	58	2	55
5	52	4	47
7	46	6	43
8	41	7	41
		8	39

11.3.24 Prove that the variance of $\hat{Y}$ can also be written

$$\text{Var}(\hat{Y}) = \frac{\sigma^2 \sum_{i=1}^{n} (x_i - x)^2}{n \sum_{i=1}^{n} (x_i - \bar{x})^2}$$

11.3.25 Show that

$$\sum_{i=1}^{n} (Y_i - \bar{Y})^2 = \sum_{i=1}^{n} (Y_i - \hat{Y}_i)^2 + \sum_{i=1}^{n} (\hat{Y}_i - \bar{Y})^2$$

for any set of points $(x_i, Y_i), i = 1, 2, \ldots, n$.

11.4 COVARIANCE AND CORRELATION

Our discussion of xy-relationships in Chapter 11 began with the simplest possible set-up from a statistical standpoint—the case where the (x_i, y_i)'s are just numbers and have no probabilistic structure whatsoever. Then we examined the more complicated (and more "inference friendly") scenario where x_i is a constant but Y_i is a random variable. Introduced in this section is the next level of complexity—problems where both X_i and Y_i are assumed to be random variables. [Measurements of the form (x_i, y_i) or (x_i, Y_i) are typically referred to as *regression data*; observations satisfying the assumptions made in this section—that is, measurements of the form (X_i, Y_i)—are more commonly referred to as *correlation data*.]

Measuring the Dependence Between Two Random Variables

Given a pair of random variables, it makes sense to inquire how one varies *with respect to the other*. If X increases, for example, does Y also tend to increase? And if so, how strong is the dependence between the two? The first step in addressing such questions is to calculate a quantity known as the *covariance*.

DEFINITION 11.4.1. Let X and Y be random variables with means μ_X and μ_Y. The *covariance of X and Y*, written $\text{Cov}(X, Y)$, is given by

$$\text{Cov}(X, Y) = E[(X - \mu_X)(Y - \mu_Y)]$$

Comment. The concept of covariance generalizes the notion of variance, since $\text{Cov}(X, X) = \text{Var}(X)$.

A sometimes more convenient form for the covariance is given in Theorem 11.4.1. The proof is trivial, following directly from the distributive property of the expected value.

THEOREM 11.4.1. For any random variables X and Y with means μ_X and μ_Y,

$$\text{Cov}(X, Y) = E(XY) - \mu_X \mu_Y$$

EXAMPLE 11.4.1

Suppose that two continuous random variables X and Y are jointly distributed according to the pdf

$$f_{X,Y}(x, y) = 8xy, \quad 0 \le x < y \le 1$$

Calculate their covariance.

Here the two marginal pdf's, $f_X(x)$ and $f_Y(y)$, are given by

$$f_X(x) = \int_{y=0}^{x} 8xy \, dy = 4x^3, \quad 0 \le x \le 1$$

and

$$f_Y(y) = \int_{x=y}^{1} 8xy \, dx = 4y - 4y^3, \quad 0 \le y \le 1$$

Therefore,

$$\mu_X = \int_0^1 x \cdot 4x^3 \, dx = \frac{4}{5}$$

and

$$\mu_Y = \int_0^1 y \cdot (4y - 4y^3)\,dy = \frac{8}{15}$$

By Theorem 11.4.1, then,

$$\text{Cov}(X, Y) = E(XY) - \mu_X\mu_Y$$

$$= \int_{x=0}^1 \int_{y=0}^x xy \cdot 8xy\,dy\,dx - \left(\frac{4}{5}\right)\left(\frac{8}{15}\right)$$

$$= \int_0^1 \frac{8x^5}{3}\,dx - \frac{32}{75}$$

$$= \frac{8}{450}$$

The Relationship Between the Covariance and Independence

If X and Y vary independently, it follows that for a given $x - \mu_X$, $Y - \mu_Y$ will sometimes be positive and other times negative, thus precipitating a certain amount of "canceling" among the set of $(x - \mu_X)(y - \mu_Y)$ values. In fact, as the next theorem proves, the absolute values of the negative terms and the positive terms are exactly the same.

THEOREM 11.4.2.   If X and Y are independent,

$$\text{Cov}(X, Y) = 0$$

Proof.   If X and Y are independent, $E(XY) = E(X) \cdot E(Y) = \mu_X\mu_Y$. The statement of the theorem follows immediately, then, from Theorem 11.4.1.

The converse of Theorem 11.4.2 is *not* true—just because the covariance of X and Y is 0, we cannot conclude that the two variables are independent. Example 11.4.2 is a case in point.

EXAMPLE 11.4.2

Consider the sample space $S = \{(-2, 4), (-1, 1), (0, 0), (1, 1), (2, 4)\}$, where each point is assumed to be equally likely. Define the random variable X to be the first component of a sample point and Y, the second. Then $X(-2, 4) = -2$, $Y(-2, 4) = 4$, and so on.

Notice that X and Y are dependent:

$$\frac{1}{5} = P(X = 1, Y = 1) \neq P(X = 1) \cdot P(Y = 1) = \frac{1}{5} \cdot \frac{2}{5} = \frac{2}{25}$$

However, the covariance of X and Y is 0:

$$E(XY) = \left[(-8) + (-1) + 0 + 1 + 8\right] \cdot \frac{1}{5} = 0$$

$$E(X) = \left[(-2) + (-1) + 0 + 1 + 2\right] \cdot \frac{1}{5} = 0$$

and

$$E(Y) = [4 + 1 + 0 + 1 + 4] \cdot \frac{1}{5} = 2$$

so

$$\text{Cov}(X, Y) = E(XY) - E(X) \cdot E(Y) = 0 - 0 \cdot 2 = 0$$

QUESTIONS

11.4.1 Suppose that two dice are thrown. Let X be the number showing on the first die and let Y be the larger of the two numbers showing. Find $\text{Cov}(X, Y)$.

11.4.2 Show that

$$\text{Cov}(aX + b, cY + d) = ac \, \text{Cov}(X, Y)$$

for any constants $a, b, c,$ and d.

11.4.3 Let U be a random variable uniformly distributed over $[0, 2\pi]$. Define $X = \cos U$ and $Y = \sin U$. Show that X and Y are dependent but that $\text{Cov}(X, Y) = 0$.

11.4.4 Let X and Y be random variables with

$$f_{X,Y}(x, y) = \begin{cases} 1, & -y < x < y, \;\; 0 < y < 1 \\ 0, & \text{elsewhere} \end{cases}$$

Show that $\text{Cov}(X, Y) = 0$ but that X and Y are dependent.

The Role of the Covariance in the Variance of a Sum

If $X_1, X_2, \ldots,$ and X_n is a set of *independent* random variables, we know from Theorem 3.13.2 that the variance of $X_1 + X_2 + \cdots + X_n$ is equal to the sum of the variances of the individual X_i's. Drawing on the notion of the covariance, that result can be generalized to include sums of *dependent* random variables.

> **THEOREM 11.4.3.** Let $X_1, X_2, \ldots, X_n$ be any set of random variables. Let $S = X_1 + X_2 + \cdots + X_n$. Then
>
> $$\text{Var}(S) = \sum_{i=1}^{n} \text{Var}(X_i) + 2 \sum_{j<k} \text{Cov}(X_j, X_k)$$

Proof. From Theorem 3.12.1, we can write

$$\text{Var}(S) = E(S^2) - [E(S)]^2$$

Replacing S with $\sum_{i=1}^{n} X_i$ gives

$$\text{Var}(S) = E\left[\left(\sum_{i=1}^{n} X_i\right)^2\right] - \left[\sum_{i=1}^{n} E(X_i)\right]^2$$

$$= E\left(\sum_{i=1}^{n} X_i^2 + 2\sum_{j<k} X_j X_k\right) - \left[\sum_{i=1}^{n} [E(X_i)]^2 + 2\sum_{j<k} E(X_j)E(X_k)\right]$$

$$= \sum_{i=1}^{n} \left[E(X_i^2) - [E(X_i)]^2\right] + 2\sum_{j<k} \left[E(X_j X_k) - E(X_j)E(X_k)\right]$$

$$= \sum_{i=1}^{n} \text{Var}(X_i) + 2\sum_{j<k} \text{Cov}(X_j, X_k)$$

[Of course, if the variables are independent, $\text{Cov}(X_i, X_j) = 0$ for all i and j, and the statement of Theorem 11.4.3 reduces to the earlier Theorem 3.12.2.]

EXAMPLE 11.4.3

Recall the hypergeometric model from Chapter 3—an urn contains N chips, r red and w white ($r + w = N$); a random sample of size n is selected without replacement and the random variable X is defined to be the number of red chips in the sample. Use Theorem 11.4.3 to calculate the variance of X.

First, for each of the n draws, define

$$X_i = \begin{cases} 1 & \text{if the } i\text{th chip drawn is red} \\ 0 & \text{otherwise} \end{cases}$$

Then $X = X_1 + X_2 + \cdots + X_n$. Clearly,

$$E(X_i) = 1 \cdot \frac{r}{N} + 0 \cdot \frac{w}{N} = \frac{r}{N}$$

and $E(X) = n\left(\dfrac{r}{N}\right) = np$, where $p = \dfrac{r}{N}$.

Since $X_i^2 = X_i$, $E(X_i^2) = E(X_i) = \dfrac{r}{N}$ and

$$\text{Var}(X_i) = E(X_i^2) - [E(X_i)]^2 = \frac{r}{N} - \left(\frac{r}{N}\right)^2 = p(1 - p)$$

Also, for any $j \neq k$,

$$\text{Cov}(X_j, X_k) = E(X_j X_k) - E(X_j)E(X_k)$$

$$= 1 \cdot P(X_j X_k = 1) - \left(\frac{r}{N}\right)^2$$

$$= \frac{r}{N} \cdot \frac{r-1}{N-1} - \frac{r^2}{N^2} = -\frac{r}{N} \cdot \frac{N-r}{N} \cdot \frac{1}{N-1}$$

From Theorem 11.4.3, then,

$$\text{Var}(X) = \sum_{i=1}^{n} \text{Var}(X_i) + 2\sum_{j<k} \text{Cov}(X_j, X_k)$$

$$= np(1-p) - 2\binom{n}{2}p(1-p) \cdot \frac{1}{N-1}$$

$$= p(1-p)\left[n - \frac{n(n-1)}{N-1}\right]$$

$$= np(1-p) \cdot \frac{N-n}{N-1}$$

The Correlation Coefficient

The covariance of X and Y necessarily reflects the *units* of both random variables, which can make it difficult to interpret. In applied settings, it helps to have a *dimensionless* measure of dependency, so that one xy-relationship can be compared to another. Dividing $\text{Cov}(X, Y)$ by $\sigma_X \sigma_Y$ accomplishes not only that objective but also scales the quotient to be a number between -1 and $+1$.

DEFINITION 11.4.2.   Let X and Y be any two random variables. The *correlation coefficient of X and Y*, denoted $\rho(X, Y)$, is given by

$$\rho(X, Y) = \frac{\text{Cov}(X, Y)}{\sigma_X \sigma_Y} = \text{Cov}(X^*, Y^*)$$

where $X^* = (X - \mu_X)/\sigma_X$ and $Y^* = (Y - \mu_Y)/\sigma_Y$.

THEOREM 11.4.4.   For any two random variables X and Y,

(a) $|\rho(X, Y)| \leq 1$.

(b) $|\rho(X, Y)| = 1$ if and only if $Y = aX + b$ for some constants a and b (except possibly on a set of probability zero).

Proof.   Following the notation of Definition 11.4.2, let X^* and Y^* denote the standardized transforms of X and Y. Then

$$0 \leq \text{Var}(X^* \pm Y^*) = \text{Var}(X^*) \pm 2\,\text{Cov}(X^*, Y^*) + \text{Var}(Y^*)$$

$$= 1 \pm 2\rho(X, Y) + 1$$

$$= 2[1 \pm \rho(X, Y)]$$

But $1 \pm \rho(X, Y) \geq 0$ implies that $|\rho(X, Y)| \leq 1$, and part (a) of the theorem is proved.

Next, suppose that $\rho(X, Y) = 1$. Then $\text{Var}(X^* - Y^*) = 0$; however, a random variable with zero variance is constant, except possibly on a set of probability 0. From the constancy of $X^* - Y^*$, it readily follows that Y is a linear function of X. The case for $\rho(X, Y) = -1$ is similar.

The converse of part (b) is left as an exercise.

QUESTIONS

11.4.5 Let X and Y have the joint pdf,

$$f_{X,Y}(x,y) = \begin{cases} \dfrac{x+2y}{22} & \text{for } (x,y) = \{(1,1),(1,3),(2,1),(2,3)\} \\ 0 & \text{elsewhere} \end{cases}$$

Find $\text{Cov}(X,Y)$ and $\rho(X,Y)$.

11.4.6 Suppose that X and Y have the joint pdf,

$$f_{X,Y}(x,y) = x+y, \qquad 0 < x < 1, 0 < y < 1$$

Find $\rho(X,Y)$.

11.4.7 If the random variables X and Y have the joint pdf

$$f_{X,Y}(x,y) = \begin{cases} 8xy, & 0 \le x \le y \le 1 \\ 0, & \text{otherwise} \end{cases}$$

$\text{Cov}(X,Y) = \frac{8}{450}$ (recall Example 11.4.1). Calculate $\rho(X,Y)$.

11.4.8 Suppose that X and Y are discrete random variables with the joint pdf

(x,y)	$f_{X,Y}(x,y)$
$(1,2)$	$\frac{1}{2}$
$(1,3)$	$\frac{1}{4}$
$(2,1)$	$\frac{1}{8}$
$(2,4)$	$\frac{1}{8}$

Find the correlation coefficient between X and Y.

11.4.9 Prove that $\rho(a+bX, c+dY) = \rho(X,Y)$ for constants a,b,c, and d where b and d are positive. Note that this result allows for a change of scale to one convenient for computation.

11.4.10 Let the random variable X take on the values $1,2,\ldots,n$, each with probability $1/n$. Define Y to be X^2. Find $\rho(X,Y)$ and $\lim_{n\to\infty} \rho(X,Y)$.

11.4.11 For random variables X and Y, show that

$$\text{Cov}(X+Y, X-Y) = \text{Var}(X) - \text{Var}(Y)$$

11.4.12 Suppose that $\text{Cov}(X,Y) = 0$. Prove that

$$\rho(X+Y, X-Y) = \frac{\text{Var}(X) - \text{Var}(Y)}{\text{Var}(X) + \text{Var}(Y)}$$

Estimating $\rho(X, Y)$: The Sample Correlation Coefficient

We conclude this section with an estimation problem. Suppose the correlation coefficient between X and Y is unknown, but we have some relevant information about its value in the form of n measurements, $(X_1, Y_1), (X_2, Y_2), \ldots$, and (X_n, Y_n). How can we use those data to estimate $\rho(X,Y)$?

Since the correlation coefficient can be written in terms of various theoretical moments,

$$\rho(X, Y) = \frac{E(XY) - E(X)E(Y)}{\sqrt{\text{Var}(X)}\sqrt{\text{Var}(Y)}}$$

it would seem reasonable to estimate each component of $\rho(X, Y)$ with its corresponding *sample* moment. That is, let $\bar{X}$ and $\bar{Y}$ approximate $E(X)$ and $E(Y)$, replace $E(XY)$ with

$$\frac{1}{n}\sum_{i=1}^{n} X_i Y_i$$

and substitute

$$\frac{1}{n}\sum_{i=1}^{n}(X_i - \bar{X})^2 \quad \text{and} \quad \frac{1}{n}\sum_{i=1}^{n}(Y_i - \bar{Y})^2$$

for $\text{Var}(X)$ and $\text{Var}(Y)$.

We define the *sample correlation coefficient*, then, to be the ratio

$$R = \frac{\dfrac{1}{n}\sum_{i=1}^{n} X_i Y_i - \bar{X}\bar{Y}}{\sqrt{\dfrac{1}{n}\sum_{i=1}^{n}(X_i - \bar{X})^2}\sqrt{\dfrac{1}{n}\sum_{i=1}^{n}(Y_i - \bar{Y})^2}} \tag{11.4.1}$$

or, equivalently,

$$R = \frac{n\sum_{i=1}^{n} X_i Y_i - \left(\sum_{i=1}^{n} X_i\right)\left(\sum_{i=1}^{n} Y_i\right)}{\sqrt{n\sum_{i=1}^{n} X_i^2 - \left(\sum_{i=1}^{n} X_i\right)^2}\sqrt{n\sum_{i=1}^{n} Y_i^2 - \left(\sum_{i=1}^{n} Y_i\right)^2}} \tag{11.4.2}$$

(Sometimes R is referred to as the *Pearson product-moment correlation coefficient* in honor of the eminent British statistician Karl Pearson).

QUESTIONS

11.4.13 Derive Equation 11.4.2 from Equation 11.4.1.

11.4.14 Let $(x_1, y_1), (x_2, y_2), \ldots, (x_n, y_n)$ be a set of measurements whose sample correlation coefficient is r. Show that

$$r = \hat{\beta}_1 \cdot \frac{\sqrt{n\sum_{i=1}^{n} x_i^2 - \left(\sum_{i=1}^{n} x_i\right)^2}}{\sqrt{n\sum_{i=1}^{n} y_i^2 - \left(\sum_{i=1}^{n} y_i\right)^2}}$$

where $\hat{\beta}_1$ is the MLE for the slope.

Interpreting *R*

The properties cited for $\rho(X, Y)$ in Theorem 11.4.4 are not sufficient to provide a useful interpretation of *R*. What does it mean, for example, to say that the sample correlation coefficient is 0.73, or 0.55, or -0.24? One way to answer such a question focuses on the *square* of *R*, rather than on *R* itself.

We know from Equation 11.3.2 that

$$\sum_{i=1}^{n} (y_i - \hat{\beta}_0 - \hat{\beta}_1 x_i)^2 = \sum_{i=1}^{n} (y_i - \bar{y})^2 - \hat{\beta}_1^2 \sum_{i=1}^{n} (x_i - \bar{x})^2$$

Using the relationship between $\hat{\beta}_1$ and *r* in Question 11.4.14—together with the fact that $\sum_{i=1}^{n} (x_i - \bar{x})^2 = \sum_{i=1}^{n} x_i^2 - \left(\sum_{i=1}^{n} x_i \right)^2 \bigg/ n$—we can write

$$\sum_{i=1}^{n} (y_i - \hat{\beta}_0 - \hat{\beta}_1 x_i)^2 = \sum_{i=1}^{n} (y_i - \bar{y})^2 - r^2 \cdot \frac{\sum_{i=1}^{n} (y_i - \bar{y})^2}{\sum_{i=1}^{n} (x_i - \bar{x})^2} \cdot \sum_{i=1}^{n} (x_i - \bar{x})^2$$

which reduces to

$$r^2 = \frac{\sum_{i=1}^{n} (y_i - \bar{y})^2 - \sum_{i=1}^{n} (y_i - \hat{\beta}_0 - \hat{\beta}_1 x_i)^2}{\sum_{i=1}^{n} (y_i - \bar{y})^2} \tag{11.4.3}$$

Equation 11.4.3 has a nice, simple interpretation. Notice that

1. $\sum_{i=1}^{n} (y_i - \bar{y})^2$ represents the *total variability* in the dependent variable—that is, the extent to which the y_i's are not all the same.

2. $\sum_{i=1}^{n} (y_i - \hat{\beta}_0 - \hat{\beta}_1 x_i)^2$ represents the variation in the y_i's *not explained* (or accounted for) by the linear regression with *x*.

3. $\sum_{i=1}^{n} (y_i - \bar{y})^2 - \sum_{i=1}^{n} (y_i - \hat{\beta}_0 - \hat{\beta}_1 x_i)^2$ represents the variation in the y_i's that *is explained* by the linear regression with *x*.

Therefore, r^2 is the *proportion of the total variation in the y_i's that can be attributed to the linear relationship with x*. So, if $r = 0.60$, we can say that *36%* of the variation in *Y* is explained by the linear regression with *X* (and 64% is associated with other factors).

CASE STUDY 11.4.1

The Scholastic Aptitude Test (SAT) is widely used by colleges and universities to help choose their incoming classes. It was never designed to measure the quality of education provided by secondary schools, but critics and supporters alike seem increasingly intent on forcing it into that role. The problem is that SAT scores reflect a variety of factors that have nothing to do with the quality of high school education.

Table 11.4.1. for example, shows the average SAT score (Y), by state, as a function of "Participation rate" (X). As Figure 11.4.1 suggests, there appears to be a strong dependency between the two measurements—as a state's participation rate goes down, its average SAT score (not surprisingly!) goes up (113). In Utah, for example, only 4% of the students eligible to take the test actually did; in New York, the participation rate was a dramatically larger 76%. The average SAT in New York was 888; in Utah, scores were 20% higher ($\bar{y} = 1067$).

TABLE 11.4.1

State	Participation Rate, x	Average SAT Score, y	State	Participation Rate, x	Average SAT Score, y
AK	49	911	MT	21	986
AL	8	1011	NE	9	1025
AZ	26	939	NV	30	913
AR	6	935	NH	69	924
CA	46	895	NJ	71	893
CO	28	969	NM	12	1003
CT	80	898	NY	76	888
DE	68	892	NC	60	860
DC	53	849	ND	5	1056
FL	49	879	OH	24	966
GA	65	844	OK	9	1019
HI	58	881	OR	53	927
ID	16	969	PA	70	879
IL	14	1024	RI	68	882
IN	60	876	SC	60	838
IA	5	1080	SD	5	1031
KS	10	1044	TN	12	1023
KY	11	997	TX	48	886
LA	9	1011	UT	4	1067
ME	68	883	VT	68	899
MD	64	908	VA	65	893
MA	79	901	WA	49	922
MI	11	1009	WV	17	921
MN	9	1057	WI	9	1044
MS	4	1013	WY	12	980
MO	10	1017			

Quantify and interpret the linear dependence between X and Y by calculating the sample correlation coefficient, r.

From Table 11.4.1, we can calculate the sums and sums of squares necessary to evaluate Equation 11.4.2:

$$\sum_{i=1}^{51} x_i = 1{,}832 \qquad \sum_{i=1}^{51} y_i = 48{,}417$$

$$\sum_{i=1}^{51} x_i^2 = 101{,}170 \qquad \sum_{i=1}^{51} y_i^2 = 46{,}198{,}947$$

$$\sum_{i=1}^{51} x_i y_i = 1{,}659{,}601$$

(continued on next page)

(Case Study 11.4.1 continued)

FIGURE 11.4.1

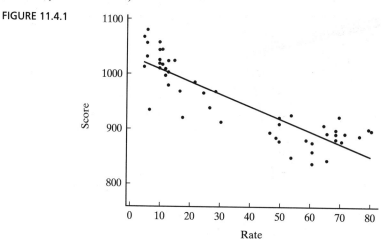

Substituting into the formula for r, then, shows that the sample correlation coefficient is -0.875:

$$r = \frac{51(1,659,601) - (1,832)(48,417)}{\sqrt{51(101,170) - (1,832)^2}\sqrt{51(46,198,947) - (48,417)^2}}$$

$$= -0.875$$

Since $r^2 = (-0.875)^2 = 0.766$, we can say that 76.6% of the variability in SATs from state to state can be attributed to the linear relationship between test scores and participation rates.

The magnitude of r^2 for these data should be a clear warning that comparing average SATs at face value from state to state or school system to school system is largely meaningless. It would make sense, though, to examine the residuals associated with $y = \hat{\beta}_0 + \hat{\beta}_1 x$. States with particularly large positive values for $y - \hat{y}$ may be doing something that other states would be well advised to copy.

CASE STUDY 11.4.2

Correlation must never be confused with causality. The presence of a large—even a perfect—correlation coefficient between a linearly related X and Y does not imply that X "causes" Y or that Y "causes" X—the relationship between the two may have no physical basis whatsoever. We call such correlations *spurious*.

Table 11.4.2 shows the number of cellular phone subscribers (X) from 1989 to 1996, as well as the total gross revenue (Y) of the top 100 U.S. law firms over that same period. As Figure 11.4.2 suggests, the relationship between X and Y is quite strong. The sample correlation coefficient, calculated from Equation 11.4.2, is *0.976*, implying that *95.3%* ($= 100 \times (0.976)^2$) of the variation in law firm revenues is "explained" by the linear relationship with cellular phone subscribers.

Is there a strong relationship between these two variables? Yes. Is there any reason to suppose that increases in cell phone subscribers are directly benefitting law firm revenues? No. Both are reflecting to no small degree the growth in the U.S. economy and the advances in communication technology, but it would be difficult to imagine that X, in any way, is influencing the value of Y.

TABLE 11.4.2

Year	Cell Phone Subscribers (thousands), x	Top U.S. Law Firms Gross Revenue (million $), y
1989	3,508.9	12,400
1990	5,283.1	13,500
1991	7,557.1	13,900
1992	11,032.8	14,300
1993	16,009.5	14,600
1994	24,134.4	15,300
1995	33,785.7	16,200
1996	44,000.0	18,000

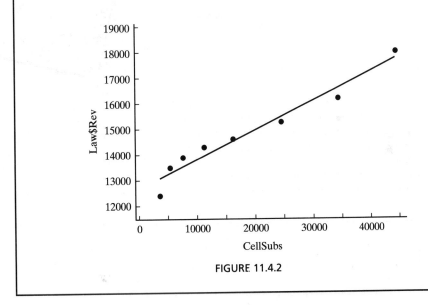

FIGURE 11.4.2

QUESTIONS

11.4.15 Some baseball fans believe that the number of home runs a team hits is markedly affected by the altitude of the club's home park. The rationale is that the air is thinner at the higher altitudes, and balls would be expected to travel farther. The following table shows the altitudes (X) of American League ballparks and the number of home runs (Y) that each team hit during a recent season (162). Calculate the sample correlation coeffient, r. What would you conclude? *Note:*

$$\sum_{i=1}^{12} x_i = 4936 \qquad \sum_{i=1}^{12} y_i = 1175$$

$$\sum_{i=1}^{12} x_i^2 = 3{,}071{,}116 \qquad \sum_{i=1}^{12} y_i^2 = 123{,}349$$

$$\sum_{i=1}^{12} x_i y_i = 480{,}565$$

Club	Altitude, x	Number of Home Runs, y
Cleveland	660	138
Milwaukee	635	81
Detroit	585	135
New York	55	90
Boston	21	120
Baltimore	20	84
Minnesota	815	106
Kansas City	750	57
Chicago	595	109
Texas	435	74
California	340	61
Oakland	25	120

11.4.16 The following table shows U.S. corn supplies (in millions of bushels) and corn prices (in dollars per bushel) for the years 1981 through 1989 (154). Calculate the sample correlation coefficient, r. *Note*:

$$\sum_{i=1}^{9} x_i = 90{,}118 \qquad \sum_{i=1}^{9} y_i = 21.69$$

$$\sum_{i=1}^{9} x_i^2 = 920{,}636{,}098 \qquad \sum_{i=1}^{9} y_i^2 = 54.1951$$

$$\sum_{i=1}^{9} x_i y_i = 212{,}111.6$$

Year	Supply, x	Price, y
1981	9,512	$2.50
1982	10,772	2.68
1983	7,700	3.25
1984	8,684	2.62
1985	10,518	2.41
1986	12,267	1.50
1987	12,016	1.94
1988	9,191	2.54
1989	9,458	2.25

11.4.17 The extent to which stress is a contributing factor to the severity of chronic illnesses was the focus of the study summarized in the following table (195). Seventeen conditions were compared on a Seriousness of Illness Rating Scale (SIRS). Patients with each of those conditions were asked to fill out a Schedule of Recent Experience (SRE) questionnaire. Higher scores on the SRE reflect presumably greater levels of stress. How much of the variation in the SIRS values can be attributed to the linear regression with SRE? *Note:*

$$\sum_{i=1}^{17} x_i = 7{,}973 \qquad \sum_{i=1}^{17} y_i = 8{,}517$$

$$\sum_{i=1}^{17} x_i^2 = 4{,}611{,}291 \qquad \sum_{i=1}^{17} y_i^2 = 5{,}421{,}917$$

$$\sum_{i=1}^{17} x_i y_i = 4{,}759{,}470$$

Admitting Diagnosis	Average SRE, x	SIRS, y
Dandruff	26	21
Varicose veins	130	173
Psoriasis	317	174
Eczema	231	204
Anemia	325	312
Hyperthyroidism	816	393
Gallstones	563	454
Arthritis	312	468
Peptic ulcer	603	500
High blood pressure	405	520
Diabetes	599	621
Emphysema	357	636
Alcoholism	688	688
Cirrhosis	443	733
Schizophrenia	609	776
Heart failure	772	824
Cancer	777	1,020

11.4.18 Among the many strategies that investors use to try to predict trends in the stock market is the "early warning" system, which is based on the premise that what the market does during the first five days in January is indicative of what it will do over the next 12 months. Listed in the following table for the 37 years from 1950 through 1986 are x, the percentage change in the market for the first five days in January, and y, the percentage change for the entire year (29). How would you quantify the strength of the linear relationship between X and Y? *Note:*

$$\sum_{i=1}^{37} x_i = 9.1 \qquad \sum_{i=1}^{37} x_i^2 = 169.47$$

$$\sum_{i=1}^{37} y_i = 324.8 \qquad \sum_{i=1}^{37} y_i^2 = 12{,}814.64$$

$$\sum_{i=1}^{37} x_i y_i = 655.11$$

Year	% Change for First 5 Days in Jan., x	% Change for Year, y	Year	% Change for First 5 Days in Jan., x	% Change for Year, y
1950	2.0	21.8	1969	−2.9	−11.4
1951	2.3	16.5	1970	0.7	0.1
1952	0.6	11.8	1971	0.0	10.8
1953	−0.9	−6.6	1972	1.4	15.6
1954	0.5	45.0	1973	1.5	−17.4
1955	−1.8	26.4	1974	−1.5	−29.7
1956	−2.1	2.6	1975	2.2	31.5
1957	−0.9	−14.3	1976	4.9	19.1
1958	2.5	38.1	1977	−2.3	−11.5
1959	0.3	8.5	1978	−4.6	1.1
1960	−0.7	−3.0	1979	2.8	12.3
1961	1.2	23.1	1980	0.9	25.8
1962	−3.4	−11.8	1981	−2.0	−9.7
1963	2.6	18.9	1982	−2.4	14.8
1964	1.3	13.0	1983	3.2	17.3
1965	0.7	9.1	1984	2.4	1.4
1966	0.8	−13.1	1985	−1.9	26.3
1967	3.1	20.1	1986	−1.6	14.6
1968	0.2	7.7			

11.5   THE BIVARIATE NORMAL DISTRIBUTION

The singular importance of the normal distribution in univariate inference procedures should, by now, be abundantly clear. In dealing with problems that involve *two* random variables—for example, the calculation of $\rho(X, Y)$—it should come as no surprise that the most frequently encountered *joint* pdf, $f_{X,Y}(x, y)$, is a bivariate version of the normal curve. Our objectives in this section are twofold: (1) to deduce the form of the bivariate normal from basic principles and (2) to identify the particular properties of that pdf that pertain to the problem of assessing the nature of the dependence between X and Y.

Generalizing the Univariate Normal pdf

How should we generalize the equation of a bell-shaped curve,

$$f_Y(y) = \frac{1}{\sqrt{2\pi}\,\sigma} e^{-\frac{1}{2}\left(\frac{y-\mu}{\sigma}\right)^2}, \quad -\infty < y < \infty,$$

to a *bivariate* "normal" pdf, $f_{X,Y}(x, y)$? What additional parameters need to be included?

As a first condition to impose, it makes sense to require that the marginal pdfs associated with $f_{X,Y}(x, y)$ be univariate normal densities. It will be sufficient to consider the case where the two marginals are *standard* normals.

If X and Y are *independent* standard normals,

$$f_{X,Y}(x, y) = \frac{1}{2\pi} e^{-\frac{1}{2}(x^2+y^2)}, \qquad \begin{array}{l} -\infty < x < \infty \\ -\infty < y < \infty \end{array} \qquad (11.5.1)$$

Notice that the simplest extension of $f_{X,Y}(x, y)$ in Equation 11.5.1 is to replace $-\frac{1}{2}(x^2 + y^2)$ with $-\frac{1}{2}c(x^2 + uxy + y^2)$, or, equivalently, with $-\frac{1}{2}c(x^2 - 2vxy + y^2)$, where c and v are constants. The desired joint pdf, then, would have the general form

$$f_{X,Y}(x, y) = Ke^{-\frac{1}{2}c(x^2-2vxy+y^2)} \qquad (11.5.2)$$

where K is the constant that makes the double integral of $f_{X,Y}(x, y)$ from $-\infty$ to ∞ equal to 1.

Now, what must be true of $K, c,$ and v if the marginal pdf's based on $f_{X,Y}(x, y)$ are to be standard normals? Note, first, that completing the square in the exponent makes

$$\begin{aligned} x^2 - 2vxy + y^2 &= x^2 - v^2x^2 + (y^2 - 2vxy + v^2x^2) \\ &= (1 - v^2)x^2 + (y - vx)^2 \end{aligned}$$

so

$$f_{X,Y}(x, y) = Ke^{-\frac{1}{2}c(1-v^2)x^2} e^{-\frac{1}{2}c(y-vx)^2}$$

The exponents, though, must be negative, which implies that $1 - v^2 > 0$, or, equivalently, $|v| < 1$.

To find K, we start by calculating

$$\int_{-\infty}^{\infty} \int_{-\infty}^{\infty} e^{-(1/2)c(1-v^2)x^2} \cdot e^{-(1/2)c(y-vx)^2} \, dy \, dx$$

$$= \int_{-\infty}^{\infty} e^{-(1/2)c(1-v^2)x^2} \left(\int_{-\infty}^{\infty} e^{-(1/2)c(y-vx)^2} \, dy \right) dx$$

$$= \int_{-\infty}^{\infty} e^{-(1/2)c(1-v^2)x^2} \left(\frac{\sqrt{2\pi}}{\sqrt{c}} \right) dx$$

$$= \frac{\sqrt{2\pi}}{\sqrt{c}} \frac{\sqrt{2\pi}}{\sqrt{c}\sqrt{1 - v^2}}$$

$$= \frac{2\pi}{c\sqrt{1 - v^2}}$$

It follows that

$$K = \frac{c\sqrt{1 - v^2}}{2\pi}$$

The constant c can be any positive value, but a convenient choice proves to be $c = 1/(1 - v^2)$. Substituting K and c, then, into Equation 11.5.2 gives

$$f_{X,Y}(x, y) = \frac{1}{2\pi\sqrt{1 - v^2}} e^{-(1/2)[1/(1-v^2)](x^2-2vxy+y^2)}$$

$$= \frac{1}{2\pi\sqrt{1 - v^2}} e^{-x^2} \cdot e^{-(1/2)[1/(1-v^2)](y-vx)^2} \qquad (11.5.3)$$

Recall that our choice of the form of $f_{X,Y}(x, y)$ was predicated on a wish for the marginal pdf's to be normal. A simple integration shows that to be the case:

$$f_X(x) = \int_{-\infty}^{\infty} f_{X,Y}(x, y)\, dy$$

$$= \frac{1}{2\pi\sqrt{1 - v^2}}\, e^{-(1/2)x^2} \int_{-\infty}^{\infty} e^{-(1/2)[1/(1-v^2)](y - vx)^2}\, dy$$

$$= \frac{1}{2\pi\sqrt{1 - v^2}}\, e^{-(1/2)x^2} \cdot \sqrt{2\pi}\sqrt{1 - v^2}$$

$$= \frac{1}{\sqrt{2\pi}}\, e^{-(1/2)x^2}$$

Since $f_{X,Y}(x, y)$ is symmetric in x and y, $f_Y(y)$ is also the standard normal.

The constant v is actually the correlation coefficient between X and Y. Since $E(X) = E(Y) = 0$,

$$\rho(X, Y) = E(XY) = \int_{-\infty}^{\infty}\int_{-\infty}^{\infty} xy\, f_{X,Y}(x, y)\, dx\, dy$$

$$= \frac{1}{\sqrt{2\pi}} \int_{-\infty}^{\infty} xe^{-(1/2)x^2} \left(\frac{1}{\sqrt{2\pi}\sqrt{1 - v^2}} \int_{-\infty}^{\infty} ye^{-(1/2)[1/(1-v^2)](y - vx)^2}\, dy \right) dx$$

$$= \frac{1}{\sqrt{2\pi}} \int_{-\infty}^{\infty} xe^{-(1/2)x^2} \cdot vx\, dx \quad \text{(why?)}$$

$$= v\, \frac{1}{\sqrt{2\pi}} \int_{-\infty}^{\infty} x^2 e^{-(1/2)x^2}\, dx = v\, \text{Var}(X) = v$$

Finally, we can replace x with $(x - \mu_X)/\sigma_X$ and y with $(y - \mu_Y)/\sigma_Y$. Doing so requires that the original pdf be multiplied by the derivative of both the X-transformation and the Y-transformation—that is, by $\dfrac{1}{\sigma_X \sigma_Y}$ [see (93)].

DEFINITION 11.5.1. Let X and Y be random variables with joint pdf

$$f_{X,Y}(x, y) = \frac{1}{2\pi\sigma_X\sigma_Y\sqrt{1 - \rho^2}}$$

$$\cdot \exp\left\{ -\frac{1}{2}\left(\frac{1}{1 - \rho^2} \right)\left[\frac{(x - \mu_X)^2}{\sigma_X^2} - 2\rho\, \frac{x - \mu_X}{\sigma_X} \cdot \frac{y - \mu_Y}{\sigma_Y} + \frac{(y - \mu_Y)^2}{\sigma_Y^2} \right] \right\}$$

for all x and y. Then X and Y are said to have the *bivariate normal distribution*.

Comment. For bivariate normal densities, $\rho(X, Y) = 0$ implies that X and Y are independent, a result not true in general (recall Example 11.4.2).

Properties of the Bivariate Normal Distribution

Francis Galton, the renowned British biologist and scientist, perhaps more than any other person was responsible for launching *regression analysis* as a worthwhile field of statistical inquiry. Galton was a redoubtable data analyst whose keen insight enabled him to intuit much of the basic mathematical structure that we now associate with correlation and regression.

One of his more famous endeavors (52) was an examination of the relationship between parents' heights (X) and their adult children's heights (Y). Those particular variables have a bivariate normal distribution, the mathematical properties of which Galton knew nothing about. Just by looking at cross-tabulations of X and Y, though, Galton postulated that (1) the marginal distributions of X and Y were both normal, (2) $E(Y|x)$ is a linear function of x, and (3) $\text{Var}(Y|x)$ is constant with x. As Theorem 11.5.1 shows, all of his empirically based deductions proved to be true.

THEOREM 11.5.1. Suppose that X and Y are random variables having the bivariate normal distribution given in Definition 11.5.1. Then

(a) $f_X(x)$ is a normal pdf with mean μ_X and variance σ_X^2; $f_Y(y)$ is a normal pdf with mean μ_Y and variance σ_Y^2

(b) $\rho(X, Y) = v = \rho$

(c) $E(Y|x) = \mu_Y + \dfrac{\rho \sigma_Y}{\sigma_X}(x - \mu_X)$

(d) $\text{Var}(Y|x) = (1 - \rho^2)\sigma_Y^2$

Proof. We have already established (a) and (b). Properties (c) and (d) will be examined for the special case $\mu_X = \mu_Y = 0$ and $\sigma_x = \sigma_y = 1$. The extension to arbitrary μ_X, μ_Y, σ_X, and σ_Y is straightforward.

First, note that

$$f_{Y|x}(y) = \frac{f_{X,Y}(x, y)}{f_X(x)}$$

$$= \frac{\dfrac{1}{2\pi\sqrt{1 - \rho^2}} e^{-(1/2)x^2} e^{-(1/2)[1/(1-\rho^2)](y-\rho x)^2}}{\dfrac{1}{\sqrt{2\pi}} e^{-(1/2)x^2}}$$

$$= \frac{1}{\sqrt{2\pi}\sqrt{1 - \rho^2}} e^{-(1/2)[1/(1-\rho^2)](y-\rho x)^2} \qquad (11.5.4)$$

By inspection, we see that Equation 11.5.4 is the pdf of a normal random variable with mean ρx and variance $1 - \rho^2$. Therefore, $E(Y|x) = \rho x$ and $\text{Var}(Y|x) = 1 - \rho^2$. Replacing Y with $(Y - \mu_Y)/\sigma_Y$ and x with $(x - \mu_X)/\sigma_X$ gives the desired results.

Comment. The term *regression line* derives from a consequence of Part (c) of Theorem 11.5.1. Suppose we make the simplifying assumption that $\mu_X = \mu_Y = \mu$ and $\sigma_X = \sigma_Y$. Then Part (c) reduces to

$$E(Y|x) - \mu = \rho(X, Y)(x - \mu)$$

But recall that $|\rho(X, Y)| \leq 1$—and, in this case, $0 < \rho(X, Y) < 1$. Here, the positive sign of $\rho(X, Y)$ tells us that, on the average, tall parents have tall children. However, $\rho(X, Y) < 1$ means (again, *on the average*) that the children's heights are closer to the mean than are the parents'. Galton called this phenomenon "regression to mediocrity."

QUESTIONS

11.5.1 Suppose that X and Y have a bivariate normal pdf with $\mu_X = 3$, $\mu_Y = 6$, $\sigma_X^2 = 4$, $\sigma_Y^2 = 10$, and $\rho = \frac{1}{2}$. Find $P(5 < Y < 6\frac{1}{2})$ and $P(5 < Y < 6\frac{1}{2}|x = 2)$.

11.5.2 Suppose that X and Y have a bivariate normal distribution with $\text{Var}(X) = \text{Var}(Y)$.
  (a) Show that X and $Y - \rho X$ are independent.
  (b) Show that $X + Y$ and $X - Y$ are independent. (*Hint*: See Question 11.4.11.)

11.5.3 Suppose that X and Y have a bivariate normal distribution.
  (a) Prove that $X + Y$ has a normal distribution when X and Y are standard normal random variables.
  (b) Find $E(cX + dY)$ and $\text{Var}(cX + dY)$ in terms of $\mu_X, \mu_Y, \sigma_X, \sigma_Y$, and $\rho(X, Y)$, where X and Y are arbitrary normal random variables.

11.5.4 Suppose that the random variables X and Y have a bivariate normal pdf with $\mu_X = 56$, $\mu_Y = 11$, $\sigma_X^2 = 1.2$, $\sigma_Y^2 = 2.6$, and $\rho = 0.6$. Compute $P(10 < Y < 10.5|x = 55)$. Suppose that $n = 4$ values were to be observed with x fixed at 55. Find $P(10.5 < \bar{Y} < 11|x = 55)$.

11.5.5 If the joint pdf of the random variables X and Y is

$$f_{X,Y}(x, y) = ke^{-(2/3)[(1/4)x^2 - (1/2)xy + y^2]}$$

find $E(X), E(Y), \text{Var}(X), \text{Var}(Y), \rho(X, Y)$, and k.

11.5.6 Give conditions on $a > 0$, $b > 0$, and u so that

$$f_{X,Y}(x, y) = ke^{-(ax^2 - 2uxy + by^2)}$$

is the bivariate normal density of random variables X and Y each having expected value zero. Also, find $\text{Var}(X), \text{Var}(Y)$, and $\rho(X, Y)$.

Testing $H_0: \rho(X, Y) = 0$

Situations arise where it is desirable to test the independence of two random variables. We are not at this point able to formulate such a test in any general context, but for the special case where X and Y are bivariate normal, independence is equivalent to $\rho(X, Y)$ being 0, and the latter can be examined without too much difficulty. Not surprisingly, the test statistic appropriate for hypotheses involving ρ, the *true* correlation coefficient, is R, the *sample* correlation coefficient (recall Equation 11.4.2). Among its other properties, R is the maximum-likelihood estimator for ρ.

THEOREM 11.5.2. Given that $f_{X,Y}(x, y)$ is a bivariate normal pdf, the maximum-likelihood estimators for $\mu_X, \mu_Y, \sigma_X^2, \sigma_Y^2$, and $\rho(X, Y)$, assuming that all are unknown, are $\bar{X}, \bar{Y}, (1/n)\sum_{i=1}^{n}(X_i - \bar{X})^2, (1/n)\sum_{i=1}^{n}(Y_i - \bar{Y})^2$, and R, respectively.

Proof. The proof is accomplished by the usual method of taking partial derivatives of the likelihood function with respect to each of the five parameters, setting those equal to 0, and solving simultaneously. The details will be omitted.

Although we have already made a case for using R to test $H_0: \rho(X, Y) = 0$, it turns out to be more convenient to use a function of R as a test statistic. The derivation of that function's density is beyond the scope of this text, but we can state the result and illustrate it with an example.

THEOREM 11.5.3.   Under the null hypothesis that $\rho(X, Y) = 0$, the statistic

$$T_{n-2} = \frac{\sqrt{n-2}\,R}{\sqrt{1-R^2}}$$

has a Student t distribution with $n - 2$ degrees of freedom.

EXAMPLE 11.5.1

Table 11.5.1 gives the mean temperature for 20 successive days in April and the average daily butterfat content in the milk of 10 cows (128). Can we conclude that temperature and butterfat content have a nonzero correlation?

TABLE 11.5.1

Date	Temperature, x	Percent Butterfat, y
3	64	4.65
4	65	4.58
5	65	4.67
6	64	4.60
7	61	4.83
8	55	4.55
9	39	5.14
10	41	4.71
11	46	4.69
12	59	4.65
13	56	4.36
14	56	4.82
15	62	4.65
16	37	4.66
17	37	4.95
18	45	4.60
19	57	4.68
20	58	4.65
21	60	4.60
22	55	4.46

Let ρ denote the true correlation coefficient between X and Y. The hypotheses to be tested are

$$H_0: \quad \rho = 0$$

versus

$$H_1: \quad \rho \neq 0$$

To accept H_0 is to conclude that X and Y are independent [assuming the (x_i, y_i) values in Table 11.5.1 are a random sample from a bivariate normal distribution].

Let $\alpha = 0.05$. We will reject the null hypothesis only if the test statistic

$$\frac{\sqrt{n-2} \cdot r}{\sqrt{1-r^2}}$$

is either too much less than zero or too much greater than zero. Since the test statistic has a Student t distribution with $20 - 2 = 18$ degrees of freedom, the measure of "too much" is $t_{.025, 18} = 2.1009$. The null hypothesis should be rejected, then, if $\dfrac{\sqrt{n-2} \cdot r}{\sqrt{1-r^2}}$ is either (1) ≤ -2.1009 or (2) ≥ 2.1009.

Since

$$\sum_{i=1}^{20} x_i = 1{,}082 \qquad \sum_{i=1}^{20} y_i = 93.5$$

$$\sum_{i=1}^{20} x_i^2 = 60{,}304 \qquad \sum_{i=1}^{20} y_i^2 = 437.6406$$

$$\sum_{i=1}^{20} x_i y_i = 5044.5$$

it follows that

$$r = \frac{20(5044.5) - (1{,}082)(93.5)}{\sqrt{20(60{,}304) - (1{,}082)^2}\,\sqrt{20(437.6406) - (93.5)^2}}$$

$$= -0.453$$

Therefore,

$$t = \frac{\sqrt{n-2}\,r}{\sqrt{1-r^2}} = \frac{\sqrt{18}\,(-0.453)}{\sqrt{1-(-0.453)^2}} = -2.156$$

Since the observed t ratio is less than the lower critical value (-2.1009), our conclusion is to *reject* the null hypothesis.

Comment.   An alternate approach to testing $H_0\colon \rho = 0$ was given by Fisher (45). He showed that the statistic

$$\frac{1}{2} \ln \frac{1+R}{1-R}$$

is asymptotically normal with mean $\frac{1}{2}\ln\left[(1+\rho)/(1-\rho)\right]$ and variance approximately $1/(n-3)$. Fisher's formulation makes it relatively easy to determine the power of a correlation test—a computation that would be much more difficult if the inference had to be based on $\sqrt{n-2}\,R/\sqrt{1-R^2}$.

QUESTIONS

11.5.7 What would the conclusion be for the test of Example 11.5.1 if $\alpha = 0.01$?

11.5.8 In a study of heart disease (65), the weight (in pounds) and the blood cholesterol (in mg/dl) of 14 men without a history of coronary incidents were recorded. At the $\alpha = 0.05$ level, can we conclude from these data that the two variables are independent?

Weight, x	Cholesterol, y
168	135
175	403
173	294
158	312
154	311
214	222
176	302
262	269
181	311
143	286
140	403
187	244
163	353
164	252

Note:

$$\sum_{i=1}^{14} x_i = 2458 \qquad \sum_{i=1}^{14} y_i = 4097$$

$$\sum_{i=1}^{14} x_i^2 = 444{,}118 \qquad \sum_{i=1}^{14} y_i^2 = 1{,}262{,}559$$

$$\sum_{i=1}^{14} x_i y_i = 710{,}499$$

11.5.9 Recall the baseball data in Question 11.4.15. Test whether home run frequency and home park altitude are independent. Let $\alpha = 0.05$.

11.5.10 Test $H_0: \rho = 0$ versus $H_1: \rho \neq 0$ on the SRE/SIRS data described in Question 11.4.17. Let 0.01 be the level of significance.

11.5.11 Use the statistic

$$\frac{1}{2} \ln \frac{1 + R}{1 - R}$$

to get an expression for an approximate $100(1 - \alpha)\%$ confidence interval for ρ.

11.5.12 Use your answer to Question 11.5.11 to construct a 90% confidence interval for the correlation coefficient between the stock market's performance early in January and its accumulated performance over the entire year (see Question 11.4.18).

APPENDIX 11.A.1   MINITAB APPLICATIONS

If a set of x_i's has been entered in column C1 and the associated y_i's in column C2, the MINITAB command

```
MTB > regress c2 1 c1
```

will compute the estimated regression line, $y = \hat{\beta}_0 + \hat{\beta}_1 x$, and provide the calculations for testing $H_0: \beta_1 = 0$ and $H_0: \beta_0 = 0$. Also printed out automatically will be r^2 and s, the square root of the unbiased estimator for σ^2 in the simple linear model. Subcommands are available for plotting the data, calculating and graphing the residuals, and constructing confidence intervals and prediction intervals.

Figure 11.A.1.1 is the printout of the REGRESS command applied to the Expenses versus Sales data described in Case Study 11.3.2. Included is a listing of the residuals (in column C3).

FIGURE 11.A.1.1
```
MTB > set c1
DATA> 1765 1942 2132 2431 2642 2895 2931 3217
DATA> end
MTB > set c2
DATA> 407 466 489 545 610 659 686 724
DATA> end
MTB > regress c2 1 c1;
SUBC> residuals c3.
```

Regression Analysis

```
The regression equation is
C2 = 24.6 + 0.220 C1
```

Predictor	Coef	Stdev	t-ratio	p
Constant	24.62	21.90	1.12	0.304
C1	0.219948	0.008620	25.51	0.000

```
s = 11.78      R-sq = 99.1%   R-sq(adj) = 98.9%

MTB > print c1 c2 c3
```

Data Display

Row	C1	C2	C3
1	1765	407	-5.8257
2	1942	466	14.2435
3	2132	489	-4.5465
4	2431	545	-14.3109
5	2642	610	4.2802
6	2895	659	-2.3665
7	2931	686	16.7154
8	3217	724	-8.1896

The entries in the "Stdev" column are based on Parts (c) and (d) of Theorem 11.3.2. The value 0.008620, for example, is the estimated standard deviation of the estimated slope. That is,

$$0.008620 = \sqrt{\frac{s^2}{\sum_{i=1}^{8}(x_i - \bar{x})^2}}$$

where $s = 11.78$ (as listed on the printout). The last entry in the "t-ratio" column is the value of T_{n-2} from Theorem 11.3.4 when $\beta_1 = 0$. That is,

$$25.51 = \frac{0.219948 - 0}{0.008620}$$

As we have seen in earlier chapters, the "conclusions" of hypothesis tests performed by computer software packages are invariably couched in terms of P-values. Here, for example, the test of $H_0: \beta_0 = 0$ versus $H_1: \beta_0 \neq 0$ yields an observed t ratio of 1.12, for which the P-value is *0.304*. Since the latter is so large, we would fail to reject $H_0: \beta_0 = 0$ at any reasonable level of α.

If SUBC > predict "x" is appended to the "regress c2 1 c1" command, MINITAB will print out the 95% confidence interval for $E(Y|x)$ and the 95% prediction interval for Y at the point x. Figure 11.A.1.2 shows the input and output that parallel the computations done in Examples 11.3.2 and 11.3.3.

```
MTB > set c1
DATA> 1765 1942 2132 2431 2642 2895 2931 3217
DATA> end
MTB > set c2
DATA> 407 466 489 545 610 659 686 724
DATA> end
MTB > regress c2 1 c1;
SUBC> predict 3500.
                    .
                    .
                    .
      Fit   Stdev. Fit       95.0%   C.I.          95.0%   P.I.
    794.43          9.62   ( 770.89,  817.97)   ( 757.21,  831.66)
```

FIGURE 11.A.1.2

Doing linear regression using MINITAB Windows

1. Enter the x_i's in C1 and the y_i's in C2.
2. Click on STAT, then on REGRESSION, then on second REGRESSION.
3. Type C2 in RESPONSE box. Then click on PREDICTOR box and type C1.
4. Click on OK.
5. To display the line, click on STAT, then on REGRESSION, then on FITTED LINE PLOT.
6. Type C2 in RESPONSE box and C1 in PREDICTOR box.
7. Click on LINEAR; then click on OK.

APPENDIX 11.A.2   A PROOF OF THEOREM 11.3.3

The strategy for the proof is to express $n\hat{\sigma}^2$ in terms of the squares of normal random variables and then apply Fisher's lemma (see Appendix 7.A.2). The random variables to be used are $\hat{\beta}_1 - \beta_1$, $W_i = Y_i - \beta_0 - \beta_1 x_i$, $i = 1, \ldots, n$, and $\bar{W} = \frac{1}{n} \sum_{i=1}^{n} W_i = \bar{Y} - \beta_0 - \beta_1 \bar{x}$. Note that

$$W_i - \bar{W} = (Y_i - \bar{Y}) - \beta_1(x_i - \bar{x})$$

or, equivalently,

$$Y_i - \bar{Y} = (W_i - \bar{W}) + \beta_1(x_i - \bar{x})$$

Next, we express $\hat{\beta}_1 - \beta_1$ as a linear combination of the W_i's. The argument begins by using Equation 11.3.1 to express $\hat{\beta}_1$:

$$\hat{\beta}_1 - \beta_1 = \frac{\sum_{i=1}^{n} (x_i - \bar{x})(Y_i - \bar{Y})}{\sum_{i=1}^{n} (x_i - \bar{x})^2} - \beta_1$$

$$= \frac{\sum_{i=1}^{n} (x_i - \bar{x})(Y_i - \bar{Y}) - \beta_1 \sum_{i=1}^{n} (x_i - \bar{x})^2}{\sum_{i=1}^{n} (x_i - \bar{x})^2}$$

$$= \frac{\sum_{i=1}^{n} (x_i - \bar{x})[(W_i - \bar{W}) + \beta_1(x_i - \bar{x})] - \beta_1 \sum_{i=1}^{n} (x_i - \bar{x})^2}{\sum_{i=1}^{n} (x_i - \bar{x})^2}$$

$$= \frac{\sum_{i=1}^{n} (x_i - \bar{x})(W_i - \bar{W})}{\sum_{i=1}^{n} (x_i - \bar{x})^2} \tag{11.A.2.1}$$

Recall from Equation 11.3.2 that

$$n\hat{\sigma}^2 = \sum_{i=1}^{n} (Y_i - \bar{Y})^2 - \hat{\beta}_1^2 \sum_{i=1}^{n} (x_i - \bar{x})^2 \tag{11.A.2.2}$$

We need to express Equation 11.A.2.2 in terms of the W_i's—that is,

$$n\hat{\sigma}^2 = \sum_{i=1}^{n} [(W_i - \bar{W}) + \beta_1(x_i - \bar{x})]^2 - \hat{\beta}_1^2 \sum_{i=1}^{n} (x_i - \bar{x})^2$$

$$= \sum_{i=1}^{n} (W_i - \bar{W})^2 + 2\beta_1 \sum_{i=1}^{n} (x_i - \bar{x})(W_i - \bar{W}) + \beta_1^2 \sum_{i=1}^{n} (x_i - \bar{x})^2$$

$$- \hat{\beta}_1^2 \sum_{i=1}^{n} (x_i - \bar{x})^2 \tag{11.A.2.3}$$

From Equation 11.A.2.1, we can write

$$\sum_{i=1}^{n} (x_i - \bar{x})(W_i - \bar{W}) = (\hat{\beta}_1 - \beta_1) \sum_{i=1}^{n} (x_i - \bar{x})^2$$

Substituting the right-hand side of the preceding expression for $\sum_{i=1}^{n} (x_i - \bar{x})(W_i - \bar{W})$ in Equation 11.A.2.3 gives

$$n\hat{\sigma}^2 = \sum_{i=1}^{n} (W_i - \bar{W})^2 + 2\beta_1(\hat{\beta}_1 - \beta_1) \sum_{i=1}^{n} (x_i - \bar{x})^2$$

$$+ \beta_1^2 \sum_{i=1}^{n} (x_i - \bar{x})^2 - \hat{\beta}_1^2 \sum_{i=1}^{n} (x_i - \bar{x})^2$$

$$= \sum_{i=1}^{n} (W_i - \bar{W})^2 + \sum_{i=1}^{n} (x_i - \bar{x})^2 [2\beta_1(\hat{\beta}_1 - \beta_1) + \beta_1^2 - \hat{\beta}_1^2]$$

$$= \sum_{i=1}^{n} (W_i - \bar{W})^2 - \sum_{i=1}^{n} (x_i - \bar{x})^2 [\hat{\beta}_1^2 - 2\hat{\beta}_1\beta_1 + \beta_1^2]$$

$$= \sum_{i=1}^{n} (W_i - \bar{W})^2 - \sum_{i=1}^{n} (x_i - \bar{x})^2 (\hat{\beta}_1 - \beta_1)^2$$

$$= \sum_{i=1}^{n} W_i^2 - n\bar{W}^2 - \sum_{i=1}^{n} (x_i - \bar{x})^2 (\hat{\beta}_1 - \beta_1)^2$$

Now, choose an orthogonal matrix, $\mathbf{M}$, whose first two rows are

$$\frac{x_1 - \bar{x}}{\sqrt{\sum_{i=1}^{n} (x_i - \bar{x})^2}} \cdots \frac{x_n - \bar{x}}{\sqrt{\sum_{i=1}^{n} (x_i - \bar{x})^2}}$$

and

$$\frac{1}{\sqrt{n}} \cdots \frac{1}{\sqrt{n}}$$

Define the random variables $Z_1, \ldots, Z_n$ through the transformation

$$\begin{pmatrix} Z_1 \\ \vdots \\ Z_n \end{pmatrix} = \mathbf{M} \begin{pmatrix} W_1 \\ \vdots \\ W_n \end{pmatrix}$$

By Fisher's lemma, the Z_i's are independent, normal random variables with mean 0 and variance σ^2, and

$$\sum_{i=1}^{n} Z_i^2 = \sum_{i=1}^{n} W_i^2$$

Also, by Equation 11.A.2.1 and the choice of the first row of $\mathbf{M}$,

$$Z_1^2 = \sum_{i=1}^{n} (x_i - \bar{x})^2 (\hat{\beta}_1 - \beta_1)^2$$

and, by the selection of the second row of **M**,

$$Z_2^2 = n\bar{W}^2$$

Thus,

$$n\hat{\sigma}^2 = \sum_{i=1}^{n} W_i^2 - Z_1^2 - Z_2^2 = \sum_{i=3}^{n} Z_i^2$$

From this follows the independence of $n\hat{\sigma}^2$, $\hat{\beta}_1$, and $\bar{Y}$.

Finally, notice that

$$\frac{n\hat{\sigma}^2}{\sigma^2} = \sum_{i=3}^{n} \left(\frac{Z_i}{\sigma} \right)^2$$

The fact that the sum has a chi-square distribution with $n - 2$ degrees of freedom proves the last part of the theorem.

CHAPTER 12

The Analysis of Variance

Ronald A. Fisher

"No aphorism is more frequently repeated in connection with field trials, than that we must ask Nature few questions or, ideally, one question, at a time. The writer is convinced that this view is wholly mistaken. Nature, he suggests, will best respond to a logical and carefully thought-out questionnaire; indeed, if we ask her a single question, she will often refuse to answer until some other topic has been discussed."

12.1 INTRODUCTION

In this chapter we take up an important extension of the two-sample location problem introduced in Chapter 9. The *completely randomized, one-factor design* is a conceptually similar k-sample location problem, but one that requires a substantially different sort of analysis than its prototype. Here, the appropriate test statistic turns out to be a ratio of variance estimates, the sampling behavior of which is described by an F distribution rather than a Student t. The name attached to this procedure, in deference to the form of its test statistic, is the *analysis of variance* (or "ANOVA," for short). A very flexible method, the analysis of variance finds many other applications, a particularly important one being the *randomized block design*, which is the subject of Chapter 13.

Comment. Credit for much of the early development of the analysis of variance goes to Sir Ronald A. Fisher. Shortly after the end of World War I, Fisher resigned a public school teaching position that he was none too happy with and accepted a post at the Rothamsted Statistical Laboratory, a facility heavily involved in agricultural research. There he suddenly found himself entangled in problems where differences in the response variable (crop yields, for example) were constantly in danger of being obscured by the high level of uncontrollable heterogeneity in the experimental environment (different soil qualities, drainage gradients, and so on). Quickly seeing that traditional techniques were hopelessly inadequate under these conditions, Fisher set out to look for alternatives and in just a few years succeeded in fashioning an entirely new statistical methodology, a panoply of data-collecting principles and mathematical tools that is today known as *experimental design*. The centerpiece of Fisher's creation—what makes it all work—is the analysis of variance.

Suppose an experimenter wishes to compare the average effects elicited by k different levels of some given factor, where k is greater than or equal to 2. The factor, for example, might be "stop-smoking" therapies and the levels, three specific methods. Or the factor might be crowdedness as it relates to aggression in captive monkeys, with the levels being five different monkey-per-square-foot densities in five separate enclosures. Still another example might be an engineering study comparing the effectiveness of four kinds of catalytic converters in reducing the concentrations of harmful emissions in automobile exhaust. Whatever the circumstances, data from a completely randomized, one-factor design will consist of k independent random samples of sizes $n_1, n_2, \ldots,$ and n_k, the total sample size being denoted $n\left(= \sum_{j=1}^{k} n_j\right)$.

We will let Y_{ij} represent the ith observation recorded for the jth level. Table 12.1.1 shows some additional notation.

The dot notation of Table 12.1.1 is standard in analysis-of-variance problems. The presence of a dot in lieu of a subscript indicates that that particular subscript has been summed over. Thus the response total for the jth sample is written

$$T_{.j} = \sum_{i=1}^{n_j} Y_{ij}$$

TABLE 12.1.1

	Factor Level			
	1	2	$\cdots$	k
	Y_{11}	Y_{12}		Y_{1k}
	Y_{21}	Y_{22}		
	$\vdots$	$\vdots$	$\cdots$	$\vdots$
	$Y_{n_1 1}$	$Y_{n_2 2}$		$Y_{n_k k}$
Sample sizes	n_1	n_2	$\cdots$	n_k
Sample totals	$T_{.1}$	$T_{.2}$		$T_{.k}$
Sample means	$\bar{Y}_{.1}$	$\bar{Y}_{.2}$		$\bar{Y}_{.k}$
True means	μ_1	μ_2		μ_k

and the corresponding sample mean,

$$\bar{Y}_{.j} = \frac{1}{n_j} \sum_{i=1}^{n_j} Y_{ij} = \frac{T_{.j}}{n_j}$$

By the same convention, $T_{..}$ and $\bar{Y}_{..}$ will denote the overall total and overall mean, respectively:

$$T_{..} = \sum_{j=1}^{k} \sum_{i=1}^{n_j} Y_{ij} = \sum_{j=1}^{k} T_{.j}$$

$$\bar{Y}_{..} = \frac{1}{n} \sum_{j=1}^{k} \sum_{i=1}^{n_j} Y_{ij} = \frac{1}{n} \sum_{j=1}^{k} n_j \bar{Y}_{.j} = \frac{1}{n} \sum_{j=1}^{k} T_{.j}$$

Appearing at the bottom of Table 12.1.1 are a set of "true means," $\mu_1, \mu_2, \ldots, \mu_k$. Each μ_j is an unknown location parameter reflecting the true average response characteristic of level j. Depending on the physical circumstances of the problem, our objective will be either to estimate the μ_j's or test their equality. The latter is perhaps the more common, and the test takes the form

$$H_0: \quad \mu_1 = \mu_2 = \cdots = \mu_k$$

versus

$$H_1: \quad \text{not all the } \mu_j \text{'s are equal}$$

In the next several sections we will propose a variance-ratio statistic for testing H_0, investigate its sampling behavior under both H_0 and H_1, and introduce a set of computing formulas to simplify its evaluation. We will also explore the possibility of testing more specific *subhypotheses* about the μ_j's—for example, their pairwise equality ($H_0: \mu_1 = \mu_2, H_0: \mu_1 = \mu_3$, and so on).

12.2 THE *F* TEST

To derive a procedure for testing $H_0: \mu_1 = \mu_2 = \cdots = \mu_k$ we could once again invoke the generalized-likelihood ratio criterion, compute $\lambda = L(\hat{\omega})/L(\hat{\Omega})$, and begin the search for a monotonic function of λ having a known distribution. But since we have already seen several examples of formal GLRT calculations in Chapters 7 and 9, the benefits of doing another would be minimal. Instead, we will deduce the test statistic on intuitive grounds and investigate its properties.

The data structure for a completely randomized one-factor design was outlined in Section 12.1. To that basic setup we now add a *distribution* assumption: The Y_{ij}'s will be presumed to be independent and normally distributed with mean μ_j, $j = 1, 2, \ldots, k$, and variance σ^2 (constant for all j)—that is,

$$f_{Y_{ij}}(y) = \frac{1}{\sqrt{2\pi}\sigma} e^{-\frac{1}{2}\left(\frac{y - \mu_j}{\sigma}\right)^2}, \quad -\infty < y < \infty$$

In analysis-of-variance problems—as was true in regression problems—distribution assumptions are usually expressed in terms of *model equations*. In the latter, the response variable is represented as the sum of one or more fixed components and one or more random components. Here, one possible model equation would be

$$Y_{ij} = \mu_j + \varepsilon_{ij}$$

where ε_{ij} denotes the "noise" associated with Y_{ij}—that is, the amount by which Y_{ij} differs from its expected value. Of course, from the distribution assumption on Y_{ij}, it follows that ε_{ij} is also normal with variance σ^2, but with mean 0.

We will denote the overall average effect associated with the n observations in the sample by the symbol μ, where $\mu = \frac{1}{n} \sum_{j=1}^{k} n_j \mu_j$. If H_0 is true, of course, μ is the value that each of the μ_j's equals.

Sums of Squares

To find an appropriate test statistic, we begin by estimating each of the μ_j's. For each $j, Y_{1j}, Y_{2j}, \ldots, Y_{n_j j}$ is a random sample from a normal distribution. By Theorem 7.2.1, the maximum-likelihood estimator of μ_j is $\bar{Y}_{.j}$. Moreover, $\frac{1}{n} \sum_{j=1}^{k} n_j \bar{Y}_{.j} = \bar{Y}_{..}$ is a good choice of an estimator for μ. It follows that

$$SSTR = \sum_{j=1}^{k} \sum_{i=1}^{n_j} (\bar{Y}_{.j} - \bar{Y}_{..})^2 = \sum_{j=1}^{k} n_j (\bar{Y}_{.j} - \bar{Y}_{..})^2$$

which is called the *treatment sum of squares*, estimates the variation among the μ_j's. (If all the μ_j's were equal, the $\bar{Y}_{.j}$'s would be similar and $SSTR$ would be small.)

Analyzing the behavior of $SSTR$ requires an expression relating the $\bar{Y}_{.j}$'s and $\bar{Y}_{..}$ to the parameter μ. But

$$SSTR = \sum_{j=1}^{k} n_j(\bar{Y}_{.j} - \bar{Y}_{..})^2 = \sum_{j=1}^{k} n_j[(\bar{Y}_{.j} - \mu) - (\bar{Y}_{..} - \mu)]^2$$

$$= \sum_{j=1}^{k} n_j[(\bar{Y}_{.j} - \mu)^2 + (\bar{Y}_{..} - \mu)^2 - 2(\bar{Y}_{.j} - \mu)(\bar{Y}_{..} - \mu)]$$

$$= \sum_{j=1}^{k} n_j(\bar{Y}_{.j} - \mu)^2 + \sum_{j=1}^{k} n_j(\bar{Y}_{..} - \mu)^2 - 2(\bar{Y}_{..} - \mu)\sum_{j=1}^{k} n_j(\bar{Y}_{.j} - \mu)$$

$$= \sum_{j=1}^{k} n_j(\bar{Y}_{.j} - \mu)^2 + n(\bar{Y}_{..} - \mu)^2 - 2(\bar{Y}_{..} - \mu)n(\bar{Y}_{..} - \mu)$$

$$= \sum_{j=1}^{k} n_j(\bar{Y}_{.j} - \mu)^2 - n(\bar{Y}_{..} - \mu)^2 \tag{12.2.1}$$

Now, with Equation 12.2.1 as background, Theorem 12.2.1 states the connection we are looking for—that the expected value of SSTR increases as the differences among the μ_j's increase.

THEOREM 12.2.1.   Let SSTR be the treatment sum of squares defined for k independent random samples of sizes $n_1, n_2, \ldots$, and n_k. Then

$$E(SSTR) = (k-1)\sigma^2 + \sum_{j=1}^{k} n_j(\mu_j - \mu)^2$$

Proof.   From Equation 12.2.1,

$$E(SSTR) = \sum_{j=1}^{k} n_j E[(\bar{Y}_{.j} - \mu)^2] - nE[(\bar{Y}_{..} - \mu)^2]$$

Since μ is the mean of $\bar{Y}_{..}$, then $E[(\bar{Y}_{..} - \mu)^2] = \sigma^2/n$. Also,

$$E[(\bar{Y}_{.j} - \mu)^2] = \text{Var}(\bar{Y}_{.j} - \mu) + [E(\bar{Y}_{.j} - \mu)]^2$$

by Theorem 3.12.1. But Theorem 3.13.1 implies that

$$\text{Var}(\bar{Y}_{.j} - \mu) = \text{Var}(\bar{Y}_{.j}) = \sigma^2/n_j$$

So, $E[(\bar{Y}_{.j} - \mu)^2] = \sigma^2/n_j + (\mu_j - \mu)^2$. Substituting these equalities in the expression for $E(SSTR)$ yields

$$E(SSTR) = \sum_{j=1}^{k} n_j \sigma^2/n_j + \sum_{j=1}^{k} n_j(\mu_j - \mu)^2 - n(\sigma^2/n)$$

or

$$E(SSTR) = (k-1)\sigma^2 + \sum_{j=1}^{k} n_j(\mu_j - \mu)^2$$

Testing H_0: $\mu_1 = \mu_2 = \cdots = \mu_k$ When σ^2 is Known

Theorem 12.2.1 suggests that SSTR can be the basis for a test of the null hypothesis that the treatment level means are all equal. When the μ_j's *are* the same, $E(SSTR) = (k-1)\sigma^2$. If the true means are not all equal, $E(SSTR)$ will be larger than $(k-1)\sigma^2$.

It follows that we should reject H_0 if $SSTR$ is "significantly large." Of course, to determine the exact location of the rejection region, for a given α, we need to know the pdf of $SSTR$, or some function of $SSTR$, when H_0 is true.

THEOREM 12.2.2.   When $H_0: \mu_1 = \mu_2 = \cdots = \mu_k$ is true, $SSTR/\sigma^2$ has a chi-square distribution with $k - 1$ degrees of freedom.

Proof.   The theorem can be proved directly at this point by an application of Fisher's lemma, similar to the approaches taken in Appendices 7.A.2 and 11.A.2. Rather than repeat those arguments, we will give a moment-generating-function derivation in Appendix 12.A.2.

If α, then, is the level of significance, *and if σ^2 is known*, we should reject $H_0: \mu_1 = \mu_2 = \cdots = \mu_k$ in favor of H_1: Not all the μ_j's are equal if $SSTR/\sigma^2 \geq \chi_{1-\alpha, k-1}$. In practice, though, comparing a set of μ_j's is seldom that easy because σ^2 is rarely known. Almost invariably, σ^2 needs to be estimated, and that changes both the nature and the distribution of the test statistic.

Testing $H_0: \mu_1 = \mu_2 = \cdots = \mu_k$ When σ^2 is Unknown

Each of the k samples provides an independent, unbiased estimator for σ^2: Specifically, the *jth sample variance* is given by

$$S_j^2 = \frac{1}{n_j - 1} \sum_{i=1}^{n_j} \left(Y_{ij} - \bar{Y}_{.j}\right)^2$$

Multiplying each S_j^2 by $n_j - 1$ and summing over j gives the numerator of the obvious "pooled" estimator for σ^2 (recall the way S_p^2 was defined in the two-sample t test). We call this quantity the *error sum of squares*, or SSE:

$$SSE = \sum_{j=1}^{k} \left(n_j - 1\right)S_j^2 = \sum_{j=1}^{k} \sum_{i=1}^{n_j} \left(Y_{ij} - \bar{Y}_{.j}\right)^2$$

THEOREM 12.2.3.   Whether or not $H_0: \mu_1 = \mu_2 = \cdots = \mu_k$ is true,

(1) SSE/σ^2 has a chi-square distribution with $n - k$ degrees of freedom.
(2) SSE and $SSTR$ are independent.

Proof.   By Theorem 7.3.3, $\left(n_j - 1\right)S_j^2/\sigma^2$ has a chi-square distribution with $n_j - 1$ degrees of freedom. By the addition property, then, of the chi-square distribution, SSE/σ^2 is a chi-square random variable with $\sum_{j=1}^{k} \left(n_j - 1\right) = n - k$ degrees of freedom.

Each S_j^2 is independent of $\bar{Y}_{.i}$ for $i \neq j$ because the underlying samples are independent. Also, each S_j^2 is independent of $\bar{Y}_{.j}$ by Theorem 7.A.2.1. Therefore, SSE and $SSTR$ are independent.

If we ignore the treatments and consider the data as one sample, then the variation about the parameter μ is estimated by the familiar $\sum_{j=1}^{k} \sum_{i=1}^{n_j} \left(Y_{ij} - \bar{Y}_{..}\right)^2$. This quantity is known as the *total sum of squares* and denoted $SSTOT$.

THEOREM 12.2.4. If n observations are divided into k samples of sizes $n_1, n_2, \ldots,$ and n_k,

$$SSTOT = SSTR + SSE$$

Proof.

$$SSTOT = \sum_{j=1}^{k} \sum_{i=1}^{n_j} \left(Y_{ij} - \bar{Y}_{..}\right)^2 = \sum_{j=1}^{k} \sum_{i=1}^{n_j} \left[(\bar{Y}_{.j} - \bar{Y}_{..}) + (Y_{ij} - \bar{Y}_{.j})\right]^2 \quad (12.2.2)$$

Expanding the right-hand side of Equation 12.2.2 gives

$$\sum_{j=1}^{k} \sum_{i=1}^{n_j} \left(\bar{Y}_{.j} - \bar{Y}_{..}\right)^2 + \sum_{j=1}^{k} \sum_{i=1}^{n_j} \left(Y_{ij} - \bar{Y}_{.j}\right)^2$$

since the cross-product term vanishes:

$$\sum_{j=1}^{k} \sum_{i=1}^{n_j} \left(\bar{Y}_{.j} - \bar{Y}_{..}\right)(Y_{ij} - \bar{Y}_{.j}) = \sum_{j=1}^{k} \left(\bar{Y}_{.j} - \bar{Y}_{..}\right) \sum_{i=1}^{n_j} \left(Y_{ij} - \bar{Y}_{.j}\right)$$

$$= \sum_{j=1}^{k} \left(\bar{Y}_{.j} - \bar{Y}_{..}\right)(0) = 0$$

Therefore,

$$\sum_{j=1}^{k} \sum_{i=1}^{n_j} \left(Y_{ij} - \bar{Y}_{..}\right)^2 = \sum_{j=1}^{k} \sum_{i=1}^{n_j} \left(\bar{Y}_{.j} - \bar{Y}_{..}\right)^2 + \sum_{j=1}^{k} \sum_{i=1}^{n_j} \left(Y_{ij} - \bar{Y}_{.j}\right)^2$$

That is, $SSTOT = SSTR + SSE$.

THEOREM 12.2.5. Suppose that each observation in a set of k independent random samples is normally distributed with the same variance σ^2. Let $\mu_1, \mu_2, \ldots,$ and μ_k be the true means associated with the k samples. Then

(a) If $H_0: \mu_1 = \mu_2 = \cdots = \mu_k$ is true,

$$F = \frac{SSTR/(k-1)}{SSE/(n-k)}$$

has an F distribution with $k - 1$ and $n - k$ degrees of freedom.

(b) At the α level of significance, $H_0: \mu_1 = \mu_2 = \cdots = \mu_k$ should be rejected if $F \geq F_{1-\alpha, k-1, n-k}$.

Proof. By Theorem 12.2.3, $SSTR$ and SSE are independent. We also know that $SSTR/\sigma^2$ and SSE/σ^2 are chi-square random variables. Part (a), then, follows from the definition of the F distribution.

To justify the location of the critical region cited in Part (b), we need to examine the behavior of the proposed test statistic when H_1 is true. From Theorem 12.2.1, we know the expected value of the numerator of F:

$$E\left(SSTR/(k-1)\right) = \sigma^2 + \frac{1}{k-1} \sum_{j=1}^{k} (\mu_j - \mu)^2 \quad (12.2.3)$$

Moreover, from Theorem 12.2.3, it follows that the expected value of the denominator of the test statistic—that is, $E(SSE/(n - k))$—is σ^2, regardless of which hypothesis is true.

Now, if H_0 is true, the expected values of both the numerator and the denominator of F will be σ^2, so the ratio is likely to be close to 1. If H_1 is true, though, the expected value of $SSTR/(k - 1)$ will be greater than the expected value of $SSE/(n - k)$, implying that the observed F ratio will tend to be larger than 1. The critical region, therefore, should be in the right-hand tail of the $F_{k-1,n-k}$ distribution. That is, we should reject $H_0\colon \mu_1 = \mu_2 = \cdots = \mu_k$ if

$$F = \frac{SSTR/(k - 1)}{SSE/(n - k)} \geq F_{1-\alpha, k-1, n-k}.$$

ANOVA Tables

The numerical information necessary to calculate an F statistic is often displayed in an *ANOVA table*. Figure 12.2.1 shows the structure of the ANOVA table that corresponds to the F test described in Theorem 12.2.5.

The *MS*, or *mean square*, column is obtained by dividing a sum of squares by its degrees of freedom. The *mean square for treatments*, then, is given by

$$MSTR = \frac{SSTR}{k - 1}$$

and the *mean square for error* becomes

$$MSE = \frac{SSE}{n - k}$$

The entry in the top row of the F column is the value of the test statistic:

$$F = \frac{MSTR}{MSE} = \frac{SSTR/(k - 1)}{SSE/(n - k)}$$

The final entry, also in the top row, is the P-value associated with the observed F. If $P < \alpha$, of course, we can reject $H_0\colon \mu_1 = \mu_2 = \cdots = \mu_k$ at the α level of significance.

Source	df	SS	MS	F	P
Treatment	$k - 1$	SSTR	MSTR	$\dfrac{\text{MSTR}}{\text{MSE}}$	$P(F_{k-1, n-k} \geq \text{observed } F)$
Error	$n - k$	SSE	MSE		
Total	$n - 1$	SSTOT			

FIGURE 12.2.1

CASE STUDY 12.2.1

Generations of athletes have been cautioned that cigarette smoking retards performance. One measure of the truth of that warning is the effect of smoking on heart rate. In one study (65) to examine that impact, six each of nonsmokers, light smokers, moderate smokers, and heavy smokers undertook sustained physical exercise. Their heart rates were measured after resting for three minutes. The results appear in Table 12.2.1. Are the differences among the $\bar{y}_{.j}$'s statistically significant? That is, if μ_1, μ_2, μ_3 and μ_4 denote the *true* average heart rates for the four groups of smokers, can we reject $H_0: \mu_1 = \mu_2 = \mu_3 = \mu_4$?

Let $\alpha = 0.05$. For these data, $k = 4$ and $n = 24$, so $H_0: \mu_1 = \mu_2 = \mu_3 = \mu_4$ should be rejected if

$$F = \frac{SSTR/(4-1)}{SSE/(24-4)} \geq F_{1-0.05,\,4-1,\,24-4} = F_{.95,\,3,\,20} = 3.10$$

(see Figure 12.2.2).

The overall sample mean, $\bar{y}_{..}$, is given by

$$\bar{y}_{..} = \frac{1}{n}\sum_{j=1}^{k} t_{.j} = \frac{374 + 379 + 430 + 490}{24}$$

$$= 69.7$$

Therefore,

$$SSTR = \sum_{j=1}^{4} n_j(\bar{y}_{.j} - \bar{y}_{..})^2 = 6\left[(62.3 - 69.7)^2 + \cdots + (81.7 - 69.7)^2\right]$$

$$= 1464.125$$

TABLE 12.2.1

	Non-Smokers	Light Smokers	Moderate Smokers	Heavy Smokers
	69	55	66	91
	52	60	81	72
	71	78	70	81
	58	58	77	67
	59	62	57	95
	65	66	79	84
$t_{.j}$	374	379	430	490
$\bar{y}_{.j}$	62.3	63.2	71.7	81.7

FIGURE 12.2.2

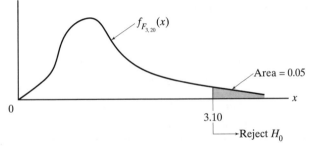

(continued on next page)

(Case Study 12.2.1 continued)

Similarly,

$$SSE = \sum_{j=1}^{4} \sum_{i=1}^{6} (y_{ij} - \bar{y}_{.j})^2 = \left[(69 - 62.3)^2 + \cdots + (65 - 62.3)^2 \right]$$

$$+ \cdots + \left[(91 - 81.7)^2 + \cdots + (84 - 81.7)^2 \right]$$

$$= 1594.833$$

The observed test statistic, then, equals *6.12*:

$$F = \frac{1464.125/(4 - 1)}{1594.833/(24 - 4)} = 6.12$$

Since $6.12 > F_{.95,3,20} = 3.10$, $H_0: \mu_1 = \mu_2 = \mu_3 = \mu_4$ should be rejected. These data support the contention that smoking influences a person's heart rate.

Figure 12.2.3 shows the analysis of these data summarized in the ANOVA table format. Notice that the small *P*-value (0.004) is consistent with the conclusion that H_0 should be rejected.

Source	df	SS	MS	F	P
Treatment	3	1464.125	488.04	6.12	0.004
Error	20	1594.833	79.74		
Total	23	3058.958			

FIGURE 12.2.3

Computing Formulas

There are easier ways to compute an *F* statistic than by using the "defining" formulas for *SSTR* and *SSE*. Let $C = T_{..}^2/n$. Then

$$SSTOT = \sum_{j=1}^{k} \sum_{i=1}^{n_j} Y_{ij}^2 - C \tag{12.2.4}$$

$$SSTR = \sum_{j=1}^{k} \frac{T_{.j}^2}{n_j} - C \tag{12.2.5}$$

and, from Theorem 12.2.4,

$$SSE = SSTOT - SSTR$$

(The proofs of Equations 12.2.4 and 12.2.5 are left as exercises.)

QUESTIONS

12.2.1 The following are the gas mileages recorded during a series of road tests on four new models of Japanese luxury sedans. Test the null hypthesis that all four models, on the average, give the same mileage. Let $\alpha = 0.05$. Will the conclusion change if $\alpha = 0.10$?

Model			
A	B	C	D
22	28	29	23
26	24	32	24
	29	28	

12.2.2 Mount Etna erupted in 1669, 1780, and 1865. When the molten lava hardens, it retains the direction of the Earth's magnetic field. Three blocks of lava were examined from each of these eruptions and the declination of the magnetic field in the block was measured (160). The results are given in the following table. Do these data suggest that the direction of the Earth's magnetic field shifted over the time period spanned by the eruptions? Let $\alpha = 0.05$.

1669	1780	1865
57.8	57.9	52.7
60.2	55.2	53.0
60.3	54.8	49.4

12.2.3 An indicator of the value of a stock relative to its earnings is its *price-earnings ratio*: the average of a given year's high and low selling prices divided by its annual earnings. The following table provides the price-earnings ratios for a sample of 30 stocks, 10 each from the financial, industrial, and utility sectors of the New York Stock Exchange. Test at the 0.01 level that the true mean price-earnings ratios for the three market sectors are the same. Use the computing formulas on page 642 to find *SSTR* and *SSE*. Use the ANOVA table format to summarize the computations; omit the *P*-value column.

Financial	Industrial	Utility
7.1	26.2	14.0
9.9	12.4	15.5
8.8	15.2	11.9
8.8	28.6	10.9
20.6	10.3	14.3
7.9	9.7	11.0
18.8	12.5	9.7
17.7	16.7	10.8
15.2	19.7	16.0
6.6	24.8	11.3

12.2.4 Each of five varieties of corn are planted in three plots in a large field. The respective yields, in bushels per acre, are in the following table.

Variety 1	Variety 2	Variety 3	Variety 4	Variety 5
46.2	49.2	60.3	48.9	52.5
51.9	58.6	58.7	51.4	54.0
48.7	57.4	60.4	44.6	49.3

Test whether the differences among the average yields are statistically significant. Show the ANOVA table. Let 0.05 be the level of significance.

12.2.5 Three pottery shards from four widely scattered and now extinct Native American tribes have been collected by a museum. Archaeologists are asked to estimate the age of the shards. Based on the results shown in the following table, is it conceivable that the four tribes were contemporaries of one another? Let $\alpha = 0.01$.

	Estimated Ages of Shards (years)		
Lakeside	Deep Gorge	Willow Ridge	Azalea Hill
1200	850	1800	950
800	900	1450	1200
950	1100	1150	1150

12.2.6 Fill in the entries missing from the following ANOVA table.

Source	df	SS	MS	F
Treatment	4			6.40
Errors			10.60	
Total		377.36		

12.2.7 Do the following data appear to violate the assumptions underlying the analysis of variance? Explain.

	Treatment		
A	B	C	D
16	4	26	8
17	12	22	9
16	2	23	11
17	26	24	8

12.2.8 Prove Equations 12.2.4 and 12.2.5.

12.2.9 Use Fisher's lemma to prove Theorem 12.2.2.

Comparing the Two-Sample *t* Test with the Analysis of Variance

The analysis of variance was introduced in Section 12.1 as a k-sample *extension* of the two-sample test. The two procedures overlap, though, when k is equal to 2. An obvious question arises: Which procedure is better for testing $H_0: \mu_X = \mu_Y$? The answer, as Example 12.2.1 shows, is "neither." The two test procedures are entirely equivalent: If one rejects H_0, so will the other.

EXAMPLE 12.2.1

Suppose that $X_1, X_2, \ldots, X_n$ and $Y_1, Y_2, \ldots, Y_m$ are two sets of independent, normally distributed random variables with the same variance, σ^2. Let μ_X and μ_Y denote their respective means. Show that the two-sample t test and the analysis of variance are equivalent for testing $H_0: \mu_X = \mu_Y$.

If H_0 were tested using the analysis of variance, the observed F ratio would be

$$F = \frac{SSTR/(k-1)}{SSE/(n+m-k)} = \frac{SSTR}{SSE/(n+m-2)} \tag{12.2.6}$$

and it would have 1 and $n + m - 2$ degrees of freedom. The null hypothesis would be rejected if $F \geq F_{1-\alpha,1,n+m-2}$.

To compare the ANOVA decision rule with a two-sample t test requires that $SSTR$ and SSE be expressed in the "X and Y" notation of t ratios. First, note that

$$SSTR = n_1(\bar{Y}_{.1} - \bar{Y}_{..})^2 + n_2(\bar{Y}_{.2} - \bar{Y}_{..})^2$$
$$= n(\bar{X} - \bar{Y}_{..})^2 + m(\bar{Y} - \bar{Y}_{..})^2$$

In this case, $\bar{Y}_{..} = \dfrac{1}{n + m}(n\bar{X} + m\bar{Y})$, so

$$SSTR = n\left[\bar{X} - \frac{1}{n + m}(n\bar{X} + m\bar{Y})\right]^2 + m\left[\bar{Y} - \frac{1}{n + m}(n\bar{X} + m\bar{Y})\right]^2$$
$$= n\left[\frac{m(\bar{X} - \bar{Y})}{n + m}\right]^2 + m\left[\frac{n(\bar{X} - \bar{Y})}{n + m}\right]^2$$
$$= \left[\frac{nm^2}{(n + m)^2} + \frac{mn^2}{(n + m)^2}\right](\bar{X} - \bar{Y})^2$$
$$= \frac{nm}{n + m}(\bar{X} - \bar{Y})^2$$

Also,

$$SSE = (n_1 - 1)S_1^2 + (n_2 - 1)S_2^2$$
$$= (n - 1)S_X^2 + (m - 1)S_Y^2$$
$$= (n + m - 2)S_P^2$$

Substituting these expressions for $SSTR$ and SSE in the F statistic of Equation 12.2.6 yields

$$F = \frac{\dfrac{nm}{n + m}(\bar{X} - \bar{Y})^2}{\dfrac{(n + m - 2)S_P^2}{(n + m - 2)}} = \frac{\dfrac{nm}{n + m}(\bar{X} - \bar{Y})^2}{S_P^2} = \frac{(\bar{X} - \bar{Y})^2}{S_P^2\left(\dfrac{1}{n} + \dfrac{1}{m}\right)} \qquad (12.2.7)$$

Notice that the right-hand expression in Equation 12.2.7 is the square of the two-sample t statistic described in Theorem 9.2.1. Moreover,

$$\alpha = P(T \leq -t_{\alpha/2, n+m-2} \quad \text{or} \quad T \geq t_{\alpha/2, n+m-2}) = P(T^2 \geq t_{\alpha/2, n+m-2}^2)$$
$$= P(F_{1, n+m-2} \geq t_{\alpha/2, n+m-2}^2)$$

But the unique value c such that $P(F_{1,n+m-2} \geq c) = \alpha$ is $c = F_{1-\alpha,1,n+m-2}$, so $F_{1-\alpha,1,n+m-2} = t_{\alpha/2, n+m-2}^2$. Thus,

$$\alpha = P(T \leq -t_{\alpha/2, n+m-2} \quad \text{or} \quad T \geq t_{\alpha/2, n+m-2}) = P(F \geq F_{1-\alpha, 1, n+m-2})$$

It follows that if one test statistic rejects H_0 at the α level of significance, so will the other.

QUESTIONS

12.2.10 Verify the conclusion of Example 12.2.1 by doing a t test and an analysis of variance on the data of Question 9.2.4. Show that the observed F ratio is the square of the observed t ratio and that the F critical value is the square of the t critical value.

12.2.11 Do an analysis of variance on the Mark Twain–Quintus Curtius Snodgrass data of Case Study 9.2.1. Verify that the observed F ratio is the square of the observed t ratio.

12.3 MULTIPLE COMPARISONS: TUKEY'S METHOD

The suspicion that smoking affects heart rates was borne out by the analysis done in Case Study 12.2.1. In retrospect, the fact that $H_0: \mu_1 = \mu_2 = \mu_3 = \mu_4$ was rejected is not surprising, given the sizeable range in the $\bar{y}_{.j}$'s (from 62.3 for nonsmokers to 81.7 for heavy smokers). But not all the treatment groups were far apart: The heart rates for nonsmokers and light smokers were fairly close—62.3 versus 63.2. That raises an obvious question: Is there some way to follow up an initial test of $H_0: \mu_1 = \mu_2 = \cdots = \mu_k$ by looking at *subhypotheses*—that is, can we test hypotheses that involve fewer than the full set of population means (for example, $H_0: \mu_1 = \mu_2$)?

The answer is "yes," but the solution is not as simple as it might appear to be at first glance. In particular, it would be inappropriate to do a series of standard two-sample t tests on different pairs of means—for example, apply Theorem 9.2.1 to μ_1 versus μ_2, then to μ_2 versus μ_3, and so on. If each of those tests was done at a certain level of significance α, the probability that *at least one* Type I error would be committed would be much larger than α. That being the case, the "nominal" value for α misrepresents the collective precision of the inferences.

Suppose, for example, we did 10 independent tests of the form $H_0: \mu_i = \mu_j$ versus $H_1: \mu_i \neq \mu_j$, each at level $\alpha = 0.05$, on a large set of population means. Even though the probability of making a Type I error on any given test is only 0.05, the chances of incorrectly rejecting a true H_0 with at least one of the 10 t tests increases dramatically to *0.40*:

$$P(\text{at least one Type I error}) = 1 - P(\text{no Type I errors})$$

$$= 1 - (0.95)^{10}$$

$$= 0.40$$

Addressing that concern, mathematical statisticians have paid a good deal of attention to the so-called *multiple comparison problem*. Many different procedures, operating under various sets of assumptions, have been developed. All have the objective of keeping the probability of committing at least one Type I error small, even when the number of tests performed is large (or even infinite). In this section, we develop one of the earliest of these techniques, a still widely used method due to John Tukey.

A Background Result: The Studentized Range Distribution

The simplest multiple-comparison problem is to test the equality of pairs of individual means—that is, to test with one procedure $H_0: \mu_i = \mu_j$ versus $H_1: \mu_i \neq \mu_j$ *for all* $i \neq j$. In Tukey's method, these tests are performed using confidence intervals for $\mu_i - \mu_j$. The derivation depends on knowing the probabilistic behavior of the ratio $\dfrac{R}{S}$, where R is the range of a set of normally distributed random variables and S is their estimated standard deviation. (Although Tukey's method can be generalized, we will apply it only in situations where each of the k sample means is based on the same number of observations.)

DEFINITION 12.3.1. Let $W_1, W_2, \ldots,$ and W_k be a set of k independent, normally distributed random variables with mean μ and variance σ^2, and let R denote their range:

$$R = \max_i W_i - \min_i W_i$$

Suppose S^2 is based on a chi-square random variable with v degrees of freedom, independent of the W_i's, where $E(S^2) = \sigma^2$. The *studentized range*, $Q_{k,v}$, is the ratio

$$Q_{k,v} = \frac{R}{S}$$

Table A.5 in the Appendix gives values of $Q_{\alpha,k,v}$, the $100(1 - \alpha)$th percentile of $Q_{k,v}$, for $\alpha = 0.05$ and 0.01, and for various values of k and v. For example, if $k = 4$ and $v = 8$, $Q_{.05,4,8} = 4.53$, meaning that $P\left(\dfrac{R}{S} \geq 4.53\right) = 0.05$, where R is the range of four normally distributed random variables whose standard deviation, S, is estimated with eight degrees of freedom (see Figure 12.3.1).

For the applications of the Studentized range that we will deal with, S^2 will be MSE and v will be $n - k$.

FIGURE 12.3.1

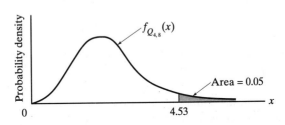

THEOREM 12.3.1. Let $\bar{y}_{.j}, j = 1, 2, \ldots, k$ be the k sample means in a completely randomized, one-factor design. Let $n_j = r$ be the common sample size, and let μ_j be the true means, $j = 1, 2, \ldots, k$. The probability is $1 - \alpha$ that all $\binom{k}{2}$ differences $\mu_i - \mu_j$ will simultaneously satisfy the inequalities

$$\bar{y}_{.i} - \bar{y}_{.j} - D\sqrt{MSE} < \mu_i - \mu_j < \bar{y}_{.i} - \bar{y}_{.j} + D\sqrt{MSE}$$

where $D = Q_{\alpha,k,rk-k}/\sqrt{r}$. If, for a given i and j, zero is not contained in the preceding inequality, $H_0: \mu_i = \mu_j$ can be rejected in favor of $H_1: \mu_i \neq \mu_j$, at the α level of significance.

Proof. Let $W_t = \bar{Y}_{.t} - \mu_t$. Then W_t is normally distributed with mean 0 and variance σ^2/r. Let max W_t and min W_t denote the maximum and minimum values, respectively, for W_t, where t ranges from 1 to k.

Take MSE/r to be the estimator for σ^2/r. From the definition of the studentized range, $\dfrac{\max W_t - \min W_t}{\sqrt{\dfrac{MSE}{r}}}$ has a $Q_{k,rk-k}$ density, which implies that

$$P\left(\frac{\max W_t - \min W_t}{\sqrt{\dfrac{MSE}{r}}} < Q_{\alpha,\,k,\,rk-k}\right) = 1 - \alpha$$

or, equivalently,

$$P(\max W_t - \min W_t < D\sqrt{MSE}) = 1 - \alpha \qquad (12.3.1)$$

where $D = Q_{\alpha,\,k,\,rk-k}/\sqrt{r}$.

Now, if Equation 12.3.1 is true, it must also be true that

$$P(|W_i - W_j| < D\sqrt{MSE}) = 1 - \alpha \quad \text{for } all \ i \text{ and } j \qquad (12.3.2)$$

Rewriting Equation 12.3.2 gives

$$P(-D\sqrt{MSE} < W_i - W_j < D\sqrt{MSE}) = 1 - \alpha \quad \text{for } all \ i \text{ and } j \qquad (12.3.3)$$

Recall that $W_t = \bar{Y}_{.t} - \mu_t$. Substituting the latter for W_i and W_j in Equation 12.3.3 yields the statement of the theorem:

$$P(\bar{Y}_{.i} - \bar{Y}_{.j} - D\sqrt{MSE} < \mu_i - \mu_j < \bar{Y}_{.i} - \bar{Y}_{.j} + D\sqrt{MSE}) = 1 - \alpha$$

for all i and j.

CASE STUDY 12.3.1

A certain fraction of antibiotics injected into the bloodstream are "bound" to serum proteins. This phenomenon bears directly on the effectiveness of the medication, because the binding decreases the systemic uptake of the drug. Table 12.3.1 lists the binding percentages in bovine serum measured for five widely prescribed antibiotics (201). Which antibiotics have similar binding properties, and which are different?

TABLE 12.3.1

	Penicillin G	Tetra-cycline	Strepto-mycin	Erythro-mycin	Chloram-phenicol
	29.6	27.3	5.8	21.6	29.2
	24.3	32.6	6.2	17.4	32.8
	28.5	30.8	11.0	18.3	25.0
	32.0	34.8	8.3	19.0	24.2
$t_{.j}$	114.4	125.5	31.3	76.3	111.2
$\bar{y}_{.j}$	28.6	31.4	7.8	19.1	27.8

To answer that question requires that we make all $\binom{5}{2} = 10$ pairwise comparisons of μ_i versus μ_j. First, MSE must be computed. From the entries in Table 12.3.1,

$$SSE = \sum_{j=1}^{5} \sum_{i=1}^{4} (y_{ij} - \bar{y}_{.j})^2 = 135.83$$

so $MSE = 135.83/(20 - 5) = 9.06$. Let $\alpha = 0.05$. Since $n - k = 20 - 5 = 15$, the appropriate cutoff from the studentized range distribution is $Q_{.05,5,15} = 4.37$. Therefore, $D = 4.37/\sqrt{4} = 2.185$ and $D\sqrt{MSE} = 6.58$.

For each different pairwise subhypothesis test, $H_0: \mu_i = \mu_j$ versus $H_1: \mu_i \neq \mu_j$, Table 12.3.2 lists the value of $\bar{y}_{.i} - \bar{y}_{.j}$, together with the corresponding 95% Tukey confidence interval for $\mu_i - \mu_j$ calculated from Theorem 12.3.1. As the last column indicates, seven of the subhypotheses are rejected (those whose Tukey intervals do not contain 0) and three are accepted.

TABLE 12.3.2

Pairwise Difference	$\bar{y}_{.i} - \bar{y}_{.j}$	Tukey Interval	Conclusion
$\mu_1 - \mu_2$	−2.8	(−9.38, 3.78)	NS
$\mu_1 - \mu_3$	20.8	(14.22, 27.38)	Reject
$\mu_1 - \mu_4$	9.5	(2.92, 16.08)	Reject
$\mu_1 - \mu_5$	0.8	(−5.78, 7.38)	NS
$\mu_2 - \mu_3$	23.6	(17.02, 30.18)	Reject
$\mu_2 - \mu_4$	12.3	(5.72, 18.88)	Reject
$\mu_2 - \mu_5$	3.6	(−2.98, 10.18)	NS
$\mu_3 - \mu_4$	−11.3	(−17.88, −4.72)	Reject
$\mu_3 - \mu_5$	−20.0	(−26.58, −13.42)	Reject
$\mu_4 - \mu_5$	−8.7	(−15.28, −2.12)	Reject

QUESTIONS

12.3.1 Use Tukey's method to make all the pairwise comparisons for the heart rate data of Case Study 12.2.1 at the 0.05 level of significance.

12.3.2 Construct 95% Tukey intervals for the three pairwise differences, $\mu_i - \mu_j$, for the data of Question 12.2.3.

12.3.3 Intravenous infusion fluids produced by three different pharmaceutical companies (Cutter, Abbott, and McGaw) were tested for their concentrations of particulate contaminants. Six samples were inspected from each company. The figures listed in the table are, for each sample, the number of particles per liter greater than 5 microns in diameter (171).

Number of Contaminant Particles		
Cutter	Abbott	McGaw
255	105	577
264	288	515
342	98	214
331	275	413
234	221	401
217	240	260

Do the analysis of variance to test $H_0: \mu_C = \mu_A = \mu_M$ and then test each of the three pairwise subhypotheses by constructing 95% Tukey intervals.

12.3.4 Construct 95% Tukey intervals for all 10 pairwise differences, $\mu_i - \mu_j$, for the data of Question 12.2.4. Summarize the results by plotting the five sample averages on a horizontal axis and drawing straight lines under varieties whose average yields are not significantly different.

12.3.5 If 95% Tukey confidence intervals tell us to reject $H_0: \mu_1 = \mu_2$ and $H_0: \mu_1 = \mu_3$, will we necessarily reject $H_0: \mu_2 = \mu_3$?

12.3.6 The width of a Tukey confidence interval is

$$2\sqrt{MSE}\,Q_{\alpha,\,k,\,n-k}\Big/\sqrt{\frac{n}{k}}$$

If k increases, but n/k and MSE stay the same, will the Tukey intervals get shorter or longer? Justify your answer intuitively.

12.4 TESTING SUBHYPOTHESES WITH ORTHOGONAL CONTRASTS

There are two general ways to test a subhypothesis, the choice depending, strangely enough, on *when H_0 can be fully specified*. If a researcher wishes to do an experiment first, and then let the results suggest a suitable subhypothesis, the appropriate analysis is any of the various multiple comparison techniques—for example, the Tukey method of Section 12.3.

If, on the other hand, physical considerations, economic factors, past experience, or any other factors suggest a particular subhypothesis *before any data are taken*, H_0 can best be tested using an *orthogonal contrast*. When they are appropriate, orthogonal contrasts provide greater power than do their multiple-comparison counterparts.

> **DEFINITION 12.4.1.** Let $\mu_1, \mu_2, \ldots, \mu_k$ denote the true means of k factor levels being sampled. A linear combination, C, of the μ_j's is said to be a *contrast* if the sum of its coefficients is zero. That is, C is a contrast if $C = \sum_{j=1}^{k} c_j \mu_j$, where the c_j's are constants such that $\sum_{j=1}^{k} c_j = 0$.

Contrasts have a direct connection with hypothesis tests. Suppose a set of data consists of five treatment levels, and we wish to test the subhypothesis $H_0: \mu_1 = \mu_2$. The latter could also be written $H_0: \mu_1 - \mu_2 = 0$, which is actually a statement about a contrast—specifically, the contrast C, where

$$C = \mu_1 - \mu_2 = (1)\mu_1 + (-1)\mu_2 + (0)\mu_3 + (0)\mu_4 + (0)\mu_5$$

As another example, suppose in Case Study 12.3.1 that there was a valid pharmacological reason for comparing the average level of serum binding for the first two antibiotics to the average level for the last three. Written as a subhypothesis, the statement of no difference would be

$$H_0: \frac{\mu_1 + \mu_2}{2} = \frac{\mu_3 + \mu_4 + \mu_5}{3}$$

As a contrast, it becomes

$$C = \frac{1}{2}\mu_1 + \frac{1}{2}\mu_2 - \frac{1}{3}\mu_3 - \frac{1}{3}\mu_4 - \frac{1}{3}\mu_5$$

In both these cases, the numerical value of the contrast will be 0 if H_0 is true. This suggests that the choice between H_0 and H_1 can be accomplished by first estimating C and then determining, via a significance test, whether that estimate is too far from 0.

We begin by considering some of the mathematical properties of contrasts and their estimates. Since $\bar{Y}_{.j}$ is always an unbiased estimator for μ_j, it seems reasonable to estimate C, a linear combination of population means, with $\hat{C}$, a linear combination of *sample* means:

$$\hat{C} = \sum_{j=1}^{k} c_j \bar{Y}_{.j}$$

(The coefficients appearing in $\hat{C}$, of course, are the same as those that defined C.) It follows that

$$E(\hat{C}) = \sum_{j=1}^{k} c_j E(\bar{Y}_{.j}) = C$$

and

$$\text{Var}(\hat{C}) = \sum_{j=1}^{k} c_j^2 \text{Var}(\bar{Y}_{.j}) = \sigma^2 \sum_{j=1}^{k} \frac{c_j^2}{n_j}$$

Comment. Replacing the unknown error variance, σ^2, by its estimate from the ANOVA table—*MSE*—gives a formula for the estimated variance of the estimated contrast:

$$S_{\hat{C}}^2 = \widehat{\text{Var}(\hat{C})} = MSE \sum_{j=1}^{k} \frac{c_j^2}{n_j}$$

The sampling behavior of $\hat{C}$ is easily derived. By Theorem 4.3.4, the normality of the Y_{ij}'s ensures that $\hat{C}$ is also normal, and by the usual Z transformation, the ratio

$$\frac{\hat{C} - E(\hat{C})}{\sqrt{\text{Var}(\hat{C})}} = \frac{\hat{C} - C}{\sqrt{\text{Var}(\hat{C})}}$$

is a *standard* normal. Therefore,

$$\left[\frac{\hat{C} - C}{\sqrt{\text{Var}(\hat{C})}}\right]^2$$

is a chi-square random variable with 1 degree of freedom. Of course, if $H_0: \mu_1 = \mu_2 = \cdots = \mu_k$ is true, C is 0, and the ratio reduces to

$$\frac{\hat{C}^2}{\sigma^2 \sum_{j=1}^{k} \frac{c_j^2}{n_j}}$$

One final property of contrasts plays a role in the significance testing of sub-hypotheses. Two contrasts,

$$C_1 = \sum_{j=1}^{k} c_{1j}\mu_j \quad \text{and} \quad C_2 = \sum_{j=1}^{k} c_{2j}\mu_j$$

are said to be *orthogonal* if

$$\sum_{j=1}^{k} \frac{c_{1j}c_{2j}}{n_j} = 0$$

Similarly, a set of q contrasts, $\{C_i\}_{i=1}^{q}$, are said to be *mutually orthogonal* if

$$\sum_{j=1}^{k} \frac{c_{sj}c_{tj}}{n_j} = 0 \quad \text{for all } s \ne t$$

(The same definitions apply, of course, to *estimated* contrasts.)

Definition 12.4.2 and Theorems 12.4.1 and 12.4.2, both stated here without proof, summarize the relationship between contrasts and the analysis of variance. In short, the treatment sum of squares can be partitioned into $k - 1$ "contrast" sums of squares, provided the contrasts are mutually orthogonal. These $k - 1$ sums of squares can then be used to form $k - 1$ F ratios—and to test $k - 1$ subhypotheses.

DEFINITION 12.4.2. Let $C_i = \sum_{j=1}^{k} c_{ij}\mu_j$ be any contrast. The sum of squares associated with C_i is given by

$$SS_{C_i} = \frac{\hat{C}_i^2}{\displaystyle\sum_{j=1}^{k} \frac{c_{ij}^2}{n_j}}$$

where $\hat{C}_i = \sum_{j=1}^{k} c_{ij}\bar{Y}_{.j}$.

THEOREM 12.4.1. Let $\left\{ C_i = \sum_{j=1}^{k} c_{ij}\mu_j \right\}_{i=1}^{k-1}$ be a set of $k - 1$ mutually orthogonal contrasts. Let $\left\{ \hat{C}_i = \sum_{j=1}^{k} c_{ij}\bar{Y}_{.j} \right\}_{i=1}^{k-1}$ be their estimators. Then

$$SSTR = \sum_{j=1}^{k} \sum_{i=1}^{n_j} (\bar{Y}_{.j} - \bar{Y}_{..})^2$$

$$= SS_{C_1} + SS_{C_2} + \cdots + SS_{C_{k-1}}$$

THEOREM 12.4.2. Let C be a contrast having the same coefficients as the sub-hypothesis $H_0: c_1\mu_1 + c_2\mu_2 + \cdots + c_k\mu_k = 0$, where $\sum_{j=1}^{k} c_j = 0$. Let $n = \sum_{j=1}^{k} n_j$ be the total sample size. Then

(a) $F = \dfrac{SS_C/1}{SSE/(n-k)}$ has an F distribution with 1 and $n - k$ degrees of freedom.

(b) $H_0: c_1\mu_1 + c_2\mu_2 + \cdots + c_k\mu_k = 0$ should be rejected at the α level of significance if $F \geq F_{1-\alpha,1,n-k}$.

Comment. Theorem 12.4.1 is not meant to imply that only mutually orthogonal contrasts can, or should, be tested. It is simply a statement of a partitioning relationship that exists between $SSTR$ and the sum of squares for mutually orthogonal C_i's. In any given experiment, the contrasts that should be singled out are those the experimenter has some prior reason to test.

CASE STUDY 12.4.1

As a rule, infants are not able to walk by themselves until they are almost 14 months old. A recent study, however, investigated the possibility of reducing that time through the use of special "walking" exercises (199). A total of 23 infants were included in the experiment—all were one-week-old white males. They were randomly divided into four groups, and for seven weeks each group followed a different training program. Group A received special walking and placing exercises for 12 minutes each day. Group B also had daily 12-minute exercise periods but were not given the special walking and placing exercises. Groups C and D received no special instruction. The progress of groups A, B, and C was checked every week; the progress of group D was checked only once, at the end of the study.

After seven weeks the formal training ended and the parents were told they could continue with whatever procedure they desired. Table 12.4.1 lists the ages (in months) at which each of the 23 children first walked alone. Table 12.4.2 shows the analysis-of-variance computations. Based on 3 and 19 degrees of freedom, the $\alpha = 0.05$ critical value is 3.13, so $H_0: \mu_A = \mu_B = \mu_C = \mu_D$ is accepted.

TABLE 12.4.1   Age When Infants First Walked Alone (Months)

	Group A	Group B	Group C	Group D
	9.00	11.00	11.50	13.25
	9.50	10.00	12.00	11.50
	9.75	10.00	9.00	12.00
	10.00	11.75	11.50	13.50
	13.00	10.50	13.25	11.50
	9.50	15.00	13.00	
$t_{.j}$	60.75	68.25	70.25	61.75
$\bar{y}_{.j}$	10.12	11.38	11.71	12.35

(continued on next page)

(Case Study 12.4.1 continued)

TABLE 12.4.2 ANOVA Computations

Source	df	SS	MS	F
Exercises	3	14.77	4.92	2.14
Error	19	43.70	2.30	
Total	22	58.47		

Comment. At this point the analysis would usually end; with the overall H_0 being accepted, there is no pressing need to look at contrasts. We will continue with the subhypothesis procedures, however, to illustrate the application of Theorem 12.4.2.

Recall that groups A and B spent equal amounts of time exercising but followed different regimens. Consequently, a test of $H_0: \mu_A = \mu_B$ versus $H_1: \mu_A \neq \mu_B$ would be an obvious way to assess the effectiveness of the special walking and placing exercises. The associated contrast, of course, would be $C_1 = \mu_A - \mu_B$. Similarly, a test of $H_0: \mu_C = \mu_D (C_2 = \mu_C - \mu_D)$ would provide an evaluation of the psychological effect of periodic progress checks.

From Definition 12.4.2 and the data in Table 12.4.1,

$$SS_{C_1} = \frac{\left[1\left(\dfrac{60.75}{6}\right) - 1\left(\dfrac{68.25}{6}\right)\right]^2}{\dfrac{1^2}{6} + \dfrac{(-1)^2}{6}} = 4.68$$

and

$$SS_{C_2} = \frac{\left[1\left(\dfrac{70.25}{6}\right) - 1\left(\dfrac{61.75}{5}\right)\right]^2}{\dfrac{1^2}{6} + \dfrac{(-1)^2}{5}} = 1.12$$

Dividing these sums of squares by the mean square for error ($= 2.30$) gives F ratios of $4.68/2.30 = 2.03$ and $1.12/2.30 = 0.49$, neither of which is significant at the $\alpha = 0.05$ level $(F_{.95,1,19} = 4.38)$ (see Table 12.4.3).

TABLE 12.4.3 Subhypothesis Computations

Subhypothesis	Contrast	SS	F
$H_0: \mu_A = \mu_B$	$C_1 = \mu_A - \mu_B$	4.68	2.03
$H_0: \mu_C = \mu_D$	$C_2 = \mu_C - \mu_D$	1.12	0.49

QUESTIONS

12.4.1 The cathode warm-up time (in seconds) was determined for three different types of X-ray tubes using 15 observations on each type. The results are listed in the following table.

Warm-Up Times (Sec)

Tube Type					
A		*B*		*C*	
19	27	20	24	16	14
23	31	20	25	26	18
26	25	32	29	15	19
18	22	27	31	18	21
20	23	40	24	19	17
20	27	24	25	17	19
18	29	22	32	19	18
35		18		18	

Do an analysis of variance on these data and test the hypothesis that the three tube types require the same average warm-up time. Include a pair of orthogonal contrasts in your ANOVA table. Define one of the contrasts so it tests $H_0: \mu_A = \mu_C$. What does the other contrast test? Check to see that the sums of squares associated with your two contrasts verify the statement of Theorem 12.4.1.

12.4.2 Test the hypothesis that the average of the true yields for the first three varieties of corn described in Question 12.2.4 is the same as the average for the last two. Let $\alpha = 0.05$.

12.4.3 In Case Study 12.2.1 test the hypothesis that the average of the heart rates for light and moderate smokers is the same as that for heavy smokers. Let the level of significance be 0.05.

12.4.4 To compare three investment funds, $2000 per year was invested in each fund during the period 1990–1994. The *total return* for such a fund is defined as the sum of equity growth plus dividends less fees. The funds are divided into three types—equity income, growth and income, and growth. The following table gives the total return for six funds of each type. Test the hypothesis that the average total return for the two growth funds is the same as the equity fund. Let $\alpha = 0.10$.

Equity Income	Growth and Income	Growth
13,288	15,738	14,790
12,782	14,249	13,827
12,812	12,369	13,680
11,713	12,822	13,150
11,201	12,117	12,669
12,233	12,605	14,267

Note: $SSE = 15{,}725{,}266$.

12.4.5 Verify that $C_3 = \frac{11}{12}\mu_A + \frac{11}{12}\mu_B - \mu_C - \frac{5}{6}\mu_D$ is orthogonal to the C_1 and C_2 of Case Study 12.4.1. Find SS_{C_3} and illustrate the statement of Theorem 12.4.1.

12.4.6 For many years sodium nitrite has been used as a curing agent for bacon, and until recently it was thought to be perfectly harmless. But now it appears that during frying, sodium nitrite induces the formation of nitrosopyrrolidine (NPy), a substance suspected of being a carcinogen. In one study focusing on this problem, measurements were made of the amount of NPy (in ppb) recovered after the frying of three slices of four commercially available brands of bacon (148). Do the analysis of variance for the data in the table and partition the treatment sum of squares into a complete set of three mutually orthogonal contrasts. Let the first contrast test

$H_0: \mu_A = \mu_B$ and the second, $H_0: (\mu_A + \mu_B)/2 = (\mu_C + \mu_D)/2$. Do all tests at the 0.05 level of significance.

NPy Recovered from Bacon (ppb)

Brand			
A	B	C	D
20	75	15	25
40	25	30	30
18	21	21	31

12.5 DATA TRANSFORMATIONS

The three assumptions required by the analysis of variance have already been mentioned: the Y_{ij}'s must be independent, normally distributed, and have the same variance for all j. In practice, these three are not equally difficult to satisfy, nor do their violations have the same consequences for the validity of the F test.

Independence is certainly a critical property for the Y_{ij}'s to have, but randomizing the order in which observations are taken (relative to the different treatment levels) tends to eliminate systematic bias—and achieve independence—quite effectively. Normality is a much more difficult property to induce or even to verify (recall Section 10.4). Fortunately, violations of that particular assumption, unless extreme, do not seriously compromise the probabilistic integrity of the analysis of variance (like the t test, the F test is *robust* against departures from normality).

If the final assumption is violated, though, and all the Y_{ij}'s do *not* have the same variance, the effect on certain inference procedures—for example, the construction of confidence intervals for individual means—can be more unsettling. However, it is possible in some situations to "stabilize" the level-to-level variances by a suitable *data transformation*.

Suppose that Y_{ij} has pdf $f_Y(y_{ij}, \mu_j)$, $i = 1, 2, \ldots, n_j$; $j = 1, 2, \ldots, k$, and a known function g exists for which $\text{Var}(Y_{ij}) = g(\mu_j)$. We wish to find a transformation, A, which, when applied to the Y_{ij}'s, will generate a new set of variables having a constant variance—that is, $A(Y_{ij}) = W_{ij}$, where $\text{Var}(W_{ij}) = c_1^2$, a constant.

By Taylor's theorem,

$$W_{ij} \doteq A(\mu_j) + (Y_{ij} - \mu_j)A'(\mu_j)$$

Of course, $E(W_{ij}) = A(\mu_j)$, since $E(Y_{ij} - \mu_j) = 0$. Also,

$$
\begin{aligned}
\text{Var}(W_{ij}) &= E[W_{ij} - E(W_{ij})]^2 \\
&= E[(Y_{ij} - \mu_j)A'(\mu_j)]^2 \\
&= [A'(\mu_j)]^2 \text{Var}(Y_{ij}) = [A'(\mu_j)]^2 g(\mu_j)
\end{aligned}
$$

Solving for $A'(\mu_j)$ gives

$$A'(\mu_j) = \frac{\sqrt{\text{Var}(W_{ij})}}{\sqrt{g(\mu_j)}} = \frac{c_1}{\sqrt{g(\mu_j)}}$$

For Y_{ij} in the neighborhood of μ_j, it follows that

$$A(Y_{ij}) = c_1 \int \frac{1}{\sqrt{g(y_{ij})}} \, dy_{ij} + c_2 \tag{12.5.1}$$

EXAMPLE 12.5.1

Suppose the Y_{ij}'s are Poisson random variables with mean μ_j, $j = 1, 2, \ldots, k$, so

$$f_Y(y_{ij}; \mu_j) = \frac{e^{-\mu_j} \mu_j^{y_{ij}}}{y_{ij}!}$$

In this case, the variance is *equal* to the mean (recall Theorem 4.2.2):

$$\mathrm{Var}(Y_{ij}) = E(Y_{ij}) = \mu_j = g(\mu_j)$$

By Equation 12.5.1, then,

$$A(Y_{ij}) = c_1 \int \frac{1}{\sqrt{y_{ij}}} \, dy_{ij} + c_2 = 2c_1 \sqrt{y_{ij}} + c_2$$

or, letting $c_1 = \frac{1}{2}$ and $c_2 = 0$ to make the transformation as simple as possible,

$$A(Y_{ij}) = Z_{ij} = \sqrt{Y_{ij}} \tag{12.5.2}$$

Equation 12.5.2 implies that if the data are known in advance to be Poisson, each of the observations should be replaced by its *square root* before we proceed with the analysis of variance.

EXAMPLE 12.5.2

Suppose each Y_{ij} is a binomial random variable with pdf

$$f_Y(y_{ij}; n, p_j) = \binom{n}{y_{ij}} p_j^{y_{ij}} (1 - p_j)^{n - y_{ij}}$$

Here, $E(Y_{ij}) = np_j = \mu_j$, which implies that

$$\mathrm{Var}(Y_{ij}) = np_j(1 - p_j) = \mu_j\left(1 - \frac{\mu_j}{n}\right) = g(\mu_j)$$

It follows that the variance-stabilizing transformation for this type of data is the *inverse sine*:

$$A(Y_{ij}) = c_1 \int \frac{1}{\sqrt{y_{ij}(1 - y_{ij}/n)}} \, dy_{ij} + c_2$$

$$= c_1 2\sqrt{n} \arcsin\left(\frac{y_{ij}}{n}\right)^{1/2} + c_2$$

or, what is equivalent,

$$A(Y_{ij}) = \arcsin\left(\frac{y_{ij}}{n}\right)^{1/2}$$

QUESTIONS

12.5.1 A commercial film processor is experimenting with two kinds of fully automatic color developers. Six sheets of exposed film are put through each developer. The number of flaws on each negative visible with the naked eye is then counted.

Number of Visible Flaws	
Developer A	Developer B
1	8
4	6
5	4
6	9
3	11
7	10

Assume the number of flaws on a given negative is a Poisson random variable. Make an appropriate data transformation and do the indicated analysis of variance.

12.5.2 An experimenter wants to do an analysis of variance on a set of data involving five treatment groups, each with three replicates. She has computed $\bar{y}_{.j}$ and s_j for each group and gotten the results listed in the following table.

	Treatment Group				
	1	2	3	4	5
$\bar{y}_{.j}$	9.0	4.0	16.0	9.0	1.0
s_j	3.0	2.0	4.0	3.0	1.0

What should the experimenter do before computing the various sums of squares necessary to carry out the F test? Be as quantitative as possible.

12.5.3 Three air-to-surface missile launchers are tested for their accuracy. The same gun crew fires four rounds with each launcher, each round consisting of 20 missiles. A "hit" is scored if the missile lands within 10 yards of the target. The following table gives the number of hits registered in each round.

Number of Hits Per Round		
Launcher A	Launcher B	Launcher C
13	15	9
11	16	11
10	18	10
14	17	8

Compare the accuracy of these three launchers by using the analysis of variance, after making a suitable data transformation. Let $\alpha = 0.05$.

APPENDIX 12.A.1   MINITAB APPLICATIONS

The MINITAB command for doing the F test of Theorem 12.2.5 is

```
MTB > aovoneway c1-ck
```

where the y_{ij}'s from the k samples have been entered in columns c1 through ck. The output appears in the ANOVA table format of Figure 12.2.1.

Displayed in Figure 12.A.1.1 are the input and output for analyzing the heart rate data described in Case Study 12.2.1. The program also prints out 95% confidence intervals for each μ_j—that is,

$$\left(\bar{y}_{\cdot j} - t_{.025, n_j - 1} \cdot \frac{s}{\sqrt{n_j}}, \bar{y}_{\cdot j} + t_{.025, n_j - 1} \cdot \frac{s}{\sqrt{n_j}} \right)$$

where s is the pooled standard deviation calculated from all k samples (see Figure 12.A.1.2).

```
MTB > set c1
DATA> 69 52 71 58 59 65
DATA> end
MTB > set c2
DATA> 55 60 78 58 62 66
DATA> end
MTB > set c3
DATA> 66 81 70 77 57 79
DATA> end
MTB > set c4
DATA> 91 72 81 67 95 84
DATA> end
MTB > aovoneway c1-c4

One-Way Analysis of Variance

Analysis of Variance
Source     DF        SS        MS        F       p
Factor      3     1464.1     488.0     6.12    0.004
Error      20     1594.8      79.7
Total      23     3059.0
```

FIGURE 12.A.1.1

```
                                  Individual 95% CIs For Mean
                                  Based on Pooled StDev
Level    N      Mean     StDev    ------+---------+---------+---------+
C1       6    62.333     7.257    (------*------)
C2       6    63.167     8.159    (------*------)
C3       6    71.667     9.158             (------*------)
C4       6    81.667    10.764                      (------*------)
                                  ------+---------+---------+---------+
Pooled StDev = 8.930                   60        70        80        90
```

FIGURE 12.A.1.2

Pairwise comparisons are also available in MINITAB, but the Tukey method requires that the data be entered differently. First, the k samples are "stacked" in a single column—say, c1. Then a second column, c2, is created whose entries identify the treatment level to which each y_{ij} in column 1 belongs. For example, c1 and c2 for the data

Level 1	Level 2
4	−1
−2	3
2	

would be

$$c1 = \begin{pmatrix} 4 \\ -2 \\ 2 \\ -1 \\ 3 \end{pmatrix} \quad \text{and} \quad c2 = \begin{pmatrix} 1 \\ 1 \\ 1 \\ 2 \\ 2 \end{pmatrix}$$

The statements

```
MTB > oneway c1 c2;
SUBC > tukey.
```

will then produce a complete set of 95% Tukey confidence intervals. *Note*: MINITAB has an expression that simplifies the writing of c2—the syntax "X(Y)" appearing in a DATA statement means that X Y's are to be entered in a designated column. For example, the c2 shown previously could be formed by typing

```
MTB > set c2
DATA > 3(1) 2(2)
```

Figure 12.A.1.3 shows the MINITAB calculation of the 95% Tukey confidence intervals for the serum binding data of Case Study 12.3.1. The lower and upper confidence interval limits for each pairwise comparison appear as entries in the lower portion of a $(k - 1) \times (k - 1)$ matrix. Intervals not containing 0, of course, correspond to null hypotheses that should be rejected.

Testing H_0: $\mu_1 = \cdots = \mu_k$ Using MINITAB Windows

1. Enter the k samples in columns C1 through Ck, respectively.
2. Click on STAT, then on ANOVA, then on ONE-WAY (UNSTACKED).
3. Type C1–Ck in RESPONSES box, and click on OK.

```
MTB > set c1
DATA> 29.6 24.3 28.5 32.0 27.3 32.6 30.8 34.8 5.8 6.2
DATA> 11.0 8.3 21.6 17.4 18.3 19.0 29.2 32.8 25.0 24.2
MTB > set c2
DATA> 4(1) 4(2) 4(3) 4(4) 4(5)
DATA> end
MTB > oneway c1 c2;
SUBC> tukey.
```

One-Way Analysis of Variance

Analysis of Variance on C1

Source	DF	SS	MS	F	p
C2	4	1480.82	370.21	40.88	0.000
Error	15	135.82	9.05		
Total	19	1616.65			

Tukey's pairwise comparisons

    Family error rate = 0.0500
Individual error rate = 0.00747

Critical value = 4.37

Intervals for (column level mean) - (row level mean)

	1	2	3	4
2	-9.350 3.800			
3	14.200 27.350	16.975 30.125		
4	2.950 16.100	5.725 18.875	-17.825 -4.675	
5	-5.775 7.375	-3.000 10.150	-26.550 -13.400	-15.300 -2.150

FIGURE 12.A.1.3

Constructing Tukey Confidence Intervals Using MINITAB Windows

1. Enter entire sample in column C1, beginning with the n_1 observations in Sample 1, followed by the n_2 observations in Sample 2, and so on.
2. In Column C2, enter n_1 1's, followed by n_2 2's, and so on.
3. Click on STAT, then on ANOVA, then on ONE-WAY.
4. Type C1 in RESPONSE box and C2 in FACTOR box.
5. Click on COMPARISONS, then on TUKEY'S FAMILY ERROR RATE. Enter the desired value for $100\,\alpha$.
6. Double click on OK.

APPENDIX 12.A.2 A PROOF OF THEOREM 12.2.2

To prove that $SSTR/\sigma^2$ has a chi-square distribution with $k - 1$ degrees of freedom, it suffices to show that the moment-generating function of $SSTR/\sigma^2$ is $\left(\dfrac{1}{1 - 2t}\right)^{(k-1)/2}$.

Note, first, that under the null hypothesis that $\mu_1 = \mu_2 = \cdots = \mu_k$,

$$SSTOT = (n - 1)S^2$$

where S^2 is the sample variance of a set of n observations from a normal distribution. Therefore, by Theorem 7.3.3,

$$M_{SSTOT/\sigma^2}(t) = \left(\frac{1}{1 - 2t}\right)^{(n-1)/2}$$

Also, from Theorem 12.2.3, SSE/σ^2 is a chi-square random variable with $n - k$ degrees of freedom, so

$$M_{SSE/\sigma^2}(t) = \left(\frac{1}{1 - 2t}\right)^{(n-k)/2}$$

Since $SSTOT/\sigma^2$ is the *sum* of two independent random variables, $SSTR/\sigma^2$ and SSE/σ^2, it follows that

$$M_{SSTOT/\sigma^2}(t) = M_{SSTR/\sigma^2}(t) \cdot M_{SSE/\sigma^2}(t)$$

or

$$\left(\frac{1}{1 - 2t}\right)^{(n-1)/2} = M_{SSTR/\sigma^2}(t) \cdot \left(\frac{1}{1 - 2t}\right)^{(n-k)/2}$$

which implies that

$$M_{SSTR/\sigma^2}(t) = \left(\frac{1}{1 - 2t}\right)^{(k-1)/2}$$

APPENDIX 12.A.3 THE DISTRIBUTION OF $\dfrac{SSTR/(k - 1)}{SSE/(n - k)}$ WHEN H_1 IS TRUE

Theorem 12.2.5 gives the distribution of the test statistic

$$F = \frac{SSTR/(k - 1)}{SSE/(n - k)}$$

when the null hypothesis is true. To calculate either the power of the analysis of variance, though, or the probability of committing a Type II error, requires that we know the pdf of the observed F *when H_1 is true*.

Recall that a similar question was pursued earlier in connection with the one-sample t test. Theorem 7.5.3 showed that when $H_0: \mu = \mu_0$ is not true, the test statistic $T = \dfrac{\bar{Y} - \mu_0}{S/\sqrt{n}}$ has a *noncentral t distribution*. Here we will show that when $H_0: \mu_1 = \mu_2 = \cdots = \mu_k$ is not true, $F = \dfrac{SSTR/(k - 1)}{SSE/(n - k)}$ has a *noncentral F distribution*.

DEFINITION 12.A.3.1.   Let V_j have a normal pdf with mean μ_j and variance 1, for $j = 1, \ldots, r$, and suppose that the V_j's are independent. Then

$$V = \sum_{j=1}^{r} V_j^2$$

is said to have the *noncentral* χ^2 *distribution* with r degrees of freedom and noncentrality parameter γ, where

$$\gamma = \sum_{j=1}^{r} \mu_j^2$$

THEOREM 12.A.3.1.   The moment-generating function for a noncentral χ^2 random variable, V, with r degrees of freedom and noncentrality parameter γ is given by

$$M_V(t) = (1 - 2t)^{-\frac{r}{2}} e^{\frac{\gamma t}{1-2t}}, \qquad t < 1/2$$

Proof.   We begin by finding the moment-generating function for the special case where $r = 1$.

Let V be a normal random variable with mean μ and variance 1, and let $V = Z + \mu$, where Z is a standard normal random variable. By definition, the moment-generating function for V^2 can be written

$$M_{V^2}(t) = E\left(e^{tV^2}\right) = E\left(e^{t(Z+\mu)^2}\right)$$

$$= \frac{1}{\sqrt{2\pi}} \int_{-\infty}^{\infty} e^{t(z+\mu)^2} e^{-\frac{1}{2}z^2} \, dz = \frac{1}{\sqrt{2\pi}} \int_{-\infty}^{\infty} e^{t(z+\mu)^2 - \frac{1}{2}z^2} \, dz$$

To evaluate the integral, we first complete the square in the exponent:

$$tz^2 + 2tz\mu + t\mu^2 - \frac{1}{2}z^2 = -\frac{1}{2}\left[(1-2t)z^2 - 4t\mu z\right] + t\mu^2$$

$$= -\frac{1}{2} \cdot \frac{z^2 - \dfrac{4t\mu}{(1-2t)}z}{1/(1-2t)} + t\mu^2$$

$$= -\frac{1}{2} \cdot \frac{z^2 - \dfrac{4t\mu}{(1-2t)}z + \dfrac{4t^2\mu^2}{(1-2t)^2}}{1/(1-2t)} + t\mu^2 + \frac{\dfrac{2t^2\mu^2}{(1-2t)^2}}{1/(1-2t)}$$

$$= -\frac{1}{2} \cdot \left[\frac{z - \dfrac{2t\mu}{(1-2t)}}{1/\sqrt{1-2t}}\right]^2 + t\mu^2 + \frac{2t^2\mu^2}{(1-2t)}$$

Therefore,

$$M_{V^2}(t) = e^{\mu^2 t + \frac{2\mu^2 t^2}{(1-2t)}} \frac{1}{\sqrt{2\pi}} \int_{-\infty}^{\infty} e^{-\frac{1}{2}\left[\frac{z - \frac{2t\mu}{(1-2t)}}{1/\sqrt{1-2t}}\right]^2} \, dz$$

$$= (1 - 2t)^{-\frac{1}{2}} e^{\mu^2 \frac{t}{1-2t}}$$

The general result, where $r \neq 1$, follows from an application of Theorem 3.16.3(b). Let $V = \sum\limits_{j=1}^{r} V_j^2$, where the V_j's are independent. Then

$$M\sum\limits_{i=1}^{k} v_i^2(t) = (1 - 2t)^{-\frac{r}{2}} e^{\sum\limits_{j=1}^{r} \mu_j^2 \frac{t}{1-2t}} = (1 - 2t)^{-\frac{r}{2}} e^{\frac{\gamma t}{1-2t}}$$

DEFINITION 12.A.3.2.   Let V_1 be a noncentral χ^2 random variable with r_1 degrees of freedom and noncentrality parameter γ. Suppose V_2 is a (central) χ^2 random variable with r_2 degrees of freedom and independent of V_1. The ratio

$$\frac{V_1/r_1}{V_2/r_2}$$

is said to have a *noncentral F distribution* with r_1 and r_2 degrees of freedom and noncentrality parameter γ.

THEOREM 12.A.3.2.   The ratio

$$\frac{SSTR/(k-1)}{SSE/(n-k)}$$

has a noncentral F distribution with $k-1$ and $n-k$ degrees of freedom and noncentrality parameter $\gamma = \dfrac{1}{\sigma^2} \sum\limits_{j=1}^{k} n_j(\mu_j - \mu)^2$.

Proof.   From Equation 12.2.1,

$$SSTR = \sum\limits_{j=1}^{k} n_j(\bar{Y}_{.j} - \mu)^2 - n(\bar{Y}_{..} - \mu)^2$$

so

$$\frac{SSTR}{\sigma^2} = \sum\limits_{j=1}^{k} \left(\frac{\bar{Y}_{.j} - \mu}{\sigma/\sqrt{n_j}}\right)^2 - \left(\frac{\bar{Y}_{..} - \mu}{\sigma/\sqrt{n}}\right)^2 \qquad (12.A.3.1)$$

Let $W_j = \dfrac{\bar{Y}_{.j} - \mu}{\sigma/\sqrt{n_j}}$, $j = 1, \ldots, k$. Since $E(\bar{Y}_{.j}) = \mu_j$, $E(W_j) = \sqrt{n_j}(\mu_j - \mu)/\sigma$. Also, $\mathrm{Var}(W_j) = \dfrac{\mathrm{Var}(\bar{Y}_{.j} - \mu)}{\sigma^2/n_j} = \dfrac{\sigma^2/n_j}{\sigma^2/n_j} = 1$. Thus, because $\bar{Y}_{.j}$ is normal, each W_j is normal with mean $\sqrt{n_j}(\mu_j - \mu)/\sigma$ and variance 1. The second component of $SSTR/\sigma^2$, $\dfrac{\bar{Y}_{..} - \mu}{\sigma/\sqrt{n}}$, is a standard normal random variable.

Now, recalling the transformation technique used in Appendix 7.A.2, choose an orthogonal matrix $\mathbf{A}$ with first row $(\sqrt{n_1/n}, \sqrt{n_2/n}, \ldots, \sqrt{n_k/n})$. Define the vector $\vec{V}$ of random variables by $\vec{V} = A(W_1, W_2, \ldots, W_k)^T$. First note that

$$V_1 = \sum_{j=1}^{k} \frac{\sqrt{n_j}}{\sqrt{n}} W_j = \sum_{j=1}^{k} \frac{\sqrt{n_j}}{\sqrt{n}} \frac{(\bar{Y}_{.j} - \mu)}{\sigma/\sqrt{n_j}}$$

$$= \frac{1}{\sigma\sqrt{n}} \sum_{j=1}^{k} n_j(\bar{Y}_{.j} - \mu) = \frac{1}{\sigma\sqrt{n}} \left(\sum_{j=1}^{k} n_j \bar{Y}_{.j} - \left(\sum_{j=1}^{k} n_j \right) \mu \right)$$

$$= \frac{1}{\sigma\sqrt{n}} (n\bar{Y}_{..} - n\mu) = \frac{\bar{Y}_{..} - \mu}{\sigma/\sqrt{n}}$$

which gives $V_1^2 = \left(\dfrac{\bar{Y}_{..} - \mu}{\sigma/\sqrt{n}} \right)^2$.

Because of the orthogonality of the matrix,

$$\sum_{j=1}^{k} V_j^2 = \sum_{j=1}^{k} W_j^2 \quad \text{or} \quad \sum_{j=2}^{k} V_j^2 = \sum_{j=1}^{k} W_j^2 - V_1^2$$

But $\sum\limits_{j=1}^{k} W_j^2 - V_1^2 = SSTR/\sigma^2$ by Equation 12.A.3.1. Moreover, each V_j is a

normal random variable for which $V_j = \sum\limits_{i=1}^{k} a_{ji} W_i$, where the a_{ji}'s are the entries

in the jth row of **A**. Therefore,

$$\text{Var}(V_j) = \sum_{i=1}^{k} \text{Var}(a_{ji} W_i) = \sum_{i=1}^{k} a_{ji}^2 \text{Var}(W_i) = \sum_{i=1}^{k} a_{ji}^2$$

since each W_j has variance 1. But the orthogonality of the matrix **A** implies that $\sum\limits_{i=1}^{k} a_{ji}^2 = 1$ for each j. So each V_j is normal with variance 1, and $\sum\limits_{j=2}^{k} V_j^2$ has a noncentral χ^2 distribution with $k-1$ degrees of freedom.

From Question 12.A.2.4, the noncentrality parameter of $\sum\limits_{j=2}^{k} V_j^2$ is

$$E\left(\sum_{j=2}^{k} V_j^2 \right) - (k-1) = E\left(\sum_{j=1}^{k} W_j^2 \right) - E(V_1^2) - (k-1)$$

$$= \sum_{j=1}^{k} \left(\text{Var}(W_j) + [E(W_j)]^2 \right) - \left(\text{Var}(V_1) + E(V_1)^2 \right) - (k-1)$$

$$= \sum_{j=1}^{k} \left(1 + [\sqrt{n_j}(\mu_j - \mu)/\sigma]^2 \right) - (1+0) - (k-1)$$

$$= \frac{1}{\sigma^2} \sum_{j=1}^{k} n_j(\mu_j - \mu)^2$$

Therefore, since SSE/σ^2 has a χ^2 distribution with $n-k$ degrees of freedom, it follows immediately from Definition 12.A.3.2 that, when H_1 is true,

$$F = \frac{\dfrac{SSTR}{k-1}}{\dfrac{SSE}{n-k}}$$

has a noncentral F distribution with $k - 1$ and $n - k$ degrees of freedom and noncentrality parameter $\gamma = \dfrac{1}{\sigma^2} \displaystyle\sum_{j=1}^{k} n_j(\mu_j - \mu)^2.$

Comment. As H_1 gets farther from H_0, as measured by γ, the noncentral F will shift more and more to the right of the central F. Accordingly, the power of the F test will increase. That is,

$$P\big(F \geq F_{1-\alpha,k-1,n-k}\big) \rightarrow 1 \qquad \text{as } \gamma \rightarrow \infty$$

The pdf for the noncentral F is not very tractable, but its integral has been evaluated by numerical approximation. This has allowed the power function for the F test to be tabulated [see, for instance, (99)].

QUESTIONS

12.A.3.1 Suppose an experimenter has taken three independent measurements on each of five treatment levels and intends to use the analysis of variance to test

$$H_0: \quad \mu_1 = \mu_2 = \mu_3 = \mu_4 = \mu_5 \, (= 0)$$

versus

$$H_1: \quad \text{not all the } \mu_j\text{'s are equal}$$

Two of the possible alternatives in H_1 are

$$H_1^*: \mu_1 = -1, \mu_2 = 2, \mu_3 = 0, \mu_4 = 1, \mu_5 = -2$$

and

$$H_1^{**}: \mu_1 = -3, \mu_2 = 2, \mu_3 = 1, \mu_4 = 0, \mu_5 = 0$$

Against which alternative will the F test have the greater power? Explain.

12.A.3.2 In the scenario of the previous question, is $H_1: \mu_1 = 2, \mu_2 = 1, \mu_3 = 1, \mu_4 = -3, \mu_5 = 0$ an "admissible" alternative hypothesis?

12.A.3.3 If the random variable V has a noncentral χ^2 distribution with r degrees of freedom and noncentrality parameter γ, use its moment-generating function to find $E(V)$.

12.A.3.4 If the random variable V has a noncentral χ^2 distribution with r degrees of freedom and noncentrality parameter γ, show that $\gamma = E(V) - r$.

12.A.3.5 Suppose $V_1, V_2, \ldots, V_n$ are independent noncentral χ^2 random variables, having $r_1, r_2, \ldots, r_n$ degrees of freedom, respectively, and with noncentrality parameters $\gamma_1, \gamma_2, \ldots, \gamma_n$. Find the distribution of $V = V_1 + V_2 + \cdots + V_n$.

CHAPTER 13

Randomized Block Designs

Pictured is a 5-by-5 Latin square laid out at Bettgelert Forest in 1929 for studying the effect of exposure on Sitka spruce, Norway spruce, Japanese larch, European larch, Pinus contorta, and beech. (A Latin square is a special type of experimental design that extends to two dimensions the important notion of "blocking" that is introduced in this chapter. Latin squares are particularly useful in agricultural research.)

13.1 INTRODUCTION

In any experiment, reducing the magnitude of the experimental error is a highly desirable objective: The smaller σ^2 is, the better will be our chances of rejecting a false null hypothesis. Basically, there are two ways to reduce experimental error. The nonstatistical approach is simply to refine the experimental technique—use better equipment, minimize subjective error, and so on. The statistical method, which can often produce results much more dramatic, is by collecting the data in "blocks," in what is referred to as a *randomized block design*.

Historically, it was Fisher who first advanced the notion of blocking. He saw it initially as a statistical defense against the obfuscating effects of soil heterogeneity in agricultural experiments. Suppose, for example, a researcher wishes to compare the yields of four different varieties of corn. Figure 13.1.1(a) shows the simplest experimental layout: Variety A is planted in the leftmost portion of the field, variety B is planted next to A, and so on. Even to a city slicker the statistical hazards involved in using this design should be obvious. Suppose, for example, there was a soil *gradient* in the field, with the best soil being in the westernmost part (where variety A was planted). Then if variety A achieved the highest yield, we would not know whether to attribute its success to its inherent quality or to its location (or to some combination of both).

A more sensible *modus operandi* is pictured in Figure 13.1.1(b). There the field is divided up into a number of smaller "blocks," each block being still further parceled into four "plots." All four varieties are planted in each block, one to a plot, with the plot assignments being chosen at random. Notice that the geographical contiguity of the four plots within a given block ensures that the environmental conditions from plot to plot will be relatively uniform and will not lead to any biasing of the observed yields. What the analysis of variance will then do is "pool" from block to block the *within*-block information concerning the treatment differences while bypassing the *between*-block differences—that is, the heterogeneity in the experimental environment. As a result, the treatment comparisons can be made with greater precision. Analytically, where the total sum of squares was partitioned into *two* components in a completely randomized, one-factor design, it will be split into *three* separate sums in a randomized block design: one for treatments, another for blocks, and a third for experimental error.

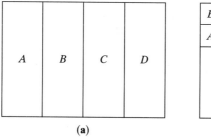
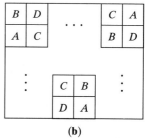

FIGURE 13.1.1 Two different experimental designs.

It did not take long for scientists to realize that the benefits of blocking could be extended well beyond the confines of agricultural experimentation. In medical research, blocks are often made up of subjects of the same age, sex, and overall physical condition. A common practice in animal studies is to form blocks out of littermates. Industrial experiments often require that "time" be a blocking criterion: Measurements taken by personnel on the day shift might be considered one block and those taken by the night shift a second block. In some sense the ultimate form of blocking, although one not always physically possible, is to apply the entire set of treatment levels to each subject, thus making each subject its own block.

Section 13.2 begins with a development of the analysis of variance for the randomized block design, where k treatment levels are administered within each of b blocks. The observations within a given block, of course, are *dependent*. As was the case in Chapter 12, the hypotheses to be tested are $H_0: \mu_1 = \mu_2 = \ldots = \mu_k$ versus H_1: not all the μ_j's are equal. The section concludes with a pair of case studies that illustrate the blocking concept in two very different settings.

We saw in the previous chapter that when $k = 2$, and the samples are independent, the F test is equivalent to a two-sample t test. A similar duality exists here. When $k = 2$ treatment levels are compared within b blocks, $H_0: \mu_1 = \mu_2$ can be tested using either the analysis of variance or a *paired t test*. The latter is described in Section 13.3.

13.2   THE *F* TEST FOR A RANDOMIZED BLOCK DESIGN

Superficially, the structure of randomized block data looks much like the format we encountered in Chapter 12—associated with each of k treatment levels is a sample of measurements. Here, though, each column has exactly the same number of observations—that is, $n_j = b$ for all j, so the data set is necessarily a $b \times k$ matrix (see Table 13.2.1).

On the other hand, from a statistical standpoint randomized block data are fundamentally different from k-sample data (recall the discussion in Section 8.2). In Chapter 12, the k samples were *independent*. Here, the observations within a given row (which corresponds to a *block*) are *dependent*, since each reflects to some extent the conditions inherent in that block. That distinction causes the analysis of variance to proceed differently.

TABLE 13.2.1

		\multicolumn{5}{c}{Treatments}			
		1	2	$\cdots$	k	Averages
	1	y_{11}	y_{12}		y_{1k}	$\bar{y}_{1.}$
	2	y_{21}	y_{22}		y_{2k}	$\bar{y}_{2.}$
Blocks	$\vdots$	$\vdots$		$\cdots$		$\vdots$
	b	y_{b1}	y_{b2}		y_{bk}	$\bar{y}_{b.}$
Averages		$\bar{y}_{.1}$	$\bar{y}_{.2}$		$\bar{y}_{.k}$	$\bar{y}_{..}$ = overall average

Our objective is to test $H_0: \mu_1 = \mu_2 = \ldots = \mu_k$, the same as it was in Chapter 12. But here the mathematical model associated with Y_{ij} has an additional term, representing the effect of the ith block. If each "block effect," β_i, is assumed to be additive, we can write

$$Y_{ij} = \mu_j + \beta_i + \varepsilon_{ij}$$

where ε_{ij} is normally distributed with mean 0 and variance σ^2, for $i = 1, 2, \ldots, b$ and $j = 1, 2, \ldots, k$. As before, we will let μ denote the overall average treatment effect associated with the bk observations—that is, $\mu = \dfrac{1}{k} \displaystyle\sum_{j=1}^{k} \mu_j$.

The basic approach followed in Chapter 12 can still be taken here, but SSE needs to be recalculated, because the "error" in a set of randomized block measurements will reflect both the block effect *and* the random error. To separate the two requires that we first estimate the set of block effects, $\beta_1, \beta_2, \ldots,$ and β_b.

Let $\bar{Y}_{i.} = \dfrac{1}{k} \displaystyle\sum_{j=1}^{k} Y_{ij}$ denote the sample average of the k observations in the ith block. Suppose the data contained no random error—that is, $\varepsilon_{ij} = 0$ for all i and j. Then

$$\bar{Y}_i = \frac{1}{k} \sum_{j=1}^{k} (\mu_j + \beta_i) = \left(\frac{1}{k} \sum_{j=1}^{k} \mu_j \right) + \frac{1}{k} k\beta_i = \mu + \beta_i$$

If $\bar{Y}_{..}$ is substituted for μ, the estimate for β_i becomes $\bar{Y}_{i.} - \bar{Y}_{..}$.

Now, adding and subtracting $\bar{Y}_{i.} - \bar{Y}_{..}$ in the expression for SSE from Chapter 12 gives,

$$\sum_{i=1}^{b} \sum_{j=1}^{k} (Y_{ij} - \bar{Y}_{.j})^2 = \sum_{i=1}^{b} \sum_{j=1}^{k} [(Y_{ij} - \bar{Y}_{.j}) + (\bar{Y}_{i.} - \bar{Y}_{..}) - (\bar{Y}_{i.} - \bar{Y}_{..})]^2$$

$$= \sum_{i=1}^{b} \sum_{j=1}^{k} [(\bar{Y}_{i.} - \bar{Y}_{..}) + (Y_{ij} - \bar{Y}_{.j} - \bar{Y}_{i.} + \bar{Y}_{..})]^2$$

$$= \sum_{i=1}^{b} \sum_{j=1}^{k} (\bar{Y}_{i.} - \bar{Y}_{..})^2 + \sum_{i=1}^{b} \sum_{j=1}^{k} (Y_{ij} - \bar{Y}_{.j} - \bar{Y}_{i.} + \bar{Y}_{..})^2$$

$$+ 2 \sum_{i=1}^{b} \sum_{j=1}^{k} (\bar{Y}_{i.} - \bar{Y}_{..})(Y_{ij} - \bar{Y}_{.j} - \bar{Y}_{i.} + \bar{Y}_{..})$$

Notice that the cross-product term can be written

$$2 \sum_{i=1}^{b} (\bar{Y}_{i.} - \bar{Y}_{..}) \sum_{j=1}^{k} (Y_{ij} - \bar{Y}_{.j} - \bar{Y}_{i.} + \bar{Y}_{..})$$

But

$$\sum_{j=1}^{k} (Y_{ij} - \bar{Y}_{.j} - \bar{Y}_{i.} + \bar{Y}_{..}) = k\bar{Y}_{i.} - k\bar{Y}_{i.} - \sum_{j=1}^{k} (\bar{Y}_{.j} - \bar{Y}_{..}) = 0$$

so

$$\sum_{i=1}^{b}\sum_{j=1}^{k}(Y_{ij} - \bar{Y}_{.j})^2 = \sum_{i=1}^{b}\sum_{j=1}^{k}(\bar{Y}_{i.} - \bar{Y}_{..})^2 + \sum_{i=1}^{b}\sum_{j=1}^{k}(Y_{ij} - \bar{Y}_{.j} - \bar{Y}_{i.} + \bar{Y}_{..})^2$$

$$(13.2.1)$$

Equation 13.2.1 is a key result. It shows that the "old" sum of squares for error from Chapter 12— $\sum_{i=1}^{b}\sum_{j=1}^{k}(Y_{ij} - \bar{Y}_{.j})^2$ —can be partitioned into the sum of two other sums of squares. The first, $\sum_{i=1}^{b}\sum_{j=1}^{k}(\bar{Y}_{i.} - \bar{Y}_{..})^2$, is called the *block sum of squares* and denoted *SSB*. The second is the "new" sum of squares measuring random error. That is, for randomized block data,

$$SSE = \sum_{i=1}^{b}\sum_{j=1}^{k}(Y_{ij} - \bar{Y}_{.j} - \bar{Y}_{i.} + \bar{Y}_{..})^2$$

The other sums of squares from Chapter 12 remain the same in the context of the randomized block design. Specifically,

$$SSTOT = \text{total sum of squares} = \sum_{i=1}^{b}\sum_{j=1}^{k}(Y_{ij} - \bar{Y}_{..})^2$$

and

$$SSTR = \text{treatment sum of squares} = \sum_{i=1}^{b}\sum_{j=1}^{k}(\bar{Y}_{.j} - \bar{Y}_{..})^2$$

Theorem 13.2.1.   Suppose that k treatment levels are measured over a set of b blocks. Then

(a) $SSTOT = SSTR + SSB + SSE$

(b) $SSTR, SSB$, and SSE are independent random variables.

Proof.   The independence of the three terms that combine to give *SSTOT* can be established using the same approach that was taken in Chapter 12. The details will be omitted.

Theorem 13.2.2.   Suppose that k treatment levels, with means $\mu_1, \mu_2, \ldots, \mu_k$, are measured over a set of b blocks, where the block effects are $\beta_1, \beta_2, \ldots, \beta_b$. Then

(a) When $H_0: \mu_1 = \mu_2 = \ldots = \mu_k$ is true, $SSTR/\sigma^2$ has a chi-square distribution with $k - 1$ degrees of freedom.

(b) When $H_0: \beta_1 = \beta_2 = \ldots = \beta_b$ is true, SSB/σ^2 has a chi-square distribution with $b - 1$ degrees of freedom.

(c) Regardless of whether the μ_j's and/or the β_i's are equal, SSE/σ^2 has a chi-square distribution with $(b - 1)(k - 1)$ degrees of freedom.

Proof.   See Appendix 12.A.2.

THEOREM 13.2.3.   Suppose that k treatment levels with means $\mu_1, \mu_2, \ldots, \mu_k$ are measured over a set of b blocks. Then

(a) If $H_0: \mu_1 = \mu_2 = \ldots = \mu_k$ is true,

$$F = \frac{SSTR/(k - 1)}{SSE/(b - 1)(k - 1)}$$

has an F distribution with $k - 1$ and $(b - 1)(k - 1)$ degrees of freedom.

(b) At the α level of significance, $H_0: \mu_1 = \mu_2 = \ldots = \mu_k$ should be rejected if $F \geq F_{1-\alpha, k-1, (b-1)(k-1)}$.

Comment.   If $H_0: \mu_1 = \mu_2 = \ldots = \mu_k$ is not true, $SSTR/\sigma^2$ will have a noncentral chi-square distribution, and the test statistic

$$F = \frac{SSTR/(k - 1)}{SSE/(b - 1)(k - 1)}$$

will be a noncentral F random variable (recall Appendix 12.A.2).

THEOREM 13.2.4.   Suppose that k treatment levels are measured over a set of b blocks, where the block effects are $\beta_1, \beta_2, \ldots$, and β_b. Then

(a) If $H_0: \beta_1 = \beta_2 = \ldots = \beta_b$ is true,

$$F = \frac{SSB/(b - 1)}{SSE/(b - 1)(k - 1)}$$

has an F distribution with $b - 1$ and $(b - 1)(k - 1)$ degrees of freedom.

(b) At the α level of significance, $H_0: \beta_1 = \beta_2 = \ldots = \beta_b$ should be rejected if $F \geq F_{1-\alpha, b-1, (b-1)(k-1)}$.

Table 13.2.2 shows the ANOVA table entries for a randomized block analysis. Notice that two F ratios are calculated, one for the treatment effect and one for the block effect.

TABLE 13.2.2

Source	df	SS	MS	F	P
Treatments	$k-1$	$SSTR$	$SSTR/(k-1)$	$\dfrac{SSTR/(k-1)}{SSE/(b-1)(k-1)}$	$P\big(F_{k-1,(b-1)(k-1)} \geq \text{obs } F\big)$
Blocks	$b-1$	SSB	$SSB/(b-1)$	$\dfrac{SSB/(b-1)}{SSE/(b-1)(k-1)}$	$P\big(F_{b-1,(b-1)(k-1)} \geq \text{obs } F\big)$
Error	$(b-1)(k-1)$	SSE	$SSE/(b-1)(k-1)$		
Total	$n-1$	$SSTOT$			

Computing Formulas

Let $C = T_{..}^2/bk$. Then

$$SSTR = \sum_{j=1}^{k} \frac{T_{.j}^2}{b} - C \tag{13.2.2}$$

$$SSB = \sum_{i=1}^{b} \frac{T_{i.}^2}{k} - C \tag{13.2.3}$$

$$SSTOT = \sum_{i=1}^{b} \sum_{j=1}^{k} Y_{ij}^2 - C \tag{13.2.4}$$

and, by Theorem 13.2.1,

$$SSE = SSTOT - SSTR - SSB$$

Equations 13.2.2, 13.2.3, and 13.2.4 are considerably easier to evaluate than their counterparts on page 671. The proofs will be left as exercises.

CASE STUDY 13.2.1

Acrophobia is a fear of heights. It can be treated in a number of different ways. Using contact desensitization, a therapist demonstrates some task that would be difficult for someone with acrophobia to do, such as looking over a ledge or standing on a ladder. Then he guides the subject through the very same maneuver, always keeping in physical contact. Another method of treatment is demonstration participation. Here the therapist tries to *talk* the subject through the task; no physical contact is made. A third technique, live modeling, requires the subject simply to *watch* the task being done—he does not attempt it himself.

These three techniques were compared in a study involving 15 volunteers, all of whom had a history of severe acrophobia (133). It was realized at the outset, though, that the affliction was much more incapacitating in some subjects than in others, and that this heterogeneity might compromise the therapy comparison. Accordingly, the experiment began with each subject being given the Height Avoidance Test (HAT), a series of 44 tasks related to ladder climbing. A subject received a "point" for each task successfully completed. On

(continued on next page)

(Case Study 13.2.1 continued)

the basis of their final scores the 15 volunteers were divided into five blocks (A, B, C, D, and E), each of size three. The subjects in Block A had the *lowest* scores (that is, the most severe acrophobia), those in block B the second lowest scores, and so on.

Each of the three therapies was then assigned at random to one of the three subjects in each block. When the counseling sessions were over, the subjects retook the HAT. Table 13.2.3 lists the *changes* in their scores (score after therapy − score before therapy). Test the hypothesis that the therapies are equally effective. Let $\alpha = 0.01$.

TABLE 13.2.3 HAT Score Changes

| | Therapy | | | |
| | Contact | Demonstration | Live | |
Block	Desensitization	Participation	Modeling	$t_{i.}$
A	8	2	−2	8
B	11	1	0	12
C	9	12	6	27
D	16	11	2	29
E	24	19	11	54
$t_{.j}$	68	45	17	130

Since $C = (130)^2/15 = 1126.7$ and $\sum_{i=1}^{5} \sum_{j=1}^{3} y_{ij}^2 = 1894$, it follows that

$$SSTOT = 1894 - 1126.7 = 767.3$$

$$SSB = \frac{(8)^2}{3} + \cdots + \frac{(54)^2}{3} - 1126.7 = 438.0$$

$$SSTR = \frac{(68)^2}{5} + \frac{(45)^2}{5} + \frac{(17)^2}{5} - 1126.7 = 260.9$$

giving an error sum of squares of 68.4:

$$SSE = 767.3 - 438.0 - 260.9 = 68.4$$

The analysis of variance is summarized in Table 13.2.4. Since the calculated value of the F statistic, 15.260, exceeds $F_{.99,2,8} = 8.65$, $H_0: \mu_1 = \mu_2 = \mu_3$ can be rejected at the 0.01 level. In fact, the P value of 0.0019 indicates that H_0 can be rejected for α as small as 0.0019.

TABLE 13.2.4

Source	df	SS	MS	F	P
Therapies	2	260.93	130.47	15.260	0.0019
Blocks	4	438.00	109.50	12.807	0.0015
Error	8	68.40	8.55		
Total	14	767.33			

The small P-value for "Blocks" (= 0.0015) implies that $H_0: \beta_1 = \beta_2 = \ldots = \beta_5$ would also be rejected. Of course, that should come as no surprise: The blocks were intentionally set up to to be as different as possible. Indeed, if $F = \dfrac{SSB/(b-1)}{SSE/(b-1)(k-1)}$ had *not* been large, we would have questioned the validity of using HAT scores to measure the severity of acrophobia.

Comment.   Using a randomized block design instead of a one-way ANOVA is a trade-off. The blocks result in *SSE* being reduced, which improves the probability of rejecting H_0 when H_0 is false. On the other hand, the degrees of freedom associated with error in the randomized block analysis $[= (b - 1)(k - 1)]$ are fewer than the degrees of freedom associated with error in the *F* ratio from Chapter 12 $[= k(b - 1)]$. The latter is an advantage of the one-way analysis because the power of a procedure diminishes as the number of degrees of freedom associated with its test statistic decreases.

Ultimately, which approach is better in a given situation depends on the magnitude of *SSB*. If the block sum of squares is significantly large, as determined by the *F* test of Theorem 13.2.4, the loss of degrees of freedom to blocks was a good investment. On the other hand, if $H_0: \beta_1 = \beta_2 = \ldots = \beta_b$ is *not* rejected, the degrees of freedom sacrificed to blocks were, in effect, wasted, implying that the *k*-sample design of Chapter 12 would have been preferable.

CASE STUDY 13.2.2

Rat poison is normally made by mixing its active chemical ingredients with ordinary cornmeal. In many urban areas, though, rats can find food that they prefer to cornmeal, so the poison is left untouched. One solution is to make the cornmeal more palatable by adding food supplements such as peanut butter or meat. Doing that is effective, but the cost is high and the supplements spoil quickly.

In Milwaukee, a study was carried out to see whether *artificial* food supplements might be a workable compromise (75). For five two-week periods, 3200 baits were placed around garbage-storage areas—800 consisted of plain cornmeal; a second 800 had cornmeal mixed with artificial butter-vanilla flavoring; a third 800 contained cornmeal mixed with artificial roast beef flavoring; and the remaining 800 were cornmeal mixed with artificial bread flavoring.

Table 13.2.5 lists, for each survey, the percentage of each type of bait that was eaten. Do the rats show any preferences for the different flavors? Were the blocks—in this case, the surveys—helpful in reducing the error sum of squares? If a follow-up study were to be done, comparing these same baits, should a *k*-sample design or a randomized block design be used?

TABLE 13.2.5

Survey Number	Plain	Butter-Vanilla	Roast Beef	Bread
1	13.8	11.7	14.0	12.6
2	12.9	16.7	15.5	13.8
3	25.9	29.8	27.8	25.0
4	18.0	23.1	23.0	16.9
5	15.2	20.2	19.0	13.7

(continued on next page)

(Case Study 13.2.2 continued)

All of these questions are answered by the F ratios shown in Table 13.2.6. The P-values for $H_0: \mu_1 = \mu_2 = \mu_3 = \mu_4 (= 0.0042)$ and $H_0: \beta_1 = \beta_2 = \beta_3 = \beta_4 = \beta_5 (=0.0000)$ are both extremely small, so both null hypotheses would be rejected. Moreover, the fact that SSB is significantly large indicates that considerable variation exists from survey to survey, irrespective of the baits. It follows that any future studies should be set up in a similar fashion—that is, using a randomized block design.

TABLE 13.2.6

Source	df	SS	MS	F	P
Flavors	3	56.38	18.79	7.58	0.0042
Surveys	4	495.32	123.83	49.93	0.0000
Error	12	29.76	2.48		
Total	19	581.46			

Tukey Comparisons for Randomized Block Data

The Tukey pairwise comparison technique of Section 12.3 can be applied to a randomized block design. The definition of D is slightly different, since the associated studentized range is no longer $Q_{k, rk-k}$ but rather $Q_{k,(b-1)(k-1)}$, a change reflecting the number of degrees of freedom available for MSE in estimating σ^2.

THEOREM 13.2.5. Let $\bar{y}_{.j}, j = 1, 2, \ldots, k$ be the sample means in a $b \times k$ randomized block design. Let μ_j be the true treatment means, $j = 1, 2, \ldots, k$. The probability is $1 - \alpha$ that all $\binom{k}{2}$ pairwise subhypotheses $H_0: \mu_s = \mu_t$ will simultaneously satisfy the inequalities

$$\bar{y}_{.s} - \bar{y}_{.t} - D\sqrt{MSE} < \mu_s - \mu_t < \bar{y}_{.s} - \bar{y}_{.t} + D\sqrt{MSE}$$

where $D = Q_{\alpha, k, (b-1)(k-1)}/\sqrt{b}$. If, for a given s and t, zero is not contained in the preceding inequality, $H_0: \mu_s = \mu_t$ can be rejected in favor of $H_1: \mu_s \neq \mu_t$ at the α level of significance.

EXAMPLE 13.2.1

Recall the comparison of the three acrophobia therapies in Case Study 13.2.1. The F test in Table 13.2.4 showed that $H_0: \mu_1 = \mu_2 = \mu_3$ can be rejected at the $\alpha = 0.05$ (or even 0.005) level of significance. Are all three therapies, though, significantly different, or is one of them simply different from the other two? Answer the question by constructing a set of 95% Tukey confidence intervals for the three pairwise comparisons.

Here,

$$D = \frac{Q_{.05, 3, 8}}{\sqrt{5}} = \frac{4.04}{2.24} = 1.81$$

and the radius of the Tukey intervals is

$$D\sqrt{MSE} = 1.81\sqrt{8.55} = 5.3$$

Table 13.2.7 summarizes the calculations called for in Theorem 13.2.5.

TABLE 13.2.7

Pairwise Difference	$\bar{y}_{.s} - \bar{y}_{.t}$	Tukey Interval	Conclusion
$\mu_1 - \mu_2$	4.6	$(-0.7, 9.9)$	Not significant
$\mu_1 - \mu_3$	10.2	$(4.9, 15.5)$	Reject
$\mu_2 - \mu_3$	5.6	$(0.3, 10.9)$	Reject

Now we have a much better picture of the relative values of these three therapies. Based on the Tukey intervals, contact desensitization (μ_1) and demonstration participation (μ_2) are *not* significantly different (at $\alpha = 0.05$). However, both contact desensitization and demonstration participation are significantly better than live modeling (μ_3).

Contrasts for Randomized Block Data

The techniques we learned in Section 12.4 for testing contrasts can be readily adapted to randomized block designs as well. If C is the contrast associated with the null hypothesis, the appropriate test statistic is

$$F = \frac{SS_C/1}{SSE/(b-1)(k-1)}$$

where F has 1 and $(b-1)(k-1)$ degrees of freedom and SSE is the error sum of squares defined for randomized block data (see page 673).

CASE STUDY 13.2.3

Case Study 1.2.3 described an investigation designed to measure the so-called Transylvania effect—that is, the influence the full moon might have on human behavior. Table 13.2.8 reproduces those data (admission rates to the emergency room of a Virginia mental health

TABLE 13.2.8

	(1) Before Full	(2) During Full	(3) After Full	
Month	Moon	Moon	Moon	$\bar{y}_{i.}$
Aug.	6.4	5.0	5.8	5.73
Sept.	7.1	13.0	9.2	9.77
Oct.	6.5	14.0	7.9	9.47
Nov.	8.6	12.0	7.7	9.43
Dec.	8.1	6.0	11.0	8.37
Jan.	10.4	9.0	12.9	10.77
Feb.	11.5	13.0	13.5	12.67
Mar.	13.8	16.0	13.1	14.30
Apr.	15.4	25.0	15.8	18.73
May	15.7	13.0	13.3	14.00
June	11.7	14.0	12.8	12.83
July	15.8	20.0	14.5	16.77
$\bar{y}_{.j}$	10.92	13.33	11.46	

Admission Rates (patients/day)

(continued on next page)

(Case Study 13.2.3 continued)

TABLE 13.2.9

Source	df	SS	MS	F
Lunar cycles	2	38.59	19.30	3.22
Months	11	451.08	41.01	
Error	22	132.08	6.00	
Total	35	621.75		

clinic); included are the month and lunar cycle averages. Here, "time," as expressed in months, is acting as the blocking variable.

Table 13.2.9 summarizes the ANOVA calculations. For 2 and 22 degrees of freedom, the 0.05 critical value for the *lunar cycle* effect is 3.44, which is greater than the observed $F(= 3.22)$. Therefore, we would fail to reject $H_0: \mu_1 = \mu_2 = \mu_3$, and the conclusion would be that a lunar effect has *not* been demonstrated.

Testing the overall $H_0: \mu_1 = \mu_2 = \mu_3$ is not the only appropriate way to analyze these data, though. An *a priori* subhypothesis is clearly suggested by the circumstances of the problem—specifically, it would make sense to test whether the admission rate during the full moon is different than the *average* rate during the rest of the month. To that end, test the subhypothesis $H_0: \mu_2 = (\mu_1 + \mu_3)/2$.

Following the procedure outlined in Section 12.4, the contrast associated with H_0 is

$$C = -\frac{1}{2}\mu_1 + \mu_2 - \frac{1}{2}\mu_3$$

while its estimate is

$$\hat{C} = -\frac{1}{2}(10.92) + 1(13.3) - \frac{1}{2}(11.46)$$

$$= 2.11$$

From Definition 12.4.2, the sum of squares associated with C is 35.62:

$$SS_C = \frac{(2.11)^2}{\dfrac{1/4}{12} + \dfrac{1}{12} + \dfrac{1/4}{12}} = 35.62$$

Dividing SS_C by the mean square for error gives an F ratio of *5.93* (with 1 and 22 degrees of freedom):

$$\frac{35.62/1}{132.08/22} = 5.93$$

For $\alpha = 0.05$, though, $F_{.95, 1, 22} = 4.30$. Therefore, contrary to our acceptance of $H_0: \mu_1 = \mu_2 = \mu_3$, we would *reject* $H_0: \mu_2 = (\mu_1 + \mu_3)/2$ and conclude that the Transylvania effect *does* exist.

Comment. It is always more than a little disconcerting when two valid statistical techniques applied to the same data lead to opposite conclusions. That such apparent contradictions occur, though, should not be unexpected. Different methods of analysis simply utilize the data in different ways. Disagreements from time to time are inevitable.

QUESTIONS

13.2.1 In recent years a number of research projects in extrasensory perception have examined the possibility that hypnosis may be helpful in bringing out ESP in persons who did not think they had any. The obvious way to test such a hypothesis is with a self-paired design: the ESP ability of a subject when he is awake is compared to his ability when hypnotized. In one study of this sort, 15 college students were each asked to guess the identity of 200 Zener cards (see Case Study 4.3.1). The same "sender"—that is, the person concentrating on the card—was used for each trial. For 100 of the trials both the student and the sender were awake; for the other 100 both were hypnotized. If chance were the only factor involved, the expected number of correct identifications in each set of 100 trials would be 20. The observed average numbers of correct guesses for subjects awake and subjects hypnotized were 18.9 and 21.7, respectively (22). Use the analysis of variance to determine whether that difference is statistically significant at the 0.05 level.

Number of Correct Responses (out of 100) in ESP Experiment

Student	Sender and Student in Waking State	Sender and Student in Hypnotic State
1	18	25
2	19	20
3	16	26
4	21	26
5	16	20
6	20	23
7	20	14
8	14	18
9	11	18
10	22	20
11	19	22
12	29	27
13	16	19
14	27	27
15	15	21
$\bar{y}_{.j}$	18.9	21.7

13.2.2 The following table shows the audience shares of the three major networks' evening news broadcasts in four major cities as reported by Arbitron. Test at the $\alpha = 0.10$ level of significance the null hypothesis that viewing levels for news are the same for ABC, CBS, and NBC.

City	ABC	CBS	NBC
A	19.7	16.1	18.2
B	18.6	15.8	17.9
C	19.1	14.6	15.3
D	17.9	17.1	18.0

13.2.3 A paint manufacturer is experimenting with an additive that might make the paint less chalky. To ensure that the additive does not affect the tint, a quality control engineer takes a sample from each of seven batches of Osage Orange. Each sample is split in half, and the additive is put into one of the two. Both samples are examined with a spectroscope, with the output read in standardized lumen units. If the tint were exactly correct the reading would be 1.00. Test that the mean spectroscope readings are the same for the two versions of Osage Orange. Let $\alpha = 0.05$.

Batch	Without Additive	With Additive
1	1.10	1.06
2	1.05	1.02
3	1.08	1.17
4	0.98	1.21
5	1.01	1.01
6	0.96	1.23
7	1.02	1.19

13.2.4 The number of new building permits can be a good indicator of the strength of a region's economic growth. The following table gives percentage increases over a four-year period for three geographical areas. Analyze the data. Let $\alpha = 0.05$. What are your conclusions?

Year	Eastern	North Central	Southwest
1990	1.1	0.1	0.9
1991	1.3	0.8	1.0
1992	2.9	1.1	1.4
1993	3.5	1.3	1.5

13.2.5 A useful measure of a stock's profitability is its yield, defined to be its dividends for the previous 12 months times 100, divided by its current market value. The following table gives the yields of the New York Stock Exchange Common Stock Index for each quarter of the years 1981 through 1985. Are yields affected by the quarter of the year? Is the variability in the yield from year to year statistically significant? State your conclusions using the $\alpha = 0.05$ level of significance.

	Quarter			
Year	First	Second	Third	Fourth
1981	5.7	6.0	7.1	6.7
1982	7.2	7.0	6.1	5.2
1983	4.9	4.1	4.2	4.4
1984	4.5	4.9	4.5	4.5
1985	4.4	4.2	4.2	3.6

13.2.6 Analyze the Transylvania effect data in Case Study 13.2.3 by calculating 95% Tukey confidence intervals for the pairwise differences among the admission rates for the three different phases of the moon. How do your conclusions agree (or differ) from those already discussed on page 678? Let $Q_{.05,3,22} = 3.56$.

13.2.7 Find the 95% Tukey intervals for the data of Question 13.2.2, and use them to test the three pairwise comparisons of ABC, CBS, and NBC.

13.2.8 A comparison was made of the efficiency of four different unit-dose injection systems. A group of pharmacists and nurses were the "blocks." For each system, they were to remove the unit from its outer package, assemble it, and simulate an injection. In addition to the standard system of using a disposable syringe and needle to draw the medication from a vial, the other systems tested were Vari-Ject (CIBA Pharmaceutical), Unimatic (Squibb), and Tubex (Wyeth). Listed in the following table are the average times (in seconds) needed to implement each of the systems (137).

Average Times (sec) for Implementing Injection Systems

Subject	Standard	Vari-Ject	Unimatic	Tubex	$t_{i.}$
1	35.6	17.3	24.4	25.0	102.3
2	31.3	16.4	22.4	26.0	96.1
3	36.2	18.1	22.8	25.3	102.4
4	31.1	17.8	21.0	24.0	93.9
5	39.4	18.8	23.3	24.2	105.7
6	34.7	17.0	21.8	26.2	99.7
7	34.1	14.5	23.0	24.0	95.6
8	36.5	17.9	24.1	20.9	99.4
9	32.2	14.6	23.5	23.5	93.8
10	40.7	16.4	31.3	36.9	125.3
$t_{.j}$	351.8	168.8	237.6	256.0	1014.2

(a) Test the equality of the means at the 0.05 level.

(b) Use Tukey's method to test all six pairwise differences of the four μ_j's. Let $\alpha = 0.05$. *Note*: $SSTOT = 2056.10$, $SSTR = 1709.60$, and $SSB = 193.53$; $Q_{.05,4,27} = 4.34$.

13.2.9 Heart rates were monitored (11) for six tree shrews (*Tupaia glis*) during three different stages of sleep: LSWS (light slow-wave sleep), DSWS (deep slow-wave sleep), and REM (rapid-eye-movement sleep).

Heart Rates (beats/5 seconds)

Tree Shrew	LSWS	DSWS	REM
1	14.1	11.7	15.7
2	26.0	21.1	21.5
3	20.9	19.7	18.3
4	19.0	18.2	17.0
5	26.1	23.2	22.5
6	20.5	20.7	18.9

(a) Do the analysis of variance to test the equality of the heart rates during these three phases of sleep. Let $\alpha = 0.05$.

(b) Because of the marked physiological difference between REM sleep and LSWS and DSWS sleep, it was decided before the data were collected to test the REM rate against the average of the other two. Test the appropriate subhypothesis with a contrast. Use the 0.05 level of significance. Also, find a second contrast orthogonal to the first and verify that the sum of the sum of squares for the two contrasts equals *SSTR*.

13.2.10 Refer to the rat-poison data of Case Study 13.2.2. Partition the treatment sum of squares into three orthogonal contrasts. Let one contrast test the hypothesis that the true acceptance percentage for the plain cornmeal is equal to the true acceptance percentage for the cornmeal with artificial roast beef flavoring. Let a second contrast compare the effectiveness of the "butter-vanilla" and "bread" baits. What does the third contrast test? Do all testing at the $\alpha = 0.10$ level of significance.

13.2.11 Prove the computing formulas given in Equations 13.2.2, 13.2.3, and 13.2.4.

13.2.12 Differentiate the function

$$L = \sum_{i=1}^{b} \sum_{j=1}^{k} \left(y_{ij} - \beta_i - \mu_j \right)^2$$

with respect to all bk parameters and calculate the least-squares estimates for the β_i's and μ_j's.

13.2.13 True or false:

(a) Does $\displaystyle\sum_{i=1}^{b} \bar{Y}_{i.} = \sum_{j=1}^{k} \bar{Y}_{.j}$?

(b) Either $MSTR$ or MSB or both are greater than or equal to MSE.

13.2.14 For a set of randomized block data comparing k treatments within b blocks, find

(a) $E(SSB)$　　　　　　　　　(b) $E(SSE)$

13.3 THE PAIRED t TEST

An important special case of a randomized block design arises when the number of treatment levels is reduced to $k = 2$. The simplicity of the data structure then allows the F test to be replaced by the one-sample t test. Specifically, if X_i and Y_i denote the responses in the ith block to treatment level 1 and treatment level 2, respectively, we will define D_i to be the within-block difference—that is, $D_i = X_i - Y_i$. If there are b blocks, the sample mean and the sample variance of the D_i's have formulas analogous to their Chapter 7 counterparts:

$$\bar{D} = \frac{1}{b} \sum_{i=1}^{b} D_i$$

and

$$S_D^2 = \frac{1}{b-1} \sum_{i=1}^{b} \left(D_i - \bar{D} \right)^2 = \frac{b \sum\limits_{i=1}^{b} D_i^2 - \left(\sum\limits_{i=1}^{b} D_i \right)^2}{b(b-1)}$$

Let μ_X and μ_Y denote the true means of levels 1 and 2, and let $\mu_D = \mu_X - \mu_Y$. Testing the null hypothesis $H_0 : \mu_X = \mu_Y$ is then the same as testing $H_0 : \mu_D = 0$. If we can assume that the D_i's are independent and normally distributed, Theorem 7.5.2 provides the appropriate critical region.

Comment. Testing $H_0 : \mu_D = 0$ is a one-sample problem analytically, but a two-sample problem conceptually. However, it is not analogous to the data structure presented in Chapter 9, because here the two samples are *dependent*, X_i and Y_i being measured on members of the same block. To emphasize that distinction, the application of Theorem 7.5.2 in this context is referred to as a *paired t test*.

CASE STUDY 13.3.1

Prior to the 1968 appearance of Kenneth Cooper's book entitled *Aerobics*, the word did not appear in Webster's Dictionary. Now the term is commonly understood to refer to sustained exercises intended to strengthen the heart and lungs. The actual benefits of such physical activities, as well as their possible detrimental effects, have spawned a great deal of research in human physiology as it relates to exercise.

TABLE 13.3.1

Subject	Before Walk, x_i	After Walk, y_i	$d_i = x_i - y_i$
A	14.6	13.8	0.8
B	17.3	15.4	1.9
C	10.9	11.3	−0.4
D	12.8	11.6	1.2
E	16.6	16.4	0.2
F	12.2	12.6	−0.4
G	11.2	11.8	−0.6
H	15.4	15.0	0.4
I	14.8	14.4	0.4
J	16.2	15.0	1.2

One such study (65) concerned changes in the blood, specifically in hemoglobin levels before and after a prolonged brisk walk. Hemoglobin helps red blood cells transport oxygen to tissues and then remove carbon dioxide. Given the stress that exercise places on the need for that particular exchange, it is not unreasonable to suspect that aerobics might alter the blood's hemoglobin levels.

Ten athletes had their hemoglobin levels measured (in g/dl) prior to embarking on a 60-kilometer walk. After they finished, their levels were measured again (see Table 13.3.1). Set up and test an appropriate H_0 and H_1.

If μ_X and μ_Y denote the true average hemoglobin levels *before* and *after* walking, respectively, and if $\mu_D = \mu_X - \mu_Y$, then the hypotheses to be tested are

$$H_0: \quad \mu_D = 0$$

versus

$$H_1: \quad \mu_D \neq 0$$

Let 0.05 be the level of significance.

From Table 13.3.1,

$$\sum_{i=1}^{10} d_i = 4.7 \quad \text{and} \quad \sum_{i=1}^{10} d_i^2 = 8.17$$

Therefore,

$$\bar{d} = \frac{1}{10}(4.7) = 0.47$$

and

$$s_D^2 = \frac{10(8.17) - (4.7)^2}{10(9)} = 0.662$$

Since $n = 10$, the critical values for the test statistic will be the 2.5th and 97.5th percentiles of the Student t distribution with 9 degrees of freedom: $\pm t_{.025,9} = \pm 2.2622$. The appropriate decision rule from Theorem 7.5.2, then, is

$$\text{Reject } H_0: \mu_D = 0 \text{ if } \frac{\bar{d}}{s_D/\sqrt{10}} \text{ is either } \begin{cases} \leq -2.2622 \\ \text{or} \\ \geq 2.2622 \end{cases}$$

(continued on next page)

> *(Case Study 13.3.1 continued)*
>
> In this case the t ratio is
>
> $$\frac{\bar{d}}{s_D/\sqrt{10}} = \frac{0.47}{\sqrt{0.662}/\sqrt{10}} = 1.83$$
>
> and our conclusion is to *accept* H_0: The difference between $\bar{d}(= 0.47)$ and the H_0 value for $\mu_D(= 0)$ is not statistically significant.

QUESTIONS

13.3.1 The Common Fund is a firm that invests funds for colleges and universities. One of its investment vehicles is a short-term note that is supposed to compete with three-month Treasury bills. The following table compares the monthly yields of the Common Fund short-term notes and three-month Treasury bills (30). Does the Common Fund have significantly higher yields than T-bills? Let $\alpha = 0.10$.

Month	Common Fund, x	Three-month T-bill, y
Jul-91	6.71	5.75
Aug-91	6.19	5.51
Sep-91	6.23	5.38
Oct-91	6.07	5.17
Nov-91	5.63	4.73
Dec-91	6.86	4.19
Jan-92	3.93	3.93
Feb-92	3.95	3.95
Mar-92	4.16	4.16
Apr-92	4.26	3.83
May-92	4.26	3.75
Jun-92	4.41	3.76

13.3.2 The following table gives the daily car rental rates charged by two rental car companies, Alamo and Avis, in 12 locations (176). The rate is for a midsize automobile rented midweek with three days advance notice. Alamo purports to be a low-budget agency. Do the prices quoted here lend credence to Alamo's claim? Test an appropriate H_0 versus H_1, letting $\alpha = 0.05$.

Airport	Alamo, x	Avis, y
Atlanta	48.99	51.99
Chicago O'Hare	49.99	55.99
Dallas–Ft. Worth	42.99	47.00
Denver	34.99	42.99
Los Angeles	42.99	44.95
Miami	33.99	38.99
Newark	59.99	69.99
Phoenix	42.89	50.99
San Francisco	47.99	49.99
St. Louis	47.99	53.99
Seattle	35.99	42.99
Washington National	44.99	44.99

13.3.3 Blood coagulates as a result of a complex sequence of chemical reactions. The protein thrombin triggers the clotting of blood under the influence of another protein called prothrombin. One measure of a person's blood clotting ability is expressed in prothrombin time, which is defined to be the interval between the initiation of the thrombin-prothrombin reaction and the formation of the clot. One study (196) looked at the effect of aspirin on prothrombin time. The following table gives, for each of 12 subjects, the prothrombin time (in seconds) *before* and *three hours after* taking two aspirin tablets (650 mg). Test the hypothesis that aspirin influences prothrombin times. Perform the test at both the $\alpha = 0.05$ and $\alpha = 0.01$ levels.

Subject	Before Aspirin, x	After Aspirin, y
1	12.3	12.0
2	12.0	12.3
3	12.0	12.5
4	13.0	12.0
5	13.0	13.0
6	12.5	12.5
7	11.3	10.3
8	11.8	11.3
9	11.5	11.5
10	11.0	11.5
11	11.0	11.0
12	11.3	11.5

13.3.4 Use a paired t test to analyze the hypnosis/ESP data given in Question 13.2.1. Let $\alpha = 0.05$.

13.3.5 Perform the hypothesis test indicated in Question 13.2.3 at the 0.05 level using a paired t test. Compare the square of the observed t with the observed F. Do the same for the critical values associated with the two procedures. What would you conclude?

13.3.6 Let $D_1, D_2, \ldots D_b$ be the within-block differences as defined in Section 13.3. Assume that the D_i's are normal with mean μ_D and variance σ_D^2, for $i = 1, 2, \ldots, b$. Derive a formula for a $100(1 - \alpha)\%$ confidence interval for μ_D. Apply this formula to the data of Case Study 13.3.1 and construct a 95% confidence interval for the true average hemoglobin difference ("before walk" − "after walk").

13.3.7 Construct a 95% confidence interval for μ_D in the prothrombin time data described in Question 13.3.3. See Question 13.3.6.

13.3.8 Show that the paired t test is equivalent to the F test in a randomized block design when the number of treatment levels is two. (*Hint*: Consider the distribution of $T^2 = b\bar{D}^2/S_D^2$.)

APPENDIX 13.A.1   MINITAB APPLICATIONS

To produce the information in a randomized block ANOVA table, MINITAB uses the command "twoway c1 c2 c3". First, the data are "stacked," treatment level over treatment level, into a single column—say, c1 (similar to the way the y_{ij}'s in a Tukey analysis are entered). Then two auxiliary columns must be created. The first, call it c2, gives the column number for each entry in c1. The second—say, c3—gives the block number (*i.e.*, the row number) for each entry in c1.

```
MTB > set c1
DATA> 8 11 9 16 24 2 1 12 11 19 -2 0 6 2 11
DATA> end
MTB > set c2
DATA> 1 1 1 1 1 2 2 2 2 2 3 3 3 3 3
DATA> end
MTB > set c3
DATA> 1 2 3 4 5 1 2 3 4 5 1 2 3 4 5
DATA> end
MTB > name c1 'HAT' c2 'Therapy' c3 'Blocks'
MTB > twoway c1 c2 c3
```

Two-way Analysis of Variance

```
Analysis of variance for HAT
Source      DF        SS        MS        F        P
Therapy      2    260.93    130.47    15.26    0.002
Blocks       4    438.00    109.50    12.81    0.001
Error        8     68.40      8.55
Total       14    767.33
```

FIGURE 13.A.1.1

Consider, again, the data in Case Study 13.2.1. Figure 13.A.1.1 is the MINITAB syntax for outputting the calculations that appear in Table 13.2.4. Notice that the Windows version reverses columns C1 and C2.

Doing a Randomized Block Analysis of Variance Using MINITAB Windows

1. Enter the entire data set in column C1, beginning with Treatment level 1, followed by Treatment level 2, and so on.
2. In column C2, enter the block number of each data point in C1; in column C3, enter the column number of each data point in C1.
3. Click on STAT, then on ANOVA, then on TWO-WAY.
4. Type C1 in RESPONSE box, C2 in ROW FACTOR box, and C3 in COLUMN FACTOR box.
5. Click on OK.

CHAPTER 14

Nonparametric Statistics

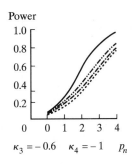

$\kappa_3 = -0.6 \quad \kappa_4 = -1 \quad p_n$

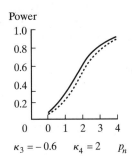

$\kappa_3 = -0.6 \quad \kappa_4 = 2 \quad p_n$

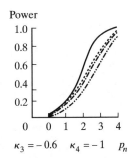

$\kappa_3 = -0.6 \quad \kappa_4 = -1 \quad p_n$

The figures show a comparison of the power functions of the one-sample t test (solid line) and the sign test (dashed lines) for three different sets of hypotheses, various degrees of nonnormality, a sample size of 10, and a level of significance of 0.05. (The parameter p_n measures the shift from H_0 to H_1; κ_3 and κ_4 measure the extent of nonnormality in the sampled population.)

14.1 INTRODUCTION

Behind every confidence interval and hypothesis test we have studied thus far have been very specific assumptions about the nature of the pdf that the data presumably represent. For instance, the usual Z test for proportions—$H_0: p_X = p_Y$ versus $H_1: p_X \neq p_Y$—is predicated on the assumption that the two samples consist of independent and identically distributed Bernoulli random variables. The most common assumption in data analysis, of course, is that each set of observations is a random sample from a *normal* distribution. This was the condition specified in every t test and F test that we have done.

The need to make such assumptions raises an obvious question: What changes when these assumptions are not satisfied? Certainly the statistic being calculated stays the same, as do the critical values that define the rejection region. What *does* change, of course, is the sampling distribution of the test statistic. As a result, the *actual* probability of committing, say, a Type I error will not necessarily equal the *nominal* probability of committing a Type I error. That is, if W is the test statistic with pdf $f_W(w | H_0)$ when H_0 is true, and C is the critical region,

$$\text{"true"} \ \alpha = \int_C f_W(w | H_0) \, dw$$

is not necessarily equal to the "nominal" α, because $f_W(w | H_0)$ is different (because of the violated assumptions) from the presumed sampling distribution of the test statistic. Moreover, there is usually no way to know the "true" functional form of $f_W(w | H_0)$ when the underlying assumptions about the data have not been met.

Statisticians have sought to overcome the problem implicit in not knowing the true $f_W(w | H_0)$ in two very different ways. One approach is the idea of *robustness*, a concept that was introduced in Section 7.5. The Monte Carlo simulations illustrated in Figure 7.5.4, for example, show that even though a set of Y_i's deviates from normality, the distribution of the t ratio,

$$T = \frac{\bar{Y} - \mu_o}{S/\sqrt{n}}$$

is likely to be sufficiently close to $f_{T_{n-1}}(t)$ that the actual α, for all practical purposes, is equal to the nominal α. The one-sample t test is not seriously compromised, in other words, if normality fails to hold.

A second way of dealing with the additional uncertainty introduced by violated assumptions is to use test statistics whose pdf's remain the same, regardless of how the population sampled may change. Inference procedures having this sort of latitude are called *nonparametric* or, more appropriately, *distribution free*.

The number of nonparametric procedures proposed since the early 1940s has been enormous and continues to grow. It is not the intention of Chapter 14 to survey this multiplicity of techniques in any comprehensive fashion. Instead, the objective here is to introduce some of the basic methodology of nonparametric statistics in the context of problems whose "parametric" solutions have already been discussed. Included in that list will be nonparametric treatments of the paired data problem, the one-sample location problem, and both of the analysis-of-variance models covered in Chapters 12 and 13.

14.2 THE SIGN TEST

Among the simplest of all nonparametric procedures is the *sign test*. It finds a number of different applications: If a set of Y_i's comes from a *symmetric* (but not necessarily normal) pdf, a sign test can be used for the one-sample location problem, $H_0: \tilde{\mu} = \tilde{\mu}_0$ versus $H_1: \tilde{\mu} \neq \tilde{\mu}_0$, where $\tilde{\mu}$ denotes the median of the population being sampled. The same test is also appropriate in a paired-data situation where the normality of the X_i's and Y_i's is questionable.

Consider the latter situation: $(X_1, Y_1), (X_2, Y_2), \ldots, (X_n, Y_n)$ is a random sample of paired observations. Let $p = P(Y_i > X_i)$. We wish to test whether or not the X's are shifted in location relative to the Y's. In terms of p, the hypotheses reduce to

$$H_0: \quad p = \tfrac{1}{2} \quad \text{(no shift in location)}$$

versus

$$H_1: \quad p \neq \tfrac{1}{2} \quad \text{(shift in location)}$$

Let each (X_i, Y_i) pair be replaced by either a plus sign or a minus sign: a plus sign if $Y_i > X_i$ and a minus sign if $Y_i < X_i$. [It will be assumed that both $f_X(x)$ and $f_Y(y)$ are continuous, so the event of a tie has probability zero.] It follows that if H_0 is true, each (X_i, Y_i) pair constitutes a Bernoulli trial, and Y_+, the number of plus signs, will have a binomial pdf with parameters n and $\tfrac{1}{2}$. The appropriate decision rule, then, is an extension of the argument given in Section 6.3: H_0 should be rejected if y_+ is either less than or equal to Y_+^* or greater than or equal to Y_+^{**}, where

$$P(Y_+ \leq Y_+^*) = P(Y_+ \geq Y_+^{**}) = \frac{\alpha}{2} \tag{14.2.1}$$

Comment. For small n, the discreteness of the binomial pdf might make it impossible to find a Y_+^* and a Y_+^{**} satisfying Equation 14.2.1 exactly. For large n, that becomes less of a problem: We simply appeal to the DeMoivre-Laplace limit theorem and approximate, say, Y_+^{**} by solving

$$z_{1-\alpha/2} = \frac{Y_+^{**} - \tfrac{1}{2} \cdot n}{\sqrt{n/4}}$$

CASE STUDY 14.2.1

Children with severe learning problems often have electroencephalograms and behavior patterns similar to those of children with petit-mal, a mild form of epilepsy. This led to speculation that drugs helpful in treating petit-mal might also be useful as "learning facilitators" (152). To test that hypothesis, 10 children, ranging in age from 8 to 14 and all having a history of learning and behavioral problems, were recruited to participate in a six-week study. For three of those weeks a child was given a placebo; for the other three weeks, ethosuximide, a widely prescribed anticonvulsant. After each three-week period the children were

(continued on next page)

(Case Study 14.2.1 continued)

given several parts of the standard Wechsler IQ test. Because a child might be expected to do better on the test the second time he or she took it, the order in which the placebo and the ethosuximide were administered was randomized: Some children were given the placebo for the first three weeks while others began the study by taking the ethosuximide.

Table 14.2.1 shows the two verbal IQ scores recorded for each subject. The last entry in the fourth column indicates the value of the test statistic, Y_+.

TABLE 14.2.1   IQ Scores in Ethosuximide Experiment

Child	IQ after Placebo, x_i	IQ after Ethosuximide, y_i	$y_i > x_i$?
1	97	113	+
2	106	113	+
3	106	101	−
4	95	119	+
5	102	111	+
6	111	122	+
7	115	121	+
8	104	106	+
9	90	110	+
10	96	126	+
			$y_+ = 9$

Suppose that we wish to test

$$H_0: \quad p = \frac{1}{2}$$

versus

$$H_1: \quad p \neq \frac{1}{2}$$

at the $\alpha = 0.10$ level of significance, where $p = P(Y_i > X_i)$. The two-sided alternative is used here to allow for the possibility that ethosuximide might actually have an adverse effect on IQ.

For the binomial pdf with parameters $n = 10$ and $p = \frac{1}{2}$,

$$P(Y_+ \leq 2) = \sum_{y=0}^{2} \binom{10}{y} \left(\frac{1}{2}\right)^y \left(\frac{1}{2}\right)^{10-y} \doteq 0.05$$

and

$$P(Y_+ \geq 8) = \sum_{y=8}^{10} \binom{10}{y} \left(\frac{1}{2}\right)^y \left(\frac{1}{2}\right)^{10-y} \doteq 0.05$$

Thus, to maintain a Type I error probability of approximately 0.10, we should reject H_0 if y_+ is either less than or equal to 2 or greater than or equal to 8. In fact, the latter was true ($y_+ = 9$), so our conclusion is to *reject* the null hypothesis: It would appear that ethosuximide *does* have an effect on IQ, and a beneficial one at that.

QUESTIONS

14.2.1 One reason cited for the mental deterioration so often seen in the very elderly is the reduction in cerebral blood flow that accompanies the aging process. Addressing itself to this notion, a study was recently done in a rest home to see whether cyclandelate, a vasodilator, might be able to stimulate the cerebral circulation and thereby slow down the rate of mental deterioration (5). The drug was given to 11 subjects on a daily basis. To measure its physiological effect, radioactive tracers were used to determine each subject's mean circulation time (MCT) at the start of the experiment and four months later when the study was discontinued. (The MCT is the length of time it takes blood to travel from the carotid artery to the jugular vein.) The results are shown in the following table. Test the appropriate hypothesis with a sign test. Use a one-sided alternative.

Cerebral Circulation Experiment

Subject	Mean Circulation Time (sec)	
	Before, x_i	After, y_i
J.B.	15	13
M.B.	12	8
A.B.	12	12.5
M.B.	14	12
J.L.	13	12
S.M.	13	12.5
M.M.	13	12.5
S.McA.	12	14
A.McL.	12.5	12
F.S.	12	11
P.W.	12.5	10

14.2.2 Recall Case Study 14.2.1. What could be concluded if the "after ethosuximide" IQs were significantly higher than the "after placebo" IQs but if all 10 children had been given the placebo first?

14.2.3 Synovial fluid is the clear, viscid secretion that lubricates joints and tendons. For some ailments, its hydrogen-ion concentration (pH) has diagnostic importance. In healthy adults, the average pH for synovial fluid is 7.39. The following table lists synovial pH values measured for fluids drawn from the knees of 44 patients with various arthritic conditions (169). Is an abnormal synovial pH a symptom of arthritis? Do a sign test on

$$H_0: \quad \tilde{\mu} = 7.39$$

versus

$$H_1: \quad \tilde{\mu} \neq 7.39$$

where $\tilde{\mu}$ denotes the synovial fluid pH typical of adults with arthritis. Let $\alpha = 0.01$.

Synovial Fluid pH

7.02	7.26	7.31	7.14	7.45	7.32	7.21	7.36	7.36
7.35	7.25	7.24	7.20	7.39	7.40	7.33	7.09	6.60
7.32	7.35	7.34	7.41	7.28	6.99	7.28	7.32	7.29
7.33	7.38	7.32	7.77	7.34	7.10	7.35	6.95	7.31
7.15	7.20	7.34	7.12	7.22	7.30	7.24	7.35	

14.2.4 Let $Y_1, Y_2, \ldots, Y_{22}$ be a random sample of normally distributed random variables with an unknown mean μ and a known variance of 6.0. We wish to test

$$H_0: \quad \mu = 10$$

versus

$$H_1: \quad \mu > 10$$

Construct a large-sample sign test having a Type I error probability of 0.05. What will the power of the test be if $\mu = 11$?

14.2.5 Suppose that $n = 7$ paired observations, (X_i, Y_i), are recorded, $i = 1, 2, \ldots, 7$. Let $p = P(Y_i > X_i)$. Write out the entire probability distribution for Y_+, the number of positive differences among the set of $Y_i - X_i$'s, $i = 1, 2, \ldots, 7$, assuming that $p = \frac{1}{2}$. What α levels are possible for testing $H_0: p = \frac{1}{2}$ versus $H_1: p > \frac{1}{2}$?

14.2.6 Analyze the Shoshoni rectangle data (Case Study 1.2.2) with a sign test. Let $\alpha = 0.05$.

14.2.7 Recall the FEV_1/VC data described in Question 7.5.11. Test $H_0: \tilde{\mu} = 0.80$ versus $H_0: \tilde{\mu} < 0.80$ using a sign test. Compare this conclusion with that of a t test of $H_0: \mu = 0.80$ versus $H_1: \mu < 0.80$. Let $\alpha = 0.10$.

14.2.8 Do a sign test on the data given in Case Study 13.3.1. Let 0.05 be the level of significance.

14.2.9 In a marketing research test, 28 adult males were asked to shave one side of their face with one brand of razor blade and the other side with a second brand. They were to use the blades for seven days and then decide which was giving the smoother shave. Suppose that 19 of the subjects preferred blade A. Use a sign test to determine whether it can be claimed, at the 0.05 level, that the two blades are significantly different.

14.2.10 Suppose that a random sample of size 36, $Y_1, Y_2, \ldots, Y_{36}$, is drawn from a uniform pdf defined over the interval $(0, \theta)$, where θ is unknown. Set up a large-sample sign test for deciding whether or not the 25th percentile of the Y-distribution is equal to 6. Let $\alpha = 0.05$. With what probability will your procedure commit a Type II error if 7 is the true 25th percentile?

14.3   THE WILCOXON SIGNED RANK TEST

Although the sign test is a bona fide nonparametric procedure, its extreme simplicity makes it somewhat atypical. The *Wilcoxon signed rank test* introduced in this section is more representative of nonparametric procedures as a whole. Like the sign test, it can be adapted to several different data structures. Here, we will pose it within the framework of a one-sample test for location, where it becomes an alternative to the one-sample t test. The procedure carries over immediately to the paired-data problem and with only minor modifications can also serve as a two-sample test for location and a two-sample test for dispersion (provided the two populations have equal locations). Historically, the Wilcoxon signed rank test was one of the first nonparametric procedures to be developed (it dates back to 1945), and it remains one of the most widely used.

Let $Y_1, Y_2, \ldots, Y_n$ be a random sample of size n from a pdf $f_Y(y)$ that is both continuous and symmetric. Let $\tilde{\mu}$ be the median of $f_Y(y)$. We wish to test

$$H_0: \quad \tilde{\mu} = \tilde{\mu}_0$$

versus

$$H_1: \quad \tilde{\mu} \neq \tilde{\mu}_0$$

where $\tilde{\mu}_0$ is some prespecified value for $\tilde{\mu}$.

The Wilcoxon statistic is based on the magnitudes, and directions, of the deviations of the Y_i's from $\tilde{\mu}_0$. Let $|Y_1 - \tilde{\mu}_0|, |Y_2 - \tilde{\mu}_0|, \ldots, |Y_n - \tilde{\mu}_0|$ denote the set of absolute deviations of the Y_i's from $\tilde{\mu}_0$. These can be ordered from smallest to largest, and we will define R_i to be the *rank* of $|Y_i - \tilde{\mu}_0|$ in the set $\{|Y_j - \tilde{\mu}_0|\}_{j=1}^n$. (The smallest $|Y_j - \tilde{\mu}_0|$ is assigned a rank of 1, the second smallest, a rank of 2, and so on up to n.) Associated with each R_i will be a sign indicator, Z_i, where

$$Z_i = \begin{cases} 0 & \text{if } Y_i - \tilde{\mu}_0 < 0 \\ 1 & \text{if } Y_i - \tilde{\mu}_0 > 0 \end{cases}$$

We will define the Wilcoxon signed rank statistic, W, to be the linear combination,

$$W = \sum_{i=1}^n Z_i R_i$$

To illustrate this terminology, consider the case where $n = 3$ and $y_1 = 6.0$, $y_2 = 4.9$, and $y_3 = 11.2$. Suppose that the problem is to test

$$H_0: \quad \tilde{\mu} = 10.0$$

versus

$$H_1: \quad \tilde{\mu} \neq 10.0$$

Note that $|y_1 - \tilde{\mu}_0| = 4.0$, $|y_2 - \tilde{\mu}_0| = 5.1$, and $|y_3 - \tilde{\mu}_0| = 1.2$. Since $1.2 < 4.0 < 5.1$, it follows that $r_1 = 2$, $r_2 = 3$, and $r_3 = 1$. Also, $z_1 = 0$, $z_2 = 0$, and $z_3 = 1$. Combining the r_i's and the z_i's we have that

$$w = \sum_{i=1}^n z_i r_i$$

$$= (0)(2) + (0)(3) + (1)(1)$$

$$= 1$$

Comment.   Notice that W is based on the *ranks* of the deviations from $\tilde{\mu}_0$ and not on the deviations themselves. For this example, the value of W would remain unchanged if y_2 were 4.9, 3.6, or $-10{,}000$. In each case, r_2 would be 3 and Z_2 would be 0. If the test statistic *did* depend on the magnitude of the deviations, it would have been necessary to specify a particular distribution for $f_Y(y)$, and the resulting procedure would no longer be nonparametric.

It should be clear that W ranges from 0 (all deviations negative) to $\sum_{i=1}^{n} i = [n(n+1)]/2$ (all deviations positive). Intuitively, if H_0 were true we would expect the Y_i's to be distributed at random above and below $\tilde{\mu}_0$, meaning that W should tend to take on values close to $[n(n+1)]/4$.

THEOREM 14.3.1. Let the observations $Y_1, Y_2, \ldots, Y_n$ have ranks $R_1, R_2, \ldots, R_n$ and sign indicators $Z_1, Z_2, \ldots, Z_n$. The pdf of $W = \sum_{i=1}^{n} Z_i R_i$ when $H_0: \tilde{\mu} = \tilde{\mu}_0$ is true is given by

$$P(W = w) = f_W(w) = \left(\frac{1}{2^n}\right) \cdot c(w)$$

where $c(w)$ is the coefficient of e^{wt} in the expansion of

$$\prod_{i=1}^{n}(1 + e^{it})$$

Proof. The statement and proof of Theorem 14.3.1 are typical of many nonparametric results. Closed-form expressions for sampling distributions are seldom possible: The combinatorial nature of nonparametric test statistics lends itself more readily to a generating-function format.

To begin, note that if H_0 is true, the distribution of $W = \sum_{i=1}^{n} Z_i R_i$ is equivalent to the distribution of $U = \sum_{i=1}^{n} U_i$, where

$$U_i = \begin{cases} 0 & \text{with probability } \frac{1}{2} \\ i & \text{with probability } \frac{1}{2} \end{cases}$$

Therefore, W and U have the same moment-generating function. Also, since the Z_i's are independent, so are the U_i's, and from Theorem 3.16.3,

$$M_U(t) = M_W(t)$$

$$= \prod_{i=1}^{n} M_{U_i}(t)$$

$$= \prod_{i=1}^{n} E(e^{U_i t})$$

$$= \prod_{i=1}^{n} \left(\frac{1}{2} e^{0t} + \frac{1}{2} e^{it}\right)$$

$$= \left(\frac{1}{2^n}\right) \prod_{i=1}^{n}(1 + e^{it}) \tag{14.3.1}$$

Now, consider the *structure* of $f_W(w)$, the pdf for the Wilcoxon statistic. In forming W, we can prefix R_1 by either a plus sign or a zero; similarly for $R_2, R_3, \ldots,$ and R_n. It follows that since each R_i can take on two different values, the total number of ways to make signed rank sums is 2^n. Under H_0, of course, each of these arrangements is equally likely so, in general terms, the probability distribution of W has the form

$$P(W = w) = f_W(w) = \frac{c(w)}{2^n} \tag{14.3.2}$$

where $c(w)$ is the number of ways to assign $+$'s and "zeros" to the first n integers so that $\sum_{i=1}^{n} Z_i R_i$ has the value w.

The conclusion of Theorem 14.3.1 follows immediately by comparing the form of $f_W(w)$ to Equation 14.3.1 and to the general expression for a moment-generating function. By definition,

$$M_W(t) = E(e^{Wt}) = \sum_{w=1}^{n(n+1)/2} e^{wt} f_W(w)$$

but from Equations 14.3.1 and 14.3.2 we can write

$$\sum_{w=1}^{n(n+1)/2} e^{wt} f_W(w) = \left(\frac{1}{2^n}\right) \prod_{i=1}^{n} (1 + e^{it}) = \sum_{w=1}^{n(n+1)/2} e^{wt} \cdot \frac{c(w)}{2^n}$$

We prove the theorem by recognizing that $c(w)$ is the coefficient of e^{wt} in the expansion of $\prod_{i=1}^{n} (1 + e^{it})$.

Calculating $f_W(w)$

It may help to clarify these ideas by considering a numerical example. Suppose $n = 4$. Then, by Equation 14.3.1, the moment-generating function for W becomes

$$M_W(t) = \left(\frac{1 + e^t}{2}\right)\left(\frac{1 + e^{2t}}{2}\right)\left(\frac{1 + e^{3t}}{2}\right)\left(\frac{1 + e^{4t}}{2}\right)$$

$$= \left(\frac{1}{16}\right)\{1 + e^t + e^{2t} + 2e^{3t} + 2e^{4t} + 2e^{5t} + 2e^{6t} + 2e^{7t} + e^{8t} + e^{9t} + e^{10t}\}$$

Thus, the probability that W equals, say, 2 is $\frac{1}{16}$ (since the coefficient of e^{2t} is 1); the probability that W equals 7 is $\frac{2}{16}$, and so on. The first two columns of Table 14.3.1 show the complete probability distribution of W, as given by the expansion of $M_W(t)$. The last column enumerates the particular assignments of $+$'s and 0's that generate each value of W.

TABLE 14.3.1 Probability Distribution of W

w	$f_W(w) = P(W = w)$	r_i 1	2	3	4
0	$\frac{1}{16}$	0	0	0	0
1	$\frac{1}{16}$	+	0	0	0
2	$\frac{1}{16}$	0	+	0	0
3	$\frac{2}{16}$	$\left\{\begin{matrix}+\\0\end{matrix}\right.$	$\begin{matrix}+\\0\end{matrix}$	$\begin{matrix}0\\+\end{matrix}$	$\left.\begin{matrix}0\\0\end{matrix}\right\}$
4	$\frac{2}{16}$	$\left\{\begin{matrix}+\\0\end{matrix}\right.$	$\begin{matrix}0\\0\end{matrix}$	$\begin{matrix}+\\0\end{matrix}$	$\left.\begin{matrix}0\\+\end{matrix}\right\}$
5	$\frac{2}{16}$	$\left\{\begin{matrix}+\\0\end{matrix}\right.$	$\begin{matrix}0\\+\end{matrix}$	$\begin{matrix}0\\+\end{matrix}$	$\left.\begin{matrix}+\\0\end{matrix}\right\}$
6	$\frac{2}{16}$	$\left\{\begin{matrix}+\\0\end{matrix}\right.$	$\begin{matrix}+\\+\end{matrix}$	$\begin{matrix}+\\0\end{matrix}$	$\left.\begin{matrix}0\\+\end{matrix}\right\}$
7	$\frac{2}{16}$	$\left\{\begin{matrix}+\\0\end{matrix}\right.$	$\begin{matrix}+\\0\end{matrix}$	$\begin{matrix}0\\+\end{matrix}$	$\left.\begin{matrix}+\\+\end{matrix}\right\}$
8	$\frac{1}{16}$	+	0	+	+
9	$\frac{1}{16}$	0	+	+	+
10	$\frac{1}{16}$	+	+	+	+
	1				

Tables of the cdf, $F_W(w)$

Cumulative tail area probabilities,

$$P\left(W \leq w_1^*\right) = \sum_{w=0}^{w_1^*} f_W(w) \quad \text{and} \quad P\left(W \geq w_2^*\right) = \sum_{w=w_2^*}^{n(n+1)/2} f_W(w)$$

are listed in Table A.6 of the Appendix for sample sizes ranging from $n = 4$ to $n = 12$. Knowing these probabilities, it is easy to construct decision rules for either one-sided or two-sided alternatives. For example, suppose n is 7 and we wish to test

$$H_0: \ \tilde{\mu} = \tilde{\mu}_0$$

versus

$$H_1: \ \tilde{\mu} \neq \tilde{\mu}_0$$

at the $\alpha = 0.05$ level of significance. The critical region would be the set of w-values less than or equal to 2 or greater than or equal to 26: $C = \{w: w \leq 2 \text{ or } w \geq 26\}$. This follows immediately from Table A.6, since

$$\sum_{w \in C} f_W(w) = 0.023 + 0.023 \doteq 0.05$$

CASE STUDY 14.3.1

Swell sharks (*Cephaloscyllium ventriosum*) are small, reef-dwelling sharks that inhabit the California coastal waters south of Monterey Bay. There is a second population of these fish living nearby in the vicinity of Catalina Island, but it has been hypothesized (58) that the two populations never mix. In between Santa Catalina and the mainland is a deep basin, which, according to the "separation" hypothesis, is an inpenetrable barrier for these particular fish.

    One way to test this theory would be compare the morphology of sharks caught in the two regions. If there were no mixing, we would expect a certain number of differences to have evolved. Table 14.3.2 lists the total length (*TL*), the height of the first dorsal fin (*HDI*), and the ratio *TL/HDI* for 10 male swell sharks caught near Santa Catalina.

    It has been estimated on the basis of past data that the median *TL/HDI* ratio for male swell sharks caught *off the coast* is 14.60. Is this figure consistent with the data of Table 14.3.2? In more formal terms, if $\tilde{\mu}$ denotes the true median *TL/HDI* ratio for the Santa Catalina population, can we reject $H_0: \tilde{\mu} = 14.60$, and thereby lend support to the separation theory?

TABLE 14.3.2   Measurements Made on Ten Sharks Caught near Santa Catalina

Total Length (mm)	Height of First Dorsal Fin (mm)	*TL/HDI*
906	68	13.32
875	67	13.06
771	55	14.02
700	59	11.86
869	64	13.58
895	65	13.77
662	49	13.51
750	52	14.42
794	55	14.44
787	51	15.43

    Table 14.3.3 gives the values of *TL/HDI* $(= Y_i)$, $Y_i - \tilde{\mu}_0 = Y_i - 14.60$, $|Y_i - 14.60|$, R_i, Z_i, and $R_i Z_i$ for the ten Santa Catalina sharks. (*Note:* When two or more numbers being ranked are equal, each is assigned the *average* of the ranks they would otherwise have received; here, $|y_6 - 14.60|$ and $|y_{10} - 14.60|$ are both competing for ranks 4 and 5.)

TABLE 14.3.3   Computations for Wilcoxon Signed Rank Test

TL/HDI $(= y_i)$	$y_i - 14.60$	$|y_i - 14.60|$	r_i	z_i	$r_i z_i$
13.32	−1.28	1.28	8	0	0
13.06	−1.54	1.54	9	0	0
14.02	−0.58	0.58	3	0	0
11.86	−2.74	2.74	10	0	0
13.58	−1.02	1.02	6	0	0
13.77	−0.83	0.83	4.5	0	0
13.51	−1.09	1.09	7	0	0
14.42	−0.18	0.18	2	0	0
14.44	−0.16	0.16	1	0	0
15.43	+0.83	0.83	4.5	1	4.5

(continued on next page)

(Case Study 14.3.1 continued)

Summing the last column of Table 14.3.3, we see that $w = 4.5$. According to Table A.6 in the Appendix, the $\alpha = 0.05$ decision rule for testing

$$H_0: \quad \tilde{\mu} = 14.60$$

versus

$$H_1: \quad \tilde{\mu} \neq 14.60$$

requires that H_0 be rejected if w is either less than or equal to 8 or greater than or equal to 47. (Why is the alternative hypothesis two-sided here?) (*Note*: The *exact* level of significance associated with $C = \{w: w \leq 8 \text{ or } w \geq 47\}$ is $0.024 + 0.024 = 0.048$.) Thus we should *reject* H_0, since the observed w was less than 8. These particular data, then, would support the separation hypothesis.

QUESTIONS

14.3.1 The average energy expenditures for eight elderly women were estimated on the basis of information received from a battery-powered heart rate monitor that each subject wore. Two overall averages were calculated for each woman, one for the summer months and one for the winter months (142), as shown in the following table. Let μ_D denote the location difference between the summer and winter energy-expenditure populations. Compute $y_i - x_i$, $i = 1, 2, \ldots, 8$, and use the Wilcoxon signed rank procedure to test

$$H_0: \quad \mu_D = 0$$

versus

$$H_1: \quad \mu_D \neq 0$$

Let $\alpha = 0.15$.

Average Daily Energy Expenditures (kcal)

Subject	Summer, x_i	Winter, y_i
1	1458	1424
2	1353	1501
3	2209	1495
4	1804	1739
5	1912	2031
6	1366	934
7	1598	1401
8	1406	1339

14.3.2 Use the expansion of

$$\prod_{i=1}^{n}(1 + e^{it})$$

to find the pdf of W when $n = 5$. What α levels are available for testing $H_0: \tilde{\mu} = \tilde{\mu}_0$ versus $H_1: \tilde{\mu} > \tilde{\mu}_0$?

A Large-Sample Wilcoxon Signed Rank Test

The usefulness of Table A.6 in the Appendix is clearly limited to tests where the sample size is small, less than or equal to 12. To accommodate a larger n, we can define a normalized test statistic, W', where

$$W' = \frac{W - E(W)}{\sqrt{\text{Var}(W)}}$$

and $E(W)$ and $\text{Var}(W)$ are the expected value and variance of W *when H_0 is true* (see Theorem 14.3.2). It can be shown that as n gets large, the distribution of W' converges to the standard normal. Furthermore, for n even as small as 13, $f_{W'}(w')$ and $f_Z(z)$ are remarkably similar. Therefore, to test

$$H_0: \quad \tilde{\mu} = \tilde{\mu}_0$$

versus

$$H_1: \quad \tilde{\mu} \neq \tilde{\mu}_0$$

at, say, the $\alpha = 0.05$ level of significance, we would reject H_0 if w' was either less than or equal to -1.96 or greater than or equal to $+1.96$.

> **THEOREM 14.3.2.** When $H_0: \tilde{\mu} = \tilde{\mu}_0$ is true, the mean and standard deviation of the Wilcoxon signed rank statistic, W, are given by
>
> $$E(W) = \frac{n(n + 1)}{4}$$
>
> and
>
> $$\text{Var}(W) = \frac{n(n + 1)(2n + 1)}{24}$$
>
> Also, for $n > 12$, the distribution of
>
> $$W' = \frac{W - [n(n + 1)]/4}{\sqrt{[n(n + 1)(2n + 1)]/24}}$$
>
> can be adequately approximated by the standard normal.

Proof. We will derive $E(W)$ and $\text{Var}(W)$; for a proof of the asymptotic normality, see (72). Recall that W has the same distribution as $U = \sum_{i=1}^{n} U_i$, where

$$U_i = \begin{cases} 0 & \text{with probability } \frac{1}{2} \\ i & \text{with probability } \frac{1}{2} \end{cases}$$

Therefore,

$$E(W) = E\left(\sum_{i=1}^{n} U_i\right) = \sum_{i=1}^{n} E(U_i)$$

$$= \sum_{i=1}^{n} \left(0 \cdot \frac{1}{2} + i \cdot \frac{1}{2}\right) = \sum_{i=1}^{n} \frac{i}{2}$$

$$= \frac{n(n+1)}{4}$$

Similarly,

$$\text{Var}(W) = \text{Var}(U) = \sum_{i=1}^{n} \text{Var}(U_i)$$

since the U_i's are independent. But

$$\text{Var}(U_i) = E(U_i^2) - \left[E(U_i)\right]^2$$

$$= \frac{i^2}{2} - \left(\frac{i}{2}\right)^2 = \frac{i^2}{4}$$

making

$$\text{Var}(W) = \sum_{i=1}^{n} \frac{i^2}{4} = \left(\frac{1}{4}\right)\left[\frac{n(n+1)(2n+1)}{6}\right]$$

$$= \frac{n(n+1)(2n+1)}{24}$$

CASE STUDY 14.3.2

Methadone is a drug widely used in the treatment of heroin addiction; another is cyclazocine. Recently a study was done (131) to evaluate the effectiveness of the latter in reducing a person's psychological dependence on heroin. The subjects were 14 males, all chronic heroin addicts. Each was asked a battery of questions that compared his feelings when he was using heroin to his feelings when he was "clean." The resultant Q-scores ranged from a possible minimum of 11 to a possible maximum of 55, as shown in Table 14.3.4. (From the way the questions were worded, higher scores represented *less* psychological dependence.)

TABLE 14.3.4   *Q*-Scores of Heroin
Addicts after Cyclazocine Therapy

51	43
53	45
43	27
36	21
55	26
55	22
39	43

The median score for addicts *not* given cyclazocine is known from past experience to be 28. Can we conclude on the basis of the data in Table 14.3.4 that cyclazocine is an effective treatment?

Since high Q-scores represent *less* dependence on heroin (and assuming cyclazocine would not tend to worsen an addict's condition), the alternative hypothesis should be one-sided *to the right*:

$$H_0: \quad \tilde{\mu} = 28$$

versus

$$H_1: \quad \tilde{\mu} > 28$$

Let α be 0.05.

Table 14.3.5 shows the computation of the test statistic: $w = 95.0$. With n being larger than 12, $W' = [W - E(W)]/\sqrt{\text{Var}(W)}$ has approximately a standard normal distribution, and the 0.05 decision rule becomes

$$\text{Reject } H_0: \quad \tilde{\mu} = 28 \quad \text{if} \quad w' \geq 1.64$$

TABLE 14.3.5 Computations to Find W

Q-Score, y_i	$(y_i - 28)$	$|y_i - 28|$	r_i	z_i	$r_i z_i$
51	+23	23	11	1	11
53	+25	25	12	1	12
43	+15	15	8	1	8
36	+8	8	5	1	5
55	+27	27	13.5	1	13.5
55	+27	27	13.5	1	13.5
39	+11	11	6	1	6
43	+15	15	8	1	8
45	+17	17	10	1	10
27	−1	1	1	0	0
21	−7	7	4	0	0
26	−2	2	2	0	0
22	−6	6	3	0	0
43	+15	15	8	1	8
					95.0

By Theorem 14.3.2, $E(W) = [14(14 + 1)]/4 = 52.5$ and $\text{Var}(W) = [14(14 + 1)(28 + 1)]/24 = 253.75$. Therefore,

$$w' = \frac{95.0 - 52.5}{\sqrt{253.75}} = 2.67$$

implying that we should *reject* H_0—it would appear that cyclazocine therapy *is* helpful in reducing heroin dependence.

QUESTIONS

14.3.3 Two manufacturing processes are available for annealing a certain kind of copper tubing, the primary difference being in the temperature required. The critical response variable is the resulting tensile strength. To compare the methods, 15 pieces of tubing were broken into pairs. One piece from each pair was randomly selected to be annealed at a moderate temperature, the other piece at a high temperature. The resulting tensile strengths (in tons/sq in.) are listed in the following table. Analyze these data with a Wilcoxon signed rank test. Use a two-sided alternative. Let $\alpha = 0.05$.

Tensile Strengths (tons/sq. in.)

Pair	Moderate Temperature	High Temperature
1	16.5	16.9
2	17.6	17.2
3	16.9	17.0
4	15.8	16.1
5	18.4	18.2
6	17.5	17.7
7	17.6	17.9
8	16.1	16.0
9	16.8	17.3
10	15.8	16.1
11	16.8	16.5
12	17.3	17.6
13	18.1	18.4
14	17.9	17.2
15	16.4	16.5

14.3.4 To measure the effect on coordination associated with mild intoxication, 13 subjects were each given 15.7 ml of ethyl alcohol per square meter of body surface area and asked to write a certain phrase as many times as they could in the space of one minute (108). The number of correctly written letters was then counted and scaled, with a scale value of 0 representing the score a subject not under the influence of alcohol would be expected to achieve. Negative scores indicate *decreased* writing speeds; positive scores, *increased* writing speeds. Use the signed rank test to determine whether the level of alcohol provided in this study has any effect on writing speed. Let $\alpha = 0.05$. Omit Subject 8 from your calculations.

Subject	Score	Subject	Score
1	−6	8	0
2	10	9	−7
3	9	10	5
4	−8	11	−9
5	−6	12	−10
6	−2	13	−2
7	20		

14.3.5 Test $H_0: \tilde{\mu} = 0.80$ versus $H_1: \tilde{\mu} < 0.80$ for the FEV_1/VC ratio data of Question 7.5.11 using a Wilcoxon signed rank test. Let $\alpha = 0.10$. Compare this test to the sign test of Question 14.2.7.

14.3.6 Do a Wilcoxon signed rank test on the hemoglobin data summarized in Case Study 13.3.1. Let α be 0.05. Compare your conclusion with the outcome of the sign test done in Question 14.2.8.

14.3.7 Suppose that the population being sampled is symmetric and we wish to test $H_0: \tilde{\mu} = \tilde{\mu}_0$. Both the sign test and the signed rank test would be valid. Which procedure, if either, would you expect to have greater power? Why?

14.4 THE KRUSKAL-WALLIS TEST

The final two sections of this chapter discuss the nonparametric counterparts for the two analysis-of-variance models introduced in Chapters 12 and 13. Neither of these procedures, the *Kruskal-Wallis test* and the *Friedman test*, will be derived. We will simply state the procedures and illustrate them with examples.

First, we consider the *k-sample problem*. Suppose that $k(\geq 2)$ independent random samples of sizes $n_1, n_2, \ldots, n_k$ are drawn, representing k populations having the same shape but possibly different locations. Our objective is to test whether the population medians are all the same—that is,

$$H_0: \quad \tilde{\mu}_1 = \tilde{\mu}_2 = \cdots = \tilde{\mu}_k$$

versus

$$H_1: \quad \text{not all the } \tilde{\mu}_j\text{'s are equal}$$

The Kruskal-Wallis procedure for testing H_0 is really quite simple, involving considerably fewer computations than the analysis of variance. The first step is to rank the entire set of $n = \sum_{j=1}^{k} n_j$ observations (from smallest to largest). Then the rank sum, $R_{.j}$, is calculated for each sample. Table 14.4.1 shows the notation we will be using: It follows the same conventions as the dot notation of Chapter 12. The only real difference is the addition of r_{ij}, the symbol for the rank corresponding to y_{ij}.

The Kruskal-Wallis statistic, B, is defined as

$$B = \frac{12}{n(n+1)} \sum_{j=1}^{k} \frac{R_{.j}^2}{n_j} - 3(n+1)$$

TABLE 14.4.1   Notation for Kruskal-Wallis Procedure

	Sample			
	1	2	$\cdots$	k
	$y_{11}(r_{11})$	$y_{12}(r_{12})$		$y_{1k}(r_{1k})$
	$y_{21}(r_{21})$			
	$\vdots$	$\vdots$	$\cdots$	$\vdots$
	$y_{n_1 1}(r_{n_1 1})$	$y_{n_2 2}(r_{n_2 2})$		$y_{n_k k}(r_{n_k k})$
Totals	$r_{.1}$	$r_{.2}$		$r_{.k}$

Notice how B resembles the computing formula for $SSTR$ in the analysis of variance. Here $\sum_{j=1}^{k}\left(R_{\cdot j}^2/n_j\right)$, and thus B, get larger and larger as the differences between the population medians increase. [Recall that a similar explanation was given for $SSTR$ and $\sum_{j=1}^{k}\left(T_{\cdot j}^2/n_j\right)$.]

THEOREM 14.4.1.   If $H_0: \widetilde{\mu}_1 = \widetilde{\mu}_2 = \cdots = \widetilde{\mu}_k$ is true,

$$B = \frac{12}{n(n+1)} \sum_{j=1}^{k} \frac{R_{\cdot j}^2}{n_j} - 3(n+1)$$

has approximately a χ_{k-1}^2 distribution and H_0 should be rejected at the α level of significance if $b > \chi_{1-\alpha, k-1}^2$.

CASE STUDY 14.4.1

On December 1, 1969, a lottery was held in Selective Service headquarters in Washington, D.C., to determine the draft status of all 19-year-old males. It was the first time such a procedure had been used since World War II. Priorities were established according to a person's birthday. Each of the 366 possible birthdates was written on a slip of paper and put into a small capsule. The capsules were then put into a large bowl, mixed, and drawn out one by one. By agreement, persons whose birthday corresponded to the first capsule drawn would have the highest draft priority; those whose birthday corresponded to the second capsule drawn, the second highest priority, and so on. Table 14.4.2 shows the order in which the 366 birthdates were drawn (147). The first date was September 14 (001); the last, June 8 (366).

We can think of the observed sequence of draft priorities as ranks from 1 to 366. If the lottery is random, the average of these ranks for each of the months should be approximately equal. If the lottery is *not* random, we would expect to see certain months having a preponderance of high ranks and other months a preponderance of low ranks.

Look at the rank totals at the bottom of Table 14.4.2. There appears to be a tendency for months late in the year to have smaller $r_{\cdot j}$'s. Address that suspicion by using the Kruskal-Wallis statistic to test the lottery for randomness.

Substituting the $r_{\cdot j}$'s into the formula for B gives

$$b = \frac{12}{366(367)} \left[\frac{(6236)^2}{31} + \cdots + \frac{(3768)^2}{31} \right] - 3(367)$$

$$= 25.95$$

By Theorem 14.4.1, B has approximately a chi-square distribution with 11 degrees of freedom (when $H_0: \widetilde{\mu}_{\text{Jan}} = \widetilde{\mu}_{\text{Feb}} = \cdots = \widetilde{\mu}_{\text{Dec}}$ is true).

Let $\alpha = 0.01$. Then H_0 should be rejected if $b \geq \chi_{.99, 11}^2 = 24.725$. But b *does* exceed that cutoff, implying that the lottery was *not* random.

An even more resounding rejecton of the randomness hypothesis can be gotten by dividing the 12 months into two half-years—the first, January through June; the second, July through December. Then the hypotheses to be tested are

$$H_0: \quad \tilde{\mu}_1 = \tilde{\mu}_2$$

versus

$$H_1: \quad \tilde{\mu}_1 \neq \tilde{\mu}_2$$

Table 14.4.3, derived from Table 14.4.2, summarizes the data appropriately. Substituting these values into the formula for the Kruskal-Wallis statistic gives a b value (with 1 degree of freedom) of *16.85*:

TABLE 14.4.2   1969 Draft Lottery, Highest Priority (001) to Lowest Priority (366)

Date	Jan.	Feb.	Mar.	Apr.	May	June	July	Aug.	Sept.	Oct.	Nov.	Dec.
1	305	086	108	032	330	249	093	111	225	359	019	129
2	159	144	029	271	298	228	350	045	161	125	034	328
3	251	297	267	083	040	301	115	261	049	244	348	157
4	215	210	275	081	276	020	279	145	232	202	266	165
5	101	214	293	269	364	028	188	054	082	024	310	056
6	224	347	139	253	155	110	327	114	006	087	076	010
7	306	091	122	147	035	085	050	168	008	234	051	012
8	199	181	213	312	321	366	013	048	184	283	097	105
9	194	338	317	219	197	335	277	106	263	342	080	043
10	325	216	323	218	065	206	284	021	071	220	282	041
11	329	150	136	014	037	134	248	324	158	237	046	039
12	221	068	300	346	133	272	015	142	242	072	066	314
13	318	152	259	124	295	069	042	307	175	138	126	163
14	238	004	354	231	178	356	331	198	001	294	127	026
15	017	089	169	273	130	180	322	102	113	171	131	320
16	121	212	166	148	055	274	120	044	207	254	107	096
17	235	189	033	260	112	073	098	154	255	288	143	304
18	140	292	332	090	278	341	190	141	246	005	146	128
19	058	025	200	336	075	104	227	311	177	241	203	240
20	280	302	239	345	183	360	187	344	063	192	185	135
21	186	363	334	062	250	060	027	291	204	243	156	070
22	337	290	265	316	326	247	153	339	160	117	009	053
23	118	057	256	252	319	109	172	116	119	201	182	162
24	059	236	258	002	031	358	023	036	195	196	230	095
25	052	179	343	351	361	137	067	286	149	176	132	084
26	092	365	170	340	357	022	303	245	018	007	309	173
27	355	205	268	074	296	064	289	352	233	264	047	078
28	077	299	223	262	308	222	088	167	257	094	281	123
29	349	285	362	191	226	353	270	061	151	229	099	016
30	164		217	208	103	209	287	333	315	038	174	003
31	211		030		313		193	011		079		100
Totals:	6236	5886	7000	6110	6447	5872	5628	5377	4719	5656	4462	3768

(continued on next page)

(Case Study 14.4.1 continued)

TABLE 14.4.3 Summary of 1969 Draft Lottery by Six-Month Periods

	Jan–June (1)	July–Dec. (2)
$r_{.j}$	37,551	29,610
n_j	182	184

$$b = \frac{12}{366(367)} \left[\frac{(37{,}551)^2}{182} + \frac{(29{,}610)^2}{184} \right] - 3(367)$$

$$= 16.85$$

The significance of 16.85 can be gauged by recalling the moments of a chi-square random variable. If B has a chi-square pdf with 1 degree of freedom, then $E(B) = 1$ and $\text{Var}(B) = 2$ (see Question 7.3.7). It follows, then, that the observed B is more than *11* standard deviations away from its mean:

$$\frac{16.85 - 1}{\sqrt{2}} = 11.2$$

Analyzed this way, there can be little doubt that the lottery was not random!

QUESTIONS

14.4.1 Recall Case Study 14.4.1. What might have accounted for the lack of randomness evident in the 1969 draft lottery?

14.4.2 Recall the fiddler crab data given in Question 9.5.3. Use the Kruskal-Wallis test to compare the times spent waving to females by the two groups of males. Let $\alpha = 0.10$.

14.4.3 Use the Kruskal-Wallis method to test at the 0.05 level that the nod swimming is different for the two types of ducks in Question 9.2.3.

14.4.4 Redo the analysis of the Quintus Curtius Snodgrass/Mark Twain data in Case Study 9.2.1, this time using a nonparametric procedure.

14.4.5 Use the Kruskal-Wallis technique to test the hypothesis of Case Study 12.2.1 concerning the effect of smoking on heart rate.

14.4.6 A sample of ten 40-W light bulbs was taken from each of three manufacturing plants. The bulbs were burned until failure. The number of hours that each remained lit is listed in the following table.

Plant 1	Plant 2	Plant 3
905	1109	571
1018	1155	1346
905	835	292
886	1152	825
958	1036	676
1056	926	541
904	1029	818
856	1040	90
1070	959	2246
1006	996	104

(a) Test the hypothesis that the median lives of bulbs produced at the three plants are all the same. Use the 0.05 level of significance.

(b) Are the *mean* lives of bulbs produced at the three plants all the same? Use the analysis of variance with $\alpha = 0.05$.

(c) Change the observation "2246" in the third column to "1500" and redo part (a). How does this change affect the hypothesis test?

(d) Change the observation "2246" in the third column to "1500" and redo part (b). How does this change affect the hypothesis test?

14.4.7 The production of a certain organic chemical requires the addition of ammonium chloride. The manufacturer can conveniently obtain the ammonium chloride in any one of three forms—powdered, moderately ground, and coarse. To see what effect, if any, the quality of the NH_4Cl has, the manufacturer decides to run the reaction seven times with each form of ammonium chloride. The resulting yields (in pounds) are listed in the following table. Compare the yields with a Kruskal-Wallis test. Let $\alpha = 0.05$.

Organic Chemical Yields (lb)

Powdered NH_4Cl	Moderately Ground NH_4Cl	Coarse NH_4Cl
146	150	141
152	144	138
149	148	142
161	155	146
158	154	139
149	150	145
154	148	137

14.4.8 Show that the Kruskal-Wallis statistic, B, as defined in Theorem 14.4.1 can also be written

$$B = \sum_{j=1}^{k} \left(\frac{n - n_j}{n} \right) Z_j^2$$

where

$$Z_j = \frac{\dfrac{R_{.j}}{n_j} - \dfrac{n + 1}{2}}{\sqrt{\dfrac{(n + 1)(n - n_j)}{12n_j}}}$$

14.5 THE FRIEDMAN TEST

The nonparametric analog of the analysis of variance for a randomized block design is *Friedman's test*, a procedure based on within-block *ranks*. Its form is similar to that of the Kruskal-Wallis statistic, and, like its predecessor, it has approximately a χ^2 distribution when H_0 is true.

> **THEOREM 14.5.1.** Suppose $k(\geq 2)$ treatments are ranked independently within b blocks. Let $r_{.j}, j = 1, 2, \ldots, k$, be the rank sum of the jth treatment. The null hypothesis that the population medians of the k treatments are all equal is rejected at the α level of significance (approximately) if
>
> $$g = \frac{12}{bk(k + 1)} \sum_{j=1}^{k} r_{.j}^2 - 3b(k + 1) \geq \chi_{1-\alpha, k-1}^2$$

CASE STUDY 14.5.1

Baseball rules allow a batter considerable leeway in how he is permitted to run from home plate to second base. Two of the possibilities are the narrow-angle and the wide-angle paths diagrammed in Figure 14.5.1. As a means of comparing the two, time trials were held involving 22 players (193). Each player ran both paths. Recorded for each runner was the time it took to go from a point 35 feet from home plate to a point 15 feet from second base. Based on those times, ranks (1 and 2) were assigned to each path for each player (see Table 14.5.1).

FIGURE 14.5.1 Batter's path from home plate to second base.

Narrow-angle

Wide-angle

TABLE 14.5.1 Times (sec) Required to Round First Base

Player	Narrow-Angle	Rank	Wide-Angle	Rank
1	5.50	1	5.55	2
2	5.70	1	5.75	2
3	5.60	2	5.50	1
4	5.50	2	5.40	1
5	5.85	2	5.70	1
6	5.55	1	5.60	2
7	5.40	2	5.35	1
8	5.50	2	5.35	1
9	5.15	2	5.00	1
10	5.80	2	5.70	1
11	5.20	2	5.10	1
12	5.55	2	5.45	1
13	5.35	1	5.45	2
14	5.00	2	4.95	1
15	5.50	2	5.40	1
16	5.55	2	5.50	1
17	5.55	2	5.35	1
18	5.50	1	5.55	2
19	5.45	2	5.25	1
20	5.60	2	5.40	1
21	5.65	2	5.55	1
22	6.30	2	6.25	1
		39		27

If $\tilde{\mu}_1$ and $\tilde{\mu}_2$ denote the true median rounding times associated with the narrow-angle and wide-angle paths, respectively, the hypotheses to be tested are

$$H_0: \quad \tilde{\mu}_1 = \tilde{\mu}_2$$

versus

$$H_1: \quad \tilde{\mu}_1 \neq \tilde{\mu}_2$$

Let $\alpha = 0.05$. By Theorem 14.5.1, the Friedman statistic (under H_0) will have approximately a χ_1^2 distribution, and the decision rule will be

Reject H_0 if $g \geq 3.84$

But

$$g = \frac{12}{22(2)(3)} \left[(39)^2 + (27)^2 \right] - 3(22)(3)$$

$$= 6.54$$

implying that the two paths are *not* equivalent. The wide-angle path appears to enable runners to reach second base quicker.

QUESTIONS

14.5.1 The following data come from a field trial set up to assess the effects of different amounts of potash on the breaking strength of cotton fibers (26). The experiment was done in three blocks. The five treatment levels—36, 54, 72, 108, and 144 lb. of potash per acre—were assigned randomly within each block. The variable recorded was the Pressley strength index.

Pressley Strength Index for Cotton Fibers

		Treatment (pounds of potash/acre)				
		36	54	72	108	144
	1	7.62	8.14	7.76	7.17	7.46
Blocks	2	8.00	8.15	7.73	7.57	7.68
	3	7.93	7.87	7.74	7.80	7.21

Compare the effects of the different levels of potash applications using Friedman's test. Let $\alpha = 0.05$.

14.5.2 Use Friedman's test to analyze the Transylvania effect data given in Case Study 13.2.3.

14.5.3 Until its recent indictment as a possible carcinogen, cyclamate was a widely used sweetener in soft drinks. The following data show a comparison of three laboratory methods for determining the percentage of sodium cyclamate in commercially produced orange drink. All three procedures were applied to each of 12 samples (144).

Percent Sodium Cyclamate (w/w)

Sample	Method		
	Picryl Chloride	Davies	AOAC
1	0.598	0.628	0.632
2	0.614	0.628	0.630
3	0.600	0.600	0.622
4	0.580	0.612	0.584
5	0.596	0.600	0.650
6	0.592	0.628	0.606
7	0.616	0.628	0.644
8	0.614	0.644	0.644
9	0.604	0.644	0.624
10	0.608	0.612	0.619
11	0.602	0.628	0.632
12	0.614	0.644	0.616

Use Friedman's test to determine whether the three methods give significantly different results. Let $\alpha = 0.05$.

14.5.4 Analyze the data in Case Study 13.3.1 using (a) a sign test and (b) Friedman's test. Let $\alpha = 0.05$.

14.5.5 Test whether the investment plans in Question 13.3.1 are equally profitable, using both Friedman's method and a Wilcoxon analysis.

14.5.6 Suppose that k treatments are to be applied within each of b blocks. Let $\bar{r}_{..}$ denote the average of the bk ranks and let $\bar{r}_{.j} = (1/b)r_{.j}$. Show that the Friedman statistic given in Theorem 14.5.1 can also be written

$$g = \frac{12b}{k(k+1)} \sum_{j=1}^{k} (\bar{r}_{.j} - \bar{r}_{..})^2$$

What analysis-of-variance expression does this resemble?

APPENDIX 14.A.1   MINITAB APPLICATIONS

The Sign Test

Figure 14.A.1.1 shows MINITAB's sign test routine applied to the ethosuximide data from Case Study 14.2.1 The basic command is

```
MTB > stest 0.0 c3;
SUBC > alternative 0.
```

where c3 contains the within-pair differences. The subcommand ALTERNATIVE 0 makes H_1 two-sided. One-sided alternative hypotheses require that ALTERNATIVE 1 (if the rejection region is to the right) or ALTERNATIVE −1 (if the rejection region is to the left) be used.

```
MTB > set c1
DATA> 97 106 106 95 102 111 115 104 90 96
DATA> end
MTB > set c2
DATA> 113 113 101 119 111 122 121 106 110 126
DATA> end
MTB > let c3 = c2 - c1
MTB > stest 0.0 c3;
SUBC> alternative 0.
```

Sign Test for Median

```
Sign test of median = 0.00000 versus N.E. 0.00000
```

	N	BELOW	EQUAL	ABOVE	P-VALUE	MEDIAN
C3	10	1	0	9	0.0215	10.00

FIGURE 14.A.1.1

Doing a Sign Test Using MINITAB Windows

1. Enter the y_i's [or the $(y_i - x_i)$'s] in C1.
2. Click on STAT, then on NONPARAMETRICS, then on ONE-SAMPLE SIGN.
3. Type C1 in the VARIABLES box.
4. Click on TEST MEDIAN and enter the H_0 value for $\tilde{\mu}$ (or for p).
5. Click on NOT EQUAL, then on whichever H_1 is desired.
6. Click on OK.

The Wilcoxon Signed Rank Test

The Wilcoxon signed rank statistic of Theorem 14.3.1 is calculated using the command MTB > wtest $\tilde{\mu}_o$ c1, where the y_i's have been entered in c1. As with the sign test, the subcommand ALTERNATIVE 0 makes H_1 two-sided. Figure 14.A.1.2 summarizes MINITAB's analysis of the shark data from Case Study 14.3.1.

```
MTB > wtest 14.6 c1;
SUBC> alternative 0.
```

Wilcoxon Signed Rank Test

```
TEST OF MEDIAN 14.60 VERSUS MEDIAN N.E. 14.60
```

	N	N FOR TEST	WILCOXON STATISTIC	P-VALUE	ESTIMATED MEDIAN
c1	10	10	4.5	0.022	13.75

FIGURE 14.A.1.2

Doing a Wilcoxon Signed Rank Test Using MINITAB Windows

1. Enter the y_i's in C1.

2. Click on STAT, then on NONPARAMETRICS, then on 1-SAMPLE WILCOXON.

3. Type C1 in VARIABLES box.

4. Click on TEST MEDIAN and enter the H_0 value for $\tilde{\mu}$.

5. Click on NOT EQUAL, then on whichever H_1 is desired.

6. Click on OK.

The Kruskal-Wallis Test

Data are entered for the Kruskal-Wallis test using the stacked format that we saw in connection with the randomized block analysis of variance in Chapter 13. The syntax, though, is different. First, the data from each treatment level are entered in a separate column. Then a *stack* command is used to transfer the y_{ij}'s to a single column (in this case, c5). Finally, an additional column—here, c6—is defined that identifies the treatment level represented by each data point in the stacked column.

Figure 14.A.1.3 shows the Kruskal-Wallis input and output for the hemoglobin data given in Case Study 12.2.1.

```
MTB > set c1
DATA> 69 52 71 58 59 65
DATA> end
MTB > set c2
DATA> 55 60 78 58 62 66
DATA> end
MTB > set c3
DATA> 66 81 70 77 57 79
DATA> end
MTB > set c4
DATA> 91 72 81 67 95 84
DATA> end
MTB > stack c1 c2 c3 c4 c5
MTB > set c6
DATA> 6(1) 6(2) 6(3) 6(4)
DATA> end
MTB > kruskal-wallis c5 c6.
```

Kruskal-Wallis Test

LEVEL	NOBS	MEDIAN	AVE. RANK	Z VALUE
1	6	62.00	8.1	-1.77
2	6	61.00	8.3	-1.67
3	6	73.50	14.0	0.60
4	6	82.50	19.6	2.83
OVERALL	24		12.5	

$H = 10.72$ d.f. = 3 $p = 0.014$
$H = 10.73$ d.f. = 3 $p = 0.014$ (adjusted for ties)

FIGURE 14.A.1.3

Doing a Kruskal-Wallis Test Using MINITAB Windows

1. Enter the entire sample in C1 using a stacked format—that is, enter the data from Treatment level 1 first, then the data from Treatment level 2, and so on.

2. In column C2, enter 1's for the data belonging to Treatment level 1, 2's for the data belonging to Treatment level 2, and so on.

3. Click on STAT, then on NONPARAMETRICS, then on KRUSKAL-WALLIS.

4. Type C1 in RESPONSE box and C2 in FACTOR box.

5. Click on OK.

The Friedman Test

The syntax for Friedman's test is similar to what is used for the Kruskal-Wallis procedure, except that an additional column identifying the block to which each y_{ij} belongs must be included. As before, the data from each treatment level are initially put into separate columns; then those columns are stacked. The final command is

```
MTB > friedman c3 c4 c5
```

where c3 is the stacked column of y_{ij}'s, c4 is a column identifying the treatment level represented by each y_{ij}, and c5 is a column giving the block location of each observation.

Figure 14.A.1.4 is the Friedman analysis of the baseball data in Case Study 14.5.1. The observed test statistic is denoted S (instead of the g on page 709).

Doing a Friedman Test Using MINITAB Windows

1. Enter the entire sample in C1 using a stacked format, beginning with the data from Treatment level 1.

2. In C2, enter the Treatment level represented by each observation in C1.

3. In C3, enter the Block number represented by each observation in C1.

4. Click on STAT, then on NONPARAMETRICS, then on FRIEDMAN.

5. Type C1 in RESPONSE box, C2 in TREATMENT box, and C3 in BLOCKS box.

6. Click on OK.

```
MTB > set c1
DATA> 5.50 5.70 5.60 5.50 5.85 5.55 5.40 5.50 5.15 5.80 5.20
DATA> 5.55 5.35 5.00 5.50 5.55 5.55 5.50 5.45 5.60 5.65 6.30
DATA> end
MTB > set c2
DATA> 5.55 5.75 5.50 5.40 5.70 5.60 5.35 5.35 5.00 5.70 5.10
DATA> 5.45 5.45 4.95 5.40 5.50 5.35 5.55 5.25 5.40 5.55 6.25
DATA> end
MTB > stack c1 c2 c3
MTB > set c4
DATA> 1 1 1 1 1 1 1 1 1 1 1 1 1 1 1 1 1 1 1 1 1 1
DATA> 2 2 2 2 2 2 2 2 2 2 2 2 2 2 2 2 2 2 2 2 2 2
DATA> end
MTB > set c5
DATA> 1 2 3 4 5 6 7 8 9 10 11 12 13 14 15 16 17 18 19 20 21 22
DATA> 1 2 3 4 5 6 7 8 9 10 11 12 13 14 15 16 17 18 19 20 21 22
DATA> end
MTB > friedman c3 c4 c5.
```

Friedman Test

```
Friedman test of C3 by C4 blocked by C5
```

$S = 6.55$ d.f. = 1 p = 0.011

C4	N	Est. Median	Sum of Ranks
1	22	5.5500	39.0
2	22	5.4500	27.0

Grand median = 5.5000

FIGURE 14.A.1.4

APPENDIX

Statistical Tables

TABLE A.1   Cumulative Areas under the Standard Normal Distribution

Z	0	1	2	3	4	5	6	7	8	9
-3.	0.0013	0.0010	0.0007	0.0005	0.0003	0.0002	0.0002	0.0001	0.0001	0.0000
-2.9	0.0019	0.0018	0.0017	0.0017	0.0016	0.0016	0.0015	0.0015	0.0014	0.0014
-2.8	0.0026	0.0025	0.0024	0.0023	0.0023	0.0022	0.0021	0.0021	0.0020	0.0019
-2.7	0.0035	0.0034	0.0033	0.0032	0.0031	0.0030	0.0029	0.0028	0.0027	0.0026
-2.6	0.0047	0.0045	0.0044	0.0043	0.0041	0.0040	0.0039	0.0038	0.0037	0.0036
-2.5	0.0062	0.0060	0.0059	0.0057	0.0055	0.0054	0.0052	0.0051	0.0049	0.0048
-2.4	0.0082	0.0080	0.0078	0.0075	0.0073	0.0071	0.0069	0.0068	0.0066	0.0064
-2.3	0.0107	0.0104	0.0102	0.0099	0.0096	0.0094	0.0091	0.0089	0.0087	0.0084
-2.2	0.0139	0.0136	0.0132	0.0129	0.0126	0.0122	0.0119	0.0116	0.0113	0.0110
-2.1	0.0179	0.0174	0.0170	0.0166	0.0162	0.0158	0.0154	0.0150	0.0146	0.0143
-2.0	0.0228	0.0222	0.0217	0.0212	0.0207	0.0202	0.0197	0.0192	0.0188	0.0183
-1.9	0.0287	0.0281	0.0274	0.0268	0.0262	0.0256	0.0250	0.0244	0.0238	0.0233
-1.8	0.0359	0.0352	0.0344	0.0336	0.0329	0.0322	0.0314	0.0307	0.0300	0.0294
-1.7	0.0446	0.0436	0.0427	0.0418	0.0409	0.0401	0.0392	0.0384	0.0375	0.0367
-1.6	0.0548	0.0537	0.0526	0.0516	0.0505	0.0495	0.0485	0.0475	0.0465	0.0455
-1.5	0.0668	0.0655	0.0643	0.0630	0.0618	0.0606	0.0594	0.0582	0.0570	0.0559
-1.4	0.0808	0.0793	0.0778	0.0764	0.0749	0.0735	0.0722	0.0708	0.0694	0.0681
-1.3	0.0968	0.0951	0.0934	0.0918	0.0901	0.0885	0.0869	0.0853	0.0838	0.0823
-1.2	0.1151	0.1131	0.1112	0.1093	0.1075	0.1056	0.1038	0.1020	0.1003	0.0985
-1.1	0.1357	0.1335	0.1314	0.1292	0.1271	0.1251	0.1230	0.1210	0.1190	0.1170
-1.0	0.1587	0.1562	0.1539	0.1515	0.1492	0.1469	0.1446	0.1423	0.1401	0.1379
-0.9	0.1841	0.1814	0.1788	0.1762	0.1736	0.1711	0.1685	0.1660	0.1635	0.1611
-0.8	0.2119	0.2090	0.2061	0.2033	0.2005	0.1977	0.1949	0.1922	0.1894	0.1867
-0.7	0.2420	0.2389	0.2358	0.2327	0.2297	0.2266	0.2236	0.2206	0.2177	0.2148
-0.6	0.2743	0.2709	0.2676	0.2643	0.2611	0.2578	0.2546	0.2514	0.2483	0.2451
-0.5	0.3085	0.3050	0.3015	0.2981	0.2946	0.2912	0.2877	0.2843	0.2810	0.2776
-0.4	0.3446	0.3409	0.3372	0.3336	0.3300	0.3264	0.3228	0.3192	0.3156	0.3121
-0.3	0.3821	0.3783	0.3745	0.3707	0.3669	0.3632	0.3594	0.3557	0.3520	0.3483
-0.2	0.4207	0.4168	0.4129	0.4090	0.4052	0.4013	0.3974	0.3936	0.3897	0.3859
-0.1	0.4602	0.4562	0.4522	0.4483	0.4443	0.4404	0.4364	0.4325	0.4286	0.4247
-0.0	0.5000	0.4960	0.4920	0.4880	0.4840	0.4801	0.4761	0.4721	0.4681	0.4641

Z	0	1	2	3	4	5	6	7	8	9
0.0	0.5000	0.5040	0.5080	0.5120	0.5160	0.5199	0.5239	0.5279	0.5319	0.5359
0.1	0.5398	0.5438	0.5478	0.5517	0.5557	0.5596	0.5636	0.5675	0.5714	0.5753
0.2	0.5793	0.5832	0.5871	0.5910	0.5948	0.5987	0.6026	0.6064	0.6103	0.6141
0.3	0.6179	0.6217	0.6255	0.6293	0.6331	0.6368	0.6406	0.6443	0.6480	0.6517
0.4	0.6554	0.6591	0.6628	0.6664	0.6700	0.6736	0.6772	0.6808	0.6844	0.6879
0.5	0.6915	0.6950	0.6985	0.7019	0.7054	0.7088	0.7123	0.7157	0.7190	0.7224
0.6	0.7257	0.7291	0.7324	0.7357	0.7389	0.7422	0.7454	0.7486	0.7517	0.7549
0.7	0.7580	0.7611	0.7642	0.7673	0.7703	0.7734	0.7764	0.7794	0.7823	0.7852
0.8	0.7881	0.7910	0.7939	0.7967	0.7995	0.8023	0.8051	0.8078	0.8106	0.8133
0.9	0.8159	0.8186	0.8212	0.8238	0.8264	0.8289	0.8315	0.8340	0.8365	0.8389
1.0	0.8413	0.8438	0.8461	0.8485	0.8508	0.8531	0.8554	0.8577	0.8599	0.8621
1.1	0.8643	0.8665	0.8686	0.8708	0.8729	0.8749	0.8770	0.8790	0.8810	0.8830
1.2	0.8849	0.8869	0.8888	0.8907	0.8925	0.8944	0.8962	0.8980	0.8997	0.9015
1.3	0.9032	0.9049	0.9066	0.9082	0.9099	0.9115	0.9131	0.9147	0.9162	0.9177
1.4	0.9192	0.9207	0.9222	0.9236	0.9251	0.9265	0.9278	0.9292	0.9306	0.9319
1.5	0.9332	0.9345	0.9357	0.9370	0.9382	0.9394	0.9406	0.9418	0.9430	0.9441
1.6	0.9452	0.9463	0.9474	0.9484	0.9495	0.9505	0.9515	0.9525	0.9535	0.9545
1.7	0.9554	0.9564	0.9573	0.9582	0.9591	0.9599	0.9608	0.9616	0.9625	0.9633
1.8	0.9641	0.9648	0.9656	0.9664	0.9671	0.9678	0.9686	0.9693	0.9700	0.9706
1.9	0.9713	0.9719	0.9726	0.9732	0.9738	0.9744	0.9750	0.9756	0.9762	0.9767
2.0	0.9772	0.9778	0.9783	0.9788	0.9793	0.9798	0.9803	0.9808	0.9812	0.9817
2.1	0.9821	0.9826	0.9830	0.9834	0.9838	0.9842	0.9846	0.9850	0.9854	0.9857
2.2	0.9861	0.9864	0.9868	0.9871	0.9874	0.9878	0.9881	0.9884	0.9887	0.9890
2.3	0.9893	0.9896	0.9898	0.9901	0.9904	0.9906	0.9909	0.9911	0.9913	0.9916
2.4	0.9918	0.9920	0.9922	0.9925	0.9927	0.9929	0.9931	0.9932	0.9934	0.9936
2.5	0.9938	0.9940	0.9941	0.9943	0.9945	0.9946	0.9948	0.9949	0.9951	0.9952
2.6	0.9953	0.9955	0.9956	0.9957	0.9959	0.9960	0.9961	0.9962	0.9963	0.9964
2.7	0.9965	0.9966	0.9967	0.9968	0.9969	0.9970	0.9971	0.9972	0.9973	0.9974
2.8	0.9974	0.9975	0.9976	0.9977	0.9977	0.9978	0.9979	0.9979	0.9980	0.9981
2.9	0.9981	0.9982	0.9982	0.9983	0.9984	0.9984	0.9985	0.9985	0.9986	0.9986
3.	0.9987	0.9990	0.9993	0.9995	0.9997	0.9998	0.9998	0.9999	0.9999	1.0000

Source: B.W. Lindgren, *Statistical Theory* (New York: Macmillan, 1962), pp. 392–393.

TABLE A.2   Upper Percentiles of Student t Distributions

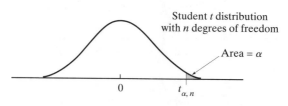

df	0.20	0.15	0.10	0.05	0.025	0.01	0.005
1	1.376	1.963	3.078	6.3138	12.706	31.821	63.657
2	1.061	1.386	1.886	2.9200	4.3027	6.965	9.9248
3	0.978	1.250	1.638	2.3534	3.1825	4.541	5.8409
4	0.941	1.190	1.533	2.1318	2.7764	3.747	4.6041
5	0.920	1.156	1.476	2.0150	2.5706	3.365	4.0321
6	0.906	1.134	1.440	1.9432	2.4469	3.143	3.7074
7	0.896	1.119	1.415	1.8946	2.3646	2.998	3.4995
8	0.889	1.108	1.397	1.8595	2.3060	2.896	3.3554
9	0.883	1.100	1.383	1.8331	2.2622	2.821	3.2498
10	0.879	1.093	1.372	1.8125	2.2281	2.764	3.1693
11	0.876	1.088	1.363	1.7959	2.2010	2.718	3.1058
12	0.873	1.083	1.356	1.7823	2.1788	2.681	3.0545
13	0.870	1.079	1.350	1.7709	2.1604	2.650	3.0123
14	0.868	1.076	1.345	1.7613	2.1448	2.624	2.9768
15	0.866	1.074	1.341	1.7530	2.1315	2.602	2.9467
16	0.865	1.071	1.337	1.7459	2.1199	2.583	2.9208
17	0.863	1.069	1.333	1.7396	2.1098	2.567	2.8982
18	0.862	1.067	1.330	1.7341	2.1009	2.552	2.8784
19	0.861	1.066	1.328	1.7291	2.0930	2.539	2.8609
20	0.860	1.064	1.325	1.7247	2.0860	2.528	2.8453
21	0.859	1.063	1.323	1.7207	2.0796	2.518	2.8314
22	0.858	1.061	1.321	1.7171	2.0739	2.508	2.8188
23	0.858	1.060	1.319	1.7139	2.0687	2.500	2.8073
24	0.857	1.059	1.318	1.7109	2.0639	2.492	2.7969
25	0.856	1.058	1.316	1.7081	2.0595	2.485	2.7874
26	0.856	1.058	1.315	1.7056	2.0555	2.479	2.7787
27	0.855	1.057	1.314	1.7033	2.0518	2.473	2.7707
28	0.855	1.056	1.313	1.7011	2.0484	2.467	2.7633
29	0.854	1.055	1.311	1.6991	2.0452	2.462	2.7564
30	0.854	1.055	1.310	1.6973	2.0423	2.457	2.7500
31	0.8535	1.0541	1.3095	1.6955	2.0395	2.453	2.7441
32	0.8531	1.0536	1.3086	1.6939	2.0370	2.449	2.7385
33	0.8527	1.0531	1.3078	1.6924	2.0345	2.445	2.7333
34	0.8524	1.0526	1.3070	1.6909	2.0323	2.441	2.7284

TABLE A.2   Upper Percentiles of Student *t* Distributions *(cont.)*

α

df	0.20	0.15	0.10	0.05	0.025	0.01	0.005
35	0.8521	1.0521	1.3062	1.6896	2.0301	2.438	2.7239
36	0.8518	1.0516	1.3055	1.6883	2.0281	2.434	2.7195
37	0.8515	1.0512	1.3049	1.6871	2.0262	2.431	2.7155
38	0.8512	1.0508	1.3042	1.6860	2.0244	2.428	2.7116
39	0.8510	1.0504	1.3037	1.6849	2.0227	2.426	2.7079
40	0.8507	1.0501	1.3031	1.6839	2.0211	2.423	2.7045
41	0.8505	1.0498	1.3026	1.6829	2.0196	2.421	2.7012
42	0.8503	1.0494	1.3020	1.6820	2.0181	2.418	2.6981
43	0.8501	1.0491	1.3016	1.6811	2.0167	2.416	2.6952
44	0.8499	1.0488	1.3011	1.6802	2.0154	2.414	2.6923
45	0.8497	1.0485	1.3007	1.6794	2.0141	2.412	2.6896
46	0.8495	1.0483	1.3002	1.6787	2.0129	2.410	2.6870
47	0.8494	1.0480	1.2998	1.6779	2.0118	2.408	2.6846
48	0.8492	1.0478	1.2994	1.6772	2.0106	2.406	2.6822
49	0.8490	1.0476	1.2991	1.6766	2.0096	2.405	2.6800
50	0.8489	1.0473	1.2987	1.6759	2.0086	2.403	2.6778
51	0.8448	1.0471	1.2984	1.6753	2.0077	2.402	2.6758
52	0.8486	1.0469	1.2981	1.6747	2.0067	2.400	2.6738
53	0.8485	1.0467	1.2978	1.6742	2.0058	2.399	2.6719
54	0.8484	1.0465	1.2975	1.6736	2.0049	2.397	2.6700
55	0.8483	1.0463	1.2972	1.6731	2.0041	2.396	2.6683
56	0.8481	1.0461	1.2969	1.6725	2.0033	2.395	2.6666
57	0.8480	1.0460	1.2967	1.6721	2.0025	2.393	2.6650
58	0.8479	1.0458	1.2964	1.6716	2.0017	2.392	2.6633
59	0.8478	1.0457	1.2962	1.6712	2.0010	2.391	2.6618
60	0.8477	1.0455	1.2959	1.6707	2.0003	2.390	2.6603
61	0.8476	1.0454	1.2957	1.6703	1.9997	2.389	2.6590
62	0.8475	1.0452	1.2954	1.6698	1.9990	2.388	2.6576
63	0.8474	1.0451	1.2952	1.6694	1.9984	2.387	2.6563
64	0.8473	1.0449	1.2950	1.6690	1.9977	2.386	2.6549
65	0.8472	1.0448	1.2948	1.6687	1.9972	2.385	2.6537
66	0.8471	1.0447	1.2945	1.6683	1.9966	2.384	2.6525
67	0.8471	1.0446	1.2944	1.6680	1.9961	2.383	2.6513
68	0.8470	1.0444	1.2942	1.6676	1.9955	2.382	2.6501
69	0.8469	1.0443	1.2940	1.6673	1.9950	2.381	2.6491
70	0.8468	1.0442	1.2938	1.6669	1.9945	2.381	2.6480
71	0.8468	1.0441	1.2936	1.6666	1.9940	2.380	2.6470
72	0.8467	1.0440	1.2934	1.6663	1.9935	2.379	2.6459
73	0.8466	1.0439	1.2933	1.6660	1.9931	2.378	2.6450
74	0.8465	1.0438	1.2931	1.6657	1.9926	2.378	2.6640
75	0.8465	1.0437	1.2930	1.6655	1.9922	2.377	2.6431
76	0.8464	1.0436	1.2928	1.6652	1.9917	2.376	2.6421
77	0.8464	1.0435	1.2927	1.6649	1.9913	2.376	2.6413
78	0.8463	1.0434	1.2925	1.6646	1.9909	2.375	2.6406
79	0.8463	1.0433	1.2924	1.6644	1.9905	2.374	2.6396

TABLE A.2   Upper Percentiles of Student *t* Distributions *(cont.)*

α

df	0.20	0.15	0.10	0.05	0.025	0.01	0.005
80	0.8462	1.0432	1.2922	1.6641	1.9901	2.374	2.6388
81	0.8461	1.0431	1.2921	1.6639	1.9897	2.373	2.6380
82	0.8460	1.0430	1.2920	1.6637	1.9893	2.372	2.6372
83	0.8460	1.0430	1.2919	1.6635	1.9890	2.372	2.6365
84	0.8459	1.0429	1.2917	1.6632	1.9886	2.371	2.6357
85	0.8459	1.0428	1.2916	1.6630	1.9883	2.371	2.6350
86	0.8458	1.0427	1.2915	1.6628	1.9880	2.370	2.6343
87	0.8458	1.0427	1.2914	1.6626	1.9877	2.370	2.6336
88	0.8457	1.0426	1.2913	1.6624	1.9873	2.369	2.6329
89	0.8457	1.0426	1.2912	1.6622	1.9870	2.369	2.6323
90	0.8457	1.0425	1.2910	1.6620	1.9867	2.368	2.6316
91	0.8457	1.0424	1.2909	1.6618	1.9864	2.368	2.6310
92	0.8456	1.0423	1.2908	1.6616	1.9861	2.367	2.6303
93	0.8456	1.0423	1.2907	1.6614	1.9859	2.367	2.6298
94	0.8455	1.0422	1.2906	1.6612	1.9856	2.366	2.6292
95	0.8455	1.0422	1.2905	1.6611	1.9853	2.366	2.6286
96	0.8454	1.0421	1.2904	1.6609	1.9850	2.366	2.6280
97	0.8454	1.0421	1.2904	1.6608	1.9848	2.365	2.6275
98	0.8453	1.0420	1.2903	1.6606	1.9845	2.365	2.6270
99	0.8453	1.0419	1.2902	1.6604	1.9843	2.364	2.6265
100	0.8452	1.0418	1.2901	1.6602	1.9840	2.364	2.6260
∞	0.84	1.04	1.28	1.64	1.96	2.33	2.58

Source: Scientific Tables, 6th ed. (Basel, Switzerland: J.R. Geigy, 1962), pp. 32–33.

TABLE A.3   Upper and Lower Percentiles of χ^2 Distributions

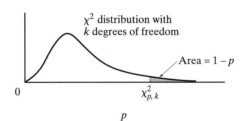

χ^2 distribution with
k degrees of freedom

Area = $1 - p$

0          $\chi^2_{p,k}$

p

df	0.010	0.025	0.050	0.10	0.90	0.95	0.975	0.99
1	0.000157	0.000982	0.00393	0.0158	2.706	3.841	5.024	6.635
2	0.0201	0.0506	0.103	0.211	4.605	5.991	7.378	9.210
3	0.115	0.216	0.352	0.584	6.251	7.815	9.348	11.345
4	0.297	0.484	0.711	1.064	7.779	9.488	11.143	13.277
5	0.554	0.831	1.145	1.610	9.236	11.070	12.832	15.086
6	0.872	1.237	1.635	2.204	10.645	12.592	14.449	16.812
7	1.239	1.690	2.167	2.833	12.017	14.067	16.013	18.475
8	1.646	2.180	2.733	3.490	13.362	15.507	17.535	20.090
9	2.088	2.700	3.325	4.168	14.684	16.919	19.023	21.666
10	2.558	3.247	3.940	4.865	15.987	18.307	20.483	23.209
11	3.053	3.816	4.575	5.578	17.275	19.675	21.920	24.725
12	3.571	4.404	5.226	6.304	18.549	21.026	23.336	26.217
13	4.107	5.009	5.892	7.042	19.812	22.362	24.736	27.688
14	4.660	5.629	6.571	7.790	21.064	23.685	26.119	29.141
15	5.229	6.262	7.261	8.547	22.307	24.996	27.488	30.578
16	5.812	6.908	7.962	9.312	23.542	26.296	28.845	32.000
17	6.408	7.564	8.672	10.085	24.769	27.587	30.191	33.409
18	7.015	8.231	9.390	10.865	25.989	28.869	31.526	34.805
19	7.633	8.907	10.117	11.651	27.204	30.144	32.852	36.191
20	8.260	9.591	10.851	12.443	28.412	31.410	34.170	37.566
21	8.897	10.283	11.591	13.240	29.615	32.671	35.479	38.932
22	9.542	10.982	12.338	14.041	30.813	33.924	36.781	40.289
23	10.196	11.688	13.091	14.848	32.007	35.172	38.076	41.638
24	10.856	12.401	13.848	15.659	33.196	36.415	39.364	42.980
25	11.524	13.120	14.611	16.473	34.382	37.652	40.646	44.314
26	12.198	13.844	15.379	17.292	35.563	38.885	41.923	45.642
27	12.879	14.573	16.151	18.114	36.741	40.113	43.194	46.963
28	13.565	15.308	16.928	18.939	37.916	41.337	44.461	48.278
29	14.256	16.047	17.708	19.768	39.087	42.557	45.722	49.588
30	14.953	16.791	18.493	20.599	40.256	43.773	46.979	50.892
31	15.655	17.539	19.281	21.434	41.422	44.985	48.232	52.191
32	16.362	18.291	20.072	22.271	42.585	46.194	49.480	53.486
33	17.073	19.047	20.867	23.110	43.745	47.400	50.725	54.776
34	17.789	19.806	21.664	23.952	44.903	48.602	51.966	56.061

TABLE A.3   Upper and Lower Percentiles of χ^2 Distributions *(cont.)*

				p				
df	0.010	0.025	0.050	0.10	0.90	0.95	0.975	0.99
35	18.509	20.569	22.465	24.797	46.059	49.802	53.203	57.342
36	19.233	21.336	23.269	25.643	47.212	50.998	54.437	58.619
37	19.960	22.106	24.075	26.492	48.363	52.192	55.668	59.892
38	20.691	22.878	24.884	27.343	49.513	53.384	56.895	61.162
39	21.426	23.654	25.695	28.196	50.660	54.572	58.120	62.428
40	22.164	24.433	26.509	29.051	51.805	55.758	59.342	63.691
41	22.906	25.215	27.326	29.907	52.949	56.942	60.561	64.950
42	23.650	25.999	28.144	30.765	54.090	58.124	61.777	66.206
43	24.398	26.785	28.965	31.625	55.230	59.304	62.990	67.459
44	25.148	27.575	29.787	32.487	56.369	60.481	64.201	68.709
45	25.901	28.366	30.612	33.350	57.505	61.656	65.410	69.957
46	26.657	29.160	31.439	34.215	58.641	62.830	66.617	71.201
47	27.416	29.956	32.268	35.081	59.774	64.001	67.821	72.443
48	28.177	30.755	33.098	35.949	60.907	65.171	69.023	73.683
49	28.941	31.555	33.930	36.818	62.038	66.339	70.222	74.919
50	29.707	32.357	34.764	37.689	63.167	67.505	71.420	76.154

Source: Scientific Tables, 6th ed. (Basel, Switzerland: J.R. Geigy, 1962), p. 36.

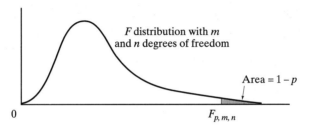

The figure above illustrates the percentiles of the F distributions shown in Table A.4. Table A.4 is used with permission from Wilfrid J. Dixon and Frank J. Massey, Jr., *Introduction to Statistical Analysis*, 2nd. ed. (New York: McGraw-Hill, 1957), pp. 389–404.

TABLE A.4   Percentiles of F Distributions

n	p	1	2	3	4	5	6	7	8	9	10	11	12	p
1	.0005	$.0^6$62	$.0^3$50	$.0^2$38	$.0^2$94	.016	.022	.027	.032	.036	.039	.042	.045	.0005
	.001	$.0^5$25	$.0^2$10	$.0^2$60	.013	.021	.028	.034	.039	.044	.048	.051	.054	.001
	.005	$.0^4$62	$.0^2$51	.018	.032	.044	.054	.062	.068	.073	.078	.082	.085	.005
	.010	$.0^3$25	.010	.029	.047	.062	.073	.082	.089	.095	.100	.104	.107	.010
	.025	$.0^2$15	.026	.057	.082	.100	.113	.124	.132	.139	.144	.149	.153	.025
	.05	$.0^2$62	.054	.099	.130	.151	.167	.179	.188	.195	.201	.207	.211	.05
	.10	.025	.117	.181	.220	.246	.265	.279	.289	.298	.304	.310	.315	.10
	.25	.172	.389	.494	.553	.591	.617	.637	.650	.661	.670	.680	.684	.25
	.50	1.00	1.50	1.71	1.82	1.89	1.94	1.98	2.00	2.03	2.04	2.05	2.07	.50
	.75	5.83	7.50	8.20	8.58	8.82	8.98	9.10	9.19	9.26	9.32	9.36	9.41	.75
	.90	39.9	49.5	53.6	55.8	57.2	58.2	58.9	59.4	59.9	60.2	60.5	60.7	.90
	.95	161	200	216	225	230	234	237	239	241	242	243	244	.95
	.975	648	800	864	900	922	937	948	957	963	969	973	977	.975
	.99	405^1	500^1	540^1	562^1	576^1	586^1	593^1	598^1	602^1	606^1	608^1	611^1	.99
	.995	162^2	200^2	216^2	225^2	231^2	234^2	237^2	239^2	241^2	242^2	243^2	244^2	.995
	.999	406^3	500^3	540^3	562^3	576^3	586^3	593^3	598^3	602^3	606^3	609^3	611^3	.999
	.9995	162^4	200^4	216^4	225^4	231^4	234^4	237^4	239^4	241^4	242^4	243^4	244^4	.9995
2	.0005	$.0^6$50	$.0^3$50	$.0^2$42	.011	.020	.029	.037	.044	.050	.056	.061	.065	.0005
	.001	$.0^5$20	$.0^2$10	$.0^2$68	.016	.027	.037	.046	.054	.061	.067	.072	.077	.001
	.005	$.0^4$50	$.0^2$50	.020	.038	.055	.069	.081	.091	.099	.106	.112	.118	.005
	.01	$.0^3$20	.010	.032	.056	.075	.092	.105	.116	.125	.132	.139	.144	.01
	.025	$.0^2$13	.026	.062	.094	.119	.138	.153	.165	.175	.183	.190	.196	.025
	.05	$.0^2$50	.053	.105	.144	.173	.194	.211	.224	.235	.244	.251	.257	.05
	.10	.020	.111	.183	.231	.265	.289	.307	.321	.333	.342	.350	.356	.10
	.25	.133	.333	.439	.500	.540	.568	.588	.604	.616	.626	.633	.641	.25
	.50	.667	1.00	1.13	1.21	1.25	1.28	1.30	1.32	1.33	1.34	1.35	1.36	.50
	.75	2.57	3.00	3.15	3.23	3.28	3.31	3.34	3.35	3.37	3.38	3.39	3.39	.75
	.90	8.53	9.00	9.16	9.24	9.29	9.33	9.35	9.37	9.38	9.39	9.40	9.41	.90
	.95	18.5	19.0	19.2	19.2	19.3	19.3	19.4	19.4	19.4	19.4	19.4	19.4	.95
	.975	38.5	39.0	39.2	39.2	39.3	39.3	39.4	39.4	39.4	39.4	39.4	39.4	.975
	.99	98.5	99.0	99.2	99.2	99.3	99.3	99.4	99.4	99.4	99.4	99.4	99.4	.99
	.995	198	199	199	199	199	199	199	199	199	199	199	199	.995
	.999	998	999	999	999	999	999	999	999	999	999	999	999	.999
	.9995	200^1	200^1	200^1	200^1	200^1	200^1	200^1	200^1	200^1	200^1	200^1	200^1	.9995
3	.0005	$.0^6$46	$.0^3$50	$.0^2$44	.012	.023	.033	.043	.052	.060	.067	.074	.079	.0005
	.001	$.0^5$19	$.0^2$10	$.0^2$71	.018	.030	.042	.053	.063	.072	.079	.086	.093	.001
	.005	$.0^4$46	$.0^2$50	.021	.041	.060	.077	.092	.104	.115	.124	.132	.138	.005
	.01	$.0^3$19	.010	.034	.060	.083	.102	.118	.132	.143	.153	.161	.168	.01
	.025	$.0^2$12	.026	.065	.100	.129	.152	.170	.185	.197	.207	.216	.224	.025
	.05	$.0^2$46	.052	.108	.152	.185	.210	.230	.246	.259	.270	.279	.287	.05
	.10	.019	.109	.185	.239	.276	.304	.325	.342	.356	.367	.376	.384	.10
	.25	.122	.317	.424	.489	.531	.561	.582	.600	.613	.624	.633	.641	.25
	.50	.585	.881	1.00	1.06	1.10	1.13	1.15	1.16	1.17	1.18	1.19	1.20	.50
	.75	2.02	2.28	2.36	2.39	2.41	2.42	2.43	2.44	2.44	2.44	2.45	2.45	.75
	.90	5.54	5.46	5.39	5.34	5.31	5.28	5.27	5.25	5.24	5.23	5.22	5.22	.90
	.95	10.1	9.55	9.28	9.12	9.01	8.94	8.89	8.85	8.81	8.79	8.76	8.74	.95
	.075	17.4	16.0	15.4	15.1	14.9	14.7	14.6	14.5	14.5	14.4	14.4	14.3	.975
	.99	34.1	30.8	29.5	28.7	28.2	27.9	27.7	27.5	27.3	27.2	27.1	27.1	.99
	.995	55.6	49.8	47.5	46.2	45.4	44.8	44.4	44.1	43.9	43.7	43.5	43.4	.995
	.999	167	149	141	137	135	133	132	131	130	129	129	128	.999
	.9995	266	237	225	218	214	211	209	208	207	206	204	204	.9995

Read $.0^3$56 as .00056, 200^1 as 2000, 162^4 as 1620000, etc.

TABLE A.4   Percentiles of *F* Distributions *(cont.)*

m \ p	15	20	24	30	40	50	60	100	120	200	500	∞	p	n
.0005	.051	.058	062	.066	.069	.072	.074	.077	.078	.080	.081	.083	.0005	1
.001	.060	.067	.071	.075	.079	.082	.084	.087	.088	.089	.091	.092	.001	
.005	.093	.101	.105	.109	.113	.116	.118	.121	.122	.124	.126	.127	.005	
.01	.115	.124	.128	.132	.137	.139	.141	.145	.146	.148	.150	.151	.01	
.025	.161	.170	.175	.180	.184	.187	.189	.193	.194	.196	.198	.199	.025	
.05	.220	.230	.235	.240	.245	.248	.250	.254	.255	.257	.259	.261	.05	
.10	.325	.336	.342	.347	.353	.356	.358	.362	.364	.366	.368	.370	.10	
.25	.698	.712	.719	.727	.734	.738	.741	.747	.749	.752	.754	.756	.25	
.50	2.09	2.12	2.13	2.15	2.16	2.17	2.17	2.18	2.18	2.19	2.19	2.20	.50	
.75	9.49	9.58	9.63	9.67	9.71	9.74	9.76	9.78	9.80	9.82	9.84	9.85	.75	
.90	61.2	61.7	62.0	62.3	62.5	62.7	62.8	63.0	63.1	63.2	63.3	63.3	.90	
.95	246	248	249	250	251	252	252	253	253	254	254	254	.95	
.975	985	993	997	100^1	101^1	101^1	101^1	101^1	101^1	102^1	102^1	102^1	.975	
.99	616^1	621^1	623^1	626^1	629^1	630^1	631^1	633^1	634^1	635^1	636^1	637^1	.99	
.995	246^2	248^2	249^2	250^2	251^2	252^2	252^2	253^2	254^2	254^2	254^2	255^2	.995	
.999	616^3	621^3	623^3	626^3	629^3	630^3	631^3	633^3	634^3	635^3	636^3	637^3	.999	
.9995	246^4	248^4	249^4	250^4	251^4	252^4	252^4	253^4	253^4	253^4	254^4	254^4	.9995	
.0005	.076	.088	.094	.101	.108	.113	.116	.122	.124	.127	.130	.132	.0005	2
.001	.088	.100	.107	.114	.121	.126	.129	.135	.137	.140	.143	.145	.001	
.005	.130	.143	.150	.157	.165	.169	.173	.179	.181	.184	.187	.189	.005	
.01	.157	.171	.178	.186	.193	.198	.201	.207	.209	.212	.215	.217	.01	
.025	.210	.224	.232	.239	.247	.251	.255	.261	.263	.266	.269	.271	.025	
.05	.272	.286	.294	.302	.309	.314	.317	.324	.326	.329	.332	.334	.05	
.10	.371	.386	.394	.402	.410	.415	.418	.424	.426	.429	.433	.434	.10	
.25	.657	.672	.680	.689	.697	.702	.705	.711	.713	.716	.719	.721	.25	
.50	1.38	1.39	1.40	1.41	1.42	1.42	1.43	1.43	1.43	1.44	1.44	1.44	.50	
.75	3.41	3.43	3.43	3.44	3.45	3.45	3.46	3.47	3.47	3.48	3.48	3.48	.75	
.90	9.42	9.44	9.45	9.46	9.47	9.47	9.47	9.48	9.48	9.49	9.49	9.49	.90	
.95	19.4	19.4	19.5	19.5	19.5	19.5	19.5	19.5	19.5	19.5	19.5	19.5	.95	
.975	39.4	39.4	39.5	39.5	39.5	39.5	39.5	39.5	39.5	39.5	39.5	39.5	.975	
.99	99.4	99.4	99.5	99.5	99.5	99.5	99.5	99.5	99.5	99.5	99.5	99.5	.99	
.995	199	199	199	199	199	199	199	199	199	199	199	200	.995	
.999	999	999	999	999	999	999	999	999	999	999	999	999	.999	
.9995	200^1	200^1	200^1	200^1	200^1	200^1	200^1	200^1	200^1	200^1	200^1	200^1	.9995	
.0005	.093	.109	.117	.127	.136	.143	.147	.156	.158	.162	.166	.169	.0005	3
.001	.107	.123	.132	.142	.152	.158	.162	.171	.173	.177	.181	.184	.001	
.005	.154	.172	.181	.191	.201	.207	.211	.220	.222	.227	.231	.234	.005	
.01	.185	.203	.212	.222	.232	.238	.242	.251	.253	.258	.262	.264	.01	
.025	.241	.259	.269	.279	.289	.295	.299	.308	.310	.314	.318	.321	.025	
.05	.304	.323	.332	.342	.352	.358	.363	.370	.373	.377	.382	.384	.05	
.10	.402	.420	.430	.439	.449	.455	.459	.467	.469	.474	.476	.480	.10	
.25	.658	.675	.684	.693	.702	.708	.711	.719	.721	.724	.728	.730	.25	
.50	1.21	1.23	1.23	1.24	1.25	1.25	1.25	1.26	1.26	1.26	1.27	1.27	.50	
.75	2.46	2.46	2.46	2.47	2.47	2.47	2.47	2.47	2.47	2.47	2.47	2.47	.75	
.90	5.20	5.18	5.18	5.17	5.16	5.15	5.15	5.14	5.14	5.14	5.14	5.13	.90	
.95	8.70	8.66	8.63	8.62	8.59	8.58	8.57	8.55	8.55	8.54	8.53	8.53	.95	
.975	14.3	14.2	14.1	14.1	14.0	14.0	14.0	14.0	13.9	13.9	13.9	13.9	.975	
.99	26.9	26.7	26.6	26.5	26.4	26.4	26.3	26.2	26.2	26.2	26.1	26.1	.99	
.995	43.1	42.8	42.6	42.5	42.3	42.2	42.1	42.0	42.0	41.9	41.9	41.8	.995	
.999	127	126	126	125	125	125	124	124	124	124	124	123	.999	
.9995	203	201	200	199	199	198	198	197	197	197	196	196	.9995	

TABLE A.4   Percentiles of F Distributions *(cont.)*

n	p	1	2	3	4	5	6	7	8	9	10	11	12	p
4	.0005	$.0^644$	$.0^350$	$.0^246$	.013	.024	.036	.047	.057	.066	.075	.082	.089	.0005
	.001	$.0^518$	$.0^210$	$.0^273$	.019	.032	.046	.058	.069	.079	.089	.097	.104	.001
	.005	$.0^444$	$.0^250$	.022	.043	.064	.083	.100	.114	.126	.137	.145	.153	.005
	.01	$.0^318$	.010	.035	.063	.088	.109	.127	.143	.156	.167	.176	.185	.01
	.025	$.0^211$	.026	.066	.104	.135	.161	.181	.198	.212	.224	.234	.243	.025
	05	$.0^244$	.052	.110	.157	.193	.221	.243	.261	.275	.288	.298	.307	.05
	.10	.018	.108	.187	.243	.284	.314	.338	.356	.371	.384	.394	.403	.10
	.25	.117	.309	.418	.484	.528	.560	.583	.601	.615	.627	.637	.645	.25
	.50	.549	.828	.941	1.00	1.04	1.06	1.08	1.09	1.10	1.11	1.12	1.13	.50
	.75	1.81	2.00	2.05	2.06	2.07	2.08	2.08	2.08	2.08	2.08	2.08	2.08	.75
	.90	4.54	4.32	4.19	4.11	4.05	4.01	3.98	3.95	3.94	3.92	3.91	3.90	.90
	.95	7.71	6.94	6.59	6.39	6.26	6.16	6.09	6.04	6.00	5.96	5.94	5.91	.95
	.975	12.2	10.6	9.98	9.60	9.36	9.20	9.07	8.98	8.90	8.84	8.79	8.75	.975
	.99	21.2	18.0	16.7	16.0	15.5	15.2	15.0	14.8	14.7	14.5	14.4	14.4	.99
	.995	31.3	26.3	24.3	23.2	22.5	22.0	21.6	21.4	21.1	21.0	20.8	20.7	.995
	.999	74.1	61.2	56.2	53.4	51.7	50.5	49.7	49.0	48.5	48.0	47.7	47.4	.999
	.9995	106	87.4	80.1	76.1	73.6	71.9	70.6	69.7	68.9	68.3	67.8	67.4	.9995
5	.0005	$.0^643$	$.0^350$	$.0^247$	.014	.025	.038	.050	.061	.070	.081	.089	.096	.0005
	.001	$.0^517$	$.0^210$	$.0^275$	.019	.034	.048	.062	.074	.085	.095	.104	.112	.001
	.005	$.0^443$	$.0^250$	.022	.045	.067	.087	.105	.120	.134	.146	.156	.165	.005
	.01	$.0^317$	.010	.035	.064	.091	.114	.134	.151	.165	.177	.188	.197	.01
	.025	$.0^211$	.025	.067	.107	.140	.167	.189	.208	.223	.236	.248	.257	.025
	.05	$.0^243$	.052	.111	.160	.198	.228	.252	.271	.287	.301	.313	.322	.05
	.10	.017	.108	.188	.247	.290	.322	.347	.367	.383	.397	.408	.418	.10
	.25	.113	.305	.415	.483	.528	.560	.584	.604	.618	.631	.641	.650	.25
	.50	.528	.799	.907	.965	1.00	1.02	1.04	1.05	1.06	1.07	1.08	1.09	.50
	.75	1.69	1.85	1.88	1.89	1.89	1.89	1.89	1.89	1.89	1.89	1.89	1.89	.75
	.90	4.06	3.78	3.62	3.52	3.45	3.40	3.37	3.34	3.32	3.30	3.28	3.27	.90
	.95	6.61	5.79	5.41	5.19	5.05	4.95	4.88	4.82	4.77	4.74	4.71	4.68	.95
	.975	10.0	8.43	7.76	7.39	7.15	6.98	6.85	6.76	6.68	6.62	6.57	6.52	.975
	.99	16.3	13.3	12.1	11.4	11.0	10.7	10.5	10.3	10.2	10.1	9.96	9.89	.99
	.995	22.8	18.3	16.5	15.6	14.9	14.5	14.2	14.0	13.8	13.6	13.5	13.4	.995
	.999	47.2	37.1	33.2	31.1	29.7	28.8	28.2	27.6	27.2	26.9	26.6	26.4	.999
	.9995	63.6	49.8	44.4	41.5	39.7	38.5	37.6	36.9	36.4	35.9	35.6	35.2	.9995
6	.0005	$.0^643$	$.0^350$	$.0^247$	.014	.026	.039	.052	.064	.075	.085	.094	.103	.0005
	.001	$.0^517$	$.0^210$	$.0^275$	.020	.035	.050	.064	.078	.090	.101	.111	.119	.001
	.005	$.0^443$	$.0^250$	.022	.045	.069	.090	.109	.126	.140	.153	.164	.174	.005
	.01	$.0^317$	.010	.036	.066	.094	.118	.139	.157	.172	.186	.197	.207	.01
	.025	$.0^211$	.025	.068	.109	.143	.172	.195	.215	.231	.246	.258	.268	.025
	.05	$.0^243$	.052	.112	.162	.202	.233	.259	.279	.296	.311	.324	.334	.05
	.10	.017	.107	.189	.249	.294	.327	.354	.375	.392	.406	.418	.429	.10
	.25	.111	.302	.413	.481	.524	.561	.586	.606	.622	.635	.645	.654	.25
	.50	.515	.780	.886	.942	.977	1.00	1.02	1.03	1.04	1.05	1.05	1.06	.50
	.75	1.62	1.76	1.78	1.79	1.79	1.78	1.78	1.78	1.77	1.77	1.77	1.77	.75
	.90	3.78	3.46	3.29	3.18	3.11	3.05	3.01	2.98	2.96	2.94	2.92	2.90	.90
	.95	5.99	5.14	4.76	4.53	4.39	4.28	4.21	4.15	4.10	4.06	4.03	4.00	.95
	.975	8.81	7.26	6.60	6.23	5.99	5.82	5.70	5.60	5.52	5.46	5.41	5.37	.975
	.99	13.7	10.9	9.78	9.15	8.75	8.47	8.26	8.10	7.98	7.87	7.79	7.72	.99
	.995	18.6	14.5	12.9	12.0	11.5	11.1	10.8	10.6	10.4	10.2	10.1	10.0	.995
	.999	35.5	27.0	23.7	21.9	20.8	20.0	19.5	19.0	18.7	18.4	18.2	18.0	.999
	.9995	46.1	34.8	30.4	28.1	26.6	25.6	24.9	24.3	23.9	23.5	23.2	23.0	.9995

TABLE A.4   Percentiles of F Distributions *(cont.)*

p \ m	15	20	24	30	40	50	60	100	120	200	500	∞	p	n
.0005	.105	.125	.135	.147	.159	.166	.172	.183	.186	.191	.196	.200	.0005	**4**
.001	.121	.141	.152	.163	.176	.183	.188	.200	.202	.208	.213	.217	.001	
.005	.172	.193	.204	.216	.229	.237	.242	.253	.255	.260	.266	.269	.005	
.01	.204	.226	.237	.249	.261	.269	.274	.285	.287	.293	.298	.301	.01	
.025	.263	.284	.296	.308	.320	.327	.332	.342	.346	.351	.356	.359	.025	
.05	.327	.349	.360	.372	.384	.391	.396	.407	.409	.413	.418	.422	.05	
.10	.424	.445	.456	.467	.478	.485	.490	.500	.502	.508	.510	.514	.10	
.25	.664	.683	.692	.702	.712	.718	.722	.731	.733	.737	.740	.743	.25	
.50	1.14	1.15	1.16	1.16	1.17	1.18	1.18	1.18	1.18	1.19	1.19	1.19	.50	
.75	2.08	2.08	2.08	2.08	2.08	2.08	2.08	2.08	2.08	2.08	2.08	2.08	.75	
.90	3.87	3.84	3.83	3.82	3.80	3.80	3.79	3.78	3.78	3.77	3.76	3.76	.90	
.95	5.86	5.80	5.77	5.75	5.72	5.70	5.69	5.66	5.66	5.65	5.64	5.63	.95	
.975	8.66	8.56	8.51	8.46	8.41	8.38	8.36	8.32	8.31	8.29	8.27	8.26	.975	
.99	14.2	14.0	13.9	13.8	13.7	13.7	13.7	13.6	13.6	13.5	13.5	13.5	.99	
.995	20.4	20.2	20.0	19.9	19.8	19.7	19.6	19.5	19.5	19.4	19.4	19.3	.995	
.999	46.8	46.1	45.8	45.4	45.1	44.9	44.7	44.5	44.4	44.3	44.1	44.0	.999	
.9995	66.5	65.5	65.1	64.6	64.1	63.8	63.6	63.2	63.1	62.9	62.7	62.6	.9995	
.0005	.115	.137	.150	.163	.177	.186	.192	.205	.209	.216	.222	.226	.0005	**5**
.001	.132	.155	.167	.181	.195	.204	.210	.223	.227	.233	.239	.244	.001	
.005	.186	.210	.223	.237	.251	.260	.266	.279	.282	.288	.294	.299	.005	
.01	.219	.244	.257	.270	.285	.293	.299	.312	.315	.322	.328	.331	.01	
.025	.280	.304	.317	.330	.344	.353	.359	.370	.374	.380	.386	.390	.025	
.05	.345	.369	.382	.395	.408	.417	.422	.432	.437	.442	.448	.452	.05	
.10	.440	.463	.476	.488	.501	.508	.514	.524	.527	.532	.538	.541	.10	
.25	.669	.690	.700	.711	.722	.728	.732	.741	.743	.748	.752	.755	.25	
.50	1.10	1.11	1.12	1.12	1.13	1.13	1.14	1.14	1.14	1.15	1.15	1.15	.50	
.75	1.89	1.88	1.88	1.88	1.88	1.88	1.87	1.87	1.87	1.87	1.87	1.87	.75	
.90	3.24	3.21	3.19	3.17	3.16	3.15	3.14	3.13	3.12	3.12	3.11	3.10	.90	
.95	4.62	4.56	4.53	4.50	4.46	4.44	4.43	4.41	4.40	4.39	4.37	4.36	.95	
.975	6.43	6.33	6.28	6.23	6.18	6.14	6.12	6.08	6.07	6.05	6.03	6.02	.975	
.99	9.72	9.55	9.47	9.38	9.29	9.24	9.20	9.13	9.11	9.08	9.04	9.02	.99	
.995	13.1	12.9	12.8	12.7	12.5	12.5	12.4	12.3	12.3	12.2	12.2	12.1	.995	
.999	25.9	25.4	25.1	24.9	24.6	24.4	24.3	24.1	24.1	23.9	23.8	23.8	.999	
.9995	34.6	33.9	33.5	33.1	32.7	32.5	32.3	32.1	32.0	31.8	31.7	31.6	.9995	
.0005	.123	.148	.162	.177	.193	.203	.210	.225	.229	.236	.244	.249	.0005	**6**
.001	.141	.166	.180	.195	.211	.222	.229	.243	.247	.255	.262	.267	.001	
.005	.197	.224	.238	.253	.269	.279	.286	.301	.304	.312	.318	.324	.005	
.01	.232	.258	.273	.288	.304	.313	.321	.334	.338	.346	.352	.357	.01	
.025	.293	.320	.334	.349	.364	.375	.381	.394	.398	.405	.412	.415	.025	
.05	.358	.385	.399	.413	.428	.437	.444	.457	.460	.467	.472	.476	.05	
.10	.453	.478	.491	.505	.519	.526	.533	.546	.548	.556	.559	.564	.10	
.25	.675	.696	.707	.718	.729	.736	.741	.751	.753	.758	.762	.765	.25	
.50	1.07	1.08	1.09	1.10	1.10	1.11	1.11	1.11	1.12	1.12	1.12	1.12	.50	
.75	1.76	1.76	1.75	1.75	1.75	1.75	1.74	1.74	1.74	1.74	1.74	1.74	.75	
.90	2.87	2.84	2.82	2.80	2.78	2.77	2.76	2.75	2.74	2.73	2.73	2.72	.90	
.95	3.94	3.87	3.84	3.81	3.77	3.75	3.74	3.71	3.70	3.69	3.68	3.67	.95	
.975	5.27	5.17	5.12	5.07	5.01	4.98	4.96	4.92	4.90	4.88	4.86	4.85	.975	
.99	7.56	7.40	7.31	7.23	7.14	7.09	7.06	6.99	6.97	6.93	6.90	6.88	.99	
.995	9.81	9.59	9.47	9.36	9.24	9.17	9.12	9.03	9.00	8.95	8.91	8.88	.995	
.999	17.6	17.1	16.9	16.7	16.4	16.3	16.2	16.0	16.0	15.9	15.8	15.7	.999	
.9995	22.4	21.9	21.7	21.4	21.1	20.9	20.7	20.5	20.4	20.3	20.2	20.1	.9995	

TABLE A.4   Percentiles of F Distributions *(cont.)*

n	p	1	2	3	4	5	6	7	8	9	10	11	12	p
7	.0005	$.0^642$	$.0^350$	$.0^248$	.014	.027	.040	.053	.066	.078	.088	.099	.108	.0005
	.001	$.0^517$	$.0^210$	$.0^276$	.020	.035	.051	.067	.081	.093	.105	.115	.125	.001
	.005	$.0^442$	$.0^250$	.023	.046	.070	.093	.113	.130	.145	.159	.171	.181	.005
	.01	$.0^317$	.010	.036	.067	.096	.121	.143	.162	.178	.192	.205	.216	.01
	.025	$.0^210$	.025	.068	.110	.146	.176	.200	.221	.238	.253	.266	.277	.025
	.05	$.0^242$	.052	.113	.164	.205	.238	.264	.286	.304	.319	.332	.343	.05
	.10	.017	.107	.190	.251	.297	.332	.359	.381	.399	.414	.427	.438	.10
	.25	.110	.300	.412	.481	.528	.562	.588	.608	.624	.637	.649	.658	.25
	.50	.506	.767	.871	.926	.960	.983	1.00	1.01	1.02	1.03	1.04	1.04	.50
	.75	1.57	1.70	1.72	1.72	1.71	1.71	1.70	1.70	1.69	1.69	1.69	1.68	.75
	.90	3.59	3.26	3.07	2.96	2.88	2.83	2.78	2.75	2.72	2.70	2.68	2.67	.90
	.95	5.59	4.74	4.35	4.12	3.97	3.87	3.79	3.73	3.68	3.64	3.60	3.57	.95
	.975	8.07	6.54	5.89	5.52	5.29	5.12	4.99	4.90	4.82	4.76	4.71	4.67	.975
	.99	12.2	9.55	8.45	7.85	7.46	7.19	6.99	6.84	6.72	6.62	6.54	6.47	.99
	.995	16.2	12.4	10.9	10.0	9.52	9.16	8.89	8.68	8.51	8.38	8.27	8.18	.995
	.999	29.2	21.7	18.8	17.2	16.2	15.5	15.0	14.6	14.3	14.1	13.9	13.7	.999
	.9995	37.0	27.2	23.5	21.4	20.2	19.3	18.7	18.2	17.8	17.5	17.2	17.0	.9995
8	.0005	$.0^642$	$.0^350$	$.0^248$	.014	.027	.041	.055	.068	.081	.092	.102	.112	.0005
	.001	$.0^517$	$.0^210$	$.0^276$	.020	.036	.053	.068	.083	.096	.109	.120	.130	.001
	.005	$.0^442$	$.0^250$	.027	.047	.072	.095	.115	.133	.149	.164	.176	.187	.005
	.01	$.0^317$	.010	.036	.068	.097	.123	.146	.166	.183	.198	.211	.222	.01
	.025	$.0^210$	.025	.069	.111	.148	.179	.204	.226	.244	.259	.273	.285	.025
	.05	$.0^242$	.052	.113	.166	.208	.241	.268	.291	.310	.326	.339	.351	.05
	.10	.017	.107	.190	.253	.299	.335	.363	.386	.405	.421	.435	.445	.10
	.25	.109	.298	.411	.481	.529	.563	.589	.610	.627	.640	.654	.661	.25
	.50	.499	.757	.860	.915	.948	.971	.988	1.00	1.01	1.02	1.02	1.03	.50
	.75	1.54	1.66	1.67	1.66	1.66	1.65	1.64	1.64	1.64	1.63	1.63	1.62	.75
	.90	3.46	3.11	2.92	2.81	2.73	2.67	2.62	2.59	2.56	2.54	2.52	2.50	.90
	.95	5.32	4.46	4.07	3.84	3.69	3.58	3.50	3.44	3.39	3.35	3.31	3.28	.95
	.975	7.57	6.06	5.42	5.05	4.82	4.65	4.53	4.43	4.36	4.30	4.24	4.20	.975
	.99	11.3	8.65	7.59	7.01	6.63	6.37	6.18	6.03	5.91	5.81	5.73	5.67	.99
	.995	14.7	11.0	9.60	8.81	8.30	7.95	7.69	7.50	7.34	7.21	7.10	7.01	.995
	.999	25.4	18.5	15.8	14.4	13.5	12.9	12.4	12.0	11.8	11.5	11.4	11.2	.999
	.9995	31.6	22.8	19.4	17.6	16.4	15.7	15.1	14.6	14.3	14.0	13.8	13.6	.9995
9	.0005	$.0^641$	$.0^350$	$.0^248$	.015	.027	.042	.056	.070	.083	.094	.105	.115	.0005
	.001	$.0^517$	$.0^210$	$.0^277$	.021	.037	.054	.070	.085	.099	.112	.123	.134	.001
	.005	$.0^442$	$.0^250$	.023	.047	.073	.096	.117	.136	.153	.168	.181	.192	.005
	.01	$.0^317$	.010	.037	.068	.098	.125	.149	.169	.187	.202	.216	.228	.01
	.025	$.0^210$	.025	.069	.112	.150	.181	.207	.230	.248	.265	.279	.291	.025
	.05	$.0^240$	.052	.113	.167	.210	.244	.272	.296	.315	.331	.345	.358	.05
	.10	.017	.107	.191	.254	.302	.338	.367	.390	.410	.426	.441	.452	.10
	.25	.108	.297	.410	.480	.529	.564	.591	.612	.629	.643	.654	.664	.25
	.50	.494	.749	.852	.906	.939	.962	.978	.990	1.00	1.01	1.01	1.02	.50
	.75	1.51	1.62	1.63	1.63	1.62	1.61	1.60	1.60	1.59	1.59	1.58	1.58	.75
	.90	3.36	3.01	2.81	2.69	2.61	2.55	2.51	2.47	2.44	2.42	2.40	2.38	.90
	.95	5.12	4.26	3.86	3.63	3.48	3.37	3.29	3.23	3.18	3.14	3.10	3.07	.95
	.975	7.21	5.71	5.08	4.72	4.48	4.32	4.20	4.10	4.03	3.96	3.91	3.87	.975
	.99	10.6	8.02	6.99	6.42	6.06	5.80	5.61	5.47	5.35	5.26	5.18	5.11	.99
	.995	13.6	10.1	8.72	7.96	7.47	7.13	6.88	6.69	6.54	6.42	6.31	6.23	.995
	.999	22.9	16.4	13.9	12.6	11.7	11.1	10.7	10.4	10.1	9.89	9.71	9.57	.999
	.9995	28.0	19.9	16.8	15.1	14.1	13.3	12.8	12.4	12.1	11.8	11.6	11.4	.9995

TABLE A.4   Percentiles of *F* Distributions *(cont.)*

p \ m	15	20	24	30	40	50	60	100	120	200	500	∞	p	n
.0005	.130	.157	.172	.188	.206	.217	.225	.242	.246	.255	.263	.268	.0005	7
.001	.148	.176	.191	.208	.225	.237	.245	.261	.266	.274	.282	.288	.001	
.005	.206	.235	.251	.267	.285	.296	.304	.319	.324	.332	.340	.345	.005	
.01	.241	.270	.286	.303	.320	.331	.339	.355	.358	.366	.373	.379	.01	
.025	.304	.333	.348	.364	.381	.392	.399	.413	.418	.426	.433	.437	.025	
.05	.369	.398	.413	.428	.445	.455	.461	.476	.479	.485	.493	.498	.05	
.10	.463	.491	.504	.519	.534	.543	.550	.562	.566	.571	.578	.582	.10	
.25	.679	.702	.713	.725	.737	.745	.749	.760	.762	.767	.772	.775	.25	
.50	1.05	1.07	1.07	1.08	1.08	1.09	1.09	1.10	1.10	1.10	1.10	1.10	.50	
.75	1.68	1.67	1.67	1.66	1.66	1.66	1.65	1.65	1.65	1.65	1.65	1.65	.75	
.90	2.63	2.59	2.58	2.56	2.54	2.52	2.51	2.50	2.49	2.48	2.48	2.47	.90	
.95	3.51	3.44	3.41	3.38	3.34	3.32	3.30	3.27	3.27	3.25	3.24	3.23	.95	
.975	4.57	4.47	4.42	4.36	4.31	4.28	4.25	4.21	4.20	4.18	4.16	4.14	.975	
.99	6.31	6.16	6.07	5.99	5.91	5.86	5.82	5.75	5.74	5.70	5.67	5.65	.99	
.995	7.97	7.75	7.65	7.53	7.42	7.35	7.31	7.22	7.19	7.15	7.10	7.08	.995	
.999	13.3	12.9	12.7	12.5	12.3	12.2	12.1	11.9	11.9	11.8	11.7	11.7	.999	
.9995	16.5	16.0	15.7	15.5	15.2	15.1	15.0	14.7	14.7	14.6	14.5	14.4	.9995	
.0005	.136	.164	.181	.198	.218	.230	.239	.257	.262	.271	.281	.287	.0005	8
.001	.155	.184	.200	.218	.238	.250	.259	.277	.282	.292	.300	.306	.001	
.005	.214	.244	.261	.279	.299	.311	.319	.337	.341	.351	.358	.364	.005	
.01	.250	.281	.297	.315	.334	.346	.354	.372	.376	.385	.392	.398	.01	
.025	.313	.343	.360	.377	.395	.407	.415	.431	.435	.442	.450	.456	.025	
.05	.379	.409	.425	.441	.459	.469	.477	.493	.496	.505	.510	.516	.05	
.10	.472	.500	.515	.531	.547	.556	.563	.578	.581	.588	.595	.599	.10	
.25	.684	.707	.718	.730	.743	.751	.756	.767	.769	.775	.780	.783	.25	
.50	1.04	1.05	1.06	1.07	1.07	1.07	1.08	1.08	1.08	1.09	1.09	1.09	.50	
.75	1.62	1.61	1.60	1.60	1.59	1.59	1.59	1.58	1.58	1.58	1.58	1.58	.75	
.90	2.46	2.42	2.40	2.38	2.36	2.35	2.34	2.32	2.32	2.31	2.30	2.29	.90	
.95	3.22	3.15	3.12	3.08	3.04	3.02	3.01	2.97	2.97	2.95	2.94	2.93	.95	
.975	4.10	4.00	3.95	3.89	3.84	3.81	3.78	3.74	3.73	3.70	3.68	3.67	.975	
.99	5.52	5.36	5.28	5.20	5.12	5.07	5.03	4.96	4.95	4.91	4.88	4.86	.99	
.995	6.81	6.61	6.50	6.40	6.29	6.22	6.18	6.09	6.06	6.02	5.98	5.95	.995	
.999	10.8	10.5	10.3	10.1	9.92	9.80	9.73	9.57	9.54	9.46	9.39	9.34	.999	
.9995	13.1	12.7	12.5	12.2	12.0	11.8	11.8	11.6	11.5	11.4	11.4	11.3	.9995	
.0005	.141	.171	.188	.207	.228	.242	.251	.270	.276	.287	.297	.303	.0005	9
.001	.160	.191	.208	.228	.249	.262	.271	.291	.296	.307	.316	.323	.001	
.005	.220	.253	.271	.290	.310	.324	.332	.351	.356	.366	.376	.382	.005	
.01	.257	.289	.307	.326	.346	.358	.368	.386	.391	.400	.410	.415	.01	
.025	.320	.352	.370	.388	.408	.420	.428	.446	.450	.459	.467	.473	.025	
.05	.386	.418	.435	.452	.471	.483	.490	.508	.510	.518	.526	.532	.05	
.10	.479	.509	.525	.541	.558	.568	.575	.588	.594	.602	.610	.613	.10	
.25	.687	.711	.723	.736	.749	.757	.762	.773	.776	.782	.787	.791	.25	
.50	1.03	1.04	1.05	1.05	1.06	1.06	1.07	1.07	1.07	1.08	1.08	1.08	.50	
.75	1.57	1.56	1.56	1.55	1.55	1.54	1.54	1.53	1.53	1.53	1.53	1.53	.75	
.90	2.34	2.30	2.28	2.25	2.23	2.22	2.21	2.19	2.18	2.17	2.17	2.16	.90	
.95	3.01	2.94	2.90	2.86	2.83	2.80	2.79	2.76	2.75	2.73	2.72	2.71	.95	
.975	3.77	3.67	3.61	3.56	3.51	3.47	3.45	3.40	3.39	3.37	3.35	3.33	.975	
.99	4.96	4.81	4.73	4.65	4.57	4.52	4.48	4.42	4.40	4.36	4.33	4.31	.99	
.995	6.03	5.83	5.73	5.62	5.52	5.45	5.41	5.32	5.30	5.26	5.21	5.19	.995	
.999	9.24	8.90	8.72	8.55	8.37	8.26	8.19	8.04	8.00	7.93	7.86	7.81	.999	
.9995	11.0	10.6	10.4	10.2	9.94	9.80	9.71	9.53	9.49	9.40	9.32	9.26	.9995	

TABLE A.4 Percentiles of F Distributions *(cont.)*

n	p	1	2	3	4	5	6	7	8	9	10	11	12	p
10	.0005	$.0^641$	$.0^350$	$.0^249$	.015	.028	.043	.057	.071	.085	.097	.108	.119	.0005
	.001	$.0^517$	$.0^210$	$.0^277$	.021	.037	.054	.071	.087	.101	.114	.126	.137	.001
	.005	$.0^441$	$.0^250$	.023	.048	.073	.098	.119	.139	.156	.171	.185	.197	.005
	.01	$.0^317$	.010	.037	.069	.100	.127	.151	.172	.190	.206	.220	.233	.01
	.025	$.0^210$	.025	.069	.113	.151	.183	.210	.233	.252	.269	.283	.296	.025
	.05	$.0^241$	.052	.114	.168	.211	.246	.275	.299	.319	.336	.351	.363	.05
	.10	.017	.106	.191	.255	.303	.340	.370	.394	.414	.430	.444	.457	.10
	.25	.107	.296	.409	.480	.529	.565	.592	.613	.631	.645	.657	.667	.25
	.50	.490	.743	.845	.899	.932	.954	.971	.983	.992	1.00	1.01	1.01	.50
	.75	1.49	1.60	1.60	1.59	1.59	1.58	1.57	1.56	1.56	1.55	1.55	1.54	.75
	.90	3.28	2.92	2.73	2.61	2.52	2.46	2.41	2.38	2.35	2.32	2.30	2.28	.90
	.95	4.96	4.10	3.71	3.48	3.33	3.22	3.14	3.07	3.02	2.98	2.94	2.91	.95
	.975	6.94	5.46	4.83	4.47	4.24	4.07	3.95	3.85	3.78	3.72	3.66	3.62	.975
	.99	10.0	7.56	6.55	5.99	5.64	5.39	5.20	5.06	4.94	4.85	4.77	4.71	.99
	.995	12.8	9.43	8.08	7.34	6.87	6.54	6.30	6.12	5.97	5.85	5.75	5.66	.995
	.999	21.0	14.9	12.6	11.3	10.5	9.92	9.52	9.20	8.96	8.75	8.58	8.44	.999
	.9995	25.5	17.9	15.0	13.4	12.4	11.8	11.3	10.9	10.6	10.3	10.1	9.93	.9995
11	.0005	$.0^641$	$.0^350$	$.0^249$	.015	.028	.043	.058	.072	.086	.099	.111	.121	.0005
	.001	$.0^516$	$.0^210$	$.0^278$	.021	.038	.055	.072	.088	.103	.116	.129	.140	.001
	.005	$.0^440$	$.0^250$	.023	.048	.074	.099	.121	.141	.158	.174	.188	.200	.005
	.01	$.0^316$	.010	.037	.069	.100	.128	.153	.175	.193	.210	.224	.237	.01
	.025	$.0^210$	.025	.069	.114	.152	.185	.212	.236	.256	.273	.288	.301	.025
	.05	$.0^241$	.052	.114	.168	.212	.248	.278	.302	.323	.340	.355	.368	.05
	.10	.017	.106	.192	.256	.305	.342	.373	.397	.417	.435	.448	.461	.10
	.25	.107	.295	.408	.481	.529	.565	.592	.614	.633	.645	.658	.667	.25
	.50	.486	.739	.840	.893	.926	.948	.964	.977	.986	.994	1.00	1.01	.50
	.75	1.47	1.58	1.58	1.57	1.56	1.55	1.54	1.53	1.53	1.52	1.52	1.51	.75
	.90	3.23	2.86	2.66	2.54	2.45	2.39	2.34	2.30	2.27	2.25	2.23	2.21	.90
	.95	4.84	3.98	3.59	3.36	3.20	3.09	3.01	2.95	2.90	2.85	2.82	2.79	.95
	.975	6.72	5.26	4.63	4.28	4.04	3.88	3.76	3.66	3.59	3.53	3.47	3.43	.975
	.99	9.65	7.21	6.22	5.67	5.32	5.07	4.89	4.74	4.63	4.54	4.46	4.40	.99
	.995	12.2	8.91	7.60	6.88	6.42	6.10	5.86	5.68	5.54	5.42	5.32	5.24	.995
	.999	19.7	13.8	11.6	10.3	9.58	9.05	8.66	8.35	8.12	7.92	7.76	7.62	.999
	.9995	23.6	16.4	13.6	12.2	11.2	10.6	10.1	9.76	9.48	9.24	9.04	8.88	.9995
12	.0005	$.0^641$	$.0^350$	$.0^249$	.015	.028	.044	.058	.073	.087	.101	.113	.124	.0005
	.001	$.0^516$	$.0^210$	$.0^278$	.021	.038	.056	.073	.089	.104	.118	.131	.143	.001
	.005	$.0^439$	$.0^250$	.023	.048	.075	.100	.122	.143	.161	.177	.191	.204	.005
	.01	$.0^316$	.010	.037	.070	.101	.130	.155	.176	.196	.212	.227	.241	.01
	.025	$.0^210$	.025	.070	.114	.153	.186	.214	.238	.259	.276	.292	.305	.025
	.05	$.0^241$	.052	.114	.169	.214	.250	.280	.305	.325	.343	.358	.372	.05
	.10	.016	.106	.192	.257	.306	.344	.375	.400	.420	.438	.452	.466	.10
	.25	.106	.295	.408	.480	.530	.566	.594	.616	.633	.649	.662	.671	.25
	.50	.484	.735	.835	.888	.921	.943	.959	.972	.981	.989	.995	1.00	.50
	.75	1.46	1.56	1.56	1.55	1.54	1.53	1.52	1.51	1.51	1.50	1.50	1.49	.75
	.90	3.18	2.81	2.61	2.48	2.39	2.33	2.28	2.24	2.21	2.19	2.17	2.15	.90
	.95	4.75	3.89	3.49	3.26	3.11	3.00	2.91	2.85	2.80	2.75	2.72	2.69	.95
	.975	6.55	5.10	4.47	4.12	3.89	3.73	3.61	3.51	3.44	3.37	3.32	3.28	.975
	.99	9.33	6.93	5.95	5.41	5.06	4.82	4.64	4.50	4.39	4.30	4.22	4.16	.99
	.995	11.8	8.51	7.23	6.52	6.07	5.76	5.52	5.35	5.20	5.09	4.99	4.91	.995
	.999	18.6	13.0	10.8	9.63	8.89	8.38	8.00	7.71	7.48	7.29	7.14	7.01	.999
	.9995	22.2	15.3	12.7	11.2	10.4	9.74	9.28	8.94	8.66	8.43	8.24	8.08	.9995

TABLE A.4   Percentiles of F Distributions *(cont.)*

p \ m	15	20	24	30	40	50	60	100	120	200	500	∞	p	n
.0005	.145	.177	.195	.215	.238	.251	.262	.282	.288	.299	.311	.319	.0005	**10**
.001	.164	.197	.216	.236	.258	.272	.282	.303	.309	.321	.331	.338	.001	
.005	.226	.260	.279	.299	.321	.334	.344	.365	.370	.380	.391	.397	.005	
.01	.263	.297	.316	.336	.357	.370	.380	.400	.405	.415	.424	.431	.01	
.025	.327	.360	.379	.398	.419	.431	.441	.459	.464	.474	.483	.488	.025	
.05	.393	.426	.444	.462	.481	.493	.502	.518	.523	.532	.541	.546	.05	
.10	.486	.516	.532	.549	.567	.578	.586	.602	.605	.614	.621	.625	.10	
.25	.691	.714	.727	.740	.754	.762	.767	.779	.782	.788	.793	.797	.25	
.50	1.02	1.03	1.04	1.05	1.05	1.06	1.06	1.06	1.06	1.07	1.07	1.07	.50	
.75	1.53	1.52	1.52	1.51	1.51	1.50	1.50	1.49	1.49	1.49	1.48	1.48	.75	
.90	2.24	2.20	2.18	2.16	2.13	2.12	2.11	2.09	2.08	2.07	2.06	2.06	.90	
.95	2.85	2.77	2.74	2.70	2.66	2.64	2.62	2.59	2.58	2.56	2.55	2.54	.95	
.975	3.52	3.42	3.37	3.31	3.26	3.22	3.20	3.15	3.14	3.12	3.09	3.08	.975	
.99	4.56	4.41	4.33	4.25	4.17	4.12	4.08	4.01	4.00	3.96	3.93	3.91	.99	
.995	5.47	5.27	5.17	5.07	4.97	4.90	4.86	4.77	4.75	4.71	4.67	4.64	.995	
.999	8.13	7.80	7.64	7.47	7.30	7.19	7.12	6.98	6.94	6.87	6.81	6.76	.999	
.9995	9.56	9.16	8.96	8.75	8.54	8.42	8.33	8.16	8.12	8.04	7.96	7.90	.9995	
.0005	.148	.182	.201	.222	.246	.261	.271	.293	.299	.312	.324	.331	.0005	**11**
.001	.168	.202	.222	.243	.266	.282	.292	.313	.320	.332	.343	.353	.001	
.005	.231	.266	.286	.308	.330	.345	.355	.376	.382	.394	.403	.412	.005	
.01	.268	.304	.324	.344	.366	.380	.391	.412	.417	.427	.439	.444	.01	
.025	.332	.368	.386	.407	.429	.442	.450	.472	.476	.485	.495	.503	.025	
.05	.398	.433	.452	.469	.490	.503	.513	.529	.535	.543	.552	.559	.05	
.10	.490	.524	.541	.559	.578	.588	.595	.614	.617	.625	.633	.637	.10	
.25	.694	.719	.730	.744	.758	.767	.773	.780	.788	.794	.799	.803	.25	
.50	1.02	1.03	1.03	1.04	1.05	1.05	1.06	1.06	1.06	1.06	1.06	1.06	.50	
.75	1.50	1.49	1.49	1.48	1.47	1.47	1.47	1.46	1.46	1.46	1.45	1.45	.75	
.90	2.17	2.12	2.10	2.08	2.05	2.04	2.03	2.00	2.00	1.99	1.98	1.97	.90	
.95	2.72	2.65	2.61	2.57	2.53	2.51	2.49	2.46	2.45	2.43	2.42	2.40	.95	
.975	3.33	3.23	3.17	3.12	3.06	3.03	3.00	2.96	2.94	2.92	2.90	2.88	.975	
.99	4.25	4.10	4.02	3.94	3.86	3.81	3.78	3.71	3.69	3.66	3.62	3.60	.99	
.995	5.05	4.86	4.76	4.65	4.55	4.49	4.45	4.36	4.34	4.29	4.25	4.23	.995	
.999	7.32	7.01	6.85	6.68	6.52	6.41	6.35	6.21	6.17	6.10	6.04	6.00	.999	
.9995	8.52	8.14	7.94	7.75	7.55	7.43	7.35	7.18	7.14	7.06	6.98	6.93	.9995	
.0005	.152	.186	.206	.228	.253	.269	.280	.305	.311	.323	.337	.345	.0005	**12**
.001	.172	.207	.228	.250	.275	.291	.302	.326	.332	.344	.357	.365	.001	
.005	.235	.272	.292	.315	.339	.355	.365	.388	.393	.405	.417	.424	.005	
.01	.273	.310	.330	.352	.375	.391	.401	.422	.428	.441	.450	.458	.01	
.025	.337	.374	.394	.416	.437	.450	.461	.481	.487	.498	.508	.514	.025	
.05	.404	.439	.458	.478	.499	.513	.522	.541	.545	.556	.565	.571	.05	
.10	.496	.528	.546	.564	.583	.595	.604	.621	.625	.633	.641	.647	.10	
.25	.695	.721	.734	.748	.762	.771	.777	.789	.792	.799	.804	.808	.25	
.50	1.01	1.02	1.03	1.03	1.04	1.04	1.05	1.05	1.05	1.05	1.06	1.06	.50	
.75	1.48	1.47	1.46	1.45	1.45	1.44	1.44	1.43	1.43	1.43	1.42	1.42	.75	
.90	2.11	2.06	2.04	2.01	1.99	1.97	1.96	1.94	1.93	1.92	1.91	1.90	.90	
.95	2.62	2.54	2.51	2.47	2.43	2.40	2.38	2.35	2.34	2.32	2.31	2.30	.95	
.975	3.18	3.07	3.02	2.96	2.91	2.87	2.85	2.80	2.79	2.76	2.74	2.72	.975	
.99	4.01	3.86	3.78	3.70	3.62	3.57	3.54	3.47	3.45	3.41	3.38	3.36	.99	
.995	4.72	4.53	4.43	4.33	4.23	4.17	4.12	4.04	4.01	3.97	3.93	3.90	.995	
.999	6.71	6.40	6.25	6.09	5.93	5.83	5.76	5.63	5.59	5.52	5.46	5.42	.999	
.9995	7.74	7.37	7.18	7.00	6.80	6.68	6.61	6.45	6.41	6.33	6.25	6.20	.9995	

TABLE A.4   Percentiles of F Distributions *(cont.)*

n	m \ p	1	2	3	4	5	6	7	8	9	10	11	12	p
15	.0005	$.0^641$	$.0^350$	$.0^249$	.015	.029	.045	.061	.076	.091	.105	.117	.129	.0005
	.001	$.0^516$	$.0^210$	$.0^279$	.021	.039	.057	.075	.092	.108	.123	.137	.149	.001
	.005	$.0^439$	$.0^250$	.023	.049	.076	.102	.125	.147	.166	.183	.198	.212	.005
	.01	$.0^316$	.010	.037	.070	.103	.132	.158	.181	.202	.219	.235	.249	.01
	.025	$.0^210$	.025	.070	.116	.156	.190	.219	.244	.265	.284	.300	.315	.025
	.05	$.0^241$	.051	.115	.170	.216	.254	.285	.311	.333	.351	.368	.382	.05
	.10	.016	.106	.192	.258	.309	.348	.380	.406	.427	.446	.461	.475	.10
	.25	.105	.293	.407	.480	.531	.568	.596	.618	.637	.652	.667	.676	.25
	.50	.478	.726	.826	.878	.911	.933	.948	.960	.970	.977	.984	.989	.50
	.75	1.43	1.52	1.52	1.49	1.48	1.47	1.46	1.46	1.45	1.44	1.44	1.43	.75
	.90	3.07	2.70	2.49	2.36	2.27	2.21	2.16	2.12	2.09	2.06	2.04	2.02	.90
	.95	4.54	3.68	3.29	3.06	2.90	2.79	2.71	2.64	2.59	2.54	2.51	2.48	.95
	.975	6.20	4.76	4.15	3.80	3.58	3.41	3.29	3.20	3.12	3.06	3.01	2.96	.975
	.99	8.68	6.36	5.42	4.89	4.56	4.32	4.14	4.00	3.89	3.80	3.73	3.67	.99
	.995	10.8	7.70	6.48	5.80	5.37	5.07	4.85	4.67	4.54	4.42	4.33	4.25	.995
	.999	16.6	11.3	9.34	8.25	7.57	7.09	6.74	6.47	6.26	6.08	5.93	5.81	.999
	.9995	19.5	13.2	10.8	9.48	8.66	8.10	7.68	7.36	7.11	6.91	6.75	6.60	.9995
20	.0005	$.0^640$	$.0^350$	$.0^250$	.015	.029	.046	.063	.079	.094	.109	.123	.136	.0005
	.001	$.0^516$	$.0^210$	$.0^279$	.022	.039	.058	.077	.095	.112	.128	.143	.156	.001
	.005	$.0^439$	$.0^250$	.023	.050	.077	.104	.129	.151	.171	.190	.206	.221	.005
	.01	$.0^316$	.010	.037	.071	.105	.135	.162	.187	.208	.227	.244	.259	.01
	.025	$.0^210$	.025	.071	.117	.158	.193	.224	.250	.273	.292	.310	.325	.025
	.05	$.0^240$	.051	.115	.172	.219	.258	.290	.318	.340	.360	.377	.393	.05
	.10	.016	.106	.193	.260	.312	.353	.385	.412	.435	.454	.472	.485	.10
	.25	.104	.292	.407	.480	.531	.569	.598	.622	.641	.656	.671	.681	.25
	.50	.472	.718	.816	.868	.900	.922	.938	.950	.959	.966	.972	.977	.50
	.75	1.40	1.49	1.48	1.47	1.45	1.44	1.43	1.42	1.41	1.40	1.39	1.38	.75
	.90	2.97	2.59	2.38	2.25	2.16	2.09	2.04	2.00	1.96	1.94	1.91	1.89	.90
	.95	4.35	3.49	3.10	2.87	2.71	2.60	2.51	2.45	2.39	2.35	2.31	2.28	.95
	.975	5.87	4.46	3.86	3.51	3.29	3.13	3.01	2.91	2.84	2.77	2.72	2.68	.975
	.99	8.10	5.85	4.94	4.43	4.10	3.87	3.70	3.56	3.46	3.37	3.29	3.23	.99
	.995	9.94	6.99	5.82	5.17	4.76	4.47	4.26	4.09	3.96	3.85	3.76	3.68	.995
	.999	14.8	9.95	8.10	7.10	6.46	6.02	5.69	5.44	5.24	5.08	4.94	4.82	.999
	.9995	17.2	11.4	9.20	8.02	7.28	6.76	6.38	6.08	5.85	5.66	5.51	5.38	.9995
24	.0005	$.0^640$	$.0^350$	$.0^250$	.015	.030	.046	.064	.080	.096	.112	.126	.139	.0005
	.001	$.0^516$	$.0^210$	$.0^279$	.022	.040	.059	.079	.097	.115	.131	.146	.160	.001
	.005	$.0^440$	$.0^250$	.023	.050	.078	.106	.131	.154	.175	.193	.210	.226	.005
	.01	$.0^316$	.010	.038	.072	.106	.137	.165	.189	.211	.231	.249	.264	.01
	.025	$.0^210$	.025	.071	.117	.159	.195	.227	.253	.277	.297	.315	.331	.025
	.05	$.0^240$	.051	.116	.173	.221	.260	.293	.321	.345	.365	.383	.399	.05
	.10	.016	.106	.193	.261	.313	.355	.388	.416	.439	.459	.476	.491	.10
	.25	.104	.291	.406	.480	.532	.570	.600	.623	.643	.659	.671	.684	.25
	.50	.469	.714	.812	.863	.895	.917	.932	.944	.953	.961	.967	.972	.50
	.75	1.39	1.47	1.46	1.44	1.43	1.41	1.40	1.39	1.38	1.38	1.37	1.36	.75
	.90	2.93	2.54	2.33	2.19	2.10	2.04	1.98	1.94	1.91	1.88	1.85	1.83	.90
	.95	4.26	3.40	3.01	2.78	2.62	2.51	2.42	2.36	2.30	2.25	2.21	2.18	.95
	.975	5.72	4.32	3.72	3.38	3.15	2.99	2.87	2.78	2.70	2.64	2.59	2.54	.975
	.99	7.82	5.61	4.72	4.22	3.90	3.67	3.50	3.36	3.26	3.17	3.09	3.03	.99
	.995	9.55	6.66	5.52	4.89	4.49	4.20	3.99	3.83	3.69	3.59	3.50	3.42	.995
	.999	14.0	9.34	7.55	6.59	5.98	5.55	5.23	4.99	4.80	4.64	4.50	4.39	.999
	.9995	16.2	10.6	8.52	7.39	6.68	6.18	5.82	5.54	5.31	5.13	4.98	4.85	.9995

TABLE A.4 Percentiles of *F* Distributions *(cont.)*

p	15	20	24	30	40	50	60	100	120	200	500	∞	p	n
.0005	.159	.197	.220	.244	.272	.290	.303	.330	.339	.353	.368	.377	.0005	**15**
.001	.181	.219	.242	.266	.294	.313	.325	.352	.360	.375	.388	.398	.001	
.005	.246	.286	.308	.333	.360	.377	.389	.415	.422	.435	.448	.457	.005	
.01	.284	.324	.346	.370	.397	.413	.425	.450	.456	.469	.483	.490	.01	
.025	.349	.389	.410	.433	.458	.474	.485	.508	.514	.526	.538	.546	.025	
.05	.416	.454	.474	.496	.519	.535	.545	.565	.571	.581	.592	.600	.05	
.10	.507	.542	.561	.581	.602	.614	.624	.641	.647	.658	.667	.672	.10	
.25	.701	.728	.742	.757	.772	.782	.788	.802	.805	.812	.818	.822	.25	
.50	1.00	1.01	1.02	1.02	1.03	1.03	1.03	1.04	1.04	1.04	1.04	1.04	.50	
.75	1.43	1.41	1.41	1.40	1.39	1.39	1.38	1.38	1.37	1.37	1.36	1.36	.75	
.90	1.97	1.92	1.90	1.87	1.85	1.83	1.82	1.79	1.79	1.77	1.76	1.76	.90	
.95	2.40	2.33	2.39	2.25	2.20	2.18	2.16	2.12	2.11	2.10	2.08	2.07	.95	
.975	2.86	2.76	2.70	2.64	2.59	2.55	2.52	2.47	2.46	2.44	2.41	2.40	.975	
.99	3.52	3.37	3.29	3.21	3.13	3.08	3.05	2.98	2.96	2.92	2.89	2.87	.99	
.995	4.07	3.88	3.79	3.69	3.59	3.52	3.48	3.39	3.37	3.33	3.29	3.26	.995	
.999	5.54	5.25	5.10	4.95	4.80	4.70	4.64	4.51	4.47	4.41	4.35	4.31	.999	
.9995	6.27	5.93	5.75	5.58	5.40	5.29	5.21	5.06	5.02	4.94	4.87	4.83	.9995	
.0005	.169	.211	.235	.263	.295	.316	.331	.364	.375	.391	.408	.422	.0005	**20**
.001	.191	.233	.258	.286	.318	.339	.354	.386	.395	.413	.429	.441	.001	
.005	.258	.301	.327	.354	.385	.405	.419	.448	.457	.474	.490	.500	.005	
.01	.297	.340	.365	.392	.422	.441	.455	.483	.491	.508	.521	.532	.01	
.025	.363	.406	.430	.456	.484	.503	.514	.541	.548	.562	.575	.585	.025	
.05	.430	.471	.493	.518	.544	.562	.572	.595	.603	.617	.629	.637	.05	
.10	.520	.557	.578	.600	.623	.637	.648	.671	.675	.685	.694	.704	.10	
.25	.708	.736	.751	.767	.784	.794	.801	.816	.820	.827	.835	.840	.25	
.50	.989	1.00	1.01	1.01	1.02	1.02	1.02	1.03	1.03	1.03	1.03	1.03	.50	
.75	1.37	1.36	1.35	1.34	1.33	1.33	1.32	1.31	1.31	1.30	1.30	1.29	.75	
.90	1.84	1.79	1.77	1.74	1.71	1.69	1.68	1.65	1.64	1.63	1.62	1.61	.90	
.95	2.20	2.12	2.08	2.04	1.99	1.97	1.95	1.91	1.90	1.88	1.86	1.84	.95	
.975	2.57	2.46	2.41	2.35	2.29	2.25	2.22	2.17	2.16	2.13	2.10	2.09	.975	
.99	3.09	2.94	2.86	2.78	2.69	2.64	2.61	2.54	2.52	2.48	2.44	2.42	.99	
.995	3.50	3.32	3.22	3.12	3.02	2.96	2.92	2.83	2.81	2.76	2.72	2.69	.995	
.999	4.56	4.29	4.15	4.01	3.86	3.77	3.70	3.58	3.54	3.48	3.42	3.38	.999	
.9995	5.07	4.75	4.58	4.42	4.24	4.15	4.07	3.93	3.90	3.82	3.75	3.70	.9995	
.0005	.174	.218	.244	.274	.309	.331	.349	.384	.395	.416	.434	.449	.0005	**24**
.001	.196	.241	.268	.298	.332	.354	.371	.405	.417	.437	.455	.469	.001	
.005	.264	.310	.337	.367	.400	.422	.437	.469	.479	.498	.515	.527	.005	
.01	.304	.350	.376	.405	.437	.459	.473	.505	.513	.529	.546	.558	.01	
.025	.370	.415	.441	.468	.498	.518	.531	.562	.568	.585	.599	.610	.025	
.05	.437	.480	.504	.530	.558	.575	.588	.613	.622	.637	.649	.669	.05	
.10	.527	.566	.588	.611	.635	.651	.662	.685	.691	.704	.715	.723	.10	
.25	.712	.741	.757	.773	.791	.802	.809	.825	.829	.837	.844	.850	.25	
.50	.983	.994	1.00	1.01	1.01	1.02	1.02	1.02	1.02	1.02	1.03	1.03	.50	
.75	1.35	1.33	1.32	1.31	1.30	1.29	1.29	1.28	1.28	1.27	1.27	1.26	.75	
.90	1.78	1.73	1.70	1.67	1.64	1.62	1.61	1.58	1.57	1.56	1.54	1.53	.90	
.95	2.11	2.03	1.98	1.94	1.89	1.86	1.84	1.80	1.79	1.77	1.75	1.73	.95	
.975	2.44	2.33	2.27	2.21	2.15	2.11	2.08	2.02	2.01	1.98	1.95	1.94	.975	
.99	2.89	2.74	2.66	2.58	2.49	2.44	2.40	2.33	2.31	2.27	2.24	2.21	.99	
.995	3.25	3.06	2.97	2.87	2.77	2.70	2.66	2.57	2.55	2.50	2.46	2.43	.995	
.999	4.14	3.87	3.74	3.59	3.45	3.35	3.29	3.16	3.14	3.07	3.01	2.97	.999	
.9995	4.55	4.25	4.09	3.93	3.76	3.66	3.59	3.44	3.41	3.33	3.27	3.22	.9995	

TABLE A.4   Percentiles of F Distributions *(cont.)*

n	p	1	2	3	4	5	6	7	8	9	10	11	12	p
30	.0005	$.0^6 40$	$.0^3 50$	$.0^2 50$	.015	.030	.047	.065	.082	.098	.114	.129	.143	.0005
	.001	$.0^5 16$	$.0^2 10$	$.0^2 80$	.022	.040	.060	.080	.099	.117	.134	.150	.164	.001
	.005	$.0^4 40$	$.0^2 50$	.024	.050	.079	.107	.133	.156	.178	.197	.215	.231	.005
	.01	$.0^3 16$	.010	.038	.072	.107	.138	.167	.192	.215	.235	.254	.270	.01
	.025	$.0^2 10$	.025	.071	.118	.161	.197	.229	.257	.281	.302	.321	.337	.025
	.05	$.0^2 40$	.051	.116	.174	.222	.263	.296	.325	.349	.370	.389	.406	.05
	.10	.016	.106	.193	.262	.315	.357	.391	.420	.443	.464	.481	.497	.10
	.25	.103	.290	.406	.480	.532	.571	.601	.625	.645	.661	.676	.688	.25
	.50	.466	.709	.807	.858	.890	.912	.927	.939	.948	.955	.961	.966	.50
	.75	1.38	1.45	1.44	1.42	1.41	1.39	1.38	1.37	1.36	1.36	1.35	1.34	.75
	.90	2.88	2.49	2.28	2.14	2.05	1.98	1.93	1.88	1.85	1.82	1.79	1.77	.90
	.95	4.17	3.32	2.92	2.69	2.53	2.42	2.33	2.27	2.21	2.16	2.13	2.09	.95
	.975	5.57	4.18	3.59	3.25	3.03	2.87	2.75	2.65	2.57	2.51	2.46	2.41	.975
	.99	7.56	5.39	4.51	4.02	3.70	3.47	3.30	3.17	3.07	2.98	2.91	2.84	.99
	.995	9.18	6.35	5.24	4.62	4.23	3.95	3.74	3.58	3.45	3.34	3.25	3.18	.995
	.999	13.3	8.77	7.05	6.12	5.53	5.12	4.82	4.58	4.39	4.24	4.11	4.00	.999
	.9995	15.2	9.90	7.90	6.82	6.14	5.66	5.31	5.04	4.82	4.65	4.51	4.38	.9995
40	.0005	$.0^6 40$	$.0^3 50$	$.0^2 50$	.016	.030	.048	.066	.084	.100	.117	.132	.147	.0005
	.001	$.0^5 16$	$.0^2 10$	$.0^2 80$	.022	.042	.061	.081	.101	.119	.137	.153	.169	.001
	.005	$.0^4 40$	$.0^2 50$	.024	.051	.080	.108	.135	.159	.181	.201	.220	.237	.005
	.01	$.0^3 16$	.010	.038	.073	.108	.140	.169	.195	.219	.240	.259	.276	.01
	.025	$.0^3 99$	.025	.071	.119	.162	.199	.232	.260	.285	.307	.327	.344	.025
	.05	$.0^2 40$	.051	.116	.175	.224	.265	.299	.329	.354	.376	.395	.412	.05
	.10	.016	.106	.194	.263	.317	.360	.394	.424	.448	.469	.488	.504	.10
	.25	.103	.290	.405	.480	.533	.572	.603	.627	.647	.664	.680	.691	.25
	.50	.463	.705	.802	.854	.885	.907	.922	.934	.943	.950	.956	.961	.50
	.75	1.36	1.44	1.42	1.40	1.39	1.37	1.36	1.35	1.34	1.33	1.32	1.31	.75
	.90	2.84	2.44	2.23	2.09	2.00	1.93	1.87	1.83	1.79	1.76	1.73	1.71	.90
	.95	4.08	3.23	2.84	2.61	2.45	2.34	2.25	2.18	2.12	2.08	2.04	2.00	.95
	.975	5.42	4.05	3.46	3.13	2.90	2.74	2.62	2.53	2.45	2.39	2.33	2.29	.975
	.99	7.31	5.18	4.31	3.83	3.51	3.29	3.12	2.99	2.89	2.80	2.73	2.66	.99
	.995	8.83	6.07	4.98	4.37	3.99	3.71	3.51	3.35	3.22	3.12	3.03	2.95	.995
	.999	12.6	8.25	6.60	5.70	5.13	4.73	4.44	4.21	4.02	3.87	3.75	3.64	.999
	.9995	14.4	9.25	7.33	6.30	5.64	5.19	4.85	4.59	4.38	4.21	4.07	3.95	.9995
60	.0005	$.0^6 40$	$.0^3 50$	$.0^2 51$	.016	.031	.048	.067	.085	.103	.120	.136	.152	.0005
	.001	$.0^5 16$	$.0^2 10$	$.0^2 80$	.022	.041	.062	.083	.103	.122	.140	.157	.174	.001
	.005	$.0^4 40$	$.0^2 50$	.024	.051	.081	.110	.137	.162	.185	.206	.225	.243	.005
	.01	$.0^3 16$	.010	.038	.073	.109	.142	.172	.199	.223	.245	.265	.283	.01
	.025	$.0^3 99$	.025	.071	.120	.163	.202	.235	.264	.290	.313	.333	.351	.025
	.05	$.0^2 40$	.051	.116	.176	.226	.267	.303	.333	.359	.382	.402	.419	.05
	.10	.016	.106	.194	.264	.318	.362	.398	.428	.453	.475	.493	.510	.10
	.25	.102	.289	.405	.480	.534	.573	.604	.629	.650	.667	.680	.695	.25
	.50	.461	.701	.798	.849	.880	.901	.917	.928	.937	.945	.951	.956	.50
	.75	1.35	1.42	1.41	1.38	1.37	1.35	1.33	1.32	1.31	1.30	1.29	1.29	.75
	.90	2.79	2.39	2.18	2.04	1.95	1.87	1.82	1.77	1.74	1.71	1.68	1.66	.90
	.95	4.00	3.15	2.76	2.53	2.37	2.25	2.17	2.10	2.04	1.99	1.95	1.92	.95
	.975	5.29	3.93	3.34	3.01	2.79	2.63	2.51	2.41	2.33	2.27	2.22	2.17	.975
	.99	7.08	4.98	4.13	3.65	3.34	3.12	2.95	2.82	2.72	2.63	2.56	2.50	.99
	.995	8.49	5.80	4.73	4.14	3.76	3.49	3.29	3.13	3.01	2.90	2.82	2.74	.995
	.999	12.0	7.76	6.17	5.31	4.76	4.37	4.09	3.87	3.69	3.54	3.43	3.31	.999
	.9995	13.6	8.65	6.81	5.82	5.20	4.76	4.44	4.18	3.98	3.82	3.69	3.57	.9995

TABLE A.4   Percentiles of *F* Distributions *(cont.)*

p \ m	15	20	24	30	40	50	60	100	120	200	500	∞	p	n
.0005	.179	.226	.254	.287	.325	.350	.369	.410	.420	.444	.467	.483	.0005	**30**
.001	.202	.250	.278	.311	.348	.373	.391	.431	.442	.465	.488	.503	.001	
.005	.271	.320	.349	.381	.416	.441	.457	.495	.504	.524	.543	.559	.005	
.01	.311	.360	.388	.419	.454	.476	.493	.529	.538	.559	.575	.590	.01	
.025	.378	.426	.453	.482	.515	.535	.551	.585	.592	.610	.625	.639	.025	
.05	.445	.490	.516	.543	.573	.592	.606	.637	.644	.658	.676	.685	.05	
.10	.534	.575	.598	.623	.649	.667	.678	.704	.710	.725	.735	.746	.10	
.25	.716	.746	.763	.780	.798	.810	.818	.835	.839	.848	.856	.862	.25	
.50	.978	.989	.994	1.00	1.01	1.01	1.01	1.02	1.02	1.02	1.02	1.02	.50	
.75	1.32	1.30	1.29	1.28	1.27	1.26	1.26	1.25	1.24	1.24	1.23	1.23	.75	
.90	1.72	1.67	1.64	1.61	1.57	1.55	1.54	1.51	1.50	1.48	1.47	1.46	.90	
.95	2.01	1.93	1.89	1.84	1.79	1.76	1.74	1.70	1.68	1.66	1.64	1.62	.95	
.975	2.31	2.20	2.14	2.07	2.01	1.97	1.94	1.88	1.87	1.84	1.81	1.79	.975	
.99	2.70	2.55	2.47	2.39	2.30	2.25	2.21	2.13	2.11	2.07	2.03	2.01	.99	
.995	3.01	2.82	2.73	2.63	2.52	2.46	2.42	2.32	2.30	2.25	2.21	2.18	.995	
.999	3.75	3.49	3.36	3.22	3.07	2.98	2.92	2.79	2.76	2.69	2.63	2.59	.999	
.9995	4.10	3.80	3.65	3.48	3.32	3.23	3.15	3.00	2.97	2.89	2.82	2.78	.9995	
.0005	.185	.236	.266	.301	.343	.373	.393	.441	.453	.480	.504	.525	.0005	**40**
.001	.209	.259	.290	.326	.367	.396	.415	.461	.473	.500	.524	.545	.001	
.005	.279	.331	.362	.396	.436	.463	.481	.524	.534	.559	.581	.599	.005	
.01	.319	.371	.401	.435	.473	.498	.516	.556	.567	.592	.613	.628	.01	
.025	.387	.437	.466	.498	.533	.556	.573	.610	.620	.641	.662	.674	.025	
.05	.454	.502	.529	.558	.591	.613	.627	.658	.669	.685	.704	.717	.05	
.10	.542	.585	.609	.636	.664	.683	.696	.724	.731	.747	.762	.772	.10	
.25	.720	.752	.769	.787	.806	.819	.828	.846	.851	.861	.870	.877	.25	
.50	.972	.983	.989	.994	1.00	1.00	1.01	1.01	1.01	1.01	1.02	1.02	.50	
.75	1.30	1.28	1.26	1.25	1.24	1.23	1.22	1.21	1.21	1.20	1.19	1.19	.75	
.90	1.66	1.61	1.57	1.54	1.51	1.48	1.47	1.43	1.42	1.41	1.39	1.38	.90	
.95	1.92	1.84	1.79	1.74	1.69	1.66	1.64	1.59	1.58	1.55	1.53	1.51	.95	
.975	2.18	2.07	2.01	1.94	1.88	1.83	1.80	1.74	1.72	1.69	1.66	1.64	.975	
.99	2.52	2.37	2.29	2.20	2.11	2.06	2.02	1.94	1.92	1.87	1.83	1.80	.99	
.995	2.78	2.60	2.50	2.40	2.30	2.23	2.18	2.09	2.06	2.01	1.96	1.93	.995	
.999	3.40	3.15	3.01	2.87	2.73	2.64	2.57	2.44	2.41	2.34	2.28	2.23	.999	
.9995	3.68	3.39	3.24	3.08	2.92	2.82	2.74	2.60	2.57	2.49	2.41	2.37	.9995	
.0005	.192	.246	.278	.318	.365	.398	.421	.478	.493	.527	.561	.585	.0005	**60**
.001	.216	.270	.304	.343	.389	.421	.444	.497	.512	.545	.579	.602	.001	
.005	.287	.343	.376	.414	.458	.488	.510	.559	.572	.602	.633	.652	.005	
.01	.328	.383	.416	.453	.495	.524	.545	.592	.604	.633	.658	.679	.01	
.025	.396	.450	.481	.515	.555	.581	.600	.641	.654	.680	.704	.720	.025	
.05	.463	.514	.543	.575	.611	.633	.652	.690	.700	.719	.746	.759	.05	
.10	.550	.596	.622	.650	.682	.703	.717	.750	.758	.776	.793	.806	.10	
.25	.725	.758	.776	.796	.816	.830	.840	.860	.865	.877	.888	.896	.25	
.50	.967	.978	.983	.989	.994	.998	1.00	1.00	1.01	1.01	1.01	1.01	.50	
.75	1.27	1.25	1.24	1.22	1.21	1.20	1.19	1.17	1.17	1.16	1.15	1.15	.75	
.90	1.60	1.54	1.51	1.48	1.44	1.41	1.40	1.36	1.35	1.33	1.31	1.29	.90	
.95	1.84	1.75	1.70	1.65	1.59	1.56	1.53	1.48	1.47	1.44	1.41	1.39	.95	
.975	2.06	1.94	1.88	1.82	1.74	1.70	1.67	1.60	1.58	1.54	1.51	1.48	.975	
.99	2.35	2.20	2.12	2.03	1.94	1.88	1.84	1.75	1.73	1.68	1.63	1.60	.99	
.995	2.57	2.39	2.29	2.19	2.08	2.01	1.96	1.86	1.83	1.78	1.73	1.69	.995	
.999	3.08	2.83	2.69	2.56	2.41	2.31	2.25	2.11	2.09	2.01	1.93	1.89	.999	
.9995	3.30	3.02	2.87	2.71	2.55	2.45	2.38	2.23	2.19	2.11	2.03	1.98	.9995	

TABLE A.4 Percentiles of F Distributions *(cont.)*

n	p	1	2	3	4	5	6	7	8	9	10	11	12	p
120	.0005	$.0^640$	$.0^550$	$.0^351$	.016	.031	.049	.067	.087	.105	.123	.140	.156	.0005
	.001	$.0^516$	$.0^210$	$.0^281$	.023	.042	.063	.084	.105	.125	.144	.162	.179	.001
	.005	$.0^439$	$.0^250$	.024	.051	.081	.111	.139	.165	.189	.211	.230	.249	.005
	.01	$.0^316$	.010	.038	.074	.110	.143	.174	.202	.227	.250	.271	.290	.01
	.025	$.0^399$	.025	.072	.120	.165	.204	.238	.268	.295	.318	.340	.359	.025
	.05	$.0^239$	.051	.117	.177	.227	.270	.306	.337	.364	.388	.408	.427	.05
	.10	.016	.105	.194	.265	.320	.365	.401	.432	.458	.480	.500	.518	.10
	.25	.102	.288	.405	.481	.534	.574	.606	.631	.652	.670	.685	.699	.25
	.50	.458	.697	.793	.844	.875	.896	.912	.923	.932	.939	.945	.950	.50
	.75	1.34	1.40	1.39	1.37	1.35	1.33	1.31	1.30	1.29	1.28	1.27	1.26	.75
	.90	2.75	2.35	2.13	1.99	1.90	1.82	1.77	1.72	1.68	1.65	1.62	1.60	.90
	.95	3.92	3.07	2.68	2.45	2.29	2.18	2.09	2.02	1.96	1.91	1.87	1.83	.95
	.975	5.15	3.80	3.23	2.89	2.67	2.52	2.39	2.30	2.22	2.16	2.10	2.05	.975
	.99	6.85	4.79	3.95	3.48	3.17	2.96	2.79	2.66	2.56	2.47	2.40	2.34	.99
	.995	8.18	5.54	4.50	3.92	3.55	3.28	3.09	2.93	2.81	2.71	2.62	2.54	.995
	.999	11.4	7.32	5.79	4.95	4.42	4.03	3.77	3.55	3.38	3.24	3.12	3.02	.999
	.9995	12.8	8.10	6.34	5.39	4.79	4.37	4.07	3.82	3.63	3.47	3.34	3.22	.9995
∞	.0005	$.0^639$	$.0^550$	$.0^351$	.016	.032	.050	.069	.088	.108	.127	.144	.161	.0005
	.001	$.0^516$	$.0^210$	$.0^281$	.023	.042	.063	.085	.107	.128	.148	.167	.185	.001
	.005	$.0^439$	$.0^250$	.024	.052	.082	.113	.141	.168	.193	.216	.236	.256	.005
	.01	$.0^316$	.010	.038	.074	.111	.145	.177	.206	.232	.256	.278	.298	.01
	.025	$.0^398$	.025	.072	.121	.166	.206	.241	.272	.300	.325	.347	.367	.025
	.05	$.0^239$	.051	.117	.178	.229	.273	.310	.342	.369	.394	.417	.436	.05
	.10	.016	.105	.195	.266	.322	.367	.405	.436	.463	.487	.508	.525	.10
	.25	.102	.288	.404	.481	.535	.576	.608	.634	.655	.674	.690	.703	.25
	.50	.455	.693	.789	.839	.870	.891	.907	.918	.927	.934	.939	.945	.50
	.75	1.32	1.39	1.37	1.35	1.33	1.31	1.29	1.28	1.27	1.25	1.24	1.24	.75
	.90	2.71	2.30	2.08	1.94	1.85	1.77	1.72	1.67	1.63	1.60	1.57	1.55	.90
	.95	3.84	3.00	2.60	2.37	2.21	2.10	2.01	1.94	1.88	1.83	1.79	1.75	.95
	.975	5.02	3.69	3.12	2.79	2.57	2.41	2.29	2.19	2.11	2.05	1.99	1.94	.975
	.99	6.63	4.61	3.78	3.32	3.02	2.80	2.64	2.51	2.41	2.32	2.25	2.18	.99
	.995	7.88	5.30	4.28	3.72	3.35	3.09	2.90	2.74	2.62	2.52	2.43	2.36	.995
	.999	10.8	6.91	5.42	4.62	4.10	3.74	3.47	3.27	3.10	2.96	2.84	2.74	.999
	.9995	12.1	7.60	5.91	5.00	4.42	4.02	3.72	3.48	3.30	3.14	3.02	2.90	.9995

TABLE A.4   Percentiles of F Distributions *(cont.)*

p \ m	15	20	24	30	40	50	60	100	120	200	500	∞	p	n
.0005	.199	.256	.293	.338	.390	.429	.458	.524	.543	.578	.614	.676	.0005	**120**
.001	.223	.282	.319	.363	.415	.453	.480	.542	.568	.595	.631	.691	.001	
.005	.297	.356	.393	.434	.484	.520	.545	.605	.623	.661	.702	.733	.005	
.01	.338	.397	.433	.474	.522	.556	.579	.636	.652	.688	.725	.755	.01	
.025	.406	.464	.498	.536	.580	.611	.633	.684	.698	.729	.762	.789	.025	
.05	.473	.527	.559	.594	.634	.661	.682	.727	.740	.767	.785	.819	.05	
.10	.560	.609	.636	.667	.702	.726	.742	.781	.791	.815	.838	.855	.10	
.25	.730	.765	.784	.805	.828	.843	.853	.877	.884	.897	.911	.923	.25	
.50	.961	.972	.978	.983	.989	.992	.994	1.00	1.00	1.00	1.01	1.01	.50	
.75	1.24	1.22	1.21	1.19	1.18	1.17	1.16	1.14	1.13	1.12	1.11	1.10	.75	
.90	1.55	1.48	1.45	1.41	1.37	1.34	1.32	1.27	1.26	1.24	1.21	1.19	.90	
.95	1.75	1.66	1.61	1.55	1.50	1.46	1.43	1.37	1.35	1.32	1.28	1.25	.95	
.975	1.95	1.82	1.76	1.69	1.61	1.56	1.53	1.45	1.43	1.39	1.34	1.31	.975	
.99	2.19	2.03	1.95	1.86	1.76	1.70	1.66	1.56	1.53	1.48	1.42	1.38	.99	
.995	2.37	2.19	2.09	1.98	1.87	1.80	1.75	1.64	1.61	1.54	1.48	1.43	.995	
.999	2.78	2.53	2.40	2.26	2.11	2.02	1.95	1.82	1.76	1.70	1.62	1.54	.999	
.9995	2.96	2.67	2.53	2.38	2.21	2.11	2.01	1.88	1.84	1.75	1.67	1.60	.9995	
.0005	.207	.270	.311	.360	.422	.469	.505	.599	.624	.704	.804	1.00	.0005	**∞**
.001	.232	.296	.338	.386	.448	.493	.527	.617	.649	.719	.819	1.00	.001	
.005	.307	.372	.412	.460	.518	.559	.592	.671	.699	.762	.843	1.00	.005	
.01	.349	.413	.452	.499	.554	.595	.625	.699	.724	.782	.858	1.00	.01	
.025	.418	.480	.517	.560	.611	.645	.675	.741	.763	.813	.878	1.00	.025	
.05	.484	.543	.577	.617	.663	.694	.720	.781	.797	.840	.896	1.00	.05	
.10	.570	.622	.652	.687	.726	.752	.774	.826	.838	.877	.919	1.00	.10	
.25	.736	.773	.793	.816	.842	.860	.872	.901	.910	.932	.957	1.00	.25	
.50	.956	.967	.972	.978	.983	.987	.989	.993	.994	.997	.999	1.00	.50	
.75	1.22	1.19	1.18	1.16	1.14	1.13	1.12	1.09	1.08	1.07	1.04	1.00	.75	
.90	1.49	1.42	1.38	1.34	1.30	1.26	1.24	1.18	1.17	1.13	1.08	1.00	.90	
.95	1.67	1.57	1.52	1.46	1.39	1.35	1.32	1.24	1.22	1.17	1.11	1.00	.95	
.975	1.83	1.71	1.64	1.57	1.48	1.43	1.39	1.30	1.27	1.21	1.13	1.00	.975	
.99	2.04	1.88	1.79	1.70	1.59	1.52	1.47	1.36	1.32	1.25	1.15	1.00	.99	
.995	2.19	2.00	1.90	1.79	1.67	1.59	1.53	1.40	1.36	1.28	1.17	1.00	.995	
.999	2.51	2.27	2.13	1.99	1.84	1.73	1.66	1.49	1.45	1.34	1.21	1.00	.999	
.9995	2.65	2.37	2.22	2.07	1.91	1.79	1.71	1.53	1.48	1.36	1.22	1.00	.9995	

TABLE A.5 Upper Percentiles of Studentized Range Distributions

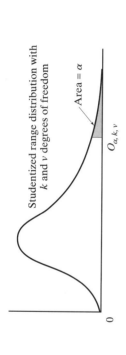

Studentized range distribution with k and v degrees of freedom

Area = α

$O_{\alpha, k, v}$

v	k	$1-\alpha$	2	3	4	5	6	7	8	9	10	11	12	13	14	15	16
1		0.95	18.0	27.0	32.8	37.1	40.4	43.1	45.4	47.4	49.1	50.6	52.0	53.2	54.3	55.4	56.3
		0.99	90.0	135	164	186	202	216	227	237	246	253	260	266	272	277	282
2		0.95	6.09	8.3	9.8	10.9	11.7	12.4	13.0	13.5	14.0	14.4	14.7	15.1	15.4	15.7	15.9
		0.99	14.0	19.0	22.3	24.7	26.6	28.2	29.5	30.7	31.7	32.6	33.4	34.1	34.8	35.4	36.0
3		0.95	4.50	5.91	6.82	7.50	8.04	8.48	8.85	9.18	9.46	9.72	9.95	10.2	10.4	10.5	10.7
		0.99	8.26	10.6	12.2	13.3	14.2	15.0	15.6	16.2	16.7	17.1	17.5	17.9	18.2	18.5	18.8
4		0.95	3.93	5.04	5.76	6.29	6.71	7.05	7.35	7.60	7.83	8.03	8.21	8.37	8.52	8.66	8.79
		0.99	6.51	8.12	9.17	9.96	10.6	11.1	11.5	11.9	12.3	12.6	12.8	13.1	13.3	13.5	13.7
5		0.95	3.64	4.60	5.22	5.67	6.03	6.33	6.58	6.80	6.99	7.17	7.32	7.47	7.60	7.72	7.83
		0.99	5.70	6.97	7.80	8.42	8.91	9.32	9.67	9.97	10.2	10.5	10.7	10.9	11.1	11.2	11.4
6		0.95	3.46	4.34	4.90	5.31	5.63	5.89	6.12	6.32	6.49	6.65	6.79	6.92	7.03	7.14	7.24
		0.99	5.24	6.33	7.03	7.56	7.97	8.32	8.61	8.87	9.10	9.30	9.49	9.65	9.81	9.95	10.1
7		0.95	3.34	4.16	4.68	5.06	5.36	5.61	5.82	6.00	6.16	6.30	6.43	6.55	6.66	6.76	6.85
		0.99	4.95	5.92	6.54	7.01	7.37	7.68	7.94	8.17	8.37	8.55	8.71	8.86	9.00	9.12	9.24
8		0.95	3.26	4.04	4.53	4.89	5.17	5.40	5.60	5.77	5.92	6.05	6.18	6.29	6.39	6.48	6.57
		0.99	4.74	5.63	6.20	6.63	6.96	7.24	7.47	7.68	7.87	8.03	8.18	8.31	8.44	8.55	8.66
9		0.95	3.20	3.95	4.42	4.76	5.02	5.24	5.43	5.60	5.74	5.87	5.98	6.09	6.19	6.28	6.36
		0.99	4.60	5.43	5.96	6.35	6.66	6.91	7.13	7.32	7.49	7.65	7.78	7.91	8.03	8.13	8.23
10		0.95	3.15	3.88	4.33	4.65	4.91	5.12	5.30	5.46	5.60	5.72	5.83	5.93	6.03	6.11	6.20
		0.99	4.48	5.27	5.77	6.14	6.43	6.67	6.87	7.05	7.21	7.36	7.48	7.60	7.71	7.81	7.91
11		0.95	3.11	3.82	4.26	4.57	4.82	5.03	5.20	5.35	5.49	5.61	5.71	5.81	5.90	5.99	6.06
		0.99	4.39	5.14	5.62	5.97	6.25	6.48	6.67	6.84	6.99	7.13	7.25	7.36	7.46	7.56	7.65
12		0.95	3.08	3.77	4.20	4.51	4.75	4.95	5.12	5.27	5.40	5.51	5.62	5.71	5.80	5.88	5.95
		0.99	4.32	5.04	5.50	5.84	6.10	6.32	6.51	6.67	6.81	6.94	7.06	7.17	7.26	7.36	7.44
13		0.95	3.06	3.73	4.15	4.45	4.69	4.88	5.05	5.19	5.32	5.43	5.53	5.63	5.71	5.79	5.86
		0.99	4.26	4.96	5.40	5.73	5.98	6.19	6.37	6.53	6.67	6.79	6.90	7.01	7.10	7.19	7.27
14		0.95	3.03	3.70	4.11	4.41	4.64	4.83	4.99	5.13	5.25	5.36	5.46	5.55	5.64	5.72	5.79
		0.99	4.21	4.89	5.32	5.63	5.88	6.08	6.26	6.41	6.54	6.66	6.77	6.87	6.96	7.05	7.12

v	k $1-\alpha$	2	3	4	5	6	7	8	9	10	11	12	13	14	15	16
15	0.95	3.01	3.67	4.08	4.37	4.60	4.78	4.94	5.08	5.20	5.31	5.40	5.49	5.58	5.65	5.72
	0.99	4.17	4.83	5.25	5.56	5.80	5.99	6.16	6.31	6.44	6.55	6.66	6.76	6.84	6.93	7.00
16	0.95	3.00	3.65	4.05	4.33	4.56	4.74	4.90	5.03	5.15	5.26	5.35	5.44	5.52	5.59	5.66
	0.99	4.13	4.78	5.19	5.49	5.72	5.92	6.08	6.22	6.35	6.46	6.56	6.66	6.74	6.82	6.90
17	0.95	2.98	3.63	4.02	4.30	4.52	4.71	4.86	4.99	5.11	5.21	5.31	5.39	5.47	5.55	5.61
	0.99	4.10	4.74	5.14	5.43	5.66	5.85	6.01	6.15	6.27	6.38	6.48	6.57	6.66	6.73	6.80
18	0.95	2.97	3.61	4.00	4.28	4.49	4.67	4.82	4.96	5.07	5.17	5.27	5.35	5.43	5.50	5.57
	0.99	4.07	4.70	5.09	5.38	5.60	5.79	5.94	6.08	6.20	6.31	6.41	6.50	6.58	6.65	6.72
19	0.95	2.96	3.59	3.98	4.25	4.47	4.65	4.79	4.92	5.04	5.14	5.23	5.32	5.39	5.46	5.53
	0.99	4.05	4.67	5.05	5.33	5.55	5.73	5.89	6.02	6.14	6.25	6.34	6.43	6.51	6.58	6.65
20	0.95	2.95	3.58	3.96	4.23	4.45	4.62	4.77	4.90	5.01	5.11	5.20	5.28	5.36	5.43	5.49
	0.99	4.02	4.64	5.02	5.29	5.51	5.69	5.84	5.97	6.09	6.19	6.29	6.37	6.45	6.52	6.59
24	0.95	2.92	3.53	3.90	4.17	4.37	4.54	4.68	4.81	4.92	5.01	5.10	5.18	5.25	5.32	5.38
	0.99	3.96	4.54	4.91	5.17	5.37	5.54	5.69	5.81	5.92	6.02	6.11	6.19	6.26	6.33	6.39
30	0.95	2.89	3.49	3.84	4.10	4.30	4.46	4.60	4.72	4.83	4.92	5.00	5.08	5.15	5.21	5.27
	0.99	3.89	4.45	4.80	5.05	5.24	5.40	5.54	5.65	5.76	5.85	5.93	6.01	6.08	6.14	6.20
40	0.95	2.86	3.44	3.79	4.04	4.23	4.39	4.52	4.63	4.74	4.82	4.91	4.98	5.05	5.11	5.16
	0.99	3.82	4.37	4.70	4.93	5.11	5.27	5.39	5.50	5.60	5.69	5.77	5.84	5.90	5.96	6.02
60	0.95	2.83	3.40	3.74	3.98	4.16	4.31	4.44	4.55	4.65	4.73	4.81	4.88	4.94	5.00	5.06
	0.99	3.76	4.28	4.60	4.82	4.99	5.13	5.25	5.36	5.45	5.53	5.60	5.67	5.73	5.79	5.84
120	0.95	2.80	3.36	3.69	3.92	4.10	4.24	4.36	4.48	4.56	4.64	4.72	4.78	4.84	4.90	4.95
	0.99	3.70	4.20	4.50	4.71	4.87	5.01	5.12	5.21	5.30	5.38	5.44	5.51	5.56	5.61	5.66
∞	0.95	2.77	3.31	3.63	3.86	4.03	4.17	4.29	4.39	4.47	4.55	4.62	4.68	4.74	4.80	4.85
	0.99	3.64	4.12	4.40	4.60	4.76	4.88	4.99	5.08	5.16	5.23	5.29	5.35	5.40	5.45	5.49

Source: Olive Jean Dunn and Virginia A. Clark, *Applied Statistics: Analysis of Variance and Regression* (New York: Wiley, 1974), pp. 371–372.

TABLE A.6   Upper and Lower Percentiles of the Wilcoxon Signed
Rank Statistic, W

	w_1^*	w_2^*	$P(W \le w_1^*) = P(W \ge w_2^*)$
$n = 4$	0	10	0.062
	1	9	0.125
$n = 5$	0	15	0.031
	1	14	0.062
	2	13	0.094
	3	12	0.156
$n = 6$	0	21	0.016
	1	20	0.031
	2	19	0.047
	3	18	0.078
	4	17	0.109
	5	16	0.156
$n = 7$	0	28	0.008
	1	27	0.016
	2	26	0.023
	3	25	0.039
	4	24	0.055
	5	23	0.078
	6	22	0.109
	7	21	0.148
$n = 8$	0	36	0.004
	1	35	0.008
	2	34	0.012
	3	33	0.020
	4	32	0.027
	5	31	0.039
	6	30	0.055
	7	29	0.074
	8	28	0.098
	9	27	0.125
$n = 9$	1	44	0.004
	2	43	0.006
	3	42	0.010
	4	41	0.014
	5	40	0.020
	6	39	0.027
	7	38	0.037
	8	37	0.049
	9	36	0.064
	10	35	0.082
	11	34	0.102
	12	33	0.125

Source: Wilfrid J. Dixon and Frank J. Massey, Jr., *Introduction to Statistical Analysis,* 2nd.
ed. (New York: McGraw-Hill, 1957), pp. 443–444.

TABLE A.6 Upper and Lower Percentiles of the Wilcoxon Signed
Rank Statistic, W *(cont.)*

	w_1^*	w_2^*	$P(W \leq w_1^*) = P(W \geq w_2^*)$
$n = 10$	3	52	0.005
	4	51	0.007
	5	50	0.010
	6	49	0.014
	7	48	0.019
	8	47	0.024
	9	46	0.032
	10	45	0.042
	11	44	0.053
	12	43	0.065
	13	42	0.080
	14	41	0.097
	15	40	0.116
	16	39	0.138
$n = 11$	5	61	0.005
	6	60	0.007
	7	59	0.009
	8	58	0.012
	9	57	0.016
	10	56	0.021
	11	55	0.027
	12	54	0.034
	13	53	0.042
	14	52	0.051
	15	51	0.062
	16	50	0.074
	17	49	0.087
	18	48	0.103
	19	47	0.120
	20	46	0.139
$n = 12$	7	71	0.005
	8	70	0.006
	9	69	0.008
	10	68	0.010
	11	67	0.013
	12	66	0.017
	13	65	0.021
	14	64	0.026
	15	63	0.032
	16	62	0.039
	17	61	0.046
	18	60	0.055
	19	59	0.065
	20	58	0.076
	21	57	0.088
	22	56	0.102
	23	55	0.117
	24	54	0.133

Answers to Selected Odd-Numbered Questions

CHAPTER 2

Section 2.2

2.2.1 $S = \{(s, s, s,), \ (s, s, f), \ (s, f, s), \ (f, s, s), \ (s, f, f), \ (f, s, f,), \ (f, f, s), \ (f, f, f)\}$; $A = \{(s, f, s,), \ (f, s, s)\}$; $\quad B = \{(f, f, f)\}$

2.2.3 $(1, 3, 4), \quad (1, 3, 5), \quad (1, 3, 6), \quad (2, 3, 4), \quad (2, 3, 5), \quad (2, 3, 6)$

2.2.5 Let p_1 and p_2 denote the two perpetrators and i_1, i_2, and i_3, the three in the lineup who are innocent. Then $S = \{(p_1, i_1), \ (p_1, i_2), \ (p_1, i_3), \ (p_2, i_1), \ (p_2, i_2), \ (p_2, i_3), \ (p_1, p_2), \ (i_1, i_2), \ (i_1, i_3), \ (i_2, i_3)\}$. The event A contains every outcome in S except (p_1, p_2).

2.2.7 In order for the shooter to win with a point of 9, one of the following (countably infinite) sequences of sums must be rolled: $(9, 9), \quad (9, \text{no } 7 \text{ or no } 9, 9), \quad (9, \text{no } 7 \text{ or no } 9, \text{no } 7 \text{ or no } 9, 9), \ldots$.

2.2.11 $A \cap B \cap C = \{x: x = 2, 3, 4\}$ $\qquad$ **2.2.13** **(a)** A_1 $\quad$ **(b)** A_k $\qquad$ **2.2.15** 40

2.2.19 **(a)** Let s be a member of $A \cup (B \cup C)$. Then s belongs to either A or $B \cup C$ (or both). If s belongs to A, it necessarily belongs to $(A \cup B) \cup C$. If s belongs to $B \cup C$, it belongs to B or C or both, so it must belong to $(A \cup B) \cup C$. Now, suppose s belongs to $(A \cup B) \cup C$. Then it belongs to either $A \cup B$ or C or both. If it belongs to C, it must belong to $A \cup (B \cup C)$. If it belongs to $A \cup B$, it must belong to either A or B or both, so it must belong to $A \cup (B \cup C)$.

Section 2.3

2.3.1 0.41 $\qquad$ **2.3.3** **(a)** $1 - P(A \cap B)$ $\quad$ **(b)** $P(B) - P(A \cap B)$

2.3.5 No. $P(A_1 \cup A_2 \cup A_3) = P(\text{at least one "6" appears}) = 1 - P(\text{no 6's appear}) = 1 - \left(\frac{5}{6}\right)^3 \neq \frac{1}{2}$. The A_i's are not mutually exclusive, so $P(A_1 \cup A_2 \cup A_3) \neq P(A_1) + P(A_2) + P(A_3)$.

2.3.7 By inspection, $B = (B \cap A_1) \cup (B \cap A_2) \cup \ldots \cup (B \cap A_n)$.

2.3.9 $\dfrac{3}{4}$ $\qquad$ **2.3.11** 0.30 $\qquad$ **2.3.13** 0.15

Section 2.4

2.4.1 $P(\text{sum} = 7) = 2P(1) \cdot P(6) + 2P(2) \cdot P(5) + 2P(3) \cdot P(4) = 2\left(\frac{1}{4}\right)\left(\frac{1}{4}\right) + 2\left(\frac{1}{8}\right)\left(\frac{1}{8}\right) +$

$2\left(\frac{1}{8}\right)\left(\frac{1}{8}\right) = 0.1875.$ When the two dice are fair, $P(\text{sum} = 7) = 6/36 = 0.1667.$ Cheaters would slip the shooter a pair of ace-six flats after the shooter's first roll had established the "point" that needed to be made. Doing so increases the chances that the shooter will lose by rolling a 7 before rolling the point.

2.4.3 3/10   **2.4.5** 3/10   **2.4.7** 12/216   **2.4.9** 1/4

Section 2.5

2.5.1 1/13   **2.5.3** 23/28   **2.5.5** $(1 - e^{-4})/(1 - e^{-9})$ **2.5.9** 1.53   **2.5.11** 0.56

Section 2.6

2.6.1 3/10   **2.6.3** 0.1   **2.6.5** 1/3   **2.6.7** 3/4   **2.6.9** $P(A) = 2/3;$ $P(B) = 1/3$

2.6.11 $P(A|B) = \dfrac{P(A \cap B)}{P(B)} = \dfrac{P(A) + P(B) - P(A \cup B)}{P(B)} = \dfrac{a + b - P(A \cup B)}{b}.$ But $P(A \cup B) \le 1,$

so $P(A|B) \ge \dfrac{a + b - 1}{b}.$

2.6.13 $P(y \ge r + t \,|\, y \ge t) = P(y \ge r + t)/P(y \ge t) = e^{-\lambda r} = P(y \ge r).$ The exponential probability function applied in this context assumes no wearout—no matter how long the bulb has already remained lit, $f(y)$ implies that it has the same probability of working for at least another r hours.

2.6.15 Let K_i be the event that the ith key tried opens the door, $i = 1, 2, \ldots, n.$ Then P(door opens first time with third key) $= P(K_1^C \cap K_2^C \cap K_3) = \dfrac{n-1}{n} \cdot \dfrac{n-2}{n-1} \cdot \dfrac{1}{n-2} = \dfrac{1}{n}.$

2.6.17 0.15   **2.6.19** 0.46   **2.6.21** 11/16

2.6.23 The optimal allocation has 1 white chip in one urn and the other 19 chips (9 white and 10 black) in the other urn. Then P(white is drawn) $= 0.74.$

2.6.25 40/100   **2.6.27** 4/7   **2.6.29** 0.85   **2.6.31** 0.486   **2.6.33** 0.027   **2.6.35** 14

Section 2.7

2.7.1 If A and B are mutually exclusive, $P(A|B) = 0 \ne P(A) > 0.$ By definition, then, A and B are not independent.

2.7.3 24   **2.7.5** 11

2.7.7 $P(A \cap B \cap C) = 0$ (since the sum of two odd numbers is necessarily even) $\ne P(A) \cdot P(B) \cdot P(C) > 0,$ so $A, B,$ and C are not mutually independent. However,

$$P(A \cap B) = \frac{9}{36} = P(A) \cdot P(B) = \frac{3}{6} \cdot \frac{3}{6}, \quad P(A \cap C) = \frac{9}{36} = P(A) \cdot P(C) = \frac{3}{6} \cdot \frac{18}{36}, \text{ and}$$

$$P(B \cap C) = \frac{9}{36} = P(B) \cdot P(C) = \frac{3}{6} \cdot \frac{18}{36}, \text{ so } A, B, \text{ and } C \text{ are pairwise independent.}$$

2.7.9 6/36

2.7.11 0.625. The solution assumes that a man's blood type is independent of the blood type of his wife. That assumption is reasonable because blood type is not a factor in the selection of a mate.

2.7.13 0.10; yes   **2.7.15** 0.56   **2.7.17** 1/18

2.7.19 $P(A_1 \cup A_2 \cup \ldots \cup A_n) = \sum_{i=1}^{n} P(A_i) - \sum_{i<j} P(A_i)P(A_j) + \sum_{i<j<k} P(A_i)P(A_j)P(A_k) - \ldots$

$\pm P(A_1)P(A_2) \ldots P(A_n)$. If all the A_i's are independent, their union can be more easily calculated using complements: $P(A_1 \cup A_2 \cup \ldots \cup A_n) = 1 - P(A_1^C \cap A_2^C \cap \ldots \cap A_n^C) = 1 - P(A_1^C)P(A_2^C) \ldots P(A_n^C)$.

Section 2.8

2.8.1 0.34   **2.8.3** 63/384   **2.8.5** $1 - \left(\dfrac{4}{7}\right)^{rm}$ **2.8.7** 25

2.8.9 $P(A \text{ throws first head}) = \dfrac{4}{7}$; $P(B \text{ throws first head}) = \dfrac{2}{7}$; $P(C \text{ throws first head}) = \dfrac{1}{7}$.

2.8.11 Put the house on Vermont Avenue, because $P(\text{opponent lands on Vermont Avenue}) = 0.166 > P(\text{opponent lands on Oriental Avenue}) = 0.147$.

2.8.13 Send m teams to Area I, where $m = \dfrac{n}{2} + \dfrac{\ln[(1-p)/p]}{2\ln(1-r)}$.

Section 2.9

2.9.1 24   **2.9.3** 45; included are *aeu* and *cdx*
2.9.5 (a) 6,760,000   (b) 3,407,040   (c) 6,759,324   **2.9.7** 256   **2.9.9** 20,000,000   **2.9.11** 3
2.9.13 4   **2.9.15** 120   **2.9.17** 2.645×10^{32} **2.9.19** 60   **2.9.21** 2880
2.9.23 (a) 576   (b) 5040   **2.9.25** $n!(m!)^n$
2.9.27 By inspection, $_nP_1 = n$. Assume that $_nP_k = n(n-1)\cdots(n-k+1)$ is the number of ways to arrange k distinct objects without repetition. Notice that $n - k$ options would be available for a $(k+1)$st object added to the sequences. By the multiplication rule, the number of ordered sequences of length $k + 1$ must be $n(n-1)\cdots(n-k+1)(n-k)$. But the latter is the formula for $_nP_{k+1}$.
2.9.29 By definition, $(n+1)! = (n+1)n!$; let $n = 0$.   **2.9.31** 300
2.9.33 (a) 4!3!3!   (b) 3!4!3!3!   (c) 10!   (d) $\dfrac{10!}{4!3!3!}$ **2.9.35** 5040   **2.9.37** $\dfrac{11!}{9!2!} \cdot \dfrac{8!}{5!3!}$
2.9.39 $(2n)!/n!(2!)^n = 1 \cdot 3 \cdot 5 \cdots (2n-1)$ **2.9.41** $11 \cdot 10!/3!$
2.9.43 Consider $k!$ objects categorized into $(k-1)!$ groups, each group being of size k. By Theorem 2.9.2, the number of ways to arrange the $k!$ objects is $(k!)!/(k!)^{(k-1)!}$, but the latter must be an integer.
2.9.45 10   **2.9.47** $\dbinom{3}{2} \cdot (4!)^2$ **2.9.49** $\dbinom{7}{5}$; order does not matter   **2.9.51** $\dbinom{16}{6} \cdot \dfrac{15!}{10!5!}$

2.9.53 Let $x = y = 1$ in the expansion $(x + y)^n = \sum_{k=0}^{n} \dbinom{n}{k} x^k y^{n-k}$. The total number of hamburgers referred to in Question 2.9.7 $(= 2^8)$ must also be equal to the number of ways to choose k condiments, $k = 0, 1, 2, \ldots, 8$—that is, $\dbinom{8}{0} + \dbinom{8}{1} + \ldots + \dbinom{8}{8}$.

2.9.55 Let $x = y = 1$ in the expansion of $(x - y)^n$. Then $0 = \sum_{k=0}^{n} \dbinom{n}{k}(-1)^{(n-k)}$, and the result follows.

2.9.57 Entropy will be maximized when $n/2$ molecules are present in each chamber.   **2.9.59** 360

Section 2.10

2.10.1 $63/210$ **2.10.3** $1 - \dfrac{37}{190}$ **2.10.5** $10/19$ (recall Bayes's rule)

2.10.7 $1/6^{n-1}$ **2.10.9** $2(n!)^2/(2n)!$

2.10.11 $7!/7^7; 1/7^6$. The assumption being made is that all possible departure patterns are equally likely, which is probably not true, since residents living on lower floors would be less inclined to wait for the elevator than would those living on the top floors.

2.10.13 $2^{10} \Big/ \dbinom{20}{10}$ **2.10.15** $\dbinom{k}{2} \cdot \dfrac{365 \cdot 364 \cdots (365 - k + 2)}{(365)^k}$ **2.10.17** $\dbinom{11}{3} \Big/ \dbinom{47}{3}$

2.10.19 $2 \Big/ \dbinom{47}{2}$; $\left[\dbinom{10}{2} - 2\right] \Big/ \dbinom{47}{2}$ **2.10.21** $\dbinom{5}{3}\dbinom{4}{2}^3\dbinom{3}{1}\dbinom{4}{2}\dbinom{2}{1}\dbinom{4}{1} \Big/ \dbinom{52}{9}$

2.10.23 $\left[\dbinom{2}{1}\dbinom{2}{1}\right]^4 \dbinom{32}{4} \Big/ \dbinom{48}{12}$

CHAPTER 3

Section 3.2

3.2.1

k	$p_X(k)$
2	1/10
3	2/10
4	3/10
5	4/10

3.2.3

k	$p_X(k)$
1	1/18
2	4/18
3	7/18
4	4/18
6	1/18
7	1/18

3.2.5

k	$p_X(k)$
0	4/10
1	3/10
2	2/10
3	1/10

3.2.7 $p_X(k) = \dfrac{\dbinom{4}{k}\dbinom{48}{5-k}}{\dbinom{52}{5}}, \quad k = 0, 1, 2, 3, 4$

3.2.9

k	$p_X(k)$
0	1/36
1	2/90
2	1/20
3	2/90
4	1/36

3.2.11 $38/64$

Section 3.3

3.3.1 $14/84$ **3.3.3** $p_X(k) = \dfrac{\dbinom{514}{k}\dbinom{3536}{65-k}}{\dbinom{4050}{65}}, \quad 0 \le k \le 65$

3.3.5 No. The probability of her getting at least 4 correct is 0.778.   **3.3.7** 2/1332   **3.3.9** 17/45

3.3.11 $P(X_1 = k_1, X_2 = k_2, \ldots, X_t = k_t) = \dfrac{\binom{n_1}{k_1}\binom{n_2}{k_2}\cdots\binom{n_t}{k_t}}{\binom{N}{n}}$

3.3.13 For incoming quality of 16 percent defective, the shipment will be accepted 50% of the time.

3.3.15 0.0064   **3.3.17** 50 bulb system: 0.923   100 bulb system: 0.867

3.3.19 The probability the plane will crash is 0.345.   The probability the boat will be disabled is 0.401.

3.3.21 The probability of two girls and two boys is 0.375.   The probability of three and one is 0.50.

3.3.23 7   **3.3.25** 0.187   **3.3.27** **(1)** 0.273   **(2)** 0.756

3.3.29 $P(X_1 = k_1, X_2 = k_2) = \dfrac{n!}{k_1!k_2!(n - k_1 - k_2)!}\, p_1^{k_1} p_2^{k_2}(1 - p_1 - p_2)^{n-k_1-k_2}$

3.3.31 $\binom{n}{r}\left(e^{-5/\theta}\right)^r\left(1 - e^{-5/\theta}\right)^{n-r}$

Section 3.4

3.4.3 For $y < 0, F_Y(y) = 0$, and for $y \geq 3$, $F_Y(y) = 1$. For other intervals   **3.4.5** 1   **3.4.7** $f_X(k) = (0.1)k, k = 1, 2, 3, 4$

$$F_Y(y) = \begin{cases} \dfrac{3}{2}y^2 - y^3 & 0 \leq y < 1 \\ 1/2 & 1 \leq y < 2 \\ \dfrac{1}{2}y - \dfrac{1}{2} & 2 \leq y < 3 \end{cases}$$

$$F_X(x) = \begin{cases} 0 & x < 1 \\ 0.10 & 1 \leq x < 2 \\ 0.30 & 2 \leq x < 3 \\ 0.60 & 3 \leq x < 4 \\ 1 & 4 \leq x \end{cases}$$

3.4.9 $P(2 < Y \leq 3)$

3.4.11 $P(-a < Y < a) = P(-a < Y \leq 0) + P(0 < Y < a)$

$$= \int_{-a}^{0} f_Y(y)\, dy + \int_{0}^{a} f_Y(y)\, dy = -\int_{a}^{0} f_Y(-y)\, dy + \int_{0}^{a} f_Y(y)\, dy$$

$$= \int_{0}^{a} f_Y(y)\, dy + \int_{0}^{a} f_Y(y)\, dy = 2[F_Y(a) - F_y(0)].$$

But by the symmetry of f_Y, $F_Y(0) = 1/2$. Thus, $2[F_Y(a) - F_Y(0)] = 2[F_Y(a) - 1/2] = 2F_Y(a) - 1$.

3.4.13 $B = (Y \neq a)$; $C = (Y = a)$ where a is an element of A.

3.4.15 $h(y) = \dfrac{(1/\lambda)e^{-y/\lambda}}{1 - (1 - e^{-y/\lambda})} = 1/\lambda$. Since the hazard rate is constant, the item does not age. Its reliability does not decrease over time.   **3.4.17** 1/2

3.4.19 If the new therapy has no effect, then $P(X > 7) = 0.00159$. The small probability of seeing 8 or more cures argues against the hypothesis that the medicine has no effect.

Section 3.5

3.5.1 1/10   **3.5.3** 6   **3.5.5** $P(X = x, Y = y) = \dfrac{\binom{3}{x}\binom{2}{y}\binom{4}{3 - x - y}}{\binom{9}{3}}, x \leq 3, y \leq 2, x + y \leq 3$

3.5.7 $13/50$ **3.5.9** **(a)** 1   **(b)** $1/8$ **3.5.11** $f_{X,Y}(x,y) = 1/4\pi, x^2 + y^2 \leq 4$ **3.5.13** $750/6561$

3.5.15 **(a)** $\{(H,1), (H,2), (H,3), (H,4), (H,5), (H,6), (T,1), (T,2), (T,3), (T,4), (T,5), (T,6)\}$ **(b)** $4/12$

3.5.17 $F_{X,Y}(x,y) = \begin{cases} 0 & 0 \leq x < 5, \quad \text{any } y \\ 1/2 & 5 \leq x < 6, \quad 2 \leq y < 3 \\ 2/3 & 5 \leq x < 6, \quad 3 \leq y \\ 2/3 & 6 \leq x, \quad 2 \leq y < 3 \\ 1 & 6 \leq x, \quad 3 \leq y \end{cases}$

3.5.19 $f_{X,Y} = 1, \quad 0 < x < 1, \quad 0 < y < 1$. The graph of $f_{X,Y}$ is a plane of height 1 over the unit square.

3.5.21 $11/32$ **3.5.23** $f_X(x) = 6x(1-x), \quad 0 < x < 1; \qquad f_Y(y) = 3(1-y)^2, \quad 0 < y < 1$

3.5.25 $f_X(x) = 1 - \dfrac{x}{2}, \quad 0 < x < 2$ **3.5.27** $f_Y(y) = 2e^{-y} - 2e^{-2y}, \quad 0 < y$ **3.5.29** 0.015 **3.5.31** $25/576$

3.5.33 $f_{W,X}(w,x) = 4wx, \quad 0 < w < 1, \quad 0 < x < 1; \qquad P(0 < W < 1/2, \quad 1/2 < X < 1) = 3/16$

Section 3.6

3.6.1 We must show that $p_{X,Y}(j, k) = p_X(j)p_Y(k)$. But for any pair (j, k), $p_{X,Y}(j, k) = 1/36 = (1/6)(1/6) = p_X(j)p_Y(k)$.

3.6.3 Note that $P(Y \geq 3/4) \neq 0$. Similarly $P(X \geq 3/4) \neq 0$. However, $(X \geq 3/4) \cap (Y \geq 3/4)$ is in the region where the density is 0. Thus, $P((X \geq 3/4) \cap (Y \geq 3/4))$ is zero, but the product $P(X \geq 3/4)P(Y \geq 3/4)$ is not zero.

3.6.5 $2/5$ **3.6.7** $1/12$

3.6.9 Take $a = c = 0$, $b = d = 1/2$. Then $P(a < X < b, \ c < Y < d) = 5/32 \neq (3/8)(1/2) = P(a < X < b)P(c < Y < d)$.

3.6.11 Let K be the region of the plane where $f_{X,Y} \neq 0$. If K is not a rectangle with sides parallel to the coordinate axes, there exists a rectangle $A = \{(x, y)|a \leq x \leq b, c \leq y \leq d\}$ with $A \cap K = \emptyset$, but for $A_1 = \{(x, y)|a \leq x \leq b, \text{all } y\}$ and $A_2 = \{(x, y)| \text{all } x, c \leq y \leq d\}, A_1 \cap K \neq \emptyset$ and $A_2 \cap K \neq \emptyset$. Then $P(A) = 0$, but $P(A_1) \neq 0$ and $P(A_2) \neq 0$. But $A = A_1 \cap A_2$, so $P(A_1 \cap A_2) \neq P(A_1)P(A_2)$.

3.6.13 **(a)** $1/16$ **(b)** 0.21 **(c)** $f_{X_2,X_2,X_3,X_4}(x_1, x_2, x_3, x_4) = 256(x_1 x_2 x_3 x_4)^3$ where $0 \leq x_1, x_2, x_3, x_4 \leq 1$ **(d)** $F_{X_2,X_3}(x_2, x_3) = x_2^4 x_3^4, \quad 0 \leq x_2, x_3 \leq 1$

Section 3.7

3.7.1 $f_Y(y) = \dfrac{\binom{4}{\frac{1}{2}y + \frac{1}{2}}\binom{3}{-\frac{1}{2}y + \frac{3}{2}}}{\binom{7}{2}}, \quad k = -1, 1, 3$ **3.7.3** $f_Y(y) = \dfrac{1}{3}, \quad -7 \leq y \leq -4$

3.7.5 $f_Y(y) = -3y^2 - 3y - 9/4, \quad -3 < y < -1$

3.7.7 **(a)** $f_Y(y) = \dfrac{1}{y^2} e^{-1/y}, \quad y > 0$ **(b)** $F_Y(y) = P(Y \leq y) = P(\ln X \leq y) = P(X \leq e^y) = F_X(e^y)$. Differentiating both sides of the equality gives $f_Y(y) = e^y e^{-e^y}, \quad -\infty < y < \infty$.

3.7.9 $f_Y(y) = \dfrac{3}{16}\sqrt{y}, \quad 0 < y < 4$ **3.7.11** $f_Y(y) = \left(\dfrac{81}{25}y + \dfrac{288}{5}\right)e^{-\left(\frac{9}{5}y+32\right)^2/2}, \quad y > -160/9$

3.7.13 First suppose that $0 < z \le 1. F_Z(z) = P(Z \le z) = P(X + Y \le Z)$. The region of integration is the right triangle with vertices at $(0,0), (0, z)$, and $(z, 0)$. Because the density is uniform, the integration is simply equal to the area of the figure. Since the region of integration is a right triangle, with sides of length z, the area is then $\dfrac{1}{2}z^2$. If $1 < z < 2$, the region of integration is the unit square minus the triangle with vertices $(1, 1), (z - 1, 1)$ and $(1, z - 1)$. The triangle is a right triangle with sides of length $2 - z$. Thus, the area of the region of integration is $1 - \dfrac{1}{2}(2 - z)^2$. In summary then

$$F_Z(z) = \begin{cases} \dfrac{1}{2}z^2, & 0 < z \le 1 \\[2mm] 1 - \dfrac{1}{2}(2 - z)^2, & 1 < z < 2 \end{cases}$$

3.7.15 $F_Z(z) = \begin{cases} \dfrac{1}{2}z, & 0 < z \le 1 \\[2mm] 1 - \dfrac{1}{2z}, & 1 < z \end{cases}$ $\qquad f_Z(z) = \begin{cases} \dfrac{1}{2}, & 0 < z \le 1 \\[2mm] \dfrac{1}{2z^2}, & 1 < z \end{cases}$

3.7.17 $f_Z(z) = \dfrac{e^{-(r+s)}}{z!}(r + s)^z, \quad z = 1, 2, 3, \dots$ This is a Poisson density with parameter $r + s$.

3.7.19 $f_Z(z) = \dfrac{z^2}{2}e^{-z}, \quad z > 0$

3.7.21 For Example 3.7.7, $f_{X+Y}(z) = \displaystyle\int_0^{\infty} f_X(x)f_Y(z - x)\, dx = \int_0^z e^{-x}e^{-(z-x)}\, dx$. The upper limit on the integral changes to z, because $f_Y(z - x) = 0$ unless $z - x > 0$, or equivalently, $x < z$. Thus, $f_{X+Y}(z) = \displaystyle\int_0^z e^{-z}\, dx = xe^{-z}\Big|_0^z = ze^{-z}, \quad z > 0.$

3.7.23 $f_Y(y) = \dfrac{2}{9}(y + 1), \quad -1 < y < 2$ **3.7.25** $f_Z(z) = \dfrac{z^2}{2}e^{-z}$

Section 3.8

3.8.1 5/16   **3.8.3** 0.64   **3.8.5** $P(Y_1' > m) = P(Y_1, \dots, Y_n > m) = \left(\dfrac{1}{2}\right)^n$

$P(Y_n' > m) = 1 - P(Y_n' < m) = 1 - P(Y_1, \dots, Y_n < m) = 1 - P(Y_1 < m) \cdot \ \dots \ \cdot P(Y_n < m) = 1 - \left(\dfrac{1}{2}\right)^n$

If $n \ge 2$, the latter probability is greater.

3.8.7 0.200   **3.8.9** $P(Y_{\min} > 20) = (1/2)^n.$ **3.8.11** 0.725; 0.95

Section 3.9

3.9.1 0.015   **3.9.3** $p_{Y|x}(y) = \dfrac{\dbinom{6}{y}\dbinom{4}{3 - x - y}}{\dbinom{10}{3 - x}}, \quad y = 0, 1, \dots, 3 - x$

3.9.5 $f_{X,Y|1}(x, y) = \dfrac{xy}{5}$, $(x, y) = (1, 1), (2, 2)$ $f_{X,Y|2}(x, y) = \dfrac{xy}{8}$, $(x, y) = (1, 2), (2, 1), (2, 2)$

3.9.7 $p_{X|z}(x) = \dfrac{\dbinom{n}{x}\dbinom{n}{z - x}}{\dbinom{2n}{z}}$, which is a hypergeometric pdf.

3.9.9   (a) 0.462   **(b)** 0, since the joint pdf is defined with y always larger than x **(c)** $f_{Y|x}(y) = e^x e^{-y}$, $0 < x < y$

3.9.11 $f_{Y|x}(y) = \dfrac{1}{1 - x}$, $0 < y < 1 - x$. For each x, the conditional pdf does not depend on y, so it is uniform.

3.9.13   (a) $f_X(x) = \dfrac{4}{5}x + \dfrac{3}{5}$, $0 < x < 1$ **(b)** $f_{Y|x}(y) = \dfrac{4x + 6y}{4x + 3}$, $0 < y < 1$ **(c)** 10/20

3.9.15   4/9   **3.9.17   (a)** $f_X(x) = \dfrac{6}{7}(2x^2 + x)$, $0 < x < 1$ **(b)** 27/224   **(c)** 55/92

Section 3.10

3.10.1   −0.144668

3.10.3   Rule A: Expected value = −49/15. Rule B: Expected value = −47/15. Neither game is fair to the player, but Rule B has the better payoff.

3.10.5   The expected number of minorities is 40.0.   **3.10.7   (a)** 1/4   **(b)** e^{-2y} **(c)** 1   **(d)** 1

3.10.9 $E(Y) = (a + b)/2$ **3.10.11** $E(X) = \displaystyle\sum_{k=1}^{20} k\binom{200}{k}0.80^k 0.20^{200-k}$ $E(X) = 200(0.80) = 160$

3.10.13   \$307,421.92   **3.10.15**

Word length, k	No. of occurrences	$p_X(k)$
1	1	1/18
2	4	4/18
3	7	7/18
4	4	4/18
5	0	0
6	1	1/18
7	1	1/18

$E(X) = 59/18$

3.10.17   1/3   **3.10.19   (a)** $c/(2 - c)$ **(b)** $2\log 2$ **3.10.21**   2

3.10.23   Let X = number of drawings to obtain a white chip, and let $p_X(k) = P$(first white is obtained on kth draw). Then $E(X) = \displaystyle\sum_{k=1}^{\infty} k \cdot p_X(k) = 1 \cdot \dfrac{1}{2} + 2 \cdot \dfrac{1}{2}\dfrac{1}{3} + 3 \cdot \dfrac{1}{2}\dfrac{2}{3}\dfrac{1}{4} + \ldots =$
$\dfrac{1}{2} + \dfrac{1}{3} + \dfrac{1}{4} + \ldots$ But the latter is a harmonic series, which diverges, so $E(X)$ does not exist.

3.10.25 $E(X) = \displaystyle\sum_{j=1}^{\infty} jf_x(j) = \sum_{j=1}^{\infty}\sum_{k=1}^{j} f_x(j) = \sum_{k=1}^{\infty}\sum_{j=k}^{\infty} f_x(j) = \sum_{k=1}^{\infty} P(X \geq k)$

3.10.27 $E(Y|X = x) = \dfrac{3x + 2}{6x + 3}$

Section 3.11

3.11.1 2   **3.11.3** $(n/8)(p - q)$ **3.11.5** 36   **3.11.7** 1/10   **3.11.9** 1.5 in^3
3.11.11 For the graph pictured to be a pdf, $t = 4$ and $f_Y(y) = y/8$. Then $E(Y^2) = 8$.
3.11.13 $2/(n + 1)$ **3.11.15** 2   **3.11.17** 1/4   **3.11.19** 12.25

Section 3.12

3.12.1 12/25   **3.12.3** 0.748   **3.12.5** 3/80   **3.12.7** 1.115
3.12.9 Johnny should pick $(a + b)/2$.
3.12.11 $E[(X - a)^2] = E[((X - \mu) + (\mu - a))^2] = E[(X - \mu)^2] + E[(\mu - a)^2] +$
$2(\mu - a)E(X - \mu) = \text{Var}(X) + (\mu - a)^2$. This is minimized when $a = \mu$, so the minimum value of
$g(a) = \text{Var}(X)$.

Section 3.13

3.13.1 **(1)** $E[(W - \mu)/\sigma] = (1/\sigma)E[(W - \mu)] = 0$
       (2) $\text{Var}[(W - \mu)/\sigma] = (1/\sigma^2)\text{Var}[(W - \mu)] = (1/\sigma^2)\sigma^2 = 1$
3.13.3 1,000,000/3   **3.13.5** $4np_X + 6mp_Y$; $16np_X(1 - p_X) + 36mp_Y(1 - p_Y)$
3.13.7 The proof of Theorem 3.13.2 demonstrated the case $n = 2$. Now suppose the theorem is true for
$n - 1$. $\text{Var}(W_1 + W_2 + \ldots W_n) = \text{Var}[(W_1 + W_2 + \ldots W_{n-1}) + W_n] = \text{Var}(W_1 + W_2 + \ldots W_{n-1}) + \text{Var}(W_n)$
by the proof of the theorem. By the induction hypothesis, $\text{Var}(W_1 + W_2 + \ldots W_{n-1}) = \text{Var}(W_1) +$
$\text{Var}(W_2) + \ldots + \text{Var}(W_{n-1})$. Thus, $\text{Var}(W_1 + W_2 + \ldots + W_n) = \text{Var}(W_1) + \text{Var}(W_2) + \ldots + \text{Var}(W_{n-1})$
$+ \text{Var}(W_n)$, which was to be shown.

3.13.9 33.178; 8.294   **3.13.11** $\dfrac{1}{2}\sqrt{\mu_h^2\sigma_a^2 + \mu_h^2\sigma_b^2 + (\mu_a + \mu_b)^2\sigma_h^2}$

Section 3.14

3.14.1 **(a)** $e^{-3} = 0.050$ **(b)** 0.25   **3.14.3** Hint: $P(Y < 52 \text{ or } X > 148) = P(|Y - 100| > 48)$

Section 3.15

3.15.1 $\dfrac{2^r}{r + 1}$; 1/7   **3.15.3** Yes, it is possible if $E(W^2) = 5/3$.   **3.15.5** **(a)** 5   **(b)** the fourth

Section 3.16

3.16.1 $M_X(t) = \displaystyle\sum_{k=1}^{\infty} e^{tk}p(1 - p)^{k-1} = pe^t \sum_{k=1}^{\infty} e^{t(k-1)}(1 - p)^{k-1}$

$= pe^t \displaystyle\sum_{k=0}^{\infty} e^{tk}(1 - p)^k = pe^t \dfrac{1}{1 - e^t(1 - p)}$

$= pe^t \dfrac{1}{1 - qe^t}, \quad 0 < qe^t < 1$

3.16.3 $\dfrac{1}{3^{10}}(2 + e^3)^{10}$ **3.16.5** $M_X(t) = \displaystyle\int_{-1}^{2} e^{tx}\dfrac{1}{3}\,dx = \dfrac{1}{3t}e^{tx}\Big|_{-1}^{2} = \dfrac{1}{3t}(e^{2t} - e^{-t})$ for $t \neq 0$.

$$M_X(0) = \lim_{t\to 0}\frac{1}{3t}\left(e^{2t} - e^{-t}\right) = \lim_{t\to 0}\frac{\dfrac{d}{dt}\left(e^{2t} - e^{-t}\right)}{\dfrac{d}{dt}\,3t}\text{ by L'Hospital's rule. Thus, } M_X(0) = \lim_{t\to 0}\frac{\left(2e^{2t} + e^{-t}\right)}{3} = 1$$

3.16.7 $M_X(t) = e^{\lambda(e^t - 1)}$

3.16.9 $M_X^{(1)}(t) = \dfrac{d}{dt}\,e^{-\lambda + \lambda e^t} = \lambda e^t e^{-\lambda + \lambda e^t}$, so $E(X) = M_X^{(1)}(0) = \lambda;\, M_X^{(2)}(t) = e^{-\lambda + \lambda e^t}\left(\lambda e^t\right)^2 +$
$e^{-\lambda + \lambda e^t}\lambda e^t$, so $E(X^2) = M_X^{(2)}(0) = \lambda^2 + \lambda$. Then $\text{Var}(X) = E(X^2) - E^2(X) = \left(\lambda^2 + \lambda\right) - \lambda^2 = \lambda$.

3.16.11 $M_X^{(1)}(t) = \dfrac{d}{dt}\,e^{at + b^2 t^2 / 2} = \left(a + b^2 t\right)e^{at + b^2 t^2 / 2}$, so $M_X^{(1)}(0) = a$
$M_X^{(2)}(t) = \left(a + b^2 t\right)^2 e^{at + b^2 t^2 / 2} + b^2 e^{at + b^2 t^2 / 2}$, so
$M_X^{(2)}(0) = a^2 + b^2$. Then $\text{Var}(X) = \left(a^2 + b^2\right) - a^2 = b^2$.

3.16.13 9   **3.16.15** 2   **3.16.17** 0.104   **3.16.19** 0.059

3.16.21 (a) Yes. It is normal with mean 3μ and variance $9\sigma^2$.   (b) Yes. It is normal with mean $3\mu + 1$ and variance $9\sigma^2$.

CHAPTER 4

Section 4.2

4.2.1 Binomial answer: 0.158;   Poisson approximation: 0.158. The agreement is not surprising because $n(= 6000)$ is so large and $p(= 1/3250)$ is so small.

4.2.3 0.602

4.2.5 For both the binomial formula and the Poisson approximation, $P(X \geq 1) = 0.10$. The exact model that applies here is the hypergeometric, rather than the binomial, because $p = P(i\text{th item must be checked})$ is a function of the previous $i - 1$ items purchased. However, the variation in p is likely to be so small that the binomial and hypergeometric distributions in this case are essentially the same.

4.2.7 0.122   **4.2.9** 6.9×10^{-12}

4.2.11 The Poisson model $p_X(k) = e^{-0.435}(0.435)^k/k!$, $k = 0, 1, \ldots$ fits the data fairly well. The expected frequencies corresponding to $k = 0, 1, 2$, and 3+ are 230.3, 100.4, 21.7, and 3.6, respectively.

4.2.13 (a) The model $p_X(k) = e^{-2.157}(2.157)^k/k!$, $k = 0, 1, \ldots$ fits the data fairly well, but there does appear to be a slight tendency for deaths to "cluster"—that is, the values 0, 5, 6, 7, 8, and 9 are all over-represented (as the table shows).

No. of deaths, k	Obs. freq.	$p_X(k) = e^{-2.157}(2.157)^k/k!$	Exp. freq.
0	162	0.1157	126.8
1	267	0.2495	273.5
2	271	0.2691	294.9
3	185	0.1935	212.1
4	111	0.1043	114.3
5	61	0.0450	49.3
6	27	0.0162	17.8
7	8	0.0050	5.5
8	3	0.0013	1.4
9	1	0.0003	0.3
10	0	0.0001	0.1

(b) Deaths may not be independent events, and the fatality rate may not be constant.

4.2.15 0.783   **4.2.17** 0.301

4.2.19 $P(3$ in two minutes$) = e^{-8.034}(8.034)^3/3! = 0.028;$ also, $P(3$ in two minutes$) = 2 \cdot P(X = 0) \cdot P(X = 3) + 2 \cdot P(X = 1) \cdot P(X = 2) = 0.028$, where $\lambda = 4.017$.

4.2.21 0.09

4.2.23 $p_{X_1|x}(x_1) = P(X_1 = x_1 | X = x) = \dfrac{P(X_1 = x_1 \text{ and } X_2 = x - x_1)}{P(X = x)}$

$$= \frac{e^{-2}2^{x_1}/x_1! \cdot e^{-2}2^{x-x_1}/(x - x_1)!}{e^{-4}4^x/x!} = \binom{x}{x_1}(\tfrac{1}{2})^{x}(1 - \tfrac{1}{2})^{x-x_1}$$

4.2.25 **(a)** Yes, because the Poisson assumptions are probably satisfied—crashes are independent events and the crash rate is likely to remain constant.   **(b)** 0.24   **(c)** 0.47   **4.2.27** 0.29

Section 4.3

4.3.1 **(a)** 0.5782   **(b)** 0.8264   **(c)** 0.9306   **(d)** 0.0000

4.3.3 **(a)** Both are the same   **(b)** $\displaystyle\int_{a-\frac{1}{2}}^{a+\frac{1}{2}} \frac{1}{\sqrt{2\pi}} e^{-z^2/2}\, dz$

4.3.5 **(a)** −0.44   **(b)** 0.76   **(c)** 0.41   **(d)** 1.28   **(e)** 0.95

4.3.7 **(a)** $\displaystyle\sum_{k=241}^{260} \binom{260}{k}(0.90)^k(0.10)^{260-k}$ **(b)** 0.0901   **4.3.9** **(a)** 0.0053   **(b)** 0.0197

4.3.11 $P(X \geq 344) \doteq P(Z \geq 13.25) = 0.0000$, which strongly discredits the hypothesis that people die randomly with respect to their birthdays.

4.3.13 No, the normal approximation is inappropriate because the values of $n(= 10)$ and $p(= 0.7)$ fail to satisfy Condition (2) specified in the Comment on p. 268.

4.3.15 **(a)** 0   **(b)** 0.5646   **4.3.17** 0.1151   **4.3.19** 0.0694

4.3.21 No, only 84% of drivers are likely to get at least 25,000 miles on the tires.

4.3.23 0.0228   **4.3.25** **(a)** 6.68%; 15.87%   **4.3.27** 434   **4.3.29** 29.85

4.3.31 0.0062. The "0.095%" driver should ask to take the test twice; the "0.11%" driver has a greater chance of not being charged by taking the test only once. As n, the number of times the test is taken, increases, the precision of the average reading increases. It is to the sober driver's advantage to have a reading as precise as possible; the opposite is true for the drunk driver.

4.3.33 Since $Z = \dfrac{Y - \mu}{\sigma}, Y = \mu + \sigma Z$. From Theorem 3.16.3, $M_Y(t) = e^{\mu t}M_Z(\sigma t) = e^{\mu t} \cdot e^{\sigma^2 t^2/2} = e^{\mu t + \sigma^2 t^2/2}$, but the latter is the moment-generating function for a normal random variable with mean μ and variance σ^2.

4.3.35 $M_Y^{(1)}(t) = e^{\mu t + \sigma^2 t^2/2} \cdot [\mu + \sigma^2 t]$ and $M_Y^{(2)}(t) = e^{\mu t + \sigma^2 t^2/2} \cdot \sigma^2 + e^{\mu t + \sigma^2 t^2/2}[\mu + \sigma^2 t]^2$. Therefore, $E(Y) = M_Y^{(1)}(0) = \mu$ and $\text{Var}(Y) = M_Y^{(2)}(0) - [M_Y^{(1)}(0)]^2 = \sigma^2 + \mu^2 - \mu^2 = \sigma^2$.

4.3.37 2663   **4.3.39** 2.28%

Section 4.4

4.4.1   0.343

4.4.3   No, the expected frequencies $\big(= 50 \cdot p_X(k)\big)$ differ considerably from the observed frequencies, especially for small values of k. The observed number of 1's, for example, is 4, while the expected number is 12.5.

4.4.5 $F_X(t) = P(X \le t) = p \sum\limits_{s=0}^{[t]} (1-p)^s$. But $\sum\limits_{s=0}^{[t]} (1-p)^s = \dfrac{1 - (1-p)^{[t]}}{1 - (1-p)} = \dfrac{1 - (1-p)^{[t]}}{p}$, and the result follows.

4.4.7   No, because $M_X(t) = M_{X_1}(t) \cdot M_{X_2}(t)$ does not have the form of a geometric moment-generating function.

4.4.9 $p_{X^*}(k) = (1-p)^k p,\ k = 0, 1, 2, \ldots;\ M_{X^*}(t) = \sum\limits_{k=0}^{\infty} (1-p)^k p e^{tk} = p \sum\limits_{k=0}^{\infty} \big[(1-p)e^t\big]^k = $

$\dfrac{p}{1 - (1-p)e^t}$. Let X denote the geometric random variable defined in Theorem 4.4.1. Then $X^* = X - 1$,

and $M_{X^*}(t) = e^{-t} M_X(t) = e^{-t} \cdot \dfrac{p e^t}{1 - (1-p)e^t} = \dfrac{p}{1 - (1-p)e^t}$.

Section 4.5

4.5.1   0.029

4.5.3   Probably not. The presumed model, $p_X(k) = \binom{k-1}{1}(\tfrac{1}{2})^2(\tfrac{1}{2})^{k-2},\ k = 2, 3, \ldots$ fits the data almost perfectly, as the table shows. Agreement this good is often an indication that the data have been fabricated.

k	$p_X(k)$	Obs. freq.	Exp. freq.
2	1/4	24	25
3	2/8	26	25
4	3/16	19	19
5	4/32	13	12
6	5/64	8	8
7	6/128	5	5
8	7/256	3	3
9	8/512	1	2
10	9/1024	1	1

4.5.5   Let Y denote the number of trials to get the rth success, and let X denote the number of trials in excess of r to get the rth success. Then $X = Y - r$. Substituting into Theorem 4.5.1 gives
$$p_X(k) = \binom{k+r-1}{r-1} p^r (1-p)^k = \binom{k+r-1}{k} p^r (1-p)^k, \quad k = 0, 1, 2, \ldots.$$

4.5.7 $M_X^{(1)}(t) = r\left[\dfrac{p e^t}{1 - (1-p)e^t}\right]^{r-1} \big[p e^t [1 - (1-p)e^t]^{-2} (1-p)e^t + [1 - (1-p)e^t]^{-1} p e^t \big]$. When

$t = 0,\ M_X^{(1)}(0) = E(X) = r\left[\dfrac{p(1-p)}{p^2} + \dfrac{p}{p}\right] = \dfrac{r}{p}$.

4.5.9 $E(X) = \sum_{k=r}^{\infty} k \binom{k-1}{r-1} p^r (1-p)^{k-r} = \frac{r}{p} \sum_{k=r}^{\infty} \binom{k}{r} p^{r+1}(1-p)^{k-r} = \frac{r}{p}.$

Section 4.6

4.6.1 Consider the integral $Q = \int_0^{\infty} \lambda^r y^{r-1} e^{-\lambda y} \, dy$. Let $u = \lambda y$, so $du = \lambda \, dy$. Then $Q = \int_0^{\infty} u^{r-1} e^{-u} \, du$.

If r is a positive integer, $Q = (r-1)!$. Therefore, $\int_0^{\infty} \frac{\lambda^r}{(r-1)!} y^{r-1} e^{-\lambda y} \, dy = 1$.

4.6.3 The 11 Y_i's comprising Y are exponential random variables, each of which is sharply skewed. In general, the convergence of sums of skewed random variables to the standard normal is slower than it is for variables whose distributions are more nearly symmetric.

4.6.5 $E(Y^m) = \int_0^{\infty} y^m \cdot \frac{\lambda^r}{(r-1)!} y^{r-1} e^{-\lambda y} \, dy = \int_0^{\infty} \frac{\lambda^r}{(r-1)!} y^{m+r-1} e^{-\lambda y} \, dy$

$= \frac{(m+r-1)!}{\lambda^m (r-1)!} \int_0^{\infty} \frac{\lambda^{m+r}}{(m+r-1)!} y^{m+r-1} e^{-\lambda y} \, dy = \frac{(m+r-1)!}{\lambda^m (r-1)!}.$

4.6.7 (a) $\Gamma(1) = \int_0^{\infty} e^{-y} \, dy = -e^{-y} \Big|_0^{\infty} = 1.$

(b) $\Gamma(r+1) = \int_0^{\infty} y^r e^{-y} \, dy$. Let $u = y^r$ and $dv = e^{-y} \, dy$. Integrating by parts shows that

$\Gamma(r+1) = r \int_0^{\infty} y^{r-1} e^{-y} \, dy$, but the latter is $r\Gamma(r)$.

(c) Let Z be a standard normal random variable. Then $E(Z^2) = \frac{1}{\sqrt{2\pi}} \int_{-\infty}^{\infty} z^2 e^{-z^2/2} \, dz =$

$\sqrt{\frac{2}{\pi}} \int_0^{\infty} z^2 e^{-z^2/2} \, dz = 1$. Let $y = z^2$. Then $E(Z^2) = \frac{2}{\sqrt{\pi}} \Gamma\left(1 + \frac{1}{2}\right) = \frac{2}{\sqrt{\pi}} \left(\frac{1}{2}\right)\Gamma\left(\frac{1}{2}\right)$, which implies that $\Gamma\left(\frac{1}{2}\right) = \sqrt{\pi}.$

CHAPTER 5

Section 5.2

5.2.1 5/8 **5.2.3** 0.122 **5.2.5** 0.733 **5.2.7** 1.69 **5.2.9** (a) 14.2 (b) $\hat{\theta}_1 = 1.8, \hat{\theta}_2 = 14.2$

5.2.11 $1/y_{\max}$ **5.2.13** $\frac{1}{n} \sum_{i=1}^{n} (y_i - \mu)^2$ **5.2.15** $2\bar{y}/(1-\bar{y})$ **5.2.17** $1/\bar{y}$

5.2.19 (a) Method of Moments estimate: $\bar{y}/(\bar{y} - k)$ (b) MLE: $\dfrac{n}{\displaystyle\sum_{i=1}^{n} \ln y_i - n \ln k}$

5.2.21 Method of Moments estimates are the same as the "MLE's"; $\hat{\mu} = \bar{y}$, $\hat{\sigma}^2 = \dfrac{1}{n} \sum_{i=1}^{n} (y_i - \bar{y})^2$

5.2.23 0.479

x	Observed frequency	Expected frequency
1	132	119.8
2	52	62.4
3	34	32.5
4	9	16.9
5	7	8.8
6	5	4.6
7	5	2.4
≥ 8	6	2.6

Section 5.3

5.3.1 Confidence interval is $(0.726, 0.807)$; the value of 0.80 is believable.   **5.3.3** 336   **5.3.5** 0.501

5.3.7 The interval given is correctly *calculated*. However, the data do not appear to be normal, so claiming that it is a 95% confidence interval would not be correct.   **5.3.9** $(0.316, 0.396)$

5.3.11 Budweiser would use the sample proportion 0.54 alone as the estimate. Schlitz would construct the 95% confidence interval $(0.36, 0.56)$ to claim that values < 0.50 are believable.

5.3.13 16,641   **5.3.15** Both intervals have confidence level approximately 50%.

5.3.17 The margin of error is correct at the 95% level. For the given data, estimates of the percentage as small as $0.30 - 0.031 = 0.269$ or as large as $0.30 + 0.031 = 0.331$ are believable.

5.3.19 In Definition 5.3.1, substitute $d = \dfrac{1.96}{2\sqrt{n}}\sqrt{\dfrac{N-n}{N-1}}$

5.3.21 For margin of error 0.06, $n = 267$. For margin of error 0.03, $n = 1068$.

5.3.23 The first case requires $n = 421$; the second, $n = 479$.   **5.3.25** 1024

Section 5.4

5.4.1 2/10   **5.4.3** 0.1841

5.4.5 **(a)** $E(\bar{X}) = E\left(\dfrac{1}{n}\sum_{i=1}^{n} X_i\right) = \dfrac{1}{n}\sum_{i=1}^{n} E(X_i) = \dfrac{1}{n}\sum_{i=1}^{n} \lambda = \lambda$ **(b)** In general, the sample mean is an unbiased estimator of the mean μ.

5.4.7 **(a)** The unbiased estimator is $\dfrac{5}{3}Y_3'$.   **(b)** 30   **(c)** Suppose the sample were 10, 14, 18, 31. The estimate for θ is 30, but the largest observation, 31, falls outside of the $[0,30]$ interval.

5.4.9 $3Y^2$ **5.4.11** The median of $\hat{\theta}$ is $\dfrac{\theta(n+1)}{n\sqrt[n]{2}}$, so the estimator is unbiased only when $n = 1$.

5.4.13 $\hat{\theta}_n = \dfrac{1}{n}\sum_{i=1}^{n}(Y_i - \bar{Y})^2$, so $E(\hat{\theta}_n) = \dfrac{n-1}{n}\sigma^2$. This estimator is asymptotically unbiased since

$\lim_{n\to\infty} E(\hat{\theta}_n) = \lim_{n\to\infty} \dfrac{n-1}{n}\sigma^2 = \sigma^2.$

5.4.15 $\text{Var}\left(\dfrac{6}{5}\cdot Y_{\max}\right) = \dfrac{\theta^2}{35}$, by example 5.4.7. By symmetry, $\text{Var}(Y_{\min}) = \text{Var}(Y_{\max}) = \dfrac{25}{36}\dfrac{\theta^2}{35} = \dfrac{5\theta^2}{252}$.
Thus, $\text{Var}(6\cdot Y_{\min}) = \dfrac{5\theta^2}{7}$, so $\dfrac{6}{5}\cdot Y_{\max}$ has smaller variance. This result makes sense intuitively, since $\text{Var}(Y_{\min}) = \text{Var}(Y_{\max})$. Thus, efficiency depends on the size of the constant needed to make the estimator unbiased.   **5.4.17** $1/n$

Section 5.5

5.5.1 $E(\hat{\theta}) = \dfrac{3}{2}E(\bar{Y}) = \dfrac{3}{2}E(Y) = \dfrac{3}{2}\left(\dfrac{2}{3}\theta\right) = \theta$

5.5.3 $\text{Var}(\hat{\lambda}) = \lambda/n$. The Cramer-Rao bound is the same: $\left[-n\left(-\dfrac{1}{\lambda}\right)\right]^{-1} = \lambda/n$

5.5.5 The Cramer-Rao bound is $\dfrac{\theta^2}{n}$. $\text{Var}(\hat{\theta}) = \dfrac{\theta^2}{n(n+2)}$, which is smaller than the Cramer-Rao bound.
This occurs because Theorem 5.5.1 is not necessarily valid if the range of the pdf depends on the parameter.

5.5.7 $E\left(\dfrac{\partial^2 \ln f_W(w;\theta)}{\partial\theta^2}\right) = \displaystyle\int_{-\infty}^{\infty} \dfrac{\partial}{\partial\theta}\left(\dfrac{\partial \ln f_W(w;\theta)}{\partial\theta}\right)f_W(w;\theta)\,dw$

$= \displaystyle\int_{-\infty}^{\infty}\dfrac{\partial}{\partial\theta}\left(\dfrac{1}{f_W(w;\theta)}\dfrac{\partial f_W(w;\theta)}{\partial\theta}\right)f_W(w;\theta)\,dw$

$= \displaystyle\int_{-\infty}^{\infty}\left[\dfrac{1}{f_W(w;\theta)}\dfrac{\partial^2 f_W(w;\theta)}{\partial\theta^2} - \dfrac{1}{(f_W(w;\theta))^2}\left(\dfrac{\partial f_W(w;\theta)}{\partial\theta}\right)^2\right]f_W(w;\theta)\,dw$

$= \displaystyle\int_{-\infty}^{\infty}\dfrac{\partial^2 f_W(w;\theta)}{\partial\theta^2}\,dw - \int_{-\infty}^{\infty}\dfrac{1}{(f_W(w;\theta))^2}\left(\dfrac{\partial f_W(w;\theta)}{\partial\theta}\right)^2 f_W(w;\theta)\,dw$

$= 0 - \displaystyle\int_{-\infty}^{\infty}\left(\dfrac{\partial \ln f_W(w;\theta)}{\partial\theta}\right)^2 f_W(w;\theta)\,dw$

The 0 occurs because $1 = \displaystyle\int_{-\infty}^{\infty} f_W(w;\theta)\,dw$, so

$$0 = \dfrac{\partial^2 \displaystyle\int_{-\infty}^{\infty} f_W(w;\theta)\,dw}{\partial\theta^2} = \int_{-\infty}^{\infty}\dfrac{\partial^2 f_W(w;\theta)}{\partial\theta^2}\,dw$$

The above argument shows that

$$E\left(\dfrac{\partial^2 \ln f_W(w;\theta)}{\partial\theta^2}\right) = -E\left(\dfrac{\partial \ln f_W(w;\theta)}{\partial\theta}\right)^2$$

Multiplying both sides of the equality by n and inverting gives the desired equality.

Section 5.6

5.6.1   We already know that $\sum_{i=1}^{n} X_i$ is Poisson with parameter $n\lambda$. Thus, $f_{\bar{x}}(\bar{x}; \lambda) = \dfrac{e^{-n\lambda}(n\lambda)^{n\bar{x}}}{(n\bar{x})!}$ by Theorem 3.7.1.

$$\prod_{i=1}^{n} \frac{e^{-\lambda}\lambda^{x_i}}{x_i!} = \frac{e^{\sum_{i=1}^{n} x_i - n\lambda}\lambda}{\prod_{i=1}^{n} x_i!} = \frac{e^{-n\lambda}\lambda^{n\bar{x}}n^{n\bar{x}}}{\left(\sum_{i=1}^{n} x_i\right)!} \cdot \frac{\left(\sum_{i=1}^{n} x_i\right)!}{\prod_{i=1}^{n} x_i! n^{n\bar{x}}}$$

$$= \frac{e^{-n\lambda}(n\lambda)^{n\bar{x}}}{(n\bar{x})!} \cdot \frac{\left(\sum_{i=1}^{n} x_i\right)!}{\prod_{i=1}^{n} x_i! n^{n\bar{x}}} = f_{\bar{x}}(\bar{x}; \lambda)s(x_1, x_2, \dots, x_n)$$

By Theorem 5.6.1, $\bar{X}$ is sufficient.

5.6.3 $P\big((1, 1, 0) \,|\, X_1 + 2X_2 + 3X_3 = 3\big)$

$$= \frac{P\big((1, 1, 0) \text{ and } X_1 + 2X_2 + 3X_3 = 3\big)}{P\big(X_1 + 2X_2 + 3X_3 = 3\big)}$$

$$= \frac{P(1, 1, 0)}{P\big((1, 1, 0), (0, 0, 1)\big)} = \frac{p^2(1 - p)}{p^2(1 - p) + p(1 - p)^2} = p.$$

Since the conditional probability does depend on the parameter p, the statistic cannot be sufficient, by Definition 5.6.1.

5.6.5 $\displaystyle\prod_{i=1}^{n} p_X(x_i; p) = \prod_{i=1}^{n} (1 - p)^{x_i} p = (1 - p)^{\left(\sum_{i=1}^{n} x_i\right) - n} p^n$

Let $g\left(\displaystyle\sum_{i=1}^{n} x_i; p\right) = (1 - p)^{\left(\sum_{i=1}^{n} x_i\right) - n} p^n$ and $u(x_1, \dots, x_n) = 1$.

By Theorem 5.6.2, the statistic $\displaystyle\sum_{i=1}^{n} X_i$ is sufficient.

5.6.7 $L = \displaystyle\prod_{i=1}^{n} f_Y(y_i; \theta) = \prod_{i=1}^{n} \theta\, y_i^{\theta - 1}$, and

$$\ln L = n \cdot \ln \theta + (\theta - 1) \sum_{i=1}^{n} \ln y_i$$

$$\frac{d \ln L}{d\theta} = \frac{n}{\theta} \ln \theta + \sum_{i=1}^{n} \ln y_i$$

Setting $\dfrac{d \ln L}{d\theta} = 0$ gives $\hat{\theta} = \dfrac{-n}{\displaystyle\sum_{i=1}^{n} \ln y_i} = \dfrac{-n}{\ln\left(\displaystyle\prod_{i=1}^{n}\right) y_i}$, which is a function of $\displaystyle\prod_{i=1}^{n} y_i$.

5.6.9 $\lambda e^{-\lambda y} = e^{\ln \lambda - \lambda y} = e^{y(-\lambda) + \ln \lambda}$. Take $K(y) = y$, $p(\lambda) = -\lambda$, $S(y) = 0$, and $q(\lambda) = \ln \lambda$. Then $\hat{\theta} = \sum_{i=1}^{n} K(y_i) = \sum_{i=1}^{n} y_i$ is sufficient.

Section 5.7

5.7.1 17

5.7.3 (a) $P(Y_1 > 2\lambda) = \int_{2\lambda}^{\infty} \lambda e^{-\lambda y} dy = e^{-2\lambda^2}$.   Then $P(|Y_1 - \lambda| < \lambda/2) < 1 - e^{-2\lambda^2} < 1$.   Thus, $\lim_{n \to \infty} P(|Y_1 - \lambda| < \lambda/2) < 1$.

(b) $P\left(\sum_{i=1}^{n} Y_i > 2\lambda \right) \geq P(Y_1 > 2\lambda) = e^{-2\lambda^2}$. The proof now proceeds along the lines of Part (a).

5.7.5 $E[(Y_{\max} - \theta)^2] = \int_0^{\theta} (y - \theta)^2 \frac{n}{\theta} \left(\frac{y}{\theta} \right)^{n-1} dy$

$$= \frac{n}{\theta^n} \int_0^{\theta} (y^{n+1} - 2\theta y^n + \theta^2 y^{n-1}) dy = \frac{n}{\theta^n} \left(\frac{\theta^{n+2}}{n+2} - \frac{2\theta^{n+2}}{n+1} + \frac{\theta^{n+2}}{n} \right)$$

$$= \left(\frac{n}{n+2} - \frac{2n}{n+1} + 1 \right) \theta^2$$

Then $\lim_{n \to \infty} E[(Y_{\max} - \theta)^2] = \lim_{n \to \infty} \left(\frac{n}{n+2} - \frac{2n}{n+1} + 1 \right) \theta^2 = 0$, and the estimator is squared error consistent.

CHAPTER 6

Section 6.2

6.2.1 (a) Reject H_0 if $\dfrac{\bar{y} - 120}{18/\sqrt{25}} \leq -1.41$; $z = -1.61$; reject H_0.   (b) Reject H_0 if $\dfrac{\bar{y} - 42.9}{3.2/\sqrt{16}}$ is either 1) ≤ -2.58 or 2) ≥ 2.58; $z = 2.75$; reject H_0.   (c) Reject H_0 if $\dfrac{\bar{y} - 14.2}{4.1/\sqrt{9}} \geq 1.13$; $z = 1.17$; reject H_0.

6.2.3 (a) No   (b) Yes   **6.2.5** No

6.2.7 (a) H_0 should be rejected if $\dfrac{\bar{y} - 12.6}{0.4/\sqrt{30}}$ is either 1) ≤ -1.96 or 2) ≥ 1.96. But $\bar{y} = 12.76$ and $z = 2.19$, suggesting that the machine should be readjusted.   (b) The test assumes that the y_i's constitute a random sample from a normal distribution. Graphed, a histogram of the 30 y_i's shows a mostly bell-shaped pattern. There is no reason to suspect that the normality assumption is not being met.

6.2.9 P-value $= P(Z \leq -0.92) + P(Z \geq 0.92) = 0.3576$; H_0 would be rejected if α had been set at any value greater than or equal to 0.3576.

6.2.11 H_0 should be rejected if $\dfrac{\bar{y} - 145.75}{9.50/\sqrt{25}}$ is 1) ≤ -1.96 or 2) ≥ 1.96. Here, $\bar{y} = 149.75$ and $z = 2.10$, so the difference between \$145.75 and \$149.75 *is* statistically significant.

Section 6.3

6.3.1 (a) $z = 0.91$, which is not larger than $z_{.05}(= 1.64)$, so H_0 would not be rejected. These data do not provide convincing evidence that transmitting predator sounds helps to reduce the number of whales in fishing waters.   **(b)** P-value $= P(Z \geq 0.91) = 0.1814$; H_0 would be rejected for any $\alpha \geq 0.1814$.

6.3.3 $z = \dfrac{72 - 120(0.65)}{\sqrt{120(0.65)(0.35)}} = -1.15$, which is not less than $-z_{.05}(= -1.64)$, so H_0: $p = 0.65$ would not be rejected.

6.3.5 Let $p = P(Y_i \leq 0.69315)$. Test H_0: $p = \frac{1}{2}$ versus H_1: $p \neq \frac{1}{2}$. Given that $x = 26$ and $n = 60$, the P-value $= P(X \leq 26) + P(X \geq 34) = 0.3030$.

6.3.7 Reject H_0 if $x \geq 4$ gives $\alpha = 0.50$; reject H_0 if $x \geq 5$ gives $\alpha = 0.23$; reject H_0 if $x \geq 6$ gives $\alpha = 0.06$; reject H_0 if $x \geq 7$ gives $\alpha = 0.01$.   **6.3.9 (a)** 0.07

Section 6.4

6.4.1 0.0735   **6.4.3** 0.3786   **6.4.5** 0.6293   **6.4.7** 95   **6.4.9** 0.23

6.4.11 $\alpha = 0.064$; $\beta = 0.107$. A Type I error (convicting an innocent defendant) would be considered more serious than a Type II error (acquitting a guilty defendant).

6.4.13 1.98   **6.4.15** $\sqrt[n]{0.95}$ **6.4.17** $1 - \beta = \left(\frac{1}{2}\right)^{\theta+1}$ **6.4.19** $\dfrac{7}{8}$ **6.4.21** 0.63

Section 6.5

6.5.1 $\lambda = \max\limits_{\omega} L(p)/\max\limits_{\Omega} L(p)$, where $\max\limits_{\omega} L(p) = p_0^n(1 - p_0)^{\sum\limits_{i=1}^{n} X_i - n}$ and

$$\max\limits_{\Omega} L(p) = \left(n\Big/\sum_{i=1}^{n} X_i\right)^n \left[1 - \left(n\Big/\sum_{i=1}^{n} X_i\right)\right]^{\sum\limits_{i=1}^{n} X_i - n}$$

6.5.3 $\lambda = \{(2\pi)^{-n/2} e^{-\frac{1}{2}\sum\limits_{i=1}^{n}(y_i - \mu_0)^2}\}/\{(2\pi)^{-n/2} e^{-\frac{1}{2}\sum\limits_{i=1}^{n}(y_i - \bar{y})^2}\} = e^{-\frac{1}{2}((\bar{y} - \mu_0)/(1/\sqrt{n}))^2}$.

Base the test on $z = (\bar{y} - \mu_0)/(1/\sqrt{n})$.

6.5.5 (a) $\lambda = \left(\frac{1}{2}\right)^n/\left[(x/n)^x(1 - x/n)^{n-x}\right] = 2^{-n}x^{-x}(n - x)^{x-n}n^n$. Rejecting H_0 when $0 < \lambda \leq \lambda^*$ is equivalent to rejecting H_0 when $x \ln x + (n - x)\ln(n - x) \geq \lambda^{**}$.
(b) By inspection, $x \ln x + (n - x)\ln(n - x)$ is symmetric in x. Therefore, the left-tail and right-tail critical regions will be equidistant from $p = \frac{1}{2}$, which implies that H_0 should be rejected if $|x - \frac{1}{2}| \geq k$, where k is a function of α.

CHAPTER 7

Section 7.2

7.2.1 (a) $\hat{\mu} = \bar{y} = 0.48$; $s^2 =$ unbiased estimate for $\sigma^2 = 0.058$

(b) $P(Y > 0.5) \doteq P\left(Z > \dfrac{0.5 - 0.48}{0.24}\right) = 0.4681$

7.2.3 93.2   **7.2.5** $f_Y(570) = 0.00246$; height of histogram $= 0.00226$

7.2.7 $\bar{y}_g = 146.4$, $s_g = 52.71$, and $P(Y \geq 99.5) = 0.8133$, so the expected frequency is 671.

7.2.9 Let $K(y) = (y - \mu)^2$, $p(\sigma) = -1/2\sigma^2$, $S(y) = 0$, and $q(\sigma) = -\ln(\sqrt{2\pi}\sigma)$; sufficient statistic $= \sum_{i=1}^{n}(y_i - \mu)^2$.

Section 7.3

7.3.1 **(a)** 23.685 **(b)** 4.605 **(c)** 2.700   **7.3.3** **(a)** 2.088 **(b)** 7.261 **(c)** 14.041 **(d)** 17.539   **7.3.5** 233.9

7.3.7 $M_{\chi_n^2}(t) = (1 - 2t)^{-n/2}$; $M_{\chi_n^2}^{(1)}(0) = E(\chi_n^2) = n$ and $M_{\chi_n^2}^{(2)}(0) - [M_{\chi_n^2}^{(1)}(0)]^2 = \text{Var}(\chi_n^2) = 2n$.

7.3.9 195   **7.3.11** 9

7.3.13 Since $E(S^2) = \sigma^2$, it follows from Chebyshev's inequality that $P(|S^2 - \sigma^2| < \varepsilon) > 1 - \dfrac{\text{Var}(S^2)}{\sigma^2}$.

But $\text{Var}(S^2) = \dfrac{2\sigma^4}{n-1} \to 0$ as $n \to \infty$. Therefore, S^2 is consistent for σ^2.   **7.3.15** $a = 5.49$; $b = 21.02$

7.3.17 Confidence intervals for σ (as opposed to σ^2) are often preferred by experimenters because they are expressed in the same units as the data, which makes them easier to interpret.

7.3.19 $H_0: \sigma^2 = 1.1$ should be rejected in favor of $H_1: \sigma^2 < 1.1$ if $\dfrac{5s^2}{1.1} \leq 1.145$. But $s^2 = 0.49$, and we fail to reject H_0.

7.3.21 **(a)** $M_Y(t) = \dfrac{1}{1 - \theta t}$. Let $X = \dfrac{2n\bar{Y}}{\theta} = \dfrac{2\sum_{i=1}^{n} Y_i}{\theta}$. Then $M_X(t) = \prod_{i=1}^{n} M_{Y_i}\left(\dfrac{2t}{\theta}\right) = \left(\dfrac{1}{1 - 2t}\right)^{2n/2}$,

implying that X is a χ_{2n}^2 random variable.

(b) $P\left(\chi_{\alpha/2,\, 2n}^2 < \dfrac{2n\bar{Y}}{\theta} < \chi_{1-\alpha/2,\, 2n}^2\right) = 1 - \alpha$, so $\left(\dfrac{2n\bar{y}}{\chi_{1-\alpha/2,\, 2n}^2}, \dfrac{2n\bar{y}}{\chi_{\alpha/2,\, 2n}^2}\right)$ is a $100(1 - \alpha)\%$ confidence interval for θ.

Section 7.4

7.4.1 **(a)** 0.983   **(b)** 0.132   **(c)** 9.00   **7.4.3** **(a)** 6.23   **(b)** 0.65   **(c)** 9   **(d)** 15   **(e)** 2.28

7.4.5 $F = \dfrac{U/m}{V/n}$, where U and V are independent χ^2 random variables with m and n degrees of freedom, respectively. Then $\dfrac{1}{F} = \dfrac{V/n}{U/m}$, which implies that $\dfrac{1}{F}$ has an F distribution with n and m degrees of freedom.

7.4.7 The 50 ratios constitute a random sample from an $F_{4,\, 4}$ distribution. The 10th, 50th, and 90th percentiles of the data are 0.32, 1.24, and 3.72, respectively. By comparison, $F_{.10,\, 4,\, 4} = 0.243$, $F_{.50,\, 4,\, 4} = 1.00$, and $F_{.90,\, 4,\, 4} = 4.11$.

7.4.9 From Question 7.4.8, $E\left(\dfrac{U}{V}\right) = \dfrac{m}{n-2}$. But $E(F_{m,\, n}) = E\left(\dfrac{U/m}{V/n}\right) = \dfrac{n}{m} E\left(\dfrac{U}{V}\right) = \dfrac{n}{n-2}$

(for $n > 2$).   **7.4.11** **(a)** 2.508   **(b)** –1.079   **(c)** 1.7056   **(d)** 4.3027

7.4.13 $(-1.397, 1.397)$; $(-1.8595, 1.8595)$ **7.4.15** $k(S) = \dfrac{2.8609 \cdot S}{\sqrt{20}}$ **7.4.17** $\pi/2$

Section 7.5

7.5.1 ($1164, $2495)

7.5.3 μ = true average daily fat intake of males in the age group 25 to 34; (93.80, 126.46)

7.5.5 Lowest annual return $\doteq \bar{y} - t_{.005, 29} \cdot s = 7.6$; highest annual return $\doteq \bar{y} + t_{.005, 29} \cdot s = 20.8$

7.5.7 No, because the length of a confidence interval for μ is a function of S as well as the confidence coefficient. If the sample standard deviation for the second sample was sufficiently small (relative to the sample standard deviation for the first sample), the 95% confidence interval would be shorter than the 90% confidence interval.

7.5.9 **(a)** 0.95   **(b)** 0.80   **(c)** 0.945   **(d)** 0.95

7.5.11 Obs. $t = -1.71$; $-t_{.05, 18} = -1.7341$; fail to reject H_0

7.5.13 Test $H_0: \mu = 40$ vs. $H_1: \mu < 40$; obs. $t = -2.25$; $-t_{.05, 14} = -1.7613$; reject H_0

7.5.15 Test $H_0: \mu = 0.0042$ vs. $H_1: \mu < 0.0042$; obs. $t = -2.48$; $-t_{.05, 9} = -1.8331$; reject H_0

7.5.17 Because of the skewed shape of $f_Y(y)$, and if the sample size were small, it would not be unusual for all the y_i's to lie close together near 0. When that happens, $\bar{y}$ will be less than μ, s will be considerably smaller than $E(S)$, and the t ratio will be further to the left of 0 than $f_{T_{n-1}}(t)$ would predict.

7.5.19 $f_Z(z)$ **7.5.21** 32   **7.5.23** **(a)** 7   **(b)** 11   **7.5.25** $1 - \beta = 0.60$

CHAPTER 8

Section 8.2

8.2.1 Paired data   **8.2.3** Categorical data   **8.2.5** Two-sample data

8.2.7 Two-sample data   **8.2.9** Paired data   **8.2.11** Randomized block data

8.2.13 One-sample data   **8.2.15** Paired data   **8.2.17** Paired data   **8.2.19** k-sample data

8.2.21 Randomized block data   **8.2.23** Regression data   **8.2.25** Randomized block data

CHAPTER 9

Section 9.2

9.2.1 Since $-t_{.05, 19} = -1.7291 < t = -1.68$, accept H_0.

9.2.3 Since $t = 3.37 > 2.9208 = t_{.005, 16}$, reject H_0.

9.2.5 Since $t = 0.96 < t_{.05, 14} = 1.7613$, accept H_0.

9.2.7 Since $t = -4.55 < -t_{.05, 148} = -z_{.05} = -1.64$, reject H_0.

9.2.9 **(a)** 22.9   **(b)** 166.97   **9.2.11** **(a)** 0.3974   **(b)** 0.2090

9.2.13 $E(S_X^2) = E(S_Y^2) = \sigma^2$ by Example 5.4.4.

$$E(S_P^2) = \frac{(n-1)E(S_X^2) + (m-1)E(S_Y^2)}{n+m-2}$$

$$= \frac{(n-1)\sigma^2 + (m-1)\sigma^2}{n+m-2} = \sigma^2$$

9.2.15 Since $t = 2.16 > t_{.05, 13} = 1.7709$, reject H_0.

Section 9.3

9.3.1 **(a)** The critical values are $F_{.025, 25, 4}$ and $F_{.975, 25, 4}$. These values are not tabulated, but in this case, we can approximate them by $F_{.025, 24, 4} = 0.296$ and $F_{.975, 24, 4} = 8.51$. The observed $F = 86.9/73.6 = 1.181$. Since $0.296 < 1.181 < 8.51$, we can accept H_0 that the variances are equal.   **(b)** Yes, we can use Theorem 9.2.2, since we have no reason to doubt that the variances are equal.

9.3.3 **(a)** The critical values are $F_{.025, 19, 19}$ and $F_{.975, 19, 19}$. These values are not tabulated, but in this case, we can approximate them by $F_{.025, 20, 20} = 0.406$ and $F_{.975, 20, 20} = 2.46$. The observed $F = 2.41/3.52 = 0.685$. Since $0.406 < 0.685 < 2.46$, we can accept H_0 that the variances are equal.   **(b)** Since $t = 2.662 > t_{.025, 38} = 2.0244$, reject H_0.

9.3.5 $F = (0.20)^2/(0.37)^2 = 0.292$. Since $0.248 = F_{.025, 9, 9} < 0.292 < 4.03 = F_{.975, 9, 9}$, accept H_0.

9.3.7 $F = 65.25/227.77 = 0.286$. Since $0.208 = F_{.025, 8, 5} < 0.286 < 6.76 = F_{.975, 8, 5}$, accept H_0. Thus, Theorem 9.2.2 is appropriate.

9.3.9 If $\sigma_X^2 = \sigma_Y^2 = \sigma^2$, the maximum likelihod estimator for σ^2 is

$$\hat{\sigma}^2 = \frac{1}{n+m} \left(\sum_{i=1}^{n} (x_i - \bar{x})^2 + \sum_{i=1}^{m} (y_i - \bar{y})^2 \right).$$

Then

$$\max L(\sigma^2, \mu_X, \mu_Y) = \left(\frac{1}{2\pi\hat{\sigma}^2} \right)^{(n+m)/2} e^{-\frac{1}{2\hat{\sigma}^2} \left(\sum_{i=1}^{n}(x_i - \bar{x})^2 + \sum_{i=1}^{m}(y_i - \bar{y})^2 \right)} = \left(\frac{1}{2\pi\hat{\sigma}^2} \right)^{(n+m)/2} e^{-(n+m)/2}$$

If $\sigma_X^2 \neq \sigma_Y^2$ the maximum likelihood estimators for σ_X^2 and σ_Y^2 are $\hat{\sigma}_X^2 = \frac{1}{n} \sum_{i=1}^{n} (x_i - \bar{x})^2$, and $\hat{\sigma}_Y^2 = \frac{1}{m} \sum_{i=1}^{m} (y_i - \bar{y})^2$. Then

$$\max L(\sigma_X^2, \sigma_Y^2, \mu_X, \mu_Y) = \left(\frac{1}{2\pi\hat{\sigma}_X^2} \right)^{(n/2)} e^{-\frac{1}{2\hat{\sigma}_X^2} \left(\sum_{i=1}^{n}(x_i - \bar{x})^2 \right)} \left(\frac{1}{2\pi\hat{\sigma}_Y^2} \right)^{(m/2)} e^{-\frac{1}{2\hat{\sigma}_Y^2} \left(\sum_{i=1}^{m}(y_i - \bar{y})^2 \right)}$$

$$= \left(\frac{1}{2\pi\hat{\sigma}_X^2} \right)^{(n/2)} e^{-m/2} \left(\frac{1}{2\pi\hat{\sigma}_Y^2} \right)^{(m/2)} e^{-n/2}$$

The ratio is $\dfrac{\left(\hat{\sigma}_X^2\right)^{n/2} \left(\hat{\sigma}_Y^2\right)^{m/2}}{\left(\hat{\sigma}^2\right)^{(n+m)/2}}$, which equates to the expression given in the statement of the question.

Section 9.4

9.4.1 Since $-1.96 < z = 1.76 < 1.96 = z_{.025}$, accept H_0.

9.4.3 Since $-1.96 < z = -0.17 < 1.96 = z_{.025}$, accept H_0 at the 0.05 level of significance.

9.4.5 $z = 1.703$, so the P value is $2(1 - 0.9554) = 0.0892$.

9.4.7 Since $z = -7.99 < -1.96 = -z_{.025}$, reject H_0.

9.4.9 Since $-2 \ln \lambda < 6.635 = \chi_{.99, 1}^2$, accept H_0.

Section 9.5

9.5.1 $(-183.4, 535.4)$

9.5.3 The confidence interval $(-15.5, 13.7)$ contains 0, so the data do *not* suggest that the dome makes a difference.

9.5.5   Equation (9.5.1) is

$$P\left(-t_{\alpha/2,\,n+m-2} \le \frac{\bar{X} - \bar{Y} - (\mu_X - \mu_Y)}{S_p\sqrt{\dfrac{1}{n} + \dfrac{1}{m}}} \le t_{\alpha/2,\,n+m-2}\right) = 1 - \alpha$$

which implies

$$P\left(-t_{\alpha/2,\,n+m-2}S_p\sqrt{\frac{1}{n} + \frac{1}{m}} \le \bar{X} - \bar{Y} - (\mu_X - \mu_Y) \le t_{\alpha/2,\,n+m-2}S_p\sqrt{\frac{1}{n} + \frac{1}{m}}\right) = 1 - \alpha,$$

or

$$P\left(-(\bar{X} - \bar{Y}) - t_{\alpha/2,\,n+m-2}S_p\sqrt{\frac{1}{n} + \frac{1}{m}} \le -(\mu_X - \mu_Y) \le -(\bar{X} - \bar{Y}) + t_{\alpha/2,\,n+m-2}S_p\sqrt{\frac{1}{n} + \frac{1}{m}}\right) = 1 - \alpha$$

Multiplying the inequality above by -1 gives the inquality of the confidence interval of Theorem 9.5.1.

9.5.7   Approximate the needed $F_{.025,\,25,\,4}$ and $F_{.975,\,25,\,4}$ by $F_{.025,\,24,\,4} = 0.296$ and $F_{.975,\,24,\,4} = 8.51$. The confidence interval is approximately $(0.251, 7.21)$. Because the confidence interval contains 1, it supports the conclusion of Question 9.3.1 to accept H_0 that the variances are equal.

9.5.9   Since $\dfrac{S_Y^2/\sigma_Y^2}{S_X^2/\sigma_X^2}$ has an F distribution with $m - 1$ and $n - 1$ degrees of freedom,

$$P\left(F_{\alpha/2,\,m-1,\,n-1} \le \frac{S_Y^2/\sigma_Y^2}{S_X^2/\sigma_X^2} \le F_{1-\alpha/2,\,m-1,\,n-1}\right) = 1 - \alpha$$

or

$$P\left(\frac{S_X^2}{S_Y^2}F_{\alpha/2,\,m-1,\,n-1} \le \frac{\sigma_X^2}{\sigma_Y^2} \le \frac{S_X^2}{S_Y^2}F_{1-\alpha/2,\,m-1,\,n-1}\right) = 1 - \alpha$$

The inquality provides the confidence interval of Theorem 9.5.2.

9.5.11   The approximate normal distribution implies that

$$P\left(-z_\alpha \le \frac{\dfrac{X}{n} - \dfrac{Y}{m} - (p_X - p_Y)}{\sqrt{\dfrac{(X/n)(1 - X/n)}{n} + \dfrac{(Y/m)(1 - Y/m)}{m}}} \le z_\alpha\right) = 1 - \alpha$$

or

$$P\left(-z_\alpha\sqrt{\frac{(X/n)(1 - X/n)}{n} + \frac{(Y/m)(1 - Y/m)}{m}} \le \frac{X}{n} - \frac{Y}{m} - (p_X - p_Y)\right.$$
$$\left. \le z_\alpha\sqrt{\frac{(X/n)(1 - X/n)}{n} + \frac{(Y/m)(1 - Y/m)}{m}}\right) = 1 - \alpha$$

which implies that

$$P\left(-\left(\frac{X}{n} - \frac{Y}{m}\right) - z_\alpha\sqrt{\frac{(X/n)(1 - X/n)}{n} + \frac{(Y/m)(1 - Y/m)}{m}} \le -(p_X - p_Y)\right.$$
$$\left. \le -\left(\frac{X}{n} - \frac{Y}{m}\right) + z_\alpha\sqrt{\frac{(X/n)(1 - X/n)}{n} + \frac{(Y/m)(1 - Y/m)}{m}}\right) = 1 - \alpha$$

Multiplying the inequality by -1 yields the confidence interval.

Appendix 9.A.2

9.A.2.1 0.48   **9.A.2.3** 0.97   **9.A.2.5** 9

CHAPTER 10

Section 10.2

10.2.1 0.000886   **10.2.3** 0.00265   **10.2.5** 0.00649

10.2.7 **(a)** $\dfrac{50!}{3!7!15!25!} (0.016)^3 (0.109)^7 (0.297)^{15} (0.578)^{25}$ **(b)** $\text{Var}(X_3) = 50(0.297)(1 - 0.297) = 10.4$

10.2.9 Assume that $M_{X_1, X_2, X_3}(t_1, t_2, t_3) = (p_1 e^{t_1} + p_2 e^{t_2} + p_3 e^{t_3})^n$. Then $M_{X_1, X_2, X_3}(t_1, 0, 0) = E(e^{t_1 X_1}) = (p_1 e^{t_1} + p_2 + p_3)^n = (1 - p_1 + p_1 e^{t_1})^n$ is the mgf for X_1. But the latter has the form of the mgf for a binomial random variable with parameters n and p_1.

Section 10.3

10.3.1

$$\sum_{i=1}^{k} \frac{(X_i - np_i)^2}{np_i} = \sum_{i=1}^{k} \frac{(X_i^2 - 2np_i X_i + n^2 p_i^2)}{np_i} = \sum_{i=1}^{k} \frac{X_i^2}{np_i} - 2\sum_{i=1}^{k} X_i + n\sum_{i=1}^{k} p_i = \sum_{i=1}^{k} \frac{X_i^2}{np_i} - n.$$

10.3.3 If the sampling is done *with* replacement, the number of white chips drawn should follow a binomial distribution (with $n = 2$ and $p = 0.4$); obs. $\chi^2 = 3.30$ with 2 df. For $\alpha = 0.10$, we would fail to reject H_0.

10.3.5 Let $p = P$(baby is born between midnight and 4 A.M.). Test H_0: $p = 1/6$ vs. H_1: $p \neq 1/6$; obs. $z = 2.73$; reject H_0 if $\alpha = 0.05$. The obs. χ^2 in Question 10.3.4 will equal the square of the obs. z. The two tests are equivalent.   **10.3.7** Obs. $\chi^2 = 12.23$ with 5 df; $\chi^2_{.95, 5} = 11.070$; reject H_0.

10.3.9 Obs. $\chi^2 = 7.71$; $\chi^2_{.90, 3} = 6.251$; reject H_0.   **10.3.11** Obs. $\chi^2 = 10.72$; $\chi^2_{.90, 4} = 7.779$; reject H_0.

Section 10.4

10.4.1 Obs. $\chi^2 = 11.72$ with $4 - 1 - 1 = 2$ df; $\chi^2_{.95, 2} = 5.991$; reject H_0.

10.4.3 Obs. $\chi^2 = 46.75$ with $7 - 1 - 1 = 5$ df; $\chi^2_{.95, 5} = 11.070$; reject H_0. The independence assumption would not hold if the infestation was contagious.

10.4.5 For the model $f_Y(y) = \lambda e^{-\lambda y}$, $\hat{\lambda} = 0.82$; obs. $\chi^2 = 4.2$ with $5 - 1 - 1 = 3$ df; $\chi^2_{.95, 3} = 7.815$; fail to reject H_0.

10.4.7 Let $p = P$(child is a boy). Then $\hat{p} = 0.533$, obs. $\chi^2 = 0.62$, and we fail to reject the binomial model because $\chi^2_{.95, 1} = 3.84$.

10.4.9 For the model $p_X(k) = e^{-3.87}(3.87)^k/k!$, obs. $\chi^2 = 12.92$ with $12 - 1 - 1 = 10$ df. But $\chi^2_{.95, 10} = 18.307$, so we fail to reject H_0.   **10.4.11** $\hat{p} = 0.26$; obs. $\chi^2 = 9.23$; $\chi^2_{.95, 3} = 7.815$; reject H_0.

Section 10.5

10.5.1 Obs. $\chi^2 = 2.77$; $\chi^2_{.90, 1} = 2.706$ and $\chi^2_{.95, 1} = 3.841$, so H_0 is rejected at the $\alpha = 0.10$ level but not at the $\alpha = 0.05$ level.

10.5.3 Obs. $\chi^2 = 42.25$; $\chi^2_{.99, 3} = 11.345$; reject H_0.   **10.5.5** Obs. $\chi^2 = 27.29$; $\chi^2_{.99, 4} = 13.277$; reject H_0.

10.5.7 Obs. $\chi^2 = 12.61$; $\chi^2_{.95, 1} = 3.84$; reject H_0.   **10.5.9** Obs. $\chi^2 = 2.20$; $\chi^2_{.95, 1} = 3.84$; fail to reject H_0.

CHAPTER 11

Section 11.2

11.2.1 $y = 25.2 + 3.3x; 84.5°F$

11.2.3

x_i	$y_i - \hat{y}_i$
0	−0.81
4	0.01
10	0.09
15	0.03
21	−0.09
29	0.14
36	0.55
51	1.69
68	−1.61

A straight line appears to fit these data.

11.2.5 The value 12 is too "far" from the data observed.

11.2.7 The least-squares line is $645.9 + 0.055x$. The residuals sorted by the size of the x values are:

x_i	$y_i - \hat{y}_i$
3591	24.9
3736	8.9
3754	50.9
3864	−105.2
3877	26.1
3947	−46.8
4002	38.2
4078	19.0
4259	−29.0
4377	−0.5
4613	8.5
5107	−5.8
5770	10.6

The linear fit for x values less than $4300 is not very good, suggesting a search for other contributing variables in the x range of $3500 to $4200.

11.2.9 $\beta_1 = \dfrac{9(7,439.37) - (41.56)(1,416.1)}{9(289.4222) - (41.56)^2} = 9.23$

$\beta_0 = \dfrac{1}{9}(1,416.1) - \dfrac{9.23}{9}(41.56) = 114.72$

11.2.11 The least-squares line is $y = 0.61 + 0.84x$, which seems inadequate.

11.2.13 When $\bar{x}$ is substituted for x in the least-squares line equation, we obtain
$y = \beta_0 + \beta_1\bar{x} = \bar{y} - \beta_1\bar{x} + \beta_1\bar{x} = \bar{y}$.

11.2.15 0.03544   **11.2.17** $y = 100 - 5.19x$ **11.2.19** **(a)** $y = 104.141e^{-0.146x}$ **(b)** 5.025

11.2.21 **(a)** $8451.472e^{-0.159x}$ **(b)** $2777   **(c)** The exponential curve, which fits the data very well, predicts that a car 0 years old will have a value of $8451, significantly less than the selling price of $9630.

11.2.23 **(a)** If $\dfrac{dy}{dx} = \beta_1 y$, then $\dfrac{1}{y}\dfrac{dy}{dx} = \beta_1$. Integrate both sides of the latter equality with respect to x:

$\displaystyle\int \frac{1}{y}\frac{dy}{dx}\,dx = \int \beta_1\,dx$ which implies that $\ln y = \beta_1 x + C$. Now apply the function e^x to both sides to get

$y = e^{\beta_1 x} e^C = \beta_0 e^{\beta_1 x}$, where $\beta_0 = e^C$.   **(b)** x on the abscissa, $\ln y$ on the ordinate.

11.2.25 **(a)** $\beta_0 = 11.99, \beta_1 = 0.876$ **(b)** $11{,}361$ **11.2.27** $\beta_0 = 1.536, \beta_1 = 19.827; y(1.32) = 16.6$

11.2.29 $\beta_0 = 5.38, \beta_1 = -1.29$

Section 11.3

11.3.1 $y = 13.8 - 1.5x$; since $-t_{.025,\,2} = -4.3027 < t = -1.59 < 4.3027 = t_{.025,\,2}$, accept H_0.

11.3.3 Since $t = 5.47 > t_{.005,\,13} = 3.0123$, reject H_0.   **11.3.5** 0.9164 **11.3.7** $(66.31, 68.70)$

11.3.9 Since $t = 4.38 > t_{.025,\,9} = 2.2622$, reject H_0.   **11.3.11** By Theorem 11.3.2, $E(\hat{\beta}_0) = \beta_0$, and

$$\mathrm{Var}(\hat{\beta}_0) = \frac{\sigma^2 \displaystyle\sum_{i=1}^n x_i}{n \displaystyle\sum_{i=1}^n (x_i - \bar{x})^2}.$$

Now $(\hat{\beta}_0 - \beta_0)/\sqrt{\mathrm{Var}(\hat{\beta}_0)}$ is normal, so

$$P\!\left(-z_{\alpha/2} < (\hat{\beta}_0 - \beta_0)/\sqrt{\mathrm{Var}(\hat{\beta}_0)} < z_{\alpha/2}\right) = 1 - \alpha.$$

Then the confidence interval is

$$\left(\hat{\beta}_0 - z_{\alpha/2}\right)\sqrt{\mathrm{Var}(\hat{\beta}_0)}, \hat{\beta}_0 + z_{\alpha/2}\sqrt{\mathrm{Var}(\hat{\beta}_0)}$$

or

$$\left(\hat{\beta}_0 - z_{\alpha/2}\frac{\sigma\sqrt{\displaystyle\sum_{i=1}^n x_i}}{\sqrt{n\displaystyle\sum_{i=1}^n (x_i - \bar{x})^2}},\ \hat{\beta}_0 + z_{\alpha/2}\frac{\sigma\sqrt{\displaystyle\sum_{i=1}^n x_i}}{\sqrt{n\displaystyle\sum_{i=1}^n (x_i - \bar{x})^2}}\right)$$

11.3.13 From Theorem 11.3.3, we know that $P\!\left(\chi^2_{\alpha/2,\,n-2} < \dfrac{n\hat{\sigma}^2}{\sigma^2} < \chi^2_{1-\alpha/2,\,n-2}\right) = 1 - \alpha$. Inverting the

inequality gives $P\!\left(\dfrac{1}{\chi^2_{1-\alpha/2,\,n-2}} < \dfrac{\sigma^2}{n\hat{\sigma}^2} < \dfrac{1}{\chi^2_{\alpha/2,\,n-2}}\right) = 1 - \alpha$ or $P\!\left(\dfrac{n\hat{\sigma}^2}{\chi^2_{1-\alpha/2,\,n-2}} < \sigma^2 < \dfrac{n\hat{\sigma}^2}{\chi^2_{\alpha/2,\,n-2}}\right) = 1 - \alpha$.

Since $s^2 = \dfrac{n}{n-2}\hat{\sigma}^2, (n-2)s^2 = n\hat{\sigma}^2$. Thus, the desired confidence interval is $\left(\dfrac{(n-2)s^2}{\chi^2_{1-\alpha/2,\,n-2}}, \dfrac{(n-2)s^2}{\chi^2_{\alpha/2,\,n-2}}\right)$.

11.3.15 **(a)** Since $-t_{.025,\,8} = -2.3060 < t = -1.66 < 2.3060 = t_{.025,\,8}$, accept H_0.   **(b)** Since $-t_{.025,\,8} = 2.3060 < t = -0.96 < 2.3060 = t_{.025,\,8}$, accept H_0.   **11.3.17** $(2.05, 2.08)$

11.3.19 The prediction interval is $(-6.04, 46.97)$ so the worst-case scenario is 47 near collisions.

11.3.21 Since $-t_{.025,\,16} = -2.1199 < t = -1.24 < 2.1199 = t_{.025,\,16}$, accept H_0. There is no statistical basis for preferring one method over the other, so it would be reasonable to choose the second, less expensive, method.   **11.3.23** Since $t = -2.59 < -t_{.025,\,7} = -2.3646$, reject H_0.

11.3.25 $\displaystyle\sum_{i=1}^{n}(\hat{Y}_i - \bar{Y})^2 = \sum_{i=1}^{n}(\hat{\beta}_0 + \hat{\beta}_1 X_i - \bar{Y})^2$

$\displaystyle\sum_{i=1}^{n}(\bar{Y} - \hat{\beta}_1 \bar{X} + \hat{\beta}_1 X_i - \bar{Y})^2 = \sum_{i=1}^{n}(\hat{\beta}_1 \bar{X} - \hat{\beta}_1 X_i)^2 = \hat{\beta}_1^2 \sum_{i=1}^{n}(X_i - \bar{X})^2$

An application of Equation 11.3.2 completes the proof.

Section 11.4

11.4.1 105/72

11.4.3 $E(X) = E(Y) = E(XY) = 0$, so $\text{Cov}(X, Y) = 0$. But X and Y are functionally dependent, $Y = \sqrt{1 - X^2}$, so they are probabilistically dependent.

11.4.5 $-8/484; -2/15\sqrt{14}$ **11.4.7** 0.492

11.4.9 $\displaystyle\rho(a + bX, c + dY) = \frac{\text{Cov}(a + bX, c + dY)}{\sqrt{\text{Var}(a + bX)\,\text{Var}(c + dY)}} = \frac{bd\,\text{Cov}(X, Y)}{\sqrt{b^2\,\text{Var}(X)d^2\,\text{Var}(Y)}}$, the equality in the numerators stemming from Question 11.4.2. Since $b > 0, d > 0$, this last expression is

$$\frac{bd\,\text{Cov}(X, Y)}{bd\sigma_X \sigma_Y} = \frac{\text{Cov}(X, Y)}{\sigma_X \sigma_Y} = \rho(X, Y).$$

11.4.11 $\text{Cov}(X + Y, X - Y) = E[(X + Y)(X - Y)] - E(X + Y)E(X - Y)$

$= E[X^2 - Y^2] - (\mu_X + \mu_Y)(\mu_X + \mu_Y)$

$= E(X^2) - \mu_X^2 - E(Y^2) + \mu_Y^2 = Var(X) - \text{Var}(X)$

11.4.13 Multiply the numerator and denominator of Equation 11.4.1 by n^2 to obtain

$$\frac{n\displaystyle\sum_{i=1}^{n}X_i Y_i - \left(\sum_{i=1}^{n}X_i\right)\left(\sum_{i=1}^{n}Y_i\right)}{\sqrt{n\displaystyle\sum_{i=1}^{n}(X_i - \bar{X})^2}\sqrt{n\displaystyle\sum_{i=1}^{n}(Y_i - \bar{Y})^2}} = \frac{n\displaystyle\sum_{i=1}^{n}X_i Y_i - \left(\sum_{i=1}^{n}X_i\right)\left(\sum_{i=1}^{n}Y_i\right)}{\sqrt{n\displaystyle\sum_{i=1}^{n}X_i^2 - \left(\sum_{i=1}^{n}X_i\right)^2}\sqrt{n\displaystyle\sum_{i=1}^{n}Y_i^2 - \left(\sum_{i=1}^{n}Y_i\right)^2}}$$

11.4.15 $r = -0.030$. The data do not suggest that altitude affects home run hitting.   **11.4.17** 58.1%

Section 11.5

11.5.1 0.1891; 0.2127

11.5.3 **(a)** $\displaystyle f_{X+Y}(t) = \frac{1}{2\pi\sqrt{1 - \rho^2}} \int_{-\infty}^{\infty} \exp\left\{-\frac{1}{2}\left(\frac{1}{1 - \rho^2}\right)[(t - y)^2 - 2\rho(t - y)y + y^2]\right\} dy$

The expression in the brackets can be expanded and rewritten as

$$t^2 + 2(1 + \rho)y^2 - 2t(1 + \rho)y = t^2 + 2(1 + \rho)[y^2 - ty]$$

$$= t^2 + 2(1 + \rho)\left[y^2 - ty + \frac{t^2}{4}\right] - \frac{1}{2}(1 + \rho)t^2$$

$$= \frac{1 - \rho}{2}t^2 + 2(1 + \rho)(y - t/2)^2.$$

Placing this expression into the exponent gives

$$f_{X+Y}(t) = \frac{1}{2\pi\sqrt{1-\rho^2}} e^{-\frac{1}{2}\left(\frac{1}{1-\rho^2}\right)\frac{1-\rho}{2}t^2} \int_{-\infty}^{\infty} e^{-\frac{1}{2}\left(\frac{1}{1-\rho^2}\right)2(1+\rho)(y-t/2)^2} dy$$

$$= f_{X+Y}(t) = \frac{1}{2\pi\sqrt{1-\rho^2}} e^{-\frac{1}{2}\left(\frac{t^2}{2(1+\rho)}\right)} \int_{-\infty}^{\infty} e^{-\frac{1}{2}\left(\frac{(y-t/2)^2}{(1+\rho)/2}\right)} dy.$$

The integral is that of a normal pdf with mean $t/2$ and $\sigma^2 = (1+\rho)/2$. Thus, the integral equals $\sqrt{2\pi(1+\rho)/2} = \sqrt{\pi(1+\rho)}$. Putting this into the expression for f_{X+Y} gives

$$f_{X+Y}(t) = \frac{1}{\sqrt{2\pi}\sqrt{2(1+\rho)}} e^{-\frac{1}{2}\left(\frac{t^2}{2(1+\rho)}\right)},$$

which is the pdf of a normal variable with $\mu = 0$ and $\sigma^2 = 2(1+\rho)$.
(b) $c\mu_X + d\mu_Y$; $c^2\sigma_X^2 + d^2\sigma_Y^2 + 2cd\sigma_X\sigma_Y\rho(X,Y)$

11.5.5 $E(X) = E(Y) = 0$; $\text{Var}(X) = 4$; $\text{Var}(Y) = 1$; $\rho(X,Y) = 1/2$; $k = 1/2\pi\sqrt{3}$

11.5.7 Since $-t_{.005,18} = -2.8784 < T_{n-2} = -2.156 < 2.8784 = t_{.005,18}$, accept H_0.

11.5.9 Since $-t_{.025,10} = -2.2281 < T_{n-2} = -0.094 < 2.2281 = t_{.025,10}$, accept H_0.

11.5.11 From the Comment on page 626, we can deduce that

$$P\left(-z_{\alpha/2} < \frac{\frac{1}{2}\ln\frac{1+R}{1-R} - \frac{1}{2}\ln\frac{1+\rho}{1-\rho}}{\sqrt{\frac{1}{n-3}}} < z_{\alpha/2}\right) = 1 - \alpha$$

To find the confidence interval, we solve the inequality for ρ:

$$-z_{\alpha/2} < \frac{\frac{1}{2}\ln\frac{1+R}{1-R} - \frac{1}{2}\ln\frac{1+\rho}{1-\rho}}{\sqrt{\frac{1}{n-3}}} < z_{\alpha/2}$$

implies

$$-z_{\alpha/2}\sqrt{\frac{1}{n-3}} < \frac{1}{2}\ln\frac{1+R}{1-R} - \frac{1}{2}\ln\frac{1+\rho}{1-\rho} < z_{\alpha/2}\sqrt{\frac{1}{n-3}}$$

or

$$e^{-z_{\alpha/2}\sqrt{\frac{1}{n-3}}} < \sqrt{\frac{1+R}{1-R}}\bigg/\sqrt{\frac{1+\rho}{1-\rho}} < e^{z_{\alpha/2}\sqrt{\frac{1}{n-3}}}.$$

Then

$$\sqrt{\frac{1-R}{1+R}}e^{-z_{\alpha/2}\sqrt{\frac{1}{n-3}}} < \sqrt{\frac{1-\rho}{1+\rho}} < \sqrt{\frac{1-R}{1+R}}e^{z_{\alpha/2}\sqrt{\frac{1}{n-3}}}.$$

Squaring the inequality gives

$$\frac{1-R}{1+R}e^{-2z_{\alpha/2}\sqrt{\frac{1}{n-3}}} < \frac{1-\rho}{1+\rho} < \frac{1-R}{1+R}e^{2z_{\alpha/2}\sqrt{\frac{1}{n-3}}},$$

or

$$\frac{1-R}{1+R}e^{-2z_{\alpha/2}\sqrt{\frac{1}{n-3}}} < -1 + \frac{2}{1+\rho} < \frac{1-R}{1+R}e^{2z_{\alpha/2}\sqrt{\frac{1}{n-3}}}.$$

Solving this inequality for ρ yields the confidence interval:

$$1 + \frac{1-R}{1+R}e^{-2z_{\alpha/2}\sqrt{\frac{1}{n-3}}} < \frac{2}{1+\rho} < 1 + \frac{1-R}{1+R}e^{2z_{\alpha/2}\sqrt{\frac{1}{n-3}}},$$

which implies

$$\frac{2}{1 + \dfrac{1-R}{1+R}e^{2z_{\alpha/2}\sqrt{\frac{1}{n-3}}}} < 1 + \rho < \frac{2}{1 + \dfrac{1-R}{1+R}e^{-2z_{\alpha/2}\sqrt{\frac{1}{n-3}}}},$$

and finally

$$-1 + \frac{2}{1 + \dfrac{1-R}{1+R}e^{2z_{\alpha/2}\sqrt{\frac{1}{n-3}}}} < \rho < -1 + \frac{2}{1 + \dfrac{1-R}{1+R}e^{-2z_{\alpha/2}\sqrt{\frac{1}{n-3}}}}$$

Note: the answer could omit the derivation and be written simply as

$$\left(-1 + \frac{2}{1 + \dfrac{1-R}{1+R}e^{z_{\alpha/2}\sqrt{\frac{1}{n-3}}}} , -1 + \frac{2}{1 + \dfrac{1-R}{1+R}e^{-2z_{\alpha/2}\sqrt{\frac{1}{n-3}}}}\right).$$

CHAPTER 12

Section 12.2

12.2.1   Obs. $F = 3.94$ with 3 and 6 df; $F_{.95, 3, 6} = 4.76$ and $F_{.90, 3, 6} = 3.29$, so H_0 would be rejected at the $\alpha = 0.10$ level, but not at the $\alpha = 0.05$ level.

12.2.3

Source	df	SS	MS	F
Sector	2	186.0	93.0	3.45
Error	27	728.2	27.0	
Total	29	914.1		

$F_{.99, 2, 30} = 5.39 < F_{.99, 2, 27} < F_{.99, 2, 24} = 5.61$, so we fail to reject H_0.

12.2.5

Source	df	SS	MS	F	P
Tribe	3	504167	168056	3.70	0.062
Error	8	363333	45417		
Total	11	867500			

Since the P-value is greater than 0.01, we fail to reject H_0.

12.2.7 The sample variances for Treatments A, C, and D are much smaller than the sample variance for Treatment B, suggesting that the assumption that σ^2 is the same for all treatment levels may not be true.

12.2.9 $SSTR/\sigma^2 = \left(1/\sigma^2\right) \sum_{j=1}^{k} n_j(\bar{Y}_{\cdot j} - \bar{Y}_{\cdot\cdot})^2 = \left(1/\sigma^2\right) \sum_{j=1}^{k} n_j[(\bar{Y}_{\cdot j} - \mu) - (\bar{Y}_{\cdot\cdot} - \mu)]^2$

$$= \left(1/\sigma^2\right) \left[\sum_{j=1}^{k} n_j(\bar{Y}_{\cdot j} - \mu)^2 - n(\bar{Y}_{\cdot\cdot} - \mu)^2 \right]$$

$$= \sum_{j=1}^{k} \left(\frac{\bar{Y}_{\cdot j} - \mu}{\sigma/\sqrt{n_j}} \right)^2 - \left(\frac{\bar{Y}_{\cdot\cdot} - \mu}{\sigma/\sqrt{n}} \right)^2.$$

Since the $\left(\dfrac{\bar{Y}_{\cdot j} - \mu}{\sigma/\sqrt{n_j}} \right)$'s are independent normal random variables, and since $\left(\dfrac{\bar{Y}_{\cdot\cdot} - \mu}{\sigma/\sqrt{n}} \right)$ can be written as a linear combination of the $\left(\dfrac{\bar{Y}_{\cdot j} - \mu}{\sigma/\sqrt{n_j}} \right)$'s, it follows from Fisher's lemma that $SSTR/\sigma^2$ has a χ^2 distribution with $k - 1$ df.

12.2.11

Source	df	SS	MS	F	P
Author	1	0.002185	0.002185	15.04	0.001
Error	16	0.002325	0.000145		
Total	17	0.004510			

From Case Study 9.2.1, obs. $t = 3.88$; except for a small rounding error, $(\text{obs. } t)^2 = (3.88)^2 = 15.05$ is the same as the obs. F.

Section 12.3

12.3.1

Pairwise difference	Tukey interval	Conclusion
$\mu_1 - \mu_2$	$(-15.27, 13.60)$	NS
$\mu_1 - \mu_3$	$(-23.77, 5.10)$	NS
$\mu_1 - \mu_4$	$(-33.77, -4.90)$	Reject
$\mu_2 - \mu_3$	$(-22.94, 5.94)$	NS
$\mu_2 - \mu_4$	$(-32.94, -4.06)$	Reject
$\mu_3 - \mu_4$	$(-24.44, 4.44)$	NS

12.3.3 Obs. $F = 5.81$ with 2 and 15 df; reject $H_0: \mu_C = \mu_A = \mu_M$ at $\alpha = 0.05$ but not at $\alpha = 0.01$.

Pairwise difference	Tukey interval	Conclusion
$\mu_1 - \mu_2$	$(-78.9, 217.5)$	NS
$\mu_1 - \mu_3$	$(-271.0, 25.4)$	NS
$\mu_2 - \mu_3$	$(-340.4, -44.0)$	Reject

12.3.5 No

Section 12.4

12.4.1

Source	df	SS	MS	F
Tube	2	510.7	255.4	11.56
Error	42	927.7	22.1	
Total	44	1438.4		

Subhypothesis	Contrast	SS	F
$H_0: \mu_A = \mu_C$	$C_1 = \mu_A - \mu_C$	264	11.95
$H_0: \mu_B = \dfrac{\mu_A + \mu_C}{2}$	$C_2 = \frac{1}{2}\mu_A - \mu_B + \frac{1}{2}\mu_C$	246.7	11.16

$H_0: \mu_A = \mu_B = \mu_C$ is strongly rejected $\left(F_{.99, 2, 42} \doteq F_{.99, 2, 40} = 5.18\right)$. Theorem 12.4.1 holds true for orthogonal contrasts C_1 and C_2 — $SS_{C_1} + SS_{C_2} = 264 + 246.7 = 510.7 = SSTR$.

12.4.3 $\hat{C} = -14.25$; $SS_C = 812.25$; obs. $F = 10.19$; $F_{.95, 1, 20} = 4.35$; reject H_0.

12.4.5

	μ_A	μ_B	μ_C	μ_D	$\displaystyle\sum_{j=1}^{4} c_j$
C_1	1	-1	0	0	0
C_2	0	0	1	-1	0
C_3	$\dfrac{11}{12}$	$\dfrac{11}{12}$	-1	$\dfrac{-5}{6}$	0

C_1 and C_3 are orthogonal because $\dfrac{1(11/12)}{6} + \dfrac{(-1)(11/12)}{6} = 0$; also C_2 and C_3 are orthogonal because $\dfrac{1(-1)}{6} + \dfrac{(-1)(-5/6)}{5} = 0$. $\hat{C}_3 = -2.293$ and $SS_{C_3} = 8.97$. But $SS_{C_1} + SS_{C_2} + SS_{C_3} = 4.68 + 1.12 + 8.97 = 14.77 = SSTR$.

Section 12.5

12.5.1 Replace each observation by its square root. At the $\alpha = 0.05$ level, $H_0: \mu_A = \mu_B$ is rejected. (For $\alpha = 0.01$, though, we would fail to reject H_0.)

Source	df	SS	MS	F	P
Developer	1	1.836	1.836	6.23	0.032
Error	10	2.947	0.295		
Total	11	4.783			

12.5.3 Since Y_{ij} is a binomial random variable based on $n = 20$ trials, each data point should be replaced by the arcsin of $(y_{ij}/20)^{1/2}$. Based on those transformed observations, $H_0: \mu_A = \mu_B = \mu_C$ is strongly rejected $(P < 0.001)$.

Source	df	SS	MS	F	P
Launcher	2	0.30592	0.15296	22.34	0.000
Error	9	0.06163	0.00685		
Total	11	0.36755			

Appendix 12.A.3

12.A.3.1 The F test will have greater power against H_1^{**} because the latter yields a larger noncentrality parameter than does H_1^*.

12.A.3.3 $M_V(t) = (1 - 2t)^{-r/2} e^{\gamma t (1-2t)^{-1}}$, so $M_V^{(1)}(t) = (1 - 2t)^{-r/2}$.

$$e^{\gamma t (1-2t)^{-1}} \left[\gamma t(-1)(1 - 2t)^{-2}(-2) + (1 - 2t)^{-1}\gamma \right] + e^{\gamma t (1-2t)^{-1}}\left(-\frac{r}{2}\right)(1 - 2t)^{-(r/2)-1}(-2).$$

Therefore $E(V) = M_V^{(1)}(0) = \gamma + r$.

12.A.3.5 $M_V(t) = \displaystyle\prod_{i=1}^{n}(1 - 2t)^{-r_i/2} e^{\gamma_i t/(1-2t)} = (1 - 2t)^{-\sum_{i=1}^{n} r_i/2} \cdot e^{\left(\sum_{i=1}^{n} \gamma_i\right)t/(1-2t)}$

which implies that V has a noncentral χ^2 distribution with $\displaystyle\sum_{i=1}^{n} r_i$ df and with noncentrality parameter $\displaystyle\sum_{i=1}^{n} \gamma_i$.

CHAPTER 13

Section 13.2

13.2.1

Source	df	SS	MS	F	P
States	1	61.63	61.63	7.20	0.0178
Students	14	400.80	28.63	3.34	0.0155
Error	14	119.87	8.56		
Total	29	582.30			

The critical value $F_{.95, 1, 14}$ is approximately 4.6. Since the F statistic $= 7.20 > 4.6$, reject H_0.

13.2.3

Source	df	SS	MS	F	P
Additive	1	0.03	0.03	4.19	0.0865
Batch	6	0.02	0.00	0.41	0.8483
Error	6	0.05	0.01		
Total	13	0.10			

Since the F statistic $= 4.19 < F_{.95, 1, 6} = 5.99$, accept H_0.

13.2.5

Source	df	SS	MS	F	P
Quarter	3	0.60	0.20	0.60	0.6272
Year	4	19.87	4.97	14.85	0.0001
Error	12	4.01	0.33		
Total	19	24.48			

Since the F statistic for treatments $= 0.60 < F_{.95, 3, 12} = 3.49$, accept H_0 that yields are not affected by the quarter. Since the F statistic for blocks $= 14.85 > F_{.95, 4, 12} = 3.26$, reject H_0; yields do depend on the year.

13.2.7

Pairwise Difference	$\bar{y}_{\cdot s} - \bar{y}_{\cdot t}$	Tukey Interval	Conclusion
$\mu_1 - \mu_2$	2.925	(0.78, 5.07)	Reject
$\mu_1 - \mu_3$	1.475	(−0.67, 3.62)	NS
$\mu_2 - \mu_3$	−1.450	(−3.60, 0.70)	NS

13.2.9 (a)

Source	df	SS	MS	F	P
Sleep stages	2	16.99	8.49	4.13	0.0493
Shrew	5	195.44	39.09	19.00	0.0001
Error	10	20.57	2.06		
Total	17	233.00			

(b) Since the observed F ratio $= 2.42 < F_{.95, 1, 10} = 4.96$, accept the subhypothesis. For the contrast $C_1 = -\dfrac{1}{2}\mu_1 - \dfrac{1}{2}\mu_2 + \mu_3$, $SS_{C_1} = 4.99$. For the contrast $C_2 = \mu_1 - \mu_2$, $SS_{C_2} = 12.00$. Then C_1 and C_2 are orthogonal and $SSTR = 16.99 = 4.99 + 12.00 = SS_{C_1} + SS_{C_2}$.

13.2.11

Equation 13.2.2:

$$SSTR = \sum_{i=1}^{b}\sum_{j=1}^{k}\left(\bar{Y}_{\cdot j} - \bar{Y}_{\cdot\cdot}\right)^2 = b\sum_{j=1}^{k}\left(\bar{Y}_{\cdot j} - \bar{Y}_{\cdot\cdot}\right)^2$$

$$= b\sum_{j=1}^{k}\left(\bar{Y}_{\cdot j}^2 - 2\bar{Y}_{\cdot j}\bar{Y}_{\cdot\cdot} + \bar{Y}_{\cdot\cdot}^2\right) = b\sum_{j=1}^{k}\bar{Y}_{\cdot j}^2 - 2b\bar{Y}_{\cdot\cdot}\sum_{j=1}^{k}\bar{Y}_{\cdot j} + bk\bar{Y}_{\cdot\cdot}^2.$$

$$= b\sum_{j=1}^{k}\frac{T_{\cdot j}^2}{b^2} - \frac{2T_{\cdot\cdot}^2}{bk} + \frac{T_{\cdot\cdot}^2}{bk} = \sum_{j=1}^{k}\frac{T_{\cdot j}^2}{b} - \frac{T_{\cdot\cdot}^2}{bk} = \sum_{j=1}^{k}\frac{T_{\cdot j}^2}{b} - c$$

Equation 13.2.3:

$$SSB = \sum_{i=1}^{b}\sum_{j=1}^{k}\left(\bar{Y}_{i\cdot} - \bar{Y}_{\cdot\cdot}\right)^2 = k\sum_{i=1}^{b}\left(\bar{Y}_{i\cdot} - \bar{Y}_{\cdot\cdot}\right)^2$$

$$= k\sum_{i=1}^{b}\left(\bar{Y}_{i\cdot}^2 - 2\bar{Y}_{i\cdot}\bar{Y}_{\cdot\cdot} + \bar{Y}_{\cdot\cdot}^2\right) = k\sum_{i=1}^{b}\bar{Y}_{i\cdot}^2 - 2k\bar{Y}_{\cdot\cdot}\sum_{i=1}^{b}\bar{Y}_{i\cdot} + bk\bar{Y}_{\cdot\cdot}^2.$$

$$= k\sum_{i=1}^{b}\frac{T_{i\cdot}^2}{k^2} - \frac{2T_{\cdot\cdot}^2}{bk} + \frac{T_{\cdot\cdot}^2}{bk} = \sum_{i=1}^{b}\frac{T_{i\cdot}^2}{k} - \frac{T_{\cdot\cdot}^2}{bk} = \sum_{i=1}^{b}\frac{T_{i\cdot}^2}{k} - c$$

Equation 13.2.4:

$$SSTOT = \sum_{i=1}^{b}\sum_{j=1}^{k}\left(Y_{ij} - \bar{Y}_{\cdot\cdot}\right)^2 = \sum_{i=1}^{b}\sum_{j=1}^{k}\left(Y_{ij}^2 - 2Y_{ij}\bar{Y}_{\cdot\cdot} + \bar{Y}_{\cdot\cdot}^2\right)$$

$$= \sum_{i=1}^{b}\sum_{j=1}^{k}Y_{ij}^2 - 2\bar{Y}_{\cdot\cdot}\sum_{i=1}^{b}\sum_{j=1}^{k}Y_{ij} + bk\bar{Y}_{\cdot\cdot}^2.$$

$$= \sum_{i=1}^{b}\sum_{j=1}^{k}Y_{ij}^2 - \frac{2T_{\cdot\cdot}^2}{bk} + \frac{T_{\cdot\cdot}^2}{bk} = \sum_{i=1}^{b}\sum_{j=1}^{k}Y_{ij}^2 - c$$

13.2.13 **(a)** False. They are equal only when $b = k$.   **(b)** False. If neither treatment levels nor blocks are significant, it is possible to have F variables

$$\frac{SSTR/(k - 1)}{SSE/(b - 1)(k - 1)} \quad \text{and} \quad \frac{SSB/(b - 1)}{SSE/(b - 1)(k - 1)} \quad \text{both} < 1.$$

In that case both $SSTR$ and SSB are less than SSE.

Section 13.3

13.3.1 Since $3.45 > 1.363 = t_{.10, 11}$, reject H_0.

13.3.3 $\alpha = 0.05$: Since $-t_{.025, 11} = -2.2010 < 0.74 < 2.2010 = t_{.025, 11}$, accept H_0.
$\alpha = 0.01$: Since $-t_{.005, 11} = -3.1058 < 0.74 < 3.1058 = t_{.005, 11}$, accept H_0.

13.3.5 Since $-t_{.025, 6} = -2.4469 < -2.0481 < 2.4469 = t_{.025, 6}$, accept H_0. The square of the observed Student t statistic $= (-2.0481)^2 = 4.1947 =$ the observed F statistic. Also, $(t_{.025, 6})^2 = (2.4469)^2 = 5.987 = F_{.95, 1, 6}$. Conclusion: the square of the t statistic for paired data is the randomized block design statistic for 2 treatments.   **13.3.7** $(-0.21, 0.43)$

CHAPTER 14

Section 14.2

14.2.1 Let $p = P(Y_i > X_i)$. For $\alpha = 0.05$, we should reject $H_0: p = 1/2$ in favor of $H_1: p < 1/2$ if $y_+ \leq 2$. This choice of critical value is because $P(Y_+ \leq 2) = 0.033$ and $P(Y_+ \leq 3) > 0.05$. Since $y_+ = 2$, reject H_0.

14.2.3 Let Y_+ denote the number of Y_i for which $Y_i - 7.39 > 0$. Omit the observation where $Y_i = 7.39$. For the 43 remaining observations, $y_+ = 4$. Since the observed Z ratio $= -5.34 < -2.58 = -z_{.005}$, reject H_0.

14.2.5

y_+	$P(Y_+ = y_+)$
0	1/128
1	7/128
2	21/128
3	35/128
4	35/128
5	21/128
6	7/128
7	1/128

Possible levels for a one-sided test: $1/128, 8/128, 29/128$, etc.

14.2.7 $P(Y_+ \leq 6) = 0.0835$; $P(Y_+ \leq 7) = 0.1796$. The closest test to one with $\alpha = 0.10$ is to reject H_0 if $y_+ \leq 6$. Since $y_+ = 9$, accept H_0. Since the observed t statistic $= -1.71 < -1.330 = -t_{.10, 18}$, reject H_0.

14.2.9 The approximate, large sample observed Z ratio is 1.89. Accept H_0, since $-z_{.025} = 1.96 < 1.89 < 1.96 = z_{.025}$.

Section 14.3

14.3.1 For the critical values of 7 and 29, $\alpha = 0.148$. Since $w = 9$, accept H_0.

14.3.3 Since the observed Z statistic $= 0.99 < 1.96 = z_{.025}$, accept H_0.

14.3.5 Since $w' = \dfrac{61.0 - 95}{\sqrt{617.5}} = -1.37 < -1.28 = -z_{.10}$, reject H_0. The sign test accepted H_0.

14.3.7 The signed rank test should have more power since it uses more of the information in the data.

Section 14.4

14.4.1 Inadequate mixing of the capsules in the bowl.

14.4.3 Since $b = 9.93 > 3.841 = \chi^2_{.95, 1}$, reject H_0.

14.4.5 Since $b = 10.72 > 7.815 = \chi^2_{.95, 3}$, reject H_0.   **14.4.7** Since $b = 12.48 > 5.991 = \chi^2_{.95, 2}$, reject H_0.

Section 14.5

14.5.1 Since $g = 8.8 < 9.488 = \chi^2_{.95, 4}$, accept H_0.   **14.5.3** Since $g = 17.0 > 5.991 = \chi^2_{.95, 2}$, reject H_0.

14.5.5 Note: In both analyses the observations where $d_i = 0$ were discarded. The Friedman statistic $g = 9.00$ exceeds $3.841 = \chi^2_{.95, 1}$, so reject H_0. With $n = 9$, a hypothesis test of approximate level $= 0.05$ rejects H_0 if $w \leq 6$ or $w \geq 39$ (see Appendix Table A.6). Since the observed Wilcoxon statistic is 45, reject H_0.

Bibliography

1. Advanced Placement Program, Summary Reports. New York: The College Board, 1996.

2. Agresti, Alan, and Winner, Larry. "Evaluating Agreement and Disagreement among Movie Reviewers." *Chance*, 10, no. 2 (1997), pp. 10–14.

3. Air Products' Culture, Annual Report. Allentown, Pa.: Air Products and Chemicals, 1992.

4. Ayala, F. J. "The Mechanisms of Evolution." *Evolution, A Scientific American Book*. San Francisco: W. H. Freeman, 1978, pp. 14–27.

5. Ball, J. A. C., and Taylor, A. R. "The Effect of Cyclandelate on Mental Function and Cerebral Blood Flow in Elderly Patients," in *Research on the Cerebral Circulation*. Edited by John Stirling Meyer, Helmut Lechner, and Otto Eichhorn. Springfield, Ill.: Thomas, 1969.

6. Barnicot, N. A., and Brothwell, D. R. "The Evaluation of Metrical Data in the Comparison of Ancient and Modern Bones," in *Medical Biology and Etruscan Origins*. Edited by G. E. W. Wolstenholme and Cecilia M. O'Connor. Boston: Little, Brown and Company, 1959, pp. 131–149.

7. Barnothy, Jeno M. "Development of Young Mice," in *Biological Effects of Magnetic Fields*. Edited by Madeline F. Barnothy. New York: Plenum Press, 1964, pp. 93–99.

8. Bartle, Robert G. *The Elements of Real Analysis*, 2nd ed. New York: John Wiley & Sons, 1976.

9. Bellany, Ian. "Strategic Arms Competition and the Logistic Curve." *Survival*, 16 (1974), pp. 228–230.

10. Bennett, W. R., Jr. "How Artificial is Intelligence?" *American Scientist*, 65, no. 6 (1977), pp. 694–702.

11. Berger, R. J., and Walker, J. M. "A Polygraphic Study of Sleep in the Tree Shrew." *Brain, Behavior and Evolution*, 5 (1972), pp. 54–69.

12. Blackman, Sheldon, and Catalina, Don. "The Moon and the Emergency Room." *Perceptual and Motor Skills*, 37 (1973), pp. 624–626.

13. Bortkiewicz, L. *Das Gesetz der Kleinen Zahlen*. Leipzig: Teubner, 1898.

14. Boyd, Edith. "The Specific Gravity of the Human Body." *Human Biology*, 5 (1933), pp. 651–652.

15. Breed, M. D., and Byers, J. A. "The Effect of Population Density on Spacing Patterns and Behavioral Interactions in the Cockroach, *Byrsotria fumigata* (Guerin)." *Behavioral and Neural Biology*, 27 (1979), pp. 523–531.

16. Brien, A. J., and Simon, T. L. "The Effects of Red Blood Cell Infusion on 10-km Race Time." *Journal of the American Medical Association*, May 22 (1987), pp. 2761–2765.

17. Brinegar, Claude S. "Mark Twain and the Quintus Curtius Snodgrass Letters: A Statistical Test of Authorship." *Journal of the American Statistical Association*, 58 (1963), pp. 85–96.

18. Buchanan, T. M.; Brooks, G. F.; and Brachman, P. S. "The Tularemia Skin Test." *Annals of Internal Medicine*, 74 (1971), pp. 336–343.

19. Bullard, Roger W., and Shumake, Stephen A. "Food Temperature Preference Response of *Desmodus rotundus*." *Journal of Mammalogy*, 54 (1973), pp. 299–302.

20. Burns, Alvin C., and Bush, Ronald F. *Marketing Research*. Englewood Cliffs, N.J.: Prentice Hall, 1995.

21. Carter, C. C. "Multifactorial Genetic Disease." *Hospital Practice*, 5 (1970), pp. 45–49.

22. Casler, Lawrence. "The Effects of Hypnosis on GESP." *Journal of Parapsychology*, 28 (1964), pp. 126–134.

23. *Chronicle of Higher Education*. April 25, 1990.

24. Clason, Clyde B. *Exploring the Distant Stars*. New York: G. P. Putnam's Sons, 1958, p. 337.

25. Cochran, W. G. "Approximate Significance Levels of the Behrens-Fisher Test." *Biometrics*, 20 (1964), pp. 191–195.

26. Cochran, W. G., and Cox, Gertrude M. *Experimental Designs*, 2nd ed. New York: John Wiley & Sons, 1957, p. 108.

27. Cohen, B. "Getting Serious About Skills." *Virginia Review*, 71 (1992).

28. Collins, Robert L. "On the Inheritance of Handedness." *Journal of Heredity*, 59, no. 1 (1968).

29. *Commercial Appeal* (Memphis). January 12, 1987.

30. *Common Fund Annual Report* (1992).

31. Cooil, B. "Using Medical Malpractice Data to Predict the Frequency of Claims: A Study of Poisson Process Models with Random Effects." *Journal of the American Statistical Association*, 86 (1991), pp. 285–295.

32. Coulson, J. C. "The Significance of the Pair-bond in the Kittiwake," in *Parental Behavior in Birds*. Edited by Rae Silver. Stroudsburg, Pa.: Dowden, Hutchinson, & Ross, 1977, pp. 104–113.

33. *CRC Standard Mathematical Tables*, 25th ed. Edited by William H. Beyer. West Palm Beach, Fla.: CRC Press, 1978, p. 414.

34. David, F. N. *Games, Gods, and Gambling*. New York: Hafner, 1962, p. 16.

35. Davis, M. "Premature Mortality among Prominent American Authors Noted for Alcohol Abuse." *Drug and Alcohol Dependence*, 18 (1986), pp. 133–138.

36. Dubois, Cora, ed. *Lowie's Selected Papers in Anthropology*. Berkeley, Calif.: University of California Press, 1960, pp. 137–142.

37. Evans, B. Personal communication.

38. Fadeley, Robert Cunningham. "Oregon Malignancy Pattern Physiographically Related to Hanford, Washington Radioisotope Storage." *Journal of Environmental Health*, 27 (1965), pp. 883–897.

39. Fagen, Robert M. "Exercise, Play, and Physical Training in Animals," in *Perspectives in Ethology*. Edited by P. P. G. Bateson and Peter H. Klopfer. New York: Plenum Press, 1976, pp. 189–219.

40. Fairley, William B. "Evaluating the 'Small' Probability of a Catastrophic Accident from the Marine Transportation of Liquefied Natural Gas," in *Statistics and Public Policy*. Edited by William B. Fairley and Frederick Mosteller. Reading, Mass.: Addison-Wesley, 1977, pp. 331–353.

41. Fairley, William B., and Mosteller, Frederick. "A Conversation about Collins," in *Statistics and Public Policy*. Edited by William B. Fairley and Frederick Mosteller. Reading, Mass.: Addison-Wesley, 1977, pp. 369–379.

42. Feller, W. "Statistical Aspects of ESP." *Journal of Parapsychology*, 4 (1940), pp. 271–298.

43. Finkbeiner, Daniel T. *Introduction to Matrices and Linear Transformations*. San Francisco: W. H. Freeman, 1960.

44. Fishbein, Morris. *Birth Defects*. Philadelphia: Lippincott, 1962, p. 177.

45. Fisher, R. A. "On the 'Probable Error' of a Coefficient of Correlation Deduced from a Small Sample." *Metron*, 1 (1921), pp. 3–32.

46. Florida Department of Commerce. February 20, 1996.

47. *Forbes Magazine*. Oct. 10, 1994.

48. ———. May 20, 1996.

49. Freund, John E. *Mathematical Statistics*, 2nd ed. Englewood Cliffs, N.J.: Prentice Hall, 1971, p. 226.

50. Fricker, Ronald D., Jr. "The Mysterious Case of the Blue M&M's." *Chance*, 9, no. 4 (1996), pp. 19–22.

51. Furuhata, Tanemoto, and Yamamoto, Katsuichi. *Forensic Odontology*. Springfield, Ill.: Thomas, 1967, p. 84.

52. Galton, Francis. *Natural Inheritance*. London: Macmillan, 1908.

53. Gendreau, Paul, et al. "Changes in EEG Alpha Frequency and Evoked Response Latency During Solitary Confinement." *Journal of Abnormal Psychology*, 79 (1972), pp. 54–59.

54. Gerber, Robert C., et al. "Kinetics of Aurothiomalate in Serum and Synovial Fluid." *Arthritis and Rheumatism*, 15 (1972), pp. 625–629.

55. Goldman, Malcolm. *Introduction to Probability and Statistics*. New York: Harcourt, Brace & World, 1970, pp. 399–403.

56. Goodman, Leo A. "Serial Number Analysis." *Journal of the American Statistical Association*, 47 (1952), pp. 622–634.

57. Griffin, Donald R.; Webster, Frederick A.; and Michael, Charles R. "The Echolocation of Flying Insects by Bats." *Animal Behavior*, 8 (1960), p. 148.

58. Grover, Charles A. "Population Differences in the Swell Shark *Cephaloscyllium ventriosum*." *California Fish and Game*, 58 (1972), pp. 191–197.

59. Gutenberg, B., and Richter, C. F. *Seismicity of the Earth and Associated Phenomena*. Princeton, N.J.: Princeton University Press, 1949.

60. Haggard, William H.; Bilton, Thaddeus H.; and Crutcher, Harold L. "Maximum Rainfall from Tropical Cyclone Systems which Cross the Appalachians." *Journal of Applied Meteorology*, 12 (1973), pp. 50–61.

61. Haight, F. A. "Group Size Distributions with Applications to Vehicle Occupancy," in *Random Counts in Physical Science, Geological Science, and Business*, vol. 3. Edited by G. P. Patil. University Park, Pa.: Pennsylvania State University Press, 1970.

62. Hankins, F. H. "Adolph Quetelet as Statistician," in *Studies in History, Economics, and Public Law*, xxxi, no. 4. New York: Longman, Green, 1908, p. 497.

63. Hansel, C. E. M. *ESP: A Scientific Evaluation*. New York: Scribner's, 1966, pp. 86–89.

64. Hare, Edward; Price, John; and Slater, Eliot. "Mental Disorder and Season of Birth: A National Sample Compared with the General Population." *British Journal of Psychiatry*, 124 (1974), pp. 81–86.

65. Hassard, Thomas H. *Understanding Biostatistics*. St Louis: Mosby Year Book, 1991.

66. Hasselblad, V. "Estimation of Finite Mixtures of Distributions from the Exponential Family." *Journal of the American Statistical Association*, 64 (1969), pp. 1459–1471.

67. Hazel, W. M., and Eglof, W. K. "Determination of Calcium in Magnesite and Fused Magnesia." *Industrial and Engineering Chemistry, Analytical Edition*, 18 (1946), pp. 759–760.

68. Heath, Clark W., and Hasterlik, Robert J. "Leukemia among Children in a Suburban Community." *The American Journal of Medicine*, 34 (1963), pp. 796–812.

69. Hendy, M. F., and Charles, J. A. "The Production Techniques, Silver Content and Circulation History of the Twelfth-Century Byzantine Trachy." *Archaeometry*, 12 (1970), pp. 13–21.

70. Hersen, Michel. "Personality Characteristics of Nightmare Sufferers." *Journal of Nervous and Mental Diseases*, 153 (1971), pp. 29–31.

71. Hill, T. P. "The First Digit Phenomenon." *American Scientist*, 86 (1998), pp. 358–363.

72. Hogg, Robert V., and Craig, Allen T. *Introduction to Mathematical Statistics*, 3rd ed. New York: Macmillan, 1970.

73. Horvath, Frank S., and Reid, John E. "The Reliability of Polygraph Examiner Diagnosis of Truth and Deception." *Journal of Criminal Law, Criminology, and Police Science*, 62 (1971), pp. 276–281.

74. Hudgens, Gerald A.; Denenberg, Victor H.; and Zarrow, M. X. "Mice Reared with Rats: Effects of Preweaning and Postweaning Social Interactions upon Adult Behaviour." *Behaviour*, 30 (1968), pp. 259–274.

75. Hulbert, Roger H., and Krumbiegel, Edward R. "Synthetic Flavors Improve Acceptance of Anticoagulant-Type Rodenticides." *Journal of Environmental Health*, 34 (1972), pp. 404–411.

76. Husni, S. A. "The Typical American Consumer Magazine of the 1980's." Presentation to the Association for Education in Journalism and Mass Communication, Annual Convention. Gainesville, Fla., 1984.

77. Huxtable, J.; Aitken, M. J.; and Weber, J. C. "Thermoluminescent Dating of Baked Clay Balls of the Poverty Point Culture." *Archaeometry*, 14 (1972), pp. 269–275.

78. Hynek, Joseph Allen. *The UFO Experience: A Scientific Inquiry*. Chicago: Rognery, 1972.

79. Ibrahim, Michel A., et al. "Coronary Heart Disease: Screening by Familial Aggregation." *Archives of Environmental Health*, 16 (1968), pp. 235–240.

80. Jacobson, Eugene, and Kosoff, Jerome. "Self-Percept and Consumer Attitudes toward Small Cars," in *Consumer Behavior in Theory and in Action*. Edited by Steuart Henderson Britt. New York: John Wiley & Sons, 1970. pp. 126–129.

81. James, Andrew, and Moncada, Robert. "Many Set Color TV Lounges Show Highest Radiation." *Journal of Environmental Health*, 31 (1969), pp. 359–360.

82. Kendall, Maurice G. "The Beginnings of a Probability Calculus," in *Studies in the History of Statistics and Probability*. Edited by E. S. Pearson and Maurice G. Kendall. Darien, Conn.: Hafner, 1970, pp. 8–11.

83. Kendall, Maurice G., and Stuart, Alan. *The Advanced Theory of Statistics*, vol. 2. New York: Hafner, 1961. pp. 39–41.

84. Kronoveter, Kenneth J., and Somerville, Gordon W. "Airplane Cockpit Noise Levels and Pilot Hearing Sensitivity." *Archives of Environmental Health*, 20 (1970), pp. 495–499.

85. Kruk-De Bruin, M.; Rost, Luc C. M.; and Draisma, Fons G. A. M. "Estimates of the Number of Foraging Ants with the Lincoln-Index Method in Relation to the Colony Size of *Formica Polyctena*." *Journal of Animal Ecology*, 46 (1977), pp. 463–465.

86. Larsen, Diane K. Personal communication.

87. Larsen, Richard J., and Marx, Morris L. *An Introduction to Probability and Its Applications*. Englewood Cliffs, N.J.: Prentice Hall, 1985.

88. Lathem, Edward Connery, ed. *The Poetry of Robert Frost*. New York: Holt, Rinehart and Winston, 1970.

89. Laurie-Ahlberg, C. C., and McKinney, F. "The Nod-Swim Display of Male Green-Winged Teal (*Anas Crecca*)." *Animal Behaviour*, 27 (1979), pp. 165–172.

90. Lavalle, Irving H. *An Introduction to Probability, Decision, and Inference*. New York: Holt, Rinehart and Winston, 1970.

91. Lemon, Robert E., and Chatfield, Christopher. "Organization of Song in Cardinals." *Animal Behaviour*, 19 (1971), pp. 1–17.

92. Li, Frederick P. "Suicide Among Chemists." *Archives of Environmental Health*, 19 (1969), pp. 518–520.

93. Lindgren, B. W. *Statistical Theory*. New York: Macmillan, 1962, pp. 109–116.

94. Linnik, Y. V. *Method of Least Squares and Principles of the Theory of Observations*. Oxford: Pergamon Press, 1961, p. 1.

95. Lockwood, L. Personal communication.

96. Lottenbach, K. "Vasomotor Tone and Vascular Response to Local Cold in Primary Raynaud's Disease." *Angiology*, 32 (1971), pp. 4–8.

97. MacDonald, G. A., and Abbott, A. T. *Volcanoes in the Sea*. Honolulu: University of Hawaii Press, 1970.

98. Maistrov, L. E. *Probability Theory—A Historical Sketch*. New York: Academic Press, 1974.

99. Mann, H. B. *Analysis and Design of Experiments*. New York: Dover, 1949.

100. Marx, Morris L. Personal communication.

101. McIntyre, Donald B. "Precision and Resolution in Geochronometry," in *The Fabric of Geology*. Edited by Claude C. Albritton, Jr. Stanford, Calif.: Freeman, Cooper, and Co., 1963, pp. 112–133.

102. "Medical News." *Journal of the American Medical Association*, 219 (1972), p. 981.

103. Miettinen, Jorma K. "The Accumulation and Excretion of Heavy Metals in Organisms," in *Heavy Metals in the Aquatic Environment*. Edited by P. A. Krenkel. Oxford: Pergamon Press, 1975, pp. 155–162.

104. Morgan, Peter J. "A Photogrammetric Survey of Hoseason Glacier, Kemp Coast, Antarctica." *Journal of Glaciology*, 12 (1973), pp. 113–120.

105. Mulcahy, R.; McGilvray, J. W.; and Hickey, N. "Cigarette Smoking Related to Geographic Variations in Coronary Heart Disease Mortality and to Expectation of Life in the Two Sexes." *American Journal of Public Health*, 60 (1970), pp. 1515–1521.

106. Munford, A. G. "A Note on the Uniformity Assumption in the Birthday Problem." *American Statistician*, 31 (1977), p. 119.

107. Nakano, T. "Natural Hazards: Report from Japan," in *Natural Hazards*. Edited by G. White. New York: Oxford University Press, 1974, pp. 231–243.

108. Nash, Harvey. *Alcohol and Caffeine*. Springfield, Ill.: Thomas, 1962, p. 96.

109. *Nashville Banner*. March 30, 1991.

110. ———. November 9, 1994.

111. *National Auto Research Black Book Official Used Car Market Guide Monthly*, April 1993. Gainesville, Ga.: Hearst Business Media Corporation.

112. *National Review*. May 10, 1993.

113. *News from the College Board*. August 25, 1994.

114. *Newsweek*. March 6, 1978.

115. Nye, Francis Iven. *Family Relationships and Delinquent Behavior*. New York: John Wiley & Sons, 1958, p. 37.

116. Olvin, J. F. "Moonlight and Nervous Disorders." *American Journal of Psychiatry*, 99 (1943), pp. 578–584.

117. Ore, O. *Cardano, The Gambling Scholar*. Princeton, N.J.: Princeton University Press, 1953, pp. 25–26.

118. Papoulis, Athanasios. *Probability, Random Variables, and Stochastic Processes*. New York: McGraw-Hill, 1965, pp. 206–207.

119. Passingham, R. E. "Anatomical Differences between the Neocortex of Man and Other Primates." *Brain, Behavior and Evolution*, 7 (1973), pp. 337–359.

120. Pearson, E. S., and Kendall, Maurice G. *Studies in the History of Statistics and Probability*. London: Griffin, 1970.

121. *Pensacola News Journal* (Florida). May 25, 1997.

122. ———. September 21, 1997.

123. Phillips, David P. "Deathday and Birthday: An Unexpected Connection," in *Statistics: A Guide to the Unknown*. Edited by Judith M. Tanur, et al. San Francisco: Holden-Day, 1972, pp. 52–65.

124. Phillips, Lawrence D. *Bayesian Statistics for Social Scientists*. London: Thomas Nelson & Sons, 1973.

125. Pierce, George W. *The Songs of Insects*. Cambridge, Mass.: Harvard University Press, 1949, pp. 12–21.

126. Porter, John W., et al. "Effect of Hypnotic Age Regression on the Magnitude of the Ponzo Illusion." *Journal of Abnormal Psychology*, 79 (1972), pp. 189–194.

127. *Profile of SAT and Achievement Test Takers*. Princeton, N.J.: The College Board, 1994.

128. Ragsdale, A. C., and Brody, S. *Journal of Dairy Science*, 5 (1922), p. 214.

129. Rahman, N. A. *Practical Exercises in Probability and Statistics*. New York: Hafner, 1972.

130. Reichler, Joseph L., ed. *The Baseball Encyclopedia*, 4th ed. New York: Macmillan, 1979, p. 1350.

131. Resnick, Richard B.; Fink, Max; and Freedman, Alfred M. "A Cyclazocine Typology in Opiate Dependence." *American Journal of Psychiatry*, 126 (1970), pp. 1256–1260.

132. Rich, Clyde L. "Is Random Digit Dialing Really Necessary?" *Journal of Marketing Research*, 14 (1977), pp. 242–250.

133. Ritter, Brunhilde. "The Use of Contact Desensitization, Demonstration-Plus-Participation and Demonstration-Alone in the Treatment of Acrophobia." *Behaviour Research and Therapy*, 7 (1969), pp. 157–164.

134. Roberts, Charlotte A. "Retraining of Inactive Medical Technologists—Whose Responsibility?" *American Journal of Medical Technology*, 42 (1976), pp. 115–123.

135. Rochat, Roger W. "Cervical Cancer Screening: The Effect of Infrequently Occurring Disease on the Accuracy of Diagnosis." Presented to the Society for Epidemiological Research. Toronto, 1976.

136. Rohatgi, V. K. *An Introduction to Probability Theory and Mathematical Statistics*. New York: John Wiley & Sons, 1976, p. 81.

137. Roulette, Amos. "An Assessment of Unit Dose Injectable Systems." *American Journal of Hospital Pharmacy*, 29 (1972), pp. 60–62.

138. Rowley, Wayne A. "Laboratory Flight Ability of the Mosquito *Culex Tarsalis Coq.*" *Journal of Medical Entomology*, 7 (1970), pp. 713–716.

139. Roy, R. H. *The Cultures of Management*. Baltimore: Johns Hopkins University Press, 1977, p. 261.

140. Rutherford, Sir Ernest; Chadwick, James; and Ellis, C. D. *Radiations from Radioactive Substances*. London: Cambridge University Press, 1951, p. 172.

141. Sagan, Carl. *Cosmos*. New York: Random House, 1980, pp. 298–302.

142. Salvosa, Carmencita B.; Payne, Philip R.; and Wheeler, Erica F. "Energy Expenditure of Elderly People Living Alone or in Local Authority Homes." *American Journal of Clinical Nutrition*, 24 (1971), pp. 1467–1470.

143. Samaras, T. T. "That Song Put Down Short People, But …" *Science Digest*, 84 (1978), pp. 76–79.

144. Saturley, B. A. "Colorimetric Determination of Cyclamate in Soft Drinks, Using Picryl Chloride." *Journal of the Association of Official Analytical Chemists*, 55 (1972), pp. 892–894.

145. Schell, E. D. "Samuel Pepys, Isaac Newton, and Probability." *The American Statistician*, 14 (1960), pp. 27–30.

146. Schoeneman, Robert L.; Dyer, Randolph H.; and Earl, Elaine M. "Analytical Profile of Straight Bourbon Whiskies." *Journal of the Association of Official Analytical Chemists*, 54 (1971), pp. 1247–1261.

147. Selective Service System. Office of the Director. Washington, D.C., 1969.

148. Sen, Nrisinha, et al. "Effect of Sodium Nitrite Concentration on the Formation of Nitrosopyrrolidine and Dimethyl nitrosamine in Fried Bacon." *Journal of Agricultural and Food Chemistry*, 22 (1974), pp. 540–541.

149. Shahidi, Syed A., et al. "Celery Implicated in High Bacteria Count Salads." *Journal of Environmental Health*, 32 (1970), p. 669.

150. Sharpe, Roger S., and Johnsgard, Paul A. "Inheritance of Behavioral Characters in F_2 Mallard × Pintail (*Anas Platyrhynchos L.* × *Anas Acuta L.*) Hybrids." *Behaviour*, 27 (1966), pp. 259–272.

151. Shore, N. S.; Greene, R.; and Kazemi, H. "Lung Dysfunction in Workers Exposed to *Bacillus subtilis* Enzyme." *Environmental Research*, 4 (1971), pp. 512–519.

152. Smith, W. Lynn. "Facilitating Verbal-Symbolic Functions in Children with Learning Problems and 14-6 Positive Spike EEG Patterns with Ethosuximide (Zarontin)," in *Drugs and Cerebral Function*. Edited by Wallace Smith. Springfield, Ill.: Thomas, 1970.

153. *State Regulations for Protection Against Radiation*. Nashville: Tennessee Department of Public Health, Division of Radiological Health, 1978, 1200-2-6-.05(3)(c).

154. *Statistical Abstract of the United States*, 110th ed. Washington, D.C.: U.S. Bureau of the Census, 1990.

155. Stroup, Donna F. Personal communication.

156. Strutt, John William (Baron Rayleigh). "On the Resultant of a Large Number of Vibrations of the Same Pitch and of Arbitrary Phase." *Philosophical Magazine*, X (1880), pp. 73–78.

157. Sukhatme, P. V. "On Fisher and Behren's Test of Significance for the Difference in Means of Two Normal Samples." *Sankhya*, 4 (1938), pp. 39–48.

158. Sutton, D. H. "Gestation Period." *Medical Journal of Australia*, 1 (1945), pp. 611–613.

159. Szalontai, S., and Timaffy, M. "Involutional Thrombopathy," in *Age with a Future*. Edited by P. From Hansen. Philadelphia: F. A. Davis, 1964, p. 345.

160. Tanguy, J. C. "An Archaeomagnetic Study of Mount Etna: The Magnetic Direction Recorded in Lava Flows Subsequent to the Twelfth Century." *Archaeometry*, 12, 1970, pp. 115–128.

161. *Tennessean* (Nashville). January 20, 1973.

162. ———. August 30, 1973.

163. ———. July 21, 1990.

164. ———. May 5, 1991.

165. ———. May 12, 1991.

166. ———. January 24, 1995.

167. ———. February 12, 1995.

168. Thorndike, Frances. "Applications of Poisson's Probability Summation." *Bell System Technical Journal*, 5 (1926), pp. 604–624.

169. Treuhaft, Paul S., and McCarty, Daniel J. "Synovial Fluid pH, Lactate, Oxygen and Carbon Dioxide Partial Pressure in Various Joint Diseases." *Arthritis and Rheumatism*, 14 (1971), pp. 476–477.

170. Trugo, L. C.; Macrae, R.; and Dick, J. "Determination of Purine Alkaloids and Trigonelline in Instant Coffee and Other Beverages Using High Performance Liquid Chromatography." *Journal of the Science of Food and Agriculture*, 34 (1983), pp. 300–306.

171. Turco, Salvatore, and Davis, Neil. "Particulate Matter in Intravenous Infusion Fluids—Phase 3." *American Journal of Hospital Pharmacy*, 30 (1973), pp. 611–613.

172. *USA Today*. March 1–3, 1991.

173. ———. July 3, 1991.

174. ———. September 20, 1991.

175. ———. January 6, 1994.

176. ———. March 14, 1994.

177. ———. April 12, 1994.

178. ———. February 10, 1995.

179. ———. March 13, 1996.

180. ———. November 18, 1996.

181. Vilenkin, N. Y. *Combinatorics*. New York: Academic Press, 1971, pp. 24–26.

182. Vogel, John H. K.; Horgan, John A.; and Strahl, Cheryl L. "Left Ventricular Dysfunction in Chronic Constrictive Pericarditis." *Chest*, 59 (1971), pp. 484–492.

183. Vogt, E. Z., and Hyman, R. *Water Witching U.S.A.* Chicago: University of Chicago Press, 1959, p. 55.

184. Walker, H. *Studies in the History of Statistical Method*. Baltimore: Williams and Wilkins, 1929.

185. Wallis, W. A. "The Poisson Distribution and the Supreme Court." *Journal of the American Statistical Association*, 31 (1936), pp. 376–380.

186. Walter, William G., and Stober, Angie. "Microbial Air Sampling in a Carpeted Hospital." *Journal of Environmental Health*, 30 (1968), p. 405.

187. Werner, Martha; Stabenau, James R.; and Pollin, William. "Thematic Apperception Test Method for the Differentiation of Families of Schizophrenics, Delinquents, and 'Normals'." *Journal of Abnormal Psychology*, 75 (1970), pp. 139–145.

188. Wilks, Samuel S. *Mathematical Statistics*. New York: John Wiley & Sons, 1962.

189. Williams, Wendy M., and Ceci, Stephen J. "How'm I Doing?" *Change*, 29, no. 5 (1997), pp. 12–23.

190. Winslow, Charles. *The Conquest of Epidemic Disease*. Princeton, N.J.: Princeton University Press, 1943, p. 303.

191. Wolf, Stewart, ed. *The Artery and the Process of Arteriosclerosis: Measurement and Modification*. Proceedings of an Interdisciplinary Conference on Fundamental Data on Reactions of Vascular Tissue in Man (Lindau, West Germany, April 19–25, 1970). New York: Plenum Press, 1972, p. 116.

192. Wood, Robert M. "Giant Discoveries of Future Science." *Virginia Journal of Science*, 21 (1970), pp. 169–177.

193. Woodward, W. F. "A Comparison of Base Running Methods in Baseball." M.Sc. Thesis, Florida State University, 1970.

194. Woolson, Robert E. *Statistical Methods for the Analysis of Biomedical Data*. New York: John Wiley & Sons, 1987, p. 302.

195. Wyler, Allen R.; Minoru, Masuda; and Holmes, Thomas H. "Magnitude of Life Events and Seriousness of Illness." *Psychosomatic Medicine*, 33 (1971), pp. 115–122.

196. Yochem, Donald; and Roach, Darrell. "Aspirin: Effect on Thrombus Formation Time and Prothrombin Time of Human Subjects." *Angiology*, 22 (1971), pp. 70–76.

197. Young, P. V., and Schmid, C. *Scientific Social Surveys and Research*. Englewood Cliffs, N.J.: Prentice Hall, 1966, p. 319.

198. Zaret, Thomas M. "Predators, Invisible Prey, and the Nature of Polymorphism in the *Cladocera* (Class *Crustacea*)." *Limnology and Oceanography*, 17 (1972), pp. 171–184.

199. Zelazo, Philip R.; Zelazo, Nancy Ann; and Kolb, Sarah. "'Walking' in the Newborn." *Science*, 176 (1972), pp. 314–315.

200. Zelinsky, Daniel. *A First Course in Linear Algebra*, 2nd ed. New York: Academic Press, 1973.

201. Ziv, G., and Sulman, F. G. "Binding of Antibiotics to Bovine and Ovine Serum." *Antimicrobial Agents and Chemotherapy*, 2 (1972), pp. 206–213.

202. Zucker, N. "The Role of Hood-Building in Defining Territories and Limiting Combat in Fiddler Crabs." *Animal Behaviour*, 29 (1981), pp. 387–395.

Photo Credits

Chapter 1 Opener
Science Photo Library/Photo Researchers, Inc.

Chapter 2 Opener
Fermat: Stock Montage, Inc./Historical Pictures Collection
Pascal: French Embassy

Chapter 3 Opener
Corbis

Chapter 4 Opener
North Wind Picture Archives

Chapter 6 Opener
Archive Photos

Chapter 9 Opener
The Granger Collection

Chapter 10 Opener
University College London

Chapter 11 Opener
Science Photo Library/Photo Researchers, Inc.

Chapter 13 Opener
United States Department of Agriculture

Index